BUSINESS STATISTICS

UNDERSTANDING POPULATIONS AND PROCESSES

MARIO F. TRIOLA
DUTCHESS COMMUNITY COLLEGE

LEROY A. FRANKLIN
INDIANA STATE UNIVERSITY

ADDISON-WESLEY PUBLISHING COMPANY

Reading, Massachusetts · Menlo Park, California · New York
Don Mills, Ontario · Wokingham, England · Amsterdam · Bonn
Sydney · Singapore · Tokyo · Madrid · San Juan · Milan · Paris

Executive Editor: **Michael Payne**
Sponsoring Editor: **Faith Sherlock**
Assistant Editor: **Maureen Lawson**
Editorial Assistant: **Adrienne L. Trager**
Senior Production Supervisor: **Loren Hilgenhurst Stevens**
Production Services: **Kathy Smith**
Senior Development Editor: **Marilyn R. Freedman**
Development Editor: **Chere Bemelmans**
Development Assistant: **Susan D. Howard**
Copy Editor: **Jackie Dormitzer**
Proofreader: **Phyllis Coyne**
Text and Cover Designer: **Paul Uhl**
Cover Design Director: **Peter M. Blaiwas**
Layout Artists: **Paul Uhl and Kathy Smith**
Art Supervisor: **Joseph Vetere**
Art Editor: **Susan London-Payne**
Technical Artist: **Scientific Illustrators**
Essay Artist: **John Burgoyne**
Photo Researcher: **Susan Van Etten**
Manufacturing Supervisor: **Roy Logan**
Composition and Film: **Black Dot Graphics**

To Ginny and my parents
M.F.T.

To my wife, Donna,
and to the memory of my parents,
Kelso and Mable Franklin
L.A.F.

Photo credits: Chapter 1, Jean-Claude Lejeune/Stock Boston; Chapter 2, Daniel Brody/Stock Boston; Chapter 3, Tony Freeman/Photo Edit; Chapter 4, Ann McQueen/Stock Boston; Chapter 5, Peter Menzel/Stock Boston; Chapter 6, Peter Vandermark/Stock Boston; Chapter 7, Wide World Photos; Chapter 8, Larry Migdale/Stock Boston; Chapter 9, © Susan Van Etten; Chapter 10, © Susan Van Etten; Chapter 11, Stacy Pick/Stock Boston; Chapter 12, Spencer Grant/Stock Boston; Chapter 13, Frank Siteman/Stock Boston; Chapter 14, © Paul Conklin; Chapter 15, Frank Siteman/Stock Boston; Chapter 16, Bill Gallery/Stock Boston; Interview #1, Bob Daemmrich/Stock Boston and courtesy of Nielsen Media Research; Interview #2, Courtesy of Boeing Aircraft Company; Interview #3, © Susan Van Etten and courtesy of Young & Rubicam Advertising.

MINITAB is a registered trademark of Minitab Inc.

Library of Congress Cataloging-in-Publication Data

Triola, Mario F.
       Business statistics: understanding populations and processes/
  Mario F. Triola, LeRoy A. Franklin.
          p.   cm.
       Includes bibliographical references and index.
       ISBN 0-201-58990-7
          1. Commercial statistics.   2. Statistics.   I. Franklin, LeRoy A.
II. Title.
HF1017.T75   1994   93-8821
519.5—dc20   CIP

Reprinted with corrections June, 1995

6 7 8 9 10 — VH — 02 01

Preface

Never before has there been such a demand for statistical thinking as there is today. With the current emphasis on quality in both the goods we manufacture and the services we provide, the study of statistics has experienced unprecedented growth.

- In 1950, quality expert W. Edwards Deming spoke to the presidents of 21 Japanese companies and told them that they could overcome their reputation for shoddy products within five years if they would use statistical analysis to improve quality. They followed the advice.
- According to the *New York Times,* Motorola introduced quality control systems at its plant in Arcade, New York, and found that "many employees lacked the mathematical skills needed to understand the new statistics-based approach."
- David Hall, division statistical manager at Boeing Commercial Airplane Group, says that "right now, American industry is crying out for people with an understanding of statistics and the ability to communicate its use."
- Jay Dean, Senior Vice President at Young & Rubicam Advertising, says that "marketing is becoming tougher and tougher today. There are more brands, increasing price competition, and more sophisticated consumers. A tougher marketing environment requires more marketing research, and that means we're using statistics more often."

The emphasis on quality and the use of statistics affects manufacturing and service industries in many ways and at many levels. Corporate executives use statistics to lower costs and increase profits, and manufacturing line workers use statistics to monitor quality. Researchers, marketers, and consumer advocates rely on statistical methods and analyses to improve production methods, determine successful sales strategies, and combat fraud and unsafe products.

UNIQUE EMPHASES ON PROCESSES, VARIABILITY, AND QUALITY

Our goal in writing *Business Statistics* was to prepare students to meet the unique challenges of today's business environment. We present a solid foundation in traditional inferential statistics, making the concepts of processes, variability, and quality unifying themes throughout the book.

- The three important features of data—center, distribution shape, and variation —for processes as well as for populations are examined. Sequence, a fourth important feature of processes, is also included. We stress the extremely important point that only when a process is stable, or under statistical control, can it be treated and statistically analyzed as a population.
- Ways of determining whether a process is statistically stable are explored. We emphasize throughout *Business Statistics* that in service and manufacturing industries, analysis of an unstable process can easily lead to incorrect, misleading, and costly decisions so we carefully develop control charts and use them as a statistical tool to track processes.

- Measurement and control of variation are emphasized. Executives from corporations such as CONRAIL and Motorola believe that the enemy of quality and profitability is variation. Techniques for measuring and understanding variation and its effect on costs and quality are detailed.

LEARNING AND MOTIVATIONAL FEATURES

We wrote *Business Statistics* for use in courses at two- and four-year colleges and universities. A strong mathematics background is not necessary, but students should have completed a year of high school algebra. Although underlying theory is often included and carefully explained, the mathematical rigor that would be more appropriate for mathematics or statistics majors is not stressed.

We achieve our goal of providing a statistics textbook for today's challenges through readable and interesting text discussions; inclusion of real business applications, scenarios, and real data; emphasis on the use of statistics for problem solving and decision making; and various learning and motivational features.

- Exercises. We provide more than 1,800 exercises. Individual exercise sets arranged in order of increasing difficulty help students to build gradually upon their concepts and skills. Exercises are separated into sections of Basic Concepts that give students the immediate practice they need to master the formulas, procedures, and applications presented in the section. Beyond the Basics provides more challenging concepts. Answers are provided for odd-numbered exercises.
- Examples. Important principles, concepts, techniques, and applications are illustrated with examples and solutions that use real-world data and scenarios to show their application in business and industry.
- From Data to Decision. These open-ended case studies are designed to develop students' problem-solving skills to make real-world decisions.
- Marginal essays. There are 98 marginal essays to motivate students by presenting them with applications of statistics in business and industry. Diverse topics include mail consistency, Mazda transmissions, jet engine failures, lie detectors, drug screening, TV ratings, product safety, and aluminum recycling.
- Flowcharts. These special figures simplify and clearly illustrate the more complicated procedures, such as the determination of the test statistic appropriate in hypothesis testing or whether a process is statistically stable with normally distributed data.
- Highlighted definitions, formulas, and notation. Major definitions, formulas, notations, and other key components are consistently set off with design features such as boxes and boldface type for easy reference.
- Chapter-opening problems. These problems will spark student interest by showing how statistics is used in real situations and practical circumstances. They include such topics as determining whether a new VCR manufacturing process works, figuring out the percentage of women who find a car's driver's seat uncomfortable, estimating the age of the U.S. commercial aircraft fleet, analyzing the discrepancy between reported rates of credit card fraud, and determining whether salaries are related to job stress.
- Chapter outlines. The first page of each chapter lists the general content.
- Chapter overviews. Each chapter begins with a statement of chapter objectives and a brief outline of the chapter contents.

- Interviews. Three interviews with a Senior Vice President at Nielsen Media Research, a Division Statistical Manager at the Boeing Commercial Airplane Group, and a Senior Vice President at Young & Rubicam Advertising demonstrate the relevance of statistics to students' future careers.
- Detachable formula/table card. This detachable card includes major formulas as well as tables of the standard normal (z) distribution, Student t distributon, and the chi-square distribution.
- Symbol table. A symbol table is included on the front inside cover for quick and easy reference to important symbols.
- Back cover tables. Tables of values for the standard normal (z) distribution and the Student t distribution are printed on the inside back cover for students' convenience.
- End-of-chapter features. Extensive end-of-chapter features include a Vocabulary List and a Review, which provide a summary of the chapter concepts; a list of Important Formulas; Review Exercises; and a Computer Project.

FLEXIBLE COMPUTER COVERAGE

Business Statistics offers flexible computer coverage. Although this text can be used without reference to computers, we have included MINITAB displays throughout the text for those instructors who choose to supplement the course with computer usage. In addition, the following items are available:

- Computer Projects. These projects use MINITAB or some other statistical package to help students understand and analyze data and become familiar with how computers are used in business for statistical problem solving and analysis. The technique of computer simulation is sometimes used to increase the student's insight into and understanding of difficult concepts, such as type I and type II errors.
- The Data Set in Appendix B is available on disk.
- *Minitab Student Laboratory Workbook*, designed specifically for this text, includes instructions and examples for using MINITAB and experiments to be conducted by students.
- *Student Edition of Minitab, Second Edition* is available from Addison-Wesley at a reasonable cost. Based on Version 8.1, it includes program software with data sets developed by Minitab Inc. and a comprehensive user manual with tutorials and a reference section written by Robert L. Schaefer of Miami University in Oxford, Ohio and Elizabeth Farber of Bucks County Community College in Newtown, Pennsylvania.
- *STAT101*, an inexpensive software package produced by Minitab Inc. and sold by Addison-Wesley, provides an excellent foundation for the more powerful MINITAB statistics software.

SUPPLEMENTS

- *Instructor's Solutions Manual:* The *Instructor's Solutions Manual* includes solutions to all text exercises, samples of course syllabi, printed test bank with answers, transparency masters, and sample quizzes with solutions.

- *Students' Solutions Manual:* The *Students' Solutions Manual* provides detailed solutions to odd-numbered exercises.
- *Computer-Generated Tests:* The testing software package, OmniTestII, available for instructors using *Business Statistics,* can help build tests complete with answer keys.

ACKNOWLEDGMENTS

The authors wish to extend their sincere thanks for the helpful suggestions made by the following reviewers:

Dr. Margaret M. Capen
East Carolina University

Professor Myron K. Cox
Wright State University

Professor Stanley R. Schultz
Cleveland State University

Professor Mark F. Batell
Washtenaw Community College

Professor Wendy J. McGuire
Santa Fe Community College

Professor Douglas A. Zahn
Florida State University

Professor Priscilla Chaffe-Stengel
California State University, Fresno

Mr. Ayshhyah Khazad
Eugene, OR

Professor Hedayeh Samavati
Indiana University, Purdue University at Fort Wayne

Professor Benny Lo
Ohlone College

Professor Diane L. Stehman
Northeastern Illinois University

Professor Don R. Robinson
Illinois State University

Professor Robert McAuliffe
Babson College

Professor Christopher H. Morrell
Loyola College

Dr. Ivan Weinel
University of Missouri, Kansas City

We also wish to thank David Hall of the Boeing Commercial Airplane Group, Barry Cook of Nielsen Media Research, and Jay Dean of Young & Rubicam Advertising. We would like to extend special thanks to Chris Franklin of the University of Georgia for her most valuable assistance in checking and preparing the solutions for the Instructor's Solutions Manual. We also wish to thank Julie Garver, Chere Bemelmans, Marilyn Freedman, Susan Howard, Michael Payne, Faith Sherlock, Maureen Lawson, Loren Hilgenhurst Stevens, Susan London-Payne, Kathy Smith, and the entire Addison-Wesley staff for their support, encouragement, and assistance. Finally, we thank our wives, Ginny and Donna, for their invaluable support when it was desperately needed.

LaGrange, New York　　　　　　　　　　　　　　　　　　　　　　　　　　M.F.T.

Terre Haute, Indiana　　　　　　　　　　　　　　　　　　　　　　　　　　L.A.F.

Contents

CHAPTER 11

ANALYSIS OF VARIANCE — 464

11.1 OVERVIEW — 466

11.2 ONE-WAY ANOVA — 468

11.3 ANOVA FOR A RANDOMIZED BLOCK DESIGN — 482

CHAPTER 12

LINEAR REGRESSION AND CORRELATION — 502

12.1 OVERVIEW — 504

12.2 SCATTER DIAGRAMS AND SIMPLE LINEAR REGRESSION — 505

BUSINESS STATISTICS

UNDERSTANDING POPULATIONS AND PROCESSES

CHAPTER 1

Introduction to Statistics

1.1 OVERVIEW

In this chapter we define the term *statistics* as well as the terms *population, process, sample, parameter,* and *statistic.* We discuss the general nature of statistics and its role in industry. Finally, we consider the impact of statistics and variability on quality.

1.2 THE NATURE OF DATA

Different ways of *arranging data* are discussed. We define the four levels of measurement (nominal, ordinal, interval, ratio), as well as discrete and continuous data.

1.3 USES AND ABUSES OF STATISTICS

Examples of beneficial uses of statistics are presented along with some of the common ways that statistics are used to deceive. Among the examples of abuses cited are the display of graphs with modified scales and the use of objects of volume.

1.4 STATISTICS AND COMPUTERS

Computers and statistical packages are briefly discussed. We also introduce some fundamentals of the Minitab statistical software package.

Same Data, Different Impressions

Currently, much attention is given to the unfair treatment of women in the work place. Biased hiring practices, sexual harassment, and lower salaries are a few of the factors that have plagued women for years. In some cases, improvements have been made on the basis of statistical data. When using statistics to pursue favorable change, we should collect data carefully and present it clearly and honestly. We can often use tricks to help create false impressions, but such methods can undermine important support and credibility. Consider the data from the Bureau of Labor Statistics that describe the mean annual earnings of husbands and wives who hold year-round full-time jobs. Figure 1.1 shows three different ways to depict the same data, with Figs. 1.1 (b) and (c) drawn to exaggerate the discrepancy. Superficial examination of Fig. 1.1 (b) could easily lead to the wrong impression that husbands earn 3 times as much as wives, but closer examination of the actual dollar amounts shows that husbands actually earn about 1.74 times as much as wives. Can you identify the trick used in Fig. 1.1 (c) to create the impression that the differences are more extreme than they really are? We will learn about these and other deceptive techniques in this chapter.

FIGURE 1.1
Comparison of Husbands' and Wives' Mean Annual Earnings

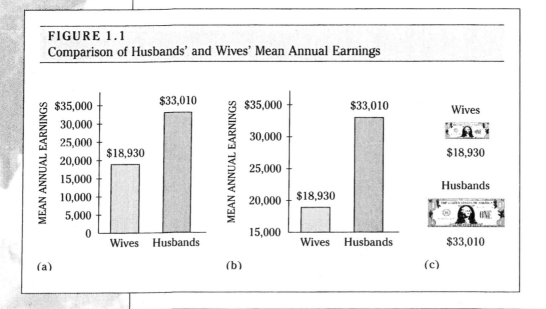

1.1 OVERVIEW

The word *statistics* has two basic meanings. We sometimes use this word when we refer to actual numbers derived from data, such as driver fatality rates, consumer price indexes, baseball attendance figures, or company profits. The second meaning refers to statistics as a subject.

> **DEFINITION**
>
> The subject of *statistics* involves the collection of methods for planning experiments, obtaining data, and then analyzing, interpreting, and drawing conclusions based on the data.

Statistics involves much more than simply collecting, tabulating, and summarizing data. In this introductory book we will learn how to develop inferences that go beyond the original data and how to form more general and more meaningful conclusions.

Chapter 1 describes the general nature of statistics and presents a small sample of its beneficial uses as well as some common abuses. Throughout the book we continue to give many examples of ways that the theories and methods of statistics have been used both for the betterment of our lives and, specifically, in business decisions. We also present some ways that statistics have been abused. We don't believe that you can prove *anything* with statistics, but we do believe that "if you torture data enough, they will confess to anything." This torturing, or manipulation, of numbers sometimes stems from ignorance or honest error, but sometimes it is the result of intentional deception. We provide a few examples of how statistics have been used to deceive. These examples will help you to become more aware and more critical when you read or hear statistical claims. As you learn more about the acceptable methods of statistics, you will be better prepared to challenge misleading statements involving statistics and more likely to recognize the "torturing of data" when it occurs.

STATISTICS IN INDUSTRY

Since the early 1920s, Walter A. Shewhart and W. Edwards Deming have had a tremendous impact on the use of statistics in business. Walter A. Shewhart was a statistician at Bell Laboratories in New York. W. Edwards Deming was a statistician at the Department of Agriculture and later joined the Census Bureau, where he introduced many of the techniques still in use today. They used statistics to monitor production processes in order to improve the consistency and quality of the final product. These techniques proved helpful to U.S. industry during World War II. After the war, however, U.S. industry largely *abandoned* these statistical techniques, partly because we were one of the few nations that could produce, and we could sell *anything* we could make. In contrast, Japan was in ruins, and its companies manufactured items notorious for their lack of quality. In 1951 Deming spoke to Japanese business leaders. They embraced his use of statistics in manufacturing and his management philosophy. Japan proceeded to make major gains in world markets by providing high-quality goods, whereas U.S. market shares declined because of lower-quality goods. U.S. industry now recognizes that statistical thinking is essential for competition and survival in today's global market.

Of particular importance to business students is the statistical concept of *variability* (how much scores differ from one another). In general, large variability implies a lack of consistency in a product or service, and this usually results in poor quality. Understanding variability and how it directly affects quality and profitability is a key topic in this text.

Someone once said that statistics means never having to say you're certain. Statistics is useful in making predictions and forming conclusions about populations or processes. But statistical conclusions involve an element of uncertainty that can lead to incorrect conclusions. For example, it is possible to get 10 consecutive heads when an ordinary coin is tossed 10 times. A statistical analysis of this experiment would lead to the incorrect conclusion that the coin is biased. Yet this conclusion is not certain. It is only "likely," reflecting the very low chance of getting 10 heads in 10 tosses. This illustrates that statistics is often inductive in nature, because conclusions are basically generalizations that may or may not correspond to reality. In most branches of mathematics we deduce or prove results, but in statistics many of our conclusions are associated with different degrees of "likelihood."

IMPORTANT TERMS

In statistics we frequently use the terms *population* and *sample* (from a population). These terms are at the very core of statistics, and we define them now.

DEFINITIONS

A *population* is the complete collection of elements (scores, people, measurements, and so on) to be studied.

A *sample* (from a population) is a subset of elements drawn from a population.

In this text we often refer to process data and a sample drawn from a process.

DEFINITIONS

Process data are data arranged according to a time sequence. They result from some combination of equipment, people, materials, methods, and conditions.

A *sample* (from a process) is a subset of elements drawn from time-ordered process data.

Closely related to the concepts of population, process, and sample are the concepts of *parameter* and *statistic*.

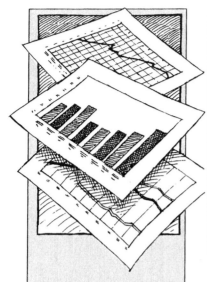

THE STATE OF STATISTICS

The word *statistics* is derived from the Latin word *status* (for "state"). Early uses of statistics involved compilations of data and graphs describing various aspects of a state or country. Modern governments and businesses rely heavily upon statistical data for guidance. Unemployment rates, inflation rates, consumer indexes, and birth and death rates continue to be carefully compiled by governments. Business leaders use the results to make decisions affecting future production levels, hiring, and expansion into new markets.

DEFINITIONS

A *parameter* is a numerical measurement describing some characteristic of a *population* or a *process*.

population or process
↕
parameter

A *statistic* is a numerical measurement describing some characteristic of a sample.

sample
↕
statistic

Let's consider an example. Of 25 students in a statistics class, 21 have credit cards. Because 21 is 84% of 25, we can say that 84% have credit cards. That 84% is a *parameter* (not a statistic) because it is based on the entire class. If we could somehow rationalize that this class is representative of all classes so that we could treat these 25 students as a *sample* drawn from a larger population, then the 84% would become a statistic.

As an example of a process, consider a machine that fills hundreds of 5-lb bags of flour every hour. Because of changing factors such as machine wear, operator adjustments, and the changing texture of the flour, this filling process should be monitored to ensure that it continues to function as desired. If we randomly select and measure 10 bags in one hour and find the average of these 10 weights, we will obtain a *statistic* from the process. But if we measure every bag, the average weight is a parameter (not a statistic).

The statistical data obtained from a process can be treated and analyzed as population data, *provided the process is statistically stable,* meaning that the fluctuations among values continue to stay within acceptable limits. If we assume that a process is statistically stable and that assumption is wrong, we can get very misleading results, and our conclusions and decisions can be wrong and costly. Because processes occur frequently in the manufacturing and service industries, we will emphasize the sequential aspect of processes and describe ways to judge statistical stability. Such judgments are necessary to ensure that industry provides high-quality goods and services.

1.2 THE NATURE OF DATA

People tend to think of collections of data as lists of numbers, such as the income levels of professional athletes or the annual profits of corporations. Yet data may be nonnumerical, and even numerical data can belong to different categories with different characteristics. For example, a market researcher may compile nonnumeric data such as the sex, race, and religion of consumers in a sample. Numeric data, instead of being in an unordered list, might be matched in pairs (discussed in

Chapters 9, 12, 15), as in the following two tables.

Pretraining productivity	99	62	74	59	70
Posttraining productivity	99	68	81	60	72

Pretraining productivity	99	62	74	59	70
Pretraining dexterity test score	174	180	171	177	168

Another common arrangement for summarizing sample data is the contingency table (discussed in Section 10.3), in which the numbers are frequencies (counts) of sample results, as in the following table.

	FACTORY		
	NY	LA	DALLAS
Defective items	293	326	158
Acceptable items	7394	8150	2844

The nature and structure of the data can affect the nature of the relevant problem and the method used for analysis. With the paired productivity data, a fundamental concern would be whether a difference exists in the pretraining and posttraining productivity levels. Analysis of these data should attempt to determine whether posttraining productivity levels are significantly higher than pretraining levels. With the paired productivity/dexterity data, the fundamental concern would be whether some relationship exists between those two factors. This requires a different method of analysis. With the contingency table, the fundamental concern would be whether the quality (measured by defective and acceptable items) is essentially the same for all three factories. This data set requires yet another method of analysis. As we consider the topics of later chapters, we will see that the structure and nature of the data affect our choice of method of analysis.

We can categorize data as either qualitative or quantitative. **Qualitative data** consist of qualities, such as political party, religion, or sex. **Quantitative data** consist of numbers representing counts or measurements. We can further categorize quantitative data by distinguishing between the discrete and continuous types.

DEFINITIONS

Discrete quantitative data result from either a finite number of possible values or a countable number of possible values.

Continuous quantitative data result from infinitely many possible values that can be associated with points on a continuous scale in such a way that there are no gaps or interruptions.

We know what a finite number of values is (1, 2, 3, and so on), but our definition of discrete data also involves the concept of a *countable* number of values. As an example, if we count the number of rolls of a pair of dice before a 7 turns up, we can get any one of the values 1, 2, 3, ... We now have an infinite number of possibilities, but they correspond to the counting numbers. Consequently, this type of infinity is called **countable.** In contrast, the number of points on a continuous scale is not countable and represents a higher degree of infinity. There is no way to count the points on a continuous scale, but we can count the number of times a die is rolled, even if the rolling seems to continue forever.

As an example, you can obtain exact counts of the numbers of Pepsi bottles in different stores, and the results will be 0, or 1, or 2, or 3, and so on. These exact bottle counts are discrete data. But if you measure the amounts (in liters) of Pepsi in different bottles, you could get values such as 1.026 or 0.99 or *any* value in between, and such measurements are continuous data. Similarly, shoe sizes (7, 9½, 8, etc.) are discrete data, whereas the actual lengths of feet (10.03 in., 11.738 in., 8.62 in., etc.) are continuous data.

Another common way to classify data is to use four *levels of measurement:* nominal, ordinal, interval, ratio.

DEFINITION

The *nominal level of measurement* is characterized by data that consist of names, labels, or categories only. The data cannot be arranged in an ordering scheme.

If we associate *nominal* with "name only," the meaning becomes easy to remember. An example of nominal data is the collection of "yes, no, undecided" responses to a survey question. We cannot arrange data at this nominal level of measurement according to some ordering scheme. That is, there is no criterion by which we can identify values as greater or less than other values. In the following example, note that the data can't be used for calculations, because the categories lack ordering or numerical meaning.

EXAMPLE   The following are other examples of sample data at the nominal level of measurement.

1. Responses consisting of 12 consumers who like a product, 15 who don't like it, and 9 who aren't sure
2. Responses consisting of 140 luxury-car owners from New York, 170 from California, 80 from Connecticut, and 70 from Florida

---

DEFINITION

The *ordinal level of measurement* involves data that may be arranged in some order, but differences between data values either cannot be determined or are meaningless.

Data categorized as "good," "better," or "best" would be at the ordinal level, but we cannot determine specific measured differences between such data. Rankings, such as 2nd, 5th, and 7th, would be at the ordinal level, and we can find differences, but the sizes of those differences don't really mean anything. The difference of 3 between ranks of 2nd and 5th isn't necessarily the same as the difference of 3 between ranks of 7th and 10th. Again, data at this level should not be used for calculations.

EXAMPLE The following are examples of data at the ordinal level of measurement.

1. In a sample of 36 batteries, 12 were rated "good," 16 were rated "better," and 8 were rated "best."
2. In a department of 19 employees, 5 required no retraining, 10 required minimal (less than a week) retraining, and 4 required extensive retraining.
3. In a class of MBA graduates, Ginny ranked 2nd, Hector ranked 5th, and Sven ranked 7th.

DEFINITION

The *interval level of measurement* is like the ordinal level, with the additional property that we can determine meaningful amounts of differences between data.

Temperature readings of 25° F and 50° F are examples of data at the interval level of measurement. Those values are ordered, and we can determine their difference (often called the *distance* between the two values). However, there is no natural starting point; the starting point was arbitrarily chosen. The value of 0° F might seem like a natural starting point, but it is arbitrary. The value of 0° F does not indicate "no heat," and it is incorrect to say that 50° F is twice as hot as 25° F. For the same reasons, temperature readings on the Celsius scale are also at the interval level of measurement.

EXAMPLE The following are other examples of data at the interval level of measurement.

1. Years in which IBM stock split
2. Room temperatures (in Celsius) of telemarketing sales offices

DEFINITION

The *ratio level of measurement* is actually the interval level modified to include the inherent zero starting point. For values at this level, differences and ratios are meaningful.

Consider two values where one value is twice the other, and ask yourself if the ratio of "twice" applies to the characteristic being measured. For example, with tree heights of 20 ft and 10 ft, it is correct to say that the taller tree is *twice as high* as the shorter tree, so *ratios* are meaningful.

EXAMPLE The following are examples of data at the ratio level of measurement.

1. Heights of trees 10 years after being planted by a lumber company
2. Volumes of helium in balloons
3. Cranking times (in minutes) of car batteries
4. Quarterly stock dividends paid by G.M. over the last 20 years

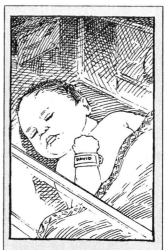

THE BIRTH OF STATISTICS

In the seventeenth century, a successful store owner named John Graunt (1620–1674) had enough spare time to pursue outside interests. His curiosity led him to study and analyze a weekly church publication, "Bills of Mortality," that listed births, christenings, and deaths and their causes. On the basis of these studies, Graunt published his observations and conclusions in a work with the catchy title "Natural and Political Observations Made upon the Bills of Mortality." This 1662 publication was the first real interpretation of social and biological phenomena based on a mass of raw data, and many people feel it marks the birth of statistics.

TABLE 1.1
Levels of Measurement

LEVEL	SUMMARY	EXAMPLE
Nominal	Categories only. Data cannot be arranged in an ordering scheme.	Market research survey about a product: 45 like 80 dislike } Categories only. 90 no opinion
Ordinal	Categories are ordered, but differences cannot be determined or they are meaningless.	Market research survey about a product: 45 low-income consumers } Data are ordered 80 middle-income consumers } by "low, middle, 90 upper-income consumers } upper" categories.
Interval	Differences between values can be found, but there may be no inherent starting point. Ratios are meaningless.	Temperatures of steel rods: 45° F 80° F } 90° F is not twice as 90° F } hot as 45° F.
Ratio	Like interval, but with an inherent starting point. Ratios are meaningful.	Lengths of steel rods: 45 cm 80 cm } 90 cm is twice 90 cm } as long as 45 cm.

In the preceding example, we can arrange each of the data collections in order, we can compute differences, and there is an inherent zero starting point. *This level is called the ratio level because the starting point makes ratios meaningful.* Because a 90 cm rod is twice as long as a 45 cm rod and 90° F is not twice as hot as 25° F, lengths are at the ratio level whereas Fahrenheit temperatures are at the interval level. See Table 1.1.

Among the four levels of measurement, the nominal is considered the lowest, followed by the ordinal level, the interval level, and the ratio level.

The following is an important guideline. **The statistics based on one level of measurement should not be used for a lower level, but can be used for a higher level.** We can, for example, calculate the average for data at the interval or ratio level, but not at the lower ordinal or nominal level. If, for data processing requirements, we assign the numbers 0, 1, and 2 to "like," "dislike," and "no opinion," respectively, and proceed to calculate the average, we are creating a meaningless statistic that can lead to incorrect conclusions.

Chapter 2 will introduce basic methods of dealing with data sets that are primarily at the interval or ratio level of measurement, and later chapters will include data sets at the other levels of measurement.

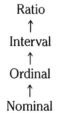

1.2 EXERCISES   BASIC CONCEPTS

In Exercises 1–10, identify each number as being *discrete* or *continuous*.

1. Among campus vending machines, 14 are found to be defective.
2. Today's records show that 25 employees were absent.

3. The car weighs 1432.76 kilograms.
4. Among 200 people surveyed, 186 recognize the Campbell's soup brand name.
5. A new Sears car battery provides 12.27 volts.
6. The car stopped in 187.3 ft.
7. Of all job applicants tested for drug use, 7 failed.
8. Of buying customers, 423 are women.
9. The crew completed refueling in 17.5 minutes.
10. Among the issues traded on the New York Stock Exchange, 327 declined.

In Exercises 11–20, determine which of the four levels of measurement (nominal, ordinal, interval, ratio) is most appropriate.

11. Cars described as subcompact, compact, intermediate, or full-size
12. Weights of a sample of machine parts
13. Colors of a sample of cars involved in alcohol-related crashes
14. Years in which the Dow Jones Industrial Average fell
15. Zip codes
16. Social security numbers
17. Total annual incomes for a sample of families
18. Job performance ratings of A, B, C, D, E
19. Body temperatures (in degrees Fahrenheit) of scuba divers testing a new wet-suit design
20. Flight instructors rated as superior, above average, average, below average, or poor

1.2 EXERCISES   BEYOND THE BASICS

21. In a final examination for a business statistics course, one student received a grade of 50, and another student received a grade of 100.
    a. If we consider these numbers to represent only the points earned on the exam, then the score of 100 is twice that of 50. What is the corresponding level of measurement?
    b. If we consider these numbers to represent the amount of the subject learned in the course, can we conclude that the one student knows twice as much as the other student? What is the level of measurement in this case?
22. Many people question what IQ scores actually measure. Assuming that IQ scores measure intelligence, is one employee with an IQ score of 150 twice as intelligent as another employee with an IQ of 75?
    a. What does an affirmative answer imply about the level of measurement corresponding to IQ scores?
    b. What does a negative answer imply about the level of those data?
23. If a recipe requires cooking something at 300° F for three hours, but you decide to cook it at 900° F for one hour, the result will be different. Explain your answer.
24. The years 1990, 1988, 1972, 1963, and 1984 form a collection of data at the interval level of measurement. Explain.

THE POWER OF YOUR VOTE

In the electoral college system, the power of a voter in a large state exceeds that of a voter in a small state. When voting power is measured as the ability to affect the outcome of an election, we see that a New Yorker has 3.312 times the voting power of a resident of the District of Columbia. This result is included in John Banzhof's article "One Man, 3.312 Votes."

As an example, the outcome of the 1916 presidential election could have been changed by shifting only 1,983 votes in California. If the same number of votes were changed in a much smaller state, the resulting change in electoral votes would not have been sufficient to alter the outcome.

1.3 USES AND ABUSES OF STATISTICS

Uses of statistics often result in changes that benefit humanity. Manufacturers can provide better products at lower costs through the effective use of statistics in quality and process control. Scientists can anticipate and control epidemics and diseases. By using statistical evidence of lower fatality rates, legislators can better justify laws such as those regulating air pollution, auto inspections, seat belt use, and drunk driving. Geologists can more accurately determine amounts and locations of oil, natural gas, and coal. Farmers can benefit from the development of better mixtures of the products they use, such as feed and fertilizer.

In contrast to these beneficial uses of statistics are the many abuses to which Benjamin Disraeli referred when he said, "There are three kinds of lies: lies, damned lies, and statistics." Some abusers of statistics are simply ignorant or careless, whereas others have personal objectives and are willing to suppress unfavorable data while emphasizing supportive data. Here are a few examples of the many ways that data can be distorted.

Many visual devices—such as bar graphs and pie charts—can be used to exaggerate or deemphasize the true nature of data. (We also discuss these in Chapter 2.) Figure 1.1 uses data from the Bureau of Labor Statistics to show figures that depict the *same data,* but part (b) is designed to exaggerate the difference between the salaries of women and men. By not starting the horizontal axis at zero, part (b) tends to produce a misleading subjective impression. Too many of us look at a graph superficially and develop intuitive impressions based on the pattern we see. Instead, we should scrutinize the graph and search for distortions of the type illustrated in Fig. 1.1. We should analyze the *numerical* information given in the graph instead of being misled by its general shape.

Drawings of objects are sometimes used to represent different quantities. For example, army tanks have been used to represent military expenditures; cows, to depict amounts of dairy production; and houses, to depict amounts of home construction. But the use of cleverly drawn two- and three-dimensional objects can be misleading. A comparison of the dollar amounts in Fig. 1.1 (c) reveals that wives earn 57% as much as their husbands do. However, if we draw the "wives'" dollar bill so that its length and width are *both* 57% as long as the length and width of the "husbands'" dollar bill, we get an area that is $0.57 \times 0.57 = 0.3249$ (or 32%) as large. We therefore create the very misleading visual impression that the wives' earnings are 32% of their husband's earnings, whereas in reality the correct value is 57%.

Another variety of statistical "lying" is often inspired by small sample results. The toothpaste preferences of only 10 dentists should not be the basis for a generalized claim such as "Caressed toothpaste is recommended by 7 out of 10 dentists." Even if the sample is large, it must be unbiased and representative of the population from which it comes; otherwise, the sample may lead to wrong results.

Sometimes the numbers themselves can be deceptive. An average annual salary of $27,735.29 sounds precise and tends to instill a high degree of confidence in its accuracy. The figure of $27,700 doesn't convey that same sense of precision and accuracy. Just because a statistic is very precise and has many decimal places does not necessarily mean that it is accurate, though.

Continental Airlines ran full-page ads boasting better service. In referring to lost baggage, the ads claimed that this is "an area where we've already improved

100% in the last six months." Do you really believe that they no longer lose any baggage at all? That's what the 100% improvement figure actually means.

"Ninety percent of all our cars sold in this country in the last 10 years are still on the road." Millions of consumers heard that commercial message and got the impression that those cars must be well built to last through those long years of driving. What the auto manufacturer failed to mention was that 90% of the cars it sold in this country were sold within the last three years. The claim was technically correct, but it was very misleading.

When discussing deceptive or misleading statistics, we cannot stress this point enough: Data collected carelessly can be absolutely worthless, even if the sample is large. It might be convenient to mail thousands of questionnaires and use only those that are returned, but such samples may be seriously biased. It might be even more convenient to set up a 900 phone number that respondents pay to call, but such sample results may be seriously biased. The person conducting the survey should select the sample subjects; the subjects should not select themselves, as they do with mailed responses or 900-number phone surveys.

The preceding examples are a small sampling of the ways in which one can use statistics deceptively. Entire books have been devoted to this subject, including Darrell Huff's *How to Lie with Statistics* and Robert Reichard's *The Figure Finaglers*. Understanding these practices will be extremely helpful in evaluating the statistical data we find in everyday situations.

1.3   EXERCISES   BASIC CONCEPTS

1. A graph similar to Fig. 1.2 appeared in *Car and Driver* magazine. What is wrong with it?
2. Seventy-two percent of Americans squeeze the toothpaste tube from the top. This and other not-so-serious findings are presented in *The First Really Impor-*

FIGURE 1.2
Car Braking Distances

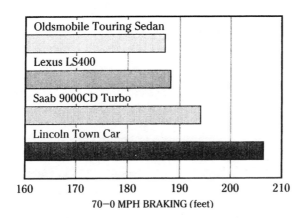

tant Survey of American Habits. Those results are based on 7000 respondents from the 25,000 mailed questionnaires. What is wrong with this survey?

3. "According to a nationwide survey of 250 hiring professionals, scuffed shoes was the most common reason for a male job seeker's failure to make a good first impression." Newspapers carried this statement based on a poll commissioned by Kiwi Brands, producers of shoe polish. Comment.

4. The Australian Minister of Labor stated, "We look forward to the day when everyone will receive more than the average wage." Comment.

5. In a study on college campus crimes committed by students under the influence of alcohol or drugs, a mail survey of 1875 students was conducted. A *USA Today* article noted, "Eight percent of the students responding anonymously say they've committed a campus crime. And 62% of that group say they did so under the influence of alcohol or drugs." Assuming that the number of students responding anonymously is 1875, how many actually committed a campus crime while under the influence of alcohol or drugs?

6. A study conducted by the Insurance Institute for Highway Safety found that the Chevrolet Corvette had the highest fatality rate—"5.2 deaths for every 10,000." The car with the lowest fatality rate was the Volvo, with only 0.6 deaths per 10,000. Does this mean that the Corvette is not as safe as a Volvo?

7. The Labor Department reported that the weekly pay of women is about 70% that of men. One reason for this is discrimination based on sex. Cite a second reason that might help to explain the discrepancy between the salaries of men and women.

8. A study by Ralph Frerichs (UCLA) showed that family incomes are related to the risk of dying because of heart disease. Higher family income levels corresponded to lower heart disease death rates.
   a. Does this imply that more earned money *causes* the risk of dying of heart disease to be lower?
   b. Identify a factor that could explain the correspondence.

9. In order to research recognition of fax machine brand names, you plan to conduct a telephone survey of 500 consumers in the United States. What would be wrong with using the telephone directory as the population from which your sample is drawn?

10. A college conducts a survey of its alumni in an attempt to determine their typical annual salary. Would alumni with very low salaries be likely to respond? How would this affect the result? Identify one other factor that might affect the result.

11. An employee earning $400 per week was given a 20% cut in pay as part of her company's attempt to reduce labor costs. After a few weeks, this employee's dissatisfaction grew and her threat to resign caused her manager to offer her a 20% raise. The employee accepted this offer because she assumed that a 20% raise would make up for the 20% cut in pay.
    a. What was the employee's weekly salary after she received the 20% cut in pay?
    b. Use the salary figure from part *a* to find the amount of the 20% increase and determine the weekly salary after the raise.
    c. Did the 20% cut followed by the 20% raise get the employee back to the original salary of $400 per week?

12. A marketing study began with 1000 consumers. A year later, 100 of the original consumers could not be located, and 300 new consumers were included. Which of the following statements about this new group are correct?

FIGURE 1.3
America's Chemical Industry: Capital Expenditures and Operating Costs for Pollution Abatement

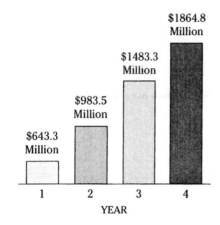

a. There are 1200 consumers in the new group.
b. The original group size, when increased by 33%, yields the size of the new group.
c. The original group size, when increased by 20%, yields the size of the new group.
d. Twenty-five percent of the group is new.

13. An article in *Forbes 400* magazine commented on the 400 wealthiest Americans. It noted that the average worth of those who were divorced at least once was $819 million, whereas those who remained with the same spouse had an average worth of only $617 million. The article stated that if you plan to remain with the same spouse, "make darn sure he or she is worth taking a $200 million hit for." Comment.

14. In an advertising supplement inserted in *Time* magazine, the increases in expenditures for pollution abatement were shown in a graph similar to Fig. 1.3. What is wrong with the figure?

1.3 EXERCISES **BEYOND THE BASICS**

15. A researcher at the Sloan-Kettering Cancer Research Center was once criticized for falsifying data. Among his data were figures obtained from 6 groups of subjects, with 20 individual subjects in each group. These values were given for the percentage of successes in each group: 53%, 58%, 63%, 46%, 48%, 67%. What's wrong?

16. If an employee is given a cut in pay of x percent, find an expression for the percent raise that would return the salary to the original amount.

17. A *New York Times* editorial criticized a chart caption that described a dental rinse as one that "reduces plaque on teeth by over 300%." What does it mean to reduce plaque by over 300%?

1.4 STATISTICS AND COMPUTERS

Computers now play a vital role in almost every aspect of statistical analysis. The widespread availability of computers and software packages has made the use of statistics possible for people of different mathematical backgrounds, but there is also greater opportunity for the misuse of statistics. It is important to recognize that statistical software and computers have a very serious limitation: they mindlessly follow instructions, even if those instructions are inappropriate or absurd. Computers don't do the necessary human reasoning or exercise judgment. An understanding of the principles of statistics is an important prerequisite for correctly interpreting computer results. Even if we don't actually employ computers in this course, it is useful to develop some skill in interpreting computer displays of statistical analyses, such as those that are found throughout this text.

Among the most popular statistical software packages are Minitab, SPSS (Statistical Package for the Social Sciences), SAS (Statistical Analysis System), and BMDP (Biomedical Data Processing). These packages tend to be extensive and expensive, but Minitab and SPSS are available in inexpensive student versions.

MINITAB

This text includes many references to Minitab statistical software. Minitab is available in a standard version that will run on microcomputers, workstations, minicomputers, and mainframes. A student edition of Minitab is also available. Originally developed as a tool for teaching introductory statistics courses, Minitab is now widely used by more than two thousand colleges as well as by many people in business and industry.

Minitab can be run with commands or a menu-driven interface. This text uses Minitab's commands because they more clearly describe the operations they perform. The procedure for loading Minitab varies with different systems, so consult with your instructor. After loading Minitab, the screen should display MTB >.

ENTERING DATA

SET C1 is the Minitab command that allows you to enter data in a column that is designated by the label C1. Minitab can store different collections of data in different columns. Each column is represented by a number, such as C1, C2, C3. For example, suppose we want to enter these values of home living areas (in square feet): 3060, 1600, 2000, 1300, and 2000. With the MTB > prompt displayed, begin by typing SET C1, then press the RETURN (or ENTER) key. Minitab will respond by displaying the prompt DATA >. Type the numbers and press the RETURN key at the end of each line. When all the data have been entered, type ENDOFDATA and press the return key. The following sequence of entries will cause the values listed above to be stored in a column identified as C1.

```
MTB > SET C1
DATA> 3060 1600 2000 1300 2000
DATA> ENDOFDATA
```

READ C1 C2 is the Minitab command that allows you to enter data in two different columns. Use READ C1 C2 C3 for three columns, and so on. With SET, you enter all the data in one operation; with READ, you enter the data one row at a time. For example, the entries of

```
MTB > READ C1 C2
DATA> 66 115
DATA> 65 107
DATA> 64 110
DATA> ENDOFDATA
```

cause three pairs of data to be entered in columns C1 and C2. Again, note that the process of entering the data is ended by the command ENDOFDATA (which can be abbreviated as END). The use of READ tends to be slower because you enter only one row at a time, but it is useful when you want to take the extra time to be sure that your data are matched correctly.

DISPLAYING DATA

PRINT C1 is the command used to display the data stored in column C1. This command is especially useful for verifying that data have been entered correctly. It's also helpful when confusion reigns and you forget which data sets are stored where. Entry of the command PRINT C1 C2 will result in a display of the values stored in columns C1 and C2.

SAVING AND RETRIEVING DATA

You can save data with the SAVE command that is used with a file name. For example, SAVE 'STATDATA' permanently stores all the current information in a computer file. The name of the file must be enclosed within single quotes, and it should be unique (different from any name already used). To save on a disk in drive B, type SAVE and the file name in this format: SAVE 'B:STATDATA'. RETRIEVE 'STATDATA' is the command that retrieves the data previously stored in a computer file. The name of the file must be enclosed within single quotes. (To retrieve from a disk in drive B, type RETRIEVE 'B:STATDATA'.)

MISCELLANEOUS NOTES

There are a few important rules that will help you work with Minitab successfully. First, *don't use commas in numbers*. For example, enter 32156.50 instead of 32,156.50. Second, if you know you have entered a wrong number, there are several ways to correct it:

1. If you haven't yet hit the RETURN key, backspace and type over the wrong entry.
2. If you have already hit the RETURN key, you can reenter the correct data set. If you prefer to replace, delete, or insert a number, use the formats suggested

AIRLINES SAMPLE

Airline companies once used an expensive accounting system to split up income from tickets that involved two or more companies. They now use a sampling method whereby a small percentage of these "split" tickets is randomly selected and used as a basis for dividing up all such revenues. The error created by this approach can cause some companies to receive slightly less than their fair share, but these losses are more than offset by the clerical savings accrued by dropping the 100% accounting method. This new system saves companies millions of dollars each year.

THE LITERARY DIGEST POLL

In the 1936 presidential race, *Literary Digest* magazine ran a poll and predicted an Alf Landon victory, but Franklin D. Roosevelt won by a landslide. Maurice Bryson notes, "Ten million sample ballots were mailed to prospective voters, but only 2.3 million were returned. As everyone ought to know, such samples are practically always biased." He also states, "Voluntary response to mailed questionnaires is perhaps the most common method of social science data collection encountered by statisticians, and perhaps also the worst." (See Bryson's "The *Literary Digest* Poll: Making of a Statistical Myth," *The American Statistician*, Vol. 30, No. 4.)

by the following examples.

LET C3(7) = 9	**Replaces** the 7th entry of column C3 with the number 9.
DELETE 3 C5	**Deletes** the entry in the 3rd row of column C5.
INSERT 5 6 C1 9	**Inserts** the number 9 in column C1 between rows 5 and 6.
ENDOFDATA	

To do arithmetic with data, use the LET command. The following examples demonstrate how to use LET.

LET C3 = C1 + C2	Creates column C3 by adding columns C1 and C2.
LET C2 = C2/5	Divides each entry of column C2 by 5.
LET C5 = C2 - C1	Creates column C5 by subtracting the column C1 values from those in column C2.
LET C6 = C1*C2	Creates column C6 by multiplying the corresponding entries from columns C1 and C2.
LET C7 = C1**2	Creates column C7 by squaring the values in column C1. The symbol ** is used for exponentiation.

1.4 EXERCISES   BASIC CONCEPTS

1. Load Minitab and use the SET C1 command to enter 2, 3, 5, 8, and 12 in column C1; then enter PRINT C1 to display them.
2. Load Minitab and enter 65, 77, 98, 67, 87, 83, 84, and 72 in column C2; then enter PRINT C2 to display them.
3. Use Minitab's READ command to enter the following scores in columns C3, C4, and C5. After entering ENDOFDATA, enter PRINT C3 C4 C5 to display those scores.

5	82	270
7	77	315
4	62	253
2	91	238

4. Use Minitab's READ command to enter the following scores in columns C6, C7, and C8; then enter PRINT C6 C7 C8 to display them.

87.3	12	3.21
95.0	16	2.92
77.9	16	2.67
85.4	17	3.02

5. After completing Exercises 1 through 4, enter the command SAVE 'EXERCISES'. Now enter the command STOP to exit Minitab, then load Minitab again and enter RETRIEVE 'EXERCISES'. Enter PRINT C1 – C8 and note the result.
6. Try to retrieve one of the data sets installed with Minitab. If using Release 8 of the standard version of Minitab, enter RETRIEVE 'TREES' and then

PRINT C1 C2 C3. If using Release 8 of the student edition of Minitab, enter
RETRIEVE 'NIELSEN' and then PRINT C1 – C6. (If unsuccessful, you
may have to consult with your instructor.) Describe the results.

7. After loading Minitab, enter the commands given below. Describe the result.

```
MTB > SET C9
DATA> 25(12.345)
DATA> ENDOFDATA
MTB > PRINT C9
```

8. Enter the command SET C10 and proceed to enter these scores:

     2   4   7   85   90   102.4,

then enter ENDOFDATA. Enter PRINT C10 to verify the scores are correct.

   a. Enter LET C11 = C10/5; then display the entries in C11 by entering
       PRINT C11. Describe the results.
   b. Enter LET C12 = C10**2; then display the entries in C12 by entering
       PRINT C12. Describe the results.

1.4 EXERCISES   BEYOND THE BASICS

9. Use the same data from Exercise 1 and enter the scores in Minitab's column
   C10. Enter each of the commands given below and, on the basis of the results
   and the name of the command, describe what each command does.
   a. MEAN C10   c. MINIMUM C10
   b. MAXIMUM C10   d. SUM C10

10. Repeat Exercise 9 after entering the Minitab command LET C10 =
    C10 * 100. How does this particular LET command affect the data stored in
    column C10? How are the results in parts *a* through *d* affected by that change?

Vocabulary List

Define and give an example of each term.

statistics	statistic	countable
population	qualitative data	nominal level of measurement
sample	quantitative data	ordinal level of measurement
process data	discrete	interval level of measurement
parameter	continuous	ratio level of measurement

Review

This chapter described the general nature of statistics along with some of its uses
and abuses, while presenting some very basic concepts dealing with the nature of
data. Section 1.1 discussed statistics as a discipline. We defined these fundamental
and important terms: *population, process, sample, parameter,* and *statistic.* The use
of statistics sometimes involves all the data in a complete population or all the data

from a process, and it sometimes involves samples drawn from a population or a process. Section 1.2 discussed the effect of different arrangements of data, such as lists or tables. We distinguished between qualitative data and quantitative data and noted that some quantitative data are *discrete,* whereas others are *continuous.* Also, data may be categorized according to one of these levels of measurement: *nominal, ordinal, interval,* and *ratio.* Section 1.3 presented uses of statistics as well as several examples of intentional or unintentional abuses. Section 1.4 discussed computer usage and introduced some fundamentals of Minitab.

Review Exercises

1. A consumers' group measures the actual horsepower of a sample of lawn mowers labeled as 12 hp. The sample is obtained by selecting 3 lawn mowers from each manufacturer.
   a.   Are the values obtained discrete or continuous?
   b.   Identify the level of measurement (nominal, ordinal, interval, ratio) for the horsepower values.
2. A process consists of filling 10-ounce potato chip bags. This process is monitored as follows: Every hour, 25 bags are randomly selected and weighed. As plant manager, why is it important that you treat the results as a sample drawn from a *process?*
3. A process corresponds to the numbers of customers entering a bank in half-hour intervals. As branch manager, why is it important to treat these numbers as process data if you wish to provide timely service to each entering customer?
4. In obtaining data on the following, determine which of the four levels of measurement (nominal, ordinal, interval, ratio) is most appropriate.
   a.   The religions of a sample of consumers
   b.   Movie ratings of 1, 2, 3, or 4 stars
   c.   The body temperature (in degrees Celsius) of runners who just completed a marathon
   d.   The weights of runners who just completed a marathon
   e.   Consumer product ratings of "recommended, acceptable, not acceptable"
5. Identify each number as being discrete or continuous.
   a.   The Minolta Corporation surveyed 703 small business owners.
   b.   The New York Metropolitan Transit Authority conducted a survey of commuting times, and the first such time is 47.23 minutes.
   c.   A consumer check of packaging revealed that a container of milk contained 30.4 ounces.
6. Census takers have found that in obtaining people's ages, they get more people of age 50 than of age 49 or 51. How might this occur?
7. A news report states that the police seized forged record albums with a value of $1 million. How do you suppose the police computed the value of the forged albums, and in what other ways can that value be estimated? Why might the police be inclined to exaggerate the value of the albums?
8. The *Poughkeepsie Journal* reported that "among 2800 stocks followed by 54 brokerages, 70 percent had consensus ratings of "buy" or "strong buy." A "buy" rating means that the stock is predicted to outperform the market as a whole. The report concluded that "70% of stocks cannot outperform the market." Do you agree with this conclusion? Explain.

ARE YOUR DATA ACCURATE?

1 If the computer project below is completed, compare your error rate to the 11.6% rate given by *PC Magazine*. Identify at least two major factors that would tend to make your error rate different from 11.6%. Describe at least one recommended procedure that would lower the error rate.

2 Refer to the 150 home selling prices in Appendix B to answer the following:

   a. Identify at least one important factor suggesting that a sample of recent home selling prices is not representative of the population of all home values.

   b. Is this a sample of discrete data or continuous data? Explain your choice.

   c. Categorize those values according to the appropriate level of measurement (nominal, ordinal, interval, ratio). Explain your choice.

3 Collect an example from a current newspaper or magazine in which data have been presented in a potentially deceptive manner. Identify the source from which the example was taken, explain briefly the way in which the data might be deceptive, and suggest how the data might be presented more fairly.

Computer Project

Use Minitab or any other available statistics software package to enter the 150 home selling prices in Appendix B. Enter the values in thousands of dollars. For example, the first entry of 179,000 would be entered as 179. Enter the data once, and make corrections only as you enter the data. Answer the following questions before checking your completed list.

1. Obtain a printed copy of the 150 scores and carefully compare them to the original 150 scores in Appendix B. How many errors did you make? (According to *PC Magazine*, "Studies have shown that the process of hand-keying data is associated with an error rate of 11.6 percent.")

2. Rank the 150 scores. The Minitab command RANK C1 AND PUT INTO C2 creates a column C2 that consists of the column C1 data arranged in order from lowest to highest. Then use the command PRINT C2 to obtain a printed copy of the 150 scores after they have been ranked by the program. Identify the lowest and highest home selling prices. Examination of these values will often reveal errors. For example, if a home selling price of $150,000 is incorrectly entered as 15, it is likely to appear near the top of the ranked list, where we would recognize that a selling price of $15,000 is not realistic.

3. After correcting any errors you made, store the data in a file named SP (for selling prices) by using the command SAVE 'SP'.

CHAPTER 2

Statistics from Populations and Processes

Data Sets: How Do We Understand Them?

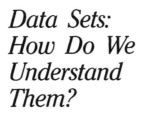 **Y**ou've just landed a job in beautiful Dutchess County, located in upstate New York. You plan to buy a home, but you don't have a good sense of what homes cost in that area. You know that the cost of comparable homes can vary by large amounts depending on their locations. A home on the beach at Malibu will cost much more than a similar home in a housing development. Because buying a home is such an expensive and important decision, you decide to do some investigation. Table 2.1 lists the actual selling prices of 150 randomly selected homes that were recently sold in Dutchess County.

A visual examination of those selling prices may provide some insight, but it is generally difficult to draw meaningful conclusions from a collection of raw data that are simply listed in no particular order. We need to look further into the data and do something with them. As one example, we might add the 150 selling prices and then divide that total by 150. The result will be an average that helps us understand the data. There are several other things we might do. The major objective of this chapter is to develop a variety of methods that will give us more insight into data sets such as the one listed in Table 2.1.

TABLE 2.1
Selling Prices (in dollars) of 150 Dutchess County Homes

179,000	126,500	134,500	125,000	142,000	164,000
146,000	129,000	141,900	135,000	118,500	160,000
89,900	169,900	127,500	162,500	152,000	122,500
220,000	141,000	80,500	152,000	231,750	180,000
185,000	265,000	135,000	203,000	141,000	159,000
182,000	208,000	96,000	156,000	185,500	275,000
144,900	155,000	110,000	154,000	151,500	141,000
119,000	108,500	126,500	302,000	130,000	140,000
123,500	153,500	194,900	165,000	179,900	194,500
127,500	170,000	160,000	135,000	117,000	235,000
223,000	163,500	78,000	187,000	133,000	125,000
116,000	135,000	194,500	99,500	152,500	141,900
139,900	117,500	150,000	177,000	136,000	158,000
211,900	165,000	183,000	85,000	126,500	162,000
169,000	175,000	267,000	150,000	115,000	126,500
215,000	190,000	190,000	113,500	116,300	190,000
145,000	269,900	135,500	190,000	98,000	137,900
108,000	120,500	128,500	142,500	72,000	124,900
134,000	205,406	217,000	94,000	189,900	168,500
133,000	180,000	139,500	210,000	126,500	285,000
195,000	97,000	117,000	150,000	180,500	160,000
181,500	124,000	125,900	165,000	122,000	132,000
145,900	156,000	136,000	142,000	140,000	144,900
133,000	196,800	121,900	126,000	164,900	172,000
100,000	129,900	110,000	131,000	107,000	165,900

2.1 OVERVIEW

In analyzing a data set, we should first determine whether we know all values for a complete population or process, or whether we know only the values for some sample. If we intend to use the data we have collected as the basis for making a general conclusion about a larger population, then what we have are known as *sample* data. That determination will affect both the methods we use and the conclusions we form.

We use methods of **descriptive statistics** to summarize or *describe* the important characteristics of a known set of data. If the 150 values given in Table 2.1 represent the selling prices of *all* homes sold in Dutchess County, then what we have are known as *population* data. We might then proceed to improve our understanding of this known population data by computing some average or by constructing a graph. In contrast to descriptive statistics, **inferential statistics** goes beyond mere description. We use inferential statistics when we use sample data to make *inferences* about a population.

Suppose we compute an average of the 150 values in Table 2.1 and obtain a value of $153,775. If exactly 150 homes are sold in Dutchess County and our list is complete, that average of $153,775 is a parameter that describes and summarizes known population data. But those values are the actual selling prices of 150 homes that were randomly selected from a larger population. Treating those 150 values as a sample drawn from a larger population, we might conclude that the average selling price for all Dutchess County homes sold is $153,775. In so doing, we have made an *inference* that goes beyond the known data.

This chapter deals with the basic concepts of descriptive statistics. Chapter 3 includes an introduction to probability theory, and the subsequent chapters deal mostly with inferential statistics. Descriptive statistics and inferential statistics are the two basic divisions of the subject of statistics.

IMPORTANT CHARACTERISTICS OF DATA

We use the tools of descriptive statistics to understand an otherwise unintelligible collection of data. The following four characteristics of data are extremely important, and they can give us considerable insight:

1. Nature or shape of the distribution, such as bell-shaped
2. Representative value, such as an average
3. Measure of scattering, or variation, or consistency of the data
4. For process data, the pattern over time

Of these characteristics, the first and second are the easiest to understand because they involve calculations and graphs that are direct and simple. In contrast, the important measure of variation or consistency involves a calculation with several steps, and its meaning can be easily lost. Although the third characteristic, variation, is the most difficult to understand, it is often the most important in business applications. The fourth characteristic, pattern over time, is present when the data are from a process.

We can learn something about the first characteristic, nature or shape of the distribution, by organizing the data and constructing graphs, as in Sections 2.2, 2.3, and 2.4. In Section 2.5 we will learn how to obtain representative scores. We will measure the extent of scattering, or variation or consistency, among data as we use the tools described in Section 2.6. In Section 2.7 we will learn about measures of position so that we can better analyze or compare various scores. In Section 2.8 we will learn about methods for exploring data sets. As we proceed through this chapter, we will refer to the 150 scores given in Table 2.1, and our insight into that data set will increase as we reveal its characteristics.

No matter how carefully we apply these descriptive techniques, if the data themselves are collected carelessly, our conclusions may be grossly incorrect. When collecting data, we must be extremely careful about the methods we use (common sense is often a critical requirement). If we plan our data collection with care and thoughtfulness, we can often learn much by using simple methods. But if our data collection is thoughtless, we may well end up with something that is misleading or worthless.

2.2 SUMMARIZING DATA

When beginning an analysis of a large set of scores, such as those listed in Table 2.1, we must often organize and summarize the data by developing tables and graphs. A **frequency table** lists classes or categories of scores along with their corresponding *frequencies*. Table 2.2 is a frequency table that summarizes the raw data in Table 2.1. A frequency table usually doesn't include the tally marks, but they are helpful in determining the frequencies that represent the numbers of scores that fall into the different classes. The following are some basic terms we can use to describe the important elements of a frequency table.

TABLE 2.2
Frequency Table for Home Selling Prices

SELLING PRICE (DOLLARS)	TALLY MARKS	FREQUENCY
50,000– 74,999	|	1
75,000– 99,999	⊩ ||||	9
100,000–124,999	⊩ ⊩ ⊩ ⊩ ||	22
125,000–149,999	⊩ ⊩ ⊩ ⊩ ⊩ ⊩ ⊩ ⊩ ⊩ ||	47
150,000–174,999	⊩ ⊩ ⊩ ⊩ ⊩ ⊩ |	31
175,000–199,999	⊩ ⊩ ⊩ ⊩ |||	23
200,000–224,999	⊩ ||||	9
225,000–249,999	||	2
250,000–274,999	|||	3
275,000–299,999	||	2
300,000–324,999	|	1

DEFINITIONS

Lower class limits are the smallest numbers that can actually belong to the different classes or categories of values (such as 50,000–74,999). (Table 2.2 has lower class limits of 50,000, 75,000, ...)

Upper class limits are the largest numbers that can actually belong to the different classes. (Table 2.2 has upper class limits of 74,999, 99,999, ...)

The *class boundaries* are obtained by increasing the upper class limits and decreasing the lower class limits by the same amount so that there are no gaps between consecutive classes. The amount to be added or subtracted is one-half the difference between the upper limit of one class and the lower limit of the following class. (In Table 2.2 the boundaries are 49,999.5, 74,999.5, ...)

The *class marks* are the midpoints of the classes. (Table 2.2 has class marks of 62,499.5, 87,499.5, ...)

The *class width* is the difference between two consecutive lower class limits (or class boundaries). (Table 2.2 has a class width of 25,000.)

The process of actually constructing a frequency table involves these key steps:

1. *Decide on the number of classes your frequency table will contain.* Guideline: The number of classes should be between 5 and 20. The actual number of classes may be affected by convenience, size of the data set, or other subjective factors. (For the data of Table 2.1, we began with 10 classes.)
2. *Find the class width* by dividing the number of classes into the range. (The range is the difference between the highest and lowest scores.) Round the result *up* to a convenient number. This rounding up (not off) is not only convenient, but it also guarantees that all the data will be included in the frequency table. (If the number of classes divides into the range evenly with no remainder, you may need to add another class for all the data to be included.)

$$\text{class width} = \text{round } up \text{ of } \frac{\text{range}}{\text{number of classes}}$$

[For the data of Table 2.1, the class width is the round up of (302,000 − 72,000)/10; we rounded 23,000 up to 25,000 for convenience.]

3. *Select as a starting point either the lowest score or a convenient value slightly less than the lowest score.* This starting point is the lower class limit of the first class. (Starting with $72,000 would be more awkward than starting with a round number like $50,000.)
4. *Add the class width to the starting point to get the second lower class limit.* Add the class width to the second lower class limit to get the third, and so on. (In Table 2.2 we used lower class limits of $50,000, $75,000, and so on.)
5. *List the lower class limits in a vertical column and enter the upper class limits,* which we can easily identify at this stage.
6. *Represent each score by a tally* in the appropriate class.
7. *Replace the tally marks in each class with the total frequency count* for that class.

When constructing frequency tables, use these guidelines:

1. *All classes should be mutually exclusive.* That is, each score must belong to exactly one class.
2. *All classes should be included,* even if the frequency is zero.
3. *All classes should use the same width.* However, it is sometimes impossible to avoid open-ended intervals such as "65 years or older."
4. *All classes should have convenient numbers for class limits.*
5. *The number of classes should be between 5 and 20.* Use a smaller number of classes for smaller data sets and a larger number of classes for larger data sets.

Note that the resulting frequency table, as shown in Table 2.2, actually has 11 classes instead of the 10 we began with. This is a result of selecting class limits that are convenient. We could have forced the table to have exactly 10 classes, but we would get messy limits such as $72,000–$96,999.

Table 2.2 provides much more useful information by making more intelligible the otherwise unintelligible list of 150 selling prices of homes. Yet we do not gain this information without some loss. In constructing frequency tables, we may lose the accuracy of the raw data. To see how this loss occurs, consider the first class of $50,000–$74,999. Table 2.2 shows that there is one score in that class, but there is no way to determine from the table exactly what that score is. We cannot reconstruct the original 150 selling prices from Table 2.2. The exact values have been compromised for the sake of comprehension.

Summarizing data generally involves a compromise between accuracy and simplicity. A frequency table with too few classes is simple but not accurate. A frequency table with too many classes is more accurate but not as easy to understand. The best arrangement is arrived at subjectively. We will overcome some of these difficulties in Section 2.8, when we discuss stem-and-leaf plots.

We can use a variation of the standard frequency table when we want to obtain cumulative totals. *The cumulative frequency for a class is the sum of the frequencies for that class and all previous classes.* Table 2.3 is an example of a **cumulative frequency table,** and it corresponds to the same 150 selling prices presented in Table 2.2. A comparison of the frequency column of Table 2.2 and the cumulative frequency column of Table 2.3 reveals that we can obtain the latter values from the former by starting at the top and adding on the successive values. For example, the cumulative frequency of 10 from Table 2.3 represents the sum 1 and 9 from Table 2.2.

Another important variation of the basic frequency table is the **relative frequency table.** We can find the relative frequency for a particular class by dividing the class frequency by the total of all frequencies.

$$\text{relative frequency} = \frac{\text{class frequency}}{\text{sum of all frequencies}}$$

Table 2.4 shows the relative frequencies for the 150 home selling prices summarized in Table 2.2. The first class has a relative frequency of $1/150 = 0.007$. (Relative frequencies can also be given as percentages.) The second class has a relative frequency of $9/150 = 0.060$, and so on. Relative frequency tables make it easier for us to compare distributions of different sets of data by using comparable relative frequencies instead of original frequencies that might be very different.

TABLE 2.3
Cumulative Frequency

SELLING PRICE (DOLLARS)	CUMULATIVE FREQUENCY
L.T. 75,000	1
L.T. 100,000	10
L.T. 125,000	32
L.T. 150,000	79
L.T. 175,000	110
L.T. 200,000	133
L.T. 225,000	142
L.T. 250,000	144
L.T. 275,000	147
L.T. 300,000	149
L.T. 325,000	150

TABLE 2.4
Relative Frequency

SELLING PRICE (DOLLARS)	FREQUENCY	RELATIVE FREQUENCY
50,000–74,999	1	0.007
75,000–99,999	9	0.060
100,000–124,999	22	0.147
125,000–149,999	47	0.313
150,000–174,999	31	0.207
175,000–199,999	23	0.153
200,000–224,999	9	0.060
225,000–249,999	2	0.013
250,000–274,999	3	0.020
275,000–299,999	2	0.013
300,000–324,999	1	0.007

(See Exercise 25.) Although Table 2.4 includes the original frequencies, they are usually omitted in a relative frequency table.

In the next section, we will explore graphic ways to depict data so that they are easy to understand. Frequency tables are necessary for some of the graphs. The graphs are often necessary for considering the way the scores are distributed; thus frequency tables are important prerequisites for other, more useful concepts.

2.2 EXERCISES   BASIC CONCEPTS

In Exercises 1–4, identify the class width, class marks, and class boundaries for the frequency table indicated.

1. Table 2.5
2. Table 2.6
3. Table 2.7
4. Table 2.8

In Exercises 5–8, construct the cumulative frequency table corresponding to the frequency table indicated.

5. Table 2.5
6. Table 2.6
7. Table 2.7
8. Table 2.8

In Exercises 9–12, construct the relative frequency table corresponding to the frequency table indicated.

9. Table 2.5
10. Table 2.6
11. Table 2.7
12. Table 2.8

TABLE 2.5		TABLE 2.6		TABLE 2.7		TABLE 2.8	
IQ	FREQUENCY	TIME (HOURS)	FREQUENCY	WEIGHT (KG)	FREQUENCY	SALES (DOLLARS)	FREQUENCY
80–87	16	0.0–7.5	16	16.2–21.1	16	0–21	2
88–95	37	7.6–15.1	18	21.2–26.1	15	22–43	5
96–103	50	15.2–22.7	17	26.2–31.1	12	44–65	8
104–111	29	22.8–30.3	15	31.2–36.1	8	66–87	12
112–119	14	30.4–37.9	19	36.2–41.1	3	88–109	14
						110–131	20

In Exercises 13–16, modify the class limits of the frequency table indicated so that the new limits make the table easier to read. Omit the frequencies, because they cannot be determined. You may have to change the number of classes.

13. Table 2.5
14. Table 2.6
15. Table 2.7
16. Table 2.8

In Exercises 17–20, use the given information to find the upper and lower limits of the first class.

17. Assume that you have a collection of scores representing the selling prices (rounded to the nearest dollar) of used cars ranging from a low of $750 to a high of $19,950. You wish to construct a frequency table with 10 classes.
18. In a study of client stock transactions, a broker has amounts ranging from $38.50 to $73,568.75. She intends to construct a frequency table with 15 classes.
19. A scientist at the Medassist Pharmaceutical Company is investigating the time (in seconds) required for a certain chemical reaction to occur. The experiment is repeated 200 times, and the results vary from 17.3 s to 42.7 s. (You wish to construct a frequency table with 12 classes.)
20. The County Auto Repair Company records service times required for brake jobs, and they vary from 41.3 min to 95.6 min. You want to construct a frequency table with 14 classes.
21. The ages of airliners cause some safety and economic concerns. Forty commercial aircraft randomly selected in the United States have the ages given below (based on data reported by Aviation Data Services). Construct a frequency table with 14 classes.

3.2	22.6	23.1	16.9	0.4	6.6	12.5	22.8
26.3	8.1	13.6	17.0	21.3	15.2	18.7	11.5
4.9	5.3	5.8	20.6	23.1	24.7	3.6	12.4
27.3	22.5	3.9	7.0	16.2	24.1	0.1	2.1
7.7	10.5	23.4	0.7	15.8	6.3	11.9	16.8

22. On page 30 are the fill weights (in ounces) of a sample of 21 flour bags collected on two days. The weights are supposed to be near 80 oz (5 lb). Construct a relative frequency table for both days and compare the performance for the two days. (Because this is a process, assume that it is statistically stable on each day.) *(continued)*

Tuesday:	80.1	80.0	79.8	80.0	79.9	79.9	80.2	79.9	80.0
	80.0	80.0	80.1	79.8	80.1	79.9	79.9	80.3	79.7
	80.0	80.1	79.8						

Thursday:	80.0	80.2	80.2	80.3	80.3	80.1	80.5	80.4	80.4
	80.4	80.3	80.5	80.1	80.2	80.2	80.2	80.3	80.3
	80.3	80.6	80.5						

23. Listed below are the actual energy consumption amounts as reported on the electric bills for one residence. Each amount is in kilowatt-hours and represents a two-month period. Construct a frequency table with 6 classes.

728	774	859	882	791	731	838	862	880	831
759	774	832	816	860	856	787	715	752	778
829	792	908	714	839	752	834	818	835	751
837									

24. Listed below are the daily sales totals (in dollars) for 44 days at a large retail outlet in Orange County, California. Construct a frequency table with 10 classes.

24,145	66,644	52,250	59,708	34,132	30,284	55,254
33,650	29,099	68,945	32,097	37,229	34,804	31,995
37,196	34,423	31,987	36,802	39,921	37,858	35,420
39,897	37,809	35,018	38,366	47,563	42,906	38,295
46,351	41,160	38,275	44,249	33,310	38,812	43,952
65,798	50,857	43,923	61,923	37,052	46,285	64,842
25,597	66,892					

2.2 EXERCISES   BEYOND THE BASICS

25. The Life Trust Insurance Company must defend its rate structure that includes higher premiums for male drivers. Part of the defense is based on gender differences related to drunk driving. The tables below include a frequency table of alcohol consumption prior to arrest of male inmates serving a sentence for DWI (driving while intoxicated) and the corresponding table for females (based on data from the U.S. Department of Justice). First construct the corresponding relative frequency tables, then use those results to compare the distributions. Note that it is difficult to compare the original frequencies, but it is much easier to compare the relative frequencies. Are the relative frequency distributions roughly the same?

ETHANOL CONSUMED BY MEN (OUNCES)	FREQUENCY
0.0– 0.9	249
1.0– 1.9	929
2.0– 2.9	1,545
3.0– 3.9	2,238
4.0– 4.9	1,139
5.0– 9.9	3,560
10.0–14.9	1,849
15.0 or more	1,546

(continued)

ETHANOL CONSUMED BY WOMEN (OUNCES)	FREQUENCY
0.0– 0.9	7
1.0– 1.9	52
2.0– 2.9	125
3.0– 3.9	191
4.0– 4.9	30
5.0– 9.9	201
10.0–14.9	43
15.0 or more	72

26. Listed below are two sets of scores that are supposed to be heights (in inches) of randomly selected adult males. One of the sets consists of real heights actually obtained from randomly selected adult males, but the other set consists of numbers that were fabricated. Construct a frequency table for each set of scores. By examining the two frequency tables, identify the set of data that you believe to be false.

70	73	70	72	72	68	71	70	73	70	72	72	67	77
71	73	71	67	71	73	69	71	66	74	76	66	76	75
68	72	67	72	71	66	77	68	75	67	68	73	74	76
71	73	72	70	71	73	67	71	77	66	69	69	67	77

27. A table in a recent issue of *USA Today* included the data shown here that were based on U.S. Bureau of the Census observations. Refer to the five guidelines for constructing frequency tables. Which of them are not followed?

AGE	U.S. POPULATION (MILLIONS)
Under 5	18.1
5–13	30.3
14–17	14.8
18–24	28.0
25–34	43.0
35–44	33.1
45–54	22.8
55–64	22.2
65–84	9.1
85/older	2.8

28. The *price-to-earnings ratio* (defined as a company's current stock price per share, divided by its annual earnings per share) is one measure of a company's most recent performance. A low price-to-earnings ratio (PE ratio) indicates a relatively low stock price compared to its annual earnings. Suppose we have recorded the PE ratio for 28 natural resource companies (gas, oil, coal, and so on) for two consecutive years. Construct a relative frequency table for both years and determine whether the proportions have changed much from the first year to the second year.

1st year:	25	35	29	9	12	42	19	16	18	20	14	19
	23	26	11	12	8	33	51	13	17	15	44	13
	26	14	7	24								

2nd year:	12	36	28	7	24	38	18	10	18	22	15	15
	24	21	10	14	16	35	53	13	9	9	41	15
	27	13	11	26								

2.3 PICTURES OF DATA

In Section 2.2 we saw that frequency tables transform a disorganized collection of raw scores into an organized and understandable summary. In this section we consider ways of presenting data in pictorial form to make them easier to understand. We attempt to show that one graphic illustration can replace a mass of data.

HISTOGRAMS

A **histogram** is a common graphic way of presenting data. Histograms are especially important because they show the shape or distribution of the data, an extremely important characteristic.

We generally construct a histogram to represent a set of scores after we have completed a frequency table. The standard format for a histogram usually involves a vertical scale for frequencies and a horizontal scale for values of the data being represented. We use bars to represent the individual classes of the frequency table. The width of each bar extends from its lower class boundary to its upper class boundary so that we can mark the class boundaries on the horizontal scale. (However, the histogram will be easier to read if we use class limits or class marks instead of class boundaries.) As an example, Fig. 2.1 is the histogram that corresponds directly to Table 2.2 in the previous section.

FIGURE 2.1
Histogram Depicting the Data in Table 2.2

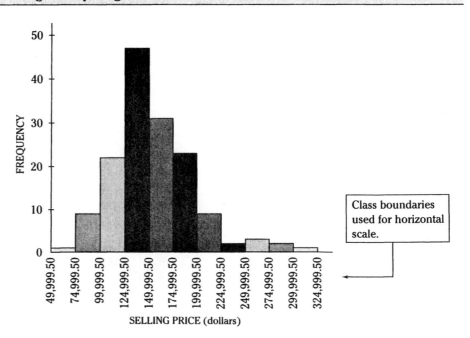

Class boundaries used for horizontal scale.

SELLING PRICE (dollars)

FIGURE 2.2
Relative Frequency Histogram of the Data in Table 2.2

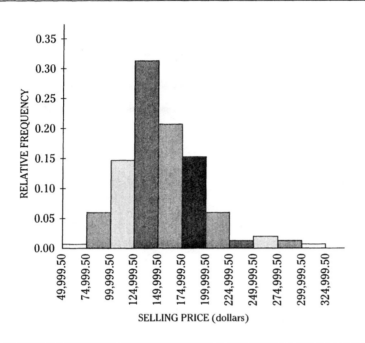

NEW DATA
COLLECTION
TECHNOLOGY

Measuring or coding
products and manually
entering results is one
way of collecting data,
but technology is now
providing us with alter-
natives that are not so
susceptible to human er-
ror. Supermarkets use
bar code readers to set
prices and analyze in-
ventory and buying hab-
its. Manufacturers are
increasingly using "di-
rect data-entry" devices,
such as electronic mea-
suring gauges connected
directly to a computer
that records results. A
third possibility is voice
data entry, such as the
Voice Data Logger. It
consists of a headset
connected to a small box
that attaches to the
speaker's belt. The box
transmits the data to a
computer.

Before we construct a histogram from a completed frequency table, we need
to consider the scales used on the vertical and horizontal axes. The maximum
frequency (or the next highest convenient number) should suggest a value for the
top of the vertical scale, with 0 at the bottom. In Fig. 2.1, we designed the vertical
scale to run from 0 to 50. The horizontal scale should accommodate all the classes
of the frequency table. Ideally, the vertical height of the histogram should be about
3/4 of the total width. Both axes should be clearly labeled.

A **relative frequency histogram** has the same shape as a histogram. The
horizontal scale is also the same, but the vertical scale is marked with *relative
frequencies* instead of actual frequencies. We can modify Fig. 2.1 to be a relative
frequency histogram by labeling the vertical scale as "relative frequency" and
changing the values on the vertical scale to range from 0 to about 0.350 or 0.040
(see Fig. 2.2). (The highest relative frequency for this data set is 0.313.)

You can use the Minitab program to design histograms. Shown below are two
different Minitab displays that you can obtain by using the HISTOGRAM command. After entering the 150 home selling prices in the column designated as C1,
enter the Minitab command HISTOGRAM C1 to get the first display. The second
display uses Minitab's high-resolution capability; you can obtain it by entering the
command GHISTOGRAM C1. The values listed in the display under "Midpoint"
are the class marks after they have been rounded to convenient numbers. For
example, the first class has a midpoint of $81,583.34 but Minitab rounds this value
to $80,000.00. The first class has a count value of 5, indicating that it contains 5
scores.

```
MTB > HISTOGRAM C1
Histogram of C1   N = 150
Midpoint   Count
    80000       5  *****
   100000       9  *********
   120000      32  ********************************
   140000      33  *********************************
   160000      29  *****************************
   180000      16  ****************
   200000      12  ************
   220000       6  ******
   240000       2  **
   260000       3  ***
   280000       2  **
   300000       1  *
```

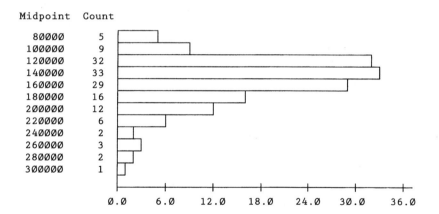

PARETO CHARTS

Histograms are bar graphs in which the horizontal scale (*x*-axis) represents a *quantitative* variable (such as the selling prices of homes). In contrast, **Pareto charts** are bar graphs for categorical or *qualitative* data. In a Pareto chart, the bars are arranged according to the frequency values so that the tallest bar is at the left; the smaller bars are farther to the right, as in Fig. 2.3. Like the histogram, the vertical axis in a Pareto chart can represent frequencies or relative frequencies. The Pareto chart is an extremely valuable tool in business applications. Because the largest frequencies appear as the leftmost bars, attention is focused on the more important categories.

Figure 2.3 depicts results similar to those that Conrail obtained in a recent study of customer desires. Conrail was about to invest millions of dollars in computers, tracking, cars, and engines in an effort to upgrade its quality of service. To its surprise, the single item customers most desired was "on-time delivery," as shown by the Pareto chart of Fig. 2.3. Because on-time delivery was at that time

FIGURE 2.3
Pareto Chart of Customer Desires

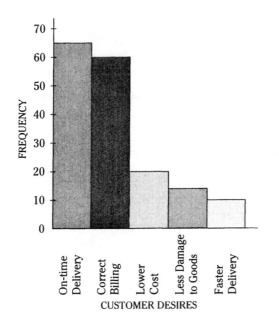

FIGURE 2.4
Pareto Chart of Causes of Late Departures

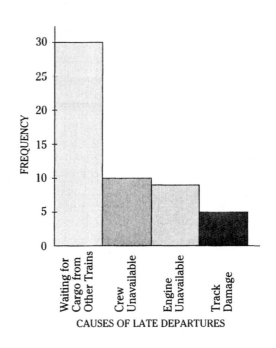

already near 90%, most Conrail managers felt that lower delivery cost or faster delivery would be more highly desired. However, "90% on-time" also implies "10% late," and each day hundreds of tons of items were not arriving on time. Further investigation of late deliveries showed that they were caused mostly by late departures.

In Fig. 2.4, the Pareto chart for causes of late departures shows that the biggest problem was delays while waiting for cargo from other trains. Investigation of all late trains revealed that one particular train (from Atlanta, Georgia, to Harrisburg, Pennsylvania) had been late *every day* for more than three years! This single train, which carried important auto parts, was holding up more than a dozen other trains out of Harrisburg, causing all of them to be late. Conrail contacted the manager of the Atlanta center and found that the late departure of that single train was due to late arrivals of UPS trucks. The Atlanta manager, now realizing the tremendous impact of that one train, contacted UPS and found that they had decided to hold back certain UPS trucks because it was simpler to let other trucks go out first. The UPS manager had no problem rearranging the order of the UPS trucks so that the Atlanta train could leave on time. This simple change cost nothing, yet it resulted in a substantial increase in on-time delivery.

In this case study, Conrail used Pareto charts often and saw directions for further investigations. Such examples are quite common, and they illustrate that even though Pareto charts are very simple tools, they can be extremely beneficial.

PIE CHARTS

FIGURE 2.5
Pie Chart of Causes of
Late Departures

Figure 2.5 shows a **pie chart** that depicts the qualitative data from the Conrail study as slices of a pie. Constructing a pie chart isn't very difficult. It merely involves slicing the pie into proper proportions. With the Conrail data, if the portion representing "waiting for cargo" is 57% of the total, then the wedge representing that category should be 57% of the total. (The central angle should be $0.57 \times 360° = 205°$.) Note that the pie chart of Fig. 2.5 and the Pareto chart of Fig. 2.4 depict the same data in different ways. If you compare the Pareto chart and the pie chart, you will see that the Pareto chart does a better job of showing the relative sizes of the different components.

Frequency tables and graphs such as histograms make it possible for us to see the distribution or shape of data. In many serious statistical analyses of data, the distribution is a critically important feature. A car designer, for example, must know something about the distribution of human heights and weights so that sales aren't lost because some drivers aren't comfortable. Many procedures in statistics require a data set with a distribution that is approximately bell-shaped, so we must often construct frequency tables and/or graphs to determine the shape of a distribution before proceeding with many methods in statistics.

FIGURE 2.5
Pie Chart of Causes of
Late Departures

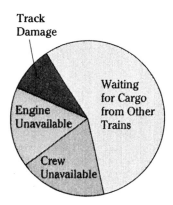

2.3 EXERCISES   BASIC CONCEPTS

1. Construct a histogram that corresponds to the frequency table given here. The data are based on information reported by Aviation Data Services.

AIRPLANE AGE (YEARS)	FREQUENCY
0.0–5.9	10
6.0–11.9	8
12.0–17.9	9
18.0–23.9	9
24.0–29.9	4

2. Construct a relative frequency histogram that corresponds to the frequency table in Exercise 1.
3. Insurance companies constantly research ages at death and causes of death. Construct a histogram that corresponds to the frequency table given here. The data are based on a *Time* magazine study of people who died from gunfire in America during one week.

AGE AT DEATH	FREQUENCY
16–25	22
26–35	10
36–45	6
46–55	2
56–65	4
66–75	5
76–85	1

4. Construct a relative frequency histogram that corresponds to the frequency table in Exercise 3.

5. Construct a histogram that corresponds to the frequency table given here. The data are based on energy consumption reported on an electric bill for 31 two-month periods.

ENERGY (KWH)	FREQUENCY
700–719	2
720–739	2
740–759	4
760–779	4
780–799	2
800–819	2
820–839	8
840–859	2
860–879	2
880–899	2
900–919	1

6. Construct a relative frequency histogram that corresponds to the frequency table in Exercise 5.

7. Construct a histogram that corresponds to the frequency table given here. The data are based on daily sales for 44 days at a large retail outlet in Orange County, California.

SALES (DOLLARS)	FREQUENCY
20,000–24,999	1
25,000–29,999	2
30,000–34,999	9
35,000–39,999	14
40,000–44,999	5
45,000–49,999	3
50,000–54,999	2
55,000–59,999	2
60,000–64,999	2
65,000–69,999	4

8. Construct a relative frequency histogram that corresponds to the frequency table in Exercise 7.

9. A utility company examines and identifies the causes of the 65 times in the past three years when a power outage occurred. The results are as follows:

CAUSE	FREQUENCY
Transformer improperly grounded	18
Power surge	4
Ice collected on lines	8
Lines shorted by tree contact	22
Traffic accident	7
Other causes	6

    a.   Construct a Pareto chart for the causes. How could the utility company use such information to improve the quality of service?   *(continued)*

b. Construct a pie chart for the given data.
c. Compare the Pareto chart and the pie chart. Which does a better job of depicting the relative size of the components?

10. Listed below are the problems found in 122 defective aluminum can lids.

PROBLEM	FREQUENCY
Lids too thick or too thin	46
Lids bent	12
Lids not round	8
Lid tabs not properly formed	36
Lids not of proper diameter	9
Other problems	11

a. Construct a Pareto chart. (Use a vertical scale of percentages.) How could management use such information to improve the quality of lids and decrease the number of defects?
b. Construct a pie chart for the given data.
c. Compare the Pareto chart with the pie chart. Which does a better job of depicting the relative size of the problems?

11. Use the following data (based on data from the U.S. Commerce Department) to construct (a) a Pareto chart and (b) a pie chart.

IMPORTS INTO THE UNITED STATES (IN BILLIONS OF DOLLARS)

Canada	81.4
Japan	95.2
Germany	27.4
Taiwan	26.3
United Kingdom	18.7
Other	212.9

12. Jobs are obtained through many different sources, including help-wanted ads, professional job placement companies, networking (making contacts through acquaintances), and mass mailing of resumes. To study the effectiveness of these approaches 400 subjects were randomly selected and the results are summarized below. (The data are based on results from the National Center for Career Strategies.)
a. Use the data to construct a pie chart.
b. Use the same data to construct a Pareto chart.
c. Compare the pie chart and the Pareto chart. Which is more effective in showing the relative importance of job sources?

JOB SOURCES OF SURVEY RESPONDENTS	NUMBER
Help-wanted ads	56
Executive search firms	44
Networking	280
Mass mailing	20

2.3   EXERCISES   BEYOND THE BASICS

13. Using a collection of sample data, we construct a frequency table with 10 classes. Then we construct the corresponding histogram. How is the histogram affected if we double the number of classes, but use the same vertical scale?

14. A **frequency polygon** is a variation of a histogram that uses line segments connected to points instead of using bars. Construct a frequency polygon for the data of Table 2.2 as follows: First, construct a vertical scale for frequencies ranging from 0 to 50, and a horizontal scale with class marks ranging from 62,499.50 to 312,499.50. Above each class mark, plot the point corresponding to the class frequency. After plotting the 11 points, extend the graph to the left and right so that it begins and ends with a frequency of 0.

15. An **ogive** (also called a **cumulative frequency polygon**) is a common graphic display that is used to show how many scores are above or below some level. Construct an ogive for the data of Table 2.2 as follows: First, construct a vertical scale of cumulative frequencies ranging from 0 to 150. With class frequencies of 1, 9, 22, . . . , 1, you can obtain the cumulative frequencies of 1, 10, 32, . . . , 150 by finding running totals as you go down the list of frequencies. For example, the third cumulative frequency of 32 is the sum of $1 + 9 + 22$. Use the class boundaries of 74,999.50, 99,999.50, . . . , 324,999.50 for the horizontal scale. Directly above each class boundary, plot a point corresponding to the cumulative frequency. After plotting the 11 points, connect them with straight line segments and then extend the graph to the left so that it begins with a cumulative frequency of 0.

2.4   PICTURES OF PROCESS DATA: RUN CHARTS

The main difference between process data and population data is the additional element of the time or sequence that is present in a process. Whereas a population is considered to be fixed, important characteristics of process data can change over time. One basic tool that we can use to graph process data is the **run chart** (or **trend chart**), in which we plot data sequentially on the horizontal time axis; then we connect the data points with line segments. The resulting graph allows us to see patterns over time so that we can better determine whether a process is running smoothly or whether undesirable changes are occurring.

As an example, consider the fill weights of 16 containers of peanut butter. Our process consists of using a machine to fill hundreds of such containers every day. Every half hour, we randomly select one jar and carefully measure its contents. Listed below are the 16 values obtained during one eight-hour shift. The data are in order by row.

| 16.1 | 16.0 | 15.9 | 16.1 | 15.8 | 15.9 | 16.2 | 16.0 |
| 16.1 | 15.9 | 16.2 | 16.0 | 15.9 | 16.0 | 16.1 | 16.0 |

The run chart generated by Minitab is shown in Fig. 2.6. Note that the sample numbers are shown on the horizontal scale. The contents (in ounces) are depicted

FIGURE 2.6
Run Chart of Filling Process

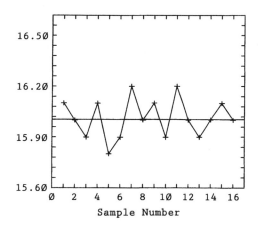

Sample Number

on the vertical scale. The first sample jar contained 16.1 oz, and it is represented by the point farthest to the left. The horizontal center line in the middle of the graph corresponds to 16.0 oz, the value that we are trying to obtain.

The run chart in Fig. 2.6 doesn't seem to reveal any obvious upward or downward trends, nor any cycles or unusual points. It displays only the natural variation present in any process. Such a process is described as being statistically stable.

DEFINITION

A process is *statistically stable* if it has only natural variation and its run chart has only random variation, with no patterns, cycles, or unusual points.

When a process is statistically stable, its data can be treated as if they came from a population; we can construct a histogram and find the values of important statistics such as the mean and the standard deviation (discussed in the following sections). Figure 2.7 is a histogram for the data listed above, and it shows that the process data have a distribution that is approximately bell-shaped. In contrast, consider this list of data collected from the *next* eight-hour shift:

| 16.0 | 15.8 | 15.9 | 16.0 | 16.2 | 16.1 | 16.3 | 16.1 |
| 16.2 | 16.3 | 16.4 | 16.3 | 16.4 | 16.5 | 16.3 | 16.5 |

The run chart (see Fig. 2.8) for this set of process data reveals an upward trend as well as natural variation. As time goes on, the second-shift process is putting more peanut butter into each jar. This example shows a process that is statistically unstable, and the first priority should be to stabilize the process. Only after

FIGURE 2.7
Histogram of Container Contents

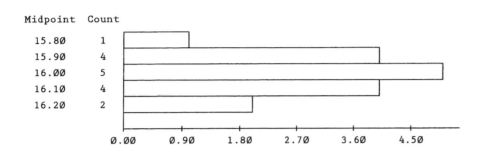

stability is achieved could we proceed to consider other important characteristics of the process. For example, is there too much variability, and too little consistency? On the whole, are the jars being overfilled or underfilled? We will address these questions later. For now, we will use run charts and subjectively judge whether the process is statistically stable, as in Fig. 2.6. Later sections will include more objective methods of analysis.

If a run chart resembles any of the graphs in Fig. 2.9, we will conclude that the process is not stable. In Fig. 2.9 (a), we have an obvious upward trend that corresponds to values that are increasing over time. If our jar-filling process were to follow this type of pattern, the jars would be filled with more and more peanut butter until they began to overflow, eventually leaving the employees knee-deep in peanut butter. This is not good.

FIGURE 2.8
Run Chart of Filling Process for the Second Shift

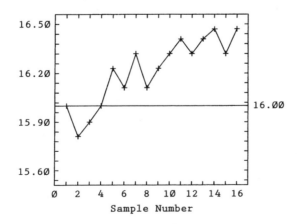

FIGURE 2.9
Run Charts Depicting Processes NOT Statistically Stable

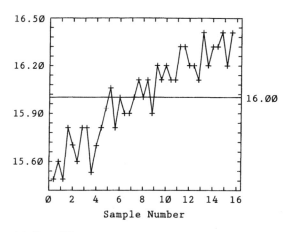

(a) Trend Up

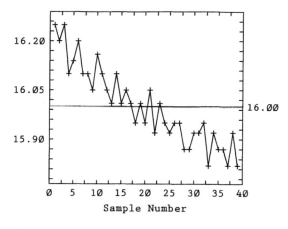

(b) Trend Down

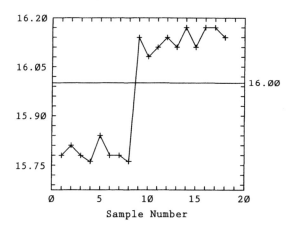

(c) Shift Up

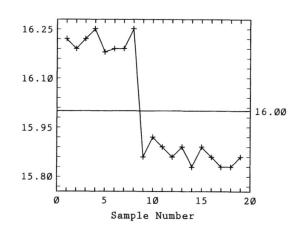

(d) Shift Down

In Fig. 2.9 (b), we have an obvious downward trend that corresponds to steadily decreasing values. Our jars would contain less and less peanut butter until they became extremely underfilled. Such a process would require a reworking of the jars to get them full enough for distribution to consumers.

In Fig. 2.9 (c), we have an upward shift. Perhaps the filling machine was adjusted after the eighth sample so that all subsequent values rose to a higher but stable value. In Fig. 2.9 (d), we have a downward shift indicating that the first few values were relatively stable; then something happened so that the last several values were relatively stable, but at a much lower level.

In Fig. 2.9 (e), we see a process that seems to be stable except for one exceptionally high value. It might be wise to investigate the cause of that unusual

FIGURE 2.9 *continued*

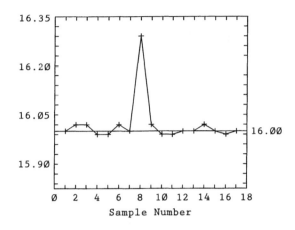

(e) Unusually High Value

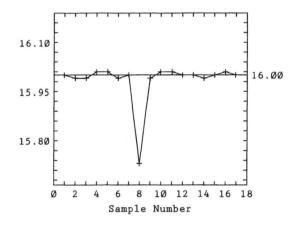

(f) Unusually Low Value

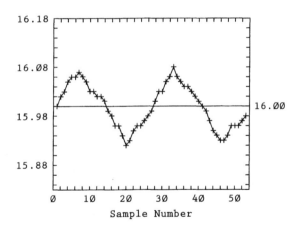

(g) Cyclical Pattern

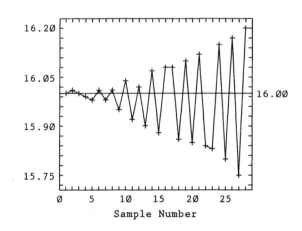

(h) Increasing Variation

value. Perhaps the jars became temporarily stuck so that some jars were filled twice instead of once. Figure 2.9 (f) shows another unusual value, but in this case it is exceptionally low.

The run chart of Fig. 2.9 (g) shows a pattern that is cyclical in the sense that there's a cycle or pattern that seems to repeat. That pattern is clearly nonrandom, and it therefore reveals a statistically unstable process. Perhaps periodic overadjustments are being made to the machinery with the effect that some desired value is continually being chased, but never captured.

In Fig. 2.9 (h), we see a common problem in quality control. The overall average value seems to remain about the same, but variability constantly increases over time. Some values become too high while others become too small, and the gap is increasing. The net effect will be products that vary more and more (such as overfilled and underfilled peanut butter jars) until almost all of them are worthless. Such trends have driven companies out of business.

Run charts are an important tool for monitoring the statistical stability of processes, and statistical stability is one of the important requirements for maintaining a process that produces quality goods and services.

2.4 EXERCISES   BASIC CONCEPTS

In Exercises 1–4, the given data represent departure times from home, as recorded by four different commuters for three consecutive weeks. In each case, construct a run chart and identify any pattern of instability that resembles any of the patterns in Fig. 2.9.

1.
M	T	W	TH	F
8:14	7:55	7:58	8:00	7:59
8:18	7:52	7:56	7:50	8:01
8:16	7:58	7:55	7:59	7:54

3.
M	T	W	TH	F
7:59	8:00	8:00	8:02	8:02
8:03	8:00	8:04	8:07	8:04
8:06	8:09	8:11	8:12	8:11

2.
M	T	W	TH	F
8:00	7:59	8:02	8:01	8:04
7:57	8:06	7:55	8:09	7:50
7:45	8:12	7:40	8:16	7:35

4.
M	T	W	TH	F
8:14	8:10	8:15	8:14	8:08
8:13	8:10	8:14	8:09	7:48
7:49	7:45	7:51	7:47	7:50

In Exercises 5–8, the given data represent the number of washing machines with chipped paint. The Telstar Appliance Company manufactures the washing machines during three 8-hr shifts each day. During each shift, workers randomly select 50 machines, inspect them carefully, and record the number of machines requiring paint repairs. Those numbers are given below for each shift on four consecutive days. In each case, construct a run chart and identify any pattern of instability that resembles any of the patterns in Fig. 2.9.

5.
Shift	1	2	3	1	2	3	1	2	3	1	2	3
Defects	3	4	8	2	3	9	5	4	11	3	5	9

6.
Shift	1	2	3	1	2	3	1	2	3	1	2	3
Defects	2	3	2	4	7	6	10	9	12	13	10	14

7.
Shift	1	2	3	1	2	3	1	2	3	1	2	3
Defects	1	2	1	2	2	1	7	8	8	9	8	8

8.
Shift	1	2	3	1	2	3	1	2	3	1	2	3
Defects	4	3	5	4	5	3	15	4	3	5	6	4

In Exercises 9–12, the given data represent the thickness of glue applied to fabric. The Flint Fabric Company supplies glued upholstery that is later installed in cars.

During the production process, workers randomly select one sample of the fabric every half hour and carefully measure the glue thickness. Each of the following exercises lists sixteen results for one work day. In each exercise, construct a run chart and identify any pattern of instability that resembles any of the patterns in Fig. 2.9. The data are listed in order by row.

9. 0.17   0.15   0.16   0.15   0.17   0.15   0.16   0.17
   0.14   0.15   0.09   0.08   0.06   0.08   0.07   0.06

10. 0.12   0.11   0.13   0.12   0.12   0.11   0.11   0.11
    0.12   0.24   0.11   0.12   0.13   0.11   0.12   0.13

11. 0.11   0.12   0.12   0.13   0.13   0.13   0.14   0.14
    0.14   0.15   0.16   0.15   0.16   0.16   0.17   0.19

12. 0.12   0.11   0.12   0.13   0.12   0.13   0.12   0.10
    0.12   0.14   0.09   0.13   0.09   0.15   0.08   0.17

In Exercises 13–16, the given data represent the diameters (in millimeters) of cylinder holes drilled for bulldozer engines. The holes are supposed to be 200 mm in diameter. The drill bit is replaced at the end of each day. Workers carefully measure every 10th hole and record the results from one day's production. Each of the following exercises lists in consecutive order the diameters of the holes selected in one day. In each case, construct a run chart and identify any pattern of instability that resembles any of the patterns in Fig. 2.9. The data are in order by row.

13. 200.1   199.9   200.0   200.1   200.0   199.8   200.2   200.0
    199.7   199.6   200.4   200.1   199.4   200.7   199.3   200.8
    199.6   199.2   199.9   199.2   200.9   199.1

14. 200.0   200.1   200.1   200.0   200.2   200.2   200.0   200.2
    200.1   200.1   200.0   199.9   199.9   200.0   199.9   199.8
    199.8   199.9   199.7   199.8   199.7   199.6

15. 200.0   200.1   200.1   199.8   199.8   200.1   199.9   199.8
    199.9   200.2   200.1   200.2   199.9   199.8   200.0   199.9
    200.1   200.2   199.8   200.2   200.1   200.0

16. 200.0   200.1   200.1   200.0   200.2   200.2   200.0   200.2
    200.1   198.7   200.0   199.9   199.9   200.0   199.9   199.9
    200.0   200.1   199.9   200.0   200.1   199.9

In Exercises 17–20, the given data represent the fill weights of a sample of 21 flour bags. The Kansas Flour Company uses a machine to fill bags of flour. During each filling production run, workers select one bag every 15 min and measure and record the weight in ounces. Each exercise lists the results for one day. In each case, construct a run chart and identify any pattern of instability that resembles any of the patterns in Fig. 2.9. The data are in order by row.

17. 80.1 80.0 80.2 80.0 79.8 79.9 80.0 80.0 79.9 79.9 80.0
    80.1 79.8 80.1 80.0 79.9 80.0 80.1 79.9 80.0 79.8

18. 80.1 80.0 80.2 80.0 79.8 79.9 80.0 80.1 79.9 79.9 80.0
    80.1 80.3 80.1 78.6 79.9 80.0 80.1 79.9 80.1 79.8

19. 81.1 81.0 81.0 80.9 80.7 80.8 80.5 80.6 80.4 80.4 80.3
    80.3 80.1 80.2 80.1 80.0 80.0 79.9 79.9 79.8 79.9

20. 79.7 79.8 79.8 79.7 79.6 79.6 79.7 79.8 79.8 81.0 81.1
    81.0 81.0 81.2 81.0 80.9 80.9 81.0 81.1 81.1 81.0

2.4   EXERCISES   BEYOND THE BASICS

21. Figure 2.9 (h) shows a process with a pattern of increasing variability. Sketch a run chart showing a pattern of decreasing variability. If you were managing the production of ball bearings to be used for aircraft wheels, would you try to change the pattern of decreasing variability? Explain.

22. The Jefferson Valley Bank monitors a new teller and records the time she requires to process customer transactions. In each of the following cases, refer to Fig. 2.9 and identify the pattern of instability that corresponds to the given circumstances.

    a. As the day passes by, the teller becomes increasingly tired and takes more time with each customer.

    b. The teller is a "morning person" who works efficiently and quickly in the morning, but is noticeably slower after lunch.

    c. The teller is new but gains confidence and experience as the day passes by and thus processes each customer faster than the preceding customer.

    d. The teller is a "night person" who works very slowly in the morning, but is noticeably faster all afternoon.

    e. The teller processes all customers in less than 5 min, except for one customer who required 25 min.

FIGURE 2.10
Histogram with the Mean as a Balance Point: If a fulcrum is placed at the position of the mean, it will balance the histogram.

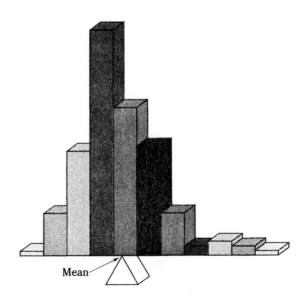

2.5 MEASURES OF CENTRAL TENDENCY

In the preceding sections, we considered frequency tables, graphs, and run charts. To identify a value that is typical or representative of the whole data set in each data picture, we need to identify a value that the sample scores tend to center around. And to do this, we need information about **measures of central tendency.** Here we discuss how to determine four measures of central tendency: the mean, the median, the mode, and the midrange.

MEAN

The arithmetic mean is the most important of all numerical descriptive measurements, and it corresponds to what most people call an *average*. As Fig. 2.10 shows, the mean is at the center of the data in the sense that it is a balance point for the data.

DEFINITION

The arithmetic mean of a list of scores is obtained by adding the scores and dividing the total by the number of scores. We will use this particular average frequently in this text, and will refer to it simply as the mean.

EXAMPLE Find the mean of the following sample of times (in minutes) for telephone calls in the technical support department of the Jefferson Valley Bank.

7   2   3   7   6   9   10   8   9   9

SOLUTION First add the scores.

$$7 + 2 + 3 + 7 + 6 + 9 + 10 + 8 + 9 + 9 = 70$$

Then divide the total by the number of scores present.

$$\frac{70}{10} = 7$$

The mean score is therefore 7 min.

Many formulas, developed for different statistics, involve the Greek letter Σ (capital sigma), which indicates summation of values. Letting x denote the value of a score, Σx means the sum of all scores. The symbol n is used to represent the **sample size,** which is the number of scores we are considering. We use the symbol N to represent the number of scores in the whole population.

HISTOGRAM GIVES CLUE TO PROBLEM

The *Journal of Quality Technology* reported a case in which a process engineer used statistics to correct a problem that became apparent through a histogram. When a large batch of transistors were measured for their individual "channel lengths," a histogram was constructed showing three distinct peaks. The process engineer wanted to determine whether the peaks were due to different tools, different types of raw material, or different people. The investigation revealed that the transistors came from three different tools, one that produced transistors with channel lengths too large, one with channel lengths too small, and one with channel lengths that were proper. The problem tools were replaced and the process was improved so the transistor channel lengths were much more consistent. The histogram provided the clue that led to an improved process.

The following formula states that the mean is the sum of all scores (Σx) divided by the number of scores.

Formula 2.1
$$\text{mean} = \frac{\Sigma x}{\text{number of scores}}$$

We can denote the result of Formula 2.1 by $\bar{x}$ if the available scores are samples from a larger population; if all scores of the population are available, then we can denote the computed mean by μ (lowercase Greek mu).

Notation

Σ	denotes *summation* of a set of values.
x	is the *variable* usually used to represent the individual raw scores.
n	represents the *number* of scores being considered in a sample.
N	represents the number of scores in a population.

$\bar{x} = \dfrac{\Sigma x}{n}$ denotes the *mean* of a set of *sample* scores.

$\mu = \dfrac{\Sigma x}{N}$ denotes the *mean* of all scores in some *population*.

Applying Formula 2.1 to the telephone-call times in the preceding example, we get the sample mean

$$\bar{x} = \frac{\Sigma x}{n} = \frac{70}{10} = 7 \text{ min}$$

According to the definition of mean, 7 is the central value of the 10 times given. Other definitions of averages involve different perceptions of how the center is determined. The median reflects another approach.

MEDIAN

DEFINITION

The *median* of a set of scores is the middle value when the scores are arranged in order of increasing magnitude.

To find the median, first *rank* the original scores (arrange them in increasing or decreasing order). Then count the number of scores.

1. If the number of scores is *odd,* the median is the number that is exactly in the middle of the list.
2. If the number of scores is *even,* you can find the median by computing the mean of the two middle numbers.

EXAMPLE Find the median of these times (in minutes) of telephone calls in the technical support department of the Jefferson Valley Bank:

7 2 3 7 6 9 10 8 9 9 10

SOLUTION Begin by arranging the scores in increasing order.

2, 3, 6, 7, 7, 8, 9, 9, 9, 10, 10

With these eleven times, the number 8 is located in the exact middle, so 8 min is the median.

EXAMPLE Find the median of these times (in minutes) of telephone calls in the technical support department of the Jefferson Valley Bank:

7 2 3 7 6 9 10 8 9 9

SOLUTION Again, begin by arranging the scores in increasing order.

2, 3, 6, 7, 7, 8, 9, 9, 9, 10

With these ten times, no single score is in the exact middle. Instead, the two scores of 7 and 8 share the middle. We therefore find the mean of those two scores.

$$\frac{7 + 8}{2} = \frac{15}{2} = 7.5$$

That is, the sample median is 7.5 min.

You can use Minitab to find the mean and median of a set of scores. After entering the scores in the column designated as C1, enter MEAN C1 and MEDIAN C1. Shown below are the Minitab results for the data in the preceding example.

```
MTB > SET C1
DATA> 7 2 3 7 6 9 10 8 9 9
DATA> END
MTB > MEAN C1
   MEAN = 7.000
MTB > MEDIAN C1
   MEDIAN = 7.500
```

Instead of entering individual commands for the mean, median, and other statistics, you could use the Minitab command DESCRIBE C1. The result of this command will be a display that includes the number of scores, the mean, the median, the minimum, the maximum, and several other statistics that will be described in the following sections.

FLORENCE NIGHTINGALE

Florence Nightingale (1820–1910) is known to many as the founder of the nursing profession, but she also saved thousands of lives by using statistics. When she encountered an unsanitary and undersupplied hospital, she improved those conditions and then used statistics to convince others of the need for more widespread medical reform. She developed original graphs to illustrate that during the Crimean War, more soldiers died as a result of unsanitary conditions than were killed in combat. Florence Nightingale pioneered the use of social statistics as well as graphics techniques.

MODE

> ## DEFINITION
>
> The *mode* is obtained from a collection of scores by selecting the score that occurs most frequently. In those cases where no score is repeated, we stipulate that there is no mode. In those cases where two scores both occur with the same greatest frequency, we say that each one is a mode, and we refer to the data set as being *bimodal*. If more than two scores occur with the same greatest frequency, each is a mode, and we refer to the data set as being *multimodal*.

EXAMPLE
  a. The scores 1, 2, 2, 2, 3, 4, 5, 6, 7, 9 have a mode of 2.
  b. The scores 2, 3, 6, 7, 8, 9, 10 have no mode because no score is repeated.
  c. The scores 1, 2, 2, 2, 3, 4, 5, 6, 6, 6, 7, 9 have modes of 2 and 6 because 2 and 6 both occur with the same highest frequency. This data set is bimodal.

Among the four measures of central tendency we are now considering, the mode is the only one that we can use with data at the nominal level of measurement, as the next example illustrates.

EXAMPLE
A research and development team consists of 12 engineers, 8 physicists, and 2 chemists. Although we cannot numerically average these disciplines, we can report that "engineer" is the modal profession because that discipline has the highest frequency.

MIDRANGE

> ## DEFINITION
>
> The midrange is the average we obtain by adding the highest score to the lowest score and then dividing the result by 2.
>
> $$\text{midrange} = \frac{\text{highest score} + \text{lowest score}}{2}$$

EXAMPLE
Find the midrange of the scores 2, 3, 6, 7, 7, 8, 9, 9, 9, 10.

$$\text{midrange} = \frac{10 + 2}{2} = 6$$

EXAMPLE For the sample of 150 home selling prices listed in Table 2.1, find the values of the (a) mean, (b) median, (c) mode, and (d) midrange.

SOLUTION a. The sum of the 150 selling prices is $23,066,256, so that

$$\bar{x} = \frac{\Sigma x}{n} = \frac{\$23,066,256}{150}$$
$$= \$153,775$$

b. After arranging the scores in increasing order, we find that the 75th and 76th scores are both $144,900, so the median is $144,900. (You can easily arrange the scores in increasing order by constructing a stem-and-leaf plot [see Section 2.8] or by using a computer program such as Minitab.)

c. The most frequent (five times) selling price is $126,500, so it is the mode. No other value occurs more than four times.

d. The midrange is found as follows:

$$\text{midrange} = \frac{\text{highest score} + \text{lowest score}}{2}$$
$$= \frac{302,000 + 72,000}{2}$$
$$= \$187,000$$

We now summarize these results.

Mean	$153,775
Median	$144,900
Mode	$126,500
Midrange	$187,000

When finding values of sample statistics, it is often misleading to express results with a greater degree of precision (or decimal places) than the original raw data warrant. We therefore use the following round-off rule.

ROUND-OFF RULE

A simple rule for rounding answers is to carry one more decimal place than was present in the original data. We should round only the final answer and not intermediate values. For example, the mean of 2, 3, 5 is expressed as 3.3. Since the original data were whole numbers, we rounded the answer to the nearest tenth. We round the mean of 2.1, 3.4, 5.7 to 3.73.

As stated in the preceding rule, we should not round numbers in the middle of our calculations. We should round only the final result.

WEIGHTED MEAN

The **weighted mean** is useful in many situations where the scores vary in degree of importance. Consider, for example, the determination of a final average for a course that includes four tests plus a final examination. If the respective grades are 70, 80, 75, 85, and 90, the mean of 80 does not reflect the greater importance placed on the final exam. Let's suppose that the instructor counts the respective tests as 15%, 15%, 15%, 15%, and 40%. The weighted mean then becomes

$$\frac{(70 \times 15) + (80 \times 15) + (75 \times 15) + (85 \times 15) + (90 \times 40)}{100}$$

$$= \frac{1050 + 1200 + 1125 + 1275 + 3600}{100}$$

$$= \frac{8250}{100} = 82.5$$

This computation suggests a general procedure for determining a weighted mean. Given a list of scores $x_1, x_2, x_3, \ldots, x_n$ and a corresponding list of weights $w_1, w_2, w_3, \ldots, w_n$, we can obtain the weighted mean by computing as follows:

Formula 2.2 $\text{weighted mean} = \dfrac{\Sigma(w \cdot x)}{\Sigma w}$ where w = weight

That is, first multiply each score by its corresponding weight; then find the total of the resulting products, thereby evaluating Σwx. Finally, add the values of the weights to find Σw and divide the latter value into the former.

MEAN FROM A FREQUENCY TABLE

We can modify Formula 2.2 so that we can approximate the mean from a frequency table. The sample of home selling price data from Table 2.1 have been entered in Table 2.9, where we use the class marks as representative scores and the frequencies as weights. Then the formula for the weighted mean leads directly to Formula 2.3, which we can use to approximate the mean of a set of scores in a frequency table.

Formula 2.3 $\bar{x} = \dfrac{\Sigma(f \cdot x)}{\Sigma f}$ where x = class mark
f = frequency

Formula 2.3 is really just a variation of Formula 2.1, $\bar{x} = \Sigma x/n$. When data are summarized in a frequency table, Σf is the total number of scores, so that $\Sigma f = n$. Also, $\Sigma(f \cdot x)$ is simply a quick way of adding up all the scores.

We can now compute the weighted mean.

$$\bar{x} = \frac{\Sigma(f \cdot x)}{\Sigma f} = \frac{23,199,925}{150} = \$154,666$$

TABLE 2.9
Finding Σf and $\Sigma (f \cdot x)$

SELLING PRICE (DOLLARS)	FREQUENCY f	CLASS MARK x	$f \cdot x$
50,000– 74,999	1	62,499.5	62,499.5
75,000– 99,999	9	87,499.5	787,495.5
100,000 124,999	22	112,499.5	2,474,989.0
125,000–149,999	47	137,499.5	6,462,476.5
150,000–174,999	31	162,499.5	5,037,484.5
175,000–199,999	23	187,499.5	4,312,488.5
200,000–224,999	9	212,499.5	1,912,495.5
225,000–249,999	2	237,499.5	474,999.0
250,000–274,999	3	262,499.5	787,498.5
275,000–299,999	2	287,499.5	574,999.0
300,000–324,999	1	312,499.5	312,499.5
Total	150		23,199,925

$$\uparrow \qquad\qquad\qquad\qquad\qquad \uparrow$$
$$\Sigma f \qquad\qquad\qquad\qquad\qquad \Sigma (f \cdot x)$$

When we used the original collection of scores to calculate the mean directly, we obtained a mean of $153,775, so the value of the weighted mean obtained from the frequency table is quite accurate. The procedure we use is justified by the fact that a class such as $50,000–$74,999 can be represented by its class mark of $62,499.5 and the frequency number of that class indicates that the representative score of $62,499.5 occurs one time. In essence, we are treating Table 2.9 as if it contained one score of $62,499.5, nine values of $87,499.5, and so on.

THE BEST MEASURE OF CENTRAL TENDENCY

Selectively choosing one of the four basic measures of central tendency (mean, median, mode, midrange) can lead to deception. Consider our 150 home selling prices that yielded these results:

Mean:	$153,775	Mode:	$126,500
Median:	$144,900	Midrange:	$187,000

Technically, someone could use any of the four preceding figures as the representative home selling price. A real estate salesperson might want to encourage a sale by emphasizing that a particular home is a bargain compared to the high value of $187,000. A wise buyer (such as you, after you've taken this course) might try to get a lower price by emphasizing the low value of $126,500. We can see that ignorance of these concepts can be very costly.

Even when we have no self-interest to promote, the selection of the most representative value is not always easy. The different measures of central tendency have different advantages and disadvantages, and there are no objective criteria that determine the one most representative for all data sets. Some of the important advantages and disadvantages are summarized in Table 2.10 and are illustrated by several of the exercises in this section.

TABLE 2.10
Comparison of Measures of Central Tendency

MEASURE	DEFINITION	HOW COMMON?	EXISTENCE	TAKES EVERY SCORE INTO ACCOUNT?	AFFECTED BY EXTREME SCORES?	MISCELLANEOUS COMMENTS
Mean	Sum of scores divided by number of scores	Most familiar	Always exists	Yes	Yes	Used throughout this book; works well with many statistical methods
Median	Middle score	Commonly used	Always exists	No	No	Often a good choice if there are some extreme scores
Mode	Most frequent score	Sometimes used	Might not exist; may be more than one mode	No	No	Appropriate for data at the nominal level
Midrange	$\dfrac{\text{high} + \text{low}}{2}$	Rarely used	Always exists	No	Yes	Very sensitive to extreme values

General comments:
- For a data collection that is approximately symmetric with one mode, the mean, median, mode, and midrange tend to be about the same.
- For a data collection that is obviously asymmetric, it would be good to report both the mean and median.
- The mean is relatively *reliable*. That is, when samples are drawn from the same population, the sample means tend to be more consistent than the other measures (consistent in the sense that the means of samples drawn from the same population don't vary as much as the other measures).

SKEWNESS

A comparison of the mean, the median, and the mode can reveal information about the characteristic of skewness, as defined below and as illustrated in Fig. 2.11.

> **DEFINITION**
>
> A distribution of data is *skewed* if it is not symmetric and extends more to one side than the other.

Data skewed to the left are said to be *negatively skewed*. The mean and the median are to the left of the mode. Also, while not always predictable, negatively skewed data generally have the mean to the left of the median. Data skewed to the right (said to be *positively skewed*) have the mean and the median to the right of the mode. Again, while not always predictable, positively skewed data generally have the mean to the right of the median. In reality, distributions skewed to the right are more common than those skewed to the left.

FIGURE 2.11
Skewness

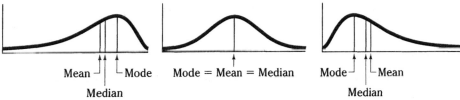

| Mean ┘│└ Mode | Mode = Mean = Median | Mode┘│└ Mean |
| Median | | Median |

(a) SKEWED TO THE LEFT
(Negatively Skewed): The
mean and median are to the
left of the mode.

(b) SYMMETRIC
(Zero Skewness): The mean,
median, and mode are the
same.

(c) SKEWED TO THE RIGHT
(Positively Skewed): The
mean and median are to the
right of the mode.

In this section we considered measures designed to identify a central or representative value. In the next section we consider the use of measures of dispersion to
describe the variation within sets of data.

2.5 EXERCISES BASIC CONCEPTS

In Exercises 1–12, find the (a) mean, (b) median, (c) mode, and (d) midrange
for the given data.

1. The following lists the amount of time (in hours) that a sample of office
   managers spent on paperwork in one day (based on data from Adia Personnel
   Services).

   | 3.7 | 2.9 | 3.4 | 0.0 | 1.5 | 1.8 | 2.3 | 2.4 | 1.0 | 2.0 |
   | 4.4 | 2.0 | 4.5 | 0.0 | 1.7 | 4.4 | 3.3 | 2.4 | 2.1 | 2.1 |

2. The article "Determining Statistical Characteristics of a Vehicle Emissions
   Audit Procedure" (by Lorenzen, *Technometrics,* Vol. 22, No. 4) includes the
   following carbon monoxide emissions data (in g/m) for vehicles.

   | 5.01 | 14.67 | 8.60 | 4.42 | 4.95 | 7.24 |
   | 7.51 | 12.30 | 14.59 | 7.98 | 11.53 | 4.10 |

3. The following are the times (in minutes) required to resolve customer complaints.

   | 8 | 1 | 2 | 4 | 12 | 7 | 8 | 10 | 10 | 11 | 10 |

4. The following are the annual salaries (in dollars) for a sample of employees at
   the Jefferson Valley Bank.

10,000	10,000	20,000	20,000	10,000	10,000	20,000	20,000
10,000	10,000	20,000	20,000	10,000	10,000	20,000	20,000
10,000	10,000	20,000	125,000				*(continued)*

In a labor dispute, which result would a labor representative be likely to use in an attempt to prove that workers are underpaid? Which would the owners use in an attempt to prove that workers are well paid? Which of the four results seems to represent the data most fairly?

5. A quality control analyst selects and weighs (in ounces) one candy bar each minute. The following *sample* consists of nine such weights. The process is statistically stable. Your goal is to produce candy bars with a net weight of 6 oz.

    6.0   6.1   6.2   5.8   5.9   6.0   6.3   5.7   6.0

6. The following sample consists of five credit card account balances (in dollars) at the Jefferson Valley Bank.

    325   675   1095   250   325

    Suppose the value of $1095 is incorrectly included as $2095. Now find the mean, median, mode, and midrange.

7. The Acton Paper Company makes reels of paper from mixtures of wood pulp and recycled paper. A sample of nine reels is obtained by selecting every 10th reel; the numbers of imperfections are counted and the results are listed below.

    8   7   4   11   6   7   8   5   9

8. The blood alcohol concentrations of 15 drivers involved in fatal accidents and then convicted with jail sentences are given below (based on data from the U.S. Department of Justice).

    0.27   0.17   0.17   0.16   0.13   0.24   0.29   0.24
    0.14   0.16   0.12   0.16   0.21   0.17   0.18

9. The 40 commercial aircraft owned by Air America are found to have the ages given below (based on data reported by Aviation Data Services). (Is this a sample or a population?)

    3.2   22.6   23.1   16.9   0.4   6.6   12.5   22.8   7.7   15.8
    26.3   8.1   13.6   17.0   21.3   15.2   18.7   11.5   10.5   6.3
    4.9   5.3   5.8   20.6   23.1   24.7   3.6   12.4   23.4   11.9
    27.3   22.5   3.9   7.0   16.2   24.1   0.1   2.1   0.7   16.8

10. A student working part time for a moving company in Boston, MA, collected the following load weights (in pounds) for 50 consecutive customers.

    8,090   3,250   12,350   4,510   8,770   5,030   12,700   12,430
    8,800   6,170   8,450   10,330   10,100   13,410   7,280   8,160
    13,490   17,810   7,470   11,450   13,260   9,310   15,970   26,580
    7,540   7,770   6,400   14,800   14,760   6,820   11,430   4,480
    7,200   13,520   16,200   10,780   10,510   17,330   7,450   6,390
    9,110   10,630   3,670   14,310   9,140   10,220   9,900   11,600
    11,860   12,010

11. Listed below are the actual energy consumption amounts as reported on the electric bills for one residence. Each amount is in kilowatt-hours and represents a two-month period.

    728   774   859   882   791   731   838   862   880   831   837
    759   774   832   816   860   856   787   715   752   778
    829   792   908   714   839   752   834   818   835   751

12. Listed below are the daily sales totals (in dollars) for 44 days at a large retail outlet in Orange County, California.

24,145	39,921	30,284	43,923	38,366	31,987	32,097
33,650	47,563	34,804	55,254	44,249	59,708	64,842
37,196	66,644	37,858	31,995	61,923	46,285	37,229
39,897	29,099	42,906	35,420	33,310	34,132	66,892
46,351	34,423	52,250	38,295	37,052	50,857	38,275
65,798	37,809	68,945	43,952	38,812	35,018	36,802
25,597	41,160					

In Exercises 13–16, use the given frequency table. (a) Identify the class mark for each class interval. (b) Find the mean using the class marks and frequencies.

13. **DISTANCES TRAVELED BY BUSES BEFORE THE FIRST MAJOR MOTOR FAILURE**

DISTANCE (IN THOUSANDS OF MILES)	FREQ
0– 39	17
40– 79	41
80–119	80
120–159	49
160–199	4

SOURCE: based on data from "Large Sample Simultaneous Confidence Intervals for the Multinomial Probabilities Based on Transformations of the Cell Frequencies," by Bailey, *Technometrics*, Vol. 22, No. 4.

14. **TIME REQUIRED TO EARN A BACHELOR'S DEGREE**

TIME (YEARS)	NUMBER
4	147
5	81
6	27
7	15
7.5–11.5	30

SOURCE: based on data from the National Center for Education Statistics.

15. **AGES OF NEW YORK DRIVERS INVOLVED IN ACCIDENTS**

AGE	NUMBER
16–20	38
21–29	110
30–39	122
40–49	91
50–59	71
60–69	82

SOURCE: based on data from the New York State Department of Motor Vehicles.

16. **INCOMES OF FAMILIES WITH INCOMES BELOW $50,000**

FAMILY INCOME (DOLLARS)	NUMBER
0–2,499	3
2,500–7,499	11
7,500–12,499	16
12,500–14,999	9
15,000–19,999	19
20,000–24,999	19
25,000–34,999	36
35,000–49,999	37

SOURCE: based on data from the Bureau of the Census.

2.5   EXERCISES   BEYOND THE BASICS

17. The following are the quarterly per share dividends (in dollars) paid by two microchip manufacturers over the past eight quarters. After calculating the four averages for each company, judge which has the "best" average quarterly performance. Which company would you prefer as a stockholder?

Company 1:   2.50   1.40   2.00   1.00   4.25   1.50   2.00   1.03
Company 2:   2.65   1.60   2.25   1.35   2.40   1.70   2.25   1.24

18. a.   Find the mean, median, mode, and midrange for the following lengths (in inches) of wood framing studs that are supposed to be 96 in. long.

96.05   95.87   96.16   96.06   95.81

   b.   Do part *a* after subtracting 95 from each score.
   c.   In general, what is the effect of subtracting a constant *k* from every score? What is the effect of adding a constant *k* to every score?
   d.   Find the mean, median, mode, and midrange of the following estimates of wealth (in dollars) of people from the list of the *Forbes 400* richest Americans.

1,700,000,000   1,400,000,000   505,000,000   2,150,000,000
876,000,000   475,000,000   390,000,000

   e.   Do part *d* after dividing each score by 1,000,000.
   f.   In general, if every score in a data set is divided or multiplied by some constant *k*, what is the effect on the mean, median, mode, and midrange?

19. a.   A student receives quiz grades of 70, 65, and 90. The same student earns an 85 on the final examination. If each quiz constitutes 20% of the final grade while the final makes up 40%, find the weighted mean.
   b.   A student earns the grades in the accompanying table. If grade points are assigned as A = 4, B = 3, C = 2, D = 1, F = 0 and the grade points are weighted according to the number of credit hours, find the weighted mean (grade-point average) rounded to three decimal places.

COURSE	GRADE	CREDIT HOURS
Math	A	4
English	C	3
Art	B	1
Physical education	A	2
Biology	C	4

20. Given a collection of *n* scores (all of which are positive), the **geometric mean** is the *n*th root of their product. For example, to find the geometric mean of 2, 3, 6, 7, 7, 8, 9, 9, 9, 10, first multiply the scores.

$$2 \cdot 3 \cdot 6 \cdot 7 \cdot 7 \cdot 8 \cdot 9 \cdot 9 \cdot 9 \cdot 10 = 102,876,480$$

Then take the 10th root of the product, because there are 10 scores.

$$\sqrt[10]{102,876,480} = 6.3$$

The geometric mean is often used in business and economics for finding average rates of change, average rates of growth, or average ratios. The *average growth factor* for money compounded at annual interest rates of 10%, 8%, 9%, 12%, and 7% can be found by computing the geometric mean of 1.10, 1.08, 1.09, 1.12, and 1.07. Find that average growth factor.

21. Refer to the data given in Exercises 1 through 5 and, in each case, identify the data as being skewed to the left, symmetric, or skewed to the right.

22. Frequency tables often have open-ended classes such as the one given here. The table shows the time spent studying by college freshmen (based on data

from *The American Freshman* as reported in *USA Today*). Formula 2.3 cannot be directly applied, because we can't determine a class mark for the class of "more than 20." Calculate the mean by assuming that this class is really (a) 21–25; (b) 21–30; (c) 21–40. What can you conclude?

HOURS STUDYING PER WEEK	FREQUENCY
0	5
1– 5	96
6–10	57
11–15	25
16–20	11
More than 20	6

23. When data are summarized in a frequency table, we can find the median by first identifying the "median class" (the class that contains the median). Then we assume that the scores in that class are evenly distributed and we can interpolate. This process can be described by

$$\text{(lower limit of median class)} + \text{(class width)} \left(\frac{\dfrac{n+1}{2} - (m+1)}{\text{frequency of median class}} \right)$$

where n is the sum of all class frequencies and m is the sum of the class frequencies that *precede* the median class. Use this procedure to find the median home selling price by referring to Table 2.9.

24. To find the 10% **trimmed mean** for a data set, first arrange the data in order. Then delete both the bottom 10% and the top 10% of the scores and calculate the mean of the remaining scores. Find the 10% trimmed mean for the data in Exercise 10. Also find the 20% trimmed mean for that data set. What advantage does a trimmed mean have over the regular mean?

2.6 VARIATION IN POPULATIONS AND PROCESSES

We have just discussed measures of *central tendency* that are supposed to identify representative or *central* scores. Now we consider measures of *variation* that are supposed to gauge the amount of dispersion or *scattering* among scores. This section is definitely one of the most important sections of the entire text (the pressure is on) because it deals with a characteristic that is so critically important to the business world. Quality goods and services not only have a good overall average level of quality, but they are also very *consistent*.

Consistency is the key to success in many businesses. For instance, many banks once had customers wait in separate lines at each teller's window. Now they have a single main waiting line. Why did they make that change? It wasn't for greater efficiency: The customers' mean waiting time didn't change with the new configuration. The banks changed to the single line because customers prefer waiting times that are much more *consistent* (have much less variation) than those they experienced with several lines. Consistency is also important in the goods you purchase. If you buy a Coke at Burger King, you would be displeased if that drink were too watery or had too much syrup; you expect a quality drink made with much consistency and little variation. If you buy a bolt labeled 1 in. long, you expect the bolt to be very close to 1 in. in length. You would be displeased with much variation from that value. Companies have gone out of business and employees have lost jobs because of an inability to control variation.

In this section we begin with a brief example to illustrate the general concept of variation among scores. Then we define important measures of variation, including the range, the standard deviation, and the variance. Among these, the standard deviation is usually the most useful. After describing the computation of the measures of variation, we consider how to understand or interpret the values we get. You may be tempted to flee this section after learning to calculate standard deviations, but we strongly recommend that you also learn to make sense out of the values you obtain. Because so many methods of statistics are based on some measure of variation, that knowledge will help you master future statistical topics.

First let's consider the general concept of variation among scores by considering the waiting times (in minutes) for samples of 10 customers at the Jefferson Valley Bank and the neighboring Bank of Providence. Those times are listed below.

Jefferson Valley Bank	6.5	6.6	6.7	6.8	7.1	7.3	7.4	7.7	7.7	7.7
Bank of Providence	4.2	5.4	5.8	6.2	6.7	7.7	7.7	8.5	9.3	10.0

Customers at the Jefferson Valley Bank enter a single waiting line that feeds three customer service stations (teller windows). Customers at the Bank of Providence can enter any one of three different lines that feed three customer service stations. If we use the methods of the preceding section to find measures of central tendency, we get these results:

	JEFFERSON VALLEY BANK	BANK OF PROVIDENCE
Mean	7.15	7.15
Median	7.20	7.20
Mode	7.7	7.7
Midrange	7.10	7.10

We don't need an advanced degree in statistical theory to see that the two banks have the same measures of central tendency, so that, on the average, customers wait the same time at both banks. Comparing the measures of central tendency alone, we can see no difference between the two banks. Yet scanning the original sample scores should reveal a fundamental difference: The waiting times at the Jefferson Valley Bank have much less variation than the times at the Bank of Providence. If all other characteristics are equal, customers are likely to prefer the Jefferson Valley Bank, where they won't become annoyed by being caught in an individual slow line.

By intuitively comparing the differences in variation between the customer waiting times at the two banks, we get a general sense for the characteristic of variation. Let's now develop some specific ways of actually *measuring* variation. We begin with the range.

LEAVE YOUR COMPUTER ON

Some people turn off their computer whenever they finish an immediate task, whereas others leave it on until they know they won't be using it again that day. The computer's circuit board and chips do suffer from repeated on/off electrical power cycles. The *mean time between failures* (MTBF) for hard-disk drives was once around 5000 hours, but it's now up to about 30,000 hours. However, the monitor can be damaged when the same image is left on a screen for very long periods of time. An image can burn itself into the screen, but you can minimize this damage by using special screen-saving programs that continually change the image or cause the screen to go blank. All angles considered, it does make sense to leave computers on until the end of the day, provided the monitor is protected with a screen-saver program. Many people use this strategy, which has evolved in part from a statistical analysis of past events.

RANGE

One measure of variability is the range, which has the advantage of being very easy to compute. The **range** is simply the difference between the highest value and the lowest value. For the Jefferson Valley Bank customers, the range is the difference between 7.7 min and 6.5 min, which is 1.2 min. The range of the Bank of Providence waiting times is $10.0 - 4.2 = 5.8$ min. This much larger range suggests greater variation or dispersion in their process.

The range is extremely easy to compute, but because it depends on only the highest and lowest scores, it's often inferior to other measures of variation that are based on the value of *every* score.

STANDARD DEVIATION

The next measure of variation or dispersion that we consider is the standard deviation, defined as follows:

> **DEFINITION**
>
> The *standard deviation* (denoted by *s*) of a set of *sample* scores is a measure of variation calculated by the following formula.

Formula 2.4
$$s = \sqrt{\frac{\Sigma(x - \bar{x})^2}{n - 1}}$$
sample standard deviation

Why define a measure of variation as in Formula 2.4? When measuring variation in a set of sample data, one reasonable approach is to begin with the individual amounts by which scores *deviate from the mean*. For a particular score x, that amount of **deviation** can be expressed as $x - \bar{x}$. The sum of all such deviations, however, is always zero. To get a measure that isn't always zero, we could take absolute values, as in $\Sigma|x - \bar{x}|$. If we find the mean of that sum, we get the **mean deviation** (or absolute deviation) described by the following expression.

$$\text{mean deviation: } \frac{\Sigma|x - \bar{x}|}{n}$$

But this approach tends to be unsuitable for the important methods of statistical inference. Instead of using absolute values, we make all deviations $(x - \bar{x})$ nonnegative by squaring them. Finally, we take the square root to compensate for that squaring. As a result, *the standard deviation has the same units of measurement as the original scores.* For example, if customer waiting times are in minutes, the standard deviation of those times will also be in minutes. Based on the format of Formula 2.4, we can describe the procedure for calculating the standard deviation as shown on the following page:

PROCEDURE FOR USING FORMULA 2.4

1. Find the mean of the scores ($\bar{x}$).
2. Subtract the mean from each individual score ($x - \bar{x}$).
3. Square each of the differences obtained from step 2. That is, multiply each value by itself. [This produces numbers of the form $(x - \bar{x})^2$.]
4. Add all of the squares obtained from step 3 to get $\Sigma(x - \bar{x})^2$.
5. Divide the total from step 4 by the number $(n - 1)$; that is, 1 less than the total number of scores present.
6. Find the square root of the result of step 5.

TABLE 2.11
Calculating Standard Deviation

x	$x - \bar{x}$	$(x - \bar{x})^2$
6.6	−0.65	0.4225
6.6	−0.55	0.3025
6.7	−0.45	0.2025
6.8	−0.35	0.1225
7.1	−0.05	0.0025
7.3	0.15	0.0225
7.4	0.25	0.0625
7.7	0.55	0.3025
7.7	0.55	0.3025
7.7	0.55	0.3025

Totals: 71.5   2.0450

$$\bar{x} = \frac{71.5}{10} = 7.15$$

$$s = \sqrt{\frac{2.0450}{10 - 1}} = \sqrt{0.2272}$$

$$= 0.48$$

EXAMPLE Find the standard deviation of the Jefferson Valley Bank customer waiting times 6.5, 6.6, 6.7, 6.8, 7.1, 7.3, 7.4, 7.7, 7.7, and 7.7 (in minutes).

SOLUTION See Table 2.11, where the following steps are executed. It is often helpful to use the same vertical format of that table.

STEP 1 Obtain the mean of 7.15 by adding the scores ($\Sigma x = 71.5$) and then dividing by the number of scores ($n = 10$).

STEP 2 Subtract the mean of 7.15 from each score to get −0.65, −0.55, . . . , 0.55. (As a quick check, these numbers must always total 0.)

STEP 3 Square each value obtained in step 2 to get 0.4225, 0.3025, . . . , 0.3025.

STEP 4 Sum all the preceding scores to get 2.045.

STEP 5 There are $n = 10$ scores, so we divide by 1 less than 10. That is, $2.045 \div 9 = 0.2272$.

STEP 6 Find the square root of 0.2272. We get a standard deviation of $\sqrt{0.2272} = 0.48$ min.

Ideally, now we would like to interpret the meaning of that result, but we will discuss such interpretations later in this section. First let us practice calculating a standard deviation by using the customer waiting times given above for the Bank of Providence. Using those times, verify that the standard deviation is 1.82 min. We can now *compare* the two standard deviations, and we note that the standard deviation of the times for the Jefferson Valley Bank is much lower than that for the Bank of Providence. This supports our intuitive observation that the Bank of Providence times have much more variation.

In our definition of standard deviation, we referred to the standard deviation of *sample* data. We use a slightly different formula to calculate the standard deviation

σ of a population: Divide by the population size N instead of the sample size n as in this expression:

$$\sigma = \sqrt{\frac{\Sigma(x - \mu)^2}{N}} \qquad \text{population standard deviation}$$

Because we will usually deal with sample data, we usually use Formula 2.4, in which we divide by $n - 1$. Many calculators do standard deviations, with division by $n - 1$ corresponding to a key labeled σ_{n-1} or s, while the key labeled σ_n or σ corresponds to division by n. For some creative but strange reason, calculators use a variety of different notations, but the following notations are very standard in statistics. These notations include reference to the *variance* of a set of scores, and we will now proceed to describe that measure of variation.

Notation

s denotes the *standard deviation* of a set of *sample* scores.

σ denotes the *standard deviation* of a set of *population* scores. (σ is the lowercase Greek sigma.)

s^2 denotes the *variance* of a set of *sample* scores.

σ^2 denotes the *variance* of a set of *population* scores.

Note: Articles in professional journals and reports often use *SD* for standard deviation and *Var* for variance.

If we omit step 6 in the procedure for calculating the standard deviation, we get the **variance,** defined as follows:

Formula 2.5 $\qquad s^2 = \dfrac{\Sigma(x - \bar{x})^2}{n - 1} \qquad$ sample variance

Similarly, we can express the population variance as

$$\sigma^2 = \frac{\Sigma(x - \mu)^2}{N} \qquad \text{population variance}$$

By comparing Formulas 2.4 and 2.5, we see that the variance is the square of the standard deviation. Although the variance will be used later in the book, we should concentrate first on the concept of standard deviation as we try to get a feeling for this statistic. A major difficulty with the variance is that it is not in the same units as the original data. For example, a data set might have a standard deviation of $3.00 and a variance of 9.00 *square* dollars. Because we can't relate well to square dollars, we find it difficult to understand variance.

ROUND-OFF RULE

As in Section 2.5, we round off answers by carrying one more decimal place than was present in the original data. We should round only the final answer and not intermediate values. (If we must round intermediate results, we should carry at least twice as many decimal places as we will use in the final answer.)

UNDERSTANDING THE STANDARD DEVIATION

We will now attempt to make some intuitive sense out of the standard deviation. First, we should clearly understand that the standard deviation measures the dispersion or variation among scores. Scores close together will yield a small standard deviation, whereas scores spread farther apart will yield a larger standard deviation. Figure 2.12 shows that as the data spread farther apart, the corresponding values of the standard deviation increase.

Because variation is such an important concept and because the standard deviation is such an important tool in measuring variation, we will consider three different ways of developing a sense for *values* of standard deviations. The first is the **range rule of thumb,** which states that *the range of a set of data is approximately four standard deviations wide.* That is,

$$\text{range} \approx 4s \text{ (for samples)}$$
$$\text{range} \approx 4\sigma \text{ (for populations)}$$

We can also express the range rule of thumb as follows:

$$s \approx \text{range}/4 \text{ (for samples)}$$
$$\sigma \approx \text{range}/4 \text{ (for populations)}$$

You may use this range rule of thumb as a check on your calculation of a standard deviation, but realize that although the approximation gets us in the general ballpark, it can be off by a fairly large amount.

For the data in the preceding example, the range is $7.7 - 6.5 = 1.2$, so we could use the range rule of thumb to get a rough estimate of s as follows:

$$s \approx \text{range}/4 = 1.2/4 = 0.3$$

We found that the standard deviation s is actually 0.48, so the range rule of thumb gives us an estimate that is a bit too low here. However, our estimate does confirm

---

FIGURE 2.12
Data Sets with Same Mean of 4, but with Different Standard Deviations

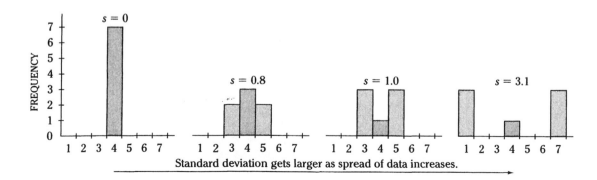

Standard deviation gets larger as spread of data increases.

that we are in the general ballpark, and we would know that a value such as 7 is probably not correct.

In attempting to understand or interpret a value of a standard deviation, we might also consider Chebyshev's theorem, which can be used with any set of data.

Chebyshev's Theorem
The *proportion* (or fraction) of any set of data lying within K standard deviations of the mean is always *at least* $1 - 1/K^2$, where K is any positive number greater than 1.

The statement of Chebyshev's theorem is abstract, but if we let $K = 2$ and then let $K = 3$, we get the following two specific results.

- At least 3/4 (or 75%) of all scores fall within the interval from two standard deviations below the mean to two standard deviations above the mean ($\bar{x} - 2s$ to $\bar{x} + 2s$).
- At least 8/9 (or 89%) of all scores fall within three standard deviations of the mean ($\bar{x} - 3s$ to $\bar{x} + 3s$).

Another rule is the **empirical rule,** which applies only to a data set having a shape or distribution that is approximately bell-shaped. This empirical rule is illustrated in Fig. 2.13. The figure shows how we can relate the mean and standard deviation of the data to the proportion of data falling within certain limits. For example, data with a bell-shaped distribution will have about 0.34, or 34%, of their values in the interval between the mean ($\bar{x}$) and one standard deviation above the mean ($\bar{x} + s$). Similarly, we can expect only about 0.001, or 0.1%, of the values to be above the point identified by $\bar{x} + 3s$ (three standard deviations above the mean). This rule is very important because statisticians often use measures based on standard deviations.

The empirical rule is often stated in an abbreviated form (sometimes called the **68-95-99 rule**) as follows:

- About 68% of all scores fall within *one* standard deviation of the mean.
- About 95% of all scores fall within *two* standard deviations of the mean.
- About 99.8% of all scores fall within *three* standard deviations of the mean.

FIGURE 2.13
Bell-shaped Distribution Illustrating the Empirical Rule

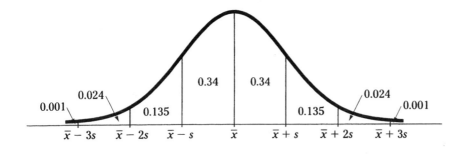

Whereas Chebyshev's theorem applies to *any* set of scores, the empirical rule applies only to scores with a bell-shaped distribution. For examples of how we can use Chebyshev's theorem and the empirical rule to understand the standard deviation, see Table 2.12.

Take the time to study the results in the table. They show us how we can use the standard deviation to get a sense for how data vary. Note that "within two standard deviations of the mean" translates to "within 2(15) of 100" or "within 30 of 100," which is really from 70 to 130. According to the empirical rule, an IQ score of 147 would be very rare, since it deviates from the mean by more than three standard deviations.

Measures of variation or dispersion are extremely important in manufacturing. Consider the Dayton Machine Company, which makes bolts that are supposed to be 1.000 in. long. The manufacturing process has a mean of 1.000 in. and a standard deviation of 0.100 in.; the distribution of bolt lengths is approximately bell-shaped. The Maxima Company is a foreign competitor that has a manufacturing process with the same mean, but the standard deviation is the much smaller value of 0.033 in. Industry specifications require that any bolts longer than 1.100 in. or shorter than 0.900 in. are unacceptable, and they are rejected as scrap.

By our empirical rule, only 68% of Dayton's bolts are acceptable; 32% are rejected as being too long or too short. (See Fig. 2.14.) Because Maxima has a much smaller process standard deviation, 99.8% of the bolts are between the specified limits and only 0.2% are rejected. Dayton has very large waste costs. We cannot detect this enormous difference in quality from the averages, because both have a mean of 1.000 in.

Whether in manufacturing or in a service area, *quality requires consistency of goods or services, and consistency corresponds to a small amount of variation, indicated by a small standard deviation.* Many companies are unclear about the role of variation. They try to improve quality by instituting more-rigorous inspections, but this results in *more* scrap and *higher* costs. W. Edwards Deming, when asked to explain his philosophy on quality, said, "Reduce variation."

TABLE 2.12
Given: IQ scores with a mean of 100, a standard deviation of 15, and a distribution that is bell-shaped

CHEBYSHEV'S THEOREM	EMPIRICAL RULE
	About 34% of all scores are between 100 and 115.
	About 47.5% of all scores are between 100 and 130.
	About 68% of all scores are between 85 and 115.
At least 75% of all scores are between 70 and 130.	About 95% of all scores are between 70 and 130.
At least 89% of all scores are between 55 and 145.	About 99.8% of all scores are between 55 and 145.

FIGURE 2.14
Distributions of Bolt Lengths

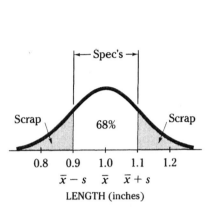

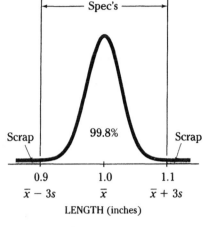

(a) Dayton Machine Company   (b) Maxima Company

SHORTCUT FORMULA AND GROUPED DATA

We now present two additional formulas for standard deviation, but these formulas do not involve a different concept; they are only different versions of Formula 2.4. First, Formula 2.4 can be expressed in the following equivalent form.

Formula 2.6
$$s = \sqrt{\frac{n(\Sigma x^2) - (\Sigma x)^2}{n(n-1)}}$$

Formulas 2.4 and 2.6 are equivalent in the sense that they will always produce the same results. Algebra can be used to show that they are equal. Formula 2.6 is called the *shortcut* formula because it tends to be convenient with messy numbers or with large sets of data. Also, Formula 2.6 is often used in calculators and computer programs because it requires only three memory registers (for n, Σx, and Σx^2) instead of one memory register for every single score. However, many instructors prefer to use only Formula 2.4 for calculating standard deviations. They argue that Formula 2.4 reinforces the concept that the standard deviation is a type of average deviation, whereas Formula 2.6 obscures that idea. Other instructors have no objections to using Formula 2.6. We have included the shortcut formula so that it is available for those who choose to use it.

For the Jefferson Valley Bank customer waiting times, we could use Formula 2.6 to find the standard deviation as in the accompanying table. Because there are 10 scores, $n = 10$. From the table we see that $\Sigma x = 71.5$ and $\Sigma x^2 = 513.27$,

x	x^2
6.5	42.25
6.6	43.56
6.7	44.89
6.8	46.24
7.1	50.41
7.3	53.29
7.4	54.76
7.7	59.29
7.7	59.29
7.7	59.29
71.5	513.27
↑	↑
Σx	Σx^2

so that

$$s = \sqrt{\frac{n(\Sigma x^2) - (\Sigma x)^2}{n(n-1)}}$$

$$= \sqrt{\frac{10(513.27) - (71.5)^2}{10(10-1)}}$$

$$= \sqrt{\frac{20.45}{90}}$$

$$= \sqrt{0.2272} = 0.48$$

We can also develop a formula for standard deviation when the data are summarized in a frequency table. The result is as follows:

$$s = \sqrt{\frac{\Sigma f \cdot (x - \bar{x})^2}{n-1}}$$

We will express this formula in an equivalent expression that usually simplifies the actual calculations.

Formula 2.7 $s = \sqrt{\dfrac{n[\Sigma(f \cdot x^2)] - [\Sigma(f \cdot x)]^2}{n(n-1)}}$ standard deviation for frequency table

where x = class mark, f = frequency, and n = sample size

Table 2.13 summarizes the work done in applying Formula 2.7 to a frequency table formed by that table's first two columns.

TABLE 2.13
Calculating Standard Deviation from Frequency Table

SCORE	FREQUENCY f	CLASS MARK x	$f \cdot x$	$f \cdot x^2$ OR $f \cdot x \cdot x$
0–8	10	4	40	160
9–17	5	13	65	845
18–26	15	22	330	7,260
27–35	3	31	93	2,883
36–44	1	40	40	1,600
Total	34		568	12,748

$$s = \sqrt{\frac{n[\Sigma(f \cdot x^2)] - [\Sigma(f \cdot x)]^2}{n(n-1)}}$$

$$= \sqrt{\frac{34(12,748) - (568)^2}{34(34-1)}}$$

$$= \sqrt{\frac{110,808}{1,122}} = \sqrt{98.759} = 9.9$$

2.6 EXERCISES | BASIC CONCEPTS

In Exercises 1–12, find the range, the variance, and the standard deviation for the given data. Unless specified otherwise, assume that the data are *sample* values.

1. The following lists the amount of time (in hours) that a sample of office managers spent on paperwork in one day (based on data from Adia Personnel Services).

   3.7   2.9   3.4   0.0   1.5   1.8   2.3   2.4   1.0   2.0
   4.4   2.0   4.5   0.0   1.7   4.4   3.3   2.4   2.1   2.1

2. The article "Determining Statistical Characteristics of a Vehicle Emissions Audit Procedure" (by Lorenzen, *Technometrics*, Vol. 22, No. 4) includes the following carbon monoxide emissions data (in g/m) for vehicles.

   5.01   14.67   8.60   4.42   4.95   7.24
   7.51   12.30   14.59   7.98   11.53   4.10

3. The following are the times (in minutes) required to resolve customer complaints.

   8   1   2   4   12   7   8   10   10   11   10

4. The following are the annual salaries (in dollars) for a sample of employees at the Jefferson Valley Bank.

   10,000   10,000   20,000   20,000   10,000   10,000   20,000
   10,000   10,000   20,000   20,000   10,000   10,000   20,000
   10,000   10,000   20,000   125,000   20,000   20,000

5. A quality control analyst selects and weighs (in ounces) one candy bar each minute. The following *sample* consists of nine such weights. The process is statistically stable. Your goal is to produce candy bars with a net weight of 6 oz.

   6.0   6.1   6.2   5.8   5.9   6.0   6.3   5.7   6.0

   A second machine led to these sample values taken at the same time as the first machine.

   6.0   6.0   6.1   6.0   5.9   6.0   6.1   6.0   5.9

   Find the mean, range, variance, and standard deviation for this second set of process scores and compare the results with those of the first machine. Which machine or process appears to be better? Why?

6. The following sample consists of five credit card account balances (in dollars) at the Jefferson Valley Bank.

   325   675   1095   250   325

   Assume that the value of $1095 is incorrectly included as $2095. Now find the range, variance, and standard deviation. Which of these statistics is least affected by the wrong entry?

7. The Acton Paper Company makes reels of paper from mixtures of wood pulp and recycled paper. A sample of nine reels is obtained by selecting every 10th reel; the numbers of imperfections are counted and the results are listed below.

   8   7   4   11   6   7   8   5   9

8. The blood alcohol concentrations of 15 drivers involved in fatal accidents and then convicted with jail sentences are given below (based on data from the U.S. Department of Justice).

0.27	0.17	0.17	0.16	0.13	0.24	0.29	0.24
0.14	0.16	0.12	0.16	0.21	0.17	0.18	

9. An investigation of the ages of the 40 commercial aircraft owned by Air America found the data given below (based on data reported by Aviation Data Services). (Is this a sample or a population?)

3.2	22.6	23.1	16.9	0.4	6.6	12.5	22.8	7.7	15.8
26.3	8.1	13.6	17.0	21.3	15.2	18.7	11.5	10.5	6.3
4.9	5.3	5.8	20.6	23.1	24.7	3.6	12.4	23.4	11.9
27.3	22.5	3.9	7.0	16.2	24.1	0.1	2.1	0.7	16.8

10. A student working part time for a moving company in Dutchess County, New York, collected the following load weights (in pounds) for 50 consecutive customers.

8,090	3,250	12,350	4,510	8,770	5,030	12,700
8,800	6,170	8,450	10,330	10,100	13,410	7,280
13,490	17,810	7,470	11,450	13,260	9,310	15,970
7,540	7,770	6,400	14,800	14,760	6,820	11,430
7,200	13,520	16,200	10,780	10,510	17,330	7,450
9,110	10,630	3,670	14,310	9,140	10,220	9,900
11,860	12,010	12,430	8,160	26,580	4,480	6,390
11,600						

11. Listed below are the actual energy consumption amounts as reported on the electric bills for one residence. Each amount is in kilowatt-hours and represents a two-month period.

728	774	859	882	791	731	838	862	880	831	837
759	774	832	816	860	856	787	715	752	778	
829	792	908	714	839	752	834	818	835	751	

12. Listed below are the daily sales totals (in dollars) for 44 days at a large retail outlet in Orange County, California.

24,145	39,921	30,284	43,923	38,366	31,987	32,097
33,650	47,563	34,804	55,254	44,249	59,708	64,842
37,196	66,644	37,858	31,995	61,923	46,285	37,229
39,897	29,099	42,906	35,420	33,310	34,132	66,892
46,351	34,423	52,250	38,295	37,052	50,857	38,275
65,798	37,809	68,945	43,952	38,812	35,018	36,802
25,597	41,160					

In Exercises 13–16, find the variance and standard deviation for the given data.

13. **AGES OF NEW YORK DRIVERS INVOLVED IN ACCIDENTS**

AGE	NUMBER
16–20	38
21–29	110
30–39	122
40–49	91
50–59	71
60–69	82

SOURCE: based on data from the New York State Department of Motor Vehicles.

14. **TIME REQUIRED TO EARN BACHELOR'S DEGREE**

TIME (YEARS)	NUMBER
4	147
5	81
6	27
7	15
7.5–11.5	30

SOURCE: based on data from the National Center for Education Statistics.

15. **DISTANCES TRAVELED BY BUSES BEFORE THE FIRST MAJOR MOTOR FAILURE**

DISTANCE (IN THOUSANDS OF MILES)	FREQ
0– 39	17
40– 79	41
80–119	80
120–159	49
160–199	4

SOURCE: based on data from "Large Sample Simultaneous Confidence Intervals for the Multinomial Probabilities Based on Transformations of the Cell Frequencies," by Bailey, *Technometrics*, Vol. 22, No. 4.

16. **INCOMES OF FAMILIES WITH INCOMES BELOW $50,000**

FAMILY INCOME (DOLLARS)	NUMBER
0–2,499	3
2,500–7,499	11
7,500–12,499	16
12,500–14,999	9
15,000–19,999	19
20,000–24,999	19
25,000–34,999	36
35,000–49,999	37

SOURCE: based on data from the Bureau of the Census.

2.6 EXERCISES   BEYOND THE BASICS

17. Refer to the data given in Exercise 11.
    a. Construct a histogram of the data.
    b. Calculate the values of $\mu - 3\sigma$ and $\mu + 3\sigma$.
    c. According to Chebyshev's theorem, what percentage of data should lie between the two values from part b?
    d. According to the empirical rule (assuming a bell-shaped distribution), what percentage of data should lie between the two values from part b?
    e. What percentage of data actually lie between the two values from part b?
    f. In this case, which gives the better results: Chebyshev's theorem or the empirical rule? Why?
    g. How well does the range rule of thumb work for this data set?

In Exercises 18 and 19, refer to the same sample data used in Exercise 1, where the mean is $\bar{x} = 2.40$, the range is 4.50, the variance is $s^2 = 1.67$, and the standard deviation is $s = 1.29$.

18. Add 10 to each score in Exercise 1 and then find the mean, range, variance, and standard deviation. Compare the results with those that apply to the original Exercise 1 data and form a general conclusion about the effect of adding a constant to all values in a data set.

19. Multiply each score in Exercise 1 by 5 and then find the mean, range, variance, and standard deviation. Compare the results with those that apply to the original Exercise 1 data and form a general conclusion about the effect of multiplying by a constant.

20. Find the range and standard deviation for each of the following two groups: Group C: 1, 20, 20, 20, 20, 20, 20, 20, 20, 20 and Group D: 2, 3, 4, 5, 6, 14, 15, 16, 17, 18. Which group has less dispersion according to the criterion of the range? Which group has less dispersion according to the criterion of the standard deviation? Which measure of dispersion is "better" in this situation: the range or the standard deviation?

21. Chebyshev's theorem states that the *proportion* (or fraction) of any set of data lying within K standard deviations of the mean is always *at least* $1 - 1/K^2$, where K is any positive number greater than 1.
    a. The mean score on the College Entrance Examination Board Scholastic Aptitude Test is 500, and the standard deviation is 100. What does Chebyshev's theorem say about the number of scores between 300 and 700?
    b. Using the data of part *a*, describe what Chebyshev's theorem says about the number of scores between 200 and 800?
22. A large set of sample scores yields a mean and standard deviation of $\bar{x} = 56.0$ and $s = 4.0$, respectively. The distribution of the histogram is roughly bell-shaped. Use the empirical rule to answer the following:
    a. What percentage of the scores should fall between 52.0 and 60.0?
    b. What percentage of the scores should fall within 8.0 of the mean?
    c. About 99.8% of the scores should fall between what two values? (The mean of 56.0 should be midway between those two values.)
23. Find the standard deviation of the 150 home selling prices by using (a) the original set of data given in Table 2.1; (b) the frequency table given in Table 2.2. Then compare the results to determine the amount of distortion caused by the frequency table.
24. Given a collection of temperatures in degrees Fahrenheit, the following statistics are calculated:

$$\bar{x} = 40.2 \qquad s = 3.0 \qquad s^2 = 9.0$$

Find the values of $\bar{x}$, s, and s^2 for the same data set after each temperature has been converted to the Celsius scale.

$$\left[C = \frac{5}{9} (F - 32) \right]$$

25. The **coefficient of variation,** expressed in percent, is used to describe the standard deviation relative to the mean. It is calculated as follows:

$$\frac{s}{\bar{x}} \cdot 100 \qquad \text{or} \qquad \frac{\sigma}{\mu} \cdot 100$$

    a. Find the coefficient of variation for the following sample scores: 2, 2, 2, 3, 5, 8, 12, 19, 22, 30.
    b. In the Taguchi method of quality engineering, a key tool is the **signal-to-noise ratio.** The simplest way to calculate this is to divide the mean by the standard deviation. Find this ratio for the sample data given in part *a*.
26. In Section 2–5, we introduced the general concept of skewness. One statistical measure of skewness is **Pearson's index of skewness:**

$$I = \frac{3(\bar{x} - \text{median})}{s}$$

If $I \geq 1.00$ or $I \leq -1.00$, the data can be considered to be *significantly skewed.* Find Pearson's index of skewness for the data given in Exercise 9 and then determine whether or not there is significant skewness.

2.7   MEASURES OF POSITION: STANDARD SCORES AND PERCENTILES

There is often a need to compare scores taken from two separate populations with different means and standard deviations. We can use the standard score (or z score) in making such comparisons. Also, we can use z scores to compare scores from the same population.

DEFINITION

The *standard score*, or *z score*, is the number of standard deviations that a given value x is above or below the mean, and it is found by

$$\text{Sample} \qquad\qquad \text{Population}$$

$$z = \frac{x - \bar{x}}{s} \quad \text{or} \quad z = \frac{x - \mu}{\sigma}$$

Round z to two decimal places.

EXAMPLE   Suppose large random samples of home selling prices are collected from two different regions and the statistics are as follows:

$$
\begin{array}{ll}
\textit{Inner City} & \textit{Suburbs} \\
\bar{x} = \$172,850 & \bar{x} = \$127,350 \\
s = \$44,650 & s = \$39,720
\end{array}
$$

A \$190,000 home in the inner city costs more than a \$160,000 home in the suburban area, but which of these two homes has the higher cost *relative to its region?*

SOLUTION   For the inner city home we get a z score of 0.38 because

$$z = \frac{x - \bar{x}}{s} = \frac{190,000 - 172,850}{44,650} = 0.38$$

For the suburban home, we get a z score of 0.82 because

$$z = \frac{x - \bar{x}}{s} = \frac{160,000 - 127,350}{39,720} = 0.82$$

That is, a price of \$190,000 in the inner city is 0.38 standard deviation above the mean, whereas a suburban home of \$160,000 is 0.82 standard deviation above the mean. This implies that the \$160,000 suburban home has a higher *relative* cost when considered in the context of its region.

We can use standard scores (or numbers of standard deviations above or below the mean) with the empirical rule and Chebyshev's theorem to help identify unusual values within a given data set. *Values with standard scores between −2 and +2 are ordinary.* Recall from the empirical rule that about 95% of the values are within two standard deviations of the mean. Also, Chebyshev's theorem states that at least 75% of the values are within two standard deviations of the mean. Figure 2.15 illustrates these concepts.

We cannot overemphasize the role that z scores or standard scores play in statistics. Statisticians typically measure in amounts that are standard deviations away from the mean (z scores), and they use the empirical rule and Chebyshev's theorem to guide them in distinguishing between ordinary scores and unusual scores in a data set.

Another method of measuring position uses quartiles, deciles, and percentiles. These measures of position are useful for comparing scores within one set of data or between different sets of data. Just as the median divides the data into two equal parts, the three quartiles, denoted by Q_1, Q_2, and Q_3, divide the ranked scores into four equal parts. Roughly speaking, the first quartile Q_1 separates the bottom 25% of the ranked scores from the top 75%; the second quartile Q_2 is the median; and the third quartile Q_3 separates the top 25% from the bottom 75%. To be more precise, at least 25% of the data will be less than or equal to Q_1, and at least 75% will be greater than or equal to Q_1. At least 75% of the data will be less than or equal to Q_3, and at least 25% will be equal to or greater than Q_3.

Similarly, there are nine **deciles,** denoted by D_1, D_2, D_3, . . . , D_9, which partition the data into 10 groups with about 10% of the data in each group. There are also 99 **percentiles,** denoted by P_1, P_2, P_3, . . . , P_{99}, which partition the data into 100 groups with about 1% of the scores in each group. (Quartiles, deciles, and percentiles are examples of *fractiles,* which partition data into parts that are approximately equal.) Percentiles are useful for converting meaningless raw scores into meaningful comparative scores. An employee taking a competitive promotion examination might learn that he or she scored in the 92nd percentile. This does not mean that the employee received a grade of 92% on the test; it indicates roughly that whatever score the employee did achieve was higher than 92% of those who took the same test (and also lower than 8% of his or her colleagues).

The process of finding the percentile that corresponds to a particular score x is fairly simple, as indicated in the following definition.

FIGURE 2.15
Interpreting z scores

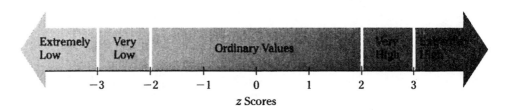

DEFINITION

$$\text{percentile of score } x = \frac{\text{number of scores less than } x}{\text{total number of scores}} \cdot 100$$

EXAMPLE   Table 2.14 lists the 150 home selling prices arranged in order from lowest to highest. Find the percentile corresponding to $100,000.

SOLUTION   From Table 2.14 we see that there are 10 selling prices less than $100,000, so that

$$\text{percentile of } \$100,000 = \frac{10}{150} \cdot 100 = 7 \qquad \text{(rounded off)}$$

The selling price of $100,000 is the 7th percentile, denoted as P_7.

There are several different methods for finding the score corresponding to a particular percentile, but the process we will use is summarized in Fig. 2.16 on page 76. In Fig. 2.16 we use L to denote the *locator*—the number representing the location or position of the score we seek.

TABLE 2.14
Ranked Selling Prices (in dollars) of 150 Dutchess County Homes

72,000	120,500	133,000	144,900	164,900	190,000
78,000	121,900	133,000	145,000	165,000	190,000
80,500	122,000	134,000	145,900	165,000	190,000
85,000	122,500	134,500	146,000	165,000	194,500
89,900	123,500	135,000	150,000	165,900	194,500
94,000	124,000	135,000	150,000	168,500	194,900
96,000	124,900	135,000	150,000	169,000	195,000
97,000	125,000	135,000	151,500	169,900	196,800
98,000	125,000	135,500	152,000	170,000	203,000
99,500	125,900	136,000	152,000	172,000	205,406
100,000	126,000	136,000	152,500	175,000	208,000
107,000	126,500	137,900	153,500	177,000	210,000
108,000	126,500	139,500	154,000	179,000	211,900
108,500	126,500	139,900	155,000	179,900	215,000
110,000	126,500	140,000	156,000	180,000	217,000
110,000	126,500	140,000	156,000	180,000	220,000
113,500	127,500	141,000	158,000	180,500	223,000
115,000	127,500	141,000	159,000	181,500	231,750
116,000	128,500	141,000	160,000	182,000	235,000
116,300	129,000	141,900	160,000	183,000	265,000
117,000	129,900	141,900	160,000	185,000	267,000
117,000	130,000	142,000	162,000	185,500	269,900
117,500	131,000	142,000	162,500	187,000	275,000
118,500	132,000	142,500	163,500	189,900	285,000
119,000	133,000	144,900	164,000	190,000	302,000

AN AVERAGE GUY

The "average" American man is named Robert. He is 31 years old and 5 ft 9½ in. tall, weighs 172 lb, wears a size 40 suit and a size 9½ shoe, and has a 34-in. waist. Each year he eats 12.3 lb of pasta, 26 lb of bananas, 4 lb of potato chips, 18 lb of ice cream, and 79 lb of beef. Each year he also watches television for 2567 hours and gets 585 pieces of mail. After eating his share of potato chips, reading some of his mail, and watching some television, he ends the day with 7.7 hours of sleep. The next day begins with a 21-minute commute to a job at which he will work for 6.1 hours.

EXAMPLE Refer to the 150 home selling prices in Table 2.14 and find the score corresponding to the 35th percentile. That is, find the value of P_{35}.

SOLUTION We refer to Fig. 2.16 and observe that the data in Table 2.14 are already ranked from lowest to highest. We now compute the locator L as follows:

$$L = \left(\frac{k}{100}\right)n = \left(\frac{35}{100}\right) \cdot 150 = 52.5$$

We answer no when asked if 52.5 is a whole number, so we are directed to round L up (not off) to 53. (In *this* procedure we round L up to the next higher integer, but in most other situations in this book we generally follow the usual process for rounding.) The 35th percentile, denoted by P_{35}, is the 53rd score, counting from the lowest. Beginning with the lowest score of $72,000, we count down the list to find the 53rd score of $134,000, so that $P_{35} = $134,000$.

In the preceding example, we can see that there are 52 scores below $134,000, so the definition of percentile indicates that the percentile of $134,000 is $(52/150) \cdot 100 = 34.7$, which is approximately 35. As the amount of data increases, these differences become smaller.

In the same example we found the 35th percentile. Because of the sample size, the locator L first became 52.5, which was rounded to 53 because L was not originally a whole number. In the next example we illustrate a case in which L does begin as a whole number. This condition will cause us to branch to the right in Fig. 2.16.

EXAMPLE Refer to the same home selling prices listed in Table 2.14. Find P_{70}, which denotes the 70th percentile.

SOLUTION Following the procedure outlined in Fig. 2.16 and noting that the data are already ranked from lowest to highest, we compute

$$L = \left(\frac{k}{100}\right)n = \left(\frac{70}{100}\right) \cdot 150 = 105$$

We now answer yes when asked if 105 is a whole number, and we then see that P_{70} is midway between the 105th and 106th scores. Since the 105th and 106th scores are $165,900 and $168,500, we get

$$P_{70} = \frac{165,900 + 168,500}{2} = $167,200$$

Once you master these calculations with percentiles, you can perform similar calculations for quartiles and deciles with the same procedures by noting the

FIGURE 2.16
Procedure for Finding the Value of the *K*th Percentile

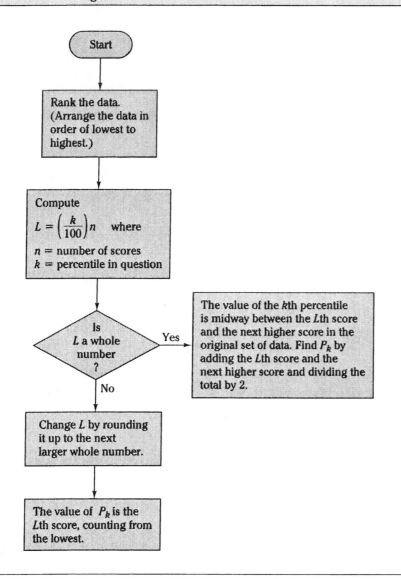

following relationships. For example, finding Q_3 is equivalent to finding P_{75}.

Quartiles   **Deciles**

$Q_1 = P_{25}$ $D_1 = P_{10}$

$Q_2 = P_{50}$ $D_2 = P_{20}$

$Q_3 = P_{75}$ $D_3 = P_{30}$

$\cdot$

$\cdot$

$\cdot$

$D_9 = P_{90}$

In addition to the measures of central tendency and the measures of dispersion already introduced, other statistics are sometimes defined using quartiles, deciles, or percentiles. For example, the **interquartile range** is a measure of dispersion obtained by evaluating $Q_3 - Q_1$. The **semi-interquartile range** is $(Q_3 - Q_1)/2$, the **midquartile** is $(Q_1 + Q_3)/2$, and the **10–90 percentile range** is defined to be $P_{90} - P_{10}$. (Remember, percentiles like P_1, P_3, or P_7 denote relatively *low* values of the data; percentiles like P_{95} or P_{97} denote relatively *high* values.)

When dealing with large collections of data, we can obtain more reliable results with greater ease if we use statistical software packages. The following Minitab computer display for the 150 home selling prices (listed in Table 2.1) shows how the computer makes it easy to find the values of the various statistics we have been discussing in this chapter.

```
MTB > SET C1
DATA> 179000 126500 134500 125000 142000 164000
DATA> 146000 129000 141900 135000 118500 160000
            .
            .
            .
DATA> 133000 196800 121900 126000 164900 172000
DATA> 100000 129900 110000 131000 107000 165900
DATA> ENDOFDATA
MTB > MEAN C1
    MEAN = 153775
MTB > STDEV C1
    ST.DEV. = 41611
MTB > MEDIAN C1
    MEDIAN = 144900
MTB > SUM C1
    SUM = 23066258
MTB > SSQ C1
    SSQ = 3.805003E + 12
MTB > MAXIMUM C1
    MAXIMUM = 302000
MTB > MINIMUM C1
    MINIMUM = 72000
```

1. SSQ is Minitab's notation for sum of squares or Σx^2.
2. The "E + 12" indicates that 3.805003 should be multiplied by 10^{12}; the effect is to move the decimal point 12 places to the right.

2.7 EXERCISES   BASIC CONCEPTS

In Exercises 1–12, express all z scores with two decimal places.

1. For a set of data, the sample mean and standard deviation are $\bar{x} = 60$ and $s = 10$, respectively. Find the z score corresponding to (a) $x = 80$, (b) $x = 40$, (c) $x = 65$, and (d) $x = 91$. (e) Which of these values is the most unusual?

2. The sample mean and standard deviation are $\bar{x} = 100$ and $s = 15$, respectively. Find the z score corresponding to (a) $x = 115$, (b) $x = 145$, (c) $x = 55$, and (d) $x = 85$. (e) Which of these values is the most unusual?

3. An investigation of the number of hours college freshmen spend studying each week found that the mean is 7.06 h and the standard deviation is 5.32 h (based on data from *The American Freshman*). Find the z score corresponding to a freshman who studies 10.00 h weekly. Is it unusually high?

4. A study of the time high school students spend working at a job each week found that the mean is 10.7 h and the standard deviation is 11.2 h (based on data from the National Federation of State High School Associations). Find the z score corresponding to a high school student who works 35.0 h each week. Is it unusually high?

5. A machine is designed to produce candy bars with a mean of 6 oz and a standard deviation of 0.1 oz. The distribution of weights is approximately bell-shaped.
   a. Find the z score corresponding to a candy bar weight of 6.14 oz. Would such a weight be ordinary, unusually heavy, or extremely heavy?
   b. Repeat part *a* for a weight of 6.21 oz.
   c. What weight corresponds to a z score of $+3.5$?

6. A process consists of a machine filling fertilizer bags with a mean of 50 lb and a standard deviation of 1 lb. The distribution of weights is bell-shaped.
   a. At the beginning of the process, three bags are selected, and their weights (in pounds) are 50.5, 49.6, and 51.2. Find the z score corresponding to each weight. Are any of them unusually heavy or light?
   b. Four hours later, three more bags are selected, and their weights (in pounds) are 54.3, 55.1, and 53.5. Find the z scores. Are any of these bags unusually heavy or light? What do these later results indicate about the process?

7. The credit card balances on the 1000 accounts at the Jefferson Valley Bank have a mean of $750, a standard deviation of $125, and a distribution that is approximately bell-shaped.
   a. What z score corresponds to a balance of $350? Is this an unusually low balance?
   b. Values with z scores between -2 and $+2$ are considered to be ordinary values. Find the lowest and highest such values.
   c. What balance would be extremely high with a z score of $+4$?

8. For men aged between 18 and 24 years, serum cholesterol levels (in mg/100 ml) have a mean of 178.1 and a standard deviation of 40.7 (based on data from the National Health Survey, USDHEW publication 78-1652). (a) Find the z score corresponding to a male, aged 18–24 years, who has a serum cholesterol level of 269.3 mg/100 ml. (b) Is this an unusually high serum cholesterol level?

9. Which of the following two scores has the better relative position?
   a. A score of 53 on a test for which $\bar{x} = 50$ and $s = 10$
   b. A score of 53 on a test for which $\bar{x} = 50$ and $s = 5$

10. Electricity consumption in a model home averages 780 kwh of electricity (for a two-month period), with a standard deviation of 60 kwh.
   a. Find the z scores for the following consumption amounts in the first year: 980 (J/F), 860 (M/A), 720 (M/J), 965 (J/A), 670 (S/O), 760 (N/D).
   b. Based on part *a*, identify any periods that seem unusually high or low.

11. Three prospective employees take equivalent tests of communicative ability. Which of the following scores corresponds to the highest relative position?
    a. A score of 60 on a test for which $\bar{x} = 50$ and $s = 5$
    b. A score of 230 on a test for which $\bar{x} = 200$ and $s = 10$
    c. A score of 540 on a test for which $\bar{x} = 500$ and $s = 15$

12. Four machines made by the Dayton Machine Company are designed to fill ice cream containers with a mean of 128 oz (or 1 gal) and a standard deviation of 1.1 oz. Two containers are randomly selected from each machine, and their weights (in ounces) are as follows:

Machine 1	Machine 2	Machine 3	Machine 4
129.4	125.5	127.5	130.4
128.5	126.0	128.2	131.2

    a. Find the eight z scores.
    b. Based on the z scores, which machine(s) seem to be operating as planned?
    c. Which machine(s) have unusually high z scores, suggesting that containers are being overfilled?
    d. Which machine(s) have unusually low z scores, suggesting that containers are being underfilled?

In Exercises 13–16, use the 150 ranked home selling prices listed in Table 2.14. Find the percentile corresponding to the given selling price.

13. $110,000
14. $125,000

15. $175,000
16. $220,000

In Exercises 17–24, use the 150 ranked home selling prices listed in Table 2.14. Find the indicated percentile, quartile, or decile.

17. P_{15}
18. P_5
19. P_{80}
20. P_{90}

21. Q_1
22. Q_2
23. Q_3
24. D_6

In Exercises 25–28, use the following data to find the percentile corresponding to the given value. These numbers are the actual weights (in pounds) of 50 consecutive loads handled by a moving company in Dutchess County, New York.

8,090	17,810	3,670	10,100	17,330
8,800	7,770	12,430	13,260	10,220
13,490	13,520	4,510	14,760	4,480
7,540	10,630	10,330	10,510	12,700
7,200	12,010	11,450	9,140	7,280
9,110	12,350	14,800	26,580	15,970
11,860	8,450	10,780	5,030	11,430
11,600	7,470	14,310	13,410	7,450
3,250	6,400	8,160	9,310	9,900
6,170	16,200	8,770	6,820	6,390

25. 5,030
26. 10,220
27. 12,430
28. 14,760

In Exercises 29–36, use the same load weights given above and find the indicated percentile, quartile, or decile.

29. P_{15}
30. P_{20}
31. P_{80}
32. P_{66}

33. Q_1
34. Q_3
35. D_3
36. D_9

2.7 EXERCISES BEYOND THE BASICS

37. Use the ranked home selling prices listed in Table 2.14.
    a. Find the interquartile range.
    b. Find the midquartile.
    c. Find the 10–90 percentile range.
    d. Does $P_{50} = Q_2$? Does P_{50} *always* equal Q_2?
    e. Does $Q_2 = (Q_1 + Q_3)/2$?
38. When finding percentiles using Fig. 2.16, if the locator L is not a whole number, we round it up to the next larger whole number. An alternative to this procedure is to *interpolate* so that a locator of 23.75 would lead to a value that is 0.75 (or 3/4) of the way between the 23rd and 24th scores. Use this method of interpolation to find Q_1, Q_3, and P_{33} for these scores:

    16   49   53   58   60   63   63   65   72   80   84   89   92   98

39. Construct a collection of data consisting of 50 scores for which $Q_1 = 20$, $Q_2 = 30$, $Q_3 = 70$.
40. Using the scores 2, 5, 8, 9, and 16, first find $\bar{x}$ and s, then replace each score by its corresponding z score. Now find the mean and standard deviation of the five z scores. Will these new values of the mean and standard deviation result from *every* set of z scores?

2.8 EXPLORATORY DATA ANALYSIS

We can use the techniques discussed in the previous sections to summarize data and find important measures, such as the mean and standard deviation. In summarizing and describing data, we should be careful to avoid overlooking important information that might be lost in our summaries. About 30 years ago, statisticians began to use an approach now referred to as **exploratory data analysis** or **EDA.** Many of the techniques used in this approach are introduced in John Tukey's book *Exploratory Data Analysis* (Addison-Wesley, 1977). EDA is more than simply a collection of new statistical techniques—it is a fundamentally different approach. With EDA we *explore* data rather than use a statistical analysis to *confirm* some claim or assumption made about the data. For data obtained from a carefully planned experiment with a very specific objective (such as comparing the mpg

MAZDA TRANSMISSIONS

Ford once asked Mazda, which it partly owns, to supply transmissions for one of its car models. Ford was producing similar transmissions at one of its American plants with the same specifications. After some time, Ford discovered that the American-made transmissions required more warranty repairs than the Japanese-made ones. When investigators inspected samples of the Japanese gearboxes, they first thought that their measuring instruments were defective because there was little variability among the Mazda gearboxes. They came to realize that although the American transmissions were built within the specifications, the Mazda transmissions were not only within the specifications, but they were consistently closer to the desired center value. By reducing variability among gearboxes, Mazda reduced the costs of inspection, scrap, rework, and warranty repair.

ratings of two different car models), traditional methods of statistics will probably be sufficient. But if you have a collection of data and a broad goal (such as trying to find out what the data reveal), then you might want to begin with exploratory data analysis. With EDA, the emphasis is on original explorations with the goals of simplifying the way the data are described and gaining deeper insight into the nature of the data. Thus it is easier to identify relevant questions that might be addressed. The table below compares EDA and traditional statistics in three major areas.

EXPLORATORY DATA ANALYSIS	TRADITIONAL STATISTICS
Used to *explore* data at a preliminary level.	Used to *confirm* final conclusions about data.
Requires few or no assumptions about the data.	Typically requires some very important assumptions about the data.
Tends to involve relatively simple calculations and graphs.	Calculations are often complex and graphs are often unnecessary.

In this section we consider two helpful devices used for exploratory data analysis: the stem-and-leaf plot and the boxplot. They are typical of EDA techniques because they involve relatively simple calculations and graphs.

STEM-AND-LEAF PLOTS

Section 2.3 discussed histograms, which are extremely useful in graphically displaying the distribution of data. By using such graphical devices, we are able to learn something about the data that is not apparent while the data remain in a list of values. This additional insight is clearly an advantage. However, in constructing histograms we also suffer the disadvantage of having distorted data because we lose some information in the process. Generally we cannot reconstruct the original data set from the histogram, which shows that some distortion has occurred. We now introduce another device, one that enables us to see the distribution of data without losing information in the process.

In a **stem-and-leaf plot** we *sort* data according to a pattern that reveals the underlying distribution. The pattern involves separating a number into two parts, usually the first digit and the other digits. The *stem* consists of the leftmost digits and *leaves* consist of rightmost digits which are arranged in order. For example, the number 23 can be separated into a stem of 2 and a leaf of 3. The method is illustrated in the following example.

EXAMPLE A corporation librarian records the number of daily microfilm uses and compiles the sample data that follow. Construct a stem-and-leaf plot for these data.

| 10 | 11 | 15 | 23 | 27 | 28 | 38 | 38 | 39 | 39 |
| 40 | 41 | 44 | 45 | 46 | 46 | 52 | 57 | 58 | 65 |

SOLUTION   We note that the numbers have first digits of 1, 2, 3, 4, 5, or 6 and
we let those values become the "stem." We then construct a vertical
line and list the "leaves" as shown. The first row represents the
numbers 10, 11, 15. In the second row we have 23, 27, 28, and so on.

STEM	LEAVES
1	015
2	378
3	8899
4	014566
5	278
6	5

By turning the page on its side, we can see a distribution of these data, which,
in this case, roughly approximates a bell shape. We have also retained all the
information in the original list. We could reconstruct the original list of values from
the stem-and-leaf plot. In the next example we illustrate the construction of a
stem-and-leaf plot for data with three digits.

EXAMPLE   An aeronautical research team investigating the stall speed of an
ultralight aircraft obtained the following sample values (in knots).
Construct a stem-and-leaf plot and the graph suggested by that plot.

21.7   24.0   22.4   22.4   24.3   22.3   22.6   25.2
24.1   21.8   23.2   23.9   23.5   23.2   23.9   23.8

SOLUTION   Note that unlike the previous example, these data are not in order, so
two sweeps will be necessary. For the first sweep, we record the data
reading across one row at a time. For the second sweep, we arrange
each row of leaves in order from low to high.

STEM	LEAVES
21.	78
22.	4436
23.	295298
24.	031
25.	2

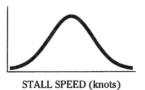

STALL SPEED (knots)

STEM	LEAVES
21.	78
22.	3446
23.	225899
24.	013
25.	2

Here we let the stem consist of the two left digits while the leaf is the
digit farthest to the right. Again, we can see the shape of the distribution by turning the page on its side and observing the columns of
digits above the line.

For some data sets, we can construct simplified stem-and-leaf plots by first rounding the values to two or three digits. If necessary, we can *condense* stem-and-leaf plots by combining adjacent rows. We can also *expand* them by subdividing rows into those with the digits 0 through 4 and those with digits 5 through 9. Note that the following two stem-and-leaf plots represent the same set of data, but the plot on the right has been stretched out to include more rows. Also note that such changes may affect the apparent shape of the distribution.

```
                                51 |          (last digits of 0 through 4)
                                51 | 6899     (last digits of 5 through 9)
         51 | 6899              52 | 034      (last digits of 0 through 4)
         52 | 0347    expand    52 | 7        (last digits of 5 through 9)
         53 | 3788   ------->   53 | 3        (last digits of 0 through 4)
                                53 | 788      (last digits of 5 through 9)
```

In the preceding example we expanded the number of rows. We can also condense a stem-and-leaf plot by combining adjacent rows as follows:

```
   50 | 01
   51 | 4             50-51 | 01*4
   52 | 56            52-53 | 56*368
   53 | 368           54-55 | 2457*3499
   54 | 2457  contract 56-57 | 0127*358
   55 | 3499  ------->  58-59 | 1269*17
   56 | 0127
   57 | 358                     ↑     ↑
   58 | 1269                    |     |
   59 | 17                    (581) (591)
```

You can use Minitab to generate stem-and-leaf plots. After entering the aircraft data in a column designated as C1, use the command STEM AND LEAF as shown below. The result is an *expanded* stem-and-leaf plot.

```
MTB > SET C1
DATA> 21.7 24.0 22.4 22.4 24.3 22.3 22.6 25.2
DATA> 24.1 21.8 23.2 23.9 23.5 23.2 23.9 23.8
DATA> ENDOFDATA
MTB > STEM AND LEAF C1

Stem-and-leaf of C1        N = 16
Leaf Unit = 0.10
    2    21 78
    5    22 344
    6    22 6
    8    23 22
    8    23 5899
    4    24 013
    1    24
    1    25 2
```

In the condensed plot, we separated digits in the "leaves" associated with the numbers in each stem by an asterisk. Every row in the condensed plot must include exactly one asterisk so that the shape of the plot is not distorted.

Another useful feature of stem-and-leaf plots is that their construction provides a fast and easy procedure for ranking data (putting data in order). Data must be ranked for a variety of statistical procedures, such as the Wilcoxon rank-sum test (Chapter 15) and finding the median of a set of data.

BOXPLOTS

When exploring a collection of numerical data, we want to be sure that we investigate (1) the value of a representative score (such as an average), (2) a measure of scattering or variation (such as the standard deviation), and (3) the nature or shape of the distribution. The distribution of data should definitely be considered because it may strongly affect other statistical methods we use and the conclusions we draw. In the spirit of exploratory data analysis, we should not simply examine a histogram and think that we understand the nature of the distribution. We should *explore.* As an example, in Fig. 2.17 (a) we show a Minitab printout of a histogram of the numbers of orders placed at the A.S.J. Computer mail order company on 20 different days. (We'll work with the actual scores later.) The last score was incorrectly entered with an extra zero: 1600 was used instead of 160. In Fig. 2.17 (b) we show the computer printout for the corrected data set. From Fig. 2.17 (b) we conclude that the data have a bell-shaped distribution, but that was not at all apparent from Fig. 2.17 (a), even though only one score was incorrect. The value of 1600 is an example of what's often called an **outlier,** which is a value that is much larger or much smaller than the other values. In this case, the outlier caused a severe distortion of the histogram. In other cases, outliers may be

FIGURE 2.17(a)
Histogram with wrong entry of 1600

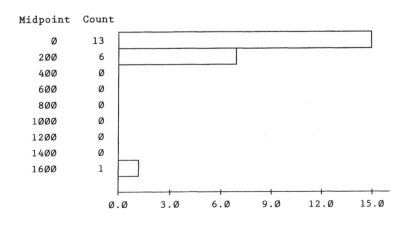

FIGURE 2.17(b)
Histogram of Corrected Data

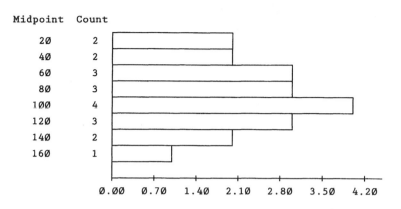

correct values but may continue to disguise the true nature of the distribution through histograms such as the one shown in Fig. 2.17 (a).

In addition to a histogram or a relative frequency histogram, we might also construct a **boxplot** (also referred to as a box-and-whisker diagram). The boxplot reveals more information about how the data are spread out. The construction of a boxplot requires that we obtain a 5-number summary, including the minimum score, the maximum score, the median, and two other values called *hinges*.

DEFINITIONS

The *lower hinge* is the median of the lower half of all scores (from the minimum score up to the original median).

The *upper hinge* is the median of the upper half of all scores (from the original median up to the maximum score).

A *5-number summary* of a set of data consists of the minimum score, the maximum score, the median, and the two hinges.

Hinges are very similar to quartiles. In fact, several texts use quartiles instead of hinges for the construction of boxplots. The differences between hinges and quartiles are usually small, especially for larger data sets. Our definition of *hinges* is consistent with John Tukey's definitions. You can easily find hinges by following these steps:

1. Arrange the data in increasing order. (Rank the data.)
2. Find the median. (With an odd number of scores, it's the middle score; with an even number of scores, the median is a new score equal to the mean of the two middle scores.)
3. List the lower half of the data from the minimum score up to and including the median found in step 2. The left hinge is the median of these scores.

4. List the upper half of the data starting with the median and including the scores up to and including the maximum. The right hinge is the median of these scores.
5. Now list the minimum, the left hinge (from step 3), the median (from step 2), the right hinge (from step 4), and the maximum.

This procedure will vary somewhat with different textbooks. The 20 scores depicted in Fig. 2.17 (a) are arranged in increasing order and listed below.

10 28 43 49 50 60 66 75 83 86 90 93 94 108 121 126 127 131 142 1600

| \

minimum   median (88)   maximum

10 28 43 49 50 (60) 66 75 83 86 88 88 90 93 94 108 (121) 126 127 131 142 1600

The *left hinge* of 60 is found by determining the median of this bottom half of the data.

The *right hinge* of 121 is found by determining the median of this top half of the data.

Note that the hinges are different from the quartiles. For this data set, $Q_1 = 55$ and $Q_3 = 123.5$, and the hinges are 60 and 121.

We will now use the 5-number summary (10, 60, 88, 121, 1600) to construct a boxplot. We begin with a horizontal scale as in Fig. 2.18 (a). We "box" in the hinges as shown and we extend lines to connect the minimum score to a hinge and the maximum score to a hinge. Figure 2.18 (b) shows the boxplot for the data set after the incorrect score of 1600 has been corrected to 160.

FIGURE 2.18
Incorrect and Correct Boxplots

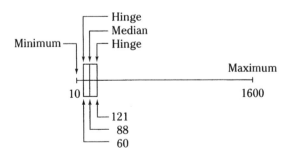

(a)

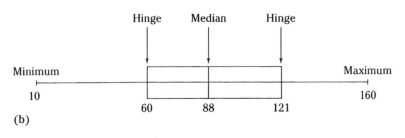

(b)

MAIL CONSISTENCY

A recent survey of 29,000 people who use the U.S. Postal Service revealed that they wanted better *consistency* in the times it takes to make a delivery. Now, a local letter could take one day or several days. *USA Today* reported a common complaint: "Just tell me how many days ahead I have to mail my mother's birthday card." The level of consistency can be measured by the standard deviation of the delivery times. A lower standard deviation reflects more consistency. The standard deviation is an important tool used to monitor and control the quality of goods and services.

FIGURE 2.19
Boxplots of Common
Distributions

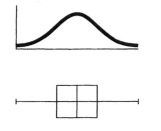

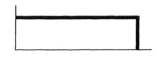

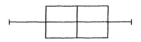

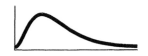

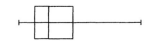

Note that by the procedures used here, approximately one-fourth of the values should fall between the low score and the left hinge, the two middle quarters are in the boxes, and approximately one-fourth of the values are between the right hinge and the maximum. The diagram therefore shows how the data are spread out. The uneven spread shown in Fig. 2.18 (a) is in strong contrast to the even spread shown in Fig. 2.18 (b). Suspecting that the numbers of orders placed at A.S.J. Computer have a bell-shaped distribution, we would expect to see a boxplot like the one in Fig. 2.18 (b), whereas the diagram in Fig. 2.18 (a) would raise suspicion and lead to further investigation. Figure 2.19 shows some common distributions along with the corresponding boxplots. You can use Minitab to create boxplots. (See the sample Minitab display of the same data.)

```
MTB > SET C1
DATA> 10 28 43 49 50 60 66 75 83 86
DATA> 90 93 94 108 121 126 127 131 142 160
DATA> ENDOFDATA
MTB > BOXPLOT C1
```

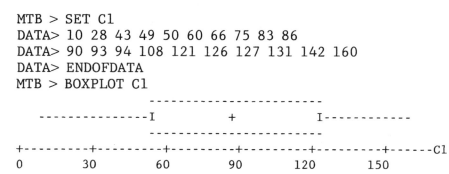

2.8 EXERCISES   BASIC CONCEPTS

In Exercises 1–4, list the original numbers in the data set represented by the given stem-and-leaf plots.

1.
STEM	LEAVES
2	00358

2.
STEM	LEAVES
1	001112278
2	3444569
3	013358

3.
STEM	LEAVES
40	6678
41	09999
42	13466
43	088

4.
STEM	LEAVES
68	45 45 47 86
69	33 38 89
70	52 59 93
71	27

In Exercises 5–7, construct the stem-and-leaf plots for the given data sets.

5. High temperatures (in degrees Fahrenheit) for the 31 days in July (recorded at Dutchess Community College):

80	68	84	86	85	77	64	81	93	94
97	93	89	82	76	75	83	90	83	84
92	94	90	92	91	84	81	84	79	80
80									

6. The amounts of sales per day at Lopez Auto Parts are given below (rounded to the nearest $10) for 20 randomly selected days.

390	350	360	390	410	400	380	390	410	420
430	380	390	400	400	410	360	420	410	390

7. Given below are the numbers of boxes of Gleason laundry detergent market-tested during a two-day period at 22 randomly selected stores in the Midwest. (Use an *expanded* stem-and-leaf plot.)

34	17	23	25	32	15	21	19	26	28	31
11	24	28	37	33	31	28	29	22	24	16

8. Candy bar weights (in ounces) from each of two machines (made by the Dayton Machine Company) are given below. Construct two separate stem-and-leaf plots and use them to compare the performances of the two machines. Is either machine better? Explain.

Machine 1:	6.1	6.0	6.1	5.9	6.0	6.1	6.0
	6.0	6.0	6.1	5.9	6.0	6.1	6.0
	5.9						
Machine 2:	6.1	6.0	6.2	6.2	6.1	6.3	6.4	6.3
	6.5	6.0	6.3	6.6	6.2	6.3	6.3	6.4
	6.2							

In Exercises 9–12, use the given data to construct boxplots. Identify the values of the minimum, maximum, median, and hinges.

9. Ages of selected full-time undergraduate students (in years):

17.2	17.9	18.6	18.8	19.3	19.3	20.0
20.1	23.4	26.3				

10. Monthly rental costs of apartments in the Northeast (in dollars):

540	545	555	560	560	570	575
590	650	730				

11. Number of words typed in a 5-min civil service test taken by 25 applicants.

174	181	219	213	213	207	106	111	143
166	350	183	198	193	190	190	185	220
229	257	243	281	308	160	221		

12. Time (in hours of operation) between failures for prototypes of computer printers:

34	22	4	9	27	36	12	40	29	32
35	25	7	9	26	36	45	43	41	2
31	31	30	14	15	18	10	27	38	21

2.8 EXERCISES   BEYOND THE BASICS

13. Filling machines are designed to put one gal (128 oz) of ice cream in each container. Figure 2.20 shows boxplots of data from two such machines.
    a. Based on the two boxplots, which machine is doing a better job of filling the containers? Explain.
    b. A production supervisor claims that because both machines put an average of a gallon of ice cream in the containers, both machines are working well. What is wrong with this claim?
    c. Listed below are the data sets corresponding to the boxplots. Which data set corresponds to the boxplot for Machine 1?

Data set A:	128.0	128.5	127.5	127.0	128.0
	127.5	128.0	128.5	129.0	
Data set B:	127.0	128.0	129.5	128.5	130.0
	129.0	128.0	126.0	127.0	

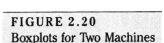

FIGURE 2.20
Boxplots for Two Machines

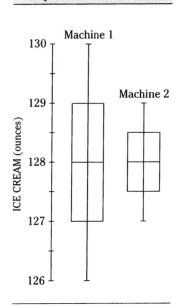

14. Assume that you have just been hired by the Soyseed Company, an agribusiness that specializes in seeds for planting soybeans. The manager has 50-lb bags of seed filled by an automatic machine bagger with three nozzles that fill three bags at a time. Listed below are data collected by selecting nine bags (one every 5 min) for each nozzle.

Nozzle 1:	50.3	50.5	49.1	52.3	51.4	48.9	51.0	49.5	51.7
Nozzle 2:	50.1	49.6	49.2	49.8	50.5	50.9	49.5	50.0	50.7
Nozzle 3:	50.7	50.9	50.5	50.1	50.0	49.6	49.8	49.5	49.2

    a. Construct a boxplot for each nozzle.
    b. Since you don't know whether the filling by each nozzle is a stable process, construct a run chart for each nozzle and identify any out-of-control patterns.
    c. Which nozzle(s) seems to be performing well, and which nozzle(s) seems to be performing poorly. Explain.

15. Two shifts of data-processing personnel produce about the same number of invoices each day. Examination of invoices from 11 randomly selected days reveals the number of invoices with typing errors. Data were gathered for the number of invoices per day that have typing errors, and the results are below.

Shift 1:	10	12	18	10	9	14	20	19	10	16	9
Shift 2:	7	8	6	4	8	7	8	6	5	7	6

    a. Construct a boxplot for each shift.
    b. Compare the performances of the two shifts.

16. Make sketches of histograms that correspond to the given boxplots.

    a. (a)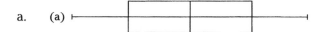

    b. (b)

    c.

    (c)

17. In "Ages of Oscar-Winning Best Actors and Actresses" (*Mathematics Teacher* magazine), Richard Brown and Gretchen Davis use stem-and-leaf plots and boxplots to compare the ages of actors and actresses when they won Oscars. Here are the results for 30 recent and consecutive winners from each category:

Actors:	32	51	33	61	35	45	55	39	76	37
	42	40	32	60	38	56	48	48	40	43
	62	43	42	44	41	56	39	46	31	47
Actresses:	80	26	41	21	61	38	49	33	74	30
	33	41	31	35	41	42	37	26	34	34
	35	26	61	60	34	24	30	37	31	27

a. Construct a "back-to-back" stem-and-leaf plot for the above data. The first two scores from each group have been entered.

ACTORS' AGES	STEM	ACTRESSES' AGES
	2	6
2	3	
	4	
1	5	
	6	
	7	
	8	0

b. Using the same scale, construct a boxplot for actors' ages and another boxplot for actresses' ages.

c. Using the results from parts *a* and *b*, compare the two different sets of data and try to explain any difference.

18. The boxplots discussed in this section are often called *skeletal* boxplots. When investigating outliers, a useful variation is to construct boxplots as follows:

a. Calculate the hinge difference, $D =$ (upper hinge) $-$ (lower hinge).

b. Draw the box with the median and hinges as usual, but when extending the lines that branch out from the box, go only as far as the scores that are within $1.5D$ of the box.

c. **Mild outliers** are scores above the upper hinge by $1.5D$ to $3D$, or below the lower hinge by $1.5D$ to $3D$. Plot them as solid dots.

d. **Extreme outliers** are scores above the upper hinge by more than $3D$ or below the lower hinge by more than $3D$. Plot them as small hollow circles.

Figure 2.21 is an example of the boxplot described here. Use this procedure to construct the boxplot for the scores 3, 15, 17, 18, 21, 21, 22, 25, 27, 30, 38, 49, and 68, and identify any mild outliers or extreme outliers.

FIGURE 2.21
Boxplot with Outliers Identified

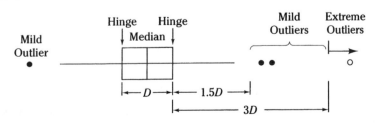

Vocabulary List

Define and give an example of each term.

descriptive statistics

inferential statistics

frequency table

lower class limits

upper class limits

class boundaries

class marks

class width

cumulative frequency table

relative frequency table

histogram

relative frequency histogram

pareto chart

pie chart

run chart

trend chart

statistically stable

average

measures of central tendency

arithmetic mean

mean

sample size

median

mode

bimodal

multimodal

midrange

weighted mean

skewed

negatively skewed

positively skewed

range

standard deviation

deviation

mean deviation

variance

range rule of thumb

Chebyshev's theorem

empirical rule

68-95-99 rule

standard score

z score

quartiles

deciles

percentiles

interquartile range

semi-interquartile range

midquartile

10–90 percentile range

exploratory data analysis (EDA)

stem-and-leaf plot

outlier

boxplot

lower hinge

upper hinge

5-number summary

Review

Chapter 2 dealt mainly with the methods and techniques of descriptive statistics. The focus was on developing the ability to organize, summarize, and illustrate data and to extract from data some meaningful measurements. Section 2.2 considered the frequency table as an excellent device for summarizing data, and Section 2.3 dealt with graphic illustrations of samples, populations, and stable processes, including histograms, relative frequency histograms, Pareto charts, and pie charts. Section 2.4 presented the run chart as a graphical technique for determining whether a process is statistically stable. All these visual illustrations help us to determine the position and distribution of a set of data. In Section 2.5 we defined the common averages or measures of central tendency. The mean, the median, the mode, and the midrange represent different ways of characterizing the central value of a collection of data. The weighted mean is used to find the average of a set of scores that may vary in importance. In Section 2.6 we presented the important measures of variation, including the range, the standard deviation, and the variance; these descriptive statistics are designed to measure the variability or consistency among a set of scores. In addition, we used two guidelines (Chebyshev's theorem and the empirical rule) to show how the proportion of data is related to the standard deviation. Section 2.7 introduced the standard score, or z score as a way of measuring the number of standard deviations by which a given score differs from the mean. We specifically used z scores for judging whether particular scores are ordinary or unusual. That section also included the common measures of position: quartiles, percentiles, and deciles. Finally, Section 2.8 presented stem-and-leaf plots and boxplots used in exploratory data analysis. The stem-and-leaf plots help us analyze the distribution of data, whereas boxplots are useful for depicting the spread of the data.

The concepts developed in this chapter should enable us to organize, present, and describe collections of data composed of single scores; to compute the key descriptive statistics that will be used in later applications; and to form a rough judgment about how extreme a single score is. We now have a better understanding of the 150 home selling prices given in Table 2.1. The histogram allowed us to see the shape of the distribution of those values. We know that the mean is $153,775, the median is $144,900, and the standard deviation is $41,611. The data are summarized in a frequency table and depicted in a histogram. Subsequent chapters will consider other ways of using sample statistics.

IMPORTANT FORMULAS

$\bar{x} = \dfrac{\Sigma x}{n}$ Sample mean

$\bar{x} = \dfrac{\Sigma (f \cdot x)}{\Sigma f}$ Computing the sample mean when the data are in a frequency table

$s = \sqrt{\dfrac{\Sigma (x - \bar{x})^2}{n - 1}}$ Standard deviation of sample data

$s^2 = \dfrac{\Sigma (x - \bar{x})^2}{n - 1}$ Variance of sample data

$s = \sqrt{\dfrac{n(\Sigma x^2) - (\Sigma x)^2}{n(n - 1)}}$ Shortcut formula for standard deviation

$s = \sqrt{\dfrac{n[\Sigma (f \cdot x^2)] - [\Sigma (f \cdot x)]^2}{n(n - 1)}}$ Computing the standard deviation when the data are in a frequency table

$z = \dfrac{x - \bar{x}}{s}$ or $\dfrac{x - \mu}{\sigma}$ Standard score or z score

AUTHORS IDENTIFIED

In 1787–88 Alexander Hamilton, John Jay, and James Madison anonymously published the famous *Federalist* papers in an attempt to convince New Yorkers that they should ratify the Constitution. The identity of most of the papers' authors became known, but the authorship of 12 of the papers was contested. Through statistical analysis of the *frequencies* of various words, we can now conclude that James Madison is the *likely* author of these 12 papers. For many of the disputed papers, the evidence in favor of Madison's authorship is overwhelming to the degree that we can be almost certain of being correct.

Review Exercises

1. The values given below are snow depths (in centimeters) measured as part of a study of satellite observations and water resources (based on sample data in *Space Mathematics* published by NASA). Find the (a) mean, (b) median, (c) mode, (d) midrange, (e) range, (f) variance, (g) standard deviation.

   19   18   12   25   22   8   8   16

2. Air America keeps a record of the numbers of incoming calls between 10:00 A.M. and 11:00 A.M. each day for 14 consecutive days. The results are given below.

   97   106   110   100   108   112   104   99   109   103   92   103   108   105

   a. Consider this sample data set to be *process data*. Construct a run chart and determine whether the process is statistically stable.
   b. Find the mean, median, mode, midrange, range, variance, and standard deviation.
   c. Construct a stem-and-leaf plot of the data. Do the data sets seem to be bell-shaped?
   d. Calculate the values of $\bar{x} - 2s$ and $\bar{x} + 2s$.
   e. Using the empirical rule, determine what proportion of scores should fall between the two values found in part d.
   f. Using Chebyshev's theorem, determine what proportion of scores should fall between the two values found in part d.
   g. Using the actual scores given, find the proportion of scores that are between the two values found in part d.

3. The given scores represent the number of cars rejected in one day at an automobile assembly plant. The 50 scores correspond to 50 different randomly selected days. Construct a frequency table with 10 classes.

29	58	80	35	30	23	88	49	35	97
12	73	54	91	45	28	61	61	45	81
83	23	71	63	47	87	36	8	94	26
95	63	86	42	22	44	8	27	20	33
28	91	87	15	67	10	45	67	26	19

4. Construct a relative frequency table (with 10 classes) for the data in Exercise 3.
5. Construct a histogram that corresponds to the frequency table from Exercise 3.
6. For the data in Exercise 3, find (a) Q_1, (b) P_{45}, and (c) the percentile corresponding to the score of 30.
7. Use the frequency table from Exercise 3 to find the mean and standard deviation for the number of rejects.
8. Use the data from Exercise 3 and the results from Exercise 7 to find the standard score or z score for these numbers of rejects: 8, 61, 97. Categorize these values as being ordinary or unusual.
9. Use the data from Exercise 3 to construct a boxplot.
10. The values given below are the living areas (in square feet) of 12 homes built during the past year in Dutchess County, New York. Treat this data set as a *sample* and find the (a) mean, (b) median, (c) mode, (d) midrange, (e) range, (f) variance, (g) standard deviation.

3060	1600	2000	1300	2000	1956
2400	1200	1632	1800	1248	2025

11. Construct a stem-and-leaf plot for the data in Exercise 10.

12. For the data given in Exercise 10, find the z score corresponding to (a) 1200 and (b) 2400.

13. Use the data given in Exercise 10 to construct a boxplot.

14. A supplier constructs a frequency table for the number of car stereo units sold daily. Use that table to find the mean and standard deviation.

NUMBER SOLD	FREQUENCY
0–3	5
4–7	9
8–11	8
12–15	6
16–19	3

15. Using the frequency table given in Exercise 14, construct the corresponding relative frequency histogram.

16. a. A set of data has a mean of 45.6. What is the mean if 5.0 is added to each score?

    b. A set of data has a standard deviation of 3.0. What is the standard deviation if 5.0 is added to each score?

    c. You just completed a calculation for the variance of a set of scores, and you got an answer of -21.3. What do you conclude?

17. At the Stewart Foods processing plant, quality control inspectors reject bags of potato chips that are underweight. Given below are the numbers of potato chip bags rejected in 24 consecutive one-hour blocks.

    23 18 21 16 20 19 17 21 19 21 20 19
    21 18 23 25 33 37 20 17 21 23 18 20

    a. Construct a run chart for this process. Does the process appear to be statistically stable?

    b. Construct a stem-and-leaf plot.

    c. Construct a boxplot.

18. Treating the data in Exercise 17 as a *sample,* find the (a) mean, (b) median, (c) mode, (d) midrange, (e) range, (f) variance, (g) standard deviation.

19. Use the data from Exercise 17 to find the z scores corresponding to these values: 18, 23, 33, 37. Are any of these values unusual?

20. Grandma's Jam Company, a maker of premium preserves, wants very few of its 16-oz jars to contain less than 16 oz of product. Management decides that 16.1 oz (on the average) will be put in the jars so that very few will be underweight. Listed below are the weights of 25 jars (one chosen every 15 min) filled by one machine during one day's shift. The data are in order by row.

    16.06   16.15   16.24   16.05   16.10   16.04   16.23   15.92   16.19
    16.02   16.14   15.96   16.14   16.29   16.02   16.07   16.10   16.28
    16.07   15.96   16.17   16.13   16.06   16.19   16.17

    a. Construct a run chart and determine whether the process is statistically stable.

    b. Construct a boxplot of the weights.

    c. Construct a histogram of the weights. Does the process appear to result in values with a bell-shaped distribution?

21. Refer to the data from Exercise 20.
    a. Use the *range rule of thumb* ($s \approx$ range/4) to estimate the sample standard deviation s.
    b. Considering the data to be a *sample,* find the mean, median, mode, midrange, range, variance, and standard deviation.
    c. Based on the results from parts *a* and *b,* how well did the range rule of thumb work in this case?
    d. Does the machine seem to be filling the jars with the desired average?
    e. Use the mean and standard deviation from part *b* to find the z scores for these weights: 16.10, 16.29, 15.95.
22. Refer to the data from Exercise 20 and assume that the mean is 16.1 oz and the standard deviation is 0.10 oz.
    a. Use the empirical rule to estimate the percentage of the jars that will be underfilled.
    b. If your plan is to adjust the mean so that only about 2.5% of the jars are underfilled, what is the value of the mean that accomplishes this? (Use the empirical rule.)
    c. Assume that engineers are able to work on the machine and process in order to decrease the standard deviation to 0.02 oz. Repeat part *b* using this assumption of a lower standard deviation.
    d. If the company produces 2 million jars each year, how many ounces could be saved by using the setting of part *c* instead of 16.2 oz?

Computer Project

Forestry planners need to estimate amounts of timber that can be obtained from different regions. Minitab has a file that includes the volumes (in cubic feet) of a sample of black cherry trees in the Alleghany National Forest in Pennsylvania. After loading Minitab, retrieve that file by entering RETRIEVE 'DATA/TREES' and proceed to display the tree volumes by entering PRINT C3. (The volumes are in column C3.) Now enter DESCRIBE C3 to find the mean, the standard deviation, the minimum, and the maximum. Obtain a histogram of the volumes by entering HISTOGRAM C3 or GHISTOGRAM C3. Describe the distribution or shape of the data. If this data set is not available on your version of Minitab, use these volumes:

10.3	10.3	10.2	16.4	18.8	19.7	15.6	18.2
21.0	21.4	21.3	19.1	22.2	33.8	27.4	25.7
36.3	38.3	42.6	55.4	55.7	58.3	51.5	51.0
22.6	19.9	24.2	24.9	34.5	31.7	77.0	

WHAT BATTERY SHOULD YOU BUY?

1 It is your job to select the battery supplier for General Motors. You are considering two different manufacturers of car batteries, and you obtain data on the lifespans (in months) for a sample of 200 batteries from each company. Analyze and compare the two data sets. Write a report that summarizes the relevant characteristics of the data and conclude with a recommendation based on your results. The data sets are summarized in the Minitab displays given below. These Minitab displays result from the command DESCRIBE, as in DESCRIBE C1, which provides the indicated statistics for the data stored in C1.

TELEKTRONIC

N	MEAN	MEDIAN	TRMEAN	STDEV	SEMEAN
200	47.885	48.000	47.861	3.038	0.215

MIN	MAX	Q1	Q3
40.000	58.000	46.000	50.000

BOSTON BATTERIES

N	MEAN	MEDIAN	TRMEAN	STDEV	SEMEAN
200	48.715	49.000	48.694	5.698	0.403

MIN	MAX	Q1	Q3
33.000	65.000	45.000	52.000

Collecting Your Own Data

2 Through observation or experimentation, compile a list of sample data that are at the interval or ratio levels of measurement. Obtain at least 40 values, and try to select data from an interesting or meaningful population.

a. Describe the nature of the data. What do the values represent?

b. What method was used to collect the values?

c. What are some possible reasons why the data might not be representative of the population? That is, what are some possible sources of bias?

d. Find the value of each of the following: sample size, minimum, maximum, mean, median, midrange, range, standard deviation, variance, and the quartiles Q_1 and Q_3.

e. Construct a frequency table, histogram, stem-and-leaf plot, and boxplot.

f. Write a brief report summarizing any important characteristics of the data.

CHAPTER 3

Probability

When Are New Processes Better Processes?

Susan Benton is a quality control manager for the Maxima Corporation, which produces video cassette recorders (VCRs). She knows that her company manufactures VCRs with a 5% rate of defects.

Tom Clarke is a production manager who claims that his department has developed a new manufacturing process that reduces defects. When 20 VCRs are manufactured with the new process, it is found that none of them is defective. Tom states that this is evidence that the new process is better. He says that "After all, a 5% rate of defects is equivalent to 1 in 20. We manufactured 20 VCRs and tested them, but there weren't any defects." Susan Benton diplomatically tells Tom that while the result is certainly encouraging, it is not sufficient evidence to conclude that the new process is better. She says that it is easy to get zero defects among 20, even if the rate of defects continues to be 5%. Susan believes that more evidence is needed before the new process is fully implemented. Tom is anxious to proceed with the new process because he believes it is better.

The issue of whether the new process can be considered better hinges on the likelihood of getting zero defects among 20, assuming that the defect rate is 5%. If that event is very unlikely, then Tom's explanation of an improved process seems plausible. However, if that event is very likely, then there isn't enough evidence to support Tom in his claim of an improved process.

We can measure amounts of likelihood with probability values. We will use probability values and basic probability rules to determine the likelihood of the event in question. We can then resolve the issue confronting Susan Benton and Tom Clarke.

3.1 OVERVIEW

Probability theory is sometimes made more difficult because correct results are sometimes very different from results we might intuitively expect. For example, in his book *Innumeracy* (a great little book), John Allen Paulos states that there is better than a 99% chance that if you take a deep breath, you will inhale a molecule that was exhaled in dying Caesar's last breath. In the same morbid spirit, consider this: If Socrates' fatal cup of hemlock was mostly water, then the next glass of water you drink will likely contain one of those same molecules. In theory, these events are very likely, but most people believe that they have almost no chance of occurring. Here, our intuition is misleading.

More positively, consider this: In this country of more than 200 million consumers, a market researcher needs to survey only 1000 people (about 0.0005% of the population) to get a good estimate of the proportion of consumers who recognize a particular brand name, such as Coca-Cola or Campbell's soup.

The preceding conclusions are based on simple principles of probability, which play a critical role in the theory of statistics. All of us now form simple probability conclusions in our daily lives. Sometimes these determinations are based on fact, whereas others are subjective. In addition to its importance in the study of statistics, probability theory is playing an increasingly important role in a society that must attempt to measure uncertainties. Before firing up a nuclear power plant, we should have some knowledge about the probability of a meltdown. Before arming a nuclear warhead, we should have some knowledge about the probability of an accidental detonation. Before opening a retail store, we should have some knowledge of the probability of achieving minimum sales goals.

In Chapter 1 we stated that inferential statistics involves the use of sample evidence in formulating inferences or conclusions about a population or a process. These inferential decisions are based on probabilities or likelihoods of events. As an example, suppose that a statistician plans to study the hiring practices of a large company. She finds that of the last 100 employees hired, all are men. Perhaps the company hires men and women at the same rate and the run of 100 men is an extremely rare chance event. Perhaps the hiring practices favor males. What should we infer? The statistician, along with most reasonable people, would conclude that men are favored. This decision is based on the very low probability of getting 100 consecutive men by chance alone.

Subsequent chapters will develop methods of statistical inference that rely on this type of thinking. It is therefore important to acquire a basic understanding of probability theory. We want to cultivate some intuitive feeling for what probabilities are, and we want to develop some very basic skills in calculating the probabilities of certain events.

This chapter begins by introducing the fundamental concept of mathematical probability, then proceeds to investigate the basic rules of probability: the addition rule, the multiplication rule, and the rule of complements. It also considers techniques of counting the number of ways an event can occur. The primary objective of this chapter is to develop a sound understanding of probability values used in subsequent chapters. A secondary objective is to develop the ability to solve simple probability problems, which are valuable in their own right, as we can use them to make decisions and better understand our world.

3.2 FUNDAMENTALS

In this section we introduce the fundamental principles of probability theory, but we begin by defining some terms commonly used in discussing probabilities. After we define the terms experiment, event, simple event, and sample space, we will then present two basic rules for finding probabilities.

> **DEFINITION**
>
> An *experiment* is any activity that allows researchers to obtain observations.
>
> An *event* is any collection of results or outcomes of an experiment.

For example, the random selection of a policyholder from an insurance company's data bank is an experiment, and the result of that policyholder being a woman is an event. Many different women can be selected, but we will soon see that some probability calculations require that we identify events that cannot be broken down into simpler outcomes.

> **DEFINITION**
>
> A *simple event* is an outcome or an event that cannot be broken down any further.

When randomly selecting an insurance policyholder, the occurrence of Gloria Steinham is a simple event that cannot be broken down any further, but the occurrence of a woman is not a simple event, because it can be broken down into the simple events corresponding to individual women.

> **DEFINITION**
>
> The *sample space* for an experiment consists of all possible simple events. That is, the sample space consists of all outcomes that cannot be broken down any further.

In the experiment of randomly selecting a policyholder, the sample space consists of all the individual policyholders.

There is no universal agreement as to the definition of the probability of an event, but among the various theories and schools of thought, two basic approaches emerge most often: the relative frequency approach and the classical approach. These approaches will be embodied in two rules for finding probabilities. In the notation we employ, P denotes probability, and capital letters such as A, B, C denote specific events. For example, A might represent the event of winning a million-dollar state lottery; $P(A)$ denotes the probability of event A occurring.

RULE 1

Relative frequency approximation of probability. Conduct (or observe) an experiment a large number of times and count the number of times that event *A* actually occurs. Then *estimate P(A)* as follows:

$$P(A) = \frac{\text{number of times } A \text{ occurred}}{\text{number of times experiment was repeated}}$$

RULE 2

Classical approach to probability. Assume that a given experiment has *n* different simple events, each of which has an *equal chance* of occurring. If event *A* can occur in *s* of these *n* ways, then

$$P(A) = \frac{s}{n} \quad \text{(requires equally likely outcomes)}$$

Note that the classical approach requires equally likely outcomes. If the outcomes are not equally likely, we must use the relative frequency estimate. Figure 3.1 illustrates this important distinction.

When determining probabilities by using Rule 1 (the relative frequency approach), we obtain an approximation instead of an exact value. As the total number of observations increases, the corresponding approximations tend to get closer to the actual probability. This idea is stated as a theorem commonly referred to as the law of large numbers.

FIGURE 3.1
Comparison of Two
Definitions of Probability

When trying to determine $P(2)$ on a "shaved" die, we must repeat the experiment of rolling it many times and then form the ratio of the number of times 2 occurred to the number of rolls. That ratio is our estimate of $P(2)$.

(a) Relative Frequency Approach (Rule 1)

With a balanced and fair die, each of the six faces has an equal chance of occurring.

$$P(2) = \frac{\text{number of ways 2 can occur}}{\text{total number of simple events}} = 1/6$$

(b) Classical Approach (Rule 2)

FIGURE 3.2
Illustration of the Law of Large Numbers

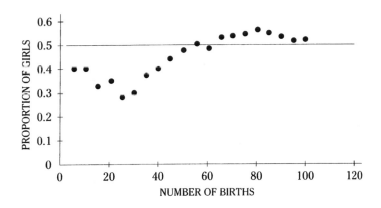

LAW OF LARGE NUMBERS

As an experiment is repeated again and again, the relative frequency probability (from Rule 1) of an event tends to approach the actual probability.

The law of large numbers tells us that the relative frequency approximations from Rule 1 tend to get better with more observations. This law reflects a simple notion supported by common sense: In only a few trials, results can vary substantially, but with a very large number of trials, results tend to be more stable and consistent. For example, it would not be unusual to get 4 girls in 4 births, but it would be extremely unusual to get 400 girls in 400 births.

Figure 3.2 illustrates the law of large numbers by showing computer-simulated results. Note that as the number of births increases, the proportion of girls approaches the 0.5 value.

Many experiments involving equally likely outcomes are so complicated that the classical approach of Rule 2 isn't practical. Instead, we can get estimates of the desired probabilities by using the relative frequency approach of Rule 1. Computer simulations are often helpful in such cases.

The following examples illustrate the use of Rules 1 and 2. In some of these examples we use the term *random.*

DEFINITION

In a *random selection* of an element, all elements available for selection have the same chance of being chosen.

This concept of random selection is extremely important in statistics. When making inferences based on samples, we must have a sampling process that is representative, impartial, and unbiased. Also, random selection is different from haphazard selection. Ask people to randomly select one of the 10 digits from 0 through 9, and they tend to favor some digits while ignoring others. Implementation of a random selection process often requires careful and thoughtful planning.

EXAMPLE   On an ACT or SAT test, a typical question has 5 possible answers. If an examinee makes a random guess on one such question, what is the probability that the response is wrong?

SOLUTION   There are 5 possible outcomes or answers, and there are 4 ways to answer incorrectly. Random guessing implies that the outcomes are equally likely, so we apply Rule 2 to get

$$P(\text{wrong answer}) = \frac{4}{5} \quad \text{or} \quad 0.8$$

In the preceding example, we know that the sample space consists of 5 different simple events corresponding to the 5 possible answers. In some other cases, the total number of simple events in the sample space is not known and must be found, as in the following example.

EXAMPLE   In an insurance study of California drivers, 561 wore seat belts and 289 did not (based on data from the National Highway Traffic Safety Administration). If one of these drivers is randomly selected, what is the probability that he or she wore a seat belt?

SOLUTION   The total number of subjects in this study is $561 + 289 = 850$. With random selection, the 850 subjects are equally likely and Rule 2 applies.

$$P(\text{wearing seat belt}) = \frac{561}{850} = 0.660 \quad \begin{array}{l}\text{number wearing seat belts} \\ \text{total number of drivers}\end{array}$$

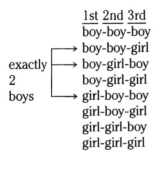

1st 2nd 3rd
boy-boy-boy
boy-boy-girl
boy-girl-boy
boy-girl-girl
girl-boy-boy
girl-boy-girl
girl-girl-boy
girl-girl-girl

exactly 2 boys

EXAMPLE   Find the probability that a couple with 3 children will have exactly 2 boys. (Assume that boys and girls are equally likely and that the sex of any child is not influenced by the sex of any other child.)

SOLUTION   In this solution we first list the sample space that identifies the 8 outcomes. Those outcomes are equally likely, so we use Rule 2. Of those 8 different possible outcomes, 3 correspond to exactly 2 boys, so that

$$P(\text{2 boys in 3 births}) = \frac{3}{8} = 0.375$$

EXAMPLE   In order to establish life insurance premiums, the Life Trust Insurance Company must find the probability of a 20-year-old male living to be 30 years of age. What is that probability?

SOLUTION Here the two outcomes of living and dying are not equally likely, so we must use the relative frequency approximation. This requires that we observe a large number of 20-year-old males and then count those who live to be 30. Suppose that we survey 10,000 20-year-old males and find that 9840 of them lived to be 30 (these are realistic figures based on U.S. Department of Health and Human Services data). Then the empirical approximation becomes

$$P(\text{20-year-old male living to 30}) = \frac{9,840}{10,000} = 0.984$$

This is the basic approach insurance companies use in the development of mortality tables.

EXAMPLE If a year is selected at random, find the probability that Thanksgiving Day will be on (a) Wednesday; (b) Thursday.

SOLUTION
a. Thanksgiving Day always falls on the fourth Thursday in November. It is therefore impossible for Thanksgiving to be on a Wednesday. When an event is impossible, we say that its probability is 0.
b. It is certain that Thanksgiving will be on a Thursday. When an event is certain to occur, we say that its probability is 1.

The probability of any impossible event is 0.
The probability of any event that is certain to occur is 1.

Because any event imaginable is impossible, certain, or somewhere in between, it is reasonable to conclude that the mathematical probability of any event is either 0, 1, or a number between 0 and 1 (see Fig. 3.3). We can express this property as follows:

$$0 \le P(A) \le 1 \qquad \text{for any event } A$$

In Fig. 3.3, the scale of 0 through 1 is shown on top, whereas the more familiar and common expressions of likelihood are shown on the bottom.

FIGURE 3.3
Possible Values for Probabilities

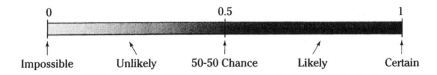

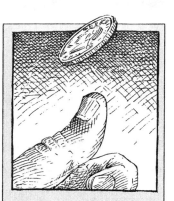

SENSITIVE SURVEYS

Survey respondents are sometimes reluctant to answer questions honestly on a sensitive topic, such as employee theft or sex. Stanley Warner (York University, Ontario) devised a scheme that leads to more accurate results in such cases. As an example, ask employees if they stole within the past year and also ask them to flip a coin. Instruct the employees to answer no if they didn't steal and the coin turns up heads. Otherwise, they should answer yes. The employees are more likely to be honest because the coin flip helps protect their privacy. You can then use probability theory to analyze responses so that you obtain more accurate results.

SUBJECTIVE PROBABILITIES

The relative frequency approach and the classical approach are two formal methods for finding probabilities of events, but another approach is simply to guess or estimate a probability. The technique of guessing is somewhat familiar to students who are sometimes not as well prepared for a test as they would like, but this technique is also used by professionals who set casino odds for sporting events. We commonly refer to a guess or an estimate based on knowledge of relevant circumstances as a **subjective probability.** A business might use a subjective probability in deciding whether to introduce a new product or to expand to a new site. Subjective probabilities of relevant events, such as those relating to sales levels and overhead costs, influence such decisions.

COMPLEMENTARY EVENTS

DEFINITION

The *complement* of event *A*, denoted by $\overline{A}$, consists of all outcomes in which event *A* does not occur.

The complement of event *A* is the event that *A* does *not* occur. If *A* represents an outcome of answering a test question correctly, then the complementary event $\overline{A}$ represents a wrong answer.

EXAMPLE A consumer test group consists of 80 persons, 30 of whom are women. If we randomly select one person from this group, find the probability of *not* getting a woman.

SOLUTION Since 30 of the 80 consumers are women, it follows that 50 of the 80 consumers are *not* women, so that

$$P \text{ (not selecting a woman)} = \frac{50}{80} = 0.625$$

ROUNDING OFF PROBABILITIES

Although it is difficult to develop a universal rule for rounding off probabilities, the following guide will apply to most problems in this text.

Either give the exact fraction representing a probability, or round off final decimal results to three significant digits.

All the digits in a number are significant except for the zeros that are included for proper placement of the decimal point. The probability of 0.00128506 can be rounded to three significant digits as 0.00129. The probability of 1/3 can be left as a fraction or rounded in decimal form to 0.333, but not 0.3.

An important concept of this section is the mathematical expression of probability as a number between 0 and 1. This type of expression is fundamental and common in statistical procedures, and we will use it throughout the remainder of this text. A typical computer output, for example, may involve a P-value expression such as "Significance less than 0.001." We will discuss the meaning of P-values later, but they are essentially probabilities of the type we discuss in this section. We should recognize that a probability of 0.001 (equivalent to 1/1000) corresponds to an event that is very rare in that it occurs an average of only once in a thousand trials.

3.2 EXERCISES | BASIC CONCEPTS

1. Which of the following values *cannot* be probabilities?

   $1.2, \quad \dfrac{77}{75}, \quad \dfrac{9}{10}, \quad 0, \quad -\dfrac{1}{2}, \quad 1, \quad 5, \quad 0.9999, \quad 1.001, \quad \sqrt{2}, \quad \sqrt{\dfrac{5}{7}}$

2. a. What is $P(A)$ if event A is certain to occur?
   b. What is $P(A)$ if event A is impossible?
   c. A sample space consists of 14 separate events that are equally likely. What is the probability of each?
   d. On a college entrance exam, each question has 5 possible answers. If an examinee makes a random guess on the first question, what is the probability that the response is correct?

3. In a sales impact study, Media General and the Associated Press surveyed 1084 adults; of these, 813 indicated support for a ban on household aerosols. Use these survey results to estimate the probability that a randomly selected adult would support such a ban.

4. Among 750 taxpayers with incomes under $100,000, 20 are audited by the IRS (based on IRS data). Use this sample to estimate the probability of a tax return being audited if the income is below $100,000.

5. A researcher for the Life Trust Insurance Company found that in a recent year, New York State reported 68,593 vehicle accidents, with 26,201 of them involving reportable property damage of $600 or more (data from the New York State Department of Motor Vehicles). Use these results to estimate the probability that a random New York State accident results in reportable property damage of at least $600.

6. If a person is randomly selected, find the probability that his or her birthday is October 18, which is National Statistics Day in Japan. Ignore leap years.

7. In a recent national election, there were 25,569,000 citizens in the 18–24 age bracket. Of these, 9,230,000 actually voted. Find the empirical probability that a person randomly selected from this group did vote in that national election.

8. In a marketing study of brand recognition, 831 consumers knew Campbell's soup and 18 did not (based on data from Total Research Corporation). Use these results to estimate the probability that a randomly selected consumer will recognize Campbell's soup.

9. A market research firm uses a computer to generate random telephone numbers. Of the numbers generated and in service, 56 are unlisted and 144 are listed in the telephone directory. If one of these telephone numbers is randomly selected, what is the probability that it is unlisted?

10. In a survey of U.S. households, 352 had home computers and 962 did not (based on data from the Electronic Industries Association). Use this sample to estimate the probability of a household having a home computer.

11. A study of consumer loans found that 37 were defaults and 1383 had all obligations satisfied (based on data from the American Bankers Association). For a consumer loan randomly selected from those studied, find the probability of a default.

12. Data collected by volunteers in the Straphangers Campaign showed that 89 New York City subway cars had broken doors and 286 cars did not. If a car is randomly selected, what is the approximate probability it will have broken doors?

13. The sales department of the Medassist Pharmaceutical Company researches Bureau of Census data and finds that in a survey of 600 people in the 18–25 age bracket, 237 people smoke. (They want to sell nicotine patches to smokers who want to quit.) If a person in that age bracket is randomly selected, find the approximate probability that he or she smokes.

14. An Environmental Protection Agency survey of cars originally equipped with catalytic converters found that 280 cars still had their converters and 12 cars had them removed. What is the approximate probability of selecting a car with a removed catalytic converter if the selection is random and is limited to cars originally assembled with converters?

15. Among 400 randomly selected drivers in the 20–24 age bracket, 136 were in a car accident during the last year (based on data from the National Safety Council). The Life Trust Insurance Company wants to find the probability of a randomly selected driver from that age being in a car accident during the next year. What is that probability?

16. The U.S. General Accounting Office recently tested the IRS for correctness of answers to taxpayers' questions. For 1733 trials, the IRS was correct 1107 times.
    a. Use these results to estimate the probability that a random taxpayer's question will be answered correctly.
    b. Use these results to estimate the probability that a random taxpayer's question will be answered incorrectly.

17. When the allergy drug Seldane was clinically tested, 70 people experienced drowsiness and 711 did not (based on data from Merrell Dow Pharmaceuticals, Inc.). Use this sample to estimate the probability of a Seldane user becoming drowsy.

18. To buy suitable advertising, supermarkets must recognize societal changes so they can remain informed about the nature of their customers. One study of married couples found that for 277 couples, the husband was responsible for grocery shopping, and for 2239 couples, the wife was responsible for that chore (based on data from a Yankelovich Clancy Shulman poll).
    a. Use these results to estimate the probability that for a randomly selected couple, the husband is responsible for grocery shopping.
    b. Use these results to estimate the probability that for a randomly selected couple, the wife is responsible for grocery shopping.

19. MasterCard International conducted a study of credit card fraud, and the accompanying table is based on their results. If one case of credit card fraud is randomly selected from the cases summarized in the table, find the probability that the fraud resulted from a lost card.

METHOD OF FRAUD	NUMBER OF CASES
Stolen card	243
Lost card	85
Counterfeit card	74
Mail or telephone order	52
Other	46

20. The accompanying table gives the number of people who receive Social Security benefits in select states (based on data from the Social Security Administration). If one of these recipients is randomly selected, find the probability of getting a Texan.

STATE	NUMBER OF SOCIAL SECURITY RECIPIENTS
New York	2,788,649
California	3,284,313
Florida	2,196,141
Maine	198,712
Texas	1,872,383

21. The accompanying table summarizes recent driver convictions for select violations in two counties (data from the New York State Department of Motor Vehicles).

COUNTY	SPEEDING	DWI
Dutchess	10,589	636
Westchester	22,551	963

If one of the convictions is randomly selected, find the probability that it is for DWI (driving while intoxicated).

22. A couple plans to have 2 children.
   a. List the different outcomes according to the sex of each child. Assume that these outcomes are equally likely.
   b. Find the probability of getting 2 girls.
   c. Find the probability of getting exactly 1 child of each sex.

3.2 EXERCISES BEYOND THE BASICS

23. The stem-and-leaf plot summarizes the time (in hours) managers spend in one day on paperwork (based on data from Adia Personnel Services). Use this sample to estimate the probability that a randomly selected manager spends more than 2.0 hours per day on paperwork.

0.	00
1.	0578
2.	00113449
3.	347
4.	445

24. In Exercise 6 we ignored leap years in finding the probability that a randomly selected person will have a birthday on October 18 (National Statistics Day in Japan). What is the probability if we assume that a leap year occurs every four years? (Express the answer as an exact fraction.) Compare this result to the result from Exercise 6.

25. A beginning finance student has reasoned that because we know nothing about the likelihood of a particular stock increasing in price, either it will or it won't, so that P (increase) = 0.5. Is this reasoning correct? Explain.

3.3 ADDITION RULE

The preceding section introduced the basic concept of probability and considered simple experiments and simple events. Many real situations involve compound events, such as the random selection of a policyholder who is a woman *or* someone who is older than age 25.

DEFINITION

Any event combining two or more simple events is called a *compound event.*

In this section we want to develop a rule for finding $P(A \text{ or } B)$, the probability that for a single outcome of an experiment, either event A or event B occurs, or both occur. (Throughout this text we use the inclusive *or*, which means either one or the other, or both. We will *not* consider the exclusive *or*, which means either one or the other, but not both.)

Notation
$P(A \text{ or } B) = P(\text{event } A \text{ occurs or event } B \text{ occurs, or they both occur})$

Let's consider the experiment results summarized in Table 3.1 (based on data from Merrell Dow Pharmaceuticals, Inc.). When exploring data consisting of frequency counts for different categories, it is helpful to arrange the data in a table such as this. (This type of table will be useful when solving several exercises in the text.)

TABLE 3.1
Clinical Test Results

	SELDANE	PLACEBO	CONTROL	
Drowsiness	70	54	113	237
No drowsiness	711	611	513	1835
Totals	781	665	626	2072

The table lists frequencies of subjects in different categories. By adding all the individual cell frequencies, we see that 2072 subjects are included in this experiment. Also, 237 of them experienced drowsiness, 1835 did not experience drowsiness, 781 took Seldane, 665 took a placebo, and 626 were in a control group who took nothing. We will use two cases as a basis for developing our rule for determining $P(A \text{ or } B)$.

CASE 1:   If one of the 2072 subjects is randomly selected, the probability of getting someone who took Seldane or a placebo is

$$\frac{781}{2072} + \frac{665}{2072} = \frac{1446}{2072} = 0.698$$

That is, $P(\text{Seldane or placebo}) = P(\text{Seldane}) + P(\text{placebo})$. This might suggest that $P(A \text{ or } B) = P(A) + P(B)$, but consider the next case.

CASE 2:   Suppose one of the 2072 subjects is randomly selected, and we want the probability of getting someone who took Seldane or experienced drowsiness. Following the same pattern of Case 1, we might write

$$\frac{781}{2072} + \frac{237}{2072} = \frac{1018}{2072} = 0.491 \qquad \text{(WRONG!)}$$

But this is wrong, because 70 subjects were counted twice. One way to compensate for that "double" counting is to subtract the 70 that was included twice. We get

$$P(\text{Seldane or drowsiness}) = \frac{781}{2072} + \frac{237}{2072} - \frac{70}{2072}$$
$$= \frac{948}{2072} = 0.458 \qquad \text{(CORRECT)}$$

This last calculation can be expressed as

$$P(\text{Seldane or drowsiness}) = P(\text{Seldane}) + P(\text{drowsiness}) - P(\text{both})$$

This is generalized in the following addition rule.

ADDITION RULE

$$P(A \text{ or } B) = P(A) + P(B) - P(A \text{ and } B)$$

where $P(A \text{ and } B)$ denotes the probability that A and B both occur at the same time as an outcome in the experiment.

FIGURE 3.4
Venn Diagram Illustrating
Overlapping Events

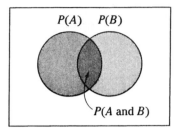

Total Area = 1

FIGURE 3.5
Venn Diagram Illustrating
Mutually Exclusive Events

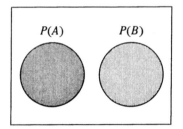

Total Area = 1

The example in Case 2 addresses this key point: **When combining the number of ways event A can occur with the number of ways B can occur, we must avoid double counting those outcomes in which A and B both happen together.**

Figure 3.4 shows a Venn diagram that visually illustrates the addition rule. In this figure we can see that the probability of A or B equals the probability of A (left circle) plus the probability of B (right circle) minus the probability of A and B (football-shaped middle region). This figure shows that the addition of areas of the two circles will cause double counting of the football-shaped middle region. This is the basic concept that underlies the addition rule. Because of this relationship between the addition rule and the Venn diagram shown in Fig. 3.4, the notation $P(A \cup B)$ is often used in place of $P(A$ or $B)$. Similarly, the notation $P(A \cap B)$ is often used in place of $P(A$ and $B)$, so that the addition rule can be expressed as

$$P(A \cup B) = P(A) + P(B) - P(A \cap B)$$

The addition rule is simplified whenever A and B cannot occur simultaneously, so that $P(A$ and $B)$ becomes zero. Figure 3.5 illustrates that with no overlapping of A and B, we have $P(A$ or $B) = P(A) + P(B)$. The following definition formalizes the lack of overlapping as shown in Fig. 3.5.

DEFINITION

Events A and B are *mutually exclusive events* if they cannot occur simultaneously.

In the experiment of rolling one die, the event of getting a 2 and the event of getting a 5 are mutually exclusive events, since no outcome can be both a 2 and a 5 simultaneously. The following pairs of events are other examples of mutually exclusive pairs in a single experiment. That is, within each of the following pairs of events, it is impossible for both events to occur at the same time.

Pairs of mutually exclusive events
$\left\{ \begin{array}{l} \text{Manufacturing a defective electronic component} \\ \text{Manufacturing a good electronic component} \end{array} \right\}$
$\left\{ \begin{array}{l} \text{Selecting a voter who is a registered Democrat} \\ \text{Selecting a voter who is a registered Republican} \end{array} \right\}$

The following pairs of events are examples that are *not* mutually exclusive in a single trial. That is, within each of the following pairs of events, it is possible that both events occur at the same time.

Pairs of events that are not mutually exclusive
$\left\{ \begin{array}{l} \text{Selecting a doctor who is a brain surgeon} \\ \text{Selecting a doctor who is a woman} \end{array} \right\}$
$\left\{ \begin{array}{l} \text{Selecting a voter who owns stock} \\ \text{Selecting a voter who is under 30 years of age} \end{array} \right\}$

We can summarize the key points of this section as follows:

1. To find $P(A$ or $B)$, begin by associating *or* with addition.
2. Consider whether events A and B are mutually exclusive. That is, can they happen at the same time? If they are not mutually exclusive (can happen at the same time), be sure to avoid or compensate for double counting when adding the relevant probabilities.

Important hint: If you *understand* the importance of not double counting when you find $P(A$ or $B)$, you don't necessarily have to calculate formally $P(A) + P(B) - P(A$ and $B)$. In finding $P(\text{Seldane or drowsiness})$ from Table 3.1, you could sum the frequencies for the Seldane column and the drowsiness row by being careful to count each cell exactly once. You would get $70 + 711 + 54 + 113 = 948$, which, when divided by the total number of subjects (2072), will yield the correct probability of 0.458. It's much better to understand what you're doing than to apply a formula blindly.

The following example further illustrates application of the addition rule.

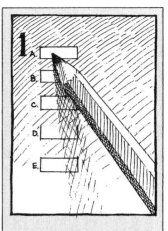

GUESS ON SATs?

EXAMPLE Survey subjects used in market research are often chosen by using computers to randomly select telephone numbers. Assume that a computer randomly generates the last digit of a telephone number. Find the probability that the outcome is (a) an 8 or a 9; (b) odd or under 4.

SOLUTION

a. The outcome of 8 and the outcome of 9 are mutually exclusive events. This means that it is impossible for both 8 and 9 to occur together when 1 digit is selected, so $P(8$ and $9) = 0$, and we apply the addition rule as follows:

$$P(8 \text{ or } 9) = P(8) + P(9) - P(8 \text{ and } 9)$$

$$= \frac{1}{10} + \frac{1}{10} - 0$$

$$= \frac{2}{10} \quad \text{or} \quad \frac{1}{5}$$

b. The outcome of an odd number and the outcome of a number under 4 are not mutually exclusive because they both happen if the result is a 1 or a 3. We must compensate for double counting, and we get

$$P(\text{odd or under } 4) = P(\text{odd}) + P(\text{under } 4) - P(\text{odd and under } 4)$$

$$= \frac{5}{10} + \frac{4}{10} - \frac{2}{10} = \frac{7}{10}$$

In this result, $P(\text{odd}) = 5/10$ because 5 of the 10 digits are odd (1, 3, 5, 7, 9). $P(\text{under } 4) = 4/10$ because 4 of them are under 4 (0, 1, 2, 3). Finally, $P(\text{odd and under } 4) = 2/10$ because 2 of the digits are both odd and under 4 (1 and 3). The correct answer is 7/10.

Errors made when applying the addition rule often involve double counting. That is, events that are not mutually exclusive are treated as if they were. One indication of such an error is a total probability that exceeds 1, but errors involving the addition rule do not always cause the total probability to exceed 1. For example, use Table 3.1 and find P(control or no drowsiness) when one person is randomly selected. The events of being in the control group and being drowsy are not mutually exclusive events, so there is danger of double-counting and getting the incorrect result of $626/2072 + 1835/2072 = 1.188$. Because this probability exceeds 1, it cannot possibly be correct and we have a definite indication that an error has occurred. (The correct answer is 0.940.) However, if the same error is made in finding P(control or drowsiness), the incorrect answer of 0.417 does not exceed 1 and might therefore seem reasonable, even though the correct answer is 0.362.

COMPLEMENTARY EVENTS

In Section 3.2 we defined the complement of event A and denoted it by $\overline{A}$. The definition of complementary events implies that they must be mutually exclusive because it is impossible for an event and its opposite to occur at the same time. Also, we can be absolutely certain that either A does or does not occur. That is, either A or $\overline{A}$ must occur. These observations enable us to apply the addition rule for mutually exclusive events as follows:

$$P(A \text{ or } \overline{A}) = P(A) + P(\overline{A}) = 1$$

We justify $P(A \text{ or } \overline{A}) = P(A) + P(\overline{A})$ by noting that A and $\overline{A}$ are mutually exclusive, and we justify the total of 1 by our absolute certainty that A either does or does not occur. This result of the addition rule leads to the following three *equivalent* forms.

RULE OF COMPLEMENTARY EVENTS

$$P(A) + P(\overline{A}) = 1$$
$$P(\overline{A}) = 1 - P(A)$$
$$P(A) = 1 - P(\overline{A})$$

FIGURE 3.6
Venn Diagram for the Complement of Event A

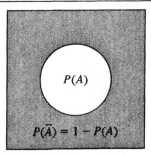

$P(A)$

$P(\overline{A}) = 1 - P(A)$

Total Area = 1

The first form comes directly from our original result, whereas the second (see Fig. 3.6) and third variations involve very simple equation manipulations.

EXAMPLE   If $P(A) = 0.4$, find $P(\overline{A})$.

SOLUTION   Using the rule of complementary events, we get

$$P(\overline{A}) = 1 - P(A) = 1 - 0.4 = 0.6$$

3.3 EXERCISES   BASIC CONCEPTS

In Exercises 1 and 2, for each pair of events given, determine whether the two events are mutually exclusive for a single experiment.

1. a. Selecting a person who owns a computer
      Selecting a person who owns a VCR
   b. Selecting a student who gets low SAT or ACT scores
      Selecting a student who succeeds in college
   c. Selecting a person with blond hair (natural or otherwise)
      Selecting a person with brown eyes
   d. Selecting a worker who has reached early-retirement age of 55
      Selecting a citizen who is too young to vote
   e. Selecting a required business course
      Selecting an elective business course

2. a. Selecting someone who colors his or her hair
      Selecting someone who has read *The Greening of America*
   b. Selecting an unmarried person
      Selecting a person with an employed spouse
   c. Selecting a high school graduate
      Selecting someone who is unemployed
   d. Selecting a voter who is a registered Democrat
      Selecting a voter who favors the Republican candidate
   e. Selecting a consumer who drives a car
      Selecting a consumer who subscribes to *Time* magazine

3. If a computer randomly generates the last digit of a telephone number, find the probability that it is odd or greater than 2.

4. A sample consists of 200 business calculators (8 of which are defective) and 150 scientific calculators (9 of which are defective). If 1 calculator is randomly selected from this sample, find the probability that it is a business calculator or is defective.

5. Among 200 seats available on one international airliner, 40 are reserved for smokers (including 16 aisle seats) and 160 are reserved for nonsmokers (including 64 aisle seats). If a late passenger is randomly assigned a seat, find the probability of getting an aisle seat or one in the smoking section.

6. A local survey asked 100 persons for their opinions on a zoning ordinance to control the growth of business. Of the 62 favorable responses, there were 40 males. Of the 38 unfavorable responses, there were 15 males. Find the probability of randomly selecting one of these subjects and getting a male or a favorable response.

7. A labor study involves a sample of 12 mining companies, 18 construction companies, 10 manufacturing companies, and 3 wholesale companies. If a company is randomly selected from this sample group, find the probability of getting a mining or construction company.

8. A study of consumer smoking habits includes 200 married people (54 of whom smoke), 100 divorced people (38 of whom smoke), and 50 adults who never married (11 of whom smoke) (based on data from the U.S. Department of Health and Human Services). If 1 subject is randomly selected from this sample, find the probability of getting someone who is divorced or smokes.

AGE	NUMBER
0–4	3,843
5–14	4,226
15–24	19,975
25–44	27,201
45–64	14,733
65–74	8,499
75 and over	16,800

Accidental deaths are of great concern to the entire insurance industry. In Exercises 9–12, refer to the data in the accompanying table, which describes the age distribution of Americans who died by accident (based on data from the National Safety Council). In each case, assume that 1 person is randomly selected from this sample group.

9. Find the probability of selecting someone under 5 or over 74.
10. Find the probability of selecting someone between 15 and 64.
11. Find the probability of selecting someone under 45 or between 25 and 74.
12. Find the probability of selecting someone under 25 or between 15 and 44.

In Exercises 13–16, use the following data. A survey of 400 randomly selected heads of households found 301 people who own cars (116 of whom are women) and 99 people who don't own cars (59 of whom are women) (based on data from the U.S. Census Bureau). In each case assume that 1 of these 400 survey respondents is randomly selected and find the probability of the given event.

13. A woman is selected.
14. A woman or someone who owns a car is selected.
15. A man or someone who doesn't own a car is selected.
16. A man or someone who owns a car is selected.

In Exercises 17–20, refer the accompanying table, which is based on data from AT&T and the Automobile Association of America. In each case assume that 1 of the 758 drivers is randomly selected.

		CAR ACCIDENT IN LAST YEAR?	
		YES	NO
Use a cellular	Yes	23	282
phone?	No	46	407

17. Find the probability that the selected driver had a car accident in the last year.
18. Find the probability that the selected driver uses a cellular phone or had a car accident in the last year.
19. Find the probability that the selected driver did not use a cellular phone.
20. Find the probability that the selected driver did not use a cellular phone or did not have an accident in the last year.

3.3   EXERCISES   BEYOND THE BASICS

21. If $P(A$ or $B) = 1/3$, $P(B) = 1/4$, and $P(A$ and $B) = 1/5$, find $P(A)$.
22. Find $P(B)$ if $P(A$ or $B) = 0.6$, $P(A) = 0.6$, and A and B are mutually exclusive events.
23. a. If $P(A) = 0.4$ and $P(B) = 0.5$, what is known about $P(A$ or $B)$ if A and B are mutually exclusive events?
    b. If $P(A) = 0.4$ and $P(B) = 0.5$, what is known about $P(A$ or $B)$ if A and B are not mutually exclusive events?
    c. $P(A$ or $B) = 0.8$ while $P(A) = 0.3$. What is known about $P(B)$? What is known about events A and B?

24. If events A and B are mutually exclusive, and events B and C are mutually exclusive, must events A and C be mutually exclusive? Give an example supporting your answer.

3.4   MULTIPLICATION RULE

In Section 3.3 we developed a rule for finding the probability that event A or B will occur in a given experiment. We now develop a rule for finding the probability that events A and B both occur. We begin with a simple example, which will suggest a preliminary multiplication rule. Then we use another example to develop a variation and ultimately obtain a generalized multiplication rule.

Probability theory is used extensively in the analysis and design of tests. Practical considerations often require that standardized tests allow only those answers that can be corrected easily, such as true-false or multiple choice. Let's assume that the first question on a test is a true-false type, whereas the second question is multiple choice with 5 possible answers (a, b, c, d, e). We will use the following two questions. Try them!

True or false:

1. The cost of the last U.S. census was about \$10 per person.
2. The father of the Taguchi methods for quality improvement is
   a.   Henry Ford
   b.   There was no father, only a mother.
   c.   Genichi Taguchi
   d.   Triola
   e.   Franklin

We want to determine the probability of getting both answers correct by making random guesses. We begin by listing the complete sample space of different possible answers.

T,a T,b T,c T,d T,e	1 case is correct
F,a F,b F,c F,d F,e	10 equally likely cases

If the answers are random guesses, then the 10 possible outcomes are equally likely. The correct answers are *true* and *c,* so that

$$P(\text{both correct}) = P(\text{true and } c) = \frac{1}{10}$$

Considering the component answers of *true* and *c,* respectively, we see that with random guesses we have $P(\text{true}) = 1/2$ while $P(c) = 1/5$. Recognizing that $1/10$ is the product of $1/2$ and $1/5$, we observe that $P(\text{true and } c) = P(T) \cdot P(c)$ and we use this observation as a basis for formulating the following preliminary rule.

Multiplication rule (preliminary): $P(A \text{ and } B) = P(A) \cdot P(B)$

INDEPENDENT JET ENGINES

Recently, a three-engine jet departed from Miami. Under normal circumstances, the probability of an engine failure was about 0.0001 for a flight. If the three engines operate independently, then the probability that all three fail on a single flight is $(0.0001)^3 =$ 0.000000000001, or one chance in a trillion. However, the flight experienced an engine failure shortly after takeoff. As the pilot turned to land, the other 2 engines failed but the pilot was able to make a safe emergency landing with no working engines. The FAA carefully studied this extremely unusual event and found that the cooling oil in the engines had been replaced by a single mechanic who mispositioned the sealing ring on the oil plug in all three engines.

One goal in using the separate engines is to increase safety through independent engines, but the use of the single mechanic allowed the engine operation to become dependent.

EXAMPLE Three disk drives are produced, and 1 of them is defective. Two are randomly selected for testing, but the first selected disk is returned and mixed in with the other two before the second selection is made. Find the probability that both disk drives are good.

SOLUTION Letting G represent the event of selecting a good disk drive, we want $P(G \text{ and } G)$. With $P(G) = 2/3$, we apply the multiplication rule to get

$$P(G \text{ and } G) = P(G) \cdot P(G) = \frac{2}{3} \cdot \frac{2}{3} = \frac{4}{9}$$

Although the preceding solution is mathematically correct, common sense suggests that we should conduct product testing without replacing the items already tested. There is always the chance that we could test the same item twice. Also, we cannot be sure of the reliability of any generalization based on a specific case, such as our preliminary multiplication rule. We would be wise to test that rule in a variety of cases to see if any errors arise. The preliminary rule is sometimes inadequate, as we will see in the improved testing procedure in the next example.

EXAMPLE Let's again assume that we have 3 disk drives, of which 1 is defective. We will again randomly select 2 disk drives, but we will *not* replace the first selection. We will find the probability of getting 2 good disk drives with this improved testing procedure.

SOLUTION To understand the sample space better, we will represent the defective disk drive by D and the 2 good disk drives by G_1 and G_2. Assuming that the first selection is not replaced, we now illustrate the different possible outcomes in Fig. 3.7, which is an example of a **tree diagram**. By examining this list of 6 equally likely outcomes, we see that only 2 cases correspond to 2 good disk drives, so that $P(G \text{ and } G) = 2/6$ or $1/3$. In contrast, our preliminary multiplication rule was used in the preceding example to produce a result of 4/9. Here, the correct result is 1/3, so the preliminary multiplication rule does *not* fit this case.

In this example, the preliminary multiplication rule does not take into account the fact that the first selection is not replaced. $P(G)$ again begins with a value of 2/3, but after getting a good disk drive on the first selection, there would be 1 good disk drive and 1 defective disk drive remaining, so that $P(G)$ becomes 1/2 on the second selection.

Here is the key concept of this last example: **Without replacement of the first selection, the second probability is affected by the first result.** There are many other cases in which a probability is affected by another event, or even by additional knowledge you may acquire. The probability of your getting to class on time may be affected by the probability of your car starting. An estimated probability of a football team winning the Super Bowl may be affected by news of an injured quarterback. Since this dependence of an event on some other event is so important, we provide a special definition.

FIGURE 3.7
Tree Diagram

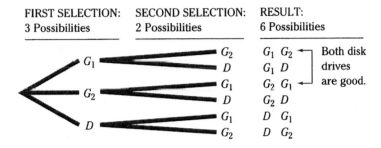

FIRST SELECTION:	SECOND SELECTION:	RESULT:
3 Possibilities	2 Possibilities	6 Possibilities

G_1 — G_2, D
G_2 — G_1, D
D — G_1, G_2

$G_1\ G_2$ ⟵ Both disk
$G_1\ D$ ⟶ drives
$G_2\ G_1$ ⟵ are good.
$G_2\ D$
$D\ G_1$
$D\ G_2$

DEFINITIONS

Two events A and B are _independent events_ if the occurrence of one does not affect the probability of the occurrence of the other. (Several events are similarly independent if the occurrence of any does not affect the probabilities of the occurrence of the others.) If A and B are not independent, they are said to be _dependent events_.

The preliminary multiplication rule holds if the events A and B are independent; in that case $P(B)$ is not affected by the occurrence of A. The preceding example suggests the following rule for dependent events. Let $P(B|A)$ represent the probability of B occurring after assuming that A has already occurred. (We can read $B|A$ as "B given A.") The multiplication rule for dependent events is: $P(A$ and $B) = P(A) \cdot P(B|A)$.

The multiplication rule for dependent events suggests these steps for finding the probability that events A and B both occur: (1) Find the probability of event A. (2) Assuming that event A has already occurred, find the probability of event B. (3) Multiply the results from steps 1 and 2.

We now have these two different multiplication rules: the multiplication rule for independent events and the multiplication rule for dependent events. Whenever events A and B are independent, we find $P(A$ and $B)$ by simply multiplying their individual probabilities. However, if the events are dependent, we must adjust probabilities by taking into account the events that have already occurred. We summarize the two different cases as follows.

MULTIPLICATION RULE

$P(A$ and $B) = P(A) \cdot P(B)$ if A and B are _independent_.
$P(A$ and $B) = P(A) \cdot P(B|A)$ if A and B are _dependent_.

In the last expression, we can easily solve for $P(B|A)$, and the result suggests the following definition.

> **DEFINITION**
>
> The *conditional probability* of B given A is
>
> $$P(B|A) = \frac{P(A \text{ and } B)}{P(A)}$$

If $P(B|A) = P(B)$, then the occurrence of event A had no effect on the probability of event B. This is often used as a test for independence. If $P(B|A) = P(B)$, then A and B are independent events. If $P(B|A) \neq P(B)$, then A and B are dependent events. Another equivalent test for independence involves checking for equality of $P(A \text{ and } B)$ and $P(A) \cdot P(B)$. If they're equal, events A and B are independent. If $P(A \text{ and } B) \neq P(A) \cdot P(B)$, then A and B are dependent events.

In some cases, the distinction between dependent and independent events is quite obvious, while in other cases it is not. Getting heads on a coin and 6 on a die clearly involves independent events. But consider the data in Table 3.2, which summarizes 60 responses to a survey question. Are the events of being a male and answering yes independent? For this group,

$$P(M \text{ and yes}) \neq P(M) \cdot P(\text{yes})$$

24 respondents are males who answered yes
$$\frac{24}{60} \neq \frac{40}{60} \cdot \frac{38}{60}$$
40 males among 60 respondents
38 yes responses out of 60

Because $P(M \text{ and yes}) \neq P(M) \cdot P(\text{yes})$, we conclude that the events of being a male and answering yes are dependent for selections from this group of 60 people. In general, if we can verify or refute the equation $P(A \text{ and } B) = P(A) \cdot P(B)$, then we can establish or disprove the independence of events A and B.

TABLE 3.2
Survey Results

		MALE	FEMALE
Do you favor the no-smoking rule on airliners?	Yes	24	14
	No	16	6

EXAMPLE Using the data in Table 3.2, find the probability of selecting someone from the group who answered yes, if we already know that the person selected is a male.

SOLUTION We want to find the probability of getting a yes answer, given that a male (M) was selected. That is, we want $P(\text{yes}|M)$.

First approach: Use Table 3.2 directly. If we know a male was selected, we know that we have 40 males, and 24 of them answered yes, so that

$$P(\text{yes}|M) = \frac{24}{40} = 0.600$$

Second approach:

$$P(\text{yes}|M) = \frac{P(M \text{ and yes})}{P(M)}$$
$$= \frac{24/60}{40/60} = \frac{24}{40} = 0.600$$

Given the condition that a male was selected, the conditional probability $P(\text{yes}|M) = 0.600$.

In the preceding example $P(\text{yes}) = 38/60 = 0.633$, but $P(\text{yes}|M) = 0.600$. Because $P(\text{yes}) \neq P(\text{yes}|M)$, we conclude that "yes" and "M" are dependent events.

So far we have discussed two events, but we can easily extend the multiplication rule to several events. In general, **the probability of any sequence of independent events is simply the product of their corresponding probabilities.** The next two examples illustrate this extension of the multiplication rule.

EXAMPLE A couple plans to have 4 children. Find the probability that all 4 children are girls. Assume that boys and girls are equally likely and that the sex of each child is independent of the sex of any other children.

SOLUTION The probability of getting a girl is 1/2 and the 4 births are independent of each other, so

$$P(\text{four girls}) = \frac{1}{2} \cdot \frac{1}{2} \cdot \frac{1}{2} \cdot \frac{1}{2} = \frac{1}{16}$$

EXAMPLE At the beginning of this chapter we presented an employee's claim that a new technique for manufacturing VCRs is better because the rate of defects is below 5%, the rate of defects in the past. When 20 VCRs are manufactured with the new technique, there are no defects. Assuming that the new manufacturing technique has the same 5% rate of defects, find the probability of getting no defects among the 20 VCRs.

SOLUTION Getting no defects means that all 20 VCRs are good, so we really want the probability of getting 20 good VCRs. If 5% are defective, it follows that 95% are good, so that $P(\text{good VCR}) = 0.95$ and

$$P(20 \text{ good VCRs}) = 0.95 \times 0.95 \times \ldots \times 0.95 \ (20 \text{ factors})$$
$$= 0.358$$

(continued)

If the new manufacturing technique has the same 5% rate of defects as the old method, there is a 0.358 chance of getting no defects among 20 VCRs. The probability of 0.358 is relatively high, and it indicates that you could *easily* get no defects when 20 VCRs are manufactured, even if the rate of defects is 5%. We don't yet have enough evidence to support the employee's claim that the new method is better. It might be better, but we would need stronger evidence to conclude that.

The preceding two examples illustrate an extension of the multiplication rule for independent events; the next example illustrates a similar extension of the multiplication rule for dependent events.

EXAMPLE The Federal Deposit Insurance Corporation assigns an accountant to audit 3 different banks to be randomly selected from a list of 5 commercial banks and 7 savings banks. Find the probability that all 3 random selections are commercial banks.

SOLUTION Let A be the event of getting a commercial bank on the first selection, while B and C represent the events of getting commercial banks on the second and third selections. These events are *dependent* because successive probabilities are affected by previous results. We can use the multiplication rule for dependent events to find the probability that the first 2 selections are commercial banks. We get

$$P(A \text{ and } B) = P(A) \cdot P(B|A)$$
$$= \frac{5}{12} \cdot \frac{4}{11} = \frac{20}{132}$$

The probability of the third selection being a commercial bank is 3/10 because, after the first 2 selections, there would be 3 commercial banks among the 10 banks that remain. In summary, we have

$$P(A \text{ and } B \text{ and } C) = P(A) \cdot P(B|A) \cdot P(C|A \text{ and } B)$$
$$= \frac{5}{12} \cdot \frac{4}{11} \cdot \frac{3}{10}$$
$$= \frac{60}{1320} = \frac{1}{22}$$

In the last example we assumed that the events are dependent because the selections are made without replacement. However, it is a common practice to treat events as independent when small samples are drawn from large populations or processes. A common guideline is to assume independence whenever the sample size is at most 5% of the size of the population. When pollsters survey 1200 adults from a population of millions, they typically assume independence, even though they sample without replacement.

When using the multiplication rule for finding probabilities in compound events, tree diagrams are sometimes helpful in determining the number of possible outcomes (see Fig. 3.7). In a tree diagram we depict schematically the possible

FIGURE 3.8
Tree Diagram

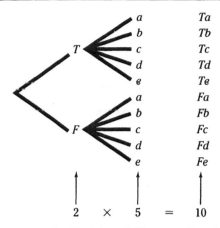

	a	Ta
	b	Tb
T	c	Tc
	d	Td
	e	Te
	a	Fa
	b	Fb
F	c	Fc
	d	Fd
	e	Fe

$$2 \quad \times \quad 5 \quad = \quad 10$$

outcomes of an experiment as line segments emanating from one starting point. Such diagrams are helpful in counting the number of possible outcomes if the number of possibilities is not too large. In cases involving large numbers of choices, the use of tree diagrams is impractical. However, they are useful as visual aids to provide insight into the multiplication rule. Returning to the situation discussed earlier in this section, if we have the true-false question and the multiple-choice question, we can use a tree diagram to summarize the outcomes (see Fig. 3.8).

Assuming that both answers are random guesses, all 10 branches are equally likely and the probability of getting the correct pair (T, c) is 1/10. For each response to the first question there are 5 responses for the second. The total number of outcomes is therefore 5 taken 2 times, or 10. The tree diagram in Fig. 3.8 illustrates the reason for the use of multiplication.

3.4 EXERCISES BASIC CONCEPTS

1. For each of the following pairs of events, classify the two events as independent or dependent.
   a. Randomly selecting a consumer having a credit card
      Randomly selecting a consumer having blue eyes
   b. Making a correct guess on the first question of a multiple-choice quiz
      Making a correct guess on the second question of the same multiple-choice quiz
   c. Randomly selecting a defective component from a bin of 15 good and 5 defective components
      Randomly selecting a second component that is defective (assume that the same bin is used and the first selection was not replaced)
   d. Events A and B, where $P(A) = 0.40$, $P(B) = 0.60$, and $P(A \text{ and } B) = 0.20$
   e. Events A and B, where $P(A) = 0.2$, $P(B) = 0.3$, and $P(A \text{ and } B) = 0.06$

2. For each of the following pairs of events, classify the two events as independent or dependent.
   a. Finding your kitchen light inoperable
      Finding your battery-operated flashlight inoperable
   b. Finding your kitchen light inoperable
      Finding your microwave oven inoperable
   c. In a stopover flight from New York to San Francisco, the flight of the first leg (New York to St. Louis) arrives on time. The flight of the second leg (St. Louis to San Francisco) arrives on time.
   d. Events A and B, where $P(A) = 0.90$, $P(B) = 0.80$, and $P(A \text{ and } B) = 0.72$
   e. Events A and B, where $P(A) = 0.36$, $P(B) = 0.50$, and $P(A \text{ and } B) = 0.15$.

3. The Wallace Clothing Store has 3 senior employees who operate independently of each other and who all average a 6% rate of absenteeism. The store cannot open if all three employees are absent on the same day.
   a. Assuming that absences are independent, find the probability that the store cannot open on a particular day. Based on this result, should the owner be concerned about not opening?
   b. Suppose the store owner knows the three employees are all close friends who enjoy fishing. Should the owner be concerned about not opening? What makes this problem different from part *a?*

4. A TV program (ABC's *Nightline*) on smoking reported that there is a 60% success rate for those trying to stop smoking through hypnosis. Find the probability that for 8 randomly selected smokers who undergo hypnosis, they all successfully stop smoking.

5. A quality control manager sets up a test of equipment to detect defects. A sample of 4 different items is to be randomly selected from a group consisting of 10 defective items and 20 items with no defects. What is the probability that all 4 items are defective? (Assume no replacement.)

6. According to a *U.S. News and World Report* article, a financial analyst for Paine Webber estimated that 35% of the computer chips manufactured by Intel are acceptable.
   a. If 3 chips are randomly selected, what is the chance of getting all good chips?
   b. If Intel increased its production yield to 70%, what is the chance that all 3 randomly selected chips will be acceptable?

7. Assume that the probability of failure in a space shuttle's O-ring is 0.023. A disaster will occur if any one of 6 such O-rings fails. Find the probability that all 6 O-rings work correctly, assuming that they are all independent. Is this probability high enough to conclude that the design is reasonably safe?

8. There are 6 defective fuses in a bin of 80 fuses. The entire bin is approved for shipping if no defects show up when 3 randomly selected fuses are tested.
   a. Find the probability of approval if the selected fuses are replaced.
   b. Find the probability of approval if the selected fuses are not replaced.
   c. Comparing the results of parts *a* and *b,* determine which procedure is more likely to reveal a defective fuse. Which procedure do you think is better?

9. Four firms using the same auditor independently and randomly select a month in which to conduct their annual audits. What is the probability that all 4 months are different?

10. Your company assembles 10 computer chips to make an electronic pager unit. All 10 chips must work for the pager to work.
    a. If 95% of the component chips are good, what is the chance that the pager will work?
    b. If 99.9% of the component chips are good, what is the chance that the pager will work?

11. The probability of a randomly selected 20-year-old male living to be 30 is 0.984 (based on data from the U.S. Department of Health and Human Services).
    a. What is the probability that two randomly selected 20-year-old males both live to age 30?
    b. What is the probability that two randomly selected 20-year-old males both die before age 30?

12. Of 2 million bulbs produced by Lectrolyte in one year, 5000 are defective. If 2 bulbs are randomly selected and tested, find the probability that they are both good in each of the following cases.
    a. The first selected bulb is replaced.
    b. The first selected bulb is not replaced.

13. A manager can identify employee theft by checking samples of shipments. Among 36 employees, 2 are stealing. If the manager checks on 4 different randomly selected employees, find the probability that neither of the thieves will be identified.

14. A life insurance company issues one-year policies to 12 men who are all 27 years of age. Based on data from the Department of Health and Human Services, each of these men has a 99.82% chance of living through the year. What is the probability that they all survive the year?

15. The Locust Tree Restaurant has found that 65% of its reservations are for nonsmoking tables, whereas 35% request tables for smoking. Find the probability that 4 randomly selected reservations are all for nonsmoking tables.

16. The mail order division of Wallace Clothing normally experiences a 7% reply rate on a flyer it sends out. There is concern about the status of one batch of 50 flyers that resulted in no returns. What is the probability of this happening by chance if the flyers were delivered and the overall reply rate really is 7%? Does the result suggest that something "unusual" has happened?

In Exercises 17–20, use the data in the accompanying table (based on data from Merrell Dow Pharmaceuticals, Inc.).

	SELDANE	PLACEBO	CONTROL
Drowsiness	70	54	113
No drowsiness	711	611	513

17. Find the probability that a subject experienced drowsiness given that he or she took Seldane.

18. Find the probability that a subject experienced drowsiness given that he or she took a placebo.

19. Find the probability that a subject was in the control group given that he or she experienced drowsiness.

20. Find the probability that a subject took Seldane given that he or she experienced drowsiness.

3.4 EXERCISES   BEYOND THE BASICS

21. Let $P(A) = 3/4$ and $P(B) = 5/6$. Find $P(A \text{ and } B)$ given that
    a. A and B are independent events
    b. $P(B|A) = 1/2$
    c. $P(A|B) = 1/3$
    d. $P(A|B) = P(A)$

22. Use a calculator or computer to compute the probability (a) that of 25 people, no 2 share the same birthday, and (b) that of 50 people, no 2 share the same birthday.

23. A poll taken on the site of a large corporation surveyed employee attitudes about a variety of issues. Fifty employees (10 females and 40 males) were polled on their involvement in volunteer work, and the results showed 20 responses of yes and 30 responses of no. This data is summarized in the table.

	YES	NO	
Male			40
Female			10
	20	30	

    a. If 1 of the 50 employees is randomly selected, find the probability of getting a male.
    b. If 1 of the 50 employees is randomly selected, find the probability of getting a female.
    c. If 1 of the 50 employees is randomly selected, find the probability of getting an employee who answered yes.
    d. If 1 of the 50 employees is randomly selected, find the probability of getting an employee who answered no.
    e. Assuming that the sex of the respondent has no effect on the response, find the probability of randomly selecting 1 of the 50 polled employees and getting a male who answered yes.
    f. Using the probability from part *e* and the fact that there are 50 respondents, what would you expect to be the number of males who answered yes?
    g. If the number from part *f* is entered in the appropriate box in the chart, can the numbers in the other boxes then be determined? If so, find those numbers.

24. A process consists of filling "50-lb" bags with salt pellets for water softeners. The process has a mean of 51 lb and a standard deviation of 1 lb, it is statistically stable, and the process yields values that have a bell-shaped distribution.
    a. Use the empirical rule from Chapter 2 to find the probability that a single randomly selected bag will contain less than 50 lb.
    b. What is the probability that 3 randomly selected bags will all contain less than 50 lb?
    c. Suppose you randomly select 3 bags and find that each contains less than 50 lb. Do you believe that the process is running as desired? Explain your answer.

3.5 PROBABILITY USED IN RUN CHARTS FOR PROCESSES

In Chapter 2 we introduced the run chart as a means of depicting statistical stability or instability in a process, and we saw several examples of processes that were out of statistical control. If the trend is dramatic (such as a large shift downward or a pronounced trend upward), then the run chart enables us to recognize the pattern, but some trends are not so obvious and it might be difficult to determine whether the process is stable. In those cases, what appears to be stable to one person might appear to be unstable to someone else. Instead of relying totally on subjective judgments, we can use probability to help make more objective conclusions.

If we are filling 16-oz jars with peanut butter, we want to have a statistically stable filling process with a mean of 16 oz. Suppose our process is statistically stable and yields normally distributed amounts (that is, a histogram of the data is approximately bell-shaped) having a mean of 16 oz, as we desire. Then P(more than 16 oz) = 0.5 and P(less than 16 oz) = 0.5. That is, there is a 50% chance that an individual jar will have more than 16 oz, and there is a 50% chance that a jar will contain less than 16 oz. The probability of getting *precisely* 16 oz is considered to be negligible. In a sense, randomly selecting a jar from this process is similar to flipping a coin and getting heads (more than 16 oz) or tails (less than 16 oz). Just as it is extremely unusual to get a run of eight heads when flipping a coin, it is also extremely unusual to get a run of eight jars with more than 16 oz. Note that when flipping a coin, the probability of getting a run of eight consecutive heads is given by

$$P(8 \text{ heads}) = P(H) \cdot P(H) \cdot P(H) \cdot P(H) \cdot P(H) \cdot P(H) \cdot P(H) \cdot P(H)$$
$$= \frac{1}{2} \cdot \frac{1}{2} \cdot \frac{1}{2} \cdot \frac{1}{2} \cdot \frac{1}{2} \cdot \frac{1}{2} \cdot \frac{1}{2} \cdot \frac{1}{2}$$
$$= 0.00391$$

Similarly, the probability of getting eight consecutive jars with more than 16 oz is also 0.00391. The probability of getting a run of eight consecutive tails is 0.00391, and the probability of getting a run of eight consecutive jars containing less than 16 oz is 0.00391. Applying the addition rule, we get

P(run of 8 jars above 16 oz or run of 8 jars below 16 oz)
= P(run of 8 jars above 16 oz) + P(run of 8 jars below 16 oz)
= 0.00391 + 0.00391 = 0.00782

Because this probability is so small, we reason that such a run of eight jars above (or below) the mean is a signal that the process is not stable.

RUN OF 8 RULE

If a process yields results with 8 consecutive values above the desired mean or 8 consecutive values below the desired mean, we conclude that the process is not statistically stable.

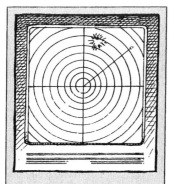

REDUNDANCY

Reliability of systems can be greatly improved with redundancy of critical components. Airplanes have two independent electrical systems, and aircraft used for instrument flight typically have two separate radios. The following is from a *Popular Science* article about stealth aircraft: "One plane built largely of carbon fiber was the Lear Fan 2100 which had to carry two radar transponders. That's because if a single transponder failed, the plane was nearly invisible to radar." Such redundancy is an application of the multiplication rule in probability theory. If one component has a 0.001 probability of failure, the probability of two independent components both failing is only 0.000001.

Note that with a stable process, even though it's very unlikely, it is possible to get a run of eight values either all above the desired mean or all below it. When this rare event does occur, we would incorrectly conclude that the process is not stable when in fact it really is stable. In effect, we would be getting a false alarm.

EXAMPLE A process consists of cutting pencils, and design specifications indicate that a mean length of 16 cm is desired. A sample of 20 consecutive pencils yields the results given below, and the corresponding run chart is depicted in Fig. 3.9. Is the process statistically stable? The data are in order by row.

15.98	16.08	16.10	16.07	15.82	15.98	15.90
15.87	15.98	16.09	15.90	15.69	15.84	15.80
15.95	15.85	15.88	15.81	15.73	15.84	

SOLUTION Examination of the run chart in Fig. 3.9 shows that the last 10 values are all below the desired mean of 16.0 cm. By applying the run of 8 rule, we conclude the process is not statistically stable. It appears that the process has changed so that the actual mean has shifted down to a value below the desired value of 16.0 cm.

Note that although the run of 8 rule is very helpful in detecting some types of process patterns (shift up/down or trend up/down), it will not detect some other patterns of instability, such as an unusually high or low value or a cyclical pattern. In Chapter 5 we will include one more rule for detecting patterns of instability that will be helpful in identifying such patterns.

FIGURE 3.9
Run Chart for Pencil-Cutting Process

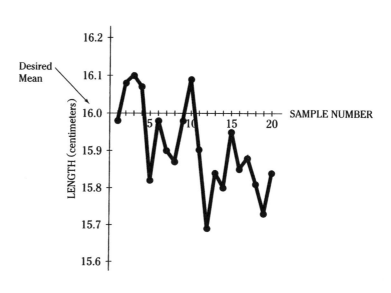

3.5 EXERCISES | BASIC CONCEPTS

In each of the following exercises, construct a run chart and then apply the run of 8 rule to determine whether it detects any patterns of statistical instability. If the process appears to be statistically unstable, identify the pattern of instability (see Fig. 3.9). Remember that there can be unstable patterns that will not be detected by the run of 8 rule. (The data are in sequence by rows.)

1. The following are the weights of 24 Swiss Delight candy bars that were randomly selected once every 20 minutes during an 8-hour shift. The desired weight is 6 oz.

6.1	6.0	5.9	6.2	5.9	5.9	6.0	6.1	6.1	6.0	6.1	5.9
5.8	5.7	5.9	5.6	5.8	5.7	5.7	5.8	5.9	5.7	5.8	5.9

2. Listed below are the fill weights of 30 flour bags, one randomly selected every minute at the Kansas Food Products Company. The desired weight is 80 oz (or 5 lb).

80.1	80.0	79.8	80.0	79.9	80.2	80.0	79.9	79.8	80.1
80.2	80.0	79.9	80.1	80.3	80.2	80.0	80.4	80.2	80.3
80.1	80.3	80.2	80.1	80.3	80.5	80.4	80.6	80.3	80.1

3. The Taylor Clothing Company manufactures shirts and wants the sleeve length to be 33 in. Listed below are the sleeve lengths, cut by a machine, for 20 shirts that were randomly selected once each 5 min.

33.1	33.2	32.8	32.7	33.3	33.0	33.2	32.8	33.0	32.7
33.1	32.9	32.7	33.2	34.1	33.0	32.9	32.7	33.3	33.0

4. Missouri Music is a mail order compact disk club that would like to deliver ordered items an average of 14 days after having received the order. Management randomly selects one order every morning and one every afternoon over a 2-week period (10 working days). The following data are the delivery times (in days).

12	14	13	15	16	13	14	12	14	13	15	12	13	14
12	15	16	14	13	15

In Exercises 5–8, the given data represent departure times from home as recorded by a commuter for 3 consecutive weeks. The desired departure time is 8:00. In each case, apply the run of 8 rule and determine whether it detects any patterns of instability. Are there *other* patterns present that are not detected by the run of 8 rule?

5.
M	T	W	Th	F
8:14	7:55	7:58	8:00	7:59
8:12	7:52	7:56	7:50	8:01
8:16	7:58	7:55	7:58	7:54

6.
M	T	W	Th	F
8:16	7:45	8:10	7:47	8:12
8:15	7:42	8:17	7:46	8:18
8:14	7:50	8:12	7:48	8:13

7.
M	T	W	Th	F
7:59	8:00	8:00	8:02	8:02
8:03	8:00	8:04	7:59	8:04
8:06	8:09	8:11	8:12	8:11

8.
M	T	W	Th	F
8:14	8:15	8:15	8:14	8:14
8:13	8:10	8:08	8:09	7:48
7:49	7:52	7:51	7:49	7:50

9. The publisher of Tom Clancy's novels wishes to monitor the quality of proof-reading in galley proofs. She selects every 10th page and records the number of proof errors with the results given below.

$$
\begin{array}{cccccccccc}
0 & 1 & 1 & 0 & 0 & 1 & 0 & 1 & 1 & 1 & 0 \\
1 & 1 & 2 & 1 & 2 & 3 & 2 & 1 & 2 & 3 & 2
\end{array}
$$

   a. Find $\bar{x}$ and consider it to be the value of the desired mean, then construct a run chart and examine it to determine whether it is statistically stable.
   b. Further investigation revealed that the original proofreader was replaced. Does that change seem to be apparent in the run chart?

10. The manager of the customer service department at the A.S.J. Computer Mail Order Company records the numbers of service calls necessary to repair computers. The results for one year are recorded in 2-wk intervals, and they are given below in consecutive order.

$$
\begin{array}{cccccccccccc}
1 & 0 & 3 & 1 & 0 & 1 & 1 & 2 & 1 & 3 & 2 & 1 \\
1 & 0 & 3 & 2 & 0 & 2 & 3 & 4 & 3 & 2 & 1 & 2 & 0 & 1
\end{array}
$$

   a. Construct a run chart about $\bar{x}$ and determine whether there is statistical stability.
   b. A process could be statistically stable about $\bar{x}$ and yet it could be undesirable. Does this example illustrate such a case?

3.5 EXERCISES   BEYOND THE BASICS

11. We have seen in this section that the run of 8 rule is associated with a probability of 0.00782 that a run of 8 process items will be either all above the mean or all below it. What corresponding probability would be associated with this rule if it were based on (a) 7 instead of 8? (b) 9 instead of 8?

12. Construct a run chart with 20 data points depicting a process that is clearly unstable (see Fig. 3.9), yet the run of 8 rule does not reveal the statistical instability.

3.6 COUNTING

In some probability problems, the biggest obstacle is determining the total number of outcomes. In this section we examine some of the efficient ways we can do this. Suppose that we use a computer to randomly select 1 of the 2 sexes (male, female) and 1 of 4 states (NY, CA, MA, IN). Let's assume that we want to know the probability of getting a male from California. We can represent this probability as $P(\text{male and CA})$ and apply the multiplication rule to get

$$
P(\text{male and CA}) = \frac{1}{2} \cdot \frac{1}{4} = \frac{1}{8}
$$

We could also arrive at the same probability by examining the tree diagram in Fig. 3.10. The tree diagram has 8 branches that, by the random computer selec-

FIGURE 3.10
Tree Diagram

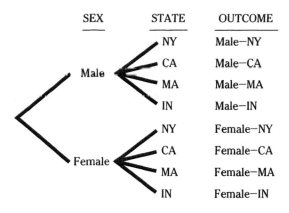

SEX	STATE	OUTCOME

tion method, are all equally likely. Because only 1 branch corresponds to P(male and CA), we get a probability of 1/8. Apart from the calculation of the probability, this solution reveals another principle, which is a generalization of the following specific observation: With 2 sexes and 4 states, there are 8 different possibilities for the compound event of selecting a sex and a state.

We now state this generalized principle:

FUNDAMENTAL COUNTING RULE

For a sequence of 2 events in which the first event can occur *m* ways and the second event can occur *n* ways, the events together can occur a total of *m* · *n* ways.

The **fundamental counting rule** easily extends to situations involving more than 2 events, as illustrated in the following example.

EXAMPLE   In designing a computer, if a byte is defined to be a sequence of 8 bits, and each bit must be a 0 or a 1, how many different bytes are possible?

SOLUTION   Since each bit can occur in 2 ways (0 or 1) and we have a sequence of 8 bits, the total number of different possibilities is given by

$$2 \cdot 2 \cdot 2 \cdot 2 \cdot 2 \cdot 2 \cdot 2 \cdot 2 = 256$$

The next three counting rules use the factorial symbol !, which denotes the product of decreasing whole numbers. For example, $5! = 5 \cdot 4 \cdot 3 \cdot 2 \cdot 1 = 120$. By special definition, $0! = 1$. (Many calculators have a factorial key.) Using the

FIGURE 3.11
Tree Diagram of Routes

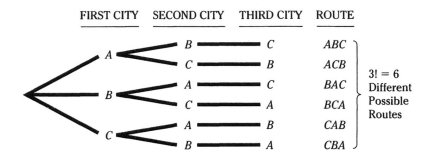

factorial symbol, we now present the factorial rule, which is actually a simple case of the permutations rule that will follow.

FACTORIAL RULE

n different items can be arranged in order n! different ways.

This **factorial rule** reflects the fact that the first item may be selected n different ways, the second item may be selected $n - 1$ ways, and so on.

EXAMPLE   Routing problems are extremely important in many applications of the factorial rule. AT&T wants to route telephone calls through the shortest networks. Federal Express wants to find the shortest routes for its deliveries. Suppose a computer salesperson must visit 3 separate cities denoted by *A, B, C.* How many routes are possible for the salesperson to travel?

SOLUTION   Using the factorial rule, we see that the 3 different cities (*A, B, C*) can be arranged in 3! = 6 different ways. In Fig. 3.11 we can see exactly why there are 6 different routes.

EXAMPLE   The business manager for a presidential candidate wants to choose a route so that her candidate visits the capital of each of the 50 states. How many different routes are possible?

SOLUTION   The 50 state capitals can be arranged 50! ways, so that the number of different routes is 50! or 30,414 *followed by 60 zeros;* that is an incredibly large number! Now we can see why the symbol ! is used for factorials!

The preceding example is a variation of a classical problem called the traveling salesman problem. It is especially interesting because the large number of possibilities precludes a direct computation for each route, even if computers are used. The time for the fastest computer to calculate directly the shortest possible route is

1,000,000,000,000,000,000,000,000,000,000,000,000,000 *centuries!*

(A Bell Laboratories mathematician claims that the shortest distance for the 48 contiguous states is 10,628 miles. See *Discover,* July 1985. See also page C1 of the *New York Times* for March 12, 1991.) Clearly, those who use computers to solve problems must be able to recognize when the number of possibilities is so large.

In the factorial counting rule, we determine the number of different possible ways we can arrange a number of items in some type of ordered sequence. Sometimes we don't want to include all the items available. When we refer to sequences, we imply that *order* is taken into account. Sequences are commonly called permutations, which explains the use of the letter *P* in the following rule.

PERMUTATIONS RULE

The number of *permutations* (or sequences) of *r* items selected from *n* available items (not allowing duplication) is

$$_nP_r = \frac{n!}{(n-r)!}$$

where *n* = total number of available items and *r* = number of items selected.

In applying the preceding permutations rule, we *must* have a total of *n* items available, we *must* select *r* of the *n* items, and we *must* consider rearrangements of the same items to be different. In the following example we are asked to find the total number of different sequences that are possible. That suggests use of the permutations rule.

EXAMPLE If a financial editor must arrange 5 articles in a magazine and there are 8 articles available, how many different arrangements are possible?

SOLUTION Here we want the number of arrangements of *r* = 5 items selected from *n* = 8 available articles, so the number of different possible arrangements is

$$_8P_5 = \frac{8!}{(8-5)!} = \frac{8!}{3!} = 6720$$

This permutation rule can be thought of as an extension of the fundamental counting rule. We can solve the preceding problem by using the fundamental

YOU BET

In the typical state lottery, the "house" keeps around 60% of the money bet; only 40% is returned as prizes. Racetracks usually keep around 15% of the money bet. In casinos, the percent kept depends on the game. It's 5.26% for roulette, 5.9% for blackjack, 1.4% for craps, and 3% to 22% for slot machines. Some professional gamblers can systematically win at blackjack by using complicated card-counting techniques. They know when a deck has disproportionately more high cards, and this is when they place large bets. Many casinos react by ejecting card counters or by shuffling the decks more frequently.

counting rule in the following way. With 8 articles available and with space for only 5 articles, we know that there are 8 choices for the first article, 7 choices for the second article, 6 choices for the third article, 5 choices for the fourth article, and 4 choices for the fifth article. The number of different possible arrangements is therefore $8 \cdot 7 \cdot 6 \cdot 5 \cdot 4 = 6720$, but $8 \cdot 7 \cdot 6 \cdot 5 \cdot 4$ is actually $8! \div 3!$. In general, whenever we select r items from n available items, the number of different possible arrangements is $n! \div (n - r)!$, and this is expressed in the permutations rule.

When we intend to select r items from n available items but *do not take order into account,* we are really concerned with possible combinations rather than permutations. That is, when **different orderings of the same items are to be counted separately, we have a permutation problem, but when different orderings are *not* to be counted separately, we have a combination problem** and may apply the following rule.

COMBINATIONS RULE

The number of *combinations* of r items selected from n available items is

$$_nC_r = \frac{n!}{(n - r)!\, r!}$$

Because choosing between the permutations rule and the combinations rule can be confusing, we provide the following example, which is intended to emphasize the difference between them.

EXAMPLE   Five students (Al, Bob, Carol, Donna, and Ed) have volunteered for service in their college's Financial Aid Office.

a. If 3 of the students are to be selected for a special *committee,* how many different committees are possible?
b. If 3 of the students are to be nominated for the offices of president, vice president, and secretary, how many different *slates* are possible?

SOLUTION   a. When forming the committee, order of selection is irrelevant. The committee of Al, Donna, and Ed is the same as that of Donna, Al, and Ed. Therefore we want the number of combinations of 5 students when 3 are selected. We get

$$_5C_3 = \frac{5!}{(5 - 3)!3!} = 10 \qquad \text{Use combinations when order is irrelevant.}$$

There are 10 different possible committees.

b. When forming slates of candidates, the order is relevant. The slate of Donna for president, Al for vice president, and Ed for secretary is different from the slate of Al, Donna, and Ed for president, vice president, and secretary, respectively. Here we want the number of permutations of 5 students when 3 are selected. We get

$$_5P_3 = \frac{5!}{(5-3)!} = 60$$

Use permutations when order is relevant.

There are 60 different possible slates.

The counting techniques presented in this section are sometimes used in probability problems. The following examples illustrate such applications.

EXAMPLE   In the New York State lottery, a player wins first prize by selecting the correct 6-number combination when 6 different numbers from 1 through 54 are drawn. If a player selects one particular 6-number combination, find the probability of winning.

SOLUTION   Since 6 different numbers are selected from 54 different possibilities, the total number of combinations is

$$_{54}C_6 = \frac{54!}{(54-6)!6!} = \frac{54!}{48!6!} = 25,827,165$$

With only 1 combination selected, the player's probability of winning is only 1/25,827,165.

EXAMPLE   The A.K.R. Security Company makes a home security device with 10 buttons that is disarmed when 3 different buttons are pushed in the proper sequence. (No button can be pushed twice.) If the correct code is forgotten, what is the probability of disarming this device by randomly pushing 3 of the buttons?

SOLUTION   The number of different possible 3-button sequences is

$$_{10}P_3 = \frac{10!}{(10-3)!} = 720$$

The probability of randomly selecting the correct 3-button sequence is therefore 1/720.

EXAMPLE   A UPS dispatcher sends a delivery truck to 8 different locations. If the order in which the deliveries are made is randomly determined, find the probability that the resulting route is the shortest possible route.

SOLUTION   With 8 locations there are 8!, or 40,320, different possible routes. Among those 40,320 different possibilities, only 2 routes will be shortest (actually the same route in 2 different directions). Hence there is a probability of only 2/40,320, or 1/20,160, that the selected route will be the shortest possible route.

In this last example, application of the appropriate counting technique made the solution easily obtainable. If we had to determine the number of routes directly by listing them, we would labor for more than 11 hours while working at the rapid rate of one route per second! Clearly, these counting techniques are extremely valuable.

The concepts and rules of probability theory presented in this chapter consist of elementary and fundamental principles. A more complete study of probability is not necessary at this time because our main objective is to study the elements of statistics, and we have already covered the probability theory that we will need. We hope that this chapter generates some interest in probability for its own sake. The importance of probability is continuing to grow as it is used by more and more political scientists, economists, biologists, actuaries, business executives, and other professionals.

3.6 EXERCISES   BASIC CONCEPTS

In Exercises 1–16, evaluate the given expressions.

1. 7!
2. 9!
3. $\dfrac{70!}{68!}$
4. $\dfrac{92!}{89!}$
5. $(9 - 3)!$
6. $(20 - 12)!$
7. $_6P_2$
8. $_6C_2$
9. $_{10}C_3$
10. $_{10}P_3$
11. $_{52}C_2$
12. $_{52}P_2$
13. $_5P_5$
14. $_5C_5$
15. $_5C_0$
16. $_5P_0$
17. In an IRS data base, data are grouped according to sex (female, male) and income level (low, middle, high). How many different possible categories are there?
18. How many different ways can 5 cars be arranged on a carrier truck with room for 5 vehicles?
19. A computer operator must select 4 jobs from among 10 available jobs waiting to be completed. How many different sequences are possible?
20. A computer operator must select 4 jobs from 10 available jobs waiting to be completed. How many different combinations are possible?
21. An IRS agent must audit 12 returns from a collection of 22 flagged returns. How many different combinations are possible?

22. A state of Florida health inspector has time to visit 7 of the 20 restaurants on a list. How many different routes are possible?

23. Using a word processor, a market research analyst develops a survey of 10 questions. She decides to rearrange the order of the questions so that any lead-in effect will be minimized. How many different versions of the survey are required if all possible sequences are included?

24. How many different 7-digit telephone numbers are possible if the first digit cannot be 0 or 1?

25. An airline mail route must be scheduled to include stops at 7 cities.
    a. How many different routes are possible?
    b. If the route is randomly selected, what is the probability that the cities will be arranged in alphabetical order?

26. A 6-member FBI investigative team is to be formed from a list of 30 agents.
    a. How many different possible combinations can be formed?
    b. If the selections are random, what is the probability of getting the 6 agents with the most time in service?

27. a. How many different Social Security numbers are possible? Each Social Security number is a sequence of 9 digits.
    b. U.S. credit card numbers consist of sequences of 16 digits. How many different credit card numbers are possible?

28. A manager for a Chevrolet dealership must randomly select 3 of 12 available people for overtime work on a Saturday. How many different groups of 3 are possible?

29. A union must elect 4 officers from 16 available candidates. How many different slates are possible if 1 candidate is nominated for each office?

30. a. How many different Zip codes are possible if each code is a sequence of 5 digits?
    b. If a computer randomly generates 5 digits, what is the probability it will produce your Zip code?

31. A typical combination lock is opened with the correct sequence of 3 numbers between 0 and 49 inclusive.
    a. How many different sequences are possible if numbers can be repeated?
    b. These sequences are commonly referred to as "combinations," but are they actually combinations or are they permutations?

32. One phase of an automobile assembly requires the attachment of 8 different parts, and they can be attached in any order. The manager decides to find the most efficient sequence by trying all possibilities. How many different sequences are possible?

33. A space shuttle crew has available 10 main dishes, 8 vegetable dishes, 13 desserts, and 3 appetizers. If the first meal includes 2 different desserts and 1 item from each of the other categories, how many different combinations are possible?

34. A password must be entered in order to access a computer file. If the password is made up of a letter followed by 5 digits (each between 0 and 9 with repetition allowed), how many different passwords are possible?

35. A television program director for the ABM cable channel has 14 shows available for Monday night and must choose 5 shows.
    a. How many different possible combinations are there?
    b. If 650 different combinations are judged to be incompatible, find the probability of randomly selecting 5 shows that are compatible.

36. A common lottery win requires that you pick the correct 6-number combination randomly selected from the numbers between 1 and 49 inclusive. Find the probability of such a win and compare it to the probability of being struck by lightning this year, which is approximately 1/700,000.

3.6 EXERCISES   BEYOND THE BASICS

37. A common computer programming rule is that names of variables must be between 1 and 8 characters long. The first character can be any of the 26 letters, while successive characters can be any of the 26 letters or any of the 10 digits. For example, allowable variable names are A, AAA, and R2D2. How many different variable names are possible?
38. a.   Five managers gather for a meeting. If each manager shakes hands with each other manager exactly once, what is the total number of handshakes?
    b.   If n managers shake hands with each other exactly once, what is the total number of handshakes?
39. a.   How many different ways can 3 negotiators be seated at a round table? (Assume that if everyone moves to the right, the seating arrangement is the same.)
    b.   How many different ways can n negotiators be seated at a round table?
40. We say that a sample is *random* if all possible samples of the same size have the same probability of being selected.
    a.   If a random sample is to be drawn from a population of size 60, find the probability of selecting any one individual sample consisting of 5 members of the population.
    b.   Write a general expression for the probability of selecting a particular random sample of size n from a population of size N.
41. Many calculators or computers cannot directly calculate 70! or higher. When n is large, $n!$ can be *approximated* by

    $$n! = 10^K \quad \text{where } K = (n + 0.5)\log n + 0.39908993 - 0.43429448n$$

    Evaluate 50! using the factorial key on a calculator and also by using the approximation given here.
42. The Bureau of Fisheries once asked Bell Laboratories for help in finding the shortest route for getting samples from 300 locations in the Gulf of Mexico. There are 300! different possible routes. If 300! is evaluated, how many digits are used in the result? (See Exercise 41.)

Vocabulary List
Define and give an example of each term.

experiment
event
simple event
sample space
relative frequency approximation of probability

classical approach to probability
law of large numbers
random selection
subjective probability
complement
compound event
addition rule
mutually exclusive events
multiplication rule
tree diagram
independent events
dependent events
conditional probability
run of 8 rule
fundamental counting rule
factorial rule
permutations
combinations

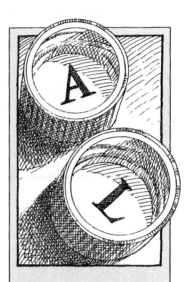

PROMOTION CONTESTS

Many contests or games have been designed to promote or sell products, but some have encountered problems. The Beatrice Company ran a contest involving matching numbers on scratch cards with scores from Monday night football games. The game cards had too few permutations, and Frank Maggio was able to identify patterns and collect around 4000 winning cards worth $21 million. The contest was canceled and lawsuits were filed. The Pepsi people ran another contest in which people had to spell out their names with letters found on bottle caps, but a surprisingly large number of people with short names like Ng forced the cancellation of this contest also.

Review

This chapter introduced the basic concept of *probability,* which is a number between 0 and 1 that expresses the likelihood of some event. In Section 3.2 we began with two rules for finding probabilities. Rule 1 represents the *relative frequency* approach, whereby we approximate the probability of an event by actually conducting or observing the experiment in question.

RULE 1

$$P(A) = \frac{\text{number of times } A \text{ occurred}}{\text{number of times experiment was repeated}}$$

Rule 2 is called the *classical* approach, and it applies only if all the outcomes are equally likely.

RULE 2

$$P(A) = \frac{s}{n} = \frac{\text{number of ways } A \text{ can occur}}{\text{total number of different outcomes}}$$

We noted that the probability of any impossible event is 0, and the probability of any certain event is 1. Also, for any event A,

$$0 \le P(A) \le 1$$

We also defined the *complement* of an event A to consist of all outcomes in which event A does not occur.

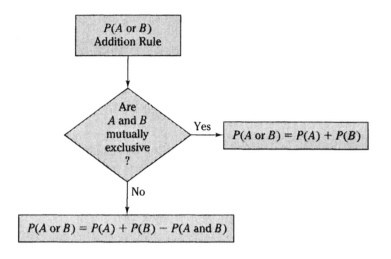

FIGURE 3.12
Finding the Probability That for a Single Trial, Either Event *A* or *B* (or Both) Will Occur

SAFETY IN NUMBERS

Some hotels have abandoned the traditional room key in favor of an electronic key made of paper and aluminum foil. A central computer changes the access code to a room as soon as a guest checks out. A typical electronic key has 32 different positions that are either punched or left untouched. This configuration allows for 2^{32}, or 4,294,967,296, different possible codes, so it is impractical to develop a complete set of keys or try to make an illegal entry by trial and error.

In Section 3.3, we considered the *addition rule* for finding the probability that *A or B* will occur. In evaluating *P(A or B)*, it is important to consider whether the events are *mutually exclusive*—that is, whether they can both occur at the same time (see Fig. 3.12). Section 3.3 also presented the rule of complements, and one form of that rule is this: $P(\overline{A}) = 1 - P(A)$.

In Section 3.4 we considered the *multiplication rule* for finding the probability that *A and B* will occur. In evaluating *P(A and B)*, it is important to consider whether the events are *independent*—that is, whether the occurrence of one event affects the probability of the other event (see Fig. 3.13).

In Section 3.5 we presented an objective rule that helps us determine whether a process is statistically unstable. The *run of 8 rule* indicates that a process is unstable if there are 8 points in a row that are all above (or all below) the desired mean for the process. This rule is based on the very low probability of such an event occurring by chance when the process is running as desired.

In Section 3.6 we considered techniques for determining the total number of different possibilities for various events. We presented the *fundamental counting rule,* the *factorial rule,* the *permutations* formula, and the *combinations* formula, all summarized below with the other important formulas from this chapter.

Most of the material that follows this chapter deals with statistical inferences based on probabilities. As an example of the basic approach used, consider a test of someone's claim that a quarter is fair. If we flip the quarter 10 times and get 10 consecutive heads, we can make one of two inferences from these sample results:

1. The coin is actually fair and the string of 10 consecutive heads is a fluke.
2. The coin is not fair.

The statistician's decision is based on the *probability* of getting 10 consecutive heads, which, in this case, is so small (1/1024) that the inference of unfairness is the better choice. Here we can see the important role that probability plays in the standard methods of statistical inference.

FIGURE 3.13
Finding the Probability That Event A Will Occur in One Trial and Event B Will Occur in Another Trial

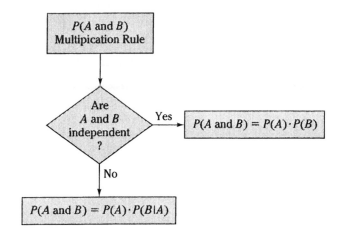

IMPORTANT FORMULAS

$0 \leq P(A) \leq 1$ for any event A

$P(A \text{ or } B) = P(A) + P(B)$ if A, B are mutually exclusive

$P(A \text{ or } B) = P(A) + P(B) - P(A \text{ and } B)$ if A, B are not mutually exclusive

$P(\overline{A}) = 1 - P(A)$

$P(A) = 1 - P(\overline{A})$

$P(A) + P(\overline{A}) = 1$

$P(A \text{ and } B) = P(A) \cdot P(B)$ if A, B are independent

$P(A \text{ and } B) = P(A) \cdot P(B|A)$ if A, B are dependent

$m \cdot n =$ the total number of ways two events can occur, if the first can occur m ways while the second can occur n ways

$n! =$ the number of ways n different items can be arranged

$_nP_r = \dfrac{n!}{(n-r)!}$ the number of *permutations* (arrangements) when r items are selected from n available items

$_nC_r = \dfrac{n!}{(n-r)!\, r!}$ the number of *combinations* when r items are selected from n available items

Review Exercises

1. A broker randomly selects 200 stocks and obtains the data summarized in the table on page 142. The data are collected for one quarter from the New York Stock

Exchange (NYSE), the American Stock Exchange (ASE), and over-the-counter (OTC) stocks.

	NYSE	ASE	OTC
Dividend declared	93	26	8
No dividend declared	27	24	22

a. If a stock is randomly selected from these 200 stocks, find the probability of selecting one from the New York Stock Exchange.
b. If a stock is randomly selected from this sample group, find the probability of selecting one from the NYSE or the ASE.
c. If a stock is randomly selected from this sample group, find the probability that a dividend was declared for the quarter.

2. Use the stock data from Exercise 1 and assume that one stock is randomly selected from this sample group.
   a. Find the probability of getting one from the NYSE that declared a dividend.
   b. Find the probability of getting one from the NYSE or one that declared a dividend.

3. Use the stock data from Exercise 1 and assume that one stock is randomly selected from this sample group.
   a. Find the probability of getting one from the NYSE given that the stock is one that did not have a dividend declared.
   b. Find the probability of getting a stock that did declare a dividend given that it is one from the NYSE.
   c. Are the events "getting a stock from the NYSE" and "declaring a dividend" independent or dependent? Explain.
   d. If you were to randomly select a stock but you want one with a dividend declared, where should you get the stock (NYSE, or ASE, or OTC)? Explain.

4. The Kansas Food Products Company decides to provide "on the average" 12.1 oz of cereal in its boxes so that customers will not complain. The filling machines are calibrated and the first 12 boxes are inspected with these results (in ounces):

   12.1   12.0   12.2   12.3   12.4   12.2   12.3   12.2   12.3   12.5   12.3   12.1

   a. Construct a run chart of this process.
   b. Does this process seem to be statistically stable around the desired value of 12.1?
   c. Calculate the probability of getting 9 consecutive points in a row that are all above the desired value. (Assume that the process is symmetrical and stable around 12.1 oz.)

5. In an experiment involving smoke detectors, an alarm was triggered after the subject fell asleep. Of the 95 sleeping subjects, 40 were awakened by the alarm, and 55 did not awaken. If 1 subject is randomly selected, find the probability that he or she is among those who were not awakened by the alarm.

6. According to Bureau of the Census data, among mothers who begin working, 30.6% have less than a high school education. If 1 working mother is randomly selected, what is the probability that she has at least a high school education?

7. Fifty-five percent of enlisted personnel are married, according to a Department

of Defense survey of 89,000 enlisted military personnel. If a crew of 6 enlisted military personnel is formed by random selection, what is the probability that none of them are married?

8. In attempting to gain access to an insurance company's computer data bank, a computer is programmed to automatically dial every phone number with the prefix 478 followed by 4 digits. How many such telephone numbers are possible?

9. The accompanying table summarizes the ratings for 6665 movies made before the NC 17 rating was introduced in 1990. (The table is based on data from the Motion Picture Association of America.)

RATING	NUMBER
G	873
PG	2505
R	2945
X	342

   a. If one of these movies is randomly selected, find the probability that it has a rating of R.
   b. If one of the movies is randomly selected, find the probability of getting one with a PG or G rating.
   c. If one movie is randomly selected, find the probability of getting one with a PG and a G rating.

10. The Automotive Supply Corporation manufactures automobile automatic transmissions that contain 125 different parts, valves, seals, and so on. This manufacturer feels confident that the product has good quality because the chance of any single part being acceptable is 0.998. (That is a common standard used in the United States for the last several years.) Calculate the probability that such a policy will result in an acceptable transmission with 125 acceptable parts (assuming that one transmission is made).

11. In one game of the New York lottery, your probability of winning by selecting the correct 6-number combination from the 54 possible numbers is 1/25,827,165. What is the probability if the rules are changed so that you must get the correct 6 numbers in the order they are selected?

12. Of 120 auto ignition circuits, 18 are defective. If 2 circuits are randomly selected, find the probability that they are both defective in each of the following cases.
   a. The first selection is replaced before the second selection is made.
   b. The first selection is not replaced.

13. a. Find $P(A \text{ and } B)$ if $P(A) = 0.2$, $P(B) = 0.4$, and A and B are independent.
   b. Find $P(A \text{ or } B)$ if $P(A) = 0.2$, $P(B) = 0.4$, and A and B are mutually exclusive.
   c. Find $P(\overline{A})$ if $P(A) = 0.2$.

14. A study conducted at a large state university involved 400 graduates of business-related programs. The grades they received in the required statistics course were determined along with their majors, and the results are given in the table.

PROGRAM	A	B	C OR LOWER
Accounting	30	40	30
Management	0	20	80
Other	30	60	110

   a. Based on these results, are the events of getting an A and being an accounting major mutually exclusive?
   b. Based on these results, are the events of getting an A and being a management major mutually exclusive?
   c. If one of these sample subjects is randomly selected, what is the probability of getting an accounting major?
   d. If one of these sample subjects is randomly selected, what is the probability of getting someone who got an A or a B?
   e. If you randomly select one of these sample subjects, what is the probability of getting someone who got an A and was an accounting major?

15. Refer to the sample data given in Exercise 14.
    a.   Find the probability of getting a student with an A, given that the selected student was an accounting major.
    b.   Find the probability of getting a student with an A, given that the selected student was a management major.
    c.   Are the events of getting an A and being a management major independent events?

16. A group of applicants for a temporary job consists of 8 men and 7 women. If 3 different applicants are randomly selected from this group, find the probability of each event.
    a.   All 3 are women.
    b.   There is at least 1 woman.

17. According to Bureau of the Census data, 52% of women aged 18 to 24 years do not live at home with their parents. If we randomly select 5 different women in that age bracket, what is the probability that none of them live at home with their parents?

18. Evaluate the following.
    a.   8!
    b. $_8P_6$
    c. $_{10}C_8$
    d. $_{80}C_{78}$

19. A market researcher claims that 12 consumers were randomly selected from a population of 200,000 consumers (30% of whom have a Sears charge card) and all 12 have a Sears charge card. The researcher claims that this could easily happen. Find the probability of getting 12 Sears card holders when 12 consumers are randomly selected from this population.

20. A major corporation has a very large pool of thousands of job applicants and 50% of them are women. If 4 employees are to be hired immediately and the selections are to be made randomly with respect to gender, find
    a.   the probability that all 4 are women;
    b.   the probability that all 4 are men;
    c.   the probability that all 4 are of the same sex.

21. A critical component in a circuit will work properly only if 3 other components all work properly. The probabilities of a failure for the 3 other components are 0.010, 0.005, and 0.012. Find the probability that at least 1 of these 3 components will fail.

22. If 7 different customers arrive for service in random order, what is the probability that they will be in alphabetical order?

Computer Project

Use Minitab to simulate the filling of 80-oz (5-lb) flour bags. The following commands simulate selecting 20 such bags from a process in which the values 70, 71, 72, . . . , 89, 90 are all equally likely.

```
RANDOM K=20 C1;
INTEGER A=70 B=90.
PRINT C1
```

    a.   Construct a run chart for your results using 80 as your desired center.
    b.   After analyzing the run chart by using the run of 8 rule, do you conclude that the process is stable?

THE VCR DEFECT CASE

he example at the beginning of this chapter involved the claim that a new technology was better because no defects were found among 20 VCRs, whereas the defect rate in the past had been 5%. In Section 3.4 we found that there isn't enough evidence to support this claim because even with a 5% rate of defects, there is a good chance (0.358) of getting 20 VCRs with no defects. We can *simulate* this problem by generating random numbers instead of actual VCRs. Since a 5% rate of defects corresponds to an average of one defect among 20, let's generate random numbers between 1 and 20 with the stipulation that a 1 represents a defect whereas 2, 3, 4, . . . , 19, 20 are all good. Use one of the following two procedures.

COMPUTER APPROACH The following Minitab commands will generate 20 numbers between 1 and 20.

```
RANDOM K=20 C3;
INTEGER A=1 B=20.
PRINT C3
```

a. Examine the results and determine whether any defects are present.
b. Repeat part *a* 9 more times. Among the 10 trials, how many times were there no defects?
c. Based on the result from part *b*, what do you conclude about the chance of getting no defects among 20 VCRs, even though the defect rate is 5%?
d. Write a response to the employee's claim that the new technology is better because no defects were found among the 20 VCRs. Refer to your simulated results as evidence supporting your position.

NONCOMPUTER APPROACH Using a telephone directory, select a page at random and use only the last two digits of telephone numbers; include only those numbers between 01 and 20. Obtain 20 such numbers by randomly selecting 20 pages. (Remember, 01 is a defect whereas 02 through 20 are all good VCRs.)

c. Use Minitab to simulate an unstable process that has shifted up 9 oz. The following commands simulate selecting 20 bags in which the values 79, 80, 81, . . . , 98, 99 are equally likely.

```
RANDOM K=20 C2;
INTEGER A=79 B=99.
PRINT C2
```

d. Construct a run chart of the results from part *c*, again using 80 as your desired center.
e. Use the run of 8 rule in analyzing the results from part *d*. Do you conclude that the process is stable?

CHAPTER 4

Probability Distributions

4.1 OVERVIEW

The chapter objectives are identified. This chapter deals with probability distributions of discrete random variables and methods for finding their means, standard deviations, and probability histograms.

4.2 RANDOM VARIABLES

Discrete and continuous random variables and probability distributions are described.

4.3 MEAN, STANDARD DEVIATION, AND VARIANCE

Given a probability distribution, methods of determining the mean, standard deviation, and variance are described, and the expected value of a probability distribution is defined.

4.4 BINOMIAL DISTRIBUTION

Probabilities in binomial experiments are calculated using a table of binomial probabilities and the binomial probability formula.

4.5 MEAN, STANDARD DEVIATION, AND VARIANCE FOR THE BINOMIAL DISTRIBUTION

Methods for calculating the mean, standard deviation, and variance for a binomial distribution are presented.

Statistics and Safety: The Twin-Engine Jet Problem

Statistics is at its best when we use it to benefit humanity in some way. Companies use statistics to become more efficient, to increase quality, to increase shareholders' profits, and to lower prices. Regulatory agencies use statistics to ensure the safety of workers and customers. In this chapter, one of the many applied examples involves factors of cost effectiveness and passenger safety. With new aircraft designs and improved engine reliability, airline companies wanted to fly transatlantic routes with twin-engine jets, but the Federal Aviation Administration (FAA) required at least three engines for such flights. If the minimum three-engine requirement were eased, less expensive two-engine jets (such as the Boeing 767) could be used. Not only are two-engine jets less

expensive to manufacture and maintain, but they consume about half the fuel of jets with three or four engines. The key issue in approving the lowered requirement is the probability of a twin-engine jet making a safe transatlantic crossing. This probability can be compared to that of three- and four-engine jets. Identifying those probabilities is essential to making a rational decision either to allow transatlantic flights with two engines or to keep the three-engine minimum requirement. The contents of this chapter will enable us to find those probabilities. Specifically, we will compute the probability that for a jet with two engines, at least one engine works successfully on a transatlantic flight. We will also compute the probability that for a jet with three engines, at least one engine works successfully on a transatlantic flight. Those probabilities will show that three-engine jets are safer, but knowing the actual probabilities will better enable us to judge if the difference justifies the FAA three-engine requirement.

4.1 OVERVIEW

In Chapter 2 we discussed the histogram as a device for showing the frequency distribution of a set of data. In Chapter 3 we discussed the basic principles of probability theory. In this chapter we combine those concepts to develop probability distributions that are basically theoretical models of the frequency distributions we produce when we collect sample data. We construct frequency tables and histograms using *observed* real scores, but we construct probability distributions by presenting possible outcomes along with their *probable* frequencies.

Suppose a casino manager suspects cheating at a dice table. The manager can compare the frequency distribution of the actual sample outcomes to a theoretical model that describes the frequency distribution likely to occur with fair dice. In this case the probability distribution serves as a model of a theoretically perfect population frequency distribution. In essence, we can determine what the frequency table and histogram would be like for a pair of fair dice rolled an infinite number of times. With this perception of the population of outcomes, we can then determine the values of important parameters such as the mean, the variance, and the standard deviation.

The concept of a probability distribution is not limited to casino management. In fact, the remainder of this book and the very core of inferential statistics depend on some knowledge of probability distributions. To analyze the effectiveness of a new drug, for example, we must know something about the probability distribution of the symptoms the drug is intended to correct. In order to determine whether a new fertilizer is effective, we must know something about the probability distribution of crop yields for the old fertilizer.

This chapter deals with discrete variables, whereas subsequent chapters involve continuous variables. We begin by examining the concept of a random variable.

4.2 RANDOM VARIABLES

In Chapter 3 we defined an experiment as any process that allows us to obtain observations. Some experiments give us observations that are quantitative (such as weights), while others give us observations that are qualitative (such as colors). We can often express qualitative outcomes with numbers. For example, the qualitative performances of Olympic divers are numerically rated by judges. If we can associate each outcome of an experiment with a single number, then we have a variable whose values are determined by chance. Such variables are called *random variables*.

DEFINITION

A *random variable* associates a single numerical value with each outcome of an experiment.

The values of a random variable are the numbers we associate with the different outcomes that make up the sample space for the experiment. As an example, consider the experiment of randomly selecting 3 consumers. We can let the random variable represent the number of those consumers who recognize the Chrysler logo. That random variable can then assume the possible values of 0, 1, 2, and 3. Even though the actual outcomes are not numbers, we can associate numbers with the results.

| EXAMPLE | A company gives job applicants a test of mathematical skills. The quiz consists of 10 multiple-choice questions. Let the random variable represent the number of correct answers. This random variable can take on the values of 0, 1, 2, 3, 4, 5, 6, 7, 8, 9, 10. |

In Section 1.3 we made a distinction between discrete and continuous data. Random variables may also be discrete or continuous, and the following two definitions are consistent with those given in Section 1.3.

DEFINITION

A *discrete random variable* has either a finite number of values or a countable number of values.

A *continuous random variable* has infinitely many values, and those values can be associated with points on a continuous scale in such a way that there are no gaps or interruptions.

Random variables that represent counts are usually discrete, whereas measurements (such as heights, weights, times, temperatures) are usually associated with continuous random variables.

As an example, if we record the number of customer complaints each week at an accounting firm, we have a *discrete* random variable that can take on any *integer* value from 0 and above. But if we measure the heights of those customers with precision carried out to many decimal places, such as 69.2476 . . . inches, we could get any number between 36 inches and 96 inches; hence we have a *continuous* random variable. It is not possible to deal with exact values of a continuous random variable, and so we round off to a limited number of decimal places, depending on the degree of precision necessary for the particular circumstances.

Inferential statistics is important in decision making in a wide variety of fields. We begin with sample data and attempt to make inferences about the population from which the sample was drawn. If the sample is very large, we may be able to develop a good estimate of the population frequency distribution, but samples are often too small for that purpose. The practical approach is to use information about the sample along with general knowledge about population distributions.

Much of this general information is included in this and the following chapters. Without a knowledge of probability distributions, users of statistics would be severely limited in the inferences they could make. We intend to develop the ability to work with discrete and continuous probability distributions, and we begin with the discrete distribution because it is simpler.

QUEUES

Queuing theory is a branch of mathematics that uses probability distributions. The study of queues, or waiting lines, is important to businesses such as supermarkets, banks, fast-food restaurants, airlines, and amusement parks. Grand Union supermarkets try to keep lines no longer than three shoppers. Wendy's introduced the "Express Pak" to expedite servicing its numerous drive-through customers. Disney conducts extensive studies of lines at its amusement parks so that it can keep patrons and plan for expansion. Bell Laboratories uses queuing theory to optimize telephone network usage, and factories use it to design efficient production lines.

A *probability distribution* gives the probability for each value of the random variable.

TABLE 4.1

x	P(x)
0	1/8
1	3/8
2	3/8
3	1/8

For example, suppose a drug is administered to 3 patients and the random variable is the number of cures (0, 1, 2, or 3). Also assume that the probability of a cure for any particular person is 1/2. (That is, each person has an equal chance of being cured or not.) Table 4.1 summarizes the probability distribution for this situation. (You can find those probabilities by listing the sample space of equally likely cases, beginning with "cure-cure-cure.") Ordinarily, the probability distribution of a random variable will be given as a table, such as Table 4.1, or a formula.

There are various ways to graph a probability distribution, but we present only the **probability histogram.** Figure 4.1 is a probability histogram that resembles the relative frequency histogram presented in Chapter 2, but the vertical scale delineates probabilities instead of actual relative frequencies.

For a discrete random variable, if two events result in different values of the random variable, those events must be mutually exclusive. As an example, if you give a drug to 3 patients, it's impossible to get *exactly* 2 cures and *exactly* 3 cures at the same time, so the events of 2 cures and 3 cures are mutually exclusive. Knowing that all the values of the random variable will cover all events of the entire sample space, and knowing that events that lead to *different* values of the random variable are mutually exclusive, we can conclude that the sum of $P(x)$ for all values of x must be 1. Also, $P(x)$ must be between 0 and 1 for any value of x.

FIGURE 4.1
Probability Histogram
Showing Distribution of
the Number of Cured
Patients among 3 Patients

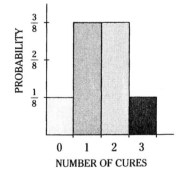

REQUIREMENTS FOR A PROBABILITY DISTRIBUTION

1. $\Sigma P(x) = 1$ where x assumes all possible values
2. $0 \leq P(x) \leq 1$ for every value of x

These two requirements for probability distributions are actually direct descendants of the corresponding rules of probabilities (discussed in Chapter 3).

EXAMPLE Does the formula $P(x) = 1/3$ (where x can be 6, 7, 8, or 9) determine a probability distribution?

SOLUTION The values of x and their probabilities $P(x)$ are shown in Table 4.2. If a probability distribution is determined, it must conform to the preceding two requirements. Since $0 \leq P(x) \leq 1$ for each x, our second requirement is met. But

$$\Sigma P(x) = P(6) + P(7) + P(8) + P(9)$$
$$= 1/3 + 1/3 + 1/3 + 1/3 = 4/3$$

so $\Sigma P(x) \neq 1$. Because the first requirement is not satisfied, we do not have a probability distribution. (See Table 4.2.)

TABLE 4.2

x	P(x)
6	1/3
7	1/3
8	1/3
9	1/3

If we change the preceding example so that $P(x) = 1/4$ for $x = 6, 7, 8,$ and 9, then we do have a probability distribution. Both of the requirements are now met. This is one example of a special probability distribution called the (discrete) **uniform distribution,** characterized by the fact that each possible value of x is just as likely as any other value of x.

EXAMPLE   Does $P(x) = x/10$ (where x can be 0, 1, 2, 3, or 4) determine a probability distribution?

SOLUTION   For the given function we conclude that

$$P(0) = \frac{0}{10} = 0 \qquad P(3) = \frac{3}{10}$$

$$P(1) = \frac{1}{10} \qquad\qquad P(4) = \frac{4}{10}$$

$$P(2) = \frac{2}{10} \qquad\qquad \left(\frac{0}{10} + \frac{1}{10} + \frac{2}{10} + \frac{3}{10} + \frac{4}{10} = 1\right.$$

$$\left. \text{so that } \Sigma P(x) = 1\right)$$

The sum of these probabilities is 1, and each $P(x)$ is between 0 and 1, so both requirements are satisfied. Consequently, we have a probability distribution.

We saw in the overview that probability distributions are extremely important in the study of statistics. We have just considered probability distributions of discrete random variables, and in later chapters we will consider important probability distributions of continuous random variables.

4.2   EXERCISES   BASIC CONCEPTS

In Exercises 1–16, determine whether a probability distribution is given. In those cases where $P(x)$ does not determine a probability distribution, identify the requirement that is not satisfied.

1. A vendor supplies refreshments at a baseball stadium and must plan for the possibility of a World Series contest. In the accompanying table (based on past results), x represents the number of games required to complete a baseball World Series contest.

x	$P(x)$
4	0.120
5	0.253
6	0.217
7	0.410

2. A national toy-store chain depends heavily on the size of the child population, and research is being conducted to learn more about it. In the accompanying table, x represents the number of children (under 18 years of age) in families. (The table is based on data from the U.S. Census Bureau.)

x	$P(x)$
0	0.48
1	0.21
2	0.19
3	0.08

3. In the accompanying table, x represents the number of long-distance telephone calls made during one hour in a telemarketing department.

x	$P(x)$
0	0.32
1	0.08
2	0.12
3	0.09
4	0.07
5	0.06
6	0.04

4. In the accompanying table, x represents the number of employees absent from the Dayton Machine Company on a given day. Why is this *not* a probability distribution? How could you change $P(x)$ to make it a probability distribution where each value of x is equally likely? Once you make this change, it becomes an example of a (discrete) uniform distribution. Construct the probability histogram of this (discrete) uniform distribution.

x	$P(x)$
0	1/5
1	1/5
2	1/5
3	1/5
4	1/5
5	1/5

5. In the accompanying table, x represents the number of chocolate chips in a cookie made by the Houston Bakery. Why isn't this a probability distribution? Modify the table so it represents a probability distribution. (There are many different ways to do this.)

x	$P(x)$
0	0.10
1	−0.70
2	0.20
3	0.30
4	1.10

6. $P(x) = 1/3$ for $x = 1, 2, 3$

7. $P(x) = x^2$ for $x = 0, 1/2, 1/3, 5/6$
8. $P(x) = x - 2.5$ for $x = 2, 3$

9. $P(x) = \dfrac{1}{2(2-x)!x!}$ for $x = 0, 1, 2$

10. $P(x) = \dfrac{3}{4(3-x)!x!}$ for $x = 0, 1, 2, 3,$

In Exercises 11–15, do each of the following:

a. List the values that the random variable x can assume.
b. Determine the probability $P(x)$ for each value of x.
c. Summarize the probability distribution as a table that follows the format of Table 4.1.
d. Construct the probability histogram that represents the probability distribution for the random variable x.

11. A drug is administered to 2 patients, and the random variable x represents the number of cures that occur. The probabilities corresponding to 0 cures, 1 cure, and 2 cures are 1/4, 1/2, and 1/4, respectively.
12. A manufacturer produces gauges in batches of 3, and the random variable x represents the number of defects in a batch. The probabilities corresponding to 0 defects, 1 defect, 2 defects, and 3 defects are found to be 0.70, 0.20, 0.09, and 0.01, respectively.
13. After carefully examining the entire hour's production of clothes dryers manufactured at the Telstar Appliance Company, you determine the chance of getting a dryer with no paint chips, one paint chip, two paint chips, or three paint chips to be 0.45, 0.25, 0.20, and 0.10, respectively.
14. The fill of 160-oz (10-lb) sugar bags purchased by the Houston Bakery is equally likely to be from 155 oz to 165 oz (inclusive) when rounded to the nearest ounce.
15. Tom Johnson, a draftsman you employ, has had difficulty arriving at work on time. You review his time card for the last year and find the following (rounded to the nearest 5 min): 10% of the time Tom arrives 5 min early; 20% of the time he is on time; he is 5 min late 30% of the time; he is 10 min late 20% of the time; he is 15 min late 20% of the time.

4.2 EXERCISES | BEYOND THE BASICS

16. If a random variable can take on any integer value starting at a and ending at b with each integer value being equally likely, we have a (discrete) uniform random variable. Assuming that $a < b$, find $P(a)$ in terms of a and b.
17. a. Let $P(x) = 1/2^x$ where $x = 1, 2, 3, \ldots$. Is $P(x)$ a probability distribution?
    b. Let $P(x) = 1/2x$ where $x = 1, 2, 3, \ldots$. Is $P(x)$ a probability distribution?
18. According to an analyst for Paine Webber, Intel's yield for computer chips is around 35%, meaning that 35% are good. Assume that we have 4 randomly selected chips and that the probability of an acceptable chip is 0.35. Let x represent the number of acceptable chips in groups of 4 and use the multiplication rule and the rule of complements (from Chapter 3) to complete the table so that you have a probability distribution.

x	$P(x)$
0	
1	0.384
2	0.311
3	
4	

y	P(y)
0	0.05
1	0.10
2	0.15
3	0.20
4	0.20
5	0.15
6	0.10
7	0.05

19. For the A.S.J. Computer Mail Order Company, the number of computers sold in one day is represented by y. Given y as a random variable with y = 0, 1, 2, 3, 4, 5, 6, or 7, the probabilities are as given in the accompanying table.
    a. Is this a probability distribution?
    b. What is the probability that y is less than 5?
    c. What is the probability that y is less than or equal to 5?
    d. What is the probability that y is between 4 and 6 inclusive?
    e. What is the probability that y is equal to 4.5?

4.3   MEAN, STANDARD DEVIATION, AND VARIANCE

A probability distribution is actually a model of a theoretically perfect population frequency distribution. The probability distribution is like a relative frequency distribution based on data that behave perfectly, without the usual imperfections of samples. Since the probability distribution allows us to perceive the population, we are able to determine the values of important parameters such as the mean, the variance, and the standard deviation. This in turn allows us to use sample data to make the inferences that are necessary for decision making in many different professions.

In Chapter 2 we saw that there are three extremely important characteristics of both population data and process data:

1. The nature or shape of the distribution of the data, such as bell-shaped
2. A measure of the center of the data, such as mean or median
3. A measure of variation or consistency of the data, such as standard deviation or range

The probability histogram we discussed in the previous section gives us insight into the nature or shape of the distribution. In this section, we will see how to find the mean, standard deviation, and variance for a probability distribution so that we can gain insight into the other two characteristics of center and variation.

We can find the mean for a probability distribution by using Formula 4.1.

Formula 4.1 $\mu = \Sigma x \cdot P(x)$ Mean for a probability distribution

We should stress that $\Sigma x \cdot P(x)$ is the same as $\Sigma[x \cdot P(x)]$. That is, multiply each value of x by its corresponding probability, and then add the resulting products. Formula 4.1 is similar in concept to the weighted mean discussed in Section 2.5. The weights in Formula 4.1 are the probabilities that reflect the frequencies of the different x values.

When we calculate the mean μ from a probability distribution, we get the average (mean) value that we would expect to get if we could repeat the trials a very large number of times or indefinitely. [This mean is sometimes called the **expected value,** denoted by $E(x)$.] We *don't* get the value we expect to occur most often. In fact, we often get a mean value that cannot occur in any one actual trial (such as 1.5 girls in 3 births).

We can also find the variance for a probability distribution by using Formula 4.2.

Formula 4.2 $\sigma^2 = \Sigma(x - \mu)^2 \cdot P(x)$ Variance for a
probability distribution

Formula 4.2 is usually manipulated into an equivalent form to make computation easier, and the result is Formula 4.3.

Formula 4.3 $\sigma^2 = [\Sigma x^2 \cdot P(x)] - \mu^2$ Variance for a
probability distribution
(shortcut version)

Formula 4.3 is a shortcut version that will always produce the same result as Formula 4.2. Formula 4.3 is usually easier to work with, whereas Formula 4.2 is easier to understand directly.

To apply Formula 4.3 to a specific case, we square each value of x and multiply that square by the corresponding probability and then add all those products. We then subtract the square of the mean. We can easily obtain the standard deviation σ by simply taking the square root of the variance. Based on Formula 4.2, the standard deviation for a probability distribution is expressed as

$$\sigma = \sqrt{\Sigma(x - \mu)^2 \cdot P(x)}$$ Standard deviation for a
probability distribution

Using the shortcut version, we can express the standard deviation as

Formula 4.4 $\sigma = \sqrt{[\Sigma x^2 \cdot P(x)] - \mu^2}$ Standard deviation for a
probability distribution
(shortcut version)

If, for example, we find that the variance for a probability distribution is 16, then the standard deviation is $\sqrt{16}$, or 4. The standard deviation gives us a measure of how much the probability distribution is spread out around the mean. A large standard deviation reflects much spread among values, and a lower standard deviation reflects lower variability, with values relatively closer to the mean.

In the following example, we find the mean, variance, and standard deviation of a random variable. We put the calculations in a well-organized table shown on the next page.

EXAMPLE   United Airlines Flight 470 from Denver to St. Louis has an on-time performance described by the probability distribution given in the first two columns of Table 4.3, where x is the number of on-time flights among 3 independent flights (based on data from the EAASY SABRE reservation system). Find the mean, variance, and standard deviation for the random variable x.

SOLUTION

TABLE 4.3
On-Time Flights

x	$P(x)$	$x \cdot P(x)$	x^2	$x^2 \cdot P(x)$
0	0.064	0	0	0
1	0.288	0.288	1	0.288
2	0.432	0.864	4	1.728
3	0.216	0.648	9	1.944
Total		1.800		3.960

In Table 4.3, the two columns on the left side describe the probability distribution, and we create the three columns on the right side for the purposes of the calculations required.

Using Formulas 4.1, 4.3, and the table results, we get $\mu = \Sigma x \cdot P(x) = 1.8$ and $\sigma^2 = [\Sigma x^2 \cdot P(x)] - \mu^2 = 3.96 - 1.8^2 = 0.72$, which is rounded to 0.7. The standard deviation is the square root of the variance, so that

$$\sigma = \sqrt{0.72} = 0.8 \qquad \text{(rounded)}$$

We now know that among 3 flights, the mean number of on-time flights is 1.8, while the variance and standard deviation are 0.7 and 0.8, respectively.

For the flights described in the preceding example, if we actually observe results for some period, such as 8 days, we might get sample results such as 2, 3, 1, 2, 3, 1, 2, and 2 for the numbers of on-time flights among the 3 flights each day. From this sample set we can find $\bar{x} = 2.0$ and $s = 0.8$. These sample statistics for $\bar{x}$ and s can be considered as short-run values whereas the mean μ and the standard deviation σ can be considered as long-run values. Samples naturally vary from their expected values.

Some of the rules introduced in Chapter 2 also apply to random variables because we can think of random variables as "long-run" accumulations of data. See the following illustrations of how Chapter 2 rules apply to the preceding example.

1. **Empirical rule** If a random variable has a bell (mound) shape for its probability histogram, then the empirical rule applies so that about 68% of the time we should get values within one standard deviation of the mean; about 95% of the time we should get values within two standard deviations of the mean, and so on. (See Section 2.6.) In the preceding example involving the numbers of on-time flights among 3 flights, we found $\mu = 1.8$ and $\sigma = 0.8$. We can now apply the empirical rule as follows: When considering groups of 3 flights, in about 95% of all such groups the number of on-time flights should be within two standard deviations of the mean. That is, in about 95% of all groups of 3 flights, the number of on-time flights will be within $2(0.8) = 1.6$ of the mean 1.8. That translates to 95% of the on-time flights falling between

0.2 and 3.4. Because $P(1) + P(2) + P(3) = 0.936$ (or 93.6%), we see that the empirical rule works quite well here.

2. **z scores** Having found that the mean number of on-time flights in groups of 3 is $\mu = 1.8$ and the standard deviation is $\sigma = 0.8$, we can also calculate z scores. As an example, the z score for 0 on-time flights (that is, $x = 0$) is given as

$$z = \frac{x - \mu}{\sigma} = \frac{0 - 1.8}{0.8} = -2.25$$

so that $x = 0$ on-time flights (among 3) is more than two standard deviations below the mean—an indication that it is rather *unusual* to have no on-time flights among 3 flights. (Recall that one criterion for being *unusual* is to differ from the mean by more than two standard deviations.)

3. **Range rule of thumb** Recall that according to the range rule of thumb for populations, the range is approximately 4σ. For our Flight 470 data, the range is $3 - 0 = 3$, so that we can estimate σ as follows:

$$\sigma \approx \frac{\text{range}}{4} = \frac{3}{4} = 0.75$$

This result agrees quite well with the computed value of $\sigma = 0.8$ and it therefore suggests that our computed value is a reasonable solution.

Issues of quality can be addressed through the use of the mean and standard deviation (or variance). For instance, bottles of Coke are noted for good quality. The *average* bottle has good taste, and the taste is very *consistent* from bottle to bottle. Quality requires a good average (mean) and very little inconsistency (that is, a small standard deviation).

4.3 EXERCISES | BASIC CONCEPTS

In Exercises 1–6, construct a probability histogram and find the mean, variance, and standard deviation of the random variable x.

1.
x	$P(x)$
0	0.2
1	0.5
2	0.3

2.
x	$P(x)$
0	0.2
1	0.7
2	0.1

3.
x	$P(x)$
1	0.05
2	0.45
3	0.45
4	0.05

4.
x	$P(x)$
5	0.20
6	0.10
7	0.45
8	0.25

5.
x	$P(x)$
5	1/4
10	1/4
20	1/4
50	1/4

6.
x	$P(x)$
5	1/20
10	3/20
20	7/20
50	9/20

7. According to an analyst for Paine Webber, Intel's yield for computer chips is around 35%. That is, 35% are good. For a batch of 6 randomly selected computer chips, the accompanying table describes the probability distribution for the number of defects. Find the mean, variance, and standard deviation for the number of defects. Graph the probability histogram and identify on it the locations of μ, $\mu - 2\sigma$, and $\mu + 2\sigma$. Calculate the z score for $x = 3$ and for $x = 0$; does either appear to be unusual?

x	$P(x)$
0	0.002
1	0.020
2	0.095
3	0.236
4	0.328
5	0.244
6	0.075

8. The Federal Deposit Insurance Corporation (FDIC) is investigating banks to determine their levels of risk attributable to various sources. In assessing credit risks, the Jefferson Valley Bank investigates the numbers of credit cards people have. Letting x represent the number of credit cards adults have, the accompanying table describes the probability distribution for a certain population (based on data from Maritz Marketing Research, Inc.). Find the mean, variance, and standard deviation for the number of credit cards.

x	$P(x)$
0	0.26
1	0.16
2	0.12
3	0.09
4	0.07
5	0.09
6	0.07
7	0.14

9. Two different commuter train lines feed into Chicago. In an effort to improve their efficiency, you monitor each line for 200 randomly selected days and you obtain the following probability distributions for x_1 and x_2, the times by which the trains miss the scheduled arrival time. (Positive values of x represent early arrivals, negative values of x represent late arrivals, and the times are all rounded to the nearest 2 min.) For each train line, find the mean and standard deviation of the arrival times. Use the range rule of thumb to estimate each σ from the range. Which line appears to be providing higher-quality service? Why? If your supervisor sees no difference between the two commuter lines, what is this supervisor ignoring?

x_1	$P(x_1)$	x_2	$P(x_2)$
-4	0.10	-2	0.10
-2	0.20	0	0.80
0	0.40	2	0.10
2	0.20		
4	0.10		

10. A manager of the Jefferson Valley Bank observed that the number of customers who come in to use the ATM machine is either 6, 7, 8, or 9 customers in
an hour, and those numbers are equally likely. Let C be the random variable
for the number of customers that use the machine during an hour; it is
represented in the accompanying table.

C	$P(C)$
6	0.25
7	0.25
8	0.25
9	0.25

a. Find μ, σ^2, and σ and construct the probability histogram.

b. The Minitab commands that would simulate 40 hours of machine users
are as follows:

```
RANDOM k = 40 C1;
INTEGER a=6 b=9.
PRINT C1
```

The data generated from one simulation are as follows:

```
7  6  6  8  8  6  8  7  6  6  6  9  8  6  9  8  9  9  6  9
9  7  9  6  9  8  7  9  8  9  7  9  8  7  6  7  6  7  7  6
```

Find $\bar{x}$, s^2, and s. Construct a relative frequency distribution for this
sample. How do these results compare to the results from part *a?*

11. Car headlight manufacturers are concerned about failure rates. One headlight
failure is an inconvenience, but if both lights fail, you can't drive at night.
Assume that the probabilities of 0, 1, or 2 failures are 0.960, 0.036, and
0.004, respectively. Find the mean and standard deviation for the number of
failures.

12. United Airlines Flight 470 from Denver to St. Louis has an on-time performance described as follows: Among 4 independent flights, the probabilities for
0, 1, 2, 3, and 4 on-time flights are 0.026, 0.345, 0.346, 0.154, and 0.129,
respectively (based on data from the EAASY SABRE reservation system).

a. Find the mean and standard deviation for the number of on-time flights
among the 4.

b. Calculate $\mu - 2\sigma$ and $\mu + 2\sigma$ and show them on a graph of the
probability histogram. What is the proportion of values actually between
these two numbers?

c. Based on the empirical rule from Section 2.6, what proportion of scores
should be between $\mu - 2\sigma$ and $\mu + 2\sigma$?

d. Use the range rule of thumb to estimate the standard deviation of the
random variable. Is it close to the actual standard deviation?

13. When 5 households are randomly selected, the probabilities of getting 0, 1, 2,
3, 4, or 5 households with VCRs are 0.009, 0.071, 0.221, 0.345, 0.270, and
0.084, respectively (based on data from the U.S. Consumer Electronics Industry). Find the mean and standard deviation for the number of households
(among 5) with VCRs.

a. Graph the probability histogram, calculate $\mu - 2\sigma$, and mark it on the graph.

b. What is the proportion of values below $\mu - 2\sigma$?

c. What proportion would you predict by the empirical rule?

d. Calculate the z score for $x = 0$ and for $x = 2$ VCRs in 5 randomly
selected households.

e. Would it be unusual to have no households (among 5) with VCRs?

f. Would it be unusual to have 2 households (among 5) with VCRs?

14. The Telektronic Company makes car batteries with two different manufacturing lines, each making batteries guaranteed for 48 months. After careful testing of 100 batteries from each line, the manufacturer develops the following probability distributions for the battery lives (rounded to the nearest month). Assume that the manufacturing process is statistically stable.
    a. Graph the probability distribution for each line.
    b. If you give a refund whenever a battery fails before 48 months, what percentage of the batteries from line 1 would require refunds? What percentage from line 2?
    c. Find the mean and standard deviation for each line. Which line has better quality?

Line 1			Line 2	
x	$P(x)$		x	$P(x)$
47	0.10		48	0.10
48	0.10		49	0.20
49	0.10		50	0.60
50	0.20		51	0.10
51	0.30			
52	0.20			

15. Air America wants to overbook flights in order to reduce the numbers of vacant seats. For a certain flight, the probabilities of 0, 1, 2, or 3 vacant seats are 0.705, 0.115, 0.090, and 0.090, respectively. Find the mean, variance, and standard deviation for the number of vacant seats. You plan to find the total number of vacant seats on 100 such flights. How many would you expect?

16. The Harold's Department Store finds that the probabilities of selling 0, 1, 2, 3, or 4 microcomputers in one day are 0.245, 0.420, 0.210, 0.095, and 0.030, respectively.
    a. Find the mean, variance, and standard deviation for the number of micro-computer sales in one day.
    b. Graph the probability histogram for that random variable. Use the range rule of thumb to estimate the standard deviation from the range.
    c. If you were to predict next year's sales from the 250 working days the store is open, how many microcomputers do you expect to sell?
    d. Calculate the standard score for $x = 4$ microcomputers in one day. Based on this and the probability distribution, would it be very unusual to sell 4 microcomputers in one day?

4.3 EXERCISES   BEYOND THE BASICS

17. The variance for the discrete random variable x is 1.25.
    a. Find the variance of the random variable $5x$. (Each value of x is multiplied by 5.)
    b. Find the variance of the random variable $x/5$.
    c. Find the variance of the random variable $x + 5$.
    d. Find the variance of the random variable $x - 5$.

18. Verify that $\sigma^2 = [\Sigma x^2 \cdot P(x)] - \mu^2$ is equivalent to $\sigma^2 = \Sigma(x - \mu)^2 \cdot P(x)$.
(*Hint:* For constant c, $\Sigma cx = c\Sigma x$. Also, $\mu = \Sigma x \cdot P(x)$.)

4.4 BINOMIAL DISTRIBUTION

On January 28, 1986, the Space Shuttle *Challenger* exploded and its seven astronauts were killed. The disaster was apparently caused by the failure of a field-joint O-ring. The Rogers Commission investigated this disaster and concluded that when the *Challenger* was launched in 31° F weather, the chance of a catastrophic failure was at least 13%; if the launch had been delayed until the temperature reached 60° F, the chance of a catastrophic failure would have been around 2%. Methods that we will discuss in this section were used in assessing risks in the redesign of space shuttles after the *Challenger* tragedy.

Component failures are examples of a broad category of events that have an element of "twoness." In manufacturing, parts either fail or they don't. In marketing and sales, a consumer either purchases a product or does not. These situations result in a special type of discrete probability distribution called the *binomial distribution*, which consists of a list of outcomes and probabilities for a binomial experiment.

DEFINITION

A *binomial experiment* is one that meets all the following requirements.

1. The experiment must have a *fixed number of trials*.
2. The trials must be *independent*. (The outcome of any individual trial doesn't affect the probabilities in the other trials.)
3. Each trial must have all outcomes classified into *two categories* (even though the sample space may have more than two simple events).
4. The probabilities associated with the two categories must remain constant for each trial.

EXAMPLE A manufacturer has a 5% rate of defects when making thermostats, which are produced in batches of 6. Let's assume that the production process involves independent events. That is, the failure of any individual thermostat does not affect the probability of failure for any other thermostat. This situation meets the requirements for a binomial experiment.

1. The number of trials (6) is fixed.
2. The trials are independent (according to the given assumption).
3. Each trial has two categories of outcome: the thermostat was manufactured successfully or it is a failure.
4. The probability of failure (0.05) remains constant for the different thermostats.

Notation

S and *F* (success and failure) denote the two possible categories of all outcomes; *p* and *q* denote the probabilities of *S* and *F*, respectively, so that

$$P(S) = p$$
$$P(F) = 1 - p = q$$

n　　　denotes the fixed number of trials.

x　　　denotes a specific number of successes in *n* trials so that *x* can be any whole number between 0 and *n*, inclusive.

p　　　denotes the probability of success in *one* of the *n* trials.

q　　　denotes the probability of failure in *one* of the *n* trials.

P(*x*)　denotes the probability of getting exactly *x* successes among the *n* trials.

The word *success* as used here need not correspond to something good. Selecting a defective parachute may be classified a success, even though the results of such a selection may be less than pleasant. We may call either of the two possible categories the success *S* as long as we identify the corresponding probability as *p*. We can always find the value of *q* by subtracting *p* from 1. If *p* = 0.95, then *q* = 1 − 0.95 = 0.05.

EXAMPLE　Again assume that thermostats are manufactured in batches of 6 with a 5% overall rate of defects. Also assume that we want to find the probability of getting 4 acceptable thermostats in a batch. Identify the values of *n*, *x*, *p*, and *q*.

SOLUTION
1. With 6 thermostats in each batch, we have *n* = 6.
2. We want 4 acceptable (successful) thermostats, so *x* = 4.
3. The probability of an acceptable (successful) thermostat is 0.95, so *p* = 0.95.
4. The probability of failure is 0.05, so *q* = 0.05.

In this section we present two methods for finding probabilities in a binomial experiment. The first method involves the use of Table A.1, and the second involves calculations using a formula. We will first describe the mechanics of both methods, then give a rationale for them.

METHOD 1: USE OF TABLE A.1 IN APPENDIX A

To use Table A.1 for finding probabilities in a binomial experiment, first locate *n* and the corresponding value of *x* that you desire. At this stage, one row of numbers should be isolated. Now align that row with the proper probability of *p* by using the column across the top. The isolated number represents the desired probability (missing its decimal point at the beginning). A very small probability such as 0.000000345 is indicated by 0 +. For example, the table indicates that for $n = 10$ trials, the probability of $x = 2$ successes when $P(S) = p = 0.05$ is 0.075. (A more precise value is 0.0746348, but the table values are approximate.)

Although the values in Table A.1 are approximate and only selected values of p are included, the use of such a table often provides quick and easy results.

EXAMPLE   Using the thermostats from the preceding example, refer to Table A.1 to find the probability of getting 4 acceptable thermostats in a randomly selected batch.

SOLUTION   In the preceding example we established that

$$n = 6 \qquad x = 4 \qquad p = 0.95 \qquad q = 0.05$$

We can now refer to Table A.1. On the first page of that table we locate $n = 6$ in the far left column. We then locate $x = 4$ and find the row entry directly below $p = 0.95$. The table shows that $P(4) = 0.031$. That is, there is a 0.031 probability that exactly 4 thermostats will be acceptable in a given batch.

Table A.1 is easy to use, but it includes only a few particular probability values, and the sample size stops at $n = 15$. Consequently, we cannot use the table in many situations. One alternative is to use Formula 4.5.

METHOD 2: USE OF THE BINOMIAL PROBABILITY FORMULA

After identifying the values of n, x, p, and q, calculate $P(x)$ by using Formula 4.5.

Formula 4.5
Binomial Probability Formula

$$P(x) = \frac{n!}{(n - x)!x!} \cdot p^x \cdot q^{n-x}$$

where n = number of trials
x = number of successes among n trials
p = probability of success in any one trial
q = probability of failure in any one trial ($q = 1 - p$)

The factorial symbol, introduced in Section 3.6, denotes the product of decreasing factors. Many calculators have a factorial key. Two examples of factorials are $3! = 3 \cdot 2 \cdot 1 = 6$ and $0! = 1$ (by definition).

PICKING LOTTERY NUMBERS

In a typical state lottery, you select six different numbers. After a random drawing, any entries with the correct combination share in the prize. Since the winning numbers are randomly selected, any choice of six numbers will have the same chance as any other choice, but some combinations are better than others. The combination of 1, 2, 3, 4, 5, 6 is a poor choice because many people tend to select it. In a Florida lottery with a $105 million prize, 52,000 tickets had 1, 2, 3, 4, 5, 6; if that combination had won, the prize would have been only $1000. It's wise to pick combinations not selected by many others. That is, while all combinations have the same probability of winning, they don't all have the same expected value of return.

EXAMPLE   Use the binomial probability formula to find the probability described in the preceding example. That is, find $P(4)$ given that $n = 6$, $x = 4$, $p = 0.95$, and $q = 0.05$.

SOLUTION   Using the given values of n, x, p, and q in Formula 4.5, we get

$$P(4) = \frac{6!}{(6-4)!\,4!} \cdot 0.95^4 \cdot 0.05^{6-4}$$

$$= \frac{720}{2 \cdot 24} \cdot 0.95^4 \cdot 0.05^2$$

$$= (15)(0.81450625)(0.0025) = 0.0305$$

Here's a reasonable strategy for choosing between the use of Table A.1 and a calculation with the binomial probability formula: Try using Table A.1 first. If you can't get the desired probability directly from that table, then use the formula. The table is quick and easy to use and it sometimes replaces several computations with the formula, as the next example illustrates.

EXAMPLE   The operation of a component in a computer system is so critical that 3 of these components are built in for backup protection. The latest quality control tests indicate that this type of component has a 10% failure rate. (For optimists, that's a 90% success rate.) Assume that this is a binomial experiment and use Table A.1 to find the probabilities of the following events.

a.   Among the 3 components, at least 1 continues to work.
b.   Among the 3 components, none continue to work.

SOLUTION   For both parts of this problem, we stipulate that a success corresponds to a component that continues to work. With 3 components and a 10% failure rate, we have

$$n = 3 \qquad p = 0.9 \qquad q = 0.1$$

Shown below is the portion of Table A.1 that relates to this problem. We have also constructed the table describing the probability distribution.

n	x	p .90		x	$P(x)$
3	0 . . .	001		0	0.001
	1 . . .	027		1	0.027
	2 . . .	243		2	0.243
	3 . . .	729		3	0.729

From Table A.1

We can now proceed to find the indicated probabilities.

a. If at least 1 component continues to work, we have $x = 1$, 2 or 3. We get

$$P(\text{at least } 1) = P(1 \text{ or } 2 \text{ or } 3)$$
$$= P(1) + P(2) + P(3) \quad \text{(addition rule)}$$
$$= 0.027 + 0.243 + 0.729 \quad \text{(from preceding table)}$$
$$= 0.999$$

The probability of at least 1 working component is 0.999.

b. The probability of no component working is represented by $P(0)$. From the preceding table we see that $P(0) = 0.001$. There is a 0.001 probability that none of the 3 components will continue to work.

To really appreciate the ease of using Table A.1, let $n = 15$ and $p = 0.6$, and find the probability of at least 8 successes using Table A.1 and the binomial probability formula. The use of Table A.1 involves looking up the 8 probabilities (for $x = 8, 9, 10, \ldots, 15$) and adding them. The use of the binomial probability formula involves using that formula 8 times, computing the 8 different probabilities, and then adding them. Given the choice in this case, most people would choose the table. However, we must use the formula when the values of n or p do not allow us to use Table A.1, as in the next example.

EXAMPLE   According to one study conducted at the University of Texas at Austin, 2/3 of all Americans can do routine computations. If an employer were to hire 8 randomly selected Americans, what is the probability that exactly 5 of them can do routine computations?

SOLUTION   Let's define "able to do routine calculations" as our success. The experiment is binomial because of the following conditions.

1. We have a fixed number of trials (8).
2. The trials are independent because the employees are randomly selected.
3. There are 2 categories because each employee either can or cannot do routine computations.
4. The probability of success is 2/3 and it remains constant from trial to trial.

We begin by identifying the values of n, p, q, and x so that we can apply the binomial probability formula. We have

$n = 8$ (number of trials)
$p = 2/3$ (probability of success)
$q = 1/3$ (probability of failure)
$x = 5$ (desired number of successes)   *(continued)*

HOLE-IN-ONE

Fundraisers sometimes run golf tournaments with big prizes for a hole-in-one. The National Hole-in-One Association provides insurance, just in case some lucky golfer actually makes one and wins the car, college scholarship, $10,000 cash, or whatever the prize is. The company estimates that when an amateur golfer tees off, the probability of a hole-in-one is 1/12,600. The insurance premium begins at $225 and goes up, depending on the number of golfers, the value of the prize, the length of the shot, and the skill involved.

TABLE 4.4	
x	*P(x)*
0	0.000
1	0.002
2	0.017
3	0.068
4	0.171
5	0.273
6	0.273
7	0.156
8	0.039

We should check for consistency by verifying that what we call a success, as counted by *x*, is the same success with probability *p*. That is, we must be sure that *x* and *p* refer to the same concept of success. Using the values for *n, p, q,* and *x* in the binomial probability formula, we get

$$P(5) = \frac{8!}{(8-5)!5!} \cdot \left(\frac{2}{3}\right)^5 \cdot \left(\frac{1}{3}\right)^{8-5}$$

$$= \frac{40,320}{(6)(120)} \cdot \frac{32}{243} \cdot \frac{1}{27}$$

$$= 0.273$$

There is a probability of 0.273 that 5 of the 8 employees can do routine computations. (Because *p* = 2/3 is not in Table A.1, we had to use the binomial probability formula.)

In the last example we found *P*(5). We could also use the binomial probability formula to find *P*(0), *P*(1), *P*(2), *P*(3), *P*(4), *P*(6), *P*(7), and *P*(8) so that the complete probability distribution for this case will be known. The results are shown in Table 4.4, where *x* denotes the number of employees who can do routine computations. (The sum of the probabilities is 0.999 and it isn't exactly equal to 1 because of rounding errors.) We can depict Table 4.4 in the form of a probability histogram, as in Fig. 4.2. The general nature of the distribution can be seen from the probability histogram.

The entries in Table A.1 are calculated by using the binomial probability formula. The following is a rationale for that formula.

FIGURE 4.2
Probability Histogram for Table 4.4

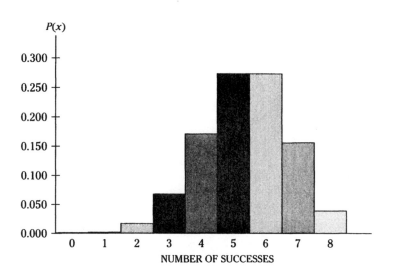

In the preceding example, we wanted the probability of getting 5 successes among the 8 trials, given a 2/3 probability of success in any 1 trial. It's correct to reason that for 5 successes among 8 trials, there must also be 3 failures. A common *error* is to conclude that the probability of 5 successes and 3 failures is as follows:

$$\overbrace{\frac{2}{3} \times \frac{2}{3} \times \frac{2}{3} \times \frac{2}{3} \times \frac{2}{3}}^{\text{5 successes}} \times \overbrace{\frac{1}{3} \times \frac{1}{3} \times \frac{1}{3}}^{\text{3 failures}} = \frac{32}{6561} = 0.00488$$

This calculation is wrong because it contains an implicit assumption that the *first* 5 employees are "successes" and the *last* 3 are failures. However, the 5 successes and 3 failures can occur in many different sequences, not only the one given above. In fact, there are 56 different sequences of 5 successes and 3 failures, each with a probability of 0.0048, so the correct probability is $56 \times 0.0048 = 0.273$.

In general, the number of ways in which it is possible to arrange x successes and $n - x$ failures is shown in Formula 4.6.

Formula 4.6 $\dfrac{n!}{(n - x)!x!}$ Number of outcomes with exactly x successes among n trials

The expression given in Formula 4.6 does correspond to $_nC_r$ as introduced in Section 3.6. (Coverage of Section 3.6 is not required for this chapter.) We won't derive Formula 4.6, but its role should be clear: It counts the number of ways you can arrange x successes and $n - x$ failures. Combining this counting device (Formula 4.6) with the direct application of the multiplication rule for independent events results in the binomial probability formula.

$$P(x) = \overbrace{\frac{n!}{(n - x)!x!}}^{\substack{\text{The number of}\\\text{outcomes with}\\\text{exactly } x \text{ successes}\\\text{among } n \text{ trials}}} \cdot \overbrace{p^x \cdot q^{n-x}}^{\substack{\text{The probability}\\\text{of } x \text{ successes}\\\text{among } n \text{ trials}\\\text{for any one particular order}}}$$

Many computer statistical packages include an option for generating binomial probabilities. Shown below is a sample of output from Minitab obtained from a binomial experiment in which $n = 3$ and $p = 0.9$. The user simply enters those values, and the probability distribution is displayed. (Compare these values with the values from Table A.1.) The Minitab command PDF (for probability distribution function) calculates probabilities for the given values. The subcommand BINOMIAL $n = 3$ $p = 0.9$ specifies that binomial probabilities be given for $n = 3$ and $p = 0.9$. This use of Minitab, or any other such statistical software package, is faster and more efficient than calculating probabilities with the binomial probability formula, and it's free of most of the limitations of Table A.1.

IS PARACHUTING SAFE?

About 30 people die each year as more than 100,000 people make about 2.25 million parachute jumps. In comparison, a typical year includes about 200 scuba diving fatalities, 7000 drownings, 900 bicycle deaths, 800 lightning deaths, and 1150 deaths from bee stings. Of course, these figures don't necessarily mean that parachuting is safer than bike riding or swimming. A fair comparison should involve fatality *rates,* not just the total number of deaths.

An author of this text, with much trepidation, made two parachute jumps but quit after missing the spacious drop zone both times. He has also flown in a hang glider, hot-air balloon, and a Goodyear blimp.

TABLE 4.5
Three Engines (*n*=3)

x	*P*(*x*)
0	0.9997872491
1	0.0002127358
2	0.0000000151
3	0.0000000000

TABLE 4.6
Two Engines (*n*=2)

x	*P*(*x*)
0	0.9998581611
1	0.0001418339
2	0.0000000050

```
MTB > PDF;
SUBC> BINOMIAL n = 3 p = 0.9.
           BINOMIAL WITH N = 3 P = 0.900000
                 K   P(X = K)
                 0   0.0010
                 1   0.0270
                 2   0.2430
                 3   0.7290
```

At the beginning of this chapter, we briefly discussed the Federal Aviation Administration's consideration of allowing twin-engine jets to make transatlantic flights. (Existing regulations required at least three engines.) A realistic estimate for the probability of an engine failing on a transatlantic flight is 1/14,100. Using that probability and the binomial probability formula, we can develop the probability distributions summarized in Tables 4.5 and 4.6, where *x* represents the number of engines that *fail* on a transatlantic flight. (Note that *x* counts engine failures, so for the purposes of this example, a "success" is an engine failure.)

Using those tables and assuming that a flight will be completed if at least one engine works, we get

$$P(\text{safe flight with three-engine jet}) = P(0, 1, \text{ or } 2 \text{ engine failures})$$
$$= 0.9997872491 + 0.0002127358 + 0.0000000151$$
$$= 1.0000000000 \text{ (rounded to 10 decimal places)}$$
$$P(\text{safe flight with twin-engine jet}) = P(0 \text{ or } 1 \text{ engine failure})$$
$$= 0.9998581611 + 0.0001418339 = 0.9999999950$$

The three-engine result of 1.0000000000 is actually a rounded-off form of the more precise result of 0.999999999996433. Comparing the two resulting probabilities, we see that the three-engine jet would be safer, as expected, but the difference doesn't seem to be too significant. All of those leading nines in the results suggest that both configurations are quite safe. The Federal Aviation Administration used this type of reasoning when it changed its regulations to allow transatlantic flights by jets with only two engines. We could analyze the implications of those final probabilities further, but this illustration does show a very useful application of the binomial probability formula.

To keep this section in perspective, remember that the binomial probability formula is only one of many probability formulas that we can use for different situations. It is, however, among the most important and most useful of all discrete probability distributions. It is often used in applications such as quality control, voter analysis, medical research, military intelligence, and advertising.

4.4 EXERCISES | BASIC CONCEPTS

1. Which of the following can be treated as binomial experiments? Why or why not?

   a. Testing a sample of 5 capacitors (with replacement) from a population of 20 capacitors, of which 40% are defective

   b. Testing a sample of 5 capacitors (without replacement) from a population of 20 capacitors, of which 40% are defective

   c. Tossing an unbiased coin 500 times

   d. Tossing a biased coin 500 times

   e. Surveying 1700 television viewers to determine whether they watched a particular show

2. Which of the following can be treated as binomial experiments? Why or why not?

   a. Surveying 1200 consumers to determine their preferences for car models

   b. Surveying 1200 consumers to determine whether they would again buy the same model of car they now drive

   c. Sampling a randomly selected group of 500 cruise ship passengers to determine whether they have been on a cruise before

   d. Sampling a randomly selected group of 500 cruise ship passengers to determine their ages

   e. Surveying 500 randomly selected new-car buyers to determine whether they would spend $300 more for an air bag

3. In a binomial experiment, a trial is repeated n times. Find the probability of x successes given the probability p of success on a given trial. (Use the given values of n, x, and p and Table A.1.)

   a. $n = 10, x = 3, p = 0.5$

   b. $n = 10, x = 3, p = 0.4$

4. In a binomial experiment, a trial is repeated n times. Find the probability of x successes given the probability p of success on a given trial. (Use the given values of n, x, and p and Table A.1.)

   a. $n = 15, x = 5, p = 0.7$

   b. $n = 12, x = 11, p = 0.6$

5. For each of the following, use Formula 4.6 to find the number of ways you can arrange x successes and $n - x$ failures.

   a. $n = 5, x = 3$

   b. $n = 5, x = 0$

6. For each of the following, use Formula 4.6 to find the number of ways you can arrange x successes and $n - x$ failures.

   a. $n = 6, x = 2$

   b. $n = 6, x = 6$

7. In a binomial experiment, a trial is repeated n times. Find the probability of x successes given the probability p of success on a single trial. Use the given values of n, x, and p and the binomial probability formula. Leave answers in the form of fractions.

   a. $n = 5, x = 3, p = 1/4$

   b. $n = 4, x = 2, p = 1/3$

8. In a binomial experiment, a trial is repeated n times. Find the probability of x successes given the probability p of success on a single trial. Use the given values of n, x, and p and the binomial probability formula. Leave answers in the form of fractions.

   a. $n = 6, x = 2, p = 1/2$

   b. $n = 3, x = 1, p = 3/7$

In Exercises 9–24, identify the values of *n, x, p,* and *q,* and find the value requested.

9. A Gallup poll showed that among convenience-store shoppers, 60% gave closeness of location as their primary reason for shopping there. Find the probability that among 5 randomly selected convenience-store customers, 3 of them give closeness of location as their primary reason for choosing that store.

10. In a study of brand recognition, 95% of consumers recognized Coke (based on data from Total Research Corporation). Find the probability that among 12 randomly selected consumers, exactly 11 will recognize Coke.

11. Porcelain sinks are cast 10 at a time. If the casting process seems statistically stable with a 75% success rate, calculate the probability of getting exactly 8 good sinks in a group of 10.

12. According to the Labor Department, 40% of adult workers have a high school diploma and no college studies. If 15 adult workers are randomly selected, find the probability that (a) exactly 10 of them have a high school diploma and no college studies, and (b) that at least 10 of them have a high school diploma and no college studies.

13. A Media General–AP poll showed that 20% of adult Americans are opposed to strict pollution controls on power plants that burn coal and oil. Assume that an environmental group launches a campaign to lower that number, and a post-campaign study begins with 15 randomly selected adults. If the 20% level of opposition hasn't changed, find the probability that among the 15 adults, fewer than 3 are opposed to strict controls. If in that postcampaign study the group finds only 1 person (among the 15) who continued to oppose strict pollution controls, does the opposition continue to be about 20% or is the percentage now lower?

14. A supplier of promotional ballpoint pens claims that 95% of the pens work properly. You randomly select 10 pens and expect most to work properly, but only 4 do so. Calculate the probability of getting 4 or fewer working pens if the 95% claim is true. Based on the result, do you believe the supplier's claim?

15. A study by the EPA (Environmental Protection Agency) showed that of the cars built with catalytic converters, 4.4% have them removed. If 50 cars built with catalytic converters are randomly selected and checked, find the probability of the following:
    a. All cars continue to have their catalytic converters.
    b. One car has the catalytic converter removed.
    c. Two cars have the catalytic converter removed.

16. The National Coffee Association reports that among individuals in the 20-to-29 age bracket, 41% drink coffee. If 5 people in that age bracket are randomly selected, find the probability of the following:
    a. They all drink coffee.
    b. Exactly 1 drinks coffee.
    c. Two drink coffee.

17. In Table A.1, the probability corresponding to $n = 3$, $x = 2$, and $p = 0.01$ is shown as $0+$. Find the exact probability represented by this $0+$.

18. The Locust Tree Restaurant owner is concerned that incorrect bills anger customers. As manager, you have found that a properly trained server makes errors on the bills only 5% of the time. You have just hired a new server and you randomly select 15 bills from the last few days. What is the chance you

will get 4 or fewer bills with errors if the server is properly trained? What is
the chance of getting 10 or more bills (among 15) with errors? If you do get
10 or more bills with errors, do you think the server has been properly trained?

19. A binomial experiment consists of 3 trials with a 1/3 probability of success in
each trial. Construct the probability distribution table for this experiment. (Use
the same format as Table 4.4.)

20. Air America has a policy of booking as many as 14 persons for an airplane
that can seat only 12. (Past studies have revealed that only 90% of the booked
passengers actually arrive for the flight.) Find the probability that if Air
America books 14 persons, enough seats won't be available.

21. A recent study by the A.C. Nielsen Company showed that 57% of all homes
have cable TV. If 10 homes are randomly selected to test an experimental
metering device, find the probability that exactly 6 of these homes have cable
TV.

22. United Airlines Flight 470 from Denver to St. Louis has an on-time performance of 60% (based on data from the EAASY SABRE reservation system).
a.   Find the probability that among 12 such flights, at least 9 arrive on time.
b.   Find the probability that among 30 such flights, exactly 20 arrive on time.

23. Data from Survey Sampling, Inc., show that in Las Vegas, 46.4% of the
telephones have unlisted numbers. If 10 residents with telephone numbers are
randomly selected, find the probability that (a) more than 8 have unlisted
numbers, and (b) 8 or more have unlisted numbers.

24. The Allied Express overnight mail delivery company claims an on-time delivery rate of 95%. If you randomly select a dozen customers, what is the
probability that exactly 10 of them have on-time delivery? What is the probability that 10 or more of them have on-time delivery?

4.4   EXERCISES   BEYOND THE BASICS

25. Suppose an experiment meets all conditions to be binomial except that the
number of trials is not fixed. Then the **geometric distribution,** which gives
us the probability of getting the first success on the xth trial, is described by
$P(x) = p(1 - p)^{x-1}$, where p is the probability of success on any one trial.
Assume that the probability of a defective computer component is 0.2. Find
the probability that the first defect is in the seventh component tested.

26. The **Poisson distribution** is used as a mathematical model describing the
probability distribution for the arrivals of entities requiring service (such as
cars arriving at a gas station, planes arriving at an airport, or people arriving
at a ride in Disney World). The Poisson distribution is defined by the equation

$$P(x) = \frac{\mu^x \cdot e^{-\mu}}{x!}$$

where x represents the number of arrivals during a given time interval (such
as 1 hour), μ is the mean number of arrivals during the same time interval,
and e is a constant approximately equal to 2.718. Assume that $\mu = 15$ cars

per hour arrive for a gas station and find the probability of each number of arrivals in an hour.

   a.   0
   b.   1
   c.   10
   d.   15
   e.   20
   f.   30

27. If we sample from a small finite population without replacement, we cannot use the binomial distribution because the events are not independent. If we sample without replacement and the outcomes belong to 1 of 2 types, we can use the **hypergeometric distribution.** If a population has A objects of one type, while the remaining B objects are of the other type, and if n objects are sampled without replacement, then the probability of getting x objects of type A and $n - x$ objects of type B is

$$P(x) = \frac{A!}{(A - x)!x!} \cdot \frac{B!}{(B - n + x)!(n - x)!} \div \frac{(A + B)!}{(A + B - n)!n!}$$

Five people are randomly selected (without replacement) from a population of 7 men and 3 women. Find the probability of getting 4 men and 1 woman.

28. Many companies monitor the quality of items supplied to them by using **acceptance sampling** based on the binomial distribution. Rubber gaskets are used to manufacture car brake components. The receiver gets large boxes of 500 gaskets and wants 99% (or more) of them to be free of defects. There is a policy of randomly selecting 25 of the 500 gaskets and testing them; this testing process destroys those 25 items. The acceptance sampling policy is to accept the whole lot if the number of defective gaskets is 0 or 1. Otherwise, the whole lot is returned. (a) If in a lot of 500 gaskets 1% are defective, what is the probability the whole lot will be accepted? (b) If in a lot of 500 gaskets 20% are defective, what is the probability the whole lot will be accepted?

4.5 MEAN, STANDARD DEVIATION, AND VARIANCE FOR THE BINOMIAL DISTRIBUTION

The binomial distribution is a probability distribution, so we can find the mean, variance, and standard deviation for the appropriate random variable from the formulas presented in Section 4.3.

Formula 4.1 $\mu = \Sigma x \cdot P(x)$

Formula 4.3 $\sigma^2 = [\Sigma x^2 \cdot P(x)] - \mu^2$

Formula 4.4 $\sigma = \sqrt{[\Sigma x^2 \cdot P(x)] - \mu^2}$

However, we can make these formulas, which apply to all probability distributions, much simpler for the special case of binomial distributions. Given the binomial probability formula and the above general formulas for the mean μ, the variance σ^2, and the standard deviation σ, we can pursue a series of somewhat complicated algebraic manipulations that ultimately lead to the following simple results.

For a binomial distribution,

Formula 4.7 $\mu = n \cdot p$ Mean for binomial distribution

Formula 4.8 $\sigma^2 = n \cdot p \cdot q$ Variance for binomial distribution

Formula 4.9 $\sigma = \sqrt{n \cdot p \cdot q}$ Standard deviation for binomial distribution

The formula for the mean does make sense intuitively. If we were to analyze 100 births, we would expect to get about 50 girls, and np in this experiment becomes $100 \cdot 1/2$, or 50. In general, if we consider p to be the proportion of successes, then the product np will give us the actual number of expected successes among n trials.

The variance and standard deviation are not so easily justified, and we prefer to omit the complicated algebraic manipulations that lead to Formula 4.8. Instead, we will show that these simplified formulas for binomial distributions (Formulas 4.7, 4.8, and 4.9) do lead to the same results as the more general formulas (Formulas 4.1, 4.3, and 4.4) that apply to *any* probability distribution.

EXAMPLE According to an analyst from Paine Webber, the Intel Corporation has a 35% yield for the computer chips it produces—35% of the chips are good and 65% are defective. Let's assume that this estimate is correct and that we have randomly selected a sample of 4 different chips. If x represents the number of good chips in such groups of 4, find its mean, variance, and standard deviation.

SOLUTION In this binomial experiment we have $n = 4$ and $P(\text{good chip}) = 0.35$. It follows that $P(\text{defective chip}) = q = 0.65$. We will find the mean and standard deviation by using two methods.

METHOD 1:

Use Formulas 4.7, 4.8, and 4.9, which apply to binomial experiments only.

$\mu = n \cdot p = 4 \cdot 0.35 = 1.4$ good chips   (Formula 4.7)

$\sigma^2 = n \cdot p \cdot q = 4 \cdot 0.35 \cdot 0.65 = 0.91$ (Formula 4.8)

$\sigma = \sqrt{n \cdot p \cdot q} = \sqrt{0.91} = 0.95$ good chips   (Formula 4.9)

METHOD 2:

Use Formulas 4.1, 4.3, and 4.4, which apply to all discrete probability distributions. (*Note:* Method 1 provided us with the solutions we sought, but we want to show that these

COMPOSITE SAMPLING

The U.S. Army once tested for syphilis by giving each inductee an individual blood test that was analyzed separately. One researcher suggested mixing pairs of blood samples. After testing the mixed pairs, syphilitic inductees could be identified by retesting the few blood samples that were in the pairs that tested positive. The total number of analyses was reduced by pairing blood specimens, so why not put them in groups of three or four or more? Probability theory was used to find the most efficient group size, and a general theory was developed for detecting the defects in any population. This technique is known as *composite sampling.*

TABLE 4.7
Calculating μ, σ, and σ^2

x	$P(x)$	$x \cdot P(x)$	x^2	$x^2 \cdot P(x)$
0	0.179	0	0	0
1	0.384	0.384	1	0.384
2	0.311	0.622	4	1.244
3	0.111	0.333	9	0.999
4	0.015	0.060	16	0.240
Total		1.399		2.867

DRIVE TO SURVIVE PAST AGE 35

Avoid cars—motor vehicle crashes are the leading cause of death among Americans under 35 years of age. If you drive, don't drink—40% of fatally injured drivers are drunk. Drive in large cars—the death rate in the largest cars (1.3 per 10,000 vehicles) is less than half the rate in the smallest cars (3.0 per 10,000 vehicles). Wear safety belts—in a study of 1126 accidents, riders wearing safety belts had 86% fewer life-threatening injuries.

same values will result from the use of the more general formulas from Section 4.3.) We begin by computing the mean using Formula 4.1: $\mu = \Sigma x \cdot P(x)$. The possible values of x are 0, 1, 2, 3, 4, but we also need the values of $P(0)$, $P(1)$, $P(2)$, $P(3)$, and $P(4)$. We use the binomial probability formula to find those values and enter them in Table 4.7.

We now use results from Table 4.7 to apply the general formulas from Section 4.3 as follows:

$$\mu = \Sigma x \cdot P(x) = 1.4 \text{ good chips} \qquad \text{(rounded off)}$$
$$\sigma^2 = [\Sigma x^2 \cdot P(x)] - \mu^2$$
$$= 2.867 - 1.4^2$$
$$= 0.91 \qquad \text{(rounded off)}$$
$$\sigma = \sqrt{0.91} = 0.95 \text{ good chips} \qquad \text{(rounded off)}$$

In the preceding example, the two methods produced the same results, except for minor discrepancies due to rounding. There are two important points to recognize. First, the simplified binomial formulas (Formulas 4.7, 4.8, and 4.9) do lead to the same results as the more general formulas that apply to all discrete probability distributions. Second, the binomial formulas are much simpler, they provide fewer opportunities for arithmetic errors, and they are generally more conducive to a positive outlook on life. If we know an experiment is binomial, we should use the simplified formulas. In the following example, we use only the simplified binomial formulas.

EXAMPLE A job aptitude test consists of 100 multiple-choice questions with possible answers of *a, b, c, d,* and *e.* For people who know nothing and guess the answer to each question, find the mean and standard deviation for the number of correct answers per person.

SOLUTION For each person, the number of trials is $n = 100$ and the probability of correctly guessing an answer is $p = 1/5$, so that $q = 4/5$. (We get $p = 1/5$ because there is 1 correct answer among the 5 possible answers.) We now proceed to find the mean and standard deviation.

FIGURE 4.3
Summary of 300 Real Experiments [Each experiment has 50 trials
($n = 50$) with $p = 0.5$.]

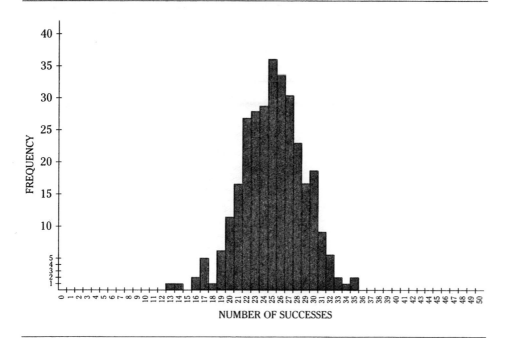

$$\mu = n \cdot p$$

$$= 100 \cdot \frac{1}{5}$$

$$= 20.0 \text{ correct answers}$$

$$\sigma = \sqrt{n \cdot p \cdot q}$$

$$= \sqrt{100 \cdot \frac{1}{5} \cdot \frac{4}{5}}$$

$$= 4.00 \text{ correct answers}$$

For the preceding example, the mean number of correct guesses is 20.0, so that a score of 20.0% on the test is actually an indication of no knowledge. We can use the value of the standard deviation to determine a reasonable range of scores for those who know nothing and guess. For example, using the empirical rule from Chapter 3, we can conclude that about 95% of all scores for guessers should be between 12 and 28 (that is, between $\mu - 2\sigma$ and $\mu + 2\sigma$). We can also conclude that for people who are guessing on every question, about 99.8% of all scores for guessers should be between 8 and 32. If some people get more than 32 correct answers, it is very *unlikely* that they are guessing at all questions. A more likely explanation is that they probably know some of the answers.

When n is large and p is close to 0.5, the binomial distribution tends to resemble the smooth curve that approximates the histograms in Figs. 4.3 and 4.4. Note that the data tend to form a bell-shaped curve. In Chapter 5, we will use this property to solve certain applied problems.

FIGURE 4.4
Summary of 300 Ideal Theoretical Experiments [Each experiment has 50 trials ($n = 50$) with $p = 0.5$.]

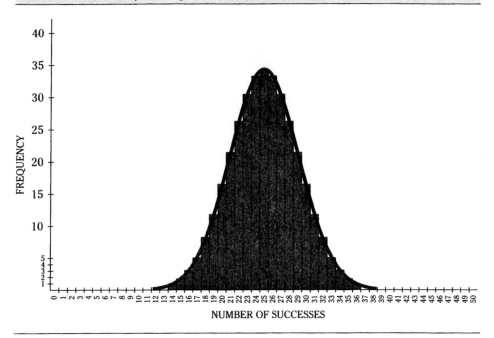

4.5 EXERCISES   BASIC CONCEPTS

In Exercises 1–12, find the mean μ, variance σ^2, and standard deviation σ for the given values of n and p. Assume that the binomial conditions are satisfied.

1. $n = 64, p = 0.5$
2. $n = 100, p = 0.5$
3. $n = 8, p = 0.6$
4. $n = 6, p = 0.3$
5. $n = 36, p = 0.25$
6. $n = 40, p = 0.85$
7. $n = 534, p = 0.173$
8. $n = 898, p = 0.392$
9. $n = 16, p = 1/5$
10. $n = 27, p = 1/4$
11. $n = 253, p = 2/3$
12. $n = 652, p = 3/8$

In Exercises 13–22, find the indicated values.

13. A supervisor gives employees a day off to watch a videotape training program at home. The supervisor then gives a follow-up true-false test of 50 questions to determine whether the employees did watch the program. Several ignored the program and all of their answers are guesses. Find the mean, variance, and standard deviation for the numbers of correct answers for such employees.

14. For a multiple-choice test with 30 questions, each question has possible answers of *a*, *b*, *c*, and *d*, one of which is correct. For people who guess at all answers, find the mean, variance, and standard deviation for the number of correct answers.

15. Porcelain bathroom sinks are cast 10 at a time in a ceramics factory. The casting process seems statistically stable with about a 75% success rate in producing usable sinks. Find the mean, variance, and standard deviation for the number of usable sinks in groups of 10.

16. According to a survey of adults by the Roper Organization, 64% of adults have money in regular savings accounts. If we plan to conduct a survey with groups of 50 randomly selected adults, find the mean, variance, and standard deviation for the numbers who have regular savings accounts.

17. According to data from the U.S. Bureau of Labor Statistics, 70.4% of women in the 20-to-24 age bracket are working. Find the mean, variance, and standard deviation for the numbers of working women in randomly selected groups of 150 women between 20 and 24 years of age.

18. A study conducted by the National Transportation and Safety Board showed that among injured airline passengers, 47% of the injuries were caused by failure of the plane's seat. Two hundred different airline passenger injuries are to be randomly selected for a study. Find the mean, variance, and standard deviation for the number of injuries caused by seat failure in such groups of 200.

19. Of all individual tax returns, 37% include errors made by the taxpayer. If IRS examiners are assigned randomly selected returns in batches of 12, find the mean and standard deviation for the number of erroneous returns per batch.

20. A Roper survey showed that 73% of adult Americans do not feel the government is doing enough to regulate toxic waste disposal. One thousand people are to be randomly selected for a related survey. Find the mean and standard deviation for the numbers in such groups of 1000 who share that same belief.

21. The Wisconsin Bottling Company claims that only 10% of its two-liter bottles of mineral water are underfilled. If you examine a case of 24 such bottles, how many do you expect to be underfilled? What would be the standard deviation?

22. In a recent year, there were 68,593 motor vehicle accidents in New York State, and 42,000 of them involved injuries (based on data from the N.Y. State Department of Motor Vehicles). An insurance analyst will randomly select different groups of accidents, with 20 in each group. Use the sample data to estimate the probability that an accident involves an injury, then find the mean and standard deviation for the number of injury accidents in such groups of 20.

4.5 EXERCISES BEYOND THE BASICS

In Exercises 23, 24, 26, and 27, consider as unusual anything that differs from the mean by more than twice the standard deviation. That is, unusual values are either less than $\mu - 2\sigma$ or greater than $\mu + 2\sigma$.

23. The Telstar Appliance Company gives away promotional ballpoint pens and claims that 95% of them work properly. The pens are shipped in boxes of 25. Determine the mean number of acceptable pens per box. Also find the variance and standard deviation. Find the values of $\mu - 2\sigma$ and $\mu + 2\sigma$ by assuming that 95% of the pens do work properly. Based on this 95% rate, would it be unusual to find only 22 good pens in a box? Would it be unusual to find only 16 good pens in a box?

24. The Dayton Machine Company employs 200 people, and you have found that on any given day about 5% can be expected to be absent. Find the mean, variance, and standard deviation for the number absent. Below are the numbers of absences for 12 randomly selected days. Identify any unusually high or low numbers of absences.

   10   13   7   6   16   11   9   10   14   8   10   5   9

25. The manager of the Denver Valley resort hotel is studying vacancy rates in order to plan a future advertising campaign. The hotel has 40 rooms, and the occupancy rate has been 80% on weekends. Find the mean, variance, and standard deviation for the numbers of occupied rooms during weekends. Find the values of $\mu - 3\sigma$ and $\mu + 3\sigma$. Would it be very unusual to have only 27 rooms occupied on a weekend? 34 rooms? (Use $\mu - 3\sigma$ and $\mu + 3\sigma$ as limits for very unusual values.)

26. The U.S. Post Office claims that 90% of the priority mail is delivered within two days. If priority letters are sent in batches of 100, find the mean, variance, and standard deviation for the numbers delivered on time in each batch. Would it be unusual to have only 85 priority letters in a batch delivered on time? Would 75 be unusual?

27. A company manufactures an appliance and gives a warranty; 95% of its appliances do not require repair before the warranty expires. Is it unusual for a buyer of 10 such appliances to require warranty repairs on 2 of the items?

28. a. If a company makes a product with an 80% yield (meaning that 80% are good), what is the minimum number of items that must be produced in order to be at least 99% sure that they have at least 5 good items?

   b. If the company produces batches of items, each with the minimum number determined in part *a*, find the mean and standard deviation for the number of good items in such batches.

Vocabulary List

Define and give an example of each term.

random variable	probability histogram
discrete random variable	uniform distribution
continuous random variable	expected value
probability distribution	binomial experiment

Review

The central concern of this chapter was the concept of a probability distribution. Here we dealt mostly with *discrete* probability distributions, whereas successive chapters deal with continuous probability distributions.

   In an experiment yielding numerical results, the *random variable* can take on those different numerical values. A *probability distribution* consists of all values of a random variable, along with their corresponding probabilities. By constructing a probability histogram, we can see a useful correspondence between those probabilities and the areas of the rectangles in the histogram.

   Of the infinite number of different probability distributions, we gave special attention to the important and useful *binomial probability distribution,* which is characterized by these properties:

1. The number of trials (denoted by n) is fixed.
2. The trials must be independent.
3. Each trial must have outcomes that can be classified in *two* categories.
4. The probabilities associated with the two categories involved must remain constant for each trial.

We saw that we can compute probabilities for the binomial distribution by using Table A.1 or by using the binomial probability formula, where n is the number of trials, x is the number of successes, p is the probability of a success, and q is the probability of a failure.

For the special case of the binomial probability distribution, we can easily compute the mean, variance, and standard deviations of the random variable by using the formulas given in the summary below.

IMPORTANT FORMULAS

Requirements for a discrete probability distribution:
1. $\Sigma P(x) = 1$ for all possible values of x.
2. $0 \le P(x) \le 1$ for any particular value of x.

For *any* discrete probability distribution:

mean $\mu = \Sigma x \cdot P(x)$

variance $\sigma^2 = \Sigma(x - \mu)^2 \cdot P(x)$

or variance $\sigma^2 = [\Sigma x^2 \cdot P(x)] - \mu^2$

standard deviation $\sigma = \sqrt{\Sigma(x - \mu)^2 \cdot P(x)}$

or $\sigma = \sqrt{[\Sigma x^2 \cdot P(x)] - \mu^2}$

Binomial probability formula: $P(x) = \dfrac{n!}{(n - x)!x!} \cdot p^x \cdot q^{n-x}$

For *binomial* probability distributions:

mean $\mu = n \cdot p$

variance $\sigma^2 = n \cdot p \cdot q$

standard deviation $\sigma = \sqrt{n \cdot p \cdot q}$

Review Exercises

1. According to the National Highway Traffic Safety Administration, 66% of California motorists use seat belts. A California Highway Patrol study involves the random selection of groups with 12 motorists each.
   a. Find the mean and standard deviation for the numbers of motorists per group who wear seat belts.
   b. Find the probability that in one group of 12 California motorists, exactly 8 wear seat belts.
2. Does $P(x) = x/12$ (for $x = 1, 2, 3, 4$) determine a probability distribution? Explain.
3. In a quality control study, it was found that 5% of all auto frames manufactured by one company had at least one defective weld. *(continued)*

a. Find the probability of getting 3 frames with defective welds when 20 frames are randomly selected.

b. Find the mean number of defective frames in groups of 20.

c. Find the standard deviation for the number of defective frames in groups of 20.

4. A study conducted by the American Resorts hotel chain showed 20% of its rooms were improperly prepared (not vacuumed, not enough towels, and so on). If one hotel has 28 rooms per floor, find (a) the mean number of improperly prepared rooms per floor, (b) the variance, and (c) the standard deviation. (d) Find the probability of having exactly 2 rooms on one floor that were improperly prepared. (e) Would it be unusual to find 14 improperly prepared rooms on one floor? Explain.

5. Does $P(x) = (x + 1)/5$ (for $x = -1, 0, 1, 2$) determine a probability distribution? Explain.

6. It has been found that the probabilities of 0, 1, 2, 3, and 4 wrong answers on a quiz are 0.20, 0.35, 0.30, 0.10, and 0.05, respectively.

a. Summarize the corresponding probability distribution.

b. Find the mean of the random variable x.

c. Find the standard deviation of the random variable x.

7. The Washington Candy Company manufactures chocolate-covered cherries and has found that 44% of the individual pieces are damaged. They are sold in boxes of 20. Find (a) the mean number of damaged pieces per box, (b) the variance for the number of damaged pieces per box, and (c) the standard deviation. (d) Would it be unusual for all the pieces in one box to be damaged?

8. Among new-car buyers in the Southeast, 40% are women, and 5 new-car buyers are randomly selected.

a. Find the probability that all 5 are women.

b. Find the probability that exactly 3 of the 5 are women.

c. Find the mean number of women in such groups of 5.

d. Find the variance of the number of women that would be selected in such groups of 5.

e. Find the standard deviation for the number of women that would be selected in such groups of 5.

x	$P(x)$
0	0.20
1	0.70
5	

9. A probability distribution $P(x)$ is described by the accompanying table.

a. Complete the table.

b. Find the mean of the random variable x.

c. Find the standard deviation of the random variable x.

d. Construct the probability histogram.

x	$P(x)$
0	0.4
1	0.4
2	0.4

10. If $P(x)$ is described by the accompanying table, does $P(x)$ form a probability distribution? Explain. Change the probability values so that we have a uniform (discrete) probability distribution (with 0, 1, 2 all equally likely).

11. The Telstar Appliance Company assembles small portable radios from purchased components that have a 0.002 rate of defects. If 40 such components are built into the radio, calculate the chance of getting a radio with no defective components. What is the chance of getting a radio with one or more defective components? (Such a radio will require repairs.) If the quality standard is raised so that only 0.0001 of the components have defects, find the probability that when a radio is made, it will contain all good components.

x	$P(x)$
-1	0.35
0	0.15
1	0.40
2	0.10

12. If $P(x)$ is described by the accompanying table, does $P(x)$ form a probability distribution? Explain.

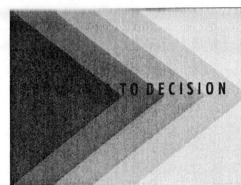

CHANGING FOR THE BETTER OR A CHIP OFF THE OLD BLOCK?

You want to improve a computer chip manufacturing process that has a 2% yield, meaning that 2% of the chips are good. If you can show that the process can be improved, then further investments will be made in it. A new process is introduced and the manager claims that the yield is now greater than 2%. You randomly select a sample of 100 chips and find that 7 of them are good. The Minitab display is based on a binomial distribution with $n = 100$ and $p = 0.02$.

a. Based on this display, what is the probability of getting 7 or more good chips?

b. Based on the result from part a, does it seem likely that the yield is now greater than 2%?

c. Write a brief report to your manager. Cite your findings and explain your conclusion. Make a recommendation either to make further investments in the process (if it can be improved) or to discontinue the process.

```
MTB > PDF;
SUBC> BINOMIAL n=100 p=0.02.
```

BINOMIAL WITH N = 100 P = 0.020000

K	P(X = K)
0	0.1326
1	0.2707
2	0.2734
3	0.1823
4	0.0902
5	0.0353
6	0.0114
7	0.0031
8	0.0007
9	0.0002
10	0.0000

Computer Projects

1. Use Minitab to find the probability that among 60 randomly selected people who go to movie theaters, there are at least 35 women. (Assume that 50% of all those who attend movies are women.)

2. a. Use Minitab to simulate the manufacture of 40 boxes of chocolate-covered cherries (see Review Exercise 7). Enter the commands

```
RANDOM k=40 C1;
BINOMIAL n=20 p=0.44.
PRINT C1
```

b. Describe what the resulting numbers represent.

c. Construct a relative frequency histogram of the results.

d. Use Minitab to calculate the probability distribution function for this problem by using the entry of

```
PDF;
BINOMIAL n=20 p=0.44.
```

e. Why aren't the two distributions (of parts c and d) identical?

BARRY COOK

SENIOR VICE PRESIDENT AT NIELSEN MEDIA RESEARCH

Barry Cook is a Senior Vice President and Chief Research Officer at Nielsen Media Research. He has taught at Yale and Hunter College and worked for NBC and the USA Cable Network. He is now in charge of Nielsen's rating system, doing research to better understand how the measurements work, as well as developing new measurement systems.

WHAT MAJOR TRENDS DO YOU SEE IN THE WAY AMERICANS WATCH TV?

In 1985 the average home received 18.8 channels. In 1990 the average home received 33.2 channels. That obviously has an effect on what people choose to view.

WHAT IS YOUR SAMPLE SIZE?

For the national survey we use "people meters" in 4000 homes with about 11,000 people. We increased the sample size because the use of television has changed. Instead of only three major sources of TV (ABC, NBC,

CBS), there are now dozens of sources of programming, many of which get only a small piece of the audience. In order to measure those smaller pieces with enough precision, a larger sample is needed. In addition, we also have meter services in 25 markets; the television sets are metered (but not the people) in 250 to 500 homes per market. Nielsen is still very big in the diary business—not for the national audience, but for measuring audiences in the 200 or so separate markets across the country. Those diaries amount to a combined sample size of 100,000, four times a year.

HAVE YOU BEEN EXPERIENCING GREATER RESISTANCE TO POLLS AND SURVEYS?

There's no question that we have seen a decline in

that probably is contributing to a decline in the cooperation rate. Also, answering machines make it harder to get through to people.

DO YOU WEIGHT SAMPLE RESULTS TO BETTER REFLECT POPULATION PARAMETERS?

We have a policy against that. We try to represent population parameters by doing the sampling correctly in the first place. We sample in a way that gives an equal probability of selection to all housing units in the 50 states. As a result, there is a known amount of sampling error and there's also an unknown amount of nonsampling error, but we've done validation research to estimate how close the samples are to measures of the population.

COULD YOU CITE A TELEVISION-PROGRAMMING STRATEGY THAT IS BASED ON SURVEY RESULTS?

The most important strategy is called "prime time." The biggest usage of television occurs in the evening hours when most people are home. The most general programming strategy is to put on your best shows when there's the greatest number of people there. With a miniseries, what you get on the first episode serves as almost a cap on what you can get after that. You want to get the maximum possible potential audience for the first installment, so Sunday night does that.

"We try to represent population parameters by doing the sampling correctly in the first place."

cooperation in both telephone and in-person contacts with people. It's across the entire survey industry. There are concerns about privacy. The data-gathering efforts are being mixed up with sales efforts, and

WHAT ARE SOME OF THE SPECIFIC STATISTICAL METHODS YOU USE?

We use a lot of statistics for our own understanding and our clients' understanding of sampling and trends. We get into hypothesis testing when we try to understand why things change. Confidence intervals are very important in interpreting the estimates of the population.

CHAPTER 5

Normal Probability Distributions

Who Can Sit in the Driver's Seat?

It's not practical to design all products to be convenient for everyone. Standard doorways have a height of 6'8"—too low for the 8'2" Don Koehler (listed in the Guinness Book of World Records) or many professional basketball players. Builders make doorways to fit most people, but not everyone. Similarly, car designers create seating areas for most people, but not for everyone.

An engineer designs a driver's seat to comfortably fit women taller than 159.0 cm (or 62.6 in.). What is the percentage of women who are shorter than 159.0 cm? This percentage of women will be excluded as buyers of this car. We can restate the problem as this: Find the probability *of randomly selecting a woman and getting someone shorter than 159.0 cm.* In Chapter 3 we solved many prob-

ability problems by using the total number of possible outcomes (n) and the number of ways (s) the event in question can occur. There are n = 104,261,000 women of driving age, but it isn't practical to actually measure and count them, so the classical definition of probability [P(A) = s/n] cannot be used. We could use the relative frequency approach by selecting a large sample of women to determine the proportion under 159.0 cm in height, but this chapter will introduce a more practical approach. We will use a theoretical model of women's heights. This approach requires knowledge of the mean, standard deviation, and shape of the distribution, but we can use results from the National Health Survey, indicating that adult women have heights with a mean of 161.5 cm, a standard deviation of 6.3 cm, and a bell-shaped distribution. This is one of many applications considered in this chapter.

FIGURE 5.1
The Normal Distribution

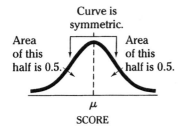

Curve is symmetric.

Area of this half is 0.5.　　Area of this half is 0.5.

μ

SCORE

5.1　OVERVIEW

Chapter 4 introduced the concept of a probability distribution and considered only *discrete* types, such as those involving a finite number of possible values. The number of defects in a roll of sheet metal and the number of customers per hour at McDonald's are examples of discrete distributions. There are also many different *continuous* probability distributions. While distributions can be described as being discrete or continuous, they can also be described by their *shape* (such as a bell shape). This chapter focuses on the normal distribution, which is extremely important because so many real applications involve data with this particular distribution. For example, a process intended to fill 8-oz containers with cologne won't put precisely 8 oz in every container; the actual amounts will probably have a normal distribution.

> **Definition**
>
> A continuous random variable has a *normal distribution* if that distribution is symmetric and bell-shaped, as in Fig. 5.1, and it can be described by Formula 5.1.

Formula 5.1
$$y = \frac{e^{-(x - \mu)^2/2\sigma^2}}{\sigma\sqrt{2\pi}}$$

Fortunately, *it is not necessary for us to use Formula 5.1,* but we might note that it is an equation relating a horizontal scale of x values to a vertical scale of y values. The symbol μ represents the mean score of an entire population, σ is the standard deviation of the population, π is approximately 3.142, and e is approximately 2.718. Formula 5.1 shows that any particular normal distribution is determined by the parameters μ and σ.

Before formally considering the normal probability distribution, let's briefly examine a simpler continuous distribution called the uniform distribution, as illustrated in Fig. 5.2. A **uniform distribution** has equally likely values over the range of possible outcomes, so its graph (called a **density curve** for continuous random variables) is always a rectangle with an enclosed area equal to 1. This property makes it very easy for us to solve probability problems. Suppose the output voltage of an electrical motor is between 5.0 volts and 9.0 volts, with all values equally likely. The uniform distribution of Fig. 5.2 describes this voltage. For example, the probability of randomly selecting a measurement of this voltage and finding a value between 7.00 V and 8.50 V is 0.375, which is the area (height × width) of the shaded region in Fig. 5.2.

Here's an important point: **For a density curve depicting the distribution of a continuous random variable, there is a correspondence between area and probability.** In Fig. 5.2, we can find the probability of a value between 7.00 V and 8.50 V by finding the area of the corresponding shaded rectangular region with dimensions 0.25 by 1.50. Normal distributions involve a more complicated curve, so it's more difficult to find areas. But the basic principle is the same: There is a correspondence between area and probability. We will describe and illustrate this important basic principle as we proceed to consider normal distributions.

FIGURE 5.2
Uniform Distribution. Area of Complete Rectangle = 0.25 × 4.00 = 1

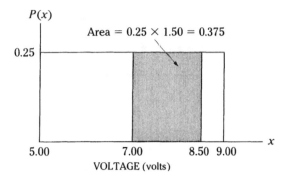

In reality, we don't usually get scores that conform to the precise relationship expressed in Formula 5.1. In a theoretically ideal normal distribution, the tails extend infinitely far in both directions as they get closer to the horizontal axis. But this property is usually inconsistent with the limitations of reality. For example, we can consider the fill levels of a 12-oz soft drink to have a distribution that is approximately normal, even though we can never have "negative ounces" of the soft drink in a can, as a true normal distribution would require.

This chapter presents the standard methods used to work with normally distributed scores, and it includes applications. In addition to the importance of the normal distribution itself, the methods are important in establishing basic patterns and concepts that will apply to other continuous probability distributions.

5.2   THE STANDARD NORMAL DISTRIBUTION

There are actually many different normal probability distributions, each dependent on only two parameters: the population mean μ and the population standard deviation σ. Figure 5.3 on the next page shows three different normal distributions of lives (in months) of car batteries, with the differences due to changes in the mean and standard deviation. A change in the value of μ causes the curve to be shifted to the right or left. A change in the value of σ causes a change in the spread or variation of the curve; the basic bell shape remains, but the curve becomes broader or narrower, depending on σ. Among the infinite possibilities, one particular normal distribution is of special interest.

DEFINITION

The *standard normal* distribution is a normal probability distribution that has a mean of 0 and a standard deviation of 1. (See Fig. 5.4.)

FIGURE 5.3
Normal Distributions of Lives of Car Batteries

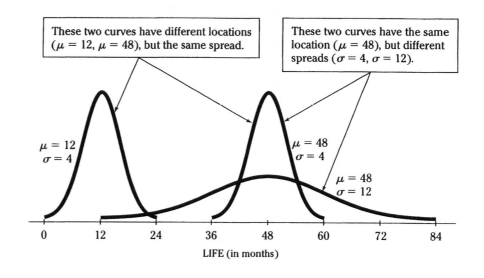

If we had to perform calculations with Formula 5.1 and we could choose any values for μ and σ, we would soon recognize that $\mu = 0$ and $\sigma = 1$ lead to the simplest form of that equation; this form is called the *standard normal* form. By letting $\mu = 0$ and $\sigma = 1$ in Formula 5.1, mathematicians were able to perform various calculations of areas. For example, the area under the curve bounded by the mean of 0 and the score of 1 is 0.3413, as shown in Fig. 5.4. The total area under the curve is 1, and this allows us to make a correspondence between area and probability, as we did in Section 5.1 when we discussed the uniform distribution of voltage levels depicted in Fig. 5.2.

FIGURE 5.4
The Standard Normal Distribution

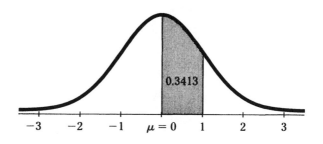

FIGURE 5.5
The Standard Normal Distribution. The area of the shaded region bounded by the mean of zero and the positive number z can be found in Table A.2.

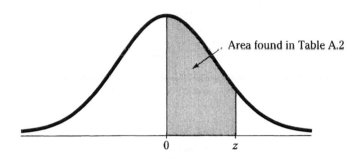

Area found in Table A.2

0   z

Although Fig. 5.4 shows only one area of 0.3413, Table A.2 (in Appendix A) includes areas (or probabilities) for many different regions. The table gives the probability corresponding to the area under the curve bounded on the left by a vertical line above the mean of 0 and bounded on the right by a vertical line above any specific positive score denoted by z (see Fig. 5.5). Note that when you use Table A.2, the hundredths part of the z score is found across the top row. To find the probability associated with a score between 0 and 1.23, for example, begin with the z score of 1.23 by locating 1.2 in the left column. Then find the value in the adjoining row of probabilities that is directly below 0.03. Thus there is a probability of 0.3907 of randomly selecting a score between 0 and 1.23. Also, there is a 0.4997 probability of randomly selecting a score between 0 and 4.0. It is essential to know that the numbers in the body of Table A.2 are probabilities or areas, whereas the z scores in the left column and across the top row are *distances*. It is also essential to remember that this table is designed only for the standard normal distribution, which has a mean of 0 and a standard deviation of 1. We will consider nonstandard cases in the next section.

Table A.2 lists probabilities corresponding to scores between 0 and 6.0. The scores between 0 and 3.09 are in steps of 0.01; the scores between 3.1 and 4.0 are in steps of 0.1; and the scores between 4.0 and 6.0 are in steps of 0.5. More complete and accurate tables are available, but Table A.2 will suffice for most purposes. For example, if you wanted to find the probability corresponding to a standard normal distribution score between 0 and 5.1, you could refer to Table A.2 and take the closest value of 5.0 to get 0.4999997133; this result would be very close to the correct answer.

The solutions to the following examples in this chapter are contingent on the values listed in Table A.2. But these values did not appear spontaneously. Mathematicians derived them through calculations that relate directly to Formula 5.1. Table A.2 serves as a convenient means of circumventing difficult computations with that equation.

Because theories concerning normal distributions originally resulted from studies of experimental errors, the examples in this section dealing with errors in measurements are particularly relevant.

EXAMPLE A manufacturer of scientific instruments produces thermometers that are supposed to give readings of 0° C at the freezing point of water. Tests on a large sample of these instruments reveal that some readings are too low (denoted by negative numbers) and some readings are too high (denoted by positive numbers). Assume that the mean reading is 0° C while the standard deviation of the readings is 1.00° C. Also assume that the frequency distribution of errors closely resembles the normal distribution. If one thermometer is randomly selected, find the probability that, at the freezing point of water, the reading is between 0° and + 1.58°.

SOLUTION We are dealing with a standard normal distribution and we are looking for the area of the shaded region in Fig. 5.5 with $z = 1.58$. We find from Table A.2 that the shaded area is 0.4429. The probability of randomly selecting a thermometer with an error between 0° and +1.58° is therefore 0.4429.

EXAMPLE With the thermometers from the preceding example, find the probability of randomly selecting one thermometer that reads (at the freezing point of water) between 0° and −2.43°.

SOLUTION We are looking for the region shaded in Fig. 5.6(a), but Table A.2 is designed to apply only to regions to the right of the mean (zero) as in Fig. 5.6(b). However, by observing that the normal probability distribution possesses symmetry about zero, we see that the shaded regions in parts (a) and (b) of Fig. 5.6 have the same area. Referring to Table A.2, we can easily determine that the shaded area of Fig. 5.6(b) is 0.4925, so the shaded area of Fig. 5.6(a) must also be 0.4925. That is, the probability of randomly selecting a thermometer with an error between 0° and −2.43° is 0.4925.

The preceding solution illustrates the important principle that whereas a z score can be negative, the area under the curve and the corresponding probability can never be negative.

Section 2.6 presented the empirical rule, which states that for bell-shaped distributions

- About 68% of all scores fall within *one* standard deviation of the mean.
- About 95% of all scores fall within *two* standard deviations of the mean.
- About 99.8% of all scores fall within *three* standard deviations of the mean.

If we refer to Fig. 5.5 and let $z = 1$, Table A.2 shows us that the shaded area is 0.3413; therefore the proportion of scores between $z = -1$ and $z = 1$ will be 0.3413 + 0.3413 = 0.6826 (because the size of the area from $z = -1$ to 0 is the same as the area from $z = 0$ to 1). That is, about 68% of all scores fall within one standard deviation of the mean. A similar calculation with $z = 2$ yields the values of 0.4772 + 0.4772 = 0.9544 (or about 95%) as the proportion of scores between $z = -2$ and $z = +2$. Similarly, the proportion of scores between $z = -3$ and $z = +3$ is 0.4987 + 0.4987 = 0.9974 (or about 99.8%). These exact values correspond

FIGURE 5.6
Positive and Negative *Z* Scores

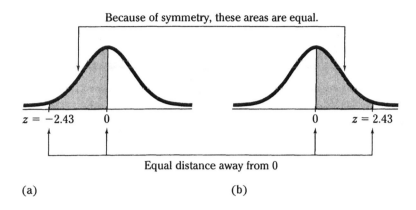

Because of symmetry, these areas are equal.

$z = -2.43$ 0   0 $z = 2.43$

Equal distance away from 0

(a)   (b)

very closely to those given in the empirical rule. In fact, the values of the empirical rule were found directly from Table A.2 and have been slightly rounded for convenience.

We incorporate an obvious but useful observation in the following example, but first go back for a minute to Fig. 5.5. A vertical line directly above the mean of 0 divides the area under the curve into two equal parts, each containing an area of 0.5. Because we are dealing with a probability distribution, the total area under the curve must be 1.

EXAMPLE   With these same thermometers, we again make a random selection. Find the probability that the chosen thermometer reads (at the freezing point of water) above +1.27°.

SOLUTION   We are again dealing with normally distributed values having a mean of 0° and a standard deviation of 1°. The probability of selecting a thermometer that reads above +1.27° corresponds to the shaded area of Fig. 5.7 on the next page. We cannot use Table A.2 to find that area directly, but we can use it to find that $z = 1.27$ corresponds to the area of 0.3980, as shown in Fig. 5.7. We can now reason that because the total area to the right of zero is 0.5, the shaded area is 0.5 − 0.3980, or 0.1020. We conclude that there is a 0.1020 probability of randomly selecting one of the thermometers with a reading above +1.27°. Another way to interpret the result is to state that if many thermometers are selected and tested, then 0.1020 (or 10.20%) of them will read above +1.27°.

We are able to determine the area of the shaded region in Fig. 5.7 by an *indirect* application of Table A.2. The following example illustrates yet another indirect use.

FIGURE 5.7
The Standard Normal Distribution

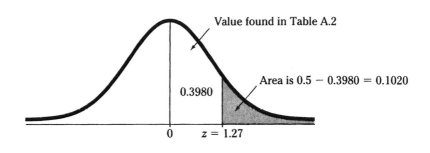

EXAMPLE   Back to the same thermometers: Assuming that one thermometer is randomly selected, find the probability that it reads (at the freezing point of water) between 1.20° and 2.30°.

SOLUTION   The probability of selecting a thermometer that reads between +1.20° and +2.30° corresponds to the shaded area of Fig. 5.8. However, Table A.2 is designed to provide only for regions bounded on the left by the vertical line above zero. We can use the table to find that $z = 1.20$ corresponds to an area of 0.3849, and $z = 2.30$ corresponds to an area of 0.4893, as shown in the figure. If we denote the area of the shaded region by A, we can see from the figure that

$$0.3849 + A = 0.4893$$

so that

$$A = 0.4893 - 0.3849$$
$$= 0.1044$$

The probability we seek is therefore 0.1044.

Notation

$P(a < z < b)$ denotes the probability that the z score is between a and b.

$P(z > a)$ denotes the probability that the z score is greater than a.

$P(z < a)$ denotes the probability that the z score is less than a.

Using this notation, the result of the last example is $P(1.20 < z < 2.30) = 0.1044$, which expresses in symbols that the probability of a z score falling between 1.20 and 2.30 is 0.1044. With a continuous probability distribution, such as the normal distribution, $P(z = a) = 0$. With *infinitely* many different possible values, the chance of getting any *one* exact value is one chance in infinity.

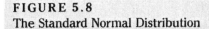

FIGURE 5.8
The Standard Normal Distribution

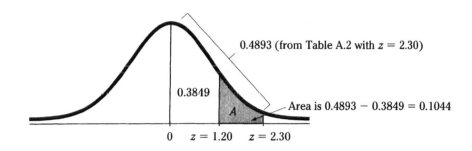

We express this as a probability of 0. For example, there is a 0 probability that $z = 1.33$ *exactly*. From this we can conclude that $P(a \leq z \leq b) = P(a < z < b)$.

The examples of this section were contrived so the mean of 0 and the standard deviation of 1 coincided exactly with the values of the standard normal distribution described in Table A.2. In reality, it would be unusual to find such a nice relationship, because typical normal distributions involve means different from 0 and standard deviations different from 1.

These nonstandard normal distributions introduce another problem. What table of probabilities can be used, since Table A.2 is designed for a mean of 0 and a standard deviation of 1? For example, IQ scores are normally distributed with a mean of 100 and a standard deviation of 15. Scores in this range are far beyond the scope of Table A.2. Section 5.3 examines these nonstandard normal distributions and the methods used in dealing with them. We will see that Table A.2 can be used with nonstandard normal distributions after performing some very simple calculations. Learning how to use Table A.2 in this section prepares us for the more practical and realistic circumstances that will be found in later sections.

5.2 EXERCISES   BASIC CONCEPTS

In Exercises 1–36, assume that the readings on the thermometers are normally distributed with a mean of 0° and a standard deviation of 1.00°. A thermometer is randomly selected and tested. In each case, draw a sketch and find the probability of each reading in degrees.

1. Between 0 and 0.25
2. Between 0 and 1.00
3. Between 0 and 1.50
4. Between 0 and 1.96
5. Between −1.00 and 0
6. Between −0.75 and 0
7. Between 0 and −1.75
8. Between 0 and −2.33

9. Greater than 1.00
10. Greater than 0.37
11. Greater than 1.83
12. Greater than 2.05
13. Less than -1.00
14. Less than -2.17
15. Less than -0.91
16. Less than -1.37
17. Greater than -1.00
18. Greater than -0.09
19. Less than 3.05
20. Less than 0.42
21. Between -1.00 and 2.00
22. Between -0.25 and 0.75
23. Between -2.00 and 1.50
24. Between -1.96 and 1.96
25. Between 1.00 and 2.00
26. Between 1.96 and 2.33
27. Between 1.28 and 2.58
28. Between 0.27 and 2.27
29. Between -0.83 and -0.51
30. Between -2.00 and -1.50
31. Between -0.25 and -1.35
32. Between -1.07 and -2.11
33. Greater than 0
34. Less than 0
35. Less than -0.50 or greater than 1.50
36. Less than -1.96 or greater than 1.96

In Exercises 37–44, assume that the readings on the thermometers are normally distributed with a mean of 0° and a standard deviation of 1.00°. Find the indicated probability where z is the reading in degrees.

37. $P(z>2.58)$
38. $P(-1.36<z<1.36)$
39. $P(z<1.28)$
40. $P(1.25<z<1.68)$
41. $P(z<-0.57)$
42. $P(0<z<1.68)$
43. $P(-2.80<z<-1.36)$
44. $P(z>-0.50)$

In Exercises 45–48, assume that a large sample of thermometers is randomly selected from a population with a normal distribution having a mean of 0° and a standard deviation of 1.00°. Find the proportion of thermometers with readings corresponding to the given z scores.

45. $-1.09<z<0$
46. $-2.73<z<2.51$
47. $z<2.45$
48. $-0.81<z<0.63$

EXERCISES BEYOND THE BASICS

49. Assume that $\mu = 0$ and $\sigma = 1$ for a normally distributed population.
    Find the percentage of data that are
    a. Within 1 standard deviation of the mean.
    b. Within 1.96 standard deviations of the mean.
    c. Between $\mu - 3\sigma$ and $\mu + 3\sigma$.
    d. Between 1 standard deviation below the mean and 2 standard deviations
       above the mean.
    e. More than 2 standard deviations away from the mean.
    f. More than 5 standard deviations away from the mean.
50. Assume that we have the same normally distributed thermometer readings
    with a mean of 0° and a standard deviation of 1.00°. If 5% of the thermome-
    ters are rejected because they read too high and another 5% are rejected
    because they read too low, what is the maximum error that will not lead to
    rejection?
51. Assume that z scores are normally distributed with a mean of 0 and a
    standard deviation of 1.
    a. If $P(0 < z < a) = 0.4778$, find a.
    b. If $P(-b < z < b) = 0.7814$, find b.
    c. If $P(z > c) = 0.0329$, find c.
    d. If $P(z > d) = 0.8508$, find d.
    e. If $P(z < e) = 0.0062$, find e.

5.3 NONSTANDARD NORMAL DISTRIBUTIONS

Section 5.2 considered only the standard normal distribution. This section extends
the same basic concepts to include nonstandard normal distributions. This inclusion will greatly expand the variety of practical applications we can make because,
in reality, most normally distributed populations will have either a nonzero mean
and/or a standard deviation different from 1.

We continue to use Table A.2, but we need a way to standardize these
nonstandard cases. We do this by converting from the nonstandard case to the
standard normal distribution by using Formula 5.2, in which z is the number of
standard deviations that a particular score x is away from the mean. We call z the
z score or **standard score,** and it is used in Table A.2 (see Fig. 5.9 on the next
page). (This same definition was presented earlier in Section 2.7.)

Formula 5.2
$$z = \frac{x - \mu}{\sigma}$$

Suppose, for example, that we are considering a normally distributed collection of
car tune-up times known to have a mean of 100 min and a standard deviation of
15 min. If we seek the probability of randomly selecting one tune-up time that is

FIGURE 5.9
Converting from a Nonstandard Normal Distribution
to a Standard Normal Distribution

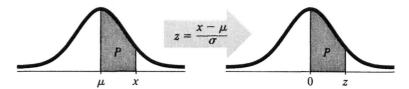

(a) Nonstandard Normal Distribution.   (b) Standard Normal Distribution.

between 100 min and 130 min, we are concerned with the area shown in Fig.
5.10. The difference between 130 min and the mean of 100 min is 30 min, or
exactly two standard deviations. The shaded area in Fig. 5.10 will therefore
correspond to the shaded area of Fig. 5.5, where $z = 2$. We get $z = 2$ either by
reasoning that 130 is two standard deviations above the mean of 100 or by
computing

$$z = \frac{x - \mu}{\sigma} = \frac{130 - 100}{15} = \frac{30}{15} = 2$$

FIGURE 5.10
Tune-up Times
(in minutes)

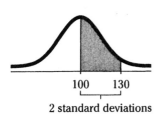

100   130

2 standard deviations

With $z = 2$, Table A.2 indicates that the shaded region we seek has an area of
0.4772, so the probability of randomly selecting a tune-up time between 100 and
130 is 0.4772. Thus we can apply Table A.2 indirectly to any normal probability
distribution if we use Formula 5.2 as the algebraic way of recognizing that the z
score is actually the number of standard deviations that x is away from the mean.
The following examples illustrate the use of Formula 5.2 as a tool that allows us to
find probabilities from Table A.2, even though we have nonstandard normal distributions.

EXAMPLE If car tune-up times are normally distributed with a mean of 100 min
and a standard deviation of 15 min, find the probability of a randomly
selected car having a tune-up time between 100 min and 133 min.

FIGURE 5.11
Tune-up Times
(in minutes)

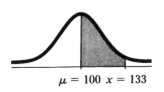

$\mu = 100$ $x = 133$

SOLUTION Referring to Fig. 5.11, we seek the probability associated with the
shaded region. To use Table A.2, we must convert the nonstandard
data to the standard normal distribution by applying Formula 5.2.

$$z = \frac{x - \mu}{\sigma} = \frac{133 - 100}{15} = \frac{33}{15} = 2.20$$

The score of 133 min therefore differs from the mean of 100 min by
2.20 standard deviations. Corresponding to a z score of 2.20, Table
A.2 indicates a probability of 0.4861. There is therefore a probability
of 0.4861 of randomly selecting a car with a tune-up time between
100 and 133.

In the preceding example, we could also express the result as $P(100 < x < 133) = 0.4861$ by using the same notation introduced in Section 5.2. Note that in this nonstandard normal distribution, we represent the score in its original units by x, not z. Note also that $P(100 < x < 133) = P(0 < z < 2.20) = 0.4861$.

When Table A.2 is used in conjunction with Formula 5.2, the nonstandard population mean corresponds to the standard mean of 0. As a result, probabilities taken directly from Table A.2 must represent regions whose left boundary is the line at the mean.

EXAMPLE   At the beginning of this chapter we described a car designer's need to find the percentage of women who would not fit comfortably in a driver's seat. For the car design being considered, women are uncomfortable in the driver's seat if they are shorter than 159.0 cm (or 62.6 in.). Based on data from the National Health Survey, we know that women's heights are normally distributed with a mean of 161.5 cm and a standard deviation of 6.3 cm. Find the percentage of women shorter than 159.0 cm.

SOLUTION   In Fig. 5.12, the shaded region corresponds to the women who are too short for this car's design. We can't find the area of the shaded region directly, but we can use Formula 5.2 to find the area of the adjacent region A.

$$z = \frac{x - \mu}{\sigma} = \frac{159.0 - 161.5}{6.3} = -0.40$$

We now use Table A.2 to find that $z = -0.40$ corresponds to an area of 0.1554. Because $A = 0.1554$, the shaded area must be $0.5 - 0.1554 = 0.3446$. Because the shaded area is 0.3446, the probability of randomly selecting a woman less than 159.0 cm tall is also 0.3446, so the percentage of women less than 159.0 cm tall is 34.46%. Because this percentage is so high, the designers will reconsider their plans, which would have resulted in cars that would be uncomfortable for such a large market share.

FIGURE 5.12
Normal Distribution of Heights (in cm) of Women

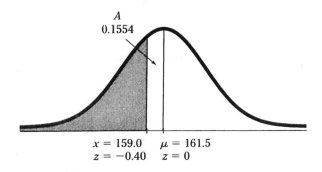

FIGURE 5.13
Contents (in oz) of Cola Cans

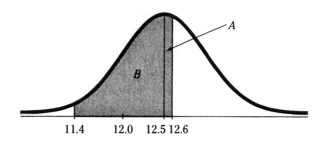

| 11.4 | 12.0 | 12.5 12.6 |

EXAMPLE   The filling of 12-oz cola cans by a company is a process. Assume that a run chart has already shown that the process is statistically stable with a mean of 12.5 oz, a standard deviation of 0.4 oz, and a distribution that is normal. Find the percentage of cans that will have between 11.4 oz and 12.6 oz of cola.

SOLUTION   Figure 5.13 shows the shaded region A corresponding to the area between 12.5 oz and 12.6 oz; region B corresponds to the area between 11.4 oz and 12.5 oz.

For area A only: $z = \dfrac{x - \mu}{\sigma} = \dfrac{12.6 - 12.5}{0.4} = 0.25$

Table A.2 shows that $z = 0.25$ corresponds to 0.0987, so area A is 0.0987.

For area B only: $z = \dfrac{x - \mu}{\sigma} = \dfrac{11.4 - 12.5}{0.4} = -2.75$

Table A.2 shows that $z = -2.75$ corresponds to 0.4970, so area B is 0.4970.

Area of A and B combined = 0.0987 + 0.4970 = 0.5957

We conclude that the percentage of cans with amounts between 11.4 oz and 12.6 oz is 59.57%.

Suppose federal regulations require manufacturers to fill at least 99% of their "12-oz" cans with levels between 11.4 oz and 12.6 oz. With the preceding production scheme, we would not be close to meeting the federal requirement. Also, with a mean of 12.5 oz, we would be wasting much of the cola, because we would be overfilling by an average of 0.5 oz; we would be wasting an average of 1 can in 24! As a manager, what could you do to improve this situation? Examine Fig. 5.13 and note that the center is at 12.5 oz instead of the desired 12.0 oz. Assume that a consultation with your engineers reveals that you can adjust the filling process so that it remains statistically stable with a normal distribution

FIGURE 5.14
Contents (in oz) of Cola Cans

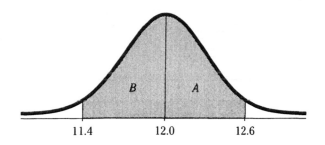

11.4   12.0   12.6

having a mean of 12.0 oz and a standard deviation of 0.4 oz. Let's find the percentage of cans that will now fall between 11.4 oz and 12.6 oz so that they meet the federal requirement. (See Fig. 5.14.)

For area *A* (between 12.0 oz and 12.6 oz) only:

$$z = \frac{x - \mu}{\sigma} = \frac{12.6 - 12.0}{0.4} = 1.50$$

In Table A.2, $z = 1.50$ corresponds to a probability of 0.4332.

For area *B* (between 11.4 oz and 12.0 oz) only:

$$z = \frac{x - \mu}{\sigma} = \frac{11.4 - 12.0}{0.4} = -1.50$$

In Table A.2, $z = -1.50$ corresponds to a probability of 0.4332.

$$\text{Area of } A \text{ and } B \text{ combined} = 0.4332 + 0.4332 = 0.8664$$

We now have about 86.6% of the cans falling between 11.4 oz and 12.6 oz. "Centering the process" exactly between the desired limits of 11.4 and 12.6 has greatly improved the production process, and we no longer have an average that constitutes an overfill. However, we do not yet meet the regulations because we do not yet have at least 99% between 11.4 oz and 12.6 oz. What do we do now? We can increase the quality of the process by reducing the variation. If we can lower the standard deviation, we will increase the percentage of cans containing between 11.4 oz and 12.6 oz. (See Exercise 20.) Try to picture this: In Fig. 5.14, a lowered standard deviation will cause the normal distribution curve to become narrower, so more of the area (or probability) will lie between 11.4 oz and 12.6 oz.

In this section we extended the concept of Section 5.2 to include more-realistic nonstandard normal probability distributions. But the use of the formula $z = (x - \mu)/\sigma$ and Table A.2 is appropriate only if the distribution of the population or stable process is approximately normal. In the following section, we will see how to determine whether a population or process is normally distributed.

5.3 **EXERCISES**   BASIC CONCEPTS

In Exercises 1–8, assume that IQ scores are normally distributed with a mean of 100 and a standard deviation of 15. An IQ score is randomly selected from this population. Draw a graph and find the indicated probability.

1. $P(100 < x < 145)$
2. $P(x < 127)$
3. $P(x > 140)$
4. $P(88 < x < 112)$
5. $P(110 < x < 120)$
6. $P(120 < x < 130)$
7. $P(x < 100)$
8. $P(85 < x < 95)$

In Exercises 9–24, answer the given questions. In each case, draw a graph.

9. At the beginning of this chapter we described the design of a driver's seat so it would comfortably fit women taller than 159.0 cm (or 62.6 in.). This would result in 34.46% of women being uncomfortable. If the engineer redesigned the seat so it would comfortably fit women taller than 150.0 cm (or 59.1 in.), what percentage of women would not be uncomfortable in the driver's seat? (Recall that women have normally distributed heights with a mean of 161.5 cm and a standard deviation of 6.3 cm.)

10. According to Nielsen Media Research, people watch television an average of 6.98 hours per day. Assume that these times are normally distributed with a standard deviation of 3.80 hours. Find the probability that a randomly selected person watches television more than 8.00 hours in a day.

11. The County Auto Repair Company plans to increase business by mailing reminder notices for oil changes, and it needs to obtain information about how far cars are driven each year. According to the Federal Highway Administration, males aged 16–24 drive an average of 10,718 mi each year. Assume that the annual mileage totals are normally distributed with a standard deviation of 3573 mi. For a randomly selected male between the ages of 16 and 24, find the probability that he drives less than 12,000 mi in a year.

12. A study of VCR owners found that their annual household incomes are normally distributed with a mean of $41,182 and a standard deviation of $19,990 (based on data from Nielsen Media Research). For households with VCRs, what is the percentage having incomes between $30,000 and $50,000?

13. A banker studying customer needs finds that the numbers of times people use automated-teller machines in a year are normally distributed with a mean of 30.0 and a standard deviation of 11.4 (based on data from Maritz Marketing Research, Inc.). (a) Find the percentage of customers who use them between 40 and 50 times. (b) Among 5000 customers, how many are expected to use them between 40 and 50 times a year?

14. By testing the lifetimes of automobile batteries you manufacture, you have found the distribution is normal with a mean of 40 months and a standard deviation of 6 months. Assume that the manufacturing process is stable.
    a. Find the probability of a battery lasting less than 36 months.
    b. If you manufacture 100,000 batteries and give free replacement for any that last less than 3 years, how many do you expect to replace?

15. A large survey of starting salaries shows that for accounting graduates accepting jobs in the Midwest, the mean is $22,500 and the standard deviation is $1400. Assuming that the distribution of these salaries is approximately normal, determine the probability of selecting one of them and finding that the starting salary is between $20,000 and $25,000.

16. A study shows that Michigan teachers have measures of job dissatisfaction that are normally distributed with a mean of 3.80 and a standard deviation of 0.95 (based on "Stress and Strain from Family Roles and Work-Role Expectations," by Cooke and Rousseau, *Journal of Applied Psychology*, Vol. 69, No. 2). If subjects with scores above 4.00 are to be given additional tests, what percentage will fall into that category?

17. Federal Express guarantees absolutely to deliver its Priority Overnight mail the next day by 10:30 A.M. Suppose management has found that the mean delivery time is 9:45 A.M. with a standard deviation of 14 min and the delivery times are normally distributed.
    a. What is the probability that a delivery will not meet the guaranteed time?
    b. In its quest for constant improvement, suppose management is able to move the mean delivery time to 9:30 while the standard deviation remains the same. What is the probability that a delivery will not meet the guaranteed time of 10:30 A.M.?
    c. If next year's goal is to reduce the standard deviation to 10 min while maintaining the mean of 9:30 achieved in part *b*, what would be the probability that a delivery will not meet the guaranteed time of 10:30 A.M.?
    d. Federal Express handles enormous volumes of daily Priority Overnight mail. If it delivers 1,000,000 pieces in one day, how many would not be delivered by the guaranteed time of 10:30 A.M. given the conditions of part *a*, then part *b*, then part *c?*

18. A shaft used in automatic transmissions must have a length between 3.470 cm and 3.530 cm to perform properly. Measuring 50 consecutive shafts shows that the process seems stable with a mean length of 3.514 cm, a standard deviation of 0.012 cm, and a distribution that is normal.
    a. What proportion of transmission shafts will be between 3.470 cm and 3.530 cm?
    b. If the engineers replace some worn parts and improve quality by decreasing the standard deviation to 0.009 cm, what proportion of transmission shafts will now fall between 3.470 cm and 3.530 cm?

19. A local bank has 4 teller windows. By monitoring the customer waiting times, the mean is found to be 3.8 min, the standard deviation is 1.5 min, and the distribution is normal. Past experience has shown that customers become irritated when the waiting time exceeds 5 min.
    a. What proportion of customers will be irritated by the present system?
    b. At a cost of $25,000 per year, another teller could be added to reduce the mean waiting time to 3.0 min. The standard deviation would remain the same. What proportion of customers would be irritated if you added the extra teller?
    c. You notice that the 4 tellers waste time using the same check-writing machine. You could provide duplicate machines (at a cost of $8000 each) with the result that the mean would decrease slightly to 3.7 min, but the standard deviation would decrease dramatically to 0.8 min. What proportion of customers would now be irritated?

20. In this section we discussed an example involving the filling of 12-oz cans of cola. By adjusting the mean, we were not able to satisfy the requirement that at least 99% of the cans have between 11.4 oz and 12.6 oz. In fact, no matter how you adjust the mean, you will never get more than 86.64% of the cans having between 11.4 oz and 12.6 oz. Some manufacturers weigh each can and reject those that do not have between 11.4 oz and 12.6 oz. Consumers would bear the costs of hiring inspectors, refilling underfilled cans, and removing cola from overfilled cans. Suppose you could decrease the standard deviation from 0.40 oz to 0.20 oz while keeping the mean at 12.00 oz. Find the proportion of cans that would meet the requirement of having between 11.4 oz and 12.6 oz. Verify that by lowering the standard deviation, we improved the process by reducing the number of cans that were underfilled or overfilled.

21. Scores on the numeric part of the Minnesota Clerical Test are normally distributed with a mean of 119.3 and a standard deviation of 32.4. This test is used to select clerical employees. (The data are based on "Modification of the Minnesota Clerical Test to Predict Performance on Video Display Terminals," by Silver and Bennett, *Journal of Applied Psychology,* Vol. 72, No. 1.) If a firm requires scores above 172, find the percentage of subjects who don't qualify.

22. In a study of employee stock ownership plans, satisfaction by employees is measured and found to be normally distributed with a mean of 4.89 and a standard deviation of 0.63 (based on "Employee Stock Ownership and Employee Attitudes: A Test of Three Models," by Klein, *Journal of Applied Psychology,* Vol. 72, No. 2). If a subject from this population is randomly selected, find the probability of a job satisfaction score less than 6.78.

23. The thickness of plastic film used to manufacture plastic bags must be between 240 microns and 300 microns to be sufficiently strong while not being so thick that it creates problems in the manufacturing machines. After measuring a roll of film at 100 different points, you determine that the manufacturing process is stable and the thicknesses are normally distributed with a mean of 275 microns and a standard deviation of 15 microns.
    a. What percentage of the roll will be outside your desired limits?
    b. If you could decrease the standard deviation to 9 microns without adjusting the mean, what percentage of a roll would now be outside your desired limits?

24. Airlines typically overbook flights because usually several passengers don't show up. Assume that one airline flies jets that seat 200 passengers, and with overbooking, the numbers of passengers that show up are normally distributed with a mean of 170 and a standard deviation of 12.
    a. What is the probability that there won't be enough seats on a flight?
    b. If a television advertising campaign raises the mean from 170 to 184 (with the same standard deviation), what is the probability that there won't be enough seats on a flight?

5.3 EXERCISES   BEYOND THE BASICS

25. The GMAT (Graduate Management Admissions Test) is given to business majors who wish to enter accredited M.B.A. programs in the United States. The scores (total of verbal and quantitative) have been scaled to provide

a mean of 500 with two-thirds of the scores falling between 400 and 600. The distribution is normal.

a. Using the fact that the mean is 500, and two-thirds of the scores are between 400 and 600, and the distribution of scores is normal, find the standard deviation of the GMAT scores.

b. Use the results from part a to find the percentage of scores that are between 350 and 650.

c. If the Harvard Business School will consider only students with scores of at least 675, what percentage of students will be eligible for consideration?

26. In the past, the Locust Tree Restaurant chain has found that customers have been dissatisfied because of slow service. In an attempt to remedy that problem, servers are trained to fill drink orders very quickly. It is believed that once customers have drinks, they won't be too concerned about the time required to serve the meal. The restaurant chain then advertises that "over 99% of its customers are served drinks between 30 sec and 90 sec after they are ordered." A study has revealed that the drink service times are normally distributed.

a. If the claim is true, what are reasonable estimates of the mean and standard deviation for the service times?

b. If the claim is true, what is the approximate probability that a randomly selected person would have a service time that exceeds 2 min (or 120 sec)?

c. Suppose you order a drink and it takes 2 min to be served. Do you believe the claim? Explain.

27. Callers to the IRS "hotline" are frequently put on hold. Suppose the times (in minutes) on hold for 20 callers are as follows:

| 3.5 | 2.4 | 1.5 | 4.2 | 3.1 | 3.4 | 2.0 | 1.3 | 1.0 | 1.6 |
| 2.7 | 3.5 | 6.1 | 3.8 | 3.2 | 4.4 | 2.9 | 5.4 | 4.6 | 4.9 |

a. Find the mean $\bar{x}$ and standard deviation s of this sample.

b. Find the actual percentage of those 20 times that are over 5.0 min.

c. Find the percentage of the population of all callers that are on hold for more than 5.0 min. What assumptions did you make to find this percentage?

28. Two machines fill 12-oz cereal boxes with bran. Ten randomly selected boxes from each machine yield the following weights (in ounces).

| Machine 1: | 12.5 | 12.2 | 11.8 | 11.5 | 11.2 | 12.6 | 12.2 | 12.0 | 11.9 | 12.1 |
| Machine 2: | 12.1 | 12.2 | 11.8 | 12.0 | 11.8 | 12.1 | 12.0 | 12.0 | 11.9 | 12.1 |

Assume that the distribution of fill weights is normal for both machines and that both processes are stable.

a. Find the mean $\bar{x}$ and standard deviation s for machine 1.

b. Estimate the proportion of boxes from machine 1 that will be below 11.5 oz.

c. Find $\bar{x}$ and s for machine 2.

d. Estimate the proportion of boxes from machine 2 that will be below 11.5 oz.

e. If you have 120,000 oz of bran in the bin, how many boxes would you expect to fill by using machine 1 only? machine 2 only?

f. Your floor manager claims there is no difference between the machines and that both are yielding boxes with 12 oz of bran. Is that claim true? What is the manager addressing?

5.4 DETERMINING NORMALITY OF POPULATION AND PROCESS DISTRIBUTIONS

Almost all the examples and exercises in Sections 5.2 and 5.3 involve a normal distribution and the use of Table A.2. If the distribution of the data from a population or a process is not approximately bell-shaped, using Table A.2 results in incorrect results and conclusions. The following example illustrates this. In Section 5.1 the output voltage of an electrical motor has a uniform distribution between 5.00 V and 9.00 V. Following are 40 measurements taken every 5 minutes in a single operating day for such a motor.

8.3	7.1	6.2	5.9	6.9	5.1	8.7	6.7	8.1	6.3
5.3	6.1	7.3	8.4	5.1	8.6	7.7	5.6	7.2	8.6
5.3	6.6	7.4	8.3	5.2	7.9	5.8	6.8	8.9	8.4
5.9	6.3	8.7	7.6	7.9	6.4	5.4	5.9	7.4	8.7

Calculation of the sample mean $\bar{x}$ and sample standard deviation s results in $\bar{x}$ = 7.000 V and s = 1.217 V. If you assumed that the distribution of the voltages is normal (which it's not) and proceeded to find the probability of a randomly selected voltage greater than 9 V, you would use $\bar{x}$ and s as estimates of μ and σ to get $z = (9.00 - 7.00)/1.217 = 1.64$. You would then use Table A.2 to find that $z = 1.64$ corresponds to an area of 0.4495, so the answer would be $0.5 - 0.4495 = 0.0505$, which is *wrong*. The voltage as shown in Fig. 5.2 can never be greater than 9.00 V, so the correct answer is 0. Very large errors are possible if you treat a population or process distribution as normal when it is not. It is therefore important that for each data set you first develop the habit of determining whether the distribution is approximately normal.

FIGURE 5.15
Histograms of Heights of Women

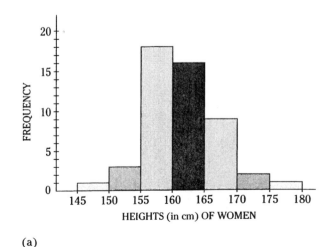

(a)

```
MTB > HISTOGRAM C1

Histogram of C1    N = 50

Midpoint        Count
     148          1    *
     152          3    ***
     156          8    ********
     160         17    *****************
     164         12    ************
     168          6    ******
     172          2    **
     176          1    *
```

(b)

POPULATION DATA

First let us consider how to determine whether the distribution of data from a *population* is approximately normal. One useful procedure is to randomly select at least 40 observations from the population and construct a histogram to see whether the shape is approximately symmetric and bell-shaped. At the beginning of the chapter we cited data from the National Health Survey: Adult women have heights with a mean of 161.5 cm, a standard deviation of 6.3 cm, and an approximately normal distribution. If this information were not available, we could measure the heights of 50 randomly selected adult women to get approximately the same information. Following is a Minitab computer-generated set of data that simulates such a random sample.

```
MTB > RANDOM k=50 C1;
SUBC> NORMAL mu=161.5 sigma=6.3.
MTB > PRINT C1
```

```
C1
    166.254    159.740    158.136    162.172    151.961    167.119    156.557
    164.590    155.336    166.685    152.368    158.460    161.188    169.405
    175.920    155.944    161.961    148.801    172.663    155.900    158.133
    159.428    166.624    165.231    158.922    160.340    157.862    163.551
    164.301    162.700    171.432    165.931    164.092    169.913    158.838
    155.507    165.631    162.528    157.117    161.066    158.821    160.574
    159.355    160.190    155.359    164.960    162.409    161.015    151.694
    158.154
```

You can calculate the sample mean and sample standard deviation to get $\bar{x} = 161.26$ cm and $s = 5.55$ cm. You could also get these results by entering the Minitab command DESCRIBE C1.

```
MTB > DESCRIBE C1
```

	N	MEAN	MEDIAN	TRMEAN	STDEV	SEMEAN
C1	50	161.26	160.79	161.14	5.55	0.78

	MIN	MAX	Q1	Q3
C1	148.80	175.92	158.07	165.03

Note that the value of $\bar{x} = 161.26$ cm is very close to the population value of $\mu = 161.5$, and $s = 5.55$ is fairly close to $\sigma = 6.3$. (We will see in Chapter 7 that σ is usually more difficult to estimate than μ and requires larger samples.)

In Fig. 5.15(a) we show a histogram of the above data; Fig. 5.15(b) shows the same data plotted in a histogram by Minitab. We can see from the figure that the shape is approximately that of a normal distribution. Advanced courses in statistics consider more-precise procedures for determining whether a data set has an approximately normal distribution, but for our purposes we can use this simple criterion: If the histogram of the sample data is approximately symmetric and has

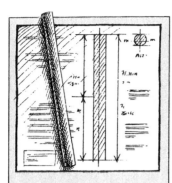

PUTTING NORMALITY TO WORK

The *Deming Dimension*, by Henry R. Neave, discussed a company manufacturing steel rods with very precise specifications. Although the rods were all within those "specs," they had low quality because many were close to the upper or lower limit. Because rods too short were useless, there was a policy of setting the machines to produce rods that were too long. The rods were measured and those longer than the upper specification limit were ground down. This resulted in many rods near the upper limit and many near the lower limit. By adjusting the machines to produce rods with a mean length midway between the upper and lower specification limits, the machinery could make the lengths with sufficiently small variation, so no reworking of the rods was necessary. The resulting rods had better quality, saving both time and money.

a single mound (or mode), then we conclude that the distribution of the sample data is approximately normal and the parent population is normally distributed as well. Using this criterion, our inspection of Fig. 5.15 leads us to conclude that the simulated sample data set is approximately normal, and we can be reasonably confident that the population from which the sample was drawn is also normally distributed. Having concluded that the population of women's heights is approximately normal, and having found the sample values of $\bar{x}$ and s, we could proceed to find the probability of randomly selecting a woman's height that is less than 159.0 cm. (Remember, we are assuming that the population parameters of μ and σ are not known.) We calculate

$$z = \frac{x - \mu}{\sigma} \approx \frac{159 - \bar{x}}{s} = \frac{159 - 161.26}{5.55} = -0.41$$

We now refer to Table A.2 (because we are satisfied that the distribution is approximately normal) to find that $z = -0.41$ corresponds to a probability of 0.1591. We now have

$$P(\text{height less than } 159.0) = 0.5 - 0.1591 = 0.3409$$

and this result, based on a sample of the population, is very close to the exact answer of 0.3446 found in Section 5.3, which we obtained when we used actual population parameters.

PROCESS DATA

The normality of the distribution of data from a process can be determined only after concluding that the process is statistically stable. If a process is statistically stable, then it can be analyzed and treated as a population. For our purposes, once we know that a process is statistically stable, we can proceed to construct a histogram of the data and inspect it to see whether it's symmetric with a single mode; that is, we can inspect the histogram to see whether it reflects a distribution of data that is approximately normal.

Remember, if a process is not stable, all other calculations and predictions are meaningless. If a process is found to be unstable, all efforts should be devoted to getting it to be under statistical control, that is, behaving in the random fashion predicted by statistical and probability rules. Achieving stability in the process might take days or weeks or longer, but to make judgments based on an unstable process is to invite disaster.

In earlier chapters we introduced methods for determining whether a process is statistically stable. In Chapter 2 we used a visual inspection of the run chart. In Chapter 3 we introduced the run of 8 rule that gives us a more quantitative and objective criterion for determining the stability of a process. (According to that rule, if 8 or more consecutive points all fall above the mean or they all fall below the mean, then we conclude that the process is not statistically stable.)

We will now present a quantitative way to judge whether a process with a known standard deviation σ is statistically stable. Using the run chart, construct a boundary at $\mu + 3\sigma$ and another one at $\mu - 3\sigma$. When we construct a run chart with boundaries of $\mu + 3\sigma$ and $\mu - 3\sigma$, the result is called a **control chart** for individual values when σ is known. The boundaries of $\mu + 3\sigma$ and $\mu - 3\sigma$ are called the upper and lower **control limits.** Other control charts for other circumstances, such as when σ is unknown, will be developed in Chapter 8. (If μ is unknown, construct the boundaries at $\bar{x} + 3\sigma$ and $\bar{x} - 3\sigma$.) According to the empirical rule from Section 2.6, about 99.8% of the data should fall between these two boundaries, assuming that the process is approximately normal and stable. According to Chebyshev's theorem, at least 88.9% of the data from the process should fall between these limits, assuming that the process is statistically stable no matter what distribution the process has. These observations suggest the following rule: *A process is stable if the points on the control chart lie between the boundaries of $\mu + 3\sigma$ and $\mu - 3\sigma$; otherwise, it is unstable.*

EXAMPLE

In Section 5.3 we described a process of using a machine to fill 12-oz cans of cola. With an improved process, the population parameters are $\mu = 12.0$ oz and $\sigma = 0.4$ oz. Use the sample data given below (listed in order by row) to construct a control chart with the control limits included, then determine whether the process is statistically stable. Following the sample values is a Minitab display of the sample statistics.

12.00	12.43	12.47	11.92	11.36	11.78	11.98
11.81	11.99	12.46	11.72	11.40	12.58	12.18
12.12	12.00	11.65	12.12	12.13	12.13	12.40
11.89	12.19	12.19	11.68	12.58	11.39	11.42
11.55	11.89	11.98	11.68	11.54	12.16	11.91
11.96	12.06	12.00	11.97	11.53		

```
MTB > DESCRIBE C8

              N      MEAN   MEDIAN   TRMEAN    STDEV   SEMEAN
C8           40    11.955   11.980   11.953    0.329    0.052


            MIN      MAX       Q1       Q3
C8       11.360   12.580   11.690   12.153
```

SOLUTION

We will proceed to apply our criterion for determining whether the above scores reflect stability. In Fig. 5.16(a) on the next page, we show the graph of the control chart for the generated data; that graph includes $\mu = 12.0$ at the center and the boundaries (or control limits) of $\mu + 3\sigma = 13.2$ and $\mu - 3\sigma = 10.8$. (In finding these boundary limits, we used $\mu = 12.0$ and $\sigma = 0.4$.)

In Fig. 5.16(a), we see that all 40 points lie between the boundaries of $\mu + 3\sigma$ and $\mu - 3\sigma$. Also, there are no consecutive "runs of 8" lying on the same side of the center line. Finally, there is no pattern of instability similar to those shown in Fig. 2.9. We therefore conclude that the process is statistically stable.

It is possible for a stable process occasionally to yield values that lie outside the boundaries of $\mu + 3\sigma$ and $\mu - 3\sigma$, but it isn't very likely. Suppose each student in a class of 30 uses Minitab to simulate the generation of the 40 cans of cola. If

FIGURE 5.16
Run Chart of Sample Data

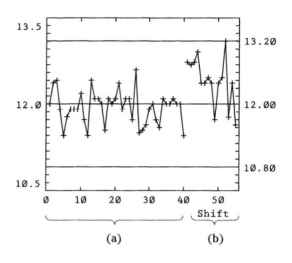

these students then proceed to construct a control chart and test for stability, the vast majority will conclude that the process is stable with no points beyond the control limits of $\mu + 3\sigma$ and $\mu - 3\sigma$. However, with $30 \times 40 = 1200$ values generated, it is very likely that a few students will get values beyond the control limits. These students would conclude that the process is not stable when it actually is stable. Statisticians call this a type I error (concluding that a process is unstable and needs adjustment, when in fact it is actually OK). We will discuss this topic further in Chapters 7 and 8.

Let's now assume that because of misadjustment, the machine begins filling the cans with $\mu = 12.5$ oz of cola, while σ remains at 0.4 oz. In the previous section we saw that this situation results in many more cans that don't meet the regulations. We would like to be able to detect this shift that indicates an unstable process. The next example includes sample data with such a shift.

EXAMPLE Use the following sample results and Minitab display to test for statistical stability. Again assume that $\mu = 12.0$ and $\sigma = 0.4$ so that the control chart boundaries are 10.8 and 13.2.

12.63	12.50	12.72	13.08	12.38	12.37	12.54	12.31	11.76
12.33	12.56	13.21	11.89	12.50	11.59			

```
MTB > DESCRIBE C4


          N     MEAN   MEDIAN   TRMEAN   STDEV   SEMEAN
C4       15   12.425   12.500   12.428   0.437    0.113

        MIN      MAX       Q1       Q3
C4   11.590   13.210   12.310   12.630
```

SOLUTION   The 15 points are plotted in the control chart of Fig. 5.16(b). Inspection of that figure reveals that the mean seems to be higher than 12.0. Next, note that the first 8 of the shifted points are above the center line; this alone is enough evidence to warrant rejection of stability. Finally, note that the 12th point is beyond the upper boundary. This too would justify the conclusion that the process is not stable. These 15 points therefore illustrate all three reasons for rejecting stability. We should stop the machine, inspect it, and have technicians fix or adjust it properly so that statistical stability can be gained.

Correcting the instability is only one problem. If we are selecting a can every 2 min, it will take $2 \times 8 = 16$ min to know we have a problem, and we might be producing thousands of cans in the interim. The first shifted value did not cause us to reject stability, so we concluded that the process was stable when, in reality, it was not stable. Statisticians call this a type II error (concluding that the process is OK when it really isn't). We will discuss type II errors further in Chapters 7 and 8. Also, Section 5.8 of this chapter will include a modified control chart that will help us identify an unstable process more quickly.

After concluding that the process is stable, we can consider whether the distribution of data is normal by using the same histogram approach used for populations. In Fig. 5.17 we show the histogram for the 40 sample values we considered in the example. The shape of that histogram does suggest that the distribution of the sample data is approximately normal.

This section included guidelines for determining normality and stability, which are summarized on the next page.

FIGURE 5.17
Histogram of Sample Data

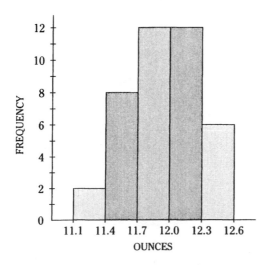

Determining normality in a population:
Using at least 40 values, construct a histogram. Examine the shape of the histogram and conclude that the distribution of the population is normal if the histogram is roughly bell-shaped.

Determining normality in a process:
1. First test for statistical stability by using the control chart. A stable process must pass all three of the following tests.

FIGURE 5.18
Determining Normality of a Population or a Process

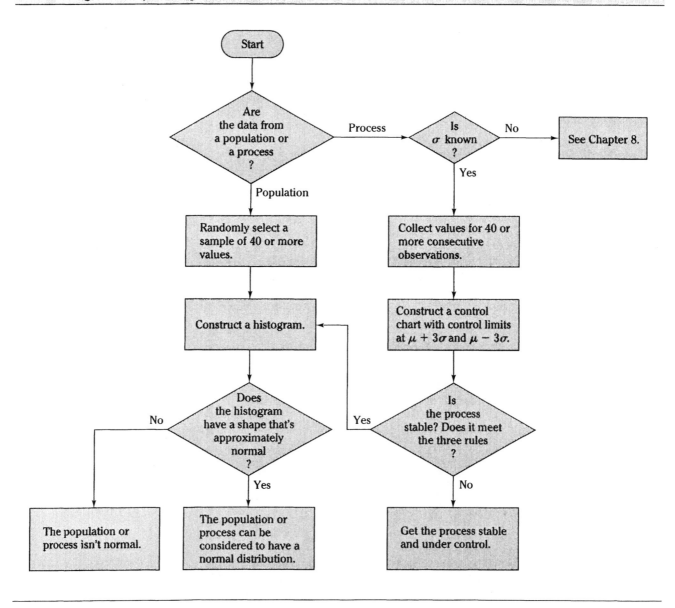

   i. Visually inspect the control chart and try to detect any patterns that are not random. Look for trends, cycles, shifts, or any other patterns of instability, such as those shown in Fig. 2.9.

  ii. Use the run of 8 rule. The process is not stable if 8 consecutive points are all above or all below the mean.

 iii. Use the control limits. The process is not stable if any points are above the upper control limit of $\mu + 3\sigma$ or below the lower control limit of $\mu - 3\sigma$. (In the absence of a desired mean μ, we can use the sample mean $\bar{x}$ as the observed central value, so the control limits are $\bar{x} + 3\sigma$ and $\bar{x} - 3\sigma$.)

2. If step 1 leads to the conclusion that the process is stable, we can now treat the process data as if they are population data. Construct a histogram of the data and conclude that the distribution of the population is normal if that histogram is roughly bell-shaped.

Figure 5.18 is a flowchart summarizing the above procedure.

5.4 EXERCISES BASIC CONCEPTS

In Exercises 1–4, the given histograms represent sample data taken from different populations. Identify the samples that seem to come from normally distributed populations.

1.

2.

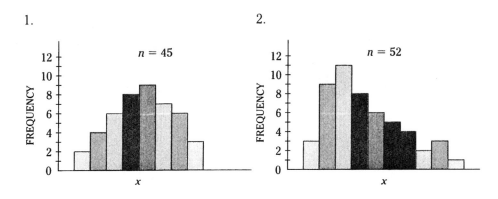

3.

4.

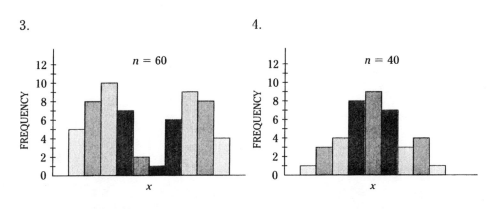

In Exercises 5–8, the given graphs consist of control charts and the corresponding histograms for different processes. In each case, determine whether the process is statistically stable or unstable. If stable, do the data seem to come from a normally distributed process?

5.

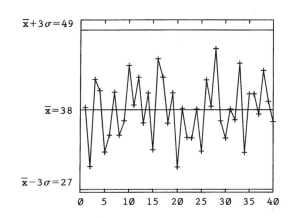
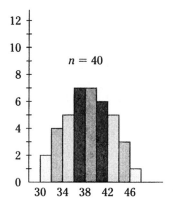

6.

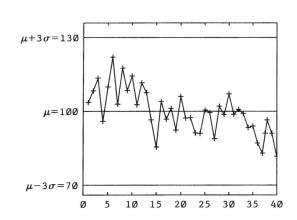
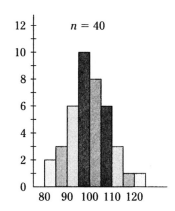

7.

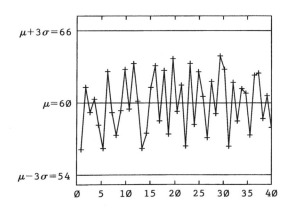
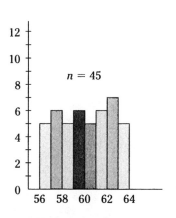

8.

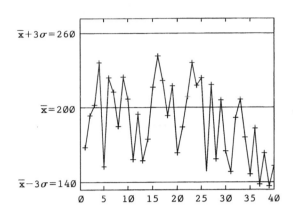
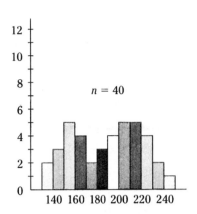

9. The accompanying data set consists of the numbers of sick days in a year for 40 randomly selected employees at the Detroit Foundry Company. Construct a histogram and determine whether the sample comes from a population having a normal distribution.

9	4	7	5	8	8	6	8	8	12
4	7	13	7	9	9	8	5	9	12
14	9	2	11	10	10	8	5	6	8
9	8	7	10	6	7	3	6	6	7

10. Exercise 9 referred to data from the Detroit Foundry Company. Eighteen months ago, the Knoxville Foundry Company instituted a pollution control program that reduces the amounts of gases that result from the casting process. Listed below are the numbers of sick days for 40 randomly selected employees in this foundry; they correspond to the same year used in Exercise 9.
   a. Construct a histogram and determine whether the sample data have a distribution suggesting that the population is approximately normally distributed.
   b. Compare the histogram from part a with the histogram constructed in Exercise 9. Does there appear to be any difference?

3	1	5	7	0	2	4	6
5	5	3	4	2	2	3	5
0	3	1	3	4	0	2	2
6	2	2	1	3	4	3	5
2	3	1	0	1	4	1	3

11. Listed below are the amounts (in dollars) charged to Visa cards during the last 60 days for 42 randomly selected bank accounts. Determine whether the sample is drawn from a population with an approximately normal distribution.

355	320	571	432	688	138	748	548	259	411	384
546	625	569	485	473	367	476	460	344	410	463
428	389	169	425	240	385	512	266	315	412	381
470	320	406	603	228	335	445	339	88		

12. At the beginning of this section, we listed 40 output voltages taken from an electrical motor every 5 min in one day. Because the measurements were taken sequentially, we are monitoring a process. Test the process for normality by constructing a control chart (with $\mu = 7$ and $\sigma = 1.1$) and a histogram.

13. Assume that a local Pillsbury facility wants to package boxes of cake mix so that the mean weight of the mix is 16.00 oz with a standard deviation of 0.2 oz. Listed below (by rows) are 42 weights (in ounces) selected in sequence from the boxing line; one box is selected every 4 min. Are we dealing with a process or a population? Test for normality.

16.28	15.99	15.95	16.14	16.09	16.21	15.80
15.96	15.76	16.29	15.85	15.90	16.03	15.78
15.94	15.89	15.71	16.02	16.23	16.05	15.81
16.26	16.21	16.26	15.86	15.79	16.10	16.03
16.31	15.91	16.21	15.73	15.94	15.96	16.22
16.02	16.34	16.02	16.11	16.19	15.81	16.23

5.4 EXERCISES   BEYOND THE BASICS

14. A telephone company employee collects data on the lengths of telephone calls; the results will be used to determine equipment purchases and to help in future planning. She plans to test for normality by randomly selecting 20 calls and recording their times. What's wrong with this plan?

15. A large shipment of 10,000 bottles used to store penicillin has been sent to a pharmaceutical manufacturer. The diameters of the bottle necks are critical in ensuring proper sealing of their contents. The manufacturer decides to check the quality of the bottles by precisely measuring the diameters of a randomly selected sample. If you want to test for normality, how many bottles should you select? Is the sample from a population or a process?

16. When compact discs are manufactured, they are plated with aluminum. The thickness of the aluminum plating is monitored through a procedure whereby every 200th disc is optically measured. If you want to test for normality of the distribution of thicknesses, how many discs must you sample? Does this test involve a population or a process? Describe the procedure for testing for normality.

FIGURE 5.19
Heights (in cm) of Women

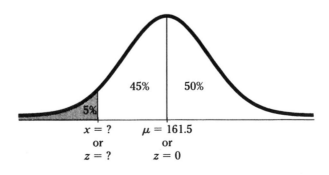

5.5   FINDING VALUES WHEN GIVEN PROBABILITIES

All examples and exercises from Sections 5.2 and 5.3 involve a normal distribution in this format: The given information includes some value for a score, and we used Table A.2 to find a corresponding probability. In this section, we reverse that format as follows: Given a probability, we will use Table A.2 to find a score. We will apply this reversed format to populations as well as statistically stable processes.

In the problem described at the beginning of this chapter, we saw a car design that was uncomfortable for women with heights under 159.0 cm (or 62.6 in.). In Section 5.3 we determined that this constitutes 34.46% of all women. Let's assume that after learning this, the engineers decide to make changes so that only 5% of all women would be uncomfortable in the driver's seat. Here's our new problem: What height separates the shortest 5% of women from the tallest 95%? Recall that National Health Survey data reveal that women have normally distributed heights with a mean of 161.5 cm and a standard deviation of 6.3 cm. Figure 5.19 depicts this situation.

We can find the z score corresponding to the x value we seek after first noting that the region containing 45% corresponds to an area of 0.4500. Referring to Table A.2, we find that 0.4500 corresponds to $z = 1.645$. Because the z score is negative whenever it is below the mean, we set $z = -1.645$. That is, the score x is 1.645 standard deviations *below* the mean of 161.5. Because the standard deviation is 6.3 cm, we conclude that 1.645 standard deviations is $1.645 \cdot 6.3$ cm = 10.3635 cm. Our x score is therefore 10.3635 cm below 161.5 cm, and we get $x = 161.5 - 10.3635 = 151.1$ cm (rounded off). That is, the height of 151.1 cm separates the shortest 5% of women from the tallest 95%. We could also state that 151.1 cm is the 5th percentile, or P_5.

We could have achieved the same result by noting that

$$z = \frac{x - \mu}{\sigma} \quad \text{becomes} \quad -1.645 = \frac{x - 161.5}{6.3}$$

when we substitute the given values for the mean μ, the standard deviation σ, and the z score corresponding to an area of 0.4500 to the left of the mean. We solve this equation by multiplying both sides by 6.3 and then adding 161.5 to both sides.

In the preceding solution, it is often too easy to make the mistake of forgetting the negative sign in -1.645. Omission of this negative sign would have led to an answer of 171.9 cm, but Fig. 5.19 should show that x can't possibly be 171.9 cm. This illustrates the importance of drawing a graph when working with the normal distribution. Always draw the graph with the relevant labels and use common sense to check that the results are reasonable.

Also note that in the preceding solution, Table A.2 led to a z score of 1.645, which is midway between 1.64 and 1.65. When using Table A.2, we can usually avoid interpolation by simply selecting the closest value. However, there are two special cases involving values that are important because they are used so often in research and business applications. These are summarized in the table shown in the margin. Except for these two special cases, we can select the closest value in the table. (If a desired value is midway between two table values, select the larger value.)

z SCORE	AREA
1.645	0.4500
2.575	0.4950

EXAMPLE An example in Section 5.3 involved the filling of 12-oz cola cans when the mean was 12.5 oz and the standard deviation was 0.4 oz (before adjustment led to an improved filling process). Find the fill amount (in ounces) that represents the 90th percentile. That is, find the amount with the property that 90% of the cans have less cola and 10% have more.

SOLUTION We illustrate the problem in Fig. 5.20. We can find the z score corresponding to the value we seek for x by noting that the region containing 40% corresponds to an area of 0.40. Referring to Table A.2, we find that 0.40 corresponds to $z = 1.28$. Substituting 1.28 for z, 12.5 for μ, and 0.4 for σ,

$$z = \frac{x - \mu}{\sigma} \quad \text{becomes} \quad 1.28 = \frac{x - 12.5}{0.4}$$

After multiplying both sides of the equation by 0.4 and then adding 12.5 to both sides, we solve for x to get $x = (1.28)(0.4) + 12.5 = 13.0$ oz. The fill level of $x = 13.0$ oz is the 90th percentile.

5.5 EXERCISES   BASIC CONCEPTS

In Exercises 1–12, assume that the errors on a scale (in meters) are normally distributed with a mean of 0 m and a standard deviation of 1 m. (The errors can be positive or negative.)

1. Ninety-five percent of the errors are below what value?
2. Ninety-nine percent of the errors are below what value?
3. Ninety-five percent of the errors are above what value?
4. Ninety-nine percent of the errors are above what value?
5. If the top 5% and the bottom 5% of all errors are unacceptable, find the minimum and maximum acceptable errors.
6. If the top 0.5% and the bottom 0.5% of all errors are unacceptable, find the minimum and maximum acceptable errors.
7. If the top 10% and the bottom 5% of all errors are unacceptable, find the minimum and maximum acceptable errors.
8. If the top 15% and the bottom 20% of all errors are unacceptable, find the minimum and maximum acceptable errors.
9. Find the value that separates the top 40% of all errors from the bottom 60%.
10. Find the value that separates the top 82% of all errors from the bottom 18%.
11. Find the value of the third quartile (Q_3), which separates the top 25% of all errors from the bottom 75%.
12. Find the value of P_{18} (18th percentile), which separates the bottom 18% of all errors from the top 82%.
13. Heights of women are normally distributed with a mean of 161.5 cm and a standard deviation of 6.3 cm (based on data from the National Health Survey). If a car design makes the driver's seat uncomfortable for the shortest 10% of women, find the height that separates the shortest 10% from the tallest 90%.

FIGURE 5.20
Contents (in oz) of Cola Cans

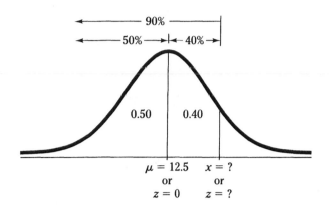

14. In Section 5.3 we found that by adjusting the center of the cola can–filling process to 12.0 oz, we came closer to meeting the federal regulation. Assume that the center is adjusted to 12.0 oz and that σ remains at 0.4 oz. Find the 90th percentile for the filling amounts in ounces.

15. The Graduate Management Admission Test (GMAT) is given for students wishing to attend a graduate business program. The scores are normally distributed with a mean of 500 and a standard deviation of 100.
    a.   Find the 60th percentile of GMAT scores and explain what it means.
    b.   If a business school admissions office uses the 70th percentile as a cutoff point, find the score that becomes the cutoff point.

16. A study of VCR owners found that their annual household incomes are normally distributed with a mean of $41,182 and a standard deviation of $19,990 (based on data from Nielsen Media Research). If an advertising campaign for a relatively expensive videotape is to be targeted at those VCR owners whose household incomes are in the top 90%, find the minimum income level for this target group.

17. A manufacturer of car tires finds that the tires last distances that are normally distributed with a mean of 35,600 mi and a standard deviation of 4275 mi. The manufacturer wants to guarantee the tires so that only 3% will be replaced because of failure before the guaranteed number of miles. For how many miles should the tires be guaranteed?

18. An insurance researcher learns that for males aged 16–24, the mean number of miles driven each year is 10,718 (based on data from the Federal Highway Administration). Assume that the annual mileage totals are normally distributed with a standard deviation of 3573 mi, and the company will impose a surcharge for those in the top 30%. Find the mileage total that separates those who will be surcharged.

19. Assume that for the Priority Overnight mail delivery, Federal Express has an average delivery time of 9:30 A.M. with a standard deviation of 14 min; the delivery times are normally distributed.
    a.   Find the 99th percentile of delivery times and explain what it means.
    b.   Find the 30th percentile of delivery times and explain what it means.

20. In manufacturing automatic transmission shafts, one machine has a statistically stable process with a mean of 3.514 cm, a standard deviation of 0.012 cm, and normally distributed values.
    a. Find the length corresponding to the shortest 1% and the length corresponding to the longest 1%.
    b. What percentage of shafts will be drilled between the two lengths found in part *a?*
    c. By using a more precise diamond-tipped drill, the standard deviation can be reduced to 0.007 cm. Now find the length corresponding to the shortest 1% and the length corresponding to the longest 1%.

21. A manufacturer has contracted to supply ball bearings. Product analysis reveals that the machine yields diameters that are normally distributed and the process is statistically stable. The process has a mean of 25.1 mm and a standard deviation of 0.2 mm. The largest 7% of the diameters and the smallest 13% of the diameters are unacceptable. Find the limits for the diameters of the acceptable ball bearings.

22. A manufacturer of color television sets tests competing brands and finds that the amounts of energy they require are normally distributed with a mean of 320 kWh and a standard deviation of 7.5 kWh. If the lowest 30% and the highest 20% are not included in a second round of tests, what are the limits for the energy amounts of the remaining sets?

23. A particular X-ray machine gives radiation dosages (in milliroentgens) that are normally distributed with a mean of 4.13 and a standard deviation of 1.27. A dosimeter is set so that it displays yellow for radiation levels that are not in the top 10% or bottom 30%. Find the lowest and highest "yellow" radiation levels.

24. A large study of new accounting graduates in the Midwest yields a mean starting salary of $22,500, a standard deviation of $1400, and a distribution that is normal.
    a. Find Q_1, the first quartile.
    b. Find Q_3, the third quartile.

5.5 EXERCISES   BEYOND THE BASICS

25. A personnel manager has been directed to investigate the possibility of early-retirement incentives as a way of trimming the number of employees from the present level of 18,500. Research shows that the mean employee age is 42 with a standard deviation of 11 years, and the ages have a distribution that is approximately normal. If there is a need to reduce the number of employees by 4,250, what age should be the cutoff for those being offered the early-retirement incentive?

26. Your business makes bags of ice labeled 10 lb. State law requires that 95% or more of the bags must have at least 10 lb of ice; only 5% can have under 10 lb. After carefully selecting a sample of 50 bags, you find that the process is normally distributed and statistically stable. Also, the mean is 10.30 lb and the standard deviation is 0.25 lb. *(continued)*

   a.   What percentage of bags will have less than 10 lb of ice?

   b.   What is the value of the 5th percentile P_5?

   c.   Based on parts *a* and *b,* are you in violation of state law?

   d.   If the answer to part *c* is yes, you want to adjust the mean so that you are in compliance with the state law. Find the lowest value of the adjusted mean that accomplishes this.

   e.   If it is possible to reduce the standard deviation to 0.10 lb, find the value of the adjusted mean that would meet the requirements of the state law.

   f.   By comparing parts *d* and *e,* describe the effect of decreasing the standard deviation and how it affects costs and savings.

27. Section 5.1 began with a discussion of the voltages of an electric motor. The voltages were uniformly distributed between 5.00 V and 9.00 V.

   a.   If you wanted to find the voltage corresponding to a given percentile, should you use Table A.2? Why or why not?

   b.   Find the 80th percentile.

   c.   Find the 10th percentile.

5.6   NORMAL APPROXIMATION TO THE BINOMIAL DISTRIBUTION

Recall from Section 4.4 that in a binomial probability distribution, we have outcomes belonging to one of two categories, and we have a fixed number n of independent trials, each having a probability p of success and a probability q of failure. The typical problem involves finding $P(x)$, the probability of x successes among n trials. In Section 4.4 we learned (we hope) how to solve binomial problems by using Table A.1 or the binomial probability formula. However, there are many important binomial problems that are not practical to solve by such methods. As an example, consider this problem:

> The Intel Corporation makes computer chips with a 35% yield, meaning that 35% of the chips are good while 65% are not (based on data from a Paine Webber analyst). What is the probability that in a batch of 150 chips, there are at least 60 good chips, which are needed to fill a special order?

This is a binomial problem with $n = 150$, $p = 0.35$, $q = 0.65$, and $x = 60, 61, 62, \ldots, 150$. Table A.1 doesn't go up to $n = 150$, so it can't be used. In theory, we could use the binomial probability formula 91 times beginning with

$$P(60) = \frac{150!}{(150 - 60)!60!} \cdot 0.35^{60} \cdot 0.65^{150 - 60}$$

The resulting 91 probabilities can be added to produce the correct result. However, these calculations would require days of work and tons of patience. Fortunately, this section introduces a simple and practical alternative: Under certain circumstances, we can approximate the binomial probability distribution by the normal distribution. The following summarizes the key point of this section.

If $np \geq 5$ and $nq \geq 5$, then the binomial random variable is approximately normally distributed with the mean and standard deviation given as

$$\mu = np$$
$$\sigma = \sqrt{npq}$$

If you go back and review Fig. 4.4 on page 176, you will see that a particular binomial distribution does have a probability histogram that has roughly the same shape as a normal distribution.

We will now use the normal approximation approach to solve our computer chip problem. (For that binomial problem we have already ruled out the use of Table A.1 or the binomial probability formula.) We first verify that $np \geq 5$ and $nq \geq 5$.

$$np = 150 \times 0.35 = 52.5 \qquad \text{(Therefore } np \geq 5.\text{)}$$
$$nq = 150 \times 0.65 = 97.5 \qquad \text{(Therefore } nq \geq 5.\text{)}$$

As a result of satisfying these two requirements, we now know that it is reasonable to approximate the binomial distribution by a normal distribution and we therefore proceed to find values for μ and σ that are needed. We get the following:

$$\mu = np = 150 \times 0.35 = 52.5$$
$$\sigma = \sqrt{npq} = \sqrt{(150)(0.35)(0.65)} = 5.84$$

CONTINUITY CORRECTION

We want the probability of getting *at least* 60 good chips in a batch of 150, so we include the probability of getting *exactly* 60. But the discrete value of 60 is approximated in the continuous normal distribution by the interval from 59.5 to 60.5. Such conversions from a discrete to a continuous distribution are called continuity corrections.

DEFINITION

When we use the continuous normal distribution as an approximation to the binomial distribution, continuity correction is made to a discrete whole-number value in a binomial distribution by both adding and subtracting 0.5.

Figure 5.21 illustrates how the discrete value of 60 is corrected for continuity when represented by the continuous normal distribution. In the problem we are

FIGURE 5.21
Distribution of the Numbers of Good Chips in Batches of 150

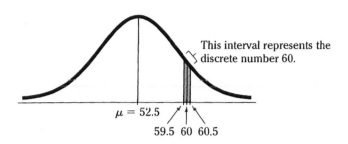

This interval represents the discrete number 60.

$\mu = 52.5$

59.5 60 60.5

considering, "at least 60" means that we include the entire interval representing 60, so 59.5 becomes the actual boundary that we use. If we ignore or forget the continuity correction, the additional error will be relatively small as long as n is large. However, the continuity correction should always be used with a normal distribution to approximate a binomial distribution.

Now let's get back to our problem of finding the probability of getting at least 60 good chips. Figure 5.22 illustrates our problem and includes the continuity correction. We need to find the shaded area. Using our usual procedures associated with normal distributions, we first find the area bound by 52.5 and 59.5. We get

$$z = \frac{x - \mu}{\sigma} = \frac{59.5 - 52.5}{5.84} = 1.20$$

Using Table A.2, we find that $z = 1.20$ corresponds to an area of 0.3849, so the shaded region has an area of $0.5 - 0.3849 = 0.1151$. The probability of getting 60 or more good chips is 0.1151. In the preceding example, if we had neglected to correct for continuity by using 60 instead of 59.5, we would have obtained $z = (60 - 52.5)/5.8 = 1.29$ and, by using Table A.2, the area would have been $0.5 - 0.4015 = 0.0985$. The result of 0.1151 is more accurate, as we will now show.

FIGURE 5.22
Distribution of the Numbers of Good Chips in Batches of 150

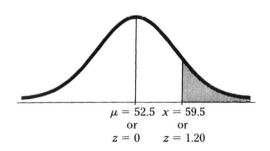

$\mu = 52.5$ $x = 59.5$
or   or
$z = 0$ $z = 1.20$

RELIABILITY AND VALIDITY

Different standard tests are used to measure IQ, job aptitude, employee performance, and qualification for promotion. In analyzing results from such tests, we should consider both reliability and validity. The reliability of data refers to the consistency with which results occur, whereas the validity of data refers to how well the data measure what they are supposed to measure. We can judge the reliability of a test by comparing scores for a test given on one date to scores for the same test given at another time. To test the validity of a standard test, we might compare the test scores to some other indicator of the quality being tested. We might compare scores on an IQ test to another indicator of intelligence, such as academic performance. Many critics charge that standard tests are reliable but not valid because they provide consistent results but don't really measure the quality they are supposed to measure.

Listed below is a Minitab computer display for the binomial probability distribution function (PDF) for $n = 150$ and $p = 0.35$. The display shows that the probabilities corresponding to 60, 61, 62, . . . good chips are 0.0296, 0.0235, 0.0182, . . . respectively. We can find the cumulative probability corresponding to 60 or more good chips by adding $0.0296 + 0.0235 + 0.0183 + \cdots + 0.0001 = 0.1160$, which is very close to the computed value of 0.1151 we obtained earlier. In this case, Minitab is a good alternative to the normal approximation. For many other problems, the normal approximation will be easier.

```
MTB > PDF;
SUBC> BINOMIAL N=150 P=0.35.

     BINOMIAL WITH N = 150 P = 0.350000
     K      P( X = K)
     31     0.0000      52     0.0681
     32     0.0001      53     0.0678
     33     0.0002      54     0.0655
     34     0.0004      55     0.0616
     35     0.0006      56     0.0563
     36     0.0011      57     0.0500
     37     0.0018      58     0.0431
     38     0.0029      59     0.0362
     39     0.0045      60     0.0296
     40     0.0067      61     0.0235
     41     0.0097      62     0.0182
     42     0.0136      63     0.0137
     43     0.0184      64     0.0100
     44     0.0240      65     0.0071
     45     0.0305      66     0.0049
     46     0.0375      67     0.0033
     47     0.0446      68     0.0022
     48     0.0516      69     0.0014
     49     0.0578      70     0.0009
     50     0.0629      71     0.0005
     51     0.0664      72     0.0003
                        73     0.0002
                        74     0.0001
                        75     0.0001
                        76     0.0000
```

Figure 5.23 summarizes the procedure for using the normal distribution as an approximation to the binomial distribution. Note that the procedure applies both to populations and to statistically stable processes that are binomial in form. We considered the batch of 150 chips as a sample from a population, but if we consider the chips to be produced one at a time, then we have a process. If the process is stable, then we can collect the 150 chips and treat them as a sample from a population and proceed to find probabilities as above. However, if the process is not statistically stable, then we must direct all our efforts to making it stable. With an unstable process, we can get strange and unpredictable results. If we look only at the overall sample and ignore the time sequence of the process, we might think that we have stability when we do not. Such an error could lead to disastrous results.

FIGURE 5.23
Solving Binomial Probability Problems

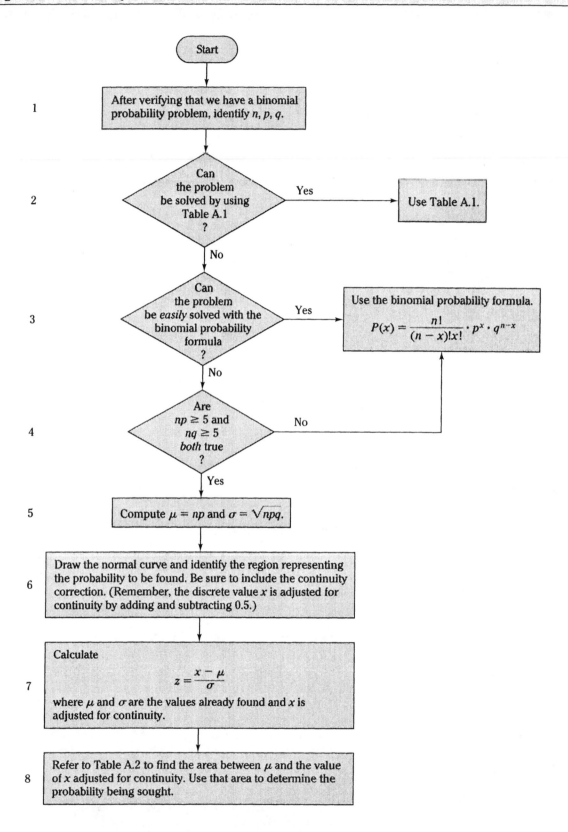

HOTTEST SPOT

A firefighter in Bullhead City, Arizona, provided daily weather statistics. One day, a Weather Service representative demanded that the thermometer be moved from the firehouse lawn to a more natural setting. The move to a drier area 100 yards away led to readings about 5° higher, which often made Bullhead City the hottest spot in the United States. As Bullhead City gained prominence in many television weather reports, some residents denounced the notoriety as a handicap to business, whereas others felt that it helped. Under more-standardized conditions, measuring instruments, such as thermometers, scales, voltmeters, and micrometers, tend to produce errors that are normally distributed.

The following example follows the procedure outlined in Fig. 5.23.

EXAMPLE According to data from the Hertz Corporation, 80% of commuters use their own vehicle. Find the probability that of 100 randomly selected commuters, *exactly* 85 use their own vehicle.

SOLUTION Refer to Fig. 5.23. In step 1 we verify that the conditions described do satisfy the criteria for the binomial distribution with $n = 100$, $p = 0.80$, $q = 0.20$, and $x = 85$. Proceeding to step 2, we see that we cannot use Table A.1 because n is too large. In step 3, the binomial probability formula applies, but

$$P(85) = \frac{100!}{(100 - 85)!85!} \cdot 0.80^{85} \cdot 0.20^{100 - 85}$$

is difficult to compute. (Many calculators cannot evaluate 70! or higher.) In step 4 we get

$$np = 100 \cdot 0.80 = 80 \geq 5 \text{ and } nq = 100 \cdot 0.20 = 20 \geq 5$$

and because np and nq are both at least 5, we conclude that the normal approximation to the binomial is satisfactory. We now go on to step 5, where we obtain the values of μ and σ as follows:

$$\mu = np = 100 \cdot 0.80 = 80.0 \text{ and } \sigma = \sqrt{npq} = \sqrt{100 \cdot 0.80 \cdot 0.20} = 4.0$$

Now we go to step 6, where we draw the normal curve shown in Fig. 5.24. The shaded region of Fig. 5.24 represents the probability we want. Use of the continuity correction results in the representation of 85 by the region extending from 84.5 to 85.5. We now proceed to step 7.

The format of Table A.2 requires that we first find the probability corresponding to the region bounded on the left by the vertical line through the mean of 80.0 and on the right by the vertical line through 85.5, so that one of the calculations required in step 7 is as follows:

$$z_2 = \frac{x - \mu}{\sigma} = \frac{85.5 - 80.0}{4.0} = 1.38$$

We also need the probability corresponding to the region bounded by 80.0 and 84.5, so we calculate

$$z_1 = \frac{x - \mu}{\sigma} = \frac{84.5 - 80.0}{4.0} = 1.13$$

Finally, in step 8 we use Table A.2 to find that a probability of 0.4162 corresponds to $z_2 = 1.38$ and 0.3708 corresponds to $z_1 = 1.13$. Consequently, the entire shaded region of Fig. 5.24 depicts a probability of $0.4162 - 0.3708 = 0.0454$. The probability that of 100 commuters exactly 85 use their own vehicle is 0.0454.

FIGURE 5.24
Numbers of Commuters (in groups of 100) Who Use Their Own Vehicle

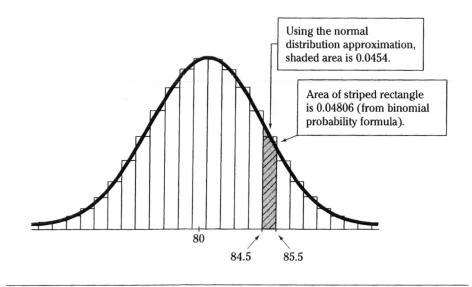

Using the normal distribution approximation, shaded area is 0.0454.

Area of striped rectangle is 0.04806 (from binomial probability formula).

80

84.5   85.5

In the preceding example, using Minitab or a calculator will result in a probability of 0.04806, while the normal approximation method resulted in a value of 0.0454. The discrepancy of 0.00266 is very small. The discrepancy occurs because we are finding the area of the shaded region in Fig. 5.24, but the actual area is a *rectangle* centered above 85. (Fig. 5.24 illustrates this discrepancy.) The area of the rectangle is 0.04806, but the area of the approximating shaded region is 0.0454.

We now have three methods for determining probabilities in binomial experiments, and they are all summarized in Fig. 5.23.

5.6 EXERCISES   BASIC CONCEPTS

In Exercises 1–4, check that $np \geq 5$ and $nq \geq 5$ to determine whether the normal distribution is a suitable approximation. In each case, also find the values of μ and σ.

1. $n = 25$, $p = 0.250$
2. $n = 50$, $p = 0.333$
3. $n = 84$, $p = 0.950$
4. $n = 125$, $p = 0.961$

In Exercises 5–8, find the indicated binomial probabilities by using (a) Table A.1 in Appendix A and (b) the normal distribution as an approximation to the binomial probability distribution.

5. With $n = 12$ and $p = 0.50$, find $P(8)$.
6. With $n = 15$ and $p = 0.40$, find $P(7)$.
7. With $n = 12$ and $p = 0.50$, find $P(\text{at least } 8)$.
8. With $n = 14$ and $p = 0.40$, find $P(\text{at most } 2)$.

9. Continental Airlines recently reported that its on-time arrival rate is 80%. Find the probability that among 100 randomly selected flights, fewer than 70 arrive on time.

10. Among U.S. households, 24% have telephone-answering machines (based on data from the U.S. Consumer Electronics Industry). If a telemarketing campaign involves 2500 households, find the probability that more than 650 have answering machines.

11. In a study by United Group Information Services, 66% of small businesses are based in homes. If a marketing study involves the random selection of 375 small businesses, find the probability that fewer than 250 are based in homes.

12. A supplier of ballpoint pens guarantees that only 2% are defective. You receive a shipment of 25,000 pens and randomly select 300 for testing.
    a. Find the probability of getting 15 or more defective pens in the sample.
    b. Assume that you test the sample of 300 pens and find 15 that are defective. Would you believe the supplier's claim?

13. Among teenagers old enough to drive, 35% have their own cars (based on data from a Rand Youth Poll). If a marketing research team randomly selects 600 teenagers of driving age, find the probability that at least 210 of them have their own cars.

14. According to Bureau of the Census data, among men aged 18 to 24, 60% live at home with their parents. If 500 men aged 18 to 24 are randomly selected, find the probability that more than 325 of them live at home with their parents.

15. Six months ago, an audit of a shipping firm revealed that 15% of the bills of lading had incorrect entries or miscalculations. That is, 15% of the bills of lading were defective. After the shipping firm promises to improve by retraining clerks, you randomly select and inspect 100 bills of lading.
    a. What is the probability of getting 5 or fewer defective bills if the error rate has remained at 15%?
    b. Assume that 5 bills are found to be defective. Does it seem likely that the error rate continues to be 15%?

16. Air America is an airline company that experiences a 7% rate of no-shows on advance reservations. Find the probability that of 250 randomly selected advance reservations, there will be at least 10 no-shows.

17. The IRS finds that of all taxpayers whose returns are audited, 70% end up paying additional taxes. Find the probability that of 500 randomly selected returns, at least 400 end up paying additional taxes.

18. A machine makes rubber valve stems for cars at the rate of 1 per sec. They are packaged in batches of 100 to a box. The manufacturer claims that the process is statistically stable with a 5% rate of defects.
    a. Find the probability of getting 12 or more defects in a box.
    b. If you did find 12 or more defects in a box, would you believe the claim that the rate of defects is 5%?

19. Of those who commute to southern Manhattan, 6.5% use commuter railroads (based on data from the New York Metropolitan Transportation Council). If we randomly select 175 people who commute to southern Manhattan, find the probability that the number who use railroads is between 10 and 15 inclusive.

20. Among workers aged 20 to 24, 26% work more than 40 hours per week (based on data from the U.S. Department of Labor). If we randomly select 350 workers aged 20 to 24, find the probability that the number who work more than 40 hours per week is between 80 and 90 inclusive.

5.6 EXERCISES   BEYOND THE BASICS

21. In a binomial experiment with $n = 15$ and $p = 0.4$, find P(at least 5) using the following:
    a. The table of binomial probabilities (Table A.1)
    b. The binomial probability formula
    c. The normal distribution approximation

22. Assume that a baseball player hits .350, so his probability of a hit is 0.350. Also assume that his hitting attempts are independent of each other.
    a. Find the probability of at least 1 hit in 4 tries in 1 game.
    b. Assuming that this batter gets up 4 times each game, find the probability of getting a total of at least 56 hits in 56 games.
    c. Assuming this batter gets up 4 times each game, find the probability of at least 1 hit in each of 56 consecutive games (Joe DiMaggio's 1941 record).
    d. What minimum batting average would be required for the probability in part c to be greater than 0.1?

23. An airline company works only with advance reservations and experiences a 7% rate of no-shows. How many reservations could be accepted for an airliner with a capacity of 250 if you want at least a 0.95 probability that all reservation holders who show will be accommodated?

24. A company manufactures integrated circuit chips with a 23% rate of defects. What is the minimum number of chips that must be manufactured to obtain at least a 90% chance that 5000 good chips can be supplied?

25. Donnelley Directory is a large national publisher of Yellow pages. Each advertisement is checked carefully for address, telephone number, spelling, and the content and clarity of any graphics. The sequence of typesetting, proofreading, and pasting up the ad copy can be considered a process. Assume that this process has been found to be statistically stable with 1% of the ads containing some type of error.
    a. How many ads must you sample to be able to use the normal approximation to the binomial distribution?
    b. Donnelley has decided to randomly select a sample of 600 ads from the thousands done each week. What is the chance that with an overall error rate of 1%, you will have no errors among the 600 ads?
    c. What is the chance that among 600 randomly selected ads, you will have 13 or more with errors?
    d. What is the chance that among 600 randomly selected ads, you will have between 1 and 12 (inclusive) with errors?
    e. If you sample 600 ads and find none with errors, does it seem likely that the error rate is really 1%? Explain.
    f. If you sample 600 ads and find 13 or more with errors, does it seem likely that the error rate is really 1%? Explain.

26. In this section we assumed that each binomial process was statistically stable and we could therefore treat the corresponding data as a sample from a population. For a given value of p, we can use a control chart to test a process for stability. The mean of $\mu = np$ can be graphed along with an upper control limit of $\mu + 3\sigma = np + 3\sqrt{npq}$ and a lower control limit of $\mu - 3\sigma = np - 3\sqrt{npq}$. Provided that $np \geq 5$ and $nq \geq 5$, the normal distribution will

serve as a good approximation to the binomial process; if the process is statistically stable, we expect to see that about 99.8% of our samples (of size *n*) lie between the upper and lower control limits, and we also expect that the run of 8 rule will hold.

Let's reconsider the Donnelley Directory problem from the preceding exercise. We will again assume an error rate of 1% and collect random samples, each containing 600 ads.

a. Draw a control chart and include the specific values for μ and the upper and lower control limits.

b. For 20 different samples (each of size 600) collected in 20 consecutive weeks, we record the numbers of defects. The results are listed below (in order by rows). Using these sample values, complete the control chart and determine whether the process is statistically stable.

```
3   7   4   6   9   4   3   8   7   5
4   5   7   5   8   4   6   7   2   6
```

5.7 THE CENTRAL LIMIT THEOREM

The central limit theorem is one of the most important and useful concepts in statistics. It will form a foundation for estimating population and stable process parameters and hypothesis testing, major topics that are discussed at length in the following chapters. Before considering this theorem, we will first try to develop an intuitive understanding of one of its most important consequences:

The distribution of sample means tends to be a normal distribution.

FIGURE 5.25
Histogram of the 300 Original Scores Randomly Selected (Between 1 and 9)

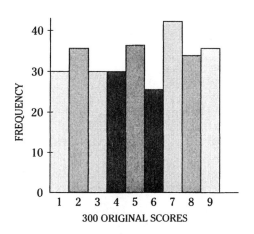

TABLE 5.1
Data for 30 Samples

SAMPLE	DATA										SAMPLE MEAN
1	2	7	5	5	2	1	7	7	9	4	4.9
2	5	8	1	1	5	7	1	4	1	4	3.7
3	7	6	9	8	5	1	6	4	7	9	6.2
4	7	3	1	7	3	6	7	9	4	3	5.0
5	9	7	7	6	1	6	8	3	4	7	5.8
6	5	3	3	4	2	5	9	9	1	9	5.0
7	5	5	3	9	5	3	1	9	1	5	4.6
8	4	3	9	5	5	9	1	7	7	8	5.8
9	2	1	7	8	6	7	7	9	8	3	5.8
10	3	4	5	6	8	4	8	3	4	5	5.0
11	5	3	2	2	6	8	1	5	5	9	4.6
12	7	5	9	6	8	2	2	7	2	1	4.9
13	3	1	4	1	7	9	3	2	3	8	4.1
14	6	2	7	4	4	5	2	6	8	6	5.0
15	9	6	2	9	4	2	6	3	5	5	5.1
16	9	2	2	3	6	2	6	6	8	3	4.7
17	5	4	2	1	9	4	2	9	4	2	4.2
18	8	1	2	1	4	3	2	8	5	4	3.8
19	5	8	9	6	2	7	9	3	8	5	6.2
20	5	6	8	7	5	9	6	4	8	7	6.5
21	7	9	9	8	3	5	5	1	4	6	5.7
22	8	4	7	8	7	8	7	7	1	8	6.5
23	5	5	1	7	5	7	7	2	9	8	5.6
24	9	5	2	5	9	2	5	3	5	8	5.3
25	4	5	8	4	2	9	2	6	6	1	4.7
26	1	7	7	3	4	7	7	2	8	7	5.3
27	8	1	1	7	6	2	2	1	4	9	4.1
28	9	4	3	7	3	7	8	4	3	2	5.0
29	1	2	9	3	8	2	4	6	2	8	4.5
30	2	9	3	3	1	2	6	7	8	7	4.8

↑ See Fig. 5.25 ↑ See Fig. 5.26

Note: Thirty samples are given here, each consisting of ten random numbers between 1 and 9. The right column consists of the corresponding sample means.

This implies that if we collect samples all of the same size and from the same population, compute their means, and then develop a histogram of those means, it will tend to assume the bell shape of a normal distribution. This is true regardless of the shape of the distribution of the original population. The central limit theorem qualifies the preceding remarks and includes additional aspects, but stop and try to understand the thrust of these remarks before continuing.

Let's begin with some concrete numbers. Table 5.1 contains a block of data consisting of 300 sample scores. These scores were generated through a computer simulation, but they could have been extracted from a telephone directory or a book of random numbers. (Now *there's* exciting reading, although the plot is a little thin.) Figure 5.25 illustrates the histogram of the 300 sample scores, showing that their distribution is essentially uniform. Now consider the 300 scores to be 30 samples, with 10 scores in each sample. The resulting 30 sample means are listed

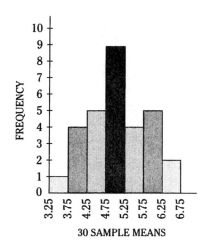

FIGURE 5.26
Histogram of the 30 Sample Means. Each sample mean is based on 10 raw scores randomly selected between 1 and 9, inclusive.

FIGURE 5.27
Central Limit Theorem

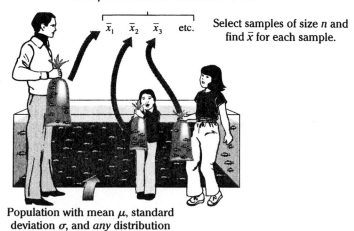

These sample means will, as *n* increases, approach a *normal* distribution with mean μ and standard deviation $\sigma/\sqrt{n}$.

$\bar{x}_1$ $\bar{x}_2$ $\bar{x}_3$ etc.

Select samples of size *n* and find $\bar{x}$ for each sample.

Population with mean μ, standard deviation σ, and *any* distribution

in Table 5.1 and illustrated in the histogram shown in Fig. 5.26. Note that the shape of Fig. 5.26 is roughly that of a normal distribution. It is important to observe that even though the original population has a uniform distribution, the sample means seem to have a normal distribution. It was observations exactly like this that led to the formulation of the central limit theorem. If our sample means were based on samples larger than 10, Fig. 5.26 would more closely resemble a normal distribution. We are now ready to consider the central limit theorem.

Let's assume that the variable x represents scores that may or may not be normally distributed, and that the mean of the x values is μ while the standard deviation is σ. Suppose we collect a sample of size n and calculate the sample mean $\bar{x}$. What do we know about the collection of all sample means that we produce by repeating this experiment, collecting a sample of size n to get the sample mean? The **central limit theorem** tells us that as n increases, the distribution of the sample means will tend to approach a normal distribution with mean μ and standard deviation $\sigma/\sqrt{n}$ (see Fig. 5.27). The distribution of sample means *tends* to be a normal distribution in the sense that as n becomes larger, the distribution of sample means gets closer to a normal distribution. This conclusion is not intuitively obvious, and it was arrived at through extensive research and analysis. The formal rigorous proof requires advanced mathematics and is beyond the scope of this text. We will illustrate the theorem and give examples of its use.

CENTRAL LIMIT THEOREM

Given:

1. The random variable x has any distribution with mean μ and standard deviation σ.
2. Samples of size n are randomly selected from this population.

Conclusions:

1. The distribution of all possible sample means $\bar{x}$ will approach a *normal* distribution as the sample size increases.
2. The *mean* of the sample means will be μ.
3. The *standard deviation* of the sample means will be $\sigma/\sqrt{n}$.

In the first conclusion, when we say that the distribution of sample means *approaches* a normal distribution, we are employing these commonly used rules:

1. For samples of size n larger than 30, the sample means can be approximated reasonably well by a normal distribution. The approximation gets better as the sample size n becomes larger.
2. If the original population is itself normally distributed, then the sample means will be normally distributed for *any* sample size n.

Notation
If all possible random samples of size n are selected from a population with mean μ and standard deviation σ, the mean of the sample means is denoted by $\mu_{\bar{x}}$ so that

$$\mu_{\bar{x}} = \mu$$

Also, the standard deviation of the sample means is denoted by $\sigma_{\bar{x}}$ so that

$$\sigma_{\bar{x}} = \frac{\sigma}{\sqrt{n}}$$

$\sigma_{\bar{x}}$ **is often called the standard error of the mean.**

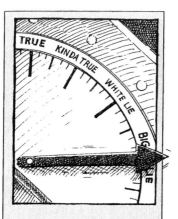

LIE DETECTORS

Businesses sometimes use lie detectors in the investigation of employee theft or sabotage. Police investigators sometimes use lie detectors, but the results are not admissible in court.

Why not require all criminal suspects to take lie detector tests and dispense with trials by jury? The Council of Scientific Affairs of the American Medical Association states, "It is established that classification of guilty can be made with 75% to 97% accuracy, but the rate of false positives is often sufficiently high to preclude use of this [polygraph] test as the sole arbiter of guilt or innocence." A "false positive" is an indication of guilt when the subject is actually innocent. Even with accuracy as high as 97%, the percentage of false positive results can be 50%, so that half of the innocent subjects incorrectly appear to be guilty.

Comparison of Figs. 5.25 and 5.26 should confirm that the original numbers have a nonnormal distribution, whereas the sample means approximate a normal distribution. The central limit theorem also indicates that the mean of *all* such sample means should be μ (the mean of the original population) and the standard deviation of all such sample means should be $\sigma/\sqrt{n}$ (where σ is the standard deviation of the original population and n is the sample size, which in this case is 10). We can find μ and σ for the original population of numbers between 1 and 9 by noting that, if those numbers were to occur with equal frequency as they should, then the population mean μ would be

$$\mu = \frac{1+2+3+4+5+6+7+8+9}{9} = 5.0$$

Similarly, we can find σ by again using 1, 2, 3, 4, 5, 6, 7, 8, 9 as an ideal or theoretical representation of the population. Following this course, σ is computed to be 2.58 by letting $N = 9$ and by letting $x = 1, 2, 3, 4, 5, 6, 7, 8, 9$ as follows

$$\sigma = \sqrt{\frac{\Sigma(x-\mu)^2}{N}} = \sqrt{\frac{\Sigma(x-5.0)^2}{9}} = 2.58$$

The mean and standard deviation of the sample means can now be found as follows:

$$\mu_{\bar{x}} = \mu = 5.0$$

$$\sigma_{\bar{x}} = \frac{\sigma}{\sqrt{n}} = \frac{2.58}{\sqrt{10}} = \frac{2.58}{3.16} = 0.82$$

For the 30 sample means shown in Table 5.1, we have a sample mean of 5.08 (close to $\mu = 5.00$) and a sample standard deviation of 0.75 (close to $\sigma/\sqrt{n} = 0.82$). We can see that our real data conform quite well to the theoretically predicted values for $\mu_{\bar{x}}$ and $\sigma_{\bar{x}}$.

FIGURE 5.28
Distribution of Customer Waiting Times (in seconds)

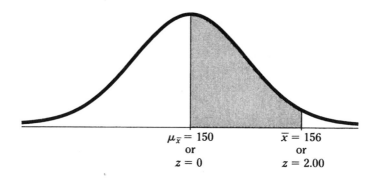

$\mu_{\bar{x}} = 150$
or
$z = 0$

$\bar{x} = 156$
or
$z = 2.00$

In the following example we use the same basic methods introduced earlier in Section 5.3, but we make some important adjustments required because our problem deals with the mean for a group of scores (instead of an individual score). Consequently, this example illustrates a method for dealing with the sampling distribution of means, instead of the sampling distribution of individual scores.

EXAMPLE   The Jefferson Valley Bank operates so that customer waiting times have a mean of 150 sec and a standard deviation of 18 sec. If 36 customers are randomly selected, find the probability that their mean waiting time is between 150 sec and 156 sec.

SOLUTION   We weren't given the distribution of the original population, but the sample size $n = 36$ exceeds 30, so we use the central limit theorem and conclude that the distribution of sample means is the normal distribution with these parameters:

$$\mu_{\bar{x}} = \mu = 150$$

$$\sigma_{\bar{x}} = \frac{\sigma}{\sqrt{n}} = \frac{18}{\sqrt{36}} = 3$$

Figure 5.28 shows the shaded area corresponding to the probability we seek. We find that area by first determining the value of the z score.

$$z = \frac{\bar{x} - \mu_{\bar{x}}}{\sigma_{\bar{x}}} = \frac{\bar{x} - \mu}{\dfrac{\sigma}{\sqrt{n}}} = \frac{156 - 150}{3} = 2.00$$

From Table A.2 we find that $z = 2.00$ corresponds to an area of 0.4772, so the probability we seek is 0.4772. That is, $P(150 < \bar{x} < 156) = P(0 < z < 2.00) = 0.4772$. There is a 0.4772 probability that when 36 customers are randomly selected, their mean waiting time is between 150 sec and 156 sec.

It is interesting to note that as the sample size increases, the sample means tend to vary less, because $\sigma_{\bar{x}} = \sigma/\sqrt{n}$ gets smaller as n gets larger. For example, assume that customer waiting times have a mean of 150 sec and a standard deviation of 18 sec. This means that if you examine many such times, about 99.8% of them will be between 96 sec and 204 sec [because $\mu - 3\sigma = 150 - 3(18) = 96$ and $\mu + 3\sigma = 150 + 3(18) = 204$]. But for samples of size $n = 36$, customer waiting times will produce sample means with $\sigma_{\bar{x}} = 18/\sqrt{36} = 3$. This implies that if you examine many sample means (with each sample of size 36), about 99.8% of them will be between 141 sec and 159 sec [because $\mu_{\bar{x}} - 3\sigma_{\bar{x}} = 150 - 3(3) = 141$ sec and $\mu_{\bar{x}} + 3\sigma_{\bar{x}} = 150 + 3(3) = 159$ sec]. If the sample size n is increased to 100, $\sigma_{\bar{x}} = 18/\sqrt{100} = 1.8$, and if you now examine many sample means (with each sample of size 100), about 99.8% will fall between 144.6 sec and 155.4 sec.

These results are supported by common sense: As the sample size increases, the corresponding sample mean will tend to be closer to the true population mean. The effect of an unusual or outstanding score tends to be diminished as it is averaged in as part of a sample.

FINITE POPULATION CORRECTION FACTOR

Our use of $\sigma_{\bar{x}} = \sigma/\sqrt{n}$ assumes that the population has infinitely many members. For instance, when we sample with replacement (that is, put back each selected item before making the next selection), the population is effectively infinite. Yet realistic applications involve sampling without replacement, so successive samples depend on previous outcomes. In manufacturing, for example, quality control inspectors typically sample items from a finite production run without replacing them. For such finite populations, we may need to adjust $\sigma_{\bar{x}}$.

Notation

Just as n denotes the *sample* size, N denotes the size of a *population* (or the size of a finite process run). For finite populations of size N, we should incorporate the *finite population correction factor* $\sqrt{(N - n) \div (N - 1)}$, so $\sigma_{\bar{x}}$ is found as follows:

$$\sigma_{\bar{x}} = \frac{\sigma}{\sqrt{n}} \sqrt{\frac{N - n}{N - 1}}$$

If the sample size n is small in comparison to the population size N, the finite population correction factor will be close to 1. Consequently its impact will be negligible and it can be ignored. Statisticians have devised the following rule of thumb.

RULE

Use the finite population correction factor when computing $\sigma_{\bar{x}}$ if the population is finite and $n > 0.05\ N$. That is, use the correction factor only if the sample size is greater than 5% of the population size.

We now have some important questions to answer when considering the use of the central limit theorem: Is the parent (original) population normally distributed? If not, are the sample sizes greater than 30? Is the population finite? If so, then are the sample sizes more than 5% of the population size? The answers to these questions affect our calculations. Figure 5.29 organizes our methods into one coherent scheme, summarizing the key points of this section.

The next example illustrates three different cases. The first case involves a simple and direct use of the normal distribution, the second case includes use of the central limit theorem, and the third case requires the central limit theorem along with the finite population correction factor.

FIGURE 5.29
Flowchart Summarizing the Decisions to Be Made When Considering a Distribution
of Sample Means

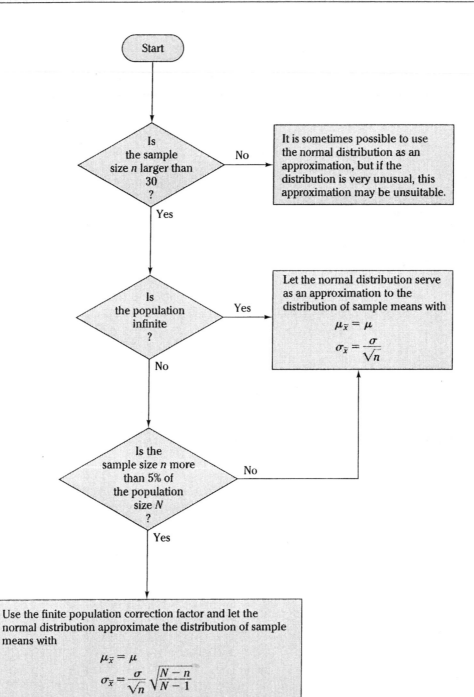

POTATO CHIP CONTROL CHARTS

In the past, quality control was simply a matter of inspecting products after they were completed. Now, manufacturers use statistical process control (SPC) to analyze samples at different points in the production process so that they know when to make adjustments and when to leave things alone. Frito Lay's bags of potato chips now have much less variability due to the use of SPC and control charts. Frito Lay aims for 1.6% salt content and continually monitors that level by using control charts.

EXAMPLE In manufacturing, a "short run" is used when a limited number of items is needed. An example would be filling an order for 750 wing support struts for Boeing 747s; 700 are needed for installation and 50 for testing. The struts are designed to have a mean bending strength of 18,000 lb with a standard deviation of 3000 lb, and the bending strengths are normally distributed. Let's consider the process to be stable so that we can treat our data as if they came from a population. In the following, assume that all samples are selected from the population of the 750 wing struts produced in the short run.

a. If one wing strut is randomly selected and tested, find the probability that it has a bending strength less than 17,250 lb.

b. If 32 wing struts are randomly selected and tested, find the probability that their mean bending strength is less than 17,250 lb.

c. If 50 struts are randomly selected and tested, find the probability that their mean bending strength is less than 17,250 lb.

SOLUTION a. *Approach:* Convert the nonstandard normal distribution to the standard normal distribution by using the z score, as in Section 5.3. We seek the area of the shaded region shown in Fig. 5.30(a), and so we calculate

$$z = \frac{x - \mu}{\sigma} = \frac{17{,}250 - 18{,}000}{3000} = -0.25$$

and then refer to Table A.2 to find that region A is 0.0987. The shaded region is therefore $0.5 - 0.0987 = 0.4013$. The probability of a single strut having a bending strength less than 17,250 lb is 0.4013. It is not unusual to select a single strut that tests below 17,250 lb; this will happen in about 40% of all such tests.

b. *Approach:* Use the central limit theorem without the finite population correction factor. Because $n > 30$, the central limit theorem indicates that the distribution of the sample means will be approximately normal, regardless of the distribution of the bending strengths. We seek the area of the shaded region in Fig. 5.30(b). Here, $\sigma_{\bar{x}} = \sigma/\sqrt{n} = 3000/\sqrt{32} = 530$ lb. We can now calculate

$$z = \frac{\bar{x} - \mu_{\bar{x}}}{\sigma_{\bar{x}}} = \frac{\bar{x} - \mu_{\bar{x}}}{\sigma/\sqrt{n}} = \frac{17{,}250 - 18{,}000}{530} = -1.42$$

Referring to Table A.2, we find that $z = 1.42$ corresponds to an area of 0.4222 for region B, so the shaded region is $0.5 - 0.4222 = 0.0778$. We can conclude that it is fairly unusual to select 32 struts, test them, and get a mean $\bar{x}$ below 17,250 lb. This should happen in only 7.78% of such cases.

c. *Approach:* Use the central limit theorem with the finite population correction factor (because the sample size of $n = 50$ does exceed 5% of 750). Again, because $n > 30$, we can be confident that the distribution of sample means is approximately normal. With $N = 750$, $n = 50$, and $\sigma = 3000$, we get

FIGURE 5.30
Distributions of Bending Strength Samples

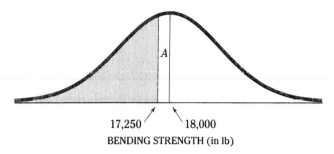

17,250   18,000
BENDING STRENGTH (in lb)

(a) Distribution of individual struts

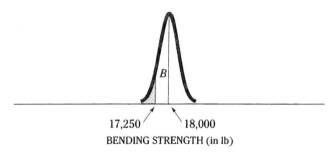

17,250   18,000
BENDING STRENGTH (in lb)

(b) Distribution of sample means ($n = 32$)

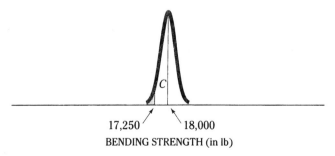

17,250   18,000
BENDING STRENGTH (in lb)

(c) Distribution of sample means ($n = 50$)

$$\sigma_{\bar{x}} = \frac{\sigma}{\sqrt{n}} \sqrt{\frac{N - n}{N - 1}} = \frac{3000}{\sqrt{50}} \sqrt{\frac{750 - 50}{750 - 1}} = 410$$

Proceed to find the shaded region of Fig. 5.30(c). We calculate

$$z = \frac{\bar{x} - \mu_{\bar{x}}}{\sigma_{\bar{x}}} = \frac{17,250 - 18,000}{410} = -1.83$$

$z = 1.83$ corresponds to an area of 0.4664, so the shaded region is $0.5 - 0.4664 = 0.0336$. It is very unlikely that 50 struts would be randomly selected with a mean bending strength less than 17,250 lb.

The central limit theorem is one of the most important and useful concepts in statistics because it allows us to use the basic normal distribution methods in a wide variety of circumstances. Many of the topics and applications in the following chapters will depend on the central limit theorem. In particular, we can use it to develop estimates of population and stable process parameters (see Chapter 6), such as the mean annual income of waiters or the mean time required to assemble cellular telephones. We can also use the theorem to test claims made about population parameters (see Chapter 7). We can, for example, test the claim that a new computer reduces the mean waiting time of bank customers.

5.7 EXERCISES   BASIC CONCEPTS

1. A large normally distributed population has a mean of 50 and a standard deviation of 10.
   a. Find the probability that a randomly selected score is between 50 and 53.
   b. If a sample of size $n = 36$ is randomly selected, find the probability that the sample mean $\bar{x}$ will be between 50 and 53.
2. A large normally distributed population has a mean of 150 and a standard deviation of 20.
   a. Find the probability that a randomly selected score is between 150 and 155.
   b. If a sample of size $n = 100$ is randomly selected, find the probability that the sample mean $\bar{x}$ will be between 150 and 155.
3. A large normally distributed population has a mean of 4.50 and a standard deviation of 1.05.
   a. Find the probability that a randomly selected score is less than 5.00.
   b. If a sample of size 40 is randomly selected, find the probability that the sample mean is less than 5.00.
4. A large normally distributed population has a mean of 640 and a standard deviation of 53.
   a. Find the probability that a randomly selected score is greater than 630.
   b. If a sample of size 65 is randomly selected, find the probability that the sample mean is greater than 630.
5. Car batteries are manufactured by Telektron with a mean life of 40 months, standard deviation of 6 months, and a distribution that is approximately normal.
   a. Find the probability that a single battery will have a life between 34 months and 46 months.
   b. If you randomly select and test 5 batteries, find the probability that their mean life will be between 34 months and 46 months.
6. A study of the time (in hours) college freshmen use to study each week found that the mean is 7.06 h and the standard deviation is 5.32 h (based on data from *The American Freshman*). If 55 freshmen are randomly selected, find the probability that their mean weekly study time exceeds 7.00 h.
7. A study of the time high school students spend working each week at a job found that the mean is 10.7 h and the standard deviation is 11.2 h (based on data from the National Federation of State High School Associations). If 42 high school students are randomly selected, find the probability that their mean weekly work time is less than 12.0 h.

8. The ages of U.S. commercial aircraft have a mean of 13.0 years and a standard deviation of 7.9 years (based on data from Aviation Data Services). If the Federation Aviation Administration randomly selects 35 commercial aircraft for special stress tests, find the probability that the mean age of this sample group is greater than 15.0 years.

9. A marketing firm for the Key Western Resort has conducted a market survey of guests and makes the claim that on average, guests spend $1850 with a standard deviation of $350. Assume that nothing is known about the nature of the distribution of the amounts spent.

    a.   Is it possible to find the probability that a single guest will spend between $1500 and $2200?

    b.   In checking the work done by the marketing firm, 32 guest records are randomly selected. Using $1850 and $350 for μ and σ respectively, find the probability of getting a sample mean between $1500 and $2200.

    c.   Assume that in randomly selecting 32 guest records, the sample mean of $1400 is obtained. Based on this result, would you believe the marketing firm's claim?

10. The times that managers spend on paperwork per day have a mean of 2.7 h and a standard deviation of 1.4 h (data from Adia Personnel Services). If a computer sales team randomly selects 75 managers, find the probability that this sample group has a mean less than 2.5 h.

11. The Grange Fertilizer Company fills 1-gal bottles of weed killer for lawns. The filling is a statistically stable process with a mean of 1.02 gal, a standard deviation of 0.06 gal, and a normal distribution.

    a.   What is the chance that a single bottle will have between 0.995 gal and 1.05 gal?

    b.   What is the chance that a single bottle will contain more than 1.10 gal?

    c.   If a shipment contains 10,000 bottles, how many are expected to contain more than 1.10 gal?

    d.   If you randomly select 8 bottles, what is the chance that their mean is between 0.995 gal and 1.05 gal?

    e.   If you randomly select 8 bottles, what is the chance that their mean is more than 1.10 gal?

12. At the beginning of this chapter, we described an electric motor with output voltages having a uniform distribution varying between 5.000 V and 9.000 V. A gauge monitors the voltage and the results constitute a statistically stable process with a mean of 7.000 V and a standard deviation of 1.154 V.

    a.   Find the probability that a single randomly selected measurement will be greater than 8.000 V. (Be careful to use the correct distribution.)

    b.   If you randomly select 40 measurements taken during an 8-hour shift (about 5 per hour), what is the probability that the mean of those 40 measurements is greater than 8.000 V?

In Exercises 13 and 14, assume that samples of size n are randomly selected from a finite population of size N. Also assume that $\sigma = 15$. Find the value of $\sigma_{\bar{x}}$. (Be sure to include the finite population correction factor whenever $n > 0.05N$.)

13. a. $N = 5000,$ $n = 200$
    b. $N = 12,000,$ $n = 1000$
    c. $N = 4000,$ $n = 500$
    d. $N = 8000,$ $n = 3000$
    e. $N = 1500,$ $n = 50$

14. a. $N = 750,$ $n = 50$
    b. $N = 673,$ $n = 32$
    c. $N = 866,$ $n = 73$
    d. $N = 50,000,$ $n = 10,000$
    e. $N = 8362,$ $n = 935$

In Exercises 15–18, be sure to check for the use of the finite population correction factor and use it whenever necessary.

15. In a study of health care costs for a population of 500 employees, it was found that the average family expense was $950 with a standard deviation of $275 and a distribution that is approximately normal.
    a. One family is randomly selected. Find the probability that their health care cost is between $900 and $1000.
    b. If 10 families are randomly selected, find the probability that their mean cost is between $900 and $1000.
    c. If 30 families are randomly selected, find the probability that their mean cost is between $900 and $1000.

16. A study involves a population of 300 women who are 6 ft tall and are between 18 and 24 years of age. This population has a mean weight of 131.5 lb and a standard deviation of 6.5 lb. If 50 members of this population are randomly selected, find the probability that the mean weight of this sample group is greater than 130.0 lb.

17. In a short production run of a stable process, 100 bus speedometers are tested at 50 mi/h and the sample mean is 48 mi/h with a standard deviation of 2 mi/h. If you randomly select and retest 35 of the speedometers, what is the probability that the mean reading (at 50 mi/h) will be 51 mi/h or higher?

18. In doing an economic impact study, a sociologist identifies a population of 1200 households with a mean annual income of $23,460 and a standard deviation of $3750. If 10% of these households are randomly selected for a more detailed survey, find the probability that the mean annual income for this sample group will fall between the acceptable limits of $23,000 and $24,000.

5.7 EXERCISES   BEYOND THE BASICS

19. A population consists of these scores:

    2   3   6   8   11   18

    a. Find μ and σ.
    b. List all samples of size $n = 2$.
    c. Find the population of all values of $\bar{x}$ by finding the mean of each sample from part b.
    d. Find the mean $\mu_{\bar{x}}$ and standard deviation $\sigma_{\bar{x}}$ for the population of sample means found in part c.
    e. Verify that

    $$\mu_{\bar{x}} = \mu \text{ and } \sigma_{\bar{x}} = \frac{\sigma}{\sqrt{n}} \sqrt{\frac{N - n}{N - 1}}$$

20. The value of $\sigma_{\bar{x}}$ can be used as a measure of how close sample means will be to the population mean μ. Assume that samples of size 36 are randomly selected from the population of IQ scores with $\mu = 100$ and $\sigma = 15$.
    a. What percentage of these sample means will fall within 2.5 IQ points of the mean?
    b. Between what two values (with the mean at the center) will 95% of these sample means fall?
21. A population has a standard deviation of 20. Samples of size n are taken randomly and the means of the samples are computed.
    a. What happens to the standard error of the mean if the sample size is increased from 100 to 400?
    b. What happens to the standard error of the mean if the sample size is decreased from 64 to 16?
22. a. Assume that a population is infinite. Find the probability that the mean of a sample of 100 differs from the population mean by more than $\sigma/4$.
    b. A sample of size 50 is randomly selected from a population of size N, with the result that the standard error of the mean is one-tenth the value of the population standard deviation. Find the size of the population.

5.8   AN APPLICATION OF THE CENTRAL LIMIT THEOREM: THE $\bar{x}$ CONTROL CHART WITH σ KNOWN

In Section 5.4 we discussed how to determine whether a population or a process is normal. For a process (with known σ), we developed the run chart for individual observations by including $\mu + 3\sigma$ and $\mu - 3\sigma$ as upper and lower control limits in a control chart. The formal name for such a chart is *control chart for individual values (when σ is known)*. In that section we considered an example of filling 12-oz cans of cola in a statistically stable process with $\mu = 12.0$ oz and $\sigma = 0.4$ oz. Figure 5.16(a) illustrated a sample of 40 values that were taken every two minutes. We then simulated a shift of the process and plotted 15 more points (shown in Fig. 5.16b) that corresponded to $\mu = 12.5$ oz and $\sigma = 0.4$ oz. We didn't detect the shift until after the eighth can was observed under the shifted conditions.

We will now show how to use the central limit theorem to make a control chart that is more efficient than the control chart for individual values. We will develop a **control chart for means** in which the points represent sample *means* instead of individual values. In particular, we will change our testing process from one of measuring a single can every 2 minutes to measuring 5 cans in 10 minutes and then finding the mean amount in those 5 cans. We will then make a run chart, but we will plot the mean for the 5 cans (instead of the amounts in the individual cans). To complete our control chart for $\bar{x}$, we need to include the control limits of $\mu_{\bar{x}} + 3\sigma_{\bar{x}}$ and $\mu_{\bar{x}} - 3\sigma_{\bar{x}}$. These limits represent deviations of plus and minus three standard deviations of $\bar{x}$. Using the central limit theorem, we get $\mu_{\bar{x}} = \mu = 12.0$ oz and $\sigma_{\bar{x}} = \sigma/\sqrt{n} = 0.4/\sqrt{5} = 0.1789$ oz. With these values, the upper and lower control limits become

$$\mu_{\bar{x}} + 3\sigma_{\bar{x}} = 12.0 + 3(0.1789) = 12.5367 \text{ oz}$$
$$\mu_{\bar{x}} - 3\sigma_{\bar{x}} = 12.0 - 3(0.1789) = 11.4633 \text{ oz}$$

FIGURE 5.31
Control Charts for Cola Cans with $\mu = 12.0$ oz

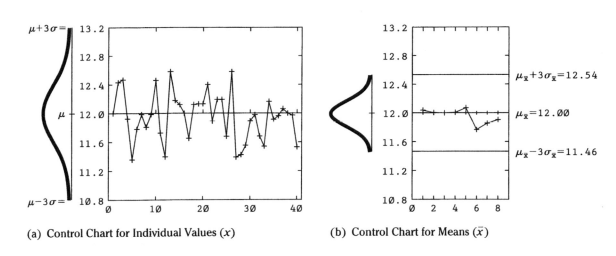

(a) Control Chart for Individual Values (x)   (b) Control Chart for Means ($\bar{x}$)

(When we constructed the control chart in Section 5.4 using individual values, we got control limits of 13.2 oz and 10.8 oz.) Table 5.2 consists of 8 simulated samples of 5 cans each.

Figure 5.31(a) has the 40 individual cans plotted on a control chart for individual values x, and Fig. 5.31(b) is the control chart for means $\bar{x}$. *Important:* Each control chart includes upper and lower limits that are three standard deviations away from the mean, but we know from the central limit theorem that the standard deviation for $\bar{x}$ is smaller than that for x. This explains why the upper and lower control limits are closer together in the $\bar{x}$ chart.

Again, both control charts of Fig. 5.31 show the process to be in statistical control around $\mu = 12.0$ oz, where we want it.

Listed below are 15 simulated values that result when the process is shifted to be out of our desired statistical control; the shifted values come from a shifted process in which $\mu = 12.5$ oz and $\sigma = 0.4$ oz. We have configured these new values to conform to Table 5.2.

Figure 5.32(a) includes a plot of the 15 individual cans, and Fig. 5.32(b) is a plot of the 3 sample means $\bar{x}$. *Note:* When using the individual-values control chart, it took 8 cans before we were able to detect the shift; but with the control chart for means, we can detect the shift with the first point representing 5 cans. This is no accident. In general, a control chart for means will detect out-of-control patterns (shifts, trends, and so on) much faster than a control chart for individual values.

Shifted Process ($\mu = 12.5$ oz)

SAMPLE	INDIVIDUAL CAN CONTENTS (x)	MEAN OF THE 5 CANS ($\bar{x}$)
1	12.63 12.50 12.72 13.08 12.38	$\bar{x}_1 = 12.662$
2	12.37 12.54 12.31 11.76 12.33	$\bar{x}_2 = 12.262$
3	12.56 13.21 11.89 12.50 11.59	$\bar{x}_3 = 12.350$

FIGURE 5.32
Control Charts for Cola Cans with $\mu = 12.5$ oz

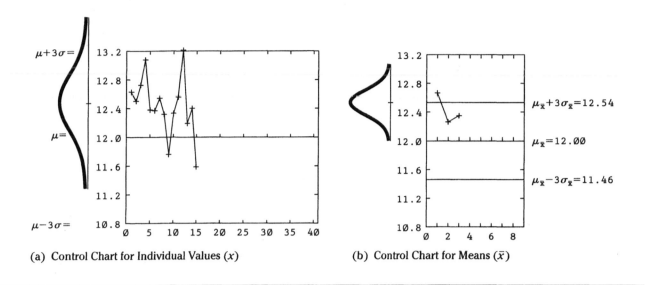

(a) Control Chart for Individual Values (x)   (b) Control Chart for Means ($\bar{x}$)

To see why the means detect the shift faster than the individual values, first note that when the process mean shifted from 12.0 oz to 12.5 oz, the individual values shifted by 0.5 oz, and this amount converts to 1.25 standard deviations, as shown below.

$$\frac{\text{shift amount}}{\text{standard deviation of } x} = \frac{0.5}{0.4} = 1.25 \text{ standard deviations for individual values}$$

When the process mean shifts from 12.0 oz to 12.5 oz, however, the sample *means* shift by an amount equivalent to 2.8 standard deviations. See the following calculation.

$$\frac{\text{shift amount}}{\text{standard deviation of } \bar{x}} = \frac{0.5}{0.1789} = 2.8 \text{ standard deviations for means}$$

TABLE 5.2
Statistically Stable Process ($\mu = 12.0$ oz)

SAMPLE	INDIVIDUAL CAN CONTENTS (x)	MEAN OF THE 5 CANS ($\bar{x}$)
1	12.00 12.43 12.47 11.92 11.36	$\bar{x}_1 = 12.036$
2	11.78 11.98 11.81 11.99 12.46	$\bar{x}_2 = 12.004$
3	11.72 11.40 12.58 12.18 12.12	$\bar{x}_3 = 12.000$
4	12.00 11.65 12.12 12.13 12.13	$\bar{x}_4 = 12.006$
5	12.40 11.89 12.19 12.19 11.68	$\bar{x}_5 = 12.070$
6	12.58 11.39 11.42 11.55 11.89	$\bar{x}_6 = 11.766$
7	11.98 11.68 11.54 12.16 11.91	$\bar{x}_7 = 11.854$
8	11.96 12.06 12.00 11.97 11.53	$\bar{x}_8 = 11.904$

The same shift of 0.5 oz converts to 1.25 standard deviations for individual values and 2.8 for means, so the means attribute much greater significance to the difference. Consequently, the control chart for means should detect a point beyond the control limits much faster than the control chart for individual values. The control chart for means is therefore more efficient in the sense that it will detect points beyond the control limits sooner than the control chart for individual values.

As the sample size increases, the sample mean $\bar{x}$ will tend to be closer and closer to the true population mean μ. Also, sample means tend to vary less than individual sample scores. As a result, a shift in $\bar{x}$ is more significant than a shift in an individual score x. The sample means are therefore better sensors for detecting a shift in the value of μ. As the sample size n increases, the ability to detect a shift in μ also increases. Statisticians refer to this ability to detect a shift in μ as the *power* of the procedure. This reflects a principle that should be somewhat intuitively clear: As the size of a sample increases, it becomes easier to determine how the population behaves. We will explore this concept in greater detail in Chapters 7 and 8.

5.8 EXERCISES   BASIC CONCEPTS

1. The plastic door handles used in a car must have a mean breaking strength of 100 lb with a standard deviation of 5 lb. Listed below are the breaking strengths for a random sample consisting of $n = 6$ handles selected every 4 hours. Find the 5 sample means and then construct a control chart for means. Use the control chart to determine whether the process is statistically stable. Assume that the distribution of the breaking strengths is normal.

SAMPLE	BREAKING STRENGTH (lb)					
1	95	102	105	94	99	107
2	92	103	101	98	100	104
3	94	97	95	105	102	101
4	106	104	100	98	103	108
5	110	101	97	94	102	100

2. The manufacturing of microchips for computers involves many processes, each critical for successful production. Several machines may perform the same process so that production proceeds more rapidly. Each machine usually has its own separate control chart, resulting in hundreds of control charts on means. Listed at the top of the following page are simulated sample data for two machines, both of which plate silicon nitride as a film 60 microns (millionths of a meter) thick with a standard deviation of 2 microns. In this plating process, several hundred chips are plated, but 3 will be randomly selected and measured for thickness. Calculate the sample means and include them in a control chart for means; then use the chart to determine whether the process is statistically stable for each of the two machines. (The numbers in parentheses identify the particular sample.)

MACHINE 1		MACHINE 2	
(1) 60 64 57	(5) 58 63 56	(9) 62 61 64	(13) 58 62 61
(2) 62 58 56	(6) 58 57 60	(10) 59 61 63	(14) 63 64 62
(3) 59 60 58	(7) 61 63 60	(11) 61 65 63	(15) 61 59 63
(4) 61 62 63	(8) 59 60 58	(12) 63 61 60	(16) 60 62 63

3. A metal lathe is used to machine power steering shafts that are to be installed in the front ends of farm tractors. They are supposed to be 1.000 in. in diameter with a standard deviation of 0.010 in. and a distribution that is normal. Listed below (in order by rows) are the diameters of 24 shafts randomly selected in 24 different hours. Construct the control chart for individual values of the diameters and use it to determine whether the process is statistically stable.

1.010	1.020	0.995	1.005	0.990	0.980
1.015	1.010	1.005	0.985	1.000	1.015
1.010	0.995	1.005	1.000	1.015	1.020
0.995	1.010	1.020	1.020	1.025	1.015

4. Refer to the same data used in Exercise 3. Treat each row as a sample of $n = 6$ measurements and find the 4 sample means. Construct the control chart for means and use it to determine whether the process is statistically stable.

5.8 EXERCISES | BEYOND THE BASICS

5. Use Minitab to simulate the filling of 12-oz cola cans. Enter the following commands to obtain a sample of 5 fill levels randomly selected from a statistically stable and normally distributed process.

```
RANDOM K = 5 C1;
NORMAL MU = 12.0 SIGMA = 0.4.
PRINT C1
```

Now repeat the above procedure 9 more times to obtain a total of 10 samples of 5 scores each.
a. Construct a control chart for individual values and identify any of the 50 individual values that were beyond the control limits. (If there are any such points, they would lead us to conclude that the process is not statistically stable when, in fact, we know it really is stable by the procedure we're using to generate the data.)
b. Construct a control chart for means ($n = 5$) and identify any points that are beyond the control limits.
c. Now generate 10 samples of 5 scores each by using these commands that result in a shift of the mean:

```
RANDOM K = 5 C2;
NORMAL MU = 12.5 SIGMA 0.4.
PRINT C2
```

(continued)

d. Construct a control chart for individual values using the data from part *c* and identify any values that are beyond the control limits.

e. Construct a control chart for means using the 10 samples of 5 scores each that were generated in part *c* and identify any points that are beyond the control limits.

f. Compare the control charts for the first data set with the control charts for the shifted data set.

Vocabulary List

Define and give an example of each term.

normal distribution
uniform distribution
density curve
standard normal distribution
z score
standard score
control chart for individual values when σ is known
control limits
continuity correction
central limit theorem
standard error of the mean
finite population correction factor
control chart for means when σ is known

Review

The main concern of this chapter is the concept of a *normal distribution,* the most important of all continuous probability distributions. Many real and natural occurrences yield data that are normally distributed or can be approximated by a normal distribution. The normal distribution, which appears bell-shaped when graphed, can be described algebraically by Formula 5.1, but the complexity of that equation usually forces us to use a table of values instead.

Table A.2 represents the *standard normal distribution,* which has a mean of 0 and a standard deviation of 1. This table relates deviations away from the mean with areas under the curve. Since the total area under the curve is 1, those areas correspond to probability values.

In the early sections of this chapter, we worked with the standard procedures used in applying Table A.2 to a variety of situations. In Section 5.3 we saw that Table A.2 can be applied to nonstandard normal distributions (that is, μ and σ are not 0 and 1, respectively). We were able to find the number of standard deviations that a score x is away from the mean μ by computing the z score: $z = (x - \mu)/\sigma$.

In Section 5.4 we saw how to use a histogram in determining whether a population has a normal distribution. We also saw how to determine whether

IMPORTANT FORMULAS

Standard normal distribution has $\mu = 0$ and $\sigma = 1$.

Standard score or z score:

$$z = \frac{x - \mu}{\sigma}$$

Prerequisites for approximating binomial by normal distribution:

$$np \geq 5 \qquad nq \geq 5$$

Parameters used when approximating binomial by normal distribution:

$$\mu = np \qquad \sigma = \sqrt{npq}$$

Parameters used when applying central limit theorem:

$$\mu_{\bar{x}} = \mu$$

$$\sigma_{\bar{x}} = \frac{\sigma}{\sqrt{n}} \qquad \text{(standard error of the mean)}$$

$$\sigma_{\bar{x}} = \frac{\sigma}{\sqrt{n}} \sqrt{\frac{N - n}{N - 1}} \qquad \text{(used when } n > 0.05N\text{)}$$

$$z = \frac{\bar{x} - \mu_{\bar{x}}}{\sigma_{\bar{x}}}$$

Control chart for individual values:

$$\text{Upper control limit (UCL)} = \mu + 3\sigma$$

$$\text{Lower control limit (LCL)} = \mu - 3\sigma$$

Control chart for means:

$$\text{Upper control limit (UCL)} = \mu_{\bar{x}} + 3\sigma_{\bar{x}} \quad \text{or} \quad \mu + 3\frac{\sigma}{\sqrt{n}}$$

$$\text{Lower control limit (LCL)} = \mu_{\bar{x}} - 3\sigma_{\bar{x}} \quad \text{or} \quad \mu - 3\frac{\sigma}{\sqrt{n}}$$

---

process data have a normal distribution: We first use control charts for individual values (a run chart with control limits at $\mu \pm 3\sigma$) to test for stability and, if the process is found to be statistically stable, we can treat the data as a population and construct a histogram that reveals whether the distribution is normal.

In Section 5.5 we considered real and practical examples as we converted from a nonstandard to a standard normal distribution. In Section 5.6 we saw that we can sometimes approximate a binomial probability distribution by a normal distribution. If both $np \geq 5$ and $nq \geq 5$, the binomial random variable x is approximately normally distributed with the mean and standard deviation given as $\mu = np$ and $\sigma = \sqrt{npq}$. Since the binomial probability distribution deals with discrete data while the normal distribution deals with continuous data, we introduced the *continuity correction,* which should be used in normal approximations to binomial distributions.

In Section 5.7 we considered the distribution of sample means that can come from normal or nonnormal populations. The *central limit theorem* asserts that the distribution of sample means $\bar{x}$ (based on random samples of size n) will, as n increases, approach a normal distribution with mean μ and standard deviation $\sigma/\sqrt{n}$. This means that if samples are of size n where $n > 30$, we can approximate the distribution of those sample means by a normal distribution. The *standard error of the mean* is $\sigma/\sqrt{n}$ as long as the population is infinite or the sample size is not more than 5% of the population or process being considered. But if n exceeds 5% of the population or process size (N), then the standard error of the mean must be adjusted by the *finite population correction factor* with $\sigma/\sqrt{n}$ multiplied by $\sqrt{(N-n)/(N-1)}$. Figure 5.29 summarizes these concepts.

Finally, in Section 5.8 we developed control charts for means (when σ is known) that are generally quicker to detect out-of-control patterns than are control charts for individual values.

Since the basic concepts of this chapter serve as critical prerequisites for the following chapters, it would be wise to master these ideas and methods now.

Review Exercises

1. Household incomes of VCR owners have a mean of $41,182 and a standard deviation of $19,990 (based on data from Nielsen Media Research). If 125 households with VCRs are randomly selected, find the probability that the mean income is between $40,000 and $45,000.

2. The heights of adult males are normally distributed with a mean of 69.0 in. and a standard deviation of 2.8 in. (based on data from the National Health Survey, USDHEW publication 79-1659). If 95% of all males satisfy a minimum height requirement for police officers, what is that requirement?

3. An insurance company finds that the ages of motorcyclists killed in crashes are normally distributed with a mean of 26.9 years and a standard deviation of 8.4 years (based on data from the U.S. Department of Transportation).
   a. If we randomly select one such motorcyclist, find the probability that he or she was under 25.
   b. If we randomly select 40 such motorcyclists, find the probability that their mean age was under 25.

4. Delta Airlines recently reported that its on-time rate was 82% (based on data from the U.S. Department of Transportation). Find the probability that among 500 randomly selected Delta flights, fewer than 400 arrive on time.

5. The Reliable Car Rental agency records data for the times required to clean and service cars in preparation for the next customer. These times are found to be normally distributed with a mean of 30 min and a standard deviation of 8 min. This agency has 250 cars.
   a. If a single car is randomly selected, find the probability that the service time exceeds 35 min.
   b. If 10 cars are randomly selected, find the probability that the mean service time exceeds 35 min.
   c. If 30 cars are randomly selected, find the probability that the mean service time exceeds 35 min.

6. Errors from voltage meter readings are normally distributed with a mean of 0 V and a standard deviation of 1 V. (The errors can be positive or negative.) One reading is randomly selected. Find the probability that the error is
   a. Between 0 V and 1.42 V.
   b. Greater than −1.05 V.
   c. Between 0.50 V and 1.50 V.
7. A study conducted by the International Council of Shopping Centers revealed that 4% of those who visit a mall or shopping center spend more than 3 hours there. If 850 people are randomly selected among those who visit malls or shopping centers, find the probability that at least 50 of them spend more than 3 hours there.
8. An employer finds that among employees categorized as level I, the numbers of years of formal education are normally distributed with a mean of 13.20 years and a standard deviation of 2.95 years.
   a. For a person randomly selected from this group, find the probability that he or she has between 13.20 and 13.50 years of education.
   b. For a person randomly selected from this group, find the probability that he or she has at least 12.00 years of education.
   c. Find the first quartile, Q_1. That is, find the value separating the lowest 25% from the highest 75%.
   d. If the employer is considering a minimum-education requirement as a criterion for upgrading employees to level II, how many years of education would be required if only the top 5% of this group qualified?
   e. If 35 employees are randomly selected from this level I group, find the probability that the mean of their years of education is at least 12.00.
9. A discount car-painting facility finds that on 24% of its cars, the paint runs. Assuming that the process is statistically stable, find the probability that in a fleet job of 100 cars, 40 or fewer have paint runs.
10. A task consists of installing an electric harness under the dashboard of a General Motors car. Assume that the times for this task are normally distributed with a mean of 100 seconds and a standard deviation of 18 seconds.
   a. If one time is randomly selected, find the probability that it will be between 100 s and 120 s.
   b. If one time is randomly selected, find the probability that it will be more than 60 s.
   c. If one time is randomly selected, find the probability that it will be between 80 s and 130 s.
   d. If 10 times are randomly selected, find the probability that their mean is between 80 s and 130 s.
   e. Find the time that is P_{80}, the 80th percentile.
11. In a study of 600 checkout times at a Caldor department store in upstate New York, the mean is found to be 1.80 min and the standard deviation is found to be 0.60 min. If 32 of these checkout times are randomly selected, find the probability that their mean is between 1.90 min and 2.00 min.
12. According to data from the American Medical Association, 10% of us are left-handed. In a freshman class of 200 students, find the probability that
   a. exactly 9 are left-handed.
   b. fewer than 9 are left-handed.
13. When Lopez Auto Parts receives an order, it then delivers the item to the front counter. One measure of quality is the speed with which the item reaches the

front counter after the order has been placed. To monitor efficiency, a manager places orders for 6 randomly selected items each day over a 7-day period. The times to reach the front counter are given in Table 5.3. Historically, these times have had a mean of 5.8 min, a standard deviation of 1.6 min, and a normal distribution. Use the data to construct a control chart for individual values and use it to determine whether the process is statistically stable.

TABLE 5.3
Times to Reach the Front Counter
(in min)

			DAY			
1	2	3	4	5	6	7
3.6	6.5	9.6	5.5	7.4	3.9	5.4
6.2	3.9	2.9	6.4	6.9	5.3	6.2
7.4	4.1	7.5	4.6	8.7	7.0	4.4
4.4	5.9	3.6	5.8	1.8	9.4	3.8
8.1	7.1	6.2	6.4	2.4	5.8	4.9
5.9	9.2	7.0	8.4	7.0	6.8	5.2

14. Refer to the same data in Exercise 13. Find the mean time for each day and construct a control chart for means; then use it to determine whether the process is statistically stable.

Computer Projects

1. a. Enter the following Minitab commands to produce 36 randomly generated numbers and to obtain a histogram for them.

   ```
   MTB > RANDOM 36 C1;
   SUBC> INTEGER 0 9.
   MTB > PRINT C1
   MTB > HISTOGRAM C1
   ```

   b. Enter the following Minitab commands to create 36 lists of random numbers, each with 30 entries. Sample statistics will be calculated for those 36 lists and the results (including the means) will be displayed.

   ```
   MTB > RANDOM 30 C1-C36;
   SUBC> INTEGER 0 9.
   MTB > DESCRIBE C1-C36
   ```

   Use Minitab's HISTOGRAM command to generate a histogram of the 36 sample means.

   c. Compare the results from parts *a* and *b*.

2. Refer to the home living areas included in the real estate data set in Appendix B. Use Minitab to enter the data and find the mean and standard deviation, then generate a histogram. Based on the histogram, do the scores appear to come from a population with values that are normally distributed?

HAS THE SECURITY OF THE TEST BEEN COMPROMISED?

A company gives prospective employees an aptitude test that produces scores that are normally distributed with a mean of 100 and a standard deviation of 15. (The company has a policy of hiring only those applicants with scores above 110.) The company has only one version of this test, and there are concerns that disclosed information about the test can help future applicants achieve higher scores. The test administrator reports that the test scores for the last 36 applicants have a mean of 106 and a standard deviation of 15.

a. Calculate the probability that a group of 36 randomly selected applicants will have test scores with a mean of 106 or greater.

b. Based on the result from part *a*, does there seem to be a reason for concern?

c. The following Minitab commands simulate a sample of 36 scores drawn from a population with a mean of 100 and a standard deviation of 15; the sample mean will be displayed. Repeat these commands until you have a good sense for how much the sample mean typically varies. Is 106 within the scope of typical means?

```
MTB > RANDOM 36 C1;
SUBC> NORMAL mu = 100 sigma = 15.
MTB > MEAN C1
```

d. Write a brief report summarizing your findings and your conclusion about the implications drawn from the results of the last 36 applicants (with a mean of 106 and a standard deviation of 16).

r after the order has been placed. To monitor efficiency, a man-
orders for 6 randomly selected items each day over a 7-day period.
reach the front counter are given in Table 5.3. Historically, these
ad a mean of 5.8 min, a standard deviation of 1.6 min, and a normal
Use the data to construct a control chart for individual values and use
ne whether the process is statistically stable.

3

each the Front Counter

	DAY			
3	4	5	6	7
6	5.5	7.4	3.9	5.4
9	6.4	6.9	5.3	6.2
5	4.6	8.7	7.0	4.4
6	5.8	1.8	9.4	3.8
2	6.4	2.4	5.8	4.9
0	8.4	7.0	6.8	5.2

he same data in Exercise 13. Find the mean time for each day and
a control chart for means; then use it to determine whether the
statistically stable.

r Projects

the following Minitab commands to produce 36 randomly generated
ers and to obtain a histogram for them.

```
> RANDOM 36 C1;
> INTEGER 0 9.
> PRINT C1
> HISTOGRAM C1
```

he following Minitab commands to create 36 lists of random num-
ach with 30 entries. Sample statistics will be calculated for those 36
d the results (including the means) will be displayed.

```
> RANDOM 30 C1-C36;
> INTEGER 0 9.
> DESCRIBE C1-C36
```

nitab's HISTOGRAM command to generate a histogram of the 36
means.
re the results from parts *a* and *b*.
home living areas included in the real estate data set in Appendix
ab to enter the data and find the mean and standard deviation,
e a histogram. Based on the histogram, do the scores appear to
population with values that are normally distributed?

imates and
mple Sizes

er introduces fundamental methods for
meters. We also briefly discuss sam-

OF MEANS

iterval are used to estimate the value
d of determining the sample size is
oution is introduced.

OF PROPORTIONS

iterval are used to estimate the value
method of determining the sample size

S OF VARIANCES

interval are used to estimate the value
ethod of determining sample size is

How Old Is the U.S. Commercial Aircraft Fleet?

The age of the U.S. commercial aircraft fleet is of great concern to many different individuals and organizations. It concerns aircraft manufacturers such as Boeing or Lockheed because they would like to build and supply new planes to replace the older ones now in use. Airline maintenance crews are concerned because they must constantly repair and replace older and worn parts. Federal Aviation Administration officials are concerned because older aircraft are more susceptible to failures arising from such factors as metal fatigue and worn equipment. The airline companies themselves are concerned because they know that commercial aircraft do not last forever and it's quite expensive to replace them. Passengers are concerned because they generally prefer newer aircraft with older pilots, instead of older aircraft with newer pilots.

When 40 U.S. commercial aircraft are randomly selected, they are found to have the following ages in years (based on data from Aviation Data Services).

3.2	22.6	23.1	16.9	0.4	6.6	12.5	22.8
26.3	8.1	13.6	17.0	21.3	15.2	18.7	11.5
4.9	5.3	5.8	20.6	23.1	24.7	3.6	12.4
27.3	22.5	3.9	7.0	16.2	24.1	0.1	2.1
7.7	10.5	23.4	0.7	15.8	6.3	11.9	16.8

$n = 40$
$\bar{x} = 13.41$
$s = 8.28$

Using only these sample results, we want to estimate the mean age of all U.S. commercial aircraft in order to determine if there is justifiable cause for concern. What is the best estimate of that mean age, and how accurate is it? In this chapter we develop methods for answering these questions.

6.1 OVERVIEW

In Chapter 1 we differentiated between the descriptive and inferential branches of statistics: With descriptive statistics we attempt to describe or understand known data, whereas with inferential statistics we use sample data to form inferences or conclusions about populations and stable processes. In Chapter 2 we considered ways of describing population or process data by using graphs (such as histograms or run charts) and measures (such as means or standard deviations). In Chapter 3 we discussed the basic principles of probability. In Chapter 4 we presented the concept of a probability distribution and considered a variety of *discrete* probability distributions, including the important binomial probability distribution. In Chapter 5 we examined the normal distribution, an extremely important *continuous* probability distribution; with this topic we began the transition to inferential statistics, which allows us to make inferences or form conclusions about populations and stable processes. In this and the following chapters we use methods of inferential statistics quite extensively.

Before using sample data to form inferences about populations and processes, we should give some thought to the methods of collecting those samples in the first place. Sampling and data collection usually require more time, effort, and money than does statistical analysis of the data. Careful planning minimizes the expenditure of precious resources. We should be especially careful with the method of sampling. The sample size must be large enough for the required purposes; however, *even large samples may be totally worthless if the data have been carelessly collected.* This is sometimes a problem among people who often believe incorrectly that large samples are good samples.

There are different types of sampling procedures. **Random sampling** gives each member of the population or process an equal chance of being selected. Random sampling is also called representative or proportionate sampling, because all groups of the population should be proportionately represented in the sample. Random sampling is very different from haphazard or unsystematic sampling. Much effort and planning must be invested to avoid any bias. One problem is that it's often difficult to identify a list of all members of the population. For example, using telephone directories would eliminate people with unlisted numbers or no telephones. Ignoring any segment of the population could produce misleading results.

In addition to random sampling, there are other methods, such as stratified, systematic, cluster, and convenience sampling. With **stratified sampling,** we first classify a population into at least two different strata (or classes) that share the same characteristics (such as sex), and we draw a sample from each stratum. With **systematic sampling,** we select some starting point and then select every *k*th (such as every 50th) member. With **cluster sampling,** we first divide the population area into sections (such as city blocks), then randomly select a few of those sections, and then choose all the members from the selected sections. With **convenience sampling,** we simply use results that are readily available. In some cases results may be quite good; in other cases they may be seriously biased. Businesses use convenience sampling when they make extensive use of census data that the U.S. Bureau of the Census has already collected.

In analyzing results, it is often helpful to discuss two kinds of errors: sampling errors and nonsampling errors. **Sampling errors** result from the actual sampling process. They derive from such factors as the small size of the sample and the fact that no sample can be expected to represent perfectly the entire population. **Nonsampling errors** arise from external factors not related to sampling, such as poorly worded questions, defective measuring instruments, or improperly entered data.

A major topic of this chapter is the development of estimates of population parameters, including means, proportions, and variances. As one example, earlier we were given the ages of 40 U.S. commercial aircraft, and our objective is to use these sample data to estimate the mean age of *all* U.S. commercial aircraft. As another example, Young and Rubicam Advertising conducts tests of commercials by first carefully selecting a sample of consumers. Their objective is to use the sample results to estimate the proportion of the entire consumer population that reacts positively to a particular commercial. In this chapter we see how to obtain such estimates and to assess their accuracy. We also develop methods for determining optimum sample sizes.

6.2   ESTIMATES AND SAMPLE SIZES OF MEANS

Consider the 40 ages of U.S. commercial aircraft given at the beginning of the chapter. Using only these sample scores, we want to estimate the mean age of *all* U.S. commercial aircraft. We could use statistics such as the sample median, midrange, or mode as estimates of the population mean μ, but the sample mean $\bar{x}$ usually provides the best estimate of a population or process mean. This is not simply an intuitive conclusion. It is based on careful study and analysis of the distributions of the different statistics that could be used as estimators. (An **estimator** is simply a likely value or range of values for some population or process parameter.) For many populations and processes, the distribution of sample means $\bar{x}$ tends to be more consistent than other sample statistics. That is, use $\bar{x}$ to estimate the population mean μ, and your errors are likely to be less than they would be with other sample statistics such as the median or the mode. For all populations and stable processes, we say that the sample mean $\bar{x}$ is an *unbiased* estimator of the population mean μ, meaning that the distribution of $\bar{x}$ tends to center about the value of μ. For these reasons, we will use $\bar{x}$ as the best estimate of μ. Because $\bar{x}$ is a single value that corresponds to a point on the number scale, we call it a point estimate.

> **DEFINITION**
>
> A *point estimate* is a likely single value (or point) of a population parameter.

EXAMPLE   Use the sample data given at the beginning of the chapter to find the best point estimate of the population mean μ of the ages of all U.S. commercial aircraft.

SOLUTION   The sample mean $\bar{x}$ is the best point estimate of μ, and for the given data we have $\bar{x} = 13.41$ years. The best point estimate of the population mean μ of all U.S. commercial aircraft is therefore 13.41 years.

In this example we see that 13.41 years is our *best* point estimate of μ, but we have no indication of just how *good* that estimate is. Suppose we had only the first two scores, 3.2 years and 22.6 years. Their mean of 12.90 years would be the best point estimate of μ, but we should not expect this best estimate to be very good, because it is based on such a small sample of only two scores. In addition to the point estimate, statisticians have developed another type of estimate that does reveal how good it is. This second type of estimate, called a confidence interval or an interval estimate, consists of a range (or an interval) of values instead of just a single value.

> **DEFINITION**
>
> A *confidence interval* (or an *interval estimate*) is a range (or an interval) of values that is likely to contain the population parameter.

Here's an example of a confidence interval that is based on the same sample data of 40 aircraft ages given earlier:

> The 95% degree of confidence interval estimate of the population mean μ is 10.84 years $< \mu <$ 15.98 years.

Before we describe how to construct such an estimate, note that it consists of a *range* of values and that it is associated with a degree of confidence. We interpret this confidence interval as follows: If we were to select many different samples of size 40 from the given population of U.S. commercial aircraft and construct similar confidence intervals, in the long run 95% of those intervals would actually contain the value of μ.

We will now describe the process for determining a confidence interval, such as the one given above. We begin with the following definition.

> **DEFINITION**
>
> The *degree of confidence* is the probability $1 - \alpha$ that the parameter is contained in the confidence interval. (The probability is often expressed as the equivalent percentage value.) The degree of confidence is also referred to as the *level of confidence* or the *confidence coefficient*. The most common choices for the degree of confidence are 0.95, 0.99, and 0.90, but other values can be used.

This definition uses the Greek letter α (alpha) to describe a probability that corresponds to an area. Refer to Fig. 6.1, where the probability α is divided equally between two tails of the standard normal distribution.

Recall from the central limit theorem that sample means $\bar{x}$ tend to be normally distributed, as in Fig. 6.1. It's *likely* that sample means will fall within the unshaded region of such a figure, and it's *unlikely* that they will fall in the shaded area. From Fig. 6.1 we can see that there is a total probability of α that a sample mean will

FIGURE 6.1
Standard Normal Distribution

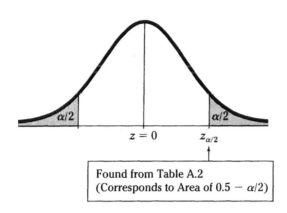

Found from Table A.2
(Corresponds to Area of $0.5 - \alpha/2$)

LARGE SAMPLE SIZE ISN'T GOOD ENOUGH

Biased sample data should not be used for inferences, no matter how large the sample is. In *Women and Love: A Cultural Revolution in Progress,* Shere Hite bases her conclusions about intimate relationships on 4500 replies received after mailing 100,000 questionnaires to various women's groups. A *random* sample of 4500 subjects would usually provide good results, but Hite's sample is biased. It is criticized for overrepresenting women who join groups and women who feel strongly about the issues addressed. Because Hite's sample is biased, her inferences are not valid, even though the sample size of 4500 might seem to be sufficiently large.

fall in either of the two shaded tails. From the rule of complements in Chapter 3, it follows that there is a probability of $1 - \alpha$ that a sample mean will fall within the unshaded region of Fig. 6.1. This is all somewhat abstract, so let's use some concrete numbers. Let's stipulate that $\alpha = 0.05$ (a very common choice). With $\alpha = 0.05$ in Fig. 6.1, there is an area of $\alpha/2 = 0.025$ in each of the two shaded tails, and an area of 0.95 in the unshaded middle region. If Fig. 6.1 is the distribution of sample means $\bar{x}$, then there is a probability of 0.95 that a sample mean will fall within the unshaded region, and it's unlikely (with a probability of only 0.05) that a sample mean will fall within either of the shaded tails. In the figure we also include the symbol $z_{\alpha/2}$, described as follows:

Notation
$z_{\alpha/2}$ **is the positive z score that separates an area of $\alpha/2$ in the right tail of the standard normal distribution.**

Because $z_{\alpha/2}$ is on the borderline separating sample means that are *likely* to occur from those that are *unlikely* to occur, it is often called a **critical score.**

 EXAMPLE If $\alpha = 0.05$, then $z_{\alpha/2} = 1.96$. That is, 1.96 is the standard z value that separates a right-tail region with an area of $0.05 \div 2$, or 0.025. We find $z_{\alpha/2}$ by noting that the region to its left (and bounded by the mean of $z = 0$) must be $0.5 - 0.025$, or 0.475. In Table A.2, an area of 0.4750 corresponds exactly to a z score of 1.96.

When we collect sets of sample data, such as the set of 40 aircraft ages, we can calculate $\bar{x}$, and those sample means are typically different from the population mean μ. We can think of those differences as errors. Using the $z_{\alpha/2}$ notation, we can now define the margin of error E as follows:

> **DEFINITION**
>
> When using sample data to estimate a population mean μ, we can obtain the *margin of error E* from Formula 6.1. There is a probability of α that a sample mean $\bar{x}$ will be in error (that is, will be different from μ) by more than *E*.

Formula 6.1
$$E = z_{\alpha/2} \cdot \frac{\sigma}{\sqrt{n}}$$

The calculation of the margin of error *E* as given in Formula 6.1 requires that you know the population standard deviation σ, but in reality it's rare to know σ when μ is not known. The following is a common practice.

If $n > 30$, we can replace σ by the *sample* standard deviation s in Formula 6.1.

If $n \leq 30$, the population must have a normal distribution and we must know σ to use Formula 6.1. [We will discuss small ($n \leq 30$) sample cases later in this section.]

Using the definition of the margin of error *E*, we can now identify the confidence interval for μ.

> **DEFINITION**
>
> The *confidence interval* (or *interval estimate*) *for the population mean* μ is given by $\bar{x} - E < \mu < \bar{x} + E$. [We will use this form for the confidence interval, but other equivalent forms are $\mu = \bar{x} \pm E$ and $(\bar{x} - E, \bar{x} + E)$.]

Once we know the sample mean $\bar{x}$ and have found the margin of error *E*, we can calculate the values of $\bar{x} - E$ and $\bar{x} + E$, which are called **confidence interval limits.**

EXAMPLE For the aircraft ages given earlier in this chapter, we have $n = 40$, $\bar{x} = 13.41$, and $s = 8.28$. For a 0.95 degree of confidence, use these statistics to find both of the following:

a. The margin of error *E*
b. The confidence interval for μ

SOLUTION a. The 0.95 degree of confidence implies that $\alpha = 0.05$, so that $z_{\alpha/2} = 1.96$. (See the previous example.)

$$E = z_{\alpha/2} \frac{\sigma}{\sqrt{n}} = 1.96 \cdot \frac{8.28}{\sqrt{40}} = 2.57$$

(Note that since σ is unknown but $n > 30$, we used $s = 8.28$ for the value of σ.)

b.   With $\bar{x}$ = 13.41 and E = 2.57, we get

$$\bar{x} - E < \mu < \bar{x} + E$$
$$13.41 - 2.57 < \mu < 13.41 + 2.57$$
$$10.84 < \mu < 15.98$$

Using the sample of 40 aircraft ages, the confidence interval for μ is 10.84 years < μ < 15.98 years, and this interval has a 0.95 degree of confidence. This means that if we were to select many different samples of size 40 and construct the confidence intervals as we did here, 95% of them would actually contain the value of μ.

Once we use sample data to find specific limits of $\bar{x} - E$ and $\bar{x} + E$, those limits either enclose the population mean μ or they do not, and we cannot determine whether they do or don't without knowing the true value of μ. It is incorrect to state that μ has a 95% chance of falling within the specific limits of 10.84 and 15.98, because μ is a constant, not a random variable, and either it will fall within those limits or it won't—and there's no probability involved in that. Although it's wrong to say that μ has a 95% chance of falling between these specific confidence interval limits, it is correct to say that in the long run, these methods will result in confidence intervals that will contain μ in 95% of the cases.

Suppose that in the preceding example the aircraft ages really come from a population with a true mean of 13.00 years. Then the confidence interval obtained from the given sample data does contain the population mean, because 13.00 is between 10.84 and 15.98. This is illustrated in Fig. 6.2 (see the first confidence interval graph).

FIGURE 6.2
Graph of Confidence Intervals. The graph shows confidence intervals, one of which does not contain μ. For 95% confidence intervals, we expect that among 100 such intervals, 5 will not contain μ = 13.00, while the other 95 will contain it.

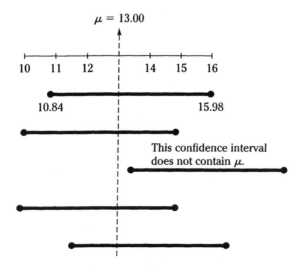

The basic idea underlying the construction of a confidence interval relates to the central limit theorem, which indicates that the distribution of sample means is approximately normal as long as the samples are large ($n > 30$). From the central limit theorem we also know that sample means have a mean of μ, while the standard deviation of means from samples of size n is $\sigma/\sqrt{n}$. That is,

$$\mu_{\bar{x}} = \mu$$

$$\sigma_{\bar{x}} = \frac{\sigma}{\sqrt{n}}$$

Because a z score is the number of standard deviations a value is away from the mean, it follows that $z_{\alpha/2}\, \sigma/\sqrt{n}$ represents a number of standard deviations away from μ. From our $z_{\alpha/2}$ notation and our margin of error E, we know that there is a probability of α that a sample mean will differ from the population mean by more than $E = z_{\alpha/2}\, \sigma/\sqrt{n}$. Conversely, there is a probability of $1 - \alpha$ that the sample mean $\bar{x}$ will be within $E = z_{\alpha/2}\, \sigma/\sqrt{n}$ of μ. Figure 6.3 illustrates this concept.

If $\bar{x}$ is within $E = z_{\alpha/2}\, \sigma/\sqrt{n}$ of the population mean μ, then μ must be between $\bar{x} - E$ and $\bar{x} + E$, and this is expressed in the general format of our confidence interval:

$$\bar{x} - E < \mu < \bar{x} + E$$

SMALL SAMPLE CASES AND THE STUDENT t DISTRIBUTION

Unfortunately, finding a confidence interval using Formula 6.1 requires either a large sample ($n > 30$) or a normally distributed population with a known value of σ. If we have a small sample ($n \leq 30$), intend to construct a confidence interval, and do not know σ, we can use the *Student t distribution* (see Table A.3) developed by William Gosset (1876–1937). Gosset was a Guinness Brewery employee who needed a distribution to use with small samples. The Irish brewery where he worked did not allow the publication of research results, so Gosset published under the pseudonym "Student." Factors such as cost and time often severely limit the size of a sample (as was the case for Gosset), so the normal distribution may not be an appropriate approximation of the distribution of means from small samples. As a result of those earlier experiments and studies of small samples, we can now use the Student t distribution instead.

If the distribution of a population is essentially normal, then the distribution of

$$t = \frac{\bar{x} - \mu}{s/\sqrt{n}}$$

is essentially a **Student t distribution** for all samples of size n. (The Student t distribution is often referred to as the **t distribution**.)

> **FIGURE 6.3**
> Distribution of Sample Means

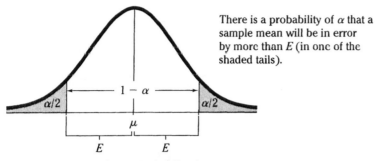

There is a probability of α that a sample mean will be in error by more than E (in one of the shaded tails).

There is a $1 - \alpha$ probability that a sample mean will be in error by less than E or $z_{\alpha/2}\sigma/\sqrt{n}$.

Table A.3 lists t scores along with corresponding areas denoted by α. We obtain values of $t_{\alpha/2}$ by locating the proper values for degrees of freedom in the left column and then proceeding across the corresponding row until we reach the number directly below the applicable value of α for two tails. Roughly stated, **degrees of freedom** correspond to the number of values that may vary after certain restrictions have been imposed on all values. For example, if 10 scores must total 50, we can freely assign values to the first 9 scores, but the 10th score would then be determined so that the sum of the 10 scores is 50. Therefore, 9 degrees of freedom are available. For the applications of this section, the number of degrees of freedom is simply the sample size minus 1.

$$\textbf{degrees of freedom} = n - 1$$

To use the Student t distribution, the distribution of the parent population must be essentially normal. The distribution does not have to be exactly normal, but if it has only one mode and is basically symmetric, we will generally get good results if we use the Student t distribution. If there is strong evidence that the population has a very nonnormal distribution, then nonparametric methods (see Chapter 15) should be used instead.

IMPORTANT PROPERTIES OF THE STUDENT *t* DISTRIBUTION

1. The Student t distribution is different for different sample sizes. (See Fig. 6.4 for the cases $n = 3$ and $n = 12$.)

2. The Student t distribution has the same general symmetric bell shape of the standard normal distribution, but it reflects the greater variability (with wider distributions) that is expected with small samples.

3. The Student t distribution has a mean of $t = 0$ (just as the standard normal distribution has a mean of $z = 0$).

4. The standard deviation of the Student t distribution varies with the sample size, but it is greater than 1 (unlike the standard normal distribution, which has $\sigma = 1$).

5. As the sample size n gets larger, the Student t distribution gets closer to the standard normal distribution. For values of $n > 30$, the differences are so small that we can use the critical z values instead of developing a much larger table of critical t values. (The values in the bottom row of Table A.3 are equal to the corresponding critical z values from the standard normal distribution.)

The following is a summary of the conditions indicating use of a t distribution instead of the standard normal distribution. These same conditions will also apply in Chapter 7.

Conditions for Student t Distribution

1. The sample is small $(n \leq 30)$; and
2. σ is unknown; and
3. The parent population has a distribution that is essentially normal.

We can now determine values for the maximum error E when a t distribution applies.

FIGURE 6.4
Student t Distributions for $n = 3$ and $n = 12$. The Student t distribution has the same general shape and symmetry as the normal distribution, but it reflects the greater variability that is expected with small samples.

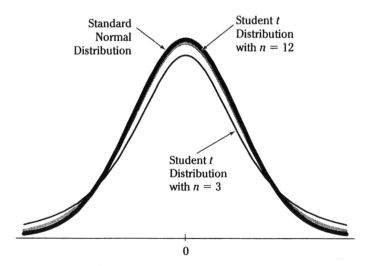

MARGIN OF ERROR FOR THE ESTIMATE FOR μ

Formula 6.2

$$E = t_{\alpha/2} \frac{s}{\sqrt{n}}$$

when **all** the following conditions are met:
1. $n \leq 30$; and
2. σ is unknown; and
3. The population is normally distributed.

In the next example we use the same aircraft age data from a previous example so that you can better compare and contrast similarities and differences between the large ($n > 30$) sample case and the small ($n \leq 30$) sample case.

EXAMPLE   Suppose we have only 10 scores representing the ages (in years) of randomly selected U.S. commercial aircraft (based on data from Aviation Data Services).

  3.2   22.6   23.1   16.9   0.4   6.6   12.5   22.8   26.3   8.1

For these scores, $n = 10$, $\bar{x} = 14.25$, and $s = 9.35$. Recognizing that this is a small sample ($n \leq 30$) and σ is unknown, construct the 95% confidence interval for the mean age of all U.S. commercial aircraft. (Assume that other studies reveal that the distribution of such ages is approximately normal.)

SOLUTION   With a small sample from a normally distributed population, and an unknown σ, we know the Student t distribution applies and we begin by calculating the margin of error E. In this calculation we use $t_{\alpha/2} = 2.262$, which is found in Table A.3 corresponding to $n - 1 = 9$ degrees of freedom and $\alpha = 0.05$ in two tails.

$$E = t_{\alpha/2} \cdot \frac{s}{\sqrt{n}} = 2.262 \cdot \frac{9.35}{\sqrt{10}} = 6.69$$

Note that this margin of error is much larger than our previous value of 2.57 because the sample size n is much smaller and we are using $t_{\alpha/2}$ instead of $z_{\alpha/2}$.
  We now substitute $E = 6.69$ and $\bar{x} = 14.25$ in

$\bar{x} - E < \mu < \bar{x} + E$ to get

$14.25 - 6.69 < \mu < 14.25 + 6.69$ or

$7.56 < \mu < 20.94$

That is, we are 95% confident that the limits of 7.56 years and 20.94 years do contain the true mean age of U.S. commercial aircraft.

CAPTURED TANK SERIAL NUMBERS REVEAL POPULATION SIZE

During World War II, Allied intelligence specialists wanted to determine the number of tanks Germany was producing. Traditional spy techniques provided unreliable results, but statisticians obtained accurate estimates by analyzing serial numbers on captured tanks. As one example, records show that Germany actually produced 271 tanks in June 1941. The estimate based on serial numbers was 244, but traditional intelligence methods resulted in the far-out estimate of 1550. (See "An Empirical Approach to Economic Intelligence in World War II," by Ruggles and Brodie, *Journal of the American Statistical Association*, Vol. 42, 1947.)

FIGURE 6.5
Choosing between Normal and *t* Distributions

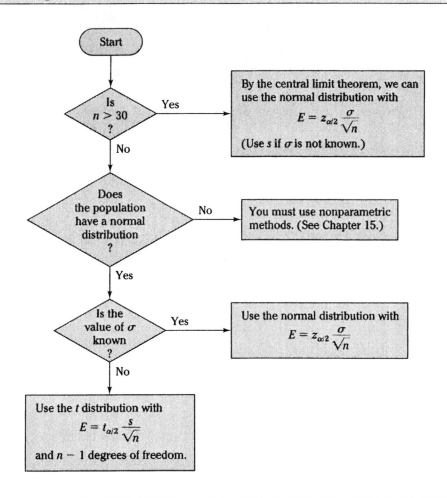

Confusion can sometimes arise when considering whether to use Formula 6.1 or 6.2 and determining when to use *s* in place of σ. The flowchart of Fig. 6.5 summarizes the key points to consider when constructing confidence intervals for estimating μ, the true population or process mean.

Shown below is the Minitab display that results from the data in the preceding example where $n = 10$ and we did not know σ. After entering the sample data, the command TINTERVAL is used on the fourth line.

```
MTB > SET C1
DATA> 3.2 22.6 23.1 16.9 0.4 6.6 12.5 22.8 26.3 8.1
DATA> ENDOFDATA
MTB > TINTERVAL with 95 percent for data in C1

        N     MEAN    STDEV    SE MEAN    95.0 PERCENT C.I.
C1      10    14.25    9.35     2.96      (  7.56,   20.94)
```

DETERMINING SAMPLE SIZE

So far we have discussed how to find point estimates and interval estimates of a population or process mean μ. We have based our procedures on known sample data, but suppose we haven't yet collected the sample. How do we know how many members of the population should be selected? This is a common problem in business and in many other fields. For example, suppose Domino's Pizza has developed a new recipe that is to be market tested. How many people should test the new recipe? When a company airs a commercial on television, the cost depends on the number of viewers. When a company like Nielsen polls viewers to estimate the number who watch a particular show, how many people should they survey? If the Merrel Dow Pharmaceutical Company believes it has a new drug that will be effective in relieving cold symptoms and the drug is to be tested, how many people should be included? Determining the appropriate size of a sample is very important because needlessly large samples waste time and money, and samples of insufficient size may lead to poor results. In many cases, we can determine the minimum sample size needed to estimate some parameter, such as μ.

If we begin with the expression for the margin of error E (Formula 6.1) and solve for the sample size n, we get

Formula 6.3
$$n = \left[\frac{z_{\alpha/2}\, \sigma}{E} \right]^2$$

This equation may be used to determine the sample size necessary to produce results accurate to a desired degree of confidence and margin of error. It should be used when we know the value of σ and want to determine the sample size necessary to establish, with a probability of $1 - \alpha$, the value of μ to within $\pm E$. The existence of such an equation is somewhat remarkable, since it implies that the sample size does not depend on the size of the population.

EXAMPLE We want to estimate the true mean age of U.S. commercial aircraft. We will allow a margin of error of 1.5 years and we want 95% confidence in our estimate. How large should our sample be? (Assume that σ is known to be 7.5 years.)

SOLUTION We seek the sample size n given that $\alpha = 0.05$ (from 95% confidence) so that $z_{\alpha/2} = 1.96$, $E = 1.5$, and $\sigma = 7.5$. Using Formula 6.3, we get

$$n = \left[\frac{z_{\alpha/2}\, \sigma}{E} \right]^2 = \left[\frac{(1.96)\,(7.5)}{1.5} \right]^2 = 9.8^2 = 96.04 = 97 \text{ (rounded } up\text{)}$$

We should therefore obtain a sample of at least 97 randomly selected U.S. commercial aircraft. For such a sample, we will be 95% confident that the sample mean $\bar{x}$ will be within 1.5 years of the true population mean μ.

ESTIMATING SUGAR IN ORANGES

In Florida, members of the citrus industry make extensive use of statistical methods. One particular application involves the way in which growers are paid for oranges used to make orange juice. An arriving truckload of oranges is first weighed at the receiving plant, then a sample of about a dozen oranges is randomly selected. The sample is weighed and squeezed, and the amount of sugar in the juice is measured. Based on the sample results, an estimate is made of the total amount of sugar in the entire truckload. Payment for the load of oranges is based on the estimate of the amount of sugar because sweeter oranges are more valuable than those less sweet, even though the amounts of juice may be the same.

If we are willing to settle for less-accurate results by using a larger margin of error, such as 2.0 years, we reduce the sample size to $n = [(1.96)\ (7.5)/2.0]^2 = 54.0225$, which is *rounded up* to 55. *We always round up in sample size computations so that the required number in the sample is at least adequate rather than slightly inadequate.* If we double the margin of error, the required sample size decreases to one-fourth its original value. Conversely, halving the margin of error would quadruple the sample size. All of this implies that if you want more-accurate results, then the sample size must be substantially increased. Because large samples generally require more time and money, there is often a need for a tradeoff between sample size and the margin of error E.

WHAT IF σ IS UNKNOWN?

Formula 6.3 requires that we substitute some value for the population standard deviation σ. The preceding example assumed that $\sigma = 7.5$ years. In reality, the value of σ might be unknown, but we may have some prior information from a previous sample so that we can use some value of s in place of σ. For example, if we want to solve the preceding example without the assumption that $\sigma = 7.5$, we could refer to the sample of 40 aircraft ages given earlier. From that sample, we can calculate $s = 8.28$ years, so that

$$n = \left[\frac{z_{\alpha/2}\ \sigma}{E}\right]^2 = \left[\frac{(1.96)\ (8.28)}{1.5}\right]^2 = 117.055 = 118 \text{ (rounded up)}$$

It may happen that we want to estimate the population mean μ but we don't know the standard deviation σ and no previous sample data are available. One practical approach is to develop an estimate of the *range* of the data and then use the range rule of thumb from Chapter 2 to estimate σ as

$$\sigma \approx \text{range}/4$$

Suppose that in the preceding example we don't know σ and the 40 sample scores are not available, but we learn that the oldest U.S. commercial aircraft is about 40 years old and the newest is 0 years. We can now estimate σ as $(40 - 0)/4 = 10$ years, so Formula 6.3 becomes

$$n = \left[\frac{z_{\alpha/2}\ \sigma}{E}\right]^2 = \left[\frac{(1.96)\ (10)}{1.5}\right]^2 = 170.738 = 171 \text{ (rounded up)}$$

Because we are estimating σ, the resulting sample size might be somewhat larger or smaller than required, but at least it gets us a "ballpark" estimate, which is better than nothing. These considerations of the required sample size are elements of what is called *experimental design*. Managers need to examine the problem carefully and consider their objectives when choosing the size of the sample they will draw.

6.2 EXERCISES   BASIC CONCEPTS

1. a.   If $\alpha = 0.05$, find $z_{\alpha/2}$.
    b.   If $\alpha = 0.02$, find $z_{\alpha/2}$.
    c.   Find $z_{\alpha/2}$ for the value of α corresponding to a confidence level of 96%.
    d.   If $\alpha = 0.05$, find $t_{\alpha/2}$ for a sample of 20 scores.
    e.   If $\alpha = 0.01$, find $t_{\alpha/2}$ for a sample of 15 scores.
2. a.   If $\alpha = 0.10$, find $z_{\alpha/2}$.
    b.   Find $z_{\alpha/2}$ for the value of α corresponding to a confidence level of 95%.
    c.   Find $z_{\alpha/2}$ for the value of α corresponding to a confidence level of 80%.
    d.   If $\alpha = 0.10$, find $t_{\alpha/2}$ for a sample of 10 scores.
    e.   If $\alpha = 0.02$, find $t_{\alpha/2}$ for a sample of 25 scores.

In Exercises 3–8, use the given data to find the margin of error E. Be sure to use the correct expression for E, depending on whether the normal distribution or the Student t distribution applies.

3. $\alpha = 0.05$, $\sigma = 15$, $n = 100$
4. $\alpha = 0.05$, $\sigma = 15$, $n = 44$
5. $\alpha = 0.01$, $\sigma = 40$, $n = 25$
6. $\alpha = 0.05$, $s = 30$, $n = 20$
7. $\alpha = 0.01$, $s = 15$, $n = 100$
8. $\alpha = 0.01$, $s = 30$, $n = 16$

In Exercises 9–12, find the indicated confidence interval. Identify those cases in which the population must have a normal distribution.

9. Find the 95% confidence interval for μ if $\sigma = 5$, $\bar{x} = 70.4$, and $n = 36$.
10. Find the 95% confidence interval for μ if $s = 7.3$, $\bar{x} = 84.2$, and $n = 40$.
11. Find the 99% confidence interval for μ if $\sigma = 2$, $\bar{x} = 98.6$, and $n = 20$.
12. Find the 90% confidence interval for μ if $s = 5.5$, $\bar{x} = 123.6$, and $n = 17$.
13. In an insurance company study of New York State licensed-drivers' ages, 570 randomly selected ages have a mean of 41.8 years and a standard deviation of 16.7 years (based on data from the New York State Department of Motor Vehicles). Construct a 99% confidence interval for the mean age of all New York State licensed drivers.
14. As the manager at a Caldor department store in upstate New York, you are considering hiring additional employees because you are concerned that customers wait too long in the check-out line. A study of 40 randomly selected check-out times results in a mean of 1.80 min and a standard deviation of 0.60 min. Construct a 90% confidence interval for the mean of all such check-out times.
15. The County Auto Repair Company is analyzing its cash flow to determine whether profitability can be increased. The owner randomly selects receipts for parts purchased on 94 different jobs. The mean is $52.32 and the standard deviation is $25.42. Construct the 95% confidence interval for the mean cost of parts for all jobs.
16. The Carolina Clothing Company is considering expanding its line to accommodate very tall people and very short people. Their research reveals that for 772 randomly selected males between the ages of 18 and 24, the mean height is 69.7 in. and the standard deviation is 2.8 in. (based on data from USDHEW

publication 79-1659). Use this sample data to find the 99% confidence interval for the mean height of all males between the ages of 18 and 24.

17. In a time-use study, 20 randomly selected managers spend a mean of 2.40 h each day on paperwork. The standard deviation of the 20 scores is 1.30 h (based on data from Adia Personnel Services). Construct the 95% confidence interval for the mean paperwork time of all managers.

18. In a study of times required for room service at a newly opened Radisson Hotel, 20 deliveries had a mean time of 24.2 min and a standard deviation of 8.7 min. Construct the 90% confidence interval for the mean of all deliveries.

19. Find the sample size necessary to estimate a population mean to within three units if $\sigma = 16$ and we want 95% confidence in our results.

20. Find the sample size necessary to estimate a population mean. Assume that $\sigma = 20$, the margin of error is 1.5, and we want 95% confidence in our results.

21. A random sample of 9 homes in Harrison Township of Vigo County, Indiana, found that a recent reassessment ordered by the state overassessed the values of homeowner properties. The amounts these homes were overassessed are as follows:

$5250 $6500 $4800 $6550 $5400 $7300 $6100 $4750 $7350

   a. Find $\bar{x}$ and s.
   b. Construct a 95% confidence interval for the mean value of overassessed homeowner properties.
   c. For the result of part b to be valid, must the population of overassessed values have a normal distribution?
   d. The state wants to find a 95% confidence interval for the mean amount the properties were overassessed. How large a sample is required if the desired margin of error is $200?

22. The manager of the Locust Tree Restaurant finds that for 7 randomly selected days, the numbers of customers served were

   289   326   264   318   306   269   352

   a. Find a 90% confidence interval for the mean number of customers per day.
   b. If you want to construct a 90% confidence interval with a margin of error of 5, how many days should be sampled?

23. The Montana Construction Supply Company makes PVC pipe that must withstand certain bending pressures. A sample item is taken every 2 min from this stable process, and 45 such items yield a sample mean of 39.8 lb. Assume that $\sigma = 6$ lb.

   a. Construct a 99% confidence interval for the true mean.
   b. How large should a sample be if we want a 99% confidence interval for μ with a margin of error of 2 lb?

24. The River Station Office Supply Company manufactures envelopes and tests the strength of the glued joints by randomly selecting an envelope every 3 min. Listed below are the strengths (in pounds) for 20 envelopes. Assume that the process is stable.

   3.4   3.1   3.0   3.2   3.4   3.4   3.5   3.1   3.3   3.4
   3.2   3.5   3.6   3.4   3.5   3.3   3.6   3.7   3.4   3.3

   a. Construct a 99% confidence interval for the true mean strength.
   b. How many envelopes must you sample if you want to be 99% confident that the margin of error is 0.1 lb?

25. We want to estimate the mean weight of one type of gold coin minted by Monrovia. How many coins must we sample from a batch of 10,000 such coins if we want to be 99% confident that the sample mean is within 0.001 oz of the true mean? Assume that a pilot study has shown that $s = 0.004$ oz can be used.

26. In a study of relationships between work schedules and family life, 29 subjects work at night. Their weekly times (in hours) spent in caring for children are measured, and the mean and standard deviation are 26.84 and 17.66, respectively. (See "Nonstandard Work Schedules and Family Life," by Staines and Pleck, *Journal of Applied Psychology*, Vol. 69, No. 3.) Use this sample data to construct the 95% confidence interval for the mean time in child care for all night workers.

6.2 EXERCISES | BEYOND THE BASICS

27. The city manager of Indianapolis wants to determine how often residents use the city bus system during a one-month period.
    a. How many residents must be surveyed if we want to develop a 95% confidence interval with a margin of error of 2 times per month? (A prior study showed that the range is from 0 to 50 times.)
    b. The city manager randomly selects 160 residents and obtains a mean of 21.3 with a standard deviation of 16.4. Using these sample results, construct a 95% confidence interval for the true mean.

28. A 95% confidence interval for the lives (in minutes) of Kodak AA batteries is $430 < \mu < 470$. Assume that this result is based on a sample of size $n = 100$.
    a. What is the value of the sample mean?
    b. What is the value of the sample standard deviation?
    c. Construct the 99% confidence interval.
    d. If the confidence interval $432 < \mu < 468$ is obtained from the same sample data, what is the degree of confidence?

29. The development of Formula 6.1 assumes that the population is infinite, or that we are sampling with replacement, or that the population is very large. If we have a relatively small population and we sample without replacement, we should modify E to include the finite population correction factor as follows:

$$E = z_{\alpha/2} \frac{\sigma}{\sqrt{n}} \sqrt{\frac{N - n}{N - 1}} \qquad \text{where } N \text{ is the population size}$$

    a. Show that the preceding expression can be solved for n to yield

$$n = \frac{N\sigma^2 [z_{\alpha/2}]^2}{(N - 1)E^2 + \sigma^2 [z_{\alpha/2}]^2}$$

    b. Do Exercise 25 assuming that the coins are selected without replacement from a population of $N = 100$ coins.

30. The standard error of the mean is $\sigma/\sqrt{n}$ provided that the population size is infinite. If the population size is finite and is denoted by N, then the correction factor

$$\sqrt{\frac{N-n}{N-1}}$$

should be used whenever $n > 0.05N$. This correction factor multiplies the standard error of the mean, as shown in Exercise 29. Find the 95% confidence interval for the mean of 100 salaries if a sample of 36 of those salaries produces a mean and standard deviation of $25,250 and $3700, respectively.

6.3   ESTIMATES AND SAMPLE SIZES OF PROPORTIONS

In this section we consider the same concepts of estimation and sample size determination discussed in Section 6.2, but we apply the concepts to *proportions* instead of means. We assume that the conditions given in Section 4.4 for the binomial distribution are satisfied. Recall from Section 4.4 that in a binomial experiment we classify all outcomes into one of two different categories, typically referred to as *success* or *failure*. Also, we have n independent trials; in each trial the probability of success is denoted by p and the probability of failure is denoted by q. The symbol x denotes the number of successes among the n trials. We also assume that the conditions $np \geq 5$ and $nq \geq 5$ are both satisfied; we saw in Section 5.6 that this assumption enables us to use the normal distribution as an approximation to the binomial distribution.

Although we make repeated references to proportions, keep in mind that the theory and procedures also apply to probabilities and percentages. Proportions and probabilities are both expressed in decimal or fraction form. If we intend to deal with percentages, we can easily convert them to proportions by deleting the percent sign and dividing by 100. The symbol p may therefore represent a proportion, a probability, or the decimal equivalent of a percentage. We continue to use p as the population proportion in the same way that we use μ to represent the population mean. We now introduce a new notation.

Notation

$$\hat{p} = \frac{x}{n}$$

In this way, p represents the population proportion, and $\hat{p}$ (called "p hat") represents the sample proportion. In previous chapters we stipulated that $q = 1 - p$, so it is natural to stipulate that $\hat{q} = 1 - \hat{p}$.

As an example, suppose that a pollster is hired to determine the proportion of adult Americans who favor a capital gains tax. Let's assume that 2000 adult Americans are surveyed, with 1347 favorable reactions. The pollster seeks the value of p, the true proportion of all adult Americans favoring a capital gains tax.

Sample results indicate that $x = 1347$ and $n = 2000$, so that

$$\hat{p} = \frac{x}{n} = \frac{1347}{2000} = 0.6735$$

Just as $\bar{x}$ was selected as the best point estimate of μ, we now select $\hat{p}$ as the **best point estimate of the population proportion** p. Of the various estimators that could be used for p, $\hat{p}$ is deemed best because it is unbiased and the most consistent. It is unbiased in the sense that the distribution of sample proportions tends to center about the value of p. It is most consistent in the sense that the variance of sample proportions tends to be smaller than the variance of any other unbiased estimators.

We assume in this section that the binomial conditions are essentially satisfied and that the normal distribution can be used as an approximation to the distribution of sample proportions. This allows us to draw from results established in Section 5.6 and to conclude that the mean number of successes μ and the standard deviation of the number of successes σ are given by

$$\mu = np \text{ and } \sigma = \sqrt{npq}$$

where p is the probability of a success. Both of these parameters pertain to n trials, and we now convert them to a "per trial" basis simply by dividing by n:

$$\text{mean of sample proportions} = \frac{np}{n} = p$$

$$\text{standard deviation of sample proportions} = \frac{\sqrt{npq}}{n} = \sqrt{\frac{npq}{n^2}} = \sqrt{\frac{pq}{n}}$$

The first result may seem trivial because we have already stipulated that the true population proportion is p. The second result is nontrivial and very useful. In the last section, we saw that the sample mean $\bar{x}$ has a probability of $1 - \alpha$ of being within $z_{\alpha/2}\, \sigma/\sqrt{n}$ of μ. Similar reasoning leads us to conclude that $\hat{p}$ has a probability of $1 - \alpha$ of being within $z_{\alpha/2}\sqrt{pq/n}$ of p. But if we already know the value of p or q, we have no need for estimates or sample size determinations. Consequently, we must replace p and q by their point estimates of $\hat{p}$ and $\hat{q}$ so that an error factor can be computed in real situations.

DEFINITION

The *margin of error for p* is given by

Formula 6.4 $$E = z_{\alpha/2}\sqrt{\frac{\hat{p}\,\hat{q}}{n}}$$

and the probability that $\hat{p}$ differs from p by less than E is $1 - \alpha$.

The *confidence interval* (or *interval estimate*) for the population proportion *p* is given by

$$\hat{p} - E < p < \hat{p} + E$$

TV RATINGS

Estimating the number of people who watch different television shows has become much more difficult now that we have VCRs, satellite receiving dishes, cable networks, and local stations. With $25 billion in advertising revenue at stake, ratings companies such as Nielsen Media Research are becoming more sophisticated. Viewers once filled out diaries. Now about 4000 participants press buttons on hand-held "people meters." A new device consists of a very sophisticated camera that can track different viewers, sense their eye movements, and record exactly who is watching the different shows. The data can be sent by telephone lines to Nielsen's computers for analysis.

The following example illustrates the construction of a confidence interval for a proportion.

EXAMPLE In a Roper Organization poll of 2000 adults, 1280 have money in regular savings accounts. Find the 95% confidence interval for the true proportion of adults who have money in regular savings accounts.

SOLUTION The sample results are $x = 1280$ and $n = 2000$, so that $\hat{p} = 1280/2000 = 0.640$ and $\hat{q} = 1 - 0.640 = 0.360$. A confidence level of 95% requires that $\alpha = 0.05$, so that $z_{\alpha/2} = 1.96$. We first calculate the margin of error E using Formula 6.4.

$$E = z_{\alpha/2} \sqrt{\frac{\hat{p}\,\hat{q}}{n}} = 1.96 \sqrt{\frac{(0.640)(0.360)}{2000}}$$
$$= 0.021$$

We can now find the confidence interval because we know that $\hat{p} = 0.640$ and $E = 0.021$.

$$\hat{p} - E \qquad < p < \hat{p} + E$$
$$0.640 - 0.021 < p < 0.640 + 0.021$$
$$0.619 \qquad < p < 0.661$$

If we wanted the 95% confidence interval for the true population *percentage,* we could express the result as $61.9\% < p < 66.1\%$. This result is often reported as follows: "Among adults, the percent with money in regular savings accounts is estimated to be 64.0%, with a margin of error of plus or minus 2.1 percentage points." The level of confidence should also be reported, but most media do not report it. Instead, they typically use 95% confidence for their interval estimates and omit any reference to the actual degree of confidence.

DETERMINING SAMPLE SIZE

Having discussed point estimates and confidence intervals for *p,* we now consider the problem of determining how large a sample should be when we want to find the approximate value of a population proportion. In the previous section we started with the expression for the error E and solved for n. Following that reasonable precedent, we begin with

$$E = z_{\alpha/2} \sqrt{\frac{\hat{p}\,\hat{q}}{n}}$$

and we solve for n to get the sample size.

SAMPLE SIZE (WHEN AN ESTIMATE $\hat{p}$ IS KNOWN)

Formula 6.5
$$n = \frac{[z_{\alpha/2}]^2 \hat{p}\,\hat{q}}{E^2}$$

In finding the sample size necessary to estimate p, Formula 6.5 requires $\hat{p}$ as an estimate of the true population proportion p. But this is circular logic, because the formula requires knowledge of the sample result $\hat{p}$ before we have determined the sample size and before the sample has been collected. However, we can sometimes make reasonable guesses of $\hat{p}$ by using previous samples or someone's special knowledge.

EXAMPLE Advertisers pay for commercial television time according to the number of viewers who watch a particular show. Suppose the Nielsen Company wants to estimate the true proportion of all TV households tuned to a particular CBS show this week. We know that last week's results revealed that the proportion was 0.218 (or 21.8%). Using that prior result, determine how many TV households must be sampled this week if we want 95% confidence that the margin of error is 0.03.

SOLUTION The 95% degree of confidence corresponds to $\alpha = 0.05$, so that $z_{\alpha/2} = 1.96$. We have $z_{\alpha/2} = 1.96$, $E = 0.03$, and $\hat{p} = 0.218$, so that

$$n = \frac{[z_{\alpha/2}]^2 \hat{p}\,\hat{q}}{E^2} = \frac{(1.96)^2(0.218)(0.782)}{(0.03)^2}$$

$$= 727.667 = 728 \text{ (rounded up)}$$

To be 95% confident that the sample proportion is within 0.03 of the true population proportion, Nielsen should survey 728 randomly selected TV households.

What do we do when we have no idea of the value of $\hat{p}$? Mathematicians have cleverly circumvented this problem by showing that, in the absence of $\hat{p}$ and $\hat{q}$, we can assign the value of 0.5 to each of those statistics and the resulting sample size will be at least sufficient. The underlying reason for the assignment of 0.5 is found in the conclusion that the product $\hat{p} \cdot \hat{q}$ achieves a maximum possible value of 0.25 when $\hat{p} = 0.5$ and $\hat{q} = 0.5$. (See the accompanying table, which lists some values of $\hat{p}$ and $\hat{q}$.) In practice, this means that lack of knowledge about $\hat{p}$ or $\hat{q}$ requires that we replace the preceding expression for n as follows:

$\hat{p}$	$\hat{q}$	$\hat{p}\,\hat{q}$
0.1	0.9	0.09
0.2	0.8	0.16
0.3	0.7	0.21
0.4	0.6	0.24
0.5	0.5	0.25
0.6	0.4	0.24
0.7	0.3	0.21
0.8	0.2	0.16
0.9	0.1	0.09

SAMPLE SIZE (WHEN NO ESTIMATE $\hat{p}$ IS KNOWN)

Formula 6.6
$$n = \frac{[z_{\alpha/2}]^2 \cdot 0.25}{E^2}$$

EXAMPLE

We want to estimate, with a maximum error of 0.03, the true proportion of all TV households tuned in to a particular show, and we want 95% confidence in our results. We have no prior information suggesting a possible value of p. How many TV households must we survey?

SOLUTION

With a confidence level of 95%, we have $\alpha = 0.05$, so that $z_{\alpha/2} = 1.96$. We are given $E = 0.03$, but in the absence of $\hat{p}$ or $\hat{q}$ we use Formula 6.6 to get

$$n = \frac{[z_{\alpha/2}]^2 \cdot 0.25}{E^2} = \frac{[1.96]^2 \cdot 0.25}{0.03^2} = 1067.11 = 1068 \text{ (rounded up)}$$

To be 95% confident that we come within 0.03 of the true proportion of TV households who watch the show, we should poll 1068 randomly selected TV households. Note that lack of knowledge about $\hat{p}$ results in our needing a larger sample (1068) to achieve the same results as the sample of 728 needed when the value of $\hat{p}$ was known.

This example shows that with a sample of 1068 randomly selected TV households, we have 95% confidence that the sample proportion is within 0.03 of the true proportion. Based on Nielsen data, there are about 93 million TV households, so that a sample size of 1068 represents about 0.001% of the population. Although that percentage is small, we are still about 95% confident that we are within 0.03 of the true value, so that the results will be quite good.

EXAMPLE

The A. J. Collins Investment Company is planning a major telephone campaign in California. The campaign will begin with an automated dialing system that delivers a message and records responses to questions. However, answering machines prove to be an obstacle to this approach. You've been hired to conduct a preliminary study for the purpose of estimating the percentage of households in California having answering machines. You want an error of no more than four percentage points and a confidence level of 99%. A previous study by the U.S. Consumer Electronics Industry indicates that the percentage should be about 24%. How large should your sample be?

SOLUTION

With a 99% confidence level, we have $\alpha = 0.01$ and $z_{\alpha/2} = 2.575$. The error of four percentage points means that $E = 0.04$, because the actual calculations use proportions. The prior study gives us $\hat{p} = 0.24$ and $\hat{q} = 0.76$. We now calculate

$$n = \frac{[z_{\alpha/2}]^2 \hat{p}\, \hat{q}}{E^2} = \frac{(2.575)^2(0.24)(0.76)}{(0.04)^2}$$

$$= 755.89 = 756 \text{ (rounded up)}$$

(continued)

Rounding *up,* we find that the sample size should be 756. (If we had no prior knowledge of the percentage, we would have used 0.25 for $\hat{p}\,\hat{q}$ and our required sample size would have been the much larger value of 1037.)

Newspaper, magazine, television, and radio reports often feature results of polls. Reporters frequently provide percentages without any indication of the sample size or degree of confidence. For example, one national newspaper reported that "the American Lung Association says that 64 percent of smokers agree they shouldn't light up near nonsmokers." Without knowing the sample size and degree of confidence, we have no real sense for how good that statistic is. In contrast, the *New York Times* published an article giving results of a poll conducted on the popularity of the president. The *Times* included a five-paragraph insert explaining that the results were "based on telephone interviews conducted Nov. 20 through Nov. 24 with 1553 adults around the U.S., excluding Alaska and Hawaii." The *Times* also explained how the telephone numbers were selected to be representative of the population. They explained how results were weighted to be representative of region, race, sex, age, and education. They explained that "in theory, in 19 cases out of 20 the results based on such samples will differ by no more than three percentage points in either direction from what would have been obtained by interviewing all adult Americans" (another way of saying "95% confident"). In general, the five-paragraph insert provided information that allowed informed readers to recognize the quality of the poll.

Polling and marketing surveys are important and common in the United States. Such surveys can affect the television shows we watch, the leaders we elect, the legislation that governs us, and the products we consume. Understanding the concepts of this section should remove much of the mystery and misunderstanding created by such samples.

We should again stress that the methods of this section require sound sampling procedures. For instance, the last example illustrated that 756 households should be surveyed, but if the sample is not carefully selected, the results could be very flawed.

6.3 EXERCISES   BASIC CONCEPTS

In Exercises 1–4, a trial is repeated n times with x successes. In each case find (a) the sample proportion of successes $\hat{p}$; (b) the sample proportion of failures $\hat{q}$; (c) the best point estimate for the value of the population proportion p; and (d) the margin of error E (assuming that $\alpha = 0.05$).

1. $n = 500, x = 100$
2. $n = 2000, x = 300$
3. $n = 1068, x = 325$
4. $n = 1776, x = 50$

In Exercises 5–8, use the given data to find the appropriate confidence interval for the population proportion p.

5. $n = 400$, $x = 100$, 95% confidence
6. $n = 900$, $x = 400$, 95% confidence
7. $n = 50$, $x = 42$, 90% confidence
8. $n = 35$, $x = 32$, 99% confidence
9. In considering the production of a new car accessory, the Telektronic Company wants to do a marketing study that includes determination of the proportion of cars with stereo tape decks. How many cars must be sampled if the manufacturer wants 92% confidence that the sample proportion is in error by no more than 0.035?
10. You want to estimate the percentage of employees who have been with their current employer for one year or less. Data from the U.S. Department of Labor suggest that this percentage is around 29%, but you must conduct a survey to be 99% confident that your randomly selected sample of employees leads to a sample percentage that is off by no more than two percentage points. How many employees must you survey?
11. The South Carolina Sports Supply Company manufactures golfing equipment and plans to advertise its new line along with general information about golfing in America. The marketing manager finds that when 1180 adults were surveyed, 79 indicated that they play golf (based on data from a Roper Organization Poll). Construct the 95% interval estimate of the true proportion of all adults who play golf.
12. a. If we want to estimate the proportion of home-accident deaths caused by falls this year, how many such deaths must we select and investigate? Use a 0.04 margin of error and a 95% degree of confidence.
    b. Do part a with the additional information that in a recent year, 23% of home-accident deaths were caused by falls.
13. You randomly select 650 home-accident deaths and find that 180 of them are caused by falls (based on data from the National Safety Council). Construct the 95% confidence interval for the true population proportion of all home-accident deaths caused by falls.
14. Mail orders placed with the Medassist Pharmaceutical Company are either error free or defective (with at least one error).
    a. A random survey of 100 orders reveals that 12 are defective. Construct a 95% confidence interval for the true population proportion of defective orders.
    b. Is the sample size of 100 large enough so that the normal approximation to the binomial distribution is suitable?
    c. How large must the sample be if we want to estimate p (the true proportion of defective orders) with a margin of error of 0.04 and a 95% degree of confidence?
15. In an Airport Transit Association poll of 4664 adults, 72% indicated that they have flown in an airplane. Find the 99% confidence interval for the percentage of all adults who have flown in an airplane.
16. In a survey of 1500 people, 63% indicated that they listened to their favorite radio station because of the music (based on data from a Strategic Radio Research poll). Construct the 90% interval estimate of the true population percentage of all people who listen to their favorite radio station because of the music.

17. You plan to conduct a poll to estimate the percentage of consumers who are satisfied with long-distance phone service. You want to be 90% confident that your sample percentage is within 2.5 percentage points of the true population value, and a Roper poll suggests that this percentage should be about 85%. How large must your sample be?

18. Labels are inked directly on compact discs by a special printer. In monitoring this process, 100 discs are selected every 10 minutes and examined for defects (smears, smudges, and so on). The results from one hour are listed below as the numbers of defective labels in 6 samples, each of size 100.

    5   8   6   7   4   6

    a. Assuming a statistically stable inking process, combine the data to get a 90% confidence interval for the proportion of defective labels.
    b. If we want to develop a 90% confidence interval with a margin of error of 0.01, how many labels must be sampled?

19. An accountant randomly selects 60 general accounts payable and examines them to determine whether they are correct. Seven accounts contain errors.
    a. Construct a 95% confidence interval for the true proportion of general accounts payable that contain errors.
    b. Is the given sample size large enough to warrant using the normal distribution as an approximation to the binomial distribution?
    c. How large must the sample be if we want 95% confidence that the margin of error is 0.06?

20. A *New York Times* article about poll results states, "In theory, in 19 cases out of 20, the results from such a poll should differ by no more than one percentage point in either direction from what would have been obtained by interviewing all voters in the United States." Find the sample size suggested by this statement.

21. The Telstar Appliance Company manufactures clothes-washing machines and is concerned about chipped exterior paint. About 9% of the units seem to have this defect. Metal grippers are replaced by soft rubber grippers to help remedy the problem.
    a. How many units must be sampled if we want to estimate the proportion of chipped units with a 95% confidence interval having a margin of error of 0.03?
    b. The manufacturer randomly selects 400 units from the stable process and finds 19 are chipped. Construct a 95% confidence interval for the true proportion of chipped units.
    c. Does it appear that the soft rubber grippers were effective in lowering the proportion of chipped units?

22. In a statistically stable process, 16 oz bags are filled with potato chips.
    a. How many bags should be selected and examined if we want to estimate the proportion of bags that are underfilled? We want to be 90% confident that the margin of error is 0.04, and we know that in the past, the proportion of underfilled bags has been around 0.06.
    b. In a random sample of 125 bags, it is found that 10 are underfilled. Construct a 90% confidence interval for the true proportion of underfilled bags.
    c. Based on the result from part *b,* does it appear that the proportion of underfilled bags has shifted?

23. According to Merrill Lynch, when 600 full-time workers in the 45–64 age bracket were surveyed, 75% of them planned to remain in their current homes after they retired. Construct the 90% confidence interval for the true proportion of all such workers with that intent.

24. A marketing study found that 312 of the 650 buyers of compact cars were women (based on data from the Ford Motor Company). Construct the 95% interval estimate for the true percentage of all compact car buyers who are women.

6.3 EXERCISES   BEYOND THE BASICS

25. In this section we developed two formulas used for determining sample size, and in both cases we assume that the population is infinite, or we are sampling with replacement, or the population is very large. If we have a relatively small population and we sample without replacement, we should modify E to include the finite population correction factor as follows:

$$E = z_{\alpha/2} \sqrt{\frac{\hat{p}\hat{q}}{n}} \sqrt{\frac{N-n}{N-1}}$$

Here N is the size of the population.

a. Show that the above expression can be solved for n to yield

$$n = \frac{N\hat{p}\hat{q}[z_{\alpha/2}]^2}{\hat{p}\hat{q}[z_{\alpha/2}]^2 + (N-1)E^2}$$

b. Do Exercise 12, part b, assuming that there is a finite population of size $N = 500$ home-accident deaths.

26. Special tables are available for finding confidence intervals for proportions involving small numbers of cases where the normal distribution approximation cannot be used. For example, given 3 successes among 8 trials, the 95% confidence interval is $0.085 < p < 0.755$. Find the confidence interval that would result if you incorrectly used the normal distribution as an approximation to the binomial distribution. Are the results reasonably close?

27. A newspaper article indicates that an estimate of the unemployment rate involves a sample of 47,000 people. If the reported unemployment rate must have an error no larger than 0.2 percentage point and the rate is known to be about 8%, find the corresponding confidence level.

28. a. If IQ scores of adults are normally distributed with a mean of 100 and a standard deviation of 15, use the methods presented in Chapter 5 to find the percentage of IQ scores above 130.

    b. Now assume that you plan to test a sample of adults with the intention of estimating the percentage of IQ scores above 130. How many adults must you test if you want to be 98% confident that your error is no more than 2.5 percentage points? (Use the result from part a.)

29. A **one-sided confidence interval** for p can be written as

$$p < \hat{p} + E \quad \text{or} \quad p > \hat{p} - E$$

where z_α replaces $z_{\alpha/2}$ in the expression for E.

If an airline company wants to report an on-time performance of "at least x percent" with 95% confidence, construct the appropriate one-sided confidence interval and then find the percentage in question. Assume that a random sample of 750 flights results in 630 that are on time.

30. Use Minitab and simulate the filling of 100 bags of potato chips labeled 16 oz. The given Minitab commands correspond to a stable process with a 6% rate of underfilled bags. In the resulting display, a 1 denotes an underfilled bag and a 0 denotes a bag with at least 16 oz.

   a. Based on the given results, construct a 90% confidence interval for the true proportion of underfilled bags. Does this confidence interval contain 0.06?

   b. Run your own simulation by entering the given Minitab commands and use your generated data to repeat part a.

```
MTB > RANDOM N = 100 C1;
SUBC> BERNOULI P = 0.06.
MTB > PRINT C1

C1
    0 0 0 0 0 0 0 0 0 0 0 0 0 0 0
    0 0 0 1 0 0 0 0 0 0 0 0 0 0 0
    0 0 1 0 0 0 0 0 1 0 0 0 0 1 0
    0 0 0 0 0 0 0 0 0 0 0 0 0 0 0
    1 0 0 0 0 0 0 0 0 0 0 0 0 0 0
    0 0 0 0 1 0 0 0 0 1 0 0 0 0 0
    0 0 0 0 0 1 0 0 0 0
```

6.4 ESTIMATES AND SAMPLE SIZES OF VARIANCES

Many real and practical situations, such as quality control in a manufacturing process, require that we estimate values of population or process variances or standard deviations. The goal of quality requires much more than simply making products that are, on the average, good. Another extremely important requirement is that products be made with *consistent* quality that doesn't run the gamut from extremely good to extremely poor. This consistency can often be measured by the variance or standard deviation, so these become vital statistics in maintaining the quality of products. In many circumstances, the variance and standard deviation might be the most critical factors. For example, when many banks changed their customer waiting lines from a separate line at each service window to one single main feeder line for all service windows, that change did not affect the mean waiting time, but it did reduce the variation among waiting times. On the average, customers were not processed any faster, but the greater consistency among waiting times resulted in happier customers who were less frustrated by being caught in an exceptionally slow line. In this case, the process was improved through a reduced standard deviation, even though the mean wasn't affected.

In this section, we assume that the population has normally distributed values. This assumption was made in earlier sections, but it is more critical here. In using the Student t distribution in Section 6.2, for example, we required that the population of values be approximately normally distributed, but we could accept deviations from normality that were not too severe. We will soon see, however, that when dealing with variances, the distribution we use is much more sensitive to departures from normality. Consequently the assumption of normality must be adhered to much more strictly. That is, we should not use the methods of this section if the distribution is very nonnormal. We should check the distribution by plotting the data in a histogram to see whether the data appear to be symmetric and bell-shaped. We describe this sensitivity by saying that inferences about the population variance σ^2 or the population standard deviation σ made with the methods of this section are not *robust* against departures from normality. In contrast, inferences made about the population mean μ based on the Student t distribution are reasonably robust, because departures from normality that are not too extreme will not lead to gross errors.

When we considered estimates of means and proportions in Sections 6.2 and 6.3, we used the normal and Student t distributions. When developing estimates of variances or standard deviations, we need another distribution, the chi-square distribution.

CHI-SQUARE DISTRIBUTION

In a normally distributed population with variance σ^2, we randomly select independent samples of size n and compute the variance s^2 for each sample. The random variable $(n - 1)s^2/\sigma^2$ has a distribution called the **chi-square distribution.**

CHI-SQUARE DISTRIBUTION

$$\chi^2 = \frac{(n - 1)s^2}{\sigma^2}$$

where

$$n = \text{sample size}$$
$$s^2 = \text{sample variance}$$
$$\sigma^2 = \text{population variance}$$

We denote chi-square by χ^2 and we pronounce it "kigh square." The specific mathematical equations used to define this distribution are not given here because they are beyond the scope of this text. Instead, you can refer to Table A.4 for required values of the chi-square distribution. We should also note that the general form of the chi-square distribution is $(df)s^2/\sigma^2$, where df represents degrees of

FIGURE 6.6
The Chi-Square Distribution

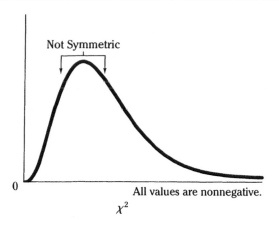

freedom. In this chapter we have $n - 1$ degrees of freedom.

$$\text{degrees of freedom} = n - 1$$

In later chapters we will encounter situations in which the degrees of freedom are not $n - 1$. For that reason, we should not universally equate degrees of freedom with $n - 1$. Here are other important properties of the chi-square distribution:

1. The chi-square distribution is not symmetric, unlike the normal and Student t distributions (see Fig. 6.6).
2. The values of chi-square can be zero or positive, but they cannot be negative (see Fig. 6.6).
3. The chi-square distribution is different for each number of degrees of freedom, which is $df = n - 1$ in this section (see Fig. 6.7).

FIGURE 6.7
Chi-Square Distributions for $df = 10$ and $df = 20$

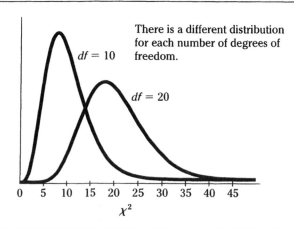

ESTIMATING CROP YIELD

Each year, the state of Florida announces the amounts of oranges and other citrus products that will be harvested. The state claims that it uses a census of Florida's entire tree population. This census is carefully maintained and updated with field workers as well as aerial photographs. When the fruit begin to ripen, field workers randomly select several trees in each grove; they randomly select limbs from those trees; and then they randomly select branches from those limbs. The number and size of the fruit on each selected branch are recorded. Using these sample results, the state can accurately predict the amount of fruit that will be harvested. Because investors buy and sell citrus futures based on the state's predictions, it is important that the state develop accurate estimates that are not divulged until an official public announcement is made.

In previous sections of this chapter we focused on the topics of estimating population parameters and determining sample size. Now we consider those topics as they relate to variances. Because of the nature of the chi-square distribution, however, the techniques discussed here do not closely parallel those in the preceding two sections.

Because sample variances tend to center on the value of the population variance, we say that the sample variance s^2 is an unbiased estimator of the population variance σ^2. Also, the variance of s^2 values tends to be smaller than the variance of the other unbiased estimators. For these reasons we conclude that among the various possible statistics we could use to estimate σ^2, the best is s^2.

The sample variance s^2 is the best **point estimate of the population variance** σ^2.

Because s^2 is the best point estimate of σ^2, it would be natural to expect s to be the best point estimate of σ, but this is not the case. For reasons we will not pursue, the sample standard deviation s is a biased estimator of the population standard deviation σ; if the sample size is large, however, the bias is small, so we can use s as a reasonably good estimate of σ.

Although the sample variance s^2 is the best point estimate of the population variance σ^2, there is no indication of how good the best estimate is. To compensate for that deficiency of the point estimate, we develop the interval estimate (or confidence interval), which is more revealing.

The **confidence interval** (or **interval estimate**) **for the population variance** σ^2 is given by

$$\frac{(n - 1)s^2}{\chi_R^2} < \sigma^2 < \frac{(n - 1)s^2}{\chi_L^2}$$

The confidence interval (or interval estimate) for σ is found by taking the square root of each component of the preceding inequality:

$$\sqrt{\frac{(n - 1)s^2}{\chi_R^2}} < \sigma < \sqrt{\frac{(n - 1)s^2}{\chi_L^2}}$$

In these expressions, χ_R^2 and χ_L^2 are notations defined as follows. (Some books use $\chi_{\alpha/2}^2$ instead of χ_R^2 and $\chi_{1-\alpha/2}^2$ for χ_L^2.)

Notation
With a total area of α divided equally between the two tails of a chi-square distribution, χ_L^2 denotes the *left-tailed critical value* and χ_R^2 denotes the *right-tailed critical value*. (See Fig. 6.8.)

In constructing a confidence interval for σ^2 by using the above expression, we must determine the values of χ_R^2 and χ_L^2, which are the critical values. In finding those values, we use Table A.4. An important feature of this table is that each critical value separates an area to the *right* that corresponds to the value given in the top row.

FIGURE 6.8
Chi-Square distribution with critical values χ_L^2 and χ_R^2. The critical values χ_L^2 and χ_R^2 separate the extreme areas corresponding to sample variances that are unlikely (with a probability α).

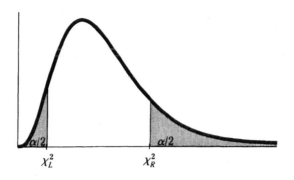

EXAMPLE Find the critical values of χ^2 that determine critical regions containing areas of 0.025 in each tail. Assume that the relevant sample size is 10 so that the degrees of freedom are $10 - 1$, or 9.

SOLUTION See Fig. 6.9 on the following page and refer to Table A.4. The critical value to the right (19.023) is obtained in a straightforward manner by locating 9 in the degrees-of-freedom column at the left and 0.025 across the top. The left critical value of 2.700 once again corresponds to 9 in the degrees-of-freedom column, but we must locate 0.975 (found by subtracting 0.025 from 1) across the top because the values in the top row are always *areas to the right* of the critical value.

First we illustrate the construction of a confidence interval in the next example, then we describe the rationale underlying confidence intervals for population variances.

EXAMPLE A container of car antifreeze is supposed to hold 3785 mL of the liquid. Realizing that fluctuations are inevitable, the quality control manager wants to be quite sure that the standard deviation is less than 30 mL. Otherwise, some containers would overflow while others would not have enough of the coolant. She randomly selects a sample with the results given below. Use these sample results to construct the 99% confidence interval for the true value of σ. Does this confidence interval suggest that the fluctuations are at an acceptable level? Assume that the distribution of fills for the containers of antifreeze is a normal distribution.

3761	3861	3769	3772	3675	3861	$n = 18$
3888	3819	3788	3800	3720	3748	$\bar{x} = 3787.0$
3753	3821	3811	3740	3740	3839	$s = 55.4$

SOLUTION   Based on the sample data, the mean of $\bar{x} = 3787.0$ appears to be acceptable because it is so close to 3785, but we will now construct the 99% confidence interval for σ^2 and then for σ. With a sample size of $n = 18$, we have $n - 1 = 17$ degrees of freedom. Because we want 99% confidence, we let $\alpha = 0.01$ and divide it equally between the two tails to get an area of 0.005 in each tail. In the 17th row of Table A.4, we find that 0.005 in the left and right tails corresponds to $\chi_L^2 = 5.697$ and $\chi_R^2 = 35.718$. With these values and $n = 18$ and $s = 55.4$, we get

$$\frac{(18 - 1)(55.4)^2}{35.718} < \sigma^2 < \frac{(18 - 1)(55.4)^2}{5.697}$$

This then becomes $1460.8 < \sigma^2 < 9158.5$. Taking the square root of each part yields $38.2 < \sigma < 95.7$. It appears that the standard deviation is too large and corrective action must be taken to ensure more-consistent container fillings. (The corrective action might involve checking line pressures, replacing worn parts, retraining operators, and so on.)

FIGURE 6.9
Finding Critical Values of the Chi-Square Distribution using Table A.4.

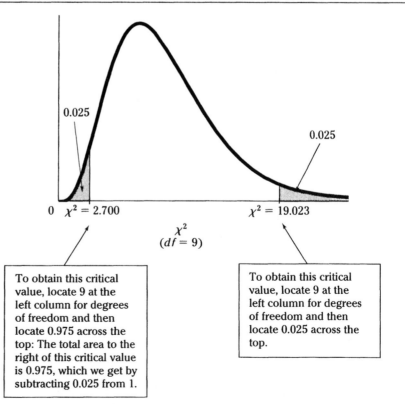

0.025

0.025

0    $\chi^2 = 2.700$ $\chi^2 = 19.023$

χ^2
$(df = 9)$

To obtain this critical value, locate 9 at the left column for degrees of freedom and then locate 0.975 across the top: The total area to the right of this critical value is 0.975, which we get by subtracting 0.025 from 1.

To obtain this critical value, locate 9 at the left column for degrees of freedom and then locate 0.025 across the top.

The rationale underlying the development of confidence intervals for population variances is based on the fact that when we collect sample data from a normally distributed population with mean μ and variance σ^2, the random variable $(n - 1)s^2/\sigma^2$ has a chi-square distribution. Note that the chi-square distribution is not the distribution of sample variances s^2. Instead, it is the distribution of the random variable $(n - 1)s^2/\sigma^2$.

Figure 6.9 shows that for a sample of $n = 10$ scores taken from a normally distributed population with mean μ and variance σ^2, the random variable $(n - 1)s^2/\sigma^2$ has a 0.05 probability of falling in the shaded area, either below 2.700 or above 19.023. In general, the random variable $(n - 1)s^2/\sigma^2$ has a probability α of falling below χ_L^2 or above χ_R^2. If we apply the rule of complements from Chapter 3, it follows that there is a $1 - \alpha$ probability that the random variable $(n - 1)s^2/\sigma^2$ will fall between χ_L^2 and χ_R^2. That is, there is a $1 - \alpha$ probability that both of the following are true.

$$\frac{(n - 1)s^2}{\sigma^2} < \chi_R^2 \quad \text{and} \quad \frac{(n - 1)s^2}{\sigma^2} > \chi_L^2$$

If we multiply both of the preceding inequalities by σ^2 and divide each inequality by the appropriate critical value of χ^2, we see that the two inequalities can be expressed in the equivalent forms

$$\frac{(n - 1)s^2}{\chi_R^2} < \sigma^2 \quad \text{and} \quad \frac{(n - 1)s^2}{\chi_L^2} > \sigma^2$$

These last two inequalities can be combined into one inequality,

$$\frac{(n - 1)s^2}{\chi_R^2} < \sigma^2 < \frac{(n - 1)s^2}{\chi_L^2}$$

There is a probability of $1 - \alpha$ that the population variance σ^2 is contained in the above interval, and this result corresponds to the definition of the confidence interval for σ^2.

DETERMINING SAMPLE SIZE

Most textbooks discuss sample size issues for cases involving means and proportions, but not standard deviations or variances. However, we feel that important implications of variation in quality control require that we include a discussion of sample size problems as they relate to the important measures of variation. The problem of determining the sample size necessary to estimate σ^2 to within given tolerances and confidence levels becomes much more complex than it was in similar problems that dealt with means and proportions. Instead of developing very complicated procedures, we supply Table 6.1, which lists approximate sample sizes (see the following page).

CAPTURE-RECAPTURE

Ecologists need to determine population sizes of endangered species. One method is to capture a sample of some species, mark each member of this sample, and then free them. Later, another sample is captured and the ratio of marked subjects, coupled with the size of the first sample, can be used to estimate the population size. This capture-recapture method was used with other methods to estimate the blue whale population, and the result was alarming: The population was as small as 1000. That led the International Whaling Commission to ban the killing of blue whales to prevent their extinction.

EXAMPLE You wish to estimate σ^2 to within 10% and you need 99% confidence in your results. How large should your sample be? Assume that the population is normally distributed.

SOLUTION From Table 6.1, 99% confidence and an error of 10% for σ^2 correspond to a sample of size 1400. You should randomly select 1400 values from the population.

TABLE 6.1
Sample Size for σ^2

TO BE 95% CONFIDENT THAT s^2 IS WITHIN	OF THE VALUE OF σ^2, THE SAMPLE SIZE n SHOULD BE AT LEAST
1%	77,210
5	3,150
10	806
20	210
30	97
40	57
50	38

TO BE 99% CONFIDENT THAT s^2 IS WITHIN	OF THE VALUE OF σ^2, THE SAMPLE SIZE n SHOULD BE AT LEAST
1%	133,362
5	5,454
10	1,400
20	368
30	172
40	101
50	67

Sample Size for σ

TO BE 95% CONFIDENT THAT s IS WITHIN	OF THE VALUE OF σ, THE SAMPLE SIZE n SHOULD BE AT LEAST
1%	19,205
5	767
10	192
20	47
30	21
40	12
50	8

TO BE 99% CONFIDENT THAT s IS WITHIN	OF THE VALUE OF σ THE SAMPLE SIZE n SHOULD BE AT LEAST
1%	33,196
5	1,335
10	336
20	85
30	38
40	22
50	14

6.4 EXERCISES | BASIC CONCEPTS

1. a. If a sample is described by the statistics $n = 100$, $\bar{x} = 146$, and $s^2 = 12$, find the best point estimate of σ^2.
   b. Use Table 6.1 to find the approximate minimum sample size necessary to estimate σ^2 with a 30% maximum error and 95% confidence.
   c. Find the χ_L^2 and χ_R^2 values for a sample of 25 scores and a confidence level of 99%.

2. a. If a sample is described by the statistics $n = 1087$, $\bar{x} = 77.3$, and $s = 4.0$, find the best point estimate of σ^2.
   b. Use Table 6.1 to find the approximate minimum sample size needed to estimate σ with a 10% maximum error and 95% confidence.
   c. Find the χ_L^2 and χ_R^2 values for a sample of 15 scores and a confidence level of 95%.

3. a. Find the χ_L^2 and χ_R^2 values for a sample of 11 scores and a confidence level of 95%.
   b. Use Table 6.1 to find the approximate minimum sample size needed to estimate σ with a 5% maximum error and 99% confidence.
   c. Find the best point estimate of σ^2 based on a sample for which $n = 17$, $\bar{x} = 69.2$, and $s = 1.2$.

4. a. Find the χ_L^2 and χ_R^2 values for a sample of 27 scores and a confidence level of 90%.
   b. Use Table 6.1 to find the approximate minimum sample size needed to estimate σ with a 10% maximum error and 99% confidence.
   c. Find the best point estimate of σ^2 based on a sample for which $n = 6$, $\bar{x} = 428.2$, and $s = 1.9$.

5. The statistics $n = 30$, $\bar{x} = 16.4$, and $s = 2.5$ are obtained from a random sample drawn from a normally distributed population. Construct the 95% confidence interval about σ^2.

6. The statistics $n = 16$, $\bar{x} = 12.37$, and $s = 1.05$ are obtained from a random sample drawn from a normally distributed population. Construct the 99% confidence interval about σ.

7. Construct a 95% confidence interval about σ^2 if a random sample of 21 scores is selected from a normally distributed population and the sample variance is 100.0.

8. Construct a 95% confidence interval about σ^2 if a random sample of 10 scores is selected from a normally distributed population and the sample variance is 225.0.

9. In a study of the relationships between work schedules and family life, 29 subjects work at night. Their times (in hours) spent in caring for children are measured, and the mean and standard deviation are 26.84 h and 17.66 h, respectively. (See "Nonstandard Work Schedules and Family Life," by Staines and Pleck, *Journal of Applied Psychology*, Vol. 69, No. 3.) Use this sample data to construct the 95% confidence interval for the standard deviation of the times in child care for all night workers.

10. The lengths of times drivers keep their cars vary with economic conditions. A knowledge of those times is important to car manufacturers so they can plan future production levels. In one study, car owners were randomly selected and asked about the length of time they plan to keep their cars. The sample mean

and standard deviation are 7.01 years and 3.74 years, respectively (based on data from a Roper poll). Assume that the sample size is 100 and construct the 95% confidence interval for the population standard deviation.

11. When working high school students are randomly selected and surveyed about the time they work at after-school jobs, the mean and standard deviation are found to be 17.6 h and 9.3 h, respectively (based on data from the National Federation of State High School Associations). Assume that these data are from a sample of 50 subjects and construct the 99% confidence interval about the standard deviation for all working high school students.

12. When using room service, hotel guests prefer quick deliveries, but they also prefer delivery times that are consistent so they need not waste time waiting. A researcher finds that the times required to fill 40 randomly selected room-service orders at a Radisson Hotel are normally distributed with mean of 24.2 min and a standard deviation of 8.7 min. Find the 99% confidence interval for the standard deviation of all room-service times at this hotel.

13. The thickness of emulsion applied to a photographic film must be very consistent. Assume that the application process is statistically stable with a standard deviation of 0.016 (in thousandths of an inch). An engineer recommends changing the temperature and pressure to get better consistency (or less variation). The changes are made, and 50 sample values result in a mean of 0.074 with a standard deviation of 0.009.
    a. Construct a 95% confidence interval for the standard deviation of the modified process. Does it seem that the changes have resulted in improved quality?
    b. What assumptions are made in part a and how could those assumptions be checked?
    c. How large must a sample be if we want to estimate σ for a 95% confidence interval to within 10% of the true value?

14. A process at the Grange Fertilizer Company consists of using a machine to fill fertilizer bags labeled 50 lb. The goal is to have a process mean equal to 50 lb while the standard deviation is 0.5 lb. During a four-hour morning shift, 31 bags are randomly selected, and they are found to have a mean of 50.1 lb and a standard deviation of 0.91 lb. Assume that the process is statistically stable.
    a. Construct a 95% confidence interval for μ.
    b. Construct a 95% confidence interval for σ^2.
    c. Construct a 95% confidence interval for σ.
    d. Based on the preceding results, does the process seem to be running as desired?

15. The values of the lives (in hours) for a sample of 14 light bulbs are as follows:

    975   1025   1010   955   1100   1070   1005
    995   1040   960   990   1030   1060   1015

    a. Construct a 99% confidence interval for σ^2 and include the units.
    b. Construct a 99% confidence interval for σ and include the units.
    c. How many bulbs must we sample if we want to be 99% confident that our estimate of σ is within 40% of the true value?

16. The following weights of cereal boxes were found from a random sample of 12 boxes labeled 13 oz (or 368 g). Assume that the weights result from a statistically stable process.

    370   375   369   360   372   365   373   374   369   371   368   369

a.   Find a 95% confidence interval for σ.

b.   What assumptions must be made in part *a?*

c.   How many boxes must be sampled if you want to estimate σ and you want to be 95% confident that s is within 30% of the true value of σ?

17. A car designer studies variations in heights of women and begins with the following values (in inches) obtained from a random sample (based on data from the National Health Survey). Construct the 95% confidence interval about σ.

60.8	63.8	64.8	64.3	62.7	68.7	62.9	61.8	66.0	63.1
64.0	61.7	61.2	64.4	65.4	60.8	59.4	66.1	66.3	63.9

18. For the Air America reservation service, telephone customer hold times are recorded for the period between 9:00 A.M. and 12:00 P.M. A sample of 16 such times (in seconds) is given below. Those who study the quality of service need to understand the variability among hold times. Construct a 95% confidence interval for the population standard deviation σ.

104   95   125   62   38   168   74   0   47   31   23   0   88   59   0   19

6.4 EXERCISES   BEYOND THE BASICS

19. A random sample is drawn from a normally distributed population and it is found that $n = 20$, $\bar{x} = 45.2$, and $s = 3.8$. Based on this sample, the following confidence interval is constructed.

$$2.8 < \sigma < 6.0$$

Find the degree of confidence.

20. A random sample of 12 scores is drawn from a normally distributed population and the 95% confidence interval is found to be

$$19.1 < \sigma < 45.8$$

Find the standard deviation of the sample.

21. In constructing confidence intervals for σ or σ^2, we use Table A.4 to find χ_L^2 and χ_R^2, but that table applies only to cases in which $n \leq 101$ so that the number of degrees of freedom is 100 or fewer. For large numbers of degrees of freedom, we can approximate χ_L^2 and χ_R^2 by

$$\chi^2 = \frac{1}{2}\left[\pm z_{\alpha/2} + \sqrt{2k - 1}\right]^2$$

Here k = number of degrees of freedom and $z_{\alpha/2}$ is as described in the preceding sections. Construct the 95% confidence interval about σ by using the following sample data. The measured heights of 772 males between the ages of 18 and 24 have a mean of 69.7 in. and a standard deviation of 2.8 in. (based on data from the National Health Survey, USDHEW publication 79-1659).

22. When 500 items are randomly selected from a normally distributed population, the mean is 253.7 and the standard deviation is 4.8. Based on this data, the following confidence interval is obtained:

$$4.5459 < \sigma < 5.0788$$

What is the degree of confidence? (*Hint:* See Exercise 21.)

23. a. Use Minitab to simulate the filling of 20 cereal boxes labeled 368 g by entering these commands that generate normally distributed results with a mean of 370 and a standard deviation of 5:

```
MTB  > RANDOM N = 20 C1;
SUBC> NORMAL MU = 370 SIGMA = 5.
MTB  > PRINT C1
MTB  > HISTOGRAM C1
MTB  > DESCRIBE C1
```

b. Use the Minitab results to construct a 95% confidence interval for σ. Does this interval contain $\sigma = 5$?

Vocabulary List

Define and give an example of each term.

random sampling
stratified sampling
systematic sampling
cluster sampling
convenience sampling
sampling errors
nonsampling errors
estimator
point estimate
confidence interval
interval estimate
degree of confidence
level of confidence
confidence coefficient
critical score
margin of error
confidence interval limits
Student t distribution
degrees of freedom
point estimate of the population proportion
point estimate of the population variance
left-tailed critical value
right-tailed critical value
chi-square distribution

Review

In this chapter we introduced important and fundamental concepts of inferential statistics. Our main objective was to develop procedures for estimating values of these population parameters: means (Section 6.2), proportions (Section 6.3), and variances or standard deviations (Section 6.4). We discussed the best *point estimates* of each of these parameters. The best point estimate for a population mean is the value of the sample mean. The best point estimate of a population proportion is the value of the sample proportion. The best point estimate of a population variance is the sample variance. (However, the best point estimate of a population standard deviation is *not* the sample standard deviation.) As single values, the point estimates don't convey any real sense of how reliable they are, so we introduced *confidence intervals* (or *interval estimates*) as more-informative estimates. We also considered ways of determining the *sample sizes* necessary to estimate parameters to within given margins of error.

This chapter also introduced the Student t and chi-square distributions. We must be careful to use the correct distribution for each set of circumstances. The following table summarizes the key concepts in this chapter.

IMPORTANT FORMULAS

PARAMETER	POINT ESTIMATE	CONFIDENCE INTERVAL		SAMPLE SIZE
μ	$\bar{x}$	$\bar{x} - E < \mu < \bar{x} + E$ where $E = z_{\alpha/2}\dfrac{\sigma}{\sqrt{n}}$	(if σ is known or if $n > 30$, in which case we use s for σ)	$n = \left[\dfrac{z_{\alpha/2}\sigma}{E}\right]^2$
		or $E = t_{\alpha/2}\dfrac{s}{\sqrt{n}}$	(if σ is unknown and $n \le 30$ and the population has a normal distribution)	
p	$\hat{p} = \dfrac{x}{n}$	$\hat{p} - E < p < \hat{p} + E$ where $E = z_{\alpha/2}\sqrt{\dfrac{\hat{p}\,\hat{q}}{n}}$	(requires $np \ge 5$ and $nq \ge 5$)	$n = \dfrac{[z_{\alpha/2}]^2\,\hat{p}\,\hat{q}}{E^2}$ or $n = \dfrac{[z_{\alpha/2}]^2 \cdot 0.25}{E^2}$
σ^2	s^2	$\dfrac{(n-1)s^2}{\chi_R^2} < \sigma^2 < \dfrac{(n-1)s^2}{\chi_L^2}$	(requires a normally distributed population)	See Table 6.1.

Review Exercises

1. Assume that the following statistics represent sample data randomly selected from a normally distributed population: $n = 60$, $\bar{x} = 83.2$ kg, $s = 4.1$ kg.
   a. What is the best point estimate of μ?
   b. Construct the 95% confidence interval about μ.
2. Use the sample data given in Exercise 1.
   a. What is the best point estimate of σ^2?
   b. Construct the 95% confidence interval about σ.
3. You want to determine the percentage of individual tax returns that include capital gains deductions. How many such returns must be randomly selected and checked? You want to be 90% confident that your sample percentage is in error by no more than four percentage points.
4. Of 1475 transportation workers randomly selected, 32.0% belong to unions (based on data from the U.S. Bureau of Labor Statistics). Construct the 95% confidence interval for the true proportion of all transportation workers who belong to unions.
5. A medical researcher wishes to estimate the serum cholesterol level (in mg/100 ml) of all women aged 18 to 24. There is strong evidence suggesting that $\sigma = 41.0$ mg/100 ml (based on data from a survey of 1524 women aged 18 to 24, as part of the National Health Survey, USDHEW publication 78-1652). If the researcher wants to be 95% confident in obtaining a sample mean that is off by no more than four units, how large must the sample be?
6. A magazine reporter is conducting independent tests to determine the distance a certain car will travel while consuming only 1 gal of gas. A sample of 5 cars is tested and a mean of 28.2 mi is obtained. Assuming that $\sigma = 2.7$ mi, find the 98% confidence interval for the mean distance traveled by all such cars using 1 gal of gas.
7. Independent tests are conducted to determine the distance a car will travel while consuming only 1 gal of gas. A sample of 5 cars is tested, and the 5 distances have a mean of 28.2 mi and a standard deviation of 2.7 mi.
   a. Construct a 99% confidence interval for the true mean μ.
   b. Construct a 99% confidence interval for the standard deviation of distances traveled for all such cars.
8. A sociologist wants to determine the mean value of cars owned by retired people. If the sociologist wants to be 96% confident that the mean of the sample group is off by no more than $250, how many retired people must be sampled? A pilot study suggests that the standard deviation is $3050.
9. In clinical trials of the allergy medication Seldane, 70 subjects experienced drowsiness while 711 did not (based on data from Merrell Dow Pharmaceuticals).
   a. Construct the 95% confidence interval for the proportion of Seldane users who experience drowsiness.
   b. How many people should be tested if we want to find a 95% confidence interval for the true proportion who experience drowsiness and we want a 0.015 margin of error?
10. A stable process consists of filling 2-liter bottles of cola. Given below are 10 randomly selected fill amounts (in liters).

    1.95   2.02   1.99   1.97   2.04   1.94   2.05   1.98   1.96   2.01

a. Construct a 95% confidence interval for μ.
b. Construct a 95% confidence interval for σ.
c. Does the process appear to be running as desired? Explain.
d. Suppose specifications require that σ be no larger than 0.01. Does the process appear to be meeting that specification?

11. a. Evaluate $z_{\alpha/2}$ for $\alpha = 0.10$.
   b. Evaluate χ_L^2 and χ_R^2 for $\alpha = 0.05$ and a sample of 10 scores.
   c. Evaluate $t_{\alpha/2}$ for $\alpha = 0.05$ and a sample of 10.
   d. What is the largest possible value of $p \cdot q$?

12. Assume that the following statistics represent sample data randomly selected from a normally distributed population of elevator passengers: $n = 16$, $\bar{x} = 83.2$ kg, $s = 4.1$ kg.
   a. What is the best point estimate of μ?
   b. Construct the 95% confidence interval about μ.

13. Use the sample data given in Exercise 12.
   a. What is the best point estimate of σ^2?
   b. Construct the 95% confidence interval about σ.

14. Based on recent data from the U.S. Bureau of the Census, the proportion of Americans below the poverty level is 0.140. A researcher wants to verify that figure by conducting an independent survey. Assuming that 0.140 is approximately correct, how many randomly selected Americans must be surveyed? The researcher wants to be 96% confident that the sample proportion is within 0.015 of the true population proportion.

15. In a Roper survey of 1,998 adults, 24% included loud commercials among the annoying aspects of television. Construct the 99% confidence interval for the proportion of all adults who are annoyed by loud commercials.

16. A botanist for the National Paper Company wants to determine the mean diameter of pine trees on land being considered for purchase. A preliminary study of 41 randomly selected trees results in a sample mean of $\bar{x} = 41.42$ cm and $s = 6.35$ cm.
   a. Construct a 95% confidence interval for the true mean diameter.
   b. Construct a 95% confidence interval for the true standard deviation of diameters.
   c. How many trees must be measured if we want to estimate the mean and we want to be 95% confident that the margin of error is no more than 1.0 cm? Do we need to assume that the diameters are normally distributed? Why?
   d. How many trees must be measured if we want to estimate the standard deviation and we want to be 95% confident that the sample standard deviation is off by no more than 10%?

17. a. Evaluate $z_{\alpha/2}$ for a confidence level of 96%.
   b. Evaluate $t_{\alpha/2}$ for a confidence level of 99% and a sample size of 16.
   c. Evaluate χ_L^2 and χ_R^2 for a confidence level of 99% and a sample size of 20.
   d. For the same set of data, confidence intervals are constructed for the 95% and 99% confidence levels. Which interval has limits that are farther apart?

18. While considering the purchase of television time for a commercial, the Bradley and Coratti Advertising Company wants to estimate the mean time spent by preschool children watching television on Saturday morning. A pilot study suggests that $\sigma = 0.8$ h. How many subjects must be surveyed for 98% confidence that the sample mean is off by no more than 0.02 h?

19. In a Gallup poll of 1004 adults, 93% indicated that restaurants and bars should refuse service to patrons who have had too much to drink. Construct the 98% confidence interval for the proportion of all adults who feel the same way.

20. A statistically stable process consists of manufacturing fishing line. Every 5 min, samples are tested for their breaking points (in pounds), and results from a particular shift are listed below.

$$\begin{array}{ccccccccccc} 20 & 23 & 14 & 12 & 18 & 19 & 13 & 23 & 19 & 20 & 16 & 26 \\ 15 & 18 & 19 & 27 & 21 & 26 & 28 & 15 & 20 & 26 & 18 & 22 \end{array}$$

    a. Construct a 95% confidence interval for μ.

    b. Construct a 95% confidence interval for σ.

    c. Construct a 95% confidence interval for the proportion of lines that break at 15 lb or lower.

    d. The fishing line is intended to break at 20 lb. Based on parts *a, b,* and *c,* does it appear that this process results in good-quality 20-lb fishing line?

Computer Projects

1. Computer software packages designed for statistics commonly provide programs for generating confidence intervals. Use Minitab to find the confidence intervals in Exercises 21, 22, and 24 from Section 6.2. (Use Minitab's TINTERVAL command.)

2. The sample scores given below are randomly selected from a population with a distribution that is very nonnormal, so the standard methods of this section don't apply. Instead, construct a 95% confidence interval about μ by using the *bootstrap* method as follows:

    a. Create 1000 new samples, each of size 10, by selecting 10 scores (with replacement) from the sample scores given below.

$$\begin{array}{cccccccccc} 2.9 & 564.2 & 1.4 & 4.7 & 67.6 & 4.8 & 51.3 & 3.6 & 18.0 & 3.6 \end{array}$$

    b. Find the means of the 1000 bootstrap samples generated in part *a.*

    c. Rank the 1000 means and then find the percentiles $P_{2.5}$ and $P_{97.5}$. These two values are the limits of the desired confidence interval. Identify the resulting confidence interval.

3. Use the bootstrap method (see Computer Project 2) to find a 95% confidence interval about the population standard deviation σ. Compare your result to the interval

$$318.4 < \sigma < 1079.6$$

This interval was obtained by incorrectly using the standard methods described in Section 6.4; the true value of σ is 232.1. Does your bootstrap interval contain $\sigma = 232.1$?

HE'S ANGRY, BUT IS HE RIGHT?

The following excerpt is taken from an actual letter written by a corporation president and sent to the Associated Press.

> "When you or anyone else attempts to tell me and my associates that 1223 persons account for our opinions and tastes here in America, I get mad as hell! How dare you! When you or anyone else tells me that 1223 people represent America, it is astounding and unfair and should be outlawed."

The writer then goes on to state that because the sample size of 1223 people represents 120 million people, his letter represents 98,000 people (120 million divided by 1223) who share the same views.

a. Given that the sample size is 1223 and the degree of confidence is 95%, find the margin of error for the proportion. Assume that there is no prior knowledge about the value of that proportion.

b. The writer is taking the position that a sample size of 1223 drawn from a population of 120 million people is too small to be meaningful. Do you agree or disagree? Write a response that either supports or refutes the writer's position that the sample is too small.

c. The writer also makes the claim that because the poll of 1223 people was projected to reflect the opinions of 120 million, then any one person actually represents 98,000 other people and, because the writer is one person, he himself represents 98,000 other people. Is this claim correct? Why or why not?

CHAPTER 7
Testing Hypotheses

Testing a Claim: Is the Mean Age of U.S. Aircraft 10 Years or Less?

Recently an Aloha Airlines flight between two Hawaiian islands survived the disturbing incident of losing part of its fuselage. A 20-ft hole left several passengers exposed to open air. The cause of the structural failure of the Boeing 737 jet was apparently due to metal fatigue; the jet had been in service for 19 years. Subsequent investigations raised concerns about the effects of aircraft age on aviation safety.

Suppose an industry representative tries to argue that U.S. commercial aircraft really aren't too old by making this claim:

"The mean age of U.S. commercial aircraft is only 10 years or less." Listed below are the ages (in years) of 40 randomly selected U.S. commercial aircraft (based on data from Aviation Data Services).

In Chapter 6 we used this collection of sample data to estimate *the mean age of U.S. commercial aircraft,* but in this chapter we use the sample data to test the claim *made by the industry representative. The*

3.2	22.6	23.1	16.9	0.4	6.6	12.5	22.8	
26.3	8.1	13.6	17.0	21.3	15.2	18.7	11.5	$n = 40$
4.9	5.3	5.8	20.6	23.1	24.7	3.6	12.4	$\bar{x} = 13.41$
27.3	22.5	3.9	7.0	16.2	24.1	0.1	2.1	$s = 8.28$
7.7	10.5	23.4	0.7	15.8	6.3	11.9	16.8	

sample data have a mean of 13.41 years, and this seems to contradict the claim that the mean age is 10 years or less. But is the sample mean of 13.41 years significantly greater than 10 years? Could it be that the population mean really is 10 years or less and the above sample results are due to chance fluctuations? This chapter provides us with the ability to answer such questions so that we can make decisions about a variety of claims.

7.1   OVERVIEW

In Chapter 6 we studied a major topic of inferential statistics—using sample statistics to *estimate* values of population parameters. In this chapter we study another major topic of inferential statistics as we use sample statistics to *test hypotheses* made about population parameters. In statistics, **a hypothesis** is a statement that something is true. The following statements are examples of hypotheses that we will test by the procedures developed in this chapter.

- An airline industry representative claims that the mean age of U.S. commercial aircraft is 10 years or less.
- A television executive claims that the majority of all adults are not annoyed by violence on television.
- A bank president claims that with a single line, customers have more-consistent waiting times, with less than the 6.2-min standard deviation for multiple waiting lines.

Before beginning Section 7.2, it would be very helpful to have a general sense of the thinking used in **hypothesis tests,** also called **tests of significance.** Try to follow the reasoning behind the following example.

Suppose you take a dime from your pocket and claim that it favors heads when it is flipped. That claim is a hypothesis, and we can test it by flipping the dime 100 times. We would expect to get around 50 heads with a fair coin. If heads occur 94 times out of 100 tosses, most people would agree that the coin favors heads. If heads occur 51 times out of 100 tosses, we should not conclude that the dime favors heads, because we could easily get 51 heads with a fair and unbiased coin. Here is the key point: We should conclude that the dime favors heads only if we get *significantly* more heads than we would expect with an unbiased dime. To most people, 51 heads out of 100 tosses is not significant, whereas 94 heads out of 100 is significant. We will establish exact criteria for identifying results that are significant.

This brief example illustrates the basic approach used in testing hypotheses. That approach involves a variety of standard terms and conditions in the context of an organized procedure. We suggest that you begin the study of this chapter by first reading Section 7.2 casually to obtain a general idea of its concepts. Then read the material more carefully to gain familiarity with the terminology. Subsequent readings should incorporate the details and refinements into the basic procedure. You are not expected to master the principles of hypothesis testing in one reading. It may take several readings for the material to become understandable. After understanding the basic principles of Section 7.2, you will understand the basic method of hypothesis testing, which you can then modify to fit many different circumstances.

Companies often place a high priority on being able to form conclusions about populations based on sample data. Nielsen Media Research continually surveys samples of television viewers to form conclusions about the population of all viewers. Automobile manufacturers conduct crash tests on a sample of new cars to form conclusions about the safety of the whole line of new cars. Pharmaceutical companies test potential new drugs on samples of people to form conclusions about their effects on the population of all people. The methods of hypothesis testing allow professionals in business, industry, and research to use sample data to form conclusions about populations. This chapter introduces those very important methods of hypothesis testing.

7.2 TESTING A CLAIM ABOUT A MEAN

We begin with the problem described at the beginning of this chapter. Here are the key components:

- An airline industry representative claims that the mean age of U.S. commercial aircraft is 10 years or less.
- A *sample* of 40 randomly selected U.S. commercial aircraft has a mean of $\bar{x} = 13.41$ years and a standard deviation of $s = 8.28$ years.

This is the key issue: Is the sample mean of 13.41 large enough for us to conclude that the population mean cannot be 10 or less as claimed? Or is the discrepancy more likely due to chance variations in samples?

In trying to answer these questions, it is easy to become entangled in a complex web of steps without ever understanding the rationale of hypothesis testing. The following concept provides the key to that understanding: **If an event can easily occur, we attribute it to chance, but if the event appears to be unusual, we attribute that significant departure to the presence of characteristics different from those assumed to be true.** If we keep this idea in mind as we examine various examples, hypothesis testing will become meaningful instead of a rote mechanical process. Before we consider our aircraft-age problem further, let's define the standard terms used in hypothesis testing.

- **Null hypothesis** (denoted by H_0): The statement of a zero or "null" difference that is directly tested. The null hypothesis is a statement about the value of a population parameter (such as the mean μ), and it must contain the condition of equality. For the mean, it will be stated in only one of three possible forms: H_0: $\mu =$ some value; H_0: $\mu \leq$ some value; or H_0: $\mu \geq$ some value. For example, the null hypothesis corresponding to the aircraft-age problem is the claim that the ages of U.S. commercial aircraft have a mean equal to 10 years or less (H_0: $\mu \leq 10$ years). The null hypothesis is tested *directly* in the sense that the final conclusion will be either a rejection of H_0 or a failure to reject H_0.
- **Alternative hypothesis** (denoted by H_1): The statement that must be true if the null hypothesis is false. For the mean, it will be stated in only one of three possible forms: $H_1 \neq$ some value; H_1: $\mu <$ some value; or H_1: $\mu >$ some value. (Note: H_1 is the opposite of H_0. For example, if H_0: $\mu \leq 10$, then it follows that the alternative hypothesis is given by H_1: $\mu > 10$.)

A very important note: Depending on how it's stated, the original claim will sometimes be the null hypothesis H_0 and sometimes the alternative hypothesis H_1. Regardless of whether the original claim corresponds to H_0 or H_1, the null hypothesis H_0 must always contain the condition of equality (with the symbolic form of $=$, $\leq$, or $\geq$).

- **Type I error:** The mistake of rejecting the null hypothesis when it is true.
- **Type II error:** The mistake of failing to reject the null hypothesis when it is false.
- **α (alpha):** Symbol used to represent the probability of a type I error.
- **β (beta):** Symbol used to represent the probability of a type II error.
- **Test statistic:** A sample statistic or a value based on the sample data. It is used in making the decision about the rejection of the null hypothesis. In this section, the test statistic will be a z score based on the sample mean.
- **Critical region:** The set of all values of the test statistic that would cause us to reject the null hypothesis.
- **Critical value(s):** The value(s) that separates the critical region from the values of the test statistic that would not lead to rejection of the null hypothesis. The critical value(s) depends on the nature of the null hypothesis, the relevant sampling distribution, and the level of significance α. In this section, the critical value(s) will be a z score(s) that acts as a cutoff point for what is significant.
- **Significance level:** The probability of rejecting the null hypothesis when it is true. Typical values selected are 0.05 and 0.01. That is, the values of $\alpha = 0.05$ and $\alpha = 0.01$ are typically used. (We use the symbol α to represent the significance level.)
- **Elation:** The feeling experienced when the techniques of hypothesis testing are mastered.

Now refer to Fig. 7.1 and follow the steps used to test the claim that the mean age of U.S. commercial aircraft is 10 years or less. Try to maintain a sense of the real issue: There is a claim that the population mean is 10 or less, but that claim is brought into question when a sample mean of $\bar{x} = 13.41$ is obtained. We need to determine whether that discrepancy is *significant* or whether it could be explained away as a typical chance fluctuation.

We will test the claim that $\mu \leq 10$ years. Refer to the steps in Fig. 7.1 and recall that our sample has $n = 40$ scores with a sample mean of $\bar{x} = 13.41$ years and a standard deviation of $s = 8.28$ years.

STEP 1:   We identify the specific claim and put it in symbolic form. The specific claim is that the mean age of U.S. commercial aircraft is 10 years or less. We express that claim in symbolic form as $\mu \leq 10$.

STEP 2:   We give the symbolic form that must be true when the original claim is false. We know that $\mu > 10$ years must be true when $\mu \leq 10$ years is false.

STEP 3:   We have H_0: $\mu \leq 10$ and H_1: $\mu > 10$ because the null hypothesis H_0 must contain the condition of equality.

STEP 4:   We select the significance level of $\alpha = 0.05$, which is a very common choice. With that choice, we select a probability of 0.05 as the value that separates significant differences from chance fluctuations. We would conclude that $\bar{x} = 13.41$ is significantly greater than 10 only if the probability of 13.41 (or greater) is less than 0.05. That is, with a population mean of $\mu = 10$, the probability of getting a sample mean $\bar{x} > 13.41$ must be less than 0.05.

FIGURE 7.1
Hypothesis Testing

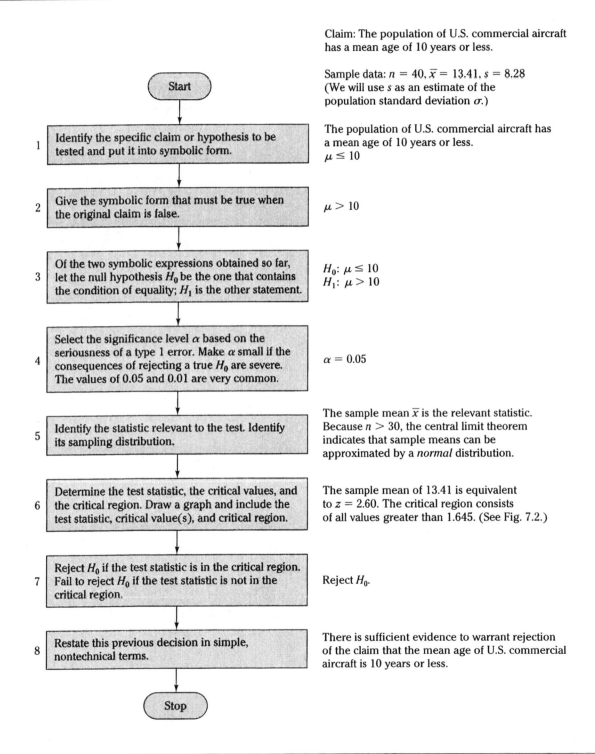

Claim: The population of U.S. commercial aircraft has a mean age of 10 years or less.

Sample data: $n = 40$, $\bar{x} = 13.41$, $s = 8.28$ (We will use s as an estimate of the population standard deviation σ.)

1 Identify the specific claim or hypothesis to be tested and put it into symbolic form.

The population of U.S. commercial aircraft has a mean age of 10 years or less.
$\mu \leq 10$

2 Give the symbolic form that must be true when the original claim is false.

$\mu > 10$

3 Of the two symbolic expressions obtained so far, let the null hypothesis H_0 be the one that contains the condition of equality; H_1 is the other statement.

H_0: $\mu \leq 10$
H_1: $\mu > 10$

4 Select the significance level α based on the seriousness of a type 1 error. Make α small if the consequences of rejecting a true H_0 are severe. The values of 0.05 and 0.01 are very common.

$\alpha = 0.05$

5 Identify the statistic relevant to the test. Identify its sampling distribution.

The sample mean $\bar{x}$ is the relevant statistic. Because $n > 30$, the central limit theorem indicates that sample means can be approximated by a *normal* distribution.

6 Determine the test statistic, the critical values, and the critical region. Draw a graph and include the test statistic, critical value(s), and critical region.

The sample mean of 13.41 is equivalent to $z = 2.60$. The critical region consists of all values greater than 1.645. (See Fig. 7.2.)

7 Reject H_0 if the test statistic is in the critical region. Fail to reject H_0 if the test statistic is not in the critical region.

Reject H_0.

8 Restate this previous decision in simple, nontechnical terms.

There is sufficient evidence to warrant rejection of the claim that the mean age of U.S. commercial aircraft is 10 years or less.

STEP 5:   We identify the relevant statistic $\bar{x}$ and note that its distribution is normal. From the central limit theorem (Section 5.7), we know that sample means tend to be normally distributed. We don't know the population standard deviation σ, but it is common with large ($n > 30$) samples to use the sample standard deviation in place of σ. Using $\mu = 10$ (from the null hypothesis) and the sample standard deviation $s = 8.28$ in place of σ, we get

$$\mu_{\bar{x}} = \mu = 10$$

$$\sigma_{\bar{x}} = \frac{\sigma}{\sqrt{n}} = \frac{8.28}{\sqrt{40}} = 1.31$$

STEP 6:   Refer to Fig. 7.2, where we show the critical value of $z = 1.645$ and the test statistic of $z = 2.60$. You will find the critical value of $z = 1.645$ in Table A.2 as the z score corresponding to an area of 0.4500. (With $\alpha = 0.05$ in the right tail, the area bounded by $z = 0$ and $z = 1.645$ is $0.5 - 0.05 = 0.4500$.) We find the test statistic as follows:

$$z = \frac{\bar{x} - \mu_{\bar{x}}}{\sigma_{\bar{x}}} = \frac{13.41 - 10}{1.31} = 2.60$$

STEP 7:   We reject the null hypothesis H_0 because Fig. 7.2 shows that the test statistic of $z = 2.60$ is in the critical region. That is, the sample mean $\bar{x} = 13.41$ is not only greater than 10, but it is *significantly* greater than 10 (using $\alpha = 0.05$).

STEP 8:   We restate in nontechnical terms the decision we made in step 7: In this example, rejection of the null hypothesis H_0 is rejection of the claim that the mean age of U.S. commercial aircraft is 10 years or less. We therefore conclude that there is sufficient evidence to warrant rejection of the claim that the mean age of U.S. commercial aircraft is 10 years or less.

In addition to knowing the general procedure outlined in Fig. 7.1, you should also be aware of some specific details. After discussing these details, we will present two examples to illustrate them.

NULL AND ALTERNATIVE HYPOTHESES

From steps 1, 2, and 3 of Fig. 7.1, we see how to determine the null and alternative hypotheses. Note that the original claim may be the null or the alternative hypothesis, depending on how it is stated. (For our aircraft-age problem, the original claim—the population of U.S. commercial aircraft has a mean age of 10 years or less—becomes H_0: $\mu \leq 10$.) If we are making our own claims, we should arrange the null and alternative hypotheses so that the most serious error is a type I error (rejecting a true null hypothesis). In this text we assume that we are testing a claim *made by someone else*. Ideally, all claims would be null hypothe-

FIGURE 7.2
Distribution of Means for Samples ($n = 40$) of U.S. Commercial Aircraft Ages

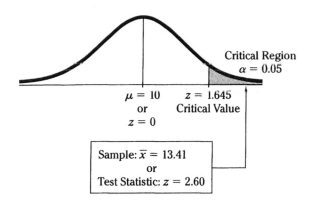

ses. Unfortunately, our world is not ideal, and there are people who make claims that are actually alternative hypotheses. This text was written with the understanding that not all original claims are as they should be. As a result, some examples and exercises involve claims that are null hypotheses, whereas others involve claims that are alternative hypotheses.

In conducting a formal statistical hypothesis test, we are *always* testing the *null hypothesis,* whether it corresponds to the original claim or not. Sometimes the null hypothesis corresponds to the original claim and sometimes it corresponds to the opposite of the original claim. *Because we always test the null hypothesis, we will be testing the original claim in some cases and the opposite of the original claim in other cases.* Carefully examine the examples in Table 7.1.

TABLE 7.1
Determining Null and Alternative Hypotheses

	ORIGINAL CLAIM					
	THE MEAN AGE IS 10	THE MEAN AGE IS NOT 10	THE MEAN AGE IS AT LEAST 10	THE MEAN AGE IS ABOVE 10	THE MEAN AGE IS AT MOST 10	THE MEAN AGE IS BELOW 10
Step 1: Symbolic form of original claim.	$\mu = 10$	$\mu \neq 10$	$\mu \geq 10$	$\mu > 10$	$\mu \leq 10$	$\mu < 10$
Step 2: Symbolic form that is true when original claim is false.	$\mu \neq 10$	$\mu = 10$	$\mu < 10$	$\mu \leq 10$	$\mu > 10$	$\mu \geq 10$
Step 3: Null hypothesis H_0 (must contain equality).	$H_0\colon \mu = 10$	$H_0\colon \mu = 10$	$H_0\colon \mu \geq 10$	$H_0\colon \mu \leq 10$	$H_0\colon \mu \leq 10$	$H_0\colon \mu \geq 10$
Step 4: Alternative hypothesis H_1 (cannot contain equality).	$H_1\colon \mu \neq 10$	$H_1\colon \mu \neq 10$	$H_1\colon \mu < 10$	$H_1\colon \mu > 10$	$H_1\colon \mu > 10$	$H_1\colon \mu < 10$

Regarding notation: Even though we may write H_0 with the symbols $\leq$ or $\geq$ as in H_0: $\mu \leq 10$ or H_0: $\mu \geq 10$, we conduct the test by assuming that H_0: $\mu = 10$ is true. We must have a fixed and specific value for μ so that we can work with one particular distribution. For our aircraft-age problem, we have H_0: $\mu \leq 10$, but we let $\mu = 10$ in Fig. 7.2.)

TYPE I AND TYPE II ERRORS

From Table 7.2 we see that the conclusion in a hypothesis test may be correct or an error. A type I error is the mistake of rejecting a true null hypothesis. A type II error is the mistake of failing to reject a false null hypothesis. The probability of a type I error is the significance level α, and the probability of a type II error is denoted by β.

It would be great if we could always have $\alpha = 0$ and $\beta = 0$, but in the real world that is not possible. The knowledgeable business professional is aware that no matter which decision is made, it could be wrong. It is therefore important to manage the α and β risk levels of making errors.

Mathematically, it can be shown that α (the probability of a type I error), β (the probability of a type II error), and n (the sample size) are all related so that when you choose or determine any two of them, the third is automatically determined. We could select both α and β, and the required sample size would then be determined; but the usual practice in research and industry is to determine in advance the values of α and n, so that the value of β is determined. Based on the seriousness of a type I error, try to use the largest α that you can tolerate. For type I errors with more-serious consequences, select smaller values of α. Common choices are $\alpha = 0.05$, $\alpha = 0.01$, or $\alpha = 0.10$. Then choose a sample size n as large as is reasonable, based on considerations of time, cost, and other relevant factors. (We discussed sample size determinations in Section 6.2.) The following practical considerations may also be relevant to some hypothesis tests:

1. For any fixed α, an increase in the sample size n will cause a decrease in β. (That is, a larger sample will lessen the chance that we fail to reject a false null hypothesis.)
2. For any fixed sample size n, a decrease in α will cause an increase in β. Conversely, an increase in α will cause a decrease in β. (See Exercise 30.)

TABLE 7.2
Type I and Type II Errors

		TRUE STATE OF NATURE	
		The null hypothesis is true.	The null hypothesis is false.
Decision	We decide to reject the null hypothesis.	Type I error	Correct decision
	We fail to reject the null hypothesis.	Correct decision	Type II error

CONCLUSIONS IN HYPOTHESIS TESTING

We have already noted that the original claim sometimes becomes the null hypothesis and sometimes it becomes the alternative hypothesis. However, our procedure requires that we always test the null hypothesis. In Step 7 of Fig. 7.1 we can see that our initial conclusion will always be one of the following:

1. Fail to reject the null hypothesis H_0.
2. Reject the null hypothesis H_0.

Some texts say that we "accept the null hypothesis" instead of "fail to reject the null hypothesis." Whether we use *accept* or *fail to reject,* we should recognize that *we are not proving the null hypothesis;* we are merely saying that the evidence provided by the sample is not strong enough to warrant rejection of the null hypothesis. It's like a jury saying that there is not enough evidence to convict a suspect. The term *accept* is somewhat misleading because it seems incorrectly to imply that the null hypothesis has been proved. The phrase *fail to reject* says, more correctly, "Let's withhold judgment because the available evidence isn't strong enough." In this text, we will use *fail to reject the null hypothesis* instead of *accept the null hypothesis.*

 We either fail to reject the null hypothesis or we reject the null hypothesis. Such a conclusion is fine for those of us with the wisdom to take a statistics course, but it's usually necessary to use simple nontechnical terms in stating what the conclusion suggests. Figure 7.3 on the following page shows how to formulate the correct wording of the final conclusion. Note that only one case leads to wording indicating that the sample data actually *support* the original claim as stated. If you want to justify some specific claim, state it in such a way that it becomes the *alternative* hypothesis, and then hope that the null hypothesis gets rejected. For example, if you want to justify the claim that we have "old planes," state the claim as follows: "U.S. commercial aircraft have a mean life *greater than 10 years.*" This claim will be an alternative hypothesis (H_1: $\mu > 10$) that will be supported if we reject the null hypothesis (H_0: $\mu \le 10$).

 If we had stated the claim as "U.S. commercial aircraft have a mean life of *at least 10 years*" (that is, 10 years or more), that claim itself becomes the null hypothesis that we either reject or fail to reject; in either case we would not be *supporting* the original claim.

LEFT-TAILED, RIGHT-TAILED, TWO-TAILED

The tails in a distribution are the extreme regions bounded by critical values. Our first example of hypothesis testing involved a right-tailed test in the sense that the critical region of Fig. 7.2 is in the extreme right region under the curve. We reject the null hypothesis H_0 if our test statistic is in the critical region, because that indicates a significant discrepancy between the null hypothesis and the sample data. Some tests will be **left-tailed,** with the critical region located in the extreme left region under the curve. Other tests may be **two-tailed** because the critical region comprises two components located in the two extreme regions under the curve. *In the two-tailed case, α is divided equally between the two tails that constitute the critical region.*

FIGURE 7.3
Stating Conclusions in Hypothesis Tests

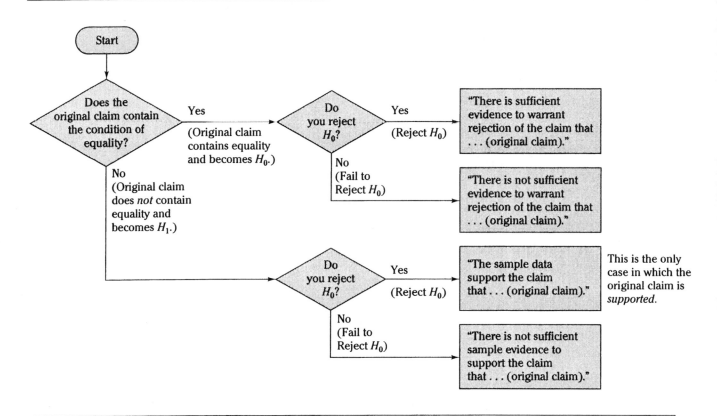

By examining the null hypothesis H_0, we should be able to *deduce* whether a test is right-tailed, left-tailed, or two-tailed. The tail will correspond to the critical region where you have the values that would conflict significantly with the null hypothesis. A useful check is summarized in the accompanying box, which shows how the inequality sign in H_1 points in the direction of the critical region. The symbol $\neq$ is often expressed in programming languages as $< >$, and this reminds us that an alternative hypothesis such as $\mu \neq 10$ corresponds to a *two*-tailed test.

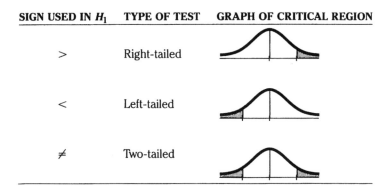

SIGN USED IN H_1	TYPE OF TEST	GRAPH OF CRITICAL REGION
$>$	Right-tailed	
$<$	Left-tailed	
$\neq$	Two-tailed	

ASSUMPTIONS

For the examples and exercises in this section, we are working with these assumptions:

1. The claim is made about the mean of a single population.
2. a. The sample is large $(n > 30)$, so that the central limit theorem applies and we can use the normal distribution. Also, we can use s if σ is unknown. Or
   b. If the sample is small $(n < 30)$, then the population is normally distributed and the value of the population standard deviation σ is known.

A potentially unrealistic feature of some examples and exercises from this section is the assumption that σ is known. Realistic tests of hypotheses must often be made without knowledge of the population standard deviation. *If the sample is large* (n > 30), *we can compute the sample standard deviation and we may be able to use that value of s as an estimate of σ.* When σ is not known and the sample is small $(n \leq 30)$, we may be able to use the t statistic discussed in Section 7.4.

> **EXAMPLE**   The Wisconsin Bottling Company distributes beer in bottles labeled 32 oz. The local Bureau of Weights and Measures randomly selects 50 of these bottles, measures their contents, and obtains a sample mean of 31.0 oz and a sample standard deviation of 0.75 oz. Is it valid at the 0.01 significance level to conclude that the bottling company is cheating consumers?

> **SOLUTION**   The bottling company is cheating consumers if it sells bottles of beer with significantly less than 32 oz. Again refer to Fig. 7.1 and follow these steps:

STEP 1:   The claim that the mean is less than 32 oz becomes $\mu < 32$ oz in symbolic form.

STEP 2:   The alternative (in symbolic form) to the original claim is $\mu \geq 32$ oz.

STEP 3:   The statement $\mu \geq 32$ oz contains the condition of equality and therefore becomes the null hypothesis H_0.

H_0: $\mu \geq 32$ oz

H_1: $\mu < 32$ oz

STEP 4:   With a 0.01 significance level, we have $\alpha = 0.01$.

STEP 5:   We use the sample mean $\bar{x} = 31$ oz to test a claim made about the population mean μ. Since $n > 30$, the central limit theorem indicates that the distribution of sample means can be approximated by a normal distribution.

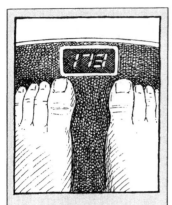

STATISTICAL SIGNIFICANCE VERSUS PRACTICAL SIGNIFICANCE

The hypothesis tests described in this text address the issue of statistical significance. We try to determine whether the observations are so unlikely that we are led to believe that differences are due to factors other than chance sample fluctuations. Experimental results can sometimes be statistically significant without being practically significant. A diet causing an average weight loss of 1/2 lb might be statistically significant if the sample size is 10,000, but such a diet would not have practical significance. Nobody would bother with a diet that resulted in a loss of only 1/2 lb.

FIGURE 7.4
Distribution of Sample Means (in oz)

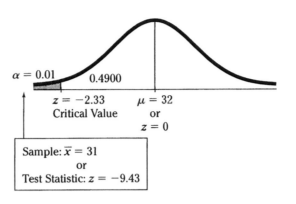

STEP 6: The test statistic, critical value, and critical region are shown in Fig. 7.4. Because $n > 30$, we can use $s = 0.75$ as a reasonable estimate of σ so that the test statistic of $z = -9.43$ is computed as follows:

$$z = \frac{\bar{x} - \mu_{\bar{x}}}{\sigma_{\bar{x}}} = \frac{31 - 32}{0.75/\sqrt{50}} = -9.43$$

We find the critical value of $z = -2.33$ in Table A.2 as the z score corresponding to an area of 0.4900.

STEP 7: From Fig. 7.4 we see that the sample mean of 31 oz does fall within the critical region, so we reject the null hypothesis H_0.

STEP 8: The sample data support the claim that the mean is less than 32 oz. The bottling company is probably cheating the consumer.

In the preceding example, the Bureau of Weights and Measures selected a sample from a large shipment of bottles, so we are really examining a *population* consisting of all bottles being shipped. If we modify the problem slightly so that 50 bottles are selected as they are being produced (such as one bottle each minute), then we could be dealing with a *process* consisting of the filling operation. Analysis of the process would require that we consider the order in which the sample is obtained, and we should begin by determining whether the process is *statistically stable* by using a control chart or a run chart. Once stability is established, we can then use the same hypothesis-testing methods described here. However, if we find that the process is not stable, our first priority should be to make it stable, because any hypothesis testing in an unstable process is meaningless and misleading.

EXAMPLE The engineering department of a car manufacturer claims that the fuel consumption rate of one model is equal to 35 mi/gal. The advertising department wants to test this claim to see whether the announced figure should be higher or lower than 35 mi/gal. The quality control group suggests that $\sigma = 4$ mi/gal, and a sample of 50 cars yields $\bar{x} = 33.6$ mi/gal. Test the claim of the engineering department using a 0.05 level of significance.

SOLUTION Refer to Fig. 7.1 and follow these steps:

STEP 1: The claim that "the mean equals 35 mi/gal" becomes $\mu = 35$ mi/gal.

STEP 2: The alternative (in symbolic form) to the original claim is $\mu \neq 35$ mi/gal.

STEP 3: The statement $\mu = 35$ mi/gal contains the condition of equality, so it becomes the null hypothesis.

H_0: $\mu = 35$ mi/gal
H_1: $\mu \neq 35$ mi/gal

STEP 4: We choose the significance level $\alpha = 0.05$ because it was specified in the statement of the problem.

STEP 5: The sample mean $\bar{x} = 33.6$ mi/gal should be used to test a claim made about the population mean μ. Because $n > 30$, the central limit theorem indicates that the distribution of sample means can be approximated by a normal distribution.

STEP 6: The test statistic, the critical values, and the critical region are shown in Fig. 7.5. The test is two-tailed because a sample mean significantly greater than 35 mi/gal (right tail) or less than 35 mi/gal (left tail) is strong evidence against the null hypothesis that $\mu = 35$ mi/gal. Our sample mean of 33.6 mi/gal is equivalent to $z = -2.47$ through the following computation:

$$z = \frac{\bar{x} - \mu_{\bar{x}}}{\sigma_{\bar{x}}} = \frac{33.6 - 35}{4/\sqrt{50}} = -2.47$$

We find the critical z scores by distributing $\alpha = 0.05$ equally between the two tails to get 0.025 in each tail. We then refer to Table A.2 (because the central limit theorem lets us assume a normal distribution) to find the z value corresponding to $0.5 - 0.025$ or 0.4750 for the right critical value. After finding $z = 1.96$, we use the property of symmetry to conclude that the left critical value is $z = -1.96$. *(continued)*

FIGURE 7.5
Distribution of Sample Means (in mi/gal)

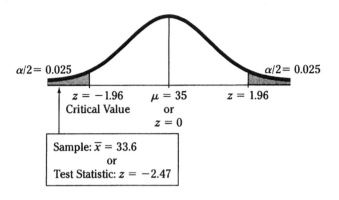

STEP 7:   Because the sample mean of 33.6 mi/gal falls within the critical region, we reject the null hypothesis H_0.

STEP 8:   There is sufficient evidence to warrant rejection of the claim that the mean fuel consumption rate is 35 mi/gal. (It may in fact be less.)

In presenting the results of a hypothesis test, it is not always necessary to show all the steps included in the last example. However, the results should include the null hypothesis, the alternative hypothesis, the calculation of the test statistic, a graph such as Fig. 7.5, the conclusion (reject H_0 or fail to reject H_0), and the final conclusion stated in nontechnical terms. The graph should show the test statistic, critical value(s), critical region, and significance level.

The method of hypothesis testing described in this section is referred to as the *classical,* or *traditional,* the approach. It is based on a comparison of the test statistic and the critical value. The following section introduces an equivalent method called the *P*-value approach, which is based on the probability of getting a sample mean at least as extreme as the one actually obtained.

7.2 EXERCISES   BASIC CONCEPTS

In Exercises 1 and 2, read the given claim and identify the null hypothesis H_0 and the alternative hypothesis H_1 as in the following example: The mean income of college professors is less than $100,000.

$$H_0: \mu \geq \$100,000$$
$$H_1: \mu < \$100,000$$

1. a. The mean age of accountants is greater than 30 years.
   b. The mean length of time managers spend on paperwork each day is more than 3 h.
   c. The mean amount charged by credit card users each month is at least $250.
   d. The mean annual household income is not $14,700.
   e. The mean monthly maintenance cost of an aircraft is $3271.
2. a. The mean annual salary of air traffic controllers is below $30,000.
   b. The mean life of radial tires is less than 35,000 mi.
   c. The mean amount of time customers spend in the Locust Tree Restaurant is 79 min.
   d. The mean length of telephone calls at Reliable Car Rental is at most 3 min.
   e. The mean cost of completing tax returns at the Allen Tax Preparation firm is at least $327.
3. Identify the type I error and the type II error corresponding to each claim in Exercise 1.
4. Identify the type I error and the type II error for each claim in Exercise 2.
5. For each claim in Exercise 1, categorize the hypothesis test as a right-tailed test, a left-tailed test, or a two-tailed test.
6. For each claim in Exercise 2, categorize the hypothesis test as a right-tailed test, a left-tailed test, or a two-tailed test.

In Exercises 7 and 8, find the critical z value for the given conditions. In each case assume that the normal distribution applies, so that you can use Table A.2. Also, draw a graph showing the critical value and critical region.

7. a. Right-tailed test; $\alpha = 0.05$
   b. Right-tailed test; $\alpha = 0.01$
   c. Two-tailed test; $\alpha = 0.05$
   d. Two-tailed test; $\alpha = 0.01$
   e. Left-tailed test; $\alpha = 0.05$
8. a. Left-tailed test; $\alpha = 0.02$
   b. Two-tailed test; $\alpha = 0.10$
   c. Right-tailed test; $\alpha = 0.005$
   d. Right-tailed test; $\alpha = 0.025$
   e. Left-tailed test; $\alpha = 0.025$

In each of the following exercises, test the given hypotheses by following the procedure suggested by Fig. 7.1. Draw the appropriate graph, as in Fig. 7.2.

9. Test the claim that $\mu \leq 100$ given a sample of $n = 81$ for which $\bar{x} = 100.8$. Assume that $\sigma = 5$, and test at the $\alpha = 0.01$ significance level.
10. Test the claim that $\mu \leq 40$ given a sample of $n = 150$ for which $\bar{x} = 41.6$ and $s = 9$. Test at the $\alpha = 0.01$ significance level.
11. Test the claim that $\mu = 20$ given a sample of $n = 100$ for which $\bar{x} = 18.7$ and $s = 3$. Test at the $\alpha = 0.05$ significance level.
12. Test the claim that $\mu \geq 15.5$ given a sample of $n = 20$ for which $\bar{x} = 12.5$. Assume that $\sigma = 5.5$ and the distribution of the data is normal. Test at the $\alpha = 0.05$ significance level.
13. Test the claim that a population mean equals 500. You have a sample of 300 items for which the sample mean is 510. Assume that $\sigma = 100$, and test at the $\alpha = 0.10$ significance level.

14. Test the claim that a population mean equals 65. You have a sample of 50 items for which the sample mean is 66.1 and the standard deviation is $s = 4$. Test at the $\alpha = 0.05$ significance level.

15. Test the claim that a population mean exceeds 40. You have a sample of 50 items for which the sample mean is 42 and the standard deviation is $s = 8$. Test at the $\alpha = 0.05$ significance level.

16. Test the claim that a population mean is less than 75.0. You have a sample of 16 items for which the sample mean is 73.8. Assume that $\sigma = 4.2$ and the distribution is normal. Test at the $\alpha = 0.10$ significance level.

17. Use the aircraft-age sample data ($n = 40$, $\bar{x} = 13.41$ years, $s = 8.28$ years) given at the beginning of the chapter. At the 0.05 level of significance, test the *Time* magazine claim that the mean age of aircraft in the U.S. fleet is 14 years. Assume that the sample standard deviation can be used for σ.

18. A brewery distributes beer in cans labeled 12 oz. The Bureau of Weights and Measures randomly selects 36 cans, measures their contents, and obtains a sample mean of 11.82 oz. Assuming that σ is known to be 0.38 oz, is it valid at the 0.01 significance level to conclude that the brewery is cheating consumers?

19. In a study of distances traveled by buses before the first major engine failure, a sample of 191 buses results in a mean of 96,700 mi and a standard deviation of 37,500 mi (based on data in *Technometrics*, Vol. 22, No. 4). At the 0.05 level of significance, test the claim that mean distance traveled before a major engine failure is more than 90,000 mi. (Assume that the sample standard deviation can be used for σ.)

20. The Medassist Pharmaceutical Company makes a nighttime cold medicine that bears a label indicating the presence of 600 mg of acetaminophen in each fluid ounce of the drug. The Food and Drug Administration randomly selects sixty-five 1-oz samples and finds that the mean acetaminophen content is 589 mg, while the standard deviation is 21 mg. With $\alpha = 0.01$, test the claim that the population mean is equal to 600 mg. (Assume that the sample standard deviation can be used for σ.)

21. A poll of 100 randomly selected car owners revealed that the mean length of time they plan to keep their car is 7.01 years and the standard deviation is 3.74 years (based on data from a Roper poll). Test the claim that the mean for all car owners is less than 7.5 years. (Assume that the sample standard deviation can be used for σ.)

22. The Regal Soap Company manufactures deodorant soaps and wants to check the actual contents of bars that are labeled as containing 5 oz. The production process appears to be stable, and every 20th bar is selected until a sample of 40 bars is obtained. This sample has a mean of 5.03 oz and a sample standard deviation of 0.19 oz. At the $\alpha = 0.05$ significance level, test the claim that the population mean equals 5 oz.

23. The mean time between failures (in hours) for a certain type of radio used in light aircraft is 420 h. Suppose 35 new radios have been modified for more reliability, and tests show that the mean time between failures for this sample is 385 h. Assume that σ is known to be 24 h and let $\alpha = 0.05$. Test the claim that the modifications improved reliability. (Note that improved reliability should correspond to a *longer* mean time between failures.)

24. In an insurance study of driving habits, 750 female drivers aged 16–24 are randomly selected, and their mean driving distance for one year is 6047 mi

(based on data from the Federal Highway Administration). Assuming that σ is known to be 2944 mi, use a 0.05 significance level to test the claim that the population mean for women in this age bracket is less than 7124 mi, which is the known mean for females in the 25–34 age bracket.

25. The Acton Paper Company employs a Human Resources manager who is given responsibility for employee benefits. She randomly selects 40 employee records for the past year and finds that the mean dental expense is $537, while the standard deviation for this sample is $78. At the $\alpha = 0.05$ significance level, test the manager's claim that the mean dental expense is $500.

26. A late-night television show is seen by a relatively large percentage of household members who videotape the show for viewing at a more convenient time. The show's marketing manager claims that the mean income of households with VCRs is greater than $40,000. Test that claim. A sample of 1700 households with VCRs produces a sample mean of $41,182 (based on data from Nielsen Media Research). Assume that σ is known to be $19,990.

7.2 EXERCISES BEYOND THE BASICS

27. The Wisconsin Bottling Company claims that the consumers are getting a mean volume equal to 32 oz in their quart bottles of mineral water. The Bureau of Weights and Measures randomly selects 36 bottles and obtains the following measures in ounces.

32.09	31.89	31.06	32.03	31.42	31.39	31.75
31.53	32.42	31.56	31.95	32.00	31.39	32.09
31.67	31.47	32.45	32.14	31.86	32.09	32.34
32.00	30.95	33.53	32.17	31.81	31.78	32.64
31.06	32.64	32.20	32.11	31.42	32.09	33.00
32.06						

Using the sample standard deviation as an estimate for σ, test the claim of the bottling company at the 0.05 significance level.

28. The Chemco Company manufactures a liquid dishwashing mixture and claims that on the average, customers are getting more than the 12 oz that is printed on the label. Listed below are the contents (in ounces) of 15 containers randomly selected (one each minute) from the production line.

12.1	12.3	11.9	12.3	12.1	12.2	12.4	11.8	12.2	11.7
12.2	12.5	11.9	12.1	12.3					

a. Construct a histogram and boxplot. Does the distribution appear to be normal?

b. Find $\bar{x}$ and s.

c. Assuming that σ is known to be 0.20 oz and the distribution is normal, test Chemco's claim. Use a 0.10 significance level.

d. Is this a process or a population? If it is a process, what should we verify before testing the claim in part c?

e. Why would Chemco like to decrease σ from 0.20 to 0.10? What benefits would be gained by that decrease? What are some specific steps Chemco might take to effect that decrease?

29. A robot sprayer paints lawn tractors, and the paint thickness is measured in microns. A sample is obtained by checking every 10th tractor until 35 tractors have been measured. The result is described by the accompanying boxplot. At the 0.05 level of significance, test the claim that the mean paint thickness is equal to 100 microns. Assume that the painting process is statistically stable.

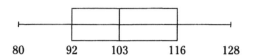

80   92   103   116   128

30. **The probability β of a type II error:** For a given hypothesis test, the probability α of a type I error is fixed, whereas the probability β of a type II error depends on the particular value of μ that is used as an alternative to the null hypothesis. For hypothesis tests of the type found in this section, we can find β as follows:

1. Find the value of $\bar{x}$ that corresponds to the critical value. In

$$z = \frac{\bar{x} - \mu_{\bar{x}}}{\sigma_{\bar{x}}}$$

substitute the critical score for z, enter the values for $\mu_{\bar{x}}$ and $\sigma_{\bar{x}}$, then solve for $\bar{x}$.
2. Given a particular value of μ that is an alternative to the null hypothesis H_0, draw the normal curve with this new value of μ at the center. Also plot the value of $\bar{x}$ found in step 1.
3. Refer to the graph from step 2 and find the area of the new critical region bounded by $\bar{x}$. This is the probability of rejecting the null hypothesis given that the new value of μ is correct.
4. The value of β is 1 minus the area from step 3. This is the probability of failing to reject the null hypothesis given that the new value of μ is correct.

The preceding steps allow you to find the probability of failing to reject H_0 when it is false. You are finding the area under the curve that *excludes* the critical region where you reject H_0; this area therefore corresponds to a failure to reject H_0 that is false, because we use a particular value of μ that goes against H_0. Refer to the aircraft-age example discussed in this section (see Figs. 7.1 and 7.2) and find the value of β corresponding to the following:
   a. $\mu = 10.50$
   b. $\mu = 11.00$
   c. $\mu = 14.00$
31. The *power* of a test is $1 - \beta$, the probability of rejecting a false null hypothesis. Refer to the aircraft-age example discussed in this section. If that test has a power of 0.8, find the mean μ (see Exercise 30).
32. a.   Using the sample data in Exercise 27, construct a 95% confidence interval about μ.
   b.   Does that interval contain 32 oz?
   c.   Describe a rule for using confidence intervals in place of the traditional methods in two-tailed hypothesis tests. What feature of a confidence interval would cause you to reject a null hypothesis?

7.3   *P-VALUES AND ALTERNATIVE WAYS TO TEST CLAIMS*

In Sections 7.1 and 7.2 we introduced the classical, or traditional, approach used to test a hypothesis or claim made about a population mean. We saw that the conclusion involved a decision either to reject or to fail to reject the null hypothesis, and that decision was determined by comparing the test statistic and the critical value. In many professional articles and software packages, we find another approach to hypothesis testing that is based on the calculation of a probability value, or *P*-value.

DEFINITION

A *P*-value is the probability of getting a value of the sample test statistic that is at least as extreme as the one found from the sample data (assuming that the hypothesized value is correct).

The *P*-value approach involves finding the *P*-value itself, then comparing it to the significance level α. The *P*-value approach uses most of the same basic procedures as the classical approach, but these steps are different:

1. Find the *P*-value. That is, find the probability of getting a value of the sample mean $\bar{x}$ that is at least as extreme as the $\bar{x}$ found from the sample data. In finding this *P*-value, we must assume that the hypothesized value of the mean is correct.
2. Report the *P*-value. Some statisticians prefer simply to report the *P*-value and leave the conclusion to the reader. Others prefer to use this decision criterion:

   - *Reject* the null hypothesis if the *P*-value is less than or equal to the significance level α.
   - *Fail to reject* the null hypothesis if the *P*-value is greater than the significance level α.

In step 2, if the conclusion is based on the *P*-value alone, the following guide may be helpful.

P-VALUE	INTERPRETATION
Less than 0.01	Highly statistically significant Very strong evidence against the null hypothesis
0.01 to 0.05	Statistically significant Adequate evidence against the null hypothesis
Greater than 0.05	Insufficient evidence against the null hypothesis

Figure 7.6 on the following page outlines key steps and decisions that lead to the *P*-value. In a right-tailed test, the *P*-value is the area to the right of the test statistic. In a left-tailed test, the *P*-value is the area to the left of the test statistic. However, we must be careful to note that in a two-tailed test, the *P*-value is *twice* the area of the extreme region bounded by the test statistic. This makes sense

FIGURE 7.6
Finding *P*-Values

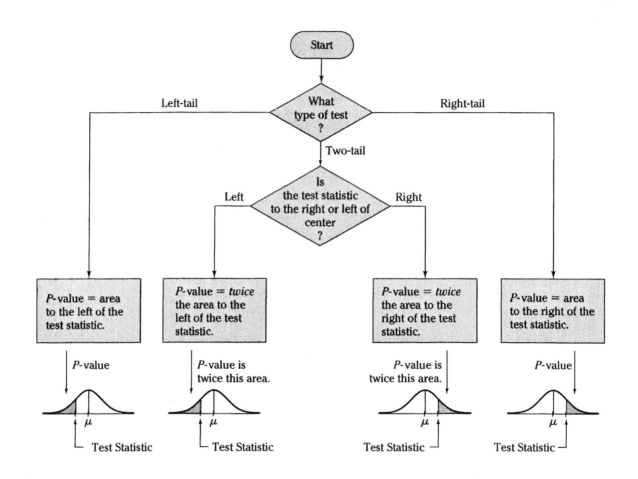

when we recognize that the *P*-value gives us the probability of getting a sample mean that is *at least as extreme* as the sample mean actually obtained, and the two-tailed case has critical or extreme regions in *both* tails.

The following example uses the *P*-value approach for the same example presented in Section 7.2 (see Figs. 7.1 and 7.2).

EXAMPLE   An airline industry representative claims that the mean age of U.S. commercial aircraft is 10 years or less. A random sample of 40 such aircraft has a mean of 13.41 years and a standard deviation of 8.28 years. At the $\alpha = 0.05$ significance level, use the *P*-value approach to test the representative's claim.

FIGURE 7.7
Distribution of Sample Means (in years)

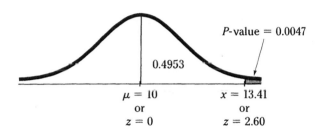

P-value $= 0.0047$

0.4953

$\mu = 10$ $x = 13.41$
or   or
$z = 0$ $z = 2.60$

SOLUTION   As in Section 7.2, we have

Null hypothesis	$H_0: \mu \leq 10$
Alternative hypothesis	$H_1: \mu > 10$
Significance level	$\alpha = 0.05$

Test statistic $z = \dfrac{\bar{x} - \mu_{\bar{x}}}{\sigma_{\bar{x}}} = \dfrac{13.41 - 10}{\dfrac{8.28}{\sqrt{40}}} = 2.60$

We will now find the P-value. Refer to Fig. 7.7 and observe that the area to the right of $\bar{x} = 13.41$ (or $z = 2.60$) can be found from Table A.2. Referring to Table A.2 with $z = 2.60$, find the area of 0.4953 as shown in Fig. 7.7. That area is subtracted from 0.5 to yield the right-tail area of 0.0047. The P-value is 0.0047 because this is the probability of getting a value at least as extreme as $\bar{x} = 13.41$.

We now observe that because the P-value of 0.0047 is less than the significance level of $\alpha = 0.05$, we reject the null hypothesis. There is sufficient evidence to warrant rejection of the claim that the mean age is 10 years or less.

In Section 7.2 we included an example of a two-tailed hypothesis test, and that example used the classical approach to hypothesis testing. In the figure on the following page we have extracted the essential components of that example to compare them to the P-value approach. (We use the decision criterion that involves a comparison of the significance level α and the P-value.) Note that the only real difference is the decision criterion, which leads to the same conclusion in both cases.

In Section 7.2, we stated that the significance level α should be selected *before* a hypothesis test is conducted. Many statisticians consider this a good practice because it helps prevent us from using the data to support subjective conclusions or beliefs. They feel that this practice becomes especially important with the *P*-value approach because we may be tempted to adjust the significance level based on the resulting *P*-value. With a 0.05 level of significance and a *P*-value of 0.06, we should fail to reject the null hypothesis, but it is sometimes tempting to say that a probability of 0.06 is small enough to warrant rejection of the null hypothesis. Consequently we should always select the significance level first. Other statisticians feel that prior selection of a significance level reduces the usefulness of *P*-values. They contend that no significance level should be specified, and the conclusion should be left to the reader. We shall use the decision criterion that involves a comparison of a significance level and the *P*-value.

INTERPRETATION OF THE OBSERVED TEST STATISTIC AND *P*-VALUE

In hypothesis testing, it is easy to get lost in the mechanics of the test and lose sight of what is really happening. We should recognize that the test statistic is just a *z* score representing the *number of standard deviations* that our sample mean $\bar{x}$ is away from the claimed population mean μ. If the claimed value of μ is in fact true, then we would expect $\bar{x}$ to be reasonably close to μ. But if $\bar{x}$ is very far away from μ, then this unusual result leads us to believe that the claimed value of μ is incorrect and so we reject the null hypothesis.

Example: Test the claim that cars of a particular model have fuel consumption equal to 35 mi/gal. The quality control group suggests that $\sigma = 4$ mi/gal and a sample of 50 cars yields $\bar{x} = 33.6$ mi/gal.

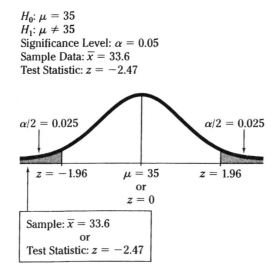

H_0: $\mu = 35$
H_1: $\mu \neq 35$
Significance Level: $\alpha = 0.05$
Sample Data: $\bar{x} = 33.6$
Test Statistic: $z = -2.47$

$\alpha/2 = 0.025$ $\alpha/2 = 0.025$

$z = -1.96$ $\mu = 35$ $z = 1.96$
                 or
                 $z = 0$

Sample: $\bar{x} = 33.6$
or
Test Statistic: $z = -2.47$

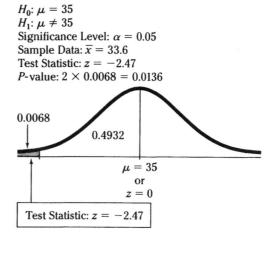

H_0: $\mu = 35$
H_1: $\mu \neq 35$
Significance Level: $\alpha = 0.05$
Sample Data: $\bar{x} = 33.6$
Test Statistic: $z = -2.47$
P-value: $2 \times 0.0068 = 0.0136$

0.0068
          0.4932

$\mu = 35$
or
$z = 0$

Test Statistic: $z = -2.47$

In the first example of this section, the sample mean of 13.41 led to a test statistic of $z = 2.60$. That is, *the sample mean is 2.60 standard deviations away from the claimed mean* of $\mu = 10$. In Chapters 2 and 5 we saw that a z score of 2.60 is relatively large and it corresponds to an unusual result (if in fact $\mu = 10$). This evidence is strong enough that it tends to make us believe that the mean is greater than 10. The critical value and critical region delineate the range of "unusual" values that cause us to reject the claimed value of μ.

After recognizing that the P-value approach to testing hypotheses is essentially equivalent to the classical approach, we might wonder why P-values are important. One reason is that most modern statistical software packages are designed to yield P-values, so the user cannot do hypothesis testing without them. Another reason comes from an interpretation of the P-value itself. Whereas the classical approach results in a "reject/fail to reject" conclusion, P-values measure how confident we are in rejecting a null hypothesis. For example, a P-value of 0.00001 would lead us to reject the null hypothesis, but it would also suggest that the sample results are *extremely* unusual if the claimed μ is in fact true. Another P-value of 0.03 might also lead us to reject the null hypothesis, but we wouldn't have quite as much confidence in our rejection as we did with a P-value of 0.00001.

The P-value is the probability of a type I error (for the given sample results), so that it is a measure of the risk of being wrong if you should reject the null hypothesis. Consider again the aircraft-age example given earlier in this section. The sample mean of $\bar{x} = 13.41$ led to a test statistic of $z = 2.60$, which in turn led to a P-value of 0.0047, and we rejected the null hypothesis. If the sample mean had been $\bar{x} = 12.23$ (instead of 13.41), the P-value would have been 0.045 (from a test statistic of $z = 1.70$), and we would again reject the null hypothesis. However, the P-value of 0.045 would indicate a much greater risk of being wrong in our rejection of the null hypothesis; the sample evidence wouldn't be as dramatic as it was with a P-value of 0.0047. The P-value of 0.0047 shows that the sample evidence ($\bar{x} = 13.41$) in favor of rejecting the null hypothesis ($\mu \leq 10$) is much stronger than the sample evidence ($\bar{x} = 12.23$) that led to a P-value of 0.045.

In Section 7.2 we described the classical, or traditional, approach to testing hypotheses, and in this section we have described the P-value approach. In addition to those two approaches, there are others, such as the following.

EXAMINING CLAIMS USING CONFIDENCE INTERVALS

In addition to the classical and P-value approaches, there are other approaches to testing claims made about population parameters such as the mean. One approach involves the use of sample data in the construction of confidence intervals (or interval estimates). Consider this brief example: An airline industry representative claims that the mean age of U.S. commercial aircraft is equal to 10 years, but a random sample of 40 such aircraft yields a mean of 13.41 years. In Section 6.2 we used that sample data to conclude that there is a 95% chance that the following interval really does contain the true mean age of U.S. commercial aircraft.

$$10.84 \text{ years} < \mu < 15.98 \text{ years}$$

DRUG SCREENING: FALSE POSITIVES

For a job applicant undergoing drug screening, a *false positive* is an indication of drug use when he or she does not use them. A *false negative* is an indication of no drug use when the applicant is a user. The *test sensitivity* is the probability of a positive indication for a drug user; the *test specificity* is the probability of a negative indication for a nonuser. Suppose that 3% of job applicants use drugs, and a test has a sensitivity of 0.99 and a specificity of 0.98. The high probabilities make the test seem reliable, but 40% of the positive indications will be false positives. The American Management Association reports that more than half of all companies test for drugs.

This implies that there is a relatively small chance of 5% or less that these limits don't contain the mean. Based on the above confidence interval, we can conclude that it is highly unlikely that the claimed mean of 10 years is correct because it is not in the confidence interval. (In recent years, editors of medical journals have been campaigning to use confidence intervals in place of hypothesis tests, and the preceding example illustrates how this is done.)

7.3 EXERCISES   BASIC CONCEPTS

In Exercises 1–4, use the P-value and significance level to choose between rejecting the null hypothesis or failing to reject the null hypothesis.

1. P-value: 0.03; significance level: $\alpha = 0.05$
2. P-value: 0.04; significance level: $\alpha = 0.01$
3. P-value: 0.405; significance level: $\alpha = 0.10$
4. P-value: 0.09; significance level: $\alpha = 0.10$

In Exercises 5–12, first find the P-value. Then either reject or fail to reject the null hypothesis by assuming a significance level of $\alpha = 0.05$.

5. H_0: $\mu \geq 152$; H_1: $\mu < 152$; test statistic: $z = -1.85$
6. H_0: $\mu \geq 100$; H_1: $\mu < 100$; test statistic: $z = -0.46$
7. H_0: $\mu \leq 15.7$; H_1: $\mu > 15.7$; test statistic: $z = 1.94$
8. H_0: $\mu \leq 428$; H_1: $\mu > 428$; test statistic: $z = 2.26$
9. H_0: $\mu = 75.0$; H_1: $\mu \neq 75.0$; test statistic: $z = 1.66$
10. H_0: $\mu = 1365$; H_1: $\mu \neq 1365$; test statistic: $z = -2.55$
11. H_0: $\mu = 2.53$; H_1: $\mu \neq 2.53$; test statistic: $z = -1.94$
12. H_0: $\mu = 12.8$; H_1: $\mu \neq 12.8$; test statistic: $z = 3.00$

In Exercises 13–16, use the P-value approach to test the given hypotheses.

13. Test the claim that $\mu \geq 100$, given a sample of $n = 45$ for which $\bar{x} = 95$. Assume that $\sigma = 15$, and test at the $\alpha = 0.05$ significance level.
14. Test the claim that $\mu \leq 500$, given a sample of $n = 35$ for which $\bar{x} = 508$. Assume that $\sigma = 90$, and test at the $\alpha = 0.01$ significance level.
15. Test the claim that $\mu = 75.6$, given a sample of $n = 81$ for which $\bar{x} = 78.8$. Assume that $s = 12.0$, and test at the $\alpha = 0.01$ significance level.
16. Test the claim that $\mu = 98.6$, given a sample of $n = 20$ for which $\bar{x} = 100.1$. Assume that $\sigma = 2.35$, the population is normal, and test at the $\alpha = 0.10$ significance level.

In Exercises 17–24, use the P-value approach to test the given hypothesis. (These exercises are also included in Section 7.2.)

17. Use the aircraft-age sample data ($n = 40$, $\bar{x} = 13.41$ years, $s = 8.28$ years) given at the beginning of the chapter. At the 0.05 level of significance, test the *Time* magazine claim that the mean age of aircraft in the U.S. fleet is 14 years. Assume that the sample standard deviation can be used for σ.
18. A brewery distributes beer in cans labeled 12 oz. The Bureau of Weights and Measures randomly selects 36 cans, measures their contents, and obtains a sample mean of 11.82 oz. Assuming that σ is 0.38 oz, is it valid at the 0.01 significance level to conclude that the brewery is cheating consumers?

19. In a study of distances traveled by buses before the first major engine failure, a sample of 191 buses results in a mean of 96,700 mi and a standard deviation of 37,500 mi (based on data in *Technometrics*, Vol. 22, No. 4). At the 0.05 level of significance, test the claim that mean distance traveled before a major engine failure is more than 90,000 mi. (Assume that the sample standard deviation can be used for σ.)

20. The Medassist Pharmaceutical Company supplies bottles of a cold medicine labeled as containing 600 mg of acetaminophen. The Food and Drug Administration randomly selects 65 samples from a large shipment and finds that the mean acetaminophen amount is 589 mg, while the sample standard deviation is 21 mg. Use a significance level of $\alpha = 0.01$ to test the claim that the population mean is equal to 600 mg. (Assume that the sample standard deviation can be used for σ.)

21. A poll of 100 randomly selected car owners revealed that the mean length of time they plan to keep their cars is 7.01 years and the standard deviation is 3.74 years (based on data from a Roper poll).
    a. Test the claim that the mean for all car owners is less than 7.5 years.
    b. Find a 90% confidence interval for the mean number of years owners plan to keep their cars.

22. The Regal Soap Company manufactures deodorant soaps and wants to check the actual contents of bars that are labeled 5 oz. The production process appears to be statistically stable, and every 20th bar is selected until a sample of 40 bars is obtained. This sample has a mean of 5.03 oz and a sample standard deviation of 0.19 oz.
    a. At the $\alpha = 0.05$ significance level, test the claim that the population mean equals 5 oz.
    b. Find a 95% confidence interval for the mean weight of the soap bars.

23. The Acton Paper Company employs a Human Resources manager who is given responsibility for employee benefits. She randomly selects 40 employee records for the past year and finds that the mean dental expense is $537, while the standard deviation is $78. At the $\alpha = 0.05$ significance level, test the manager's claim that the mean dental expense is equal to $500.

24. A late-night television show is seen by a relatively large percentage of household members who videotape the show for viewing at a more convenient time. The show's marketing manager claims that the mean income of households with VCRs is greater than $40,000. Test that claim. A sample of 1700 households with VCRs produces a sample mean of $41,182 (based on data from Nielsen Media Research). Assume that σ is known to be $19,990.

7.3 EXERCISES   BEYOND THE BASICS

25. This exercise involves the difference between *statistical significance* and *practical significance*. Repeat Exercise 22 after changing the sample size from 40 to 400. Compare the results using $n = 400$ to those obtained in Exercise 22 with $n = 40$. If we now reject the null hypothesis of $\mu = 5.0$ oz, does the difference between the desired mean (5.0 oz) and the actual mean (estimated to be 5.03 oz) warrant actions to correct the apparent overfilling?

26. A robot sprayer paints lawn tractors, and the paint thickness is measured in microns. A sample is obtained by checking every 10th tractor until 35 tractors have been measured. The result is described by the accompanying boxplot.
    a. At the 0.05 level of significance, test the claim that the mean paint thickness is equal to 100 microns. (Assume that the painting process is statistically stable.) Also, comment on the magnitude of the P-value.
    b. Find a 95% confidence interval for the mean paint thickness.

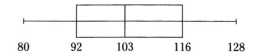

        80   92   103   116   128

27. Find the smallest mean above $23,460 that leads to a rejection of the claim that the mean annual household income is $23,460. Assume a 0.02 significance level, and assume that $\sigma = \$3750$. The sample consists of 50 randomly selected households.

In Sections 7.2 and 7.3 we introduced the general method for testing hypotheses, but all the examples and exercises involved situations in which we could use the normal distribution. The population standard deviations were given for normally distributed data or the samples were large (or both), and each hypothesis tested related to a population mean. In those cases, we can apply the central limit theorem and use the normal distribution as an approximation to the distribution of sample means. A very unrealistic feature of those examples and exercises is the assumption that the population standard deviation σ is known. If σ is unknown and the sample is large, we can treat the sample standard deviation s as if it were σ and proceed as in Section 7.2 or 7.3. This estimation of σ by s is reasonable because large random samples tend to be representative of the population. But small random samples tend to be more erratic, so that s is not a satisfactory replacement for σ. **In this section we consider tests of hypotheses about a population mean when the samples are small, σ is unknown, and the data are normally distributed.** We begin by referring to Fig. 7.8, which outlines the theory we are describing.

Starting at the top of Fig. 7.8, we see that our immediate concerns lie only with the hypotheses made about one population mean. (In following sections we will consider hypotheses made about population parameters other than the mean.) Figure 7.8 summarizes the following observations.

1. In *any* population, the distribution of sample means can be approximated by the normal distribution as long as the random samples are large. This is justified by the central limit theorem.

2. In populations with distributions that are essentially normal, samples of *any* size will yield means having a distribution that is approximately normal. The value of the population mean μ would correspond to the null hypothesis, and the value of the population standard deviation σ must be known. If σ is unknown and the samples are large, we can use the sample standard deviation

FIGURE 7.8
Choosing between the Normal and Student Distributions

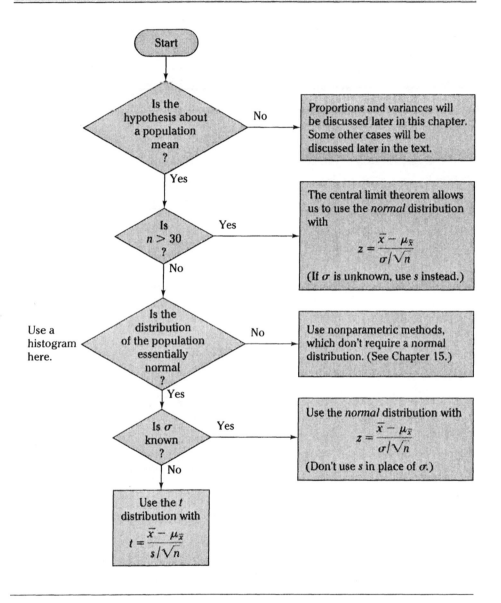

s as a substitute for σ, because large random samples tend to be representative of the populations from which they come.

3. In populations with distributions that are essentially normal, assume that we randomly select *small* samples and we do not know the value of σ. For this case, we can use *s* instead of σ and we can use the Student *t* distribution, first introduced in Section 6.2.

4. If our random samples are small, σ is unknown, and the population distribution is grossly nonnormal, then we can use nonparametric methods, some of which are discussed in Chapter 15.

In Section 6.2 we introduced the Student t distribution and noted several important features. Those features particularly relevant to this section are given below.

Conditions for Using the Student t Distribution

1. The sample is small $(n \leq 30)$; and
2. The value of σ is unknown; and
3. The parent population is essentially normal.

TEST STATISTIC

If the distribution of the population is essentially normal, then the distribution of

$$t = \frac{\bar{x} - \mu}{s/\sqrt{n}}$$

is essentially a *Student t distribution* for all samples of size *n*. (The Student *t* distribution is often referred to as the *t distribution*.)

Critical Values

1. Critical values are found in Table A.3.
2. Degrees of freedom = $n - 1$.

Important Properties

1. The Student t distribution is different for different sample sizes (see Fig. 6.4 in Section 6.2).
2. The Student t distribution has the same general bell shape of the normal distribution, but its wider shape reflects the greater variability expected with small samples.
3. The Student t distribution has a mean of $t = 0$ (just as the standard normal distribution has a mean of $z = 0$).
4. The standard deviation of the Student t distribution varies with the sample size and is greater than 1 (unlike the standard normal distribution, which has $\sigma = 1$).
5. As the sample size n gets larger, the Student t distribution gets closer to the normal distribution. For values of $n > 30$, the differences are so small that we can use the critical z values instead of developing a much larger table of critical t values. (The values in the bottom row of Table A.3 are equal to the corresponding critical z values from the normal distribution.)

EXAMPLE   The Carolina Tobacco Company claims that its best-selling cigarettes contain at most an average of 40 mg of nicotine per cigarette. Test this claim at the 0.01 significance level by using the results of 15 randomly selected cigarettes for which $\bar{x} = 42.6$ mg and $s = 3.7$ mg. Other evidence suggests that the distribution of nicotine contents is a normal distribution.

SOLUTION   We list the solution according to the steps outlined in Fig. 7.1, which summarizes the classical procedure for testing hypotheses.

STEP 1:   The original claim in symbolic form is $\mu \le 40$.

STEP 2:   The opposite of the original claim is $\mu > 40$.

STEP 3: H_0 must contain the condition of equality so we get

H_0: $\mu \le 40$ (null hypothesis)

H_1: $\mu > 40$ (alternative hypothesis)

STEP 4:   The significance level is $\alpha = 0.01$.

STEP 5:   Use the sample mean in testing a claim about a population mean. Because the sample is small, σ is unknown, and the distribution of nicotine levels is normal, we use the Student t distribution.

STEP 6:   The test statistic is $t = \dfrac{\bar{x} - \mu}{s/\sqrt{n}} = \dfrac{42.6 - 40}{3.7/\sqrt{15}} = 2.722$

Using $n - 1 = 14$ degrees of freedom, we get a critical value of $t = 2.625$. The test statistic and critical value are shown in Fig. 7.9.

STEP 7:   Because the test statistic of $t = 2.722$ does fall in the critical region, we reject H_0.

STEP 8:   There is sufficient evidence to warrant rejection of the tobacco company's claim. These cigarettes appear to have a mean significantly greater than 40 mg of nicotine.

FIGURE 7.9
Distribution of Cigarette Nicotine Mean Amounts

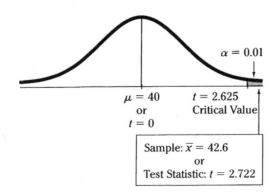

Note in the preceding example that the claim of "at most" 40 mg of nicotine translated into a null hypothesis of $\mu \leq 40$. The referrence to "at most" 40 mg implies that the nicotine levels are below 40 mg or they are equal to 40 mg, but they do not exceed 40 mg. We must be very careful to correctly interpret such key words, because their implications can be quite dramatic. For example, if we make the simple error of expressing "at most" as $\mu \leq 40$, we would incorrectly conclude that we have a left-tailed test, whereas the correct interpretation results in a right-tailed test.

The correct interpretation of the stated claim in the preceding example leads to a right-tailed test, but we might consider how two-tailed and left-tailed tests are handled. If this example had been based on the claim that the mean nicotine content is *equal* to 40 mg, then the test would have been two-tailed and there would have been two critical values ($t = -2.977$ and $t = 2.977$) corresponding to 14 degrees of freedom with $\alpha = 0.01$ divided equally between two tails. The test statistic of $t = 2.722$ would not fall within the critical region, and we would fail to reject the claim that the mean equals 40 mg.

If the tobacco company had claimed that the mean nicotine content was below 50 mg, then we would have a left-tailed test with the test statistic

$$t = \frac{\bar{x} - \mu_{\bar{x}}}{s/\sqrt{n}} = \frac{42.6 - 50}{3.7/\sqrt{15}} = -7.746$$

and critical value $t = -2.625$ found from Table A.3. The test statistic would fall within the critical region, and we would support the claim that the mean is less than 50 mg.

P-Values and the *t* Distribution

In the example presented in this section, we used the classical approach to hypothesis testing. However, much of the literature and many computer packages use the *P*-value approach. Shown here, for example, is the Minitab display for our last example. The first set of numbers comprises the nicotine contents for the $n = 15$ randomly selected and tested cigarettes. The command DESCRIBE C1 reveals that $\bar{x} = 42.600$ and $s = 3.702$. The command TTEST mu = 40 C1 gives the result of the *t* test for the hypothesis $H_0: \mu = 40$; the subcommand of ALTERNATIVE=1 specifies a right-tailed test. (The subcommand ALTERNATIVE=-1 specifies a left-tailed test, and a two-tailed test is conducted when the subcommand is omitted.) The observed test statistic is $t = 2.72$ with a *P*-value of 0.0083. Because this *P*-value is less than $\alpha = 0.01$, we reject the null hypothesis, just as we did with the classical approach.

```
MTB > SET C1
DATA> 39.7 41.3 45.8 43.2 44.2 40.6 46 44.9
DATA> 46.3 39.2 38.3 46.9 37.6 48.0 37
DATA> ENDOFDATA
MTB > DESCRIBE C1
```

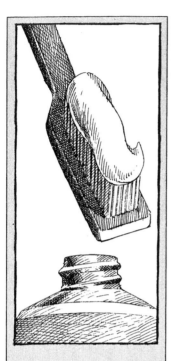

PRODUCT TESTING

The United States Testing Company in Hoboken, New Jersey, is the world's largest independent product-testing laboratory. It's often hired to verify advertising claims. A vice president has said that the most difficult part of his job is "telling a client when his product stinks. But if we didn't do that, we'd have no credibility." He says that there have been a few clients who wanted results fabricated, but most clients want honest results. United States Testing Company evaluates detergents, cosmetics, insulation materials, zippers, pantyhose, football helmets, toothpaste, fertilizer, and a wide variety of other products.

	N	MEAN	MEDIAN	TRMEAN	STDEV	SEMEAN
C1	15	42.600	43.200	42.615	3.702	0.956

	MIN	MAX	Q1	Q3
C1	37.000	48.000	39.200	46.000

MTB > TTEST MU=40 C1;
SUBC> ALTERNATIVE=1.

TEST OF MU = 40.000 VS MU G.T. 40.000

	N	MEAN	STDEV	SEMEAN	T	P VALUE
C1	15	42.600	3.702	0.956	2.72	0.0083

Because the t distribution table (Table A.3) includes only selected values of α, we cannot usually find the specific P-value from Table A.3. Instead, we can use that table to identify limits that contain the P-value. In the last example we found the test statistic to be $t = 2.722$, and we know that the test is one-tailed with 14 degrees of freedom. By examining the row of Table A.3 corresponding to 14 degrees of freedom, we see that the test statistic of 2.722 falls between the table values of 2.977 and 2.625, which, in a one-tailed test, correspond to $\alpha = 0.005$ and $\alpha = 0.01$. Although we cannot determine the exact P-value from Table A.3, we do know that it must fall between 0.005 and 0.01, so that

$$0.005 < P\text{-value} < 0.01$$

With a significance level of 0.01 and a P-value less than 0.01, we would reject the null hypothesis as we did in the classical approach. (Some calculators and computer programs allow us to find exact P-values.)

So far, we have discussed tests of hypotheses made about population means only. In the next section we learn how to test hypotheses made about population proportions or percentages. In the last section of this chapter we learn how to test hypotheses made about population variances or standard deviations. This chapter is limited to hypothesis tests involving a single population, but subsequent chapters will deal with cases involving two or more populations, as well as different arrangements of data.

7.4   EXERCISES   BASIC CONCEPTS

In Exercises 1 and 2, find the critical t value suggested by the given data.

1. a. $H_0: \mu = 12$ b. $H_0: \mu \leq 50$ c. $H_0: \mu \geq 1.36$
       $n = 27$ $n = 17$ $n = 6$
       $\alpha = 0.05$ $\alpha = 0.10$ $\alpha = 0.01$

2. a. $H_0: \mu \leq 100$ b. $H_1: \mu \neq 500$ c. $H_1: \mu < 67.5$
       $n = 27$ $n = 16$ $n = 12$
       $\alpha = 0.10$ $\alpha = 0.05$ $\alpha = 0.05$

In Exercises 3–6 assume that the population is normally distributed. In each case, test the given claim and find the approximate P-value.

3. Test the claim that $\mu \le 10$, given a sample of 9 for which $\bar{x} = 11.54$ and $s = 2.00$. Use a significance level of $\alpha = 0.05$.

4. Test the claim that $\mu \ge 100$, given a sample of 22 for which $\bar{x} = 95$ and $s = 18$. Use a 5% level of significance.

5. Test the claim that $\mu = 75$, given a sample of 15 for which $\bar{x} = 77.6$ and $s = 5$. Use a significance level of $\alpha = 0.05$.

6. Test the claim that $\mu = 500$, given a sample of 20 for which $\bar{x} = 565.4$ and $s = 115$. Use a significance level of $\alpha = 0.10$.

In Exercises 7–20, test the given hypothesis by following the procedure suggested by Fig. 7.1. Draw the appropriate graph. In each case, assume that the population or process has a distribution that is approximately normal.

7. The Taylor Clothing Company randomly selects 24 eleven-year-old girls and records various measurements. Their heights have a mean of 147.6 cm and the standard deviation is 7.85 cm (based on data from the National Health Survey). At the 0.02 significance level, test a clothing designer's claim that the mean height of all eleven-year-old girls is equal to 157.6 cm.

8. The Ryan and Greco accounting firm audits the Acton Paper Company and finds that for a random sample of $n = 20$ transactions, the undocumented expenses have a mean of $27.25 (per transaction) and a standard deviation of $12.50. At the 0.05 level of significance, test Acton's claim that undocumented expenses average $20 or less per transaction.

9. The skid properties of a snow tire have been tested and the mean skid distance of 154 ft has been established for standardized conditions. A new, more expensive tire is developed, but tests on a sample of 20 new tires yield a mean skid distance of 141 ft with a standard deviation of 12 ft. Because of the cost involved, the new tires will be purchased only if they skid less at the $\alpha = 0.005$ significance level. Based on the sample, will the new tires be purchased?

10. An aircraft manufacturer randomly selects 12 planes of the same model and tests them to determine the distance (in meters) they require for takeoff. The sample mean and standard deviation are computed to be 524 m and 23 m, respectively. At the 0.05 level of significance, test the claim that the mean for all such planes is more than 500 m.

11. The Medassist Pharmaceutical Company has a process that produces pills that are supposed to contain 20.0 mg of phenobarbitol. A random sample of 25 pills taken from the assembly line yields a mean and standard deviation of 20.5 mg and 1.5 mg, respectively. Test the claim that the mean is 20.0 mg and use a 0.05 level of significance. Assume that the process is statistically stable.

12. One vacuum cleaner brand is supposed to produce suction of 8 lb/in.^{2} or greater. The quality control supervisor randomly selects 10 vacuum cleaners from the assembly line and finds that the mean suction is 7.2 lb/in.^{2} and the standard deviation is 1.1 lb/in.^{2}. Test the manufacturer's claim. Use $\alpha = 0.05$ and assume that the process is statistically stable.

13. In a study of consumer credit, 25 randomly selected credit card holders were surveyed. The mean amount they charged in the past 12 months was found to be $1756, and the standard deviation was $843. Use a 0.025 level of significance to test the claim that the mean amount charged by all credit card holders was greater than $1500.

14. A study was conducted to determine whether or not a standard clerical test would need revision for use on video display terminals (VDT). The VDT scores of 22 subjects have a mean of 170.2 and a standard deviation of 35.3 (based on data from "Modification of the Minnesota Clerical Test to Predict Performance on Video Display Terminals," by Silver and Bennett, *Journal of Applied Psychology,* Vol. 72, No. 1). At the 0.05 level of significance, test the claim that the mean for all subjects differs from the mean of 243.5 for the standard printed version of the text.

15. A high school senior is concerned about attending college because she knows that many college students require more than four years to earn a bachelor's degree. At the 0.10 level of significance, test the claim of a guidance counselor who states that the mean time is greater than five years. Sample data consist of 28 randomly selected college graduates who had a mean of 5.15 years and a standard deviation of 1.68 years (based on data from the National Center for Education Statistics).

16. The Allen Tax Preparation Company is considering the introduction of a new training program and refers to a study that was conducted to determine the effects of mental training in organizations. (See "Routinization of Mental Training in Organizations: Effects on Performance and Well-Being," by Larsson, *Journal of Applied Psychology,* Vol. 72, No. 1.) For an experimental group of 20 subjects, a performance exam resulted in scores with a mean of 79.12 and a standard deviation of 17.49. At the 0.10 level of significance, test the claim that the experimental group comes from a population with a mean less than 85.70.

17. The Florida Fruit Supply Company uses bottles that are labeled as containing 23 oz of orange juice. A random sample of $n = 18$ such bottles shows that the sample mean and standard deviation are 22.75 oz and 0.64 oz, respectively. Assume that this filling process is statistically stable.
    a.   Test the claim that the bottles contain an average of 23 oz. Use a 0.05 level of significance.
    b.   Find a 95% confidence interval for the true mean of the contents.

18. The Medassist Pharmaceutical Company supplies vitamin pills and claims that its pills have at least 18 mg of iron (100% of the recommended daily allowance). A sample of 25 pills results in a mean of 17.1 mg and a standard deviation of 1.4 mg. Assume that the production process is statistically stable.
    a.   Use a 0.05 significance level to test the given claim.
    b.   Find a 95% confidence interval for the true mean amount of iron per pill.

19. A sample of beer cans labeled 16 oz is randomly selected and the actual contents accurately measured. The results (in ounces) are as follows. Is the consumer being cheated?

       15.8   16.2   16.3   15.9   15.5
       15.9   16.0   15.6   15.8

20. The Ryan and Greco accounting firm randomly selects 12 accounts receivable for a small shipping firm and finds the following differences when recorded amounts are subtracted from audited amounts.

       $0 $34 $240 $0 $278   −$38 $0 $218 $0 $0 $97 $0

    a.   Test the firm's claim that the mean difference is $0. Use a 0.10 level of significance.
    b.   Find a 90% confidence interval for the true mean difference.

---

21. For certain conditions, a hypothesis test requires the Student t distribution, as described in this section. Assume that the standard normal distribution is incorrectly used instead. Using the standard normal distribution, are you more likely to reject the null hypothesis, less likely, or does it make no difference? Explain.

22. What do you know about the P-value in each of the following cases?
    a. H_0: $\mu \le 5.00$; $n = 10$; test statistic: $t = 2.205$
    b. H_0: $\mu = 5.00$; $n = 20$; test statistic: $t = 2.678$
    c. H_0: $\mu \ge 5.00$; $n = 16$; test statistic: $t = -1.234$

23. Some computer programs approximate critical t values by

$$t = \sqrt{DF \cdot (e^{A^2/DF} - 1)}$$

where

$$DF = n - 1$$
$$e = 2.718$$
$$A = z\left(\frac{8\,DF + 3}{8\,DF + 1}\right)$$

and z is the critical z score.

   Use this approximation to find the critical t score corresponding to $n = 10$ and a significance level of 0.05 in a right-tailed case. Compare the results to the critical t found in Table A.3.

24. Refer to Exercise 13 and assume that you're testing the null hypothesis of $\mu \le \$1500$. Find β, the probability of a type II error, given that $\mu = \$1600$. (See Exercise 30 from Section 7.2 and use s as an estimate of σ.)

7.5 TESTING A CLAIM ABOUT A PROPORTION

In Section 7.2 we learned the basic method for testing hypotheses. It is not difficult to modify that procedure for many other circumstances. In this section we consider a method for testing hypotheses made about a population proportion. The particular assumptions for this section are listed below.

Assumptions

1. We are testing a claim made about a population *proportion, probability,* or *percentage.*
2. The conditions for a *binomial experiment* are satisfied. (That is, we have a fixed number of independent trials having constant probabilities, and each trial has two outcome categories.)

3. The conditions **$np \geq 5$** and **$nq \geq 5$** are both satisfied, so that **the binomial distribution of sample proportions can be approximated by a normal distribution** with $\mu = np$ and $\sigma = \sqrt{npq}$.

If $np \geq 5$ and $nq \geq 5$ are not both true, we may be able to use Table A.1 or the binomial probability formula described in Section 4.4, but this section deals only with situations in which the normal distribution is a suitable approximation for the distribution of sample proportions.

If these three conditions are all satisfied, we can find the value of the test statistic by computing z, as follows:

TEST STATISTIC

$$z = \frac{\hat{p} - p}{\sqrt{\dfrac{pq}{n}}}$$

where **n = number of trials**
p = population proportion (given in the null hypothesis)
$q = 1 - p$
$\hat{p} = x/n$ (sample proportion)

We find the **critical value** from Table A.2 by using the same procedures described in Section 7.2.

The above test statistic is justified by noting that when using the normal distribution to approximate a binomial distribution, we substitute $\mu = np$ and $\sigma = \sqrt{npq}$ to get

$$z = \frac{x - \mu}{\sigma} = \frac{x - np}{\sqrt{npq}}$$

Here x is the number of successes among n trials. Divide the numerator and denominator of this last expression by n, then replace x/n by the symbol $\hat{p}$, and you get the test statistic given above. In other words, the above test statistic is simply $z = (x - \mu)/\sigma$ modified for the binomial notation; the distribution of sample proportions $\hat{p}$ is approximately a normal distribution with mean p and standard deviation $\sqrt{pq/n}$.

We can now test hypotheses made about population proportions. Simply follow the same general steps listed in Fig. 7.1 and use the test statistic given above.

> **EXAMPLE** An auditor for the U.S. Postal Service wants to examine its special Two Day Priority mail handling to determine the proportion of parcels that actually require longer than two days for delivery. A randomly selected sample of 150 such parcels is found to contain nine that required longer than two days. Use a 0.05 level of significance to test the auditor's claim that the percentage of late parcels exceeds 4%.

DRUG APPROVAL

The Pharmaceutical Manufacturing Association has reported that the development and approval of a new drug costs around $87 million and takes about eight years. Extensive laboratory testing is followed by FDA approval for human testing, which is done in three phases. Phase I human testing involves about 80 people, and phase II involves about 250 people. In phase III, between 1000 and 3000 volunteers are used. Overseeing such a complex, extensive, and time-consuming process would be enough to give anyone a headache, but the process does protect us from dangerous or worthless drugs. Although companies must bear very high research, development, and testing costs, the process helps ensure that only safe and effective drugs are approved.

SOLUTION   We will follow the steps outlined in Fig. 7.1.

STEP 1: The original claim is that the rate of late Priority parcels exceeds 4%. We express this in symbolic form as $p > 0.04$.

STEP 2: The opposite of the original claim is $p \leq 0.04$.

STEP 3: Because $p \leq 0.04$ contains equality, we have

H_0: $p \leq 0.04$ (null hypothesis)
H_1: $p > 0.04$ (alternative hypothesis)

STEP 4: The significance level is $\alpha = 0.05$.

STEP 5: The statistic relevant to this test is the sample proportion of late parcels: $\hat{p} = 9/150 = 0.06$. The sampling distribution of sample proportions is approximated by the normal distribution. [The requirements that $np \geq 5$ and $nq \geq 5$ are satisfied because $np = (150)(0.04) = 6$ and $nq = (150)(0.96) = 144$.]

STEP 6: The test statistic is

$$z = \frac{\hat{p} - p}{\sqrt{\frac{pq}{n}}} = \frac{0.06 - 0.04}{\sqrt{\frac{(0.04)(0.96)}{150}}} = 1.25$$

In Section 5.6 we included a correction for continuity, but we ignore it here because its effect is negligible with such a large sample. The critical value of $z = 1.645$ is found from Table A.2. The critical value corresponds to a table entry of 0.4500, which is equivalent to a right-tail area of $\alpha = 0.05$ (see Fig. 7.10).

STEP 7: Because the test statistic does not fall within the critical region, we fail to reject the null hypothesis.

STEP 8: There is not sufficient evidence to support the claim that the rate of late Priority mail parcels exceeds 4%. We lack sufficient evidence to conclude that the proportion of late Priority mail is greater than 0.04, or 4%.

The claim in the preceding example involved a percentage, but when calculating the test statistic we must use the equivalent decimal or fraction form. We can use the methods presented in this section to test claims made about proportions, probabilities, or percentages. Whether we have a proportion, a percentage, or a probability, the value of p must be between 0 and 1, and the sum of p and q must be exactly 1. (Yogi Berra revealed that he lacked formal training in statistics when he said, "Baseball is 90% mental; the other half is physical.")

FIGURE 7.10
Distribution of Sample Proportions of Late Parcels

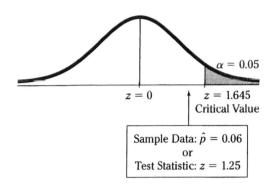

$\alpha = 0.05$

$z = 0$ $z = 1.645$
Critical Value

Sample Data: $\hat{p} = 0.06$
or
Test Statistic: $z = 1.25$

P-VALUES AND CLAIMS ABOUT PROPORTIONS

The example in this section followed the traditional approach to hypothesis testing, but it would be easy to use the P-value approach, because the test statistic is a z score. The P-value is obtained by using the same procedure described in Section 7.3. In a right-tailed test, the P-value is the area to the right of the test statistic. In a left-tailed test, the P-value is the area to the left of the test statistic. In a two-tailed test, the P-value is twice the area of the extreme region bounded by the test statistic (see Fig. 7.6). We reject the null hypothesis if the P-value is less than the significance level.

The preceding example was right-tailed, so the P-value is the area to the right of the test statistic $z = 1.25$. (That is, we are 1.25 standard deviations above the expected proportion value.) Table A.2 indicates that the area between $z = 0$ and $z = 1.25$ is 0.3944, so the P-value is $0.5 - 0.3944 = 0.1056$. Because the P-value of 0.1056 is greater than the significance level of 0.05, we fail to reject the null hypothesis and again conclude that there is not sufficient sample evidence to support the claim that the proportion of late Priority mail is greater than 0.04, or 4%. Again, the P-value approach is another way of arriving at the same conclusion.

7.5 EXERCISES   BASIC CONCEPTS

In Exercises 1–16, test the given hypotheses. Include the steps listed in Fig. 7.1, and draw the appropriate graph.

1. At the 0.05 significance level, test the claim that the proportion of defects p for road flares equals 0.3. Sample data consist of $n = 100$ randomly selected flares, of which 45 are defective.
2. At the 0.05 significance level, test the claim that the proportion of women employed in the clothing industry equals 0.6. Sample data consist of $n = 80$ randomly selected clothing industry employees, 54 of whom are women.

3. In a survey by Media General and the Associated Press, 813 of the 1084 respondents indicated support for a ban on household aerosols. At the 0.01 significance level, test the claim that more than 70% of the population supports the ban.

4. In a Roper Organization poll of 2000 adults, 1280 have money in regular savings accounts. Use this sample data to test the claim that less than 65% of all adults have money in regular savings accounts. Use a 0.05 level of significance.

5. According to a Harris Poll, 71% of Americans believe that the overall cost of lawsuits is too high. If a random sample of 500 people results in 74% who hold that belief, test the claim that the actual percentage is 71%. Use a 0.10 significance level.

6. In clinical studies of the allergy drug Seldane, 70 of the 781 subjects experienced drowsiness (based on data from Merrell Dow Pharmaceuticals, Inc.). Test the claim that more than 8% of Seldane users experience drowsiness. Use a 0.05 significance level.

7. Test the claim that more than one-fourth of all white-collar criminals have attended college. Sample data (from U.S. Bureau of Justice statistics) consist of 1400 randomly selected white-collar criminals, with 33% of them having attended college. Use a 0.02 level of significance.

8. The Ryan and Greco accounting firm found that among 200 randomly selected transactions, 18 contained errors. Test the claim that 5% of the transactions contained errors. Use a significance level of $\alpha = 0.10$.

9. Recently, TWA reported an on-time arrival rate of 78.4%. Assume that a later random sample of 750 flights results in 630 that are on time. If TWA were to claim that its on-time arrival rate is now higher than 78.4%, would that claim be supported at the 0.01 level of significance?

10. An airline reservations system suffers from a 7% rate of no-shows. A new procedure is instituted whereby reservations are confirmed on the day preceding the actual flight, and a study is then made of 5218 randomly selected reservations made under the new system. If 333 no-shows are recorded, test the claim that the no-show rate is lower with the new system.

11. The Medassist Pharmaceutical company tests 550 vitamin bottles for their resistance to tampering. Among those bottles tested, 12 were found to be sealed incorrectly so that tampering was possible. At the $\alpha = 0.05$ significance level, test the claim that no more than 1% are incorrectly sealed. Assume that the manufacturing process is statistically stabled.

12. The A. J. Collins Investment Company plans to conduct a telemarketing campaign in San Francisco and is concerned about unlisted telephone numbers. Test the claim that fewer than one-half of San Francisco residential telephones have unlisted numbers. A random sample of 400 such phones results in an unlisted rate of 39%. Use a 0.01 level of significance. Identify the P-value for this hypothesis test.

13. In a randomly selected group of people who bought compact cars, 312 were women and 338 were men (based on data from the Ford Motor Company). Test the claim that men constitute more than half the buyers of compact cars and identify the P-value for this hypothesis test.

14. In a survey of randomly selected households, 288 had computers, while 962 did not (based on data from the Electronic Industries Association).

a. At the 0.01 level of significance, test the claim that computers are in 20% of all households.
b. Identify the *P*-value.
c. Find a 99% confidence interval for the proportion of households with computers.

15. A study of randomly selected loans revealed that 37 were defaulted, while 1383 had all obligations satisfied.
    a. At the 0.01 level of significance, test the claim that the loan default rate is less than 4%.
    b. Identify the *P*-value.
    c. Find a 90% confidence interval for the loan default rate.

16. In a study of brand recognition, 831 subjects recognized the Campbell's soup brand, while 18 did not.
    a. Use this sample data to test the claim that the recognition rate is equal to 98%. Use a 0.10 level of significance.
    b. Identify the *P*-value.
    c. Find a 90% confidence interval for the recognition rate.

7.5 EXERCISES   BEYOND THE BASICS

17. A supplier of chemical waste containers finds that 3% of a sample of 500 units are defective. Being somewhat devious, he wants to make a claim that the defective rate is no more than some specified percentage, and he doesn't want that claim rejected at the 0.05 level of significance if the sample data are used. What is the *lowest* defective rate he can claim under these conditions?

18. A reporter claims that 10% of the residents of her city feel that the mayor is doing a good job. Test her claim if it is known that, in a random sample of 15 residents, there are none who feel that the mayor is doing a good job. Use a 5% level of significance. Since $np = 1.5$ and is not at least 5, the normal distribution is not a suitable approximation of the distribution of sample proportions.

19. The Wisconsin Bottling Company is a manufacturer of 2-L plastic cola bottles and wants to sample from the production process to determine whether fewer than 4% have scratch defects.
    a. What is the smallest sample that can be taken to ensure that the normal approximation to the binomial distribution will be a good approximation?
    b. At the 0.10 significance level, test the claim that the rate of scratch defects is under 4%. Assume that the manufacturing process is statistically stable and that in a random sample of 300 bottles, 7 had scratch defects.
    c. Find a 95% confidence interval for the proportion of bottles with scratch defects.

20. Refer to the example in this section that relates to Two Day Priority mail handling. If the true value of *p* is 0.05, find β, the probability of a type II error. (See Exercise 30 in Section 7.2.) *Hint:* In step 3, use the values of $p = 0.05$ and $\sqrt{pq/n} = \sqrt{(0.05)(0.95)/150}$.

7.6 TESTING A CLAIM ABOUT A VARIANCE OR STANDARD DEVIATION

Many applications of statistics involve decisions or inferences about variances or standard deviations. In manufacturing, quality control engineers want to ensure that a product is, on the average, acceptable. But they also want to produce items of *consistent* quality so there will be few defective products. Consistency is often measured by variance or standard deviation.

In this section we discuss tests of hypotheses made about a population variance σ^2 or standard deviation σ. Because σ is the square root of σ^2, if we know the value of one, we also know the value of the other. As a result, we can use the same procedure for testing claims about σ or σ^2. The preceding sections used the normal distribution and the Student t distribution. Tests of claims about σ^2 or σ again require that the population have normally distributed values, so the discussions of this section are made with the following assumptions.

Assumptions

1. We are testing a hypothesis made about a population variance σ^2 or standard deviation σ.
2. The population has values that are normally distributed.

Given these assumptions, the following test statistic has a **chi-square distribution** with $n - 1$ degrees of freedom and critical values given in Table A.4.

TEST STATISTIC

$$\chi^2 = \frac{(n-1)s^2}{\sigma^2}$$

where n = sample size
s^2 = sample variance
σ^2 = population variance (given in the null hypothesis)

FIGURE 7.11
Properties of the Chi-Square Distribution

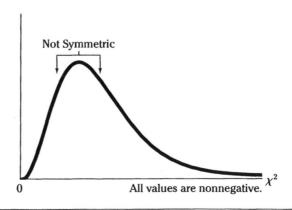

Not Symmetric

0   All values are nonnegative. χ^2

The **critical value** is found from Table A.4. The number of degrees of freedom is $n - 1$. The chi-square distribution was introduced in Section 6.4, where we noted these important properties:

Properties of the Chi-Square Distribution

1. All values of χ^2 are nonnegative and the distribution is not symmetric (see Fig. 7.11).
2. There is a different distribution for each number of degrees of freedom (see Fig. 7.12).
3. The critical values are found in Table A.4, where degrees of freedom = $n - 1$. In using Table A.4, it is essential to note that each critical value separates an *area to the right* that corresponds to the value given in the top row.

As in Section 6.4, we should again note that later chapters will involve cases in which the degrees of freedom are not $n - 1$, so we should not universally equate degrees of freedom with $n - 1$. Once we have determined degrees of freedom, the significance level α, and the type of test (left-tailed, right-tailed, or two-tailed), we can use Table A.4 to find the critical chi-square values.

In a right-tailed test, the value of α will correspond exactly to the areas given in the top row of Table A.4. In a left-tailed test, the value of $1 - \alpha$ will correspond exactly to the areas given in the top row of Table A.4. In a two-tailed test, the values of $\alpha/2$ and $1 - \alpha/2$ will correspond exactly to the areas given in the top row of Table A.4. (See Fig. 6.9 and note the example on page 283.)

We have noted that in manufacturing, quality control engineers want to ensure that a product is, on the average, acceptable and that the items have *consistent* quality. Let's consider aircraft altimeters. Because of mass-production techniques and various other factors, these altimeters don't give readings that are exactly correct; some errors are to be expected. Federal Aviation Regulation 91.36 requires that aircraft altimeters be tested and calibrated to give a reading "within 125 feet (on a 95-percent probability basis)." Even if the mean altitude reading is exactly correct, an excessively large standard deviation will result in individual

DELAYING DEATH

University of California sociologist David Phillips has studied the ability of people to postpone their death until after some important event. Analyzing death rates of Jewish men who died near Passover, he found that the death rate dropped dramatically in the week before Passover, but rose the week after. He found a similar phenomenon occurring among Chinese-American women: Their death rate dropped the week before their important Harvest Moon Festival, then rose the week after.

FIGURE 7.12
Chi-Square Distributions for $df = 10$ and $df = 20$

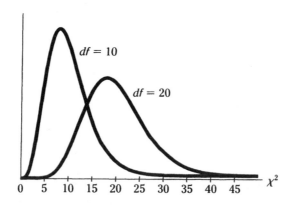

readings that are dangerously low or high. Such a large standard deviation would indicate that production is out of control and that unacceptable and dangerous altimeters are being manufactured. See the following example.

EXAMPLE The Stewart Aviation Products Company has been successfully manufacturing aircraft altimeters with errors that have a mean of 0 ft (achieved by calibration) and a standard deviation of 43.7 ft. After installing new production equipment, 30 altimeters are randomly selected from the new line. This sample group has errors with a standard deviation of $s = 54.7$ ft. At the 0.05 level of significance, test the claim that the new population has errors with a standard deviation equal to 43.7 ft. (Assume that the new process is statistically stable and the calibration errors are normally distributed.)

SOLUTION We will follow the same general steps listed in Fig. 7.1.

STEP 1:   The claim is that the new production method has resulted in a population with a standard deviation equal to 43.7 ft. In symbolic form we have $\sigma = 43.7$ ft.

STEP 2:   If the original claim is false, then $\sigma \neq 43.7$ ft.

STEP 3:   Because the null hypothesis must contain equality, we have

$H_0: \sigma = 43.7$
$H_1: \sigma \neq 43.7$

STEP 4:   The significance level is $\alpha = 0.05$.

STEP 5:   Because this claim is about σ, we will use the chi-square distribution.

STEP 6:   The test statistic is

$$\chi^2 = \frac{(n-1)s^2}{\sigma^2} = \frac{(30-1)(54.7)^2}{43.7^2} = 45.437$$

The critical values are 16.047 and 45.772. They are found in Table A.4, in the 29th row (degrees of freedom = $n - 1 = 29$) in the columns corresponding to 0.975 and 0.025. See Fig. 7.13, where the test statistic and critical values are shown.

STEP 7:   Because the test statistic is not in the critical region, we fail to reject the null hypothesis.

STEP 8:   There is not sufficient evidence to warrant rejection of the claim that the standard deviation is equal to 43.7 ft. However, the results suggest that it would be wise to continue monitoring and testing the new product line.

FIGURE 7.13
Chi-Square Distribution for Altimeters

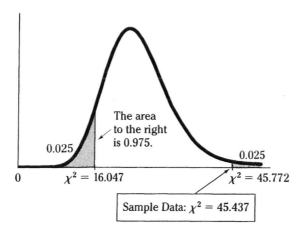

The area to the right is 0.975.

0.025

0.025

0

$\chi^2 = 16.047$

$\chi^2 = 45.772$

Sample Data: $\chi^2 = 45.437$

We emphasize throughout this text that "quality" and "competitive edge" relate to averages *and* variation. In many businesses, variation is the most important but least understood property. Variation is a major concern in providing high-quality service for the waiting lines of banks. As we have already noted, in the past customers traditionally entered a bank and selected one of several lines formed at different windows. Now many banks have a single main waiting line that feeds the various windows as vacancies occur. The average (mean) waiting time isn't reduced, but the variation among waiting times is decreased. It follows that there is also a decrease in the irritation of being stuck in an unusually slow line.

EXAMPLE   With individual lines at its various windows, the Jefferson Valley Bank finds that the standard deviation for normally distributed waiting times on Friday afternoons is 6.2 min. The bank experiments with a single main waiting line and finds that for a random sample of 25 customers, the waiting times have a standard deviation of 3.8 min. At the $\alpha = 0.05$ significance level, test the claim that a single line causes lower variation (or standard deviation) among the waiting times.

SOLUTION   We wish to test $\sigma < 6.2$ based on a sample of $n = 25$ for which $s = 3.8$. We begin by identifying the null and alternative hypotheses.

H_0: $\sigma \geq 6.2$
H_1: $\sigma < 6.2$

The significance level of $\alpha = 0.05$ has already been selected, so we proceed to compute the value of χ^2 based on the given data:

$$\chi^2 = \frac{(n-1)s^2}{\sigma^2} = \frac{(25-1)(3.8)^2}{(6.2)^2} = 9.016$$

FIGURE 7.14
Chi-Square Distribution for Waiting Times

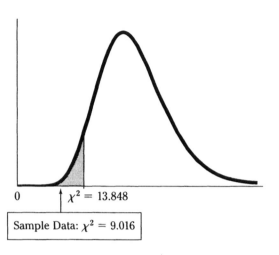

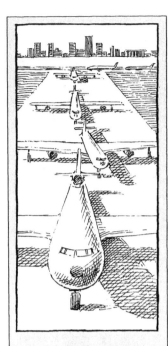

This test is left-tailed because H_0 will be rejected only for small values of χ^2; with $\alpha = 0.05$ and $n = 25$, we go to Table A.4 and align 24 degrees of freedom with an area of 0.95 to obtain the critical χ^2 value of 13.848 (see Fig. 7.14). Because the test statistic falls within the critical region, we reject H_0 and conclude that the 3.8-min standard deviation is significantly less than the 6.2-min standard deviation that corresponds to multiple waiting lines. The sample data support the claim of lower variation. That is, the single main line does appear to lower the variation among waiting times.

Figure 7.15 illustrates visually what is happening here. The old multiline system has the same mean as the new single-line system, but the old system has much more variation, as indicated by a distribution with more spread. In contrast, the narrower distribution reflects greater consistency of waiting times.

P-VALUES AND CLAIMS ABOUT VARIANCES

We can use the *P*-value approach to hypothesis testing to test claims made about population standard deviations or variances. Because the chi-square distribution table (Table A.4) includes only selected values of α, we cannot usually find the specific *P*-value from that table. Instead, we can use the table to identify limits that contain the *P*-value. In the last example we found the test statistic to be $\chi^2 = 9.016$ and we know the test is left-tailed with 24 degrees of freedom. By examining the 24th row of Table A.4, we see that the test statistic of 9.016 is less than the lowest table value of 9.886, so the *P*-value must be less than 0.005. With a significance level of $\alpha = 0.05$, we reject the null hypothesis as we did in the classical approach used in the example given.

FIGURE 7.15
Distributions of Waiting Times

WAITING TIMES

(a) Old Multi-line System With More Variability

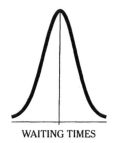

WAITING TIMES

(b) New One-line System With Less Variability

7.6 EXERCISES   BASIC CONCEPTS

In Exercises 1 and 2, use Table A.4 to find the critical values of χ^2 based on the given data.

1. a. $\alpha = 0.05$
      $n = 20$
      $H_0: \sigma = 16$
   b. $\alpha = 0.05$
      $n = 20$
      $H_0: \sigma^2 \geq 256$
   c. $\alpha = 0.01$
      $n = 23$
      $H_0: \sigma^2 \leq 10$

2. a. $\alpha = 0.10$
      $n = 6$
      $H_1: \sigma < 10$
   b. $\sigma = 0.05$
      $n = 41$
      $H_1: \sigma^2 > 500$
   c. $\alpha = 0.05$
      $n = 71$
      $H_1: \sigma^2 \neq 31.5$

In Exercises 3–16, test the given hypotheses. Follow the pattern outlined in Fig. 7.1 and draw the appropriate graph. In all cases, assume that the population is normally distributed.

3. At the $\alpha = 0.05$ significance level, test the claim that $\sigma^2 > 100$ if a random sample of 27 yields $s^2 = 194$.

4. At the $\alpha = 0.05$ significance level, test the claim that $\sigma^2 = 100$ if a random sample of 27 yields a variance of 57.

5. At the $\alpha = 0.05$ significance level, test the claim that a population has a variance less than or equal to 9.00. A random sample of 81 items yields a variance of 12.25.

6. At the $\alpha = 0.025$ significance level, test the claim that a population has a standard deviation less than 98.6. A random sample of 51 items yields a standard deviation of 79.0.

7. The Stewart Aviation Products Company uses a new production method to manufacture aircraft altimeters. A random sample of 81 altimeters results in errors with a standard deviation of $s = 52.3$ ft. At the 0.05 level of significance, test the claim that the new production line has errors with a standard deviation equal to 43.7 ft., which was the standard deviation for the old production method.

8. If the standard deviation for the weekly downtimes of a computer is low, then availability of the computer is predictable and planning is facilitated. If 12 weekly downtimes for a computer are randomly selected and the standard deviation is computed to be 2.85 h, at the 0.025 significance level, test the claim that $\sigma > 2.00$ h.

9. The Medassist Pharmaceutical Company uses a machine to pour medicine into bottles in such a way that the standard deviation of the weights is 0.15 oz. A new machine is tested by randomly selecting 71 bottles from the pouring station, and the standard deviation for this group is 0.12 oz. At the 0.05 significance level, test the claim that the new machine produces less variance. Assume that the filling process is statistically stable and find the P-value for this test.

10. The Fulton Manufacturing Company uses a machine to produce plastic bottles with necks having diameters that are normally distributed with a mean of 40 mm and a standard deviation of 1.10 mm. To test the performance of the molding machine, 81 bottles are randomly selected from the process, and the sample statistics are found to be $\bar{x} = 40.03$ mm and $s = 1.48$ mm. The process appears to be statistically stable. Use a 0.05 significance level to test the claim that the standard deviation of the process is greater than 1.10 mm. Include the P-value.

11. The Kansas Farm Products Company uses a machine to fill 50-lb corn-seed bags. In the past, the machine has had a standard deviation of 0.75 lb. In an attempt to get more-consistent weights (and therefore a higher-quality product), mechanics and engineers have replaced some worn machine parts. A random sample of 61 bags taken from the repaired machinery produces a sample mean of 50.13 lb and a sample standard deviation of 0.48 lb. Assume that the process is statistically stable. At the $\alpha = 0.05$ significance level, test the claim that the standard deviation is lower with the repaired machinery than it was in the past. Identify the P-value.

12. When 22 bolts are tested for hardness, their indexes have a standard deviation of 65.0. Test the claim that the standard deviation of the hardness indexes for all such bolts is greater than 50.0. Test at the 0.025 level of significance.

13. In a study of the wide ranges in the academic success of college freshmen, an obvious factor is the amount of time spent studying. At the 0.05 significance level, test the claim that the standard deviation is more than 4.00 h. Sample data consist of 70 randomly selected freshmen who have a standard deviation of 5.33 h (based on data reported by *USA Today*).

14. The caffeine contents (in mg) are given below for a dozen cans of King Cola randomly selected from a statistically stable manufacturing process. At the 0.05 level of significance, test the claim that the standard deviation for all such cans is less than 2.0 mg. Identify the *P*-value.

    34.2   33.7   31.9   34.3   31.6   32.7
    33.1   35.2   31.6   32.9   33.0   32.4

15. Listed below are the total electric energy consumption amounts (in kWh) for the author Triola's home during seven years. At the 0.10 significance level, test the claim that the standard deviation for all such years is equal to 1000 kWh.

    11,943   11,463   10,789   9907   9012   9942   11,153

16. At the Washington sawmill, wood-framing studs are cut into lengths that are supposed to be 8 ft, or 96 in. In the course of monitoring this process, you observe that it is statistically stable, but some pieces are shorter and others are longer than 96 in. You supply a contractor who specifies a standard deviation no larger than 0.25 in. You randomly select 15 framing studs and obtain the lengths given below (in inches). At the $\alpha = 0.05$ significance level, test the claim that the standard deviation is greater than 0.25 in. Include the *P*-value.

    95.96   96.75   95.77   96.24   96.00   95.24   96.41   95.30
    96.65   95.94   95.58   96.49   95.73   96.04   95.86

7.6 EXERCISES   BEYOND THE BASICS

17. For large numbers of degrees of freedom, we can approximate values of χ^2 as follows:

$$\chi^2 = \frac{1}{2}[z + \sqrt{2k - 1}]^2$$

    Here k = number of degrees of freedom and z = the critical score, found in Table A.2.

    For example, if we want to approximate the two critical values of χ^2 in a two-tailed hypothesis test with $\alpha = 0.05$ and a sample size of 150, we let $k = 149$ with $z = -1.96$, followed by $k = 149$ and $z = 1.96$.

    a. Use this approximation to estimate the critical values of χ^2 in a two-tailed hypothesis test when $n = 101$ and $\alpha = 0.05$. Compare the results to those found in Table A.4.

    b. Use this approximation to estimate the critical values of χ^2 in a two-tailed hypothesis test when $n = 150$ and $\alpha = 0.05$.

18. What do you know about the *P*-value in each of the following cases?

    a. $H_1: \sigma > 15.0$; $n = 10$; test statistic is $\chi^2 = 19.735$.

    b. $H_1: \sigma < 45.0$; $n = 20$; test statistic is $\chi^2 = 7.337$.

    c. $H_0: \sigma = 1.52$; $n = 30$; test statistic is $\chi^2 = 54.603$.

19. The Houston Bakery uses a cake-mix–filling process designed to have a standard deviation of 2 grams or less. Two quality control analysts obtain samples in an attempt to monitor the standard deviation. The first analyst obtains a sample of size 10 for which $s_1 = 2.61$, and the second analyst obtains a sample of size 51 for which $s_2 = 2.59$. Both find that the process is statistically stable.

    a. Using the sample data from the first analyst, test the claim that the standard deviation is greater than 2 grams. Use a 0.05 level of significance.

    b. Repeat part a for the second set of sample data.

    c. Write a brief report of the two sets of results and conclusions. Comment on any apparent discrepancies. Include references to P-values.

Vocabulary List

Define and give an example of each term.

hypothesis
hypothesis tests
tests of significance
null hypothesis
alternative hypothesis
type I error
type II error
test statistic
critical region
critical value
significance level
right-tailed test
left-tailed test
two-tailed test
P-value
Student t distribution
t distribution
chi-square distribution

Review

Chapters 6 and 7 introduce two of the most important methods used in working with sample data to make inferences about a population. Whereas the major objective of Chapter 6 was estimating the values of population parameters, this chapter focused on methods for testing hypotheses made about population parameters. We considered claims made about population means, proportions, variances, and standard deviations. Hypothesis tests are also called tests of significance, reflecting the fact that we decide whether sample differences are due to chance fluctuations or whether the differences are so dramatic that they are not likely to occur by chance. We are able to select exact *levels of significance;* 0.05 and 0.01 are common values. Sample results are said to reflect significant differences when their occurrences have probabilities or P-values less than the chosen level of significance (α).

Section 7.2 presented in detail the procedure for testing hypotheses. The essential steps are summarized in Fig. 7.1. We defined *null hypothesis, alternative hypothesis, type I error, type II error, test statistic, critical region, critical value,* and *significance level.* All these standard terms are commonly used in discussing tests of hypotheses. We also identified the three basic types of tests: *right-tailed, left-tailed,* and *two-tailed.*

We introduced the method of testing hypotheses in Section 7.2 by using examples in which only the normal distribution applies, and we introduced other distributions in subsequent sections. The following table summarizes the hypothesis tests covered in this chapter.

Section 7.2 outlined the *classical approach* to testing hypotheses, and Section 7.3 presented the *P-value* approach. In the classical approach, we make a decision about the null hypothesis by comparing the test statistic and critical value. With the *P*-value approach, we base that decision on a comparison of the significance level and the *P*-value, which represents the probability of getting a sample that is at least as extreme as the one obtained.

We also noted that a *P*-value indicates the degree of confidence or the risk involved in rejecting the null hypothesis. A very small *P*-value (such as a value below 0.05) indicates low risk in being wrong if you reject H_0.

Finally, we noted that for tests involving means and proportions, the *z* score for the test statistic represents the number of standard deviations the sample is from the claimed value. A large positive or negative *z* score (such as +3.20 or −2.97) indicates an unusual result, assuming that the null hypothesis is true. The *P*-value is a precise measure of just how unusual the result is.

IMPORTANT FORMULAS

PARAMETER TO WHICH HYPOTHESIS REFERS	APPLICABLE DISTRIBUTION	ASSUMPTION	TEST STATISTIC	TABLE OF CRITICAL VALUES
μ (population mean)	Normal	σ is known and population is normally distributed.	$z = \dfrac{\bar{x} - \mu}{\sigma/\sqrt{n}}$	Table A.2
	Normal	$n > 30$ (If σ is not known, use s for σ.)	$z = \dfrac{\bar{x} - \mu}{\sigma/\sqrt{n}}$	Table A.2
	Student t	σ is unknown, $n \leq 30$ and population is normally distributed.	$t = \dfrac{\bar{x} - \mu}{s/\sqrt{n}}$	Table A.3
p (population proportion)	Normal	$np \geq 5$ and $nq \geq 5$	$z = \dfrac{\hat{p} - p}{\sqrt{pq/n}}$ where $\hat{p} = \dfrac{x}{n}$	Table A.2
σ^2 (population variance) σ (population standard deviation)	Chi-square	Population is normally distributed.	$\chi^2 = \dfrac{(n-1)s^2}{\sigma^2}$	Table A.4

Review Exercises

In Exercises 1 and 2, find the appropriate critical values.

1. a. $\alpha = 0.05$
       $n = 160$
       $H_0: p \geq 0.5$
   b. $\alpha = 0.01$
       $n = 35$
       $H_0: \mu \leq 16.5$
   c. $\alpha = 0.01$
       $n = 12$
       $H_0: \mu = 38.4$
   d. $\alpha = 0.01$
       $n = 25$
       $H_0: \sigma^2 \geq 225$
   e. $\alpha = 0.05$
       $n = 30$
       $H_0: \sigma^2 = 84.3$

2. a. $\alpha = 0.10$
       $n = 15$
       $H_0: \mu = 1.23$
   b. $\alpha = 0.10$
       $n = 15$
       $H_0: \sigma^2 = 123$
   c. $\alpha = 0.06$
       $n = 100$
       $H_0: \mu = 72.3$
   d. $\alpha = 0.05$
       $n = 10$
       $H_0: \sigma = 15$
   e. $\alpha = 0.01$
       $n = 30$
       $H_1: \sigma < 5.8$

In Exercises 3 and 4, respond to each of the following:
   a.   Give the null hypothesis in symbolic form.
   b.   Is this test left-tailed, right-tailed, or two-tailed?
   c.   In simple nontechnical terms, describe the type I error.
   d.   In simple nontechnical terms, describe the type II error.
   e.   What is the probability of making a type I error?

3. At the 0.01 level of significance, the claim is that the mean treatment time for a dentist is at least 20.0 min.

4. At the 0.05 level of significance, the claim is that the mean customer service time is 6.2 min.

In Exercises 5–8, test the given claims, state any assumptions being made, and note how those assumptions could be checked.

5. At the $\alpha = 0.05$ significance level, test the claim that the proportion of fraudulent credit card applicants is less than 0.15. A sample of $n = 600$ reveals that 12.5% of them are fraudulent (based on data from the American Banker's Association).

6. At the 0.05 significance level, test the claim that the mean annual household income in Alaska is $40,000. Sample data consist of 100 Alaskan households for which $\bar{x}$ = $37,941 and s = $14,100 (based on data from the U.S. Census Bureau).

7. At the 0.01 level of significance, test the claim that lawnmowers produce less than 55 g of smog-producing emissions when operated for one hour. Sample data consist of 25 lawnmowers, for which $\bar{x}$ = 50.2 g and s = 4.4 g (based on data from *USA Today*).

8. Refer to the same sample data in Exercise 7 and test the claim that $\sigma^2 > 10.0$ by using a significance level of $\alpha = 0.05$.

9. At the 0.05 significance level, test the claim that fewer than 1/4 of all income tax returns have the presidential donation box checked. A random sample of 80 returns shows that 16 of them have that box checked (based on data from *USA Today*).

10. The Houston Bakery quality control manager randomly selects 300 packaged loaves and inspects the air tightness seal. In the past, 2% were not tightly sealed. For this sample, 13 are not tightly sealed. Test the claim that the proportion of loaves not tightly sealed is the same as in the past. Use a significance level of $\alpha = 0.10$. Identify the *P*-value and comment on its magnitude.

11. The New England Insurance Company sponsors a study of drinking and driving. Under standard conditions, sober drivers have a mean braking reaction time of 0.75 s and a standard deviation of 0.22 s. Among drivers who had each consumed four beers, a random sample of 29 is taken and the mean and standard deviation are found to be 1.38 s and 0.62 s, respectively.
   a. At the $\alpha = 0.05$ level of significance, test the claim that the population who had consumed four beers has a mean greater than 0.75 s.
   b. Identify the test statistic and the *P*-value for the hypothesis test of part *a*. Interpret both values by commenting on their magnitudes.
   c. At the $\alpha = 0.10$ level of significance, test the claim that the population who had consumed four beers has a standard deviation greater than 0.22 s.
   d. Comment on the *P*-value for the hypothesis test of part *c*.
   e. Based on the preceding results, write a brief statement describing the apparent effect that four beers have on braking reaction times.

12. The Dayton Machine Company uses a plating process that is intended to deposit a mean of 88.9 micrometers (μm) of platinum on catalytic converter parts, with a standard deviation of 12.7 μm. If the deposit is too much below 88.9 μm, the part won't work properly. If it's too much above 88.9 μm, there is too much waste of the expensive platinum. A random sample of 41 converters yields a sample mean and standard deviation of 92.7 μm and 20.8 μm, respectively. The process is found to be statistically stable.
   a. Test the claim that the mean is equal to 88.9 μm. Use a significance level of $\alpha = 0.10$ and identify the *P*-value. Comment on the magnitude of the *P*-value.
   b. Test the claim that the standard deviation is equal to 12.7 μm. Use a significance level of $\alpha = 0.10$.
   c. Write a brief statement that assesses the quality of the product based on the sample results.

13. A television executive claims that "less than half of all adults are annoyed by the violence on television." (That is, violence in television shows, not atop

television sets.) Test this claim using the sample data from a Roper poll in which 48% of 1,998 surveyed adults indicated their annoyance with television violence. Use a 0.05 significance level.

14. Test the claim that less than half of those earning a bachelor's degree in business are women. A random sample of 200 business graduates earning a bachelor's degree includes 80 women and 120 men. Find and interpret the P-value.

15. Listed below are the numbers of chocolate chips found in a sample of 11 randomly selected special birthday cookies made by the Houston Bakery. A goal is to have a mean of 30 chips with a standard deviation of 5 chips. Assume that the process is statistically stable.

    29   38   24   43   18   35   21   19   39   37   23

    a. Find $\bar{x}$ and s.
    b. Test the claim that the mean is 30 chips. Use a 0.05 significance level.
    c. Test the claim that the standard deviation is greater than 5 chips. Use a 0.05 significance level.
    d. Write a brief statement describing the behavior of the process in terms of the given specifications.

Computer Projects

1. One of the advantages of using statistical software is that we can often simulate processes to better understand how they work when they run as planned. Consider, for example, the Western Food Company that produces ketchup in jars that are supposed to be filled so that the contents have an average of 48 oz with a standard deviation of 16 oz. In this project we use Minitab to simulate a process that is statistically stable with the desired mean, standard deviation, and normal distribution.

    a. Simulate a statistically stable, normally distributed, and properly functioning filling process by entering the following Minitab commands.

```
MTB > RANDOM n = 5 C1;
SUBC> NORMAL mu = 48 sigma = 1.6.
MTB > PRINT C1
MTB > DESCRIBE C1
```

    b. Using the displayed sample statistics, test the claim that the mean equals 48 oz. Use a 0.05 significance level and include the P-value.
    c. For the number of students in your statistics-course section, how many would you expect to make the type I error of rejecting H_0 ($\mu = 48$) even though it is true? Explain.
    d. What steps might be taken to reduce the probability of a type I error in hypothesis tests of the type given in part b?

2. a. Repeat part a of the preceding computer project after changing the Minitab commands so that 48 is replaced by 47. That is, the simulated containers are being underfilled with a mean of 47 oz.
   b. Describe a type II error and how it relates to this simulation.

3. Repeat the simulation in Computer Project 2, but in addition to changing the mean from 48 to 47, also change the sample size from 5 to 25. How is a type II error affected by the increased sample size?

TESTING THE CLAIM: THE RELOCATION CASE

1

a. Refer to the real estate data in Appendix B. For the same time period during which the 150 homes were sold, *U.S. Housing Markets* reported that the average price of a home in the United States was $121,000. Test the claim that the sample of the 150 homes comes from a population with a mean selling price that is greater than the national average of $121,000.

b. As the manager for a corporation, you have been directed to investigate several different regions of the country to find a suitable relocation site for a major research unit. Identify at least one important consequence of selecting a location with a mean selling price for homes that is substantially above the national average.

c. Based on the results from parts *a* and *b*, write a brief report that summarizes your results. Conclude with a recommendation about using this region as a relocation site.

CHAPTER 8

Statistical Quality Control

8.1 OVERVIEW

The importance of quality control is discussed.

8.2 TOOLS OF STATISTICAL QUALITY CONTROL

Previously discussed topics of quality control are briefly reviewed. Random variation and assignable variation in a process are defined. Specific criteria are identified for determining when a control chart indicates that a process is not statistically stable.

8.3 CONTROL CHARTS FOR MEANS (with σ unknown)

This section describes the construction of control charts that can be used to monitor the center or *mean* of a process. In Section 5.8 we discussed these control charts for cases in which the process standard deviation σ is known, but in this section we assume that σ is unknown. We develop two types of $\bar{x}$ control charts: $\bar{x}$ charts based on sample standard deviations and $\bar{x}$ charts based on sample ranges.

8.4 CONTROL CHARTS FOR VARIATION

This section describes the use of control charts for monitoring the *variation* in a process. R charts (based on ranges) and s charts (based on standard deviations) will be introduced.

8.5 CONTROL CHART FOR ATTRIBUTES

This section describes the construction of p charts, which are control charts used to monitor the *proportion* of process items having some attribute, such as being defective.

"All of our representatives are busy. Please stand by."

The A. S. J. Computer Mail Order Company uses a process that consists of receiving telephone customer orders and sending the necessary information to the assembly, billing, and shipping departments. If that process is statistically stable, then labor requirements vary little and the need for employees is predictable. With an unstable process, too much variation occurs, so that sometimes the system is underloaded, wasting employee time and company money, and at other times the system is over-loaded and customers are not serviced. Many of us are quite familiar with this repeating telephone message: "All of our representatives are busy. Please stand by."

During each working hour at A. S. J., a sample of 5 telephone-order–processing times is carefully selected. Table 8.1 summarizes the results from 20 consecutive working hours. Is this telephone-ordering process statistically stable? If it is not stable, improving process stability should be a top priority to maintain quality. A stable process is also more cost-effective by minimizing employee idle times. Companies have gone out of business because they failed to monitor and correct processes that became unstable. In this chapter we develop control charts that will help A. S. J. avoid that mistake.

TABLE 8.1
A.S.J. Telephone Order Processing Times

SAMPLE	PROCESSING TIMES (MINS)					MEAN $\bar{x}$	RANGE R	STANDARD DEVIATION s
1	17	18	17	20	15	17.4	5	1.82
2	23	26	34	8	29	24.0	26	9.82
3	18	20	20	31	3	18.4	28	10.01
4	45	10	27	26	3	22.2	42	16.39
5	32	37	41	29	7	29.2	34	13.24
6	25	13	30	17	16	20.2	17	7.05
7	16	16	30	20	19	20.2	14	5.76
8	24	25	25	34	24	26.4	10	4.28
9	31	33	8	26	29	25.4	25	10.06
10	33	17	31	20	12	22.6	21	9.07
11	31	27	34	15	27	26.8	19	7.22
12	25	23	26	21	30	25.0	9	3.39
13	18	29	19	31	27	24.8	13	5.93
14	16	32	23	25	26	24.4	16	5.77
15	26	14	33	20	31	24.8	19	7.85
16	12	37	15	23	37	24.8	25	11.84
17	30	25	27	32	9	24.6	23	9.13
18	22	26	29	19	27	24.6	10	4.04
19	19	20	35	26	24	24.8	16	6.38
20	26	20	30	20	29	25.0	10	4.80

8.1 OVERVIEW

Since the 1920s, Walter A. Shewhart and W. Edwards Deming have had a tremendous impact on the use of statistics and quality control in business. Shewhart was a statistician at Bell Laboratories in New York. Deming was at the Department of Agriculture and later joined the Census Bureau, where he introduced many of the techniques still in use today. Their methods used statistics to monitor production processes to improve the consistency and quality of the final product. United States industry found these techniques helpful during World War II. After the war, U.S. industry largely abandoned these statistical techniques, partly because we were one of the few nations that could produce anything, and we could sell anything we could make. In contrast, Japan was in ruins and its companies manufactured items notorious for their lack of quality. In 1951 Deming spoke to Japanese leaders. They embraced his use of statistics in manufacturing and his management philosophy in general. Japan soon began to make major gains in world markets by providing high-quality goods, whereas U.S. market shares declined because of lower-quality goods.

United States industry is now recognizing that statistical thinking is essential for competition and survival in today's global market. That recognition is paying off in improved quality of goods and services as well as improved profit margins. AMP, Inc., saved $75 million over the last several years by training employees in statistical procedures and by instituting a quality improvement plan. In a recent five-year period, Motorola estimated that it saved over $2 billion through the use of quality control methods. The Perstorp Components Corporation reduced its waste by more than two-thirds through the use of quality control methods. L. L. Bean's quality improvement efforts now allow that company to enjoy a very profitable mail order business that is fostered by a 99.92% error-free rate of shipping orders. In some cases, quality control is becoming a requirement for doing business. As one example, Motorola is requiring its suppliers to justify their quality claims. Those suppliers must apply for a national quality award or they could be dropped by Motorola.

What exactly is quality? A spokesperson for the Perstorp Components Company said that "customer satisfaction is as good a definition of quality as there is. The key to pleasing customers is not shipping mistakes." Other definitions of quality include conformance to requirements or specifications, meeting customer requirements, and achieving the highest manufacturing or service standards.

How do we control or improve quality? Quality control experts are quick to point out that there is no single approach that works for everyone. For some organizations, quality improvement efforts should be aimed at reducing cycle time—the total time it takes to make a product or supply a service. In other cases, companies might benefit from "benchmarking"—copying ideas from other companies that run processes better. For example, Motorola once sent employees to observe Japanese production of calculators and computers. There's now a benchmark clearing house to help match companies. Quality can sometimes be improved through "quality control circles" that consist of meetings of workers discussing their roles and ways to implement improvements. These different approaches tend to have three common goals: Reduce variation and thereby reduce cost, waste, and defects; make customers happy with reliable and defect-free goods and services; and continually monitor processes and seek ways to improve them.

In this chapter we present some of the basic tools that are commonly used to monitor processes and quality. We begin with $\bar{x}$ charts used to monitor the mean, followed by the s and R charts that are used to monitor variation. Finally, we consider p charts that are used to monitor the proportion of defective items.

8.2   TOOLS OF STATISTICAL QUALITY CONTROL

We noted in the Overview that the quality of goods and services can be improved by several different approaches, and there is no single technique that works for everyone. We also cited some particular methods for improving quality, including the reduction of cycle time and the use of benchmarking and quality control circles. Many quality control improvement methods are based on statistical concepts. Although this chapter focuses on statistical methods of quality control, this is not the first time we have discussed such topics. Several methods described earlier, including the following, are often used in quality control applications.

- *Pareto charts* (Section 2.3) are bar charts arranged according to height. Pareto charts are particularly helpful in identifying the most important causes of defects or problems in a process.
- *Histograms* (Section 2.3) are bar graphs that are useful in determining the nature of the distribution of values from a process. Once we have established that a process is stable, a histogram can reveal its distribution to ensure that it's suitable.
- *Means and standard deviations* (Sections 2.5 and 2.6) are measures of data important in monitoring process results and verifying that those results center on a desired value and have an acceptably small amount of variation.
- *Run charts* (Section 2.4) show process data plotted sequentially over time. Run charts are useful for determining whether a process is statistically stable. (Figure 2.9 illustrates several different patterns in which processes are not statistically stable.) An unstable process must be fixed as soon as possible.
- *Control charts for individual values* (Section 5.4) are run charts that include upper and lower control limits at $\mu + 3\sigma$ and $\mu - 3\sigma$. These control limits provide additional help in determining whether a process is statistically stable or whether it is unstable.
- *Control charts for means* (Section 5.8) plot sample process means sequentially over time. They include upper and lower control limits at $\mu_{\bar{x}} + 3\sigma_{\bar{x}}$ and $\mu_{\bar{x}} - 3\sigma_{\bar{x}}$. (We assume in Section 5.8 that the population mean μ and standard deviation σ are known, so that by the central limit theorem we have $\mu_{\bar{x}} = \mu$ and $\sigma_{\bar{x}} = \sigma/\sqrt{n}$.) In general, control charts for means will detect out-of-control patterns faster than control charts for individual values. Recognizing problems sooner allows us to fix them sooner.
- *Confidence intervals* (Chapter 6) enable us to use sample data to estimate some population parameter, such as μ, σ, or the population proportion p. From such estimates, we can determine whether a process is working as desired.
- *Hypothesis tests* (Chapter 7) enable us to test claims made about populations. For example, we can test the claim that the population of coins made from a new machine has less variability than the coins made with the old machine.

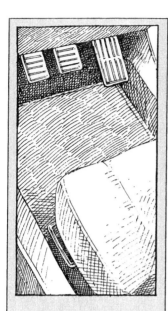

QUALITY CONTROL AT PERSTORP

Perstorp Components, Inc., uses a computer that automatically generates control charts for monitoring thicknesses of the floor insulation it makes for Ford Rangers and Jeep Grand Cherokees. The $20,000 cost of the computer was offset by a first-year savings of $40,000 in labor that had been employed to manually generate the control charts the company used to ensure insulation thicknesses between the specifications of 2.912 mm and 2.988 mm. Through the use of control charts and other quality control methods, Perstorp has reduced its waste by more than two-thirds.

In addition to these tools of quality control, earlier chapters also presented the important definition and concept of statistical stability and variation.

- A process is *statistically stable* if it has only natural variation. That is, the process has no cycles, unusual points, or patterns that aren't random. When a process is statistically stable, we can treat its data as if they came from a population. We can calculate statistics such as the mean and standard deviation; construct confidence intervals; test hypotheses, and so on. The absence of statistical stability, however, indicates that conditions are changing, so we will obtain misleading results if we treat the data as if they came from a population.

One common goal of many different methods of quality control is to reduce variation in a product or service. When Ford was having trouble with its U.S. transmissions, an inspection was made of the same types of transmissions made by Mazda in Japan. Ford found that the Mazda transmissions had substantially less variation in the gearbox components. Even though the Ford transmissions were built to be within allowable limits, too many required warranty repair. In contrast, the Mazda transmissions were more reliable (and of higher quality) because of their lower variation. Variation in a process can be described in terms of two types of causes.

DEFINITION

Random variation is due to chance; it is the type of variation inherent in any process not capable of producing every good or service exactly the same way every time.

Assignable variation results from causes that are assignable in the sense that we can identify them.

EXAMPLE The U.S. Mint has a stable process that produces new quarters. The physical characteristics of those quarters (weight, diameter, thickness, roundness) continue to stay within specifications, and the result is a high-quality product. The quarters do vary in weight, diameter, thickness, and roundness, but the variation is very small and it results from random variation.

Suppose that a machine is damaged so that the diameters of the quarters gradually increase. In addition to the random variation already present, we would also have assignable variation—the variation due to the specific cause of a damaged machine.

HOW TO USE CONTROL CHARTS

The mean is an important measure of central tendency; the standard deviation is an important measure of variation; the histogram is an important tool for determining the nature or shape of a distribution; and the control chart is an important tool for identifying patterns over time. A nonrandom pattern in a control chart

FIGURE 8.1
Control Chart

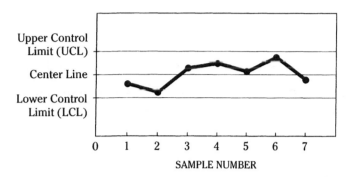

signals the presence of *assignable variation* (such as damaged machines or improperly trained employees). After identifying causes of assignable variation and eliminating them, we have a statistically stable process that contains only *random variation.* Yet even with a statistically stable process it is important to continue monitoring with control charts so that stability is maintained.

After achieving stability by eliminating all assignable variation, businesses use control charts for the next phase of increasing quality by reducing the random variation in a process. This second phase tends to be more expensive and time consuming because specific causes of random variation are usually much more difficult to identify.

Figure 8.1 illustrates the general format for a control chart. It includes a center line, an upper control limit (UCL), and a lower control limit (LCL). The major objective of a control chart is to monitor a process to determine whether it is within statistical control (with only random variation) or out of statistical control (with nonrandom patterns, trends, or cycles, or with unusual points).

INTERPRETING CONTROL CHARTS

Before we consider control charts in more detail, it is very important to note that the upper and lower control limits are based on the *actual* variation in the process, not the *desired* variation. We can state this concept as follows.

> A control chart describes how a process *is* behaving, not how we might *want* it to behave.

A particular control chart by itself might suggest that a process is statistically stable, but failure to meet manufacturing specifications and customer requirements could make that same process totally worthless.

Finally, we should clearly understand the criteria for determining whether a process is in statistical control (that is, whether it is statistically stable). In Section 2.4, Fig. 2.9 illustrated several different patterns of instability in a run chart. We used this subjective criterion: A process is not statistically stable if the run chart is as depicted in Fig. 2.9. In Section 3.5 we presented the objective run of 8 rule which states that a process is not statistically stable if 8 consecutive points are all above the center line or all below the center line. In Section 5.4 we presented another objective rule by using a control chart with an upper control limit and a lower control limit, and we noted that a process is not statistically stable if a point lies beyond either of those limits. Based on the preceding criteria, we now summarize the criteria we will use for determining statistical stability from a control chart. If any of these criteria apply, we conclude that the process is not statistically stable, or that it is *out of statistical control.*

Criteria for Determining that a Process Is Not Statistically Stable (is out of statistical control)

1. Any single point lies beyond the upper or lower control limits.
2. Run of 8 rule: Eight consecutive points are all above or all below the center line.
3. A pattern, trend, or cycle exists that is visually observed as not random (such as those depicted in Fig. 2.9).

Although we will use only the three criteria listed above to determine whether a process is out of statistical control, some companies use additional criteria, such as these:

- Six consecutive points are all increasing or all decreasing.
- Fourteen consecutive points are all alternating between up and down (that is, up, down, up, down, and so on).
- Two of 3 consecutive points are beyond control limits that are two standard deviations from the center line.
- Four of 5 consecutive points are beyond control limits that are one standard deviation from the center line.

 **8.2 EXERCISES** | BASIC CONCEPTS

In Exercises 1–8, identify the type of variation as being either random or assignable. If the variation is of the assignable type, briefly describe (a) a procedure to detect the problem and (b) at least one way to correct the problem.

1. A bank teller becomes increasingly fatigued so that his customer transaction times are consistently increasing.
2. A bank teller works very consistently, but customer service times vary because of the nature of the individual transactions.
3. The exact amounts of liquid soap placed in containers marked 8 oz vary because the filling machinery has an inherent variability that depends on chance.

4. The exact amounts of liquid soap placed in containers marked 8 oz are gradually increasing because the nozzle in the filling machine is gradually becoming larger through extensive wear.

5. At the Allen Tax Preparation Service, a process consists of completing tax returns. The times required to complete those tax returns have dramatically increased because the head preparer resigned to become a statistics teacher and she was replaced by a new employee with no experience.

6. At the Allen Tax Preparation Service, the times required to complete tax returns vary because of the varying complexity of the information supplied with individual returns.

7. At the County Auto Repair shop, the times required to replace fuel pumps vary because of differences both in rust on the retaining bolts and in the location of the fuel pump on different cars.

8. At the County Auto Repair shop, a process consists of rotating tires. The times required for that process have increased because the air-powered automatic tool has broken and the lug nuts must now be removed and replaced manually with a lug wrench.

In Exercises 9–16, briefly describe how the given statistical tools can be used to improve or maintain quality in this process: The A. S. J. Computer Mail Order company receives mail and telephone orders, assembles the ordered computers, tests them, and then ships them.

9. Pareto chart
10. Histogram
11. Mean
12. Standard deviation
13. Run chart
14. Control chart for individual values
15. $\bar{x}$ chart
16. Confidence interval

In Exercises 17–20, examine each control chart for individual values and determine whether the corresponding process is in statistical control by using the three criteria given in this section. If the process does not appear to be in statistical control, identify which of the criteria lead to that conclusion.

17.

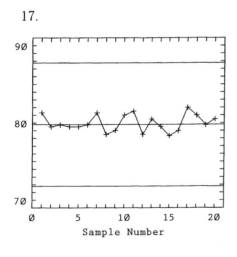

Sample Number

18.

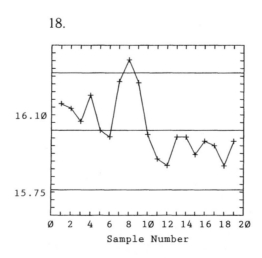

Sample Number

19.   20.

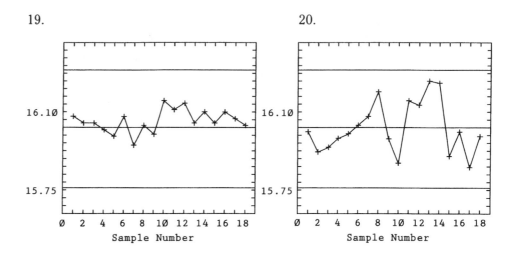

8.2 EXERCISES   BEYOND THE BASICS

21. We have noted that when a process is statistically stable, its data can be treated as population data. Suppose a process of filling milk cartons labeled 32 oz begins in statistical control, but machine wear causes the process to go out of control, filling the containers with increasing amounts of milk. Describe how this process would affect (a) a run chart, (b) an $\bar{x}$ chart, (c) a histogram, (d) the mean, and (e) the standard deviation.

22. Refer to the same process described in Exercise 21. If we incorrectly conclude that the process is stable after a long run and we proceed to calculate a mean, what corrective action would be suggested by that result alone? If that corrective action is taken, would the process become statistically stable? If the process is not monitored and no corrective action is taken, what effect will this have on the consumer? The company filling the containers?

8.3 CONTROL CHARTS FOR MEANS (with σ unknown)

In Section 2.4 we introduced the *run chart* in which *individual* values were plotted sequentially, with time represented on the horizontal axis. In Section 5.4 we used the run chart to examine the *statistical stability* (or lack thereof) of a process; we used *control limits* of $\mu + 3\sigma$ and $\mu - 3\sigma$ and constructed a *control chart for individual values when the process standard deviation σ is known*. Then, in Section 5.8, we used sample means instead of individual values and we employed control limits of $\mu_{\bar{x}} + 3\sigma_{\bar{x}}$ and $\mu_{\bar{x}} - 3\sigma_{\bar{x}}$ to develop an $\bar{x}$ chart with the process standard deviation σ known. We noted that a control chart for *means* will generally detect out-of-control patterns much faster than the control chart for *individual* values. In this section we develop an $\bar{x}$ chart with σ unknown.

For a process with unknown mean μ and unknown standard deviation σ, the following apply to a control chart for sample means.

Notation

Given: The process data consist of a sequence of samples all of the same size, and the distribution of the process data is essentially normal.

n = size of each sample (this sample is often called a *subgroup*)

k = number of samples (to get usable control limits, we recommend that $k \geq 20$)

$\bar{\bar{x}}$ = mean of the sample means (that is, find the sum of the sample means, then divide by k)

$\bar{s}$ = mean of the sample standard deviations (that is, find the sum of the sample standard deviations, then divide by k)

Control Chart for $\bar{x}$ (with σ unknown) Based on Sample Standard Deviations

Center line: $\bar{\bar{x}}$

Upper control limit (UCL): $\bar{\bar{x}} + A_3\bar{s}$

Lower control limit (LCL): $\bar{\bar{x}} - A_3\bar{s}$

where the values of A_3 are given in Table 8.2.

TABLE 8.2
Control Chart Constants

OBSERVATIONS IN SUBGROUP, n	$\bar{x}$		$\bar{s}$		$\bar{R}$	
	A_2	A_3	B_3	B_4	D_3	D_4
2	1.880	2.659	0.000	3.267	0.000	3.267
3	1.023	1.954	0.000	2.568	0.000	2.574
4	0.729	1.628	0.000	2.266	0.000	2.282
5	0.577	1.427	0.000	2.089	0.000	2.114
6	0.483	1.287	0.030	1.970	0.000	2.004
7	0.419	1.182	0.118	1.882	0.076	1.924
8	0.373	1.099	0.185	1.815	0.136	1.864
9	0.337	1.032	0.239	1.761	0.184	1.816
10	0.308	0.975	0.284	1.716	0.223	1.777
11	0.285	0.927	0.321	1.679	0.256	1.744
12	0.266	0.886	0.354	1.646	0.283	1.717
13	0.249	0.850	0.382	1.618	0.307	1.693
14	0.235	0.817	0.406	1.594	0.328	1.672
15	0.223	0.789	0.428	1.572	0.347	1.653
16	0.212	0.763	0.448	1.552	0.363	1.637
17	0.203	0.739	0.466	1.534	0.378	1.622
18	0.194	0.718	0.482	1.518	0.391	1.608
19	0.187	0.698	0.497	1.503	0.403	1.597
20	0.180	0.680	0.510	1.490	0.415	1.585
21	0.173	0.663	0.523	1.477	0.425	1.575
22	0.167	0.647	0.534	1.466	0.434	1.566
23	0.162	0.633	0.545	1.455	0.443	1.557
24	0.157	0.619	0.555	1.445	0.451	1.548
25	0.153	0.606	0.565	1.435	0.459	1.541
More than 25		$3/\sqrt{n}$	$1 - 3/\sqrt{2n}$	$1 + 3/\sqrt{2n}$		

SOURCE: Adapted from *ASTM Manual on the Presentation of Data and Control Chart Analysis* (Philadelphia: ASTM 1976), pp. 134–36. Copyright ASTM.

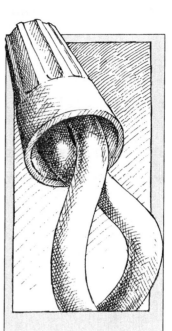

AMP, INC.

AMP, Inc., is a Pennsylvania company that makes electrical connectors. In 1983 it instituted a quality improvement plan that so far has resulted in savings of about $75 million. While some companies continue to use a system of management decree by higher-level supervisors, AMP and many other successful companies are committed to the total involvement of employees. One aspect of that total involvement is that each of the more than 10,000 AMP employees receives training in statistical procedures related to control of processes.

We will use the expressions given above for finding the control limits, but other approaches are possible, including the following:

Upper control limit: $\bar{\bar{x}} + 3\,\dfrac{\bar{s}}{\sqrt{n}}$ Lower control limit: $\bar{\bar{x}} - 3\,\dfrac{\bar{s}}{\sqrt{n}}$

(Note that A_3 is approximately equal to $3/\sqrt{n}$, and Table 8.2 indicates that $A_3 = 3/\sqrt{n}$ when $n > 25$.)

For the center line and control limits, we are using the mean $\bar{\bar{x}}$ of all available sample scores as an estimate of the process mean μ, and we are using the mean $\bar{s}$ of all sample standard deviations as an estimate of the process standard deviation σ. In Chapter 5 the central limit theorem showed that the standard deviation of sample means is given by $\sigma_{\bar{x}} = \sigma/\sqrt{n}$. In Chapters 6 and 7 we saw that for large ($n > 30$) samples, we can use the sample standard deviation s to estimate the population standard deviation σ, and

$$z = \frac{\bar{x} - \mu}{\dfrac{s}{\sqrt{n}}}$$

has a distribution that is approximately normal. When $n < 30$ and the population distribution is normal, the statistic

$$t = \frac{\bar{x} - \mu}{\dfrac{s}{\sqrt{n}}}$$

has a Student t distribution. We calculate the values of A_3 by using a Student t distribution (because we are using s instead of σ and $n \le 30$), and they take into account the factor of $\sqrt{n}$ as well as another adjustment included because s is a biased estimator of σ.

EXAMPLE   Using the A. S. J. Computer Mail Order process data from Table 8.1, construct a control chart for $\bar{x}$ based on the sample standard deviations.

SOLUTION   We will plot the 20 points corresponding to the 20 values of $\bar{x}$, and we will use the format of the control chart shown in Fig. 8.1. We must first find the value for the center line and the values for the control limits. We get

Center line: $\bar{\bar{x}} = \dfrac{17.4 + 24.0 + \ldots + 25.0}{20} = 23.780$ min

$\bar{s} = \dfrac{1.82 + 9.82 + \ldots + 4.80}{20} = 7.693$ min

Referring to Table 8.2 for $n = 5$, we find that $A_3 = 1.427$. We can now find the control limits.

Upper control limit: $\bar{\bar{x}} + A_3\bar{s} = 23.780 + (1.427)(7.693) = 34.758$
Lower control limit: $\bar{\bar{x}} - A_3\bar{s} = 23.780 - (1.427)(7.693) = 12.802$

The resulting control chart for $\bar{x}$ will be as shown in the Minitab display of Fig. 8.2. Fig. 8.2 results from entering the 100 values in column C1 and these Minitab commands:

```
GXBARCHART C1 5;
HLINES 12.802 23.780 34.758.
```

The prefix of G in GXBARCHART specifies high-resolution graphics; the 5 indicates the sample (or subgroup) size; and the subcommand HLINES specifies the locations of the horizontal lines in the control chart. You can simply enter GXBARCHART C1 5, and Minitab will automatically generate an $\bar{x}$ control chart with an upper control limit of 35.14 and a lower control limit of 12.42. These values are slightly different from the control limits we have calculated.

Examination of the Minitab control chart (Fig. 8.2) shows that there is an out-of-control pattern: Eight points are above the center line. Inspection of the control chart shows that variation seems to be decreasing, but the average processing time seems to have increased. Perhaps employees have adopted a policy of spending at least 24 min on each order, whether they need that time or not. Whatever the cause, A. S. J. management should immediately seek ways to identify and correct this situation.

The control limits we have described are based on the sample standard deviations. In the 1920s and 1930s, when Walter Shewhart developed the concept of a control chart, all calculations were done manually because calculators and computers were not yet available. Because the calculations of standard deviations are very complex, the early control charts for $\bar{x}$ were based on the sample ranges $\bar{R}$ as measures of variability. See the following page.

FIGURE 8.2
Control Chart for $\bar{x}$

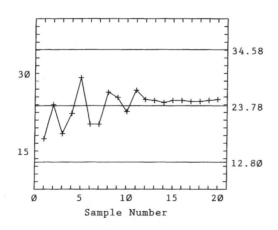

U.S. COMPANIES STRIVE FOR QUALITY

U.S. companies are finding that quality control programs can greatly reduce the numbers of defects among products or services. This reduction in defects results in savings through reduction of inspection, scrap, reworking, and repair costs. Eastman Kodak now produces Kodacolor film with a defect rate of less than 1 in a million. L. L. Bean is a famous Maine catalog company that fills orders with less than 1 error in each 1000 orders. Motorola now produces several electronics communications products with a defect rate of less than 4 per million. In one recent five-year period, Motorola estimated that it saved more than $2 billion through the use of its quality control methods.

DON'T TAMPER!

Nashua Corp. had trouble with its paper-coating machine and considered spending a million dollars to replace it. The machine was working well with a stable process, but samples were taken every so often and, based on the results, adjustments were made. These overadjustments, called *tampering*, caused shifts away from the distribution that had been good. The effect was an increase in defects. When W. Edwards Deming studied the process, he recommended that no adjustments be made unless warranted by a signal that the process had shifted or had become unstable. The company was better off with no adjustments than with the tampering that took place.

Notation

$\overline{R}$ = mean of the sample ranges (that is, find the sum of the sample ranges, then divide by the number of samples k)

Control Chart for $\overline{x}$ (with σ unknown) Based on Sample Ranges

Center line: $\overline{\overline{x}}$
Upper control limit (UCL): $\overline{\overline{x}} + A_2\overline{R}$
Lower control limit (LCL): $\overline{\overline{x}} - A_2\overline{R}$
where the values of A_2 are given in Table 8.2.

EXAMPLE Using the data from Table 8.1, construct the $\overline{x}$ chart based on sample ranges.

SOLUTION From Table 8.1 we have $\overline{\overline{x}} = 23.780$, $n = 5$ (the sample or subgroup size), and $k = 20$. We find the value of $\overline{R}$ as follows:

$$\overline{R} = \frac{5 + 26 + \ldots + 10}{20} = 19.100 \text{ min}$$

Referring to Table 8.2, we find that $A_2 = 0.577$ corresponds to $n = 5$. Knowing the values of $\overline{\overline{x}}$, A_2, and $\overline{R}$, we can now find the control limits.

Upper control limit: $\overline{\overline{x}} + A_2\overline{R} = 23.780 + (0.577)(19.10) = 34.801$
Lower control limit: $\overline{\overline{x}} - A_2\overline{R} = 23.780 - (0.577)(19.10) = 12.759$

Using the center line and control limit values of 23.780, 34.801, and 12.759, and using the values of the sample ranges listed in Table 8.1, we can plot a control chart that will be very similar to Fig. 8.2.

   Note that these control limit values are very close to the values found in the preceding example that involved the $\overline{x}$ chart based on sample standard deviations. The $\overline{x}$ chart based on sample ranges is similar to the $\overline{x}$ chart based on sample standard deviations.

We now have three different methods for constructing an $\overline{x}$ chart: (1) Base the control chart on sample standard deviations; (2) base the control chart on sample ranges; and (3) use Minitab's GXBARCHART command. For the data of Table 8.1, the three results differ by small amounts. Whichever approach is used, the intent is the same. We want to establish control limits based on a 99.73% (3 standard deviations) confidence interval about the mean. Using these methods, we expect about 99.73% of our $\overline{x}$ points to fall within the control limits. A point beyond those limits is either a *very* rare exception or (much more likely) a signal that the process is not behaving as we would expect.

   Again, it is extremely important to note that *our control chart for $\overline{x}$ describes how the process* is *behaving, not the way in which we might* want *it to behave*. In particular, the center line is at $\overline{\overline{x}}$, and this is where the process mean seems to be, not necessarily where we might like it to be. The control chart is used to monitor statistical stability in a process; it does not show whether the center or variation of the process conforms to desired specifications. Suppose that for planning purposes, the A. S. J. Computer Mail Order Company wants the process to have a mean between 15 min and 30 min. Because these specifications refer to individual times, it would be meaningful to include them on a control chart for individual values. However, those specification limits should *not* be included on the $\bar{x}$ chart, because it deals with means, not individual values. Inclusion of specification limits on an $\bar{x}$ chart could lead to the very dangerous and costly mistake of concluding that the process is fine because the sample means are within the specifications. Even though the sample means are within specifications, many individual values may not be. If including specification limits is necessary or desirable, include them only in run charts or control charts for *individual* values.

We use control charts to monitor some characteristic of a process. Although we can identify when a process has gone out of control, the control chart cannot reveal the cause. It might, however, provide some strong clues, especially if we record relevant changes, such as "new machine operator began work at 2:00 P.M. on Nov. 27" or "drill bit changed at 5:00 P.M. on March 5."

In this section we presented the $\bar{x}$ chart as a device for monitoring the mean. In the next section we introduce charts for monitoring the variation in a process.

8.3   EXERCISES   BASIC CONCEPTS

1. Windsor Export Supply is an overseas supplier for Ford automobile and truck parts made in North America. Orders are taken from foreign manufacturing and assembly plants, and parts are purchased from Ford supply plants. Windsor arranges for the shipment and collection of payments. In the early 1980s, Windsor began to use control charts to monitor several operations. One operation was the time it took from the receiving of a freight invoice by Windsor to when their Oakville bank issued a check to the freight shipper. Suppose we randomly select 6 invoices each day for 24 consecutive days; the resulting times (in days) are given in Table 8.3 on page 364. Construct an $\bar{x}$ chart based on standard deviations. What do you conclude about the statistical stability of the process mean?

2. Using the same data from Exercise 1, construct an $\bar{x}$ chart based on sample ranges. What do you conclude about statistical stability of the process mean?

3. The Wisconsin Bottling Company uses a machine to fill bottles with cola. The bottles are supposed to contain 16 oz. Each hour, a sample of 4 bottles is tested; the results for 20 consecutive hours are given in Table 8.4 on page 364. Construct an $\bar{x}$ chart based on standard deviations and determine whether the process mean is in statistical control.

4. Use the same data from Exercise 3 and construct an $\bar{x}$ chart based on ranges. Based on the result, is the process mean in statistical control?

5. The Anderson Company makes vinyl-coated aluminum replacement windows for older homes. The vinyl coating must have a thickness between certain limits, because a coating too thick would cause the window to jam, and a coating too thin would not seal properly. Suppose a thickness of 15 mm is desired. Assume that we randomly select 4 windows each hour over a 24-hour work day and measure the vinyl thicknesses, with the results given in Table 8.5 on page 365. Construct an $\bar{x}$ chart based on the sample ranges. Does the process mean seem to be in statistical control?

TABLE 8.3
Times for Windsor to Issue Checks

SAMPLE		DAYS	LAPSED				MEAN	RANGE	STANDARD DEVIATION
1	26	12	25	12	17	23	19.17	14.0	6.37
2	14	25	24	28	24	13	21.33	15.0	6.25
3	22	27	12	29	25	27	23.67	17.0	6.19
4	24	25	10	17	14	21	18.50	15.0	5.89
5	24	27	27	30	10	29	24.50	20.0	7.40
6	18	10	11	30	28	11	18.00	20.0	9.01
7	12	27	19	15	10	29	18.67	19.0	7.87
8	17	24	16	14	14	19	17.33	10.0	3.78
9	16	17	20	14	14	30	18.50	16.0	6.06
10	23	18	21	13	20	24	19.83	11.0	3.97
11	15	18	20	19	11	11	15.67	9.0	3.98
12	27	12	23	23	29	18	22.00	17.0	6.20
13	26	15	12	23	26	16	19.67	14.0	6.09
14	26	30	25	25	23	21	25.00	9.0	3.03
15	27	22	24	27	16	19	22.50	11.0	4.42
16	28	20	25	28	22	30	25.50	10.0	3.89
17	27	11	13	17	18	10	16.00	17.0	6.26
18	11	13	17	23	23	10	16.17	13.0	5.81
19	30	29	13	10	23	24	21.50	20.0	8.26
20	10	24	19	30	29	25	22.83	20.0	7.41
21	16	17	14	21	17	30	19.17	16.0	5.78
22	17	20	29	23	25	27	23.50	12.0	4.46
23	12	17	11	12	11	28	15.17	17.0	6.68
24	13	29	30	26	13	28	23.17	17.0	7.99

$\bar{\bar{x}} = 20.306$ $\bar{R} = 14.958$ $\bar{s} = 5.960$

TABLE 8.4
Amounts (in ounces) in Cola Bottles

SAMPLE		AMOUNT			MEAN	RANGE	STANDARD DEVIATION
1	15.7	15.7	16.0	15.8	15.800	0.3	0.141
2	16.2	16.1	15.9	16.1	16.075	0.3	0.126
3	16.2	15.9	15.8	15.9	15.950	0.4	0.173
4	15.7	16.0	16.0	16.3	16.000	0.6	0.245
5	15.9	15.7	15.4	16.1	15.775	0.7	0.299
6	16.1	16.6	16.2	16.0	16.225	0.6	0.263
7	16.0	16.1	16.0	15.9	16.000	0.2	0.082
8	16.2	15.9	16.2	16.2	16.125	0.3	0.150
9	15.7	16.0	15.8	15.9	15.850	0.3	0.129
10	16.0	15.8	16.2	16.0	16.000	0.4	0.163
11	16.3	16.0	16.3	16.0	16.150	0.3	0.173
12	16.2	16.2	16.0	15.9	16.075	0.3	0.150
13	15.9	15.8	15.9	15.8	15.850	0.1	0.058
14	15.9	15.8	16.0	16.1	15.950	0.3	0.129
15	16.1	15.8	16.0	15.7	15.900	0.4	0.183
16	15.9	15.8	15.8	15.9	15.850	0.1	0.058
17	16.1	16.0	15.8	16.1	16.000	0.3	0.141
18	16.3	15.9	16.1	16.3	16.150	0.4	0.191
19	16.2	16.1	16.1	16.0	16.100	0.2	0.082
20	15.9	15.8	15.7	15.9	15.825	0.2	0.096

TABLE 8.5
Thickness of Vinyl Window Coatings

SAMPLE	THICKNESS OF COATING				MEAN	RANGE	STANDARD DEVIATION
1	13	18	15	14	15.00	5.0	2.160
2	16	12	13	14	13.75	4.0	1.708
3	18	16	13	18	16.25	5.0	2.360
4	15	15	13	17	15.00	4.0	1.633
5	12	13	12	16	13.25	4.0	1.893
6	16	17	16	17	16.50	1.0	0.577
7	15	17	15	12	14.75	5.0	2.060
8	18	15	16	14	15.75	4.0	1.708
9	15	15	15	13	14.50	2.0	1.000
10	13	14	16	14	14.25	3.0	1.258
11	14	13	13	16	14.00	3.0	1.414
12	17	15	16	14	15.50	3.0	1.291
13	17	13	13	16	14.75	4.0	2.060
14	16	13	16	17	15.50	4.0	1.732
15	5	19	10	7	10.25	14.0	6.185
16	21	18	17	5	15.25	16.0	7.042
17	8	6	15	22	12.75	16.0	7.274
18	23	13	22	14	18.00	10.0	5.228
19	20	9	25	21	18.75	16.0	6.850
20	6	23	8	22	14.75	17.0	8.995
21	7	15	12	6	10.00	9.0	4.243
22	24	13	14	19	17.50	11.0	5.066
23	13	9	14	18	13.50	9.0	3.697
24	14	15	16	6	12.75	10.0	4.573

TABLE 8.6
Strengths of Spot Welds on Bicycle Frames

SAMPLE	STRENGTH (IN LB)					MEAN	RANGE	STANDARD DEVIATION
1	495	501	500	495	487	495.6	14	5.55
2	490	496	489	500	500	495.0	11	5.29
3	504	501	505	504	508	504.4	7	2.51
4	489	496	500	503	503	498.2	14	5.89
5	504	490	502	504	504	500.8	14	6.10
6	500	503	497	504	487	498.2	17	6.83
7	499	501	510	506	500	503.2	11	4.66
8	495	502	492	501	499	497.8	10	4.21
9	501	505	507	506	495	502.8	12	4.92
10	496	501	503	494	498	498.4	9	3.65
11	506	507	505	501	504	504.6	6	2.30
12	513	494	497	505	498	501.4	19	7.64
13	501	502	512	497	503	503.0	15	5.52
14	496	495	498	496	486	494.2	12	4.71
15	504	502	505	501	505	503.4	4	1.82
16	504	498	506	494	498	500.0	12	4.90
17	500	503	497	496	500	499.2	7	2.77
18	502	497	490	498	507	498.8	17	6.30
19	495	506	513	488	503	501.0	25	9.72
20	481	486	485	485	493	486.0	12	4.36

TABLE 8.7
Distance between Holes on Fax Machines

SAMPLE	DISTANCE					MEAN	RANGE
1	4.98	5.02	4.98	4.88	4.99	4.970	0.14
2	5.04	5.03	5.03	5.02	5.03	5.030	0.02
3	4.96	4.89	5.05	5.02	4.98	4.980	0.16
4	5.05	4.95	4.96	4.96	4.95	4.974	0.10
5	5.04	4.96	4.96	5.01	4.98	4.990	0.08
6	5.00	4.93	4.96	4.95	5.02	4.972	0.09
7	4.99	5.01	5.08	5.01	5.03	5.024	0.09
8	4.96	4.93	5.00	5.02	5.04	4.990	0.11
9	4.91	4.93	4.97	4.92	4.99	4.944	0.08
10	4.96	4.97	5.03	4.98	5.08	5.004	0.12
11	4.97	5.07	5.05	5.01	4.94	5.008	0.13
12	4.83	4.44	4.94	5.22	5.73	5.032	1.29
13	4.92	5.19	4.70	5.02	4.91	4.948	0.49
14	5.38	4.71	5.10	4.85	5.73	5.154	1.02
15	5.18	4.71	5.95	5.03	5.55	5.284	1.24
16	4.68	4.84	6.15	4.85	5.30	5.164	1.47
17	4.56	5.59	5.03	4.81	4.81	4.960	1.03
18	5.53	5.20	5.26	4.91	5.40	5.260	0.62
19	5.96	5.50	5.25	5.23	4.54	5.296	1.42
20	5.39	5.28	5.90	5.31	5.10	5.396	0.80

6. The Dayton Machine Company uses a manufacturing process that consists of applying spot welds to bicycle frames. During each work shift, a random sample of 5 spot welds is obtained, and each weld in the sample is tested for shear strength. The results (in lb) for 20 work shifts are given in Table 8.6 on page 365. Construct the $\bar{x}$ chart based on sample ranges. Is the process mean in statistical control?

7. Use the same data from Exercise 6 to construct an $\bar{x}$ chart based on sample standard deviations. Is the process mean in statistical control?

8. In the process of manufacturing a fax machine, two holes are to be drilled 5.00 cm apart. During each hour, a random sample of 5 pairs of holes is selected and the distances between the holes are measured. Table 8.7 lists the results from 20 consecutive hours. Construct an $\bar{x}$ chart based on sample ranges. Is the process mean in statistical control?

8.3 EXERCISES   BEYOND THE BASICS

9. Do Exercise 1 using control limits of

$$\bar{\bar{x}} + 3\frac{\bar{s}}{\sqrt{n}} \quad \text{and} \quad \bar{\bar{x}} - 3\frac{\bar{s}}{\sqrt{n}}$$

Compare the results with those obtained in Exercises 1 and 2.

10. Table 8.1 contains a subgroup of size 5, meaning that there are 5 values in each sample. But suppose we had 24 values in each sample, find the value of A_3 from Table 8.2 that would be used in constructing a control chart based on standard deviations. How close is that value to the value of $3/\sqrt{n}$ that would be used by another method for constructing $\bar{x}$ charts?

11. Refer to Exercise 6.
    a. Identify practical consequences that would result from the process being out of statistical control.
    b. Suppose safety specifications require that the welds have a shear strength greater than 485 lb. How many of the sample means are equal to or less than 485 lb? How many individual spot welds are equal to or less than 485 lb? Does the process result in welds that conform to the specifications?

8.4 CONTROL CHARTS FOR VARIATION

Section 8.3 explained the use of $\bar{x}$ charts for monitoring the mean in a process. This section introduces the **R chart** (or range chart) and the **s chart** (or standard deviation chart) for monitoring the *variation* in a process. (Don't confuse the R chart with the control chart for $\bar{x}$ based on sample ranges. The R chart plots sample ranges and is used to monitor variation, whereas the $\bar{x}$ chart plots sample means and is used to monitor the central value of the process. As in Section 8.3, we assume that the population standard deviation σ is not known.) A process may well have a stable mean that stays within statistical control, while the variation might be increasing so that individual items vary more, with the effect that more of the items are defective. For example, suppose a process is intended to cut boards to a length of 8 ft, but half the boards are cut to 6 ft and the other half are cut to 10 ft. Samples could have means close to the target value of 8 ft so the sample means seem to be fine, but the large variation results in all the individual boards being defective because they are far too long or too short. Businesses generally want to have a process with both a stable mean and a stable variation. Hence it is very common to produce both $\bar{x}$ charts and R charts together.

R CHARTS

The basic format of the R chart (with σ not known) includes points plotted in sequence, a center line, and upper and lower control limits. The $\bar{x}$ chart of Section 8.2 plots the sample means $\bar{x}$; the R chart plots the sample ranges.

Notation

$\bar{R}$ = mean of the sample ranges (that is, first find the range of each sample, then calculate the mean of those results)

D_3 = value found from Table 8.2

D_4 = value found from Table 8.2

MOTOROLA AND THE SIX-SIGMA (σ) QUALITY STANDARD

From the 1950s to the 1970s, U.S. manufacturers sought to make 99.8% of their components good, with only 0.2% defective. This rate corresponds to a "three-sigma" level of tolerance. This seems to be a high level of quality, but Motorola recognized that when many such components are *combined,* the chance of getting a defective product is quite high. The company sought to reduce the variation in all processes by one-half. This standard became known as the "six-sigma" program. A six-sigma level corresponds to about two defects per *billion* items. Motorola found that it could achieve this level with many components and processes. The extra cost of this increased quality was more than offset by reduced costs of repair, scrap, and warranty work. In 1988 Motorola won the first Malcolm Baldridge National Quality Award.

Control Chart for R

Center line: $\overline{R}$
Upper control limit: $D_4\overline{R}$
Lower control limit: $D_3\overline{R}$

EXAMPLE Using the process data from Table 8.1, construct a control chart for R.

SOLUTION We first find the value of the mean of the available sample ranges $\overline{R}$ as follows:

$$\overline{R} = \frac{5 + 26 + 28 + \cdots + 10}{20} = 19.1$$

The center line for our R chart is at $\overline{R} = 19.1$. To find the upper and lower control limits, we must first find the values of D_3 and D_4; referring to Table 8.2 for $n = 5$, we get $D_3 = 0$ and $D_4 = 2.114$. The control limits are as follows:

Upper control limit: $D_4\overline{R} = 2.114 \times 19.1 = 40.38$
Lower control limit: $D_3\overline{R} = 0 \times 19.1 = 0$

Using a center-line value of $\overline{R} = 19.1$ and control limits of 0 and 40.38, we can now plot the sample *ranges.* The result is shown in Fig. 8.3, which you can obtain with these Minitab commands:

```
GRCHART C1 5;
RBAR.
```

The 5 in the command GRCHART C1 5 indicates the sample (or subgroup) size, and the subcommand RBAR tells Minitab to use $\overline{R}$ as the center line. Without the RBAR subcommand, Minitab would use a slightly different center line.

As with $\bar{x}$ charts, we can interpret R charts by applying the out-of-control criteria identified in Section 8.2. Applying the three listed criteria to Fig. 8.3, we conclude that this process is out of control because a point exists beyond the upper control limit. We therefore conclude that the *variation* (and not necessarily the mean) of the process is out of statistical control; the range seems to be too large during the start of our sampling and this is consistent with what we noted on the $\bar{x}$ chart.

s CHARTS

In monitoring process variation, an alternative to using R charts is to use s charts that plot the sample standard deviations instead of the sample ranges. The s charts involve messy calculations, but statistical software has effectively eliminated that obstacle. For example, Minitab can be used to produce s charts. The center line and control limits for the **s chart** are as follows:

FIGURE 8.3
Control Chart for R

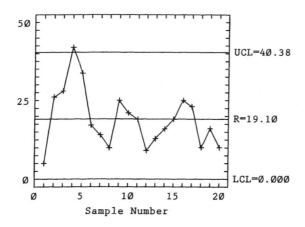

Sample Number

Notation

$\bar{s}$ = mean of the sample standard deviations (that is, first find the standard deviation of each sample, then calculate the mean of those results)

B_3 = value found from Table 8.2

B_4 = value found from Table 8.2

Control Chart for s

Center line: $\bar{s}$
Upper control limit: $B_4\bar{s}$
Lower control limit: $B_3\bar{s}$

EXAMPLE   Use the process data from Table 8.1 to construct an s chart.

SOLUTION   We first find the value of the mean of the sample standard deviation as follows:

$$\bar{s} = \frac{1.82 + 9.82 + 10.0 + \cdots + 4.80}{20} = 7.693$$

The center line for the s chart is at 7.693. To find the upper and lower control limits, we must first find the values of B_3 and B_4. Referring to Table 8.2 for $n = 5$, we get $B_3 = 0$ and $B_4 = 2.089$. We can now find the values of the control limits as follows:

Upper control limit: $B_4\bar{s} = (2.089)(7.693) = 16.07$
Lower control limit: $B_3\bar{s} = (0)(7.693) = 0$ *(continued)*

FIGURE 8.4
Control Chart for *s*

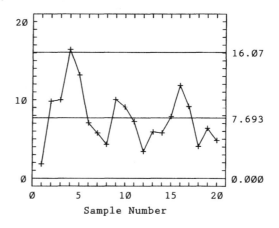

With a center line at 7.693 and control limits at 0 and 16.07, the *s* chart will appear as shown in Fig. 8.4. That display was obtained by entering these Minitab commands:

```
GSCHART C1 5;
HLINES 0 7.693 16.07.
```

The prefix of G in GSCHART indicates that the chart will be displayed in high-resolution graphics; the 5 indicates the sample (or subgroup) size; and the HLINES command specifies the location of the horizontal lines for the lower control limit, the center line, and the upper control limit, respectively. If we want to avoid the calculations and accept Minitab's approach to constructing the *s* chart, we can simply enter the data in column C1 and then enter the command GSBARCHART C1 5. Because Minitab's calculations are slightly different, the resulting display will be slightly different from the display shown here.

Applying our three out-of-control criteria, we conclude that the process is out of statistical control because there is a point beyond the upper control limit; in fact, it is the same point as in the *R* chart of Fig. 8.3. Both the *R* and the *s* charts indicate that the process *variation* seems to be out of statistical control around the fourth sample. We need to investigate and correct that occurrence.

Because these control charts were developed in the 1920s and 1930s, when computers and calculators were not available, the *R* chart was favored because it involved much easier calculations. The *R* chart has been the most widely taught and continues to be the most widely used control chart for monitoring process variation, even though the *s* chart has some theoretical advantages.

STRATEGY FOR USING CONTROL CHARTS

When using control charts to monitor a process, it's wise first to ensure that variation is in statistical control, because out-of-control variation can easily make the $\bar{x}$ chart appear to be out of control. In such a case, the problem might appear to be lack of control in the process *center,* when in fact the real problem is lack of control in variation. Only after the process variation seems stable should we proceed to monitor the process center. Consequently, a good strategy is to *use an* R *chart or an* s *chart first, and only if variation seems stable should we proceed to develop an* $\bar{x}$ *chart for monitoring the process center.* Also, if we use an R chart to monitor variation, then we should monitor the process center by using an $\bar{x}$ chart based on ranges. If instead we use an s chart to monitor variation, then we should use an $\bar{x}$ chart based on sample standard deviations to monitor the process center.

8.4 **EXERCISES** **BASIC CONCEPTS**

In Exercises 1–4, examine the R chart. Determine whether the process is within statistical control. If it is not, identify which of the three out-of-control criteria apply.

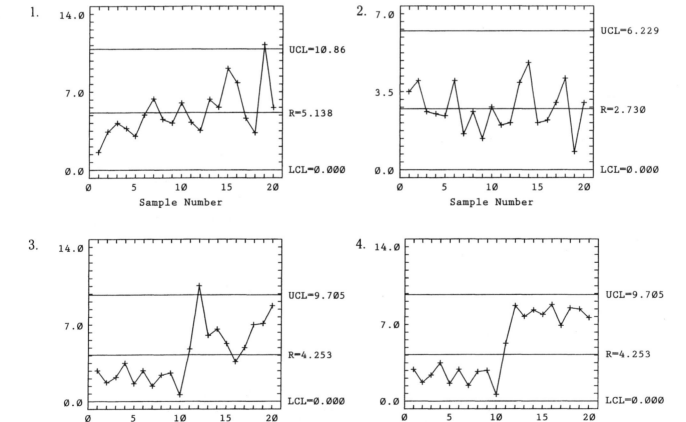

In Exercises 5–14, use the given process data from Section 8.3 to construct the indicated control charts for variation. Determine whether the process is within statistical control. If it is not, identify which of the three out-of-control criteria apply.

5. Refer to Exercise 1 in Section 8.3 for the Windsor Export Supply data. Construct an R chart for variation.

6. Refer to Exercise 1 in Section 8.3 for the Windsor Export Supply data. Construct an s chart for variation.

7. Refer to the Wisconsin Bottling Company data given in Exercise 3 of Section 8.3. Construct an s chart for variation.

8. Refer to the Wisconsin Bottling Company data given in Exercise 3 of Section 8.3. Construct an R chart for variation.

9. Refer to the process data given in Exercise 5 of Section 8.3. Construct an R chart for variation.

10. Refer to the process data given in Exercise 5 of Section 8.3. Construct an s chart for variation.

11. Refer to the Dayton Machine Company data given in Exercise 6 of Section 8.3. Construct an s chart for variation.

12. Refer to the Dayton Machine Company data given in Exercise 6 of Section 8.3. Construct an R chart for variation.

13. Refer to the hole-drilling data given in Exercise 8 of Section 8.3. Construct an R chart for variation.

14. Refer to the hole-drilling data given in Exercise 8 of Section 8.3. Construct an s chart for variation.

8.4   EXERCISES   BEYOND THE BASICS

15. Refer to the control charts for Exercises 1 and 2 of Section 8.3 and Exercises 5 and 6 of this section. Those control charts should suggest that the Windsor Export Supply data (given in Exercise 1 of Section 8.3) come from a process that is statistically stable for both the center and variation. We can therefore treat the sample data as if they came from a population. Combine all the data, and (a) with $\alpha = 0.05$, test the claim that the population mean μ is greater than 15 days; (b) construct a 95% confidence interval for μ; and (c) with $\alpha = 0.05$, test the claim that the population standard deviation σ is greater than 3 days. (Hint: See Exercise 17 of Section 7.6.)

16. Refer to the example of this section. Using Minitab, enter the same data and then enter the command GRCHART C1 5. This command estimates σ using a "pooled" standard deviation of the sample data. Compare the resulting R chart with the one given in this section.

17. Examine the $\bar{x}$ chart for the data in Exercise 8 of Section 8.3 and the R chart for Exercise 13 of this section. Those charts refer to the same data set. Write a brief summary of what seems to be occurring with both the center and variation of the drilling process. Include any recommendations for further investigation or corrective action.

8.5 CONTROL CHART FOR ATTRIBUTES

In this section we construct a control chart for an attribute, such as the proportion p of defective items. The objective is to monitor a process to maintain quality, but instead of tracking the quantitative characteristics of mean and variation, we now consider the qualitative attribute of whether an item has some particular characteristic (such as being defective). We will describe control charts for the attribute of "being defective," but it could also be some other attribute, such as "being nonconforming." A good or a service is nonconforming if it doesn't meet specifications or requirements. (Nonconforming goods are sometimes called seconds and are sold at reduced prices.) As before, we select samples at regular time intervals and plot points in a sequential graph with a center line and control limits. The relevant notation and control chart are as follows:

Notation

$\bar{p}$ = pooled estimate of the proportion of defects in the process

$$= \frac{\text{total number of defects found among all items sampled}}{\text{total number of items sampled}}$$

$\bar{q}$ = $1 - \bar{p}$

Control Chart for p

Center line: $\bar{p}$
Upper control limit: $\bar{p} + 3\sqrt{\dfrac{\bar{p}\,\bar{q}}{n}}$

Lower control limit: $\bar{p} - 3\sqrt{\dfrac{\bar{p}\,\bar{q}}{n}}$

We use $\bar{p}$ for the center line because it is the best estimate of the proportion of defects from the process. The expression for the control limits corresponds to three standard deviations away from the center line. In Section 6.3 we noted that the standard deviation of sample proportions is

$$\sqrt{\frac{\bar{p}\,\bar{q}}{n}}$$

and this is expressed in the above control limits.

EXAMPLE The Paris Cosmetics Company manufactures lipstick tubes that dispense (you guessed it) lipstick. Each day, 200 tubes are randomly selected and tested. The results are given below for 20 consecutive days listed by row. Construct and interpret a **p chart** for the proportion of defective units.

$$
\begin{array}{cccccccccc}
4 & 2 & 3 & 6 & 1 & 4 & 3 & 0 & 5 & 5 \\
2 & 1 & 9 & 3 & 4 & 1 & 0 & 2 & 6 & 3
\end{array}
$$

TAGUCHI METHODS OF QUALITY CONTROL

Genichi Taguchi developed methods for improving quality and reducing costs through a reduction in process variability. The Japanese company INAX used Taguchi methods to analyze problems in its process of baking tiles in a kiln. The tile defect rate was about 30% because lack of uniform baking causes wide variation in tile size. Using Taguchi methods, the production team identified seven "control factors" believed to affect the problem. For each factor, the team recommended a new performance level that would improve the process and bring the product closer to the target value. Engineers ran experiments on the kiln, with each control factor at the old performance level and at the new recommended level. Based on the results, the company made inexpensive changes that lowered the defect rate from 30% to 1%.

FIGURE 8.5
p Chart for Lipstick Tubes

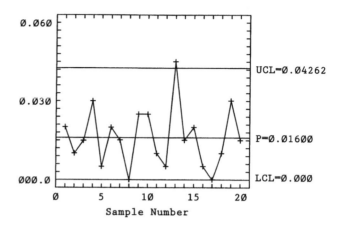

SOLUTION The center line for our control chart is at

$$\bar{p} = \frac{\text{total number of defective items from all samples combined}}{\text{total number of items sampled}}$$

$$= \frac{4 + 2 + 3 + \cdots + 3}{20 \times 200}$$

$$= \frac{64}{4000} = 0.016$$

Because $\bar{p} = 0.016$, it follows that $\bar{q} = 1 - 0.016 = 0.984$. Using $\bar{p} = 0.016$, $\bar{q} = 0.984$, and $n = 200$, we find the control limits as follows:

Upper control limit:

$$\bar{p} + 3\sqrt{\frac{\bar{p}\,\bar{q}}{n}} = 0.016 + 3\sqrt{\frac{(0.016)(0.984)}{200}}$$

$$= 0.016 + 0.027$$
$$= 0.043$$

Lower control limit:

$$\bar{p} - 3\sqrt{\frac{\bar{p}\,\bar{q}}{n}} = 0.016 - 3\sqrt{\frac{(0.016)(0.984)}{200}}$$

$$= 0.016 - 0.027$$
$$= -0.011$$

Because it's impossible to have a negative proportion, we will use 0 for the lower control limit so in this case we can never have an out-of-control signal from a point that is below the lower control limit. Having found the values for the center line and control limits, we can proceed to plot the daily proportion of defects. The Minitab command GPCHART C1 C2 results in the chart displayed in Fig. 8.5; the column C1 consists of the numbers of defects (4, 2, 3, 6, . . .) and the column C2 consists of the sample sizes (200, 200, 200, 200, . . .). Figure 8.5 plots the sample proportions consisting of the C1 values divided by the corresponding C2 values.

We can interpret the *p* chart by considering the out-of-control criteria listed in Section 8.2. Using those criteria, we conclude that this process is out of statistical control because a point falls above the upper control limit. Recall that those limits represent values that are three standard deviations away from the center, so that 99.73% of all points should fall between them. Because we have a point beyond those limits, it's either an extremely rare exception or an indication that the process is not behaving as we would expect.

A variation of the *p* chart is the **np chart,** in which the actual *numbers* of defects are plotted instead of the *proportions* of defects. The *np* chart will have a center-line value of $n\bar{p}$, and the control limits will have values of $n\bar{p} + 3\sqrt{n\bar{p}\bar{q}}$ and $n\bar{p} - 3\sqrt{n\bar{p}\bar{q}}$. The *p* chart and the *np* chart differ only in the scale of values used for the vertical axis.

8.5   EXERCISES   BASIC CONCEPTS

In Exercises 1–4, examine the given *p* chart and determine whether the process is within statistical control. If it is not, identify which of these three out-of-control criteria apply: (1) There is a point beyond the control limits; (2) Eight consecutive points are all above or all below the center line; (3) There is a pattern, trend, or cycle that is not random (such as those in Fig. 2.9).

1.

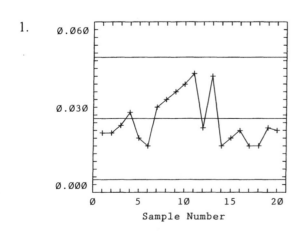

2.

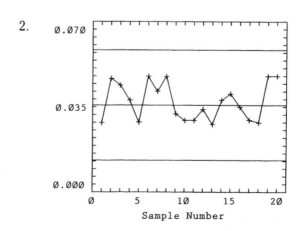

3.   4.

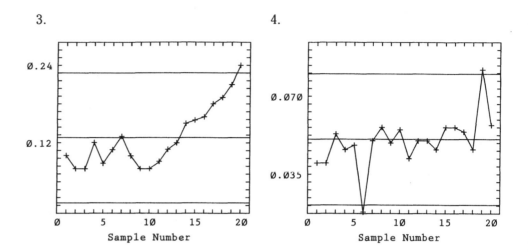

In Exercises 5–8, use the given process data to construct a control chart for p, the proportion of defects. In each case, use the three out-of-control criteria listed in Section 8.2 and determine whether the process is within statistical control. If it is not, identify which of the three out-of-control criteria apply.

5. Columbia House runs a music club from Terre Haute, Indiana, and uses p charts to monitor proportions of CD and tape orders that are incorrectly filled. Suppose 300 orders are randomly selected and monitored each day; the results for 21 consecutive days are given below. If further investigation revealed that on the sixth and seventh days temporary employees were hired to fill in for vacationing employees, what would you recommend?

   3   2   4   7   3   15   18   2   6   4   3
   5   4   6   5   2   4   3   6   1   5

6. The Telektronic Company produces 20-amp fuses used to protect car radios from too much electrical power. Each day 400 fuses are randomly selected and tested; the results (numbers of defects) for 20 consecutive days (listed by row) are given below.

   10   8   7   6   6   9   12   5   4   7
   9   6   11   4   6   5   10   5   9   11

7. The Riverside Building Supply Company manufactures concrete blocks to be used for home foundations. During each production run, which lasts for 6 hours, a random sample of 120 blocks is tested. The numbers of defective blocks for 18 consecutive production runs are given below.

   4   3   3   2   5   4   3   16   6   3   3   2   5   7   8   4   6   5

8. A manager for the Gleason Supermarket monitors customer waiting times at the checkout counter and considers a wait of more than 5 min to be a defect. Each week, 100 customers are randomly selected and timed at the checkout counter. Given below are the numbers of defects found in 24 consecutive weeks (listed by row).

   8   7   11   13   10   8   9   8   7   12   14   6
   5   9   11   8   7   10   9   8   10   7   11   10

8.5 EXERCISES   BEYOND THE BASICS

9. Refer to the data in Exercise 6. The control chart should indicate statistical stability so that the data can be treated as if they came from a population.
   a. Using all the data combined, construct a 95% confidence interval for the proportion of defects.
   b. Using a 0.05 significance level, test the claim that the rate of defects is 1% or less.
10. Construct the *np* chart for the lipstick-tube example of this section. Compare the result with the control chart for *p* given in this section.
11. a. Identify the locations of the center line and control limits for a *p* chart representing a process that has been having a 5% rate of nonconforming items, based on samples of size 100.
    b. Repeat part *a* after changing the sample size to 300.
    c. Compare the two sets of results. What are the advantages and disadvantages of each? Which chart would be better in detecting a shift from 5% to 10%?

Vocabulary List

Define and give an example of each term.

random variation
assignable variation
control chart
within statistical control
control chart for $\bar{x}$ based on sample standard deviations
control chart for $\bar{x}$ based on sample ranges

R chart
s chart
p chart
np chart

Review

In this chapter we introduced different types of *control charts* to monitor processes. By sampling from a process at regular periods, we can identify when production begins to go out of statistical control so we know that corrective action must be taken.

In the Overview, we discussed the nature and importance of quality control. In Section 8.2 we reviewed some of the quality control tools presented earlier in this book. We defined random variation and assignable variation. We reviewed the basic format of a control chart, which consists of points plotted in sequence, a center line, and lines representing upper and lower control limits. We also identified specific criteria for determining whether a process is out of statistical control. We noted that the control charts presented in this chapter describe how a process *is behaving,* not how we might *like it to behave* because of such factors as manufacturer specifications.

IMPORTANT FORMULAS

	CONTROL CHART VALUES		
CHARACTERISTIC	CENTER LINE	UPPER CONTROL LIMIT	LOWER CONTROL LIMIT
MEAN			
$\bar{x}$ chart (if $n > 25$)	$\bar{\bar{x}}$	$\bar{\bar{x}} + 3\dfrac{\bar{s}}{\sqrt{n}}$	$\bar{\bar{x}} - 3\dfrac{\bar{s}}{\sqrt{n}}$
$\bar{x}$ chart (if $n \leq 25$) based on standard deviations	$\bar{\bar{x}}$	$\bar{\bar{x}} + A_3\bar{s}$	$\bar{\bar{x}} - A_3\bar{s}$
$\bar{x}$ chart (if $n \leq 25$) based on ranges	$\bar{\bar{x}}$	$\bar{\bar{x}} + A_2\bar{R}$	$\bar{\bar{x}} - A_2\bar{R}$
VARIATION			
R chart	$\bar{R}$	$D_4\bar{R}$	$D_3\bar{R}$
s chart	$\bar{s}$	$B_4\bar{s}$	$B_3\bar{s}$
PROPORTION OF DEFECTS			
p chart	$\bar{p}$	$\bar{p} + 3\sqrt{\dfrac{\bar{p}\,\bar{q}}{n}}$	$\bar{p} - 3\sqrt{\dfrac{\bar{p}\,\bar{q}}{n}}$

In Section 8.3 we discussed $\bar{x}$ *charts*. Sample means are plotted in an attempt to monitor the characteristic of the process mean or center. An $\bar{x}$ chart can be based on sample standard deviations or sample ranges. In Section 8.4 we plotted sample ranges in *R charts* in an attempt to monitor process variation. We also introduced *s charts* that can be used to monitor variation. In Section 8.5 we plotted sample proportions in *p charts* as we attempted to monitor the defects or nonconforming goods or services in a process.

The accompanying flowchart in Figure 8.6 should be helpful in determining which control charts should be used and the order in which they should be used.

Review Exercises

In Exercises 1–4, examine the given control chart and determine whether the corresponding process is within statistical control. If it is not, identify the relevant out-of-control criteria. Exercise 1 is an $\bar{x}$ chart, Exercise 2 is an R chart, and Exercises 3 and 4 are p charts.

1.
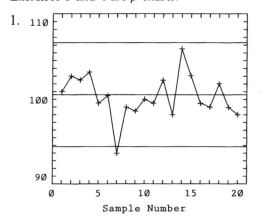

2.
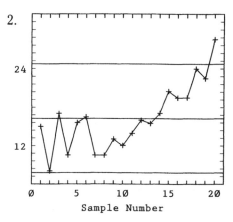

FIGURE 0.6
Using Control Charts to Monitor Process Data

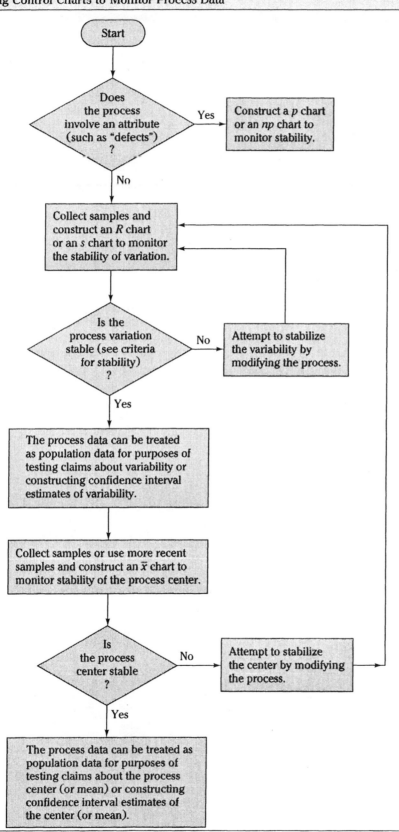

3.   4.

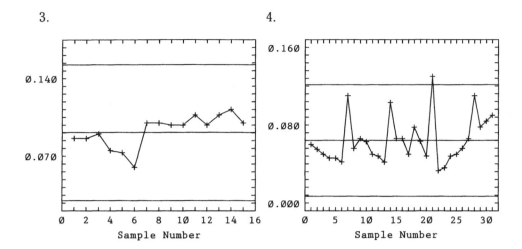

Sample Number   Sample Number

5. The Telstar Appliance Company uses a process consisting of painting refrigerators with a coat of enamel. During each shift, a sample of 5 refrigerators is randomly selected and the thickness of the paint (in mils) is determined. If the enamel coat is too thin, it will not provide enough protection. If it's too thick, it will result in an uneven appearance with running and wasted paint. Table 8.8 lists the results from 20 consecutive shifts. Construct an R chart to determine whether variation is in statistical control.

6. Using the same sample data from Exercise 5, construct an $\bar{x}$ chart based on ranges. On the basis of this result, is the process center in statistical control?

TABLE 8.8
Thicknesses of Enamel on Refrigerators

SAMPLE			THICKNESS			MEAN	RANGE	STANDARD DEVIATION
1	2.7	2.3	2.6	2.4	2.7	2.54	0.4	0.182
2	2.6	2.4	2.6	2.3	2.8	2.54	0.5	0.195
3	2.3	2.3	2.4	2.5	2.4	2.38	0.2	0.084
4	2.8	2.3	2.4	2.6	2.7	2.56	0.5	0.207
5	2.6	2.5	2.6	2.1	2.8	2.52	0.7	0.259
6	2.2	2.3	2.7	2.2	2.6	2.40	0.5	0.235
7	2.2	2.6	2.4	2.0	2.3	2.30	0.6	0.224
8	2.8	2.6	2.6	2.7	2.5	2.64	0.3	0.114
9	2.4	2.8	2.4	2.2	2.3	2.42	0.6	0.228
10	2.6	2.3	2.0	2.5	2.4	2.36	0.6	0.230
11	3.1	3.0	3.5	2.8	3.0	3.08	0.7	0.259
12	2.4	2.8	2.2	2.9	2.5	2.56	0.7	0.288
13	2.1	3.2	2.5	2.6	2.8	2.64	1.1	0.404
14	2.2	2.8	2.1	2.2	2.4	2.34	0.7	0.279
15	2.4	3.0	2.5	2.5	2.0	2.48	1.0	0.356
16	3.1	2.6	2.6	2.8	2.1	2.64	1.0	0.365
17	2.9	2.4	2.9	1.3	1.8	2.26	1.6	0.702
18	1.9	1.6	2.6	3.3	3.3	2.54	1.7	0.783
19	2.3	2.6	2.7	2.8	3.2	2.72	0.9	0.327
20	1.8	2.8	2.3	2.0	2.9	2.36	1.1	0.483

7. The Telektronic Company manufactures electronic automatic shutoff devices for irons. During each work shift, 100 of these devices are randomly selected and tested. Listed below are the numbers of defects for 15 consecutive work shifts. Construct a control chart for p and then determine whether the process is within statistical control. If it is not, identify which criteria apply.

9   4   11   12   8   8   8   7   0   16   6   13   5   12   7

8. The Medassist Pharmaceutical Company provides discounted prescription medicine to retirees of several corporations. Orders are placed by mail each day and they are filled by three groups of workers in consecutive 8-hour shifts. In an attempt to monitor the quality of service, 50 orders are randomly selected every 2 hours and they are examined for correctness (correct drug, correct amount, and so on). The number of nonconforming orders was recorded for each shift over 2 consecutive days, and the results are given below. Use a control chart to determine whether the process is statistically stable. Should any corrective action be taken to improve the process?

Shift   A A A B B B B C C C C A A A A B B B B C C C C
Number   2 6 3 4 11 10 9 12 2 3 4 2 3 5 4 6 12 10 11 12 5 2 3 4

9. A manufacturing process at the Portland Machine Company requires the drilling of cylinder holes for bulldozer engines. The holes are supposed to be 200 mm in diameter. During each working hour, a sample of 4 holes is selected; the results are given in Table 8.9 for 20 consecutive hours. Construct an s chart to monitor the process variation. Does the process variation seem to be in statistical control?

10. Use the same process data from Exercise 9. Construct an $\bar{x}$ chart based on standard deviations. Does the process center seem to be in statistical control?

TABLE 8.9
Diameters of Bulldozer Engine Cylinder Holes

SAMPLE	DIAMETER				MEAN	RANGE	STANDARD DEVIATION
1	199.90	201.10	199.40	201.20	200.400	1.8	0.891
2	201.10	199.90	199.10	200.80	200.225	2.0	0.907
3	200.90	198.80	200.50	199.40	199.900	2.1	0.970
4	198.60	199.00	199.80	200.70	199.525	2.1	0.929
5	198.90	199.00	199.60	199.30	199.200	0.7	0.316
6	197.80	199.50	199.80	199.00	199.025	2.0	0.881
7	199.35	198.55	199.25	198.75	198.975	0.8	0.386
8	200.20	200.80	200.00	197.50	199.625	3.3	1.457
9	200.10	202.40	199.30	199.70	200.375	3.1	1.389
10	199.10	200.00	200.00	202.10	200.300	3.0	1.273
11	199.60	200.60	198.60	199.70	199.625	2.0	0.818
12	201.40	198.30	201.30	200.20	200.300	3.1	1.440
13	200.60	200.10	201.20	199.60	200.375	1.6	0.685
14	200.30	199.60	199.40	201.80	200.275	2.4	1.087
15	199.40	198.30	199.10	200.10	199.225	1.8	0.746
16	199.10	200.70	199.20	200.50	199.875	1.6	0.842
17	200.90	198.80	200.80	200.50	200.250	2.1	0.981
18	201.20	200.00	199.60	199.90	200.175	1.6	0.704
19	199.40	198.80	199.60	201.00	199.700	2.2	0.931
20	199.30	200.10	200.10	199.50	199.750	0.8	0.412

Computer Projects

1. a.   The Chemco Company fills containers of liquid cleaning detergents. The filling process is supposed to be stable with a mean of 80.0 oz and a standard deviation of 0.3 oz (so that 99.73% of the containers are between 79.1 oz and 80.9 oz). Simulate 25 samples, each consiting of 5 containers, by entering the following Minitab commands.

```
RANDOM k = 5 C1-C24;
NORMAL 80 0.3.
PRINT C1-C25
DESCRIBE C1-C25
```

   b.   Construct an $\bar{x}$ chart for the means of the 25 samples and determine whether the process is within statistical control.
   c.   Simulate an additional 10 samples assuming that variation has increased so that the standard deviation is 0.9 instead of 0.3.
   d.   Combine the data generated from parts a and c to construct a control chart for the 35 samples. Determine whether the process is within statistical control.

2. a.   Simulate 20 days of manufacturing lipstick tubes with a 1% nonconforming rate. Sample 200 tubes each day by entering the following Minitab commands.

```
RANDOM k = 20 C1;
BINOMIAL n = 200 p = 0.01.
PRINT C1
```

   b.   Construct a p chart for the proportion of nonconforming tubes and determine whether the process is within statistical control. Because we know the process is actually stable with $p = 0.01$, concluding it is not stable would be a type I error. That is, we would have a false alarm causing us to believe that the process needs to be adjusted when in fact it should be left alone.
   c.   Simulate an additional 10 days of manufacturing lipstick tubes with a nonconforming rate of 3%. (See the above Minitab commands and modify them for the change from 1% to 3%.)
   d.   Combine the data generated from parts a and c to represent a total of 30 days of sample results. Construct a p chart for this combined data set. Is the process out of control? If we conclude that the process is not out of control, we are making a type II error. That is, we would believe that the process is OK when in fact it should be repaired or adjusted to correct the shift to the 3% nonconforming rate.

ARE ALL JEEPS CREATED EQUAL?

In manufacturing crankshafts for Jeeps, specifications require that crankshafts have endplay between 35 ten-thousandths of an inch and 80 ten-thousandths of an inch. Each hour, a random sample of 4 crankshafts is obtained; the results are given in the table. Analyze the stability of this process. Include a plot of a histogram of all sample values, a plot of the $\bar{x}$ chart, and a plot of the R chart. Write a report that summarizes your results and include any recommendations about whether the process needs to be modified.

SAMPLE	ENDPLAY			
1	51	65	52	47
2	62	49	66	60
3	79	73	79	61
4	119	96	104	110
5	79	64	69	73
6	72	60	32	41
7	68	55	64	72
8	66	49	55	62
9	54	48	55	71
10	60	66	43	49
11	48	58	66	55
12	65	51	74	49
13	53	58	61	62
14	68	70	59	80
15	61	68	62	59
16	51	61	52	70

DAVID HALL

DIVISION STATISTICAL MANAGER
AT THE BOEING COMMERCIAL
AIRPLANE GROUP

David Hall is Division Statistical Manager, Renton Division, Boeing Commerical Airplane Group. He manages the Statistical Methods Organization, which focuses on applying statistical and other quality technology techniques to continuous quality improvement. Before joining Boeing, he worked at Battelle Pacific Northwest Laboratories, where he was manager of a statistical applications group.

HOW EXTENSIVE IS THE USE OF STATISTICS AT BOEING, AND IS IT INCREASING, DECREASING, OR REMAINING ABOUT THE SAME?

The use of statistics is extensive and definitely increasing. I'm sure that this is true of the aircraft industry in general. People are becoming very aware of the need to improve, and to improve you must have data. Statistics is riding the wave of quality improvement. The use of control charts and, more generally, statistical process control, is increasing. Designed experiments are very common. In the beginning, 99% of the useful (statistical) tools are very, very simple. As the processes get refined and understanding in-

*We naturally have a great many
engineers at Boeing and almost
all of them have studied some
statistics. We are now expecting
our managers to have more familiarity with statistics than ever
before. They are expected to understand variation and how to
effectively use data.*

**DO YOU HAVE ANY ADVICE FOR TODAY'S
STUDENTS?**

*When I get new statisticians just
out of school, whether they have
a B.S., M.S., or Ph.D., they still
have a tremendous amount to
learn before they are effective in
the organizational environment
here at Boeing. Most of what
they need involves people skills,
team building, experience, planning, and communication. Right
now, American industry is crying out for people with an*

*creases, more sophisticated tools
are required. Regression and
correlation analysis, analysis of
variance, contingency tables, hypothesis testing, confidence intervals, and time series analysis
—virtually all techniques are
used at some time.*

HOW DO YOU SAMPLE AT BOEING?

*Our Quality Assurance Depart-
ment uses many of the well-
known sampling schemes for inspection. Currently, we check
the daylights out of everything.
However, sampling is also involved in statistical process control applications.*

*The sampling can be quite
complex and is handled on a
case-by-case basis.*

**COULD YOU CITE A SPECIFIC EXAMPLE OF
HOW THE USE OF STATISTICS WAS HELP-
FUL AT BOEING?**

*We were working with our Fab-
rication Division to produce
more consistent hydropress
formed parts. Through the use
of designed experiments, we
found that the type of rubber*

"Statistics is riding the wave of quality improvement."

*placed over the blanks during
forming could drasticallly reduce
the part-to-part variation. That's
one simple example of what
goes on all the time. An example of a more sophisticated application was the use of boot-
strapping to estimate the
variability in wind tunnel tests.*

*understanding of statistics and
the ability to communicate its
use to their colleagues.*

385

CHAPTER 9

Inferences from Two Samples

9.1 OVERVIEW

Chapter objectives are identified. This chapter extends the methods of inferential statistics to two populations. Both hypothesis testing and the construction of confidence intervals are discussed.

9.2 COMPARING TWO VARIANCES

The method for testing hypotheses made about two population variances or standard deviations is presented.

9.3 INFERENCES ABOUT TWO MEANS

Methods for testing hypotheses about the means of two populations are presented. Methods for constructing confidence intervals as estimates of the differences between two population means are also presented.

9.4 INFERENCES ABOUT TWO PROPORTIONS

Pooled estimates of p_1 and p_2 are used to test hypotheses made about the population proportions p_1 and p_2. Confidence intervals used to estimate the difference between two population proportions are also constructed.

Stolen Credit Cards: Are the Numbers Wrong?

Credit card fraud is a serious problem affecting all consumers as well as the banks that issue credit cards. Citibank, Bank of New York, Maryland Bank of North America, and Chemical Bank are only a few of the large banks that issue credit cards, and those banks lose about $15 million each year from credit card fraud. Because those losses are so large, the banks continually research this problem and seek corrective measures that will help reduce the losses. Some credit cards now include a photo of the cardholder. Many banks now require that cardholders call in to confirm their identity before the account is activated. These strategies are guided by research revealing the seriousness of different types of fraud: stolen cards, counterfeit cards, lost cards, mail order fraud, and fraud through telephone orders. It is therefore important to have good research data available so

banks know where to apply their efforts.

USA Today *recently ran two separate reports that contained this information:*

- 22% of fraudulent credit card uses result from cards stolen from the mail (based on data from the American Bankers Association).
- 16% of fraudulent credit card uses result from cards stolen from the mail or from the factories where they are made (based on data from MasterCard International).

In comparing these two percentages, it's reasonable to expect the second percentage to be **larger** *because it represents thefts from both the mail and factories, whereas the first one represents mail thefts only. It seems that a discrepancy exists. Even if we ignore the fact that there is a difference in categories (mail only vs. mail/factory), we might question the discrepancy between 22% and 16%. We know that samples fluctuate, so perhaps that difference isn't really significant and can be explained by chance sample variation. In this chapter we test the claim that the difference is not statistically significant.*

9.1 OVERVIEW

We use inferential statistics when we use sample data to form conclusions about populations. Chapters 6 and 7 introduced two of the most important and practical topics in the field of inferential statistics: estimating population and stable process parameters (Chapter 6) and testing hypotheses about those parameters (Chapter 7). Both chapters shared this feature: All examples and exercises involved the use of *one* sample to form an inference about *one* population or process. In reality, many business situations involve the comparison of *two* sets of data. The following are typical cases.

- Determine whether the rate of defects from a new robotic production method is lower than the rate from the current manual production method.
- Determine whether two different strategies for placing telephone customers on hold result in a difference in the variability of waiting times.
- Determine whether the mean life of Sears Diehard car batteries differs from the mean life of Montgomery Ward Quickstart batteries.

This chapter presents methods for using data from two samples to make inferences about the populations from which they came.

We began Chapters 6 and 7 by examining means, followed by proportions, then variances. In this chapter we depart from that order because we will sometimes use results of tests comparing two variances as a prerequisite for tests comparing two means. Consequently, we begin with a discussion of the method for comparing two variances.

9.2 COMPARING TWO VARIANCES

HYPOTHESIS TESTS

Variation is a critically important characteristic of data because it affects such factors as defect rates, the ability to meet specifications, and quality in general. Consumers prefer goods that are *consistent,* and this consistency can be measured by the variance or standard deviation. When buying a "60-month" car battery, for example, consumers recognize that the battery will not last *precisely* 60 months. Although they expect some variation, consumers want it to be small. They don't want to gamble on a new battery that might last anywhere from 6 months to 66 months. In Chapter 6 we considered inferences made about variation when we examined methods of constructing confidence intervals for population variances and standard deviations. In Chapter 7 we discussed methods for testing hypotheses about the variance or standard deviation of a single population. Whereas Chapters 6 and 7 involved cases with a single population, this chapter deals with cases in which we want to compare two populations. This section presents a method for using two samples to compare the variances of the populations from which the samples are drawn. The method we use requires the following assumptions.

Assumptions

When we test a hypothesis about the **variances** of two populations, we assume that:

1. The two samples are **independent** of each other.
2. The two populations are each **normally distributed.**

> **DEFINITION**
>
> Two samples are *independent* if the sample selected from one population is not related to the sample selected from the other population. If one sample is related to the other, the samples are *dependent.*

The second assumption—that both populations have normal distributions—is critical for the test presented in this section. The relevant test statistic is very sensitive to departures from normality, and this extreme sensitivity does not diminish with large samples. Other tests in the following sections of this chapter are not so sensitive to departures from normality.

For an example, see the two groups of sample data in Table 9.1. A manufacturer of car batteries wants to compare two production methods. From the statistics included in the table, we can see that both groups of batteries seem to last the same length of time, but the batteries produced by method A show much less consistency. The different degrees of consistency are reflected in the different sample variances of 3.59 and 0.05. Because not all comparisons of variances are so obvious, we need more-standardized procedures. Even for the data in Table 9.1, the difference between the sample variances of 3.59 and 0.05 must be weighed against the sample sizes to determine whether this "obvious" difference is statisti-

TABLE 9.1
Life of Car Batteries (in years)

PRODUCTION METHOD A	PRODUCTION METHOD B
2.0	3.6
2.1	3.7
2.5	3.9
3.0	3.9
3.3	3.9
4.2	4.0
4.2	4.0
4.3	4.0
6.8	4.1
7.6	4.2
	4.3
	4.4
$n_1 = 10$	$n_2 = 12$
$\bar{x}_1 = 4.00$	$\bar{x}_2 = 4.00$
$s_1^2 = 3.59$	$s_2^2 = 0.05$

FIGURE 9.1
F Distribution

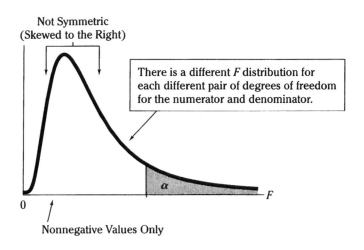

Not Symmetric
(Skewed to the Right)

There is a different *F* distribution for
each different pair of degrees of freedom
for the numerator and denominator.

α

F

0

Nonnegative Values Only

cally significant. We will now consider a procedure for determining whether such differences in variances are statistically significant.

Extensive analyses have shown that **for two normally distributed populations with equal variances (that is, $\sigma_1^2 = \sigma_2^2$), the sampling distribution of the following test statistic is the *F* distribution illustrated in Fig. 9.1 with critical values listed in Table A.5.** That is, if you continue to repeat an experiment of randomly selecting samples from two normally distributed populations with equal variances, the distribution of the ratio s_1^2/s_2^2 of the sample variances is the *F* **distribution.** See Fig. 9.1 and note that this distribution is not symmetric, its values cannot be negative, and its exact shape depends on two different degrees of freedom.

TEST STATISTIC

$$F = \frac{s_1^2}{s_2^2}$$

We can simplify our computations by stipulating that s_1^2 represents the larger of the two sample variances. This stipulation presents no logical difficulties because the identification of the samples through subscript notation is arbitrary. We choose the following notation.

Notation
s_1^2 = *larger* of the two *sample variances*
n_1 = size of the sample with the *larger* variance
σ_1^2 = variance of the *population* from which the sample was drawn
The symbols s_2^2, n_2, and σ_2^2 correspond to the other population and sample.

If the two populations really do have equal variances, then $F = s_1^2/s_2^2$ tends to be close to 1 because s_1^2 and s_2^2 tend to be close in value. But if the two populations have radically different variances, s_1^2 and s_2^2 tend to be very different numbers. Denoting the larger of the sample variances by s_1^2, we see that the ratio s_1^2/s_2^2 will be a large number whenever s_1^2 and s_2^2 are far apart in value. Consequently, a value of F near 1 will be evidence in favor of the conclusion that $\sigma_1^2 = \sigma_2^2$. A large value of F will be evidence against the conclusion of equality of the population variances.

When we use Table A.5, we obtain *critical F values* that are determined by the following three values:

1. The significance level α (Table A.5 has six pages of critical values for $\alpha = 0.01, 0.025,$ and 0.05.)
2. The **degrees of freedom for the numerator,** $(n_1 - 1)$
3. The **degrees of freedom for the denominator,** $(n_2 - 1)$

When using Table A.5, be sure that n_1 corresponds to the sample having variance s_1^2, while n_2 is the size of the sample with variance s_2^2. Identify a level of significance and determine whether the test is one-tailed or two-tailed. For a one-tailed test (H_0: $\sigma_1^2 \le \sigma_2^2$), use the significance level found in Table A.5. (Because we stipulate that the larger sample variance is s_1^2, all one-tailed tests will be right-tailed.) For a two-tailed test (H_0: $\sigma_1^2 = \sigma_2^2$), first divide the area of the critical region (equal to the significance level) equally between the two tails and refer to that part of Table A.5 representing *one-half* of the significance level. In that part of Table A.5, intersect the column representing the degrees of freedom for s_1^2 with the row representing the degrees of freedom for s_2^2. (Unlike the normal and Student t distributions, the F distribution is not symmetric and does not have 0 at its center. Consequently, left-tail critical values *cannot* be found by using the negative of the right-tail critical values. Instead, left-tail critical values can be found by using the reciprocal of the right-tail value with the numbers of degrees of freedom reversed. See Exercise 17.)

EXAMPLE When a consumer buys a car battery advertised to last 4 years (or 48 months), he or she expects it to last 4 years, give or take some relatively small amount of variation. The consumer does *not* want to gamble with a battery that might last anywhere from a week to 6 years. Car batteries with such high variation would soon alienate customers.

Table 9.1 lists the lives (in years) of car batteries produced by two different production methods. The statistics are given below with extra decimal places included. At the 0.05 significance level, test the claim that the variance of all battery lives from production method A is equal to the variance for production method B. Prior measurements on batteries from the two production methods have resulted in histograms strongly suggesting that each set of sample data comes from a normally distributed population.

PRODUCTION METHOD A   **PRODUCTION METHOD B**

$n_1 = 10$ $n_2 = 12$

$\bar{x}_1 = 4.0000$ $\bar{x}_2 = 4.0000$

$s_1^2 = 3.5911$ $s_2^2 = 0.0527$

SOLUTION Because the larger variance is already denoted by s_1^2, we use the same subscript notation given above. (If s_2^2 had been larger, we would have interchanged the subscripts so that s_1^2 would be the larger variance.) We now proceed to follow the steps for hypothesis testing as outlined in Fig. 7.1.

STEP 1   The claim of equal variances is expressed in symbolic form as $\sigma_1^2 = \sigma_2^2$.

STEP 2   If the original claim is false, then $\sigma_1^2 \neq \sigma_2^2$.

STEP 3   Because the null hypothesis must contain equality, we have

$$H_0: \sigma_1^2 = \sigma_2^2$$
$$H_1: \sigma_1^2 \neq \sigma_2^2$$

STEP 4   The significance level is $\alpha = 0.05$.

STEP 5   Because this test involves two population variances, we use the F distribution.

STEP 6   The test statistic is

$$F = \frac{s_1^2}{s_2^2} = \frac{3.5911}{0.0527} = 68.1423$$

For the critical values, we first note that this is a two-tailed test with 0.025 in each tail. As long as we are stipulating that the larger variance is placed in the numerator of the F test statistic, we need to find only the right-tail critical value. In Table A.5, refer to the pages for which $\alpha = 0.025$ and find 3.5879, which corresponds to 9 degrees of freedom for the numerator and 11 degrees of freedom for the denominator (see Fig. 9.2).

STEP 7   Figure 9.2 shows that the test statistic does fall well within the critical region, so we reject the null hypothesis.

STEP 8   The evidence is sufficient to warrant rejection of the claim that the two variances are equal.

We can reasonably conclude that the batteries from the two production methods have significantly different amounts of variation. Because the means are the same but the amounts of variability are so different, production method B apparently yields more-consistent and therefore higher-quality batteries.

If the preceding test had been based on the claim that the variance for production method A is *greater* than that for method B, then the test would have been

FIGURE 9.2
F Distribution for Example

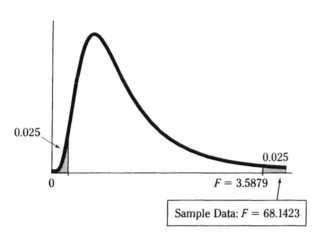

0.025

0.025

0

$F = 3.5879$

Sample Data: $F = 68.1423$

PRODUCT SAFETY

Product safety is often enhanced through statistical analysis of such factors as injuries requiring emergency room care. Topping the list of products directly linked with hospital treatment is the category of bicycles, followed by knives; then the category of nails, screws, and tacks; then power and hand saws, followed by drinking glasses and then ladders (based on data from the U.S. Consumer Product Safety Commission). Manufacturers often attempt to avoid paying court-awarded damages by placing warning labels on their products. A car sun shield contains this warning: "Do not drive with sun shield in place. Remove from windshield before starting ignition." That certainly seems like sound advice. One survey showed that 88% of consumers saw the warning labels, but only 46% read them. There is now concern that an avalanche of warning labels will be counterproductive as consumers lose interest and ignore them.

right-tailed instead of two-tailed (with H_0: $\sigma_1^2 \leq \sigma_2^2$ and H_1: $\sigma_1^2 > \sigma_2^2$), and we would have obtained a critical value of $F = 2.8962$ for a right-tailed area of 0.05.

We can use the same procedures to test claims about two population standard deviations. Any claim about two population standard deviations can be restated in terms of the corresponding variances. For example, suppose we want to test the claim that $\sigma_1 = \sigma_2$, and we are given the following sample data taken from normal populations.

SAMPLE 1	SAMPLE 2
$n_1 = 16$	$n_2 = 10$
$s_1 = 15$	$s_2 = 10$

Restating the claim as $\sigma_1^2 = \sigma_2^2$, we get $s_1^2 = 15^2 = 225$ and $s_2^2 = 10^2 = 100$, and we can proceed with the F test in the usual way. Rejection of $\sigma_1^2 = \sigma_2^2$ is equivalent to rejection of $\sigma_1 = \sigma_2$. Failure to reject $\sigma_1^2 = \sigma_2^2$ implies failure to reject $\sigma_1 = \sigma_2$.

When referring to Table A.5 for critical values of F, we sometimes have numbers of degrees of freedom that are not included in that table. We can use linear interpolation to approximate the missing values, but in most cases that's not necessary because the F test statistic is either less than the lowest possible critical value or greater than the largest possible critical value. For example, Table A.5 shows that for $\alpha = 0.025$ in the right tail, 20 degrees of freedom for the numerator, and 34 degrees of freedom for the denominator, the critical F score is between 2.0677 and 2.1952. Any F test statistic below 2.0677 will result in failure to reject the null hypothesis, whereas any F test statistic above 2.1952 will result in rejection of the null hypothesis. Interpolation would be necessary here only if the F test statistic were between 2.0677 and 2.1952.

Note that in all tests of hypotheses made about population variances and standard deviations, the values of the means are irrelevant. In the next section we consider tests comparing two population means, and we will see that some of those tests require that the populations have equal variances. We can verify that requirement by using the hypothesis-testing method just described.

CONFIDENCE INTERVALS

When comparing two population variances, hypothesis tests are used much more often than confidence intervals. Confidence intervals (or interval estimates) of the ratio σ_1^2/σ_2^2 can be constructed by using

$$\frac{s_1^2}{s_2^2} \cdot \frac{1}{F_R} < \frac{\sigma_1^2}{\sigma_2^2} < \frac{s_1^2}{s_2^2} \cdot \frac{1}{F_L}$$

Here F_L and F_R are as described in Exercise 17 (see Exercises 17 and 18). The confidence intervals in the following sections are generally more important, and we will examine them more closely.

9.2 EXERCISES   BASIC CONCEPTS

In Exercises 1–4, test the claim that the two samples come from populations having equal variances. Use a significance level of $\alpha = 0.05$ and assume that all populations are normally distributed. Follow the pattern suggested by Fig. 7.1 and draw the appropriate graphs.

1. Sample A: $n = 10$, $s^2 = 50$
   Sample B: $n = 10$, $s^2 = 25$
2. Sample A: $n = 10$, $s^2 = 50$
   Sample B: $n = 15$, $s^2 = 25$
3. Sample A: $n = 5$, $\bar{x} = 372, s = 14.3$
   Sample B: $n = 15$, $\bar{x} = 298, s = 1.1$
4. Sample A: $n = 25$, $\bar{x} = 583, s = 3.9$
   Sample B: $n = 10$, $\bar{x} = 648, s = 6.3$

In Exercises 5–8, test the claim that the variance of population A exceeds that of population B. Use a 0.05 level of significance and assume that all populations are normally distributed. Follow the pattern outlined in Fig. 7.1 and draw the appropriate graphs.

5. Sample A: $n = 10$, $\bar{x} = 200, s^2 = 48$
   Sample B: $n = 10$, $\bar{x} = 180, s^2 = 12$
6. Sample A: $n = 50$, $\bar{x} = 75.3, s^2 = 18.2$
   Sample B: $n = 20$, $\bar{x} = 75.9, s^2 = 8.7$
7. Sample A: $n = 16$, $\bar{x} = 124, s^2 = 225$
   Sample B: $n = 200$, $\bar{x} = 128, s^2 = 160$
8. Sample A: $n = 35$, $\bar{x} = 238, s^2 = 42.3$
   Sample B: $n = 25$, $\bar{x} = 254, s^2 = 16.2$

In Exercises 9–16, assume that the samples are independent and come from normally distributed populations.

9. The Telektronic Company uses two different production methods to manufacture AA batteries. The battery lives (in hours) are found for a sample of each process with the results given below. (Assume that both production processes are statistically stable.) At the 0.05 significance level, test the claim that the two production methods yield batteries with the same variance.

   Production method A: $n = 25$, $\bar{x} = 3.70$, $s = 0.37$
   Production method B: $n = 28$, $\bar{x} = 4.00$, $s = 0.31$

10. The Gleason Supermarket manager experiments with two methods for checking out customers. One method requires that the cashier manually key each price into the register, whereas the other method uses a scanner that automatically registers prices. Sample data are given below. At the 0.02 significance level, test the claim that $\sigma_1^2 = \sigma_2^2$.

SAMPLE A	SAMPLE B
$n_1 = 16$	$n_2 = 10$
$s_1^2 = 225$	$s_2^2 = 100$

11. The Riverside Building Supply Company uses two different lines for filling containers that are supposed to hold 3785 ml (or 1 gal) of paint. A random sample of 25 containers is obtained from the first line, while another sample of 30 containers is obtained from the second line. Both filling processes are statistically stable. The sample results are as follows:

LINE 1	LINE 2
$n_1 = 25$	$n_2 = 30$
$\bar{x}_1 = 3789$ ml	$\bar{x}_2 = 3780$ ml
$s_1 = 29$ ml	$s_2 = 15$ ml

   a. Test the hypothesis that the first line has a larger standard deviation than the second line. Use a 0.05 level of significance.
   b. Both lines seem to be providing a mean fill amount near the desired level of 3785 ml. Describe why a smaller standard deviation would result in a higher-quality product.

12. In a study of the effect of job previews on work expectation, 60 newly hired bank tellers were given specific job previews and another group of 40 newly hired bank tellers had no previews. Their initial expectations for promotion were measured and the group with previews had a mean of 19.14 and a standard deviation of 6.56. For the "no preview" sample group of 40 subjects, the mean is 20.81 and the standard deviation is 4.90. (The data are based on "Effects of Realistic Job Previews on Hiring Bank Tellers," by Dean and Wanous, *Journal of Applied Psychology,* Vol. 69, No. 1.) At the 0.10 level of significance, test the claim that the two sample groups come from populations with the same standard deviation.

13. In an insurance study of pedestrian deaths in New York State, monthly fatalities are totaled for two different time periods. Sample data for the first time period are summarized by these statistics: $n = 12$, $\bar{x} = 46.42$, $s = 11.07$. Sample data for the second time period are summarized by these statistics: $n = 12$, $\bar{x} = 51.00$, $s = 10.39$ (based on data from the New York State Department of Motor Vehicles). At the 0.05 significance level, test the claim that both time periods have the same variance.

14. The actual amounts of corn chips in "16-oz" bags are measured by randomly selecting 25 bags from each of 3 shifts. Sample results from the 3 statistically stable processes are as follows:

SHIFT 1	SHIFT 2	SHIFT 3
$n_1 = 25$	$n_2 = 25$	$n_3 = 25$
$\bar{x}_1 = 16.04$ oz	$\bar{x}_2 = 15.72$ oz	$\bar{x}_3 = 16.28$
$s_1 = 0.41$ oz	$s_2 = 0.36$ oz	$s_3 = 0.97$ oz

Test each of the following 3 hypotheses. Use a 0.05 level of significance.
a. H_0: $\sigma_1^2 = \sigma_2^2$
b. H_0: $\sigma_2^2 = \sigma_3^2$
c. H_0: $\sigma_1^2 = \sigma_3^2$

15. The Telstar Appliance Company and the American Home Appliance Company use two different methods for assembling standard residential refrigerators. The numbers of units produced at Telstar are recorded for 21 randomly selected days, and the numbers of units produced at American are recorded for 19 randomly selected days.

TELSTAR					AMERICAN			
227	211	225	210	224	229	203	211	194
220	222	219	220		202	200	230	242
218	226	221	226		199	246	224	232
215	208	231	212		240	190	203	216
230	220	219	217		227	242	236	

Test the hypothesis that both methods have the same variation. If both methods have approximately the same mean, which method would you recommend?

16. A prospective home buyer is investigating home selling-price differences between zone 1 (southern Dutchess County) and zone 7 (northern Dutchess County). The given random sample data are in thousands of dollars. (This will not affect the value of the test statistic F, but it allows us to work with more-manageable numbers.) At the 0.05 significance level, test the claim that both zones have the same variance. Assume that the sample data come from normally distributed populations. (In many cases, home selling prices might not be normally distributed. But histograms show that the assumption of normal distributions is reasonable here.) The data are listed at the top of the following page.

ZONE 7 (NORTH)		ZONE 1 (SOUTH)	
270.000		115.000	
107.000		136.900	
148.000		121.000	
125.000		164.000	
127.500	$n = 11$	175.000	
125.500	$\bar{x} = 142.32$	128.500	
126.000	$s^2 = 2122$	147.500	$n = 14$
109.000		147.000	$\bar{x} = 138.24$
113.500		105.000	$s^2 = 455$
147.000		163.750	
167.000		115.000	
		149.165	
		120.500	
		147.000	

9.2 EXERCISES BEYOND THE BASICS

17. For hypothesis tests in this section that were two-tailed, we found only the upper critical value. Let's denote that value by F_R, where the subscript suggests the right side. The lower critical value F_L (for the left side) can be found by first interchanging the degrees of freedom and then taking the reciprocal of the resulting F value found in Table A.5. (F_R is often denoted by $F_{\alpha/2}$ while F_L is often denoted by $F_{1 - \alpha/2}$.) Find the critical values F_L and F_R for two-tailed hypothesis tests based on the following values.
    a. $n_1 = 10$, $n_2 = 10$, $\alpha = 0.05$
    b. $n_1 = 10$, $n_2 = 7$, $\alpha = 0.05$
    c. $n_1 = 7$, $n_2 = 10$, $\alpha = 0.05$
    d. $n_1 = 25$, $n_2 = 10$, $\alpha = 0.02$
    e. $n_1 = 10$, $n_2 = 25$, $\alpha = 0.02$
18. In addition to testing claims involving σ_1^2 and σ_2^2, we can also construct interval estimates of the ratio σ_1^2/σ_2^2 using the following:

$$\frac{s_1^2}{s_2^2} \cdot \frac{1}{F_R} < \frac{\sigma_1^2}{\sigma_2^2} < \frac{s_1^2}{s_2^2} \cdot \frac{1}{F_L}$$

Here F_L and F_R are as described in Exercise 17. Construct the 95% interval estimate for the ratio of the zone 7 variance to the zone 1 variance for the data in Exercise 16.
19. Sample data consist of temperatures recorded for two different groups of car catalytic converters that were produced by two different production techniques. A quality control specialist plans to analyze the results. She begins by testing for equality of the two population standard deviations.
    a. If she adds the same constant to every temperature from both groups, is the value of the test statistic F affected? Explain.
    b. If she uses the same constant to multiply every score from both groups, is the value of the test statistic F affected? Explain.
    c. If she converts all temperatures from the Fahrenheit scale to the Celsius scale, is the value of the test statistic F affected? Explain.

20. a. Two samples of equal size produce variances of 37 and 57. At the 0.05 significance level, we test the claim that the variance of the second population exceeds that of the first, and that claim is upheld by the data. What is the approximate minimum size of each sample?

    b. A sample of 21 scores produces a variance of 67.2 and another sample of 25 produces a variance that causes rejection of the claim that the two populations have equal variances. If this test is conducted at the 0.02 level of significance, find the maximum variance of the second sample if you know that it is smaller than that of the first sample.

9.3   INFERENCES ABOUT TWO MEANS

When using samples to compare two different populations, it's usually important to compare their means as well as their amounts of variation. If the California Highway Patrol is to replace its fleet of police cars and the field of prospective car models has been reduced to two, fuel consumption (in mi/gal) would be one of several relevant factors to consider. Samples could be obtained from each model and we could then compare their means to determine whether the difference between the two population means is significant.

In the preceding section we considered a method for testing hypotheses about two population variances; in this section we consider methods for testing hypotheses about two population means as well as methods for constructing confidence intervals for the differences between two population means. The following assumption applies.

Assumption

When we *test a hypothesis* about the means of two populations or construct an *interval estimate* of the difference between the means of two populations, we assume that either we have sample data from each of two *normally distributed* populations or the two sample sizes are each greater than 30 (or both).

The particular methods we use will be affected by the presence or absence of a relationship between the two samples. Recall that in Section 9.2 we defined dependent and independent samples and, according to those definitions, two samples are dependent if one is related to the other. Consider the following sample data. The sample of pretraining weights and the sample of posttraining weights for five randomly selected persons are two *dependent* samples because each pair is matched according to the person involved. Such "before-and-after" data are usually matched and are usually dependent. (The table is based on data from the *Journal of Applied Psychology,* Vol. 62, No. 1.)

Pretraining weights (kg)	99	62	74	59	70	73
Posttraining weights (kg)	94	62	66	58	70	76

For the following data, however, the two samples are *independent* because the sample of females is completely independent of the sample of males. The data are not matched as they are in the table above.

Weights of females (lb)	115	107	110	128	130		
Weights of males (lb)	128	150	160	140	163	155	175

When dealing with two dependent samples, it is very wasteful to reduce the sample data to $\bar{x}_1$, s_1, n_1, $\bar{x}_2$, s_2, and n_2 because the relationship between matched pairs of values would be completely lost. Instead, we compute the *differences* (d) between the pairs of data as follows:

x	99	62	74	59	70	73
y	94	62	66	58	70	76
$d = x - y$	5	0	8	1	0	-3

Notation

Let $\bar{d}$ denote the mean value of d or $x - y$ for the paired *sample* data.
Let μ_d denote the mean value of $x - y$ for the *population* of paired data.
Let s_d denote the standard deviation of the d values for the paired sample data.
Let n denote the number of *pairs* of data.

For the d values of 5, 0, 8, 1, 0, and -3 taken from the preceding table, we get

$$\bar{d} = \frac{\Sigma d}{n} = \frac{5 + 0 + 8 + 1 + 0 - 3}{6} = \frac{11}{6} = 1.8$$

For the d values of 5, 0, 8, 1, 0, and -3, we get $s_d = 4.0$ as follows:

$$s_d = \sqrt{\frac{\Sigma(d - \bar{d})^2}{n - 1}} = \sqrt{\frac{78.83}{5}} = 4.0$$

For the data of the last table, $n = 6$.

HYPOTHESIS TESTS

In repeated random sampling of two dependent samples from normally distributed populations in which the population mean of the paired differences is μ_d, the following test statistic possesses a Student t distribution with $n - 1$ degrees of freedom.

TEST STATISTIC

$$t = \frac{\bar{d} - \mu_d}{s_d / \sqrt{n}}$$

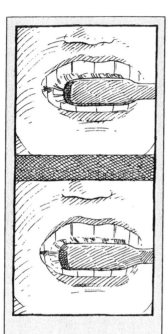

CREST AND DEPENDENT SAMPLES

In the late 1950s, Procter and Gamble introduced Crest as the first toothpaste with fluoride. To test the effectiveness of Crest in reducing cavities, experiments were conducted with several sets of twins. One of the twins was given Crest with fluoride while the other twin continued to use ordinary toothpaste without fluoride. Researchers assumed that each pair of twins would have similar eating and brushing habits and similar genetic characteristics. Results showed that the twins who used Crest developed significantly fewer cavities than those who did not. This use of twins as dependent samples allowed the researchers to control many of the different variables affecting cavities.

Note that the involved populations must be normally distributed. If the populations depart radically from normal distributions, we should not use the methods given in this section. Instead, we may be able to apply nonparametric tests such as the sign test or the Wilcoxon signed-ranks test discussed in Chapter 15.

If we claim that there is no difference between the two population means, then we are claiming that $\mu_d = 0$. This makes sense if we recognize that $\overline{d}$ should be around 0 if there is no difference between the two population means.

In the following example we illustrate a complete hypothesis test for a situation involving dependent samples.

EXAMPLE The Malloy and Clinton Advertising Company has prepared two different television commercials for Taylor women's jeans. One commercial is humorous and the other is serious. A test screening involves 8 consumers who are tested for their reactions; the results are listed below. At the 0.05 significance level, test the claim that the humorous commercials receive higher scores (that is, have a larger mean).

Consumer	A	B	C	D	E	F	G	H
Humorous commercial	26.2	20.3	25.4	19.6	21.5	28.3	23.7	24.0
Serious commercial	24.1	21.3	23.7	18.0	20.1	25.8	22.4	21.4
Difference	2.1	−1.0	1.7	1.6	1.4	2.5	1.3	2.6

SOLUTION Because both commercials were watched by each consumer, we have paired data and can conclude that the above sample values are dependent. If the humorous commercials result in larger scores, we would expect positive differences, so that $\overline{d}$ would tend to be positive and significantly greater than 0. We therefore have the null hypothesis H_0: $\mu_d \le 0$ and the alternative hypothesis H_1: $\mu_d > 0$.

We can find the mean and standard deviation of the differences as follows:

$$\overline{d} = \frac{\Sigma d}{n} = \frac{2.1 + (-1.0) + 1.7 + 1.6 + 1.4 + 2.5 + 1.3 + 2.6}{8}$$

$$= \frac{12.2}{8} = 1.525$$

$$s_d = \sqrt{\frac{\Sigma(d - \overline{d})^2}{n-1}} = \sqrt{\frac{(2.1 - 1.525)^2 + \cdots + (2.6 - 1.525)^2}{7}}$$

$$= \sqrt{\frac{8.915}{7}} = 1.129$$

With $\overline{d} = 1.525$, $s_d = 1.129$, and $n = 8$, we find the value of the test statistic to be

$$t = \frac{\overline{d} - \mu_d}{s_d / \sqrt{n}} = \frac{1.525 - 0}{1.129 / \sqrt{8}} = 3.821$$

With $\alpha = 0.05$, the critical region from Table A.3 is $t = 1.895$ (because this is a right-tailed test and there are $8 - 1 = 7$ degrees of freedom). Because the test statistic of $t = 3.821$ falls within the critical region, we reject the null hypothesis. Our P-value [for $P(t > 3.821)$] is less than 0.005, so we can be very confident in rejecting H_0. (See Section 7.3 for a review of P-values.) Because we rejected the null hypothesis, we have sufficient evidence to support the claim that the humorous commercials receive higher scores.

The preceding test could also be conducted as a t test for a single population mean μ_d. When using Minitab, enter the humorous commercial scores in C1, enter the serious commercial scores in C2, then enter "LET C3 = C1 - C2." The commands and output are presented below. The test is run with the option "ALTERNATIVE = +1" (the Minitab code for a hypothesis test that is right-tailed).

```
MTB > SET C1
DATA> 26.2 20.3 25.4 19.6 21.5 28.3 23.7 24.0
DATA> ENDOFDATA
MTB > SET C2
DATA> 24.1 21.3 23.7 18.0 20.1 25.8 22.4 21.4
DATA> ENDOFDATA
MTB > LET C3 = C1 -C2
MTB > TTEST MU = 0 C3;
SUBC> ALTERNATIVE = +1.

TEST OF MU = 0.000 VS MU G.T. 0.000

       N    MEAN   STDEV   SE MEAN      T   P VALUE
C3     8   1.525   1.129     0.399   3.82    0.0033
```

The preceding example involved the means of two dependent populations. As we consider other tests of hypotheses about two population means, we begin to encounter a maze that can easily lead to confusion. Questions must be answered regarding the independence of samples, knowledge of σ_1 and σ_2, and sample size before the correct procedure can be selected. You can avoid most of the confusion by referring to Fig. 9.3 on page 403, which summarizes the procedures discussed in this section. We illustrate the use of Fig. 9.3 through specific examples. Since we have already presented an example involving dependent populations, our next examples will involve independent populations. We begin with an example for which both samples are large ($n_1 > 30$ and $n_2 > 30$) and both population standard deviations (σ_1 and σ_2) are known.

EXAMPLE Two machines fill bulk packages of golf tees and both processes seem statistically stable. Samples are selected from each machine. Denoting the package weights from machine A as group 1 and those from machine B as group 2, we have

MACHINE A	MACHINE B
$n_1 = 50$	$n_2 = 100$
$\bar{x}_1 = 4.53$ kg	$\bar{x}_2 = 4.01$ kg

If the standard deviations of the contents filled by machines A and B are known to be 0.80 kg and 0.60 kg, respectively, test the claim that both machines have the same mean. Use a 0.05 level of significance.

SOLUTION The two samples are independent, and n_1 and n_2 are both greater than 30. Referring to Fig. 9.3, we see that we should use a normal distribution test with

$$z = \frac{(\bar{x}_1 - \bar{x}_2) - (\mu_1 - \mu_2)}{\sqrt{\frac{\sigma_1^2}{n_1} + \frac{\sigma_2^2}{n_2}}} = \frac{(4.53 - 4.01) - 0}{\sqrt{\frac{0.80^2}{50} + \frac{0.60^2}{100}}} = 4.06$$

(Note that both σ_1 and σ_2 are known.)

With the null and alternative hypotheses described as

$$H_0: \mu_1 = \mu_2 \qquad (\text{or } \mu_1 - \mu_2 = 0)$$
$$H_1: \mu_1 \neq \mu_2 \qquad (\text{or } \mu_1 - \mu_2 \neq 0)$$

and $\alpha = 0.05$, we conclude that the test involves two tails. From Table A.2 we extract the critical z values of 1.96 and -1.96. The test statistic of 4.06 is well into the critical region, and we therefore reject H_0 and conclude that the population means corresponding to the two machines are not equal. It appears that machine A fills with amounts that are significantly greater than those of machine B.

Although not always necessary, it is often a good strategy to **identify the data set with the larger sample variance as group 1,** and to identify the data set with the smaller sample variance as group 2. This is the same procedure followed in Section 9.2. If it becomes necessary to use the F test of $\sigma_1^2 = \sigma_2^2$, this identification will be helpful.

The preceding example is somewhat contrived because we seldom know the values of σ_1 and σ_2. It is rare to sample from two populations with unknown means but known standard deviations. To cover more-realistic cases involving independent samples with unknown standard deviations or variances, we next examine the sizes of the two samples, as suggested by Fig. 9.3. In this next example and the remaining examples of this section, the samples must come from normally distributed populations. If this condition is not satisfied, we may be able to use nonparametric methods, some of which are discussed later in Chapter 15.

If both samples are greater than 30, we can estimate σ_1 and σ_2 by s_1 and s_2. We can then proceed as in the last example. If either sample is small, however, we must apply the F test to determine whether the two sample variances are significantly different so that we can use the appropriate test statistic. (If the variances appear to be equal, we estimate their common value with a weighted average of the sample variances. Otherwise, the variance of the differences between sample means is estimated as the sum of their individual variances.) The next example illustrates these points because the populations are independent, both samples are small ($n_1 \leq 30$ and $n_2 \leq 30$), both populations have normal distributions, and both population standard deviations are unknown.

We will see in the next example that the F test suggests the two population variances are not equal, and from Fig. 9.3 we see that the circumstances of the example cause us to turn right at the last diamond.

FIGURE 9.3
Testing Hypotheses about the Means of Two Populations

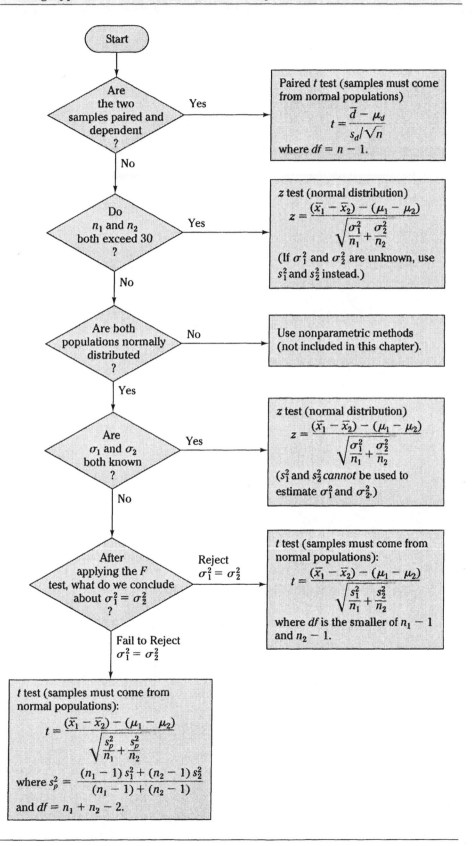

EXAMPLE

Random samples of home selling prices are obtained from two zones in Dutchess County. Results are summarized below.

ZONE 7 (NORTH)	ZONE 1 (SOUTH)
$n_1 = 11$	$n_2 = 14$
$\bar{x}_1 = \$142,318$	$\bar{x}_2 = \$138,237$
$s_1 = \$46,068$	$s_2 = \$21,336$

At the 0.05 significance level, test the claim that the two zones have the same mean selling price. (We are assuming that the two distributions of selling prices are both approximately normal.)

SOLUTION

Because the zone-7 results have a larger variance, we made them the first sample. Because the samples are independent, both samples are small, both populations are normally distributed, and neither standard deviation is known, Fig. 9.3 indicates that we begin by applying the F test discussed in Section 9.2. We want to decide whether $\sigma_1^2 = \sigma_2^2$, so we formulate the following null and alternative hypotheses.

H_0: $\sigma_1^2 = \sigma_2^2$

H_1: $\sigma_1^2 \neq \sigma_2^2$

With $\alpha = 0.05$, we do a complete hypothesis test to decide whether $\sigma_1^2 = \sigma_2^2$. We then do another complete hypothesis test of the claim that $\mu_1 = \mu_2$ using the appropriate Student t distribution. For the preliminary test we get

$$F = \frac{s_1^2}{s_2^2} = \frac{(46,068)^2}{(21,336)^2} = 4.6620$$

The critical F value obtained from Table A.5 is 3.2497. (The test involves two tails with $\alpha = 0.05$, and the degrees of freedom for the numerator and the denominator are 10 and 13, respectively.) These results cause us to reject the null hypothesis of equal variances, that is, we reject $\sigma_1^2 = \sigma_2^2$. In Fig. 9.3 we test the claim that $\mu_1 = \mu_2$ by using the Student t distribution and the test statistic given in the box to the *right* of the fifth diamond. With

H_0: $\mu_1 = \mu_2$ (or $\mu_1 - \mu_2 = 0$)

H_1: $\mu_1 \neq \mu_2$ (or $\mu_1 - \mu_2 \neq 0$)

$\alpha = 0.05$

we compute the test statistic based on the sample data.

$$t = \frac{(\bar{x}_1 - \bar{x}_2) - (\mu_1 - \mu_2)}{\sqrt{\dfrac{s_1^2}{n_1} + \dfrac{s_2^2}{n_2}}} = \frac{(142,318 - 138,237) - 0}{\sqrt{\dfrac{46,068^2}{11} + \dfrac{21,336^2}{14}}}$$

$$= 0.272$$

This is a two-tailed test with $\alpha = 0.05$ and 10 degrees of freedom (the smaller of $n_1 - 1 = 10$ and $n_2 - 1 = 13$), so the critical t values obtained from Table A.3 are $t = 2.228$ and $t = -2.228$. The computed t value of 0.272 does not fall within the critical region and we fail to reject the null hypothesis of equal means. Based on the available sample data, we cannot reject the claim that the two zones have the same mean selling price. However, our analysis does reveal that the variation of zone-7 prices is different from the variation of the zone-1 prices.

The next example illustrates a hypothesis test comparing two means for a situation featuring the following characteristics.

- The two samples are independent.
- Both populations are normally distributed.
- σ_1 and σ_2 are unknown.
- Both sample sizes are small (≤ 30).
- The sample variances suggest, through the F test, that $\sigma_1^2 = \sigma_2^2$.

The conditions inherent in this next example cause us to follow the path leading to the bottom of the flowchart in Fig. 9.3. That case incorporates use of the **pooled variance** $s_p{}^2$, which is a weighted average of the two sample variances.

EXAMPLE

The intent of a new manufacturing process is to increase the lives of alkaline flashlight batteries (so flashlights will no longer be known as containers in which to store dead batteries). A random sample of 16 of these new batteries is tested along with a sample of 12 batteries made by the old process. Test the claim that the new process has a mean life greater than that of the old process. Use $\alpha = 0.05$. For the following sample data, we stipulate that the larger sample variance be identified as group 1.

GROUP 1 (NEW)	GROUP 2 (OLD)
$n_1 = 16$	$n_2 = 12$
$\bar{x}_1 = 17.64$ h	$\bar{x}_2 = 11.93$ h
$s_1 = 4.54$ h	$s_2 = 3.69$ h

SOLUTION

Referring to Fig. 9.3, we begin by questioning the independence of the two samples and we conclude that they are independent because separate samples of batteries are used. We continue with the flowchart by noting that neither n_1 nor n_2 exceeds 30, so we need to assume that the two distributions of battery lives are both normal. (We can check this with a histogram.) Finally, because σ_1 and σ_2 are not known, we need to apply the F test to determine whether σ_1 and σ_2 are equal. With H_0: $\sigma_1^2 = \sigma_2^2$, H_1: $\sigma_1^2 \neq \sigma_2^2$, and $\alpha = 0.05$, we compute the test statistic as

$$F = \frac{s_1^2}{s_2^2} = \frac{4.54^2}{3.69^2} = 1.5138$$

(continued)

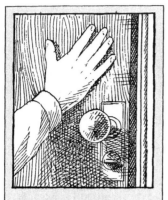

POLL RESISTANCE

Surveys based on relatively small samples can be quite accurate, provided the sample is random or representative of the population. However, increasing survey refusal rates are now making it more difficult to obtain random samples. The Council of American Survey Research Organizations reported that in a recent year, 38% of consumers refused to respond to surveys. The head of one market research company said, "Everyone is fearful of self-selection and worried that generalizations you make are based on cooperators only." Results from the multibillion-dollar market research industry affect the products we buy, the television shows we watch, and many other facets of our lives.

With $\alpha = 0.05$ in a two-tailed F test and with $n_1 - 1 = 15$ and $n_2 - 1 = 11$ degrees of freedom for the numerator and the denominator, respectively, we use Table A.5 to find the critical value of $F = 3.3299$. Because the computed test statistic of $F = 1.5138$ is not within the critical region, we fail to reject the null hypothesis of equal variances. Although this does not *prove* the variances are equal, it does suggest that their values are fairly close. Leaving the last diamond in Fig. 9.3, we proceed downward to the bottom and apply the required t test as follows:

H_0: $\mu_1 \leq \mu_2$ (or $\mu_1 - \mu_2 \leq 0$)

H_1: $\mu_1 > \mu_2$ (or $\mu_1 - \mu_2 > 0$)

First we find the pooled or combined estimate of the variance.

$$s_p^2 = \frac{(n_1 - 1)s_1^2 + (n_2 - 1)s_2^2}{(n_1 - 1) + (n_2 - 1)} = \frac{(16 - 1)(4.54)^2 + (12 - 1)(3.69)^2}{(16 - 1) + (12 - 1)}$$

$$= \frac{458.951}{26} = 17.652$$

Because s_p^2 is calculated by combining both samples, we get combined degrees of freedom

$$(n_1 - 1) + (n_2 - 1) = 15 + 11 = 26$$

The test statistic is

$$t = \frac{(\bar{x}_1 - \bar{x}_2) - (\mu_1 - \mu_2)}{\sqrt{\frac{s_p^2}{n_1} + \frac{s_p^2}{n_2}}} = \frac{(17.64 - 11.93) - 0}{\sqrt{\frac{17.652}{16} + \frac{17.652}{12}}}$$

$$= \frac{5.71}{\sqrt{2.574}} = 3.559$$

Noting that $\mu_1 > \mu_2$ is equivalent to $\mu_1 - \mu_2 > 0$, we can see more clearly that the test is right-tailed. With $\alpha = 0.05$ in this right-tailed t test and with 26 degrees of freedom, we obtain a critical t value of 1.706. Because the computed or observed test statistic $t = 3.559$ falls within the critical region, we reject H_0. We conclude that the sample evidence is sufficient to support the claim that the mean life of the batteries made by the new production process (group 1) is longer than the old mean life (group 2).

The calculations in this last example might seem somewhat complex, but calculators and computers can be used to ease that burden. Minitab, for example, can be used to conduct this test if the original scores are known. The 16 batteries manufactured by the new technique are in C1 and the 12 batteries manufactured by the old technique are in C2. The following is the Minitab display that results from these commands.

```
MTB > TWOSAMPLE C1 C2;
SUBC> ALTERNATIVE = +1;
SUBC> POOLED.
```

The subcommand "ALTERNATIVE = +1" is Minitab's code for a hypothesis test that is right-tailed, and the subcommand "POOLED" indicates that the two sample variances will be pooled or combined to form an estimate of a variance common to both populations.

Note that a 95% confidence interval for $\mu_1 - \mu_2$ is also included in the display. We will discuss confidence intervals later in this section.

```
MTB > SET C1
DATA> 18.2 10.4 12.6 18.0 11.7 15.0 25.9 17.3
DATA> 23.8 16.4 24.2 18.9 14.7 21.6 19.0 14.5
DATA> ENDOFDATA
MTB > SET C2
DATA> 12.1 7.5 8.3 13.7 7.2 15.0
DATA> 17.5 9.1 16.8 12.9 8.5 14.5
DATA> ENDOFDATA
MTB > DESCRIBE C1 C2
```

	N	MEAN	MEDIAN	TRMEAN	STDEV	SEMEAN
C1	16	17.64	17.65	17.56	4.54	1.13
C2	12	11.93	12.50	11.84	3.69	1.07

	MIN	MAX	Q1	Q3
C1	10.40	25.90	14.55	20.95
C2	7.20	17.50	8.35	14.87

```
MTB > TWOSAMPLE C1 C2;
SUBC> ALTERNATIVE = +1;
SUBC> POOLED.
```

```
TWOSAMPLE T FOR C1 VS C2
```

	N	MEAN	STDEV	SE MEAN
C1	16	17.64	4.54	1.1
C2	12	11.93	3.69	1.1

```
95 PCT CI FOR MU C1 - MU C2: (2.4, 9.0)

TTEST MU C1 = MU C2 (VS GT): T = 3.56 P=0.0007 DF= 26

POOLED STDEV =        4.20
```

One of the most difficult aspects of tests comparing two means is the determination of the correct test statistic to use. Careful and consistent use of Fig. 9.3 should help us avoid using the wrong procedures for a situation involving a hypothesis test. We risk being overwhelmed by the work involved in the five different cases considered here. However, we can use Fig. 9.3 to decompose a complex problem into simpler components that can be treated individually.

P-Values

The comments made in Section 7.3 about *P*-values apply to this section as well. (See Fig. 7.6, which summarizes key decisions to be made in determining *P*-values.) The preceding example is right-tailed with a test statistic of $t = 3.559$ and 26 degrees of freedom. Refer to the 26th row of Table A.3, where we can see that a test statistic of $t = 3.594$ corresponds to a *P*-value less than 0.005. Note that Minitab provides the exact *P*-value of 0.0007. We can now see that our risk of being wrong if we reject H_0 is very small and we can therefore be very confident in rejecting H_0.

Confidence Intervals

Figure 9.4 summarizes the decisions and choices to be made when constructing confidence intervals for the difference between two population means. If you compare the confidence interval flowchart (Fig. 9.4) to the hypothesis-testing flowchart (Fig. 9.3), you will see very strong similarities. The same underlying theory for hypothesis tests also applies to confidence intervals.

The following four examples use the same data as the corresponding four examples of hypothesis testing given earlier in this section. They illustrate the same cases included in Fig. 9.4.

EXAMPLE   Eight consumers view a humorous commercial and a serious commercial for Taylor women's jeans and they then score the effectiveness of the commercials. The sample results are given below. Construct a 95% confidence interval for the mean of the differences between the two scores for each consumer.

Consumer	A	B	C	D	E	F	G	H
Humorous commercial	26.2	20.3	25.4	19.6	21.5	28.3	23.7	24.0
Serious commercial	24.1	21.3	23.7	18.0	20.1	25.8	22.4	21.4
Difference	2.1	−1.0	1.7	1.6	1.4	2.5	1.3	2.6

SOLUTION   Because we are dealing with dependent samples, Fig. 9.4 indicates that we should use the formula to the right of the first diamond. In our previous hypothesis test involving the same data, we found that $n = 8$, $\overline{d} = 1.525$, and $s_d = 1.129$. From Table A.3 we find that $t_{\alpha/2} = 2.365$ corresponds to $n - 1 = 7$ degrees of freedom and an area of 0.05 in two tails (with 95% confidence). Using these results, we first evaluate the margin of error E.

$$E = t_{\alpha/2} \frac{s_d}{\sqrt{n}} = 2.365 \frac{1.129}{\sqrt{8}} = 0.944$$

With $\overline{d} = 1.525$ and $E = 0.944$,

$$\overline{d} - E < \mu_d < \overline{d} + E$$

(continued)

FIGURE 9.4
Confidence Intervals for the Difference between Two Population Means

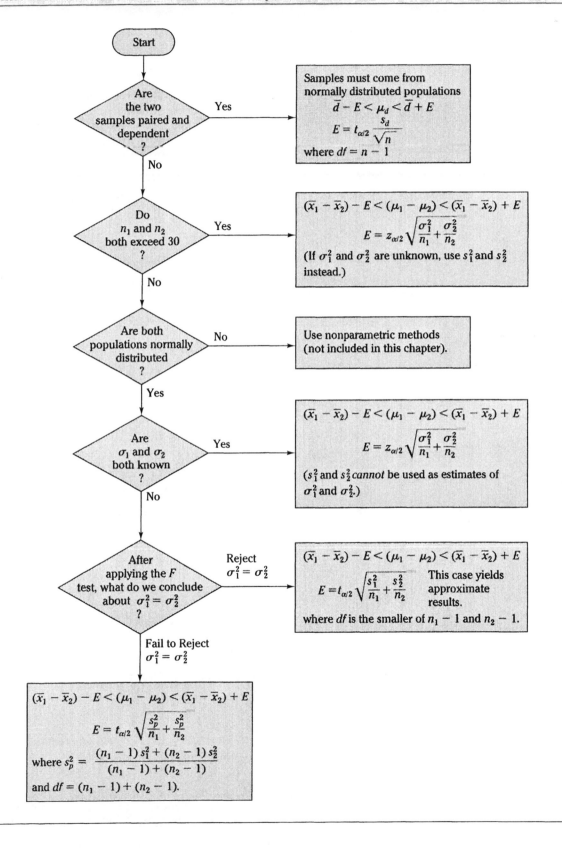

becomes $1.525 - 0.944 < \mu_d < 1.525 + 0.944$

or $0.581 < \mu_d < 2.469$

We are 95% confident that the limits of 0.581 and 2.469 actually do contain the true mean difference μ_d. That is, the humorous commercial seems to receive scores that are an average of 0.581 to 2.469 greater than those for the serious commercial.

EXAMPLE On page 401 we conducted a test of the claim that two machines provide the same mean amount of package contents. The sample data shown below were given along with these values for the population standard deviations: $\sigma = 0.80$ for machine A; $\sigma = 0.60$ for machine B. Use the same data to construct a 95% confidence interval for the difference between the two population means. (Assume that both filling processes are statistically stable.)

MACHINE A	MACHINE B
$n_1 = 50$	$n_2 = 100$
$\bar{x}_1 = 4.53$ kg	$\bar{x}_2 = 4.01$ kg

SOLUTION These samples are independent, both n_1 and n_2 exceed 30, and the population standard deviations are known, so Fig. 9.4 leads us to the fourth rectangle for the form of the confidence interval and the margin of error E. We first evaluate E.

$$E = z_{\alpha/2} \sqrt{\frac{\sigma_1^2}{n_1} + \frac{\sigma_2^2}{n_2}} = 1.96 \sqrt{\frac{0.80^2}{50} + \frac{0.60^2}{100}} = 0.25$$

With $\bar{x}_1 = 4.53$, $\bar{x}_2 = 4.01$, and $E = 0.25$, the confidence interval

$$(\bar{x}_1 - \bar{x}_2) - E < (\mu_1 - \mu_2) < (\bar{x}_1 - \bar{x}_2) + E$$

becomes

$$(4.53 - 4.01) - 0.25 < (\mu_1 - \mu_2) < (4.53 - 4.01) + 0.25$$

or

$$0.27 \text{ kg} < (\mu_1 - \mu_2) < 0.77 \text{ kg}$$

We are 95% confident that machine A is providing an average of 0.27 kg to 0.77 kg more than machine B.

Note that the above confidence interval for $\mu_1 - \mu_2$ does not contain 0, suggesting that $\mu_1 - \mu_2 \neq 0$. This is consistent with the previous hypothesis test based on the same data; there we concluded that the two means are not equal, so it follows that $\mu_1 - \mu_2 \neq 0$, and this is affirmed by the fact that the above confidence interval does not contain 0. Here we have a direct correspondence between the 95% confidence interval and the two-tailed hypothesis test with a 0.05 significance level.

EXAMPLE

Random samples of home selling prices are obtained from two zones in Dutchess County. Results are summarized below.

ZONE 7 (NORTH)	ZONE 1 (SOUTH)
$n_1 = 11$	$n_2 = 14$
$\bar{x}_1 = \$142,318$	$\bar{x}_2 = \$138,237$
$s_1 = \$46,068$	$s_2 = \$21,336$

Construct a 95% confidence interval for the difference between the two population means.

SOLUTION

This same collection of data was considered in the hypothesis test illustrated on page 404. The samples are independent, both populations are small, we're assuming that both populations have normal distributions, neither population standard deviation is known, and the preliminary F test caused us to reject $\sigma_1^2 = \sigma_2^2$. (Figure 9.4 indicates that we turn right at the fifth diamond.) We now calculate

$$E = t_{\alpha/2} \sqrt{\frac{s_1^2}{n_1} + \frac{s_2^2}{n_2}} = 2.228 \sqrt{\frac{46,068^2}{11} + \frac{21,336^2}{14}} = 33,453$$

In the above calculation, $t_{\alpha/2} = 2.228$ corresponds to 0.05 in two tails (95% confidence) and 10 degrees of freedom (the smaller of 10 and 13). With $\bar{x}_1 = 142,318$, $\bar{x}_2 = 138,237$, and $E = 33,453$,

$$(\bar{x}_1 - \bar{x}_2) - E < (\mu_1 - \mu_2) < (\bar{x}_1 - \bar{x}_2) + E$$

becomes

$$-\$29,372 < (\mu_1 - \mu_2) < \$37,534$$

Note that the above confidence interval for $\mu_1 - \mu_2$ does contain 0. This is consistent with the previous hypothesis test based on the same data; we failed to reject equality of the two population means. If $\mu_1 = \mu_2$, then $\mu_1 - \mu_2 = 0$, and the above confidence interval does contain 0. In particular, we are 95% confident that the zone-7 prices could be *larger* than those in zone 1 by as much as $37,534 or they could be *smaller* by as much as $29,372. We have a direct correspondence between the confidence interval and the two-tailed hypothesis test.

EXAMPLE

We have already used the following sample data for hypothesis testing. Recall that the group-1 statistics refer to a new method of manufacturing alkaline batteries. Construct a 95% confidence interval for the difference between the two population means.

GROUP 1 (NEW)	GROUP 2 (OLD)
$n_1 = 16$	$n_2 = 12$
$\bar{x}_1 = 17.64$ h	$\bar{x}_2 = 11.93$ h
$s_1 = 4.54$ h	$s_2 = 3.69$ h

BETTER RESULTS WITH SMALLER CLASS SIZE

An experiment at the State University of New York at Stony Brook found that students did significantly better in classes limited to 35 students than in large classes with 150 to 200 students. For a calculus course, failure rates were 19% for the small classes compared to 50% for the large classes. The percentages of A's were 24% for the small classes and 3% for the large classes. These results suggest that students benefit from smaller classes, which allow for more direct interaction between students and teachers.

SOLUTION   The samples are independent, the sample sizes small ($n_1 \leq 30$ and $n_2 \leq 30$), we assume that both populations are normally distributed, and the population standard deviations are not known, so Fig. 9.4 directs us to conduct the F test with H_0: $\sigma_1^2 = \sigma_2^2$. Recall that we have already failed to reject H_0, so we now have the case located at the bottom of Fig. 9.4. We next calculate

$$s_p^2 = \frac{(n_1 - 1)s_1^2 + (n_2 - 1)s_2^2}{(n_1 - 1) + (n_2 - 1)} = \frac{(16-1)(4.54)^2 + (12-1)(3.69)^2}{(16-1) + (12-1)}$$

$$= 17.652$$

and

$$df = (n_1 - 1) + (n_2 - 1) = (16 - 1) + (12 - 1) = 26$$

From Table A.3 we get $t_{\alpha/2} = 2.056$ (because 95% corresponds to $\alpha = 0.05$ in two tails and we have 26 degrees of freedom). We now find that

$$E = t_{\alpha/2} \sqrt{\frac{s_p^2}{n_1} + \frac{s_p^2}{n_2}} = 2.056 \sqrt{\frac{17.652}{16} + \frac{17.652}{12}} = 3.30$$

With $\bar{x}_1 = 17.64$ h, $\bar{x}_2 = 11.93$ h, and $E = 3.30$ h, the confidence interval

$$(\bar{x}_1 - \bar{x}_2) - E < (\mu_1 - \mu_2) < (\bar{x}_1 - \bar{x}_2) + E$$

becomes

$$(17.64 - 11.93) - 3.30 < (\mu_1 - \mu_2) < (17.64 - 11.93) + 3.30$$

or

$$2.41 \text{ h} < (\mu_1 - \mu_2) < 9.01 \text{ h}$$

We are 95% confident that the new method results in a mean life that is from 2.41 h to 9.01 h longer than the mean for the old method. Note that the Minitab display for the previous hypothesis test included the confidence interval limits of (2.4, 9.0) and they agree with the results shown here.

The corresponding hypothesis test that used the same data was a one-tailed test, so a direct comparison between this confidence interval (which is two-tailed) and that test is not appropriate. A direct comparison between the hypothesis test and the confidence interval is best done only when the hypothesis test is two-tailed. Although it's a bit tricky, we can compare a one-tailed hypothesis test with significance level α (such as 0.05) to a confidence interval with degree of confidence $1 - 2\alpha$ (such as 0.90). For example, we can compare a right-tailed hypothesis test with a 0.05 significance level to a 0.90 confidence interval. The data in the last example will result in this 0.90 confidence interval:

$$2.97 \text{ h} < \mu_1 - \mu_2 < 8.45 \text{ h}$$

In testing the hypothesis (at the 0.05 significance level) that $\mu_1 > \mu_2$ (or $\mu_1 - \mu_2 > 0$), the above 0.90 confidence interval shows that this claim of $\mu_1 - \mu_2 > 0$ is supported. (Because $\mu_1 - \mu_2$ is probably greater than 2.97, it is also probably greater than 0.) That is, the evidence is sufficient to support the claim that the mean for the new manufacturing method is greater than that for the old method.

9.3 EXERCISES | BASIC CONCEPTS

In Exercises 1–4, use a 0.05 significance level to test the claim that $\mu_1 = \mu_2$. In each case, the two samples are independent and are randomly selected from populations with normal distributions.

1. **CONTROL GROUP** **EXPERIMENTAL GROUP**

    $n_1 = 40$ $n_2 = 40$
    $\bar{x}_1 = 79.6$ $\bar{x}_2 = 88.2$
    $s_1 = 12.4$ $s_2 = 11.8$

2. **BRAND X**   **BRAND Y**

    $n_1 = 16$ $n_2 = 14$
    $\bar{x}_1 = 64.3$ $\bar{x}_2 = 65.1$
    $\sigma_1 = 2.50$ $\sigma_2 = 2.30$

3. **TREATED**   **UNTREATED**

    $n_1 = 16$ $n_2 = 20$
    $\bar{x}_1 = 91.4$ $\bar{x}_2 = 98.6$
    $s_1 = 8.60$ $s_2 = 4.20$

4. **PRODUCTION METHOD A**   **PRODUCTION METHOD B**

    $n_1 = 20$ $n_2 = 25$
    $\bar{x}_1 = 127.4$ $\bar{x}_2 = 108.3$
    $s_1 = 15.6$ $s_2 = 14.3$

In Exercises 5–8, use the data in the indicated exercise to construct a 95% confidence interval for the difference $\mu_1 - \mu_2$. In each case, the two samples are independent and are randomly selected from populations with normal distributions.

5. Exercise 1
6. Exercise 2
7. Exercise 3
8. Exercise 4

In Exercises 9–28, assume that any independent and small ($n \leq 30$) samples come from normally distributed populations.

9. The Medassist Pharmaceutical Company plans to advertise the effectiveness of the drug captopril, which is designed to lower systolic blood pressure. The drug is administered to 10 randomly selected volunteers, with the following

results. Construct the 95% confidence interval for μ_d, the mean of the differences between the before and after scores.

Before pill	120	136	160	98	115	110	180	190	138	128
After pill	118	122	143	105	98	98	180	175	105	112

10. Using the sample data from Exercise 9, test the claim that systolic blood pressure is not affected by the pill. Use a 0.05 significance level.
11. The Telektronic Company manufactures AA batteries by two different production methods. The battery lives (in hours) are found for a sample from each statistically stable process, and the results are as follows:

    Production method A: $n = 25$, $\bar{x} = 3.70$, $s = 0.37$
    Production method B: $n = 28$, $\bar{x} = 4.00$, $s = 0.31$

    At the 0.05 level of significance, test the claim that there is no difference in the two population means. Identify the P-value.
12. Use the sample data from Exercise 11 to construct a 95% confidence interval for the difference between the two population means.
13. In a study of the effect of job previews on work expectation, 60 newly hired bank tellers were given specific job previews and another group of 40 newly hired bank tellers had no previews. Their initial expectations for promotion were measured and the group with the previews had a mean of 19.14 and a standard deviation of 6.56. For the "no preview" sample group of 40 subjects, the mean is 20.81 and the standard deviation is 4.90. (See "Effects of Realistic Job Previews on Hiring Bank Tellers," by Dean and Wanous, *Journal of Applied Psychology*, Vol. 69, No. 1.) At the 0.10 level of significance, test the claim that the two sample groups come from populations with the same mean.
14. Use the sample data from Exercise 13 to construct a 90% confidence interval for the difference between the population means $(\mu_1 - \mu_2)$, where μ_1 is the mean score for all subjects given specific job previews and μ_2 is the mean for the "no preview" population.
15. An investor considering two possible locations for a new restaurant commissions a study of the pedestrian traffic at both sites. At each location, the pedestrians are observed in 1-hour units and, for each hour, an index of desirable characteristics is compiled (see the sample results below). Construct a 95% confidence interval for the difference between the two mean indexes.

EAST	WEST
$n = 35$	$n = 50$
$\bar{x} = 421$	$\bar{x} = 347$
$s = 122$	$s = 85$

16. Use the sample data from Exercise 15 to test the claim that the East site has a higher mean for pedestrian traffic than the West site. Include the P-value. Use a 0.05 significance level.
17. The A. J. Collins Investment Company is analyzing costs of switching to a different long-distance telephone company. It collects sample data on the lengths of telephone calls (in minutes) made by employees in two different

divisions, and the results are given below. At the 0.02 level of significance, test the claim that there is no difference between the mean times of all long-distance calls made in the two divisions.

SALES DIVISION	CUSTOMER SERVICE DIVISION
$n_1 = 40$	$n_2 = 20$
$\bar{x}_1 = 8.26$	$\bar{x}_2 = 6.93$
$s_1 = 5.65$	$s_2 = 3.93$

18. Use the sample data in Exercise 17 to construct a 98% confidence interval for the difference between the two population means.

19. Twelve different and independent samples from each of two competing cold medicines are tested for the amount of acetaminophen, and the results (in milligrams) are given below. At the 0.05 significance level, test the claim that the mean amount of acetaminophen is the same in each brand.

Brand X	472	487	506	512	489	503	511	501	495	504	494	462
Brand Y	562	512	523	528	554	513	516	510	524	510	524	508

20. Using the data from Exercise 19, construct a 95% confidence interval for this difference: the mean of the brand Y levels minus the mean of the brand X levels.

21. A company training program is designed to reduce the numbers of defects created by employees on an assembly line for answering machines. Sample results for randomly selected employees are given below for randomly selected work days. At the 0.05 significance level, test the claim that the training program had no effect on the numbers of defects.

Employee	A	B	C	D	E	F	G	H	I
Defects before program	24	24	27	19	31	29	33	20	26
Defects after program	17	22	9	12	16	21	15	15	19

22. Refer to the same data given in Exercise 21 and construct a 95% confidence interval for the mean difference of the before values minus the after values.

23. The actual amounts of corn chips in "16-oz" bags are measured by randomly selecting 25 bags from each of 3 shifts. Sample results from the 3 statistically stable processes are as follows:

SHIFT 1	SHIFT 2	SHIFT 3
$n_1 = 25$	$n_2 = 25$	$n_3 = 25$
$\bar{x}_1 = 16.04$ oz	$\bar{x}_2 = 15.72$ oz	$\bar{x}_3 = 16.28$ oz
$s_1 = 0.41$ oz	$s_2 = 0.36$ oz	$s_3 = 0.97$ oz

Assume we have already established that the variances for shifts 1 and 2 are not significantly different, whereas the variance for shift 3 is significantly different from either of the other two. Test the claim that shifts 1 and 2 have the same mean.

24. Refer to the same data from Exercise 23 and test the claim that shifts 1 and 3 have the same mean.

25. Refer to the same data from Exercise 23 and test the claim that shifts 2 and 3 have the same mean.
26. Use the data from Exercise 23 to construct a 95% confidence interval for $\mu_1 - \mu_2$.
27. Use the data from Exercise 23 to construct a 95% confidence interval for $\mu_1 - \mu_3$.
28. Use the data from Exercise 23 to construct a 90% confidence interval for $\mu_2 - \mu_3$.

9.3 EXERCISES   BEYOND THE BASICS

29. The sample size needed to estimate the difference between two population means to within E, with confidence level $1 - \alpha$, can be found as follows: First, in the expression

$$E = z_{\alpha/2} \sqrt{\frac{\sigma_1^2}{n_1} + \frac{\sigma_2^2}{n_2}}$$

replace n_1 and n_2 by n. (We're assuming that both samples will have the same size n.) Use σ_1 and σ_2 if those values are known, or use s_1 and s_2 as estimates of them. Now calculate

$$n = \frac{z_{\alpha/2}^2 (\sigma_1^2 + \sigma_2^2)}{E^2}$$

Refer to the data from Exercise 1 and use this approach to determine how many subjects should be randomly selected from each of the two groups to estimate the difference between their means. We want 95% confidence that we are within 1.5.

30. Refer to Exercise 1. If the actual difference between the population means is $\mu_1 - \mu_2 = -6.0$, find β, the probability of a type II error. (See Exercise 30 in Section 7.2.) *Hint:* In step 1, replace $\bar{x}$ by $(\bar{x}_1 - \bar{x}_2)$, replace $\mu_{\bar{x}}$ by 0, and replace $\sigma_{\bar{x}}$ by

$$\sqrt{\frac{\sigma_1^2}{n_1} + \frac{\sigma_2^2}{n_2}}$$

31. a. Find the variance for this *population* of x scores: 5, 10, 15.
    b. Find the variance for this *population* of y scores: 1, 2, 3.
    c. List the population of all possible $x - y$ scores, then find the variance of this population.
    d. Use the results from parts *a, b,* and *c* to verify that

$$\sigma_{x-y}^2 = \sigma_x^2 + \sigma_y^2$$

(This principle is used to derive the test statistic and confidence interval for several cases in this section.)

9.4 INFERENCES ABOUT TWO PROPORTIONS

In this section we consider inferences about two population proportions. The methods of this section are quite useful and important in business applications. The concepts and procedures we develop can be used to answer questions such as the following:

- When a television commercial for Bayer aspirin is market-tested in two different geographic regions, is there a difference between the percentages of people who react favorably?
- When the A. S. J. Computer Mail Order Company tries to improve its order-tracking process through more employee training, is the error rate for the new process lower than the error rate for the old process?

In the examples and exercises of this section, we are dealing with *proportions* (instead of means or standard deviations) because we have qualitative data consisting of attributes (such as the number of defects) instead of quantitative data consisting of measurements (such as weights). In this section we make the following assumptions.

Assumptions

The methods we use to *test a hypothesis* or to construct a *confidence interval* for the difference between two population proportions are based on these assumptions:

1. We have two *independent* sets of sample data.
2. For both samples, the conditions $np \geq 5$ and $nq \geq 5$ are satisfied.

We also use the following notation first introduced in Chapter 6.

Notation
For population 1 we let:

p_1 denote the population proportion
n_1 denote the size of the sample
x_1 denote the number of successes

$$\hat{p}_1 = \frac{x_1}{n_1}$$

The corresponding meanings are attached to p_2, n_2, x_2, and $\hat{p}_2$, which come from population 2.

HYPOTHESIS TESTS

We know from Section 5.6 that if $n_1 p_1 \geq 5$ and $n_1 q_1 \geq 5$, then we can approximate the binomial distribution by the normal distribution. This applies to the second population as well. As a result, our test statistic will be approximately normally distributed. **We will be testing only claims including the assumption that $p_1 = p_2$,** and we will use the following pooled (or combined) estimate of their common value. (For other cases, see the exercises of this section.)

The **pooled estimate of p_1 and p_2** is denoted by $\bar{p}$ and is given by

$$\bar{p} = \frac{x_1 + x_2}{n_1 + n_2}$$

$$\bar{q} = 1 - \bar{p}$$

With a null hypothesis of $p_1 = p_2$, or $p_1 \geq p_2$, or $p_1 \leq p_2$, we can use the following test statistic.

TEST STATISTIC

(For H_0: $p_1 = p_2$, H_0: $p_1 \geq p_2$, or H_0: $p_1 \leq p_2$)

$$z = \frac{(\hat{p}_1 - \hat{p}_2) - (p_1 - p_2)}{\sqrt{\dfrac{\bar{p}\bar{q}}{n_1} + \dfrac{\bar{p}\bar{q}}{n_2}}}$$

where

$$(p_1 - p_2) = 0$$

and

$$\hat{p}_1 = \frac{x_1}{n_1} \qquad \hat{p}_2 = \frac{x_2}{n_2}$$

$$\bar{p} = \frac{x_1 + x_2}{n_1 + n_2}$$

$$\bar{q} = 1 - \bar{p}$$

We will first illustrate the procedure for testing hypotheses, then we will justify the test statistic given above.

EXAMPLE In the credit card–fraud problem described at the beginning of this chapter, we noted that samples of fraud cases led to these results:

- 22% of fraudulent credit card uses result from cards stolen from the mail (based on data from the American Bankers Association).
- 16% of fraudulent credit card uses result from cards stolen from the mail or the factories where they are made (based on data from MasterCard International).

Ignore the discrepancy between categories (mail only vs. mail/factory) and test the claim that there is no significant difference between the results from the two studies. Assume that the American Bankers Association study is based on a sample of size 2000, and the MasterCard study is based on a sample of size 1000. (Samples of these sizes are very common.) Use a 0.05 significance level.

SOLUTION We begin by identifying the specific claim and representing it in symbolic form. The claim of "no significant difference" between the two percentages is expressed as $p_1 = p_2$. We arbitrarily stipulate that the 22% result is from sample 1, and the 16% result is from sample 2. We must now conduct this test using proportions instead of percentages, so the sample data are summarized as follows:

$n_1 = 2000$ $\qquad\qquad$ $n_2 = 1000$
$\hat{p}_1 = 0.22$ $\qquad\qquad$ $\hat{p}_2 = 0.16$
$x_1 = 22\%$ of $2000 = 440$ $\qquad$ $x_2 = 16\%$ of $1000 = 160$

Because our claim of $p_1 = p_2$ contains equality, we have

$H_0: p_1 = p_2$ $\qquad$ (or $p_1 - p_2 = 0$)
$H_1: p_1 \neq p_2$ $\qquad$ (or $p_1 - p_2 \neq 0$)

We will find the value of the test statistic, but we must first find the value of the pooled estimate of p_1 and p_2 as follows:

$$\bar{p} = \frac{x_1 + x_2}{n_1 + n_2} = \frac{440 + 160}{2000 + 1000} = \frac{600}{3000} = 0.2$$

$$\bar{q} = 1 - \bar{p} = 1 - 0.2 = 0.8$$

We can now find the value of the test statistic as follows:

$$z = \frac{(\hat{p}_1 - \hat{p}_2) - 0}{\sqrt{\frac{\bar{p}\bar{q}}{n_1} + \frac{\bar{p}\bar{q}}{n_2}}} = \frac{(0.22 - 0.16) - 0}{\sqrt{\frac{(0.2)(0.8)}{2000} + \frac{(0.2)(0.8)}{1000}}}$$

$$= 3.87$$

With a significance level of $\alpha = 0.05$ in this two-tailed test, the critical values of $z = -1.96$ and $z = 1.96$ are found from Table A.2. The test statistic and critical values are shown in Fig. 9.5. The test statistic is well within the critical region, so we reject the null hypothesis. The evidence is sufficient to warrant rejection of the claim that no significant difference exists between the results from the two studies. A significant discrepancy does appear to exist between the two studies. If we also consider that the 22% statistic represented credit card thefts from the mail only, whereas the 16% statistic represented thefts from both the mail and factories, we conclude that the discrepancy is even greater than our results suggest.

Because there does seem to be a discrepancy, banks cannot proceed with the knowledge that they have a sound data base. They should conduct further research before planning their strategies to combat credit card fraud. Perhaps that research could be facilitated by hiring students who have had the wisdom to take a statistics course.

FIGURE 9.5
Differences between Proportions

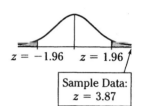

$z = -1.96$ $\qquad$ $z = 1.96$

Sample Data:
$z = 3.87$

We hope that the symbols x_1, x_2, n_1, n_2, $\hat{p}_1$, $\hat{p}_2$, $\bar{p}$, and $\bar{q}$ have become more meaningful through this example. Note that in the preceding example, sample data consisted of $n_1 = 2000$, $n_2 = 1000$, $\hat{p}_1 = 0.22$, and $\hat{p}_2 = 0.16$, but the values of

x_1, x_2, $\bar{p}$, and $\bar{q}$ were not given. We can easily find the value of x_1 by noting that $\hat{p}_1 = x_1/n_1$ implies that $x_1 = \hat{p}_1 \times n_1$. In the preceding example, we have $x_1 = \hat{p}_1 \times n_1 = 0.22 \times 2000 = 440$. The same approach resulted in $x_2 = 0.16 \times 1000 = 160$.

Note also that under the assumption of equal proportions, the best estimate of the common proportion is obtained by pooling both samples into one larger sample. Then

$$\bar{p} = \frac{x_1 + x_2}{n_1 + n_2}$$

becomes a more obvious estimate of the common population proportion.

EXAMPLE   A long-distance telephone company examines 2000 randomly selected bills and finds that 2.90% of them contain errors. Six months later, after reviewing procedures and modifying equipment, another sample of 2000 bills is randomly selected with the result that 1.75% of them contain errors. At the 0.05 significance level, test the claim that the two proportions are equal. That is, test the claim that the corrective actions have had no effect.

SOLUTION   The claim of equal proportions is expressed as H_0: $p_1 = p_2$. The alternative hypothesis is H_1: $p_1 \neq p_2$. Because $\hat{p}_1 = x_1/n_1$ and $\hat{p}_1 = 0.029$ (from 2.90%), it follows that $x_1 = \hat{p}_1 \times n_1 = 0.029 \times 2000 = 58$. A similar calculation shows that $x_2 = 0.0175 \times 2000 = 35$. We can now find $\bar{p}$ and $\bar{q}$ as follows:

$$\bar{p} = \frac{x_1 + x_2}{n_1 + n_2} = \frac{58 + 35}{2000 + 2000} = \frac{93}{4000} = 0.02325$$

$$\bar{q} = 1 - \bar{p} = 0.97675$$

We continue by computing the value of the test statistic.

$$z = \frac{(\hat{p}_1 - \hat{p}_2) - 0}{\sqrt{\dfrac{\bar{p}\bar{q}}{n_1} + \dfrac{\bar{p}\bar{q}}{n_2}}}$$

FIGURE 9.6
Differences between Proportions

$$= \frac{(0.0290 - 0.0175) - 0}{\sqrt{\dfrac{(0.02325)(0.97675)}{2000} + \dfrac{(0.02325)(0.97675)}{2000}}} = 2.41$$

With $\alpha = 0.05$ in this two-tailed test, we use Table A.2 to obtain the critical z values of -1.96 and 1.96 (see Fig. 9.6). Because the test statistic falls within the critical region, we reject the null hypothesis. We conclude that the sample evidence is sufficient to warrant rejection of the claim that the two proportions are equal. Although this evidence doesn't prove that the changes in procedure and equipment directly affect the error rate, it strongly suggests that those modifications were effective.   *(continued)*

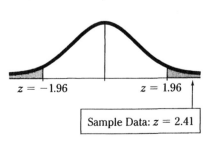

$z = -1.96$ $z = 1.96$

Sample Data: $z = 2.41$

The P-value can be found by using Table A.2. The test statistic of $z = 2.41$ corresponds to an area of 0.4920. Because this test is two-tailed, the P-value is $2 \times (0.5000 - 0.4920) = 0.016$. Because the P-value of 0.016 is less than the significance level of 0.05, we should reject the null hypothesis of equal proportions.

The test statistic we are using can be justified as follows:

1. With $n_1 p_1 \geq 5$ and $n_1 q_1 \geq 5$, the distribution of $\hat{p}_1$ can be approximated by a normal distribution with mean p_1, standard deviation $\sqrt{p_1 q_1/n_1}$ and variance $p_1 q_1/n_1$. These conclusions follow from Sections 5.6 and 6.3. They also apply to the second sample and population.

2. Because $\hat{p}_1$ and $\hat{p}_2$ are each approximated by a normal distribution, $\hat{p}_1 - \hat{p}_2$ will also be approximated by a normal distribution with mean $p_1 - p_2$ and variance.

$$\sigma^2_{(\hat{p}_1 - \hat{p}_2)} = \sigma^2_{\hat{p}_1} + \sigma^2_{\hat{p}_2} = \frac{p_1 q_1}{n_1} + \frac{p_2 q_2}{n_2}$$

3. Because the values of p_1, p_2, q_1, and q_2 are typically unknown, and from the null hypothesis we assume that $p_1 = p_2$, we can pool the sample data. The pooled estimate of the common value of p_1 and p_2 is

$$\bar{p} = \frac{x_1 + x_2}{n_1 + n_2}$$

If we replace p_1 and p_2 by $\bar{p}$, and replace q_1 and q_2 by $\bar{q} = 1 - \bar{p}$, the variance from step 2 above leads to this standard deviation:

$$\sigma_{(\hat{p}_1 - \hat{p}_2)} = \sqrt{\frac{\bar{p}\bar{q}}{n_1} + \frac{\bar{p}\bar{q}}{n_2}}$$

4. We now know that the distribution of $\hat{p}_1 - \hat{p}_2$ is approximately normal, with mean $p_1 - p_2$ and standard deviation as given above. This corresponds to the test statistic

$$z = \frac{\text{(sample statistic)} - \text{(population mean)}}{\text{(population standard deviation)}}$$

or

$$z = \frac{(\hat{p}_1 - \hat{p}_2) - (p_1 - p_2)}{\sqrt{\frac{\bar{p}\bar{q}}{n_1} + \frac{\bar{p}\bar{q}}{n_2}}}$$

which is the test statistic given earlier.

Remember, to use this test statistic we must assume that $p_1 = p_2$, $p_1 \leq p_2$, or $p_1 \geq p_2$. With this assumption, $p_1 - p_2$ in the test statistic will always be 0. For testing claims that the difference $p_1 - p_2$ is equal to a nonzero constant, we use a different test statistic (see Exercise 19).

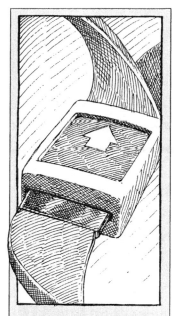

BUCKLE UP

S tatistical analysis of data can lead to changes in public policy. The Highway Users Federation estimated that if we all used safety belts, each year there would be 1200 fewer highway deaths and 330,000 fewer disabling injuries. One study of 1126 accidents showed that riders wearing safety belts had 86% fewer life-threatening injuries. Some people don't use safety belts because they know of cases where a serious injury was avoided when an unbelted rider was thrown clear of the wreck. Although there are cases where the safety belt had a negative effect, they are far outnumbered by cases in which it was clearly helpful. The wisest strategy is to buckle up.

CONFIDENCE INTERVALS

In this section we have discussed hypothesis testing, but we sometimes need an estimate of the actual difference between two proportions. Suppose an advertising specialist uses hypothesis testing and concludes that there is a difference between the proportion of men and the proportion of women who react favorably to a television commercial for Jeeps. The next logical question might be, How large is the difference? Is the difference large enough to address with different advertising campaigns targeted at the different market segments? We can estimate the size of the difference by constructing a confidence interval.

With the same assumptions given at the beginning of this section, we can construct a confidence interval for the difference between population proportions p_1 and p_2 by evaluating

$$(\hat{p}_1 - \hat{p}_2) - E < (p_1 - p_2) < (\hat{p}_1 - \hat{p}_2) + E$$

where

$$E = z_{\alpha/2} \sqrt{\frac{\hat{p}_1 \hat{q}_1}{n_1} + \frac{\hat{p}_2 \hat{q}_2}{n_2}}$$

We will first give an example illustrating the construction of a confidence interval, then we will justify the format given above.

EXAMPLE Use the sample data given in the preceding example to construct the 95% confidence interval for the difference between the proportions of errors before and after changes in procedures and equipment.

BEFORE	AFTER
$n_1 = 2000$	$n_2 = 2000$
$x_1 = 58$	$x_2 = 35$

SOLUTION With a 95% degree of confidence, $z_{\alpha/2} = 1.96$ (from Table A.2). With $\hat{p}_1 = 58/2000 = 0.0290$ and $\hat{p}_2 = 35/2000 = 0.0175$, we first evaluate the margin of error E.

$$E = z_{\alpha/2} \sqrt{\frac{\hat{p}_1 \hat{q}_1}{n_1} + \frac{\hat{p}_2 \hat{q}_2}{n_2}}$$

$$= 1.96 \sqrt{\frac{(0.0290)(0.9710)}{2000} + \frac{(0.0175)(0.9825)}{2000}} = 0.0093$$

With $\hat{p}_1 = 0.0290$, $\hat{p}_2 = 0.0175$, and $E = 0.0093$, the confidence interval

$$(\hat{p}_1 - \hat{p}_2) - E < (p_1 - p_2) < (\hat{p}_1 - \hat{p}_2) + E$$

becomes $(0.0290 - 0.0175) - 0.0093 < (\hat{p}_1 - \hat{p}_2)$

$$< (0.0290 - 0.0175) + 0.0093$$

or $0.0022 < (p_1 - p_2) < 0.0208$

(continued)

We can conclude, with 95% confidence, that the limits of 0.0022 and 0.0208 actually do contain the "before-after" difference in proportions. This suggests that the "after" values are lower, so the corrective actions do seem to have been effective in lowering the billing-error rate.

We should be careful when interpreting confidence intervals. Because p_1 and p_2 have fixed values and are not variables, it is wrong to state that there is a 95% chance that the value of $p_1 - p_2$ falls between 0.0022 and 0.0208. It is correct to state that if we repeat the same sampling process and construct 95% confidence intervals, in the long run 95% of the intervals will actually contain the value of $p_1 - p_2$.

In the preceding example, if we had reversed the order of the samples, the result would have been

$$-0.0208 < (p_1 - p_2) < -0.0022$$

When there does appear to be a difference, be sure you know which proportion is larger.

The form of the confidence interval comes directly from the test statistic if we use the variance

$$\sigma^2_{(\hat{p}_1 - \hat{p}_2)} = \sigma^2_{\hat{p}_1} + \sigma^2_{\hat{p}_2} = \frac{p_1 q_1}{n_1} + \frac{p_2 q_2}{n_2}$$

to estimate the standard deviation as

$$\sqrt{\frac{\hat{p}_1 \hat{q}_1}{n_1} + \frac{\hat{p}_2 \hat{q}_2}{n_2}}$$

(We don't use pooled estimates of proportions because we're not assuming from a null hypothesis that $p_1 = p_2$.) In the test statistic

$$z = \frac{(\hat{p}_1 - \hat{p}_2) - (p_1 - p_2)}{\sqrt{\frac{\hat{p}_1 \hat{q}_1}{n_1} + \frac{\hat{p}_2 \hat{q}_2}{n_2}}}$$

let z be positive and negative (for two tails) and solve for $p_1 - p_2$. The result is the confidence interval given earlier.

9.4 EXERCISES | BASIC CONCEPTS

1. Let samples from two populations be such that $x_1 = 45$, $n_1 = 100$, $x_2 = 115$, and $n_2 = 200$.
   a. Compute the z test statistic based on the given data.
   b. If the significance level is 0.05 and the test is two-tailed, find the critical z values.
   c. Test the claim that the two populations have equal proportions using the significance level of $\alpha = 0.05$.
   d. Find the P-value.
   e. Find the 95% confidence interval for $p_1 - p_2$.

2. Samples taken from two populations yield the data $x_1 = 90$, $n_1 = 750$, $x_2 = 44$, and $n_2 = 800$.
   a. Compute the z test statistic based on the given data.
   b. If the significance level is 0.01 and the test is right-tailed, find the critical z value.
   c. Test the claim that the first population has a higher proportion than the second population.
   d. Find the P-value.
   e. Find the 99% confidence interval for $p_1 - p_2$.

3. Some companies rely heavily on market research conducted through consumer surveys, and they are becoming increasingly concerned about potential respondents refusing to cooperate. When 294 central city residents were surveyed, 28.9% refused to respond. A survey of 1015 residents not in a central city resulted in a 17.1% refusal rate (based on data from "I Hear You Knocking But You Can't Come In," by Fitzgerald and Fuller, *Sociological Methods and Research*, Vol. 11, No. 1). At the 0.01 significance level, test the claim that the central city refusal rate is the same as the refusal rate in other areas.

4. Using the sample data in Exercise 3, construct a 99% confidence interval for the difference between the proportions of refusals in a central city and elsewhere.

5. On examining 500 randomly selected transactions, a C.P.A. finds that 52 of them involved errors. The sales clerks who do the transactions are given a training session and then another sample of 400 randomly selected transactions is examined with the result that 23 of them involved errors. At the $\alpha = 0.10$ significance level, test the claim that the error rate is lower after the training session. Compute the P-value for this hypothesis test.

6. Use the data from Exercise 5 to construct a 95% confidence interval for the difference in proportions (pretraining minus posttraining).

7. The *Independent Gentleman* is a new magazine designed specifically for young men living alone. The market research department finds that in a recent survey of 500 males aged 14–24, 3.6% of them were living alone. In a 1960 survey of 750 males aged 14–24, 1.6% were living alone (based on data from the U.S. Bureau of the Census). Construct a 99% confidence interval for the difference between the two proportions of males living alone.

8. Refer to the sample data in Exercise 7. At the 0.01 level of significance, test the claim that the more recent rate is greater than the rate in 1960.

9. The Chemco Company manufactures plastic trash bags. The quality control manager randomly selects 300 bags during the first hour of production and finds that 19 of them have holes. After modifying the raw plastic used in the process, another check of 400 bags shows that 8 have holes. At the 0.10 level of significance, test the claim that the modification has no effect on the rate of bags with holes. Include the P-value.

10. Refer to the sample data from Exercise 9 and construct a 90% confidence interval for the difference between the population proportions.

11. The American College Testing Program provides data showing that 30% of four-year public college freshmen drop out, and the dropout rate at four-year private colleges is 26%. Assume that these results are based on observations of 1000 four-year public college freshmen and 500 four-year private college freshmen. At the 0.05 significance level, test the claim that four-year public and private colleges have the same freshman dropout rate.

12. Use the data from Exercise 11 to construct a 95% confidence interval for the difference between the proportion of dropout rates for four-year public and private colleges.
13. In initial tests of the Salk vaccine, 33 of 200,000 vaccinated children later developed polio. Of 200,000 children vaccinated with a placebo, 115 later developed polio. At the 1% level of significance, test the claim that the Salk vaccine is effective in lowering the polio rate.
14. An actuary for the Life Trust Insurance Company is responsible for adjusting automobile insurance rates based on DWI convictions. The New York State Department of Motor Vehicles provided her with the following motor vehicle conviction data for a recent year.

	ALBANY COUNTY	QUEENS COUNTY
Total convictions	24,384	166,197
DWI convictions	558	1,214

At the 0.01 level of significance, test the claim that the proportion of DWI (driving while intoxicated) convictions is lower in Queens County. Assume that the given data represent random samples drawn from a larger population.
15. The Medassist Pharmaceutical Company obtains a random sample of 550 vitamin bottles and finds that 12 have their tamper-proof seals improperly attached. When 400 bottles are randomly selected from a second production process, the company finds that only 7 have that same defect. Both processes appear to be statistically stable. At the $\alpha = 0.05$ level, test the hypothesis that the two proportions of defects are different. Include the P-value.
16. Refer to the data in Exercise 15 and construct a 95% confidence interval for the difference between the two proportions of defects.
17. An advertiser studies the proportion of radio listeners who prefer country music. In region A, 38% of the 250 listeners surveyed indicated a preference for country music. In region B, country music was preferred by 14% of the 400 listeners surveyed. Construct a 98% confidence interval for the difference between the proportions of listeners who prefer country music.
18. Using the data from Exercise 17, and using a 0.02 significance level, test the claim that region A has a greater proportion of listeners who prefer country music.

9.4 EXERCISES BEYOND THE BASICS

19. To test the null hypothesis that the difference between two population proportions is equal to a nonzero constant c, use

$$z = \frac{(\hat{p}_1 - \hat{p}_2) - c}{\sqrt{\frac{\hat{p}_1(1 - \hat{p}_1)}{n_1} + \frac{\hat{p}_2(1 - \hat{p}_2)}{n_2}}}$$

(continued)

As long as n_1 and n_2 are both large, the sampling distribution of the above test statistic z will be approximately the standard normal distribution. Suppose a winery is conducting market research in New York and California. In a sample of 500 New Yorkers, 120 like the wine, while a sample of 500 Californians shows that 210 like the wine. Use a 0.05 level of significance to test the claim that the percentage of Californians who like the wine is 25% more than the percentage of New Yorkers who like it.

20. Sample data are randomly drawn from three independent populations. The sample sizes and the numbers of successes follow.

POPULATION 1	POPULATION 2	POPULATION 3
$n = 100$	$n = 100$	$n = 100$
$x = 40$	$x = 30$	$x = 20$

   a. At the 0.05 significance level, test the claim that $p_1 = p_2$.
   b. At the 0.05 significance level, test the claim that $p_2 = p_3$.
   c. At the 0.05 significance level, test the claim that $p_1 = p_3$.
   d. In general, if hypothesis tests result in failure to reject both $p_1 = p_2$ and $p_2 = p_3$, does it follow that the decision $p_1 = p_3$ will be reached under the same conditions?

21. The **sample size** needed to estimate the difference between two population proportions to within E with a confidence level of $1 - \alpha$ can be found as follows: In the expression

$$E = z_{\alpha/2} \sqrt{\frac{p_1 q_1}{n_1} + \frac{p_2 q_2}{n_2}}$$

replace n_1 and n_2 by n (assuming that both samples have the same size) and replace each of p_1, q_1, p_2, and q_2 by 0.5, assuming that their values are not known. (If the values of p_1, q_1, p_2, and q_2 can be estimated, you could enter those estimated values in the above equation.) Then solve for n.

   Use this approach to find the size of each sample if you want to estimate the difference between the proportions of men and women who own cars. Assume that you want 95% confidence that your error is no more than 0.03.

Vocabulary List

Define and give an example of each term.

independent samples
dependent samples
F distribution
degrees of freedom for the numerator
degrees of freedom for the denominator
interval estimates
pooled variance
pooled estimate of p_1 and p_2

Review

In Chapters 6 and 7 we introduced two major concepts of inferential statistics: the estimation of population or stable process parameters and the methods of testing hypotheses made about population or stable process parameters. The examples and exercises in Chapters 6 and 7 were restricted to cases involving a *single* sample drawn from a single population. This chapter extended our coverage to include *two* samples drawn from two populations or two stable processes.

We began by presenting a test for comparing two population variances (or standard deviations) that come from two independent populations having normal distributions. We compared two variances or standard deviations first because such a test is sometimes used as part of an overall test for comparing two population means. In Section 9.2 we saw that when $\sigma_1^2 = \sigma_2^2$, the sampling distribution of the ratio s_1^2/s_2^2 is the F distribution, for which Table A.5 was computed. We briefly discussed the construction of confidence intervals for the ratio of two population variances.

In Section 9.3 we considered various situations that can occur when we want to use a hypothesis test for comparing two means. We begin such a test by determining whether the two populations are *dependent,* or related in some way. When comparing population means that come from two dependent and normal populations, we compute the differences between corresponding pairs of values. Those differences have a sample mean and sample standard deviation denoted by $\bar{d}$ and s_d, respectively. In repeated random samplings, the values of $\bar{d}$ possess a Student t distribution with mean μ_d, standard deviation $\sigma_d/\sqrt{n}$, and $n - 1$ degrees of freedom.

When using hypothesis tests to compare two population means from independent populations, we encounter four situations that can be summarized best by Fig. 9.3. These cases incorporate standard deviations reflecting the property that, if one random variable x has variance σ_x^2 and another independent random variable y has variance σ_y^2, the random variable $x - y$ will have variance $\sigma_x^2 + \sigma_y^2$.

Section 9.3 also included confidence intervals that serve as estimates of differences between population means. Figure 9.4 can be used to determine the appropriate form of the confidence interval for the four different cases that occur.

In Section 9.4 we considered hypothesis tests and confidence intervals for proportions, probabilities, or percentages that come from two independent populations. We saw that the sample proportions have differences

$$\frac{x_1}{n_1} - \frac{x_2}{n_2} \quad \text{or} \quad \hat{p}_1 - \hat{p}_2$$

that tend to have a distribution that is approximately normal, with mean $p_1 - p_2$ and a standard deviation estimated by

$$\sqrt{\frac{\bar{p}\bar{q}}{n_1} + \frac{\bar{p}\bar{q}}{n_2}}$$

when $p_1 = p_2$. Also, $\bar{q} = 1 - \bar{p}$ and $\bar{p}$ is the pooled proportion $(x_1 + x_2)/(n_1 + n_2)$.

Figure 9.7 provides a reference chart for locating the appropriate material. One of the most difficult aspects of inferential statistics is the identification of the most appropriate distribution and the selection of the proper test statistic or confidence interval. Figure 9.7 should help in that determination.

AIRLINE CHILD SAFETY SEATS

Recently, a consumer's group lobbied for special safety seats to be made available for children on airliners. The Federal Aviation Administration responded with this argument: If babies are placed in their special safety seats, they will require their own seat on the plane instead of being held by a parent. If babies require their own seats, they must be charged a fare. If you charge a fare for babies, the extra cost will force many parents to drive instead of fly. The fatality rate for cars is much higher than the rate for airliners. Therefore, in the long run it's safer to let babies continue to fly in people's laps without requiring special safety seats.

FIGURE 9.7
Confidence Intervals and Hypothesis Tests

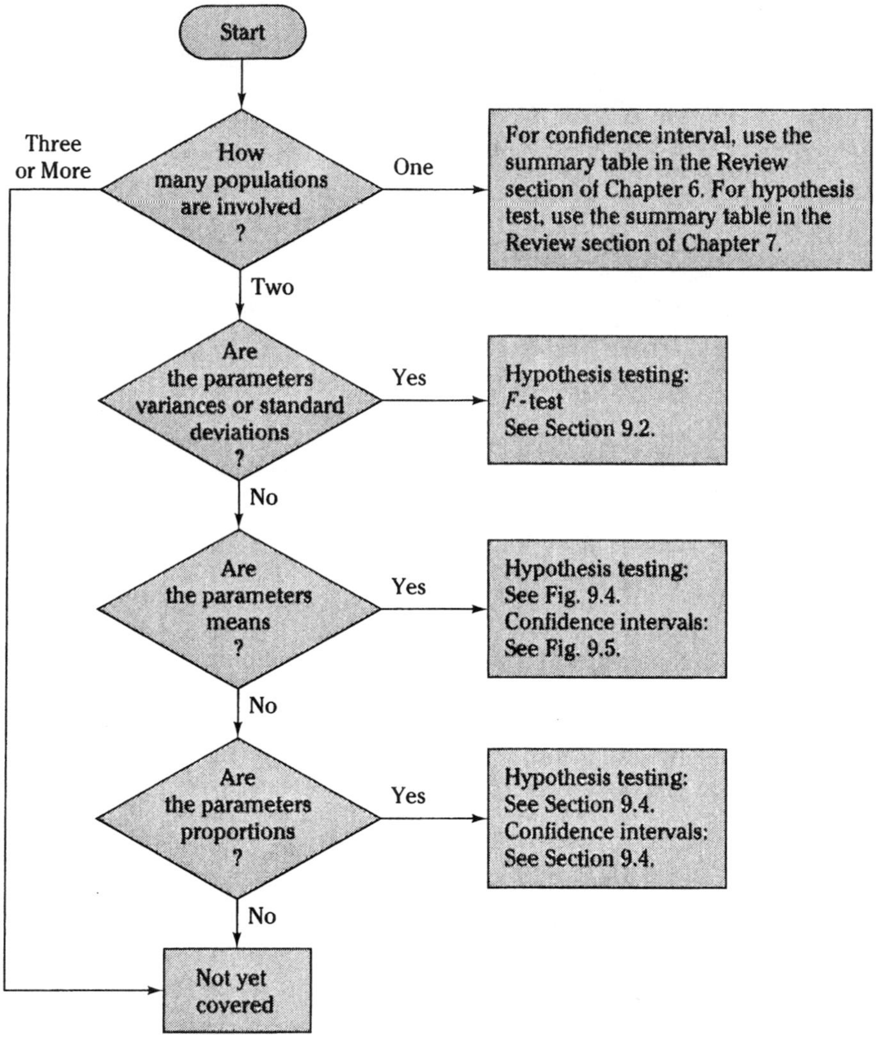

Review Exercises

1. The Houston Bakery produces cake mixes. In an experiment, 16 boxes labeled "16 oz" are randomly selected. The actual weights (in ounces) are listed near the bottom of page 429. After reducing the humidity in the processing area by 20%, a second random sample of 21 boxes is obtained, and the results are also listed on the next page. In both cases, the process is statistically stable with a normal distribution.

   a. Find the mean and variance for each of the two samples.

   b. Test the claim that both populations have the same variance. Use a 0.05 level of significance.   *(continued)*

Important Formulas

PARAMETERS	APPLICABLE DISTRIBUTION	TESTING HYPOTHESES (TEST STATISTIC)	CONFIDENCE INTERVALS	TABLE OF CRITICAL VALUES
σ_1, σ_2 (two standard deviations) or σ_1^2, σ_2^2 (two variances)	F	$F = \dfrac{s_1^2}{s_2^2}$ where $s_1^2 > s_2^2$	See Exercises 17 and 18 in Section 9.2.	Table A.5
μ_1, μ_2 (two means): dependent samples	Student t	$t = \dfrac{\bar{d} - \mu_d}{s_d/\sqrt{n}}$	$\bar{d} - E < \mu_d < \bar{d} + E$ where $E = t_{\alpha/2}\dfrac{s_d}{\sqrt{n}}$	Table A.3
independent *samples* (*hypothesis tests*: see Fig. 9.3; confidence intervals: see Fig. 9.4)	Normal or Student t	$z = \dfrac{(\bar{x}_1 - \bar{x}_2) - (\mu_1 - \mu_2)}{\sqrt{\dfrac{\sigma_1^2}{n_1} + \dfrac{\sigma_2^2}{n_2}}}$	$(\bar{x}_1 - \bar{x}_2) - E < (\mu_1 - \mu_2)$ $< (\bar{x}_1 - \bar{x}_2) + E$ where $E = z_{\alpha/2}\sqrt{\dfrac{\sigma_1^2}{n_1} + \dfrac{\sigma_2^2}{n_2}}$	Table A.2
		$t = \dfrac{(\bar{x}_1 - \bar{x}_2) - (\mu_1 - \mu_2)}{\sqrt{\dfrac{s_1^2}{n_1} + \dfrac{s_2^2}{n_2}}}$	or $E = t_{\alpha/2}\sqrt{\dfrac{s_1^2}{n_1} + \dfrac{s_2^2}{n_2}}$	Table A.3
		$t = \dfrac{(\bar{x}_1 - \bar{x}_2) - (\mu_1 - \mu_2)}{\sqrt{\dfrac{s_p^2}{n_1} + \dfrac{s_p^2}{n_2}}}$ where $s_p^2 = \dfrac{(n_1 - 1)s_1^2 + (n_2 - 1)s_2^2}{(n_1 - 1) + (n_2 - 1)}$	or $E = t_{\alpha/2}\sqrt{\dfrac{s_p^2}{n_1} + \dfrac{s_p^2}{n_2}}$	Table A.3
p_1, p_2 (two proportions)	Normal	$z = \dfrac{(\hat{p}_1 - \hat{p}_2) - (p_1 - p_2)}{\sqrt{\dfrac{\bar{p}\bar{q}}{n_1} + \dfrac{\bar{p}\bar{q}}{n_2}}}$	$(\hat{p}_1 - \hat{p}_2) - E < (p_1 - p_2)$ $< (\hat{p}_1 - \hat{p}_2) + E$ where $E = z_{\alpha/2}\sqrt{\dfrac{\hat{p}_1\hat{q}_1}{n_1} + \dfrac{\hat{p}_2\hat{q}_2}{n_2}}$	Table A.2

ORIGINAL SAMPLE				SAMPLE AFTER HUMIDITY REDUCTION					
15.8	14.8	15.4	15.5	16.3	14.7	16.3	15.8	16.6	16.4
14.9	16.9	16.0	17.3	14.8	15.6	16.5	16.5	16.4	
18.5	18.3	15.1	18.1	16.8	16.4	15.5	15.6	16.8	
14.7	18.4	15.6	15.9	16.8	15.6	16.5	15.6	16.7	

c. Test the claim that both populations have the same mean. Use a 0.05 level of significance.

d. Write a brief statement summarizing your conclusions about any effects from the reduced humidity.

2. Given below are summary statistics for sample data obtained from two popular drugs. Both samples consist of times (in minutes) required to experience relief from headaches.

DRUG A	DRUG B
$n = 50$	$n = 45$
$\bar{x} = 10.3$ min	$\bar{x} = 13.1$ min
$s = 2.4$ min	$s = 3.8$ min

   a. Test the hypothesis that the two drugs have the same standard deviation. Use a 0.10 level of significance.
   b. Test the claim that drug A has a mean below that of drug B. Use a 0.10 level of significance.
   c. Construct a 95% confidence interval for the difference between the two means $(\mu_A - \mu_B)$.
   d. Assume that drug B is the market leader and you work for the pharmaceutical company producing drug A. Use the results from parts a, b, and c to write a brief statement outlining the advantages and disadvantages of drug A.

3. In a survey of 450 persons who commute by car, 339 ride alone. After a long advertising campaign intended to encourage car pooling, a second survey of 500 car commuters shows that 371 ride alone. Test the claim that the campaign was successful in lowering the rate of commuters who ride alone. Use a 0.05 level of significance and identify the P-value.

4. Automobiles are selected at random and tested for fuel economy with each of two different carburetors. The following results show the distance traveled on 1 gal of gas.
   a. At the 0.05 level of significance, test the claim that both carburetors produce the same mean mileage.
   b. Construct a 95% confidence interval for the mean of the differences.

Car	1	2	3	4	5	6	7	8	9
Distance—carburetor A	16.1	21.3	19.2	14.8	29.3	20.2	18.6	19.7	16.4
Distance—carburetor B	18.2	23.4	19.7	14.7	28.7	23.4	19.0	21.2	18.2

5. In a study of union and nonunion migrant farm workers, hourly wages are recorded for randomly selected members of each group, and the results are summarized below.

UNION	NONUNION
$n = 20$	$n = 25$
$\bar{x} = \$4.95$	$\bar{x} = \$4.45$
$s = \$0.92$	$s = \$1.07$

   a. Test the claim that the wages of the two groups have the same variance. Use a 0.05 level of significance.
   b. Test the claim that the union workers have a higher mean hourly wage. Use a 0.10 significance level and identify the P-value.
   c. Construct a 95% confidence interval for the difference between the two population means.

6. The Life Trust Insurance Company is studying the possibility of offering medical malpractice insurance to surgeons. Various demographic data are being collected, including the following: Among 200 randomly selected female physicians, 2.5% are surgeons. Among 250 randomly selected male physicians, 19.2% are surgeons. (The data are based on information provided by the American Medical Association.)

   a. At the 0.05 significance level, test the claim that the percentage of male surgeons is greater than the percentage of female surgeons.

   b. Construct a 95% confidence interval for the difference between the two proportions.

7. Two different firms manufacture garage door springs that are designed to produce a tension of 68 kg. Random samples are selected from each of these two suppliers, and tension test results are as follows:

FIRM A	FIRM B
$n = 20$	$n = 32$
$\bar{x} = 66.0$ kg	$\bar{x} = 68.3$ kg
$s = 2.1$ kg	$s = 0.4$ kg

   a. At the 5% level of significance, test the claim that both firms produce the same standard deviation.

   b. Test the claim that both firms' springs produce the same mean tension. Use a 0.05 level of significance.

   c. Construct a 95% confidence interval for the difference between the mean for firm A and the mean for firm B.

8. Researchers studying commercial air-filtering systems for noise pollution reported the following sample results. At the 5% level of significance, test the claim that there is no difference in the mean noise levels.

UNIT A	UNIT B
$n = 8$	$n = 6$
$\bar{x} = 87.5$	$\bar{x} = 91.3$
$s = 0.8$	$s = 1.1$

9. The board of directors of the Jefferson Valley Bank wants improvements in service. A manager records the times required for transactions by customers using the drive-up windows. After making several physical and personnel changes, the manager records those times for a second sample of customers. Both sets of randomly selected results are shown with all times in minutes.

BEFORE CHANGES					AFTER CHANGES				
3.84	1.57	4.31	2.69	2.54	4.59	0.90	2.24	3.14	2.48
2.21	3.69	3.16	4.60	3.41	2.55	2.09	2.07	1.84	2.65
2.79	5.98	2.69	1.49	2.44	2.27	1.66	4.24	1.70	2.85
2.53	4.19	3.18	3.54	4.72	3.64	3.28	2.28	2.23	1.29
1.63	4.02	3.32	2.86	4.50	3.83	2.07	2.42	1.74	0.94

   a. Find the mean and standard deviation for each sample.

   b. Test the claim that the variation in times was not affected by the changes. Use a 0.05 level of significance. (continued)

c. Test the claim that the mean time has changed. Use a 0.05 level of significance.
d. Find a 90% confidence interval for the difference between the two population means (before minus after). Explain or interpret the result by writing a brief statement.
e. Write a brief statement to the bank's board of directors. Include a description of any changes in the waiting times and conclude with a recommendation either to keep the changes or to return to the original procedures.

10. The New York State Department of Motor Vehicles provided the following motor vehicle conviction data for a recent year.

	ALBANY COUNTY	MONROE COUNTY
Total convictions	24,384	60,961
Speeding convictions	10,292	26,074

a. At the 0.10 significance level, test the claim that the proportion of speeding convictions is the same for both counties. Assume that the given data represent random samples drawn from a larger population.
b. Construct a 90% confidence interval for the difference between the proportions of speeding convictions in both counties.

11. The A. J. Collins Investment Company gives a test of billing-procedure skills before and after a training session. The results are given below. At the 0.025 level of significance, test the claim that the training session was effective in increasing the test scores.

Employee	A	B	C	D	E	F	G	H
Before	6	8	5	4	3	5	4	7
After	9	10	8	9	6	8	7	10

12. The manager of a movie theater conducts a study of the ages of those who view two different movies. The study yields the following sample results.

MOVIE X	MOVIE Y
$n = 45$	$n = 65$
$\bar{x} = 22.6$ years	$\bar{x} = 31.0$ years
$s = 5.8$ years	$s = 4.7$ years

a. At the 0.025 level of significance, test the claim that there is no difference between the two population means.
b. Construct a 97.5% confidence interval for the difference between the mean age for movie X and the mean age for movie Y.

Computer Projects

1. We will simulate two processes that involve filling ice cream containers labeled "one gallon" (or 128 oz). The first set of Minitab commands (see below) simulates a sample of size $n = 26$ taken from a population with a mean of 128 and a standard deviation of 1.5. The second set of Minitab commands simulates a sample of size $n = 23$ taken from a population with a mean of 126 and a standard deviation of 1.9. Both populations are normally distributed.

a. After rounding all values to the nearest ounce, construct a stem-and-leaf plot for each of the two simulated sets of sample data. Do you see any differences from a comparison of the two diagrams?

b. Test the claim that the two production methods have the same standard deviation. Use a 0.05 level of significance. We know from our Minitab commands that the first sample has a standard deviation of 1.5 and the second sample has a standard deviation of 1.9. Does the hypothesis test recognize the difference?

c. After completing the test in part b, test the claim that the two population mean fill weights are the same. Use a 0.05 level of significance. We know from our Minitab commands that the first mean is 128 oz and the second mean is 126 oz. Does our hypothesis test recognize that difference? Explain.

d. Construct a 95% confidence interval for the difference between the mean fill of the two production lines.

```
MTB > RANDOM k=26 C1;
SUBC> NORMAL mu=128 sigma=1.5.
MTB > PRINT C1

C1
   128.024  127.586  125.278  128.310  128.224  129.229  127.556
   128.540  127.067  127.135  130.415  131.244  129.247  129.973
   127.586  129.017  126.633  128.591  129.509  128.306  127.382
   128.196  128.109  129.544  126.077  126.680

MTB > RANDOM k=23 C2;
SUBC> NORMAL mu=126 sigma=1.9.
MTB > PRINT C2

C2
   124.942  126.980  124.784  124.440  125.095  127.366  128.218
   124.678  125.129  127.799  125.031  125.166  124.414  125.819
   128.886  130.152  127.342  122.964  127.545  126.904  127.039
   125.983  126.789

MTB > DESCRIBE C1 C2

                N    MEAN  MEDIAN  TRMEAN  STDEV  SEMEAN
C1             26  128.21  128.21  128.21   1.36    0.27
C2             23  126.24  125.98  126.21   1.70    0.35

              MIN     MAX      Q1      Q3
C1         125.28  131.24  127.32  129.23
C2         122.96  130.15  124.94  127.37
```

   Does the confidence interval contain the true difference between the two means (2 oz)?

e. Use Minitab to generate your own simulated data. Enter the two sets of commands given below and then repeat parts a, b, c, and d using your own data.

2. Simulate results for a presidential election poll in which the incumbent is favored by exactly 51% of the voters. Given below are the Minitab commands along with sample results coded so that 1 indicates a vote for the incumbent and 0 is a vote against the incumbent.

```
MTB > RANDOM k=200 C4;
SUBC> BERNOULI p=.51.
MTB > PRINT C4
C4
    1  1  0  1  1  0  0  1  0  1  1  0  1  0  1
    1  0  0  1  1  0  1  0  0  0  0  1  1  0  1
    1  0  0  1  0  1  0  1  1  0  0  1  1  0  0
    1  0  0  0  0  1  0  0  0  0  0  1  0  1  1
    0  0  1  1  0  1  0  0  0  1  1  1  1  0  0
    0  0  0  0  1  0  1  0  1  0  0  1  1  0  0
    1  1  1  1  0  1  1  1  0  1  1  0  0  0  0
    0  0  1  0  0  1  0  1  0  0  0  1  1  1  0
    1  1  1  1  1  0  1  1  1  1  1  1  1  1  0
    0  0  0  0  1  0  1  1  1  0  0  1  1  0  0
    1  1  1  1  0  0  0  1  0  1  1  0  0  0  1
    1  1  0  1  1  1  0  1  0  0  1  1  1  1  1
    0  1  0  1  1  1  0  1  0  0  1  1  1  1  1
    0  0  0  0  0
```

```
MTB > HISTOGRAM C4
```

Histogram of C4 N = 200
Each * represents 5 obs.

```
Midpoint  Count
     0      97    *******************
     1     103    ********************
```

After a televised debate between the incumbent and a challenger, there is no change in voting preferences, so the next set of Minitab commands and results simulates the postdebate poll.

```
MTB > RANDOM k=200 C5;
SUBC> BERNOULI p=.51.
MTB > PRINT C5
C5
    1  1  1  1  1  0  0  0  1  1  1  1  1  0  1
    0  1  0  1  1  1  0  1  1  0  1  1  0  0  1
    1  0  1  1  1  1  1  0  1  1  1  1  1  0  1
    1  0  0  1  0  0  0  0  0  1  0  0  0  1  1
    0  0  0  0  1  0  0  0  0  0  1  0  1  0  1
    1  0  1  0  1  1  1  0  0  0  1  0  1  1  0
    0  1  1  0  0  1  0  1  1  1  1  1  0  0  0
    1  1  1  1  0  1  0  1  1  1  1  1  0  1  1
    0  0  1  1  1  1  0  0  1  1  0  1  1  0  0
    0  1  0  0  1  0  0  1  0  1  0  1  1  0  1
    1  0  1  0  0  0  0  1  1  0  1  0  1  0  0
    1  1  0  1  1  1  1  0  0  1  0  0  0  0  0
    0  0  0  0  0  0  1  1  1  0  1  1  1  0  1
    0  1  0  0  1
```

(continued)

HOUSING COSTS: THE PLOT THICKENS

1 You're considering the purchase of a home on a 3-acre lot. Your real estate agent claims that you are getting a good buy because the lot is so large. It might seem reasonable to believe that homes on larger lots should sell for more than comparable homes on smaller lots. Some regions have smaller lots in more-populated areas with greater housing demand and higher prices, however, whereas larger lots are often found in more-rural areas where land is much less expensive. (a) Refer to the real estate data in Appendix B. Find the mean of the 150 lot sizes and form these two samples: sample A, consisting of lots smaller than the mean; sample B, consisting of lots larger than the mean. (b) Test the claim that the mean home selling price is greater for sample B. (c) Based on the results of the hypothesis test in part *b*, is the real estate agent's claim supported? Explain. (d) If you were undecided about buying this house, and this issue of getting a good buy because of the large lot is extremely important to you, what should you decide?

```
MTB > HISTOGRAM C5
Histogram of C5   N = 200
Each * represents 5 obs.

Midpoint  Count
       0     94  *******************
       1    106  ********************
```

a. Test the claim that the proportion of voters supporting the incumbent does not change after the debate. Use a 0.05 level of significance. We know from the Minitab commands that the proportion did not change. Does the result of the hypothesis test support this knowledge?

b. Construct a 95% confidence interval for the difference in the proportions before and after the debate. Does the interval contain the true difference between the population proportions (which we know is zero)?

c. Use Minitab to simulate your own polls (with $p = 0.51$) before and after the debate, then repeat parts *a* and *b* using your data.

CHAPTER 10

Multinomial Experiments and Contingency Tables

10.1 OVERVIEW

Chapter objectives are identified. This chapter introduces some methods for dealing with data from more than two sample groups.

10.2 MULTINOMIAL EXPERIMENTS

This section presents a procedure for testing hypotheses about more than two proportions from a population. We define and consider multinomial experiments.

10.3 CONTINGENCY TABLES

Hypotheses that the row and column variables of contingency tables are independent are tested.

Does the Punishment Fit the Crime?

The banking industry is concerned about "white-collar" crimes. Kate Malloy, president of the Jefferson Valley Bank, claims that the justice system imposes light sentences on those convicted of such crimes. She also claims that the different categories of white-collar crimes are not punished equally as they should be. A researcher randomly selects 400 convictions for such crimes and obtains the results summarized in the table (based on data from the U.S. Department of Justice).

There are really two issues here. First, Ms. Malloy claimed that the sentences are too light. The data in the table show that 172 of the 400 convictions (or 43%) resulted in jail sentences. We can't use methods of statistics here, because arguments that the 43% jail rate is too low are based on subjective opinion. We might note, however, that other Department of Justice data show that there's a 40% jail rate for those convicted of other types of larceny or theft. This suggests that convicts of white-collar crime are jailed at a rate that's not lower than the rate for other similar crimes.

The second issue involves Ms. Malloy's claim that the different categories of white-collar crimes

	SENT TO JAIL	NOT SENT TO JAIL
Embezzlement	22	57
Fraud	130	146
Forgery	20	25

are not punished equally as they should be. The data show that the jail rates are as follows: 28% for convicted embezzlers; 47% for persons convicted of fraud; 44% for convicted forgers. These results do seem to be different. But are those differences significant? Is the sentence (jail or no jail) independent of the type of white-collar crime? We address that question in this chapter.

10.1 OVERVIEW

We noted in Chapter 1 that the nature and configuration of data dramatically affect the type of statistical analyses that can and should be used. For data at the interval or ratio levels of measurement, we can often use methods involving sample statistics such as the mean and standard deviation. For data at the nominal or ordinal levels of measurement (such as pencils categorized as defective or acceptable), we can often use proportions or other tools that make it possible to do some type of statistical analysis. In this chapter we consider data at the nominal or ordinal levels of measurement. In particular, the data will consist of frequency counts for different categories. The configuration of those frequency counts will either be a single row or column (Section 10.2) or a table (Section 10.3). Unlike many methods involving interval or ratio levels of data, the methods of this chapter do not require that the populations in question have a normal distribution or any other particular distribution.

In Section 10.2 we begin by considering a method for testing a hypothesis made about a multinomial experiment, which involves several population proportions. Instead of working with the sample proportions, we deal directly with the frequencies with which the events occur. Our objective is to test for the significance of the differences between observed frequencies and the frequencies we would expect in theory. Because we test for how well an observed frequency distribution conforms to (or "fits") some theoretical distribution, this procedure is often referred to as a goodness-of-fit test. This section introduces the test statistic that measures the differences between observed frequencies and expected frequencies. Using the methods of Section 10.2, we could test claims such as these:

- Defective (or nonconforming) products occur on the different days of the work week in the same proportion.
- Different machines or production methods have the same rate of defects.

In Section 10.3 we analyze tables of frequencies called contingency tables or two-way tables. In these tables, the rows represent categories of one variable, and the columns represent categories of another variable. We test the hypothesis that the two classification variables are independent in the sense that no relationship exists between them. We will determine whether there is a statistically significant difference between the observed sample frequencies and the frequencies we would expect in theory if the two variables are independent. Contingency tables are *extremely* important in many different fields. We can use them to address questions such as these:

- Are sentences (jail or no jail) independent of the types of white-collar crime (embezzlement, fraud, forgery)? (See Table 10.1.)
- Is the quality of Ford transmissions (defective or acceptable) independent of the plants in which they are manufactured (those in the United States or Japan)?

Multinomial experiments and contingency tables (the two major topics of this chapter) share some common elements. They both have test statistics that are approximated by the chi-square distribution (named for the Greek letter chi, or χ) used earlier in Chapters 6 and 7. We should recall these important properties of the chi-square distribution:

FIGURE 10.1
Chi-Square Distribution

FIGURE 10.1
Chi-Square Distribution

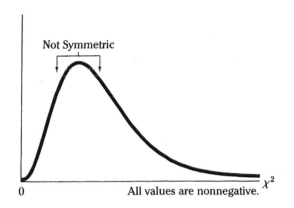

FIGURE 10.2
Two Chi-Square Distributions

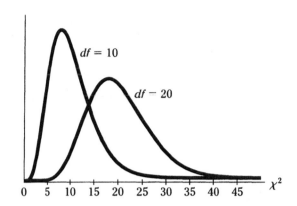

1. Unlike the normal and Student t distributions, the chi-square distribution is not symmetric. (See Fig. 10.1.)
2. The values of the chi-square distribution can be 0 or positive, but they cannot be negative. (See Fig. 10.1.)
3. The chi-square distribution is different for each number of degrees of freedom. (See Fig. 10.2.)

Critical values of the chi-square distribution are found in Table A.4.

10.2   MULTINOMIAL EXPERIMENTS

In Chapter 4 we introduced the binomial probability distribution and indicated that each trial must have all outcomes classified into exactly one of two categories. This requirement for two categories is reflected in the prefix *bi,* which begins the term *binomial.* In this section we consider *multinomial experiments,* which require each trial to yield outcomes belonging to one of several categories. Except for this difference, binomial and multinomial experiments are essentially the same.

DEFINITION

A *multinomial experiment* is one that meets these conditions:

1. The number of trials is fixed.
2. The trials are independent.
3. Each trial must have all outcomes classified into exactly one of several categories.
4. The probabilities for the different categories remain constant for each trial.

TABLE 10.1
Distribution of Industrial Accidents

Day	MON.	TUES.	WED.	THURS.	FRI.
Observed accidents	31	42	18	25	31

We have already discussed methods for testing hypotheses made about one population proportion (Section 7.5) and two population proportions (Section 9.4). However, there is often a need to deal with cases involving a population with more than two proportions. Consider the case involving a study of 147 industrial accidents that required medical attention. The sample data are summarized in Table 10.1, and we will test the claim that accidents occur on the five days with equal frequencies. (The data are based on results from "Counted Data CUSUM's," by Lucas, *Technometrics*, Vol. 27, No. 2.) Because this claim involves equality, it will become the null hypothesis (H_0: $p_1 = p_2 = p_3 = p_4 = p_5$). The alternative hypothesis will be H_1: At least one of the proportions is different.

If accidents occur with equal frequencies on the five different days, the 147 accidents would average out to 29.4 per day. **The expected frequency of an outcome is the product of the probability of that outcome and the total number of trials.** If there are 5 possible outcomes that are supposed to be equally likely, the probability of each outcome is 1/5. For 147 trials and 5 equally likely outcomes, the expected frequency of each outcome is $1/5 \times 147 = 29.4$. Table 10.2 lists the observed frequencies along with the expected frequencies.

We know that samples deviate from what we theoretically expect, so we now present the key question: Do the differences between the actual *observed* values and the theoretically *expected* values occur just by chance, or are the differences statistically significant? To answer this question, we need some way of measuring the significance of the differences between the observed values and the theoretical values.

In testing for the differences among the five sample proportions, one approach might be to compare them two at a time by using the methods given in Section 9.4, but that would involve 10 different pairings and 10 different hypothesis tests. With 10 hypothesis tests, there would be a serious distortion of the significance level because the presence of a difference would be indicated by rejection of the null hypothesis of equality in any one of the 10 tests. Instead of pairing off samples, we will develop one comprehensive test that uses all the data. We will use a test statistic that measures the disagreement between the observed frequencies and the expected frequencies. This test statistic, based on observed and expected frequencies (instead of proportions), is as follows:

TEST STATISTIC

$$\chi^2 = \sum \frac{(O - E)^2}{E}$$

where

O = the *observed frequency* of an outcome
E = the theoretical or *expected frequency* of an outcome

TABLE 10.2
Observed and Expected Industrial Accidents

Day	MON.	TUES.	WED.	THURS.	FRI.
Observed accidents	31	42	18	25	31
Expected accidents	29.4	29.4	29.4	29.4	29.4

From Table 10.2, we see that the O values are 31, 42, 18, 25, and 31, and the corresponding values of E are 29.4, 29.4, 29.4, 29.4, and 29.4. There are five categories.

Simply summing the differences between observed and expected frequencies does not lead to a good measure. That sum is always 0 because ΣO and ΣE are each equal to the total number of all scores combined, denoted by n.

$$\Sigma(O - E) = \Sigma O - \Sigma E = n - n = 0$$

Squaring the $O - E$ values provides a better statistic, which does reflect the differences between observed and expected frequencies, but $\Sigma(O - E)^2$ reflects only the total magnitude of the differences. That sum could be large for two reasons: (1) there are very substantial and significant differences between observed and expected frequencies; and (2) the data sets are very large and the differences between observed and expected frequencies appear to be large, even though those differences are not really significant. We need a measure that expresses a value that is sensitive to only one factor: the differences between observed and expected frequencies. We can effectively eliminate the effect of large sample sizes by using a type of average: Divide each term of $(O - E)^2$ by the expected frequency E. This approach is expressed in the form of the above test statistic. For our accident data, Table 10-2 shows that for Monday, the observed frequency is 31 while the expected frequency is 29.4, so that

$$\frac{(O - E)^2}{E} = \frac{(31 - 29.4)^2}{29.4} = \frac{1.6^2}{29.4} = 0.0871$$

Proceeding in a similar manner with the remaining data, we get

$$\chi^2 = \Sigma \frac{(O - E)^2}{E}$$

$$= \frac{(31 - 29.4)^2}{29.4} + \frac{(42 - 29.4)^2}{29.4} + \frac{(18 - 29.4)^2}{29.4}$$

$$\quad + \frac{(25 - 29.4)^2}{29.4} + \frac{(31 - 29.4)^2}{29.4}$$

$$= 0.0871 + 5.4000 + 4.4204 + 0.6585 + 0.0871$$

$$= 10.653$$

The theoretical distribution of $\Sigma(O - E)^2/E$ is a discrete distribution because the number of possible values is limited. However, this distribution can be approximated by a chi-square distribution. This approximation is generally considered acceptable, provided that all values of E are at least 5. We include this requirement with the assumptions that apply to this section. These assumptions refer to the number of different categories, which we denote by k.

MAGAZINE SURVEYS

Magazines often boost sales through reader surveys, but such surveys are usually biased and reflect only the views of the respondents. A *Time* article on magazine surveys noted that when wives were asked if they had ever had an extramarital affair, the results were 21% yes for *Ladies Home Journal*, 34% yes for *Playboy*, and 54% yes for *Cosmopolitan*. One pollster suggested that a *Reader's Digest* survey "would probably find that *nobody* had any extramarital affairs." When people decide whether or not to include themselves in a survey, the survey is "self-selected" and cannot be considered representative of a larger population.

DID MENDEL FUDGE HIS DATA?

R. A. Fisher analyzed the results of Mendel's experiments in hybridization. Fisher noted that the data were unusually close to theoretically expected outcomes. He says, "The data have evidently been sophisticated systematically, and after examining various possibilities, I have no doubt that Mendel was deceived by a gardening assistant, who knew only too well what his principal expected from each trial made." Fisher used chi-square tests and concluded that only about a 0.00004 probability exists of such close agreement between expected and reported observations.

ASSUMPTIONS

The following assumptions apply when we test a hypothesis that for the k categories of outcomes in a multinomial experiment, the population proportion for each of the k categories is as claimed.

1. The sample data consist of frequency counts for the k different categories, and the data constitute a random sample.
2. For every one of the k categories, the expected frequency is at least 5.

In Section 5.6 we saw that the continuous normal probability distribution can reasonably approximate the discrete binomial probability distribution, provided that np and nq are both at least 5. We now see that the continuous chi-square distribution can reasonably approximate the discrete distribution of $\Sigma(O - E)^2/E$, provided that all values of E are at least 5. There are ways of circumventing the problem of an expected frequency that is less than 5. One procedure simply involves combining categories so that all expected frequencies are at least 5. (See Exercise 15.)

When we use the chi-square distribution as an approximation, we obtain the critical value from Table A.4 after determining the level of significance α and the number of degrees of freedom. In a multinomial experiment with k possible outcomes, the number of degrees of freedom is $k - 1$.

degrees of freedom = $k - 1$

This reflects the fact that for n trials, the frequencies of $k - 1$ outcomes can be freely varied provided they're (1) nonnegative and (2) not so large that the sum of the frequencies doesn't exceed the sample size n. Once the frequencies for $k - 1$ outcomes are determined, the frequency of the last outcome is determined. Our 147 accidents are distributed among 5 categories or cells, but we can freely vary the frequencies of only 4 cells because the last cell would be 147 minus the total of the first 4 cell frequencies. In this case, we say that the number of degrees of freedom is 4.

Note that close *agreement* between observed and expected values will lead to a *small* value of χ^2. A large value of χ^2 will indicate strong disagreement between observed and expected values. A significantly large value of χ^2 will therefore cause rejection of the null hypothesis of no difference between observed and expected frequencies. Our test is right-tailed because the critical value and critical region are located at the extreme right of the distribution. Unlike previous hypothesis tests in which we had to determine whether the test was left-tailed, right-tailed, or two-tailed, **these multinomial tests are all right-tailed.**

For the sample accident data, we have determined the value of the test statistic ($\chi^2 = 10.653$) and the number of degrees of freedom (4). Let's assume a 0.05 level of significance so that $\alpha = 0.05$. With 4 degrees of freedom and $\alpha = 0.05$, Table A.4 indicates a critical value of 9.488.

Figure 10.3 indicates that our test statistic of 10.653 falls within the critical region, so we reject the null hypothesis that accidents occur on the different weekdays with equal frequencies. Examination of the five terms that make up the χ^2 sum of 10.653 shows that Tuesday (5.4000) and Wednesday (4.4204) have the largest differences between observed and expected frequencies and so they contribute most to the total value of χ^2. Further examination of the actual frequencies

FIGURE 10.3
Chi-Square Distribution: Industrial Accident Data

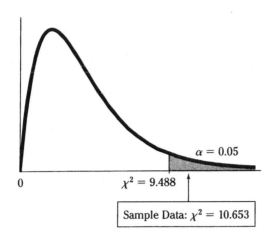

$\alpha = 0.05$

0

$\chi^2 = 9.488$

Sample Data: $\chi^2 = 10.653$

seems to show that Tuesday has a higher accident rate and Wednesday has a lower accident rate. However, such conclusions require additional statistical analysis, such as the methods presented in Chapters 6 and 7 that deal with a single proportion.

The first example of this section dealt with the null hypothesis that the frequencies of accidents on the five working days were all equal. This can be represented as H_0: $p_1 = p_2 = p_3 = p_4 = p_5$, with the alternative hypothesis H_1 being the statement that at least one of the proportions is different. The theory and methods we present here can also be used in cases where the claimed frequencies are different, as in the next example.

EXAMPLE Use a 0.05 significance level and the industrial accident data in Table 10.1 to test the claim that the accidents are distributed on workdays as follows: 30% on Monday, 15% on Tuesday, 15% on Wednesday, 20% on Thursday, and 20% on Friday.

SOLUTION The null hypothesis is the claim that the stated percentages are correct. This leads to the following null and alternative hypotheses:

H_0: $p_1 = 0.30$ and $p_2 = 0.15$ and $p_3 = 0.15$ and $p_4 = 0.20$ and $p_5 = 0.20$.
H_1: At least one of the preceding proportions is not equal to the value claimed.

Before computing the test statistic, we must first determine the values of expected frequency E. According to the claim, we expect 30% of the accidents to occur on Monday. Because 30% of 147 is $0.30 \times 147 = 44.1$, we have $E = 44.1$ for Monday. The expected value E for Tuesday is found by taking 15% of 147, and so on.   *(continued)*

CLASS ATTENDANCE *DOES* HELP

A study of 424 undergraduates at the University of Michigan found that students with the worst attendance records tended to get the lowest grades. (Is anybody surprised?) Those who were absent less than 10% of the time tended to receive grades of B or above. The study also showed that students who sit in the front of the class tend to get significantly better grades.

Day	MON.	TUES.	WED.	THURS.	FRI.
TABLE 10.3 Distribution of Industrial Accidents					
Observed accidents	31	42	18	25	31
Expected accidents	44.1	22.05	22.05	29.4	29.4

Using the observed and expected frequencies from Table 10.3, we now compute the test statistic.

$$\chi^2 = \sum \frac{(O - E)^2}{E}$$

$$= \frac{(31 - 44.1)^2}{44.1} + \frac{(42 - 22.05)^2}{22.05} + \frac{(18 - 22.05)^2}{22.05}$$

$$+ \frac{(25 - 29.4)^2}{29.4} + \frac{(31 - 29.4)^2}{29.4}$$

$$= 3.8914 + 18.0500 + 0.7439 + 0.6585 + 0.0871$$

$$= 23.431$$

This is a right-tailed test with $\alpha = 0.05$ and $5 - 1 = 4$ degrees of freedom, so the critical value from Table A.4 is 9.488. Because the test statistic of $\chi^2 = 23.431$ falls within the critical region, we reject the null hypothesis. The evidence is sufficient to warrant rejection of the claim that the accidents are distributed according to the given percentages.

P-VALUES

The preceding solution follows the traditional approach to hypothesis testing, but the *P*-value approach can also be used. When testing claims involving multinomial experiments, we can find *P*-values by using the same methods introduced in earlier chapters. For example, the preceding example resulted in a test statistic of $\chi^2 = 23.431$, and the critical value was found by using four degrees of freedom. By referring to Table A.4, we see that the test statistic of $\chi^2 = 23.431$ exceeds all the critical values in the row for four degrees of freedom so that the *P*-value for this right-tailed test must be less than 0.005. This implies that there is a very small (less than 0.005) probability of being wrong if we reject the null hypothesis. You can find more-exact *P*-values by using software such as Minitab.

GOODNESS OF FIT

The techniques of this section can be used to test for how well an observed frequency distribution conforms or ''fits'' some theoretical frequency distribution. Such tests are referred to as **goodness-of-fit tests.** When we first considered the employee accident data considered in this section, we used a goodness-of-fit test to decide whether the observed accidents conformed to a uniform distribution, and we found that the differences were significant. It appears that the observed frequencies do not make a good fit with a uniform distribution. Because many statistical analyses require a normally distributed population, we can use the chi-square test in this section to determine whether given samples are drawn from normally distributed populations. (See Exercises 16 and 17.)

10.2 EXERCISES   BASIC CONCEPTS

1. The following table is obtained from a random sample of 100 employee absences at the Acton Paper Company. At the $\alpha = 0.01$ significance level, test the claim that absences occur on the 5 days with equal frequency.

Day	MON.	TUES.	WED.	THURS.	FRI.
Number absent	27	19	22	20	12

   a. Find the χ^2 value based on the sample data.
   b. Find the critical value of χ^2.
   c. What do you conclude about the claim?

2. The Life Trust Insurance Company provides auto insurance in Montana and is analyzing data obtained from fatal crashes. A sample of motor vehicle deaths in Montana is randomly selected for a recent year. The numbers of fatalities are listed below for the different days of the week (based on data from the Insurance Institute for Highway Safety). At the 0.05 significance level, test the claim that accidents occur on the different days with equal frequency.

Day	SUN.	MON.	TUES.	WED.	THURS.	FRI.	SAT.
Number of fatalities	31	20	20	22	22	29	36

3. The Life Trust Insurance Company requires physical exams for life insurance applicants. There is a concern that the exam results from Dr. Lindson are carelessly obtained or are not accurate. One common test for authenticity of data is to analyze the frequencies of digits. When people are weighed and their weights are rounded to the nearest pound, we expect that the digits (0, 1, 2, . . . , 9) will occur with about the same frequency. In contrast, if we *ask* people how much they weigh, the digits 0 and 5 tend to occur at higher rates. When 80 cases are randomly selected from Dr. Lindson's reports and only the last digits are recorded, the results below are obtained. At the 0.01 significance level, test the claim that the last digits occur with the same frequency. Is there sufficient evidence to reject Dr. Lindson's claim that she is actually weighing the patients?

Last digit	0	1	2	3	4	5	6	7	8	9
Frequency	35	0	2	1	4	24	1	4	7	2

4. The Nevada Gaming Supply Company manufactures dice that are supplied to Las Vegas casinos, and it must ensure that the dice are fair and unbiased in the sense that the 6 outcomes are all equally likely. One die is randomly selected from the assembly line and is rolled 100 times with the following results. Test the claim that all 6 outcomes are equally likely. Use a 0.05 level of significance.

Outcome of die	1	2	3	4	5	6
Frequency	17	20	15	16	14	18

5. Given below are outcomes for 100 tosses of a die seized by Baltimore police in a raid on an illegal gambling operation. Test the claim that all 6 outcomes are equally likely. Use a 0.05 level of significance.

Outcome of die	1	2	3	4	5	6
Frequency	7	14	12	18	15	34

6. The Gleason Supermarket manager must decide how much of each flavor of ice cream he should stock so that customer demands are satisfied but unwanted flavors don't result in waste. The ice cream supplier claims that among the 4 most popular flavors, customers have these preference rates: 62% prefer vanilla, 18% prefer chocolate, 12% prefer neapolitan, and 8% prefer vanilla fudge. (The data are based on results from the International Association of Ice Cream Manufacturers.) A random sample of 200 customers produces the results below. At the $\alpha = 0.05$ significance level, test the claim that the percentages given by the supplier are correct.

Flavor	VANILLA	CHOCOLATE	NEAPOLITAN	VANILLA FUDGE
Number preferring	120	40	18	22

7. Among the defective home-video games the Telektronic Company produces, 300 are randomly selected and identified according to the production line that manufactured them. The results are given below. At the 0.05 significance level, test the claim that defects are equally distributed among the different production lines.

Production line	A	B	C	D	E
Number of defects	68	62	57	49	64

8. The Gleason Supermarket manager must make work assignments one week in advance, and he makes them according to the numbers of shoppers expected on different days. A marketing specialist claims that among supermarket shoppers who prefer a particular day, these rates apply: 7% prefer Sunday, 5% prefer Monday, 9% prefer Tuesday, 11% prefer Wednesday, 19% prefer Thursday, 24% prefer Friday, and 25% prefer Saturday. (The data are based on results from the Food Marketing Institute.) Sample results are given here. At the 0.05 significance level, test the claim that the given percentages are correct.

Day	SUN.	MON.	TUES.	WED.	THURS.	FRI.	SAT.
Number preferring	9	6	10	8	19	23	28

9. Nicorette, a chewing gum designed to help people stop smoking cigarettes, was tested for adverse reactions. Among subjects with mouth or throat soreness, 129 are randomly selected and categorized as shown in the table below (based on data from Merrell Dow Pharmaceuticals, Inc.). If the chewing gum and placebo produce the same effect, we would expect (because of different sample sizes) that the given categories have 30.9%, 19.1%, 30.9%, and 19.1% of the subjects, respectively. At the 0.05 significance level, test the claim that the actual frequencies agree with the expected rates.

Subject	CHEWING GUM (U.S.)	CHEWING GUM (BRITISH)	PLACEBO (U.S.)	PLACEBO (BRITISH)
Number with soreness	35	33	30	31

10. Among drivers who have had an accident in the last year, 88 are randomly selected and categorized by age, with the results listed below (based on data from the Insurance Information Institute). If all ages have the same accident rate, we would expect (because of the age distribution of licensed drivers) that the given categories have 16%, 44%, 27%, and 13% of the subjects, respectively. At the 0.05 significance level, test the claim that the actual frequencies agree with the expected rates.

Age	UNDER 25	25–44	45–64	Over 64
Number	36	21	12	19

11. Every car manufacturer must decide how many cars to paint with each available color. A study of the color choices for buyers of compact cars claims that among the 5 most frequent choices, these preference rates apply: 22% prefer light red/brown, 22% prefer white, 20% prefer light blue, 18% prefer dark blue, and 18% prefer red. (The data are based on results from the Automotive Information Center.) When 270 compact cars are randomly selected, the following results are found. At the 0.05 level of significance, test the claim that the given percentages are correct.

Color	LT. RED/BROWN	WHITE	LT. BLUE	DK. BLUE	RED
Frequency	60	61	43	41	65

12. NBC is told by a consulting firm that its 8 leading TV shows are favored according to the percentages given in the following table. A separate and independent sample is obtained by another consulting firm. Do the figures from the second consultant agree with the percentages claimed by the first consultant? Assume a significance level of 0.05.

Show	A	B	C	D	E	F	G	H
First consultant	22%	18%	12%	12%	10%	9%	9%	8%
Second consultant (number of respondents favoring show)	29	30	20	16	9	17	10	19

13. An employee in the telemarketing department of the Delaney and Taylor Advertising Company records orders for advertisements to be placed in the Yellow pages of a telephone directory. After reviewing 5000 such ads, she found that 78% had no errors, 12% had exactly one error, 7% had exactly two errors, and 3% had three or more errors. A new order form is designed in an attempt to improve quality by reducing the numbers of errors. After reviewing 200 randomly selected ads placed with the new form, the following results are obtained.

Number of errors	0	1	2	3 or more
Number of orders	182	14	3	1

Test the claim that the new form doesn't affect the error rates. Use a 0.05 significance level.

14. The Wilson Drugstore chain has 5 stores in the Chicago area. Unhappy customers can file complaints with the national office. A regional manager randomly selects 90 such complaints from the Chicago area and classifies them according to the stores from which they came. The results follow.

Store	1	2	3	4	5
Number of complaints	15	31	20	17	7

a. Test the claim that when a complaint from the Chicago area is randomly selected, there is the same chance that it comes from any one of the 5 stores. Use a 0.05 level of significance.

b. Construct a 95% confidence interval for the proportion of complaints from the store that appears to be the worst, and also construct a 95% confidence interval for the proportion of complaints from the store that appears to be the best.

10.2 EXERCISES   BEYOND THE BASICS

15. In a survey of radio listeners, data are collected for different time slots, beginning at 1:00 P.M. The results are listed along with the expected frequencies based on past surveys. We cannot use the chi-square distribution, because all expected values are not at least 5. However, we can combine some columns so that all expected values do equal or exceed 5. Use this suggestion to test the claim that the observed and expected frequencies are compatible. Try to combine categories in a meaningful way.

Time slot	1	2	3	4	5	6	7	8	9	10
Observed frequency	2	8	8	9	3	5	3	0	12	3
Expected frequency	4	5	8	7	4	6	5	2	9	3

16. An observed frequency distribution of IQ scores is shown on the following page, and we will test for goodness of fit with a normal distribution with a mean of 100 and a standard deviation of 15.

a.   Assuming a normal distribution with $\mu = 100$ and $\sigma = 15$, use the methods given in Chapter 5 to find the probability of a randomly selected subject belonging to each class. (The class boundaries are 79.5, 95.5, 110.5, 120.5.)

b.   Using the probabilities found in part a, find the expected frequency for each category.

c.   Use a 0.01 level of significance to test the claim that the IQ scores were randomly selected from a normally distributed population with $\mu = 100$ and $\sigma = 15$.

IQ score	UNDER 80	80–95	96–110	111–120	ABOVE 120
Frequency	20	20	80	40	40

17. An observed frequency distribution is given below, and we will test for goodness of fit with a binomial distribution for which $n = 3$ and $p = 1/3$.

a.   Assuming a binomial distribution with $n = 3$ and $p = 1/3$, use the binomial probability formula to find the probability corresponding to each category of the table.

b.   Using the probabilities found in part a, find the expected frequency for each category.

c.   Use a 0.05 level of significance to test the claim that the observed frequencies fit a binomial distribution for which $n = 3$ and $p = 1/3$.

Number of successes	0	1	2	3
Frequency	89	133	52	26

d.   Show that

$$\sum \frac{(O - E)^2}{E} = \left(\sum \frac{O^2}{E} \right) - n$$

where n is the sum of all frequencies, then repeat part c using this latter form of the test statistic.

18. In this exercise we will show that a hypothesis test involving a multinomial experiment with only two categories is equivalent to a hypothesis test for a proportion (Section 7.5). Assume that a particular multinomial experiment has only two possible outcomes A and B with observed frequencies of f_1 and f_2, respectively.

a.   Find an expression for the χ^2 test statistic and find the critical value for a 0.05 significance level. Assume that we are testing the claim that both categories have the same frequency $(f_1 + f_2)/2$.

b.   The test statistic

$$z = \frac{\hat{p} - p}{\sqrt{\dfrac{pq}{n}}}$$

is used to test the claim that a population proportion is equal to some value p. With the claim that $p = 0.5$, with $\alpha = 0.05$, and with

$$\hat{p} = \frac{f_1}{f_1 + f_2}$$

show that z^2 is equivalent to χ^2 (from part a). Also show that the square of the critical z score is equal to the critical χ^2 value from part a.

10.3 CONTINGENCY TABLES

Section 10.2 involved frequencies listed in a single row (or column) according to category, and this section also involves frequencies listed according to category, but here we consider cases with at least two rows and at least two columns. For example, Table 10.4 on page 452 has two rows (jail, no jail) and three columns (embezzlement, fraud, forgery). Tables similar to Table 10.4 are generally called contingency tables or two-way tables.

> **DEFINITION**
>
> A *contingency table* (or *two-way table*) consists of rows representing categories of one variable, columns representing categories of a second variable, and entries consisting of *frequencies* corresponding to the various rows and columns. It is used to analyze the dependence between the two variables.

In this context, the word *contingency* refers to dependence, but it is only a statistical dependence that cannot be used to establish a direct cause-effect link between the two variables in question. For example, after analyzing the data of Table 10.4, we might conclude that a relationship exists between the sentence and the category of crime, but that doesn't mean that the crime category is a direct *cause* of the sentence.

ASSUMPTIONS

When working with data in the form of a contingency table, we test the hypothesis that the row variable and the column variable are *independent,* and the following assumptions apply. (Note that those assumptions do *not* require the parent population to have a normal distribution or any other particular distribution.)

1. The sample data are randomly selected.
2. For every cell in the contingency table, the *expected* frequency E is at least 5.

Our hypothesis test uses the following test statistic.

> **TEST STATISTIC**
>
> $$\chi^2 = \sum \frac{(O - E)^2}{E}$$

This test statistic allows us to measure the degree of disagreement between the frequencies actually observed and those that we would theoretically expect when the two variables are independent. The reasons underlying the development of the χ^2 statistic in the previous section also apply here. In repeated large samplings, *the distribution of the test statistic χ^2 can be approximated by the chi-square distribution provided that all expected frequencies are at least 5.* We include this requirement with the assumptions that apply to this section.

The critical values are found in Table A.4. There are two important items to consider.

1. **Tests of independence with contingency tables involve only right-tailed critical regions.**
2. In a contingency table with r rows and c columns, the number of degrees of freedom is given by the following:

$$\text{degrees of freedom} = (r - 1)(c - 1)$$

Small values of the χ^2 test statistic support the claimed independence of the two variables. That is, χ^2 is small if observed and expected frequencies are close. Large values of χ^2 are to the right of the chi-square distribution, and they reflect significant differences between observed and expected frequencies. The number of degrees of freedom $(r - 1)(c - 1)$ reflects the fact that because we know the total of all frequencies in a contingency table, we can freely assign frequencies to only $r - 1$ rows and $c - 1$ columns before the frequency for every cell is determined. (We say that we can "freely" assign frequencies to $r - 1$ rows and $c - 1$ columns, but we cannot have negative frequencies nor can we have frequencies so large that their sum exceeds the total of the frequencies for all cells combined.)

In the preceding section we knew the corresponding probabilities and could easily determine the expected values, but the typical contingency table does not come with the relevant probabilities. Consequently, we need to devise a method for obtaining the corresponding expected values. We will first describe the procedure for finding the values of the expected frequencies, and then proceed to justify the procedure. For each cell in the frequency table, the expected frequency E can be calculated by using the following:

$$\text{Expected frequency } E = \frac{(\text{row total}) \cdot (\text{column total})}{(\text{grand total})}$$

Here *grand total* refers to the total number of observations in the table. For example, in the upper left cell of Table 10.4, we see the observed frequency of 22. The total of all frequencies for that row is 172, the total of the column frequencies is 79, and the total of all frequencies in the table is 400, so the expected frequency for that upper left cell is computed as follows:

$$E = \frac{(172)\,(79)}{400} = 33.97$$

TABLE 10.4
Contingency Table: Observed and Expected Frequencies

	EMBEZZLEMENT	FRAUD	FORGERY	
Sent to jail	22 (33.97)	130 (118.68)	20 (19.35)	172
Not sent to jail	57 (45.03)	146 (157.32)	25 (25.65)	228
	79	276	45	(Grand total: 400)

TABLE 10.5
Finding Expected Frequencies

	EMBEZZLEMENT	FRAUD	FORGERY	
Sent to jail				172
Not sent to jail				228
	79	276	45	(Grand total: 400)

In the upper left cell, the *observed* frequency is 22, and the *expected* frequency is 33.97. Table 10.4 shows the expected frequencies inserted in parentheses. As in Section 10.2, we require all expected frequencies to be at least 5 before we can conclude that the chi-square distribution serves as a suitable approximation to the distribution of the test statistic χ^2 values.

To better understand the rationale for this procedure, let's pretend that we know only the row and column totals and that we must determine the cell frequencies by assuming that sentence and category of crime are independent. (That is, there is no relationship between the two variables involved. See Table 10.5.)

We begin with the cell in the upper left corner that corresponds to embezzlers who were jailed. Because 172 of the 400 convicts were jailed, we have $P(\text{jail}) = 172/400$. Similarly, 79 of the 400 convicts are embezzlers, so that $P(\text{embezzler}) = 79/400$. Because we assume that sentence and category of crime are independent, we conclude that

$$P(\text{jail and embezzler}) = \frac{172}{400} \times \frac{79}{400}$$

This follows from the multiplication rule of probability whereby $P(A \text{ and } B) = P(A) \times P(B)$ if A and B are independent events. To obtain the expected value for the upper left cell, we simply multiply the probability for that cell by the total number of subjects available to get

$$\frac{172}{400} \times \frac{79}{400} \times 400 = 33.97$$

The form of this product suggests a general way to obtain the expected frequency of a cell when we assume there is no relationship between the row and column variables:

$$\text{Expected frequency } E = \frac{(\text{row total})}{(\text{grand total})} \cdot \frac{(\text{column total})}{(\text{grand total})} \cdot (\text{grand total})$$

The above expression can be simplified by using division to cancel out the common factor of "grand total." The result is shown below and it is the expression we use for finding the expected frequency for an individual category (or cell).

$$E = \frac{(\text{row total}) \cdot (\text{column total})}{(\text{grand total})}$$

We can now proceed to use contingency table data for testing hypotheses, as in the following example that uses the data given in the problem described at the beginning of the chapter.

EXAMPLE At the 0.05 significance level, use the data in Table 10.4 to test the claim that the sentence (jail, no jail) is independent of the category of crime (embezzlement, fraud, forgery).

SOLUTION The null and alternative hypotheses are as follows:

H_0: The sentence and crime category are independent.
H_1: The sentence and crime category are dependent.

The significance level is $\alpha = 0.05$. Because the data are in the form of a contingency table, we use the χ^2 distribution with this test statistic:

$$\chi^2 = \sum \frac{(O - E)^2}{E}$$

$$= \frac{(22 - 33.97)^2}{33.97} + \frac{(130 - 118.68)^2}{118.68} + \cdots + \frac{(25 - 25.65)^2}{25.65}$$

$$= 4.2179 + 1.0797 + \cdots + 0.0165$$

$$= 9.332$$

The critical value of $\chi^2 = 5.991$ is found from Table A.4 by noting that $\alpha = 0.05$ in the right tail and the number of degrees of freedom is $(r - 1)(c - 1) = (2 - 1)(3 - 1) = 2$. The test statistic and critical value are shown in Fig. 10.4. Because the test statistic falls within the critical region, we reject the null hypothesis that the sentence and the crime category are independent. It appears that the sentence and the category of crime are dependent. That is, the chances of going to jail appear to vary, depending on the category of crime that has been committed.

FIGURE 10.4
Chi-Square Distribution for Crime Data

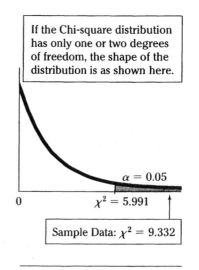

If the Chi-square distribution has only one or two degrees of freedom, the shape of the distribution is as shown here.

$\alpha = 0.05$

0          $\chi^2 = 5.991$

Sample Data: $\chi^2 = 9.332$

Because of the large number of calculations required, it is often helpful to use a statistical software package for tests of the type discussed in this section. The accompanying Minitab display shows the results obtained for the data of Table 10.4. Note that the test statistic of $\chi^2 = 9.332$ is included along with the row totals, column totals, grand total, expected values, and degrees of freedom. Note that neither the critical value nor the P-value is included.

```
MTB > READ C1 C2 C3
DATA> 22 130 20
DATA> 57 146 25
DATA> ENDOFDATA
DATA> ENDOFDATA     2 ROWS READ
MTB > CHISQUARE C1 C2 C3

Expected counts are printed below observed counts

            C1        C2        C3     Total
    1       22       130        20       172
          33.97    118.68     19.35

    2       57       146        25       228
          45.03    157.32     25.65

Total       79       276        45       400

ChiSq = 4.218 + 1.080 + 0.022 +
        3.182 + 0.815 + 0.016 = 9.332
df = 2
```

P-VALUES

The preceding example used the traditional approach to hypothesis testing, but we can again find P-values by using the same methods introduced earlier. The preceding example resulted in a test statistic of $\chi^2 = 9.332$ and the critical value involved two degrees of freedom. Refer to Table A.4 and note that for the row with two degrees of freedom, the test statistic of $\chi^2 = 9.332$ falls between the critical values of 9.210 and 10.597 so that the P-value must fall between the corresponding areas of 0.01 and 0.005. We can express this as follows:

$$0.005 < P\text{-value} < 0.01$$

Based on this relatively small P-value, we again reject the null hypothesis and conclude that the sample evidence is sufficient to warrant rejection of the claim that the sentence and the category of crime are independent. It appears that they are dependent. If the P-value had been greater than the significance level of 0.05, then we would have failed to reject the null hypothesis of independence.

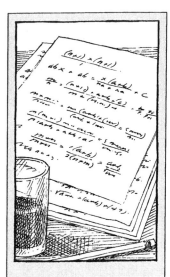

CHEATING SUCCESS

Eighteen students from a high school in a depressed area of Los Angeles took an Advanced Placement test in calculus and they all passed. Representatives of the Educational Testing Service challenged the validity of 14 students' results. A retest of 12 of the students confirmed the original scores; the students knew their calculus. What appeared to be cheating was actually the result of hard work by a group of dedicated students and an exceptional teacher, Jaime Escalante. His accomplishments were later dramatized in the movie *Stand and Deliver.*

10.3 EXERCISES   BASIC CONCEPTS

1. Nicorette is a chewing gum designed to help people stop smoking cigarettes. Tests for adverse reactions yield the results given in the accompanying table (based on data from Merrell Dow Pharmaceuticals, Inc.). At the 0.05 significance level, test the claim that the treatment (drug or placebo) is independent of the reaction (whether or not mouth or throat soreness was experienced).

	DRUG	PLACEBO
Soreness	43	35
No soreness	109	118

2. In the judicial case *United States* v. *City of Chicago,* fair employment practices were challenged. A minority group (group A) and a majority group (group B) took the Fire Captain Examination. At the 0.05 significance level, use the given results and test the claim that success on the test is independent of the group.

	PASS	FAIL
Group A	10	14
Group B	417	145

3. Companies such as Campbell Soup and Procter & Gamble want to target their advertising to the consumers who actually do the shopping. The marketing manager for *Independent Gentleman* magazine tries to attract more advertising by claiming that more men shop now than in the past and the type of item purchased isn't related to the gender of the buyer. Given below are sample survey results (based on data from Nielsen Homescan). At the 0.05 significance level, test the claim that the category of the item purchased is independent of the gender of the shopper.

	FROZEN FOODS	DETERGENT	SOUP
Female	203	73	142
Male	97	27	58

4. Four separate machines mold the same plastic parts that are used in cellular telephones. A random sample of 400 such parts is obtained, and each part is identified according to its machine and whether it is acceptable or defective. The results are given below. At the 0.05 level of significance, test the claim that the machine is independent of whether a part is acceptable or defective. Identify the *P*-value.

	MACHINE A	MACHINE B	MACHINE C	MACHINE D
Defective	9	7	10	16
Acceptable	111	103	105	39

5. A study of car accidents and drivers who use cellular phones provided the following sample data. (The data are based on results from AT&T and the Automobile Association of America.) At the 0.05 level of significance, test the claim that the occurrence of accidents is independent of the use of cellular phones.

	HAD ACCIDENT IN LAST YEAR	HAD NO ACCIDENT IN LAST YEAR
Cellular phone user	23	282
Not a cellular phone user	46	407

6. A random sample of 500 one-gallon containers of antifreeze is taken from a Chemco Company production process that uses two filling machines. The contents are categorized as underfilled, acceptable, or overfilled, and the results are summarized in the table below. Use the accompanying Minitab display to test the claim that the category of filling is independent of the machine. Use a 0.05 level of significance.

	UNDERFILLED	ACCEPTABLE	OVERFILLED
Machine A	11	205	14
Machine B	47	181	42

```
MTB > READ C4 C5 C6
DATA> 11 205 14
DATA> 47 181 42
DATA> END OF DATA
      2 ROWS READ
MTB > CHISQUARE C4 C5 C6

Expected counts are printed below observed counts
            C4          C5          C6      Total
    1       11         205          14        230
          26.68      177.56       25.76

    2       47         181          42        270
          31.32      208.44       30.24

Total       58         386          56        500

ChiSq = 9.215 + 4.241 + 5.369 +
        7.850 + 3.612 + 4.573 = 34.860
df = 2
```

7. A quality control manager randomly selects 275 defective office chairs requiring rework before shipment. The defects are classified according to type and according to the shift during which they were made. The results are summarized in the table on the next page. Use the accompanying Minitab display to test the claim that the category of defect is independent of the shift. Use a 0.05 level of significance.

	SHIFT 1	SHIFT 2	SHIFT 3
Material cutting defect	15	26	22
Defective assembly	37	37	16
Finishing defect	45	69	8

```
MTB > CHISQUARE C1 C2 C3
Expected counts are printed below observed counts

          C1        C2        C3      Total
    1      15        26        22       63
        22.22     30.24     10.54

    2      37        37        16       90
        31.75     43.20     15.05

    3      45        69         8      122
        43.03     58.56     20.41

Total     97       132        46      275
ChiSq = 2.347 + 0.594 + 12.466 +
        0.870 + 0.890 + 0.059 +
        0.090 + 1.861 + 7.543 = 26.721
df = 4
```

8. Many companies make extensive use of surveys, and there is an increasing concern that growing numbers of potential survey respondents are refusing to cooperate. A study of people who refused to answer survey questions provided the sample data in the table (based on data from "I Hear You Knocking But You Can't Come In," by Fitzgerald and Fuller, *Sociological Methods and Research,* Vol. 11, No. 1). Use the accompanying Minitab display to test the claim that the cooperation of the subject (response/refuse) is independent of the age category. Use a 0.01 significance level.

	AGE (YEARS)					
	18–21	22–29	30–39	40–49	50–59	60 and over
Responded	73	255	245	136	138	202
Refused	11	20	33	16	27	49

```
MTB > READ C1 C2 C3 C4 C5 C6
DATA> 73 255 245 136 138 202
DATA> 11 20 33 16 27 49
DATA> END OF DATA
      2 ROWS READ
MTB > CHISQUARE C1 C2 C3 C4 C5 C6
```

(continued)

SIMPSON'S PARADOX

Suppose a random sample of 400 watches from a Detroit factory has 16 that are defective, and a sample of 1000 watches from an Orlando factory has 60 defects. The *Detroit* factory seems better because its 4% rate of defects is lower than Orlando's 6%. But the Detroit sample has 300 men's watches (with 8 defects) and 100 women's watches (with 8 defects), whereas the Orlando sample has 300 men's watches (with 6 defects) and 700 women's watches (with 54 defects). Now it seems that the *Orlando* factory is doing better because its defect rates (2% for men and 7.7% for women) are lower than those rates for the Detroit factory (2.7% for men and 8% for women). This is an example of Simpson's paradox.

Expected counts are printed below observed counts

	C1	C2	C3	C4	C5	C6	Total
1	73	255	245	136	138	202	1049
	73.13	239.40	242.01	132.32	143.64	218.51	
2	11	20	33	16	27	49	156
	10.87	35.60	35.99	19.68	21.36	32.49	
Total	84	275	278	152	165	251	1205

ChiSq = 0.000 + 1.017 + 0.037 + 0.102 + 0.221 + 1.247 +
        0.001 + 6.837 + 0.248 + 0.687 + 1.489 + 8.384
      = 20.271
df = 5

9. The following table provides sample data from a study of dropout rates among college freshmen. At the 0.05 significance level, test the claim that the type of college is independent of the dropout rate. (The sample data are based on results from the American College Testing Program.)

	FOUR-YEAR PUBLIC	FOUR-YEAR PRIVATE	TWO-YEAR PUBLIC	TWO-YEAR PRIVATE
Freshmen dropouts	10	9	15	9
Freshmen who stay	26	28	18	27

10. The following table summarizes results from randomly selected drivers convicted of motor vehicle violations in New York State. (The data are based on results from the New York State Department of Motor Vehicles.) At the 0.05 significance level, test the claim that the county is independent of the type of violation. (DWI is driving while intoxicated and DTD is driving with a disabled traffic device, such as a broken tail light.)

	ALBANY	MONROE	ORANGE	WESTCHESTER
DWI	6	19	6	10
Speeding	103	261	160	226
DTD	60	152	25	174

11. A marketing study is conducted to determine whether Maine Muffins' appeal is affected by geographical region. Given the sample data in the following table, use a 0.01 significance level to test the claim that the consumer's opinion is independent of region.

	LIKE	DISLIKE	UNCERTAIN
Northeast	30	15	15
Southeast	10	30	20
West	40	60	15

12. A tobacco industry marketing strategist conducts a study to determine the rates of smokers among persons from different age groups. The study led to the following sample data (based on data from the National Center for Health Statistics). At the 0.05 significance level, test the claim that smoking is independent of the four listed age groups.

	AGE (YEARS)			
	20–24	25–34	35–44	45–64
Smoke	18	15	17	15
Don't smoke	32	35	33	35

10.3   EXERCISES   BEYOND THE BASICS

13. The chi-square distribution is continuous, whereas the test statistic used in this section is actually discrete. Some statisticians use **Yates' correction for continuity** in cells with an expected frequency less than 10 or in all cells of a contingency table with two rows and two columns. With Yates' correction, we replace

$$\sum \frac{(O - E)^2}{E} \quad \text{with} \quad \sum \frac{(|O - E| - 0.5)^2}{E}$$

Given the accompanying contingency table, find the value of the χ^2 test statistic with and without Yates' correction. In general, what effect does Yates' correction have on the value of the test statistic?

	X	Y
A	5	25
B	65	5

14. If each observed frequency in a contingency table is multiplied by a positive integer K (where $K \geq 2$), how is the value of the test statistic affected? How is the critical value affected?

15. a. For the contingency table shown here, verify that the test statistic becomes

$$\chi^2 = \frac{(a + b + c + d)(ad - bc)^2}{(a + b)(c + d)(b + d)(a + c)}$$

	COLUMN	
	1	2
Row 1	a	b
Row 2	c	d

b. Let $\hat{p}_1 = a/(a + c)$ and let $\hat{p}_2 = b/(b + d)$ and show that the test statistic

$$z = \frac{(\hat{p}_1 - \hat{p}_2) - 0}{\sqrt{\bar{p}\bar{q}\left(\frac{1}{n_1} + \frac{1}{n_2}\right)}}$$

is such that $z^2 = \chi^2$ (the same result from part a). This shows that the chi-square test involving a 2 × 2 table is equivalent to the test for the difference between two proportions, as described in Section 9.4.

Vocabulary List

Define and give an example of each term.

multinomial experiment
observed frequency
expected frequency
goodness-of-fit tests
contingency table
two-way table

Review

We began this chapter by developing methods for testing hypotheses made about more than two population proportions. For *multinomial experiments* we tested for goodness of fit or agreement between observed and expected frequencies by using the chi-square test statistic given in the table that follows. In repeated large samplings, the distribution of the χ^2 test statistic can be approximated by the chi-square distribution. This approximation is generally considered acceptable as long as all expected frequencies are at least 5. In a multinomial experiment with k cells or categories, the number of degrees of freedom is $k - 1$.

In Section 10.3 we used the sample χ^2 test statistic to measure disagreement between observed and expected frequencies in *contingency tables*. A contingency table contains frequencies; the rows correspond to categories of one variable and the columns correspond to categories of another variable. With contingency tables, we test the hypothesis that the two variables of classification are independent. In this test of independence, we can again approximate the sampling distribution of that statistic by the chi-square distribution as long as all expected frequencies are at least 5. In a contingency table with r rows and c columns, the number of degrees of freedom is $(r - 1)(c - 1)$.

Chapter 7 introduced the important method of hypothesis testing, but that chapter was limited to cases involving a single population. In this chapter we again discussed hypothesis testing, but we considered these very different configurations of data: frequency counts in multinomial experiments and frequency counts in contingency tables.

Important Formulas

APPLICATION	APPLICABLE DISTRIBUTION	TEST STATISTIC	DEGREES OF FREEDOM	TABLE OF CRITICAL VALUES
Multinomial	Chi-square	$\chi^2 = \sum \dfrac{(O - E)^2}{E}$	$k - 1$	Table A.4
Contingency table	Chi-square	$\chi^2 = \sum \dfrac{(O - E)^2}{E}$ where $E = \dfrac{(\text{row total})(\text{column total})}{(\text{grand total})}$	$(r - 1)(c - 1)$	Table A.4

Review Exercises

1. A Gleason Supermarket advertisement claims that "people are twice as likely to use our generic brand (A) of toothpaste over brands B or C." Results from a random sample of 400 persons are summarized in the following table. Test the advertising claim ($p_A = 0.50$, $p_B = 0.25$, $p_C = 0.25$) by using a 0.05 significance level.

Brand	A (GENERIC)	B	C
Number preferring	209	97	94

2. Clinical tests of the allergy drug Seldane were conducted. Among subjects who experienced drowsiness, 212 were randomly selected and categorized as shown in the table below (based on data from Merrell Dow Pharmaceuticals, Inc.). At the 0.05 significance level, test the claim that those who experience drowsiness are equally distributed among the three categories.

Group	SELDANE USERS	PLACEBO USERS	CONTROL
Experienced drowsiness	54	49	109

3. Clinical tests of the allergy drug Seldane yielded results summarized in the table (based on data from Merrell Dow Pharmaceuticals, Inc.). At the 0.05 significance level, test the claim that the occurrence of headaches is independent of the group (Seldane/placebo/control).

	SELDANE USERS	PLACEBO USERS	CONTROL
Headache	49	49	24
No headache	732	616	602

4. The Magellan Travel Agency uses 4 agents to book trips. In a random survey of 350 clients, results are categorized according to the degree of satisfaction and according to the agent who did the booking. The results are summarized below along with the Minitab display. Test the claim that the degree of satisfaction is independent of the booking agent. Identify the P-value.

	AGENT A	AGENT B	AGENT C	AGENT D
Very satisfied	50	39	20	35
Satisfied	54	46	47	32
Dissatisfied	6	5	13	3

```
MTB > CHISQUARE C1 C2 C3 C4
     .
     .
     .

ChiSq =  0.497 + 0.105 + 5.067 + 1.335 +
         0.091 + 0.000 + 0.905 + 0.403 +
         0.728 + 0.544 + 7.556 + 1.067 = 18.297
df = 6
```

5. The quality control manager of a photocopy machine production process is concerned about the high cost of reworking defective machines. In attempting to determine causes of defects, she collects the following sample data. Test the claim that the day of the week is independent of product quality.

	MON.	TUES.	WED.	THURS.	FRI.
Acceptable products	80	100	95	93	82
Defective products	15	5	5	7	12

6. In the Northeast, a survey of companies that officially declared bankruptcy during the past year yielded the following sample data. Of the 120 small bankrupt businesses, 72 advertised in weekly newspapers. Of the 65 medium-sized bankrupt businesses, 25 advertised in weekly newspapers, while 8 of the 15 large bankrupt businesses did so. At the 0.05 level of significance, test the claim that the size of the bankrupt company is independent of whether it advertised in weekly newspapers.

Computer Project

Let's stipulate that the numbers 1, 2, and 3 represent three different types of pizza dough that are being tested on consumers. Each consumer tastes all three dough types and selects the one preferred. Minitab and other statistical software packages can be used to simulate this multinomial distribution. Given below are the Minitab commands that will generate 100 sample results from a multinomial distribution having possible outcomes of 1, 2, and 3 with the corresponding probabilities of 0.30, 0.50, and 0.20, respectively.

a. Use the displayed results to test the claim that consumers like all three types of pizza dough equally. Use a 0.05 level of significance. Identify the P-value.
b. Find the pizza dough type with the highest sample proportion and construct a 95% confidence interval for this single proportion.
c. Use Minitab to run your own simulation of 100 consumers who taste the three types of pizza dough. Using your data, repeat parts a, b, and c.

```
MTB > READ C1 C2
DATA> 1 .300
DATA> 2 .500
DATA> 3 .200
DATA> END OF DATA
     3 ROWS READ
MTB > RANDOM n=100 C5;
SUBC> DISCRETE VALUES C1 prob C2.
MTB > PRINT C5

C5
    1  2  3  1  3  1  1  1  2  2  2  2  2  3  2
    2  3  2  3  2  1  3  1  1  2  2  2  1  1  2
    3  1  3  1  2  1  1  2  2  3  3  2  1  1  2
    2  1  3  3  1  1  2  3  2  2  2  1  1  1  3
    2  2  2  2  2  2  2  1  3  2  2  1  1  2  2
    1  2  2  2  1  1  3  2  2  2  2  1  1  1  2
    2  2  1  1  1  2  1  2  1  3
```

MUST A LARGE HOME HAVE MORE THAN ONE BATHROOM?

A real estate agent is trying to convince you to buy a large home that has only one bathroom. She argues that the number of bathrooms has nothing to do with the size of the home.

a. Using the Appendix B data for homes sold, enter the frequencies in the table below.

	1 OR 1.5 BATHS	2 OR MORE BATHS
Under 2000 sq ft		
2000 sq ft or more		

Use this data to test the claim that the number of baths is independent of the living area.

b. Based on the data and your results, are you inclined to agree with the agent's claim that the number of bathrooms has nothing to do with the size of the home? Write a brief response that either supports the agent's claim or refutes it.

c. Identify one important and practical consequence of making a type I error. (Type I errors are described in Section 7.2.)

d. Identify one important and practical consequence of making a type II error. (Type II errors are described in Section 7.2.)

CHAPTER 11

Analysis of Variance

11.1 OVERVIEW

Chapter objectives are identified. This chapter introduces methods for testing the hypothesis that several population means are equal, so the differences among the sample means are due only to chance.

11.2 ONE-WAY ANOVA

This section deals with cases involving three or more populations or stable processes. A random sample is drawn from each population, and we proceed to use analysis of variance (ANOVA) to test the claim that three or more population means are equal. The *t* test for two *independent* population means was presented in Chapter 9, and in this section we extend that test to one-way ANOVA as a way of testing for equality of three or more population means.

11.3 ANOVA FOR A RANDOMIZED BLOCK DESIGN

In this section the technique of analysis of variance is extended to include blocking, in which data are arranged according to one characteristic, and then samples for each type of a second characteristic are selected. This will allow us to better control the variability caused by one characteristic so that we can better compare the effects of the second characteristic. This technique serves as an extension of the Chapter 9 *t* test for two *dependent* samples; this section will involve testing the equality of three or more population means.

Which Type of Minivan Should Be Bought?

It is a common belief that vehicles with manual transmissions get much better gas mileage than those with automatic transmissions. Is that actually true? Let's consider the specific case of a utility company considering the purchase of a minivan fleet. The company has concerns about the fuel consumption rates (in mi/gal). Tests are conducted and it is found that three different transmission types are used in a sample group of 12 different minivans, all having 6 cylinders and an engine size of 3.0 liters. Among the 12 minivans, 4 have automatic transmissions (denoted by A), 5 have manual transmissions (denoted by M), and 3 have lockup torque converters (denoted by L). For each vehicle, the fuel consumption (in mi/gal) is measured under iden-tical highway conditions and the results are given below (based on data from the Environmental Protection Agency). Does the type of transmission have an effect on fuel consumption? The sample means of 21.75, 25.60, and 24.67 are different, but are those differences statistically significant?

A	M	L
23	27	24
23	29	26
20	25	24
21	23	
	24	

$n_1 = 4$	$n_2 = 5$	$n_3 = 3$
$\bar{x}_1 = 21.75$	$\bar{x}_2 = 25.60$	$\bar{x}_3 = 24.67$
$s_1^2 = 2.25$	$s_2^2 = 5.80$	$s_3^2 = 1.33$

The problem we have described might seem similar to problems we have already discussed in Chapter 9. However, in Chapter 9 we tested for equality between two means, whereas this problem requires a test for equality among three means. We might expect that we could use the same methods from Chapter 9, but that is not the case. This chapter will present a new method that can be used with problems such as the one described here.

OVERVIEW

In Section 9.3 we developed procedures for testing the hypothesis that two population means are equal (H_0: $\mu_1 = \mu_2$). In this chapter we develop methods for using sample variances to test the hypothesis that differences among three or more sample means are due to chance.

DEFINITION

***Analysis of variance* (ANOVA) involves methods for testing equality of sample means by analyzing sample variances.**

Among applications of ANOVA are the following:

- When minivans are arranged into three different groups according to the type of transmission they have, we can test for equality of their mean fuel consumption amounts.
- When three different work shifts make the same paint mixtures, we can test for a difference in the mean time required to produce a case of four 1-gal cans.
- When four different telemarketing teams attempt to sell subscriptions to *Independent Gentleman* magazine, we can test to determine whether there is a difference in the mean time each team requires to obtain an order.
- When six fields of corn are each subdivided into six plots that are given different fertilizer treatments, we can test for equality of crop yields.

The method of analysis of variance derives its name from the fact that we focus on analyzing different types of variation among the data. By comparing different types

---

FIGURE 11.1
The *F* Distribution

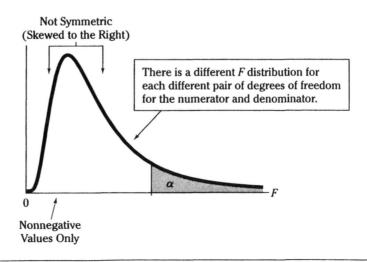

of variances, we can form conclusions about whether the *means* of the populations are equal.

We might wonder why we should bother with this new procedure when we can test for equality of *two* means by using the methods described in Section 9.3. For example, suppose we need to test for equality of three means, each with a 0.05 significance level so that there is 95% confidence in not making a type I error. Why not simply pair them off and do two at a time by testing H_0: $\mu_1 = \mu_2$ and H_0: $\mu_1 = \mu_3$ and H_0: $\mu_2 = \mu_3$? With that approach (doing two at a time), the degree of confidence in making no type I errors could be as low as $0.95 \times 0.95 \times 0.95 = 0.857$. In general, as we increase the number of individual tests of significance, we increase the likelihood of finding a difference by chance alone. The risk of a type I error of finding a difference in one of the pairs, when no such difference actually exists, would be excessively high. The method of analysis of variance enables us to avoid that particular pitfall by using *one* test for equality of several means.

F DISTRIBUTION

The following sections introduce test statistics having the *F* distribution, which was introduced in Section 9.2. Recall that the *F* distribution has these important properties (see Fig. 11.1):

1. The *F* distribution is not symmetric; it is skewed to the right.
2. The values of *F* can be 0 or positive, but they cannot be negative.
3. There is a different *F* distribution for each pair of degrees of freedom for the numerator and denominator.

Critical values of *F* are given in Table A.5.

We begin with a description of one-way analysis of variance in Section 11.2. The term *one-way* is used because the sample data are separated into groups according to one criterion or factor. The minivan-selection problem described at the beginning of the chapter, for example, involves sample data separated into three different groups according to the criterion of transmission type. The method of Section 11.2 can be applied to cases in which the sample data are obtained from *independent and random* samples. With independent and random samples, however, results are sometimes affected by another characteristic that is overrepresented in some groups. For example, refer again to the data on the minivans and note that the minivans with automatic transmissions had the worst fuel consumption mean of 21.8 mi/gal. It's possible that, by chance, the four minivans with automatic transmissions are the heaviest and that weight is another factor (in addition to transmission type) affecting fuel consumption. In randomized block analysis of variance (Section 11.3), we first arrange the sample items into *similar* groups (or *blocks*) before assigning the different criteria. For example, we might first arrange minivans into similar weight classes (light, average, heavy), then select samples of each transmission type from each weight class. This would allow us to better compare the effects of the different transmission types because the effects of different weights would be reduced. The creation of the similar weight groups is an example of the blocking technique introduced in the randomized block design of Section 11.3.

11.2 ONE-WAY ANOVA

In this section we consider **one-way analysis of variance** (or single-factor analysis of variance). The methods we consider allow us to test hypotheses that assert equality of more than two means, as in H_0: $\mu_1 = \mu_2 = \mu_3$. The alternative hypothesis H_1 is the statement that the means are not all equal.

ASSUMPTIONS

When we use one-way ANOVA methods to test the hypothesis that three or more samples come from populations with the same mean, the following assumptions apply.

1. The populations being considered have normal distributions.
2. The populations being considered have the same variance (or standard deviation).
3. The samples are randomly selected from each population.
4. The samples are independent of one another.

The requirements of normality and equal variances are somewhat loose because the methods in this chapter work reasonably well unless a distribution is very nonnormal or the population variances differ by large amounts. The University of Wisconsin statistician George E. P. Box showed that as long as the sample sizes are equal (or nearly equal), the variances can be up to nine times as large and the results of the ANOVA would continue to be essentially reliable.

We will now introduce the basic concepts underlying the method of analysis of variance for one treatment. We begin by introducing relevant terminology and notation. We then present the essential components used in the hypothesis test, followed by an example that illustrates the procedure.

> **DEFINITION**
>
> A *treatment* is a property or characteristic that allows us to distinguish the different populations from one another.

For example, the minivan-selection problem involves a single treatment: the type of transmission. The three different groups of data are distinguished according to the types of transmission they have, so the data are broken down according to the single treatment of transmission type. The term *treatment* is used because early applications of ANOVA involved analysis of agricultural experiments in which different plots of farmland were treated with different fertilizers, seed types, insecticides, and so on.

Notation

$\bar{\bar{x}}$ = overall mean (sum of all sample scores divided by the total number of scores)

$t =$ **number of population means being compared (t is commonly used because it suggests the number of different treatment types.)**

$n_j =$ **number of values in the jth sample**

$n =$ **total number of values in all samples combined (so that $n = n_1 + n_2 + \cdots + n_t$)**

The key components in the ANOVA method are identified below.

SSTotal (or total sum of squares) is a measure of the total variation (around $\bar{\bar{x}}$) in all the sample data combined.

Formula 11.1 $$\textbf{SSTotal} = \Sigma(x - \bar{\bar{x}})^2$$

SSTotal can be broken down into the components of *SSTreatment* and *SSError,* described as follows:

SSTreatment is a measure of the variability among the sample means.

Formula 11.2 $$\textbf{SSTreatment} = n_1(\bar{x}_1 - \bar{\bar{x}})^2 + n_2(\bar{x}_2 - \bar{\bar{x}})^2 + \cdots + n_t(\bar{x}_t - \bar{\bar{x}})^2$$

If the population means ($\mu_1, \mu_2, \cdots, \mu_t$) are equal, then $\bar{x}_1, \bar{x}_2, \cdots, \bar{x}_t$ will all tend to be close together and also close to $\bar{\bar{x}}$. The result will be a relatively small value of SSTreatment. However, if the population means are not all equal, then at least two of $\bar{x}_1, \bar{x}_2, \cdots, \bar{x}_t$ will tend to be far apart from each other and also far apart from $\bar{\bar{x}}$. The result will be a relatively large value of *SSTreatment*. In one-way ANOVA, *SSTreatment* is sometimes referred to as *SSFactor*. Because it's a measure of variability *between* the sample means, it is also referred to as *SS* (*between* groups) or *SS*(*between* samples).

SSError is a sum of squares representing the **variability that is assumed to be common to all the populations being considered.**

Formula 11.3 $$\textbf{SSError} = (n_1 - 1)\, s_1^2 + (n_2 - 1)s_2^2 + \cdots + (n_t - 1)\, s_t^2$$

SSError is the numerator of the expression for the *pooled variance* s_p^2 from Section 9.3. Because *SSError* is a measure of the variance within groups, it is sometimes denoted as *SS*(*within* groups) or *SS*(*within* samples).

Given the above expressions for *SSTotal*, *SSTreatment*, and *SSError,* the following relationship will always hold.

Formula 11.4 $$SSTotal = SSTreatment + SSError$$

Because of the relationship expressed in Formula 11.4, we can consider *SSError* to be that part of the total variability that is not explained by differences between the sample means.

SSTreatment and *SSError* are each sums of squares, and if we divide them each by their corresponding number of degrees of freedom, we get *mean squares,* as defined below.

MSTreatment is a mean square for treatments obtained as follows:

Formula 11.5 $\text{MSTreatment} = \dfrac{\text{SSTreatment}}{t - 1}$

MSError is a mean square for error obtained as follows:

Formula 11.6 $\text{MSError} = \dfrac{\text{SSError}}{n - t}$

MSTotal is a mean square for the total variability obtained as follows:

Formula 11.7 $\text{MSTotal} = \dfrac{\text{SSTotal}}{n - 1}$

We can now use the above measures to identify the test statistic that is relevant to this section.

TEST STATISTIC

In testing the null hypothesis H_0: $\mu_1 = \mu_2 = \cdots = \mu_t$ against the alternative that those means are not all equal, the test statistic

Formula 11.8 $F = \dfrac{\text{MSTreatment}}{\text{MSError}}$

has an *F* distribution (when the null hypothesis H_0 is true) with degrees of freedom given by

degrees of freedom (numerator) = $t - 1$
degrees of freedom (denominator) = $n - t$

INTERPRETING THE *F* TEST STATISTIC

In the test statistic *F* given above, the denominator depends only on the sample variances that measure variability within the treatments, and it is not affected by the differences among the sample means. In contrast, the numerator does depend on differences between the sample means. If the differences among the sample means are extreme, they will cause the numerator to be very large so that *F* in turn will also be very large. Consequently, **very large values of *F* suggest unequal means, and the ANOVA test is therefore right-tailed.** For example, see the accompanying Minitab display that depicts *dotplots* of four different data sets corresponding to C1, C2, C3, and C4. The dotplots show the distribution and location of the data. All four data sets appear to have the same amount of spread or variability. Data sets C1, C3, and C4 also appear to have about the same mean, but data set C2 appears to have consistently lower values so that its mean is different from the other three. If we were to exclude the values in C2, we would expect a small value of the F test statistic (it is actually $F = 0.08$), because there are only small differences between C1, C3, and C4. The inclusion of all four data sets, however, would result in a large value ($F = 147.36$) of the test statistic F due to the large differences among the means of those four data sets.

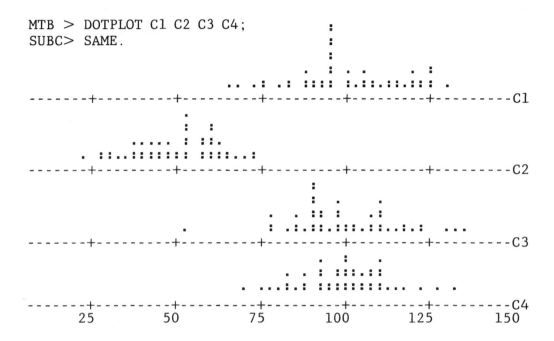

```
MTB > DOTPLOT C1 C2 C3 C4;
SUBC> SAME.
```

EXAMPLE A utility company considering the purchase of a fleet of minivans is concerned about the fuel consumption (in mi/gal). Three different transmission types are used in a sample of 12 different minivans, all having 6-cylinder engines and an engine size of 3.0 liters. The fuel consumption (in mi/gal) is found for highway conditions with the results given below (based on data from the Environmental Protection Agency). The letters A, M, L represent automatic, manual, and lockup torque converter, respectively. At the 0.05 significance level, test the claim that the mean fuel consumption values are the same for all three transmission types.

A	M	L
23	27	24
23	29	26
20	25	24
21	23	
	24	
$n_1 = 4$	$n_2 = 5$	$n_3 = 3$
$\bar{x}_1 = 21.75$	$\bar{x}_2 = 25.60$	$\bar{x}_3 = 24.67$
$s_1^2 = 2.25$	$s_2^2 = 5.80$	$s_3^2 = 1.33$

QUALITY AT FORD

In the early 1980s, the Ford Motor Company began to invest over $3 billion in its development of the Taurus model. The subsequent sales of the Taurus proved this to be a successful gamble, as Ford losses were turned into profits. The success of the Taurus is largely attributable to the priority placed on quality. One quality approach issue was to develop a measurable standard referred to as "Best in Class." Fifty foreign and domestic car models in the same class were analyzed for their best features. Four hundred features were identified, and the Taurus team set out to incorporate as many of them as possible. As one example, seats from a dozen competing cars were tested with women and men drivers of all ages. Analysis of the results enabled the Taurus team to develop a seat design that was as good as or better than the best in its class. Statistical analysis of results of this type is often accomplished with analysis-of-variance techniques.

SOLUTION

In Chapter 7 we identified eight specific steps for testing hypotheses. Following those same steps, we get the following:

STEP 1: The claim that the mean fuel consumption values are the same for all three transmission types can be expressed as

$$\mu_A = \mu_M = \mu_L \text{ (or } \mu_1 = \mu_2 = \mu_3)$$

STEP 2: The opposite of the given claim is the statement that the means are not all equal.

STEP 3: Because the original claim includes the condition of equality, it becomes the null hypothesis, and we have

H_0: $\mu_A = \mu_M = \mu_L$ (or $\mu_1 = \mu_2 = \mu_3$)
H_1: The preceding means are not all equal.

STEP 4: The significance level is $\alpha = 0.05$.

STEP 5: Because of the nature of the data and the claim being tested, we use the F distribution in analysis of variance.

STEP 6: We proceed to calculate the test statistic as follows:

Number of treatments or samples: $t = 3$
$\bar{\bar{x}}$ = mean of all 12 sample scores = $289/12 = 24.08$

We now evaluate *SSTreatment* and then *MSTreatment* by using Formulas 11.2 and 11.5.

$$\begin{aligned}
SSTreatment &= n_1(\bar{x}_1 - \bar{\bar{x}})^2 \ n_2(\bar{x}_2 - \bar{\bar{x}})^2 + n_3(\bar{x}_3 - \bar{\bar{x}})^2 \\
&= 4(21.75 - 24.08)^2 + 5(25.60 - 24.08)^2 \\
&\quad + 3(24.67 - 24.08)^2 \\
&= 21.7156 + 11.552 + 1.0443 \\
&= 34.3119
\end{aligned}$$

$$MSTreatment = \frac{SSTreatment}{t - 1} = \frac{34.3119}{3 - 1} = 17.156$$

Next, we evaluate *SSError* and *MSError* by using Formulas 11.3 and 11.6.

$$\begin{aligned}
SSError &= (n_1 - 1)\, s_1{}^2 + (n_2 - 1)s_2{}^2 + (n_3 - 1)s_3{}^2 \\
&= (4 - 1)\,(2.25) + (5 - 1)\,(5.80) + (3 - 1)\,(1.33) \\
&= 32.61
\end{aligned}$$

$$MSError = \frac{SSError}{n - t} = \frac{32.61}{12 - 3} = 3.623$$

We can now calculate the value of the F test statistic.

$$F = \frac{MSTreatment}{MSError} = \frac{17.156}{3.623} = 4.735$$

FIGURE 11.2
F Distribution for Minivan Data

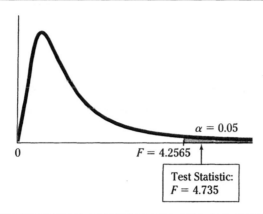

$\alpha = 0.05$

0                               $F = 4.2565$

Test Statistic:
$F = 4.735$

The critical value of $F = 4.2565$ is obtained from Table A.5 by noting that $\alpha = 0.05$, and the degrees of freedom are as follows:

degrees of freedom (numerator) $= t - 1 = 3 - 1 = 2$
degrees of freedom (denominator) $= n - t = 12 - 3 = 9$

STEP 7:   Because the test statistic of $F = 4.735$ does exceed the critical value of $F = 4.2565$ (see Fig. 11.2), we reject the null hypothesis that the means are equal.

STEP 8:   The sample evidence is sufficient to warrant rejection of the claim that the three population means are equal. The mean fuel consumption is apparently not the same for all three transmission types.

It may seem strange to test for equality of several *means* by analyzing only *variances,* but the values of the sample means directly affect the value of the test statistic F. To illustrate this, let's modify the data from the last example by adding 4 mi/gal to each of the automatic transmission values. This change will alter the mean $\bar{x}_1$, but it will not affect the variance s_1^2. After making this change, the sample statistics are as shown below.

A (MODIFIED)	M	L
$n_1 = 4$	$n_2 = 5$	$n_3 = 3$
$\bar{x}_1 = 25.75$	$\bar{x}_2 = 25.60$	$\bar{x}_3 = 24.67$
$s_1^2 = 2.25$	$s_2^2 = 5.80$	$s_3^2 = 1.33$

This modification results in three sample means that are now much closer. For this modified set of data, we repeat the same procedures used in the preceding example and obtain a test statistic of $F = 0.32$, so that we will now *fail to reject* the null hypothesis of equal means. Note that by adding 4 to each of the automatic

TABLE 11.1
ANOVA Table

SOURCE OF VARIATION	SUM OF SQUARES SS	DEGREES OF FREEDOM	MEAN SQUARE MS	TEST STATISTIC
Treatment	$SSTreatment$	$t-1$	$MSTreatment$ $= \dfrac{SSTreatment}{t-1}$	
Error	$SSError$	$n-t$	$MSError$ $= \dfrac{SSError}{n-t}$	$F = \dfrac{MSTreatment}{MSError}$
Total	$SSTotal$	$n-1$	$MSTotal$ $= \dfrac{SSTotal}{n-1}$	

COMMERCIALS

Television networks have their own clearance departments for screening commercials and verifying claims. The National Advertising Division, a branch of the Council of Better Business Bureaus, investigates advertising claims. The Federal Trade Commission and local district attorneys also become involved. In the past, Firestone had to drop a claim that its tires resulted in 25% faster stops, and Warner Lambert had to spend $10 million informing customers that Listerine doesn't prevent or cure colds. Many deceptive ads are voluntarily dropped and many others escape scrutiny simply because the regulatory mechanisms can't keep up with the flood of commercials.

transmission values, the F test statistic changes from 4.735 to 0.32. This shows that the F test statistic is very sensitive to sample *means,* even though it is obtained through estimates of variation. (You might also verify that $SSTreatment$ changes from 34.3119 to 2.2851, $MSTreatment$ changes from 17.156 to 1.1426, but $SSError$ and $MSError$ don't change.)

Table 11.1 is a standard and convenient format for summarizing key results in ANOVA calculations. We will now describe the use of Minitab and present a Minitab display resulting from the data we are considering. Note that the display includes a format very similar to that of Table 11.1.

USING MINITAB FOR ONE-WAY ANOVA

Examination of the calculations for $SSTreatment$, $SSError$, $MSTreatment$, $MSError$, and the test statistic F reveals that making mistakes when performing manual calculations would be quite easy. Fortunately, many statistical software packages include programs that yield these results. Shown below is the Minitab printout for our minivan-selection problem. Note that Minitab uses the term *factor* instead of the term *treatment*. Under the column heading of SS, we therefore have $SSTreatment = 34.30$, $SSError = 32.62$, and $SSTotal = 66.92$. Also, $MSTreatment = 17.15$ and $MSError = 3.62$.

```
MTB > SET C1
DATA> 23 23 20 21
DATA> ENDOFDATA
MTB > SET C2
DATA> 27 29 25 23 24
DATA> ENDOFDATA
MTB > SET C3
DATA> 24 26 24
DATA> ENDOFDATA
```

Minitab uses *factor* instead of *treatment.*

```
MTB > AOVONEWAY C1 C2 C3
                             ┌─── Degrees of freedom
 ANALYSIS OF VARIANCE    ┌── Sum of squares     ┌─ Test statistic
 SOURCE      DF      SS        MS        F         p   ← P-value
 FACTOR       2    34.30     17.15     4.73     0.039
 ERROR        9    32.62      3.62
 TOTAL       11    66.92
```

Compare to Table 11.1.

```
                                INDIVIDUAL 95 PCT CI'S FOR MEAN
                                BASED ON POOLED STDEV
   LEVEL       N      MEAN     STDEV   --+---------+---------+---------+----
   C1          4    21.750     1.500   (--------*--------)
   C2          5    25.600     2.408                    (------*-------)
   C3          3    24.667     1.155             (---------*---------)
                                       --+---------+---------+---------+----
 POOLED STDEV =         1.904          20.0      22.5      25.0      27.5
```

Individual sample means — Individual sample standard deviations

Note the use of the key Minitab command AOVONEWAY C1 C2 C3, where the automatic transmission values have been entered in column C1, the manual transmission values have been entered in column C2, and the lockup transmission values have been entered in column C3. Following the AOVONEWAY C1 C2 C3 command is the standard format of the ANOVA table given above (except for the order of the columns for *df* and *SS*).

Again referring to the Minitab display, note that the *P*-value of 0.039 is included. For our one-way ANOVA, the *P*-value is the probability of getting sample means that differ from one another by at least as much as those differences actually obtained. Because the *P*-value of 0.039 (based on the assumption of equal means) is less than the significance level of $\alpha = 0.05$, we again reject the null hypothesis of equal means. The low *P*-value suggests that we are safe in concluding that the means are not equal.

CONFIDENCE INTERVALS

The lower portion of the Minitab display includes the individual sample means, standard deviations, and 95% confidence intervals for each of the three samples. These confidence intervals are computed by the same methods described in Chapter 6, except that the pooled variance s_p^2 or *MSError* is used in place of the individual sample variances. The last entry shows that the pooled standard deviation is $s_p = 1.904$. We can generalize this by expressing the confidence interval estimate of μ_j (the mean of the *j*th population) as shown below.

CONFIDENCE INTERVAL FOR μ_j FROM ANOVA

$$\bar{x}_j - E < \mu_j < \bar{x}_j + E \quad \text{where} \quad E = t_{\alpha/2}\frac{s_p}{\sqrt{n_j}}$$

and $t_{\alpha/2}$ has $n - t$ degrees of freedom and $s_p = \sqrt{SSError/(n - t)} = \sqrt{MSError}$.

EXAMPLE Construct a 95% confidence interval for the L (lockup) transmission mean.

SOLUTION We have $n - t = 12 - 3 = 9$ degrees of freedom, $n_3 = 3$, $\bar{x}_3 = 24.67$, and $s_p = \sqrt{3.623} = 1.903$. (Minitab's result is 1.904 and the discrepancy is due to rounding error.) Referring to Table A.3 with 9 degrees of freedom and $\alpha = 0.05$ in two tails (from 95% confidence), we find that $t_{\alpha/2} = 2.262$, so that

$$E = t_{\alpha/2}\frac{s_p}{\sqrt{n_j}} = 2.262\,\frac{1.903}{\sqrt{3}} = 2.49$$

and $\bar{x}_3 - E < \mu_3 < \bar{x}_3 + E$ becomes $22.18 < \mu_3 < 27.16$. That is, we are 95% confident that the limits of 22.18 mi/gal and 27.16 mi/gal actually do contain the true value of the mean mileage for the lockup transmission. This confidence interval is graphically illustrated in the preceding Minitab display as the line corresponding to C3.

When we use ANOVA and reject the null hypothesis of equal means, we might be interested in trying to identify which particular means are significantly different. We can compare confidence intervals for individual populations. Also, we can construct confidence intervals for *differences* between population means. If a confidence interval for the difference between two means contains 0, then the difference between those two means is not significant. Conversely, if a confidence interval for the difference between two means does *not* contain 0, then those two means apparently are significantly different, and we have an estimate of the magnitude of the difference between them. Such confidence intervals can be constructed as follows:

CONFIDENCE INTERVAL FOR $\mu_i - \mu_j$ FROM ANOVA

$$(\bar{x}_i - \bar{x}_j) - E < \mu_i - \mu_j < (\bar{x}_i - \bar{x}_j) + E \quad \text{where} \quad E = t_{\alpha/2}\sqrt{\frac{s_p^2}{n_i} + \frac{s_p^2}{n_j}}$$

and $t_{\alpha/2}$ has a Student t distribution with $n - t$ degrees of freedom and $s_p^2 = \text{MSError}$.

EXAMPLE Construct a 95% confidence interval for $\mu_2 - \mu_1$ (the manual transmission mean minus the automatic transmission mean).

SOLUTION As in the preceding example, we have $t_{\alpha/2} = 2.262$ (from Table A.3 with $n - t = 9$ degrees of freedom and $\alpha = 0.05$ in two tails). We get a margin of error of

DISCRIMINATION CASE USES STATISTICS

Statistics often play a key role in discrimination cases. One such case involved Matt Perez and more than 300 other FBI agents who won a class action suit charging that Hispanics in the FBI were discriminated against in the areas of promotions, assignments, and disciplinary actions. The plaintiff employed statistician Gary Lafree, who showed that the FBI's upper management positions had significantly low proportions of Hispanic employees. Statistics were instrumental in the plaintiff's victory in this case.

$$E = t_{\alpha/2}\sqrt{\frac{s_p^2}{n_2} + \frac{s_p^2}{n_1}} = (2.262)\sqrt{\frac{3.623}{5} + \frac{3.623}{4}} = 2.89$$

so the confidence interval becomes

$(25.6 - 21.75) - 2.89 < \mu_2 - \mu_1 < (25.6 - 21.75) + 2.89$ or
$0.96 < \mu_2 - \mu_1 < 6.74$

Because this confidence interval does not contain 0, we conclude that the manual transmission population mean is different from the automatic transmission population mean. In fact, we are 95% confident that the minivans with manual transmissions will get higher fuel mileage levels than the minivans with automatic transmissions, and the difference between the means is as little as 0.96 mi/gal or as great as 6.74 mi/gal.

By constructing confidence intervals for individual means and for differences between pairs of means, we can better determine which means are different and which means are the same. When we construct such confidence intervals and try to compare means, we are using some of the many different *multiple comparison procedures* that are available. The use of such procedures is somewhat controversial, but we suggest that (1) we not use any of the confidence intervals if ANOVA leads to the conclusion that we fail to reject equality of the population means, and (2) even when we do reject equality of the means, we then construct only a few confidence intervals. The construction of every possible confidence interval could lead to severe distortions of the significance level being used and the degree of confidence we have in our confidence intervals.

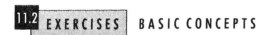

11.2 EXERCISES | BASIC CONCEPTS

In Exercises 1–18, assume that the population or process being sampled has a normal distribution.

1. The Telektronic Corporation tests 3 different methods for manufacturing video display screens for computers. Random samples are collected from each of the methods and the display screens are tested for longevity. The sample statistics are given below in thousands of hours. At the $\alpha = 0.05$ significance level, test the claim that the 3 methods produce display screens with the same mean life.

METHOD 1	METHOD 2	METHOD 3
$n_1 = 14$	$n_2 = 12$	$n_3 = 13$
$\bar{x}_1 = 17.54$ h	$\bar{x}_2 = 11.93$ h	$\bar{x}_3 = 16.21$ h
$s_1^2 = 20.32$ h^2	$s_2^2 = 13.69$ h^2	$s_3^2 = 17.64$ h^2

2. Repeat Exercise 1 after changing $\bar{x}_2$ from 11.93 to 16.55.

3. The Florida Sugar Company uses 3 machines to fill packages labeled "5 pounds," or 80 oz. The 3 filling processes appear to be statistically stable, and random samples from each machine are collected. The results are given below. At the 0.05 significance level, test the claim that the 3 machines have the same mean.

MACHINE 1	MACHINE 2	MACHINE 3
$n_1 = 8$	$n_2 = 8$	$n_3 = 8$
$\bar{x}_1 = 80.2$ oz	$\bar{x}_2 = 81.8$ oz	$\bar{x}_3 = 79.9$ oz
$s_1^2 = 1.4$ oz^2	$s_2^2 = 1.8$ oz^2	$s_3^2 = 1.5$ oz^2

4. Refer to the data in Exercise 3 and construct a 95% confidence interval for the mean of the second machine.

5. Refer to the data in Exercise 3 and construct a 95% confidence interval for the difference $\mu_2 - \mu_3$.

6. Refer to the data in Exercise 3 and construct a 95% confidence interval for the difference $\mu_2 - \mu_1$.

7. The Dallas Financial Consulting Company conducts a survey of the state's manufacturing, retail, banking, and education industries to estimate next year's projected salary increases. Five companies within each group were asked to provide data, and all agreed except for one bank. The results are summarized below. At the 0.05 level of significance, test the claim that the 4 different industries have the same mean projected increase.

MANUFACTURING	RETAIL	BANKING	EDUCATION
$n_1 = 5$	$n_2 = 5$	$n_3 = 4$	$n_4 = 5$
$\bar{x}_1 = 4.6\%$	$\bar{x}_2 = 3.2\%$	$\bar{x}_3 = 3.3\%$	$\bar{x}_4 = 2.3\%$
$s_1 = 1.6\%$	$s_2 = 1.3\%$	$s_3 = 1.4\%$	$s_4 = 0.8\%$

8. The Fisher Company manufactures vacuum cleaners and uses electric motors from 3 different suppliers. Six motors are randomly selected from each supplier, and all of these sample motors are run until a failure occurs. The results are given below in hundreds of hours. At the 0.05 level of significance, test the claim that the 3 suppliers have the same MTBF (mean time before failure).

RYAN ELECTRICAL SUPPLY CO.			MANCUSO ELECTRONICS			RELIABLE MOTORS		
7.3	6.4	7.0	7.1	6.2	7.0	5.6	6.3	6.0
6.5	7.0	7.2	6.4	6.8	6.7	5.7	6.2	5.0

9. Refer to the data in Exercise 8 and find a 95% confidence interval for the mean from Reliable Motors.

10. Refer to the data in Exercise 8 and find a 95% confidence interval for the difference between the means of Ryan Electrical Supply and Reliable Motors.

11. A preliminary study is conducted to determine whether there is any relationship between education and income. The sample results are as follows. The figures represent, in thousands of dollars, the lifetime incomes of randomly selected workers from each category. At the $\alpha = 0.05$ level of significance, test the claim that the samples come from populations with equal means. The data are listed at the top of the following page.

	YEARS OF EDUCATION			
8 OR LESS	9–11	12	13–15	16 OR MORE
300	270	400	420	570
210	330	430	480	640
260	380	370	510	590
330	310	390	390	700
		420	470	620
				660

12. Refer to the data in Exercise 11 and find a 95% confidence interval for the mean lifetime income of those with a high school (12 years) education.

13. Refer to the data in Exercise 11 and find a 95% confidence interval for the difference between the means for college graduates (16 or more years) and those with a high school education (12 years).

14. The Lincoln Cellular Phone Company must buy rechargeable batteries. Three different brands of varying cost are being considered, and results (in hours before recharging is necessary) are given below for samples from each brand.

TELEBATTERY	PHONE CELL	RYAN ELECTRICAL SUPPLY CO.
26.0	29.0	30.0
28.5	28.8	26.3
27.3	27.6	29.2
25.9	28.1	27.1
28.2	27.0	29.8

Shown below is the Minitab display resulting from the analysis of variance for the data given above.

a. Identify the mean and standard deviation for each sample.

b. Use a 0.05 significance level to test the claim that the 3 population means are the same.

c. If the cost of one battery from each of the 3 brands is $14.00, $13.50, and $19.00, respectively, which brand should be purchased?

```
MTB > AOVONEWAY C1 C2 C3
ANALYSIS OF VARIANCE
SOURCE      DF        SS        MS        F         p
FACTOR      2        4.47      2.23      1.35     0.295
ERROR      12       19.82      1.65
TOTAL      14       24.28

                                 INDIVIDUAL 95 PCT CI'S FOR MEAN
                                 BASED ON POOLED STDEV
LEVEL       N       MEAN      STDEV    ----+---------+---------+---------+--
C1          5      27.180     1.207    (---------*----------)
C2          5      28.100     0.831          (---------*----------)
C3          5      28.480     1.675            (---------*----------)
                                      ----+---------+---------+---------+--
POOLED STDEV =    1.285               26.4      27.6      28.8      30.0
```

In Exercises 15–18, use the accompanying data. The data represent 30 different homes recently sold in Dutchess County, New York. The zones (1, 4, 7) correspond to different geographical regions of the county. The values of SP are the selling prices in thousands of dollars. The values of LA are the living areas in hundreds of square feet. The Acres values are the lot sizes in acres, and the Taxes values are the annual tax bills in thousands of dollars. For example, the first home is in zone 1, it sold for \$147,000, it has a living area of 2000 square feet, it is on a 0.50-acre lot, and the annual taxes are \$1900.

ZONE	SP	LA	ACRES	TAXES
1	147	20	0.50	1.9
1	160	18	1.00	2.4
1	128	27	1.05	1.5
1	162	17	0.42	1.6
1	135	18	0.84	1.6
1	132	13	0.33	1.5
1	181	24	0.90	1.7
1	138	15	0.83	2.2
1	145	17	2.00	1.6
1	165	16	0.78	1.4
4	160	18	0.55	2.8
4	140	20	0.46	1.8
4	173	19	0.94	3.2
4	113	12	0.29	2.1
4	85	9	0.26	1.4
4	120	18	0.33	2.1
4	285	28	1.70	4.2
4	117	10	0.50	1.7
4	133	15	0.43	1.8
4	119	12	0.25	1.6
7	215	21	3.04	2.7
7	127	16	1.09	1.9
7	98	14	0.23	1.3
7	147	23	1.00	1.7
7	184	17	6.20	2.2
7	109	17	0.46	2.0
7	169	20	3.20	2.2
7	110	14	0.77	1.6
7	68	12	1.40	2.5
7	160	18	4.00	1.8

15. Sue Jackson is a real estate agent who claims that homes in zones 1, 4, and 7 have the same mean selling prices. Test her claim of equal means by using a significance level of 0.05.

16. After viewing homes in different geographical regions, you suspect that homes in zones 1, 4, and 7 are about the same size. Test the claim of the real estate agent that homes in those three zones have the same mean living areas. Use a significance level of 0.05.

17. At the 0.05 significance level, test the claim that the means of the lot sizes (in acres) are the same in zones 1, 4, and 7.

18. At the 0.05 significance level, test the claim that the means of the tax amounts are the same in zones 1, 4, and 7.

11.2 EXERCISES | BEYOND THE BASICS

19. Instead of using the formulas given in this section, you can use shortcut formulas for *SSTreatment, SSError,* and *SSTotal.* These shortcut formulas facilitate calculations, but they tend to conceal the meaning of the statistics they represent. Define T_j to be the total of the sample scores in the jth treatment and let GT represent the grand total of $T_1 + T_2 + \cdots + T_t.$ Show that when you apply the following formulas to the minivan example of this section, they will yield the same values obtained in that example.

$$SSTreatment = \sum \frac{T_j^2}{n_j} - \frac{(GT)^2}{n}$$

$$SSError = \sum x^2 - \sum \frac{T_j^2}{n_j}$$

$$SSTotal = \sum x^2 - \frac{(GT)^2}{n}$$

20. A study is made of three police precincts to determine the time (in seconds) required for a police car to be dispatched after a crime is reported. Sample results are given in the margin.
    a. At the 0.05 level of significance, test the claim that $\mu_1 = \mu_2.$ Use the methods discussed in Chapter 9.
    b. At the 0.05 level of significance, test the claim that $\mu_2 = \mu_3.$ Use the methods discussed in Chapter 9.
    c. At the 0.05 level of significance, test the claim that $\mu_1 = \mu_3.$ Use the methods discussed in Chapter 9.
    d. At the 0.05 level of significance, test the claim that $\mu_1 = \mu_2 = \mu_3.$ Use analysis of variance.
    e. Compare the methods and results of parts *a, b,* and *c* to part *d.*

PRECINCT 1

$n_1 = 50$
$\bar{x}_1 = 170$ s
$s_1 = 18$ s

PRECINCT 2

$n_2 = 50$
$\bar{x}_2 = 202$ s
$s_2 = 20$ s

PRECINCT 3

$n_3 = 50$
$\bar{x}_3 = 165$ s
$s_3 = 23$ s

21. a. Complete the following ANOVA table resulting from 3 samples with sizes of 5, 7, and 7, respectively.

SOURCE OF VARIATION	SUM OF SQUARES SS	DEGREES OF FREEDOM	MEAN SQUARE MS	TEST STATISTIC
Treatments	?	?	?	
Error	112.57	?	?	$F = ?$
Total	114.74	?		

   b. Use a 0.05 significance level to test the claim that the means are equal.

22. a. Complete the following ANOVA table that resulted from samples of sizes 12, 25, 50, and 32.

SOURCE OF VARIATION	SUM OF SQUARES SS	DEGREES OF FREEDOM	MEAN SQUARE MS	TEST STATISTIC
Treatments	21.34	?	?	
Error	144.45	?	?	$F = ?$
Total	?	?		

   b. Use a 0.05 significance level to test the claim that the means are equal.

23. In this exercise we will verify that when we have two sets of sample data, the t test for independent samples and the ANOVA method of this section are equivalent. Refer to the real estate data used in Exercises 15–18, but exclude the zone-7 data.

    a. Use a 0.05 level and the method of Section 9.3 to test the claim that zones 1 and 4 have the same mean living areas.
    b. Use a 0.05 level and the ANOVA method of this section to test the same claim in part a.
    c. Verify that the squares of the t test statistic and critical value from part a are equal to the F test statistic and critical value from part b.

11.3 ANOVA FOR A RANDOMIZED BLOCK DESIGN

In Section 11.2 we used one-way analysis of variance for testing the claim that three or more population means are equal. In that section, our data collection was broken up into different groups according to one criterion, referred to as a *treatment*. The methods of Section 11.2 were used under the assumption that the sample data were obtained from independent and random samples. With independent and random samples, however, results are sometimes affected by another characteristic that might affect some groups more than others. Suppose we want to collect data describing insurance rates from three different companies so that we can test the claim that those companies have the same mean rate. It is possible that, by chance, the randomly selected policies from the first company will include only male drivers under 25 years of age—a group known to have disproportionately higher rates than other groups. We could analyze the data and incorrectly conclude that the three insurance companies have different mean rates when the differences are actually due to the overrepresentation of young males in one sample group. Recognizing that the sex and age of the driver will affect the insurance premium, it would be good to configure our sample data as in Table 11.2 so that effects from sex and age are controlled. The use of *blocks* will allow us to reduce or eliminate the variability due to such other factors.

> **DEFINITION**
>
> In analysis of variance, *blocks* are similar groupings of data that allow us to better compare the effects of treatments by reducing the variation due to causes other than the treatments themselves.

For example, suppose that we first establish sex/age categories such as females younger than 25, females 25 or older, males younger than 25, and males 25 or older. We can then randomly select policies from each of these "block" categories for each of three different insurance companies. The sex/age categories are the blocks, and the different insurance companies are the treatments. This approach allows us to better focus on the differences among the rates charged by the different companies; the comparisons are not so clouded by rate differences

TABLE 11.2
Semiannual Premiums (dollars)

	INSURANCE COMPANY			
SEX/AGE CLASSIFICATION	FIDELITY	EASTERN TRUST	IOWA TRUST	
Female younger than 25	186	170	190	$\overline{B}_1 = 182$
Female 25 and older	174	160	179	$\overline{B}_2 = 171$
Male younger than 25	259	240	260	$\overline{B}_3 = 253$
Male 25 and older	233	218	227	$\overline{B}_4 = 226$
	$\overline{x}_1 = 213$	$\overline{x}_2 = 197$	$\overline{x}_3 = 214$	

due to the different sex/age categories. When we arrange the data into similar groups (or blocks) and then assign the different treatments, we are using an analysis-of-variance technique referred to as a **randomized block design.**

ASSUMPTIONS

When we use ANOVA methods with a randomized block design, the following assumptions apply.

1. The populations being considered have normal distributions.
2. The populations being considered have the same variance (or standard deviation).
3. The samples are drawn randomly.

We will use the same notation for $\overline{\overline{x}}$ (the mean of all scores), t (the number of treatments), and n (the total number of values in all samples combined). We introduce new notation relevant to this section.

Notation
$b =$ **the number of blocks**
  (**$b = n_i$ because each treatment will have the same number of blocks so that b or n_i is the sample size common to each of the treatments.**)
$\overline{B}_i =$ **the mean of the items in the ith block**

As in the preceding section, we again test claims such as H_0: $\mu_1 = \mu_2 = \mu_3$, and our ANOVA will again be based on a ratio of two different measures of variability, but some of the calculations will be adjusted to account for the presence of blocks. We begin with *SSTotal*. As in the preceding section, *SSTotal* is the total sum of squares and it is a measure of the total variation (around $\overline{\overline{x}}$) in all the sample data combined.

Formula 11.9 $\text{SSTotal} = \Sigma \, (x - \overline{\overline{x}})^2$

SSTreatment is a measure of the variability among the treatment means.

Formula 11.10 $\text{SSTreatment} = b(\bar{x}_1 - \bar{\bar{x}})^2 + b(\bar{x}_2 - \bar{\bar{x}})^2 + \cdots + b(\bar{x}_t - \bar{\bar{x}})^2$

SSBlock is a measure of the variability among the block means.

Formula 11.11 $\text{SSBlock} = t(\bar{B}_1 - \bar{\bar{x}})^2 + t(\bar{B}_2 - \bar{\bar{x}})^2 + \cdots + t(\bar{B}_b - \bar{\bar{x}})^2$

The following is a measure of the common variation within samples that is due to chance.

$$\text{SSError} = \Sigma \, (x - \bar{x}_j - \bar{B}_i + \bar{\bar{x}})^2$$

Given the above expressions, the following relationship will always hold.

$$\textit{SSTotal} = \textit{SSTreatment} + \textit{SSBlock} + \textit{SSError}$$

We can take advantage of this last expression and enjoy the simpler calculations required if we evaluate *SSError* using the following:

$$\textbf{SSError} = \textit{SSTotal} - \textit{SSTreatment} - \textit{SSBlock}$$

SSTreatment, SSBlock, and *SSError* represent *sums of squares,* and if we divide each of them by the corresponding numbers of degrees of freedom, we get *mean squares,* as follows: First, *MSTreatment* is a mean square for treatments.

Formula 11.12 $\text{MSTreatment} = \dfrac{\text{SSTreatment}}{t - 1}$

MSBlock is a mean square for blocks obtained as follows:

Formula 11.13 $\text{MSBlock} = \dfrac{\text{SSBlock}}{b - 1}$

MSError is a mean square for error obtained as follows:

Formula 11.14 $\text{MSError} = \dfrac{\text{SSError}}{(b - 1)\,(t - 1)}$

We can now use the above measures to identify the test statistics that are relevant to the randomized block ANOVA of this section. Instead of one simple (?!) test of the claim that $\mu_1 = \mu_2 = \cdots = \mu_t$, we will now conduct *two* separate tests.

1. Test the claim that the *treatment* means are equal. That is, test H_0: $\mu_1 = \mu_2 = \cdots = \mu_t$ where these means correspond to the t different treatments.
2. Test the claim that the *block* means are equal. That is, test H_0: $\mu_1 = \mu_2 = \cdots = \mu_b$ where these means correspond to the b different blocks.

The test statistics for the above two cases are as follows:

TEST STATISTICS

1. In testing the null hypothesis that the *treatment* means are equal, the test statistic

Formula 11.15
$$F = \frac{\text{MSTreatment}}{\text{MSError}}$$

has an F distribution (when the null hypothesis of equal treatment means is true) with degrees of freedom given by

degrees of freedom (numerator) = $t - 1$
degrees of freedom (denominator) = $(b - 1)(t - 1)$

2. In testing the null hypothesis that the *block* means are equal, the test statistic

Formula 11.16
$$F = \frac{\text{MSBlock}}{\text{MSError}}$$

has an F distribution (when the null hypothesis of equal block means is true) with degrees of freedom given by

degrees of freedom (numerator) = $b - 1$
degrees of freedom (denominator) = $(b - 1)(t - 1)$

INTERPRETING THE F TEST STATISTIC

As in the preceding section, both of the above tests will always be *right-tailed* because only relatively *large* values of F test statistics reflect extreme differences among the means being considered. Conversely, small values of the F test statistic suggest that the means are relatively close to one another.

EXAMPLE   The semiannual insurance premiums (in dollars) have been identified for four different sex/age classifications and, for each classification, the premiums were obtained from each of three different insurance companies. The results are summarized in Table 11.2, where we also provide some of the important statistics. In this example, the treatments (columns) are the different insurance companies, and the blocks (rows) are the different sex/age classifications. (a) Test the claim that the three insurance companies charge premiums that are, on the average, the same. (b) Test the claim that the premiums for the four sex/age classifications are, on the average, the same. In both cases, use a significance level of $\alpha = 0.05$.

STATISTICS AND BASEBALL STRATEGY

Statisticians are using computers to develop very sophisticated measures of baseball performance and strategy. They have found, for example, that sacrifice bunts, sacrifice fly balls, and stolen bases rarely help win games and that it is seldom wise to have a pitcher intentionally walk the batter. They can identify the ball-parks that favor pitchers and those that favor batters. Instead of simply comparing the batting averages of two different players, they can develop better measures of offensive strength by taking into account such factors as pitchers faced, position in the lineup, ballparks played, and weather conditions.

SOLUTION We begin by finding some of the key components needed for our calculations. From Table 11.2 we find that

$\bar{\bar{x}}$ = mean of all scores = 208

$t = 3$ (the number of treatments or the number of columns; in this case, there are three different treatments or insurance companies)

$b = 4$ (the number of blocks or rows; in this case, there are four different blocks or sex/age classifications)

The values of *SSTotal, SSTreatment, SSBlock,* and *SSError* must be found so that the relevant test statistics can be computed. We get

$$SSTotal = \Sigma(x - \bar{\bar{x}})^2$$
$$= (186 - 208)^2 + (174 - 208)^2 + \cdots + (227 - 208)^2$$
$$= 13{,}968$$

$$SSTreatment = b(\bar{x}_1 - \bar{\bar{x}})^2 + b(\bar{x}_2 - \bar{\bar{x}})^2 + \cdots + b(\bar{x}_t - \bar{\bar{x}})^2$$
$$= 4(213 - 208)^2 + 4(197 - 208)^2 + 4(214 - 208)^2$$
$$= 728$$

$$SSBlock = t(\bar{B}_1 - \bar{\bar{x}})^2 + t(\bar{B}_2 - \bar{\bar{x}})^2 + \cdots + t(\bar{B}_b - \bar{\bar{x}})^2$$
$$= 3(182 - 208)^2 + 3(171 - 208)^2 + 3(253 - 208)^2$$
$$+ 3(226 - 208)^2$$
$$= 13{,}182$$

$$SSError = SSTotal - SSTreatment - SSBlock$$
$$= 13{,}968 - 728 - 13{,}182$$
$$= 58$$

$$MSTreatment = \frac{SSTreatment}{t - 1} = \frac{728}{3 - 1} = 364$$

$$MSBlock = \frac{SSBlock}{b - 1} = \frac{13{,}182}{4 - 1} = 4394$$

$$MSError = \frac{SSError}{(b - 1)(t - 1)} = \frac{58}{(4 - 1)(3 - 1)} = 9.6667$$

Having identified the necessary components, we can now proceed to test the two given claims.

a. To test the claim that the three insurance companies charge premiums that are, on average, the same (that is, the *treatment* means are equal), we use the test statistic

$$F = \frac{MSTreatment}{MSError} = \frac{364}{9.6667} = 37.655$$

This F test statistic has an F distribution with degrees of freedom given by

degrees of freedom (numerator) $= t - 1 = 3 - 1 = 2$

degrees of freedom (denominator) $= (b - 1)(t - 1)$
$$= (4 - 1)(3 - 1) = 6$$

Referring to Table A.5 with the above degrees of freedom and with $\alpha = 0.05$ in this right-tailed test, we find the critical value of $F = 5.1433$. Because the test statistic of $F = 37.655$ exceeds the critical value, we reject the claim of equal treatment (insurance company) means. It appears that the mean insurance premiums for the three insurance companies are not equal.

b. To test the claim that the *block* means are equal, we use the test statistic

$$F = \frac{\text{MSBlock}}{\text{MSError}} = \frac{4394}{9.6667} = 454.55$$

This F test statistic has an F distribution with degrees of freedom given by

degrees of freedom (numerator) $= b - 1 = 4 - 1 = 3$
degrees of freedom (denominator) $= (b - 1)(t - 1)$
$$= (4 - 1)(3 - 1) = 6$$

Referring to Table A.5 with the above degrees of freedom and with $\alpha = 0.05$ in this right-tailed test, we find the critical value of $F = 4.7571$. Because the test statistic of $F = 454.55$ exceeds the critical value, we reject the claim of equal block (classification) means. The mean insurance premiums for the four sex/age classifications apparently are not all equal.

ANOVA TABLE FOR RANDOMIZED BLOCK DESIGN

We can summarize key results from our ANOVA calculations in a table such as Table 11.3. That table is similar to the ANOVA table described in Section 11.2, but it includes an extra row for the block results. Also, it contains two test statistics corresponding to the two hypothesis tests of equal treatment means and equal block means. We will now proceed to discuss the use of Minitab, and we will provide a Minitab display with the same general format as that of Table 11.3.

TABLE 11.3
ANOVA Table

SOURCE OF VARIATION	SUM OF SQUARES *SS*	DEGREES OF FREEDOM	MEAN SQUARE *MS*	TEST STATISTIC
Treatment	*SSTreatment*	$t - 1$	$MSTreatment = \dfrac{SSTreatment}{t - 1}$	$F = \dfrac{MSTreatment}{MSError}$
Block	*SSBlock*	$b - 1$	$MSBlock = \dfrac{SSBlock}{b - 1}$	$F = \dfrac{MSBlock}{MSError}$
Error	*SSError*	$(b - 1)(t - 1)$	$MSError = \dfrac{SSError}{(b - 1)(t - 1)}$	
Total	*SSTotal*	$n - 1$		

USING STATISTICAL SOFTWARE FOR A RANDOMIZED BLOCK DESIGN

We can simplify the calculations required for a randomized block design by using shortcut formulas or by using suitable software. Shown below is the Minitab display corresponding to the preceding example. Note that the format for entering the sample data is very different from the format used in Section 11.2. Here, we enter the sample score in column C1, then enter its row and column numbers in C2 and C3, respectively. For example, the entry of 240 is in the 3rd row and 2nd column, so we enter 240 3 2 for that value. The key Minitab command is TWOWAY C1 C2 C3 where the data have been entered in C1, while C2 and C3 contain the position identifiers for the rows (blocks) and columns (treatments). By ending the TWOWAY C1 C2 C3 command with a semicolon and including the subcommand MEANS C2 C3 (followed by a period), we are entering the subcommand that will provide confidence intervals for the classification blocks (C2) and the insurance company treatments (C3).

The "ANALYSIS OF VARIANCE" section of the display does not provide the F test statistics nor does it provide P-values, but it does provide the values of *MSTreatment, MSBlock,* and *MSError* that we need. Using Minitab's notation, we can easily find the test statistics by noting that:

C2 corresponds to "block."
C3 corresponds to "treatment."

From the Minitab display, we therefore have *SSBlock* = 13182.00, *SSTreatment* = 728.00, and *SSError* = 58.00. We could now use those results and proceed to obtain the other necessary statistics by performing relatively simple calculations. For example, *MSTreatment* = *SSTreatment*/$(t - 1)$ = 728.00/2 = 364. The value of *MSError* is 58/6 = 9.67, so that the test statistic is F = *MSTreatment/MSError* = 364/9.67 = 37.64. Most of the messier calculations are replaced by reference to the Minitab display.

```
MTB > READ C1 C2 C3
DATA> 186 1 1
DATA> 174 2 1
DATA> 259 3 1
DATA> 233 4 1
DATA> 170 1 2
DATA> 160 2 2
DATA> 240 3 2    ←240 is in the 3rd row and 2nd column.
DATA> 218 4 2
DATA> 190 1 3
DATA> 179 2 3
DATA> 260 3 3
DATA> 227 4 3
DATA> END OF DATA
MTB > TWOWAY C1 C2 C3;
SUBC> MEANS C2 C3.
```

(continued)

```
ANALYSIS OF VARIANCE  C1

SOURCE         DF        SS         MS
C2←Block        3    13182.00    4394.00      ⎤   Most of the entries
C3←Treatment    2      728.00     364.00      |   for Table 11.3 can
ERROR           6       58.00       9.67      |   be found here.
TOTAL          11    13968.00                 ⎦
```

```
                     Individual 95% CI
    C2    Mean    ----+---------+---------+---------+-------
     1    182.0        (-*-)
     2    171.0      (*-)
     3    253.0                                  (-*-)
     4    226.0                          (*-)
                  ----+---------+---------+---------+-------
                   175.0     200.0     225.0     250.0
```

```
                     Individual 95% CI
    C3    Mean    ---------+---------+---------+---------+--
     1    213.0                              (-----*-----)
     2    197.0    (-----*------)
     3    214.0                               (------*-----)
                  ---------+---------+---------+---------+--
                       198.0     204.0     210.0     216.0
```

It's enlightening to see what happens if we use the same data in the preceding example, but ignore blocking and use Minitab's AOVONEWAY command. That is, we treat the data as if we randomly select four different policies from each of the three insurance companies. The Minitab display would include a test statistic of $F = 0.25$ and a P-value of 0.786, so that we *fail* to reject the null hypothesis of equal means. This suggests that we do not have sufficient evidence to conclude that there is a difference in the mean rates charged by the three insurance companies. With blocking, however, the sample evidence is sufficient to conclude that there is a difference. In general, with blocking we usually need a smaller sample to show significant differences in means. By controlling other sources of variation (such as sex/age categories) with blocking, we have a more efficient experiment that can detect significant differences among means with fewer sample values.

CONFIDENCE INTERVALS

If we have used ANOVA in a randomized block design and rejected the null hypothesis of equal population means, we will find that confidence intervals are valuable in comparing the population means. The lower portion of the Minitab display includes a display of the confidence intervals for the four blocks (C2) and the three treatments (C3). In general, such confidence intervals can be found from the formulas shown on the following page.

> ## CONFIDENCE INTERVAL FOR THE *j*TH *TREATMENT* MEAN IN RANDOMIZED BLOCK DESIGN:
>
> $$\bar{x}_j - E < \mu_j < \bar{x}_j + E$$
>
> $$\text{where } E = t_{\alpha/2} \frac{s_p}{\sqrt{b}}$$
>
> and $t_{\alpha/2}$ has $(b - 1)(t - 1)$ degrees of freedom and
>
> $$s_p = \sqrt{\frac{SSError}{(b - 1)(t - 1)}}$$

> ## CONFIDENCE INTERVAL FOR THE *i*TH *BLOCK* MEAN IN RANDOMIZED BLOCK DESIGN:
>
> $$\bar{B}_i - E < \mu_i < \bar{B}_i + E$$
>
> $$\text{where } E = t_{\alpha/2} \frac{s_p}{\sqrt{t}}$$
>
> and $t_{\alpha/2}$ has $(b - 1)(t - 1)$ degrees of freedom and
>
> $$s_p = \sqrt{\frac{SSError}{(b - 1)(t - 1)}}$$

As in Section 11.2, we again illustrate the construction of confidence intervals for individual population treatment (insurance company) means as well as differences between population block (age/sex) means. Later we will also show construction of confidence intervals for differences between population means.

EXAMPLE   Again referring to the sample data in Table 11.2, find a 95% confidence interval for the Eastern Trust mean premium over all sex/age categories.

SOLUTION   Because Eastern Trust is one of the three *treatments,* we use the format of a confidence interval for a treatment mean as given above. We get (using 6 degrees of freedom)

$$E = t_{\alpha/2} \frac{s_p}{\sqrt{b}} = 2.447 \frac{3.109}{\sqrt{4}} = 3.80$$

so that $\bar{x}_2 - E < \mu_2 < \bar{x}_2 + E$

becomes

$$197 - 3.80 < \mu_2 < 197 + 3.80 \quad \text{or} \quad 193.20 < \mu_2 < 200.80$$

That is, we are 95% confident that the limits of $193.20 and $200.80 actually do contain the true Eastern Trust mean premium. This confidence interval is graphically displayed near the bottom of the Minitab computer printout (see the second display under C3).

Confidence intervals useful for comparing two means follow the same patterns from the preceding section.

CONFIDENCE INTERVAL FOR THE DIFFERENCE $\mu_i - \mu_j$ BETWEEN TWO *TREATMENT* MEANS IN RANDOMIZED BLOCK DESIGN:

$$(\bar{x}_i - \bar{x}_j) - E < \mu_i - \mu_j < (\bar{x}_i - \bar{x}_j) + E$$

$$\text{where } E = t_{\alpha/2}\sqrt{\frac{s_p^2}{b} + \frac{s_p^2}{b}}$$

and $t_{\alpha/2}$ has $(b - 1)(t - 1)$ degrees of freedom and

$$s_p^2 = \frac{SSError}{(b - 1)(t - 1)}$$

CONFIDENCE INTERVAL FOR THE DIFFERENCE $\mu_i - \mu_j$ BETWEEN TWO *BLOCK* MEANS IN RANDOMIZED BLOCK DESIGN:

$$(\bar{B}_i - \bar{B}_j) - E < \mu_i - \mu_j < (\bar{B}_i - \bar{B}_j) + E$$

$$\text{where } E = t_{\alpha/2}\sqrt{\frac{s_p^2}{t} + \frac{s_p^2}{t}}$$

and $t_{\alpha/2}$ has $(b - 1)(t - 1)$ degrees of freedom and

$$s_p^2 = \frac{SSError}{(b - 1)(t - 1)}$$

EXAMPLE

From the sample data of Table 11.2, we can see that the Iowa Trust sample mean exceeds the Eastern Trust sample mean by $17. Find a 95% confidence interval for this difference: the mean μ_3 of the Iowa Trust premiums minus the mean μ_2 of the Eastern Trust premiums. Does the confidence interval suggest that the Iowa Trust premiums actually do exceed those for Eastern Trust?

SOLUTION

Referring to Table 11.2, we find that $\bar{x}_3 = \$214$ and $\bar{x}_2 = \$197$. With $(b - 1)(t - 1) = 6$ degrees of freedom and with $\alpha = 0.05$, we refer to Table A.2 to find that $t_{\alpha/2} = 2.447$. We find the confidence interval for the difference between two treatment means by first evaluating the margin of error E as shown on the following page:

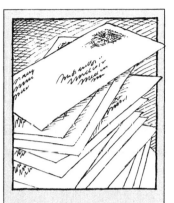

ZIP CODES REVEAL MUCH

The Claritas Corporation has developed a way of obtaining considerable information about people from their Zip codes. Zip code data are extracted from a variety of mailing lists, purchase orders, warranty cards, census data, and market research surveys. With people of the same social and economic levels tending to live in the same areas, it is possible to match Zip codes with such factors as purchase patterns, types of cars driven, foods preferred, leisure-time activities, and television-viewing choices. The company helps clients target their advertising efforts to regions that are most likely to accept particular products.

$$E = t_{\alpha/2}\sqrt{\frac{s_p^2}{b} + \frac{s_p^2}{b}} = 2.447\sqrt{\frac{9.667}{4} + \frac{9.667}{4}} = 5.38$$

With $\bar{x}_3 = \$214$ and $\bar{x}_2 = \$197$ and $E = \$5.38$, our confidence interval

$$(\bar{x}_3 - \bar{x}_2) - E < \mu_3 - \mu_2 < (\bar{x}_3 - \bar{x}_2) + E$$

becomes $\$11.62 < \mu_3 - \mu_2 < \$22.38$.

That is, we are 95% confident that the limits of $11.62 and $22.38 actually do contain the true difference between the mean Iowa Trust premium and the mean Eastern Trust premium. This suggests that we can be 95% confident that the mean Iowa Trust premium is higher than the mean Eastern Trust premium by as little as $11.62 or as much as $22.38.

The examples of this section are based on the sample data in Table 11.2, which involves a very small sample size. We deliberately kept the sample size small so that the calculations would not become too difficult, but real cases typically involve much larger data sets. When you apply the ANOVA techniques to larger cases, we strongly recommend the use of statistical software such as Minitab.

11.3 EXERCISES   BASIC CONCEPTS

1. Engineers design 4 different spark plugs that are tested in 3 different cars, each having a different engine size. The sample results for fuel consumption (in mi/gal) are given in the table below. Use ANOVA for a randomized block design and test the claim that the plug types have the same mean fuel consumption. Use a 0.05 level of significance.

| | **PLUG TYPE** | | | |
SIZE	A	B	C	D
2.0 L	27	28	31	26
2.5 L	24	25	29	24
3.0 L	21	22	24	19

In Exercises 2–6, use the same sample data given in the table for Exercise 1.

2. Find a 95% confidence interval for the mean fuel consumption of the type C spark plugs.

3. Currently, the type B plug is sold as the premium model and the type C spark plug is a new platinum-tipped model that is undergoing tests. Find a 95% confidence interval for the type B plug mean minus the type C plug mean.

4. At the 0.05 significance level, test the claim that the engine sizes have the same mean fuel consumption rate.

5. Find a 95% confidence interval for the mean fuel consumption of the 3.0-L engines.
6. Find a 95% confidence interval for the mean of the 2.0-L engines minus the mean of the 2.5-L engines.
7. Starting salaries are obtained for a sample of 20 students who graduated from a midwestern business school. Those salaries (in thousands of dollars) are arranged according to major and grade point average, as shown in the table below. The Minitab display for this sample is also given. In that Minitab display, C1 corresponds to the salaries, C2 corresponds to the grade point average, and C3 corresponds to the major. Use the Minitab display and test the claim that the mean starting salaries of the 5 majors are all equal. Use a 0.01 level of significance.

GRADE POINT AVERAGE	MAJOR				
	FINANCE	ACCOUNTING	MARKETING	MANAGEMENT	MIS
Above 3.50	26.0	29.5	25.8	24.2	29.0
3.00–3.50	24.8	27.2	25.1	23.0	27.5
2.51–2.99	23.9	25.5	23.6	22.5	25.0
2.00–2.50	22.7	24.0	22.2	21.0	24.3

```
MTB > TWOWAY C1 C2 C3;
SUBC> MEANS C2 C3.

ANALYSIS OF VARIANCE   C1

SOURCE     DF        SS        MS
C2          3     46.268    15.423
C3          4     43.543    10.886
ERROR      12      3.637     0.303
TOTAL      19     93.448

                      Individual 95% CI
   C2     Mean    --+---------+---------+---------+---------
    1    26.90                                   (--*---)
    2    25.52                         (--*---)
    3    24.10               (---*--)
    4    22.84       (--*---)
                   --+---------+---------+---------+---------
                 22.50      24.00     25.50     27.00

                      Individual 95% CI
   C3     Mean    ---+---------+---------+---------+---------
    1    24.35                (---*---)
    2    26.55                          (---*---)
    3    24.17                (---*---)
    4    22.67        (---*---)
    5    26.45                            (---*---)
                   ---+---------+---------+---------+---------
                  22.50      24.00     25.50     27.00
```

In Exercises 8–12, use the same data given in Exercise 7.

8. Find a 95% confidence interval for the mean starting salary of finance majors.
9. Find a 95% confidence interval for this difference: the mean starting salaries of accounting majors minus the mean starting salaries of marketing majors. What does the result suggest about those two majors?
10. Use a 0.01 significance level to test the claim that the 4 categories of grade point average have the same mean starting salary.
11. Find a 95% confidence interval for this difference: the mean starting salary for grade point averages above 3.50 minus the mean starting salary for grade point averages in the 2.00–2.50 category. What does the result suggest?
12. Find a 95% confidence interval for the mean starting salary of MIS (Management Information Systems) majors.

Exercises 13–16 refer to the sample data below and the corresponding Minitab display. The table entries are the times (in minutes) required to complete a document. The same document was entered by 4 different typists using each of 3 different word processors.

	WORD PROCESSOR		
TYPIST	I	II	III
A	16	21	13
B	20	25	16
C	18	21	14
D	19	22	15

ROW	C1	C2	C3
1	16	1	1
2	20	2	1
3	18	3	1
4	19	4	1
5	21	1	2
6	25	2	2
7	21	3	2
8	22	4	2
9	13	1	3
10	16	2	3
11	14	3	3
12	15	4	3

```
MTB > TWOWAY C1 C2 C3;
SUBC> MEANS C2 C3.
```

ANALYSIS OF VARIANCE C1

SOURCE	DF	SS	MS
C2	3	22.000	7.333
C3	2	120.167	60.083
ERROR	6	2.500	0.417
TOTAL	11	144.667	

(continued)

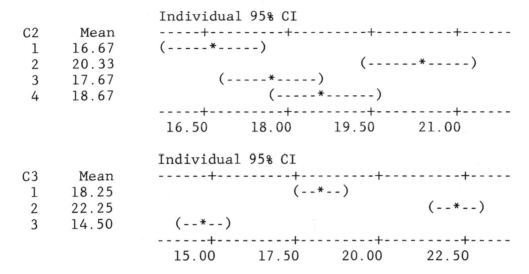

```
                    Individual 95% CI
    C2      Mean    -----+---------+---------+---------+------
    1      16.67    (-----*-----)
    2      20.33                              (------*-----)
    3      17.67           (-----*-----)
    4      18.67               (-----*------)
                    -----+---------+---------+---------+------
                       16.50     18.00     19.50     21.00

                    Individual 95% CI
    C3      Mean    ------+---------+---------+---------+-----
    1      18.25                      (--*--)
    2      22.25                                  (--*--)
    3      14.50           (--*--)
                    ------+---------+---------+---------+-----
                       15.00     17.50     20.00     22.50
```

13. At the 0.05 level of significance, test the claim that the choice of word processor has no effect on the mean typing time.

14. Find a 95% confidence interval for this difference: the mean typing time for word processor I minus the mean for word processor II. What does the result suggest?

15. At the 0.05 level of significance, test the claim that the choice of typist has no effect on the mean typing time.

16. Find a 95% confidence interval for this difference: the mean typing time for typist 2 minus the mean for typist 1. Does the result suggest that the typing time for typist 2 has a mean greater than that for typist 1?

11.3 EXERCISES BEYOND THE BASICS

17. A direct calculation of SSError can be made by using

$$SSError = \Sigma(x - \bar{x}_j - \bar{B}_i + \bar{\bar{x}})^2$$

 a. Refer to the data of Table 11.2 and calculate SSError using the above expression.

 b. Verify that $SSTotal = SSTreatment + SSBlock + SSError$.

18. Instead of using the formulas given in this section, you can use shortcut formulas for $SSBlock$, $SSTreatment$, and $SSTotal$. These shortcut formulas facilitate calculations, but they tend to conceal the meaning of the statistics they represent. Define T_j to be the total of the sample scores of the jth treatment and let GT represent the grand total of $T_1 + T_2 + \cdots + T_t$. Show that when you apply the following formulas to the example of this section, they will yield the same values obtained in that example.

$$SSBlock = \Sigma\frac{B_i^2}{t} - \frac{(GT)^2}{bt} \qquad SSTreatment = \Sigma\frac{T_j^2}{b} - \frac{(GT)^2}{bt}$$

$$SSTotal = \Sigma x^2 - \frac{(GT)^2}{bt}$$

19. Refer to the insurance premium sample data given in Table 11.2 and *transpose* the data by interchanging the rows and columns so that the classifications become treatments and the insurance companies become blocks. How are the ANOVA results affected?

20. Refer to the insurance premium sample data given in Table 11.2 and add 10 to each entry. How are the ANOVA results affected?

21. Refer to the insurance premium sample data given in Table 11.2 and multiply each entry by 10. How are the ANOVA results affected?

22. Refer to the insurance premium sample data given in Table 11.2 and exclude the last column of values. That is, delete the Iowa Trust data.

   a. Use the *t* test method (for dependent samples) of Section 9.3 to test the claim that the mean for Fidelity is equal to the mean for Eastern Trust. Use a 0.05 significance level.

   b. Use the randomized block ANOVA method of this section to test the same claim given in part *a*.

   c. Show that the tests in parts *a* and *b* are equivalent by showing that the squares of the *t* test statistic and critical value are equal to the ANOVA *F* test statistic and critical value.

Vocabulary List

Define and give an example of each term.

analysis of variance
ANOVA
one-way analysis of variance
treatment
blocks
randomized block design

Review

In this chapter we used *analysis of variance* to determine whether differences among sample means are due to chance fluctuations or whether the differences are significant. This method requires (1) normally distributed populations, (2) populations with the same standard deviation (or variance), and (3) random samples that are independent of one another for one-way ANOVA (but dependent samples are used for randomized block ANOVA).

Our test statistics are based on the ratio of two different estimates of the common population variance. In repeated samplings, the distribution of the *F* test statistic can be approximated by the *F* distribution, which has critical values given in Table A.5.

In Section 11.2 we considered one-way or one-factor analysis of variance. We also discussed multiple comparison procedures based on *t* tests from Chapters 7 and 9 to construct confidence intervals for one mean or to compare two means.

In Section 11.3 we considered randomized block analysis of variance for cases involving two factors. We categorized the data according to two different factors, one of which is often of lesser interest and is used to help control the variation in the data that is due to that factor. This factor is called a block and it results in a table that has one entry per cell. Finally, we discussed multiple comparison procedures for randomized block analysis of variance, and we obtained confidence intervals as in Section 11.2.

IMPORTANT FORMULAS

APPLICA-TION	DISTRIBU-TION	TEST STATISTIC	DEGREES OF FREEDOM	CRITICAL VALUES
One-Way ANOVA	F	$F = \dfrac{MSTreatment}{MSError}$ where	num.: $t - 1$ den.: $n - t$	Table A.5

t = number of populations
$\bar{\bar{x}}$ = mean of all sample scores combined
n = total number of values in all samples combined
n_j = number of values in the jth sample
$\bar{x}_j$ = mean of values in the jth sample

$SSTotal = SSTreatment + SSError$
$SSTotal = \Sigma(x - \bar{\bar{x}})^2$ $n - 1$
$SSTreatment = n_1(\bar{x}_1 - \bar{\bar{x}})^2 + n_2(\bar{x}_2 - \bar{\bar{x}})^2 +$ $t - 1$
     $\cdots + n_t(\bar{x}_t - \bar{\bar{x}})^2$
$SSError = (n_1 - 1)s_1^2 + (n_2 - 1)s_2^2 +$ $n - t$
     $\cdots + (n_t - 1)s_t^2$

$MSTreatment = \dfrac{SSTreatment}{t - 1}$

$MSError = \dfrac{SSError}{n - t}$

$MSTotal = \dfrac{SSTotal}{n - 1}$

| Randomized Block Design | F | Treatment
 $F = \dfrac{MSTreatment}{MSError}$ | num.: $t - 1$
 den.: $(b - 1)(t - 1)$ | Table A.5 |
| | | Block
 $F = \dfrac{MSBlock}{MSError}$
 where | num.: $b - 1$
 den.: $(b - 1)(t - 1)$ | Table A.5 |

t = number of treatments
b = number of blocks
$n = bt$ = total number of scores in all samples combined
$\bar{x}_j$ = mean of values in the jth treatment
$\bar{B}_i$ = mean of values in the ith block
$\bar{\bar{x}}$ = mean of all sample scores combined

$SSTotal = SSTreatment + SSBlock + SSError$ $n - 1 = bt - 1$
     $SSTotal = \Sigma(x - \bar{\bar{x}})^2$
$SSTreatment = b(\bar{x}_1 - \bar{\bar{x}})^2 + b(\bar{x}_2 - \bar{\bar{x}})^2 +$ $t - 1$
     $\cdots + b(\bar{x}_t - \bar{\bar{x}})^2$
$SSBlock = t(\bar{B}_1 - \bar{\bar{x}})^2 + t(\bar{B}_2 - \bar{\bar{x}})^2 + \cdots + t(\bar{B}_b - \bar{\bar{x}})^2$ $b - 1$
$SSError = SSTotal - SSTreatment - SSBlock$ $(b - 1)(t - 1)$

$MSTreatment = \dfrac{SSTreatment}{t - 1}$

$MSBlock = \dfrac{SSBlock}{b - 1}$

$MSError = \dfrac{SSError}{(b - 1)(t - 1)}$

Review Exercises

1. An international manufacturer of tennis balls tests 4 methods of sealing the balls to lengthen the time before they lose acceptable levels of bounce. Several lots of balls are made by each of the 4 methods, and they are stored for 3 months when 30 balls from each process are randomly selected. Each selected ball is dropped from a fixed platform, and the height of the bounce is recorded, with the sample results summarized below. Use a 0.05 level of significance to test the claim that the 4 sealing methods have the same mean bounce height.

I	II	III	IV
$n_1 = 30$	$n_2 = 30$	$n_3 = 30$	$n_4 = 30$
$\bar{x}_1 = 28.4$ in.	$\bar{x}_2 = 29.1$ in.	$\bar{x}_3 = 32.2$ in.	$\bar{x}_4 = 27.9$ in.
$s_1 = 3.5$ in.	$s_2 = 3.2$ in.	$s_3 = 2.9$ in.	$s_4 = 3.5$ in.

2. Use the same sample data given in Exercise 1. Construct a 95% confidence interval for the mean height for method I.

3. Use the same sample data given in Exercise 1. Construct a 95% confidence interval for the difference between the mean for method III and the mean for method I. What does the result suggest?

4. Three methods of teaching accounting are used with 3 groups of randomly selected business students. All students in the sample group take the same final exam, and the Minitab ANOVA results are given below. At the 0.05 significance level, test the claim that the 3 teaching methods result in the same mean final exam score.

```
MTB > AOVONEWAY C1 C2 C3

ANALYSIS OF VARIANCE
SOURCE      DF      SS      MS      F        P
FACTOR       2     250     125    1.02    0.365
ERROR       63    7680     122
TOTAL       65    7930
                                 INDIVIDUAL  95  PCT CI'S  FOR MEAN
                                 BASED ON POOLED STDEV
   LEVEL      N    MEAN    STDEV  ----+---------+---------+---------+--
   C1        21   80.00     9.21                 (-----------*-----------)
   C2        22   75.23    11.96   (-----------*-----------)
   C3        23   78.13    11.64        (----------*-----------)
                                 ----+---------+---------+---------+--
POOLED STDEV =   11.04          72.0      76.0      80.0      84.0
```

5. A bank manager records the number of checks processed by 3 employees, each of whom works on 3 different check-processing machines. Given below are sample results from a 10-min test period.

	MACHINE I	MACHINE II	MACHINE III
Employee 1	47	39	37
Employee 2	50	37	42
Employee 3	56	44	50

Using the machine type as treatment and the employee as block, conduct a randomized block analysis of variance to test the claim that the machines have the same mean. Use a 0.05 level of significance.

6. Use the same data from Exercise 5 to construct a 95% confidence interval for this difference: the mean for machine I minus the mean for machine III.

7. Use the same data from Exercise 5 to test the claim that the 3 employees have the same mean check-processing rate. Use a 0.05 level of significance.

8. Use the same data from Exercise 5 to construct a 95% confidence interval for the mean number of checks processed by employee 2.

Computer Projects

1. Listed below are weights (in grams) of a sample of M&M candies. Use Minitab and the methods of this chapter to test the claim that the different colored candies have the same mean weight.

RED	ORANGE	YELLOW	BROWN	TAN	GREEN
0.864	0.921	0.890	0.848	0.957	0.894
0.952	0.882	0.927	0.831	0.942	0.922
0.941	0.939	0.912	0.936	0.886	0.842
0.817	0.927	0.971	0.843	0.950	0.893
0.957	0.935	0.920	0.888	0.957	0.947
0.920	0.918	0.890	0.946	0.876	0.900
0.958	0.893	0.914	0.949	1.003	0.871
0.933	0.938	0.986	0.932	0.935	0.802
0.870	0.914	0.925	0.949	0.890	0.940
0.871		0.929	0.941	0.947	
0.921		0.892	0.924	0.899	
0.896		0.845	0.976		
0.913		0.958	0.946		
0.844		0.930	0.924		
0.931		0.922	0.972		
0.909		0.914	0.942		
0.876		0.912	0.889		
		0.936	0.905		
		0.822	0.936		
		0.861	1.027		
		0.912	0.922		
		0.935	0.824		
		0.905	0.888		
		0.931	0.992		
			0.978		
			0.963		
			0.966		
			0.961		
			0.955		
			0.816		

Simulation of ANOVA and Type I Error

2. Given below is a set of Minitab commands that simulate 3 diets, all assumed to have the same effect consisting of weight losses (over a 3-month period) that are normally distributed with a mean of 11 lb and a standard deviation of 3 lb. Fifteen people (5 for each diet) are simulated. The ANOVA display is included in the printout below.

   a. Use a 0.05 level of significance to test the claim that the 3 diets have the same mean. (Note that we are generating the sample data with the condition that $\mu_1 = \mu_2 = \mu_3$; that is, the 3 diets have the same mean weight loss.)

   b. Repeat the given Minitab commands to generate your own set of sample results and run your own ANOVA. Then repeat the same test described in part a. Rejecting H_0: $\mu_1 = \mu_2 = \mu_3$ would be a type I error. In a class of 40 students, how many of these type I errors would you expect if each student runs this simulation?

```
MTB > RANDOM k=5 C1;
SUBC> NORMAL mu=11 sigma=3.
MTB > RANDOM k=5 C2;
SUBC> NORMAL mu=11 sigma=3.
MTB > RANDOM k=5 C3;
SUBC> NORMAL mu=11 sigma=3.
MTB > PRINT C1 C2 C3

ROW          C1           C2           C3

 1       15.8561       9.8109      12.6394
 2       11.5258      14.3574       4.2556
 3        8.7116      13.1469      11.4744
 4       10.9366      11.6373       8.2604
 5       10.9430      11.1449      11.5859


MTB > AOVONEWAY C1 C2 C3

ANALYSIS OF VARIANCE
SOURCE      DF         SS         MS        F        P
FACTOR       2      16.06       8.03     1.11    0.362
ERROR       12      86.90       7.24
TOTAL       14     102.96
                                       INDIVIDUAL 95 PCT CI'S FOR MEAN
                                       BASED ON POOLED STDEV
   LEVEL     N      MEAN      STDEV    --+---------+---------+---------+----
C1           5    11.595      2.614               (---------*----------)
C2           5    12.019      1.770                 (---------*----------)
C3           5     9.643      3.429     (----------*---------)
                                       --+---------+---------+---------+----
POOLED STDEV =    2.691               7.5       10.0       12.5       15.0
```

IS THE REAL ESTATE AGENT BEING HONEST?

You are considering the purchase of a home with a selling price that is well above average for its region. You are concerned that although the cost is well above average, the home has only 1.5 baths. Your real estate agent claims that the number of baths doesn't really affect the value or selling price of a home. You suspect that this argument isn't correct, but you would like to obtain some factual data. Using the Appendix B data for homes sold, enter the selling prices in the appropriate column below. Then test the claim that the samples in all three categories come from populations having the same mean. Do the results of the test support the real estate agent or are they contradictory? Write a brief report summarizing your findings.

NUMBER OF BATHS

1 or 1.5	2 or 2.5	3 or more

CHAPTER 12
Linear Regression and Correlation

12.1 OVERVIEW

12.2 SCATTER DIAGRAMS AND SIMPLE LINEAR REGRESSION

Scatter diagrams are presented to illustrate graphically the relationships between two variables. We then show how to describe the linear relationship with an equation of the regression line, and we illustrate how that equation can be used for making predictions. The determination of the equation for the regression line is based on the least-squares property, which is described in this section.

12.3 MEASURING VARIATION AROUND THE REGRESSION LINE

This section shows the assumptions of regression that allow us to make inferences from our regression line. Also, we analyze the *variation* between *predicted* and *observed* values. The *coefficient of determination R^2* is discussed as a measure of how well a regression line fits the data.

12.4 HYPOTHESIS TESTING AND CONFIDENCE INTERVALS FOR THE SLOPE β_1

Methods for *hypothesis testing* and for constructing *confidence intervals* for the slope β_1 of the regression line are presented. Also, a typical computer printout for simple linear regression is presented and discussed.

12.5 CONFIDENCE INTERVALS FOR PREDICTED VALUES

Instructions are given for constructing *confidence intervals* for the mean predicted value and *prediction intervals* for individual predicted values.

12.6 CORRELATION

The *linear correlation coefficient* is used to determine whether a linear relationship exists between two variables.

Can a Home's Living Area Be Used to Predict Its Selling Price?

B ecause the purchase of a home is the largest investment most of us ever make, home buyers are naturally concerned about the price. Almost no home buyers pay the asking price. Instead, they try to estimate the home's value and they negotiate a lower price accordingly. A homeowner selling a house naturally wants the highest possible price, but if the asking price is set too high, the home might be on the market too long. In establishing an asking price, what factors should the homeowner take into account? The living area, usually measured in square feet, is clearly an important factor. Larger homes require more materials and more labor costs, so they tend to have higher selling prices. Table 12.1 lists the actual living areas and selling prices for eight homes sold in Dutchess County, New York. The living areas are given in hundreds of square feet and the selling prices are in thousands of dollars. Using the given data, can we conclude that there is a relationship between

TABLE 12.1

Living area	15	38	23	16	16	13	20	24
Selling price	145	228	150	130	160	114	142	265

selling price and living area? If so, what is the relationship and can we use it to predict the selling price of a home with 1800 sq ft? An objective of this chapter is to analyze such relationships. We will show that there is a relationship between selling price and living area, we will identify that relationship, we will determine the predicted selling price of a home with 1800 sq ft, and we will show how accurate that prediction is.

In business and industry, we often need to analyze relationships between variables. Consider, for example, the following issues.

- For American Airlines, is the volume of ticket sales related to the prices charged? If so, what is that relationship? If it's necessary to increase ticket prices by 4%, can the effect on ticket sales be predicted?
- For the Merrill Lynch investment company, is there a relationship between the volume of business (measured in dollars) and the amount spent on advertising? If so, what is that relationship? If next month's advertising budget is increased by $10,000, can the effect on business volume be predicted?

These are only two examples of the many different circumstances in which we might need to analyze relationships between variables. In Chapter 10 we described a method of testing for a relationship between two variables, but we considered categorical data only, such as gender and yes/no response to a survey question. Also, the method of Chapter 10 enables us to conclude only that a relationship does or does not exist. In this chapter we again consider relationships between two variables, but we now deal with data at the interval or ratio level of measurement. In addition to determining whether there is a relationship, we will proceed to describe the relationship (if it exists) with an equation that can be used for making predictions.

In using statistical methods, it is extremely important to understand that both the arrangement and nature of data as well as the question you want answered can dramatically affect the particular methods that can and should be used. Examine Table 12.2. It consists of a sample of six paired data, but the actual nature of the data determines the statistical approach that should be used. Consider the following scenarios.

SCENARIO 1   In Table 12.2 the *x*-*y* pairs represent times (in minutes) required for six technicians to enter a document into two different word processing systems. The first technician required 110 min on the *x* system and 108 min on the *y* system. One reasonable and sensible question is this: "Are the *y* times *significantly less* than the *x* times?" If yes, then the *y* word processing system appears to be the more efficient one. A relevant method of analysis is the test of the hypothesis $\mu_x > \mu_y$, where the two populations are dependent. (See Section 9.3.)

SCENARIO 2   Suppose that in Table 12.2 the *x*-*y* pairs represent the number of telephone calls (*x*) and the dollar value (*y*) of sales for six members of a magazine telemarketing team. A reasonable and sensible question is this: "Is there a *relationship* between the number of calls and the dollar value of sales?" The relevant method of analysis will be presented in this chapter.

We begin the next section by graphing sample paired data in a scatter diagram. Then we proceed to use methods of regression analysis for describing the relationship between the two variables and for predicting the value of one variable

TABLE 12.2
$x - y$ Paired Data

x	110	103	105	98	140	112
y	108	104	101	96	135	107

given some particular value of the other variable. Finally, we discuss the concept of correlation, which is used to determine whether a significant linear relationship exists between two variables.

Throughout this chapter we deal only with *linear* relationships (relationships that can be described by a straight-line equation or graph). The next chapter will involve linear relationships between more than two variables, as well as some nonlinear relationships.

12.2   SCATTER DIAGRAMS AND SIMPLE LINEAR REGRESSION

The scatter diagram is one tool that we can use to analyze linear (straight-line) relationships between two variables, such as the selling price of a home and its living area, or the sales for a company and the amount spent on advertising.

DEFINITION

A scatter diagram is a graph consisting of a horizontal axis representing the x variable, a vertical axis representing the y variable, and a point plotted for each x-y pair of sample data.

See Fig. 12.1 on page 506 for the scatter diagram that corresponds to the data in Table 12.1. Based on that scatter diagram, does there seem to be a linear relationship between the selling price and living area? Because the points in the scatter diagram seem to follow an upward pattern, we might conclude that a relationship does exist between x (living area) and y (selling price). Other examples of scatter diagrams are shown in Fig. 12.2 on page 507. In general, scatter diagrams are easy to plot and often reveal patterns. But conclusions drawn from them tend to be subjective, and some of us might see patterns where others do not. Fortunately, more precise and objective methods have been developed. We now consider one such method.

THE REGRESSION LINE

Given a set of sample paired data, such as the data of Table 12.1 depicted in Fig. 12.1, we can identify a special straight line that fits the points "best." (Later, we will describe the criterion for what we now casually refer to as "best.") Because this chapter deals only with *linear* relationships between two variables, the straight line will have an equation similar to the equation of $y = mx + b$ we have all come to know and love from high school courses.

FIGURE 12.1
Scatter Diagram for Table 12.1

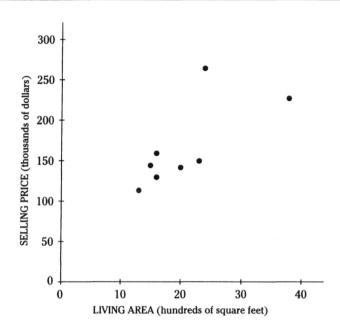

DEFINITION

Given a collection of sample paired data, the *regression line* is the straight line that best fits the data. The regression line is described algebraically by the *regression equation* (see Formula 12.1) that expresses the relationship between the two variables.

Formula 12.1

$$\hat{y} = \hat{\beta}_0 + \hat{\beta}_1 x$$

$$\uparrow \qquad \uparrow$$

$$\text{y-intercept} \quad \text{slope}$$

Notation

$\hat{y}$	Predicted value of y
β_0	y-intercept of the regression line for all the paired population data (β_0 is a population parameter.)
$\hat{\beta}_0$	Sample estimate of the y-intercept β_0 ($\hat{\beta}_0$ is a sample statistic.)
β_1	Slope of the regression line for all the paired population data (β_1 is a population parameter.)
$\hat{\beta}_1$	Sample estimate of the slope β_1 ($\hat{\beta}_1$ is a sample statistic.)

Formula 12.1 is based on a collection of sample paired data, and the formula $y = \beta_0 + \beta_1 x$ is the regression equation for the population of paired data.

We have noted that in high school math courses, a straight line is commonly represented by the equation $y = mx + b$, where m is the slope and b is the

FIGURE 12.2
Scatter Diagrams

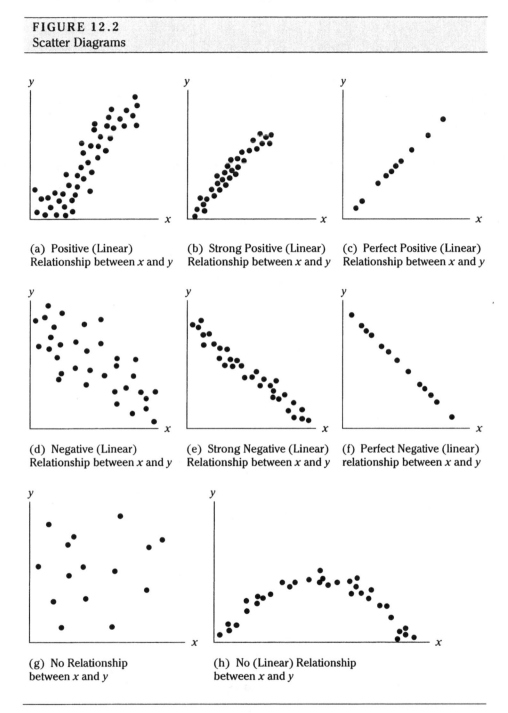

(a) Positive (Linear)
Relationship between x and y

(b) Strong Positive (Linear)
Relationship between x and y

(c) Perfect Positive (Linear)
Relationship between x and y

(d) Negative (Linear)
Relationship between x and y

(e) Strong Negative (Linear)
Relationship between x and y

(f) Perfect Negative (linear)
relationship between x and y

(g) No Relationship
between x and y

(h) No (Linear) Relationship
between x and y

RISING TO NEW HEIGHTS

The concept of regression was introduced in 1877 by Sir Francis Galton. His research showed that when tall parents have children, those children tend to have heights that "regress," or revert to the mean height of the population.

Stanford University's Dr. Darrell Wilson reported on a correlation between height and intelligence. Taller children tend to earn higher scores on intelligence tests as well as on achievement tests. The correlation was found to be significant, but the test scores of tall people were not very much higher than those of shorter people.

y-intercept. Formula 12.1 is another form of $y = mx + b$. The symbol $\hat{\beta}_0$ represents the y-intercept, $\hat{\beta}_1$ represents the slope, and we use $\hat{y}$ to denote a *predicted* value of y. Remember, one important use of a regression line is to predict the value of one variable given some particular value of the other variable. Given the living area of a home, for example, we might want to find the value of $\hat{y}$, the predicted selling price of that home.

On first exposure to Formula 12.1, you might wonder why we're using seemingly messy notation like $\hat{\beta}_0$ and $\hat{\beta}_1$, and you might wonder how you can find those values. Just as $\bar{x}$ is a sample estimate of the population mean μ, the symbol $\hat{\beta}_0$ represents a sample estimate of the population parameter β_0, and $\hat{\beta}_1$ is a sample estimate of the population parameter β_1. To find values for $\hat{\beta}_0$ and $\hat{\beta}_1$, we use Formulas 12.2 and 12.3, which will be presented shortly. First, we introduce the notation that will be used in those formulas and throughout this chapter.

Notation

n	denotes the *number of pairs* of data present. In Table 12.1, $n = 8$.
Σ	denotes the addition of the items indicated.
Σx	denotes the sum of all x scores.
Σx^2	indicates that each x score should be squared, and then those squares added.
$(\Sigma x)^2$	indicates that the x scores should be added and the total then squared. It is extremely important to avoid confusion between Σx^2 and $(\Sigma x)^2$.
Σxy	indicates that each x score should be multiplied by its corresponding y score. After obtaining all such products, find their sum.
$SSx = \Sigma(x - \bar{x})^2$	indicates that we first subtract the mean $\bar{x}$ from each x score, then square all those differences, and then find the sum of those squares. (Note that this is the numerator of the sample variance of the x values; it measures the total amount of variation for the x values.) It can be expressed in a "shortcut" form as $SSx = \Sigma x^2 - (\Sigma x)^2/n$.
$SSy = \Sigma(y - \bar{y})^2$	indicates that we first subtract the mean $\bar{y}$ from each y score, then square all those differences, and then find the sum of those squares. (Note that this is the numerator of the sample variance of the y values; it measures the total amount of variation for the y values.) It can be expressed in a "shortcut" form as $SSy = \Sigma y^2 - (\Sigma y)^2/n$.
$SSxy = \Sigma(x - \bar{x})(y - \bar{y})$	indicates that for each $x - y$ pair of data, subtract the mean $\bar{x}$ from x, subtract the mean $\bar{y}$ from y, then multiply those two results; after obtaining all such products, find their sum. $SSxy$ is a measure of the total variation for the x and y values together. It can be expressed in a "shortcut" form as $SSxy = \Sigma xy - (\Sigma x)(\Sigma y)/n$.

Using the above notation, we now present the formulas for the slope $\hat{\beta}_1$ and y-intercept $\hat{\beta}_0$ of the regression line that best fits sample data. We give the formula for the slope first because it is used in finding the value of the y-intercept.

Formula 12.2 $\hat{\beta}_1 = \dfrac{SSxy}{SSx}$ (estimated slope)

where $SSxy$ and SSx are as given above.

The following formula is equivalent to Formula 12.2. That is, both formulas will yield the same results. However, this formula generally involves simpler computations and is therefore a "shortcut" version of Formula 12.2.

Shortcut version of Formula 12.2 $\hat{\beta}_1 = \dfrac{\Sigma xy - \dfrac{(\Sigma x)(\Sigma y)}{n}}{\Sigma x^2 - \dfrac{(\Sigma x)^2}{n}}$

While Formula 12.2 provides the value of the estimated slope of the regression line, the following formula can be used to find the estimated y-intercept.

Formula 12.3 $\hat{\beta}_0 = \bar{y} - \hat{\beta}_1\bar{x}$ (estimated y-intercept)

mean of the   found from   mean of the
y values   Formula 12.2   x values

   Employing the above formulas, we can use sample paired data to find the equation of the regression line. Such an equation can then be used for describing a relationship between two variables and for predicting the value of one variable given some value for the other variable. In the following example, we will use the real estate sample data in Table 12.1 to find the equation of the regression line. That equation will algebraically describe the relationship between living area and selling price. Then we will present another example in which we predict the selling price of a home with a living area of 1800 sq ft.

EXAMPLE   Using the real estate sample data in Table 12.1, find: $\hat{\beta}_1$ (the value of the sample estimate of the slope), $\hat{\beta}_0$ (the sample estimate of the y-intercept), and the equation of the regression line ($\hat{y} = \hat{\beta}_0 + \hat{\beta}_1 x$).

SOLUTION   For the sample paired data in Table 12.1 we get $n = 8$ because there are 8 pairs of data. The other components required in Formulas 12.2 and 12.3 are found from the calculations in the table below. Note how this vertical format makes the calculations easier.

LIVING AREA x	SELLING PRICE y	$x \cdot y$	x^2	y^2
15	145	2,175	225	21,025
38	228	8,664	1,444	51,984
23	150	3,450	529	22,500
16	130	2,080	256	16,900
16	160	2,560	256	25,600
13	114	1,482	169	12,996
20	142	2,840	400	20,164
24	265	6,360	576	70,225
Total: 165	1,334	29,611	3,855	241,394
Σx	Σy	Σxy	Σx^2	Σy^2

Using these calculated values, we can now find $\hat{\beta}_1$ as follows:

$$\hat{\beta}_1 = \frac{SSxy}{SSx} = \frac{\Sigma xy - \dfrac{(\Sigma x)(\Sigma y)}{n}}{\Sigma x^2 - \dfrac{(\Sigma x)^2}{n}} = \frac{29{,}611 - \dfrac{(165)(1334)}{8}}{3855 - \dfrac{(165)^2}{8}} = \frac{2097.25}{451.875}$$

$$= 4.6412$$

Using $\hat{\beta}_1 = 4.6412$, we can now calculate $\hat{\beta}_0$ by using Formula 12.3.

$$\hat{\beta}_0 = \bar{y} - \hat{\beta}_1\bar{x} = \frac{1334}{8} - (4.6412)\left(\frac{165}{8}\right) = 71.025$$

(For accuracy, we should carry at least 5 digits in intermediate calculations, and round only at the end.) Having found $\hat{\beta}_0$ and $\hat{\beta}_1$, we can now express the equation of the regression line as

$$\hat{y} = 71.0 + 4.64x$$

That is, the selling price (in thousands of dollars) can be predicted by adding 71.0 to the product of 4.64 and the living area (in hundreds of square feet). Note that the slope $\hat{\beta}_1$ of 4.64 is *positive,* and this agrees with the apparent upward trend of the data in the scatter diagram of Fig. 12.1.

In the preceding solution, we found $\hat{\beta}_1$ by using the shortcut version of Formula 12.2. We could also use the other version by noting the following, which yield the same results found earlier.

$SSx = \Sigma(x - \bar{x})^2 = (15 - 20.625)^2 + \cdots + (24 - 20.625)^2 = 451.875$

$SSxy = \Sigma(x - \bar{x})(y - \bar{y})$

$\qquad = (15 - 20.625)(145 - 166.75) + \cdots + (24 - 20.625)(265 - 166.75)$

$\qquad = 2097.25$

$\hat{\beta}_1 = SSxy/SSx = \dfrac{2097.25}{451.875} = 4.64$

Most students tend to find the longer form more tedious because many digits of accuracy must be carried to prevent rounding errors that can dramatically affect final results for $\hat{\beta}_1$ and $\hat{\beta}_0$. Although even the shortcut version of Formula 12.2 appears messy, it's quite easy once we know the values of n, Σx, Σy, Σx^2, Σy^2, and Σxy. In fact, almost all the calculations in this chapter involve those terms. (Some inexpensive calculators will automatically provide values for the slope $\hat{\beta}_1$ and the y-intercept $\hat{\beta}_0$ after you have entered the data. Check the manual for your particular calculator and see if it includes a reference to regression. Many computer software packages also allow you to obtain the important results.)

What can we do with the regression equation once it is found? We can graph it on the scatter diagram, as in Fig. 12.3. Just select at least two convenient values of x, substitute them into the regression equation to find the corresponding values of $\hat{y}$, plot them, and sketch the straight line passing through them. We can also use the regression equation to make predictions.

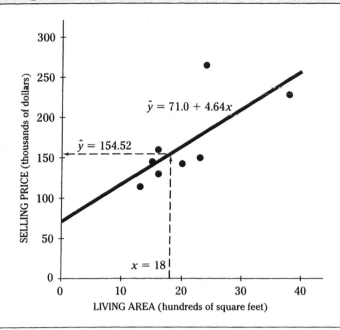

FIGURE 12.3
Plotting the Regression Line for Table 12.1

MAKING PREDICTIONS

Given some value of x, we can often use the regression equation to find the predicted value of $\hat{y}$ by simply substituting the given value of x into the regression equation. However, **we should use the regression equation only if there is a significant linear relationship between the two variables. In the absence of a significant linear relationship, our best estimate of y is simply the sample mean $\bar{y}$.** Later in the chapter we will present objective procedures for determining whether there is a significant linear relationship between the two variables (that is, whether the regression line fits the points well). For now, we can use the scatter diagram to judge whether a significant linear relationship exists. Because the scatter diagram of Fig. 12.1 does seem to reveal an upward linear pattern, we will use the regression equation for making predictions. With this approach, we can now answer the question posed at the beginning of the chapter: "What selling price would you predict for a home that has a living area of 1800 square feet?" See the following example.

EXAMPLE   We have found that the sample data of Table 12.1 lead to the regression equation $\hat{y} = 71.0 + 4.64x$. (Recall that the values of x represent living areas in hundreds of square feet, and values of $\hat{y}$ represent selling prices in thousands of dollars.) Given a home with a living area of 1800 sq ft, what is the predicted selling price?

> **SOLUTION** Because the living area is 1800 sq ft, we let $x = 18$. We have
> concluded from the scatter diagram that a significant linear relation-
> ship exists between x and y, so we will use the regression equation
> for predictions. (If we had concluded that there is no significant linear
> relationship, our best estimate of y would simply be $\bar{y} = 1334/8 =$
> 166.8, regardless of the value for x.) Substituting 18 for x in the
> regression equation, we get
>
> $$\hat{y} = 71.0 + 4.64(18) = 154.52$$
>
> which corresponds to a selling price of \$154,520. That is, based on
> our sample data, we predict that a home with a living area of 1800 sq
> ft will have a selling price of \$154,520. (Using the more precise
> values, before rounding, of $\hat{\beta}_0 = 71.025$ and $\hat{\beta}_1 = 4.6412$, we get a
> predicted selling price of \$154,567.)

We can also use the regression equation to see the effect on one variable when the
other variable changes by some specific amount.

DEFINITION

**When working with two variables related by a regression equation, the
marginal change in a variable is the amount it changes when the other
variable changes by one unit.**

The slope in the regression equation represents the marginal change in y resulting
when x changes by one unit. For our real estate data, we can see that an increase
in x of one unit will cause $\hat{y}$ to change by 4.64 units (or \$4640). That is, if you
increase the living area by 100 sq ft, the predicted selling price increases by
\$4640. Such information is clearly important to anyone considering an addition to
their home. The cost of the addition can be compared to the increase in selling
price so that the value of the addition can be analyzed in terms of a return on
investment.

LEAST-SQUARES PROPERTY

When defining the terms *regression line* and *regression equation*, we referred to the
straight line that fits the points "best." The best-fitting line satisfies the **least-
squares property:**

> **The sum of the squares of the vertical deviations of the sample
> points from the regression line is the smallest sum possible.**

This least-squares property can be understood (believe it or not!) by examining
Fig. 12.4 and the text that follows. Figure 12.4 shows the paired data contained in
the following table.

FIGURE 12.4
Differences between Observed and Predicted y Values

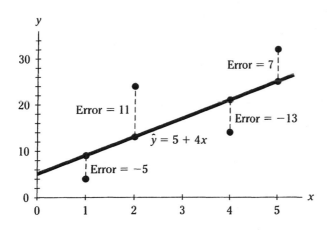

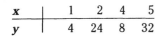

x	1	2	4	5
y	4	24	8	32

Figure 12.4 also shows the regression line, with equation $\hat{y} = 5 + 4x$, found by using the formulas for $\hat{\beta}_1$ and $\hat{\beta}_0$. The distances identified as errors in Fig. 12.4 are the differences between the actual *observed* y values and the *predicted* $\hat{y}$ values on the regression line. The least-squares property guarantees that the sum of the squares of those vertical errors

$$(-5)^2 + (11)^2 + (-13)^2 + (7)^2 = 364$$

is the *minimum* sum that is possible with the given data. Any other line will yield a sum of squares larger than 364. It is in this sense that the line $\hat{y} = 5 + 4x$ fits the data best. (For example, the line $\hat{y} = 8 + 3x$ will have vertical errors of -7, 10, -12, and 9, and the sum of their squares is 374, which exceeds the minimum of 364.)

Fortunately, we need not deal directly with the least-squares property when we want to find the equation of the regression line. Calculus has been used to build the least-squares property into our formulas for $\hat{\beta}_0$ and $\hat{\beta}_1$. Because the derivations of those formulas require calculus, we don't include the derivations in this text.

12.2   EXERCISES   BASIC CONCEPTS

In Exercises 1 and 2, determine whether you expect a positive association (or slope), a negative association (or slope), or no association for each of the given sets of variables.

CORRELATION DOES NOT IMPLY CAUSALITY

A study conducted in Holland in the 1950s revealed a very strong positive correlation between the number of storks in a town and the number of babies born in that town. However, this correlation doesn't necessarily imply that the storks were causing babies. In fact, an increase in the stork population was fostered by an increase in the type of housing in which storks like to build nests. As the town's population grew, more homes were built and more storks came to nest in them.

Causation is usually very difficult to establish. Representatives of the tobacco industry are quick to point out that a high correlation between smoking and lung cancer does not necessarily imply that smoking *causes* cancer. In general, a statistical correlation between two variables does not necessarily imply that one variable has a causal effect on the other.

1. a.   The ages of cars and their resale values
   b.   The monthly amounts spent by Coca-Cola on advertising and the sales of Coca-Cola products
   c.   The amount of china made in England and the price of tea in China
   d.   The years of education and the incomes of taxpayers
   e.   The weights of cars and fuel consumption as measured in miles per gallon

2. a.   The prices of American Airline tickets and the numbers of tickets sold
   b.   Annual per capita income for different nations and per capita entertainment expenditures for those nations
   c.   Hours spent studying for tests and the resulting test scores
   d.   The times spent training different workers and the costs of repairing the car transmissions they build
   e.   The maintenance costs of American Airlines jets and the lengths of delays due to inclement weather

3. Based on a sample of 10 homes, the Central Valley Utility Company develops the regression equation $\hat{y} = -830 + 1.78x$, where $\hat{y}$ is the number of kilowatt hours of electricity used in a month and x is the living area in square feet. Assume that the regression line fits the sample data points well and use this equation to predict the number of kilowatt hours of electricity to be used in one month by a home with (a) 1500 sq ft of living area and (b) 2000 sq ft of living area.

4. Based on a sample of 15 homes, the Central Valley Utility Company develops the regression equation $\hat{y} = -980 + 1.92x$, where $\hat{y}$ is the number of kilowatt hours of electricity used in a month and x is the living area in square feet. Assume that the regression line fits the data well and use this equation to predict the number of kilowatt hours of electricity to be used in one month by a home with (a) 1500 sq ft of living area and (b) 2000 sq ft of living area.

In Exercises 5–8, find the equation of the regression line by using the given values of n, Σx, Σx^2, Σy, and Σxy obtained from sample paired data relating time spent trying to reduce variation in a process (x) and the dollar value saved because of fewer defects (y).

5. $n = 6$, $\Sigma x = 73$, $\Sigma x^2 = 935$, $\Sigma y = 39$, and $\Sigma xy = 497$
6. $n = 7$, $\Sigma x = 63$, $\Sigma x^2 = 571$, $\Sigma y = 109$, and $\Sigma xy = 985$
7. $n = 8$, $\Sigma x = 49.0$, $\Sigma x^2 = 319.5$, $\Sigma y = 133.0$, and $\Sigma xy = 774.2$
8. $n = 12$, $\Sigma x = 15.4$, $\Sigma x^2 = 126.3$, $\Sigma y = 55.8$, and $\Sigma xy = 73.1$

In Exercises 9–18, use the given list of paired data.

   a.   Construct the scatter diagram.
   b.   Determine the values of n, Σx, Σx^2, Σy, Σy^2, Σxy, $SSxy$, and SSx.
   c.   Find $\hat{\beta}_1$.
   d.   Find $\hat{\beta}_0$.
   e.   Find the equation of the regression line.

9.

x (advertising units)	1	1	2	3	4	4	5
y (sales units)	1	5	4	2	7	8	10

10.

x (hours of training)	1	2	2	3	4	5
y (production units)	6	8	12	14	15	20

11.

x (number of telephone inquiries received per day)	0	1	1	2	5
y (number of mail orders received per day)	3	3	4	5	6

12.

x (customer complaints)	1	3	3	4	5	5
y (units sold)	5	3	2	2	0	1

13. For randomly selected homes recently sold in Dutchess County, New York, the annual tax amounts (in thousands of dollars) are listed along with the selling prices (in thousands of dollars). If you use your regression equation for predictions, what is the predicted selling price of a home with taxes of $3500?

Taxes	1.9	2.4	1.4	1.4	1.5	1.8	2.4	4.0
Selling price	145	228	150	130	160	114	142	265

14. The table below lists the value of exports (in billions of dollars) and the value of imports (in billions of dollars) for several different years (based on data from the U.S. Department of Commerce). If you use your regression equation for predictions, what is the predicted value of imports for a year when U.S. exports were valued at $200 billion?

Exports	10	20	43	221	218	218
Imports	9	15	40	245	326	370

15. The following table summarizes sample data for 7 pregnant women taken at an urban hospital. If you use your regression equation for predictions, what is the predicted weight of a baby born to a nonsmoking woman? A woman who smokes 30 cigarettes per day?

Cigarettes smoked per day	0	10	0	30	0	25	40
Weight of baby (pounds)	8.5	6.5	7.2	5.8	8.0	6.3	6.0

16. At an auction, a national car rental agency sold 5 comparably equipped two-year-old Chevrolet Corsica sedans. The table lists the mileage (in thousands) and the auction price (in thousands of dollars). If you use the regression line for predictions, what is the estimated selling price of another Chevrolet Corsica if its mileage is 10,000 miles? 25,000 miles?

Mileage	35	22	32	18	25
Selling price	7.0	8.5	7.0	8.9	7.6

17. Emissions data are given (in grams per meter) for a sample of different vehicles. (See "Determining Statistical Characteristics of a Vehicle Emissions Audit Procedure," by Lorenzen, Technometrics, Vol. 22, No. 4.) If you use the regression equation for predictions, what is the estimated carbon monoxide level if the hydrocarbon level is 0.50 grams/m?

HC	0.65	0.55	0.72	0.83	0.57	0.51	0.43	0.37
CO	14.7	12.3	14.6	15.1	5.0	4.1	3.8	4.1

18. For randomly selected homes recently sold in Dutchess County, New York, the living areas (in hundreds of square feet) are listed along with the annual tax amounts (in thousands of dollars). If the living area of a home is 1900 sq ft, what is the predicted value of taxes?

Living area	15	38	23	16	16	13	20	24
Taxes	1.9	2.4	1.4	1.4	1.5	1.8	2.4	4.0

12.2 **EXERCISES**   BEYOND THE BASICS

19. a. Construct the scatter diagram for the data in the table given below.
    b. Find the equation of the regression line.
    c. Plot the regression line on the scatter diagram.
    d. How does the sign of $\hat{\beta}_1$ relate to the scatter diagram?

x	3	4	5	6	7
y	8	10	12	10	8

20. a. Construct the scatter diagram for the data in table given below. Note any unusual shape or pattern.
    b. Try to find $\hat{\beta}_1$ and $\hat{\beta}_0$. What is happening?
    c. Is there a straight line that best fits the data? If so, sketch it on the scatter diagram and identify its equation.

x	3	3	3	3	3
y	7	10	5	15	13

21. The regression line must always pass through the point $(\bar{x}, \bar{y})$ called the **centroid.**
    a. Verify this for the data of Table 12.1.
    b. Use Formulas 12.2 and 12.3 to show that the centroid $(\bar{x}, \bar{y})$ always lies on the regression line.

12.3 **MEASURING VARIATION AROUND THE REGRESSION LINE**

From Section 12.2 we know how to use sample paired data to find the equation of the regression line and we know how to use that regression equation for making predictions. But one data set and its regression equation may lead to accurate predictions, whereas a different data set and its regression equation may lead to very inaccurate predictions. The accuracy of prediction depends on the strength of the relationship between the two variables.

Suppose that a company plans to spend additional thousands of dollars for advertising because *you* predicted that the increase in advertising will pay off with increased sales. It would be useful to have some indication of how good your prediction is likely to be. Nobody wants to be asked, "Hey, we spent $50,000 more for advertising this month as you recommended, so why didn't sales increase as you predicted?" In this section we introduce some statistical tools that will help us judge how well the regression equation fits the sample data. If the regression equation fits the sample data extremely well, then we expect our predictions to be very accurate. Conversely, if the regression equation doesn't fit the data well, then we can't expect our predictions to be very accurate.

For *any* set of paired data, it is possible to find an equation of the regression line that fits the points best according to the least-squares property described in the preceding section. Although the line of "best" fit sometimes fits the points quite well, it sometimes fits the points very poorly. Consider the contrasting examples for salesperson 1 and salesperson 2 below, where x represents the number of clients visited in a week and y represents the number of units of software sold during the week. For each salesperson we have four pairs of data representing four weeks. Here's some personal information about them: Salesperson 1 is affectionately called Ms. Reliability because she is an organized, systematic, and reliable employee whose methods and results have been very consistent; salesperson 2 is affectionately known as Ms. Unpredictable because she is impulsive and disorganized, and her methods and results have been very inconsistent, ranging from extremely poor to exceptionally good. In the long run, they both average about the same number of sales.

	Salesperson 1 Regression line fits *well*					Salesperson 2 Regression line fits *poorly*			
Original data	x	10	10	20	20	x	10	10	20	20
	y	23	27	44	46	y	10	40	25	65

Regression equation: $\hat{y} = 5 + 2x$
Scatter diagram: Fig. 12.5 (a)

$\hat{y} = 5 + 2x$
Fig. 12.5 (b)

Examination of the two scatter diagrams in Fig. 12.5 reveals that the regression line for salesperson 1 fits the points quite well, whereas the regression line for salesperson 2 fits the data poorly. Suppose that we want to find the predicted $\hat{y}$ value for the number of software units sold in a week given that $x = 10$ customers are visited. In both cases we get $\hat{y} = 5 + 2(10) = 25$ software units. But 25 units is a *good* predicted value for salesperson 1 (because the regression line fits well);

FIGURE 12.5
Regression Lines Fitting Well and Poorly

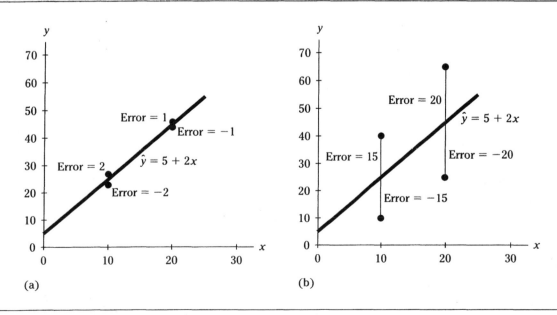

(a)

(b)

POWER LINES CORRELATE WITH CANCER

Several scientific studies suggest that there is a correlation between exposure to electromagnetic fields and the occurrence of cancer. Epidemiologists from Sweden's Karolinska Institute researched the 500,000 people who lived within 300 meters of a high-tension power line in Sweden during a 25-year period. They found that children had a higher than usual incidence of leukemia. The findings have led Sweden's government to consider regulations that would reduce housing in close proximity to high-tension power lines.

In an article on this study, *Time* magazine reported that "Although the research does not prove cause and effect, it shows an unmistakable correlation between the degree of exposure and the risk of childhood leukemia."

the number of units actually sold by salesperson 1 is likely to be close to 25. In contrast, 25 units is a *poor* predicted value for salesperson 2; the number of units actually sold may be considerably lower or greater than 25. If we are going to place software orders for next week based on our predictions, we would like to justify those predictions by using a more objective approach than an intuitive eyeball examination of a scatter diagram. After all, the software packages cost several hundred dollars each and they could quickly become obsolete in the rapidly changing software field. We don't want to order too many units because unsold units might result in very large losses.

SSERROR

In the preceding section we described the least-squares criterion by which the regression line is the line of best fit. We saw that the regression line results in the minimum possible sum obtained when we add the squares of the vertical distances between the original data points and the regression line. That same sum, which we will refer to as *SSError,* is useful in judging how well a regression line fits data, and the formula for finding *SSError* is as follows:

Formula 12.4 $$\text{SSError} = \Sigma(y - \hat{y})^2$$

Notation

$\Sigma(y - \hat{y})^2$ **indicates that we first subtract each predicted $\hat{y}$ value from the actual observed y value, then square each difference, and then find the total of those squares.**

If you want to get a good sense for *SSError,* look at Fig. 12.4, which shows the vertical (y) errors of -5, 11, -13, and 7. *SSError* is the sum of the squares of those errors, so that

$$\text{SSError} = (-5)^2 + 11^2 + (-13)^2 + 7^2 = 364$$

From Fig. 12.4 and from the above calculation, we can see that *SSError* is a sum of squares (*SS*) of the *errors* (or differences) between the actual data points and the regression line.

We can also express *SSError* in the following equivalent form that generally requires easier calculations.

$$\text{SSError} = SSy - \hat{\beta}_1 SSxy \qquad \text{(shortcut form of Formula 12.4)}$$

where $\hat{\beta}_1$ is found from Formula 12.2 and *SSy* and *SSxy* have been presented earlier as:

$$SSy = \Sigma(y - \bar{y})^2 = \Sigma y^2 - \frac{(\Sigma y)^2}{n}$$

and

$$SSxy = \Sigma(x - \bar{x})(y - \bar{y}) = \Sigma xy - \frac{(\Sigma x)(\Sigma y)}{n}$$

TABLE 12.3
Sample Data for Salesperson 1

x	y	$x \cdot y$	x^2	y^2
10	23	230	100	529
10	27	270	100	729
20	44	880	400	1936
20	46	920	400	2116
60	140	2300	1000	5310
$\uparrow$	$\uparrow$	$\uparrow$	$\uparrow$	$\uparrow$
Σx	Σy	Σxy	Σx^2	Σy^2

EXAMPLE

We would like to verify the regression equation for salesperson 1 because we will use it for predicting sales and want to be sure it's correct. Also, we want to get some measure of how good our weekly predictions are likely to be, so we will begin by finding the value of *SSError*, which is a measure of how well the regression line fits the sample data. Therefore, we use the sample paired data given for salesperson 1 to:

a.   Verify that the regression equation is $\hat{y} = 5 + 2x$.

b.   Find the value of *SSError*.

SOLUTION

The values of $\hat{\beta}_0$, $\hat{\beta}_1$, and *SSError* can be found from n, Σx, Σy, Σx^2, Σy^2, and Σxy. We begin by finding those values from Table 12.3.

a.   We can find $\hat{\beta}_1$ and $\hat{\beta}_0$ by first finding *SSxy* and *SSx* and then using Formulas 12.2 and 12.3 from the preceding section. We get

$$\hat{\beta}_1 = \frac{SSxy}{SSx} = \frac{\Sigma xy - \dfrac{(\Sigma x)(\Sigma y)}{n}}{\Sigma x^2 - \dfrac{(\Sigma x)^2}{n}} = \frac{2300 - \dfrac{(60)(140)}{4}}{1000 - \dfrac{(60)^2}{4}} = \frac{200}{100} = 2$$

$$\hat{\beta}_0 = \bar{y} - \hat{\beta}_1\bar{x} = \frac{140}{4} - 2\left(\frac{60}{4}\right) = 5$$

Regression equation: $\hat{y} = \hat{\beta}_0 + \hat{\beta}_1 x$
$$= 5 + 2x$$

b. $SSError = SSy - \hat{\beta}_1 SSxy$

$\llcorner$ 200   (see part *a*)
2   (see part *a*)

$$\Sigma y^2 - \frac{(\Sigma y)^2}{n} = 5310 - \frac{(140)^2}{4} = 410$$

$$= 410 - (2)(200) = 10$$

It might be helpful to stop here and verify that for the sample paired data for salesperson 2, *SSError* = 1250. Note that the well-fitting regression equation for salesperson 1 results in a relatively small value of *SSError* = 10, whereas the poorly fitting regression equation for salesperson 2 results in the very large value of *SSError* = 1250. These results suggest that if we make predictions of sales for each salesperson, the predicted number of units for salesperson 1 is likely to be much more accurate than the predicted number for salesperson 2. The software units stocked for salesperson 2 involve a much larger gamble and a much greater potential for loss.

DEVIATION, VARIATION, AND SSREGRESSION

Let's consider the sample paired data for salesperson 1, but let's focus on one particular pair of values: (20, 46). Those coordinates indicate that when salesperson 1 visited $x = 20$ customers in one particular week, she sold $y = 46$ units of software. Refer to Fig. 12.6 to see how the following definitions apply.

DEFINITIONS

Given a collection of paired data, the *total deviation, explained deviation, and unexplained deviation* (from the mean) for a particular point (x, y) are as follows:

total deviation = $y - \bar{y}$
explained deviation = $\hat{y} - \bar{y}$
unexplained deviation = $y - \hat{y}$

If we were totally ignorant of regression concepts and wanted to predict a value of y given that $x = 20$, our best guess would be the sample mean $\bar{y} = 35$. But we are not totally ignorant of regression concepts: We know that in this case (when a linear relationship exists), the way to predict the value of y when $x = 20$ is to use the regression equation, which yields $\hat{y} = 5 + 2(20) = 45$. Because of the linear association between x and y, when $x = 20$, y *should* be the predicted value of 45, and not the mean value of 35, so the difference of $\hat{y} - \bar{y} = 45 - 35 = 10$ is "explained" by the regression line prediction. But although y *should* be 45, *it is actually* 46, and that difference between the predicted value of 45 and the actual sample value of 46 cannot be explained by the regression line and is called an *unexplained deviation, error,* or *residual*. The specific case of one data point of Fig. 12.6 can be generalized as follows:

(total deviation) = (explained deviation) + (unexplained deviation)
or
$(y - \bar{y})$ $= (\hat{y} - \bar{y})$ $+ (y - \hat{y})$

This last expression can be further generalized and modified to include all the pairs of sample data as follows. (By popular demand, we omit the intermediate algebraic manipulations.)

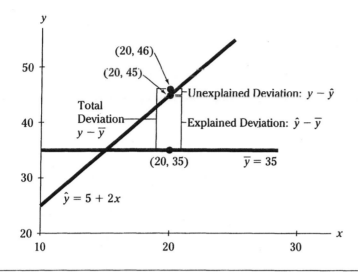

FIGURE 12.6
Unexplained, Explained, and Total Deviations

Formula 12.5

(total variation of y) = (explained variation of y) + (unexplained variation of y)
or
$$\Sigma(y - \bar{y})^2 \qquad = \Sigma(\hat{y} - \bar{y})^2 \qquad + \Sigma(y - \hat{y})^2$$

Explained variation is often referred to as *SSRegression* because it is a sum of squares (*SS*) and it represents the portion of the variation that is explained or accounted for by the regression equation.

DEFINITION

For a collection of paired sample data, the amount of the variation of y that is explained by the regression equation is as follows:

Formula 12.6 $$\text{SSRegression} = \Sigma(\hat{y} - \bar{y})^2$$

SSRegression can also be expressed as

$$SSRegression = \hat{\beta}_1\, SSxy$$

which is a "shortcut" formula because it generally involves easier calculations.

Using the definition of *SSRegression*, we can now rewrite Formula 12.5 as follows:

Formula 12.7 $$SSy = SSRegression + SSError$$

This formula tells us that the total variation (SSy) is the sum of variation that is explained by the regression line ($SSRegression$) and the variation that is unexplained ($SSError$).

EXAMPLE   Use the sample paired data for salesperson 1 (Ms. Reliability) to (a) find $SSRegression$ and (b) verify that $SSy = SSRegression + SSError$.

SOLUTION   a.   Using the values from Table 12.3, we get the results shown below.

x	y	PREDICTED VALUE $\hat{y} = 5 + 2x$	EXPLAINED DEVIATION $\hat{y} - \bar{y}$	EXPLAINED VARIATION $(\hat{y} - \bar{y})^2$
10	23	$5 + 2(10) = 25$	$25 - 35 = -10$	100
10	27	$5 + 2(10) = 25$	$25 - 35 = -10$	100
20	44	$5 + 2(20) = 45$	$45 - 35 = 10$	100
20	46	$5 + 2(20) = 45$	$45 - 35 = 10$	100

$\bar{x} = 30$ $\bar{y} = 35$ $\Sigma(\hat{y} - \bar{y})^2 = 400$

We therefore have $SSRegression = \Sigma(\hat{y} - \bar{y})^2 = 400$.

b.   In the solution to the preceding example, we have already found that $SSy = 410$ and $SSError = 10$, so that

$$SSy = SSRegression + SSError$$
or $410 = 400 + 10$

and this is the verification we sought. Note that the total variation is $SSy = 410$ and the amount that can be explained by the regression equation is $SSRegression = 400$, so that very little of the variation in y remains unexplained. This indicates that for salesperson 1, the title of "Ms. Reliability" is appropriate because her work is very predictable in the sense that very little of it involves variability that is unexplainable.

COEFFICIENT OF DETERMINATION R^2

The value of $SSError$ can be used to judge how well the regression line fits the data when we are comparing one $SSError$ to another $SSError$ from a different data set with the same number of pairs of data. For example, because $SSError = 10$ for salesperson 1 and $SSError = 1250$ for salesperson 2, we conclude that salesperson 1 has a much lower error and so the regression line for salesperson 1 will fit the data better. When working with a single set of paired data, no such comparison can be made and we may have to rely on a subjective interpretation of the magnitude of $SSError$, which may be difficult. Instead, we present the coefficient of determination, denoted by R^2, a better measure of how well the regression line fits the data.

The **coefficient of determination** R^2 is given by

Formula 12.8
$$R^2 = \frac{SSRegression}{SSy}$$

Here's how we can interpret the values of R^2: First, use the equation $SSy = SSRegression + SSError$ to rewrite Formula 12.8 as

Formula 12.9
$$R^2 = \frac{SSRegression}{SSRegression + SSError}$$

and note that in this expression, if $SSError$ is close to 0 (which happens when the sample points are very close to the regression line), the value of R^2 will be close to 1. Conversely, if $SSError$ is a very large number (which happens when the sample points are very far from the regression line), the value of R^2 will be close to 0. That is, **a value of R^2 near 1 indicates a well-fitting regression line, but a value of R^2 near 0 indicates a regression line that doesn't fit the data well.** (These somewhat subjective judgments of "close to" 1 or 0 will be replaced in Section 12.4 by much more objective procedures.) Also, algebra can be used to prove that the coefficient of determination R^2 has the property that

$$0 \leq R^2 \leq 1$$

While $SSError$ and $SSRegression$ can both be used to measure how well a regression line fits the sample points, R^2 has the important advantage of yielding numbers between 0 and 1 that can be interpreted with much greater ease.

EXAMPLE Use the sample paired data for salesperson 1 and find the value of the coefficient of determination R^2. Is the result close to 1, confirming that the regression line fits the data well?

SOLUTION We have already found that $SSy = 410$, $SSRegression = 400$, and $SSError = 10$, so we can use either of the above two formulas for R^2. Using Formula 12.9, we get

$$R^2 = \frac{SSRegression}{SSRegression + SSError} = \frac{400}{400 + 10} = 0.976$$

Because 0.976 is very close to 1, we conclude that the regression line for salesperson 1 fits the sample data very well and predictions we make based on that regression equation are likely to be quite good. In contrast, the coefficient of determination for the data from salesperson 2 results in $R^2 = 0.242$, which suggests a poorly fitting regression equation. Any predictions for salesperson 2 are likely to be much less reliable.

Also, in finding that $R^2 = 0.976$ for the salesperson-1 data, we can conclude that 97.6% of the variation in the y values (software units sold) can be explained or accounted for by the regression line, and only 2.4% of that variation remains unexplained (because Formula 12.8 expresses R^2 as the ratio of explained variation to total variation).

Assumptions in Simple Linear Regression

Those who use the regression methods we have discussed recognize that sample paired data rarely consist of points all lying perfectly along some straight line. When developing a mathematical equation (often referred to as a *model*) describing the association between x and y, we therefore include a random error variable e as described below and illustrated in Fig. 12.7.

For *linear* relationships, the complete regression model is

$$y = \beta_0 + \beta_1 x + e$$

where e is assumed to be a random variable that has a normal distribution with a mean of zero and a constant standard deviation denoted by σ_e.

The above model involves these assumptions:

1. We are investigating only *linear* relationships.
2. For each x value, y is a random variable having a normal distribution. All of these y distributions have the same standard deviation. Also, all of these y distributions have means that lie on the regression line.
3. The y values are statistically *independent,* meaning that when we obtain sample data, the y values for one particular x value do not affect or depend on the y values for any other x value.

FIGURE 12.7
Distribution of the Random Error Variable e

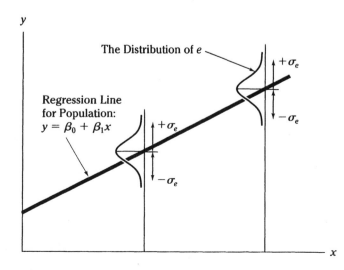

These assumptions need not be strictly met. We can get reasonably good results if departures from the normal distributions and equal variances are not too extreme.

We can estimate the standard deviation of the error variable e, σ_e, by using $\hat{\sigma}_e$, defined as follows:

Formula 12.10 $\hat{\sigma}_e = \sqrt{\dfrac{SSError}{n-2}}$ (sometimes denoted as s_e)

In evaluating *SSError* in the above expression, the differences $(y - \hat{y})$ are squared, summed, and divided by $n - 2$, and we get an expression very much like the variance of the y values:

$$s_y^2 = \frac{\Sigma(y - \bar{y})^2}{n - 1}$$

The reason we divide by $n - 2$ in Formula 12.10 relates to the fact that we have n pairs of data that we use to estimate *two* parameters (β_0 and β_1).

EXAMPLE   Use the sample paired data from salesperson 1 and find the value of $\hat{\sigma}_e$.

SOLUTION   We have already found that *SSError* = 10 and, because $n = 4$, we have

$$\hat{\sigma}_e = \sqrt{\frac{SSError}{n-2}} = \sqrt{\frac{10}{4-2}} = \sqrt{5} = 2.236$$

In contrast to this relatively small standard deviation, the sample paired data for salesperson 2 result in $\hat{\sigma}_e = 25$. As we might expect, the estimate $\hat{\sigma}_e$ for salesperson 2 is much larger than for salesperson 1 because the points for salesperson 2 are located much farther away from the regression line. That is, the salesperson-2 regression line misses the points by larger error amounts and thus indicates that salesperson 2 has a larger $\hat{\sigma}_e$.

We've encountered several formulas that could be overwhelming, but remember that our calculations can be based on the simple components of n, Σx, Σy, Σx^2, Σy^2, and Σxy. Let's now reconsider the data from the real estate problem described at the beginning of the chapter so that we can see how those simple components are used for finding important results.

EXAMPLE   For the real estate data of Table 12.1, we have already found that

$n = 8$ $\Sigma x = 165$ $\Sigma y = 1334$
$\Sigma x^2 = 3855$ $\Sigma y^2 = 241{,}394$ $\Sigma xy = 29{,}611$
$SSxy = 2097.25$ $\hat{\beta}_1 = 4.6412$ $\hat{\beta}_0 = 71.025$

Find the values of (a) *SSy*, the total variation in the y values; (b) *SSError*, the sum of the squares of the differences (errors) between

SAVINGS AND NUCLEAR WAR

Is there a correlation between savings rates and the perceived likelihood of nuclear war? If consumers believe the probability of nuclear war is low, they save more for future consumption because they believe there will be a future in which to consume. But if consumers believe the probability of nuclear war is relatively high, they tend to save less. One study collected data on savings rates and "times before midnight," as determined by the *Bulletin of Atomic Scientists*. In recent years, that "doomsday" clock has indicated times ranging from 2 minutes before midnight (for a very high threat of nuclear war) to 12 minutes before midnight (for a lesser threat). Data for a recent 20-year period suggest that there is a significant correlation, which in turn suggests that savings rates are affected by perceptions about the likelihood of nuclear war.

the actual observed y values and the y values predicted by the regression equation; (c) *SSRegression*, the variation of the y values that is explained by the regression equation; (d) the coefficient of determination R^2; and (e) $\hat{\sigma}_e$, the standard deviation of the random error variable e in the regression model.

SOLUTION

a. $SSy = \Sigma y^2 - \dfrac{(\Sigma y)^2}{n} = 241{,}394 - \dfrac{(1334)^2}{8} = 18{,}949.5$

b. $SSError = SSy - \hat{\beta}_1 SSxy = 18{,}949.5 - (4.6412)(2097.25)$

   $= 9215.743$

c. $SSRegression = \hat{\beta}_1 SSxy = (4.6412)(2097.25) = 9733.76$
   (Note that $SSy = SSRegression + SSError$.)

d.   We now find the value of the coefficient of determination R^2 to get some sense for how well the regression line fits the data (and how good it will be for making predictions). Using Formula 12.8, we get

   $$R^2 = \frac{SSRegression}{SSy} = \frac{9733.76}{18{,}949.5} = 0.5137$$

That is, 51.37% of the variation in the y values (selling prices) is explained by the regression line; 48.63% of the variation remains unexplained. This is only a moderately good R^2. In the next section we will consider more-objective procedures for determining whether a regression line with $R^2 = 0.5137$ is useful for predictions.

e. $\hat{\sigma}_e = \sqrt{\dfrac{SSError}{n-2}} = \sqrt{\dfrac{9215.743}{8-2}} = \sqrt{1535.957} = 39.19$

12.3   EXERCISES   BASIC CONCEPTS

1. For each of the following values, identify the numbers that are possible values of R^2. For the numbers that are possible values of R^2, select those that seem to indicate that the regression line fits the data well.
   a.   0.888
   b.   0.116
   c.   −0.146
   d.   0.926
   e.   1.256
   f.   0.231

2. Given the following sample data, find the total variation SSy by using (a) $SSy = \Sigma(y - \bar{y})^2$ and (b) $SSy = \Sigma y^2 - (\Sigma y)^2/n$. Verify that both results are the same.

x (minutes spent with customer)	2	4	5	7	8
y (amount of cologne sold)	8	10	14	14	16

In Exercises 3–12, use the given list of paired data to find the indicated values. (In Section 12.2 we used the same sets of data to find n, Σx, Σx^2, Σy, Σy^2, Σxy, $SSxy$, and SSx.)

    a.   Total variation: SSy
    b.   Total variation of x and y values together: $SSxy$
    c.   Unexplained variation: $SSError$
    d.   Standard deviation of the error variable: $\hat{\sigma}_e$
    e.   Explained variation: $SSRegression$
    f.   Coefficient of determination: R^2

3.
x (advertising units)	1	1	2	3	4	4	5
y (sales units)	1	5	4	2	7	8	10

4.
x (hours of training)	1	2	2	3	4	5
y (production units)	6	8	12	14	15	20

5.
x (number of telephone inquiries received per day)	0	1	1	2	5
y (number of mail orders received per day)	3	3	4	5	6

6.
x (customer complaints)	1	3	3	4	5	5
y (units sold)	5	3	2	2	0	1

7.
Taxes	1.9	2.4	1.4	1.4	1.5	1.8	2.4	4.0
Selling price	145	228	150	130	160	114	142	265

8.
Exports	10	20	43	221	218	218
Imports	9	15	40	245	326	370

9.
Cigarettes smoked per day	0	10	0	30	0	25	40
Weight of baby (pounds)	8.5	6.5	7.2	5.8	8.0	6.3	6.0

10.
Mileage	35	22	32	18	25
Selling price	7.0	8.5	7.0	8.9	7.6

11.
HC	0.65	0.55	0.72	0.83	0.57	0.51	0.43	0.37
CO	14.7	12.3	14.6	15.1	5.0	4.1	3.8	4.1

12.
Living area	15	38	23	16	16	13	20	24
Taxes	1.9	2.4	1.4	1.4	1.5	1.8	2.4	4.0

13. A sample collection of $n = 12$ pairs of data yields a total variation of $SSy = \Sigma(y - \bar{y})^2 = 3000$.
    a.   Find the values of R^2 and $\hat{\sigma}_e$ if the unexplained variation is $SSError = 500$. Would this indicate a good or a bad fit of the regression line to the data?
    b.   Find the values of R^2 and $\hat{\sigma}_e$ if the unexplained variation is $SSError = 2400$. Would this indicate a good or a bad fit of the regression line to the data?

14. For a sample of paired data with $n = 9$ observations, $\bar{y} = 25$, $SSy = \Sigma(y - \bar{y})^2 = 2400$, $\bar{x} = 10$, $SSx = \Sigma(x - \bar{x})^2 = 400$. Find the values of $\hat{\beta}_1$ and $\hat{\beta}_0$, then find $SSError$, $\hat{\sigma}_e^2$, $SSRegression$, and R^2 given that
   a. $SSxy = 920$
   b. $SSxy = -840$
   c. $SSxy = 120$
   d. $SSxy = -150$

12.3   EXERCISES   BEYOND THE BASICS

15. In this section we defined $SSRegression$ as $\hat{\beta}_1 SSxy$ and $SSError$ as $SSy - \hat{\beta}_1 SSxy$. (a) Show algebraically that $SSy = SSRegression + SSError$. (b) Use the salesperson-2 data in this section to find SSx, $SSxy$, SSy, $\hat{\beta}_0$, and $\hat{\beta}_1$. (c) Use the regression equation $\hat{y} = 5 + 2x$ and find the four predicted $\hat{y}$ values corresponding to the observed values of $x = 10, 10, 20,$ and 20 for salesperson 2.

16. Given the accompanying Minitab display that results from the data of salesperson 1 in this section, identify those parts of the display that correspond to $\hat{\beta}_1$, $\hat{\beta}_0$, SSy, $SSError$, $SSRegression$, R^2, and $\hat{\sigma}_e$.

```
MTB > REGRESSION C2 1 C1

The regression equation is
C2 = 5.00 + 2.00 C1

Predictor        Coef       Stdev     t-ratio         p
Constant        5.000       3.536        1.41     0.293
C1             2.0000      0.2236        8.94     0.012

s = 2.236     R-sq = 97.6%     R-sq(adj) = 96.3%

Analysis of Variance

SOURCE          DF          SS          MS         F         p
Regression       1      400.00      400.00     80.00     0.012
Error            2       10.00        5.00
Total            3      410.00
```

12.4   HYPOTHESIS TESTING AND CONFIDENCE INTERVALS FOR THE SLOPE β_1

In the preceding section we introduced the coefficient of determination of R^2 as a tool for assessing how well the regression line fits the data. We noted that values of R^2 "close to" 1 suggest a good fit and values of R^2 "close to" 0 suggest a poor fit.

We would like to make those subjective criteria much more objective. First, note that if the x and y values in a sample of paired data are completely *unrelated*, then in our regression equation

$$y = \beta_0 + \beta_1 x + e$$

introduced in the preceding section, y should not change as x changes, so that the slope β_1 must be 0. Conversely, if y is related to the value of x, then the slope β_1 must be nonzero. We can test the claim that $\beta_1 = 0$, and this will be equivalent to testing the claim that there is no linear association between x and y. If we reject H_0: $\beta_1 = 0$, then we conclude that there is an association between x and y, and the regression equation is therefore a good fit that is useful for making predictions. Hence it is very important to test the claim that $\beta_1 = 0$, and we now consider that test.

TESTING CLAIMS ABOUT β_1 (SLOPE OF THE REGRESSION LINE)

We can test the claim that β_1 (the slope of the regression line) is equal to some constant b (or $\beta_1 \geq b$ or $\beta_1 \leq b$). Although we can test the hypothesis that b is any constant, by far the most frequently chosen value is $b = 0$. With $b = 0$, we are testing that the regression line is horizontal and, indirectly, that there is no linear association between x and y. In testing $\beta_1 = b$ (or $\beta_1 \geq b$ or $\beta_1 \leq b$), the following test statistic applies.

TEST STATISTIC

Formula 12.11
$$t = \frac{\hat{\beta}_1 - b}{s_{\hat{\beta}_1}}$$

where
$$s_{\hat{\beta}_1} = \frac{\hat{\sigma}_e}{\sqrt{SSx}}$$

The **critical values** are found in Table A.3; the number of degrees of freedom is $n - 2$.

> **EXAMPLE**   Given the sample real estate data of Table 12.1, test the claim that $\beta_1 = 0$. Use a 0.05 level of significance. Based on the given sample data, is there a linear association between living area and selling price? Rejection of $\beta_1 = 0$ would suggest that there is an association because a nonzero slope indicates that the selling prices (y) depend on the values of the living areas (x).

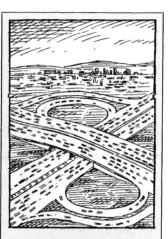

LOS ANGELES OZONE

The South Coast Air Quality Management District monitors the ozone levels for the Los Angeles basin region. The ozone levels are affected by weather as well as by pollutants from the infamous stream of dense traffic in the Los Angeles area. One useful indicator of an ozone problem is its level in parts per million for the worst hour of the year. Regression analysis shows a downward trend in that indicator, suggesting that despite a large increase in people and cars, ozone levels are actually decreasing to about half the level of 40 years ago. The downward trend is seen in the "worst-hour" levels for six recent and consecutive years: 0.32, 0.32, 0.25, 0.21, 0.22, and 0.22. Such statistical analyses help verify the impact of clean-air legislation and raise issues of the cost effectiveness of new legislation.

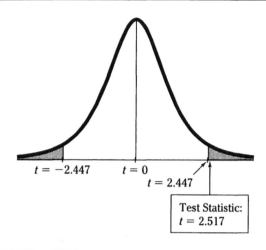

FIGURE 12.8
Testing $\beta_1 = 0$ for Data of Table 12.1

$t = -2.447$ $t = 0$

$t = 2.447$

Test Statistic:
$t = 2.517$

SOLUTION We have H_0: $\beta_1 = 0$, H_1: $\beta_1 \neq 0$, and $\alpha = 0.05$. The test statistic is

$$t = \frac{\hat{\beta}_1 - b}{\dfrac{\hat{\sigma}_e}{\sqrt{SSx}}} = \frac{4.6412 - 0}{\dfrac{39.19}{\sqrt{451.875}}} = 2.517$$

With H_0: $\beta_1 = 0$, the test is two-tailed because a sample value of $\hat{\beta}_1$ significantly above 0 or below 0 would lead to rejection of H_0. The critical values of $t = -2.447$ and $t = 2.447$ can be found from Table A.3 by noting that we have $n - 2 = 8 - 2 = 6$ degrees of freedom and $\alpha = 0.05$ in two tails. The test statistic of $t = 2.517$ does fall within the critical region, so we reject the null hypothesis and conclude that $\beta_1 \neq 0$ (see Fig. 12.8). The P-value is less than 0.05 and it leads to the same conclusion. Because we reject $\beta_1 = 0$, we conclude that the regression line fits the data well and it is usable for predictions. This decision criterion is much more objective than one based on judging whether R^2 is "close to" 1, as in Section 12.3.

CONFIDENCE INTERVAL FOR β_1
(SLOPE OF THE REGRESSION LINE)

The value of β_1 (the slope of the regression line) is useful for determining how much y is likely to change for each unit change in x. In addition to testing some claim about the value of β_1, we might want to use sample data to estimate its value. In general, the best point estimate of β_1 is $\hat{\beta}_1$. For the sample data of Table 12.1, the best point (single-number) estimate of β_1 is $\hat{\beta}_1 = 4.6412$. The general interval estimate or confidence interval for β_1 is as follows:

CONFIDENCE INTERVAL FOR β_1

$$\hat{\beta}_1 - E < \beta_1 < \hat{\beta}_1 + E$$

where the margin of error E is given by

$$E = t_{\alpha/2}\, s_{\hat{\beta}_1} = t_{\alpha/2} \frac{\hat{\sigma}_e}{\sqrt{SSx}}$$

and $t_{\alpha/2}$ has $n - 2$ degrees of freedom.

This interval estimate of β_1 has a $1 - \alpha$ degree of confidence.

EXAMPLE   Using the sample real estate data from Table 12.1, construct the 90% confidence interval for β_1.

SOLUTION   We can begin by finding the margin of error E. We will use $t_{\alpha/2} = 1.943$ because $\alpha = 0.10$ (corresponding to 90% confidence) in two tails, and the number of degrees of freedom is $n - 2 = 8 - 2 = 6$; refer to Table A.3. We have already found that $\hat{\sigma}_e = 39.19$ and $SSx = 451.875$. We first evaluate the margin of error.

$$E = t_{\alpha/2} \frac{\hat{\sigma}_e}{\sqrt{SSx}} = 1.943 \frac{39.19}{\sqrt{451.875}} = 3.582$$

Knowing that $E = 3.582$ and using our previous result of $\hat{\beta}_1 = 4.6412$, we can now construct the desired confidence interval.

$$\hat{\beta}_1 - E < \beta_1 < \hat{\beta}_1 + E$$
$$4.6412 - 3.582 < \beta_1 < 4.6412 + 3.582$$
$$1.059 < \beta_1 < 8.223$$

That is, we are 90% confident that the limits 1.059 and 8.223 contain the true value of β_1. This is a relatively large range, mainly because we have a relatively small sample size of $n = 8$.

We can also test claims about β_0 (the y-intercept of the regression line) and construct confidence intervals for β_0, but hypothesis tests and confidence intervals for β_1 are much more common and important. See Exercises 19 and 20 for procedures that apply to β_0.

INTERPRETING COMPUTER OUTPUT

The calculations of this chapter can be quite messy. In real applications with larger data sets, we would soon find that calculators and computer software are vital tools that allow us to obtain quick results so that we can focus on interpreting them.

Given below is a Minitab printout of our Table 12.1 data. We have entered several annotations referring to results we obtained earlier in this chapter.

Note that Minitab does the calculations necessary for testing the following two null hypotheses.

H_0: $\beta_1 = 0$ (claim about the slope)
H_0: $\beta_0 = 0$ (claim about the y-intercept)

Although the Minitab results always correspond to two-tailed tests for $\beta_1 = 0$ and $\beta_0 = 0$, the software package also provides the components needed for other cases. To test the claim that $\beta_1 = 1$, for example, the test statistic is $t = (\hat{\beta}_1 - 1)/s_{\hat{\beta}_1}$, and Minitab provides the values of $\hat{\beta}_1 = 4.641$ and $s_{\hat{\beta}_1} = 1.844$, so that we are required to do only a very simple calculation of $(4.641 - 1)/1.844$. Similarly, confidence intervals can be easily calculated for β_1 and β_0 by using the Minitab results. For example, we have seen that the confidence interval for β_1 has limits of $\hat{\beta}_1 - E$ and $\hat{\beta}_1 + E$, where

$$E = t_{\alpha/2} s_{\hat{\beta}_1}$$

Minitab provides us with $s_{\hat{\beta}_1} = 1.844$, and we need to find $t_{\alpha/2}$ from Table A.3. Once that value is found, we can easily complete the construction of the confidence interval. Even though Minitab might not directly give us the confidence interval limits, we can use the Minitab results to greatly simplify the required calculations.

```
              x values   y values
                 ↓        ↓
         MTB > READ C1 C2
         DATA> 15 145
         DATA> 38 228
         DATA> 23 150
         DATA> 16 130                    Data
         DATA> 16 160                    entered
         DATA> 13 114                    here
         DATA> 20 142
         DATA> 24 265
         DATA> ENDOFDATA
         MTB > REGRESSION C2 1 C1   ←The Key Minitab command

         The regression equation is
         C2 = 71.0 + 4.64 C1        ←This is ŷ = β̂₀ + β̂₁x.

         Predictor     Coef          Stdev        t-ratio      p
         Constant      71.02 ←β̂₀     40.47 ←s_β₀     1.75     0.130
         C1      σ̂_e   4.641 ←β̂₁     1.844 ←s_β₁     2.52     0.045
                  ↓
         s = 39.19    R-sq = 51.4%    R-sq(adj) = 43.3%
                            ↑
         Analysis of Variance          R² coefficient of determination
```

(continued)

SOURCE	DF	SS	MS	F	p
Regression	1	9734 ←SSReg 9734		6.34	0.045
Error	6	9216 ←SSError 1536			
Total	7	18949 ←SSy			

COMMON ERRORS

When doing a regression analysis for the purpose of making predictions, use the following guidelines to avoid making some common errors.

1. If we fail to reject the claim that $\beta_1 = 0$, we should not use the regression equation to make predictions. (Testing the claim that $\beta_1 = 0$ is our most objective criterion for deciding whether to use the regression equation for making predictions.)
2. *When using the regression equation for predictions, stay within the scope of the available sample data.* For our real estate data, it would be unwise to predict the selling price of a home with 5000 sq ft because the largest home in our sample had only 3800 sq ft.
3. *A regression equation based on old data is not necessarily valid now.* If we use selling prices and living areas of homes in 1970 to predict selling prices of homes today, we may obtain results with substantial errors.
4. *Don't make predictions about a population that is different from the population from which the sample data were drawn.* If we use selling prices and living areas of homes in Dutchess County, New York, the results should not be used to predict selling prices of homes in North Dakota.

12.4 EXERCISES   BASIC CONCEPTS

In Exercises 1–4, use the given sample statistics to find (a) $\bar{x}$, (b) $\bar{y}$, (c) SSx, (d) SSy, (e) $SSxy$, and (f) the equation of the regression line. Then test the claim that $\beta_1 = 0$ by using a 0.05 significance level. In each case, x represents time spent to reduce variation and y represents the dollar value saved because of fewer defects.

1. $n = 6$, $\Sigma x = 73$, $\Sigma x^2 = 935$, $\Sigma y = 39$, $\Sigma y^2 = 265$, $\Sigma xy = 497$
2. $n = 7$, $\Sigma x = 63$, $\Sigma x^2 = 571$, $\Sigma y = 109$, $\Sigma y^2 = 1709$, $\Sigma xy = 985$
3. $n = 8$, $\Sigma x = 49.0$, $\Sigma x^2 = 319.5$, $\Sigma y = 133.0$, $\Sigma y^2 = 2341.0$, $\Sigma xy = 774.2$
4. $n = 12$, $\Sigma x = 15.4$, $\Sigma x^2 = 126.3$, $\Sigma y = 55.8$, $\Sigma y^2 = 1709$, $\Sigma xy = 73.1$

In Exercises 5–8, construct a 95% confidence interval for β_1. Use the sample statistics in the exercise identified.

5. Exercise 1
6. Exercise 2
7. Exercise 3
8. Exercise 4

In Exercises 9–18, use the given sample data reproduced from Section 12.2.

a.   Use a 0.05 significance level to test the claim that $\beta_1 = 0$. Based on your conclusion, determine whether the regression line can be used for making predictions.

b.   Construct a 95% confidence interval for β_1.

9.
x (advertising units)	1	1	2	3	4	4	5
y (sales units)	1	5	4	2	7	8	10

10.
x (hours of training)	1	2	2	3	4	5
y (production units)	6	8	12	14	15	20

11.
x (number of telephone inquiries received per day)	0	1	1	2	5
y (number of mail orders received per day)	3	3	4	5	6

12.
x (customer complaints)	1	3	3	4	5	5
y (units sold)	5	3	2	2	0	1

13.
Taxes	1.9	2.4	1.4	1.4	1.5	1.8	2.4	4.0
Selling price	145	228	150	130	160	114	142	265

14.
Exports	10	20	43	221	218	218
Imports	9	15	40	245	326	370

15.
Cigarettes smoked per day	0	10	0	30	0	25	40
Weight of baby (pounds)	8.5	6.5	7.2	5.8	8.0	6.3	6.0

16.
Mileage	35	22	32	18	25
Selling price	7.0	8.5	7.0	8.9	7.6

17.
HC	0.65	0.55	0.72	0.83	0.57	0.51	0.43	0.37
CO	14.7	12.3	14.6	15.1	5.0	4.1	3.8	4.1

18.
Living area	15	38	23	16	16	13	20	24
Taxes	1.9	2.4	1.4	1.4	1.5	1.8	2.4	4.0

12.4 EXERCISES   BEYOND THE BASICS

19.   When testing a claim that β_0 (the y-intercept of the regression line) is equal to some constant b, the test statistic is $t = (\hat{\beta}_0 - b)/s_{\hat{\beta}_0}$ where

$$s_{\hat{\beta}_0} = \hat{\sigma}_e \sqrt{\frac{\Sigma x^2}{n(SSx)}}$$

The test statistic has a t distribution with $n - 2$ degrees of freedom. Refer to the sample data in Table 12.1 and test the claim that $\beta_0 = 0$.

20. A confidence interval for β_0 (the y-intercept of the regression line) can be found from

$$\hat{\beta}_0 - E < \beta_0 < \hat{\beta}_0 + E$$

$$\text{where } E = t_{\alpha/2} \hat{\sigma}_e \sqrt{\frac{\Sigma x^2}{n(SSx)}}$$

and $t_{\alpha/2}$ has $n - 2$ degrees of freedom. Refer to the sample data in Table 12.1 and construct the 95% confidence interval for β_0.

21. Use the Table 12.1 sample data for the following:
   a. At the $\alpha = 0.05$ significance level, test the claim that $\beta_1 = 5.00$.
   b. At the $\alpha = 0.05$ significance level, test the claim that $\beta_0 = 50.0$.

22. Refer to the accompanying Minitab display that resulted from entering randomly selected paired data. The data represent 150 homes sold in Dutchess County, where x is the living area (in square feet) and y is the selling price (in dollars).
   a. Identify $\hat{\beta}_0$, $\hat{\beta}_1$, and the regression equation.
   b. Identify the values of R^2, $SSRegression$, $SSError$, SSy, and $\hat{\sigma}_e$.
   c. At the $\alpha = 0.05$ significance level, test the claim that $\beta_1 = 0$.
   d. Based on the result from part c, does the regression line fit the data well, so that it is usable for predictions?

```
MTB > REGRESSION C2 1 C1

The regression equation is
C2 = 311 + 0.00983 C1

Predictor          Coef         Stdev      t-ratio          p
Constant           311.1        132.5         2.35      0.020
C1              0.0098344    0.0008321        11.82      0.000

s = 422.6      R-sq = 48.6%      R-sq(adj) = 48.2%

Analysis of Variance

SOURCE          DF          SS            MS          F          p
Regression       1     24951298      24951298     139.70      0.000
Error          148     26434374        178611
Total          149     51385672
```

12.5 CONFIDENCE INTERVALS FOR PREDICTED VALUES

In Section 12.4 we considered a method for constructing confidence intervals for β_1 (the slope of the regression line). In this section we discuss two other types of confidence intervals that are also very important because they give us some sense for how much our predictions might be in error:

1. Confidence interval for the mean of all y values for some given fixed value of x
2. Confidence interval for an individual y value for some given fixed value of x

In Section 12.3 we used the regression equation

$$\hat{y} = 71.0 + 4.64x$$

to make a prediction. Specifically, we found that if the living area is 1800 sq ft (or $x = 18$), we get a predicted selling price of \$154,520 (or $\hat{y} = 154.52$). Having made that prediction, we might proceed to construct interval estimates so we can judge how dependable it is. There are two different formats for such cases, depending on whether we want to estimate a single y value (such as the selling price of one home) or the mean of all y values (such as the mean of all homes in Dutchess County). See the following two interval estimates.

CONFIDENCE INTERVAL

Given the fixed value of x_0, the *confidence interval for the mean of all y values* is

$$\hat{y} - E < \mu_y < \hat{y} + E$$

where

$$E = t_{\alpha/2}\hat{\sigma}_e\sqrt{\frac{1}{n} + \frac{(x_0 - \bar{x})^2}{SSx}}$$

and

x_0 represents the given value of x,
$t_{\alpha/2}$ has $n - 2$ degrees of freedom,
$\hat{\sigma}_e$ is given in Formula 12.10.

It is common to use the term *prediction interval* when referring to a confidence interval for an individual predicted value of y.

PREDICTION INTERVAL

Given the fixed value of x_0, the *prediction interval for an individual value y* is

$$\hat{y} - E < y < \hat{y} + E$$

where

$$E = t_{\alpha/2}\hat{\sigma}_e\sqrt{1 + \frac{1}{n} + \frac{(x_0 - \bar{x})^2}{SSx}}$$

and

x_0 represents the given value of x,
$t_{\alpha/2}$ has $n - 2$ degrees of freedom,
$\hat{\sigma}_e$ is given in Formula 12.10.

EXAMPLE   Given the same Table 12.1 real estate data, and given that a particular home has a living area of 1800 sq ft, find

    a. A 95% confidence interval for the *mean* selling price of homes with living areas of 1800 sq ft.

    b. A 95% prediction interval for the selling price of an *individual* home with a living area of 1800 sq ft.

SOLUTION   a. First let's find the value of $t_{\alpha/2}$. With $\alpha = 1-0.95 = 0.05$ and with the number of degrees of freedom given by $n - 2 = 8 - 2 = 6$, we refer to Table A.3 to find that $t_{\alpha/2} = 2.447$ corresponds to 0.05 (two tails) and 6 degrees of freedom. Earlier in this chapter we showed that $\hat{\sigma}_e = 39.19$, $\bar{x} = 165/8 = 20.625$, and $SSx = 451.875$. Substituting these values along with $x_0 = 18$, we calculate the value of the margin of error E as follows:

**STUDENT
RATINGS
OF TEACHERS**

$$E = t_{\alpha/2}\,\hat{\sigma}_e\sqrt{\frac{1}{n} + \frac{(x_0 - \bar{x})^2}{SSx}}$$

$$= (2.447)(39.19)\sqrt{\frac{1}{8} + \frac{(18 - 20.625)^2}{451.875}}$$

$$= (2.447)(39.19)(0.3745) = 35.91$$

Our 95% confidence interval for the mean predicted selling price y (for homes with living areas of 1800 sq ft) is

$$\hat{y} - E < \mu_y < \hat{y} + E$$
$$154.52 - 35.91 < \mu_y < 154.52 + 35.91$$
$$118.61 < \mu_y < 190.43$$

Because the selling price is in thousands of dollars and the living area is in hundreds of square feet, we see that for homes with living areas of 1800 sq ft, we are 95% confident that the mean selling price is contained within the limits of $118,610 and $190,430. This range shows that the mean selling price can vary considerably.

    b. As in part *a*, we again substitute $x_0 = 18$, $t_{\alpha/2} = 2.447$, $\hat{\sigma}_e = 39.19$, $\bar{x} = 165/8 = 20.625$, and $SSx = 451.875$ to find the margin of error E for this case. We get

$$E = t_{\alpha/2}\,\hat{\sigma}_e\sqrt{1 + \frac{1}{n} + \frac{(x_0 - \bar{x})^2}{SSx}}$$

$$= (2.447)(39.19)\sqrt{1 + \frac{1}{8} + \frac{(18 - 20.625)^2}{451.875}}$$

$$= (2.447)(39.19)(1.068) = 102.42 \qquad \text{(continued)}$$

Many colleges equate high student ratings of teachers with good teaching—an equation often fostered by the fact that student evaluations are easy to administer and measure.

However, one study that compared student evaluations of teachers with the amount of material learned found a strong *negative* correlation between the two factors. Teachers rated highly by students seemed to induce less learning.

In a related study, an audience gave a high rating to a lecturer who conveyed very little information but was interesting and entertaining.

Our 95% confidence interval for an individual predicted y value (given that $x = 18$) becomes

$$\hat{y} - E < y < \hat{y} + E$$
$$154.52 - 102.42 < y < 154.52 + 102.42$$
$$52.10 < y < 256.94$$

We now conclude that for a home with a living area of 1800 sq ft, we are 95% confident that the interval from \$52,100 to \$256,940 does contain the true predicted selling price. Another way of stating this is that 95 of 100 intervals similarly constructed would contain the true selling price. That range of selling prices is so wide mainly because our sample is so small ($n = 8$).

In the preceding example, be careful to distinguish between the two different types of interval estimates. In part *a*, we conclude that if we examine many homes with areas of 1800 sq ft, we can expect (with 95% confidence) the *mean* selling price to be between \$118,610 and \$190,430. In part *b*, we conclude that for an *individual* home with an area of 1800 sq ft, its predicted selling price is between \$52,100 and \$256,940 (with 95% confidence).

INTERPRETING COMPUTER OUTPUT

Such interval estimates are extremely useful when employing regression analysis for making predictions. Unfortunately, the manual calculations can be quite cumbersome, especially for large data sets. Fortunately, Minitab and other statistical software packages can be used to obtain quick and reliable results. See the accompanying Minitab display and note that the use of the PREDICT 18 subcommand results in the 95% confidence interval and the 95% prediction interval corresponding to $x = 18$ (or 1800 sq ft). See parts *a* and *b* of the preceding example. (There are small discrepancies due to rounding errors.)

```
MTB > READ C1 C2
DATA> 15 145
DATA> 38 228
DATA> 23 150           Enter
DATA> 16 130           data.
DATA> 16 160
DATA> 13 114
DATA> 20 142
DATA> 24 265
DATA> ENDOFDATA
MTB > REGRESSION C2 1 C1;     The semicolon indicates that more
SUBC> PREDICT 18.            related commands will follow.

The regression equation is
C2 = 71.0 + 4.64 C1
```

(continued)

```
Predictor      Coef    Stdev     t-ratio          p
Constant       71.02   40.47        1.75      0.130
C1             4.641   1.844        2.52      0.045

s = 39.19    R-sq = 51.4%    R-sq(adj) = 43.3%
```

Analysis of Variance

```
SOURCE            DF         SS      MS       F         p
Regression         1       9734    9734    6.34     0.045
Error              6       9216    1536
Total              7      18949
```

```
   Fit  Stdev.Fit        95% C.I.            95% P.I.
  154.6      14.7   (  118.6,   190.5)   (  52.1,   257.0)
    ↑                     ↑                    ↑
Predicted           95% confidence interval   95% prediction interval
value ŷ             for the mean              for the selling price
given that          selling price of homes    of an individual home
x = 18              with 1800 sq ft           with 1800 sq ft
```

12.5 EXERCISES   BASIC CONCEPTS

In Exercises 1–4, refer to the sample data in Table 12.1. (See the example of this section.) In each case, use the given living area to find (a) the predicted selling price of a home, (b) a 95% confidence interval for the mean selling price of homes with living areas equal to the value given, and (c) a 95% prediction interval for the selling price of a home with the given living area.

1. 2500 sq ft
2. 1500 sq ft
3. 2000 sq ft
4. 2650 sq ft
5. Use the given data to find (a) the predicted selling price of a home with taxes of $2000 ($x = 2.0$), (b) a 95% confidence interval for the mean selling price μ_y of homes with taxes of $2000 ($x = 2.0$), and (c) a 95% prediction interval for the selling price y of a home with taxes of $2000 ($x = 2.0$).

Taxes	1.9	2.4	1.4	1.4	1.5	1.8	2.4	4.0
Selling price	145	228	150	130	160	114	142	265

6. Use the given data to find (a) the predicted value of imports when exports are $100 billion ($x = 100$), (b) a 95% confidence interval for the mean value of imports μ_y when exports are $100 billion ($x = 100$), and (c) a 95% prediction interval for the value of imports y when the export value is $100 billion ($x = 100$).

Exports	10	20	43	221	218	218
Imports	9	15	40	245	326	370

7. Use the given data to find (a) the predicted weight of a baby born to a mother who doesn't smoke ($x = 0$ cigarettes smoked per day), (b) a 95% confidence interval for the mean weight of babies (μ_y) born to mothers who don't smoke ($x = 0$), and (c) a 95% prediction interval for the weight of a baby (y) born to a mother who doesn't smoke ($x = 0$).

Cigarettes smoked per day	0	10	0	30	0	25	40
Weight of baby (pounds)	8.5	6.5	7.2	5.8	8.0	6.3	6.0

8. Use the given data to find (a) the predicted selling price of a car with 30,000 miles ($x = 30$), (b) a 95% confidence interval for the mean selling price μ_y of cars with 30,000 miles ($x = 30$), and (c) a 95% prediction interval for the selling price y of a car with 30,000 miles ($x = 30$).

Mileage	35	22	32	18	25
Selling price	7.0	8.5	7.0	8.9	7.6

9. Use the given data to find (a) the predicted CO level of a vehicle with an HC level of 0.50, (b) a 95% confidence interval for the mean CO level μ_y of vehicles with an HC level of 0.50, and (c) a 95% prediction interval for the CO level of a vehicle with an HC level of 0.50.

HC	0.65	0.55	0.72	0.83	0.57	0.51	0.43	0.37
CO	14.7	12.3	14.6	15.1	5.0	4.1	3.8	4.1

10. Use the given data to find (a) the predicted taxes for a home with a living area of 3000 sq ft ($x = 30$), (b) a 95% confidence interval for the mean tax bill μ_y for homes with living areas of 3000 sq ft ($x = 30$), and (c) a 95% prediction interval for the tax bill for a home with a living area of 3000 sq ft ($x = 30$).

Living area	15	38	23	16	16	13	20	24
Taxes	1.9	2.4	1.4	1.4	1.5	1.8	2.4	4.0

12.5 EXERCISES BEYOND THE BASICS

11. A soft-drink container consists of a black plastic bottom that is glued by machine onto a clear plastic bottle. Too much glue would ooze out and would be wasteful and costly as well as unappealing to consumers, whereas too little glue would cause the bottom to fall off during processing, shipping, or use. Listed below are sample values representing x (glue nozzle pressure in lb/in²) and y (amount of glue applied in oz). The Minitab display for this data set is also given.

x	20	20	22	24	24	26	28	28	30	30
y	1.4	1.6	1.6	1.7	1.9	2.0	2.2	2.5	2.9	2.7

```
MTB > PLOT C2 C1
```

```
              -                                              *
     C2       -                                        *
              -
              -
     2.50+                                       *
              -
              -
              -                              *
              -
     2.00+                            *
              -                  *
              -
              -              *
              -        *        *
     1.50+
              -     *
              -
           ----+---------+---------+---------+---------+---------+--C1
             20.0      22.0      24.0      26.0      28.0      30.0
```

```
MTB > REGRESSION C2 1 C1;
SUBC> PREDICT 23;
SUBC> PREDICT 24;
SUBC> PREDICT 25;
SUBC> PREDICT 26.
```

```
The regression equation is
C2 = -1.18 + 0.128 C1
```

Predictor	Coef	Stdev	t-ratio	p
Constant	-1.1778	0.3698	-3.19	0.013
C1	0.12809	0.01453	8.82	0.000

```
s = 0.1654    R-sq = 90.7%    R-sq(adj) = 89.5%
```

Analysis of Variance

SOURCE	DF	SS	MS	F	p
Regression	1	2.1262	2.1262	77.75	0.000
Error	8	0.2188	0.0273		
Total	9	2.3450			

Fit	Stdev.Fit	95% C.I.	95% P.I.
1.7682	0.0613	(1.6268, 1.9096)	(1.3614, 2.1750)
1.8963	0.0551	(1.7692, 2.0234)	(1.4942, 2.2984)
2.0244	0.0524	(1.9036, 2.1452)	(1.6243, 2.4245)
2.1525	0.0536	(2.0289, 2.2760)	(1.7515, 2.5534)

a. Based on the scatter diagram, does a linear relationship appear to exist between the glue nozzle pressure and the amount of glue?

b. At the 0.05 significance level, test the claim that $\beta_1 = 0$.

c. Identify a 95% confidence interval for β_1.   (continued)

d. Based on the Minitab regression results, should the regression equation be used to make predictions?

e. Specifications indicate that the amount of glue applied should have a mean of 2.0 oz, with no less than 1.6 oz and no more than 2.5 oz applied to any one bottle. Which of the following nozzle pressures seems to be best: 23, 24, 25, or 26? Explain.

12. Sample data are collected from 9 randomly selected accounting majors who graduated from a midwestern business school. The GPA (grade point average) x and starting salary (in thousands of dollars) y is given for each student. Minitab results for these data are also given.

a. Based on the scatter diagram, does a linear relationship appear to exist between x and y?

b. Identify a 95% confidence interval for the mean predicted salary for students with GPAs of 2.5, identify a 95% prediction interval for the salary of someone with a GPA of 2.5, and explain the difference between the two types of interval estimates.

c. Test the claim that $\beta_1 = 2$. Use a 0.05 level of significance.

d. Find a 95% confidence interval for β_1.

e. If an accounting major raised her GPA from 2.0 to 3.0, how much *more* starting salary can she expect? Give a point estimate and an interval estimate.

x (GPA)	2.7	3.6	3.5	3.0	2.5	2.5	2.3	3.2	3.1
y (salary)	25.5	27.5	28.0	26.2	24.0	22.4	20.7	26.5	25.0

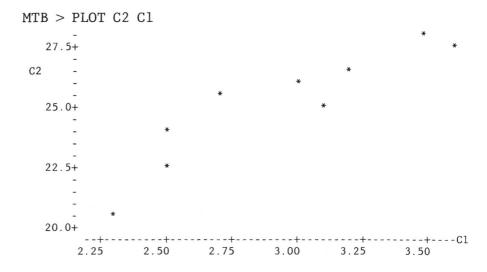

```
MTB > PLOT C2 C1
```

```
MTB > REGRESSION C2 1 C1;
SUBC> PREDICT 2.5;
SUBC> PREDICT 3.0;
SUBC> PREDICT 3.5.
```

```
The regression equation is
C2 = 11.3 + 4.71 C1
```

(continued)

```
Predictor        Coef      Stdev     t-ratio          p
Constant       11.262      2.369       4.75      0.000
C1             4.7137     0.7990       5.90      0.000

s = 1.042     R-sq = 83.3%     R-sq(adj) = 80.9%
```

Analysis of Variance

```
SOURCE            DF          SS          MS          F          p
Regression         1      37.773      37.773      34.81      0.000
Error              7       7.596       1.085
Total              8      45.369

    Fit   Stdev.Fit          95% C.I.              95% P.I.
 23.046       0.490   ( 21.886, 24.206)   ( 20.323, 25.770)
 25.403       0.351   ( 24.572, 26.234)   ( 22.803, 28.003)
 27.760       0.571   ( 26.410, 29.110)   ( 24.951, 30.569)
```

12.6   CORRELATION

In Section 12.4 we saw that we can objectively test for the presence of a linear relationship between two variables by testing the claim that $\beta_1 = 0$, where β_1 is the slope of the true regression line. If we fail to reject H_0: $\beta_1 = 0$, then we conclude that there is no significant linear relationship. If we reject H_0: $\beta_1 = 0$, then we conclude that there is a significant linear relationship between the two variables. In this section we introduce another *equivalent* method for determining whether a significant linear relationship is present. This method is equivalent to the preceding one in the sense that both methods will always lead to the same conclusion under the same circumstances. This new method is based on the linear correlation coefficient.

DEFINITIONS

The *sample linear correlation coefficient*, denoted by r, measures the strength of the linear association or relationship between the paired x and y values in a *sample*. r is a sample statistic.

The *population linear correlation coefficient*, denoted by ρ (rho), measures the strength of the linear association or relationship between the paired x and y values in a *population*. ρ is a population parameter.

For a set of paired sample data, the linear correlation coefficient r is given by

Formula 12.12
$$r = \frac{SSxy}{\sqrt{(SSx)(SSy)}}$$

Formula 12.12 can also be expressed as follows to make the calculations easier.

$$r = \frac{\Sigma xy - \dfrac{(\Sigma x)(\Sigma y)}{n}}{\sqrt{\left[\Sigma x^2 - \dfrac{(\Sigma x)^2}{n}\right]\left[\Sigma y^2 - \dfrac{(\Sigma y)^2}{n}\right]}}$$

EXAMPLE Use the sample paired real estate data in Table 12.1 to calculate r, the sample linear correlation coefficient.

SOLUTION Using the sample data in Table 12.1, we have already found that SSx = 451.875, SSy = 18,949.5, and $SSxy$ = 2097.25. Using these values, we calculate r as follows:

$$r = \frac{SSxy}{\sqrt{(SSx)(SSy)}} = \frac{2097.25}{\sqrt{(451.875)(18,949.5)}}$$

$$= \frac{2097.25}{2926.22} = 0.7167$$

Interpretation of this result will be discussed in the following text.

We can easily obtain computer results with the Minitab command CORRELA-TION. After entering the data in columns C1 and C2, enter that command as shown below.

```
MTB > CORRELATION C1 C2

Correlation of C1 and C2 = 0.717
```

After calculating r, how do we interpret the result? Given the way that Formula 12.12 was derived, it can be shown that r must always fall between -1 and $+1$ inclusive.

$$-1 \le r \le 1$$

A strong *positive* linear association between the two variables is reflected by a value of r "close to" 1, whereas a strong *negative* linear association is reflected by a value of r "close to" -1. If r is "close to" 0, we conclude that there is no significant linear relationship between the two variables. We can make this decision process much more objective by conducting a formal hypothesis test of the claim that $\rho = 0$. When testing H_0: $\rho = 0$ (or $\rho \le 0$ or $\rho \ge 0$), the following test statistic applies.

TEST STATISTIC

$$t = \frac{r - 0}{s_r} \quad \text{where} \quad s_r = \sqrt{\frac{1 - r^2}{n - 2}}$$

MANATEES SAVED

Manatees are large mammals that like to float just below the water's surface, where they are in danger from powerboat propellers. A Florida study of the number of powerboat registrations and the number of accidental manatee deaths confirmed that there was a significant positive correlation. As a result, Florida created coastal sanctuaries where powerboats are prohibited so that manatees can thrive. This is one of many examples of the beneficial use of statistics.

The critical value is found in Table A.3; use $n - 2$ degrees of freedom.

EXAMPLE | At the $\alpha = 0.05$ significance level, use the sample data in Table 12.1 to test the claim that $\rho = 0$.

SOLUTION | We have H_0: $\rho = 0$, H_1 $\rho \neq 0$, and $\alpha = 0.05$ in two tails. The test statistic is

$$t = \frac{r - 0}{s_r} = \frac{r - 0}{\sqrt{\dfrac{1 - r^2}{n - 2}}} = \frac{0.7167 - 0}{\sqrt{\dfrac{1 - (0.7167)^2}{8 - 2}}}$$

$$= \frac{0.7167}{0.2847} = 2.517$$

The critical values of $t = -2.447$ and $t = 2.447$ are found in Table A.3 by using $n - 2 = 8 - 2 = 6$ degrees of freedom and 0.05 in two tails. Because the test statistic falls in the critical region (see Fig. 12.9), we reject H_0 and conclude that there is a significant linear correlation.

If we compare the above test statistic to the test statistic for $\beta_1 = 0$ (see Section 12.4), we see that they are both $t = 2.517$. This is no coincidence. The test results for $\rho = 0$ and for $\beta_1 = 0$ will always be identical provided that we use the same significance level and the same type of test (two-tailed, left-tailed, or right-tailed). See Exercise 29.

If our only concern is whether a significant linear relationship is present between two variables, then we need only calculate the linear correlation coeffi-

---

FIGURE 12.9
Testing $\rho = 0$ for Data of Table 12.1

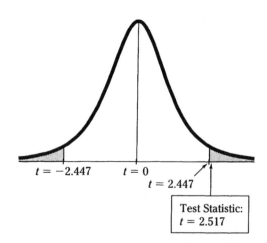

$t = -2.447$ $t = 0$

$t = 2.447$

Test Statistic:
$t = 2.517$

cient r. In business and industry, it is usually the case that in addition to determining whether a linear relationship exists, we also want to predict outcomes when there is such a relationship. It is for that reason that we have emphasized regression instead of correlation. However, in the *absence* of a significant linear correlation, we should not use the regression methods discussed earlier.

We noted that a test of H_0: $\beta_1 = 0$ is equivalent to a test of H_0: $\rho = 0$, and that equivalence establishes a link between regression and correlation. Another link is found in the values of R^2 and r. It can be shown that

$$R^2 = r^2$$

$$\uparrow \quad \uparrow$$

coefficient of   square of the linear
determination   correlation coefficient

To illustrate this relationship between R^2 and r^2, recall that for the data of Table 12.1, we have found that $R^2 = 0.5136$ and $r = 0.7167$. Using those values, we have

$$r^2 = 0.7167^2 = 0.5136 = R^2$$

Other comparisons between regression and correlation can be made from the following properties of r and of $\hat{\beta}_1$.

Properties of r

1. *The value of r is always between -1 and 1.* That is, $-1 \leq r \leq 1$.
2. *The value of r does not change if all values of either variable are converted to a different scale.* For example, if the units of x are so large that they cause calculator errors, you can divide them all by a constant number, such as 1000, and the value of r will not change.
3. *The value of r is not affected by the choice of x or y.* Interchange all x and y values, and the value of r will not change.
4. *r measures the strength of a linear relationship.* It is not designed to measure the strength of a relationship that is not linear.

Properties of $\hat{\beta}_1$

1. $\hat{\beta}_1$ can be any real number.
2. The value of $\hat{\beta}_1$ *does* change if all values of either variable are converted to a different scale. (See Exercise 28.)
3. If you interchange variables, the value of $\hat{\beta}_1$ *does* change. (See Exercise 27.)
4. $\hat{\beta}_1$ measures the strength of a *linear* relationship. It is not designed to measure the strength of a relationship that is not linear. (See Chapter 13.)

Relationships between r and $\hat{\beta}_1$

1. r and $\hat{\beta}_1$ will always have the same sign. (That is, they are both positive, or both negative, or both zero.)
2. Given the same significance level α and the same type of test (two-tailed, left-tailed, right-tailed), the test of $\beta_1 = 0$ is equivalent to the test of $\rho = 0$.

COMMON ERRORS

We now identify three of the most common errors made in interpreting results involving correlation.

1. *We must be careful to avoid concluding that a significant linear correlation between two variables is proof that there is a cause-effect relationship between them.* The statistical correlation between smoking and cancer is not proof that smoking *causes* cancer. The techniques in this chapter can be used only to establish a linear relationship. We cannot establish the existence or absence of any inherent cause-effect relationship between the variables. This problem is for the various professionals, such as medical researchers, psychologists, sociologists, biologists, and others.

2. *Another source of potential error arises with data based on rates or averages.* When we use rates or averages for data, we suppress the variation among the individuals or items, and this may easily lead to an inflated correlation coefficient. One study produced a 0.4 linear correlation coefficient for paired data relating income and education among *individuals,* but the correlation coefficient became 0.7 when regional *averages* were used.

3. *A third error involves the property of linearity.* The conclusion that there is no significant linear correlation does not mean that x and y are not related in any way. The data depicted in the last (lower right) scatter diagram of Fig. 12.2 earlier would result in a value of $r = 0$, an indication of no *linear* relationship between the two variables. However, we can easily see from the figure that there *is* a pattern showing a very strong (nonlinear) relationship. Chapter 13 will discuss such cases.

In this section we considered another method for determining whether a significant linear relationship is present between two variables. We can make that determination by testing the claim that the slope $\beta_1 = 0$ or that the population correlation coefficient $\rho = 0$. When making predictions, remember the important point that **we should use the regression equation only if there is a significant linear relationship between the two variables. In the absence of a significant linear relationship, our best estimate of y is simply the sample mean $\bar{y}$.** We illustrate this point with the following example.

EXAMPLE   For a particular collection of sample data, we find the following:

$n = 25$ $\bar{x} = 4.50$ $\bar{y} = 12.00$
Regression equation: $\hat{y} = 3.00 + 2.00x$

Find the best predicted point estimate of y when $x = 5.00$ given the following computed values of the linear correlation coefficient.

a. $r = 0.987$
b. $r = 0.013$

SOLUTION   a.   When testing the claim that $\rho = 0$, the value of r leads to a test statistic of $t = 29.452$, which, for any reasonable significance level such as 0.05, will fall within the critical region. We therefore reject the claim that $\rho = 0$ and conclude that there is a significant linear relationship between the two variables. *Because there is a significant linear correlation between the two variables, we use the regression equation to find predicted values.* We substitute $x = 5.00$ into the regression equation to get

$$\hat{y} = 3.00 + 2.00(5.00) = 13.00$$

as the best predicted point estimate of y.

b. When testing the claim that $\rho = 0$, the value of $r = 0.013$ leads to a test statistic of $t = 0.062$, which, for any reasonable significance level such as 0.05, will not fall within the critical region. We therefore fail to reject the claim that $\rho = 0$ and conclude that there is not a significant linear relationship between the two variables. *Because there is not a significant linear relationship between the two variables, we should not use the regression equation for predictions; instead, our best estimate of y is simply the mean $\bar{y}$.* We therefore conclude that given $x = 5.00$, the best predicted point estimate of y is $\bar{y} = 12.00$.

12.6 EXERCISES   BASIC CONCEPTS

In Exercises 1–8, use the given statistics to conduct the relevant hypothesis test.

1. H_0: $\rho = 0$; $\alpha = 0.05$; $n = 20$; $r = 0.833$
2. H_0: $\rho = 0$; $\alpha = 0.05$; $n = 22$; $r = 0.370$
3. H_1: $\rho \neq 0$; $\alpha = 0.05$; $n = 75$; $r = 0.370$
4. H_1: $\rho \neq 0$; $\alpha = 0.05$; $n = 10$; $r = -0.847$
5. H_1: $\rho > 0$; $\alpha = 0.05$; $n = 25$; $r = 0.503$
6. H_1: $\rho < 0$; $\alpha = 0.10$; $n = 20$; $r = -0.751$
7. H_1: $\rho < 0$; $\alpha = 0.05$; $n = 15$; $r = -0.234$
8. H_1: $\rho > 0$; $\alpha = 0.05$; $n = 8$; $r = 0.500$

In Exercises 9–18, use the given data reproduced from Section 12.2.

a. Find the value of the linear correlation coefficient r.
b. Test the claim that $\rho = 0$. Use a 0.05 significance level.
c. Is there a significant linear relationship between the two variables?
d. Verify that $r^2 = R^2$.

9.
x (advertising units)	1	1	2	3	4	4	5
y (sales units)	1	5	4	2	7	8	10

10.
x (hours of training)	1	2	2	3	4	5
y (production units)	6	8	12	14	15	20

11.
x (number of telephone inquiries received per day)	0	1	1	2	5
y (number of mail orders received per day)	3	3	4	5	6

12.

x (customer complaints)	1	3	3	4	5	5
y (units sold)	5	3	2	2	0	1

13.

Taxes	1.9	2.4	1.4	1.4	1.5	1.8	2.4	4.0
Selling price	145	228	150	130	160	114	142	265

14.

Exports	10	20	43	221	218	218
Imports	9	15	40	245	326	370

15.

Cigarettes smoked per day	0	10	0	30	0	25	40
Weight of baby (pounds)	8.5	6.5	7.2	5.8	8.0	6.3	6.0

16.

Mileage	35	22	32	18	25
Selling price	7.0	8.5	7.0	8.9	7.6

17.

HC	0.65	0.55	0.72	0.83	0.57	0.51	0.43	0.37
CO	14.7	12.3	14.6	15.1	5.0	4.1	3.8	4.1

18.

Living area	15	38	23	16	16	13	20	24
Taxes	1.9	2.4	1.4	1.4	1.5	1.8	2.4	4.0

In Exercises 19–22, assume that a collection of sample paired data yields a regression equation of $\hat{y} = 10.0 + 50.0x$ and the sample means are $\bar{x} = 0.30$ and $\bar{y} = 25.0$. In each case, use the additional information to (a) test the claim that $\rho = 0$ by using a 0.05 level of significance, and (b) find the best predicted point estimate of y when $x = 2.0$.

19. $n = 10$; $r = 0.005$
20. $n = 15$; $r = 0.902$
21. $n = 25$; $r = 0.887$
22. $n = 22$; $r = 0.567$

12.6   EXERCISES | BEYOND THE BASICS

In Exercises 23 and 24, use the given sample statistics to find the value of r.

23. a. $R^2 = 0.964$; $\hat{\beta}_1 = 3.207$
    b. $R^2 = 0.964$; $\hat{\beta}_1 = -3.207$
24. a. $R^2 = 0.648$; $\hat{\beta}_1 = -1.776$
    b. $R^2 = 0.521$; $\hat{\beta}_1 = 2.002$

In Exercises 25 and 26, use the information given in the Minitab display for the indicated exercises.

a. Calculate the value of the linear correlation coefficient r.
b. At the $\alpha = 0.05$ significance level, test the claim that $\rho = 0$.
c. Is there a significant linear relationship between the two variables? Explain.
25. Section 12.5, Exercise 11
26. Section 12.5, Exercise 12

27. In the example of this section, we let x = living area (in hundreds of square feet) and y = selling price (in thousands of dollars). Interchange those two variables.
    a. Plot the scatter diagram.
    b. Find the new equation of the regression line.
    c. Use the regression equation to predict the living area of a home with a selling price of $150,000.
    d. Calculate the value of r, the linear correlation coefficient.
28. In the example of this section, we let x = living area (in hundreds of square feet) and y = selling price (in thousands of dollars). Change the values of x to be in square feet by using 1500, 3800, and so on.
    a. Find the new equation of the regression line. How are $\hat{\beta}_0$ and $\hat{\beta}_1$ affected by the change in scale for x?
    b. Calculate R^2 and compare the result to the value of $R^2 = 0.5136$ found earlier.
    c. Calculate r and compare the result to the value of $r = 0.717$ found earlier.
    d. Test the claim that $\beta_1 = 0$. Compare results to those given in Section 12.4.
29. Equivalence of testing $\beta_1 = 0$ and $\rho = 0$: Show that the following test statistics are equivalent. (*Hint:* Use $SSError = SSy - \hat{\beta}_1 SSxy$.)

Test for $\hat{\beta}_1 = 0$

$$t = \frac{\hat{\beta}_1 - 0}{\sqrt{\dfrac{SSError}{n-2} \div SSx}}$$

Test for $\rho = 0$

$$t = \frac{r - 0}{\sqrt{\dfrac{1 - r^2}{n-2}}}$$

Vocabulary List
Define and give an example of each term.

scatter diagram
regression line
regression equation
marginal change
least-squares property
total deviation
explained deviation
unexplained deviation
coefficient of determination
confidence interval for the slope β_1
confidence interval for the mean of all y values
prediction interval for an individual y value
sample linear correlation coefficient
population linear correlation coefficient

Review
This chapter considered methods for using sample paired data to analyze the relationship between the corresponding two variables. In Section 12.2 we began with *scatter diagrams* that can be used to make subjective judgments about the presence of a linear relationship between variables. We also presented a method

IMPORTANT FORMULAS

$$SSx = \Sigma(x - \bar{x})^2 = \Sigma x^2 - \frac{(\Sigma x)^2}{n}$$

$$SSy = \Sigma(y - \bar{y})^2 = \Sigma y^2 - \frac{(\Sigma y)^2}{n}$$

$$SSxy = \Sigma(x - \bar{x})(y - \bar{y}) = \Sigma xy - \frac{(\Sigma x)(\Sigma y)}{n}$$

$$\hat{y} = \hat{\beta}_0 + \hat{\beta}_1 x \qquad \text{Equation of regression line}$$

$$\hat{\beta}_1 = \frac{SSxy}{SSx} \qquad \text{Slope of regression line}$$

$$\hat{\beta}_0 = \bar{y} - \hat{\beta}_1\bar{x} \qquad \text{y-intercept of regression line}$$

$$SSy = SSRegression + SSError$$

$$SSError = \Sigma(y - \hat{y})^2 = SSy - \hat{\beta}_1 SSxy$$

$$SSRegression = \Sigma(\hat{y} - \bar{y})^2 = \hat{\beta}_1 SSxy$$

$$R^2 = \frac{SSRegression}{SSy} = \frac{SSy - SSError}{SSy} \qquad \text{Coefficient of determination}$$

$$\hat{\sigma}_e = \sqrt{\frac{SSError}{n - 2}} \qquad \text{Estimated standard deviation of random error } e$$

$$t = \frac{\hat{\beta}_1 - b}{s_{\hat{\beta}_1}} \quad \text{where} \quad s_{\hat{\beta}_1} = \frac{\hat{\sigma}_e}{\sqrt{SSx}} \qquad \begin{array}{l}\text{Test statistic for claim about} \\ \beta_1 \ (df = n - 2)\end{array}$$

$$\hat{\beta}_1 - E < \beta_1 < \hat{\beta}_1 + E \quad \text{where} \quad E = t_{\alpha/2}\frac{\hat{\sigma}_e}{\sqrt{SSx}} \qquad \begin{array}{l}\text{Confidence interval for} \\ \beta_1 \ (df = n - 2)\end{array}$$

$$\hat{y} - E < \mu_y < \hat{y} + E \quad \text{where} \quad E = t_{\alpha/2}\hat{\sigma}_e\sqrt{\frac{1}{n} + \frac{(x_0 - \bar{x})^2}{SSx}} \qquad \begin{array}{l}\text{Confidence interval for mean} \\ \text{predicted } y \text{ value given } x_0 \ (df = n - 2)\end{array}$$

$$\hat{y} - E < y < \hat{y} + E \quad \text{where} \quad E = t_{\alpha/2}\hat{\sigma}_e\sqrt{1 + \frac{1}{n} + \frac{(x_0 - \bar{x})^2}{SSx}} \qquad \begin{array}{l}\text{Prediction interval for individual} \\ \text{value } y \text{ given } x_0 \ (df = n - 2)\end{array}$$

$$r = \frac{SSxy}{\sqrt{(SSx)(SSy)}} \qquad \text{Linear correlation coefficient}$$

$$= \frac{\Sigma xy - \dfrac{(\Sigma x)(\Sigma y)}{n}}{\sqrt{\left[\Sigma x^2 - \dfrac{(\Sigma x)^2}{n}\right]\left[\Sigma y^2 - \dfrac{(\Sigma y)^2}{n}\right]}}$$

$$t = \frac{r - 0}{s_r} \quad \text{where} \quad s_r = \sqrt{\frac{1 - r^2}{n - 2}} \qquad \begin{array}{l}\text{Test statistic for claim} \\ \text{that } \rho = 0 \ (df = n - 2)\end{array}$$

for finding the equation of the *regression line*, or line of "best" fit. That equation can be useful in predicting the value of one variable when given some value for the other variable. If no relationship exists between the two variables, then we should not use the regression equation for predicting the value of one variable when given the value of the other variable; instead, we simply use the mean of the other variable.

In Section 12.3 we introduced *SSError* and the *coefficient of determination* as measures of how well a regression line fits sample data. In addition, we introduced the concept of *total variation,* with components of explained and unexplained variation. We also considered the assumptions used in our regression model.

Section 12.4 included hypothesis testing and confidence intervals for the slope β_1. Testing the claim that $\beta_1 = 0$ is equivalent to testing the claim that the regression line is a *good* fit of the sample data to determine whether it can then be used for predictions.

In Section 12.5 we developed a confidence interval for the mean predicted y value. We also developed a "prediction interval," which is a confidence interval for an individual predicted y value.

Finally, Section 12.6 introduced the concept of (linear) *correlation*. We used the linear correlation coefficient as a measure of the strength of the linear relationship between two variables. Testing the claim that a population of paired data has a linear correlation coefficient equal to zero is equivalent to testing the claim that the regression line has a slope of zero. We identified important properties of the linear correlation coefficient as well as the slope of the regression line.

Figure 12.10 outlines some of the important procedures in this chapter.

Review Exercises

In Exercises 1–7, use the sample data described below. (Let the independent variable x represent the measures of satisfaction.) In a study of employee stock ownership plans, data on satisfaction with the plan and the amount of organizational commitment were collected at 8 companies. Results are given in the accompanying table, which is based on "Employee Stock Ownership and Employee Attitudes: A Test of Three Models," by Klein, *Journal of Applied Psychology,* Vol. 72, No. 2.

Satisfaction	5.05	4.12	5.39	4.17	4.00	4.49	5.40	4.86
Commitment	5.37	4.49	5.42	4.45	4.24	5.34	5.62	4.90

1. Construct the scatter diagram. Based on the result, does there appear to be a relationship between satisfaction and commitment?
2. Find the values of $\hat{\beta}_1$ and $\hat{\beta}_0$, then identify the equation of the regression line.
3. Find the values of *SSRegression, SSError,* the coefficient of determination R^2, and the linear correlation coefficient r.
4. Construct a 95% confidence interval for $\hat{\beta}_1$.
5. At the 0.05 level of significance, test the claim that $\beta_1 = 0$. Based on the test results, determine whether the regression line fits the data well or poorly.
6. At the 0.05 level of significance, test the claim that the population correlation coefficient ρ is equal to 0.
7. a. Given a satisfaction value of 5.00, find the best predicted value of commitment.
   b. For employees with satisfaction levels of 5.00, find the 95% confidence interval for the mean predicted commitment value.
   c. For an individual employee with a satisfaction level of 5.00, find the 95% prediction interval for the predicted value of commitment.

In Exercises 8–14, use the sample data described below. (Let the independent variable x represent the measures of productivity.)

FIGURE 12.10
Summary of Important Procedures

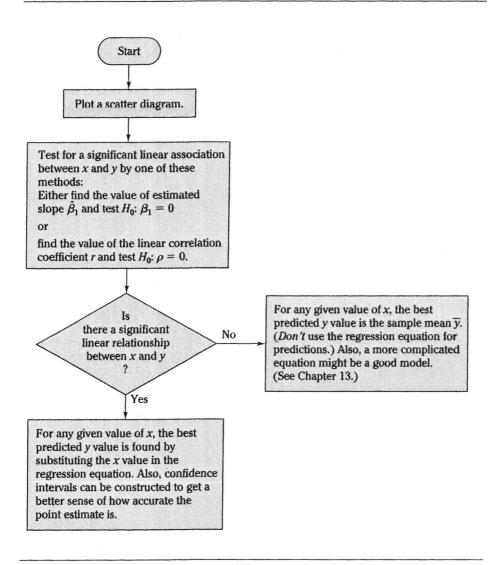

A manager in a factory randomly selects 15 assembly-line workers and develops scales to measure their dexterity and productivity levels. The results are listed in the following table.

Productivity	63	67	88	44	52	106	99	110	75	58	77	91	101	51	86
Dexterity	2	9	4	5	8	6	9	8	9	7	4	10	7	4	6

8. Construct the scatter diagram. Based on the result, does there appear to be a relationship between productivity and dexterity?
9. Find the values of $\hat{\beta}_1$ and $\hat{\beta}_0$, then identify the equation of the regression line.

10. Find the values of *SSRegression, SSError,* the coefficient of determination R^2, and the linear correlation coefficient *r*.
11. Construct a 95% confidence interval for $\hat{\beta}_1$.
12. At the 0.05 level of significance, test the claim that $\beta_1 = 0$. Based on the test results, determine whether the regression line fits the data well or poorly.
13. At the 0.05 level of significance, test the claim that the population correlation coefficient ρ is equal to 0.
14. Given a productivity level of 80, find the best predicted value of dexterity.

In Exercises 15 and 16, assume that a collection of sample paired data yields a regression equation of $\hat{y} = 50.0 - 20.0x$ and the sample means are $\bar{x} = 0.50$ and $\bar{y} = 40.0$. In each case, use the additional information to (a) test the claim that $\rho = 0$ by using a 0.05 level of significance, and (b) find the best predicted point estimate of *y* when $x = 1.00$.

15. $n = 20; r = -0.403$
16. $n = 15; r = -0.836$

Computer Project

In the examples and exercises of this chapter, we typically began with sample paired data and proceeded to make inferences using such factors as $\hat{\beta}_0$, $\hat{\beta}_1$, R^2, and *r*. In this project we *assume that we already know that the true population regression equation is*

$$y = 40 + 60x + e$$

where the random error variable *e* is normally distributed with a mean of 0 and a standard deviation of $\sigma_e = 10$. The variable *x* is the amount (in thousands of dollars) spent for advertising in a month by a large carpet retailer, and *y* represents the gross sales (in thousands of dollars).

a. We can generate 12 values of *e* from a normally distributed population with a mean of 0 and a standard deviation of 10 by entering these Minitab commands:

```
MTB > RANDOM 12 C1;
SUBC> NORMAL MU = 0 SIGMA = 10.
MTB > PRINT C1
```

Either enter those commands to get 12 values of *e* or use these values: -3.4, 2.5, -11.5, 5.5, -3.7, 13.9, 12.8, 2.0, -17.5, 11.6, 6.9, and 0.9. Given that the generated values of *e* correspond to $x = 1.4$, 0.8, 0.8, 1.5, 0.9, 0.7, 1.1, 0.6, 1.0, 1.2, 0.9, and 0.8, find the 12 corresponding values of *y*.
b. Construct a scatter diagram of the 12 paired *x–y* values. (If the 12 pairs of data are entered in Minitab as columns C1 for *x* and C2 for *y*, use the command PLOT C2 C1.)
c. Using the 12 pairs of data, find the estimated equation of the regression line ($\hat{y} = \hat{\beta}_0 + \hat{\beta}_1 x$), then plot it on the scatter diagram along with the population regression equation $y = 40 + 60x$. Compare the estimated regression line to the true regression line. (Use Minitab's command REGRESSION C2 1 C1 to find the equation of the estimated regression line.)
d. Find the values of *SSx, SSError,* $\hat{\sigma}_e$, R^2, and *r*.

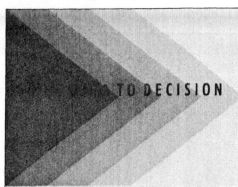

PREDICTING SELLING PRICES OF HOMES: THE PLOT THICKENS

Y ou have been hired to manage a housing construction project, and in order to establish home selling prices, you need to know something about the relationship between lot size and selling price in Dutchess County. It might seem that homes on larger lots should have higher selling prices, but other factors cloud that simple relationship. For example, some very large lots are found in more rural parts of the county where the selling prices tend to be lower. This chapter considered the relationship between living area and selling price, but this project will involve lot size (in acres) and selling price. For the sample data, refer to Appendix B and randomly select a sample of 20 homes. Let x = lot size and let y = selling price (in thousands of dollars).

a. Plot the scatter diagram. Does a relationship appear to exist between lot size and selling price?

b. Find the equation of the regression line and then plot it on the scatter diagram.

c. Find the values of SSx, $SSError$, $\hat{\sigma}_e$, R^2, and r.

d. At the 0.05 level of significance, test the claim that the regression line has a slope of zero ($\beta_1 = 0$). Based on the conclusion, does the estimated regression equation fit the data well or poorly?

e. Based on the sample data, what is the best predicted value for the selling price of a home on a 1.00-acre lot? How was that value determined?

f. Based on the preceding results, write a brief report summarizing your conclusions about the relationship between lot size and selling price. Include a recommendation about how much the variable of lot size should be considered in setting the selling prices of homes in Dutchess County. In addition to living area and lot size, identify any other important factors that one might seriously consider for newly constructed homes.

e. Using the paired $x-y$ data, test the claim that $\beta_1 = 0$ by using a 0.05 level of significance. Based on the conclusion, does the estimated regression equation fit the data well or poorly?

f. Use the paired $x-y$ data to construct the 95% confidence interval for β_1. We know from our model that the true value of β_1 is 60. Does the confidence interval contain the true value of β_1?

g. Given that $1000 ($x = 1.0$) is spent on advertising in one month, find:

i. The predicted value of gross sales.

ii. A 95% confidence interval about the mean predicted value of sales for months in which $1000 is spent on advertising. We know from our model that the true mean predicted value of sales for $x = 1.0$ is $y = 40 + 60(1.0) = 100$. Does the confidence interval contain that true value of the mean?

iii. A 95% prediction interval for the predicted sales value in an individual month with $1000 spent on advertising.

(Use the Minitab command REGRESSION along with the subcommand PREDICT as illustrated in Section 12.5.)

JAY DEAN

SENIOR VICE PRESIDENT AT
THE SAN FRANCISCO OFFICE OF
YOUNG & RUBICAM ADVERTISING

Jay Dean is Director of the Consumer Insights Department at the San Francisco office of Young & Rubicam. He has worked with many well-known advertisers, including AT&T, Chevron, Clorox, Coors, Dr. Pepper, Ford Motor Co., General Foods, Gillette, Gulf Oil, H. J. Heinz, Kentucky Fried Chicken, and Warner-Lambert.

HOW EXTENSIVE IS YOUR USE OF STATISTICS AT YOUNG & RUBICAM?

We use statistics every day. I'm now working on a typical design, an advertising test for Take Heart salad dressing, one of the brands we handle for the Clorox Company. Two commercials were shown to independent samples of consumers. We then asked questions about what was being communicated by each commercial, perceptions of the brand, likes and dislikes, and so on. Significance testing will be used to compare the results and to choose the best commercial.

On larger surveys we use multivariate techniques such as factor analysis and multiple re-

gression. Marketing is becoming tougher and tougher today. There are more brands, increasing price competition, and more-sophisticated consumers. A tougher marketing environment requires more marketing research, and that means we're using statistics more often as well.

COULD YOU CITE A CASE IN WHICH THE USE OF STATISTICS WAS INSTRUMENTAL IN DETERMINING A SUCCESSFUL STRATEGY?

We recently conducted a major creative exploratory for Pine-Sol, another Clorox brand. About half a dozen commercials were produced in rough form and shown to independent samples of consumers. Statistics helped us to identify the best commercial for the new Pine-Sol advertising campaign. Early marketplace results are very encouraging. At Y&R we believe consumer research helps us to produce the most effective advertising. Statistics help us to make informed decisions based upon the results of the research.

HOW DO YOU TYPICALLY COLLECT DATA FOR STATISTICAL ANALYSIS?

There are many ways to collect data, but typically it's either random telephone sampling for survey work or, if you want to show people something like a commercial, we use a central location interview. For example, respondents are intercepted in a shopping mall by an interviewer, screened for eligibility, asked to

go into a testing facility to be shown a commercial, and so on.

DO YOU FIND IT DIFFICULT TO OBTAIN REPRESENTATIVE AND UNBIASED SAMPLES?

Yes. The marketing research industry now is very concerned about the growing refusal rate among the general public. That is driven in part by salespeople who use marketing research as a guise for selling. Mail surveys are subject to a huge self-selection bias, and response rates are typically quite low. Shopping mall interviews have other problems. Not everyone goes to malls, and there is a certain degree of interviewer bias in approaching prospective respondents.

WHAT IS YOUR TYPICAL SAMPLE SIZE?

For a national survey, the rule of thumb is about a thousand people, although you might go with as few as 600 in some cases. For an advertising test, a sample on the order of 200 would be a pretty healthy sample size—sometimes as few as a hundred.

DO YOU FEEL THAT JOB APPLICANTS IN YOUR FIELD ARE VIEWED MORE FAVORABLY IF THEY HAVE STUDIED SOME STATISTICS?

Yes, absolutely. Everyone has to understand and use statistics at some level. It's very important for entry-level people to know statistics well because they do much of our research project work.

> **"If I could go back to school, I would certainly study more math, statistics, and computer science."**

DO YOU HAVE ANY ADVICE FOR TODAY'S STUDENTS?

If I could go back to school, I would certainly study more math, statistics, and computer science. I studied a lot of it, but I would like to know even more. There's an enormous data explosion in business these days. All businesses are becoming much more quantitative than they ever were in the past. Today, there is more information than you know what to do with, and you've got to have the analytical tools and knowledge to deal with this information if you want to be successful.

CHAPTER 13

Multiple Regression

13.1 OVERVIEW

13.2 THE MULTIPLE REGRESSION EQUATION

This section presents the basic concept of multiple regression, illustrates how it is related to simple linear regression, and shows how predictions can be made. The interpretation of the coefficients of the variables in the multiple regression equation is described, and the least-squares property used in determining the multiple regression equation is identified. The assumptions used for the methods of this chapter are also identified.

13.3 MEASURING VARIATION AND OVERALL QUALITY OF THE MULTIPLE REGRESSION EQUATION

A test on the coefficient of determination R^2 that can be used to judge how well a multiple regression equation fits sample data is described.

13.4 HYPOTHESIS TESTING AND CONFIDENCE INTERVALS FOR COEFFICIENTS

This section shows how computer displays can be used to develop a hypothesis test and confidence interval for each coefficient of the multiple regression equation.

13.5 CONFIDENCE INTERVALS FOR PREDICTED VALUES

The construction of confidence intervals for the predicted mean value μ_y and prediction intervals for individual y values is described. Emphasis is on the interpretation of computer displays.

13.6 EXTRAPOLATION, ESTIMABILITY, AND MULTICOLLINEARITY

This section describes some common pitfalls and problems associated with multiple regression.

Price Too High?

The Jefferson Valley Bank carefully scrutinizes mortgage applications and appraises each home. We will consider the problem of predicting the selling price of a home with a living area of 1800 sq ft and an annual tax bill of $1500. A couple wants to buy this home for $190,000 and has applied for a mortgage.

In Chapter 12 we used a regression equation to predict the selling price of a home with a specific living area. Our actual results confirmed that there is a relationship between living area and selling price. We might also expect that in addition to living area, other factors can be used to predict a home's selling price. In Table 13.1 we list the same data used in Chapter 12, but we include the additional variable of tax bill (in thousands of dollars). Because the tax bill is supposedly based on the value of the real estate, it's reasonable to expect that there should be a very high (if not perfect) correlation between tax bill and selling price. But in Table 13.1 the tax rates are not all the same; they vary from 0.9% to 1.7%.

We could use the methods of Chapter 12 to determine whether the tax bill by itself would be a good predictor of selling price

TABLE 13.1
Data for Homes Sold

Living area (x_1)	15	38	23	16	16	13	20	24
Tax bill (x_2)	1.9	2.4	1.4	1.4	1.5	1.8	2.4	4.0
Selling price (y)	145	228	150	130	160	114	142	265

(see Exercise 13 in Section 12.6), but in this chapter we want to determine whether it would be better to use **both** the living area and tax bill. Given the sample data of Table 13.1, what is the best predicted value of the selling price for a home with a living area of 1800 sq ft and a tax bill of $1500? How does the predicted selling price compare to the $190,000 selling price negotiated by the buyers?

13.1 OVERVIEW

Chapter 12 included discussions of a regression equation that relates *two* variables; in this chapter we deal with regression equations that relate more than two variables.

> ### DEFINITION
>
> A *multiple regression equation* expresses a linear relationship between a dependent variable y and two or more independent variables $(x_1, x_2, \ldots, x_k)$.

When attempting to predict values for the variable y (such as home selling price), many variables might be relevant. In this chapter we see how to use computer software to find a multiple regression equation and how to use that equation for making predictions. We discuss the underlying assumptions for multiple regression and show how we can use a hypothesis test to determine whether the multiple regression equation fits the data well. Next, we show how a hypothesis test and confidence interval can be made for each coefficient in the multiple regression equation, and how to get confidence intervals for the predicted mean y value μ_y and prediction intervals for individual y values. Finally, we discuss some problems that can occur in multiple regression, and we use computer displays to illustrate some of them.

13.2 THE MULTIPLE REGRESSION EQUATION

Multiple regression is an extension of the simple linear regression discussed in Chapter 12. In Chapter 12 we found that for a set of sample paired data, there is a statistically significant linear relationship between Dutchess County home selling price and living area. We obtained the regression equation $\hat{y} = 71.0 + 4.64x$. In this equation, x is the living area (in hundreds of square feet) and $\hat{y}$ is the predicted selling price (in thousands of dollars). We predicted that for a home with a living area of 1800 sq ft, the selling price is $\hat{y} = 71.0 + 4.64(18) = 154.52$ (or \$154,520). The estimate of the slope ($\hat{\beta}_1 = 4.64$) can be interpreted as the marginal change in $\hat{y}$ for one additional unit of x. That is, if you increase the living area by one unit (or 100 sq ft), the predicted selling price increases by $1 \times 4.64 = 4.64$ (or \$4640). We found the coefficient of determination to be $R^2 = 0.514$, which is only moderately good because it indicates that 51.4% of the total variation in the selling price is explained by the regression line; 48.6% of the variation remains unexplained. Finally, we found a 95% confidence interval for the mean selling price of homes with living areas of 1800 sq ft. We obtained this result: $\$118,610 < \mu_y < \$190,430$. Instead of dealing with only two variables, we will now consider more than two variables. Many of the concepts, assumptions, tests, and estimators of simple linear regression also apply to multiple regression.

It was not too surprising to find a significant linear relationship between selling price and living area. After all, large homes cost more to build, and that increased cost is reflected in increased value. In the problem described at the beginning of the chapter, we noted that several other important factors might be considered in trying to predict the selling price of a home. Let us consider the data of the annual tax bill (in thousands of dollars) as another variable (x_2) and see whether it could be included with our variable of living area (x_1) to produce a much improved prediction equation. Because the dependent variable is the selling price y and the independent variables are living area (x_1) and tax bill (x_2), the form of that equation will be as follows:

Formula 13.1
$$\hat{y} = \hat{\beta}_0 + \hat{\beta}_1 x_1 + \hat{\beta}_2 x_2$$

This formula fits the form of a multiple regression equation because it expresses a linear relationship between y and two or more independent variables.

Throughout this chapter, the following notation and terminology will be used. Some of the notation was already introduced in Chapter 12 but is included here for review.

Notation

n = sample size

k = number of *independent* variables, or the number of *predictor* variables, or the number of *slope coefficients,* or the number of *x* variables

$\hat{y}$ = predicted value of the dependent variable y

$x_1, x_2, \ldots, x_k$ are the independent variables

β_0 = constant

$\hat{\beta}_0$ = sample *estimate* of the constant β_0

$\beta_1, \beta_2, \ldots, \beta_k$ are the coefficients of the independent variables x_1, $x_2, \ldots, x_k$

$\hat{\beta}_1, \hat{\beta}_2, \ldots, \hat{\beta}_k$ are the sample *estimates* of the coefficients $\beta_1, \beta_2, \ldots, \beta_k$

We want to use the sample data of Table 13.1 to find the multiple regression equation of the form given in Formula 13.1, and so we need to find values for $\hat{\beta}_0$, $\hat{\beta}_1$, and $\hat{\beta}_2$. The actual process for manually finding these values is extremely complex and involves calculations that are extensive, time consuming, and error-prone. Fortunately, we can use inexpensive statistical software packages, such as Minitab, SAS, or SPSS. These values are now almost always found by using such software packages instead of manual calculations. Our procedure for finding the values of those coefficients is to obtain them from a computer display. The Minitab display for the Table 13.1 data is given here. Note that the key Minitab REGRES-SION command for multiple regression is very similar to the corresponding command used in Chapter 12 for simple linear regression; the resulting display is also quite similar.

PLASTIC PEOPLE

When counting people, the Census Bureau often misses some, so that population totals are too low for some communities. Because those totals affect more than $100 billion in government allocations, representation in Congress, and redistricting of local governments, many civic leaders and government officials are understandably concerned in demanding the totals be correct. The Census Bureau has used a variety of methods in attempts to rectify the problem of undercounting. In one case, the Census Bureau requested that the University of Arizona's research of garbage be used to estimate population sizes. After considering many variables, such as the weight of paper, the weight of plastic, or the total weight of the garbage, researchers found that the best predictor was a single variable: the weight of plastic. The regression equation is $\hat{y} = 0.282x$, where $\hat{y}$ is the predicted number of people and x is the weight (in lbs) of plastic collected in 5 weeks.

```
MTB > READ C1 C2 C3
DATA> 15 1.9 145
DATA> 38 2.4 228
DATA> 23 1.4 150
DATA> 16 1.4 130          Data from Table 13.1
DATA> 16 1.5 160          entered here
DATA> 13 1.8 114
DATA> 20 2.4 142
DATA> 24 4.0 265
DATA> ENDOFDATA
      8 ROWS READ                            Data for $x_1$ and $x_2$
MTB > REGRESSION C3 2 C1 C2
        Data for $y$                    We must indicate the
The regression equation is     number of $x$ variables.
C3 = 24.2 + 3.01 C1 + 38.3 C2   ← Multiple regression equation


Predictor      Coef      Stdev    t-ratio        p
Constant      24.17      27.52       0.88    0.420
C1            3.014      1.189       2.54    0.052
C2           38.29      11.02        3.48    0.018

s = 23.23    R-sq = 85.8%    R-sq(adj) = 80.1%

Analysis of Variance

SOURCE         DF         SS         MS        F        p
Regression      2     16251.1     8125.5    15.06    0.008
Error           5      2698.4      539.7
Total           7     18949.5

SOURCE         DF     SEQ SS
C1              1     9733.8
C2              1     6517.3
```

EXAMPLE If we use the data of Table 13.1, we will get the accompanying Minitab display. Refer to that display and the original data set to identify (a) the multiple regression equation, and (b) the values of n, k, $\hat{\beta}_0$, $\hat{\beta}_1$, and $\hat{\beta}_2$.

SOLUTION
a. From the Minitab display, we see that the multiple regression equation is given as C3 = 24.2 + 3.01C1 + 38.3C2. Using our notation, we express this multiple regression equation as

$$\hat{y} = 24.2 + 3.01x_1 + 38.3x_2$$

b. Referring to Table 13.1, we see that there are 8 triplets of data, so that $n = 8$. The multiple regression equation has two independent or predictor variables or x variables, so that $k = 2$. From the multiple regression equation given in part a, we see that $\hat{\beta}_0 =$

24.2, $\hat{\beta}_1 = 3.01$, and $\hat{\beta}_2 = 38.3$. Note also that the Minitab display includes a column labeled "Coef" and the entries consist of $\hat{\beta}_0$, $\hat{\beta}_1$, and $\hat{\beta}_2$ with an extra decimal place (24.17, 3.014, and 38.29).

MAKING PREDICTIONS

We now know that we can obtain multiple regression equations by using software packages such as Minitab. Once a multiple regression equation is identified, it becomes quite easy for us to use it for making predictions. Given particular values for the independent variables $(x_1, x_2,$ and so on), we can substitute them into the multiple regression equation to find the predicted value $\hat{y}$.

EXAMPLE Using the data of Table 13.1 and Minitab, we have found that the multiple regression equation is $\hat{y} = 24.2 + 3.01x_1 + 38.3x_2$. Find the predicted selling price of a home with a living area of 1800 sq ft and a tax bill of $1500.

SOLUTION Recall that the given multiple regression equation has living area expressed in hundreds of square feet, while selling price and tax bill are in thousands of dollars. We therefore substitute 18 for x_1 and 1.5 for x_2, and we get

$$\hat{y} = 24.2 + 3.01x_1 + 38.3x_2$$
$$= 24.2 + 3.01(18) + 38.3(1.5)$$
$$= 135.83 \quad \text{(or } \$135,830\text{)}$$

That is, a home with a living area of 1800 sq ft and a tax bill of $1500 has a predicted selling price of $135,830.

In our opening problem we noted that a couple is applying for a bank mortgage on a home with a living area of 1800 sq ft and a tax bill of $1500, and a selling price of $190,000 has been negotiated. In predicting (appraising) the value of the home for the bank, we get $135,830 by using the available sample data. There appears to be a large discrepancy. Initially, it seems that the bank should not approve a mortgage based on a predicted selling price much higher than $135,830. The bank needs to protect its loan by being able to sell the house, if necessary, and recover its money.

In the above example, if we change the living area from $x_1 = 18$ to $x_1 = 19$ while holding the tax bill constant at $x_2 = 1.5$, we will see that $\hat{y}$ changes from 135.83 to 138.84 (an increase of 3.01). That is, a unit change in the value of x_1 (while holding x_2 constant) causes a marginal change of 3.01 in the value of $\hat{y}$. In general, the coefficient of $\hat{\beta}_1 = 3.01$ can be interpreted as the marginal change in $\hat{y}$ per unit change in x_1, while holding x_2 constant. Similarly, the coefficient of $\hat{\beta}_2 = 38.3$ can be interpreted as the marginal change in $\hat{y}$ per unit change in x_2,

TABLE 13.2
Data for Homes Sold

Living area (x_1)	15	38	23	16	16	13	20	24
Tax bill (x_2)	1.9	2.4	1.4	1.4	1.5	1.8	2.4	4.0
Swimming pool (x_3)	1	0	0	0	1	0	0	0
Selling price (y)	145	228	150	130	160	114	142	265

while holding x_1 constant. In contrast, for the simple linear regression equation (from Chapter 12) of $\hat{y} = 71 + 4.64x$, we have $\hat{\beta}_1 = 4.64$, so that the marginal change in selling price per unit change in living area is 4.64. But when x_1 (living area) and x_2 (tax bill) are both included, we get the very different value of $\hat{\beta}_1 = 3.01$. Thus the impact of one unit of x_1 changes according to which other variables are used in the regression equation.

DUMMY VARIABLES

So far, we have considered only the continuous variables of selling price, living area, and tax bill. However, it is sometimes necessary to include data that do not consist of numbers, such as whether a home has or doesn't have a swimming pool. Such data can be included as a dummy variable.

DEFINITION

A *dummy variable* has a value of 1 or 0, depending on whether a particular characteristic is present or is not present.

In Table 13.2 we extend the data of Table 13.1 by including the dummy variable x_3, where 1 indicates that the home has a swimming pool and 0 indicates that it does not have a swimming pool.

The accompanying Minitab display results from the data of Table 13.2, which includes the dummy variable x_3. Note from the display that the regression equation is now $\hat{y} = 2.3 + 3.53x_1 + 40.5x_2 + 26.7x_3$, and the coefficient for the dummy variable is $\hat{\beta}_3 = 26.7$. This seems to imply that if we hold the variables x_1 and x_2 constant, the predicted value of the home should increase by \$26,700 if there is a swimming pool (that is, $x_3 = 1$), but the predicted value of the home does not change if there is no swimming pool (that is, $x_3 = 0$). Thus the value of $\hat{\beta}_3 = 26.7$ seems to indicate that a swimming pool adds \$26,700 to the predicted value of a home.

In the following Minitab display, note that the READ command is used for entering the data into the columns designated as C1, C2, C3, and C4. The SET command could have been used, but the READ command is better with data that are matched, as in Table 13.2. After entering the data for the eight homes, the command REGRESSION C4 3 C1 C2 C3 is entered. This is the key command that calls for multiple regression with the variable for column C4 (selling prices) included as the dependent variable, and the 3 variables for columns C1, C2, and C3 included as the independent variables.

```
MTB > READ C1 C2 C3 C4
DATA> 15 1.9 1 145
DATA> 38 2.4 0 228
DATA> 23 1.4 0 150
DATA> 16 1.4 0 130
DATA> 16 1.5 1 160
DATA> 13 1.8 0 114
DATA> 20 2.4 0 142
DATA> 24 4.0 0 265
DATA> ENDOFDATA
        8 ROWS READ
MTB > REGRESSION C4 3 C1 C2 C3

The regression equation is
C4 = 2.3 + 3.53 C1 + 40.5 C2 + 26.7 C3
```

Predictor	Coef	Stdev	t-ratio	p
Constant	2.33	29.72	0.08	0.941
C1	3.526	1.151	3.06	0.038
C2	40.48	10.23	3.96	0.017
C3	26.69	19.16	1.39	0.236

```
s = 21.31    R-sq = 90.4%    R-sq(adj) = 83.2%
```

Analysis of Variance

SOURCE	DF	SS	MS	F	p
Regression	3	17132.6	5710.9	12.57	0.017
Error	4	1816.9	454.2		
Total	7	18949.5			

SOURCE	DF	SEQ SS
C1	1	9733.8
C2	1	6517.3
C3	1	881.5

The values for the coefficients $\hat{\beta}_0$, $\hat{\beta}_1$, $\hat{\beta}_2$, . . . , $\hat{\beta}_k$ are determined by the same least-squares criterion introduced in Section 12.2. That is, the values of $\hat{\beta}_0$, $\hat{\beta}_1$, $\hat{\beta}_2$, . . . , $\hat{\beta}_k$ are those which result in the smallest possible sum of the squares of the differences between the actual observed y sample values and $\hat{y}$ values predicted from the regression equation. As in Chapter 12, that sum is also expressed as

$$SSError = \Sigma(y - \hat{y})^2$$

where y is the actual observed selling price and $\hat{y}$ is the predicted selling price found by substituting the $x_1, x_2, . . . , x_k$ values into the regression equation. As in Chapter 12, this least-squares criterion results in the equation that "best" fits the sample data.

It is important to note again that $\hat{\beta}_0$, $\hat{\beta}_1$, $\hat{\beta}_2$, . . . , $\hat{\beta}_k$ are estimates of the true coefficients $\beta_0, \beta_1, \beta_2, . . . , \beta_k$ and are based on a particular sample. A different set of sample data would yield different values for those estimates.

ASSUMPTIONS FOR MULTIPLE REGRESSION

The assumptions underlying multiple regression are natural extensions of the assumptions presented in Chapter 12 for simple linear regression. Specifically, for the general multiple regression equation involving k independent predictor variables, these assumptions apply:

1. The true regression equation is

$$y = \beta_0 + \beta_1 x_1 + \beta_2 x_2 + \cdots + \beta_k x_k + e$$

2. The e in the true regression equation is a random error variable that, for any one set of x values, satisfies these properties:
   i. e has a normal distribution with mean 0 and constant standard deviation given by σ_e.
   ii. All e's are independent of one another.

Just as we use $\hat{\beta}_0, \hat{\beta}_1, \ldots, \hat{\beta}_k$ as sample estimates of $\beta_0, \beta_1, \ldots, \beta_k$, we can also get an estimate for the population standard deviation σ_e, which measures the amount of dispersion of the sample data points from the graph of the regression equation. It is found from the following:

Formula 13.2
$$\hat{\sigma}_e = \sqrt{\frac{SSError}{n - (k + 1)}}$$

where n is the sample size and k is the number of slope coefficients (or independent variables). The value of $\hat{\sigma}_e$ is used in constructing the confidence intervals discussed in the following sections, but Minitab will include $\hat{\sigma}_e$ in its calculations, so we will not deal directly with the values of $\hat{\sigma}_e$.

13.2 EXERCISES   BASIC CONCEPTS

In Exercises 1–4, use the following regression equation.

$$\hat{y} = 34.8 + 1.21x_1 + 0.23x_2$$

Here $\hat{y}$ is the predicted calculus grade, x_1 is the score on an algebra placement test, and x_2 is the high school rank expressed as a percentile. (The equation is based on data from "Factors Affecting Achievement in the First Course in Calculus," by Edge and Friedberg, *Journal of Experimental Education*, Vol. 52, No. 3.)

1. Find the predicted calculus grade if the score on the algebra pretest (x_1) is 24 and the high school rank is the 92nd percentile.
2. Find the predicted calculus grade if the score on the algebra pretest (x_1) is 12 and the high school rank is the 71st percentile.

TABLE 13.3
Data for Sold Chevrolet Corsicas

x_1	35	22	32	18	25	36	33	17	26	21
x_2	0	1	0	1	0	1	1	0	1	0
x_3	22	19	19	21	18	20	19	18	15	24
y	7.0	8.5	7.0	8.9	7.6	7.4	7.3	8.6	7.9	8.0

3. Find the predicted calculus grade if the score on the algebra pretest (x_1) is 18 and the high school rank is the 81st percentile.
4. Find the predicted calculus grade if the score on the algebra pretest (x_1) is 31 and the high school rank is the 99th percentile.

In Exercises 5–8, use the data of Table 13.3 and the Minitab display. The data represent 10 Chevrolet Corsicas randomly selected from those sold by a national car rental agency. The selling prices y (entered as column C4) are in thousands of dollars, the mileages x_1 (in column C1) are in thousands of miles, the variable x_2 (in column C2) is coded so that 1 represents a car with cruise control and 0 represents a car without cruise control, and x_3 (in column C3) is the age of the car in months.

```
MTB > REGRESSION C4 3 C1 C2 C3

The regression equation is
C4 = 9.49 - 0.0899 C1 + 0.483 C2 + 0.0240 C3

Predictor           Coef         Stdev      t-ratio          p
Constant          9.4927        0.5287        17.95      0.000
C1             -0.089884      0.008060       -11.15      0.000
C2                0.4834        0.1134         4.26      0.005
C3               0.02398       0.02422         0.99      0.361

s = 0.1704     R-sq = 95.8%     r-sq(adj) = 93.7%

Analysis of Variance

SOURCE          DF          SS          MS          F          p
Regression       3      3.9418      1.3139      45.24      0.000
Error            6      0.1742      0.0290
Total            9      4.1160
```

5. Identify the multiple regression equation that expresses the selling price in terms of mileage, cruise control, and age.
6. Use the multiple regression equation to predict the selling price of a car with 30,000 mi, no cruise control, and an age of 16 months.
7. Use the multiple regression equation to predict the selling price of a car with 30,000 mi, cruise control, and an age of 16 months.
8. Use the multiple regression equation to predict the selling price of a car with 27,000 mi, cruise control, and an age of 20 months.

TABLE 13.4
Plastic Shelves

x_1	5	2	1	3	4	3
x_2	10	8	7	11	7	5
x_3	2	3	4	3	1	4
y	25	13	16	13	10	40

In Exercises 9–12, use the data of Table 13.4 and Minitab to find the indicated multiple regression equation. Also, find the predicted y value for $x_1 = 2$, $x_2 = 9$, and $x_3 = 3$. The variable y is the weight in pounds that can be supported by plastic refrigerator shelves, x_1 is a measure of the pressure, x_2 is the time in the mold, and x_3 is the temperature setting on the machine which makes the shelves.

9. Express the weight variable in terms of the pressure and time variables. That is, find the multiple regression equation of the form $\hat{y} = \hat{\beta}_0 + \hat{\beta}_1 x_1 + \hat{\beta}_2 x_2$.

10. Express the weight variable in terms of the pressure and temperature variables. That is, find the multiple regression equation of the form $\hat{y} = \hat{\beta}_0 + \hat{\beta}_1 x_1 + \hat{\beta}_3 x_3$.

11. Express the weight variable in terms of the time and temperature variables. That is, find the multiple regression equation of the form $\hat{y} = \hat{\beta}_0 + \hat{\beta}_2 x_2 + \hat{\beta}_3 x_3$.

12. Express the weight variable in terms of the pressure, time, and temperature variables. That is, find the multiple regression equation of the form $\hat{y} = \hat{\beta}_0 + \hat{\beta}_1 x_1 + \hat{\beta}_2 x_2 + \hat{\beta}_3 x_3$.

In Exercises 13–16, use the sample data of Table 13.5 and Minitab. The data are based on sales of homes in Dutchess County, New York. Selling prices and taxes are in thousands of dollars. The living areas are in hundreds of square feet and the acreage amounts are in acres.

13. a. Find the multiple regression equation that expresses the tax bill in terms of selling price and living area.
   b. Using the result from part *a*, find the predicted tax bill for a home with a selling price of $230,000 and a living area of 3600 sq ft.

14. a. Find the multiple regression equation that expresses the selling price in terms of living area, acreage, and number of rooms.
   b. Using the result from part *a*, find the predicted selling price for a home with a living area of 1700 sq ft and 7 rooms on a lot of 0.8 acre.

15. a. Find the multiple regression equation that expresses the taxes in terms of living area, acreage, and number of rooms.
   b. Using the result from part *a*, find the predicted taxes for a home with 2100 sq ft and 8 rooms on a lot of 1.2 acres.

TABLE 13.5
Data for Homes Sold

Living area	15	38	23	16	16	13	20	24
Taxes	1.9	2.4	1.4	1.4	1.5	1.8	2.4	4.0
Acreage	2.0	3.6	1.8	0.53	0.50	0.31	0.75	2.0
Rooms	5	11	9	7	7	7	9	7
Selling price	145	228	150	130	160	114	142	265

16. a. Find the multiple regression equation that expresses the selling price in terms of living area, taxes, acreage, and number of rooms.
    b. Using the result from part a, find the predicted selling price of a home with 2200 sq ft, 8 rooms, taxes of $1900, and a lot size of 1.5 acres.

13.2 EXERCISES | BEYOND THE BASICS

17. We claimed that using the data of Table 13.1, we would find that the equation $\hat{y} = 24.2 + 3.01x_1 + 38.3x_2$ is the line of best fit according to the least-squares criterion.
    a. Using the 8 pairs of tax-bill and living-area sample data from Table 13.1, find the 8 corresponding values of $\hat{y}$ (predicted selling price) by using the above equation.
    b. Find the value of $SSError = \Sigma(y - \hat{y})^2$, where y is the selling price actually observed and $\hat{y}$ is the predicted selling price.
    c. Repeat parts a and b by using this multiple regression equation: $\hat{y} = 40 + 2x_1 + 40x_2$. Show that the resulting value of $SSError$ is *larger* than the value obtained by using the original multiple regression equation that satisfies the *least*-squares criterion.

13.3 MEASURING VARIATION AND OVERALL QUALITY OF THE MULTIPLE REGRESSION EQUATION

In Section 13.2 we used the sample data of Table 13.1 and Minitab to find the multiple regression equation $\hat{y} = 24.2 + 3.01x_1 + 38.3x_2$, which in turn led to a predicted selling price of $\hat{y} = \$135,830$ for a home with a living area of 1800 sq ft and a tax bill of $1500. In Chapter 12 the regression equation $\hat{y} = 71.0 + 4.64x$ led to a predicted selling price of $\hat{y} = \$154,520$ for a home with a living area of 1800 sq ft. Which predicted value is better? Which of the two equations generally fits the data better? To answer these questions, we need first to recall some important elements introduced in Chapter 12 that also apply to multiple regression.

$SSError = \Sigma(y - \hat{y})^2$ is the total amount of variation between the actual observed values of y and the values predicted by the regression equation.

$SSRegression = \Sigma(\hat{y} - \bar{y})^2$ is the amount of variation that is explained by the regression equation.

$SSy = \Sigma(y - \bar{y})^2$ is the total amount of variation for the y values.

$SSy = SSRegression + SSError$ expresses the relationship among SSy (total variation), $SSRegression$ (explained variation), and $SSError$ (unexplained variation).

EXPLAINED VARIATION AND R^2

Because the above formulas come from Chapter 12 and also apply to multiple regression, the following expression for the coefficient of determination R^2 also applies to multiple regression.

$$R^2 = \frac{SSRegression}{SSy}$$

As in Chapter 12, *the value of* R^2 *can be interpreted as the proportion of variation in the y values (about* $\bar{y}$*) that is explained by the regression equation.* Also as in Chapter 12, it is a property of R^2 that

$$0 \le R^2 \le 1$$

EXAMPLE Using the Minitab display for the data of Table 13.1, find the value of the coefficient of determination R^2 by (a) locating it directly from the Minitab display, and (b) calculating it using *SSRegression* and *SSy* found from the Minitab display.

SOLUTION
a. Refer to the first Minitab display in Section 13.2 and note that it includes R-sq = 85.8%. The decimal equivalent of that result is $R^2 = 0.858$.
b. Refer to the same Minitab display and note that under the *SS* column and corresponding to the rows labeled "Regression" and "Total" we get these values: *SSRegression* = 16251.1 and *SSy* = 18949.5. (Recall that Minitab's *SSTotal* is the same as *SSy*.) We can now calculate R^2 as follows:

$$R^2 = \frac{SSRegression}{SSy}$$

$$= \frac{16251.1}{18949.5} = 0.858$$

That is, 85.8% of the total variation in the selling prices can be explained in terms of the relationship to living areas and tax bills, and only 14.2% of the total variation remains unexplained.

It might seem that we could simply compare the coefficients of determination R^2 and conclude that the multiple regression equation is better because its R^2 is 0.858, which is greater than $R^2 = 0.514$ for the simple linear regression case (Chapter 12), but that is not so. *When we include an additional variable in any regression equation, the value of* R^2 *will increase.* (Actually, R^2 could remain the same, but it usually increases. R^2 remains the same when the additional variable has a slope coefficient of 0.) We will now explain why R^2 remains the same or increases whenever another variable is included.

TABLE 13.6
Comparison of Regression Equations

	SIMPLE LINEAR REGRESSION (CHAPTER 12)	MULTIPLE REGRESSION (CHAPTER 13)	MULTIPLE REGRESSION (CHAPTER 13)
Variable	Selling price Living area	Selling price Living area Taxes	Selling price Living area Taxes Swimming pool
Regression equation	$\hat{y} = 71.0 + 4.64x$	$\hat{y} = 24.2 + 3.01x_1 + 38.3x_2$	$\hat{y} = 2.3 + 3.53x_1 + 40.5x_2 + 26.7x_3$
Coefficient of Determination	$R^2 = 0.514$	$R^2 = 0.858$	$R^2 = 0.904$
SSRegression	9733.756	16251.1	17132.6
SSError	9215.744	2698.4	1816.9
SSy	18949.5	18949.5	18949.5

EFFECTS OF ADDED VARIABLES

In Table 13.6 we list the values of R^2 along with other comparable items from this chapter and Chapter 12. The values shown for the multiple regression parts of that table can be found from the Minitab displays in Section 13.2. It is important to note from the table that the total variation SSy is the same for all three cases because $SSy = \Sigma (y - \bar{y})^2$ is calculated from the same eight y values of home selling prices. However, the $SSError$ values are different because the different regression equations fit the sample data differently and with different errors.

Consider this: Our regression methods yield the best equation $\hat{y} = \hat{\beta}_0 + \hat{\beta}_1 x$ for simple linear regression, but if we include another independent variable, we then get the best equation $\hat{y} = \hat{\beta}_0 + \hat{\beta}_1 x_1 + \hat{\beta}_2 x_2$ for multiple regression. This last equation could result in $\hat{\beta}_2 = 0$, so that the best-fitting regression equation could be $\hat{y} = \hat{\beta}_0 + \hat{\beta}_1 x_1 + 0$ (the same as the linear regression case). That extra $\hat{\beta}_2 x_2$ term provides the opportunity for an improved fit that is at least as good as the fit obtained from $\hat{y} = \hat{\beta}_0 + \hat{\beta}_1 x$. Consequently, R^2 usually increases (although it could remain constant) when we include another independent variable. When we add another variable, the improved fit also causes $SSError$ to decrease (although it could remain the same). It also follows that the addition of another variable usually causes $SSRegression = SSy - SSError$ to increase (although it could remain the same). In summary, when we include additional variables, the following effects occur.

SSy remains constant.
$SSError$ usually decreases (it could remain constant).
$SSRegression$ usually increases (it could remain constant).
R^2 usually increases (it could remain the same).

In the following section we will discuss the determination of the best regression equation. First, we consider a hypothesis test that allows us to distinguish between a regression equation that fits the data *well* and a regression equation that fits the data *poorly*.

HYPOTHESIS TEST FOR THE OVERALL SIGNIFICANCE OF THE MULTIPLE REGRESSION EQUATION

By using Minitab computer displays, it becomes relatively easy to develop formal hypothesis tests that reveal whether a regression equation fits sample data well and is therefore useful for predictions. The hypothesis test will be based on the null hypothesis that all the slope coefficients (β_1, β_2, . . . , β_k) are equal to zero, so that there is no relationship between the dependent variable y and the independent variables. The hypothesis test has these key components:

HYPOTHESIS TEST FOR THE OVERALL SIGNIFICANCE OF THE MULTIPLE REGRESSION EQUATION

Null Hypothesis: H_0: The coefficients β_1, β_2, . . . , β_k are all zero. (That is, $\beta_1 = \beta_2 = \cdots = \beta_k = 0$.)

Alternative Hypothesis: H_1: At least one of those slope coefficients is not zero.

Test statistic:
$$F = \frac{SSRegression/k}{SSError/[n - (k + 1)]}$$

where k = the number of *slope* coefficients (β_1, β_2, . . . , β_k) being tested
n = sample size

Critical value: This test is always *right-tailed*. Use Table A.5 (critical F values) with numerator degrees of freedom = k and denominator degrees of freedom = $n - (k + 1)$.

EXAMPLE   We have seen that the sample data of Table 13.1 resulted in the multiple regression equation of $\hat{y} = 24.2 + 3.01x_1 + 38.3x_2$. At the 0.05 level of significance, test the claim that $\beta_1 = \beta_2 = 0$. Also, use the resulting P-value to determine how confident we are in our conclusions.

SOLUTION   We have H_0: $\beta_1 = \beta_2 = 0$, and H_1 is the claim that at least one of those two slope coefficients is not zero. The test statistic is found by first noting that the sample size is $n = 8$ and the number of coefficients being tested is $k = 2$ (for living area and tax bill). The other components required for the test statistic are found in the Minitab computer display for the data of Table 13.1. (See Section 13.2.) We get

$$F = \frac{SSRegression/k}{SSError/[n - (k + 1)]} = \frac{16251.1/2}{2698.4/5} = 15.056$$

FIGURE 13.1
F Distribution and Test Statistic for Data of Table 13.1

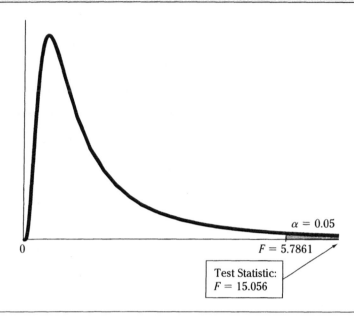

$\alpha = 0.05$

0    $F = 5.7861$

Test Statistic:
$F = 15.056$

The critical value of $F = 5.7861$ is found from Table A.5 by noting that we have $\alpha = 0.05$ and the numbers of degrees of freedom are as follows:

numerator degrees of freedom $= k = 2$
denominator degrees of freedom $= n - (k + 1) = 8 - (2 + 1) = 5$

In Fig. 13.1 we show the test statistic and critical value. Because the test statistic falls within the critical region, we reject the null hypothesis and conclude that at least one of β_1 and β_2 is nonzero. (In the next section we will see how to determine which one is nonzero or whether both are nonzero.) Because at least one of β_1 and β_2 is nonzero, a relationship exists between y and at least one of the variables x_1 and x_2. Also, the Minitab display shows this same test and a *P*-value of 0.008. The low *P*-value indicates that we have great confidence in rejecting the null hypothesis of $\beta_1 = \beta_2 = 0$. Based on these sample results, we conclude that the given regression equation fits the data well (instead of poorly) and is therefore useful for making predictions. However, this doesn't imply that the given equation is the *best*-fitting regression equation that can be found from the sample data.

In contrast to the preceding example, if we were to use the Table 13.2 data and express the dependent variable of selling price y in terms of living area x_1 and the dummy variable x_3 for swimming pool, we get this regression equation:

$$\hat{y} = 60.2 + 4.98x_1 + 15.0x_3$$

For this regression equation, the hypothesis test of H_0: $\beta_1 = \beta_3 = 0$ is *not* rejected, because the *P*-value is 0.152, which exceeds the significance level of $\alpha = 0.05$. This regression equation therefore fits the data poorly and should not be used for predictions. Here's a key point: *To judge the usefulness of a regression equation for making predictions, we should begin by testing for the overall significance of the regression equation.*

The hypothesis test we have described in this section can be used to distinguish between regression equations that are good (and usable for predictions) and those that are poor. Considering the three regression equations in Table 13.6, their computer printouts have their overall significances with *P*-values of 0.045, 0.008, and 0.017, respectively. This suggests that the three regression equations in Table 13.6 fit the data well and each can be used for predictions, but the fourth regression equation given above ($\hat{y} = 60.2 + 4.98x_1 + 15.0x_3$) should not be used for predictions, because it does not fit the data well. In the next section we determine which of those three equations is best. In particular, we will see that the third one is not as good as its overall significance and R^2 values seem to suggest.

PREDICTING WINE BEFORE ITS TIME

Princeton University economist Orley Ashenfelter applies regression analysis to use weather as a predictor of the quality and price of vintage wines. He includes these variables: rainfall preceding the growing season, average growing season temperature, and rainfall during harvest. Ashenfelter states: "Predicting the quality and price of a wine could be like predicting any other market item. All you need is the right equation and the right values for your variables." He successfully tested his multiple regression equation on past results, finding that wine auction prices confirmed his prediction of quality.

13.3 EXERCISES   BASIC CONCEPTS

In Exercises 1–4, use the accompanying Minitab display. The Minitab variables *C1*, *C2*, and *C3* correspond to the variables x_2 (hours of labor), x_2 (cost of raw materials), and $\hat{y}$ (cost of producing one circuit board).

```
MTB > REGRESSION C3 2 C1 C2

The regression equation is
C3 = -0.48 + 6.17 C1 - 0.076 C2

Predictor        Coef      Stdev     t-ratio        p
Constant       -0.483      1.315       -0.37    0.724
C1             6.1744      0.2363       26.12    0.000
C2            -0.0764      0.1470       -0.52    0.620

s = 1.913     R-sq = 99.4%     R-sq(adj) = 99.3%

Analysis of Variance

SOURCE         DF         SS         MS         F        p
Regression      2     4454.0     2227.0    608.82    0.000
Error           7       25.6        3.7
Total           9     4479.6

SOURCE         DF     SEQ SS
C1              1     4453.0
C2              1        1.0
```

1. Identify the multiple regression equation.
2. Identify the value of the coefficient of determination.
3. Test the hypothesis that all the slope coefficients are zero. Use a 0.05 level of significance. Also, find the P-value.
4. What percentage of the variation in the y values (stored in the column designated as C3) can be explained by the variables included in the sample data (in columns C1 and C2)?

For Exercises 5–8, refer to the data and Minitab display given for Table 13.3 in the exercises of Section 13.2. In each case use Minitab to generate the items needed.

5. a. Consider the multiple regression equation in which selling price is expressed in terms of mileage, cruise control, and age. At the 0.05 significance level, test the claim that the three slope coefficients are all zero.
   b. What is the P-value for the test in part a?
   c. What proportion of the variation in selling price can be explained by mileage, cruise control, and age?
6. a. Consider the multiple regression equation in which selling price is expressed in terms of mileage and age. At the 0.05 significance level, test the claim that the two slope coefficients are both zero.
   b. What is the P-value for the test in part a?
   c. What proportion of the variation in selling price can be explained by mileage and age?
7. a. Consider the multiple regression equation in which selling price is expressed in terms of mileage and cruise control. At the 0.05 significance level, test the claim that the two slope coefficients are both zero.
   b. What is the P-value for the test in part a?
   c. What proportion of the variation in selling price can be explained by mileage and cruise control?
8. a. Consider the multiple regression equation in which mileage is expressed in terms of selling price, cruise control, and age. At the 0.05 significance level, test the claim that the three slope coefficients are all zero.
   b. What is the P-value for the test in part a?
   c. What proportion of the variation in mileage can be explained by selling price, cruise control, and age?

For Exercises 9–12, refer to the sample data of Table 13.5 in the exercises of Section 13.2. In each case use Minitab to generate the items needed.

9. a. Consider the regression equation in which the tax bill is expressed in terms of selling price and living area. At the 0.05 level of significance, test the claim that the two slope coefficients are both zero.
   b. What is the P-value for the test in part a?
   c. What is the proportion of the variation in tax bill that can be explained by selling price and living area?
10. a. Consider the regression equation in which the selling price is expressed in terms of living area, acreage, and number of rooms. At the 0.05 level of significance, test the claim that the three slope coefficients are all zero.
    b. What is the P-value for the test in part a?
    c. What is the proportion of the variation in selling price that can be explained by living area, acreage, and number of rooms?

11. a. Consider the regression equation in which taxes are expressed in terms of living area, acreage, and number of rooms. At the 0.05 level of significance, test the claim that the three slope coefficients are all zero.
   b. What is the P-value for the test in part a?
   c. What is the proportion of the variation in taxes that can be explained by living area, acreage, and number of rooms?

12. a. Consider the regression equation in which selling price is expressed in terms of living area, taxes, acreage, and number of rooms. At the 0.05 level of significance, test the claim that the four slope coefficients are all zero.
   b. What is the P-value for the test in part a?
   c. What is the proportion of the variation in selling price that can be explained by living area, taxes, acreage, and number of rooms?

13. Use the data of Table 13.2 and Minitab to find the regression equation in which selling price (y) is expressed in terms of living area (x_1) and the dummy variable representing swimming pool (x_3).
   a. Verify that the regression equation is $\hat{y} = 60.2 + 4.98x_1 + 15.0x_3$, as we claimed in this section.
   b. Find the values of *SSRegression* and *SSError* and use them to verify that $R^2 = 0.529$.
   c. At the 0.05 level of significance, test the claim that the true slope coefficients are both zero.

13.3 EXERCISES   BEYOND THE BASICS

14. When we are trying to use different combinations of independent variables for finding the best multiple regression equation, the value of R^2 alone is sometimes misleading because the largest R^2 is achieved by using all the variables. The *adjusted* R^2 is often used instead.

$$\text{adjusted } R^2 = 1 - \frac{(n-1)}{[n-(k+1)]}(1 - R^2)$$

   where k = number of independent variables included
   n = number of observations

   For the data of Table 13.5, the inclusion of lot size as a third independent variable x_3 increases R^2 from 0.858 to 0.865. (a) Find the adjusted R^2 values corresponding to those two R^2 values that are based on 8 observations. (b) Does the value of the adjusted R^2 increase when we include x_3? (c) Does the regression equation with x_1, x_2, and x_3 seem better than the regression equation with x_1 and x_2 only?

15. **Nonlinear regression:** The accompanying table lists the percentage yield of U.S. Treasury bonds along with the time (in months) to maturity (based on past data from Shearson-Lehman Hutton).

y (yield)	3.24	3.34	3.55	4.65	5.63	6.70	7.07	7.54
x_1 (time)	3	6	12	36	60	120	240	360

a. Plot the scatter diagram (see Section 12.2) and note the nonlinear pattern.

b. Find the simple linear regression equation of the form $\hat{y} = \hat{\beta}_0 + \hat{\beta}_1 x_1$ and find the corresponding R^2 and P-value in the F test of the claim that $\beta_1 = 0$.

c. Create another independent variable x_2, where each value of x_2 is simply the square of the corresponding x_1 value. That is, the values of x_2 are 9, 36, 144, and so on. Find the regression equation of the form $\hat{y} = \hat{\beta}_0 + \hat{\beta}_2 x_2$. (This will be the equation of the parabola with vertex on the y-axis that best fits the data.) Find R^2 and the P-value in the F test of the claim that $\beta_2 = 0$.

d. Find the multiple regression equation of the form $\hat{y} = \hat{\beta}_0 + \hat{\beta}_1 x_1 + \hat{\beta}_2 x_2$. (This will be the equation of the parabola that best fits the data.) Find R^2 and the P-value in the F test of the claim that $\beta_1 = \beta_2 = 0$.

e. Compare the preceding results and identify the best model. Why is it best? Graph this equation on the scatter diagram from part a.

13.4 HYPOTHESIS TESTING AND CONFIDENCE INTERVALS FOR COEFFICIENTS

In the preceding section we developed a method for testing for the overall significance of a multiple regression equation. We used that method with the data of Table 13.1 and found, using Minitab displays, that the equations

$$\hat{y} = 24.2 + 3.01x_1 + 38.3x_2$$

and

$$\hat{y} = 2.3 + 3.53x_1 + 40.5x_2 + 26.7x_3$$

both fit the data well and appear to be useful for predictions, such as the predicted selling price y that the Jefferson Valley Bank needs for appraising the value of a home with 1800 sq ft ($x_1 = 18$), a tax bill of $1500 ($x_2 = 1.5$), and a pool or no pool ($x_3 = 1$ or 0). While we know that the above multiple regression equations do have *overall* significance (based on the hypothesis test examples given in Section 13.3), we don't know anything about the significance of each of the individual regression coefficients of 3.01 and 38.3 for the first equation, and 3.53, 40.5, and 26.7 for the second equation. It sometimes happens that a particular multiple regression equation has overall significance, but some of the individual slope coefficients are not significant. For example, if we include the distance between the front door and the mailbox as a new variable, we might find that the regression equation has overall significance, even though that distance really has no relationship to the selling price of the home. In this section we develop a procedure for testing the significance of each individual variable. We will again take the approach typically used by business professionals: We emphasize the use of computer-generated displays. We begin with hypothesis tests of claims made about the values of the regression coefficients $\beta_0, \beta_1, \beta_2, \ldots, \beta_k$.

HYPOTHESIS TESTS

The same general method of testing hypotheses will apply to each of the regression coefficients, so we denote an arbitrary regression coefficient by β_i. We are usually interested in whether β_i is equal to zero, but our test could involve any arbitrary constant we denote by b. (Testing the claim that $\beta_i = 0$ is really the same as testing the claim that the variable x_i has no relationship to the dependent variable y.) In testing the claim that $\beta_i = b$ (or $\beta_i \le b$ or $\beta_i \ge b$), the following test statistic applies.

TEST STATISTIC

For H_0: $\beta_i = b$ **(or $\beta_i \le b$ or $\beta_i \ge b$)**

$$t = \frac{\hat{\beta}_i - b}{s_{\hat{\beta}_i}}$$

where $s_{\hat{\beta}_i}$ is the estimate of the standard deviation of $\hat{\beta}_i$.

The above test statistic has a t distribution, and the critical value is found in Table A.3, where the number of degrees of freedom is given by

$$df = n - (k + 1) \qquad (n = \text{sample size} \quad \text{and} \quad k = \text{number of independent } x \text{ variables})$$

Rejecting H_0: $\beta_i = 0$ suggests that the variable x_i is significant and should be included in the regression equation. Failure to reject H_0: $\beta_i = 0$ suggests that the variable x_i is unimportant and should not be included. But some professionals recommend that if there is a sound theoretical reason for including a variable, then include it even if it's not significant.

FIGURE 13.2
Testing $\beta_2 = 0$

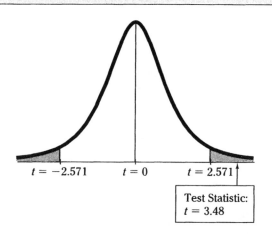

$t = -2.571$ $t = 0$ $t = 2.571$

Test Statistic:
$t = 3.48$

EXAMPLE

Consider the multiple regression equation of our chapter problem. Given below is the relevant portion of the Minitab display included in Section 13.2. Recall that β_2 corresponds to the variable of annual tax bill. At the $\alpha = 0.05$ significance level, test the claim that $\beta_2 \neq 0$. (Testing the claim that $\beta_2 \neq 0$ is really testing the claim that the tax bill has some linear effect on the predicted selling price.)

```
The regression equation is
C4 = 24.2 + 3.01 C1 + 38.3 C2
```

Predictor	Coef	Stdev	t-ratio	p
Constant	24.17	27.52	0.88	0.420
C1	3.014	1.189	2.54	0.052
C2	38.29	11.02	3.48	0.018

SOLUTION

We have $H_0: \beta_2 = 0$ and $H_1: \beta_2 \neq 0$. The test statistic is found by using these Minitab results: $\beta_2 = 38.29$ and $s_{\hat{\beta}_2} = 11.02$. We get

$$t = \frac{\hat{\beta}_2 - b}{s_{\hat{\beta}_2}} = \frac{38.29 - 0}{11.02} = 3.475$$

The same test statistic of $t = 3.48$ (rounded off) is included in the Minitab display under the column heading of "t-ratio." The critical values of $t = -2.571$ and $t = 2.571$ are found from Table A.3 by using $n - (k + 1) = 8 - (2 + 1) = 5$ degrees of freedom and $\alpha = 0.05$ in two tails. See Fig. 13.2. The test statistic does fall in the critical region, so we reject the null hypothesis. There is sufficient evidence to warrant rejection of the claim that the tax bill coefficient is equal to zero. (Note also that Minitab displays the two-tailed P-value of 0.018; because this P-value is less than the significance level of $\alpha = 0.10$, we again reject $H_0: \beta_2 = 0$.) In addition to knowing that the regression equation has overall significance, we also now know that the tax bill coefficient is significant when included with living area. It appears that the tax bill variable should be included in predictions of the selling price.

EXAMPLE

Use the data of Table 13.2, which includes the dummy variable of x_3 for swimming pools. Use a significance level of $\alpha = 0.05$ to test the claim that $\beta_3 = 0$ (that is, a swimming pool has no effect on the selling price of a home). Shown below is the relevant portion of the Minitab display.

```
The regression equation is
C4 = 2.3 + 3.53 C1 + 40.5 C2 + 26.7 C3
```

Predictor	Coef	Stdev	t-ratio	p
Constant	2.33	29.72	0.08	0.941
C1	3.526	1.151	3.06	0.038
C2	40.48	10.23	3.96	0.017
C3	26.69	19.16	1.39	0.236

SOLUTION The null hypothesis is H_0: $\beta_3 = 0$ and the alternative hypothesis is H_1: $\beta_3 \neq 0$. The test statistic of $t = 1.39$ can be found in the Minitab display (or it can be computed by noting that $\hat{\beta}_3 = 26.69$ and $s_{\hat{\beta}_3} = 19.16$). The critical values of $t = -2.776$ and $t = 2.776$ are found from Table A.3 by using $n - (k + 1) = 8 - (3 + 1) = 4$ degrees of freedom and 0.05 in two tails. With a test statistic of $t = 1.39$ and critical values of $t = -2.776$ and $t = 2.776$, the test statistic does not fall in the critical region and we therefore fail to reject the null hypothesis. The evidence is not sufficient to reject the null hypothesis of $\beta_3 = 0$. The displayed P-value of 0.236 supports the same conclusion. Even though the multiple regression equation based on Table 13.2 has overall significance, the individual slope coefficient of β_3 is not significant. This suggests that a swimming pool does not seem important in determining the selling price of a home.

In the preceding example, we concluded that the slope coefficient for the swimming pool variable (β_3) is not significant, but that does not *prove* that having a swimming pool (or not having one) affects the value of the home. Rather, it suggests that the swimming pool variable x_3 should not be included in the regression equation used to predict the selling price. Many professionals would recommend that x_3 now be removed from the regression equation because its slope coefficient (β_3) does not seem to be significant in the presence of the other variables.

CHOOSING AMONG GOOD REGRESSION EQUATIONS

In Section 13.3 we presented a hypothesis test for the overall significance of a multiple regression equation, and we have presented in this section a method for testing for the significance of individual slope coefficients. Those tests are included among the following properties, which serve as criteria for identifying the best multiple regression equation among other such equations. Ideally, the best multiple regression equation satisfies these properties.

1. The best multiple regression equation should have overall significance, determined by using the hypothesis-testing procedure described in Section 13.3.
2. Instead of including almost every available variable, the best multiple regression equation should include relatively few independent (or predictor) variables.
3. The coefficient of determination R^2 is largest for the given number of independent variables. That is, no other combination of the same number of independent variables will yield a larger value of R^2.
4. The inclusion of another independent variable will not lead to a substantial increase in R^2.
5. Each of the individual slope coefficients is significant or nearly significant when tested with the null hypothesis H_0: $\beta_i = 0$. If a slope coefficient is found to be not significant (through failure to reject H_0: $\beta_i = 0$), consider eliminating that variable from the equation.

EXAMPLE Use the preceding five criteria to compare the simple linear regression equation from Chapter 12 with the multiple regression equation based on Table 13.1. That is, which regression equation is better: the equation relating selling price and living area or the equation relating selling price, living area, and tax bill?

SOLUTION (1) We have already seen that both equations have overall significance. (2) Both equations contain relatively few independent variables. (3) If we are simply comparing the two given regression equations, the third criterion doesn't really apply, but if we are free to use the data of Table 13.1 as we desire, we would find that $R^2 = 0.514$ for the selling-price/living-area equation, but $R^2 = 0.675$ for a selling-price/tax-bill equation. This would suggest that for a single independent variable, the tax bill is a better choice than the living area. (4) The inclusion of the tax-bill variable causes R^2 to increase from 0.514 to 0.858, and that is a substantial increase. This suggests that we should include that additional variable. (5) In considering the multiple regression equation with independent variables for living area and tax bill, the tax-bill slope coefficient β_2 is significant at the $\alpha = 0.05$ level, but the living-area slope coefficient β_1 is not significant at that level. Should we therefore exclude the variable x_1? Excluding x_1 seems consistent with the fifth criterion, but with a P-value of 0.052 it is *very* close to being significant at the 0.05 level. (In testing $\beta_1 = 0$, it would be significant at the 0.10 level, and in testing $\beta_1 > 0$, it would be significant at the 0.05 level.) Also, excluding x_1 would be in conflict with the fourth criterion. Finally, it is probably due to the small sample size that β_1 does not appear to be significant. Very likely, a larger sample size (which we avoided in Chapter 12 for simplification of calculations) would show that β_1 is significant. Furthermore, it seems reasonable (as most real estate sales personnel would suggest) that the selling price of a home is affected by its living area.

In general, the fifth criterion should be examined very carefully and weighed against the other criteria as well as against any special knowledge that might be available. Exclusion of the variable x_1 would result in a much poorer prediction equation. Hence we have stated in the fifth criterion that the slope coefficient β_i should be "significant or nearly significant." In this case, we therefore conclude that the multiple regression equation is better than the simple linear regression equation. Although both equations could be used to predict selling price, the multiple regression equation is likely to result in a much better prediction.

The preceding example shows that it is not always easy to identify the regression equation that is best. Some situations involve many independent variables, so the considerations and choices become very complex. Many statistical software packages can automatically consider several variables in an attempt to find the best combination. In particular, many of these software packages use a method called *stepwise regression,* whereby various independent variables are

PREDICTORS FOR SUCCESS

When a college accepts a new student, it would like to have some positive indication that the student will be successful in his or her studies. College admissions deans consider SAT scores, standard achievement tests, rank in class, difficulty of high school courses completed, high school grades, and extracurricular activities. In one study of the characteristics that make good predictors of success in college, investigators found that class rank and scores on standard achievement tests are better predictors than SAT scores. A multiple regression equation with college grade point average predicted by high school rank and achievement test score was not improved by including another variable for SAT score, suggesting that SAT scores should not be included among the college admissions criteria. But supporters of SAT scores argue that they are useful for comparing students from different geographic locations and high school backgrounds.

tested for inclusion in the regression equation. This might seem the ideal way to get the best combination of variables, but strange results sometimes occur with the stepwise regression method. Because of this, some professionals recommend that all possible combinations of variables be considered, tested, and compared.

When using the preceding five criteria for finding the best regression equation, care and common sense should be applied to prevent costly errors. Consider any practical implications and any special knowledge that might be available. For example, if the Jefferson Valley Bank does begin to include tax bills as an important factor in predicting (appraising) home values, there is a danger that some homeowners might petition for an *increase* in their tax bill so that they could make their homes easier to sell because there's a bank willing to lend more money based on higher predicted values. No statistical analysis would reveal that problem, but it's the type of important problem that creates great difficulty when blindly applying formulas without considering practical consequences.

CONFIDENCE INTERVALS

The general form for a confidence interval for any individual regression coefficient β_i (with all other variables included in the regression equation) is given by the following:

CONFIDENCE INTERVALS

$$\hat{\beta}_i - E < \beta_i < \hat{\beta}_i + E$$

where the margin of error E is given by

$$E = t_{\alpha/2}\, s_{\hat{\beta}_i}$$

and $t_{\alpha/2}$ has $n - (k + 1)$ degrees of freedom.

EXAMPLE Using the Table 13.1 data, find a 95% confidence interval for β_2, the slope coefficient for the tax bill, with living area included in the regression equation. (This can be an alternative to testing for the significance of β_2. If the confidence interval contains 0, then we would fail to reject H_0: $\beta_2 = 0$.)

SOLUTION We know from previous results that $\hat{\beta}_2 = 38.29$. We now proceed to find the margin of error E. The value of E is found by using $t_{\alpha/2} = 2.571$, which is obtained from Table A.3. [Use $\alpha = 0.05$ in two tails and use $df = n - (k + 1) = 8 - (2 + 1) = 5$.] Also, $s_{\hat{\beta}_2} = 11.02$, which is obtained from the Minitab display. We now get

$$E = t_{\alpha/2}\, s_{\hat{\beta}_2}$$
$$= (2.571)(11.02) = 28.33$$

Our 95% confidence interval for $\hat{\beta}_2$ is given by

$$
\hat{\beta}_2 - E < \beta_2 < \hat{\beta}_2 + E
$$
$$
38.29 - 28.33 < \beta_2 < 38.29 + 28.33
$$
$$
9.96 < \beta_2 < 66.62
$$

We can be 95% confident that the limits of 9.96 and 66.62 contain the true slope for the tax bill coefficient *when the living area* x_1 *is held constant.* This relatively wide interval is due primarily to the relatively small size of our sample. Because that interval does not contain zero, we conclude that β_2 is significantly different from 0 (at $\alpha = 0.05$) and that the tax bill is an important variable to consider when predicting the selling price of a home with an equation that also includes living area.

13.4 EXERCISES   BASIC CONCEPTS

In Exercises 1–8, use the sample data of Table 13.1 and the corresponding Minitab display (for living area and tax bill) in Section 13.2.

1. At the 0.05 significance level, test the claim that the living area coefficient (β_1) is equal to zero.
2. At the 0.05 significance level, test the claim that the tax bill coefficient (β_2) is greater than zero.
3. At the 0.05 significance level, test the claim that the tax bill coefficient (β_2) is equal to 30.0.
4. At the 0.05 significance level, test the claim that the intercept constant β_0 is equal to zero.
5. Construct the 90% confidence interval for β_2, the tax bill coefficient.
6. Construct the 95% confidence interval for β_1, the living area coefficient.
7. Construct the 90% confidence interval for β_0, the intercept constant.
8. Construct the 99% confidence interval for β_2, the tax bill coefficient.

In Exercises 9–15, use the data and Minitab display for Table 13.3 given in Section 13.2.

9. At the 0.05 significance level, test the claim that the mileage coefficient is equal to zero.
10. Construct a 95% confidence interval estimate of the slope coefficient that corresponds to the variable representing mileage.
11. Construct a 90% confidence interval for the true intercept constant (which we denote by β_0).
12. Test the claim that the age coefficient is positive. Use a significance level of $\alpha = 0.10$.
13. Construct a 95% confidence interval for the slope coefficient representing age.
14. At the 0.05 significance level, test the claim that the cruise-control slope coefficient is positive.
15. Construct a 95% confidence interval for the cruise-control slope coefficient.

13.4 EXERCISES   BEYOND THE BASICS

16. Compare the results from the hypothesis test in Exercise 9 and the confidence interval in Exercise 10. Establish a direct relationship between those two sets of results.

17. Based on the results from Exercises 9, 12, and 14 and the guidelines listed in this section, it would seem wise to find a regression equation for predicting selling price based on mileage and cruise control. Use Minitab and eliminate the variable representing age of the car to answer the following.

    a. Find the multiple regression equation for selling price expressed in terms of mileage and cruise control.
    b. What is the value of R^2 for the case with mileage and cruise control included, but age excluded? What is the value of R^2 for the case with mileage, cruise control, and age all included?
    c. Repeat Exercises 9 and 14 for the multiple regression equation from part *a*.
    d. Which multiple regression equation seems better: the one with age included or the one with age excluded?

13.5 CONFIDENCE INTERVALS FOR PREDICTED VALUES

In this section we parallel Section 12.5 and extend the concepts from that section (which considered only linear regression) to multiple regression. We construct both confidence intervals for the predicted *mean* value μ_y and "prediction intervals" for predicted *individual* values.

In this chapter we have worked with the sample data of Table 13.1 and derived the multiple regression equation of

$$\hat{y} = 24.17 + 3.014x_1 + 38.29x_2$$

with $R^2 = 0.858$. An *F*- test of the claim that the slope coefficients are zero yielded a *P*-value of 0.008, and that, along with the value of R^2 and our testing for significance of the individual slope coefficients, suggests that our equation fits the data well and is therefore useful for making predictions. We showed that for a home with 1800 sq ft of living area and an annual tax bill of $1500, the predicted selling price is

$$\hat{y} = 24.17 + 3.014\,(18) + 38.29\,(1.5) = 135.857$$

or $135,857. But, as we noted in Chapter 12, such an estimate is really the predicted or estimated mean selling price of many homes, each with 1800 sq ft and a $1500 tax bill. In Chapter 6 we noted that an estimate consisting of a single number, such as $135,857, is referred to as a *point* estimate. Point estimates generally have the serious disadvantage of not conveying any sense of how accurate or inaccurate they might be. In Chapter 6 we introduced interval estimates (confidence intervals) that largely overcome that disadvantage. One of the main objectives in using regression methods is to be able to predict values of the dependent variable y. It would be unwise to spend the time and effort required to obtain a good regression equation and then use it to obtain only a point estimate of y. It would be much better to obtain interval estimates because they reveal so much more about the quality of the estimate. Let's consider the Jefferson Valley Bank's problem of trying to decide whether to approve the mortgage for a home with a living area of 1800 sq ft and a tax bill of $1500. We now know that the predicted selling price of such a home is $135,857 and this seems to differ substantially from the $190,000 selling price the mortgage applicants have negotiated. But knowing that samples vary, we might question the accuracy of that $135,857 predicted value. In Section 12.5, the linear regression version of this section, we provided the manual calculations for finding the confidence interval, but the calculations required for multiple regression are too complex for manual calculations. Instead, we again emphasize the use of computer results. With Minitab, it is quite easy to generate the interval estimates we want.

EXAMPLE Using Minitab for the data of Table 13.1, we enter the living areas (x_1) in column C1, the tax bills (x_2) in column C2, and the selling prices (y) in column C3. We now enter the following Minitab commands:

```
MTB > REGRESSION C3 2 C1 C2;
SUBC> PREDICT 18 1.5.
```

The Minitab display will include the results shown below. Refer to those results and identify (a) a 95% confidence interval for the mean predicted selling price y, and (b) a 95% prediction interval for the predicted selling price of an individual home. (Note that for part a, the estimate is based on homes with living areas of 1800 sq ft and tax bills of $1500, whereas part b is based on an individual home with a living area of 1800 sq ft and a tax bill of $1500.)

```
   Fit   Stdev.Fit        95% C.I.            95% P.I.
135.86       10.23   (109.56, 162.17)   (  70.59, 201.13)
```

SOLUTION a. Based on the Minitab display under "95% C.I.," we conclude that for homes with 1800 sq ft and a $1500 tax bill, we are 95% confident that the *mean* selling price is between $109,560 and $162,170. This is formally expressed as

$$\$109,560 < \mu_y < \$162,170$$

b. Based on the Minitab display under "95% P.I.," we conclude that for an *individual* home with 1800 sq ft and a $1500 tax bill, we are 95% confident that the selling price is between $70,590 and $201,130. This is formally expressed as

$$\$70,590 < y < \$201,130$$

The Jefferson Valley Bank can now use the results from parts a and b in its consideration of the mortgage application. What should the bank decide? The part b results show that for an individual home with a living area of 1800 sq ft and a tax bill of $1500, we are 95% confident that the selling price should be between $70,590 and $201,130. That's a wide range (due largely to the small sample size), but it does include the $190,000 selling price the home buyers have negotiated. On this basis, the application should not be immediately rejected. However, using common sense, we might note that the $190,000 is really pushing the upper limit of a confidence interval that is very wide because of the small sample size. Under these circumstances, the bank would be foolish to approve the mortgage application without further justification based on other factors. For example, if the couple plans to make a down payment of $140,000 and needs a mortgage of only $50,000, and the couple has a stable source of income and an excellent credit history, then the bank could approve the mortgage because their $50,000 loan would be very secure. Should there be a need to foreclose, our prediction interval suggests that the selling price should be well above the bank's investment of $50,000.

In the preceding use of Minitab, note that the same subcommand of PREDICT is used here for multiple regression as was used for the simple linear regression in Chapter 12. However, because the multiple regression equation here has *two* independent or predictor (x) variables, we must provide a value for x_1 and another value for x_2, as we did in the above command of PREDICT 18 1.5.

The interval estimates obtained in the preceding example are much narrower than the corresponding interval estimates from Chapter 12 that were based on one independent variable (living area) instead of two. This is because our simple linear regression equation had a coefficient of determination of $R^2 = 0.514$, and so it accounted for only 51.4% of the variation in the y values. But our multiple regression equation has $R^2 = 0.858$, and so it accounts for 85.8% of the variation in the y values. With less variation left unexplained, we get more accuracy in our predictions. This is a good practical reason to try and develop multiple regression equations with high R^2 values: Our predictions are more accurate with narrower confidence intervals.

13.5 EXERCISES   BASIC CONCEPTS

In Exercises 1–4, refer to the accompanying Minitab display, which results from these commands:

```
MTB > REGRESSION C4 3 C1 C2 C3;
SUBC> PREDICT 30 0 15;
SUBC> PREDICT 25 1 20.
```

The sample data are from Table 13.3 in Section 13.2, where C4 (or y) is car selling price in thousands of dollars, C1 (or x_1) is mileage in thousands of miles, C2 (or x_2) is cruise control (1 = equipped, 0 = not equipped), and C3 (or x_3) is age in months. Exercises 1–4 can be solved by referring to the Minitab display.

```
The regression equation is
C4 = 9.49 - 0.0899 C1 + 0.483 C2 + 0.0240 C3
```

Predictor	Coef	Stdev	t-ratio	p
Constant	9.4927	0.5287	17.95	0.000
C1	-0.089884	0.008060	-11.15	0.000
C2	0.4834	0.1134	4.26	0.005
C3	0.02398	0.02422	0.99	0.361

```
s = 0.1704     R-sq = 95.8%     R-sq(adj) = 93.7%
```

Analysis of Variance

SOURCE	DF	SS	MS	F	p
Regression	3	3.9418	1.3139	45.24	0.000
Error	6	0.1742	0.0290		
Total	9	4.1160			

SOURCE	DF	SEQ SS
C1	1	3.4110
C2	1	0.5023
C3	1	0.0284

Fit	Stdev.Fit	95% C.I.	95% P.I
7.1558	0.1520	(6.7838, 7.5278)	(6.5969, 7.7147)
8.2085	0.0834	(8.0044, 8.4127)	(7.7442, 8.6729)

1. a. What is the predicted selling price of a car with 30,000 miles, no cruise control, and an age of 15 months?
   b. What is the 95% confidence interval for the predicted mean selling price of cars with 30,000 mi, no cruise control, and an age of 15 months?
   c. What is the 95% prediction interval for an individual car with 30,000 mi, no cruise control, and an age of 15 months?
2. a. What is the predicted selling price of a car with 25,000 mi, cruise control, and an age of 20 months?
   b. What is the 95% confidence interval for the predicted mean selling price of cars with 25,000 mi, cruise control, and an age of 20 months?
   c. What is the 95% prediction interval for an individual car with 25,000 mi, cruise control, and an age of 20 months?
3. What is the Minitab command for finding the 95% confidence interval for the mean selling price of a car with 27,000 mi, no cruise control, and an age of 16 months?
4. What is the Minitab command for finding the 95% confidence interval for the mean selling price of a car with 24,000 mi, cruise control, and an age of 14 months?

In Exercises 5–12, use Minitab with the data of Table 13.1 and the values given in the exercises to find (a) the best estimate of selling price, (b) a 95% confidence interval for the mean predicted selling price of homes with the given living areas and tax bills, and (c) a 95% prediction interval for the estimated selling price of an individual home with the given living area and tax bill.

5. Living area: 1900 sq ft; tax bill: $1500
6. Living area: 2700 sq ft; tax bill: $2100
7. Living area: 2400 sq ft; tax bill: $1700
8. Living area: 3000 sq ft; tax bill: $2500
9. Living area: 3000 sq ft; tax bill: $2600
10. Living area: 1750 sq ft; tax bill: $2100
11. Living area: 1450 sq ft; tax bill: $1800
12. Living area: 2175 sq ft; tax bill: $1800

13.5   EXERCISES   BEYOND THE BASICS

We can analyze the **marginal effect** of an independent variable by changing it by one unit while holding the other independent variables constant. In Exercises 13 and 14, use Minitab with the data of Table 13.1.

13. If the living area is held constant at 1800 sq ft while the tax bill is increased from $1500 to $1600, how are the corresponding 95% confidence intervals and prediction intervals affected?
14. If the tax bill is held constant at $1500 while the living area is increased from 1800 sq ft to 1900 sq ft, how are the corresponding 95% confidence intervals and prediction intervals affected?
15. It sometimes happens that a single point or two may not be suitable for inclusion in the regression analysis. Perhaps an error has been made in recording a result or perhaps some special circumstances have led to an unusual result. Such points can often be identified through an analysis of **residuals,** or values of $y - \hat{y}$ (or observed y value minus predicted y value). The accompanying Minitab display corresponds to the same data of Table 13.1, except that the selling price of 145 has been entered incorrectly as 415. The additional Minitab command of BRIEF 3 causes the program to display more results, including those relating to residuals. In particular, note that Minitab has marked the incorrect data point with an R because it has a "standard residual" of 2.19, which is more than two standard deviations away from its predicted value. Identify any residuals that Minitab marks as having a large standard residual by using (a) the data of Table 13.1, (b) the data of Table 13.2 with a selling price of 145 entered incorrectly as 415, and (c) the data of Table 13.1 with the y value of 114 incorrectly entered as 11.

```
MTB > BRIEF 3
MTB > REGRESSION C3 2 C1 C2

  The regression equation is
  C3 = 124 - 0.45 C1 + 40.7 C2
```

. (part of display omitted)

CONTINUE? yes

Obs.	C1	C6	Fit	Stdev.Fit	Residual	St.Resid
1	15.0	415.0	194.9	49.6	220.1	2.19R
2	38.0	228.0	204.9	102.6	23.1	0.51
3	23.0	150.0	171.0	59.5	-21.0	-0.22
4	16.0	130.0	174.1	53.7	-44.1	-0.45
5	16.0	160.0	178.2	51.3	-18.2	-0.18
6	13.0	114.0	191.7	56.5	-77.7	-0.80
7	20.0	142.0	213.0	43.4	-71.0	-0.69
8	24.0	265.0	276.3	103.1	-11.3	-0.25

R denotes an obs. with a large st. resid.

13.6 EXTRAPOLATION, ESTIMABILITY, AND MULTICOLLINEARITY

Multiple regression is a powerful and important tool for many business applications. However, we need to be aware of some potential problems, which are discussed in this section. We begin with extrapolation.

EXTRAPOLATION

Using the Table 13.1 sample data, we developed a multiple regression equation that used x_1 (living area) and x_2 (tax bill) to predict selling prices of homes. The sample data for living area varied from 1300 sq ft to 3800 sq ft, while the annual tax bill varied from $1400 to $4000. In general, as long as we predict selling prices for homes within these ranges, we can be reasonably confident that our estimates will be reliable and our interpretations of 95% confidence intervals for μ_y and 95% prediction intervals for y will be accurate. Such estimates based on values within the range of the sample data are called interpolations. When estimates are based on values beyond the range of the sample data, they are referred to as extrapolations.

DEFINITIONS

Interpolation involves predicting a value of a dependent variable y when the values of the independent (predictor) variables are all within the range of the sample data.

Extrapolation involves predicting a value of the dependent variable y when the values of the independent (predictor) variables go beyond the range of the sample data.

WAGE GENDER GAP

Many articles note that, on average, full-time female workers earn about 70¢ for each $1 earned by full-time male workers. Researchers at the Institute for Social Research at the University of Michigan analyzed the effects of various key factors and found that about one-third of the discrepancy can be explained by differences in education, seniority, work interruptions, and job choices. The other two-thirds remains unexplained by such labor factors.

Extrapolations have the potential for yielding predictions that are way off. For example, we could easily use the same methods described earlier to predict the selling price of a home with 4500 sq ft and an annual tax bill of $7000, but that would be risky and could result in a substantial error. However, predictions based on values that are only slightly outside our range of sample data can often be made with a fair degree of confidence.

Issues of extrapolation are present in many areas of industry and government. For example, given the most recent three years of economic data, economists are often able to provide very accurate forecasts of unemployment and growth in the gross national product *for the next quarter*. But using that data to predict what will happen two years from now is very risky extrapolation because so many unknown and unexpected events could occur. Similar pitfalls can be expected from attempts to predict sales or demand too far into the future.

ESTIMABILITY

Estimability is a sophisticated title for a relatively simple concept. For the mathematics of the method of least squares to work in developing a regression equation, each variable must take on several different values. For example, in our Table 13.1 data, the living areas (in square feet) are 1500, 3800, 2300, and so on. If, by some accident or other twist of fate, all the homes in our data set had the same living area, then we would not be able to estimate the slope coefficient β_1 for the variable x_1. Such a strange occurrence (getting the same value) doesn't happen very often if the data are randomly selected. It could happen if the sample isn't random or if the sample is drawn from some population in which one of the variables always has the same value. For example, if our eight sample homes were all selected from the same housing subdivision, they might all have exactly the same living area, and we would have the estimability problem. Table 13.7 lists such a data set, and the corresponding Minitab display is also provided. Minitab recognizes this estimability problem and automatically eliminates the problem variable (in this case x_1) from the regression equation before proceeding.

```
MTB > REGRESSION C3 2 C1 C2
*        C1 is (essentially) constant
*        C1 has been removed from the equation

The regression equation is
C3 = 55.4 + 71.2 C2

Predictor      Coef     Stdev    t-ratio         p
Constant      55.38     15.55       3.56     0.012
C2            71.25     10.35       6.89     0.000

s = 2.926     R-sq = 88.8%     R-sq(adj) = 86.9%

Analysis of Variance

SOURCE         DF        SS         MS         F       p
Regression      1    406.13     406.13     47.43   0.000
Error           6     51.37       8.56
Total           7    457.50
```

TABLE 13.7
Estimability Problem

y (selling price)	165	150	176	170	160	158	162	157
x_1 (living area)	16	16	16	16	16	16	16	16
x_2 (tax bill)	1.5	1.4	1.7	1.6	1.5	1.4	1.5	1.4

Another estimability problem occurs when the number of coefficients being estimated in the multiple regression equation $(\hat{\beta}_0, \hat{\beta}_1, \hat{\beta}_2, \ldots, \hat{\beta}_k)$ is greater than or equal to the sample size n. The mathematics of least squares requires one degree of freedom (or one sample point) for each coefficient being estimated ($k + 1$ of them when you remember to count $\hat{\beta}_0$), and the required number of degrees of freedom is subtracted from the sample size n to yield the remaining number of degrees of freedom $[n - (k + 1)]$ used in *SSError* to provide an estimate for σ_e.

Table 13.8 lists a data set illustrating this second type of estimability problem. We have these four independent or predictor variables that we want to include in our regression equation: x_1 = living area, x_2 = tax bill, x_3 = acreage, and x_4 = number of rooms. We also have a sample size of only $n = 5$. Because we are trying to estimate $\hat{\beta}_0, \hat{\beta}_1, \hat{\beta}_2, \hat{\beta}_3$, and $\hat{\beta}_4$ simultaneously, we have

$$n - (k + 1) = 5 - (4 + 1) = 0$$

degrees of freedom remaining to be used in estimating σ_e. In effect, we have such an abundance of predictor variables that we get a *perfect* fit to the data. We present the Minitab display of the output for this case. With four independent variables and a sample size of $n = 5$, the regression equation will *always* have a perfect fit to the data points. But we really know nothing about how the independent variables affect the dependent variable. This display warns of the problem with the statement that a variable "is highly correlated with other predictor variables." Also note that the F test statistic and P-value are not computed. They require some positive estimate of σ_e, but we don't have a large enough sample to provide such an estimate.

TABLE 13.8
Estimability Problem

y (selling price)	145	228	150	130	160
x_1 (living area)	15	38	23	16	16
x_2 (tax bill)	1.9	2.4	1.4	1.4	1.5
x_3 (acreage)	2.0	3.6	1.8	0.53	0.50
x_4 (rooms)	5	11	9	7	7

$$y \quad x_1 \quad x_2 \quad x_3 \quad x_4$$
$$\downarrow \quad \downarrow \quad \downarrow \quad \downarrow \quad \downarrow$$

```
MTB > REGRESSION C5 4 C1 C2 C3 C4
  * NOTE *        C1 is highly correlated with other predictor variables
  * NOTE *        C2 is highly correlated with other predictor variables
  * NOTE *        C4 is highly correlated with other predictor variables
```

(continued)

```
The regression equation is

C5 = - 540 - 33.3 C1 + 309 C2 + 29.3 C3 + 108 C4

Predictor          Coef      Stdev     t-ratio      p
Constant       -540.489      0.000         *        *
C1             -33.2927      0.0000        *        *
C2              308.798      0.000         *        *
C3              29.3275      0.0000        *        *
C4              107.902      0.000         *        *

s = *
Analysis of Variance

SOURCE             DF            SS            MS      F     p
Regression          4      5815.200      1453.800      *     *
Error               0             *             *
Total               4      5815.200

SOURCE      DF      SEQ SS
C1           1     4962.808
C2           1      355.819
C3           1      204.259
C4           1      292.314
```

There is no *SSError*.

$n - (k + 1) = 0$, so there's nothing left for *SSError*.

MAKING MUSIC WITH MULTIPLE REGRESSION

Sony International's Digital Audio Disc Corporation manufactures millions of compact disks in Terre Haute, Indiana. One step in the manufacturing process uses a laser to expose a photographic plate so that a musical signal is transferred into a digital signal coded with zeros and ones. This photographic process was statistically analyzed with a goal of identifying the effects of different variables, such as length of exposure and thickness of the photographic emulsion. Methods of multiple regression were used and, among all of the variables considered, four of them were most significant. The photographic process was adjusted for optimal results based on the four critical variables. As a result, the percent of defective discs dropped while the tone quality was maintained. The use of multiple regression methods led to lower production costs and better process control.

This second estimability problem can create an impossible situation if the number of predictor (x) variables is equal to or greater than the sample size. If such a regression were attempted by Minitab, it would yield a response of "*ERROR* Not enough data in the column." This case can be better understood by considering an attempt to fit a regression line ($y = \beta_0 + \beta_1 x_1$) to sample data consisting of only one point. Infinitely many lines pass through the single point, so we would need more data before our regression methods could work correctly. The two types of estimability problems are summarized in the following definition.

DEFINITION

When attempting to construct a regression equation, the inability to estimate some or all of the parameters $\beta_0, \beta_1, \beta_2, \ldots, \beta_k$ is referred to as the *estimability* problem, and it occurs when the sample values for a variable are all the same or when the sample size is too small.

Note that whereas Minitab does provide cautions, notes, and warnings, some other statistical software packages do not. The user could be kept ignorant of the fact that there are major problems, and dangerous or costly prediction errors could result.

MULTICOLLINEARITY

One of the most troublesome, peculiar, and overlooked problems that can occur in multiple regression is **multicollinearity.** This phenomenon has many complex manifestations and causes, but we will consider only the most easily recognized and most common form, in which *two independent or predictor variables are highly correlated with each other.* In the most desirable circumstances, we want all the predictor or independent (x) variables to be uncorrelated and independent of one another. Unfortunately, it often happens in reality that some of the x variables have at least a small correlation among them. Because many of the features of the least-squares method are not overly sensitive to such problems, this small correlation usually presents only minor problems. But variables that are highly correlated can present big problems.

We illustrate this by considering our previous real estate data (see Table 13.5) with the three independent variables of x_1 (living area in column C1), x_2 (tax bill in column C2), and x_3 (acreage in column C3); the dependent variable is again y (selling price in column C4). We use the Minitab command CORRELATION to show the correlations that are present. See the resulting Minitab display.

```
              C1          C2          C3
C2         0.394
C3         0.864       0.392
C4         0.717       0.821       0.696
```

The Minitab display of correlation coefficients shows that the selling price correlates reasonably well with living area (0.717), tax bill (0.821), and acreage (0.696). This suggests that x_1, x_2, and x_3 are all good candidates for inclusion in the multiple regression model. If some other variable had a very low correlation with selling price, we would be inclined to exclude it.

Now note in the Minitab display the high correlation (0.864) between acreage (C3) and living area (C1). This high correlation between two independent variables is a sign of multicollinearity and is a likely source of trouble when we try to obtain a good regression equation for making predictions.

Suppose we consider all seven possible regressions for our Table 13.5 data of selling prices, living areas, tax bills, and lot sizes in acres, as shown in Table 13.9. The first three cases involve simple linear regressions and show that each one of

TABLE 13.9
Possible Regressions for x_1, x_2, x_3

VARIABLES	REGRESSION EQUATION	R^2	P-VALUE
y, x_1	$\hat{y} = 71.0 + 4.64x_1$	0.514	0.045
y, x_2	$\hat{y} = 63.2 + 49.3x_2$	0.675	0.012
y, x_3	$\hat{y} = 121 + 32.1x_3$	0.484	0.055
y, x_1, x_2	$\hat{y} = 24.2 + 3.01x_1 + 38.3x_2$	0.858	0.008
y, x_1, x_3	$\hat{y} = 85.9 + 2.95x_1 + 14.0x_3$	0.537	0.146
y, x_2, x_3	$\hat{y} = 55.8 + 38.9x_2 + 20.4x_3$	0.840	0.010
y, x_1, x_2, x_3	$\hat{y} = 33.5 + 2.07x_1 + 37.7x_2 + 8.1x_3$	0.865	0.032

Aluminum Recycling

Commonwealth Aluminum of Lewisport, Kentucky, recycles scrap aluminum by rolling it into thin sheets, some of which is used for aluminum cans. A critical property of cans is *earing*, a measure of unevenness around the top rim. In a study aimed at reducing earing, 150 variables were identified as possibly affecting it. Rolling temperatures were believed to be highly important, but a statistical analysis showed only a small correlation. However, further investigation revealed that the measurement device had high variability and was difficult to calibrate. A better system of temperature measurement was installed, and a much higher correlation between temperature and earing was found. Commonwealth Aluminum was then able to reduce earing and thereby improve product quality, but the concept of correlation was instrumental in identifying an important problem in measurement accuracy.

TABLE 13.10
Effects of Combining x_1 and x_3

REGRESSION EQUATION VARIABLES	R^2	HYPOTHESIS TEST ($\alpha = 0.05$) OF SLOPE COEFFICIENT = 0
x_1 alone:	$R^2 = 0.514$	$t = 2.52$; P-value = 0.045: β_1 is significant
x_3 alone:	$R^2 = 0.484$	$t = 2.37$; P-value = 0.055: β_3 is close to significant
	Only a slight increase ↓	
x_1 and x_3:	$R^2 = 0.537$	$t_1 = 0.75$; P-value = 0.485: β_1 not significant
		$t_3 = 0.50$; P-value = 0.637: β_3 not significant

the three independent variables is promising as a good predictor. Noteworthy is the variable x_2 (tax bill) with $R^2 = 0.675$. The next three cases are all multiple regressions that are possible with two independent variables. Among them, the combinations of x_1 with x_2 (for which $R^2 = 0.858$) and x_2 with x_3 (for which $R^2 = 0.840$) seem very promising. The last case involves all the independent variables x_1, x_2, and x_3, but it results in $R^2 = 0.865$, which is only a slight increase over $R^2 = 0.858$ for the case involving x_1 and x_2. This slight increase in R^2, along with less significance (see the P-values), indicates that the last model is probably not as good as the model using x_1 and x_2.

Let's now focus on the fifth case, which involves x_1 and x_3, so that we can see some of the effects of multicollinearity. By combining x_1 and x_3, we increase R^2 by only a slight amount (over x_1 alone or x_3 alone), and strange things seem to happen with the significance of the slope coefficients. See Table 13.10.

It seems as though we are saying that x_1 is very important by itself and x_3 seems fairly important by itself, but when we put them in the same equation, the combination of x_1 and x_3 is not important. This can be clarified and better understood if we recall that the coefficients in a multiple regression equation signify the effect of one particular x variable *while holding the other* x *variables constant*. Here the correct conclusion is that the variable x_1 in the presence of x_3 is not significant, even though x_1 might be significant by itself. That is, when holding x_3 constant, the variable x_1 has little effect. Similarly, when holding x_1 constant, the variable x_3 has little effect. With this form of multicollinearity, it is best to eliminate one of the highly correlated variables. We choose to eliminate x_3 (acreage) because it is less significant than x_1.

Other examples of multicollinearity exist where the inclusion of one x variable causes another x variable not only to change significance but also to change sign and dramatically affect the size of the other coefficient (such as a change from -1.82 to $+ 36.84$).

Multiple regression is part science and part art. If we are working with a fairly complicated regression project, we should seriously consider getting help from a professional statistician. In our quality-oriented and data-driven environment, many corporations and institutions now employ such people, and this has proved to be a wise investment.

13.6 EXERCISES   BASIC CONCEPTS

In Exercises 1–4, analyze the given data set and identify any problems with extrapolation, estimability, and multicollinearity. In each case, you plan to predict the total cost y (in dollars) of producing a printed agenda for a corporate board of directors meeting. The variable x_1 represents the time (in minutes) required to type the agenda; x_2 represents the number of copies needed. In Exercises 1 and 2, you want to predict the value of y for $x_1 = 12$ and $x_2 = 50$.

1.

y	54	63	71	72	85	67	27	49
x_1	12	14	16	16	18	14	7	11
x_2	32	24	26	26	28	24	27	21

2.

y	54	63	71	72	85	67	27	49
x_1	12	14	16	16	18	14	7	11
x_2	25	25	25	25	25	25	25	25

3.

y	54	63	71	72
x_1	12	14	16	16
x_2	32	51	49	47
x_3	6	5	7	9
x_4	17	23	21	20

4.

y	54	63	71	72	79
x_1	12	14	16	16	18
x_2	32	51	49	47	43
x_3	6	5	7	9	8
x_4	17	23	21	20	25

5. Using the data of Table 13.1, you plan to predict the selling price of an individual home with a living area of 5000 sq ft and a tax bill of $8300. Identify any problems with extrapolation, estimability, and multicollinearity.

6. Use the data of Table 13.1, but change the x_2 (tax bill) values to be one-tenth of the living area values. (This corresponds to a tax bill of $1 per square foot.) Identify any problems with extrapolation, estimability, and multicollinearity.

7. Using the data of Table 13.3, predict the mean selling price of Corsicas with 50,000 mi, cruise control, and an age of 48 months. Identify any problems with extrapolation, estimability, and multicollinearity.

8. Use the data of Table 13.3, but change x_2 so that all the cars have cruise control. Predict the mean selling price of Corsicas with 25,000 mi, no cruise control, and an age of 48 months. Identify any problems with extrapolation, estimability, and multicollinearity.

13.6 EXERCISES   BEYOND THE BASICS

In Exercises 9–12, construct a set of values for the dependent variable y and the independent variables x_1 and x_2 that satisfy the stated condition.

9. The data set has a problem of multicollinearity but not of estimability.
10. The data set has a problem of estimability but not of multicollinearity.
11. The data set has problems of both estimability and multicollinearity.
12. The data set has no problems with either estimability or multicollinearity.

Vocabulary List

Define and give an example of each term.

multiple regression equation	multicollinearity	extrapolation
dummy variable	interpolation	estimability

Review

The concepts presented in Chapter 12 allow us to analyze a linear relationship between one independent variable and one dependent variable. In this chapter we extended those concepts to include two or more independent variables. Because of the complexity of the calculations, we used a computer-oriented approach.

In Section 13.2 we identified the basic format for a general multiple regression equation. We also noted that the least-squares criterion from Chapter 12 also applies to this chapter as well; given a choice of specific independent variables, the least-squares criterion is used to determine which multiple regression equation best fits the available sample data. We saw that making predictions simply involves substitution into the multiple regression equation.

In Section 13.3 we considered values of R^2 and hypothesis tests as tools that allow us to judge how well a multiple regression equation fits sample data. The P-value from the F test reveals the significance of the equation, while the coefficient of determination R^2 is the proportion of the variation in y values (about $\bar{y}$) that is explained by the multiple regression equation. Section 13.3 also discussed the assumptions underlying the methods of this chapter.

In Section 13.4 we presented methods for testing claims about the values of the individual slope coefficients $\beta_1, \beta_2, \ldots, \beta_k$, as well as methods for developing confidence interval estimates of those slope coefficients. In Section 13.5 we developed procedures for finding confidence interval estimates of μ_y (the mean predicted value) and prediction interval estimates for y (an individual predicted value).

Finally, in Section 13.6 we discussed three different types of problems that can occur with multiple regression analysis: extrapolation, estimability, and multicollinearity. Figure 13.3 summarizes some of the major points of this chapter.

IMPORTANT FORMULAS

$$\hat{y} = \hat{\beta}_0 + \hat{\beta}_1 x_1 + \hat{\beta}_2 x_2 + \cdots + \hat{\beta}_k x_k$$

General multiple regression equation estimated from sample data

$$SSError = \Sigma (y - \hat{y})^2$$

$$F = \frac{SSRegression/k}{SSError/[n - (k + 1)]}$$

Test statistic for H_0: All slope coefficients $(\beta_1, \beta_2, \ldots, \beta_k)$ are zero. n = sample size; k = number of slope coefficients; numerator $df = k$; denominator $df = n - (k + 1)$

$$\hat{\sigma}_e = \sqrt{\frac{SSError}{n - (k + 1)}}$$

Estimate of σ_e (standard deviation of error in the regression equation)

$$R^2 = \frac{SSRegression}{SSy}$$

Coefficient of determination

$$t = \frac{\hat{\beta}_i - b}{s_{\hat{\beta}_i}}$$

Test statistic for H_0: $\beta_i = b$ (or $\beta_i \leq b$ or $\beta_i \geq b$) t has $n - (k + 1)$ degrees of freedom

$$\hat{\beta}_i - E < \beta_i < \hat{\beta}_i + E$$

Confidence interval for β_i: $E = t_{\alpha/2}\, s_{\hat{\beta}_i}$ and $t_{\alpha/2}$ has $n - (k + 1)$ degrees of freedom

FIGURE 13.3
Multiple Regression

597

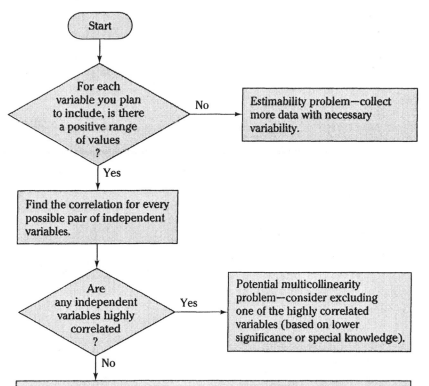

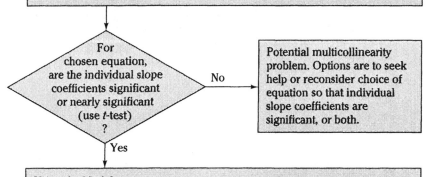

Review Exercises

In Exercises 1–8, use the data in the accompanying table and the given Minitab display. (A more complete data set is included in Release 8 of *The Student Edition of Minitab*.) The variable y (column C5) is home radon measurements in picocuries; x_1 is the age of the home in years; x_2 is the number of days a radon kit was exposed; x_3 is the thickness of insulation (coded as 0 = poor, 1 = average, 2 = excellent); and x_4 indicates whether the radon sample was taken near a sump pump (0 = yes; 1 = no). The Minitab display results from a regression analysis using the dependent variable y and the independent variables x_1, x_2, x_3, and x_4 (corresponding to columns C1, C2, C3, and C4, respectively).

y (radon level)	2.40	2.60	2.90	5.22	2.52	7.38	4.68	27.00	2.70	5.70
x_1 (age)	1	1	1	2	5	4	5	4	1	3
x_2 (exposure)	5	5	7	6	6	8	9	3	5	4
x_3 (insulation)	2	2	1	2	2	1	1	1	2	1
x_4 (sump pump)	0	0	1	1	1	0	1	0	1	1

```
MTB > REGRESSION C5 4 C1 C2 C3 C4;
SUBC> PREDICT 3 4 0 1.

The regression equation is
C5 = 27.6 + 1.69 C1 - 2.46 C2 - 6.04 C3 - 4.20 C4

Predictor      Coef      Stdev     t-ratio        p
Constant     27.599      9.568        2.88    0.034
C1            1.692      1.172        1.44    0.209
C2           -2.461      1.052       -2.34    0.067
C3           -6.043      3.720       -1.62    0.165
C4           -4.200      3.521       -1.19    0.286

s = 5.246    R-sq = 72.6%    R-sq(adj) = 50.6%

Analysis of Variance

SOURCE         DF          SS         MS        F        p
Regression      4      363.89      90.97     3.31    0.111
Error           5      137.62      27.52
Total           9      501.51

SOURCE         DF      SEQ SS
C1              1       65.32
C2              1      177.36
C3              1       82.04
C4              1       39.17

Unusual Observations
Obs.        C1         C5       Fit   Stdev.Fit   Residual   St.Resid
   8      4.00      27.00     20.94        4.40       6.06      2.12R

R denotes an obs. with a large st. resid.
```

(continued)

```
    Fit   Stdev.Fit        95% C.I.          95% P.I.
   18.63       6.61  (   1.63,  35.63)  (  -3.07, 40.33) X
```

X denotes a row with X values away from the center

1. Identify the multiple regression equation that expresses the radon level in terms of age, exposure, insulation, and sump pump.
2. a.   Identify the value of the coefficient of determination.
   b.   What proportion of the variation in the radon level can be explained by the combination of the age, exposure, insulation, and sump pump variables?
3. Using the multiple regression equation, find the predicted radon level of a home that is 3 years old, has the radon kit exposed for 5 days, has average insulation, and does not have a sump pump.
4. a.   An individual home is 3 years old, has the radon kit exposed for 4 days, has poor insulation, and the sample was not taken near a sump pump. What is the predicted value of the radon measurement?
   b.   For homes having the same characteristics described in part a, find a 95% confidence interval for the mean predicted radon measurement.
   c.   For the individual home described in part a, find a 95% prediction interval for the predicted radon measurement.
   d.   Observe that parts a, b, and c all involve a home with poor insulation, but none of the homes in the sample has poor insulation. Is this a problem of extrapolation, estimability, or multicollinearity? Recognizing this problem, describe how it affects the results from parts a, b, and c.
5. a.   At the 0.05 significance level, test the null hypothesis that the four slope coefficients $(\beta_1, \beta_2, \beta_3, \beta_4)$ are all equal to zero.
   b.   What is the P-value for the test in part a?
6. At the 0.05 significance level, test the claim that the age coefficient β_1 is equal to zero.
7. Construct a 95% confidence interval for the slope β_1.
8. Construct a 95% confidence interval for the slope β_2.

In Exercises 9–16, use the same data set given above, but exclude the insulation and sump pump variables. That is, use only the radon level, age, and number of days the radon kit was exposed.

9. Find the multiple regression equation that expresses the radon level in terms of age and exposure time.
10. a.   Identify the value of the coefficient of determination.
    b.   What proportion of the variation in the radon level can be explained by age and exposure?
11. Using the multiple regression equation, find the predicted radon level of a home that is 3 years old and has the radon kit exposed for 5 days.
12. a.   An individual home is 3 years old and has the radon kit exposed for 4 days. What is the predicted value of the radon measurement?
    b.   For homes having the same characteristics described in part a, find a 95% confidence interval for the mean predicted radon measurement.
    c.   For the individual home described in part a, find a 95% prediction interval for the predicted radon measurement.

13. a.   At the 0.05 significance level, test the null hypothesis that the two slope coefficients (β_1, β_2) are both equal to zero.
    b.   What is the P-value for the test in part a?
14. At the 0.05 significance level, test the claim that the age coefficient is equal to zero.
15. The slope β_1 corresponds to the variable x_1, the age of the home in years. Construct a 95% confidence interval for this slope.
16. The slope β_2 corresponds to the variable x_2, the number of days the radon kit was exposed. Construct a 95% confidence interval for that slope.

Computer Project

Various versions of Minitab include different data sets. Choose one of a, b, and c below and do problems 1–5 that follow.

a.   Release 8 of the *Student Edition of Minitab* includes the data set TECHN, which includes employee salary (C1); years employed (C2); years of prior experience (C3); years of college education (C4); company ID number (C5); sex (0 = female and 1 = male) (C6); department (1 = sales, 2 = purchasing, 3 = advertising, 4 = engineering) (C7); and number of supervisors (C8) for employees at the Technitron Company. Ignore the data in columns C5 and C7 because those values are only codes for data at the nominal level of measurement.

b.   Release 8 of the standard version of Minitab includes the data set FURNACE, which includes chimney area (C2), chimney height in feet (C4), house age in years (C7), average energy consumption with vent damper in (C8), and average energy consumption with vent damper out (C9). Ignore the other columns of data because they consist of codes for data at the nominal level of measurement.

c.   Use any other Minitab data set that is suitable for multiple regression analysis.

1. Use Minitab to retrieve the data set TECHN or FURNACE or any other data set that is suitable for multiple regression analysis. (Try the command RETRIEVE 'TECHN' or RETRIEVE 'DATA/TECHN'.) Choose an appropriate dependent variable (such as salary or energy consumption) and at least two independent variables.
2. Use Minitab to find the multiple regression equation and the coefficient of determination R^2.
3. At the 0.05 level of significance, test the claim that all the slope coefficients are zero.
4. Construct a 95% confidence interval for each of the slope coefficients.
5. Working with *all* the variables available, try to find the best multiple regression equation. (You might try using the STEPWISE command. For example, if your dependent variable is in column C4 and your independent variables are in C1, C2, C3, and C5, enter the Minitab command STEPWISE C4 C1 C2 C3 C5 and consult a Minitab manual for help in interpreting the results and for obtaining more details about the STEPWISE command.) Identify the equation you consider to be best and explain your choice. How well does your best regression equation fit the sample data? Explain.

SHOULD SHE MAJOR IN ACCOUNTING?

Y ou are a faculty advisor working with a student who is undecided about being an accounting major. Consider the accompanying table of sample data from a college of business in a midwestern university. In that table, let y = starting salary (in thousands of dollars); let x_1 = sex (1 = male; 0 = female); let x_2 = grade point average (GPA); let x_3 = age at graduation; and let x_4 = major (1 = accounting; 0 = other).

a. Identify each of the 15 different possible regression models.

b. Based on the results from part a, identify the model that you consider to be best. Write a brief explanation justifying your choice.

c. What are the factors that seem to be most important in affecting salary? A student can't normally do anything about his or her sex, but what advice would you give about GPA, age, and being an accounting major?

d. You are working with a female student who has a GPA of 3.3, plans to graduate at age 24, and is an accounting major. For all such students meeting those criteria, what is the 95% confidence interval for the mean predicted starting salary? Identify the interval and write a brief statement that interprets this result.

e. For a female student with a GPA of 3.3 who plans to graduate at age 24 and is an

accounting major, find the 95% prediction interval for her starting salary. Identify the prediction interval and write a brief statement that interprets this result.

f. Using the given sample data, explore and identify any problems of estimability and multicollinearity. Write a brief statement summarizing your results.

g. For a female student with a GPA of 3.3 who plans to graduate shortly at age 49 and is an accounting major, find the 95% prediction interval for her starting salary. Identify this prediction interval, write a brief statement that interprets the result, and write a brief statement that comments on any problems associated with this particular prediction estimate.

SALARY	SEX	GPA	AGE	ACCOUNTING MAJOR
23	1	2.4	25	0
27	0	3.5	23	0
30	0	3.6	24	1
25	1	2.9	24	0
27	1	2.8	23	1
24	0	2.6	24	0
26	1	2.6	23	1
24	0	2.7	22	0
29	1	3.5	24	1
24	0	2.5	23	0

CHAPTER 14

Time Series

New Housing Construction: What's the Forecast?

You've just been hired to coordinate sales activity for Hampton and Windsor Real Estate Development Company. In planning for the future, you know that the level of new housing construction will have a dramatic effect on the resources your firm will require, and accurately forecasting that level would be extremely helpful.

Table 14.1 lists values (in billions of dollars) of new housing units for each quarter of the most recent four-year period (based on data from the U.S.

Department of Commerce and the Bureau of the Census).

Given the data in Table 14.1, you would like to determine if there is any long-term pattern of increasing or decreasing values. Identifying such a pattern would be extremely helpful in forecasting future values. You would also like to know of any short-term patterns. For example, you know that the level of housing construction drops off in the colder months and rises in the warmer months, but you would like to have more specific knowledge of such seasonal changes. Just how much does it drop during the cold months and how much does it rise during the warm months? You also want to forecast the values of housing starts for the next year. Such a forecast, along with a knowledge of long-term and short-term patterns, could be extremely helpful as you plan for your firm's needs.

What patterns are present and how do we use them to make a forecast for the following year? We will answer these questions as we proceed through this chapter.

TABLE 14.1
Value of New Housing Units by Quarter

QUARTER	VALUE (BILLIONS OF DOLLARS)
1st year 1	16.0
2	23.0
3	28.6
4	27.1
2nd year 1	23.1
2	29.3
3	32.6
4	28.9
3rd year 1	23.6
2	29.1
3	32.4
4	29.6
4th year 1	25.5
2	33.7
3	39.0
4	35.0

14.1 OVERVIEW

In the early chapters of this book, we dealt mostly with collections of data consisting of single values, such as the set of home selling prices in Chapter 2. In the more recent chapters we considered different configurations of data, such as the contingency tables in Chapter 10 and the paired data of home selling prices and living areas in Chapter 12. In this chapter we investigate sets of data called *time series,* which consist of values corresponding to different time intervals.

Such collections of data are extremely important in many applications, especially those involving business or economics. For example, investors and securities analysts work hard at trying to predict stock and bond performances. The new owner of a store wants to predict sales activity with seasonal fluctuations and long-term trends taken into account. A prospective home builder may alter the startup date because of business expectations. Time series data are useful in all these applications.

A major objective of this chapter is to examine past time series data and use our observations to *forecast,* or predict, future values. Although many different models can be used to represent a time series, we will examine only the multiplicative model with trend, cyclical, seasonal, and irregular components. We will learn how to take a time series and break it down into its four basic components, and how to obtain *seasonally adjusted* values. We will also learn one of the many different methods of forecasting. Because some components of our time series model are index numbers, and index numbers are commonly used in business and industry, we begin with a discussion of them.

14.2 INDEX NUMBERS

It is often helpful or necessary to compare scores by using some appropriate basis for comparison. We have already seen (in Chapter 2) that *z scores* can be used to compare scores from separate populations with different means and standard deviations, and *percentile* scores can be used to compare scores within the same set of data or between different sets of data. In this section we introduce *index numbers,* which allow us to measure and compare changes over time in prices, costs, inventory, production output, and other quantities used in business applications.

> **DEFINITION**
>
> An *index number* reflects changes in values for different time periods. A value for one particular time period is used as a basis for comparison, and the index number for another time period is obtained by forming a ratio that is usually multiplied by 100, as shown below.

$$\text{Index number for time period } t = \frac{(\text{value for time period } t)}{(\text{value for base time period})} \times 100$$

We began by defining index numbers and price indexes. Now we proceed to consider the Laspeyres price index, the Paasche price index, and Fisher's ideal price index.

PRICE INDEXES

A price index is often referred to as a measure of the cost of living.

> **DEFINITION**
>
> A *price index* (or price relative) is a value representing changes in the price of some set of goods and/or services, as expressed below.
>
> $$\text{Price index} = \frac{P_t}{P_0} \times 100$$
>
> where P_t = price in time period t
> P_0 = price in the base time period

EXAMPLE Suppose we wish to compare over time the prices of 19-inch color television sets. In Table 14.2 we list prices for years in the last decade (based on data from the U.S. Department of Labor, Bureau of Labor Statistics). Using 1982 as the base time period, find the price index for 1990.

SOLUTION Because 1982 is designated as the base year, we have P_0 = \$432. Because we want the price index for 1990, we have P_t = \$307. We now calculate the price index as follows:

$$\text{Price index} = \frac{P_t}{P_0} \times 100 = \frac{\$307}{\$432} \times 100 = 71.1$$

This result can be interpreted as follows: The price of 19-inch color televisions in 1990 is 71.1% of the price in 1982. (Televisions, computers, and calculators are among those rare items whose prices have been *decreasing* over the last several years.)

We suggest that you stop here and verify that the price index for 1985 (with a base year of 1982) is 82.9.

TABLE 14.2
Prices of 19-Inch Color Television Sets

Year	1981	1982	1983	1984	1985	1986	1987	1988	1989	1990
Price of TV (dollars)	441	432	417	389	358	342	327	323	318	307

The preceding example used 1982 as the base year, but sometimes a period of more than one year is used as the base time period. Suppose we want to use 1982–84 as the base period. We can proceed to find the mean of the prices for those years. Thus P_0 is calculated as follows:

$$P_0 = \frac{432 + 417 + 389}{3} = 412.7$$

Using 1982–84 as the base time period, the price index for 1990 becomes

$$\text{Price index} = \frac{P_t}{P_0} \times 100$$

$$= \frac{\$307}{\$412.7} \times 100 = 74.4$$

The time period 1982–84 has been used by the Bureau of Labor Statistics in developing some price indexes. The selection of a base period is not arbitrary; it should be carefully selected as a time period of relative stability with no major disruptive influences, such as wars or stock market crashes. The base period should be changed when there is a dramatic change in consumer spending patterns. Using these guidelines, the Bureau of Labor Statistics has used base periods of 1982–84, 1967, 1957–59, 1947–49, 1935–39, and 1925–29.

THE LASPEYRES PRICE INDEX

The preceding example illustrates the construction of a simple price index for the prices of 19-inch color televisions. With consumers buying hundreds of different items each year, it would be confusing to develop separate price indexes for each type of item. Instead, it is generally better to combine items. The **consumer price index (CPI)** is a well-known and commonly used index designed to reveal changes in prices of a fixed market basket of hundreds of goods and services, including such items as milk, lettuce, rent, cablevision rates, and babysitting costs. To illustrate the method used in developing the CPI, we will use a "market basket" consisting of only milk, sugar, and coffee, instead of the hundreds of items actually included in the CPI. We will use 1982 as the base year. Consider the data given in Tables 14.3, 14.4, and 14.5 (based on data from the U.S. Department of Agriculture, Economic Research Service).

TABLE 14.3
Milk Prices and Per Capita Consumption

Year	1981	1982	1983	1984	1985	1986	1987	1988	1989	1990
Whole-milk price (dollars/gal)	1.72	1.73	1.73	1.79	1.76	1.80	1.82	1.91	2.14	2.19
Per capita consumption (gallons)	15.7	15.5	15.1	14.7	14.3	13.5	12.9	12.2	11.1	10.5

TABLE 14.4
Sugar Prices and Per Capita Consumption

Year	1981	1982	1983	1984	1985	1986	1987	1988	1989	1990
Sugar price (dollars/lb)	0.44	0.45	0.46	0.48	0.49	0.50	0.51	0.54	0.56	0.58
Per capita consumption (pounds)	79.4	75.3	71.0	67.6	63.4	60.8	62.4	62.0	62.2	64.2

TABLE 14.5
Coffee Prices and Per Capita Consumption

Year	1981	1982	1983	1984	1985	1986	1987	1988	1989	1990
Coffee price (dollars/lb)	1.66	1.74	1.73	1.84	1.85	2.27	1.95	2.06	2.04	2.07
Per capita consumption (pounds)	10.3	10.1	10.0	10.2	10.4	10.5	10.1	9.3	10.3	10.2

Any meaningful price index based on the combined data of Tables 14.3 through 14.5 should take the consumption quantities into account. The Laspeyres price index takes consumption quantities into account.

DEFINITION

The *Laspeyres price index*, based on a combination of several items, weights prices according to quantities consumed in the *base* year. It is calculated as follows:

$$\text{Laspeyres price index} = \frac{\Sigma P_t Q_0}{\Sigma P_0 Q_0}(100)$$

where P_t = price of a good or service in year t
P_0 = price of a good or service in the base time period
Q_0 = *quantity* of a good or service consumed in the base time period

The Laspeyres price index is an example of a *weighted aggregate index*. It is weighted in the sense that each price is multiplied by a quantity. It is aggregate in the sense that several items are combined.

EXAMPLE   Using the data of Tables 14.3 through 14.5 for milk, sugar, and coffee, and using 1982 as the base year, find the Laspeyres price index for 1990.

SOLUTION   Because we want the Laspeyres price index for 1990, we have $\Sigma P_t Q_0 = 98.526$ as calculated on the following page.

1990	P_t	Q_0	P_tQ_0
Milk	2.19	15.5	33.945
Sugar	0.58	75.3	43.674
Coffee	2.07	10.1	20.907
		$\Sigma P_tQ_0 =$	98.526

1990 prices
1982 quantities

Because 1982 is the base year, we have $\Sigma P_0Q_0 = 78.274$ as shown below.

1982	P_0	Q_0	P_0Q_0
Milk	1.73	15.5	26.815
Sugar	0.45	75.3	33.885
Coffee	1.74	10.1	17.574
		$\Sigma P_0Q_0 =$	78.274

1982 prices
1982 quantities

Having found both ΣP_tQ_0 and ΣP_0Q_0, we now compute

$$\text{Laspeyres price index} = \frac{\Sigma P_tQ_0}{\Sigma P_0Q_0}\,(100) = \frac{98.526}{78.274}\,(100) = 125.9$$

That is, if the same quantities of milk, sugar, and coffee that were bought in 1982 were again purchased in 1990, it would cost 25.9% more than it did in 1982.

One advantage of the Laspeyres price index is that the *quantities* of goods are held constant from the base year. Changing tastes, demands, and other factors could have dramatic effects on the quantities purchased. For example, as the price of an item goes up, consumers may tend to buy less of it, so that per capita consumption decreases. Yet the Laspeyres price index is based on the same quantity that was purchased in the base year, so the Laspeyres price index is somewhat distorted. However, that same property is also an advantage in the sense that we can use the same base quantities Q_0 year after year; we don't need to conduct a new study of consumption quantities every year. The CPI is an example of a Laspeyres price index. It is periodically adjusted with a new base time period so that the fixed initial quantities don't get too far out of line with current conditions.

THE PAASCHE PRICE INDEX

The Laspeyres price index assumes that the same quantities purchased in the base time period will also be purchased in successive years. The Paasche price index uses the actual *current* quantities for the base time period as well as the current year.

DEFINITION

The *Paasche price index*, based on a combination of several items, weights prices according to quantities consumed in the *current* year. It is calculated as follows:

$$\text{Paasche price index} = \frac{\Sigma P_t Q_t}{\Sigma P_0 Q_t}(100)$$

where P_t = price of a good or service in year t
P_0 = price of a good or service in the base time period
Q_t = quantity of a good or service in the year t

EXAMPLE   Using the data of Tables 14.3 through 14.5 for milk, sugar, and coffee, and using 1982 as the base year, find the Paasche price index for 1990.

SOLUTION   For 1990 we get $\Sigma P_t Q_t = 81.345$, as shown below.

1990	P_t	Q_t	$P_t Q_t$
Milk	2.19	10.5	22.995
Sugar	0.58	64.2	37.236
Coffee	2.07	10.2	21.114
		$\Sigma P_t Q_t =$	81.345

We also find $\Sigma P_0 Q_t = 64.803$ by using the base year (1982) prices and the 1990 quantities as shown in the table below.

	P_0	Q_t	$P_0 Q_t$
Milk	1.73	10.5	18.165
Sugar	0.45	64.2	28.890
Coffee	1.74	10.2	17.748
		$\Sigma P_0 Q_t =$	64.803

Having found $\Sigma P_t Q_t$ and $\Sigma P_0 Q_t$, we now compute the Paasche price index.

$$\text{Paasche price index} = \frac{\Sigma P_t Q_t}{\Sigma P_0 Q_t}(100) = \frac{81.345}{64.803}(100) = 125.5$$

That is, by purchasing the 1990 quantities of milk, sugar, and coffee at the 1990 prices, you spend 25.5% more than you would have spent for the same quantities back in 1982.

When calculating the Paasche price index for each year, you weight the prices by using the quantities for the current year. (This is in contrast to the Laspeyres price index, which weights prices according to the same quantities for the base

THE CONSUMER PRICE INDEX

The *consumer price index (CPI)* was begun around 1917, a time during World War I when prices increased dramatically. According to the U.S. Department of Labor, "the CPI measures the average change in prices over time for a fixed market basket of goods and services." The CPI is calculated from a sample of prices of goods and services that people require for daily living. Most of these prices are obtained through visits to about 21,000 retail establishments and 60,000 housing units. Changes in the CPI affect government policy, wages of millions of employees, and incomes of about 60 million people who benefit from social programs such as Social Security, food stamps, and the School Lunch Program.

time period.) The Paasche price index therefore has the advantage of reflecting the latest quantity levels used by consumers, but it has the disadvantage of requiring that the quantity values Q_t be updated each year. If you're listing Paasche price indexes for a series of several years, all those values must be recalculated.

FISHER'S IDEAL PRICE INDEX

It is fairly common to have a period of several years in which prices rise while consumers decrease the quantities they use. For example, car prices have climbed dramatically in recent years, leading to the term "sticker shock" to describe the surprise of prospective car-buyers when they learn how much costs have increased since their last purchase of a new car. Car sales dropped as drivers kept their old cars longer. The Laspeyres price index would tend to overstate the problem of rising car prices, because it would continue to use the same higher quantities of car purchases from the base time period; the effect on consumers would therefore be exaggerated because they are softening the impact of higher prices by delaying purchases. The Paasche price index would tend to understate the problem because the current lower levels of quantities would be used; the effect on consumers would appear less than it really is. In a period of falling prices and rising quantities of consumption, the Laspeyres price index would tend to understate the effect on consumers, whereas the Paasche price index would tend to overstate it.

Because the Laspeyres price index and the Paasche price index are ratios, we can balance their opposing distortions of understating and exaggerating by finding the geometric mean of those two values. (The *geometric mean* of two scores is the square root of their product. The geometric mean is used to find an average of ratios.) This balance, known as Fisher's ideal price index, is expressed as follows:

Fisher's ideal price index $= \sqrt{(\text{Laspeyres price index})\ (\text{Paasche price index})}$

EXAMPLE In the preceding examples we used 1982 and 1990 prices and quantities for milk, sugar, and coffee to find the Laspeyres price index of 125.9 and the Paasche price index of 125.5. Use those results to find Fisher's ideal price index.

SOLUTION Fisher's ideal price index

$= \sqrt{(\text{Laspeyres price index})\ (\text{Paasche price index})}$

$= \sqrt{(125.9)\ (125.5)}$

$= 125.7$

Although this index seems to be theoretically ideal, it is rarely used in practice because it has the same major disadvantage as the Paasche price index: New quantities must be determined every year, and that would be a major project. In practice, the Laspeyres price index is used much more than either the Paasche price index or Fisher's ideal price index.

INTERPRETING PRICE INDEXES

An earlier example used 1982 and 1990 prices and quantities for milk, sugar, and coffee. Based on those values, the Laspeyres price index was 125.9. If people lived on only milk, sugar, and coffee (not too unrealistic for some college students), their CPI for 1990 would be 125.9, meaning that it would cost 25.9% more than in the base year of 1982. If we again use 1982 as the base year but include the entire collection of hundreds of goods and services that constitute the government's definition of the "market basket," we get these values (based on data from the U.S. Department of Labor, Bureau of Labor Statistics):

YEAR	CPI
1982	100.0
1989	128.5
1990	135.4

If we include all items (not only milk, sugar, and coffee), in 1990 it would cost 35.4% more to buy the market basket of 1982. In 1989 it would cost 28.5% more to buy the 1982 market basket of goods and services. We might say that in 1989 the cost of living increased by 28.5% when compared to 1982. However, we must be careful when comparing 1989 and 1990. It is correct to say that from 1989 to 1990 the CPI increased by $135.4 - 128.5 = 6.9$ *percentage points* (based on 1982), but it would be *wrong* to say that there was a 6.9% increase from 1989 to 1990. The 1990 prices can be expressed as a percentage of 1989 prices as shown below.

$$\frac{1990 \text{ CPI}}{1989 \text{ CPI}} (100\%) = \frac{135.4}{128.5} (100\%) = 105.4\%$$

We can now see that there was a 5.4% increase in prices from 1989 to 1990.

Another way to interpret the CPI is to determine the purchasing power of the dollar, defined as follows:

DEFINITION

Purchasing power of the dollar $= \dfrac{1}{\text{CPI}} (100)$

EXAMPLE   Extend the preceding table of CPI values for 1982, 1989, and 1990 to include a column representing purchasing power of the dollar for those years.

SOLUTION   Purchasing power of dollar in 1982 $= \dfrac{1}{\text{CPI}} (100) = \dfrac{1}{100} (100) = \$1.00$

Purchasing power of dollar in 1989 $= \dfrac{1}{\text{CPI}} (100) = \dfrac{1}{128.5} (100) = \$0.78$

Purchasing power of dollar in 1990 $= \dfrac{1}{\text{CPI}} (100) = \dfrac{1}{135.4} (100) = \$0.74$

(continued)

We include these results below.

YEAR	CPI	PURCHASING POWER OF THE DOLLAR
1982	100.0	$1.00
1989	128.5	$0.78
1990	135.4	$0.74

A 1990 dollar had the purchasing power of only 74 cents when compared to a 1982 dollar.

This section began with the concept of a general index number and proceeded to include different *price indexes.* A price index is a measure of the "cost of living." There are also other indexes that can be used to measure the "standard of living," which is based on changes in the *quantities* of goods and services consumed. See Exercise 29.

Although these various indexes seem to yield very exact numerical results, there are major problems affecting their validity. For the CPI, new car prices are difficult to establish because of discounts, trade-ins, special low-interest rates, and changes in standard equipment. Improved technology leads to better products, but how do you measure the value of computerized fuel injectors that replace carburetors, or the value of a digital fuel display that replaces a needle gauge? A multitude of subjective factors tend to prevent price indexes from being perfectly valid and reliable measures of the cost of living. Although price indexes might appear to be somewhat exact, in reality they are not; nevertheless, we must often proceed with the best information available.

14.2 EXERCISES   BASIC CONCEPTS

In Exercises 1–8, use the data of Table 14.2, use the given base year, and find the price index of televisions for the indicated year.

1. Base year = 1982; reference year = 1983
2. Base year = 1982; reference year = 1986
3. Base year = 1982; reference year = 1988
4. Base year = 1982; reference year = 1981
5. Base year = 1981; reference year = 1982
6. Base year = 1981; reference year = 1985
7. Base year = 1990; reference year = 1982
8. Base year = 1985; reference year = 1990

In Exercises 9–16, use the data of Tables 14.3 through 14.5 for milk, sugar, and coffee, and use the given base year to find the Laspeyres price index for the given reference year.

9. Base year = 1982; reference year = 1983
10. Base year = 1982; reference year = 1985
11. Base year = 1982; reference year = 1987
12. Base year = 1982; reference year = 1981
13. Base year = 1981; reference year = 1982
14. Base year = 1981; reference year = 1985

15. Base year = 1990; reference year = 1982
16. Base year = 1985; reference year = 1990

In Exercises 17–20, use the data of Tables 14.3 through 14.5 for milk, sugar, and coffee, and use the given base year to find the Paasche price index for the given reference year.

17. Base year = 1982; reference year = 1983
18. Base year = 1982; reference year = 1985
19. Base year = 1990; reference year = 1982
20. Base year = 1985; reference year = 1990

In Exercises 21–24, use the data of Table 14.6 (based on data from the U.S. Department of Labor, Bureau of Labor Statistics) with 1982 as the base year. Find the purchasing power of the dollar in the given year.

TABLE 14.6
The Consumer Price Index

Year	1981	1982	1983	1984	1985	1986	1987	1988	1989	1990
CPI	94.2	100.0	103.2	107.7	111.5	113.6	117.7	122.6	128.5	135.4

21. 1983
22. 1985
23. 1981
24. 1986

14.2 EXERCISES BEYOND THE BASICS

In Exercises 25–27, refer to the data of Table 14.6.

25. Find the percentage increase in the CPI from 1984 to 1990.
26. If the purchasing power of a dollar in 1985 is $1.00, what is it in 1987?
27. Table 14.6 was constructed with 1982 as the base period. To *shift the base year*, divide each index by the index for the new base year, then multiply by 100. Reconstruct Table 14.6 so that the base year is 1987.
28. Use Table 14.2 and a base time period of 1981–83 to find the price index of the televisions for 1990.
29. Whereas a price index represents an attempt to measure the cost of living, a quantity index represents an attempt to measure the *standard of living*. The following are quantity indexes.

$$\text{Laspeyres quantity index} = \frac{\Sigma Q_t P_0}{\Sigma Q_0 P_0} (100)$$

$$\text{Paasche quantity index} = \frac{\Sigma Q_t P_t}{\Sigma Q_0 P_t} (100)$$

Fisher's ideal quantity index =
$$\sqrt{(\text{Laspeyres quantity index}) \ (\text{Paasche quantity index})}$$

(continued)

Refer to Tables 14.3 through 14.5 for the milk, sugar, and coffee data. Use 1982 as the base time period and find (a) the Laspeyres quantity index for 1990, (b) the Paasche quantity index for 1990, (c) Fisher's ideal quantity index for 1990, and (d) the total cost index for 1990, which is defined as follows:

$$\textbf{total cost index} = \frac{\Sigma P_t Q_t}{\Sigma P_0 Q_0}\,(100)$$

30. In 1982, unleaded regular gas cost $1.30 per gallon and the per car consumption was 576 gallons. In 1988, unleaded regular gas cost $0.95 per gallon and the per car consumption was 507 gallons (based on data from the U.S. Federal Highway Administration). Include this information with the data of Tables 14.3 through 14.5 to find the Laspeyres price index for 1988. Use 1982 as the base year.

14.3   TIME SERIES COMPONENTS

The preceding section used index numbers to measure and compare *past* changes in such factors as prices or costs, but in many situations it is helpful, profitable, or necessary to predict some *future* activity. Textbook publishers must predict sales to print enough copies for students. Ford must predict sales volumes to make just enough cars to satisfy demand and preclude the need for major price cuts. Financial advisors must predict a variety of economic factors so they can give investors sound advice on stocks, bonds, and other investment opportunities. Local, state, and national governments must predict future economic activity to combat excessive inflation, unemployment, recession, and other conditions that voters dislike. We *forecast* a future event when we attempt to predict its outcome. In this section we begin by examining the concept of a time series, which will help us forecast or predict future events.

> **DEFINITION**
>
> A *time series* consists of a collection of observations of values that correspond to consecutive time intervals.

In Table 14.1 we listed values (in billions of dollars) of new housing units along with the corresponding time intervals. Because we have observed values listed with consecutive time intervals, we have an example of a time series. In Fig. 14.1 we depict these data in a graph. From the graph we can easily see that as we move farther to the right, the points generally tend to be higher, forming a pattern of increasing values. However, there are other patterns that are not quite so obvious. As one example, examine Fig. 14.1 closely for changes in revenues from the third quarter to the fourth quarter of each year. Try to see this pattern: In each year, the fourth quarter values were *less than* those for the third quarter. For each of the four years, there was a fourth-quarter drop in values of new housing units.

FIGURE 14.1
Time Series Graph for Table 14.1 Data

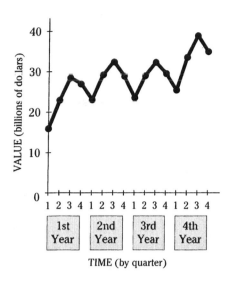

We now know of two different patterns in this time series:

1. The general overall pattern of increasing values
2. The fourth-quarter drop in values

Once we recognize these two patterns, we might wonder whether there are other patterns as well. Instead of trying to identify all patterns through a subjective and intuitive examination of the graph, we will develop a more systematic procedure.

Specifically, we will describe the different patterns in terms of four distinct *types of variation* that occur in time series: trend, cyclical variation, seasonal variation, and irregular variation (or random variation).

DEFINITIONS

The *trend* in a time series consists of a long-term increasing or decreasing pattern. (See Fig. 14.2a.)

The *cyclical variation* in a time series consists of patterns that *repeat* over time periods that exceed one year. (See Fig. 14.2b.)

The *seasonal variation* in a time series consists of patterns that *repeat* over time periods of one year or less. That is, the effects from seasonal influences are completed in a time period of one year, then they repeat on a yearly basis. (See Fig. 14.2c.)

The *irregular variation* (or random variation) in a time series consists of fluctuations that are not predictable, because they result from unusual events (such as war) or chance fluctuations. (See Fig. 14.2d.)

HELP WANTED ADVERTISING INDEX

The Conference Board is a business research group that uses the number of newspaper help-wanted ads as a basis for the Help Wanted Advertising Index. This monthly index is intended to gauge the status of job growth in the labor market. A drop in the Help Wanted Advertising Index suggests that the state of the labor market has declined, whereas a rise in this index suggests an improved labor market. It currently uses 1967 as a base year with an index of 100.

Notation

We denote the four components of a time series as follows:

T denotes trend.
C denotes the cyclical variation.
S denotes the seasonal variation.
I denotes the irregular (or random) variation.

The trend *T*, cyclical *C*, seasonal *S*, and irregular *I* components are illustrated in Fig. 14.2, but the patterns need not be (and usually aren't) as perfect as those shown in this figure.

It is not difficult to think of real cases that illustrate the four different components of a time series. There is a *trend* in the number of television sets owned in this country; that number has increased over the past several years. An Olympic fund-raising committee is likely to experience *cyclical variation* that corresponds to the Olympic events that occur once every two or four years. A manufacturer of women's perfume is likely to experience *seasonal variation* that includes increased sales around Christmas and Mother's Day. A clothing store devastated by an earthquake—and just about everyone else—is likely to experience some degree of *irregular variation* that follows no predictable pattern.

Figure 14.2 illustrates the four different components of time series, but actual time series typically consist of combinations of these components. Table 14.1 and Fig. 14.1 correspond to a time series comprising a combination of components, and the following sections will show how we can identify such components. We will consider time series in which the *Y* values are expressed as a product of the trend *T*, cyclical *C*, seasonal *S*, and irregular *I* components. We will represent the time series with the format of

$$Y = T \times C \times S \times I$$

and will proceed to *decompose* (break down) the product of $T \times C \times S \times I$. The following section focuses on a method for finding the combined trend and cyclical components.

14.3 EXERCISES   BASIC CONCEPTS

In Exercises 1–8, identify the time series pattern as trend, cyclical variation, seasonal variation, or irregular variation.

1. A manufacturer of men's neckties experiences an increase in sales during December of each year.
2. A company that produces integrated circuits for computers finds that the number of units sold has grown steadily over the past decade.
3. When analyzing the number of returned items, a retail store owner finds that the number fluctuates up and down without any predictable pattern.
4. A supplier of campaign promotional products has a surge in revenue that corresponds to the month preceding each presidential election.
5. A manager observes that over the past several years there has been a small but steady decrease in annual production.

FIGURE 14.2
Time Series Components

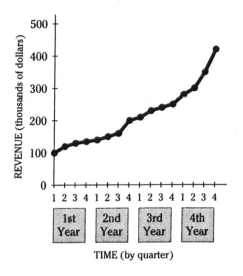

(a) Trend (Long-term Increase)

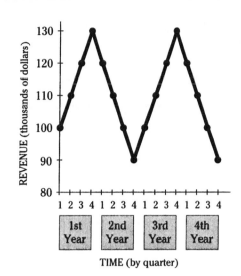

(b) Cyclical Variation

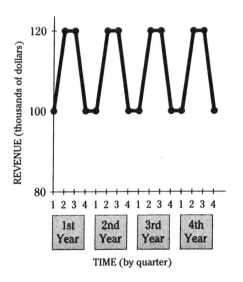

(c) Seasonal Variation

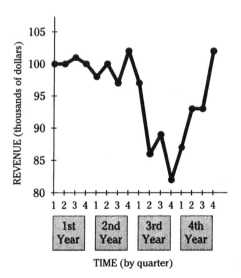

(d) Irregular Variation

6. For a certain bus route, the number of passengers rises and falls in a way that is unpredictable and without any pattern.

7. A pilot experiences increased expenses once every two years as she prepares for the biennial flight review required by the Federal Aviation Administration.

8. A farmer has losses for most months of the year, but larger gains at the end of each growing season.

In Exercises 9–16, refer to the figure and identify the time series pattern as trend, cyclical variation, seasonal variation, or irregular variation.

9.

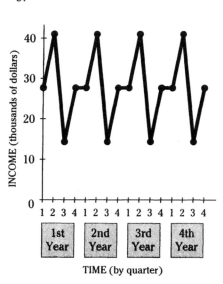

10.

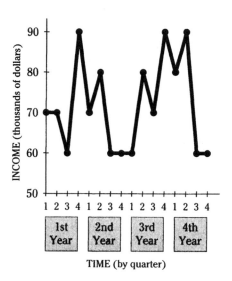

11.

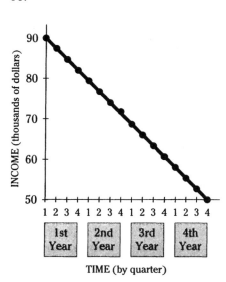

12.

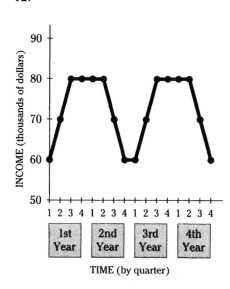

13.

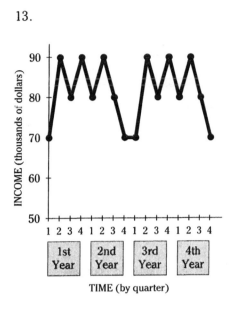

14.

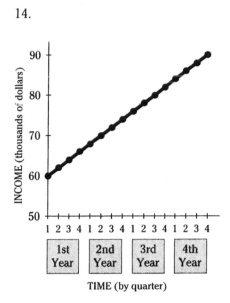

15.

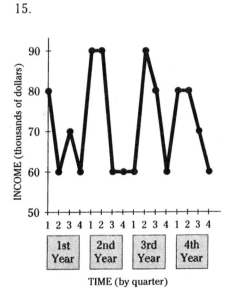

16.

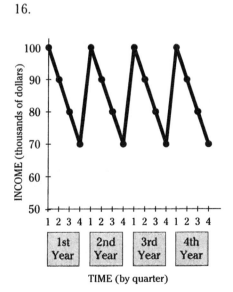

In Exercises 17–24, use the given time series data to construct a graph and identify the time series pattern as trend, cyclical variation, seasonal variation, or irregular variation. In each case, the data are listed in rows by consecutive quarters.

17. 600   570   542   514   489   464   441   419
     398   378   359   341   324   308   293   278

18. 600   570   542   514   489   464   441   419
     419   441   464   489   514   542   570   600

19.	600	620	625	610	650	560	570	540
	615	605	630	570	580	585	575	615
20.	600	570	542	514	600	570	542	514
	600	570	542	514	600	570	542	514
21.	367	386	350	405	367	386	350	405
	367	386	350	405	367	386	350	405
22.	350	367	386	405	425	447	469	492
	517	543	570	600	629	660	693	728
23.	492	469	447	425	405	386	367	350
	350	367	386	405	425	447	469	492
24.	517	386	447	660	543	350	492	693
	728	469	367	570	600	629	405	425

14.3 EXERCISES   BEYOND THE BASICS

In Exercises 25–28, use the given time series data to construct a graph and identify the time series pattern as trend, cyclical variation, seasonal variation, or irregular variation. The 48 cost values correspond to 48 consecutive months (listed by rows), beginning with the first month of the first year.

25.	84	81	121	119	115	71	92	150	141	98	70	108
	133	89	77	105	107	103	91	97	108	90	93	78
	76	79	103	100	108	92	130	75	111	133	147	76
	70	110	84	75	127	100	84	93	129	125	97	87
26.	27.6	27.3	27.1	27.0	26.8	26.6	26.5	26.2	25.9	25.6	25.2	
	24.9	24.6	24.4	24.2	24.0	23.8	23.5	23.2	22.9	22.6	22.3	
	22.0	21.8	21.8	22.0	22.3	22.6	22.9	23.2	23.5	23.8	24.0	
	24.2	24.4	24.6	24.9	25.2	25.6	25.9	26.2	26.5	26.6	26.8	
	27.0	27.1	27.3	27.6								
27.	71	73	77	81	84	89	94	50	103	108	114	120
	126	131	134	139	142	145	149	154	157	162	165	171
	177	183	188	191	194	200	203	208	212	216	221	227
	230	234	238	243	249	253	257	262	265	271	274	278
28.	5.8	5.6	5.9	6.2	6.6	5.9	5.9	6.4	6.6	6.0	5.8	5.7
	5.8	5.6	5.9	6.2	6.6	5.9	5.9	6.4	6.6	6.0	5.8	5.7
	5.8	5.6	5.9	6.2	6.6	5.9	5.9	6.4	6.6	6.0	5.8	5.7
	5.8	5.6	5.9	6.2	6.6	5.9	5.9	6.4	6.6	6.0	5.8	5.7

14.4 DECOMPOSITION: TREND AND CYCLICAL COMPONENTS COMBINED

In Section 14.3 we identified and described the four basic patterns that occur in time series. Forecasting requires that the time series follow some pattern that can be identified and used. In Section 14.3 we saw examples of variation involving only one of the four basic patterns. In reality, a time series typically includes a combination of the four patterns.

We will assume that a time series comprises all four types of patterns. We further assume that the time series values are represented by Y and the time series model has the following format.

$$Y = T \times C \times S \times I$$

Value   Trend   Cyclical   Seasonal   Irregular
variation   variation   variation

This model is called *multiplicative* because the components are multiplied. There are other models, such as the additive model

$$Y = T + C + S + I$$

Other possibilities include models such as $Y = T \times C \times S + I$. A major advantage of the multiplicative model is that it makes it easier to isolate the four different components. (This isolation of the four components assumes that they result from different causes.) Also, the multiplicative model is the one most commonly used in business and economics applications.

In the multiplicative model, the values of T, C, S, and I are expressed as follows:

T: Expressed in the same units as Y (such as dollars)

C: Expressed as an index number, such as 1.05 or 0.90, that multiplies T

S: Expressed as an index number that multiplies T

I: Expressed as an index number that multiplies T

We will develop a method for beginning with a known time series and *decomposing* it (breaking it down) into the four components of trend, cyclical variation, seasonal variation, and irregular variation. We can then use these results to make forecasts. For example, given a time series describing the value of new housing units over the last few years, we can isolate the trend effect, the effect due to cyclical variation, the effect due to seasonal variation, and the effect due to irregular variation. In this section we isolate the combined trend and cyclical components, and in the following sections we isolate the individual trend, cyclical, seasonal, and irregular components.

In Table 14.7 on page 622 and Fig. 14.3 on page 623 we present the same time series data (given at the beginning of the chapter) for a recent four-year period (based on data from the U.S. Department of Commerce and the Bureau of the Census). The listed values of 16.0, 23.0, . . . , 35.0 can be considered values of Y, so that each is the product of the four time series components $T \times C \times S \times I$.

We begin the process by isolating the combined trend and cyclical components, denoted by $T \times C$. The isolation of $T \times C$ is based on this observation:

> If we average the data for a one-year period, the resulting average will tend to exclude the effects due to seasonal and irregular variations.

TABLE 14.7
Value of New Housing Units by Quarter

	QUARTER	VALUE (BILLIONS OF DOLLARS)
1st year	1	16.0
	2	23.0
	3	28.6
	4	27.1
2nd year	1	23.1
	2	29.3
	3	32.6
	4	28.9
3rd year	1	23.6
	2	29.1
	3	32.4
	4	29.6
4th year	1	25.5
	2	33.7
	3	39.0
	4	35.0

(The mean is actually the average referred to above, and *mean* is a better term than *average,* but it is common to use the latter when discussing a time series. Throughout this chapter, "average" will refer to the mean.) As a practical example, housing construction tends to decrease during the colder seasons. If we analyze housing starts by looking at yearly totals or averages (instead of quarterly values), we eliminate the seasonal variation and can focus on long-term trends.

SMOOTHING WITH CENTERED MOVING AVERAGES

Because our data in Table 14.7 are listed by quarters, we can effectively isolate the combined trend and cyclical component of $T \times C$ by combining four quarters, thereby eliminating the seasonal effects and reducing the effects from random variation. That is, we are "smoothing" out the little bumps that occur within each year. To isolate the combined $T \times C$ component, we first calculate moving totals as shown in Table 14.8. Each **moving total** is the sum of the nearest four quarters in the column of $T \times C \times S \times I$ values. In Table 14.8 we show that 112.1 is the sum of 27.1, 23.1, 29.3, and 32.6. These totals are called *moving* totals because we sum the first four quarters, move down to sum the next sequence of four consecutive quarters, and so on. See the table below.

$T \times C \times S \times I$ FOUR-QUARTER MOVING TOTALS

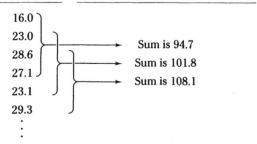

FIGURE 14.3
Time Series Graph for Table 14.7 Data

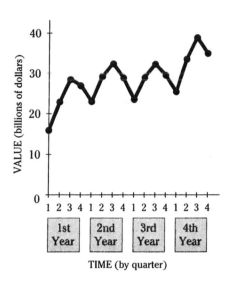

In Table 14.8 on page 624 we can see that the **moving averages** are simply the moving totals divided by the number of time periods in a year. Because this time series has data listed by quarter and there are four quarters in each year, the moving averages are found by dividing the moving totals by 4. For example, the first moving average of 23.675 is found by evaluating 94.7 ÷ 4. Note that the moving totals and moving averages all fall *between* quarters instead of being aligned with particular quarters.

Each **centered moving average** is the mean of two consecutive moving averages (the two nearest moving averages located to the left). For example, Table 14.8 shows that the centered moving average of 24.56 is found by using the values of 23.675 and 25.450. Note that each centered moving average does *center* on a particular quarter, instead of falling between two quarters. This centering will prove very useful in future calculations. *The column of centered moving averages* (farthest to the right in Table 14.8) *represents estimates of the combined trend and cyclical components, which we denote as $T \times C$.* This makes sense when we realize that the values in this rightmost column are essentially averages taken over periods one year in length. Such averages tend to eliminate the effects of seasonal and irregular components so that effects of only the trend and cyclical components remain.

Given time series data listed by quarters, we can therefore decompose the values of Y (or $T \times C \times S \times I$) into an estimate of the combined $T \times C$ component by this procedure:

1. Calculate the moving totals by finding the sum of each sequence of four consecutive quarters.
2. Calculate the moving averages by dividing each moving total by 4.
3. Isolate $T \times C$ by finding the centered moving averages. This is done by calculating the average (mean) of each pair of consecutive moving averages.

TABLE 14.8
Finding Centered Moving Averages

	QUARTER	VALUE OF NEW HOUSING UNITS OR $T \times C \times S \times I$	MOVING TOTALS	MOVING AVERAGES	$T \times C$ CENTERED MOVING AVERAGES
1st year	1	16.0			
	2	23.0			
	3	28.6	94.7	23.675	
					24.56
	4	27.1	101.8	25.450	
					26.24
			108.1	27.025	
2nd year	1	23.1			27.53
			112.1	28.025	
	2	29.3			28.25
			113.9	28.475	
	3	32.6			28.54
			114.4	28.600	
	4	28.9			28.58
			114.2	28.550	
3rd year	1	23.6			28.53
			114.0	28.500	
	2	29.1			28.59
			114.7	28.675	
	3	32.4			28.91
			116.6	29.150	
	4	29.6			29.73
			121.2	30.300	
4th year	1	25.5			31.13
			127.8	31.950	
	2	33.7			32.63
			133.2	33.300	
	3	39.0			
	4	35.0			

Add → 94.7 $\xrightarrow{\div \text{ by } 4}$ 23.675 } Average → 24.56

The above procedure can be easily modified to apply to time series data with time intervals other than quarters (such as months or weeks). With months, for example, we would (1) calculate the moving totals by finding the sum of each sequence of 12 consecutive months, (2) calculate the moving averages by dividing each moving total by 12, and (3) isolate $T \times C$ by finding the centered moving averages [calculate the average (mean) of each given pair of consecutive moving averages].

Recognizing that the trend T is a long-term increasing or decreasing pattern and cyclical variation C is a pattern that repeats over time periods longer than one year, we see that the combined effect of the $T \times C$ component is a long-term effect. That is, the $T \times C$ component effectively eliminates the short-term effects from seasonal and irregular variations. Consider the graphs of Figs. 14.4 (a) and (b). In Fig. 14.4 (a) we show the original time series data for the values of new housing units, while Fig. 14.4 (b) shows the combined trend and cyclical components ($T \times C$) by using centered moving averages. A comparison of the two graphs should reveal that the short-term fluctuations present in the original data have been "smoothed" by the $T \times C$ values. Figure 14.4 (b) therefore gives us

FIGURE 14.4
Smoothing Data with Centered Moving Averages

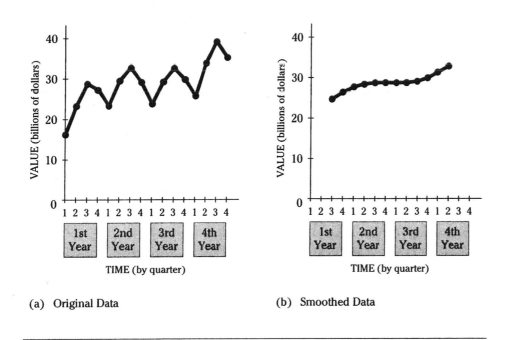

(a) Original Data

(b) Smoothed Data

the long-term picture that reflects the combined effect of the trend and cyclical components.

Using the methods of this section, we can now isolate $T \times C$, the long-term combined effect of the trend and cyclical components. In the following section we will further decompose $T \times C$ so that we can obtain the individual trend T and cyclical C components. We will then have a better understanding of the trend effect and the cyclical variation.

ROUNDING OFF

When calculating values of the various components, the following round-off guidelines may be helpful.

COMPONENT	ROUNDING OFF
Moving totals	Same number of decimal places as original values
Forecast values (Section 14.7)	Same number of decimal places as original values
Moving averages	Two more decimal places than original values
Centered moving averages	One more decimal place than original values
$T \times C$	One more decimal place than original values
T	One more decimal place than original values
$C, S \times I, S, I$	Three decimal places, as in 1.258 or 0.897

14.4 EXERCISES   BASIC CONCEPTS

In Exercises 1–8, use the given time series data to find the moving totals, moving averages, and centered moving averages. Construct a table that follows the same format as Table 14.8.

1. The values of *Y* represent amounts of consumer credit (in billions of dollars) held by commercial banks (based on data from the Board of Governors of the Federal Reserve System).

	QUARTER	Y		QUARTER	Y
1st year	1	149	3rd year	1	219
	2	152		2	226
	3	161		3	235
	4	172		4	245
2nd year	1	178	4th year	1	246
	2	192		2	253
	3	202		3	260
	4	212		4	265

2. The values *Y* represent amounts of consumer credit (in billions of dollars) held by credit unions (based on data from the Board of Governors of the Federal Reserve System).

	QUARTER	Y		QUARTER	Y
1st year	1	47.1	3rd year	1	66.9
	2	48.7		2	69.3
	3	51.1		3	71.4
	4	53.5		4	72.7
2nd year	1	56.4	4th year	1	72.3
	2	60.3		2	74.0
	3	63.3		3	76.9
	4	66.2		4	78.5

3. The values *Y* represent the amounts (in billions of dollars) spent on new road construction (based on data from the U.S. Department of Commerce and the Bureau of the Census).

	QUARTER	Y		QUARTER	Y
1st year	1	1.99	3rd year	1	2.51
	2	4.07		2	5.79
	3	6.61		3	7.88
	4	4.53		4	5.57
2nd year	1	2.14	4th year	1	2.98
	2	4.67		2	6.37
	3	6.95		3	8.54
	4	5.02		4	5.47

4. The values Y represent the indexes of industrial production for mining and utilities (based on data from the Board of Governors of the Federal Reserve System).

	QUARTER	Y		QUARTER	Y
1st year	1	99.4	3rd year	1	110.5
	2	99.8		2	109.2
	3	107.7		3	111.3
	4	108.9		4	111.8
2nd year	1	109.9	4th year	1	104.5
	2	111.4		2	102.1
	3	112.9		3	101.9
	4	111.0		4	102.4

5. The values Y represent the indexes of total industrial production (based on data from the U.S. Department of Commerce, Bureau of Economic Analysis).

	QUARTER	Y		QUARTER	Y
1st year	1	98.3	4th year	1	111.9
	2	103.1		2	107.3
	3	104.2		3	110.9
	4	99.1		4	107.9
2nd year	1	103.1	5th year	1	112.0
	2	109.7		2	114.3
	3	111.3		3	114.6
	4	107.7		4	104.5
3rd year	1	111.7	6th year	1	106.0
	2	113.8		2	105.1
	3	113.5		3	104.4
	4	107.9		4	97.6

6. The values Y represent the numbers of failures by industrial and commercial enterprises (based on data from the U.S. Department of Commerce, Bureau of Economic Analysis).

	QUARTER	Y		QUARTER	Y
1st year	1	1729	4th year	1	3454
	2	1696		2	4429
	3	1592		3	4381
	4	1602		4	4530
2nd year	1	1919	5th year	1	5477
	2	2044		2	6275
	3	1806		3	6579
	4	1795		4	6577
3rd year	1	2331			
	2	3137			
	3	3076			
	4	3198			

7. The values *Y* represent the consumer price indexes for housing (based on data from the U.S. Department of Commerce, Bureau of Economic Analysis).

	QUARTER	Y		QUARTER	Y
1st year	1	196.7	4th year	1	282.6
	2	202.0		2	292.2
	3	207.5		3	303.7
	4	211.5		4	305.2
2nd year	1	217.5	5th year	1	306.7
	2	225.5		2	317.5
	3	234.6		3	319.7
	4	243.6		4	316.3
3rd year	1	254.5			
	2	266.7			
	3	267.7			
	4	276.9			

8. The values *Y* represent the amounts of energy (in kWh) used in the home of one of the authors.

	QUARTER	Y		QUARTER	Y
1st year	1	3819	5th year	1	2305
	2	2869		2	2481
	3	2599		3	1959
	4	2656		4	2269
2nd year	1	3115	6th year	1	3024
	2	3131		2	2683
	3	2452		3	1999
	4	2730		4	2236
3rd year	1	3571	7th year	1	3135
	2	2924		2	2914
	3	2063		3	2598
	4	2231		4	2508
4th year	1	3105			
	2	2619			
	3	2108			
	4	2077			

14.4 EXERCISES   BEYOND THE BASICS

9. The end of this section included three steps for isolating the combined $T \times C$ component of a time series. Those three steps are based on a time series in which the data are listed by quarters. As stated, those three steps do not apply to weekly data. Restate those three steps so they apply to weekly data instead of quarterly data.
10. Use the given time series data to find the moving totals, moving averages, and centered moving averages. Note that the data are listed by month instead of by quarter. The values of *Y* are amounts (in billions of dollars) of new housing units (based on data from the U.S. Department of Commerce and the Bureau of the Census). The data are at the top of the following page.

	MONTH	Y		MONTH	Y
1st year	1	4.93	3rd year	1	7.75
	2	5.00		2	7.33
	3	6.07		3	8.51
	4	6.72		4	9.01
	5	7.61		5	9.74
	6	8.62		6	10.33
	7	9.18		7	10.71
	8	9.68		8	10.89
	9	9.77		9	10.76
	10	9.65		10	10.67
	11	9.38		11	10.15
	12	8.03		12	8.80
2nd year	1	7.31	4th year	1	8.28
	2	7.36		2	7.94
	3	8.43		3	9.25
	4	8.89		4	10.10
	5	9.89		5	11.24
	6	10.50		6	12.35
	7	10.88		7	12.96
	8	10.95		8	13.04
	9	10.76		9	12.98
	10	10.52		10	12.82
	11	9.91		11	12.04
	12	8.42		12	10.18

11. Use the given time series data to find the moving totals, moving averages, and centered moving averages. Note that the data are listed by month instead of by quarter. The values of Y are indexes of industrial production for mining and utilities (based on data from the Board of Governors of the Federal Reserve system).

	MONTH	Y		MONTH	Y
1st year	1	106.8	3rd year	1	114.3
	2	104.9		2	117.3
	3	99.4		3	110.5
	4	98.6		4	106.3
	5	97.1		5	105.1
	6	99.8		6	109.2
	7	102.7		7	107.9
	8	108.0		8	111.2
	9	107.7		9	111.3
	10	105.4		10	106.8
	11	106.2		11	107.6
	12	108.9		12	111.8
2nd year	1	115.2	4th year	1	113.1
	2	112.9		2	110.8
	3	109.9		3	104.5
	4	107.9		4	101.1
	5	107.3		5	98.5
	6	111.4		6	102.1
	7	112.0		7	102.1
	8	114.6		8	103.8
	9	112.9		9	101.9
	10	106.8		10	99.1
	11	109.3		11	101.4
	12	111.0		12	102.4

12. For a particular time series, suppose you find that the values of the centered moving averages are all the same, even though the original values are not all equal. What can you conclude about the effects of trend, cyclical variation, seasonal variation, and irregular variation?

13. In this section we used centered moving averages to isolate the combined $T \times C$ component, and this enabled us to "smooth" the time series data by eliminating the short-term effects of seasonal and irregular variation. **Exponential smoothing,** another technique for reducing short-term variation, uses weighted averages of observed time series values and previous exponentially smoothed values. The exponentially smoothed value for time period x is denoted by E_x and is found by

$$E_x = \alpha Y_x + (1 - \alpha) E_{x-1}$$

where α is a smoothing constant $(0 \le \alpha \le 1)$, Y_x is the time series value for time period x, and E_{x-1} is the exponentially smoothed value for the time period preceding x. The choice of α is subjective and is based on the amount of smoothing desired. Begin the process by letting E_1 be the first value in the time series. Let $\alpha = 0.04$ and find the exponentially smoothed values for the time series data of Table 14.1. Begin with $E_1 = 16.0$ and proceed to find E_2, E_3, ..., E_{16}. Plot the exponentially smoothed values on Fig. 14.4(a).

14. Repeat Exercise 13 using a smoothing constant of $\alpha = 0.9$. Compare the resulting graph to the one obtained in Exercise 13. Which value of α led to more smoothing?

 SEPARATING THE TREND AND CYCLICAL COMPONENTS

SEPARATING THE TREND COMPONENT T

Given a time series represented by $Y = T \times C \times S \times I$, we saw that we could use moving averages to estimate the combined $T \times C$ component. In this section we take the combined $T \times C$ component and separate it into the individual components of T and C so that we can see the effect of trend and the separate effect of cyclical variation. We begin by isolating the trend component T from the combined $T \times C$ component by using simple linear regression, as discussed in Chapter 12. We determine the regression line that best fits the paired data consisting of the $T \times C$ values and the values of time. In Table 14.9 we reproduce the original data in the time series described in Table 14.1 and repeated in Table 14.7. We also include a column of the values of $T \times C$ found in Section 14.4. We enter a column of x values, corresponding to the values of $T \times C$, that represent the quarters coded to be consecutive integers. Letting the values of $T \times C$ correspond to y and using the indicated x values, we can use Formulas 12.2 and 12.3 to find the slope $\hat{\beta}_1$ and y-intercept $\hat{\beta}_0$ (see Table 14.10) of the straight line that best fits the paired x–y data. This is the same straight line that best fits the points shown in Fig. 14.4(b). (In some cases, the best-fitting curve might not be a straight line; it could be a parabola or an exponential curve, for example. In this chapter our use of regression will be limited to straight lines.)

TABLE 14.9
Centered Moving Averages Matched with
Consecutive Integers

	QUARTER	VALUE OF NEW HOUSING UNITS (BILLIONS)	x	$T \times C$
1st year	1	16.0		
	2	23.0		
	3	28.6	1	24.56
	4	27.1	2	26.24
2nd year	1	23.1	3	27.53
	2	29.3	4	28.25
	3	32.6	5	28.54
	4	28.9	6	28.58
3rd year	1	23.6	7	28.53
	2	29.1	8	28.59
	3	32.4	9	28.91
	4	29.6	10	29.73
4th year	1	25.5	11	31.13
	2	33.7	12	⌊32.63⌋
	3	39.0		
	4	35.0		

Original data
from Table 14.1

Found in
Section 14.4

Quarters coded
to be consecutive
integers

TABLE 14.10
Calculations for Slope and Intercept

x	y (or $T \times C$)	$x - \bar{x}$	$y - \bar{y}$	$(x - \bar{x})(y - \bar{y})$	$(x - \bar{x})^2$
1	24.56	−5.5	−4.04	22.22	30.25
2	26.24	−4.5	−2.36	10.62	20.25
3	27.53	−3.5	−1.07	3.75	12.25
4	28.25	−2.5	−0.35	0.88	6.25
5	28.54	−1.5	−0.06	0.09	2.25
6	28.58	−0.5	−0.02	0.01	0.25
7	28.53	0.5	−0.07	−0.04	0.25
8	28.59	1.5	−0.01	−0.02	2.25
9	28.91	2.5	0.31	0.78	6.25
10	29.73	3.5	1.13	3.96	12.25
11	31.13	4.5	2.53	11.39	20.25
12	32.63	5.5	4.03	22.17	30.25
Total 78	343.22			75.81	143.00

$$\hat{\beta}_1 = \frac{SSxy}{SSx} = \frac{\Sigma(x - \bar{x})(y - \bar{y})}{\Sigma(x - \bar{x})^2} = \frac{75.81}{143.00} = 0.530$$

$$\hat{\beta}_0 = \bar{y} - \hat{\beta}_1 \bar{x} = \frac{343.22}{12} - (0.530)\left(\frac{78}{12}\right) = 25.157$$

The preceding calculations result in the trend equation $\hat{y} = 25.157 + 0.530x$. In general, the **trend equation** is the equation of the regression line found by using values of $T \times C$ paired with values of time coded as consecutive integers.

If we now use the trend equation to find the predicted value $\hat{y}$ for each value of x from 1 through 12, we will obtain estimates of the trend component T. This makes sense when we recognize that the trend equation represents only long-term trend; cyclical variations are represented by the deviations of the $T \times C$ values away from the trend line. We can therefore find the values of T by evaluating

$$T = 25.157 + 0.530x$$

for $x = 1, 2, 3, \ldots, 12$. The resulting values of T are listed below.

x	1	2	3	4	5	6	7	8	9	10	11	12
T	25.69	26.22	26.75	27.28	27.81	28.34	28.87	29.40	29.93	30.46	30.99	31.52

Having found T, we now summarize the steps that allowed us to isolate the trend component:

1. List the values of the $T \times C$ component found by using the methods of Section 14.4.
2. Let x represent the values of time, where x is coded so that its values are consecutive integers $(1, 2, 3, \ldots)$
3. Let the values of $T \times C$ correspond to y and let the values of x be as described in step 2. Use Formulas 12.2 and 12.3 with the paired $x-y$ values to find the trend equation.
4. Substitute each value of x into the trend equation to find the values of the trend component T.

SEPARATING THE CYCLICAL COMPONENT C

Recall that the cyclical component involves a pattern that repeats over time periods longer than a year. After finding the trend component T, we can easily estimate the cyclical component C by noting that

$$C = \frac{T \times C}{T}$$

That is, we obtain values of C by dividing the values of $T \times C$ by the values of T. For example, the first value of C was found from Table 14.11 as follows:

$$C = \frac{T \times C}{T} = \frac{24.56}{25.69} = 0.956$$

The second value of C was found as follows:

$$C = \frac{T \times C}{T} = \frac{26.24}{26.22} = 1.001$$

TABLE 14.11
Separating the Trend and Cyclical Components

	QUARTER	$T \times C \times S \times I$	$T \times C$	T	C
1st year	1	16.0			
	2	23.0			
	3	28.6	24.56	25.69	0.956
	4	27.1	26.24	26.22	1.001
2nd year	1	23.1	27.53	26.75	1.029
	2	29.3	28.25	27.28	1.036
	3	32.6	28.54	27.81	1.026
	4	28.9	28.58	28.34	1.008
3rd year	1	23.6	28.53	28.87	0.988
	2	29.1	28.59	29.40	0.972
	3	32.4	28.91	29.93	0.966
	4	29.6	29.73	30.46	0.976
4th year	1	25.5	31.13	30.99	1.005
	2	33.7	32.63	31.52	1.035
	3	39.0			
	4	35.0			

Recall that the values of C are expressed as index numbers that multiply the corresponding values of T. (The values of T are expressed in the same units as the original values of the data in the time series.)

In Table 14.11 we list the original values of housing starts along with the values of $T \times C$ (found in Section 14.4), the values of T (found above), and the values of C (found by dividing $T \times C$ by T).

Like the values of the seasonal and irregular variation components to be found later, the values of C are index numbers that multiply T. The value of 0.956 shows that for the third quarter of the first year, the cyclical variation has the effect of reducing the value of T to 95.6% of its original value. Similar interpretations can be given to the other index numbers S and I.

USING COMPUTER DISPLAYS

Some software packages will take time series data and provide the components T, C, S, and I in the multiplicative model $Y = T \times C \times S \times I$. Minitab does not do this directly, but Minitab commands can be used to obtain the required results. Shown in the accompanying display are the Minitab commands and results for the data of Table 14.1. The LAG command is used to shift values. The command LAG 1 C1 C2 says, "Shift the values in column C1 down one position and put the results in column C2." (To see the effect of the command LAG 1 C1 C2, see the Minitab display that follows and notice how the column labeled C2 is actually a copy of column C1 with all values shifted down one position. After the shift, the last value of 35.0 is deleted and the first entry is replaced by an asterisk.) Note that the Minitab display includes the centered moving averages (or $T \times C$) in column C7 and the values of the trend component T are listed in the column labeled "Fit" at the bottom.

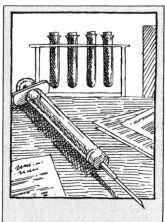

```
MTB > SET C1
DATA> 16.0 23.0 28.6 27.1 23.1 29.3 32.6 28.9    ⎤ Time series data of
DATA> 23.6 29.1 32.4 29.6 25.5 33.7 39.0 35.0    ⎦ Table 14.1 entered here.
DATA> ENDOFDATA
MTB > LAG 1 C1 C2
MTB > LAG 2 C1 C3
MTB > LAG 3 C1 C4
MTB > LET C5=(C1+C2+C3+C4)/4   ← C5 values are moving averages.
MTB > LAG 1 C5 C6
MTB > LET C7=(C5+C6)/2   ← C7 values are centered
MTB > SET C8              ⎤         moving averages or T × C.
DATA> 1:16               ⎥ Creates column C9
DATA> ENDOFDATA          ⎥ as displayed below.
MTB > LAG 4 C8 C9        ⎦
MTB > PRINT C1-C9
```

$$T \times C$$
$$\downarrow$$

ROW	C1	C2	C3	C4	C5	C6	C7	C8	C9
1	16.0	*	*	*	*	*	*	1	*
2	23.0	16.0	*	*	*	*	*	2	*
3	28.6	23.0	16.0	*	*	*	*	3	*
4	27.1	28.6	23.0	16.0	23.675	*	*	4	*
5	23.1	27.1	28.6	23.0	25.450	23.675	24.5625	5	1
6	29.3	23.1	27.1	28.6	27.025	25.450	26.2375	6	2
7	32.6	29.3	23.1	27.1	28.025	27.025	27.5250	7	3
8	28.9	32.6	29.3	23.1	28.475	28.025	28.2500	8	4
9	23.6	28.9	32.6	29.3	28.600	28.475	28.5375	9	5
10	29.1	23.6	28.9	32.6	28.550	28.600	28.5750	10	6
11	32.4	29.1	23.6	28.9	28.500	28.550	28.5250	11	7
12	29.6	32.4	29.1	23.6	28.675	28.500	28.5875	12	8
13	25.5	29.6	32.4	29.1	29.150	28.675	28.9125	13	9
14	33.7	25.5	29.6	32.4	30.300	29.150	29.7250	14	10
15	39.0	33.7	25.5	29.6	31.950	30.300	31.1250	15	11
16	35.0	39.0	33.7	25.5	33.300	31.950	32.6250	16	12

```
MTB > REGRESSION C7 1 C9;   ← Command for regression equation
SUBC> PREDICT C8.   ← Subcommand for predicted values using the regression equation

The regression equation is
C7 = 25.2 + 0.530 C9   ← Trend equation
```

[Part of Minitab display deleted here]

Fit	Stdev.Fit	95% C.I.	95% P.I.
25.686	0.454	(24.674, 26.698)	(23.565, 27.806)
26.215	0.397	(25.332, 27.099)	(24.153, 28.278)
26.745	0.344	(25.979, 27.511)	(24.730, 28.760)
27.275	0.298	(26.611, 27.939)	(25.296, 29.253)
27.804	0.263	(27.218, 28.391)	(25.851, 29.758)
28.334	0.244	(27.791, 28.878)	(26.393, 30.275)
28.864	0.244	(28.320, 29.407)	(26.923, 30.805)

(continued)

29.393	0.263	(28.807, 29.980)	(27.440, 31.347)
29.923	0.298	(29.259, 30.587)	(27.945, 31.901)
30.453	0.344	(29.687, 31.219)	(28.438, 32.468)
30.983	0.397	(30.099, 31.866)	(28.920, 33.045)
31.512	0.454	(30.500, 32.524)	(29.392, 33.633)
32.042	0.515	(30.895, 33.189)	(29.854, 34.230)
32.572	0.577	(31.285, 33.858)	(30.307, 34.836)
33.101	0.641	(31.672, 34.531)	(30.752, 35.450)
33.631	0.707	(32.056, 35.206)	(31.191, 36.071)

↑
Values of trend component T

So far, we have presented methods for decomposing a time series of the type $Y = T \times C \times S \times I$ into the trend (T) and cyclical (C) components. In the next section we will present methods for separating the seasonal (S) and irregular (I) components.

14.5 EXERCISES BASIC CONCEPTS

In Exercises 1–4, the combined trend and cyclical components ($T \times C$) are listed along with time periods coded to be integers in consecutive order. In each case find (a) the trend equation, (b) the values of the trend component T, and (c) the values of the cyclical component C.

1. x	$T \times C$	2. x	$T \times C$	3. x	$T \times C$	4. x	$T \times C$
1	52.0	1	10.0	1	709	1	393
2	54.0	2	22.0	2	715	2	390
3	56.0	3	34.0	3	718	3	388
4	58.0	4	46.0	4	726	4	384
5	60.0	5	58.0	5	728	5	383
6	62.0	6	70.0	6	733	6	380
7	64.0	7	82.0	7	739	7	377
8	66.0	8	94.0	8	745	8	375
9	68.0	9	106.0	9	752	9	371
10	70.0	10	118.0	10	755	10	368
11	72.0	11	130.0	11	761	11	369
12	74.0	12	142.0	12	766	12	362
				13	769	13	359
				14	777	14	361
				15	782	15	356
				16	787	16	350

In Exercises 5–12, the given values are quarterly amounts Y that correspond to the time series described in Exercises 1–8 from Section 14.4. In each case find (a) the trend equation, (b) the values of the trend component T, and (c) the values of the cyclical component C.

5. 149 152 161 172 178 192 202 212 219 226 235 245
   246 253 260 265

6. | 47.1 | 48.7 | 51.1 | 53.5 | 56.4 | 60.3 | 63.3 | 66.2 | 66.9 | 69.3 |
   | 71.4 | 72.7 | 72.3 | 74.0 | 76.9 | 78.5 | | | | |

7. | 1.99 | 4.07 | 6.61 | 4.53 | 2.14 | 4.67 | 6.95 | 5.02 | 2.51 | 5.79 |
   | 7.88 | 5.57 | 2.98 | 6.37 | 8.54 | 5.47 | | | | |

8. | 99.4 | 99.8 | 107.7 | 108.9 | 109.9 | 111.4 | 112.9 | 111.0 | 110.5 |
   | 109.2 | 111.3 | 111.8 | 104.5 | 102.1 | 101.9 | 102.4 | | |

9. | 98.3 | 103.1 | 104.2 | 99.1 | 103.1 | 109.7 | 111.3 | 107.7 | 111.7 |
   | 113.8 | 113.5 | 107.9 | 111.9 | 107.3 | 110.9 | 107.9 | 112.0 | |
   | 114.3 | 114.6 | 104.5 | 106.0 | 105.1 | 104.4 | 97.6 | | |

10. | 1729 | 1696 | 1592 | 1602 | 1919 | 2044 | 1806 | 1795 | 2331 | 3137 |
    | 3076 | 3198 | 3454 | 4429 | 4381 | 4530 | 5477 | 6275 | 6579 | 6577 |

11. | 196.7 | 202.0 | 207.5 | 211.5 | 217.5 | 225.5 | 234.6 | 243.6 |
    | 254.5 | 266.7 | 267.7 | 276.9 | 282.6 | 292.2 | 303.7 | 305.2 |
    | 306.7 | 317.5 | 319.7 | 316.3 | | | | |

12. | 3819 | 2869 | 2599 | 2656 | 3115 | 3131 | 2452 | 2730 | 3571 | 2924 |
    | 2063 | 2231 | 3105 | 2619 | 2108 | 2077 | 2305 | 2481 | 1959 | 2269 |
    | 3024 | 2683 | 1999 | 2236 | 3135 | 2914 | 2598 | 2508 | | |

14.5 EXERCISES   BEYOND THE BASICS

13. The example of this section is based on a time series with quarterly data. How are the procedures for separating the trend and cyclical components affected if a time series consists of monthly data?

14. The given values are the *monthly* amounts for housing starts in the time series described in Exercise 10 of the preceding section. Find (a) the trend equation, (b) values of the trend component T, and (c) values of the cyclical component C.

4.93	5.00	6.07	6.72	7.61	8.62	9.18	9.68	9.77	9.65	9.38
8.03	7.31	7.36	8.43	8.89	9.89	10.50	10.88	10.95	10.76	10.52
9.91	8.42	7.75	7.33	8.51	9.01	9.74	10.33	10.71	10.89	10.76
10.67	10.15	8.80	8.28	7.94	9.25	10.10	11.24	12.35	12.96	13.04
12.98	12.82	12.04	10.18							

15. The given values are the *monthly* indexes of industrial production described in Exercise 11 of the preceding section. Find (a) the trend equation, (b) values of the trend component T, and (c) values of the cyclical component C.

106.8	104.9	99.4	98.6	97.1	99.8	102.7	108.0	107.7	105.4
106.2	108.9	115.2	112.9	109.9	107.9	107.3	111.4	112.0	114.6
112.9	106.8	109.3	111.0	114.3	117.3	110.5	106.3	105.1	109.2
107.9	111.2	111.3	106.8	107.6	111.8	113.1	110.8	104.5	101.1
98.5	102.1	102.1	103.8	101.9	99.1	101.4	102.4		

16. For a particular time series, you find that the slope in the trend equation is zero. What can you conclude about the effects of trend, cyclical variation, seasonal variation, and irregular variation?

Given a time series represented by $Y = T \times C \times S \times I$, we saw that we could isolate the combined $T \times C$ component, then we could isolate the trend component T and the cyclical component C. Having discussed methods for separating T and C, we now proceed to consider the separation of the seasonal and irregular components. The ability to decompose $Y = T \times C \times S \times I$ into the four individual components will allow us to see the effect of each, and we can then consider some important applications. For example, knowing the effect of the seasonal component S will allow us to "deseasonalize" time series data so we can better compare values from different time periods. If Ford wants to compare sales from the first quarter of this year to those from the second quarter, the sales amounts must be deseasonalized because the first-quarter sales tend to be lower due to colder weather. The seasonal component is also an important ingredient used in forecasting future values. If Ford wants to forecast sales for next year to establish production levels, the seasonal component must be identified. The following section will use the seasonal component in developing forecasts of future values. This section deals with the determination of the seasonal component and the irregular component.

SEPARATION OF THE COMBINED $S \times I$ COMPONENT

It is very easy to estimate the combined $S \times I$ component by noting that

$$S \times I = \frac{T \times C \times S \times I}{T \times C}$$

In Section 14.4 we saw how to use moving averages to estimate the combined $T \times C$ component, so the denominator in the above expression can be found. As an example, Table 14.12 includes the original values of housing starts along with the estimated values of $T \times C$ found in Section 14.4. We also included the $S \times I$ column, where each value is found by dividing the corresponding $T \times C \times S \times I$ value by the $T \times C$ value. We will now proceed to separate the seasonal component S.

SEPARATION OF THE SEASONAL COMPONENT S

We separate the seasonal component S by finding a *seasonal index* for each quarter. We must assume that for each of the four quarters, the effect of S is the same every year. That is, the effect of S in the first quarter is the same each year; the effect of S in the second quarter is the same each year, and so on. A consequence of this assumption is that variations in the values of $S \times I$ for the same quarter in different years is attributed to the irregular component I.

TABLE 14.12
Separating the Combined $S \times I$ Component

	QUARTER	VALUE OF NEW HOUSING STARTS $(T \times C \times S \times I)$	$T \times C$	$S \times I$
1st year	1	16.0		
	2	23.0		
	3	28.6 ÷	24.56 =	1.164
	4	27.1	26.24	1.033
2nd year	1	23.1	27.53	0.839
	2	29.3	28.25	1.037
	3	32.6	28.54	1.142
	4	28.9	28.58	1.011
3rd year	1	23.6	28.53	0.827
	2	29.1	28.59	1.018
	3	32.4	28.91	1.121
	4	29.6	29.73	0.996
4th year	1	25.5	31.13	0.819
	2	33.7	32.63	1.033
	3	39.0		
	4	35.0		

Divide

Since we assume that S has the same effect in the first quarter of each year, let's examine all the first-quarter values of $S \times I$ for the data of Table 14.12. Those values are 0.839, 0.827, and 0.819. Remember, we are assuming that the variations in those numbers are attributable to the irregular component I. If we calculate their mean, we tend to eliminate the effect of the irregular variations, which tend to average out. That is,

$$\frac{0.839 + 0.827 + 0.819}{3} = \frac{2.485}{3} = 0.8283$$

is an estimate of S for the first quarter, and this estimate tends to exclude the effect of I. Applying this same procedure to the other quarters, we get averages of 1.0293, 1.1423, and 1.0133 for the second, third, and fourth quarters, respectively.

Since S is a seasonal variation with the long-term effects of trend and cyclical variation eliminated, the mean of the four S values should be 1 and the sum of the four S values should therefore be 4. Because the sum of the four quarterly averages is

$$0.8283 + 1.0293 + 1.1423 + 1.0133 = 4.0132$$

we must adjust those four values so that the sum becomes 4. We can multiply each quarterly average by an adjustment factor calculated as follows:

$$\text{Adjustment} = \frac{4}{0.8283 + 1.0293 + 1.1423 + 1.0133} = 0.9967$$

Note that $0.9967 \times 4.0132 = 4$, so that the multiplication of each quarterly average by the adjustment of 0.9967 will result in a total of 4 that corresponds to the desired average of 1. We need to scale down each of the four quarterly averages so their total is 4 instead of 4.0132, and the adjustment of 0.9967 does the job.

> ### DEFINITION
>
> The *seasonal index* for each quarter is the mean of the values for that quarter, multiplied by an adjustment factor. (The adjustment factor causes the sum of the four seasonal indexes to be 4.)

When we multiply each quarterly average by the adjustment of 0.9967, the result is called the seasonal index. Shown below are the four seasonal indexes for the data under consideration.

	(QUARTERLY AVERAGE)	×	(ADJUSTMENT)	=	SEASONAL INDEX
First quarter	0.8283	×	0.9967	=	0.826
Second quarter	1.0293	×	0.9967	=	1.026
Third quarter	1.1423	×	0.9967	=	1.139
Fourth quarter	1.0133	×	0.9967	=	1.010

We now summarize the steps used in determining the values of the seasonal indexes (based on quarterly data).

1. Beginning with the original time series data, find the centered moving averages as described in Section 14.4. The original data include the values of $T \times C \times S \times I$, and the centered moving averages are estimates of $T \times C$.
2. Divide the values of $T \times C \times S \times I$ by the estimated values of $T \times C$ to get the estimated values of $S \times I$. That is,

$$S \times I = \frac{T \times C \times S \times I}{T \times C}$$

3. For each of the four quarters, find the mean of the $S \times I$ values. This eliminates the effect of the irregular variation.
4. Adjust each of the above four means by multiplying by the following adjustment factor.

$$\text{Adjustment} = \frac{4}{(\text{sum of the four quarterly averages})}$$

The results of this process are adjusted quarterly averages called quarterly seasonal indexes that estimate the seasonal variation S. These steps can be easily modified for time series data that are monthly, weekly, or by some other time period that is not quarterly.

In the next section we will show how the original values in a time series can be divided by the seasonal indexes to yield values that are "deseasonalized" or "seasonally adjusted." We will first end this section with a very simple procedure for identifying the irregular component I.

UNUSUAL ECONOMIC INDICATORS

Forecasting and predicting are important goals of statistics. Investors seek indicators that can be used to forecast stock market behavior. Some of them are quite colorful. The hemline index is based on heights of women's skirts; rising hemlines supposedly precede a rise in the Dow Jones Industrial Average. According to the Super Bowl omen, a Super Bowl victory by a team with NFL origins is followed by a year in which the New York Stock Exchange index rises; otherwise, it falls. This indicator has been correct in 21 of the past 23 years. Other indicators: aspirin sales, limousines on Wall Street, and elevator traffic at the New York Stock Exchange.

TABLE 14.13
Separating the Irregular Component *I*

	QUARTER	VALUE OF NEW HOUSING STARTS $(T \times C \times S \times I)$	$S \times I$		*S* (SEASONAL INDEX)		*I*
1st year	1	16.0					
	2	23.0					
	3	28.6	1.164	÷	1.139	=	1.022
	4	27.1	1.033		1.010		1.023
2nd year	1	23.1	0.839		0.826		1.016
	2	29.3	1.037		1.026		1.011
	3	32.6	1.142		1.139		1.003
	4	28.9	1.011		1.010		1.001
3rd year	1	23.6	0.827		0.826		1.001
	2	29.1	1.018		1.026		0.992
	3	32.4	1.121		1.139		0.984
	4	29.6	0.996		1.010		0.986
4th year	1	25.5	0.819		0.826		0.992
	2	33.7	1.033		1.026		1.007
	3	39.0					
	4	35.0					

Divide

SEPARATING THE IRREGULAR COMPONENT *I*

The final (hooray!) step in the decomposition is very easy (hooray again). If we have estimated values of $S \times I$ and estimated values of *S*, we can isolate the values of *I* through the simple process of division by noting that

$$I = \frac{S \times I}{S}$$

In Table 14.13 we include the original data along with the combined $S \times I$ component and the seasonal indexes found earlier in this section. The column farthest to the right consists of values of *I*. For example, the *I* value of 1.022 is found by evaluating 1.164 ÷ 1.139.

We have now completed the process of decomposing time series data into the four components of trend (*T*), cyclical variation (*C*), seasonal variation (*S*), and irregular variation (*I*). In the next section we examine applications made possible by such decomposition.

14.6   EXERCISES   BASIC CONCEPTS

In Exercises 1–4, use the given quarterly values of the combined $S \times I$ component to find (a) the value of the adjustment factor, and (b) the values of the four seasonal indexes.

1.

	VALUES OF $S \times I$		
1ST QUARTER	**2ND QUARTER**	**3RD QUARTER**	**4TH QUARTER**
0.903	1.145	1.050	0.857
0.921	1.100	1.152	0.888
0.905	1.161	1.167	0.820

2.

	VALUES OF $S \times I$		
1ST QUARTER	**2ND QUARTER**	**3RD QUARTER**	**4TH QUARTER**
1.356	0.936	1.191	1.233
1.248	0.917	1.091	1.207
1.325	0.942	1.143	1.209

3.

	VALUES OF $S \times I$		
1ST QUARTER	**2ND QUARTER**	**3RD QUARTER**	**4TH QUARTER**
0.796	0.946	0.982	1.143
0.802	0.939	1.035	1.161
0.788	0.949	1.106	1.164
0.797	0.972	0.972	1.128
0.804	0.961	0.993	1.147

4.

	VALUES OF $S \times I$		
1ST QUARTER	**2ND QUARTER**	**3RD QUARTER**	**4TH QUARTER**
0.685	1.044	1.135	0.847
0.703	1.038	1.147	0.833
0.715	1.102	1.098	0.852
0.698	1.096	1.116	0.839
0.721	1.115	1.169	0.846

In Exercises 5–8, use the given time series data to find (a) the values of the combined $S \times I$ components, (b) the seasonal index for each of the four quarters, and (c) the values of the irregular component I.

5.

	QUARTER	PRODUCTION $(T \times C \times S \times I)$	$T \times C$
1st year	1	132.0	
	2	130.0	
	3	126.0	126.500
	4	123.0	123.625
2nd year	1	122.0	120.375
	2	117.0	117.000
	3	113.0	113.250
	4	109.0	109.250
3rd year	1	106.0	105.125
	2	101.0	100.500
	3	96.0	95.500
	4	89.0	90.375
4th year	1	86.0	85.250
	2	80.0	80.875
	3	76.0	
	4	74.0	

6.

	QUARTER	SALES $(T \times C \times S \times I)$	$T \times C$
1st year	1	19.6	
	2	20.2	
	3	21.2	21.2875
	4	22.2	22.3875
2nd year	1	23.5	23.6375
	2	25.1	24.9375
	3	26.3	26.1375
	4	27.5	27.1375
3rd year	1	27.8	28.0250
	2	28.8	28.7875
	3	29.7	29.4125
	4	30.2	29.9500
4th year	1	30.1	30.4875
	2	30.8	31.0875
	3	32.0	
	4	32.7	

7.

	QUARTER	INCOME $(T \times C \times S \times I)$	$T \times C$
1st year	1	235.2	
	2	230.4	
	3	221.7	223.7250
	4	216.6	219.3750
2nd year	1	217.2	215.4750
	2	213.6	211.6125
	3	207.3	207.1500
	4	200.1	201.7125
3rd year	1	198.0	195.3375
	2	189.3	188.1375
	3	180.6	179.4750
	4	169.2	170.0625
4th year	1	159.6	161.0250
	2	152.4	153.0750
	3	145.2	
	4	141.0	

8.

	QUARTER	INVENTORY $(T \times C \times S \times I)$	$T \times C$
1st year	1	109.4	
	2	170.8	
	3	127.4	117.050
	4	59.6	115.650
2nd year	1	111.4	112.550
	2	157.6	109.925
	3	115.8	107.375
	4	50.2	103.675
3rd year	1	100.4	98.550
	2	139.0	94.825
	3	93.4	92.675
	4	42.8	90.600
4th year	1	90.6	88.250
	2	132.2	86.375
	3	81.4	
	4	39.8	

In Exercises 9–16, the given values are quarterly amounts Y that correspond to the time series described in Exercises 1–8 from Section 14.4. In each case, find (a) the values of the combined $S \times I$ component, (b) the values of the seasonal indexes, and (c) the values of the irregular component I.

9. 149   152   161   172   178   192   202   212   219   226   235   245
   246   253   260   265

10. 47.1   48.7   51.1   53.5   56.4   60.3   63.3   66.2   66.9   69.3
    71.4   72.7   72.3   74.0   76.9   78.5

11. 1.99   4.07   6.61   4.53   2.14   4.67   6.95   5.02   2.51   5.79
    7.88   5.57   2.98   6.37   8.54   5.47

12. 99.4   99.8   107.7   108.9   109.9   111.4   112.9   111.0   110.5
    109.2   111.3   111.8   104.5   102.1   101.9   102.4

13. 98.3   103.1   104.2   99.1   103.1   109.7   111.3   107.7   111.7
    113.8   113.5   107.9   111.9   107.3   110.9   107.9   112.0   114.3
    114.6   104.5   106.0   105.1   104.4   97.6

14. 1729   1696   1592   1602   1919   2044   1806   1795   2331   3137
    3076   3198   3454   4429   4381   4530   5477   6275   6579   6577

15. 196.7   202.0   207.5   211.5   217.5   225.5   234.6   243.6
    254.5   266.7   267.7   276.9   282.6   292.2   303.7   305.2
    306.7   317.5   319.7   316.3

16. 3819   2869   2599   2656   3115   3131   2452   2730   3571   2924
    2063   2231   3105   2619   2108   2077   2305   2481   1959   2269
    3024   2683   1999   2236   3135   2914   2598   2508

14.6 EXERCISES   BEYOND THE BASICS

17. This section lists four steps that lead to values of seasonal indexes. Modify those four steps so they apply to *monthly* data.

18. The values below are *monthly* amounts for housing starts in the time series in Exercise 10 of Section 14.4. Find the values of the (a) $S \times I$ component, (b) seasonal indexes, and (c) irregular component.

4.93   5.00   6.07   6.72   7.61   8.62   9.18   9.68   9.77   9.65   9.38
8.03   7.31   7.36   8.43   8.89   9.89   10.50   10.88   10.95   10.76   10.52
9.91   8.42   7.75   7.33   8.51   9.01   9.74   10.33   10.71   10.89   10.76
10.67   10.15   8.80   8.28   7.94   9.25   10.10   11.24   12.35   12.96   13.04
12.98   12.82   12.04   10.18

19. The given values are the *monthly* indexes of industrial production described in Exercise 11 of Section 14.4. Find (a) the values of the $S \times I$ component, (b) the values of the seasonal indexes, and (c) the values of the irregular component.

106.8   104.9   99.4   98.6   97.1   99.8   102.7   108.0   107.7   105.4
106.2   108.9   115.2   112.9   109.9   107.9   107.3   111.4   112.0   114.6
112.9   106.8   109.3   111.0   114.3   117.3   110.5   106.3   105.1   109.2
107.9   111.2   111.3   106.8   107.6   111.8   113.1   110.8   104.5   101.1
 98.5   102.1   102.1   103.8   101.9   99.1   101.4   102.4

20. For a particular time series of quarterly data, the values of $S \times I$ are all equal to I. Does this imply that there are no effects due to seasonal and irregular variations? Explain.

14.7 SEASONAL ADJUSTMENTS AND FORECASTING

The preceding sections allowed us to decompose a time series into its trend, cyclical, seasonal, and irregular components. In this section we use results of such a decomposition to consider the two important applications of seasonal adjustments and forecasting.

SEASONAL ADJUSTMENTS

When presenting time series data, it is very common to provide values that have been **seasonally adjusted** (or deseasonalized) by dividing the original time series values by the seasonal indexes S. In such data the effect of seasonal variations is removed, thereby allowing more direct and equitable comparisons of results from different time periods. When analyzing the values of housing starts, for example, it wouldn't make much sense to compare a first-quarter value to a second-quarter value, because housing starts are historically lower in the colder first quarter than in the warmer second quarter. However, we can compare those values if the seasonal effect has been removed.

TABLE 14.14
Calculating Seasonally Adjusted Values

	QUARTER	VALUE OF NEW HOUSING STARTS $(T \times C \times S \times I)$		S		SEASONALLY ADJUSTED VALUES
1st year	1	16.0				
	2	23.0				
	3	28.6	÷	1.139	=	25.1
	4	27.1		1.010		26.8
2nd year	1	23.1		0.826		28.0
	2	29.3		1.026		28.6
	3	32.6		1.139		28.6
	4	28.9		1.010		28.6
3rd year	1	23.6		0.826		28.6
	2	29.1		1.026		28.4
	3	32.4		1.139		28.4
	4	29.6		1.010		29.3
4th year	1	25.5		0.826		30.9
	2	33.7		1.026		32.8
	3	39.0				
	4	35.0				

Divide

Section 14.6 presented a method for obtaining seasonal indexes. To obtain seasonally adjusted time series data, simply divide the original data by the corresponding seasonal index. That is,

$$\text{seasonally adjusted value} = \frac{\text{original value}}{\text{seasonal index}}$$

In Table 14.14 we list the original values of housing starts along with the seasonal indexes found in Section 14.6. The column farthest to the right consists of seasonally adjusted values.

In Table 14.14, examine the first and second quarters of the third year. The actual values of housing starts rose from $23.6 billion to $29.1 billion. However, when seasonal influences are taken into account, we see that the second quarter reflects a relatively *lower* level. That is, the actual increase from $23.6 billion to $29.1 billion was not as large as it should have been for the second quarter. The direct comparison of $23.6 billion to $29.1 billion is hindered by seasonal variation, but we can directly compare the seasonally adjusted values of $28.6 billion and $28.4 billion.

FORECASTING

We can forecast values by assuming that past patterns and conditions will remain constant into the future. A **forecast** value in a time series is a predicted value for a time period beyond those for which values are known. Forecasting future values in a time series is a major reason for estimating the trend, cyclical, seasonal, and irregular components. However, not all those components will be used in developing a forecast. We ignore the irregular component I because its effect cannot be predicted. Also, inclusion of the cyclical component C is beyond the scope of this book because including it would require enough data to find and project an identifiable cyclical pattern. We therefore base our forecasts on the trend and seasonal components. Specifically, a forecast value $\hat{Y}$ is found for a particular time period by using

$$\hat{Y} = T \times S$$

where T is the value of the trend component for the time period and S is the corresponding seasonal index. Figure 14.5 describes a procedure in which the decomposition of a time series (as presented in Section 14.4 through 14.6) into the trend and seasonal components can be used for forecasting.

Using the method of Section 14.4, we first isolate the combined $T \times C$ component. Then we use the methods of Section 14.5 to isolate the trend component T and to identify the trend equation $\hat{y} = \hat{\beta}_0 + \hat{\beta}_1 x$. That same trend equation can now be used to find the predicted values of T for the time periods desired. Recall that these time periods are x values coded as consecutive integers. Next, we find the seasonal index for each desired period by using the methods of Section 14.6. Finally, for each time period for which a forecast is desired, we multiply the predicted value of T by the corresponding seasonal index S. The forecast values are the products of the T and S components. The following example illustrates this forecasting technique.

FORECASTING LOTTERY NUMBERS

You can spend a small fortune buying books, computer software, or magazine subscriptions that are supposed to help you select lottery numbers. These "aids" are apparently blind to the fact that lottery numbers are randomly selected and the outcomes are independent of previous results. The aids typically recommend some numbers as "hot" because they have been coming up often. Others are recommended as "due" because they haven't been coming up often. Other approaches involve numerology, astrology, dreams, and numbers that have "appeared or talked to" a seeress, as one book claims. It's all worthless in predicting winning lottery numbers. In time series terms, there is no trend, cyclical, or seasonal component. The changes in the winning numbers result from irregular variance of chance fluctuations.

EXAMPLE Forecast the quarterly values for the fifth year of the time series described by the first four years in Table 14.15.

SOLUTION In Section 14.5 we used this same time series to find the trend equation: $T = 25.157 + 0.530x$. In that equation, x represents quarters coded to be consecutive integers. We find the predicted values of the trend component T by substituting 15, 16, 17, and 18 for x.

TABLE 14.15
Forecasting Fifth Year Values

	QUARTER	VALUE OF NEW HOUSING UNITS $(T \times C \times S \times I)$	x	S
1st year	1	16.0		
	2	23.0		
	3	28.6	1	1.139
	4	27.1	2	1.010
2nd year	1	23.1	3	0.826
	2	29.3	4	1.026
	3	32.6	5	1.139
	4	28.9	6	1.010
3rd year	1	23.6	7	0.826
	2	29.1	8	1.026
	3	32.4	9	1.139
	4	29.6	10	1.010
4th year	1	25.5	11	0.826
	2	33.7	12	1.026
	3	39.0	13	1.139
	4	35.0	14	1.010
5th year	1	?	15	0.826
	2	?	16	1.026
	3	?	17	1.139
	4	?	18	1.010

In the table below, we show the calculations leading to the forecast values of 27.3, 34.5, 38.9, and 35.0. That is, for the fifth year we forecast the values of new housing units (in billions of dollars) to be 27.3 for the first quarter, 34.5 for the second quarter, 38.9 for the third quarter, and 35.0 for the fourth quarter.

	QUARTER	x	$T = 25.157 + 0.530x$	S	$T \times S$
5th year	1	15	33.107	0.826	27.3
	2	16	33.637	1.026	34.5
	3	17	34.167	1.139	38.9
	4	18	34.697	1.010	35.0

Substitute for x Multiply

The above forecast was based on the time series model, but other models are available for different situations. A **causal model** has a variable that is dependent on (or caused by) other variables. For example, a dairy farmer may be able to

FIGURE 14.5
Forecasting

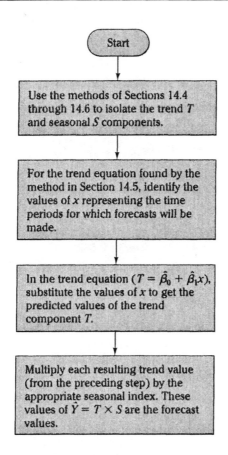

forecast weekly milk production accurately by simply knowing the number of cows that are available. A **naive model** is one that is extremely simple and does not require sophisticated statistical techniques. As one example, the Internal Revenue Service allows taxpayers to forecast their tax bill for the next year by simply using the amount paid in the current year.

    Business indicators can be extremely helpful in forecasting. Such indicators allow us to measure and predict general business and economic conditions. **Leading indicators** tend to lead or precede a change in business conditions. For example, the values of new orders are considered to be leading indicators of business conditions. A drop in new orders tends to precede a drop in the level of business activity. **Coinciding indicators** tend to coincide (what else?) with changes in business conditions. The gross national product and the income earned by retail stores tend to reflect the current state of business activity. **Lagging indicators** tend to follow (lag behind) changes in the state of the economy. A lowered level of business activity tends to be followed by lower expenditures on plant and capital equipment.

Forecasting is tricky business. In this chapter we used time series with relatively few observations. Time series covering longer spans of time with many more observations will tend to produce much better results. Also, we should realize that a forecast becomes less reliable when it is made for a time period farther into the future. The reliability of the forecast is dependent on the assumption that past patterns and conditions will remain constant in the future. Fires, earthquakes, wars, recessions, new technology, and pure chance are only a few of the factors that can cause a forecast to be in error by embarrassing amounts.

14.7 EXERCISES   BASIC CONCEPTS

In Exercises 1–4, use the given time series values and seasonal indexes to find the corresponding seasonally adjusted values.

1. For the second quarter of a year, a company's revenues total $856,750. The seasonal index for the second quarter is 1.183.
2. For the month of June, a company had orders for 672 microwave ovens. The seasonal index for June is 0.893.
3. For one year, the quarterly net earnings for a company are $82,600, $105,200, $96,700, and $93,800. The corresponding seasonal indexes are 0.873, 1.112, 1.022, and 0.992.
4. For one year, the quarterly energy consumption levels (in kWh) for an office building are 34,600, 27,800, 32,700, and 25,100. The corresponding seasonal indexes are 1.151, 0.918, 1.127, and 0.804.

In Exercises 5–8, use the given trend equation and seasonal indexes to forecast values for the indicated time periods.

5. The coded time period of $x = 15$ corresponds to the seasonal index of 1.050, and the trend equation is $T = 12.6 + 2.57x$. Forecast the value of the time series corresponding to the time period represented by $x = 15$.
6. The coded time period of $x = 16$ corresponds to the seasonal index of 0.906, and the trend equation is $T = 93.6 + 45.8x$. Forecast the value of the time series corresponding to the time period represented by $x = 16$.
7. The coded time periods of $x = 15, 16, 17,$ and 18 correspond to the seasonal indexes of 1.050, 0.885, 0.955, and 1.110, respectively. The trend equation is $T = -34.7 + 6.22x$. Forecast the values of the time series corresponding to the time periods represented by the given values of x.
8. The coded time periods of $x = 15, 16, 17,$ and 18 correspond to the seasonal indexes of 1.095, 1.132, 0.948, and 0.825, respectively. The trend equation is $T = -20.3 + 85.6x$. Forecast the values of the time series corresponding to the time periods represented by the given values of x.

In Exercises 9–16, the given values are quarterly amounts that correspond to the time series described in Exercises 1–8 from Section 14.4. (a) Find the seasonally adjusted values. (b) Forecast the values for the four quarters of the next year.

9. 149 152 161 172 178 192 202 212 219 226 235 245
    246 253 260 265

10. 47.1   48.7   51.1   53.5   56.4   60.3   63.3   66.2   66.9   69.3
     71.4   72.7   72.3   74.0   76.9   78.5

11. 1.99   4.07   6.61   4.53   2.14   4.67   6.95   5.02   2.51   5.79
     7.88   5.57   2.98   6.37   8.54   5.47

12. 99.4   99.8   107.7   108.9   109.9   111.4   112.9   111.0   110.5
     109.2   111.3   111.8   104.5   102.1   101.9   102.4

13. 98.3   103.1   104.2   99.1   103.1   109.7   111.3   107.7   111.7
     113.8   113.5   107.9   111.9   107.3   110.9   107.9   112.0   114.3
     114.6   104.5   106.0   105.1   104.4   97.6

14. 1729   1696   1592   1602   1919   2044   1806   1795   2331   3137
     3076   3198   3454   4429   4381   4530   5477   6275   6579   6577

15. 196.7   202.0   207.5   211.5   217.5   225.5   234.6   243.6
     254.5   266.7   267.7   276.9   282.6   292.2   303.7   305.2
     306.7   317.5   319.7   316.3

16. 3819   2869   2599   2656   3115   3131   2452   2730   3571   2924
     2063   2231   3105   2619   2108   2077   2305   2481   1959   2269
     3024   2683   1999   2236   3135   2914   2598   2508

14.7 EXERCISES   BEYOND THE BASICS

17. The examples and discussion of this section related to time series data consist-
    ing of quarterly values. Given a time series with *monthly* data, determine how
    the method for finding seasonally adjusted values is affected, and how the
    method for forecasting is affected.

18. The given values are the *monthly* amounts for housing starts in the time series
    described in Exercise 10 of Section 14.4. (a) Find the seasonally adjusted
    values. (b) Forecast the values for the 12 months of the next year.

    4.93   5.00   6.07   6.72   7.61   8.62   9.18   9.68   9.77   9.65   9.38
    8.03   7.31   7.36   8.43   8.89   9.89   10.50   10.88   10.95   10.76   10.52
    9.91   8.42   7.75   7.33   8.51   9.01   9.74   10.33   10.71   10.89   10.76
    10.67   10.15   8.80   8.28   7.94   9.25   10.10   11.24   12.35   12.96   13.04
    12.98   12.82   12.04   10.18

19. The given values are the *monthly* indexes of industrial production described in
    Exercise 11 of Section 14.4. (a) Find the seasonally adjusted values. (b)
    Forecast the values for the 12 months of the next year.

    106.8   104.9   99.4   98.6   97.1   99.8   102.7   108.0   107.7   105.4
    106.2   108.9   115.2   112.9   109.9   107.9   107.3   111.4   112.0   114.6
    112.9   106.8   109.3   111.0   114.3   117.3   110.5   106.3   105.1   109.2
    107.9   111.2   111.3   106.8   107.6   111.8   113.1   110.8   104.5   101.1
    98.5   102.1   102.1   103.8   101.9   99.1   101.4   102.4

20. The accompanying table describes a time series for the amount of total
    outstanding consumer credit (in billions of dollars) for a recent four-year
    period (based on data from the U.S. Department of Commerce, Bureau of
    Economic Analysis). The trend equation is $T = 258.5 + 4.351x$. (a) Forecast

LONG-RANGE WEATHER FORECASTING

A high school teacher in Millbrook, New York, created a controversy by conducting a classroom experiment in which long-range weather forecasts were made by throwing darts. The dart method resulted in 7 correct predictions among 20 winter storms, while a nearby private forecasting service correctly predicted only 6 of the storms. The teacher claimed that whereas short-range weather forecasts are usually quite accurate, long-range forecasts are not.

the values for the four quarters of the fifth year. (b) Given that the *actual* values for the fifth year were 312, 318, 323, and 332, find the **mean squared error** (MSE) by evaluating

$$MSE = \frac{\Sigma(y - \hat{y})^2}{n}$$

where y is the actual value, $\hat{y}$ is the forecast (predicted) value, and n is the number of periods in the forecast. The mean squared error is a measure of how well the time series model of $Y = T \times C \times S \times I$ fits the data, and it could be used to compare this model with some other model, such as the additive model $Y = T + C + S + I$.

	QUARTER	CONSUMER CREDIT ($T \times C \times S \times I$)	x	T	S
1st year	1	226			
	2	241			
	3	253	1	262.8	1.003
	4	265	2	267.2	1.012
2nd year	1	268	3	271.5	0.991
	2	280	4	275.9	0.994
	3	291	5	280.2	1.003
	4	300	6	284.6	1.012
3rd year	1	297	7	288.9	0.991
	2	294	8	293.3	0.994
	3	296	9	297.6	1.003
	4	300	10	302.0	1.012
4th year	1	297	11	306.3	0.991
	2	304	12	310.7	0.994
	3	312			
	4	316			

Vocabulary List

Define and give an example of each term.

index number
price index
consumer price index (CPI)
Laspeyres price index
Paasche price index
Fisher's ideal price index
purchasing power of the dollar
time series
trend
cyclical variation
seasonal variation
irregular variation
moving total
moving averages
centered moving average
trend equation

seasonal index
seasonally adjusted values
forecast
causal model
naive model
business indicators
leading indicators
coinciding indicators
lagging indicators

Review

In this chapter we began by considering index numbers. We described price indexes, including the Laspeyres price index, the Paasche price index, Fisher's ideal price index, and purchasing power. We then studied methods for analyzing a *time series*. We used the multiplicative model

$$Y = T \times C \times S \times I$$

where T is the *trend component, C* is the *cyclical component, S* is the *seasonal component,* and I is the *irregular component.* In Sections 14.4 through 14.6 we presented procedures for *decomposition* of a time series into the four individual components. That process is summarized in Fig. 14.6.

In Section 14.7 we considered two applications. We can *seasonally adjust* time series values by dividing them by the corresponding seasonal indexes. We can also *forecast* values by multiplying the projected trend value T (found from the trend equation) by the appropriate seasonal index.

IMPORTANT FORMULAS

$Y = T \times C \times S \times I$	Multiplicative time series model
$\hat{y} = \hat{\beta}_0 + \hat{\beta}_1 x$	Trend equation used to find estimates of the trend component T
$C = \dfrac{T \times C}{T}$	Isolation of cyclical component
$S \times I = \dfrac{T \times C \times S \times I}{T \times C}$	Isolation of $S \times I$ component
$I = \dfrac{S \times I}{S}$	Isolation of irregular component
$\hat{Y} = T \times S$	Forecast value of Y

Seasonal index = (quarterly average) × (adjustment)

$$\text{Seasonally adjusted value} = \frac{\text{original value}}{\text{seasonal index}}$$

Review Exercises

In Exercises 1–4, identify the time series pattern as trend, cyclical variation, seasonal variation, or irregular variation.

1. A manufacturer of golf equipment experiences a large increase in orders during the second quarter of each year.
2. A Washington, D.C., restaurant has a surge of customers during the inaugurations of the president every four years.
3. A Washington, D.C., restaurant finds that the number of canceled reservations fluctuates without any pattern.
4. A supplier of laser disks finds that the number of units shipped has dropped steadily over the last several years.

FIGURE 14.6
Decomposition of Time Series

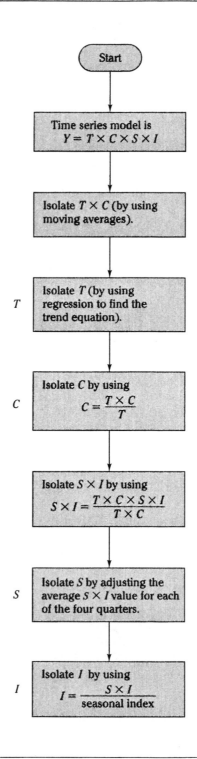

In Exercises 5–8, refer to the figure and identify the time series pattern as trend, cyclical variation, seasonal variation, or irregular variation.

5.

6.

7.

8.

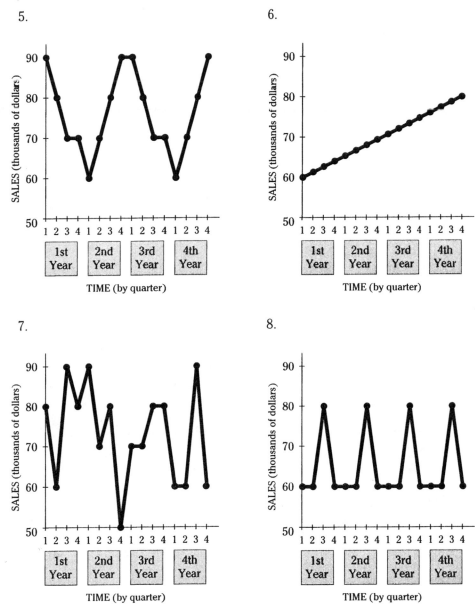

In Exercises 9–16, use the time series data in Table 14.16 (*Standard and Poor's composite price index for a recent four year period*).

9. Use moving averages to find the values of the combined trend and cyclical component $T \times C$.
10. Identify the trend equation, and find the values of the trend component T.
11. Find the values of the cyclical component C.
12. Find the values of the combined seasonal and irregular component $S \times I$.
13. Find the values of the seasonal indexes for each quarter.

TABLE 14.16 Composite Price Index			TABLE 14.17 Liquor Sales		
	QUARTER	$(T \times C \times S \times I)$		QUARTER	$(T \times C \times S \times I)$
1st year	1	100.11	1st year	1	4.14
	2	101.73		2	4.58
	3	108.60		3	4.85
	4	107.78		4	5.54
2nd year	1	104.69	2nd year	1	4.07
	2	114.55		2	4.38
	3	126.51		3	4.59
	4	133.48		4	5.21
3rd year	1	133.19	3rd year	1	4.19
	2	133.28		2	4.65
	3	118.27		3	5.02
	4	123.79		4	5.63
4th year	1	110.84	4th year	1	4.47
	2	109.70		2	4.86
	3	122.43		3	4.99
	4	139.37		4	5.48

14. Find the values of the irregular component I.
15. Find the seasonally adjusted values for the given time series.
16. Forecast the value of the four quarters for the fifth year.

In Exercises 17–24, use the time series data in Table 14.17. The values of $T \times C \times S \times I$ are the amounts (in billions of dollars) of sales from liquor stores.

17. Use moving averages to find the values of the combined trend and cyclical component $T \times C$.
18. Identify the trend equation. Also, use that trend equation to find the values of the trend component T.
19. Find the values of the cyclical component C.
20. Find the values of the combined seasonal and irregular component $S \times I$.
21. Find the values of the seasonal indexes for each quarter.
22. Find the values of the irregular component I.
23. Find the seasonally adjusted values for the given time series.
24. Forecast the value of the four quarters for the fifth year.

In Exercises 25 through 28, refer to Tables 14.2 through 14.5 found in Section 14.2.

25. Using 1983 as the base year, find the price index of televisions for the reference year of 1985.
26. Using 1987 as the base year, find the price index of milk for the reference year of 1982.
27. Using 1983 as the base year and 1987 as the reference year, find the Laspeyres price index for milk, sugar, and coffee.
28. Using 1983 as the base year and 1987 as the reference year, find the Paasche price index for milk, sugar, and coffee.

CAN HIGHER PRICES BE AVOIDED BY STOCKPILING SUPPLIES?

R efer to the time series data given in Table 14.18 in the Computer Project. Using only the first ten years, forecast the twelve values for the eleventh year by applying the methods of this chapter. Compare your forecast values to the actual values for the eleventh year. Your company is considering the stockpiling of supplies in anticipation of higher prices. That decision will be based at least partly on the projected consumer price indexes for transportation. Based on your results, do you think that those projections are reliable? Write a brief report summarizing your findings and include a recommendation regarding the inclusion of the consumer price indexes for transportation.

Computer Project

In Section 14.5 we provided Minitab commands and a display for time series data listed by quarter. The given display includes the combined $T \times C$ values, the trend equation, and the values of the trend component T. Monthly consumer price indexes for transportation for an eleven year period are shown in Table 14.18 (based on data from the U.S. Department of Commerce, Bureau of Economic Analysis). (a) Modify the Minitab commands shown in Section 14.5 so they apply to monthly data instead of quarterly data; then use those commands for the data given in Table 14.18 and run Minitab to obtain the combined $T \times C$ values, the trend equation, and the values of the trend component T. (b) If we have a time series with data listed by year, there is no seasonal variation, so our forecast of $\hat{Y} = T \times S$ becomes $\hat{Y} = T$. That is, our forecast value is found from the trend equation that is found by the same regression methods used in Chapter 12. For the time series data given in Table 14.18, use the December indexes for the first ten years to find the trend equation. Use that equation to forecast the index for the eleventh year and compare the forecast result with the actual result. Use Minitab's REGRESSION command to find the trend equation.

TABLE 14.18
Monthly Consumer Price Indexes for Transportation

YEAR	JAN	FEB	MARCH	APR	MAY	JUNE	JULY	AUG	SEPT	OCT	NOV	DEC
1	118.9	118.3	118.4	118.6	119.5	119.8	120.2	120.5	121.0	121.2	121.4	121.3
2	121.0	121.1	121.5	122.6	123.5	124.6	124.8	124.5	123.9	125.0	125.8	126.7
3	128.1	129.3	132.0	133.7	136.3	138.8	140.6	141.3	142.2	142.9	143.4	143.5
4	143.2	143.5	144.8	146.2	147.4	149.8	152.6	153.6	155.4	156.1	157.4	157.6
5	158.1	158.5	159.8	161.3	163.5	165.9	167.6	168.5	169.5	170.9	171.4	171.4
6	172.2	173.2	174.7	176.7	178.1	179.1	179.2	178.8	178.4	178.6	178.7	178.8
7	179.0	179.4	179.9	181.1	183.2	185.5	187.2	188.1	188.7	189.7	191.4	192.6
8	193.9	195.6	198.1	202.9	207.7	212.6	216.6	219.6	221.4	222.7	224.9	227.7
9	233.5	239.6	243.7	246.8	249.0	249.7	251.0	252.7	254.7	256.1	259.0	261.1
10	264.7	270.9	273.5	275.3	277.8	279.9	282.6	283.7	285.2	287.2	289.1	289.8
11	289.9	288.0	285.1	282.9	285.6	292.8	296.1	296.2	295.3	295.5	295.8	294.8

CHAPTER 15

Nonparametric Statistics

15.1 OVERVIEW

15.2 SIGN TEST

The sign test can be used to test the claim that two sets of dependent data have the same median.

15.3 WILCOXON SIGNED-RANKS TEST FOR TWO DEPENDENT SAMPLES

The Wilcoxon signed-ranks test can be used to test the claim that two sets of dependent data come from identical populations.

15.4 WILCOXON RANK-SUM TEST FOR TWO INDEPENDENT SAMPLES

The Wilcoxon rank-sum test can be used to test the claim that two independent samples come from identical populations.

15.5 KRUSKAL-WALLIS TEST

The Kruskal-Wallis test can be used to test the claim that several independent samples come from identical populations.

15.6 RANK CORRELATION

The rank correlation coefficient can be used to test for an association between two sets of paired data.

15.7 RUNS TEST FOR RANDOMNESS

The runs test can be used to test for randomness in the way data are selected.

Are Salaries Related to Job Stress?

Employees like to believe that their salaries are fair. They want to be fairly compensated for their efforts, abilities, stress levels, and physical demands. Let's consider the relationship between salary and level of stress. In Table 15.1 we list randomly selected jobs along with rankings (with 1 for highest and 10 for lowest) for salary and stress levels (based on data from **The Jobs Rated Almanac**). Among these ten jobs, stockbrokers have the second highest salary and the second highest stress level. Zoologists have the sixth highest salary and the seventh highest stress level. Commercial airline pilots have the highest levels of stress and they also have the highest salaries.

Is there a relationship between a job's salary and its level of stress? In questioning the presence or absence of a relationship between two variables, we are really asking whether there is a correlation between them. We have already discussed (in Chapter 12) the correlation between two variables, but one of the assumptions involved normally distributed values for the two variables. However, because the data in Table 15.1 consist of ranks, we cannot satisfy that requirement of normal distributions. Specifically, the Table 15.1 salary values and stress values of 1, 2, 3, . . . , 10 are not normally distributed and they do not come from a normally distributed population. Consequently, we cannot use the linear correlation coefficient. Although we can't use the methods of Chapter 12, we can use an alternative method that can be applied to data consisting of ranks, such as the data in Table 15.1.

In Section 15.6 we will apply the concept of rank correlation to the data in Table 15.1 as we test for a relationship between job salary and stress level. We will determine whether there is a correlation between the stress levels of jobs and the corresponding salaries.

TABLE 15.1
Jobs Ranked by Salary and Stress

JOB	SALARY RANK	STRESS RANK
Stockbroker	2	2
Zoologist	6	7
Electrical engineer	3	6
School principal	5	4
Hotel manager	7	5
Bank officer	10	8
Occupational safety inspector	9	9
Home economist	8	10
Psychologist	4	3
Commercial airline pilot	1	1

15.1 OVERVIEW

Most of the methods of inferential statistics covered before Chapter 10 can be called *parametric methods* because their validity is based on sampling from a population with particular parameters such as the mean, standard deviation, or proportion. Parametric methods can usually be applied only to circumstances in which some fairly strict requirements are met. One typical requirement is that the sample data come from a normally distributed population. What do we do when the necessary requirements are not satisfied? This chapter introduces inferential methods consisting of hypothesis tests that are classified as nonparametric.

> **DEFINITIONS**
>
> *Parametric tests* require assumptions about the nature or shape of the populations involved. *Nonparametric tests* do not require assumptions about the nature or shape of the populations involved; for this reason, nonparametric tests of hypotheses are often called *distribution-free tests.* (Actually, some nonparametric tests do depend on a parameter such as the median, but they don't require a particular distribution. Although "distribution-free" is a more accurate description, the term *nonparametric* is commonly used. Sorry about that.)

In addition to being an alternative to parametric methods, nonparametric techniques are frequently valuable in their own right. In this chapter we introduce six of the more popular nonparametric methods currently used. These methods have advantages and disadvantages.

ADVANTAGES OF NONPARAMETRIC METHODS

1. Nonparametric methods can be applied to a wider variety of situations because they do not have the more rigid requirements of their parametric counterparts. In particular, nonparametric methods do not require normally distributed populations.
2. Unlike the parametric methods, nonparametric methods can often be applied to nominal data that lack exact numerical values.
3. Nonparametric methods usually involve computations that are simpler than the corresponding parametric methods and are therefore easier to understand.

If all of these terrific advantages could be gained without any significant disadvantages, we could ignore the parametric methods and enjoy much simpler procedures. Unfortunately, there are some disadvantages.

DISADVANTAGES OF NONPARAMETRIC METHODS

Nonparametric methods tend to waste information because exact numerical data are sometimes reduced to a qualitative form. As an example of the way that information is wasted, in one nonparametric test (the sign test) weight losses by dieters are recorded simply as negative signs. With this particular method, a weight loss of only 1 pound receives the same representation as a weight loss of 50 pounds. This would not thrill dieters.

A second disadvantage concerns the test's **efficiency,** which is its sensitivity when compared to the corresponding parametric test. With a nonparametric test, we generally need "stronger evidence" (such as a larger sample or greater differences) before we reject a null hypothesis. Although nonparametric tests are less sensitive than their parametric counterparts, this can be compensated for by an increased sample size. The efficiency of a nonparametric method is one concrete measure of its sensitivity. Section 15.6 deals with a concept called the *rank correlation coefficient,* which has an efficiency rating of 0.91 when compared to the linear correlation coefficient of Chapter 12. This means that with all things being equal, this nonparametric approach would require 100 sample observations to achieve the same results as 91 sample observations analyzed through the parametric approach, assuming the stricter requirements for using the parametric method are met. Not bad! The point, though, is that an increased sample size can overcome lower sensitivity. Table 15.2 lists the nonparametric methods covered in this chapter, along with the corresponding parametric approach and efficiency rating. You can see from this table that the lower efficiency rating might not be a critical factor. However, because nonparametric tests have lower efficiency ratings than their parametric counterparts, we recommend the parametric tests when their required assumptions are satisfied.

In choosing between a parametric method and a nonparametric method, the key factors that should govern our decision are cost, time, efficiency, amount of data available, type of data available, method of sampling, nature and distribution of the population, and probabilities (α and β) of making type I and type II errors. In one experiment we might have abundant data with strong assurances that all the requirements of a parametric test are satisfied, and we would probably be wise to choose that parametric test. But given another experiment with relatively few cases drawn from some mysterious population, we would probably fare better with a nonparametric test. Sometimes we don't really have a choice. Only nonparametric methods can be used on data consisting of observations that can only be ranked.

TABLE 15.2
Efficiency of Nonparametric Tests

APPLICATION	PARAMETRIC TEST	NONPARAMETRIC TEST	EFFICIENCY OF NONPARAMETRIC TEST WITH NORMALLY DISTRIBUTED POPULATION
Two dependent samples	t test or z test	Sign test Wilcoxon signed-ranks test	0.63 0.95
Two independent samples	t test or z test	Wilcoxon rank-sum test	0.95
Several independent samples	Analysis of variance (F test)	Kruskal-Wallis test	0.95
Correlation	Linear correlation	Rank correlation	0.91
Randomness	No parametric test	Runs test	No basis for comparison

RANKS

Ranked data have been referred to earlier in this text. The procedure for finding the median of a set of values begins with ranking the data. In Section 2.7 we considered a procedure for finding a score that corresponds to a percentile, and that procedure also began with a ranking of the data. Those earlier uses of ranked data simply involved arranging the data in order, but this chapter includes some tests that are based on data consisting of ranks. Instead of describing ranks in each section and making some sections dependent on others, we will now discuss ranks so that we will be prepared to use them wherever they are required.

DEFINITION

Data are *ranked* when they are arranged according to some criterion, such as size (smallest to largest) or quality (best to worst). A *rank* is a number assigned to an individual sample item according to its order in the ranked list. The first sample item is assigned a rank of 1, the second sample item is assigned a rank of 2, and so on.

For example, the numbers 5, 3, 40, 10, and 12 can be arranged from lowest to highest as 3, 5, 10, 12, and 40, and these numbers have ranks of 1, 2, 3, 4, 5, respectively (see the following illustration). If a tie in ranks should occur, the usual procedure is to find the mean of the ranks involved and then assign that mean rank to each of the tied items. The numbers 3, 5, 5, 10, and 12 would be given ranks of 1, 2.5, 2.5, 4, and 5, respectively. In this case, there is a tie for ranks 2 and 3, so we find the mean of 2 and 3 (which is 2.5) and assign it to the scores that created the tie. As another example, the scores 3, 5, 5, 7, 10, 10, 10, and 15 would be ranked 1, 2.5, 2.5, 4, 6, 6, 6, and 8, respectively. From these examples we can see how to convert numbers to ranks. In many situations, however, the original data consist of ranks. If a judge ranks five piano contestants, we get ranks of 1, 2, 3, 4, 5 corresponding to five names; it's this type of data that precludes the use of parametric methods and demonstrates the importance of nonparametric methods.

Scores	5	3	40	10	12
Scores in order	3	5	10	12	40
	↑	↑	↑	↑	↑
Ranks	1	2	3	4	5

Scores	3	5	5	10	12
	↑	↑	↑	↑	↑
Ranks	1	2.5	2.5	4	5

(2 and 3 are tied)

15.2 SIGN TEST

The **sign test** is one of the easiest nonparametric tests to use, and it is applicable to several different situations. One application is to the paired data that form the basis for hypothesis tests involving *two dependent samples*. We considered such cases by using parametric tests in Section 9.3. There we used the parametric Student *t* test for dependent samples, but in this section we apply the nonparametric sign test, which can be used to determine whether two sets of data have equal medians. We begin the sign test by working with each pair of values: Subtract each value of the second variable from the corresponding value of the first variable, but record only the *sign* of the difference. In our sign test procedure, we exclude any ties (represented by zeros). (For other ways to handle ties, see Exercise 18.) Exclude ties and record the positive and negative signs. The key concept underlying the sign test is this: **If the two sets of data have equal medians, the number of positive signs should be approximately equal to the number of negative signs.** For consistency and ease, we will stipulate the following:

Notation

x The test statistic *x* *is the number of times the less frequent sign occurs.*

n **The total number of positive and negative signs combined.**

Because the results fall into two categories (positive sign, negative sign) and we have a fixed number of independent cases (or pairs of values), we could use the binomial probability distribution (Section 4.4) to determine the likelihood of getting the test statistic *x* described above. Instead, we have already used the binomial probability formula to construct a separate table (Table A.7) that lists critical values for the sign test.

EXAMPLE An example from Section 9.3 refers to the Malloy and Clinton Advertising Company that prepared a humorous commercial and a serious commercial for Taylor women's jeans. Listed in Table 15.3 are sample results from eight consumers tested for their reactions. At the $\alpha = 0.05$ significance level, test the claim that the humorous commercials receive higher scores.

TABLE 15.3
Consumer Reactions to Television Commercials

Subject	A	B	C	D	E	F	G	H
Humorous commercial	26.2	20.3	25.4	19.6	21.5	28.3	23.7	24.0
Serious commercial	24.1	21.3	23.7	18.0	20.1	25.8	22.4	21.4
Sign of difference (humorous−serious)	+	−	+	+	+	+	+	+

> **SOLUTION**
>
> The claim that the humorous commercials receive higher scores is the alternative hypothesis, while the null hypothesis is the claim that the humorous commercials have scores equal to or below those for the serious commercials.
>
> H_0: The humorous scores are equal to or below the serious scores.
> H_1: The humorous scores are higher.
>
> With the above null hypothesis, we assume that positive signs and negative signs occur with equal frequency, so P (positive sign) = P (negative sign) = 0.5. (The null hypothesis includes the possibility of lower humorous scores, but we continue to assume that positive signs and negative signs are equally likely.) For the data of Table 15.3, we can conclude that the humorous scores are higher if we see an excess of positive signs and a deficiency of negative signs. From Table 15.3 we see that we have $n = 8$ pairs of data and the test statistic is $x = 1$ (the smaller of 1 and 7). We now pose this specific question: Do the 7 positive signs in Table 15.3 *significantly* outnumber the 1 negative sign? Or, to put it another way, is the number of negative signs small enough to be significant?
>
> Our test is one-tailed with $\alpha = 0.05$, and Table A.7 indicates that the critical value is 1. Table A.7 (see note 2 in that table) indicates that we should reject the null hypothesis only if the test statistic is less than or equal to 1. With a test statistic of $x = 1$, we do reject the null hypothesis of equal or lower scores. It appears that the humorous commercial has higher scores.

Shown below is an annotated Minitab display for the preceding example. Note the use of the STEST command for sign test.

```
MTB > READ C1 C2 ⎫
DATA> 26.2 24.1 ⎪
DATA> 20.3 21.3 ⎪
DATA> 25.4 23.7 ⎪
DATA> 19.6 18.0 ⎪
DATA> 21.5 20.1 ⎬ Data entered here
DATA> 28.3 25.8 ⎪
DATA> 23.7 22.4 ⎪
DATA> 24.0 21.4 ⎪
DATA> ENDOFDATA ⎭
DATA> ENDOFDATA      8 ROWS READ
MTB > LET C3=C1-C2   ← C3 represents differences of C1-C2.
MTB > STEST MEDIAN=0 C3;   ← Minitab command for sign test
SUBC> ALTERNATIVE=+1.   ← Indicates a right-tailed test

SIGN TEST OF MEDIAN = 0.00000 VERSUS  G.T.  0.00000
```

Because P-value is less than 0.05, reject null hypothesis.

	N	BELOW	EQUAL	ABOVE	P-VALUE	MEDIAN
C3	8	1	0	7	0.0352	1.650

TABLE 15.4
Consumer Reactions to Television Commercials

Subject	A	B	C	D	E	F	G	H
Humorous commercial	23.2	20.3	25.4	19.6	21.5	28.3	23.7	24.0
Serious commercial	24.1	21.3	23.7	18.0	20.1	25.8	22.4	21.4
Difference	−0.9	−1.0	+1.7	+1.6	+1.4	+2.5	+1.3	+2.6
Sign of difference (humorous−serious)	−	−	+	+	+	+	+	+

In the preceding example we arrived at the same conclusion obtained in Section 9.3. We will now illustrate our previous assertion that nonparametric tests lack the sensitivity of parametric tests, so stronger evidence tends to be required before a null hypothesis is rejected. Consider the new data set given in Table 15.4.

This data set contains 2 negative signs and 6 positive signs. If we use the sign test, the test statistic is $x = 2$, and we fail to reject the null hypothesis of equal or lower scores. But if we use the Student t test for dependent data from Section 9.3, we get

$$t = \frac{\bar{d} - 0}{s_d / \sqrt{n}}$$
$$= \frac{1.15 - 0}{1.38 / \sqrt{8}} = 2.357$$

This causes *rejection* of the null hypothesis because the test statistic of $t = 2.357$ is in the critical region bounded by the critical t score of 1.895. An intuitive analysis of Table 15.4 suggests that the "serious" scores are significantly lower, but the sign test is blind to the *magnitude* of the changes. This shows that the nonparametric sign test lacks the sensitivity of the corresponding parametric Student t test.

When applying the sign test, we should be careful to avoid making the wrong conclusion when one sign occurs significantly more often than the other, but the sample data seem to *support* the null hypothesis. For example, suppose we change only the claim in the preceding example so that we get the following:

H_0: The humorous scores are equal to or greater than the serious scores.
H_1: The humorous scores are lower.

The test statistic continues to be $x = 1$ and the critical value from Table A.7 continues to be 1, so it would seem that we should again reject the null hypothesis and conclude that the humorous scores are lower. *This would be a wrong conclusion* because the sample data seem to *support* the null hypothesis, so the null hypothesis should not be rejected under any circumstances. Here again, it's important to use common sense and not apply procedures or formulas blindly. Always check to be sure the sample data are in conflict with the null hypothesis, and proceed with the test to determine whether that conflict is significant so that the null hypothesis is actually rejected. In Fig. 15.1 we summarize the procedure for the sign test and we include this check.

A FAIR JURY?

Some statistical tests, such as the sign test, can be used to analyze categorical data, such as gender. In one case a statistician showed that a certain judge had a consistently lower proportion of women jurors than the other six judges in the same federal judicial district. That judge presided over a trial of Dr. Benjamin Spock, a famous author of books on the care of babies and children. Spock was convicted of conspiracy to encourage resistance to the military draft during the Vietnam War. The defense appealed the conviction and argued that Dr. Spock was handicapped because all 12 jurors were men. Women would have been more inclined to be sympathetic because opposition to the war was greater among women and Spock was well known to many mothers. Spock's conviction was overturned for other reasons, but we now randomly select federal court jurors.

In the preceding example we found the critical value in Table A.7, but examination of that table shows that it can be used only for values of n up to 25. When $n > 25$, we use a normal approximation to obtain critical values. For $n > 25$, the test statistic x is converted to a z score as follows:

$$\textbf{Test statistic (for } \textbf{\textit{n}} \textbf{ > 25):} \; z = \frac{(x + 0.5) - (n/2)}{\sqrt{n}/2}$$

The critical value corresponding to this test statistic is found in Table A.2. The next example involves a sample size greater than 25.

CLAIMS INVOLVING NOMINAL DATA

The example below illustrates the use of the sign test with nominal data. Recall that nominal data consist of names or categories only. Because this example involves a sample size greater than 25, the normal approximation will be used.

EXAMPLE   A company claims that its hiring practices are fair, it does not discriminate on the basis of sex, and the fact that 40 of the last 50 new employees are men is just a fluke. The company acknowledges that applicants are about half men and half women, and all have met the basic job qualification standards. Test the null hypothesis that men and women are hired equally by this company. Use a significance level of 0.05.

SOLUTION H_0: $p_1 = p_2$ (the proportions of men and women are equal)
H_1: $p_1 \neq p_2$
If we denote hired women by $+$ and hired men by $-$, we have 10 positive signs and 40 negative signs. Refer now to the flowchart in Fig. 15.1. The test statistic x is the smaller of 10 and 40, so $x = 10$. This test involves two tails because a disproportionately low number of either sex will cause us to reject the claim of equality. The sample data do not support the null hypothesis of equality because 10 and 40 are not precisely equal.
Continuing with the procedure in Fig. 15.1, we note that the value of $n = 50$ is above 25, so the test statistic x is converted to the test statistic z as follows:

$$z = \frac{(x + 0.5) - (n/2)}{\sqrt{n}/2}$$

$$= \frac{(10 + 0.5) - (50/2)}{\sqrt{50}/2} = -4.10$$

With $\alpha = 0.05$ in a two-tailed test, the critical values are $z = -1.96$ and 1.96. The test statistic $z = -4.10$ is less than these critical values (see Fig. 15.2 on page 664), so we reject the null hypothesis of equality. There is sufficient sample evidence to warrant rejection of the claim that the hiring practices are fair.

FIGURE 15.1
Sign Test Procedure

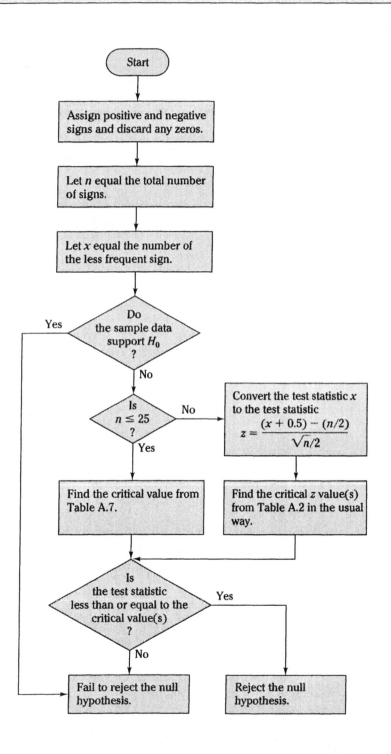

FIGURE 15.2
Sign Test of Fair Hiring Practices

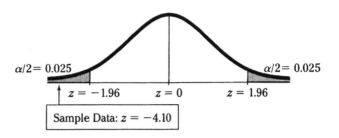

When $n > 25$, the test statistic z is based on a normal approximation to the binomial probability distribution with $p = q = 1/2$. In Section 5.6 we saw that the normal approximation to the binomial distribution is acceptable when both $np \geq 5$ and $nq \geq 5$. Also, in Section 4.5 we saw that $\mu = np$ and $\sigma = \sqrt{n \cdot p \cdot q}$ for binomial experiments. Because this sign test assumes that $p = q = 1/2$, we meet the $np \geq 5$ and $nq \geq 5$ prerequisites whenever $n \geq 10$; we have a table of critical values (Table A.7) for n up to 25, so that we need the normal approximation only for values of n above 25. Also, with the assumption that $p = q = 1/2$, we get $\mu = np = n/2$ and $\sigma = \sqrt{n \cdot p \cdot q} = \sqrt{n/4} = \sqrt{n}/2$, so that

$$z = \frac{x - \mu}{\sigma} \quad \text{becomes} \quad z = \frac{x - \left(\dfrac{n}{2}\right)}{\dfrac{\sqrt{n}}{2}}$$

Finally, we replace x by $x + 0.5$ as a correction for continuity. That is, the values of x are discrete, but because we are using a continuous probability distribution, a discrete value such as 10 is actually represented by the interval from 9.5 to 10.5. Because x represents the less frequent sign, we need to concern ourselves only with $x + 0.5$; we thus get the test statistic z as given above and in Fig. 15.1.

CLAIMS ABOUT A MEDIAN

The previous examples involved application of the sign test to a comparison of *two* sets of data, but we can also use the sign test to investigate a claim made about the median of one set of data, as the next example shows.

EXAMPLE   Use the sign test to test the claim that the median IQ of pilots is at least 100 if a sample of 50 pilots contained exactly 22 members with IQs of 100 or higher.

SOLUTION The null hypothesis is the claim that the median is equal to or greater than 100; the alternative hypothesis is the claim that the median is less than 100.

H_0: Median is at least 100. (Median $\geq$ 100)
H_1: Median is less than 100. (Median < 100)

We select a significance level of 0.05, and we use + to denote each IQ score that is at least 100. We therefore have 22 positive signs and 28 negative signs. We can now determine the significance of getting 22 positive signs out of a possible 50. Referring to Fig. 15.1, we note that $n = 50$ and $x = 22$ (the smaller of 22 and 28). The sense of the data is against the null hypothesis because a median of at least 100 would require at least 25 (half of 50) scores of 100 or higher. The value of n exceeds 25, so we convert the test statistic x to the test statistic z.

$$z = \frac{(x + 0.5) - (n/2)}{\sqrt{n}/2}$$

$$= \frac{(22 + 0.5) - (50/2)}{\sqrt{50}/2}$$

$$= \frac{22.5 - 25}{\sqrt{50}/2} = -0.71$$

In this one-tailed test with $\alpha = 0.05$, we use Table A.2 to get the critical z value of -1.645. From Fig. 15.3 we can see that the computed value of -0.71 does not fall within the critical region. We therefore fail to reject the null hypothesis. Based on the available sample evidence, we don't have enough evidence to reject the claim that the median IQ is at least 100. A corresponding parametric test may or may not lead to the same conclusion, depending on the specific values of the 50 sample scores.

FIGURE 15.3
Sign Test that Median Is at Least 100

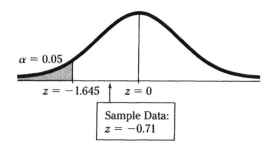

We have shown that the sign test wastes information because it uses only information about the direction of the differences between pairs of data, while the magnitudes of those differences are ignored. The next section introduces the Wilcoxon signed-ranks test, which largely overcomes that disadvantage.

15.2 EXERCISES   BASIC CONCEPTS

In Exercises 1–16, use the sign test.

1. A container-filling process at the Kansas Food Products Company involves a machine with two nozzles that are each supposed to supply 14 oz of cereal. The machine fills 2 boxes at a time (one from each nozzle). During one day, 10 pairs of boxes were sampled, and their weights are given below. At the 0.05 level of significance, test the claim that there is no difference between the filling weights of the two nozzles.

Nozzle 1	14.1	13.9	14.1	14.0	14.0	13.8	13.9	14.0	14.0	13.8
Nozzle 2	14.3	14.0	14.0	14.2	14.1	13.9	14.2	14.1	14.2	13.8

2. The Medassist Pharmaceutical Company manufactures a drug intended to provide relief from migraine headaches. A new drug (A) is tested against the old drug (B) in an experiment involving 10 persons who chronically suffer from migraine headaches. Each of the 10 persons uses the old drug and the new drug in different headache events, and they rate effectiveness on a scale from 1 (no effect) to 5 (extremely effective). The results are given below. Because the data are not normally distributed, the paired t test is not appropriate here. Use the sign test at the 0.05 level of significance and test the claim that there is no difference between the two drugs.

Subject	1	2	3	4	5	6	7	8	9	10
Drug A	4	3	4	5	3	4	2	4	3	2
Drug B	2	2	1	3	3	2	3	3	2	1

3. Two different firms design their own IQ tests, and a psychologist administers both tests to randomly selected subjects. The results are given below. At the 0.05 level of significance, test the claim that there is no significant difference between the two tests.

Subject	A	B	C	D	E	F	G	H	I	J
Test I	98	94	111	102	108	105	92	88	100	99
Test II	105	103	113	98	112	109	97	95	107	103

4. A pill designed to lower systolic blood pressure is administered to 12 randomly selected volunteers. The results follow. At the $\alpha = 0.05$ significance level, test the claim that systolic blood pressure is not affected by the pill. That is, test the claim that the before and after values are equal.

Before pill	120	136	160	98	115	110	180	190	138	128	118	122
After pill	118	122	143	105	98	98	180	175	105	112	112	114

5. A test of driving ability is given to a random sample of 10 student drivers before and after they have completed a formal driver education course conducted by the Dallas Driving School. The results follow. At the $\alpha = 0.05$ significance level, test the claim that the course does not affect scores.

Before course	100	121	93	146	101	109	149	130	127	120
After course	136	129	125	150	110	138	136	130	125	129

6. A firm is using 12 subjects in market testing 2 different pie fillings. Each subject samples both fillings and rates them on a scale of 1 (repulsive) to 10 (excellent). The results are listed below. At the 0.05 level of significance, test the claim that the 2 fillings are preferred equally.

Subject	1	2	3	4	5	6	7	8	9	10	11	12
Filling A	7	8	6	7	9	7	8	9	5	7	9	8
Filling B	9	10	7	7	10	8	7	9	7	10	10	9

7. The following chart lists a random sampling of the ages of married couples. The age of each husband is listed above the age of his wife. At the 0.01 significance level, test the claim that there is no difference between the ages of husbands and wives.

Husband	28.1	33.0	29.8	53.1	56.7	41.6	50.6	21.4	62.0	19.7
Wife	28.4	27.6	32.7	52.0	58.1	41.2	50.7	20.6	61.1	18.1

8. Ten randomly selected volunteers test a new diet, with the following results. At the 0.01 level of significance, test the claim that the diet is effective—that is, that weights (in kilograms) are lower after the diet.

Subject	A	B	C	D	E	F	G	H	I	J
Weight before diet	68	54	59	60	57	62	62	65	88	76
Weight after diet	65	52	52	60	58	59	60	63	78	75

9. A television commercial advertises that 7 out of 10 dentists surveyed prefer Covariant toothpaste over the leading competitor. Assume that 10 dentists are surveyed and 7 do prefer Covariant, while 3 favor the other brand. Is this a reasonable basis for making the claim that most (more than half) dentists favor Covariant toothpaste? Use the sign test with a significance level of 0.05.

10. Use the sign test to test the claim that the median life of a Telektronic Company battery is at least 40 hours if a random sample of 75 includes exactly 32 that last 40 hours or more. Assume a significance level of 0.05.

11. The Grange Fertilizer Company is experimenting with new fertilizer at 50 different locations. In 32 of the locations there is an increase in production, while in 18 locations there is a decrease. At the 0.05 level of significance, use the sign test to test the claim that production is increased by the new fertilizer.

12. A new diet is designed to lower cholesterol levels. In six months, 36 of the 60 subjects on the diet have lower cholesterol levels, 22 have slightly higher levels, and 2 register no change. At the 0.01 level of significance, use the sign test to test the claim that the diet produces no change in cholesterol levels.

13. In a large shipment of lumber framing studs, the seller claims that the average number of knots per stud is 2 or less. Studs with more than 2 such defects are sold at a lower price. A random selection of 28 studs includes 20 with more than 2 knots. At the 0.05 significance level, test the claim that the median number of knots is 2 or less.

14. Liquid industrial solvents are poured into containers labeled 5 gal (or 640 oz). A sample is obtained from the filling process by selecting one container every 10 min, and the results are listed below. At the 0.05 level of significance, test the claim that the median fill amount is at least 640 oz.

    642   646   640   642   638   634   632   635
    631   638   636   628   625   630   623

15. Of 50 voters surveyed, 28 favor a tax revision bill before Congress, while all the others are opposed. At the 0.10 level of significance, use the sign test to test the claim that the majority (more than half) of voters favor the bill.

16. A standardized aptitude test yields a mathematics score M and a verbal score V for each person. Among 15 male subjects, $M - V$ is positive in 12 cases, negative in 2 cases, and 0 in 1 case. At the 0.05 level of significance, use the sign test to test the claim that males do better on the mathematics portion of the test than on the verbal portion.

15.2   EXERCISES   BEYOND THE BASICS

17. Given n sample scores sorted in ascending order $(x_1, x_2, \ldots, x_n)$, if we wish to find the approximate $1 - \alpha$ confidence interval for the population median M, we get

$$x_{k+1} < M < x_{n-k}$$

Here k is the critical value (Table A.7) for the number of signs in a two-tailed hypothesis test conducted at the significance level of α. Find the approximate 95% confidence interval for the population median M by using the sample scores listed below.

    3   8   6   2   1   7   9   11   17   23   25   10   14   8   30

18. **Differences of zero:** In the sign test procedure described in this section, we excluded ties (represented by 0 instead of a sign of $+$ or $-$). A second approach is to treat half the zeros as positive signs and half as negative signs. (If there are an odd number of zeros, exclude one so they can be divided equally.) With a third approach, in two-tailed tests we make half the zeros positive and half negative; in one-tailed tests we make all zeros either positive or negative, whichever supports the null hypothesis. Assume that in using the

sign test of a claim that the median score is at least 100, we get 60 scores below 100, 40 scores above 100, and 21 scores equal to 100. Identify the test statistic and conclusion for the three different ways of handling differences of zero. Assume a 0.05 significance level in all three cases.

19. Of n subjects tested for high blood pressure, a majority of exactly 50 provide negative results. (That is, their blood pressure is not high.) This is sufficient for us to apply the sign test and reject (at the 0.01 level of significance) the claim that the median blood pressure level is high. Find the largest value n can assume.

20. Table A.7 lists critical values for limited choices of α. Use Table A.1 to add a new column in Table A.7 (down to $n = 15$) that would represent a significance level of 0.03 in one tail or 0.06 in two tails. For any particular n we use $p = 0.5$ because the sign test requires the assumption that

$$P(\text{positive sign}) = P(\text{negative sign}) = 0.5$$

The probability of x or fewer like signs is the sum of the probabilities up to and including x.

15.3   WILCOXON SIGNED-RANKS TEST FOR TWO DEPENDENT SAMPLES

In the preceding section we used the sign test to analyze the differences between sample paired data. The sign test used only the signs of the differences and ignored the actual magnitudes of the differences. In this section we introduce the **Wilcoxon signed-ranks test** to be used with sample paired data, but this test will take the magnitudes of the differences into account. Because the test incorporates and uses more information than the ordinary sign test, it tends to yield better results than the sign test. However, the Wilcoxon signed-ranks test requires the assumption that the population of differences (found from the pairs of data) has a distribution that is approximately symmetric. Unlike the Student t test for paired data (see Section 9.3), the Wilcoxon signed-ranks test does *not* require normal distributions.

In general, the null hypothesis will be the claim that both samples come from the same population distribution. We summarize here the procedure for using the Wilcoxon signed-ranks test with paired data.

1. For each pair of data, find the difference d by subtracting the second score from the first. Retain signs, but discard any pairs for which $d = 0$.

2. Ignoring the signs of the differences, rank them from lowest to highest. When differences have the same numerical value, assign to them the mean of the ranks involved in the tie. (See Section 15.1 for the method of ranking data.)

3. Assign to each rank the sign of the difference from which it came.

4. Find the sum of the absolute values of the negative ranks. Also find the sum of the positive ranks.

5. Let T be the smaller of the two sums found in step 4.   *(continued)*

Notation

T **Smaller of these two sums:**
   1. The sum of the absolute values of the negative ranks
   2. The sum of the positive ranks
n **Number of *pairs* of data after excluding any pairs in which both values are the same**

6. Let n be the number of pairs of data for which the difference d is not zero.
7. If $n \leq 30$, use Table A.8 to find the critical value of T. Reject the null hypothesis if the sample data yield a value of T less than or equal to the value in Table A.8. Otherwise, fail to reject the null hypothesis. If $n > 30$, compute the test statistic z by using the following:

Test Statistic

$$z = \frac{T - \dfrac{n(n+1)}{4}}{\sqrt{\dfrac{n(n+1)(2n+1)}{24}}} \quad \text{(for } n > 30\text{)}$$

When the above test statistic is used, the critical z values are found by using Table A.2 in the usual way. Again reject the null hypothesis if the test statistic z is less than or equal to the critical value(s) of z. Otherwise, fail to reject the null hypothesis.

EXAMPLE   Consider the sample data in Table 15.5. The 13 programmers are given a test for logical thinking. They are then given a tranquilizer and retested. Use the Wilcoxon signed-ranks test to test the claim that the tranquilizer has no effect, so there is no significant difference between before and after scores. Use a 0.05 level of significance.

TABLE 15.5
Tests of Logic for Programmers

SUBJECT	BEFORE	AFTER	DIFFERENCE	RANKS OF DIFFERENCES	SIGNED RANKS
A	67	68	−1	1	−1
B	78	81	−3	2	−2
C	81	85	−4	3	−3
D	72	60	+12	10	+10
E	75	75	0	—	—
F	92	81	+11	8.5	+8.5
G	84	73	+11	8.5	+8.5
H	83	78	+5	4	+4
I	77	84	−7	5	−5
J	65	56	+9	6	+6
K	71	61	+10	7	+7
L	79	64	+15	11	+11
M	80	63	+17	12	+12

SOLUTION   Based on the given claim, we have the following hypotheses.

H_0: The tranquilizer has no effect on logical thinking.
H_1: The tranquilizer has an effect on logical thinking.
We will follow the seven steps listed in the above procedure.

STEP 1   In Table 15.5 the column of differences is obtained by subtracting each "after" score from the corresponding "before" score. Differences of zero are discarded. See the fourth column of the table.

STEP 2   Ignoring their signs, we then rank the differences from lowest to highest, treating ties in the manner described in Section 15.1. See the fifth column of Table 15.5.

STEP 3   The signed-ranks column is then created by applying to each rank the sign of the corresponding difference. The results are listed in the last column of Table 15.5. If the tranquilizer really has no effect, we would expect the sum of the positive ranks to be approximately equal to the sum of the negative ranks. If the tranquilizer tends to lower scores, then the sum of the ranks of positive sign would tend to be greater than the sum of the ranks of negative sign. If the tranquilizer tends to raise scores, then the sum of the ranks of negative sign would tend to be greater than the sum of the ranks of positive sign. We can detect a domination by either sign through analysis of the rank sums.

STEP 4   Now find the sum of the absolute values of the negative ranks and the sum of the positive ranks. For the data of Table 15.5, we get

sum of absolute values of negative
ranks $= 1 + 2 + 3 + 5 = 11$
sum of positive ranks
$= 10 + 8.5 + 8.5 + 4 + 6 + 7 + 11 + 12 = 67$

STEP 5   We will base our test on the smaller of those two sums, denoted by T. For the given data we have $T = 11$.

STEP 6 $n = 12$ because there are 12 pairs of data with nonzero differences.

STEP 7   Whenever $n \leq 30$, we use Table A.8 to find the critical values. If $n > 30$, we can use a normal approximation with the z test statistic given earlier and the critical values given in Table A.2. As in Section 15.2, we would be justified in using the normal approximation whenever $n \geq 10$, but we have a table of critical values for values of n up to 30 so that we really need the normal approximation only for $n > 30$. Because the data of

Table 15.5 yield $n = 12$, we use Table A.8 to get the critical value of 14. ($\alpha = 0.05$ and the test is two-tailed because our null hypothesis is the claim that the scores have not changed significantly.) Because $T = 11$ is less than or equal to the critical value of 14, we reject the null hypothesis. It appears that the drug does affect scores.

Shown below is an annotated Minitab display for the preceding example. Note the use of the WTEST command that runs this Wilcoxon signed-ranks test.

```
MTB > READ C1 C2
DATA> 67 68
DATA> 78 81
DATA> 81 85
DATA> 72 60
DATA> 75 75
DATA> 92 81
DATA> 84 73          Data entered here
DATA> 83 78
DATA> 77 84
DATA> 65 56
DATA> 71 61
DATA> 79 64
DATA> 80 63
DATA> ENDOFDATA
DATA> ENDOFDATA      13 ROWS READ
MTB > LET C3=C2-C1   ← C3 represents differences of C2 − C1.
MTB > WTEST C3   ← Minitab command for Wilcoxon signed-ranks test
```

TEST OF MEDIAN = 0.000000 VERSUS MEDIAN N.E. 0.000000

	N	N FOR TEST	WILCOXON STATISTIC	↓ P-VALUE	ESTIMATED MEDIAN
C3	13	12	11.0	0.031	-5.500

Because *P*-value is less than significance level of 0.05, reject the null hypothesis.

In the example given above, the unsigned ranks of 1 through 12 have a total of 78. If the two sets of data have no significant differences, each of the two signed-rank totals should be in the neighborhood of $78 \div 2$, or 39. However, for the given sample data we got 11 for one total and 67 for the other; this 11-67 split was a significant departure from the 39-39 split expected with a true null hypothesis. The table of critical values shows that at the 0.05 level of significance with 12 pairs of data, a 14-64 split represents a significant departure from the null hypothesis, and any split farther apart (such as 13-65 or 12-66) will also represent a significant departure from the null hypothesis. Conversely, splits like 15-63, 16-62, or 38-40 do not represent significant departures away from a 39-39 split, and they would not be a basis for rejecting the null hypothesis. The Wilcoxon signed-ranks test is based on the lower rank total, so that instead of analyzing both numbers that constitute the split, it is necessary to analyze only the lower number.

The sum of all the ranks $1 + 2 + 3 + \cdots + n$ is equal to $n(n + 1)/2$. If this is a rank sum to be divided equally between two categories (positive and negative), each of the two totals should be near $n(n + 1)/4$, which is $n(n + 1)/2$ after it is halved. Recognition of this principle helps us understand the test statistic given in this section. The denominator in that formula represents a standard deviation of T and is based on the principle that

$$1^2 + 2^2 + 3^2 + \cdots + n^2 = n(n + 1)(2n + 1)/6.$$

If we were to apply the ordinary sign test (Section 15.2) to the example given in this section, we would fail to reject the null hypothesis of no change in before and after scores. This is not the same conclusion reached through the Wilcoxon signed-ranks test, which is more sensitive to the magnitudes of the differences and is therefore more likely to be correct.

The Wilcoxon signed-ranks test can be used for paired data only, but the next section involves a rank-sum test that can be applied to two sets of data that are not paired.

15.3 EXERCISES   BASIC CONCEPTS

In Exercises 1–4, first arrange the given data in order of lowest to highest and then find the rank of each entry.

1. 5, 8, 12, 15, 10
2. 6, 8, 8, 9, 12, 20
3. 6, 8, 8, 8, 9, 12, 20
4. 36, 27, 27, 27, 41, 39, 58, 63, 63

In Exercises 5 and 6, use the given before and after test scores in the Wilcoxon signed-ranks test procedure to do the following:

a. Find the differences d.
b. Rank the differences while ignoring their signs.
c. Find the signed ranks.
d. Find T.

5.

Before	103	98	112	94	118	99	90	101
After	100	105	114	98	119	99	100	116

6.

Before	52	49	37	45	50	48	39	49	55	42	40
After	44	46	40	35	41	43	41	34	35	35	40

In Exercises 7–10, assume a 0.05 level of significance in a two-tailed hypothesis test. Use the given statistics to find the critical score from Table A.8, then form a conclusion about the null hypothesis H_0.

7. a. $T = 24, n = 15$
   b. $T = 25, n = 15$

8. a. $T = 26, n = 15$
   b. $T = 81, n = 24$
9. a. $T = 25, n = 17$
   b. $T = 8, n = 10$
10. a. $T = 5, n = 10$
    b. $T = 15, n = 12$

In Exercises 11–18, use the Wilcoxon signed-ranks test.

11. The Allen Tax Preparation Company wants to test the claim that two different tests of tax knowledge produce the same results. Both tests are given to a sample of 9 randomly selected employees, with the results given below. At the 0.05 level of significance, test the claim that both tests produce the same results.

Test A	100	111	93	92	99	85	117	110	98
Test B	106	112	95	90	107	100	126	105	110

12. The Kansas Food Supply Company tests a new pig-feed enzyme that is intended to increase weight. Thirteen pairs of pigs (each pair from the same litter) are selected, and in each pair one pig is given the regular feed and the other pig is given the feed with the new enzyme. Each pig is weighed, and the results are listed below. At the 0.05 level of significance, test the claim that the enzyme has no effect on weight.

Pair	1	2	3	4	5	6	7	8	9	10	11	12	13
With enzyme	99.6	92.8	90.2	101.6	109.3	97.4	104.0	89.4	107.7	95.1	87.4	102.9	96.8
Without enzyme	90.2	86.4	91.3	96.2	92.5	93.5	92.5	89.0	100.3	90.8	82.6	94.7	88.0

13. The Riverside Building Supply Company manufactures paint and wants to determine whether a new additive helps make the paint last longer. Fourteen homes are randomly selected from different regions, and half of each home is painted with the standard paint while the other half is painted with the mixture containing the new additive. At the end of two years, each half of each home is rated from 1 (extremely bad) to 50 (extremely good). Test the claim that there is no difference between the two types of paint.

Home	1	2	3	4	5	6	7	8	9	10	11	12	13	14
Additive	36	38	44	31	34	40	42	39	43	31	33	41	40	26
No additive	42	39	47	39	44	38	44	40	48	42	39	47	45	39

14. To test the effect of smoking on pulse rate, a researcher compiled data consisting of pulse rate before and after smoking. The results are given below. At the 0.05 level of significance, test the claim that smoking does not affect pulse rate.

Before smoking	68	72	69	70	70	74	66	71
After smoking	69	76	68	73	72	76	66	71

15. When the A. J. Collins Investment Company hires new employees, it gives a test for anxiety about mathematics before and after an intensive program in which required mathematical skills are identified along with the company's hiring and firing policies. Sample results are given below. Test the claim that the program has no effect on the anxiety level.

Subject	1	2	3	4	5	6	7	8	9	10	11	12	13
Before program	104	97	60	88	39	82	91	87	41	43	82	58	67
After program	83	64	58	72	40	70	87	79	25	43	64	40	52

16. Two types of cooling systems are being tested in preparation for the construction of a nuclear power plant. Eight different standard experimental situations yield the temperature in degrees Fahrenheit of water expelled by each of the cooling systems, and the results follow. At the 0.05 level of significance, test the claim that both cooling systems produce the same results.

Type A	72	78	81	77	84	76	79	74
Type B	75	71	71	72	73	74	70	74

17. A study of assessed values of business properties in Indiana involves evaluations by an independent firm. Listed below are the assessed values (in thousands of dollars) for 12 properties. At the 0.05 level of significance, test the claim that there is no difference between the assessed values as determined by the county assessor and the independent firm.

Property	A	B	C	D	E	F	G	H	I	J	K	L
County assessor	106	152	88	100	257	300	144	275	225	170	350	280
Independent firm	124	175	95	90	299	355	195	300	245	210	400	325

18. Randomly selected executives are surveyed in an attempt to measure their attitudes toward two different minority groups, and the sample results follow. At the 0.05 level of significance, test the claim that there is no difference in their attitudes toward the two groups.

Group A	420	490	380	570	630	710	425	576	550	610	580	575
Group B	520	510	450	530	600	705	415	600	625	730	500	530

15.3 EXERCISES   BEYOND THE BASICS

19. a.   Two checkout systems are being tested at a department store. One system uses an optical scanner to record prices, while the other system has prices manually entered by the clerk. Randomly selected customers are paid to use both checkout systems, and their processing times are recorded. Listed here are the differences (in seconds) obtained when the times for

the scanner system are subtracted from the corresponding times for the manual system. At the 0.01 significance level, use the Wilcoxon signed-ranks test to test the claim that both systems require the same times.

30	33	27	0	-5	-3	18	10	16	12	3	52	14	-8
-27	0	42	26	19	35	72	14	5	1	12	-6	23	52
47	33	19	16	0	-12	44	40	29	59	38			

   b. Part *a* is a two-tailed test. Now test the claim that the scanner times are lower. That is, the distribution of scanner times is shifted to the left of the distribution of times for the manual system. Use the same 0.01 significance level.

20. a. With $n = 8$ pairs of data, find the lowest and highest possible values of T.
     b. With $n = 10$ pairs of data, find the lowest and highest possible values of T.
     c. With $n = 50$ pairs of data, find the lowest and highest possible values of T.

21. Use the z test statistic given in this section to find the critical value of T for a two-tailed hypothesis test with a significance level of 0.05. Assume that there are $n = 100$ pairs of data with no differences of zero.

22. The Wilcoxon signed-ranks test can be used to test the claim that a sample comes from a population with a specified median. This use of the Wilcoxon signed-ranks test requires that the population distribution be approximately symmetric. That is, when the population distribution is separated in the middle, the left half approximates a mirror image of the right half. The procedure for testing hypotheses is the same as the one described in this section, except that the differences (step 1) are obtained by subtracting the value of the hypothesized median from each score. At the 0.05 level of significance, test the claim that the values below are drawn from a population with a median of 10,000 lb. The scores are the weights (in pounds) of 50 different loads handled by a moving company in Dutchess County, New York.

8,090	9,110	17,810	12,350	3,670
14,800	10,100	26,580	17,330	15,970
8,800	11,860	7,770	8,450	12,430
10,780	13,260	5,030	10,220	11,430
13,490	11,600	13,520	7,470	4,510
14,310	14,760	13,410	4,480	7,450
7,540	3,250	10,630	6,400	10,330
8,160	10,510	9,310	12,700	9,900
7,200	6,170	12,010	16,200	11,450
8,770	9,140	6,820	7,280	6,390

15.4 WILCOXON RANK-SUM TEST FOR TWO INDEPENDENT SAMPLES

While Section 15.3 used ranks to analyze dependent or paired data, this section introduces the **Wilcoxon rank-sum test,** which can be applied to situations involving two samples that are *independent* and not paired. This test is equivalent to the **Mann-Whitney U test** found in some other books (see Exercise 14). The basis for the procedure used in the Wilcoxon rank-sum test is the principle that if two samples are drawn from identical populations and the individual scores are all *ranked* as one combined collection of values, then the high and low ranks should be dispersed evenly between the two samples. If we find that the low ranks are found predominantly in one sample and the high ranks are found predominantly in the other sample, we suspect that the two populations are not identical.

The procedure for using the Wilcoxon rank-sum test begins by ranking all the sample data combined. We then find the sum of the ranks for one of the samples. In the following notation, either sample can be chosen as the "first" sample.

Notation

n_1	Size of the first sample
n_2	Size of the second sample
R_1	Sum of ranks for the first sample
R_2	Sum of ranks for the second sample
R	Same as R_1 (sum of ranks for the sample considered to be first)
μ_R	Mean of the sample R values
σ_R	Standard deviation of the sample R values

When testing the null hypothesis of identical populations and with both sample sizes greater than 10, the sampling distribution of R is approximately normal with mean μ_R, standard deviation σ_R, and the test statistic as given below.

TEST STATISTIC

$$z = \frac{R - \mu_R}{\sigma_R}$$

where

$$\mu_R = \frac{n_1(n_1 + n_2 + 1)}{2}$$

$$\sigma_R = \sqrt{\frac{n_1 n_2(n_1 + n_2 + 1)}{12}}$$

The expression for μ_R is a variation of a result of mathematical induction, which states that the sum of the first n positive integers is given by $1 + 2 + 3 + \cdots + n = n(n + 1)/2$, and the expression for σ_R is a variation of a result that states that the integers $1, 2, 3, \ldots, n$ have standard deviation $\sqrt{(n^2 - 1)/12}$.

Because the test statistic is based on the normal distribution, critical values can be found in Table A.2. Note that our procedure requires that each of the two samples have more than 10 scores. That requirement is included among the other assumptions necessary for the Wilcoxon rank-sum test.

ASSUMPTIONS

1. We have two independent samples.
2. We are testing the null hypothesis that the two independent samples come from the same distribution; the alternative hypothesis is the claim that the two distributions are different in some way.

(continued)

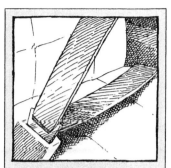

SEAT BELT USE LOWERS HOSPITAL COSTS

The Wilcoxon rank sum test can be used to compare hospital costs for drivers who wear seat belts and those who do not. An article in the *Boston Globe* noted that "if all the car crash victims treated last year at three major trauma centers in Massachusetts had worn seat belts, the hospitals could have saved 33% of the cost of treating them, according to new data . . . in favor of a new bill requiring seat belt use." No matter how compelling such statistical evidence may be, there will always be those who refuse to wear seat belts as well as those who oppose laws requiring their use. The *Boston Globe* article quoted radio talk show host Jerry Williams as saying, "I never got involved in the swapping of statistics with respect to a mandatory seat belt law. I look upon it as a police intrusion. They could come up with all the statistics they want."

3. Each of the two samples has more than 10 scores. (For cases with samples having 10 or fewer values, special tables are available in more advanced books.)
4. Unlike the corresponding hypothesis test in Section 9.3, the Wilcoxon rank-sum test does *not* require normally distributed populations.
5. Unlike the corresponding hypothesis test in Section 9.3, the Wilcoxon rank-sum test *can* be used with data at the ordinal level of measurement, such as data consisting of ranks.

In Section 15.1 we noted that the Wilcoxon rank-sum test has a 0.95 efficiency rating when compared to the parametric t test or z test. Because this test has such a high efficiency rating and involves easier calculations, it is often preferred over the parametric tests presented in Section 9.3, even when the condition of normality is satisfied.

We will illustrate the procedure used for the Wilcoxon rank-sum test with the following example.

EXAMPLE Random samples of teachers' salaries from Massachusetts and Pennsylvania are as follows. (The data are based on a survey by the National Education Association.) At the 0.05 level of significance, test the claim that the salaries of teachers are the same in both states.

MASSACHUSETTS	PENNSYLVANIA	
\$32,100 (8)	\$30,800 (1)	
36,500 (23)	36,300 (21)	
36,700 (25)	31,000 (3)	
31,400 (4)	31,900 (5.5) ←	⌐
35,200 (19)	33,200 (11)	Tie between
34,100 (16)	33,400 (13)	5 and 6
36,600 (24)	31,900 (5.5) ←	⌐
33,300 (12)	32,800 (10)	
42,600 (29)	36,000 (20)	
36,400 (22)	35,100 (18)	
38,200 (28)	37,100 (26)	
	37,600 (27)	
	30,900 (2)	
	33,800 (14)	
	32,000 (7)	
	34,400 (17)	
	32,600 (9)	
	33,900 (15)	

$$n_1 = 11 \qquad n_2 = 18$$
$$R_1 = 210 \qquad R_2 = 225$$

SOLUTION H_0: The populations of salaries are identical.
H_1: The populations are not identical.

We may be tempted to use the Student t test to compare the means of two independent samples (as in Section 9.3), but there may be a question about the normality of the distribution of teachers' salaries. We therefore use the Wilcoxon rank-sum test, which does not require normal distributions.

We rank all 29 salaries, beginning with a rank of 1 (assigned to the lowest salary of $30,800). The ranks corresponding to the various salaries are shown in parentheses in the above table. Note that the tie between the fifth and sixth scores results in assigning the rank of 5.5 to each of those two salaries. We denote by R the sum of the ranks for the sample we choose as "first." If we choose the Massachusetts salaries, we get

$$R = 8 + 23 + 25 + 4 + 19 + 16 + 24 + 12 + 29 + 22 + 28$$
$$= 210$$

Because there are 11 Massachusetts salaries, we have $n_1 = 11$. Also, $n_2 = 18$ because there are 18 Pennsylvania salaries. We can now determine the values of μ_R, σ_R, and z.

$$\mu_R = \frac{n_1(n_1 + n_2 + 1)}{2} = \frac{11(11 + 18 + 1)}{2} = 165.00$$

$$\sigma_R = \sqrt{\frac{n_1 n_2(n_1 + n_2 + 1)}{12}}$$

$$= \sqrt{\frac{(11)(18)(11 + 18 + 1)}{12}} = 22.25$$

$$z = \frac{R - \mu_R}{\sigma_R} = \frac{210 - 165.00}{22.25} = 2.02$$

A large positive value of z would indicate that the higher ranks are disproportionately found in the Massachusetts salaries, whereas a large negative value of z would indicate that Massachusetts has a disproportionate share of lower ranks. In either case, we would have strong evidence against the claim that the Massachusetts and Pennsylvania salaries are identical. The test is therefore two-tailed.

The significance of the test statistic z can now be treated in the same manner as in previous chapters. We are now testing (with $\alpha = 0.05$) the hypothesis that the two populations are the same, so we have a two-tailed test with critical z values of 1.96 and -1.96. The test statistic of $z = 2.02$ falls within the critical region and we therefore reject the null hypothesis that the salaries are the same in both states. Massachusetts appears to have significantly higher teacher salaries than Pennsylvania.

We can verify that if we interchange the two sets of salaries and consider Pennsylvania to be first, we will now find that $R = 225$, $\mu_R = 270.0$, $\sigma_R = 22.25$, and $z = -2.02$, so that the same conclusion will be reached.

Shown on the following page is an annotated Minitab display for the preceding example. Note the use of the command MANN-WHITNEY for this Wilcoxon rank-sum test for two independent samples, which is equivalent to the Mann-Whitney test.

GENDER GAP IN DRUG TESTING

A study of the relationships between heart attacks and doses of aspirin involved 22,000 male physicians. This study, like many others, excluded women. The General Accounting Office recently criticized the National Institutes of Health for not including both sexes in many studies, because results of medical tests on males do not necessarily apply to females. For example, women's hearts are different from men's in many important ways. When forming conclusions based on sample results, we should be wary of an inference that extends to a population larger than the one from which the sample was drawn.

```
MTB > SET C1
DATA> 32100 36500 36700 31400 35200 34100
DATA> 36600 33300 42600 36400 38200
DATA> SET C2
DATA> 30800 36300 31000 31900 33200 33400          Data entered
DATA> 31900 32800 36000 35100 37100 37600          here
DATA> 30900 33800 32000 34400 32600 33900
DATA> ENDOFDATA
MTB > MANN-WHITNEY C1 C2    ← Minitab command for the Mann-Whitney
                              test, which is equivalent to the Wilcoxon
Mann-Whitney Confidence Interval and Test        rank-sum test

C1    N =  11    Median =          36400              With significance
C2    N =  18    Median =          33300              level of 0.05,
Point estimate for ETA1-ETA2 is    2150              reject the
95.5 pct c.i. for ETA1-ETA2 is (100,4300)           null hypothesis.
W = 210.0  ← Test Statistic
Test of ETA1 = ETA2 vs. ETA1 n.e. ETA2 is significant at 0.0455 ←┘
The test is significant at 0.0455 (adjusted for ties)
```

Like the Wilcoxon signed-ranks test, the rank-sum test also considers the relative magnitudes of the sample data, whereas the sign test does not. In the sign test, a weight loss of 1 lb or 50 lb receives the same sign, so the actual magnitude of the loss is ignored. While rank-sum tests do not directly involve quantitative differences between data from two samples, changes in magnitude do cause changes in rank, and these in turn affect the value of the test statistic. For example, if we change the Pennsylvania salary of $30,800 to $40,800, then the value of the rank-sum R will change, and the value of the z test statistic will also change.

15.4 EXERCISES   BASIC CONCEPTS

In Exercises 1–12, use the Wilcoxon rank-sum test.

1. Random samples of teachers' salaries (in hundreds of dollars) from California and Maryland are as follows. (The data are based on a survey by the National Education Association.) At the 0.05 significance level, test the claim that salaries of teachers are the same in both states.

California	271	306	323	336	364	390	391	405	408	409	417	464
Maryland	287	312	323	326	334	339	341	344	387	396	403	405
	439	443	459	478								

2. The values listed in the table below are selling prices (in thousands of dollars) of randomly selected homes sold in Dutchess County, New York. Test the claim that the selling prices are the same in homes with seven rooms as they are in homes with eight rooms. Use a 0.05 significance level.

Seven rooms	154	142	119	160	136	122	114	135	127	138	134
Eight rooms	215	165	127	170	153	172	164	205	190	135	145
	197	124	212								

3. Listed below are the starting salaries (in thousands of dollars) of 14 accounting majors and 10 marketing majors randomly selected from the recent graduates of a midwestern business school. At the 0.05 level of significance, test the claim that the populations of salaries are identical.

Accounting	26.4	25.8	27.2	26.9	23.0	28.5	27.7			
	24.5	27.4	28.0	28.3	28.0	26.2	29.0			
Marketing	23.5	22.7	22.0	23.0	25.8	23.0	24.1	23.7	25.4	24.4

4. The shipping manager for the Dayton Machine Company must send many shipments from the central warehouse to the city in which the assembly takes place, and she wants to determine the faster of two railroad routes. A search of past records provides the following data. (The shipment times are in hours.) At the 0.05 level of significance, determine whether the difference between the routes is significant.

Route A	98	102	83	117	128	92	112	108	108	100	93	72	95	91
Route B	96	132	121	87	106	102	116	95	99	76	97	104	115	114

5. Alkaline flashlight batteries are manufactured at the Telektronic Company by two different production methods. The lives (in hours) are found for a random sample of batteries from each production method, and the results are given below. At the 0.05 level of significance, test the claim that there is no difference between the lives of batteries from each method. Assume that both processes are stable.

Method A	3.20	3.51	3.84	3.11	3.68	3.44	3.57	3.69	3.72	3.75	
Method B	4.11	4.25	4.06	3.96	4.22	3.90	4.07	4.13	3.87	3.92	4.06	4.15

6. Two coffee-vending machines are studied to determine whether they distribute the same amounts. Samples are obtained, and the contents (in liters) are as follows. At the 0.05 level of significance, test the claim that the machines distribute the same amount.

Machine A	0.210	0.213	0.206	0.195	0.180	0.250	0.212	0.217
	0.213	0.222	0.201	0.205	0.209			
Machine B	0.229	0.224	0.221	0.247	0.270	0.233	0.237	0.235
	0.238	0.200	0.198	0.216	0.241	0.273	0.205	

7. An investor is considering two possible locations for a computer software store. Given below are measurements of pedestrian traffic at each site for randomly selected time periods. Use a 0.05 significance level to test the claim that both sites have identical populations of pedestrian traffic.

Site 1	56	72	79	83	66	70	59	90	87	64	75
Site 2	46	61	53	60	41	49	52	56	63	36	

8. In a study of crop yields, two different fertilizer treatments are tested on parcels with the same area and soil conditions. Listed below are the yields (in bushels of corn) for sample plots. Use a 0.05 significance level and determine

whether there is a difference between the treatments.

Treatment A	132	137	129	142	160	139	143	147	145	140	131	136
Treatment B	162	180	149	157	159	159	152	167	163	165	180	156
	158	151										

9. A consumer investigator obtains prices from mail order companies and computer stores. Listed below are the prices (in dollars) quoted for boxes of 10 floppy disks from various manufacturers. Use a 0.05 level of significance to test the claim that there is no difference between mail order and store prices.

Mail order	23.00	26.00	27.99	31.50	32.75	27.00
	27.98	24.50	24.75	28.15	29.99	29.99
Computer store	30.99	33.98	37.75	38.99	35.79	33.99
	34.79	32.99	29.99	33.00	32.00	

10. A quality control manager examines samples of cola cans, with 3 cans in each sample. The contents are measured in ounces. Given below are the means and standard deviations for 10 such samples taken before control charts were used and for 10 samples taken after control charts were used.
   a. At the 0.05 level of significance, test the claim that the populations of means are identical.
   b. At the 0.05 level of significance, test the claim that the populations of standard deviations are identical.
   c. Write a brief description of what has happened, if anything, after the introduction of control charts.

BEFORE CONTROL CHARTS

Sample	1	2	3	4	5	6	7	8	9	10
Mean	16.20	15.67	16.57	15.69	16.42	16.81	15.28	15.54	16.10	16.45
Standard deviation	1.02	1.13	1.35	1.24	1.49	1.06	1.20	1.37	1.04	1.16

AFTER CONTROL CHARTS

Sample	1	2	3	4	5	6	7	8	9	10
Mean	16.13	15.92	15.94	16.08	16.16	16.00	15.89	16.07	16.04	16.11
Standard deviation	0.46	0.52	0.63	0.59	0.64	0.57	0.49	0.62	0.55	0.58

11. The Kansas Food Products Company produces soybeans for farmers. In an attempt to improve germination rates, the quality control manager suggests increasing drying temperature while shortening the drying time. This change is tested in an experiment involving 12 random samples of 100 soybeans each from the old drying method and 12 random samples of 100 soybeans each from the new, faster drying method. Given on the next page are the numbers of seeds that germinated in each sample. Test the claim that the new drying technique produces the same population of germination rates as the old technique. Use a 0.05 level of significance.

Sample	1	2	3	4	5	6	7	8	9	10	11	12
Old method	97	94	96	98	100	95	93	94	97	100	96	95
New method	89	93	88	90	95	91	92	88	90	88	89	95

12. The arrangement of test items was studied for its effect on anxiety. Sample results are given below. At the 0.05 level of significance, test the claim that the two samples come from populations with the same scores. (The data are based on "Item Arrangement, Cognitive Entry Characteristics, Sex and Test Anxiety as Predictors of Achievement Examination Performance," by Klimko, *Journal of Experimental Education,* Vol. 52, No. 4.)

EASY TO DIFFICULT					DIFFICULT TO EASY			
24.64	39.29	16.32	32.83		33.62	34.02	26.63	30.26
28.02	33.31	20.60	21.13		35.91	26.68	29.49	35.32
26.69	28.90	26.43	24.23		27.24	32.34	29.34	33.53
7.10	32.86	21.06	28.89		27.62	42.91	30.20	32.54
28.71	31.73	30.02	21.96					
25.49	38.81	27.85	30.29					
30.72								

15.4 EXERCISES   BEYOND THE BASICS

13. a. The *ranks* for group I are 1, 2, . . . , 15 and the *ranks* for group II are 16, 17, . . . , 30. At the 0.05 level of significance, use the Wilcoxon rank-sum test to test the claim that both groups come from the same population.
   b. The *ranks* for group I are 1, 3, 5, 7, . . . , 29 and the *ranks* for group II are 2, 4, 6, . . . , 30. At the 0.05 level of significance, use the Wilcoxon rank-sum test to test the claim that both groups come from the same population.
   c. Compare parts *a* and *b*.
   d. What changes occur when the rankings of the two groups in part *a* are interchanged?
   e. Use the two groups in part *a* and interchange the ranks of 1 and 30 and then note the changes that occur.
14. The Mann-Whitney U test is equivalent to the Wilcoxon rank-sum test for independent samples in the sense that they both apply to the same situations and they always lead to the same conclusions. In the Mann-Whitney U test we calculate

$$z = \frac{U - \dfrac{n_1 n_2}{2}}{\sqrt{\dfrac{n_1 n_2 (n_1 + n_2 + 1)}{12}}}$$

where

$$U = n_1 n_2 + \frac{n_1 (n_1 + 1)}{2} - R$$

(continued)

Show that if the expression for U is substituted into the preceding expression for z, we get the same test statistic (with opposite sign) used in the Wilcoxon rank-sum test for two independent samples.

15. Assume that we have two treatments (A and B) that produce measurable results, and we have only two observations for treatment A and two observations for treatment B. We cannot use the test statistic given in this section because both sample sizes do not exceed 10.

   a. Complete the accompanying table by listing the other five rows corresponding to the other five cases, and enter the corresponding rank sums for treatment A.

| | RANK | | | (RANK SUM FOR |
1	2	3	4	TREATMENT A)
A	A	B	B	3

   b. List the possible values of R along with their corresponding probabilities. (Assume that the rows of the table from part a are equally likely.)
   c. Is it possible, at the 0.10 significance level, to reject the null hypothesis that there is no difference between treatments A and B? Explain.

16. Do Exercise 15 for the case involving a sample of size 3 for treatment A and a sample of size 3 for treatment B.

15.5 KRUSKAL-WALLIS TEST

In Chapter 11 we used one-way analysis of variance to test hypotheses that differences among several samples are due to chance. That particular F test requires that all the involved populations possess normal distributions with variances that are approximately equal. In this section we introduce the **Kruskal-Wallis test** (also called the H test) as a nonparametric alternative that does not require normal distributions. Assumptions for the Kruskal-Wallis test are as follows:

ASSUMPTIONS

1. We have at least three samples, all of which are random.
2. We want to test the null hypothesis that the samples come from the same or identical populations.
3. Each sample has at least five observations. (For cases involving samples with fewer than five observations, refer to more advanced books for special tables of critical values.)
4. Unlike the corresponding one-way analysis-of-variance method used in Chapter 11, the Kruskal-Wallis test does *not* require normally distributed populations. It does require equal variances, so this test shouldn't be used if the different samples have variances that are very far apart.

5. Unlike the corresponding one-way analysis-of-variance method in Chapter 11, the Kruskal-Wallis test can be used with data at the ordinal level of measurement, such as data consisting of ranks.

In applying the Kruskal-Wallis test, we compute the test statistic H, **which has a distribution that can be approximated by the chi-square distribution as long as each sample has at least five observations.** When we use the chi-square distribution in this context, the number of degrees of freedom is $k - 1$, where k is the number of samples. (For a quick review of the key features of the chi-square distribution, see Section 6.4.)

TEST STATISTIC

$$H = \frac{12}{N(N + 1)}\left(\frac{R_1^2}{n_1} + \frac{R_2^2}{n_2} + \cdots + \frac{R_k^2}{n_k}\right) - 3(N + 1)$$

where degrees of freedom = $k - 1$

and N = total number of observations in all samples combined
 R_1 = sum of ranks for the first sample
 R_2 = sum of ranks for the second sample
 R_k = sum of ranks for the kth sample
 k = the number of samples

In using the Kruskal-Wallis test, we replace the original scores by their corresponding ranks. We then proceed to calculate the test statistic H, which is basically a measure of the variance of the rank sums $R_1, R_2, \ldots, R_k$. If the ranks are distributed evenly among the sample groups, then H should be a relatively small number. If the samples are very different, then the ranks will be excessively low in some groups and high in others, with the net effect that H will be large. Consequently, only large values of H lead to rejection of the null hypothesis that the samples come from identical populations. **The Kruskal-Wallis test is therefore a right-tailed test.**

Begin by considering all observations together, and then assign a rank to each one. We rank from lowest to highest, and we also treat ties as we did in the previous sections of this chapter—the mean value of the ranks is assigned to each of the tied observations. Then take each individual sample and find the sum of the ranks and the corresponding sample size. We will illustrate the Kruskal-Wallis test in the following example. The Kruskal-Wallis test is especially appropriate here because there may be some doubt that home selling prices are normally distributed. We will see similarities between the Kruskal-Wallis test and Wilcoxon's rank-sum test because both are based on rank sums.

EXAMPLE   A real estate investor randomly selects homes recently sold in three different zones of the same county. The selling prices (based on data from homes recently sold in Dutchess County, New York) are listed here. At the 0.05 significance level, test the claim that selling prices are the same in all three zones.

SELLING PRICES (DOLLARS)

ZONE 1	ZONE 4	ZONE 7
$147,000 (15.5)	$160,000 (17.5)	$215,000 (24)
160,000 (17.5)	140,000 (14)	127,000 (8)
128,000 (9)	173,000 (21)	98,000 (2)
162,000 (19)	113,000 (4)	147,000 (15.5)
135,000 (12)	85,000 (1)	184,000 (23)
132,000 (10)	120,000 (7)	109,000 (3)
181,000 (22)	285,000 (25)	169,000 (20)
138,000 (13)	117,000 (5)	
	133,000 (11)	
	119,000 (6)	

$$n_1 = 8 \qquad n_2 = 10 \qquad n_3 = 7$$
$$R_1 = 118 \qquad R_2 = 111.5 \qquad R_3 = 95.5$$

SOLUTION

H_0: The populations are identical.

H_1: The populations are not identical.

STEP 1 Rank the combined samples from lowest to highest. Begin with the lowest observation of $85,000, which is assigned a rank of 1. Ranks are shown in parentheses with the original data in the preceding list.

STEP 2 For each individual sample, find the number of observations and the sum of the ranks. The first sample (zone 1) has eight observations, so $n_1 = 8$. Also, $R_1 = 15.5 + 17.5 + \ldots + 13 = 118$. The values of n_2, R_2, n_3, and R_3 are shown above. Because the total number of observations is 25, we have $N = 25$.

STEP 3 Compute the value of the test statistic H.

$$H = \frac{12}{N(N+1)}\left(\frac{R_1^2}{n_1} + \frac{R_2^2}{n_2} + \frac{R_3^2}{n_3}\right) - 3(N+1)$$

$$= \frac{12}{25(26)}\left(\frac{118^2}{8} + \frac{111.5^2}{10} + \frac{95.5^2}{7}\right) - 3(26)$$

$$= \frac{12}{650}(1740.5 + 1243.225 + 1302.893) - 78$$

$$= 1.138$$

STEP 4 Because each sample has at least five observations, the distribution of H is approximately a chi-square distribution with $k - 1$ degrees of freedom. The number of samples is $k = 3$, so we get $3 - 1$, or 2, degrees of freedom. Refer to Table A.4 to find the critical value of 5.991, which corresponds to 2 degrees of freedom and a significance level of $\alpha = 0.05$. (This use of the chi-square distribution is always right-tailed because only large values of H reflect disparity in the distribution of ranks among the samples.)

STEP 5 The test statistic $H = 1.138$ is less than the critical value of 5.991, so we fail to reject the null hypothesis of identical populations. We reject the null hypothesis of identical populations only when H exceeds the critical value. The three zones appear to have selling prices that are not significantly different.

Shown below is the Minitab display for the preceding example. When using the KRUSKAL-WALLIS C4 C5 command, all the sample data must be stored in column C4, while column C5 consists of subscripts or numbers that identify the different samples. After entering the three sets of sample scores in columns C1, C2, and C3, we proceed to STACK the 25 scores into one big column C4. The first 8 scores are from column C1, the second 10 are from column C2, and the last 7 are from column C3. Column C5 consists of these 25 sample identifiers:

$$1\ 1\ 1\ 1\ 1\ 1\ 1\ 1\ 2\ 2\ 2\ 2\ 2\ 2\ 2\ 2\ 2\ 2\ 3\ 3\ 3\ 3\ 3\ 3\ 3$$

The Minitab display includes the test statistic of $H = 1.14$ and the P-value of 0.566. Because the P-value is not less than the significance level of 0.05, we fail to reject the null hypothesis.

```
MTB > SET C1
DATA> 147000 160000 128000 162000 135000
DATA> 132000 181000 138000
DATA> SET C2
DATA> 160000 140000 173000 113000  85000      Data entered
DATA> 120000 285000 117000 133000 119000      here
DATA> SET C3
DATA> 215000 127000  98000 147000 184000
DATA> 109000 169000
DATA> ENDOFDATA
MTB > STACK C1 C2 C3 C4;
SUBC> SUBSCRIPTS C5.
MTB > KRUSKAL-WALLIS C4 C5
```

LEVEL	NOBS	MEDIAN	AVE. RANK	Z VALUE
1	8	142500	14.8	0.82
2	10	126500	11.1	-1.03
3	7	147000	13.6	0.27
OVERALL	25		13.0	

⌐ Test statistic
H = 1.14 d.f. = 2 p = 0.566
H = 1.14 d.f. = 2 p = 0.566 (adj. for ties)

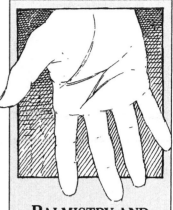

PALMISTRY AND INSURANCE COMPANIES

Rates for life insurance policies are based on such factors as age, health, and smoking habits. Palm readers claim that longevity can be predicted by the length of a person's palm "life line." If that claim were true, life insurance companies could increase profits through better predictions. In a letter published in the *Journal of the American Medical Association*, authors M. E. Wilson and L. E. Mather refuted that claim with a study of cadavers. Ages at death were recorded along with the lengths of palm life lines. The authors concluded that there is no significant correlation between age at death and length of palm life line. Palmistry lost, hands down.

The test statistic H, as presented earlier, is the rank version of the test statistic F used in the analysis of variance discussed in Chapter 11. When dealing with ranks R instead of raw scores x, many components are predetermined. For example, the sum of all ranks can be expressed as $N(N + 1)/2$, where N is the total number of scores in all samples combined. The expression

$$H = \frac{12}{N(N + 1)} \Sigma n_i (\overline{R}_i - \overline{\overline{R}})^2$$

where

$$\overline{R}_i = \frac{R_i}{n_i}$$

and

$$\overline{\overline{R}} = \frac{\Sigma R_i}{\Sigma n_i}$$

combines weighted variances of ranks in a test statistic that is algebraically equivalent to the H test statistic, which is easier to work with.

In comparing the procedures of the parametric F test for analysis of variance and the nonparametric Kruskal-Wallis test, we see that the Kruskal-Wallis test is much simpler to apply. We need not compute the sample variances and sample means. We do not require normal population distributions. Life becomes so much easier. However, the Kruskal-Wallis test is not as efficient as the F test, and it may require more dramatic differences for the null hypothesis to be rejected.

15.5 EXERCISES BASIC CONCEPTS

In Exercises 1–10, use the Kruskal-Wallis test.

1. An experiment conducted by the Iowa Food Cooperative involves raising samples of corn under identical conditions except for the type of fertilizer used. Yields are obtained for 3 different fertilizers, and those values are ranked with the results shown here.
   a. Find the value of the test statistic H.
   b. Does there seem to be a difference in yields? Assume a 0.05 significance level.

TREATMENT		
A	**B**	**C**
1	2	3
6	4	5
7	8	9
12	11	10
14	15	13

2. Do Exercise 1 after replacing the given ranks with those listed below.

TREATMENT		
A	**B**	**C**
1	6	11
2	7	12
3	8	13
4	9	14
5	10	15

3. A plant manager for the Washington Candy Company examines 3 lines of machines filling bags of Halloween candy that are labeled 32 oz. She randomly selects bags from each line, and the weights are listed below. At the 0.05 level of significance, test the claim that the samples come from identical populations.

Line 1	30.8	31.1	30.9	31.0	30.4	31.3	30.2
Line 2	31.7	31.6	32.4	31.9	32.0	31.5	31.7
Line 3	32.4	31.7	32.0	31.6	32.5	32.1	32.4

4. Three different transmission types are installed on different cars, all having 6 cylinders and an engine size of 3.0 liters. The fuel consumption (in mi/gal) is found for highway conditions with the results given here (based on data from the Environmental Protection Agency). The letters *A, M, L* represent automatic, manual, and lockup torque converter, respectively.
   a. At the 0.05 significance level, test the claim that the fuel consumption values are the same for the three transmission types.
   b. Which transmission seems to be different from the others? How?

A	M	L
23.2	27.0	24.1
23.2	29.8	26.1
20.7	25.7	24.8
21.6	23.5	25.6
22.9	24.3	26.5

5. A store owner records the gross receipts for days randomly selected from periods during which she used only newspaper advertising, only radio advertising, or no advertising. The results are listed here. At the 0.05 level of significance, test the claim that the receipts are the same, regardless of advertising.

NEWSPAPER	RADIO	NONE
845	811	612
907	782	574
639	749	539
883	863	641
806	872	666

6. Starting salaries are randomly selected from the population of workers at the A. J. Collins Investment Company who recently earned bachelor's degrees in accounting. The results are listed below (in dollars) according to geographic location of the company's offices.
   a. At the 0.05 significance level, test the claim that the 4 locations have the same distribution of starting salaries.
   b. Do any particular locations seem to have lower or higher values?

West	30,700	31,200	33,000	32,900	30,200	31,700
Central	26,500	27,700	29,800	30,500	28,400	29,900
Southeast	29,500	30,400	28,450	27,500	29,100	28,500
Northeast	34,100	33,100	30,100	30,800	32,400	31,300

7. The accompanying data represent 25 different homes sold in Dutchess County, New York. The zones (1, 4, 7) correspond to different geographic regions of the county. LA values are living areas in hundreds of square feet, Acres values are lot sizes in acres, and Taxes values are the annual tax bills in thousands of dollars. At the 0.05 significance level, test the claim that living areas are the same in all three zones.

8. Use the data from Exercise 7. At the 0.05 level of significance, test the claim that lot sizes (as measured in acres) are the same in all three zones.

9. Use the data from Exercise 7. At the 0.05 level of significance, test the claim that taxes are the same in all three zones.

10. Refer to the data from Exercise 7 and change the zone 7 Tax values to the following: 3.0, 1.8, 1.1, 1.4, 2.3, 2.0, 2.4. Note that the mean Tax amount does not change, but these values vary more. Now repeat Exercise 9 with this modified data set and note the effect of increasing the spread of the values in one of the samples.

ZONE	LA	ACRES	TAXES
1	20	0.50	1.9
1	18	1.00	2.4
1	27	1.05	1.5
1	17	0.42	1.6
1	18	0.84	1.6
1	13	0.33	1.5
1	24	0.90	1.7
1	15	0.83	2.2
4	18	0.55	2.8
4	20	0.46	1.8
4	19	0.94	3.2
4	12	0.29	2.1
4	9	0.26	1.4
4	18	0.33	2.1
4	28	1.70	4.2
4	10	0.50	1.7
4	15	0.43	1.8
4	12	0.25	1.6
7	21	3.04	2.7
7	16	1.09	1.9
7	14	0.23	1.3
7	23	1.00	1.7
7	17	6.20	2.2
7	17	0.46	2.0
7	20	3.20	2.2

15.5 EXERCISES　BEYOND THE BASICS

11. a. Simplify the expression of the test statistic H for the special case of 8 samples, all consisting of exactly 6 observations each.

　　b. In general, how is the value of the test statistic H affected if a constant is added to (or subtracted from) each score?

　　c. In general, how is the value of the test statistic H affected if each score is multiplied (or divided) by a positive constant?

12. For three samples, each of size 5, what are the largest and smallest possible values of H?

13. In using the Kruskal-Wallis test, the following correction factor should be applied whenever there are many ties: Divide H by

$$1 - \frac{\Sigma T}{N^3 - N}$$

Here $T = t^3 - t$. For each group of tied scores, find the number of observations that are tied and represent this number by t. Then compute $t^3 - t$ to find the value of T. Repeat this procedure for all cases of ties and find the total of the T values, which is ΣT. For the example presented in this section, use this procedure to find the corrected value of H.

14. Show that for the case of two samples, the Kruskal-Wallis test is equivalent to the Wilcoxon rank-sum test. This can be done by showing that for the case of two samples, the test statistic H equals the square of the test statistic z used in the Wilcoxon rank-sum test. Also note that with one degree of freedom, the critical values of χ^2 correspond to the square of the critical z score.

15.6   RANK CORRELATION

In Chapter 12 we considered the concept of correlation, and we introduced the *linear correlation coefficient* as a measure of the strength of the association between two variables. In this section we study rank correlation, the nonparametric counterpart of that parametric measure. In Chapter 12 we computed values for the linear correlation coefficient r, but here we will be computing values for the *rank correlation coefficient*. The method presented here has the following distinct advantages over the parametric methods discussed in Chapter 12.

1. With rank correlation, we can analyze some types of data that can be ranked but not measured; yet such data could not be considered with the parametric linear correlation coefficient r of Chapter 12.

2. Rank correlation can be used to detect some relationships that are not linear. An example illustrating this will be given later in this section.

3. The computations for rank correlation are much simpler than those for the linear correlation coefficient r. This can be readily seen by comparing Formula 15.1 in this section to Formula 12.12. With many calculators you can get the value of r easily, but if you did not have a calculator or a computer, you would probably find that the rank correlation coefficient is easier to compute.

4. Rank correlation can be used when some of the more restrictive requirements of the linear correlation approach are not met. That is, the nonparametric approach can be used in a wider variety of circumstances than can the parametric method. For example, the parametric approach requires that the involved populations have normal distributions; the nonparametric approach does not require normality. We do assume that we have a random sample. If a sample is not random, it may be totally worthless.

A disadvantage of rank correlation is its efficiency rating of 0.91, as described in Section 15.1. This efficiency rating indicates that with all circumstances being equal, the nonparametric approach of rank correlation would require 100 pairs of sample data to achieve the same results as only 91 pairs of sample observations analyzed through the parametric approach, assuming the stricter requirements of the parametric approach are met.

Given a collection of sample paired data, if we want to test for a relationship between the two variables, we can use the **rank correlation coefficient,** which can be calculated by using Formula 15.1.

Formula 15.1

$$r_s = 1 - \frac{6\Sigma d^2}{n(n^2 - 1)}$$

where

r_s = rank correlation coefficient
n = number of *pairs* of data
d = difference between ranks for the
    two observations within a pair

We use the notation r_s for the *rank* correlation coefficient so that we don't confuse it with the *linear* correlation coefficient r. The subscript s is commonly used in honor of Charles Spearman (1863–1945), who originated the rank correlation approach. In fact, r_s is often called **Spearman's rank correlation coefficient**. The subscript s has nothing to do with standard deviation, and for that we should be thankful. Just as r is a sample statistic that can be considered an estimate of the population parameter ρ (the Greek letter rho), we can also consider r_s to be an estimate of the population parameter ρ_s, the rank correlation coefficient for all the population data.

Formula 15.1 is a shortcut formula for r_s, but r_s can also be found by replacing the original sample values by their corresponding ranks and then using those ranks to calculate the linear correlation coefficient r as described in Section 12.7.

When converting original sample values to ranks, ties can be handled as in the preceding sections: Find the mean of the ranks involved in the tie and then assign that mean rank to each of the tied items. Formula 15.1 yields the exact value of r_s only if there are no ties. With a relatively small number of ties, Formula 15.1 results in a good approximation of r_s. (When ties occur, we can get an exact value of r_s by ranking the data and then using Formula 12.12 for the linear correlation coefficient; after finding the value of r_s, we could then continue with the procedures of this section.) After finding the test statistic r_s, we can find the critical value by referring to Table A.9.

EXAMPLE   Consider the data in Table 15.6, which is based on results in *The Jobs Rated Almanac* (presented at the beginning of the chapter). Randomly selected jobs are ranked according to salary and stress. Does a relationship exist between salary and stress? We can't use the linear correlation coefficient r because the data consist of ranks and therefore do not satisfy the normal distribution requirement described in Chapter 12. Instead, find the value of the rank correlation coefficient and use it to test the claim that there is no relationship between salary and stress. Use a 0.05 level of significance.

SOLUTION The claim of no relationship between salary and stress can be expressed as $\rho_s = 0$, and we therefore have the null and alternative hypotheses given as $H_0: \rho_s = 0$ and $H_1: \rho_s \neq 0$. In Table 15.6 we show the calculation of the differences d and their squares d^2 that result in a value of $\Sigma d^2 = 24$. With $n = 10$ (for 10 pairs of data) and with $\Sigma d^2 = 24$, we can now find the value of the test statistic r_s.

TABLE 15.6
Jobs Ranked by Salary and Stress

JOB	SALARY RANK	STRESS RANK	DIFFERENCE d	d^2
Stockbroker	2	2	0	0
Zoologist	6	7	−1	1
Electrical engineer	3	6	−3	9
School principal	5	4	1	1
Hotel manager	7	5	2	4
Bank officer	10	8	2	4
Occupational safety inspector	9	9	0	0
Home economist	8	10	−2	4
Psychologist	4	3	1	1
Commercial airline pilot	1	1	0	0
			Total: $\Sigma d^2 = 24$	

With $n = 10$ and $\Sigma d^2 = 24$, we get

$$r_s = 1 - \frac{6\Sigma d^2}{n(n^2 - 1)}$$

$$= 1 - \frac{6(24)}{10(10^2 - 1)}$$

$$= 1 - 0.145$$

$$= 0.855$$

If we now refer to Table A.9 for the critical value, we will see that with $n = 10$ and $\alpha = 0.05$, the critical value of r_s is 0.648. Because the test statistic $r_s = 0.855$ exceeds the critical value of 0.648, we reject the null hypothesis of no correlation. There appears to be a positive correlation between salary and stress.

The hypothesis-testing procedure we use here is very similar to the one used in Chapter 12, except for the calculation of the test statistic and the table used for the critical value. See Fig. 15.4 on the following page, which summarizes this procedure.

Shown below is the Minitab display for the preceding example. The Minitab command CORRELATION will yield the rank correlation coefficient when the original data are already in the form of ranks. If the original data are not in the form of ranks, we can enter the data in columns C1 and C2, but the following two lines must be entered before the CORRELATION command.

```
RANK C1 AND PUT INTO C3
RANK C2 AND PUT INTO C4
```

FIGURE 15.4
Rank correlation Test of H_0: $\rho_s = 0$

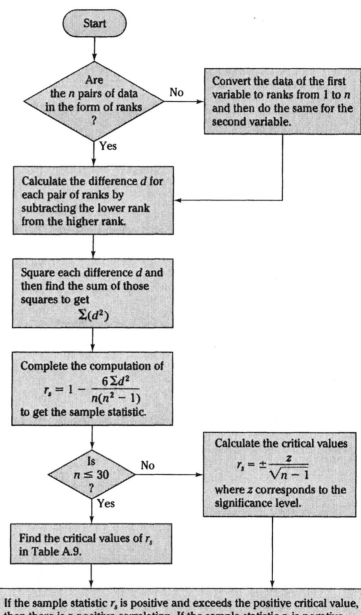

Then enter the command CORRELATION C3 C4 to obtain the rank correlation coefficient.

```
MTB > READ C1 C2
DATA> 2 2
DATA> 6 7
DATA> 3 6
DATA> 5 4
DATA> 7 5
DATA> 10 8
DATA> 9 9
DATA> 8 10
DATA> 4 3
DATA> 1 1
DATA> ENDOFDATA
DATA> ENDOFDATA      10 ROWS READ
MTB > CORRELATION C1 C2

Correlation of C1 and C2 = 0.855
```

For practical reasons, we are omitting the theoretical derivation of Formula 15.1, but we can gain some insight by considering the following three cases. If we intuitively examine Formula 15.1, we can see that strong agreement between the two sets of ranks will lead to values of d near 0, so that r_s will be close to 1 (see Case I). Conversely, when the ranks of one set tend to be at opposite extremes when compared to the ranks of the second set, then the values of d tend to be high, which will cause r_s to be near -1 (see Case II). If there is no relationship between the two sets of ranks, then the values of d will be neither high nor low and r_s will tend to be near 0 (see Case III).

Cases I and II illustrate the most extreme cases, so that the following property applies.

$$-1 \leq r_s \leq 1$$

When the number of pairs of ranks n exceeds 30, the sampling distribution of r_s is approximately a normal distribution with mean 0 and standard deviation $1/\sqrt{n-1}$. We therefore get

$$z = \frac{r_s - 0}{\frac{1}{\sqrt{n-1}}} = r_s\sqrt{n-1}$$

In a two-tailed case we would use the positive and negative z values. Solving for r_s, we then get the *critical values* by evaluating

Formula 15.2 $$r_s = \frac{\pm z}{\sqrt{n-1}} \qquad \text{(when } n > 30\text{)}$$

The value of z would correspond to the significance level.

DANGEROUS TO YOUR HEALTH

■n 1965 the first warning labels were put on cigarette packs, and in 1969 cigarette commercials were banned from television and radio. Reports of the surgeon general include many convincing statistics showing that smoking greatly increases the danger of cancer. The Tobacco Institute contests these reports. Horace Kornegay, the Tobacco Institute's chairman, says, "While many people believe a causal link between smoking and cancer is a given, scientific research has not been able to establish that link." Critics note that not a single case has shown smoking to be the cause of cancer, but the evidence clearly indicates a significant correlation.

Case I: Perfect Positive Correlation			
RANK x	**RANK** y	**DIFFERENCE** d	d^2
1	1	0	0
3	3	0	0
5	5	0	0
4	4	0	0
2	2	0	0
			$\Sigma d^2 = 0$

$$r_s = 1 - \frac{6(0)}{5(5^2 - 1)} = 1$$

Case II: Perfect Negative Correlation			
RANK x	**RANK** y	**DIFFERENCE** d	d^2
1	5	4	16
2	4	2	4
3	3	0	0
4	2	2	4
5	1	4	16
			$\Sigma d^2 = 40$

$$r_s = 1 - \frac{6(40)}{5(5^2 - 1)} = -1$$

Case III: No Correlation			
RANK x	**RANK** y	**DIFFERENCE** d	d^2
1	2	1	1
2	5	3	9
3	3	0	0
4	1	3	9
5	4	1	1
			$\Sigma d^2 = 20$

$$r_s = 1 - \frac{6(20)}{5(5^2 - 1)} = 0$$

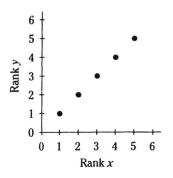

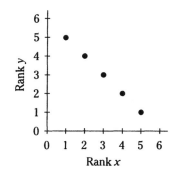

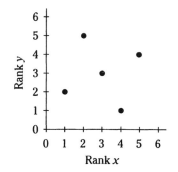

EXAMPLE Find the critical values of Spearman's rank correlation coefficient r_s when the data consist of 40 pairs of ranks. Assume a two-tailed case with a 0.05 significance level.

SOLUTION Because there are 40 pairs of data, $n = 40$. Because n exceeds 30, we use Formula 15.2 instead of Table A.9. With $\alpha = 0.05$ in two tails, we let $z = 1.96$ to get

$$r_s = \frac{\pm 1.96}{\sqrt{40 - 1}} = \pm 0.314$$

In the next example, the data are graphed in the scatter diagram shown in Fig. 15.5. The pattern is not linear, but watch what happens.

EXAMPLE Ten students study for a test; the table below lists the number of hours studied (x) and the corresponding number of correct answers (y). At the 0.05 level of significance, use Spearman's rank correlation approach to determine whether a relationship exists between hours studied and the number of correct answers.

x	5	9	17	1	2	21	3	29	7	100
y	6	16	18	1	3	21	7	20	15	22

SOLUTION   We will test the null hypothesis of no rank correlation ($\rho_s = 0$).

H_0: $\rho_s = 0$
H_1: $\rho_s \neq 0$

Refer to Fig. 15.4, which we will follow in this solution. The given data are not ranks, so we convert them into ranks as shown in the table below. (Section 15.1 describes the procedure for converting scores into ranks.)

x	4	6	7	1	2	8	3	9	5	10
y	3	6	7	1	2	9	4	8	5	10
d	1	0	0	0	0	1	1	1	0	0
d^2	1	0	0	0	0	1	1	1	0	0

After expressing all data as ranks, we next calculate the differences, d, and then we square them. The sum of the d^2 values is 4. We now calculate

$$r_s = 1 - \frac{6\Sigma d^2}{n(n^2 - 1)}$$
$$= 1 - \frac{6(4)}{10(10^2 - 1)}$$
$$= 1 - 0.024$$
$$= 0.976$$

Proceeding with Fig. 15.4, $n = 10$, so we answer yes when asked if $n \leq 30$. We use Table A.9 to get the critical values of -0.648 and 0.648. Finally, the sample statistic of 0.976 exceeds 0.648, so we conclude that there is significant positive correlation. More hours of study appear to be associated with higher grades. (You didn't really think we would suggest otherwise, did you?)

If we compute the linear correlation coefficient r (using Formula 12.12) for the original data in this last example, we get $r = 0.629$, which leads to the conclusion that there is no significant *linear* correlation at the 0.05 level of significance. If we examine the scatter diagram in Fig. 15.5 on the following page, we can see that there does seem to be a relationship, but it's not linear. This last example is intended to illustrate two advantages of the nonparametric approach over the parametric approach. We have already noted the advantage of detecting some relationships that are not linear. The example also illustrates this additional advantage: *Spearman's rank correlation coefficient* r_s *is less sensitive to a value that is very far out of line*, such as the 100 hours in the preceding data.

FIGURE 15.5
Nonlinear Relationship Between Hours Studied
and Number of Correct Responses

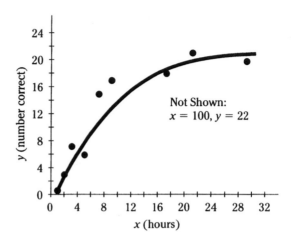

15.6 EXERCISES   BASIC CONCEPTS

In Exercises 1 and 2, find the critical value for r_s by using Table A.9 or Formula 15.2 as appropriate. Assume two-tailed cases where α represents the level of significance and n represents the number of pairs of data.

1. a. $n = 20, \alpha = 0.05$
   b. $n = 50, \alpha = 0.05$
   c. $n = 40, \alpha = 0.02$
   d. $n = 25, \alpha = 0.02$
   e. $n = 37, \alpha = 0.04$
2. a. $n = 82, \alpha = 0.04$
   b. $n = 15, \alpha = 0.01$
   c. $n = 50, \alpha = 0.01$
   d. $n = 37, \alpha = 0.01$
   e. $n = 43, \alpha = 0.05$

In Exercises 3 and 4, compute the sample statistic r_s by using Formula 15.1.

3.
x	1	2	3	4
y	4	2	3	1

4.
x	28	28	35	37	40
y	16	17	12	19	20

In Exercises 5–16:
    a. Compute the rank correlation coefficient r_s for the given sample data.
    b. Assume that $\alpha = 0.05$ and find the critical value of r_s from Table A.9 or Formula 15.2.
    c. Based on the results of parts *a* and *b*, decide whether there is significant correlation. In each case, assume a significance level of 0.05.

5. Table 15.6 in this section includes paired salary and stress level ranks for 10 randomly selected subjects. The physical demands of those jobs were also ranked; the salary and physical demand ranks are given below (based on data from *The Jobs Rated Almanac*).

Salary	2	6	3	5	7	10	9	8	4	1
Physical demand	5	2	3	8	10	9	1	7	6	4

6. Listed below are the grade point averages and starting salaries (in thousands of dollars) of 9 randomly selected accounting majors who graduated from a midwestern business school.

GPA	2.7	3.6	3.5	3.0	2.5	2.5	2.3	3.2	3.1
Salary	25.5	27.5	28.0	26.2	24.0	22.4	20.7	26.5	25.0

7. Listed below are the selling prices (in thousands of dollars) and the mileage readings (in thousands of miles) for a sample of 7 used and comparably equipped compact cars.

Selling price	7.0	8.5	7.2	8.9	8.6	8.4	6.8
Mileage	35	22	32	18	25	28	40

8. In studying the effects of heredity and environment on intelligence, scientists have learned much by analyzing IQs of identical twins who were separated soon after birth. Identical twins share identical genes inherited from the same fertilized egg. By studying identical twins reared apart, we can eliminate the variable of heredity and can better isolate the effects of environment. The following are the IQs of identical twins (older twins are x) reared apart (based on data from "IQ's of Identical Twins Reared Apart," by Arthur Jensen, *Behavioral Genetics*).

x	107	96	103	90	96	113	86	99	109	105	96	89
y	111	97	116	107	99	111	85	108	102	105	100	93

9. *Consumer Reports* tested VHS tapes used in VCRs. Given below are performance scores and prices (in dollars) of randomly selected tapes.

Performance	91	92	82	85	87	80	94	97
Price	4.56	6.48	5.99	7.92	5.36	3.32	7.32	5.27

10. Ten jobs are randomly selected and ranked according to stress level and physical demand, with the results given below (based on data from *The Jobs Rated Almanac*).

Stress level	2	7	6	4	5	8	9	10	3	1
Physical demand	5	2	3	8	10	9	1	7	6	4

11. A wholesale liquor distributor wants to investigate the relationship between wine and beer consumption. For randomly selected states, the following table lists the per capita beer consumption (in gallons) and the per capita wine consumption (in gallons) (based on data from *Statistical Abstract of the United States*).

Beer	32.2	29.4	35.3	34.9	29.9	28.7	26.8	41.4
Wine	3.1	4.4	2.3	1.7	1.4	1.2	1.2	3.0

12. The following table lists the times (in months) to maturity of U.S. Treasury bonds along with their percentage yield (based on recent data from Shearson-Lehman Hutton).

Time	3	6	12	36	60	120	240	360
Yield	3.24	3.34	3.55	4.65	5.63	6.70	7.07	7.54

13. For randomly selected homes recently sold in Dutchess County, New York, the living areas (in hundreds of square feet) are listed along with the annual tax amounts (in thousands of dollars).

Living area	15	38	23	16	16	13	20	24
Taxes	1.9	3.0	1.4	1.4	1.5	1.8	2.4	4.0

14. For randomly selected homes recently sold in Dutchess County, New York, the annual tax amounts (in thousands of dollars) are listed along with the selling prices (in thousands of dollars).

Taxes	1.9	3.0	1.4	1.4	1.5	1.8	2.4	4.0
Selling price	145	228	150	130	160	114	142	265

15. Listed below are data describing the mean rates of return of common stock portfolios for 10 mutual funds for one 5-yr period and their values 10 years later. All values are in millions of dollars.

Mean rate of return	17.25	16.89	16.33	15.45	15.25	14.61	14.22	13.27	13.05	12.11
Value 10 yr later	88.9	92.6	124.7	106.8	180	95.6	207.4	226.3	420.2	355.8

16. In a study of employee stock ownership plans, data on satisfaction with the plan and the amount of organizational commitment were collected at 8 companies. Results are given below. (See "Employee Stock Ownership and Employee Attitudes: A Test of Three Models," by Klein, *Journal of Applied Psychology*, Vol. 72, No. 2.)

Satisfaction	5.05	4.12	5.39	4.17	4.00	4.49	5.40	4.86
Commitment	5.37	4.49	5.42	4.45	4.24	5.34	5.62	4.90

15.6 EXERCISES   BEYOND THE BASICS

17. Two judges each rank 3 contestants, and the ranks from the first judge are 1, 2, and 3, respectively.

a. List all possible ways that the second judge can rank the same 3 contestants. (No ties allowed.)

b. Compute r_s for each of the cases found in part a.

c. Assuming that all the cases from part a are equally likely, find the probability that the sample statistic r_s is greater than 0.9.

18. One alternative to using Table A.9 involves an approximation of critical values for r_s given as

$$r_s = \pm \sqrt{\frac{t^2}{t^2 + n - 2}}$$

Here t is the t score from Table A.3 corresponding to the significance level and $n - 2$ degrees of freedom. Apply this approximation to find critical values of r_s for the following cases.

a. $n = 8$, $\alpha = 0.05$

b. $n = 15$, $\alpha = 0.05$

c. $n = 30$, $\alpha = 0.05$

d. $n = 30$, $\alpha = 0.01$

e. $n = 8$, $\alpha = 0.01$

19. a. Given the sample paired data depicted in the scatter diagram, which would be more likely to detect the relationship between x and y: the linear correlation coefficient r or the rank correlation coefficient r_s? Explain.

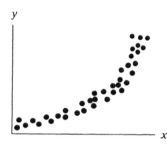

b. How is r_s affected if one variable is ranked from low to high while the other variable is ranked from high to low?

c. One researcher ranks both variables from low to high, while another researcher ranks both variables from high to low. How will their values of r_s compare?

d. Using the job salary/stress level data given in Table 15.6, test the claim that there is a *positive* correlation. That is, test the claim that $\rho_s > 0$. Use a 0.05 significance level.

20. Assume that a set of paired data has been converted to ranks according to the procedure described in this section, and also assume that no ties occur. Show that Formula 15.1 (for r_s) and Formula 12.17 (for r) will provide the same result when the ranks are used as the x and y values.

15.7 RUNS TEST FOR RANDOMNESS

A classic example of the misuse of statistics involved a company president who was convinced that employees were stealing some of the pantyhose being produced. Further investigations showed that production figures were based on samples obtained with newly serviced machinery, which produced a finer mesh and more pantyhose. The production level dropped when the machinery became worn; there was no employee theft. The initial sampling with only newly serviced machinery was not random, and it led to misleading results and embarrassment for the poor president who had proclaimed that pantyhose were being pilfered.

In many of the examples and exercises in this book, we have assumed that data were randomly selected. In this section we describe the **runs test,** which is a systematic and standard procedure for testing the randomness of data. (The runs test of this section is very different from the run charts of Section 2.4.)

> **DEFINITION**
>
> A *run* is a sequence of data that exhibit the same characteristic; the sequence is preceded and followed by different data or no data at all.

As an example, consider the cola choice of consumers in a market research project. We let D denote a consumer who prefers *diet* cola, while R indicates a consumer who prefers *regular* cola. The following sequence contains exactly four runs.

$$\underbrace{D\,D\,D\,D}_{\text{1st run}} \quad \underbrace{R\,R}_{\text{2nd run}} \quad \underbrace{D\,D\,D}_{\text{3rd run}} \quad \underbrace{R}_{\text{4th run}}$$

We would use the runs test in this situation to test for the randomness with which diet and regular occur. Let's use common sense to see how runs relate to randomness. Examine the sequence below and then stop to consider how randomly diet and regular occur. Also count the number of runs.

$$D\,D\,D\,D\,D\,D\,D\,D\,D\,R\,R\,R\,R\,R\,R\,R\,R\,R$$

In this example, it is reasonable to conclude that diet and regular occur in a sequence that is *not* random. Note that in the sequence of 20 data, there are only two runs. This example might suggest that if the number of runs is very low, randomness may be lacking. Now consider the sequence of 20 data given below. Try again to form your own conclusion about randomness before you continue reading.

$$D\,R\,D\,R\,D\,R\,D\,R\,D\,R\,D\,R\,D\,R\,D\,R\,D\,R\,D\,R$$

In this example, it should be apparent that the sequence of diet and regular is again *not* random, because there is a distinct, predictable pattern. In this case, the number of runs is 20. The example suggests that *randomness is lacking when the number of runs is too high.*

It is important to note that **this test for randomness is based on the *order* in which the data occur. This runs test is *not* based on the *frequency* of the data.** For example, a particular sequence containing 3 men and 20 women might lead to the conclusion that the sequence is random. The issue of whether or not 3 men and 20 women constitute a *biased* sample is another issue not addressed by the runs test.

The last two sequences given above are obvious in their lack of randomness, but most sequences are not so obvious; we therefore need more-sophisticated techniques for analysis. We begin by introducing some notation.

Notation

n_1 Number of elements in the sequence that have the same characteristic
n_2 Number of elements in the sequence that have the other characteristic
G Number of runs

We use G to represent the number of runs because n and r have already been used for other statistics, and G is a relatively innocuous letter that deserves more attention.

EXAMPLE   In the sequence $D, D, D, D, R, R, D, D, D, R, R, R, R, D$, we obtain the following values for n_1, n_2, and G.

$n_1 = 8$ because there are 8 diet cola consumers
$n_2 = 6$ because there are 6 regular cola consumers
$G = 5$ because there are 5 runs

We can now revert to our standard procedure for hypothesis testing. **The null hypothesis H_0 will be the claim that the sequence is random;** the alternative hypothesis H_1 will be the claim that the sequence is *not* random. The flowchart in Fig. 15.6 summarizes the mechanics of the procedure. That flowchart directs us to Table A.10 of critical G values when the following three conditions are *all* met.

1. $\alpha = 0.05$, and
2. $n_1 \leq 20$, and
3. $n_2 \leq 20$.

If all these conditions are not satisfied, we use the fact that G has a distribution that is approximately normal with mean and standard deviation as follows:

Formula 15.3 $\mu_G = \dfrac{2n_1 n_2}{n_1 + n_2} + 1$ Mean number of runs

Formula 15.4 $\sigma_G = \sqrt{\dfrac{(2n_1 n_2)(2n_1 n_2 - n_1 - n_2)}{(n_1 + n_2)^2 (n_1 + n_2 - 1)}}$ Standard deviation for number of runs

When this normal approximation is used, the test statistic is

Formula 15.5 $z = \dfrac{G - \mu_G}{\sigma_G}$

and the critical values are found by using the procedures introduced in Chapter 6. This normal approximation is quite good. If the entire table of critical values (Table A.10) had been computed using this normal approximation, no critical value would be off by more than one unit.

We now illustrate the use of the runs test for randomness by presenting examples of complete tests of hypotheses.

EXAMPLE   The president of an investment firm has observed that men and women have been hired in the following sequence: $M, M, M, W, M, M, M, M, W, W, W, M$. At the 0.05 level of significance, test the personnel officer's claim that the sequence of men and women is random. [Note that we are not testing for a *bias* in favor of one sex over the other (there are 8 men and 4 women), but we are testing only for the *randomness* in the way they appear in the given sequence.]

FIGURE 15.6
Runs Test for Randomness

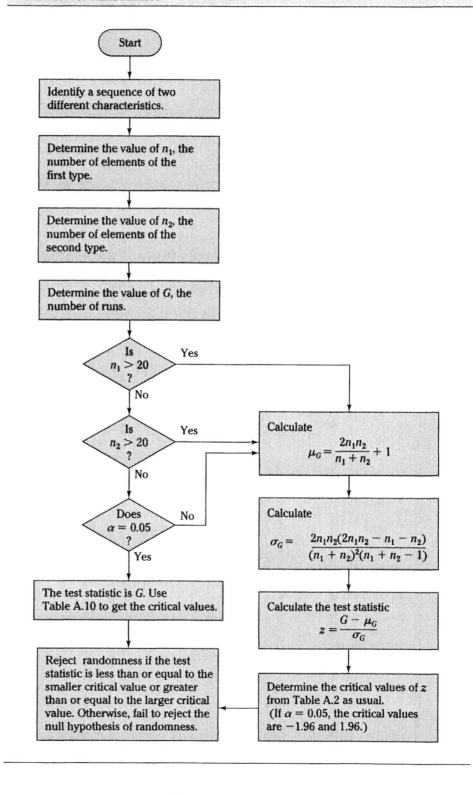

FIGURE 15.7
Runs Test for Randomness

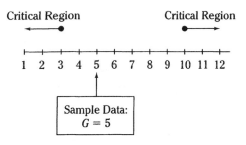

SOLUTION The null hypothesis is the claim of randomness, so we get:

H_0: The 8 men and 4 women have been hired in a random sequence.
H_1: The sequence is not random.

The significance level is $\alpha = 0.05$. Figure 15.6 summarizes the procedure for the runs test, so we refer to that flowchart. We now determine the values of n_1, n_2, and G for the given sequence.

n_1 = number of men = 8
n_2 = number of women = 4
G = number of runs = 5

Continuing with Fig. 15.6, we answer no when asked if $n_1 > 20$ (because $n_1 = 8$), no when asked if $n_2 > 20$ (because $n_2 = 4$), and yes when asked if $\alpha = 0.05$. The test statistic is $G = 5$, and we refer to Table A.10 to find the critical values of 3 and 10. Figure 15.7 shows that the test statistic $G = 5$ does not fall in the critical region. We therefore fail to reject the null hypothesis that the given sequence of men and women is random. That is, there is not sufficient evidence to reject randomness.

The next example illustrates the procedure to be followed when Table A.10 cannot be used and the normal approximation must be used instead.

EXAMPLE A machine produces defective (D) items and acceptable (A) items in the following sequence.

$D A A A A D A A A A D A A A A$
$D A A A A D A A A A D A A A A$

At the 0.05 level of significance, test the claim that the sequence is random.

H_0: The sequence is random.
H_1: The sequence is not random.

STOCKS, SPORTS, AND HOT STREAKS

It is a common belief that athletes often have "hot streaks," or short periods of extraordinary success. The Stanford University psychologist Amos Tversky and other researchers used statistics to analyze thousands of shots taken by the Philadelphia 76ers. They found that the number of hot streaks was no different than would be expected from random trials. In sports and in business, people often "see" patterns where they don't actually exist. Many investment specialists claim that individual stock performances behave randomly instead of according to predictable scheme. Those claims have been supported by many documented cases in which stock portfolios selected by random methods (such as throwing darts) have performed better than portfolios carefully selected by market experts.

Here $\alpha = 0.05$, and the statistic relevant to this test is G. Referring to the flowchart in Fig. 15.6, we determine the values of n_1, n_2, and G as follows:

n_1 = number of defective items = 6
n_2 = number of acceptable items = 24
G = number of runs = 12

Continuing with the flowchart, we answer no when asked if $n_1 > 20$ (because $n_1 = 6$) and yes when asked if $n_2 > 20$ (because $n_2 = 24$). The flowchart now directs us to calculate μ_G. Because of the sample sizes involved, we are on our way to using a normal approximation.

$$\mu_G = \frac{2n_1 n_2}{n_1 + n_2} + 1$$

$$= \frac{2(6)(24)}{6 + 24} + 1$$

$$= \frac{288}{30} + 1 = 9.6 + 1 = 10.6$$

The next step requires the computation of σ_G.

$$\sigma_G = \sqrt{\frac{(2n_1 n_2)(2n_1 n_2 - n_1 - n_2)}{(n_1 + n_2)^2 (n_1 + n_2 - 1)}}$$

$$= \sqrt{\frac{2(6)(24)[2(6)(24) - 6 - 24]}{(6 + 24)^2 (6 + 24 - 1)}}$$

$$= \sqrt{\frac{288(258)}{900(29)}} = \sqrt{\frac{74,304}{26,100}}$$

$$= \sqrt{2.847} = 1.69$$

We now calculate the test statistic z.

$$z = \frac{G - \mu_G}{\sigma_G} = \frac{12 - 10.6}{1.69} = 0.83$$

At the 0.05 level of significance, the critical values of z are -1.96 and 1.96. The test statistic $z = 0.83$ does not fall in the critical region, so we fail to reject the null hypothesis that the sequence is random. This is a good example of why we do not say "accept the null hypothesis," because examination of the data reveals that there is a consistent pattern that is clearly not random, but the sample evidence isn't strong enough to reject randomness.

RANDOMNESS ABOVE AND BELOW
THE MEAN OR MEDIAN

In each of the preceding examples, the data clearly fit into two categories, but we can also test for randomness in the way numerical data fluctuate above or below a mean or median. That is, in addition to analyzing sequences of nominal data of the type already discussed, we can also analyze sequences of data at the interval or ratio levels of measurement (see Section 1.2), as in the following example.

EXAMPLE An investor wants to analyze long-term trends in the stock market. The annual high points of the Dow Jones Industrial Average for a recent sequence of 10 years are given below.

1071 1287 1287 1553 1956 2722 2184 2791 3000 3169

At the 0.05 significance level, test for randomness above and below the median.

SOLUTION For the given data, the median is 2070. Let B denote a value *below* the median of 2070 and let A represent a value *above* 2070. We can rewrite the given sequence as follows. (If a value is equal to the median, we simply delete it from the sequence.)

B	B	B	B	B	A	A	A	A	A
↓	↓	↓	↓	↓	↓	↓	↓	↓	↓
1071	1287	1287	1553	1956	2722	2184	2791	3000	3169

It is helpful to write the A's and B's directly above the numbers they represent. This makes checking easier and also reduces the chance of having the wrong number of letters. After finding the sequence of letters, we can proceed to apply the runs test in the usual way. We get

n_1 = number of B's = 5
n_2 = number of A's = 5
G = number of runs = 2

From Table A.10, the critical values of G are found to be 2 and 10. At the 0.05 level of significance, we reject a null hypothesis of randomness above and below the median if the number of runs is 2 or lower, or 10 or more. Because $G = 2$, we reject the null hypothesis of randomness above and below the median. It isn't necessary to be a financial wizard to recognize that the yearly high levels of the Dow Jones Industrial Average appear to be following an upward trend. This example illustrates one way to recognize such trends, especially those that are not so obvious.

We could also test for randomness above and below the *mean* by following the same procedure (after we have deleted from the sequence any values that are equal to the mean).

RUNS TEST AND CONTROL CHARTS

The runs test of this section can be easily applied to control charts by denoting points above the center line by A and points below the center line by B. A process that is statistically stable and in control should produce points that are positioned about the center line in a random manner. We saw in earlier chapters that an upward trend is one example of a nonrandom pattern. An upward trend will be depicted with a control chart having many of the early data points below the center line, while the latest points are above the center line, as in the following sequence.

$$B\ B\ B\ B\ B\ B\ B\ B\ B\ B\ A\ A\ A\ A\ A\ A\ A\ A\ A\ A$$

This particular upward-trend sequence results in $n_1 = 10$, $n_2 = 10$, and $G = 2$ runs, which is below the Table A.10 critical value of 6, so the null hypothesis of randomness is rejected. The runs test can therefore be used as another way of detecting the presence of variation due to assignable causes. However, the runs test cannot replace the control chart analysis because it does not address all the out-of-control criteria we described in Chapter 8. For example, a point beyond the upper or lower control limit will be recorded as an ordinary A or B and will not signal an out-of-control condition, as it should.

Economists use the runs test for randomness above and below the median in an attempt to identify trends or cycles. An upward economic trend would contain a predominance of B's in the beginning and A's at the end, so that the number of runs would be small, as in the preceding example. A downward trend would have A's dominating the beginning and B's at the end, with a low number of runs. A cyclical pattern would yield a sequence that systematically changes, so that the number of runs would tend to be large.

15.7 EXERCISES   BASIC CONCEPTS

In Exercises 1–4, use the given sequence to determine the values of n_1, n_2, the number of runs G, and the appropriate critical values from Table A.10. (Assume a 0.05 significance level.)

1. $A, B, B, B, A, A, A, A,$
2. $A, A, A, B, A, B, A, A, B, B$
3. $A, B, B, B, A, B, B, B, B, B, A, B, A, A, A, A, A, B, A, A$
4. $A, A, A, B, B, B, B, A, A, A, A, A, B, B, B, B, B, A, A, A, B, B, B, B, B, B, A, A, A, A, A$

In Exercises 5–8, use the given sequence to answer the following:

   a. Find the mean.
   b. Let B represent a value below the mean and let A represent a value above the mean. Rewrite the given numerical sequence as a sequence of A's and B's.
   c. Find the values of n_1, n_2, and G.

d. Assuming a 0.05 level of significance, use Table A.10 to find the appropriate critical values of G.

e. What do you conclude about the randomness of the values above and below the mean?

5. 3, 8, 7, 7, 9, 12, 10, 16, 20, 18
6. 2, 2, 3, 2, 4, 4, 5, 8, 4, 6, 7, 9, 9, 12
7. 15, 12, 12, 10, 17, 11, 8, 7, 7, 5, 6, 5, 5, 9
8. 3, 3, 4, 4, 4, 8, 8, 8, 9, 7, 10, 4, 4, 3, 2, 4, 4, 10, 10, 12, 9, 10, 10, 11, 5, 4, 3, 3, 4, 5

In Exercises 9–12, use the given sequence to answer the following for the given numbers of customer complaints on consecutive days of business.

a. Find the median.

b. Let B represent a value below the median and let A represent a value above the median. Rewrite the given numerical sequence as a sequence of A's and B's.

c. Find the values of n_1 (the number of scores below the median), n_2 (the number of scores above the median), and also find G (the number of runs).

d. Assuming a 0.05 level of significance, use Table A.10 to find the appropriate critical values of G.

e. What do you conclude about the randomness of the values above and below the median?

9. 3, 8, 7, 7, 9, 12, 10, 16, 20, 18
10. 2, 2, 3, 2, 4, 4, 5, 8, 4, 6, 7, 9, 9, 12
11. 3, 3, 4, 5, 8, 8, 8, 9, 9, 9, 10, 15, 14, 13, 16, 18, 20
12. 19, 17, 3, 2, 2, 15, 4, 12, 14, 13, 9, 7, 7, 7, 8, 8, 8
13. Engineers at the Phillips Medical Supply Company have built a new machine that produces digital thermometers. The machine produces defective (D) and acceptable (A) items in the sequence below. At the 0.05 level of significance, test the claim that the sequence is random.

$$A\,A\,A\,D\,A\,A\,A\,A\,D\,A\,A\,A\,A\,A\,D\,A$$
$$A\,A\,A\,A\,A\,D\,A\,A\,A\,A\,A\,A\,A\,D\,D\,D$$
$$A\,D\,D\,D\,D\,A\,A\,A\,A\,D\,D\,D\,D$$

14. The owner of the Scott Autopark car dealership wants to determine whether his salesman Marc Taylor has random occurrences of sales among the potential customers he works with. Given below are the results for one week coded as follows: S = car was sold, N = no sale. Use a 0.05 level of significance to test the claim that sales occur in random order.

$$N\,N\,S\,N\,N\,N\,S\,N\,S\,N\,N\,N\,N\,N\,S\,S\,N\,N\,N$$

15. The number of housing starts for the more recent consecutive years in Washington County are listed below (by rows). At the 0.05 level of significance, test the claim of randomness of those values above and below the *median*.

| 973 | 1067 | 856 | 971 | 1456 | 903 | 899 | 905 |
| 812 | 630 | 720 | 676 | 731 | 655 | 598 | 617 |

16. The gold reserves of the United States (in millions of fine troy ounces) for a recent 12-year sequence are given here (based on data from the International Monetary Fund). At the 0.05 significance level, test for randomness above (*A*) and below (*B*) the median. (The data are arranged in chronological order by rows.)

> 274.71   274.68   277.55   276.41   264.60   264.32
> 264.11   264.03   263.39   262.79   262.65   262.04

17. The thicknesses of glue (in mm) applied to fabric are listed below for samples randomly selected once each half hour. At the 0.05 level of significance, test for randomness above and below the median. (Data are in order by rows.)

> 0.17   0.18   0.16   0.19   0.17   0.18   0.16   0.17   0.16   0.14
> 0.15   0.12   0.09   0.08   0.06   0.08   0.07   0.06   0.07   0.08

18. A teacher develops a true-false test with these answers:

> *T*   *F*   *F*   *F*   *F*   *T*   *T*   *T*   *T*   *T*   *T*   *F*   *F*   *F*
> *F*   *T*   *T*   *T*   *T*   *T*   *T*   *T*   *F*   *F*   *F*   *F*   *F*   *F*
> *F*   *F*   *F*   *T*   *T*   *T*   *T*   *T*   *T*   *F*   *F*   *F*

At the 0.05 level of significance, test the claim that the sequence of answers is random.

19. Test the claim that the sequence of World Series wins by American League and National League teams is random. Use a 0.05 level of significance. Given below are recent results with American and National league teams represented by *A* and *N*, respectively.

> *A*   *N*   *A*   *N*   *N*   *N*   *A*   *A*   *A*   *A*   *N*   *A*   *A*   *A*   *A*   *N*   *A*   *N*
> *N*   *A*   *A*   *N*   *N*   *A*   *A*   *A*   *A*   *N*   *A*   *N*   *N*   *A*   *A*   *A*   *A*   *A*
> *N*   *A*   *N*   *A*   *N*   *A*   *N*   *A*   *A*   *A*   *A*   *A*   *A*   *A*   *N*   *N*   *A*   *N*
> *A*   *N*   *N*   *A*   *A*   *N*   *N*   *N*   *A*   *N*   *A*   *N*   *A*   *N*   *A*   *A*   *A*   *N*
> *N*   *A*   *A*   *N*   *N*   *N*   *N*   *A*   *A*   *A*   *N*   *A*   *N*   *A*   *N*

20. A *New York Times* article about the calculation of decimal places of π noted that "mathematicians are pretty sure that the digits of π are indistinguishable from any random sequence." Given below are the first 100 decimal places of π. At the 0.05 level of significance, test for randomness of odd (*O*) and even (*E*) digits.

> 1   4   1   5   9   2   6   5   3   5   8   9   7   9   3   2   3   8   4   6
> 2   6   4   3   3   8   3   2   7   9   5   0   2   8   8   4   1   9   7   1
> 6   9   3   9   9   3   7   5   1   0   5   8   2   0   9   7   4   9   4   4
> 5   9   2   3   0   7   8   1   6   4   0   6   2   8   6   2   0   8   9   9
> 8   6   2   8   0   3   4   8   2   5   3   4   2   1   1   7   0   6   7   9

15.7 EXERCISES   BEYOND THE BASICS

21. The number of customers arriving at the Jefferson Valley Bank each hour are recorded for 5 consecutive days.
    a. At the 0.05 level of significance, test the claim that the number of customers per hour is random above and below the mean. (Use this order: Monday at 8:00, Monday at 9:00, . . . , Friday at 3:00.)

b.   What is happening? (*Hint:* Construct a run chart to see whether any
     pattern can be identified.)

	MONDAY	TUESDAY	WEDNESDAY	THURSDAY	FRIDAY
8:00	8	7	5	6	9
9:00	9	6	8	9	7
10:00	11	10	7	6	10
11:00	9	8	9	7	8
12:00	26	24	25	23	34
1:00	14	12	13	12	12
2:00	8	8	7	8	8
3:00	5	6	8	8	23

22. Using A, A, B, B, what is the minimum number of possible runs that can be
    arranged? What is the maximum number of runs? Now refer to Table A.10 to
    find the critical G values for $n_1 = n_2 = 2$. What do you conclude about this
    case?

23. Let $z = 1.96$ and $n_1 = n_2 = 20$, and then compute μ_G and σ_G. Use those
    values in Formula 15.5 to solve for G. What is the importance of this result?
    How does this result compare to the corresponding value found in Table A.10?
    How do you explain any discrepancy?

24. The Williamstown Industrial Components Company makes sensors that are
    tested and rated A (for excellent) or B (for barely acceptable). A sequence of
    9 sensors is produced and tested with the results given below.

    $$A\ A\ A\ B\ B\ B\ B\ B\ B$$

    a.   Using all of the above elements, list the 84 different possible sequences.
    b.   Find the number of runs for each of the 84 sequences.
    c.   Assuming that each sequence has a probability of 1/84, find $P(2 \text{ runs})$,
         $P(3 \text{ runs})$, $P(4 \text{ runs})$, and so on.
    d.   Use the results of part c to establish your own critical G values in a
         two-tailed test with 0.025 in each tail.
    e.   Compare your results to those given in Table A.10.
    f.   Assuming that the 84 sequences from part a are all equally likely, use the
         results from part b to find the mean number of runs. Compare your result
         to the result obtained by using Formula 15.3.

25. The Williamson Industrial Components Company makes sensors that are test-
    ed and rated as A (for excellent) or B (for barely acceptable). A sequence of
    12 sensors is produced and tested with the results given below.

    $$A\ A\ A\ B\ B\ B\ B\ B\ B\ B\ B\ B$$

    a.   Using all of the above elements, it is possible to have 220 different
         sequences. List all of the sequences that have exactly 3 runs.
    b.   Using your result from part a, find $P(3 \text{ runs})$.
    c.   Using your answer to part b, determine whether $G = 3$ should be in the
         critical region. Use a 0.05 significance level.
    d.   Find the lower critical value from Table A.10.
    e.   Find the lower critical value by using the normal approximation.

26. Refer to the example in this section that involved defective (D) and acceptable
    (A) items. Assume that the given sequence repeats itself four more times so
    that $n_1 = 30$ and $n_2 = 120$. Now test the claim that the sequence is random.

Vocabulary List

Define and give an example of each term.

parametric tests

nonparametric tests

distribution-free tests

efficiency

ranked data

rank

sign test

Wilcoxon signed-ranks test

Wilcoxon rank-sum test

Kruskal-Wallis test

rank correlation coefficient

Spearman's rank correlation coefficient

runs test

run

Review

In this chapter we examined six different *nonparametric* methods for analyzing statistics. Besides excluding involvement with population parameters like μ and σ, nonparametric methods are not encumbered by many of the restrictions placed on parametric methods, such as the requirement that data come from normally distributed populations. Although nonparametric methods generally lack the sensitivity of their parametric counterparts, they can be used in a wider variety of circumstances and can accommodate more types of data. Also, the computations required in nonparametric tests are generally much simpler than the computations required in the corresponding parametric tests.

In Table 15.7, we list the nonparametric tests presented in this chapter, along with their functions. The table also lists the corresponding parametric tests. Following it is a listing of the important formulas from this chapter.

TABLE 15.7
Summary of Nonparametric Tests

NONPARAMETRIC TEST	FUNCTION	PARAMETRIC TEST
Sign test (Section 15.2)	Test for claimed value of average with one sample	*t* test or *z* test (Sections 7.2, 7.3, 7.4)
	Test for a difference between two dependent samples	*t* test or *z* test (Section 9.3)
Wilcoxon signed-ranks test (Section 15.3)	Test for difference between two dependent samples	*t* test or *z* test (Section 9.3)
Wilcoxon rank-sum test (Section 15.4)	Test for difference between two independent samples	*t* test or *z* test (Section 9.3)
Kruskal-Wallis test (Section 15.5)	Test for more than two independent samples coming from identical populations	Analysis of variance (Sections 11.2, 11.3)
Rank correlation (Section 15.6)	Test for a relationship between two variables	Linear correlation (Section 12.7)
Runs test (Section 15.7)	Test for randomness of sample data	(No parametric test)

IMPORTANT FORMULAS

TEST	TEST STATISTIC	DISTRIBUTION
Sign test	x = number of times the less frequent sign occurs Test statistic when $n > 25$: $$z = \frac{(x + 0.5) - \left(\frac{n}{2}\right)}{\frac{\sqrt{n}}{2}}$$	If $n \le 25$, see Table A.7. If $n > 25$, use the normal distribution (Table A.2).
Wilcoxon signed-ranks test for two dependent samples	T = smaller of the rank sums Test statistic when $n > 30$: $$z = \frac{T - \frac{n(n + 1)}{4}}{\sqrt{\frac{n(n + 1)(2n + 1)}{24}}}$$	If $n \le 30$, see Table A.8. If $n > 30$, use the normal distribution (Table A.2).
Wilcoxon rank-sum test for two independent samples	$$z = \frac{R - \mu_R}{\sigma_R}$$ where R = sum of ranks of the sample with size n_1 $$\mu_R = \frac{n_1(n_1 + n_2 + 1)}{2}$$ $$\sigma_R = \sqrt{\frac{n_1 n_2(n_1 + n_2 + 1)}{12}}$$	Normal distribution (Table A.2) (Requires that $n_1 > 10$ and $n_2 > 10$.)
Kruskal-Wallis test	$$H = \frac{12}{N(N + 1)}\left(\frac{R_1^2}{n_1} + \frac{R_2^2}{n_2} + \cdots + \frac{R_k^2}{n_k}\right) - 3(N + 1)$$ where N = total number of sample values R_k = sum of ranks for the kth sample k = the number of samples	Chi-square with $k - 1$ degrees of freedom (Requires that each sample has at least five values.)
Rank correlation	$$r_s = 1 - \frac{6\Sigma d^2}{n(n^2 - 1)}$$	If $n \le 30$, use Table A.9. If $n > 30$, critical values are $$r_s = \frac{\pm z}{\sqrt{n - 1}}$$ where z is from the normal distribution.
Runs test for randomness	Test statistic when $n > 20$: $$z = \frac{G - \mu_G}{\sigma_G}$$ where $\mu_G = \frac{2n_1 n_2}{n_1 + n_2} + 1$ $$\sigma_G = \sqrt{\frac{(2n_1 n_2)(2n_1 n_2 - n_1 - n_2)}{(n_1 + n_2)^2(n_1 + n_2 - 1)}}$$	If $n_1 \le 20$ and $n_2 \le 20$, use Table A.10. If $n_1 > 20$ or $n_2 > 20$, use the normal distribution (Table A.2)

Review Exercises

In Exercises 1–24, use the indicated test. If no particular test is specified, use the appropriate nonparametric test from this chapter.

1. A telephone solicitor writes a report listing *N* for unanswered calls and *Y* for answered calls. At the 0.05 level of significance, test the claim that the sample listed below is random.

    N N N N N N N N Y Y N N N N N Y Y
    Y Y Y Y N N N N N N N N N N N

2. The manager for the New England Insurance Company claims office suspects overcharging by a particular auto repair shop. During a period of 4 months, 11 randomly selected cars are taken in for estimates at the suspect auto shop as well as another shop in the same town. The estimates (in dollars) are listed below. At the 0.05 level of significance, use the Wilcoxon signed-ranks test of the claim that there is no difference between the estimates obtained from the two shops.

Car	A	B	C	D	E	F	G	H	I	J	K
Shop 1	625	895	1450	2550	950	1775	1125	2850	1545	825	1010
Shop 2	765	927	1565	2400	1075	1950	1350	2900	1725	950	1150

3. A ranking of randomly selected cities according to population density (people per square mile) and crime rate (crimes per 100,000 people) yielded the results given below (based on data from *USA Today*). At the 0.05 level of significance, use the rank correlation coefficient to determine whether there is a positive correlation, a negative correlation, or no correlation.

City	AUSTIN	LONG BEACH	SAN DIEGO	DETROIT	BALTIMORE	TAMPA	BOSTON
Population density	1	4	3	5	6	2	7
Crime rate	4	2	1	6	3	7	5

4. The city manager's office conducts a study of the response time of police cars after dispatching occurs. Sample results for 3 precincts are given below in seconds. At the 0.05 level of significance, test the claim that precincts 1 and 2 have the same response times.

Precinct 1	160	172	176	176	178	191	183	177	173	179	180	185
Precinct 2	165	174	180	181	184	186	190	200	176	192	195	201
Precinct 3	162	175	177	179	187	195	210	215	216	220	222	

5. Using the sample data given in Exercise 4, test the claim that the three precincts have the same response times.

6. In a marketing taste test between two popular colas, 50 persons were asked to state their preference. Twenty-eight preferred cola A, 16 preferred cola B, and 6 had no preference. Use the sign test to test the claim that there is no difference in preference between the two colas. Use a 0.05 significance level.

7. The Jacobsen Testing Center offers training for a CPA exam and claims that its course increases scores. The median score for a particular exam is 78. Twelve randomly selected students took the training course and received the CPA exam scores given below. At the 0.05 level of significance, test the claim that those taking the course have a median score greater than 78.

Student	1	2	3	4	5	6	7	8	9	10	11	12
Score	80	76	75	78	90	84	70	65	85	69	81	92

8. A manager of health care benefits wishes to compare the medical costs incurred by a standard benefit package and a "cost guard" program involving copayments and deductibles. Thirty families from the standard program are matched with 30 families from the cost guard program according to age, family size, and past medical history. The total costs (in hundreds of dollars) for the 30 families are recorded for 12 months, with the results given below. Use the Wilcoxon signed-ranks test at the 0.05 significance level to test the claim that there is no difference in cost between the two programs.

Month	1	2	3	4	5	6	7	8	9	10	11	12
Standard	6.9	5.4	6.5	4.7	4.6	5.2	4.0	8.7	5.8	6.3	4.9	5.5
Cost guard	5.3	3.2	7.6	4.4	3.9	5.0	2.8	4.2	3.8	6.0	4.9	4.6

9. A police academy gives an entrance exam; sample results for applicants from two different counties follow. Use the Wilcoxon rank-sum test to test the claim that there is no difference between the scores from the two counties. Assume a significance level of 0.05.

Orange County	63	39	26	14	75	60	62	79	86	70	66	
Westchester County	54	35	39	27	40	78	17	7	5	10	48	50	49

10. Professor Townsend hypothesizes that students who complete and submit their final exams early tend to have lower grades than those who stay longer. She realizes that the exams are arranged in sequence with the first completed exam located on the bottom of the pile. She records the grades listed below in order by row. At the 0.05 level of significance, test for randomness above and below the mean.

45	50	92	87	79	89	93	75	76	74	76
73	65	68	69	70	78	60	60	60	55	100

11. A study of 10 randomly selected towns in Indiana reveals the following numbers of bars and churches.
    a. At the 0.05 significance level, test for a correlation between these two variables.
    b. If there is a significant correlation, would this prove that bars cause churches or that churches cause bars?

Town	1	2	3	4	5	6	7	8	9	10
Bars	41	11	4	2	26	28	85	15	7	0
Churches	32	17	8	5	22	30	103	23	19	2

12. The Milton Novelty Store specializes in items such as bumper stickers and key chains. When a large order is received, the manager decides to purchase a new machine for making key chains. She finds three different machines available and she obtains sample data listing the output for different randomly selected days. The results are given below. Using a 0.05 level of significance, test the claim that the machines produce the same amount.

Machine A	660	690	690	672	683
Machine B	590	588	560	570	592
Machine C	520	572	578	553	564

13. Randomly selected cars are tested for fuel consumption and then retested after a tune-up. The measures of fuel consumption follow. At the 0.05 significance level, use the Wilcoxon signed-ranks test to test the claim that the tune-up has no effect on fuel consumption.

Before tune-up	16	23	12	13	7	31	27	18	19	19	19	11	9	15
After tune-up	18	23	16	17	8	29	31	21	19	20	24	13	14	18

14. Refer to the data given in Exercise 13. At the 0.05 level of significance, use rank correlation to test for a relationship between the before and after values.

15. Refer to the data given in Exercise 13. At the 0.05 level of significance, use the sign test to test the claim that the tune-up has no effect on fuel consumption.

16. Three groups of men were selected for an experiment designed to measure their blood alcohol levels after consuming 5 drinks. Members of group A were tested after 1 hour, members of group B were tested after 2 hours, and members of group C were tested after 4 hours. The results are given below. At the 0.05 level of significance, use the Kruskal-Wallis test to test the claim that the 3 groups come from identical populations.

A	B	C
0.11	0.08	0.04
0.10	0.09	0.04
0.09	0.07	0.05
0.09	0.07	0.05
0.10	0.06	0.06
		0.04
		0.05

17. Samples of equal amounts of two brands of a food substance were randomly selected and the amounts of carbohydrates were measured (in grams). The results are listed below. Use the Wilcoxon rank-sum test to test the claim that both brands are the same when compared on the basis of carbohydrate content. Use a 0.05 level of significance.

Brand X	20.3	21.2	19.3	19.2	19.1	19.0	22.6	23.6	22.9	20.7	20.7
Brand Y	18.9	18.8	19.1	21.0	20.0	18.6	20.4	23.3	20.1	17.9	17.7

18. A market researcher is hired to collect data from 30 randomly selected consumers. As the data are turned in, the sexes of the interviewed subjects are noted and the sequence below is obtained. At the 0.05 level of significance, test the claim that the sequence is random.

M M M M M M M M F M M M M F F F
F F F F F F M M M M M M M M

19. A unit on business law is taught to 5 different classes of randomly selected students. A different teaching method is used for each group, and sample final test data are given below. The scores represent the final averages of the individual students. Test the claim that the 5 methods are equally effective. Use a 0.05 level of significance.

TRADITIONAL	PROGRAMMED	AUDIO	AUDIOVISUAL	VISUAL
76.2	85.2	67.3	75.8	50.5
78.3	74.3	60.1	81.6	70.2
85.1	76.5	55.4	90.3	88.8
63.7	80.3	72.3	78.0	67.1
91.6	67.4	40.0	67.8	77.7
87.2	67.9		57.6	73.9
	72.1			
	60.4			

20. The following scores were randomly selected from last year's college entrance examination scores. Use the Wilcoxon rank-sum test to test the claim that the performance of New Yorkers equals that of Californians. Assume a significance level of 0.05.

New York	520	490	571	398	602	475	557	621	737	403	511	598
California	508	563	385	617	704	401	409	527	393	478	521	536

21. Two judges grade entries in a science fair. The grades for 8 randomly selected contestants are given below. Use the data to test the claim that there is no difference between their scoring. Use the Wilcoxon signed-ranks test at the 0.05 level of significance.

Judge A	6.3	7.2	6.6	8.5	9.7	7.0	7.3	8.8
Judge B	7.1	6.5	8.2	8.6	9.0	6.1	6.3	8.8

22. An annual sales award was won by women in 30 out of 40 regions. At the 0.05 significance level, use the sign test to test the claim that men and women are equal in their abilities to win this award.

23. The Dakota Metal Company has a large roller for rolling sheet metal used in molding. A troublesome defect has been appearing in certain rolls of thin sheet metal. To test for the randomness of this defect's occurrence, 70 ft of the roll are marked into 1-ft sections, and each section is denoted by *A* (acceptable) or *D* (defective), with the results given below in row order.

a. At the 0.05 level of significance, test the claim that the defects occur randomly in the roll.

```
A   A   A   D   A   A   A   A   A   D   A   A   A   A   A   D
A   A   A   A   A   D   A   D   A   A   A   D   A   A   A   A
A   D   A   A   A   A   A   D   A   A   A   A   A   D   A   A
A   A   A   D   A   A   A   A   A   D   A   A   A   A   A   D
A   A   A   A   A   D
```

b. Based on visual inspection, is there any obvious pattern in the occurrence of defective items?

24. Several cities were ranked according to number of hotel rooms and amount of office space. The results are as follows. With a 0.05 significance level, use rank correlation to test for a relationship between office space and hotel rooms.

City	NY	Ch	SF	Ph	LA	At	Mi	KC	NO	Da	Ba	Bo	Se	Ho	SL
Office rank	1	3	2	7	6	10	14	15	11	9	12	4	8	5	13
Hotel rank	1	2	3	8	6	7	14	15	4	10	13	5	9	11	12

Computer Project

We can use Minitab's RANDOM command to generate random numbers. Shown below are the commands resulting in 50 integers randomly selected between 1 and 99 inclusive.

```
MTB > RANDOM 50 C1;
SUBC> INTEGERS 1 99.
MTB > PRINT C1

C1
    64   98   60   83   47   43   41   52   22   21   54   78   12
    48   33    8   22   73   33   10   55   97   29   85   66   79
    88   87   60   46    2   38    5   94   10   98   52   95    3
    85   38   68   33   79   69   58   26   27   50   87
```

These random numbers are generated in such a way that the 99 possible integers are all equally likely.

a. Load Minitab and enter the same commands listed above. Obtain a printout of the resulting scores.

b. Now exit Minitab by entering the command STOP, then restart Minitab and proceed to enter the above commands a second time. Obtain a printout of the second set of generated values.

c. Use the rank correlation coefficient to test for a relationship between your first set of generated numbers and your second set. What does the result of that test suggest about Minitab's random number generator? Does it appear to be working as it should?

d. Use the Wilcoxon rank-sum test to test the claim that your two samples come from the same population. Based on the result of the Wilcoxon rank-sum test, does Minitab's random number generator appear to be working as it should?

e. Now enter the above commands a third time and obtain a printout of the 50 numbers. Use the Kruskal-Wallis test to test the claim that your three samples come from the same population. Based on the result of the Kruskal-Wallis test, does Minitab's random number generator appear to be working as it should?

WAS THE DRAFT LOTTERY RANDOM?

I n 1970 the U.S. Army needed many soldiers to fight in Vietnam, and men were drafted through a process that was claimed to be random. The selection process began with capsules containing the 366 different possible birthdays. The capsules were mixed and selected so that priority numbers were established according to birth dates. Men were then drafted in order according to their priority numbers. For example, the first selected date of September 14 was given draft priority number 1, so that men born on that date were drafted first. Listed below are the 366 priority numbers selected in the 1970 Selective Service draft lottery.

a. Use the runs test to test the sequence for randomness above and below the median of 183.5.

b. Use the Kruskal-Wallis test to test the claim that the 12 months have priority numbers drawn from the same population.

c. Calculate the 12 monthly means. Then plot those 12 means on a graph. (The horizontal scale lists the 12 months and the vertical scale ranges from 100 to 260.) Note any pattern suggesting that the original priority numbers are not randomly selected.

d. Based on the preceding results, do you conclude that the 1970 selections are truly random? Write a brief statement summarizing your conclusion. If the process does not appear to be truly random, also write a recommendation describing a process that would yield draft priority numbers that are truly random.

Jan.	305	159	251	215	101	224	306	199	194	325	329	221	318	238	017	121
	235	140	058	280	186	337	118	059	052	092	355	077	349	164	211	
Feb.	086	144	297	210	214	347	091	181	338	216	150	068	152	004	089	212
	189	292	025	302	363	290	057	236	179	365	205	299	285			
Mar.	108	029	267	275	293	139	122	213	317	323	136	300	259	354	169	166
	033	332	200	239	334	265	256	258	343	170	268	223	362	217	030	
Apr.	032	271	083	081	269	253	147	312	219	218	014	346	124	231	273	148
	260	090	336	345	062	316	252	002	351	340	074	262	191	208		
May	330	298	040	276	364	155	035	321	197	065	037	133	295	178	130	055
	112	278	075	183	250	326	319	031	361	357	296	308	226	103	313	
June	249	228	301	020	028	110	085	366	335	206	134	272	069	356	180	274
	073	341	104	360	060	247	109	358	137	022	064	222	353	209		
July	093	350	115	279	188	327	050	013	277	284	248	015	042	331	322	120
	098	190	227	187	027	153	172	023	067	303	289	088	270	287	193	
Aug.	111	045	261	145	054	114	168	048	106	021	324	142	307	198	102	044
	154	141	311	344	291	339	116	036	286	245	352	167	061	333	011	
Sept.	225	161	049	232	082	006	008	184	263	071	158	242	175	001	113	207
	255	246	177	063	204	160	119	195	149	018	233	257	151	315		
Oct.	359	125	244	202	024	087	234	283	342	220	237	072	138	294	171	254
	288	005	241	192	243	117	201	196	176	007	264	094	229	038	079	
Nov.	019	034	348	266	310	076	051	097	080	282	046	066	126	127	131	107
	143	146	203	185	156	009	182	230	132	309	047	281	099	174		
Dec.	129	328	157	165	056	010	012	105	043	041	039	314	163	026	320	096
	304	128	240	135	070	053	162	095	084	173	078	123	016	003	100	

CHAPTER 16 Decision Analysis

16.1 OVERVIEW

The objectives of this chapter are identified.

16.2 COMPONENTS OF THE DECISION PROBLEM

The four main components of actions, states of nature, outcomes, and objective variables are identified. The construction of payoff tables is described.

16.3 OPPORTUNITY LOSS TABLES AND DECISION TREES

Methods for summarizing the key data in a decision problem are presented. The methods of constructing payoff tables, opportunity loss tables, and decision trees are described.

16.4 DECISION MAKING UNDER UNCERTAINTY

If a decision problem does not have probabilities associated with states of nature, we can use the maximax, maximin, or minimax decision strategies.

16.5 DECISION MAKING UNDER RISK

If a decision problem has probabilities associated with states of nature, we can use expected values of payoff and the expected payoff criterion to determine the best decision.

Repair or Replace?

The Dayton Machine Company manufactures auto parts and has received a $245,000 contract to produce and supply auto parts for General Motors. Dayton has submitted a bid to win a second order. Unfortunately, the machinery breaks down. Management must now choose to repair it, replace it, or lease machinery. A key factor is the profit or loss that will result from the decision, and that profit or loss is dramatically affected by whether the bid on the second order is won or lost. What should the company do? Should it repair, replace, or lease?

In making a decision, a good beginning is to collect any additional relevant data. Roberta

	BID IS WON	BID IS LOST
Repair old machinery	$40,000 profit	$0 (break even)
Purchase new machinery	$70,000 profit	$5000 loss
Lease new machinery	$50,000 profit	$70,000 loss

Simpson is an executive at the Dayton Machine Company and her research has revealed that if the machinery is repaired, the company will make a $40,000 profit if the second bid is won and it will break even if the bid is not won. If the machinery is replaced by new equipment, there will be a $70,000 profit if the new bid is won and a $5000 loss if the bid is not won. She also determines that if machinery is leased, there will be a $50,000 profit if the new bid is won and a $70,000 loss if the new bid is not won. We can summarize the choices in the table shown here. This decision problem will be analyzed in the sections that follow.

16.1 OVERVIEW

In several of the preceding chapters we use hypothesis testing to either reject or fail to reject the null hypothesis. Hypothesis testing allows only two different possibilities, however, and the conditions must also fall into one of only two categories. But there are many real and practical situations involving multiple choices, such as "buy, sell, or hold." Also, hypothesis testing does not directly take into account the amounts of money (or other quantity) that are gained or lost as a result of different courses of action. The analysis of decision problems, as discussed in this chapter, largely overcomes these hypothesis-test limitations.

A **decision problem** includes at least two different possible courses of action, and we must choose one of them. Each of us frequently encounters decision problems that involve a variety of factors we should consider. The quality of our decisions may affect not only our personal lives but our professional status and income as well. Corporate chief executive officers, securities analysts, insurance underwriters, oil well drillers, clothing buyers, income tax specialists, home builders, land speculators, song promoters, and book publishers are only a few of the many professionals whose success or failure hinges on their ability to make sound decisions about issues such as whether to invest in a particular company, to underwrite an insurance policy, to drill an oil well, to buy a line of clothes, and so on. In this chapter we focus on the process of making quality decisions.

Decision problems can be made under very different circumstances. We will consider three categories:

1. Decision problems with certainty
2. Decision problems under risk
3. Decision problems under uncertainty

Some decision problems are well defined with clear, concise, and objective factors that can be easily analyzed. If you plan to buy a car and your local dealer charges $1000 less than your car salesman cousin in Dubuque, your decision is easy. This is an example of a **decision problem with certainty,** which is characterized by the fact that you *know* the result of each possible choice. You may have already solved some business problems involving decisions with certainty, such as this problem: A furniture manufacturer wants to determine how many tables and chairs should be produced each week to maximize profit. The manufacturer knows the amounts of raw material and labor that are available. The costs of those items are also known. When the profits per table and per chair are known, the problem can then be solved by using *linear programming*. Such problems are usually considered in a finite mathematics course or a course in operations research or linear programming.

In this chapter we deal with decision problems that involve some form of uncertainty. Such problems are characterized by solutions that are affected by chance. As an example, let's reconsider the above furniture problem. Suppose that the exact costs of manufacturing a table or a chair are *not known,* but it is known that the costs per table will be either $100, $125, or $130 and the costs per chair will be either $30, $40, or $45, depending on the results of current union contract negotiations. Now we are dealing with a decision problem wherein the data and decisions involve uncertainty. If we determine that the probabilities of the three different costs are 0.5, 0.3, and 0.2, respectively, then we are dealing with a

decision problem under risk. However, if we don't know the complete probability distribution for the three probabilities, then we are dealing with a **decision problem under uncertainty.**

16.2 COMPONENTS OF THE DECISION PROBLEM

In Section 16.1 we discussed the specific types of decision problem to be considered in this chapter. To better understand the particular types of problem, we will identify and define the fundamental components and then consider a specific decision problem.

DEFINITIONS

The *actions* are the different alternatives the decision-maker has available.

The *states of nature* are the *chance* events that determine the outcome of an action.

The *outcomes* (or *payoffs*) are the results corresponding to all actions for each different state of nature.

The *objective variable* is the quantity that is measured when the outcomes are described.

A *payoff table* lists the outcomes (or payoffs) for all possible actions (listed in rows) corresponding to each different state of nature (listed in columns).

EXAMPLE

A 27-year-old woman is trying to decide whether to buy a one-year term life insurance policy with coverage of $100,000. The cost of this policy is $156 (based on an actual premium). Identify the actions, states of nature, outcomes, and objective variable. Summarize the outcomes for the different combinations of actions and states of nature in the form of a payoff table.

SOLUTION

This decision problem involves two actions and two states of nature, described as follows:

ACTIONS
1. The woman buys the insurance.
2. She doesn't buy the insurance.

STATES OF NATURE
1. The woman lives through the year.
2. She dies within the year.

Note in the preceding definition that outcomes are results corresponding to all actions for each different state of nature. This example involves two actions and two states of nature, so we must describe four different cases. For each case we describe the net change in the woman's wealth. *(continued)*

CASE	OUTCOME (NET CHANGE IN WEALTH)
She buys policy and lives.	$156 loss
She buys policy and dies.	$100,000 − $156 = $99,844 gain
She doesn't buy policy and lives.	0 (no change)
She doesn't buy policy and dies.	0 (no change)

These cases and outcomes can be summarized in the form of a payoff table, such as the following:

	SHE LIVES	SHE DIES
She buys policy	−$156	$99,844
She doesn't buy policy	0 (no change)	0 (no change)

In considering a life insurance policy, the woman's objective is to provide financial security for her beneficiaries. That objective was recognized when we described the outcomes in terms of net monetary changes in the woman's wealth. The quantity of "net change in wealth" is therefore the objective variable. We have now identified the important elements of this decision problem.

In the following sections we will find it helpful to represent actions and states of nature by symbols. The following notation will be used.

Notation
$A1$, $A2$, $A3$, . . . denote the first action, the second action, and so on.
$S1$, $S2$, $S3$, . . . denote the first state of nature, the second state of nature, and so on.

ASSUMPTIONS

1. The problem involves decision making under uncertainty. That is, the decision-maker does not know which state of nature will result, and the state of nature depends on chance instead of the action of a competitor.
2. The objective variable can be measured and described with numbers.

Further, although some decision problems may involve large numbers of actions or states of nature, the examples and exercises of this chapter will generally involve relatively small numbers of possibilities. In the last example we presented a real decision problem, but one of the actions (not buying the insurance) led to two outcomes of zero. In many cases we make decisions by default; that is, we choose an action involving no change. By default, we may decide not to buy a lottery ticket, not to interview for a new job, or not to take a course. Such inaction often has outcomes of zero-zero corresponding to no loss and no gain. However, many other situations occur in which all the actions have some positive or negative effect. The next example illustrates such a case.

EXAMPLE

An executive for the Dayton Machine Company, a manufacturer of auto parts, has already made a contractual commitment to sell one large batch, and she has submitted a bid for a second large order. The required machinery breaks, and this executive must choose between repairing it or replacing it. Analysis is made of the repair, maintenance, and replacement costs along with the efficiency of the new and old machinery. When that information is considered with the profits from the orders, the results can be summarized as shown in Table 16.1. All entries in the table describe amounts of profit; the negative entry of −$5000 is actually a *loss* of $5000. Identify the actions, states of nature, outcomes, and objective variable.

TABLE 16.1
Payoff Table

	S1: BID IS WON	S2: BID IS LOST
A1: Repair old machinery	$40,000	$0
A2: Purchase new machinery	$70,000	−$5000
A3: Lease machinery	$50,000	−$70,000

SOLUTION

This decision problem involves the following three actions and two states of nature:

ACTIONS   A1: Repair old machinery
            A2: Purchase new machinery
            A3: Lease machinery

STATES OF   S1: The bid on the second order is won.
 NATURE   S2: The bid on the second order is lost.

The table below summarizes the six outcomes.

CASE	OUTCOME (PROFIT)
She repairs old machinery and bid is won.	$40,000
She repairs old machinery and bid is lost.	$0 (break even)
She buys new machinery and bid is won.	$70,000
She buys new machinery and bid is lost.	−$5000 (loss)
She leases new machinery and bid is won.	$50,000
She leases new machinery and bid is lost.	−$70,000 (loss)

The executive's objective is to earn a profit for her company, and the outcomes are measured in terms of the amount of profit in dollars. This quantity of profit is therefore the objective variable. The four elements of this decision problem have now been identified.

In this example we simply identified the elements of the decision problem and made no attempt to actually make the decision. In the following sections we will pursue actual decision-making strategies. We note that after formulating the payoff

LET'S MAKE A DEAL

In recent years there has been much discussion about a decision problem based on an old television game show called "Let's Make a Deal." Here's the problem: You are a contestant in a game show and you have chosen one of three available curtains. One of the curtains hides a new car, but the other two hide small, empty rooms. After identifying your selection, the game show host (knowing where the car is) opens one of the other curtains, shows that it is empty, then gives you this choice: You can stick with your original selection or you can switch to the other unopened curtain. Should you stick or should you switch? *Chance Magazine* notes that "some prestigious business schools" use the puzzle to educate their students in decision making. The solution? Switch, because you then have a probability of 2/3 of winning the car.

table, however, it may include an action that should never be selected, regardless of which state of nature might occur. In our example, action 3 (to lease) always results in a worse financial outcome than action 2 (to purchase), regardless of whether the bid is won or lost. Action 3 is said to be *dominated* by action 2. Such dominated actions should not be considered as possible options; hence they are referred to as **inadmissible actions.** By eliminating any inadmissible actions, we can reduce the calculations needed to arrive at the optimal decision.

DEFINITION

An action *A1 dominates* an action *A2* if, for each state of nature, the outcome value of *A1* is greater than or equal to the outcome value for *A2*.

Refer to Table 16.1 and note that the second row dominates the third row.

 BASIC CONCEPTS

In each of the following exercises, identify the actions, states of nature, outcomes, and objective variable. Also, construct the payoff table. Save the payoff tables for further analyses in the following sections.

1. A 64-year-old man is considering the purchase of a one-year term life insurance policy with $50,000 coverage. The cost of the policy is $87.
2. The operator of a food booth at a county fair can set up the booth with or without a rented tent. If the tent is not rented, a $300 profit is expected in good weather, but if it rains, the lack of a tent will discourage customers, so that a $100 loss is expected. If the tent is rented, a $150 profit is expected in good weather and a $50 profit in rainy weather.
3. A defendant in a product liability case must choose between settling out of court for a loss of $150,000 or going to trial and either losing nothing (if found not guilty) or losing $500,000 (if found guilty).
4. The owner of a bookstore is trying to decide whether to add a VCR rental area. If demand is sufficient, profits will increase by $15,000. If demand is not sufficient, a loss of $10,000 can be expected.
5. An executive in charge of advertising must decide whether to use television or print media, or both. For those three options, a successful campaign will increase profits by $250,000, $175,000, and $300,000, respectively. For those three options, an unsuccessful campaign will decrease profits by $80,000, $60,000, and $140,000, respectively.
6. A company plans to open a service station with 1, 2, or 3 service bays. If the station is successful, the profits will be $20,000, $35,000, and $45,000, respectively. If the station is unsuccessful, the losses will be $50,000, $100,000, and $150,000, respectively.
7. An investor is trying to decide whether to buy a safe blue-chip stock or a speculative stock. It is estimated that a healthy economy would result in a

$5000 profit from the blue-chip stock and a $12,000 profit from the speculative stock. An unhealthy economy would lead to losses of $3000 and $15,000 for the blue-chip stock and the speculative stock, respectively.

8. A builder knows that a large corporation is considering a major expansion into a particular region. The builder is trying to decide whether to exercise an option on the purchase of a large parcel of land. If the option is exercised, the builder will gain $500,000 (if the corporation moves in) or will lose $150,000 (if the corporation does not move in). If the option is not exercised, the builder loses $25,000 whether or not the company comes.

9. A concert promoter can schedule an event in a large outdoor stadium or a smaller indoor arena. If the outdoor stadium is chosen, the event will yield a profit of $200,000 in good weather or a loss of $100,000 in rain. With the indoor arena, it will yield a $40,000 profit, regardless of the weather.

10. The owner of a small publishing firm is considering the possibility of starting a local magazine. Depending on its success, the magazine can yield a $400,000 profit or a $250,000 loss. If the owner decides against the magazine, there is no profit or loss.

11. A cable company authorizes the use of cable TV decoders that are sold to retailers in groups of five. One particular retailer must order either 0, 5, 10, or 15 units. If the TV signal doesn't change, those four options will produce profits of $0, $300, $600, or $900, respectively. If the TV signal does change, those four options will produce losses of $0, $450, $900, or $1350, respectively.

12. The owner of a fitness center is trying to decide whether to expand, and the options are 0, 1, or 2 additional sites. Depending on whether the state of local economic and health awareness factors is positive or negative, those three options will either lead to additional profits of $0, $70,000, or $120,000 or result in losses of $0, $140,000, or $250,000, respectively.

16.2   EXERCISES   BEYOND THE BASICS

13. In Table 16.1 the second row dominates the third.
    a. Modify the values in the second row so that no row dominates another row.
    b. After modifying the second row as described in part *a*, add a fourth row in such a way that no row dominates any other row.
    c. Use the result of part *b* and add a fifth row in such a way that no row dominates any other row.
    d. After completing parts *a*, *b*, and *c*, consider the maximum possible number of rows constructed so that no row dominates another row. Is there a maximum number?

14. In a payoff table, if row *A*1 dominates row *A*2, and row *A*2 dominates row *A*3, must row *A*1 also dominate row *A*3? Explain.

15. In a payoff table, assume that row *A*1 dominates both row *A*2 and row *A*3. Must it follow that for rows *A*2 and *A*3, one of them must dominate the other? Give an example.

16.3 OPPORTUNITY LOSS TABLES AND DECISION TREES

In Section 16.2 we discussed the general nature of decision problems and we identified the major components of actions, states of nature, outcomes, and objective variables. We also introduced the payoff table, which summarizes outcomes in a concise and convenient format. Table 16.1 in the preceding section is one example of a payoff table. In general, such tables clarify key data and relationships between actions and states of nature.

The payoff table shown in Table 16.2 represents the decision problem described in Table 16.1, but the inadmissible action $A3$ has been deleted. Recall that $A1$ and $A2$ denote the different possible actions, and $S1$ and $S2$ denote the different possible states of nature.

Table 16.2 has two rows and two columns, but other decision problems may involve more than two rows and more than two columns. Also, while this payoff table has positive, negative, and zero entries, other decision problems may lead to payoff tables with positive entries only, or negative entries only, or any other combination of positive, negative, and zero entries.

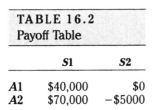

TABLE 16.2
Payoff Table

	S1	*S2*
A1	$40,000	$0
A2	$70,000	−$5000

OPPORTUNITY LOSS TABLES

Just as some people see a glass of water as half full while others see it as half empty, some of us see the actual payoffs in a decision problem while others think about what might have been. For example, suppose we choose to repair the old machinery (action $A1$) in the preceding payoff table, and the bid is won (state of nature $S1$). The corresponding outcome of a $40,000 gain can also be thought of in terms of losing the opportunity to gain $30,000 more by purchasing new machinery (action $A2$) instead of repairing the old machinery. The executive might boast that her decision led to a $40,000 gain, but a critic might point out that she lost $30,000 because action $A2$ would have resulted in a $70,000 gain. The executive did lose the opportunity for gaining $30,000 more. This $30,000 amount is commonly referred to as the *opportunity loss* that corresponds to action $A1$ and state of nature $S1$. This particular case suggests the following general definition.

> **DEFINITION**
>
> The *opportunity loss* corresponding to a particular action and state of nature is the maximum of all values for that state of nature minus the payoff for the particular action/state combination.

This definition can be condensed into the following formula, which refers to a payoff table with actions corresponding to rows and states of nature corresponding to columns, as in Table 16.2.

Formula 16.1   **Opportunity loss for a cell =**
(maximum column value) − (cell value)

In this expression the maximum column value is actually the best possible result for a particular state of nature. The cell value is the payoff for a specific action. By subtracting, we find the amount of lost opportunity, or the *additional* amount that we could have realized had we made the best possible decision. The "best" decision is the one that results in the greatest possible gain; if all decisions must result in a loss, then the "best" decision is the one that results in the least possible loss.

If we determine the opportunity loss value for each cell in a payoff table, we can then construct an opportunity loss table as shown in Table 16.3. In the middle part we show the arithmetic that allows us to convert each payoff value into an opportunity loss value. For each cell, we are using Formula 16.1 as given above.

DEFINITION

An *opportunity loss table* lists the values of opportunity loss for all possible actions (listed in rows) corresponding to each different state of nature (listed in columns).

Given the way that opportunity loss is defined, the following three properties must apply.

1. No opportunity loss value can ever be negative.
2. For each state of nature (or column), the opportunity loss corresponding to the best decision is zero.
3. The number of rows and columns in an opportunity loss table are exactly the same as in the corresponding payoff table.

The first property makes sense when we realize that opportunity loss is found by subtracting a specific column number from the maximum column value. In Formula 16.1 the cell value must be less than or equal to the maximum column value, so the subtraction can never lead to a negative result.

The second property makes sense when we see that the "best" decision is the one that leads to the maximum payoff for a particular state of nature. This means that in Formula 16.1 the cell value will be equal to the maximum column value, and the opportunity loss will therefore be zero.

The third property reflects the fact that each opportunity loss value is found from a corresponding outcome (payoff) in a payoff table.

| EXAMPLE | Given the payoff table summarized in Table 16.4, find the corresponding opportunity loss table.

TABLE 16.4
Payoff Table

	S1	S2	S3	S4
A1	0	−5	−4	8
A2	−3	2	−6	7

TABLE 16.3
Opportunity Loss Table

Payoff Table (Table 16.2)

	S1	S2
A1	$40,000	$0
A2	$70,000	−$5000

↓

	S1	S2
A1	70,000	0
	−40,000	−0
	30,000	0
A2	70,000	0
	−70,000	−(−5000)
	0	5000

↓

	S1	S2
A1	$30,000	$0
A2	$0	$5000

TABLE 16.5
Opportunity Loss Table

	S1	*S2*	*S3*	*S4*
A1	⓪	−5	⑴−4⑴	⑧
A2	−3	②	−6	7

Column maximums are circled.

	S1	*S2*	*S3*	*S4*
A1	$0 - 0 = 0$	$2 - (-5) = 7$	$-4 - (-4) = 0$	$8 - 8 = 0$
A2	$0 - (-3) = 3$	$2 - 2 = 0$	$-4 - (-6) = 2$	$8 - 7 = 1$

Formula 16.1 is used in each cell.

Payoff Table
(Table 16.4)

$\longrightarrow$

	S1	*S2*	*S3*	*S4*
A1	0	7	0	0
A2	3	0	2	1

SOLUTION   Using Formula 16.1, we find the value of opportunity loss for each outcome in the payoff table. Remember, for each entry of Table 16.4 we find the opportunity loss by subtracting the entry from the maximum column value. That difference represents the opportunity for greater gain that would be lost by the decision-maker because of the action selected.

The middle table shows the arithmetic that allows us to convert the payoff table into an opportunity loss table. The result of that arithmetic is the opportunity loss table we wanted to construct. It's important to note that unlike a payoff table, the entries in this table are not values of outcomes. Instead, they are *opportunity loss* values.

In Section 16.2 we noted that if an action in the payoff table is dominated by one or more of the other actions, then the *dominated* action should be dropped from consideration; it is inadmissible. In the payoff table below, for example, row *A1* is dominated by row *A2*, so it should be dropped. However, if an action in the opportunity loss table dominates one or more of the other actions, then the *dominating* action should be eliminated because it results in a larger loss, regardless of the state of nature. In the opportunity loss table shown below, row *A1* should be dropped because it always results in a larger loss than row *A2*. For both payoff tables and opportunity loss tables, we are eliminating options that should never be selected.

Payoff Table

	S1	*S2*
A1	1	2
A2	3	4

← Delete the dominated row.

Opportunity Loss Table

	S1	*S2*
A1	2	2
A2	0	0

← Delete the dominating row.

DECISION TREES

For a given decision problem, we can illustrate the different combinations of possibilities by constructing either a payoff table or an opportunity loss table. We can also use a third format, the decision tree, defined as follows:

DEFINITION

A *decision tree* is a tree diagram in which the leftmost branches correspond to actions and the rightmost branches correspond to states of nature.

We illustrate this definition with an example that uses the same decision problem given in Section 16.2.

EXAMPLE   An executive must choose between repairing old machinery and purchasing new machinery. She has already made a contractual commitment for one order and has bid on a second order. The outcomes are summarized in the payoff table below. Construct the corresponding decision tree.

	BID IS WON	BID IS LOST
Repair old machinery	$40,000	$0
Purchase new machinery	$70,000	−$5000

SOLUTION   In Fig. 16.1 we show the decision tree for the given decision problem. This figure graphically displays the different alternatives and states of nature. The symbol ☐ at the left of the figure indicates that a

FIGURE 16.1
Decision Tree

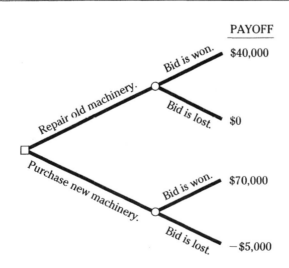

PAYOFF

Repair old machinery.
Bid is won. $40,000
Bid is lost. $0

Purchase new machinery.
Bid is won. $70,000
Bid is lost. −$5,000

BUY FLIGHT INSURANCE?

Most airports lease space to companies that sell aircraft flight insurance for specific flights. In a typical arrangement, Mutual of Omaha installs a small self-service counter where airline passengers can spend between $5 (for a $150,000 policy) and $17 (for a $500,000 policy). How many people buy them? *Smart Money* magazine noted that Mutual of Omaha sells about one million such policies each year for more than $8 million. In a recent crash resulting in 270 deaths, only 5 of those who died had bought flight insurance. Critics argue that flight insurance is overpriced and passengers don't really need it because the airline company can be sued if a passenger loses his or her life.

decision must be made. The symbol ◯ represents the different states of nature, which are determined by chance. To the right of the branches we list the payoff values, but we could also list the opportunity loss values.

Using payoff tables, opportunity loss tables, and decision trees, we can summarize and illustrate decision problems to gain a better understanding of the relevant actions, states of nature, and results of actions. In the following sections we develop strategies for actually making decisions.

16.3 EXERCISES   BASIC CONCEPTS

In Exercises 1–8, use the given payoff tables and construct the corresponding opportunity loss tables.

1.

	S1	S2
A1	10	−2
A2	6	3

2.

	S1	S2
A1	0	−2
A2	−3	5

3.

	S1	S2	S3
A1	3	1	−2
A2	3	5	4

4.

	S1	S2
A1	−2	4
A2	3	5
A3	8	7

5.

	S1	S2	S3
A1	20	−10	5
A2	15	−20	0
A3	30	−30	−5

6.

	S1	S2	S3
A1	50	−40	20
A2	30	−60	−50
A3	−10	20	−80

7.

	S1	S2	S3	S4
A1	16	−3	6	0
A2	4	−7	−5	−8

8.

	S1	S2	S3
A1	27	−12	−6
A2	0	−5	−8
A3	−3	7	−15
A4	9	3	−20

In Exercises 9–12, use the payoff table from the indicated exercise and construct the corresponding decision tree.

9. Exercise 1
10. Exercise 2
11. Exercise 3
12. Exercise 4

In Exercises 13–16, use the given decision trees and construct the corresponding opportunity loss tables.

13.

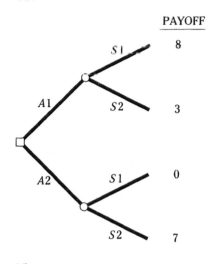

14.

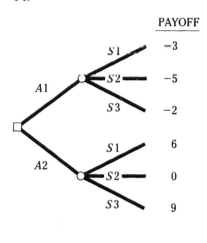

15.

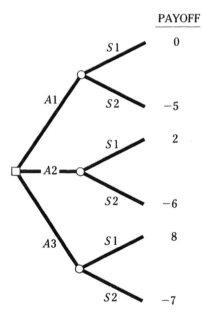

16.

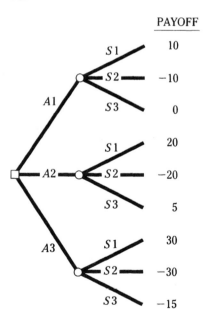

In Exercises 17–20, construct the opportunity loss tables for the decision problems given in the indicated exercise from Section 16.2.

17. Exercise 1
18. Exercise 2
19. Exercise 3
20. Exercise 4

In Exercises 21–24, construct the decision tree for the decision problems given in the indicated exercise from Section 16.2.

21. Exercise 5
22. Exercise 6
23. Exercise 7
24. Exercise 8

16.3 EXERCISES   BEYOND THE BASICS

25. Construct the opportunity loss table corresponding to the payoff tables in parts *a* and *b*.

a.

	S1	*S2*	*S3*
A1	5	−2	−3
A2	8	6	−10

b.

	S1	*S2*	*S3*
A1	17	−12	30
A2	20	−4	23

c. We know we can convert a payoff table into an opportunity loss table. Can we find a procedure for converting an opportunity loss table into the original payoff table?

26. A decision problem might contain a number of actions that are inadmissible because they are dominated by other actions. Recall that in a payoff table, we eliminate *dominated* actions, but in an opportunity loss table, we eliminate *dominating* actions.

    For the payoff tables in parts *a* and *b*, reduce the problem to one with no dominated actions. What can you conclude about the best choice of action for the table in part *b?*

a.

	S1	*S2*	*S3*	*S4*
A1	1	0	−1	4
A2	2	5	8	4
A3	6	1	3	5

b.

	S1	*S2*	*S3*
A1	1	0	−1
A2	2	1	5
A3	3	6	7
A4	2	1	6

27. For the opportunity loss tables in parts *a* and *b*, reduce the problem to one with no dominating actions. What can you conclude about the best choice of action for the table in part *b?*

a.

	S1	*S2*	*S3*
A1	2	0	0
A2	3	1	1
A3	2	0	1
A4	0	1	3

b.

	S1	*S2*	*S3*
A1	4	1	3
A2	0	0	0
A3	5	1	3

16.4 DECISION MAKING UNDER UNCERTAINTY

In the preceding sections we discussed decision problems and their major components (actions, states of nature, outcomes, objective variable). We saw that we
could illustrate relationships among those components by constructing a payoff
table, an opportunity loss table, or a decision tree. In this and the following sections
we consider strategies for determining which action is best. In this section we
consider those situations in which the decision-maker cannot obtain probability
values for the different states of nature, and in the following section we consider
cases in which those probabilities can be found or estimated.

   In this section we describe three strategies for making decisions without the
probabilities of the states of nature. The first two decision strategies are based
on payoff values, whereas the third is based on opportunity loss values.

MAXIMAX DECISION STRATEGY

If we are extreme optimists and tend to believe that the best will happen, then we
want the maximax strategy. It is called maximax because we must first find the
maximum payoff for each action, and then choose the action corresponding to the
maximum of those maximums. The word *maximax* is therefore an abbreviation
for "maximum of the maximums." This might sound like double-talk, but we can
simplify this rule by recognizing that the maximum of the maximums is simply the
largest outcome value in the entire payoff table. Using this simplified version, we
get the following definition.

DEFINITION

The *maximax decision strategy* is to choose the action that corresponds to
the maximum value in the payoff table.

EXAMPLE   Given payoff Table 16.6, use the maximax decision strategy to determine the best action.

TABLE 16.6
Payoff Table

	S1: BID IS WON	*S2*: BID IS LOST
A1: Repair old machinery	$40,000	$0
A2: Buy new machinery	$70,000	−$5000

SOLUTION   Examining the payoffs (outcome values) in Table 16.6, we see that
the maximum value is $70,000. Because that maximum value corre-
sponds to action *A2,* **we choose action *A2* and purchase the
new machinery.**

The philosophy underlying the maximax decision rule can be summarized as follows: Identify the possible results that could occur, and then throw all caution to the wind and go for the maximum possible result.

MAXIMIN DECISION STRATEGY

Whereas the maximax is an optimistic approach, the maximin is very pessimistic and conservative. The philosophy underlying the maximin strategy is this: Things will go badly and the worst will occur, so choose the best of all the worst cases. This approach is reflected in the following definition.

DEFINITION

The *maximin decision strategy* is to select the largest of the minimum outcomes for each action.

The procedure for identifying the maximin decision strategy for a payoff table can be summarized as follows:

1. For each action, find the lowest payoff (outcome value).
2. Choose the action corresponding to the largest value found in step 1.

From this procedure we can see that we are really finding the action that has the maximum of the minimum payoffs. Abbreviating "maximum of the minimums" leads to "maximin."

EXAMPLE

Given payoff Table 16.7, use the maximin decision strategy to determine the best action.

TABLE 16.7
Payoff Table

	$S1$: Bid is won	$S2$: Bid is lost	Min
A1: Repair old machinery	$40,000	$0	$0
A2: Buy new machinery	$70,000	−$5000	−$5000
		Maximin:	$0

SOLUTION

Examining the payoffs in Table 16.7, we apply step 1 in the above procedure to get these minimums:

Action $A1$: Minimum payoff is $0.
Action $A2$: Minimum payoff is −$5000.

We can now proceed to step 2, where we identify the largest value from step 1; that largest value is $0. We should therefore choose action $A1$ because it corresponds to the maximum of the minimum values listed above. That is, we should choose to repair the old machinery.

MINIMAX DECISION STRATEGY

The preceding two decision strategies are based on payoff (outcome) values in a payoff table, but the next strategy is based on opportunity loss values. Remember, these values represent amounts of payoffs that were lost by not choosing the best action. Unlike payoff values, opportunity loss values are unfavorable, and we therefore want to minimize them. This strategy is reflected in the following definition.

> **DEFINITION**
>
> The *minimax decision strategy* is to choose the action with the lowest of the maximum values of opportunity loss.

The minimax decision strategy can be determined by this procedure:

1. Construct the opportunity loss table and for each action, find the *maximum* value of *opportunity loss.*
2. Choose the action corresponding to the lowest value found in step 1.

With this approach we are minimizing the maximum values of opportunity loss, and the abbreviation of "minimizing the maximums" leads to "minimax."

EXAMPLE Given payoff Table 16.8, use the minimax decision strategy to determine the best action.

TABLE 16.8
Payoff Table

	S1: Bid is won	*S2*: Bid is lost
A1: Repair old machinery	$40,000	$0
A2: Buy new machinery	$70,000	−$5000

SOLUTION Because the minimax strategy is based on opportunity loss values, we must first construct the opportunity loss table. For each cell of the payoff table, we find the opportunity loss value by subtracting the cell value from the maximum column value, as described in Section 16.3. Corresponding to payoff Table 16.8 is opportunity loss Table 16.9.

TABLE 16.9
Opportunity Loss Table

	S1: Bid is won	*S2*: Bid is lost	Max
A1: Repair old machinery	$30,000	$0	$30,000
A2: Buy new machinery	$0	$5000	$5000
		Minimax:	$5000

BRAND LOYALTY DECLINING

Instead of selecting well-advertised brands of goods with recognizable names, growing numbers of consumers are selecting the brands of goods that are cheapest. The brand-name companies must decide how to react to this market shift. Some companies are successfully competing by pursuing ways to lower costs so they can lower their prices, but many other companies have decided to do nothing. A *Business Week* article quotes the Berkeley professor David Aaker as saying, "Companies are really dragging their heels, since it's so painful to forgo short-term profits and think strategically." The problem is so serious that some companies will be forced to close if they fail to make rational and strategic decisions. The use of statistical methods, such as those included in this chapter, can help in the formulation of good decisions.

Because we have opportunity loss values for each action, we can now proceed to apply the minimax decision strategy. In step 1 we find the maximum value of opportunity loss for each action and list the results.

Action $A1$: Maximum opportunity loss is $30,000.
Action $A2$: Maximum opportunity loss is $5000.

In step 2 we now choose action $A2$ because it corresponds to the lowest value listed above. Using this minimax decision strategy, we choose to purchase the new machinery.

After examining all three of these decision strategies, it might not be clear that they are all distinct and have different criteria. In the following example we will show that the three different strategies all lead to different actions.

EXAMPLE

You and two friends have just graduated from college, and the three of you are planning to start a management consulting firm that will specialize in one industry. You have narrowed the industries (or actions) that you are considering down to three:

$A1$: Sports and leisure activities industry
$A2$: Automobile industry
$A3$: Generic (no name) products industry

All three of these industries offer different potentials for growth, depending on the state of economy over the next few years (the states of nature):

$S1$: Economy grows
$S2$: Economy stays the same
$S3$: Economy takes a dive

You calculate the business's expected profit or loss in thousands of dollars for the first year for the various actions and states of nature, and construct the following payoff table.

TABLE 16.10
Payoff Table

	S1	S2	S3	Max	Min
A1	30	−20	−10	30	−20
A2	20	−10	−10	20	−10
A3	10	−30	20	20	−30

Each partner recommends an industry for the consulting firm. Each partner, however, uses a different strategy to come to a decision: maximax, maximin, and minimax. Using each of these strategies, which industry is selected?

SOLUTION

Maximax decision strategy: You choose the sports and leisure activities industry because that profit is the maximum value in the payoff table.

LIFE INSURANCE

Americans spend an average of 15% of their incomes on health insurance, property and liability insurance, and life insurance. About 2500 companies provide life insurance that produces premiums of $300 billion each year. In fact, life insurance is the largest single source of income and profit for the insurance industry. The decision to buy life insurance should take into account the cost of the premiums, the face value of the policy, and various personal factors. Some common recommendations are that single people don't need life insurance, but a working parent should have an amount of life insurance equal to roughly six times annual income. Rates for mail order insurance companies tend to be relatively high, but fortunately (or unfortunately) many agents would delight in trying to sell any one of a wide variety of life insurance policies.

Maximin decision strategy: You choose the automobile industry because that profit corresponds to the maximum of the minimum values.
Minimax decision strategy: You choose the generic food industry. To determine that the generic food industry is best by the minimax decision rule, first construct the opportunity loss table shown in Table 16.11.

Using the opportunity loss table, list the maximum value of opportunity loss for each action:

A1 (sports and leisure activities industry):
  Maximum opportunity loss is 30.
A2 (automobile industry):
  Maximum opportunity loss is 30.
A3 (generic or no name products industry):
  Maximum opportunity loss is 20.

Your business chooses the generic products industry because the loss generated corresponds to the lowest of the maximum opportunity loss values. That is, it is best according to the minimax criterion.

We can summarize the results of this example as follows:

DECISION STRATEGY	BEST ACTION (OR INDUSTRY)
Maximax	Sports and leisure products
Maximin	Automobile
Minimax	Generic food products

TABLE 16.11
Opportunity Loss Table

	S1	S2	S3	Max
A1	0	10	30	30
A2	10	0	30	30
A3	20	20	0	20

Minimax = 20

In this section we considered the maximax, maximin, and minimax decision tools to arrive at a "best" decision when we don't know the probabilities of the different states of nature. In the next section we consider a strategy that can be used when those probabilities are known.

16.4 EXERCISES   BASIC CONCEPTS

In Exercises 1–8, use the given payoff table to find the action that is best according to the (a) maximax, (b) maximin, and (c) minimax decision strategies.

1.

	S1	S2
A1	10	−2
A2	6	3

2.

	S1	S2
A1	0	−2
A2	−3	5

3.

	S1	S2	S3
A1	3	1	−2
A2	3	5	4

4.

	S1	S2
A1	−2	4
A2	3	5
A3	8	7

5.

	S1	S2	S3
A1	20	−10	5
A2	15	−20	0
A3	30	−30	−5

6.

	S1	S2	S3
A1	50	−40	20
A2	30	−60	−50
A3	−10	20	−80

7.

	S1	S2	S3	S4
A1	16	-3	6	0
A2	4	-7	-5	-8

8.

	S1	S2	S3
A1	27	-12	-6
A2	0	-5	-8
A3	-3	7	-15
A4	9	3	-20

In Exercises 9–20, refer to the indicated decision problems in Section 16.2 to find the actions that are best according to the (a) maximax, (b) maximin, and (c) minimax decision strategies.

9. Exercise 1   12. Exercise 4   15. Exercise 7   18. Exercise 10
10. Exercise 2   13. Exercise 5   16. Exercise 8   19. Exercise 11
11. Exercise 3   14. Exercise 6   17. Exercise 9   20. Exercise 12

16.4 EXERCISES   BEYOND THE BASICS

21. In this section we saw that the minimax decision strategy is based on opportunity loss values. Can the maximax or maximin decision strategies be determined by using an opportunity loss table?
22. A first action *dominates* a second action if the first action produces a greater payoff for each state of nature. Can a dominated action ever be chosen as best by either the maximax, the maximin, or the minimax decision strategies?
23. In a decision problem with three actions and three states of nature, all nine payoff values are different. Is it possible that the maximax, maximin, and minimax decision strategies result in the same action being chosen as best? If so, construct such a payoff table.
24. Describe the effect on the maximax, maximin, and minimax decision strategies when a payoff table is changed as follows:
    a. The same constant is added to every payoff value.
    b. Every payoff value is multiplied by the same positive constant.
    c. Every payoff value is multiplied by the same negative constant.

16.5 DECISION MAKING UNDER RISK

We have noted that in a decision problem, the states of nature depend on chance. In some cases it is possible to assign probabilities to the different states of nature, and decisions in such cases are referred to as *decisions under risk*. For example, if a university plans to hold its commencement outside, it can gamble on no rain and pay nothing for tent rental, or it can spend $8000 to rent a large tent. If the probability of rain (based on past experience) is known to be 0.1, then we have a decision problem under risk.

We begin our decision-making process by assigning weights to payoffs according to their probabilities. That is, for each action we multiply each payoff by the probability (weight) corresponding to the different states of nature. The following notation will be used.

Notation

$E(A)$ denotes the *expected value of payoff* from action *A*.

$E(A)$ is often referred to simply as the *expected value* of *A*.

$E(A1)$ is the expected value for action *A1*, $E(A2)$ is the expected value for action *A2*, and so on.

x denotes an outcome, or payoff, in a decision problem.

Using this notation, we express the expected value of an action as follows:

The **expected value of payoff** from action A is given by

$$E(A) = \Sigma x \cdot P(x)$$

where x represents the payoff values for action A and $P(x)$ represents the probabilities corresponding to the different states of nature.

EXAMPLE One action in a decision problem has payoffs of $70,000 and −$5000. For these payoffs, if we know that the states of nature have probabilities of 0.200 and 0.800, then we can find $E(x)$, the expected value for this particular action.

SOLUTION The table below is not a payoff table or an opportunity loss table; it simply shows the calculations required to find the expected value of payoff from the given action. From this table we see that for this action, the expected value of payoff is

$$E(A) = \Sigma x \cdot P(x) = \$10,000$$

x	$P(x)$	$x \cdot P(x)$
70,000	0.200	14,000
−5,000	0.800	−4,000
	Total:	10,000

$$E(A) = \Sigma x \cdot P(x) = 10,000$$

If we select the particular action being considered in this example, we don't know which state of nature will occur, but using the given probabilities, we now know that the expected value is 10,000. If this action is selected many times, the first state of nature will occur about 20% of the time (with a $70,000 gain), the second state of nature will occur about 80% of the time (with a $5000 loss), but the average payoff will be $10,000.

The expression for $E(A)$ might seem familiar (then again, it might not) because the mean of a discrete random variable was given in Chapter 4 as $\mu = \Sigma x \cdot P(x)$. In fact, this mean and the expected value are essentially the same. When we calculate the expected value of payoff $E(A)$, we are actually finding the mean payoff that would result if this action were to be selected infinitely many times. In a decision problem, the decision-maker wants to select the "best," or optimal, decision. The objective is to make the choice that results in the greatest possible gain; if all decisions result in a loss, then we want to make the choice that results in the least possible loss. If we know the probabilities for the different states of nature, we can find the expected value for each action; we can then use those expected values to find the best action by using the criterion given in the following definition.

DEFINITION

The *expected payoff criterion* indicates that we should choose the action that has the highest expected value of payoff.

For example, if a decision problem has actions $A1$ and $A2$ with expected values of $163 and $172, respectively, we choose action $A2$ because its expected value is larger.

Given a decision problem for which the states of nature have probabilities that can be identified, we now have a decision-making strategy summarized by these steps:

1. Identify the actions, states of nature, outcomes, objective variable, and the probability of each state of nature.
2. Calculate the expected value of payoff for each action by using $E(A) = \Sigma x \cdot P(x)$.
3. Choose the action resulting in the largest expected value.
4. It's important to use common sense to be sure that you don't mess up.

GAME THEORY

Game Theory is a branch of mathematics begun around 1927 with the work of John von Neumann (1903–1957). In 1944 von Neumann and Oscar Morgenstern published *Theory of Games and Economic Behavior,* in which a new approach was used for analysis in economics. Von Neumann and Morgenstern showed that certain human events can be approximated by games of strategy that can be analyzed mathematically. Game theory involves principles of decision theory as well as principles of probability theory. In the subject of game theory, a game is not merely an amusement or a recreational pastime; it is a problem of strategy in the context of a competitive situation. The players are not necessarily individuals; they can be nations, corporations, or groups of consumers.

EXAMPLE   Let's again consider the example from Section 16.2 in which an executive for the Dayton Machine Company must choose between repairing old machinery and buying new machinery. The company manufactures auto parts and has already made a contractual commitment to sell one large batch and has submitted a bid for a second large order. The outcomes are summarized in the payoff table given in Table 16.2.

TABLE 16.12
Payoff Table

	*S*1: BID IS WON	*S*2: BID IS LOST
*A*1: Repair old machinery	$40,000	$0
*A*2: Buy new machinery	$70,000	−$5000

In addition to the information given in Section 16.2, let's also assume that the probability of winning the bid is 0.200, while the probability of losing it is (you guessed it) 0.800. These probabilities could be based on past results. Use the expected payoff criterion to find the best choice.

SOLUTION Our solution will follow the steps listed above.

1. The objective variable is the amount of profit. The actions, states of nature, and outcomes are given in Table 16.12. The probabilities of the states of nature are given in the statement of the problem.
2. The expected value for action $A2$ (purchase new machinery) was calculated in the preceding example so that $E(A2) = \$10,000$. The expected value for action $A1$ (repair old machinery) is calculated as follows:

x	$P(x)$	$x \cdot P(x)$
40,000	0.200	8000
0	0.800	0
	Total:	8000

$$E(A1) = \Sigma x \cdot P(x) = 8000$$

3. We choose action $A2$ (purchase new machinery) because its expected value of $10,000 is greater than the expected value of $8000 for action $A1$ (repair old machinery). That is, the executive should choose to purchase new machinery.
4. The preceding conclusion takes into account only the information given. New technologies, changing market demands, and other relevant factors should be considered. However, based on the information available and using the expected-payoff criterion, our decision to buy the new machinery seems reasonable.

In the last example we used outcomes (or payoffs) when we calculated the expected values for each decision. The values of these payoffs could have come from the original problem statement, the payoff table, or a decision tree. However, we could also use the values of opportunity loss. *When we use opportunity loss values, our calculations will be similar and the end result will always be the same.* However, when using opportunity loss values, we should choose the action that leads to the *lowest* expected value. The most favorable result is achieved by minimizing the amount of opportunity loss. Shown in Table 16.13 are the calculations that result in expected values of opportunity loss for the preceding example. Because action $A2$ produces a *lower* expected value of opportunity loss, we should choose that action. We are led to the same conclusion: Buy the new machinery.

To use this tool for decision making under risk (that is, with *known* probabilities assigned to the states of nature), it might be helpful to indicate how the probability values are obtained. One way to estimate these probabilities is to use information on the relative occurrence of these different states of nature in the past. Such values are called *relative frequency probabilities,* as defined in Chapter 3. For example, suppose we are choosing the site of this year's graduation ceremony and both the outdoor stadium and the indoor auditorium are available. Weather is a major factor. If past records show that it rained on 15 of the past 50 graduation days, then the relative frequency estimate of no rain becomes 35/50 = 0.7. The probability of using the auditorium for the graduation ceremony becomes 0.3, while the probability of using the outdoor stadium is 0.7.

TABLE 16.13
Action $A1$ (repair the old machinery)

x	$P(x)$	$x \cdot P(x)$
30,000	0.200	6000
0	0.800	0
	Total:	6000 ←

Action $A2$ (purchase new machinery)

x	$P(x)$	$x \cdot P(x)$
0	0.200	0
5000	0.800	4000
	Total:	4000 ←

A second way to estimate probabilities of the various states of nature is to use the subjective judgment of those believed to be knowledgeable about the given circumstances. If we again consider the example of choosing a graduation site, the final decision, including a possible last-minute change, is to be made by the college president. Members of the graduation committee may believe that the ceremony will be moved indoors if any clouds appear on the morning of graduation day. Because they know that on past graduation days it was cloudy for 20 of the 50 days, they assign a probability of $20/50 = 0.4$ to the likelihood that the ceremony will be indoors (0.6 for outdoors). Note that in general, subjective information is usually combined with relative frequency information to arrive at the probability estimate for the states of nature. Considerable care should be made in estimating these probabilities. If they are in error by large amounts, then the quality of our decision making will suffer.

The different decision-making strategies discussed in this chapter often fail to take into account the decision-maker's outlook toward *risk*. In many situations the expected payoff criterion leads to a choice of action that might not be best when we take risk into account. For example, in a typical state lottery, if we calculate expected values for the actions of buying a ticket and not buying one, we will see that the larger expected value of 0 indicates that we should not choose to buy a lottery ticket. But because only $1 is at risk, it's not a big deal, and we could easily choose the action of buying a lottery ticket even though that's contrary to the strategy determined by the expected payoff criterion.

Now let's think about the lottery problem another way. Suppose someone offers you $1 to act as the state and run your own lottery. If the bettor loses, you get to keep his $1, but if he wins, you must shell out $1,000,000 or everything you own. The expected payoff criterion would lead to the conclusion that you should take the bet, but almost nobody would be willing to risk everything in order to win $1. The risk is unacceptable. There are more formal methods for including risk in the decision-making strategy, but we won't pursue them in this book. However, common sense is a valuable resource in making reasonable decisions.

16.5 EXERCISES   BASIC CONCEPTS

In Exercises 1–8, find the expected value of payoff for the given actions and probabilities.

1. Action $A1$ has outcomes of 280, 360, and -120. The corresponding states of nature have probabilities of 0.250, 0.600, and 0.150, respectively.
2. Action $A2$ has outcomes of $45, $38, $-$21, and $16. The corresponding states of nature have probabilities of 0.145, 0.440, 0.380, and 0.035, respectively.
3. Action $A3$ has payoffs of 28.2, -36.4, 49.1, and 0. The corresponding states of nature have probabilities of 0.137, 0.204, 0.086, and 0.573, respectively.
4. Action $A4$ has payoffs of 578, 419, -212, -647, and 0. The corresponding states of nature have probabilities of 0.243, 0.184, 0.337, 0.209, and 0.027, respectively.
5. A 27-year-old woman decides to pay $156 for a one-year life insurance policy with coverage of $100,000. The probability of her living through the year is

0.9995. (Based on data from the U.S. Department of Health and Human
Services and AFT Group Life Insurance.)

6. A gambler buys a $1 lotto ticket. If she wins, her net profit will be $499. If she
loses, her loss is the cost of the ticket. Because she must select the correct
three-digit number, her probability of winning is 0.001.

7. A contractor has decided to bid on a job to construct a building. The probability of making a $340,000 profit is 0.7, the probability of losing $125,000 is
0.2, the probability of breaking even is 0.1.

8. An airport fixed-base operator has decided to open a flight school that makes
a profit of $200 on fair days, but loses $150 for each day of bad weather. If
the probability of bad weather is 0.183, what is the expected value of payoff
for a single day?

In Exercises 9–12, use the given payoff tables and the given probabilities to find
(a) the expected value of payoff for each action, and (b) the action that is best
according to the expected payoff criterion.

9.

	$S1$	$S2$
$A1$	10	−2
$A2$	6	3

$P(S1) = 0.6$; $P(S2) = 0.4$

10.

	$S1$	$S2$
$A1$	0	−2
$A2$	−3	5

$P(S1) = 0.250$; $P(S2) = 0.750$

11.

	$S1$	$S2$	$S3$
$A1$	3	1	−2
$A2$	3	5	4

$P(S1) = 0.452$;
$P(S2) = 0.249$;
$P(S3) = 0.299$

12.

	$S1$	$S2$
$A1$	−2	4
$A2$	3	5
$A3$	8	7

$P(S1) = 0.642$; $P(S2) = 0.358$

In Exercises 13–16, use the given payoff tables and probabilities to find (a) the
expected value of opportunity loss for each action, and (b) the action that is best.

13.

	$S1$	$S2$	$S3$
$A1$	20	−10	5
$A2$	15	−20	0
$A3$	30	−30	−5

$P(S1) = 0.300$;
$P(S2) = 0.500$;
$P(S3) = 0.200$

14.

	$S1$	$S2$	$S3$
$A1$	50	−40	20
$A2$	30	−60	−50
$A3$	−10	20	−80

$P(S1) = 0.200$;
$P(S2) = 0.700$;
$P(S3) = 0.100$

15.

	$S1$	$S2$	$S3$	$S4$
$A1$	16	−3	6	0
$A2$	4	−7	−5	−8

$P(S1) = 0.225$;
$P(S2) = 0.246$;
$P(S3) = 0.317$;
$P(S4) = 0.212$

16.

	$S1$	$S2$	$S3$
$A1$	27	−12	−6
$A2$	0	−5	−8
$A3$	−3	7	−15
$A4$	9	3	−20

$P(S1) = 0.323$;
$P(S2) = 0.479$;
$P(S3) = 0.198$

In Exercises 17–28, use the given decision problems to find (a) the expected value of payoff for each action, and (b) the action that is best according to the expected payoff criterion.

17. A 64-year-old man is considering the purchase of a one-year term life insurance policy with $50,000 coverage. The cost of the policy is $87. The probability that a 64-year-old man will live through his next year is 0.980 (based on data from the U.S. Department of Health and Human Services).

18. The operator of a food booth at a county fair must choose between renting a tent or not renting one. If the tent is not rented, a $300 profit is expected in good weather and a $100 loss in rainy weather. If the tent is rented, a $150 profit is expected in good weather and a $50 profit in rainy weather. Based on past records, the probability of rain is 0.125.

19. A defendant in a product liability case must choose between settling out of court for a loss of $150,000 or going to trial and either losing nothing (if found not guilty) or losing $500,000 (if found guilty). The attorney estimates that the probability of a not-guilty verdict is 0.8.

20. The owner of a bookstore is trying to decide whether to add a VCR rental area. If demand is sufficient, profits will increase by $15,000. If demand is not sufficient, a loss of $10,000 can be expected. The owner estimates that the probability of sufficient demand is 0.7.

21. An executive in charge of advertising must decide whether to use television or print media, or both. For those three options, a successful campaign will increase profits by $250,000, $175,000, and $300,000, respectively. An unsuccessful campaign will decrease profits by $80,000, $60,000, and $140,000, respectively. Based on past results, the probability of a successful campaign is 0.6.

22. A company plans to open a service station with either 1, 2, or 3 service bays. If the station is successful, the profits will be $20,000, $35,000, and $45,000, respectively. If the station is unsuccessful, the losses will be $50,000, $100,000, and $150,000, respectively. It is estimated that the probability of success is 0.9.

23. An investor is trying to decide whether to buy a safe blue-chip stock or a speculative stock. It is estimated that a healthy economy would result in a $5000 profit from the blue-chip stock and a $12,000 profit from the speculative stock. An unhealthy economy would lead to losses of $3000 and $15,000 for the blue-chip stock and the speculative stock, respectively. The probability of an unhealthy economy is estimated to be 0.7.

24. A builder knows that a large corporation is considering a major expansion into a particular region. The builder is trying to decide whether to exercise an option on the purchase of a large parcel of land. If the option is exercised, the builder will gain $500,000 (if the corporation moves in) or will lose $150,000 (if the corporation does not move in). If the option is not exercised, the builder loses $25,000 whether or not the company comes. Based on the latest available information, the probability that the corporation will come is 0.1.

25. A concert promoter can schedule an event in a large outdoor stadium or a smaller indoor arena. If the outdoor stadium is chosen, the event will yield a profit of $200,000 in good weather or a loss of $100,000 in rain. With the

indoor arena, it will yield a $40,000 profit, regardless of the weather. The probability of rain is 0.125.

26. The owner of a small publishing firm is considering the possibility of starting a local magazine. Depending on its success, the magazine can yield a $400,000 profit or a $250,000 loss. If the owner decides against the magazine, there is no profit or loss. Based on similar ventures elsewhere, the probability of success is estimated to be 0.4.

27. Cable TV decoders are sold to retailers in groups of five. One particular retailer must order either 0, 5, 10, or 15 units. If the TV signal doesn't change, those four options will produce profits of $0, $300, $600, or $900, respectively. If the TV signal does change, those four options will produce losses of $0, $450, $900, or $1350, respectively. The probability of a changing signal is 0.2.

28. The owner of a fitness center is trying to decide whether to expand, and the options are 0, 1, or 2 additional sites. Depending on the state of local economic and health awareness factors, those three options will either lead to additional profits of $0, $70,000, or $120,000 or result in losses of $0, $140,000, or $250,000, respectively. The probability that the factors will be favorable is 0.6.

16.5 EXERCISES   BEYOND THE BASICS

29. Given the accompanying payoff table and probabilities find the opportunity loss table, the expected value of payoff for each action, the expected opportunity loss for each action, and the best action.

$P(S1)$ =   0.285
$P(S2)$ =   0.335
$P(S3)$ =   0.380

	S1	S2	S3
A1	−12.6	18.3	10.6
A2	15.4	−1.4	2.1
A3	17.2	−7.9	8.9

30. Action $A1$ leads to an expected value of payoff of 5, and action $A2$ leads to an expected value of opportunity loss of 4. Based on this information, can the most favorable action be determined? If so, which is it? Explain.

31. Describe the effect on the expected value when a payoff table is changed as follows:
    a.   Every payoff value is multiplied by the same positive constant.
    b.   Every payoff value is multiplied by the same negative constant.

32. Describe the effect on the expected value when a payoff table is changed as follows:
    a.   Every payoff value has the same positive constant added to it.
    b.   Every payoff value has the same positive constant subtracted from it.

PRICE WARS

Consider this dilemma: Exxon and Texaco gas stations are located on opposite corners and they are run by independent owners. They now charge the same price for a gallon of gas, but if either one charges a little less, then that station will win many more customers and the other station will lose business. The Exxon station owner lowers the price by two cents per gallon, so the Texaco station retaliates with a similar reduction in price. The Exxon station counters with another reduction that is also matched by the Texaco station. As the two stations continue to lower prices, neither wins nor loses customers, but they both lose income in this price war. The ideal solution for the involved parties may require collusion, which in many cases is outlawed by antitrust legislation. The analysis of problems often involves a branch of mathematics called *game theory,* which isn't as frivolous as its title suggests.

Vocabulary List
Define and give an example of each term.

decision problem
decision problem with certainty
decision problem under risk
decision problem under uncertainty
actions
states of nature
outcomes
payoffs
objective variable
payoff table
inadmissible actions
dominates
opportunity loss
opportunity loss table
decision tree
maximax decision strategy
maximin decision strategy
minimax decision strategy
expected value of payoff
expected payoff criterion

Review

The central concern of this chapter is the process of decision making when the decision problem has an element of uncertainty, in that the results are affected by conditions that depend on chance. In Section 16.2 we saw that the decision problem has the major components of *actions, states of nature, outcomes* (or payoffs), and an *objective variable;* the *payoff table* can be used to represent those components. The actions are the available alternatives, the states of nature are the chance events, the outcomes are the measured results, and the objective variable is the quantity being considered. In Section 16.3 we saw how to illustrate relevant data in the form of an *opportunity loss table* or a *decision tree.*

We began the actual process of determining the best decision strategy in Section 16.4, where we considered three different decision strategies for decision problems in which probabilities are not assigned to the states of nature. The *maximax decision strategy* involves selecting the action with the largest payoff. With the *maximin strategy* we choose the action with the highest of the minimum payoffs for the different actions. With the *minimax strategy* we choose the action with the lowest of the maximum values of opportunity loss.

In Section 16.5 we saw that if we can assign a probability value to each state of nature, then we can calculate the *expected value of payoff* for each action. The *expected payoff criterion* indicates that we should choose the action that yields the highest expected payoff value (or the lowest expected opportunity loss value).

IMPORTANT FORMULAS

Opportunity loss for a cell = (maximum column value) − (cell value)
$E(A) = \Sigma x \cdot P(x)$ Expected value of action A

Review Exercises

1. In each of the following, determine the decision strategy that is being used.

    a. In deciding whether to bet $5 on roulette, a slot machine, or the lottery, a gambler chooses the lottery because its payoff of $1 million is highest.

    b. In deciding whether to bet $5 on the lottery or $25 on a raffle ticket for a new car, an accountant chooses the lottery so that she will lose less.

    c. Three options can provide profits or (depending on conditions) losses of $5000, $6000, or $7000, respectively. The first option is chosen so that no more than $5000 will be lost.

2. Given the accompanying payoff table, construct the corresponding opportunity loss table.

	S1	S2	S3
A1	38	−15	7
A2	−12	−17	19
A3	0	25	−8

3. Given the payoff table in Exercise 2, find the action that is best according to the (a) maximax, (b) maximin, and (c) minimax decision strategies.

4. A decision problem has the payoff table given in Exercise 2. Also, $P(S1) = 0.634$, $P(S2) = 0.127$, and $P(S3) = 0.239$. Find the expected value of payoff for each action and then find the action that is best according to the expected payoff criterion.

5. A taxpayer is being billed for an additional $10,000 and is trying to decide whether to pay it or contest it in court. A favorable court ruling will result in $2000 lost to legal expenses, whereas an unfavorable ruling will result in a total loss of $12,000. Identify the actions, states of nature, outcomes, and the objective variable.

6. Construct the payoff table for the decision problem in Exercise 5.

7. Construct the opportunity loss table for the decision problem in Exercise 5.

8. Construct the decision tree for the decision problem given in Exercise 5.

9. For the decision problem of Exercise 5, find the action that is best according to the (a) maximax, (b) maximin, and (c) minimax decision strategies.

10. For the decision problem of Exercise 5, a study of similar cases suggests that the probability of a favorable court ruling is 0.3. Find the expected value of payoff for each action and then find the action that is best according to the expected payoff criterion.

11. The manager of a fuel oil supply company finds that a pump on a truck is working very slowly. He is trying to decide whether to fix the pump, replace it, or leave it as is. He also knows that the owner might buy a new truck. The manager estimates that fixing the pump will cost $300 whether the truck is kept or sold. A new pump will cost $1000 if the truck is kept and $800 if the truck is sold. Leaving the pump as is would cost $2000 if the truck is kept and nothing if it is sold. Identify the actions, states of nature, outcomes, and objective variable.

12. Construct the payoff table for the decision problem given in Exercise 11.

13. Construct the opportunity loss table for the decision problem given in Exercise 11.

14. Construct the decision tree for the problem given in Exercise 11.

15. For the decision problem given in Exercise 11, find the action that is best according to the (a) maximax, (b) maximin, and (c) minimax decision strategies.

16. For the decision problem of Exercise 11, the sale of the truck depends on chance conditions, and it is estimated that $P(\text{sale}) = 0.8$. Find the expected value of payoff for each action that is best according to the expected payoff criterion.

Computer Project

This chapter discussed some basic techniques of decision making, but technology makes possible other approaches. Specifically, computer simulations sometimes allow us to investigate a problem in ways that would otherwise be impractical or impossible. Pilots are trained to make potentially life-saving decisions by using computer-controlled flight simulators. Operators of nuclear power plants use computer simulations to be prepared for various emergencies that could occur. City managers use computer simulations to test the effects of different planning strategies. In this Computer Project we use a computer simulation to determine the most profitable ordering strategy for a relatively simple situation.

Suppose you can buy newspapers for 30 cents each and you can sell them for 50 cents each. Any newspapers you sell will result in a profit of 20 cents each, but any newspapers you buy and don't resell will result in a loss of 30 cents each. Your objective is to maximize profit, but how do you decide how many newspapers to order? This decision should be based on the distribution of customers wanting to buy newspapers. Enter the Minitab commands below to simulate the number of customers for 20 days. Those commands randomly generate 20 numbers from a uniform distribution with a mean of $\mu = 40$.

```
MTB > RANDOM 20 C1;
SUBC> INTEGERS 30 50.
MTB > PRINT C1
```

In reality, you won't know in advance the number of customers that will arrive, so choose some number of newspapers to be ordered (such as 30) for each of the 20 days and then calculate the net profit. (Remember, you make a profit of 20 cents on each newspaper sold, but if the number of newspapers ordered is less than the number of customers, you will lose 30 cents for each unsold newspaper.) Use trial and error to find the number of newspapers that should be ordered. The best choice is the number that produces that largest profit.

SELL OR STAY?

Assume that you own a home in Dutchess County and you have a living area of 3100 square feet. You learn that 20 homes with areas of at least 3000 square feet will be randomly selected and considered for possible condemnation as housing sites for dependent adults. You estimate that you will lose $20,000 in real estate value if your home is one of the 20 selected, so you consider selling your home before the selection is made. This decision problem involves these two actions: Sell or don't sell. There are two states of nature: Your home is selected or it isn't.

a. Construct the payoff table and identify the actions that are best according to the maximax, maximin, and minimax decision strategies.

b. Refer to Appendix B and use the 150 homes to estimate the proportion of homes with living areas of at least 3000 square feet.

c. Given that there are 64,357 homes in the county, use the result from part b to find the expected number of homes with living areas of at least 3000 square feet.

d. Use the result from part c and the fact that 20 homes will be selected to estimate the probability that your home will be chosen.

e. Use the result from part d to find the expected payoff for each action.

f. Using the results from part e, determine the action that is best according to the expected payoff criterion.

g. Using the results from parts a and f, determine the decision that seems the most sensible.

Appendix A: Tables

TABLE A.1
Binomial Probabilities

n	x	.01	.05	.10	.20	.30	.40	.50	.60	.70	.80	.90	.95	.99	x
2	0	980	902	810	640	490	360	250	160	090	040	010	002	0+	0
	1	020	095	180	320	420	480	500	480	420	320	180	095	020	1
	2	0+	002	010	040	090	160	250	360	490	640	810	902	980	2
3	0	970	857	729	512	343	216	125	064	027	008	001	0+	0+	0
	1	029	135	243	384	441	432	375	288	189	096	027	007	0+	1
	2	0+	007	027	096	189	288	375	432	441	384	243	135	029	2
	3	0+	0+	001	008	027	064	125	216	343	512	729	857	970	3
4	0	961	815	656	410	240	130	062	026	008	002	0+	0+	0+	0
	1	039	171	292	410	412	346	250	154	076	026	004	0+	0+	1
	2	001	014	049	154	265	346	375	346	265	154	049	014	001	2
	3	0+	0+	004	026	076	154	250	346	412	410	292	171	039	3
	4	0+	0+	0+	002	008	026	062	130	240	410	656	815	961	4
5	0	951	774	590	328	168	078	031	010	002	0+	0+	0+	0+	0
	1	048	204	328	410	360	259	156	077	028	006	0+	0+	0+	1
	2	001	021	073	205	309	346	312	230	132	051	008	001	0+	2
	3	0+	001	008	051	132	230	312	346	309	205	073	021	001	3
	4	0+	0+	0+	006	028	077	156	259	360	410	328	204	048	4
	5	0+	0+	0+	0+	002	010	031	078	168	328	590	774	951	5
6	0	941	735	531	262	118	047	016	004	001	0+	0+	0+	0+	0
	1	057	232	354	393	303	187	094	037	010	002	0+	0+	0+	1
	2	001	031	098	246	324	311	234	138	060	015	001	0+	0+	2
	3	0+	002	015	082	185	276	312	276	185	082	015	002	0+	3
	4	0+	0+	001	015	060	138	234	311	324	246	098	031	001	4
	5	0+	0+	0+	002	010	037	094	187	303	393	354	232	057	5
	6	0+	0+	0+	0+	001	004	016	047	118	262	531	735	941	6
7	0	932	698	478	210	082	028	008	002	0+	0+	0+	0+	0+	0
	1	066	257	372	367	247	131	055	017	004	0+	0+	0+	0+	1
	2	002	041	124	275	318	261	164	077	025	004	0+	0+	0+	2
	3	0+	004	023	115	227	290	273	194	097	029	003	0+	0+	3
	4	0+	0+	003	029	097	194	273	290	227	115	023	004	0+	4
	5	0+	0+	0+	004	025	077	164	261	318	275	124	041	002	5
	6	0+	0+	0+	0+	004	017	055	131	247	367	372	257	066	6
	7	0+	0+	0+	0+	0+	002	008	028	082	210	478	698	932	7
8	0	923	663	430	168	058	017	004	001	0+	0+	0+	0+	0+	0
	1	075	279	383	336	198	090	031	008	001	0+	0+	0+	0+	1
	2	003	051	149	294	296	209	109	041	010	001	0+	0+	0+	2
	3	0+	005	033	147	254	279	219	124	047	009	0+	0+	0+	3
	4	0+	0+	005	046	136	232	273	232	136	046	005	0+	0+	4
	5	0+	0+	0+	009	047	124	219	279	254	147	033	005	0+	5
	6	0+	0+	0+	001	010	041	109	209	296	294	149	051	003	6
	7	0+	0+	0+	0+	001	008	031	090	198	336	383	279	075	7
	8	0+	0+	0+	0+	0+	001	004	017	058	168	430	663	923	8

NOTE: 0+ represents a positive probability less than 0.005.

(continued)

TABLE A.1 (cont.)

n	x	.01	.05	.10	.20	.30	.40	.50	.60	.70	.80	.90	.95	.99	x
9	0	914	630	387	134	040	010	002	0+	0+	0+	0+	0+	0+	0
	1	083	299	387	302	156	060	018	004	0+	0+	0+	0+	0+	1
	2	003	063	172	302	267	161	070	021	004	0+	0+	0+	0+	2
	3	0+	008	045	176	267	251	164	074	021	003	0+	0+	0+	3
	4	0+	001	007	066	172	251	246	167	074	017	001	0+	0+	4
	5	0+	0+	001	017	074	167	246	251	172	066	007	001	0+	5
	6	0+	0+	0+	003	021	074	164	251	267	176	045	008	0+	6
	7	0+	0+	0+	0+	004	021	070	161	267	302	172	063	003	7
	8	0+	0+	0+	0+	0+	004	018	060	156	302	387	299	083	8
	9	0+	0+	0+	0+	0+	0+	002	010	040	134	387	630	914	9
10	0	904	599	349	107	028	006	001	0+	0+	0+	0+	0+	0+	0
	1	091	315	387	268	121	040	010	002	0+	0+	0+	0+	0+	1
	2	004	075	194	302	233	121	044	011	001	0+	0+	0+	0+	2
	3	0+	010	057	201	267	215	117	042	009	001	0+	0+	0+	3
	4	0+	001	011	088	200	251	205	111	037	006	0+	0+	0+	4
	5	0+	0+	001	026	103	201	246	201	103	026	001	0+	0+	5
	6	0+	0+	0+	006	037	111	205	251	200	088	011	001	0+	6
	7	0+	0+	0+	001	009	042	117	215	267	201	057	010	0+	7
	8	0+	0+	0+	0+	001	011	044	121	233	302	194	075	004	8
	9	0+	0+	0+	0+	0+	002	010	040	121	268	387	315	091	9
	10	0+	0+	0+	0+	0+	0+	001	006	028	107	349	599	904	10
11	0	895	569	314	086	020	004	0+	0+	0+	0+	0+	0+	0+	0
	1	099	329	384	236	093	027	005	001	0+	0+	0+	0+	0+	1
	2	005	087	213	295	200	089	027	005	001	0+	0+	0+	0+	2
	3	0+	014	071	221	257	177	081	023	004	0+	0+	0+	0+	3
	4	0+	001	016	111	220	236	161	070	017	002	0+	0+	0+	4
	5	0+	0+	002	039	132	221	226	147	057	010	0+	0+	0+	5
	6	0+	0+	0+	010	057	147	226	221	132	039	002	0+	0+	6
	7	0+	0+	0+	002	017	070	161	236	220	111	016	001	0+	7
	8	0+	0+	0+	0+	004	023	081	177	257	221	071	014	0+	8
	9	0+	0+	0+	0+	001	005	027	089	200	295	213	087	005	9
	10	0+	0+	0+	0+	0+	001	005	027	093	236	384	329	099	10
	11	0+	0+	0+	0+	0+	0+	0+	004	020	086	314	569	895	11
12	0	886	540	282	069	014	002	0+	0+	0+	0+	0+	0+	0+	0
	1	107	341	377	206	071	017	003	0+	0+	0+	0+	0+	0+	1
	2	006	099	230	283	168	064	016	002	0+	0+	0+	0+	0+	2
	3	0+	017	085	236	240	142	054	012	001	0+	0+	0+	0+	3
	4	0+	002	021	133	231	213	121	042	008	001	0+	0+	0+	4
	5	0+	0+	004	053	158	227	193	101	029	003	0+	0+	0+	5
	6	0+	0+	0+	016	079	177	226	177	079	016	0+	0+	0+	6
	7	0+	0+	0+	003	029	101	193	227	158	053	004	0+	0+	7
	8	0+	0+	0+	001	008	042	121	213	231	133	021	002	0+	8
	9	0+	0+	0+	0+	001	012	054	142	240	236	085	017	0+	9
	10	0+	0+	0+	0+	0+	002	016	064	168	283	230	099	006	10
	11	0+	0+	0+	0+	0+	0+	003	017	071	206	377	341	107	11
	12	0+	0+	0+	0+	0+	0+	0+	002	014	069	282	540	886	12

NOTE: 0+ represents a positive probability less than 0.005.

(continued)

TABLE A.1 (cont.)

n	x	.01	.05	.10	.20	.30	.40	.50	.60	.70	.80	.90	.95	.99	x
13	0	878	513	254	055	010	001	0+	0+	0+	0+	0+	0+	0+	0
	1	115	351	367	179	054	011	002	0+	0+	0+	0+	0+	0+	1
	2	007	111	245	268	139	045	010	001	0+	0+	0+	0+	0+	2
	3	0+	021	100	246	218	111	035	006	001	0+	0+	0+	0+	3
	4	0+	003	028	154	234	184	087	024	003	0+	0+	0+	0+	4
	5	0+	0+	006	069	180	221	157	066	014	001	0+	0+	0+	5
	6	0+	0+	001	023	103	197	209	131	044	006	0+	0+	0+	6
	7	0+	0+	0+	006	044	131	209	197	103	023	001	0+	0+	7
	8	0+	0+	0+	001	014	066	157	221	180	069	006	0+	0+	8
	9	0+	0+	0+	0+	003	024	087	184	234	154	028	003	0+	9
	10	0+	0+	0+	0+	001	006	035	111	218	246	100	021	0+	10
	11	0+	0+	0+	0+	0+	001	010	045	139	268	245	111	007	11
	12	0+	0+	0+	0+	0+	0+	002	011	054	179	367	351	115	12
	13	0+	0+	0+	0+	0+	0+	0+	001	010	055	254	513	878	13
14	0	869	488	229	044	007	001	0+	0+	0+	0+	0+	0+	0+	0
	1	123	359	356	154	041	007	001	0+	0+	0+	0+	0+	0+	1
	2	008	123	257	250	113	032	006	001	0+	0+	0+	0+	0+	2
	3	0+	026	114	250	194	085	022	003	0+	0+	0+	0+	0+	3
	4	0+	004	035	172	229	155	061	014	001	0+	0+	0+	0+	4
	5	0+	0+	008	086	196	207	122	041	007	0+	0+	0+	0+	5
	6	0+	0+	001	032	126	207	183	092	023	002	0+	0+	0+	6
	7	0+	0+	0+	009	062	157	209	157	062	009	0+	0+	0+	7
	8	0+	0+	0+	002	023	092	183	207	126	032	001	0+	0+	8
	9	0+	0+	0+	0+	007	041	122	207	196	086	008	0+	0+	9
	10	0+	0+	0+	0+	001	014	061	155	229	172	035	004	0+	10
	11	0+	0+	0+	0+	0+	003	022	085	194	250	114	026	0+	11
	12	0+	0+	0+	0+	0+	001	006	032	113	250	257	123	008	12
	13	0+	0+	0+	0+	0+	0+	001	007	041	154	356	359	123	13
	14	0+	0+	0+	0+	0+	0+	0+	001	007	044	229	488	869	14
15	0	860	463	206	035	005	0+	0+	0+	0+	0+	0+	0+	0+	0
	1	130	366	343	132	031	005	0+	0+	0+	0+	0+	0+	0+	1
	2	009	135	267	231	092	022	003	0+	0+	0+	0+	0+	0+	2
	3	0+	031	129	250	170	063	014	002	0+	0+	0+	0+	0+	3
	4	0+	005	043	188	219	127	042	007	001	0+	0+	0+	0+	4
	5	0+	001	010	103	206	186	092	024	003	0+	0+	0+	0+	5
	6	0+	0+	002	043	147	207	153	061	012	001	0+	0+	0+	6
	7	0+	0+	0+	014	081	177	196	118	035	003	0+	0+	0+	7
	8	0+	0+	0+	003	035	118	196	177	081	014	0+	0+	0+	8
	9	0+	0+	0+	001	012	061	153	207	147	043	002	0+	0+	9
	10	0+	0+	0+	0+	003	024	092	186	206	103	010	001	0+	10
	11	0+	0+	0+	0+	001	007	042	127	219	188	043	005	0+	11
	12	0+	0+	0+	0+	0+	002	014	063	170	250	129	031	0+	12
	13	0+	0+	0+	0+	0+	0+	003	022	092	231	267	135	009	13
	14	0+	0+	0+	0+	0+	0+	0+	005	031	132	343	366	130	14
	15	0+	0+	0+	0+	0+	0+	0+	0+	005	035	206	463	860	15

NOTE: 0+ represents a positive probability less than 0.005.
SOURCE: From Mosteller, *Probability with Statistical Applications*, 2/e, © 1970 Addison-Wesley Publishing Co., Reading, MA. Reprinted by permission.

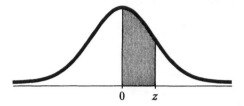

TABLE A.2
The Standard Normal (z) Distribution

z	.00	.01	.02	.03	.04	.05	.06	.07	.08	.09
0.0	.0000	.0040	.0080	.0120	.0160	.0199	.0239	.0279	.0319	.0359
0.1	.0398	.0438	.0478	.0517	.0557	.0596	.0636	.0675	.0714	.0753
0.2	.0793	.0832	.0871	.0910	.0948	.0987	.1026	.1064	.1103	.1141
0.3	.1179	.1217	.1255	.1293	.1331	.1368	.1406	.1443	.1480	.1517
0.4	.1554	.1591	.1628	.1664	.1700	.1736	.1772	.1808	.1844	.1879
0.5	.1915	.1950	.1985	.2019	.2054	.2088	.2123	.2157	.2190	.2224
0.6	.2257	.2291	.2324	.2357	.2389	.2422	.2454	.2486	.2517	.2549
0.7	.2580	.2611	.2642	.2673	.2704	.2734	.2764	.2794	.2823	.2852
0.8	.2881	.2910	.2939	.2967	.2995	.3023	.3051	.3078	.3106	.3133
0.9	.3159	.3186	.3212	.3238	.3264	.3289	.3315	.3340	.3365	.3389
1.0	.3413	.3438	.3461	.3485	.3508	.3531	.3554	.3577	.3599	.3621
1.1	.3643	.3665	.3686	.3708	.3729	.3749	.3770	.3790	.3810	.3830
1.2	.3849	.3869	.3888	.3907	.3925	.3944	.3962	.3980	.3997	.4015
1.3	.4032	.4049	.4066	.4082	.4099	.4115	.4131	.4147	.4162	.4177
1.4	.4192	.4207	.4222	.4236	.4251	.4265	.4279	.4292	.4306	.4319
1.5	.4332	.4345	.4357	.4370	.4382	.4394	.4406	.4418	.4429	.4441
1.6	.4452	.4463	.4474	.4484	.4495 *	.4505	.4515	.4525	.4535	.4545
1.7	.4554	.4564	.4573	.4582	.4591	.4599	.4608	.4616	.4625	.4633
1.8	.4641	.4649	.4656	.4664	.4671	.4678	.4686	.4693	.4699	.4706
1.9	.4713	.4719	.4726	.4732	.4738	.4744	.4750	.4756	.4761	.4767
2.0	.4772	.4778	.4783	.4788	.4793	.4798	.4803	.4808	.4812	.4817
2.1	.4821	.4826	.4830	.4834	.4838	.4842	.4846	.4850	.4854	.4857
2.2	.4861	.4864	.4868	.4871	.4875	.4878	.4881	.4884	.4887	.4890
2.3	.4893	.4896	.4898	.4901	.4904	.4906	.4909	.4911	.4913	.4916
2.4	.4918	.4920	.4922	.4925	.4927	.4929	.4931	.4932	.4934	.4936
2.5	.4938	.4940	.4941	.4943	.4945	.4946	.4948	.4949 *	.4951	.4952
2.6	.4953	.4955	.4956	.4957	.4959	.4960	.4961	.4962	.4963	.4964
2.7	.4965	.4966	.4967	.4968	.4969	.4970	.4971	.4972	.4973	.4974
2.8	.4974	.4975	.4976	.4977	.4977	.4978	.4979	.4979	.4980	.4981
2.9	.4981	.4982	.4982	.4983	.4984	.4984	.4985	.4985	.4986	.4986
3.0	.4987	.4987	.4987	.4988	.4988	.4989	.4989	.4989	.4990	.4990

z	area
3.1	.49903
3.2	.49931
3.3	.49952
3.4	.49966
3.5	.49977
3.6	.49984
3.7	.49989
3.8	.49993
3.9	.49995
4.0	.49997
4.5	.4999966023
5.0	.4999997133
5.5	.4999999810
6.0	.4999999990

Above 6.0: Use 0.4999999990

Notes:
1. For values of z above 6.0, use 0.4999999990 for the area.
2.*Use these common values that result from interpolation:

z SCORE	AREA
1.645	0.4500
2.575	0.4950

SOURCE: From Mosteller/Rourke, *Sturdy Statistics*, 1973, Addison-Wesley Publishing Co. Reprinted with permission of Frederick Mosteller.

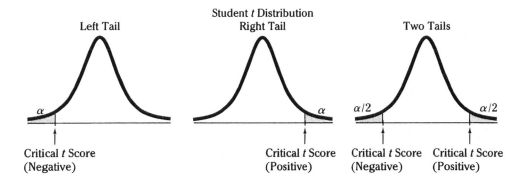

Student t Distribution

Left Tail — α — Critical t Score (Negative)

Right Tail — α — Critical t Score (Positive)

Two Tails — $\alpha/2$ ... $\alpha/2$ — Critical t Score (Negative) Critical t Score (Positive)

TABLE A.3
t Distribution

	α					
DEGREES OF FREEDOM	.005 (ONE TAIL) .01 (TWO TAILS)	.01 (ONE TAIL) .02 (TWO TAILS)	.025 (ONE TAIL) .05 (TWO TAILS)	.05 (ONE TAIL) .10 (TWO TAILS)	.10 (ONE TAIL) .20 (TWO TAILS)	.25 (ONE TAIL) .50 (TWO TAILS)
1	63.657	31.821	12.706	6.314	3.078	1.000
2	9.925	6.965	4.303	2.920	1.886	.816
3	5.841	4.541	3.182	2.353	1.638	.765
4	4.604	3.747	2.776	2.132	1.533	.741
5	4.032	3.365	2.571	2.015	1.476	.727
6	3.707	3.143	2.447	1.943	1.440	.718
7	3.500	2.998	2.365	1.895	1.415	.711
8	3.355	2.896	2.306	1.860	1.397	.706
9	3.250	2.821	2.262	1.833	1.383	.703
10	3.169	2.764	2.228	1.812	1.372	.700
11	3.106	2.718	2.201	1.796	1.363	.697
12	3.054	2.681	2.179	1.782	1.356	.696
13	3.012	2.650	2.160	1.771	1.350	.694
14	2.977	2.625	2.145	1.761	1.345	.692
15	2.947	2.602	2.132	1.753	1.341	.691
16	2.921	2.584	2.120	1.746	1.337	.690
17	2.898	2.567	2.110	1.740	1.333	.689
18	2.878	2.552	2.101	1.734	1.330	.688
19	2.861	2.540	2.093	1.729	1.328	.688
20	2.845	2.528	2.086	1.725	1.325	.687
21	2.831	2.518	2.080	1.721	1.323	.686
22	2.819	2.508	2.074	1.717	1.321	.686
23	2.807	2.500	2.069	1.714	1.320	.685
24	2.797	2.492	2.064	1.711	1.318	.685
25	2.787	2.485	2.060	1.708	1.316	.684
26	2.779	2.479	2.056	1.706	1.315	.684
27	2.771	2.473	2.052	1.703	1.314	.684
28	2.763	2.467	2.048	1.701	1.313	.683
29	2.756	2.462	2.045	1.699	1.311	.683
Large (z)	2.575	2.327	1.960	1.645	1.282	.675

SOURCE: From Triola, *Elementary Statistics* 5/e, © 1992 Addison-Wesley Publishing Co., Reading, MA. Reprinted by permission.

TABLE A.4
Chi-Square (χ^2) Distribution

DEGREES OF FREEDOM	AREA TO THE RIGHT OF THE CRITICAL VALUE									
	0.995	0.99	0.975	0.95	0.90	0.10	0.05	0.025	0.01	0.005
1	—	—	0.001	0.004	0.016	2.706	3.841	5.024	6.635	7.879
2	0.010	0.020	0.051	0.103	0.211	4.605	5.991	7.378	9.210	10.597
3	0.072	0.115	0.216	0.352	0.584	6.251	7.815	9.348	11.345	12.838
4	0.207	0.297	0.484	0.711	1.064	7.779	9.488	11.143	13.277	14.860
5	0.412	0.554	0.831	1.145	1.610	9.236	11.071	12.833	15.086	16.750
6	0.676	0.872	1.237	1.635	2.204	10.645	12.592	14.449	16.812	18.548
7	0.989	1.239	1.690	2.167	2.833	12.017	14.067	16.013	18.475	20.278
8	1.344	1.646	2.180	2.733	3.490	13.362	15.507	17.535	20.090	21.955
9	1.735	2.088	2.700	3.325	4.168	14.684	16.919	19.023	21.666	23.589
10	2.156	2.558	3.247	3.940	4.865	15.987	18.307	20.483	23.209	25.188
11	2.603	3.053	3.816	4.575	5.578	17.275	19.675	21.920	24.725	26.757
12	3.074	3.571	4.404	5.226	6.304	18.549	21.026	23.337	26.217	28.299
13	3.565	4.107	5.009	5.892	7.042	19.812	22.362	24.736	27.688	29.819
14	4.075	4.660	5.629	6.571	7.790	21.064	23.685	26.119	29.141	31.319
15	4.601	5.229	6.262	7.261	8.547	22.307	24.996	27.488	30.578	32.801
16	5.142	5.812	6.908	7.962	9.312	23.542	26.296	28.845	32.000	34.267
17	5.697	6.408	7.564	8.672	10.085	24.769	27.587	30.191	33.409	35.718
18	6.265	7.015	8.231	9.390	10.865	25.989	28.869	31.526	34.805	37.156
19	6.844	7.633	8.907	10.117	11.651	27.204	30.144	32.852	36.191	38.582
20	7.434	8.260	9.591	10.851	12.443	28.412	31.410	34.170	37.566	39.997
21	8.034	8.897	10.283	11.591	13.240	29.615	32.671	35.479	38.932	41.401
22	8.643	9.542	10.982	12.338	14.042	30.813	33.924	36.781	40.289	42.796
23	9.260	10.196	11.689	13.091	14.848	32.007	35.172	38.076	41.638	44.181
24	9.886	10.856	12.401	13.848	15.659	33.196	36.415	39.364	42.980	45.559
25	10.520	11.524	13.120	14.611	16.473	34.382	37.652	40.646	44.314	46.928
26	11.160	12.198	13.844	15.379	17.292	35.563	38.885	41.923	45.642	48.290
27	11.808	12.879	14.573	16.151	18.114	36.741	40.113	43.194	46.963	49.645
28	12.461	13.565	15.308	16.928	18.939	37.916	41.337	44.461	48.278	50.993
29	13.121	14.257	16.047	17.708	19.768	39.087	42.557	45.772	49.588	52.336
30	13.787	14.954	16.791	18.493	20.599	40.256	43.773	46.979	50.892	53.672
40	20.707	22.164	24.433	26.509	29.051	51.805	55.758	59.342	63.691	66.766
50	27.991	29.707	32.357	34.764	37.689	63.167	67.505	71.420	76.154	79.490
60	35.534	37.485	40.482	43.188	46.459	74.397	79.082	83.298	88.379	91.952
70	43.275	45.442	48.758	51.739	55.329	85.527	90.531	95.023	100.425	104.215
80	51.172	53.540	57.153	60.391	64.278	96.578	101.879	106.629	112.329	116.321
90	59.196	61.754	65.647	69.126	73.291	107.565	113.145	118.136	124.116	128.299
100	67.328	70.065	74.222	77.929	82.358	118.498	124.342	129.561	135.807	140.169

SOURCE: From Owen, *Handbook of Statistical Tables,* © 1962 Addison-Wesley Publishing Co., Reading, MA. Reprinted by permission.

TABLE A.4 (*cont.*)

Right Tail

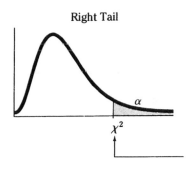

To find this value, use the column with the area α given at the top of the table.

Left Tail

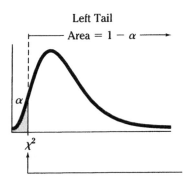

To find this value, determine the area of the region to the right of this boundary (the unshaded area) and use the column with this value at the top. If the left tail has area α, use the column with the value of $1 - \alpha$ at the top of the table.

Two Tails

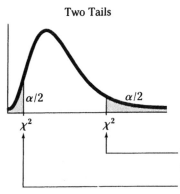

To find this value, use the column with area $\alpha/2$ at the top of the table.

To find this value, use the column with area $1 - \alpha/2$ at the top of the table.

TABLE A.5
F Distribution ($\alpha = 0.01$ in the right tail)

NUMERATOR DEGREES OF FREEDOM

df_2 \ df_1	1	2	3	4	5	6	7	8	9
1	4052.2	4999.5	5403.4	5624.6	5763.6	5859.0	5928.4	5981.1	6022.5
2	98.503	99.000	99.166	99.249	99.299	99.333	99.356	99.374	99.388
3	34.116	30.817	29.457	28.710	28.237	27.911	27.672	27.489	27.345
4	21.198	18.000	16.694	15.977	15.522	15.207	14.976	14.799	14.659
5	16.258	13.274	12.060	11.392	10.967	10.672	10.456	10.289	10.158
6	13.745	10.925	9.7795	9.1483	8.7459	8.4661	8.2600	8.1017	7.9761
7	12.246	9.5466	8.4513	7.8466	7.4604	7.1914	6.9928	6.8400	6.7188
8	11.259	8.6491	7.5910	7.0061	6.6318	6.3707	6.1776	6.0289	5.9106
9	10.561	8.0215	6.9919	6.4221	6.0569	5.8018	5.6129	5.4671	5.3511
10	10.044	7.5594	6.5523	5.9943	5.6363	5.3858	5.2001	5.0567	4.9424
11	9.6460	7.2057	6.2167	5.6683	5.3160	5.0692	4.8861	4.7445	4.6315
12	9.3302	6.9266	5.9525	5.4120	5.0643	4.8206	4.6395	4.4994	4.3875
13	9.0738	6.7010	5.7394	5.2053	4.8616	4.6204	4.4410	4.3021	4.1911
14	8.8616	6.5149	5.5639	5.0354	4.6950	4.4558	4.2779	4.1399	4.0297
15	8.6831	6.3589	5.4170	4.8932	4.5556	4.3183	4.1415	4.0045	3.8948
16	8.5310	6.2262	5.2922	4.7726	4.4374	4.2016	4.0259	3.8896	3.7804
17	8.3997	6.1121	5.1850	4.6690	4.3359	4.1015	3.9267	3.7910	3.6822
18	8.2854	6.0129	5.0919	4.5790	4.2479	4.0146	3.8406	3.7054	3.5971
19	8.1849	5.9259	5.0103	4.5003	4.1708	3.9386	3.7653	3.6305	3.5225
20	8.0960	5.8489	4.9382	4.4307	4.1027	3.8714	3.6987	3.5644	3.4567
21	8.0166	5.7804	4.8740	4.3688	4.0421	3.8117	3.6396	3.5056	3.3981
22	7.9454	5.7190	4.8166	4.3134	3.9880	3.7583	3.5867	3.4530	3.3458
23	7.8811	5.6637	4.7649	4.2636	3.9392	3.7102	3.5390	3.4057	3.2986
24	7.8229	5.6136	4.7181	4.2184	3.8951	3.6667	3.4959	3.3629	3.2560
25	7.7698	5.5680	4.6755	4.1774	3.8550	3.6272	3.4568	3.3239	3.2172
26	7.7213	5.5263	4.6366	4.1400	3.8183	3.5911	3.4210	3.2884	3.1818
27	7.6767	5.4881	4.6009	4.1056	3.7848	3.5580	3.3882	3.2558	3.1494
28	7.6356	5.4529	4.5681	4.0740	3.7539	3.5276	3.3581	3.2259	3.1195
29	7.5977	5.4204	4.5378	4.0449	3.7254	3.4995	3.3303	3.1982	3.0920
30	7.5625	5.3903	4.5097	4.0179	3.6990	3.4735	3.3045	3.1726	3.0665
40	7.3141	5.1785	4.3126	3.8283	3.5138	3.2910	3.1238	2.9930	2.8876
60	7.0771	4.9774	4.1259	3.6490	3.3389	3.1187	2.9530	2.8233	2.7185
120	6.8509	4.7865	3.9491	3.4795	3.1735	2.9559	2.7918	2.6629	2.5586
∞	6.6349	4.6052	3.7816	3.3192	3.0173	2.8020	2.6393	2.5113	2.4073

Denominator degrees of freedom

SOURCE: From Maxine Merrington and Catherine M. Thompson, "Tables of Percentage Points of the Inverted Beta (F) Distribution," *Biometrika* 33 (1943): 80–84. Reproduced with permission of the Biometrika Trustees.

TABLE A.5 (*cont.*)

df_2 \ df_1	10	12	15	20	24	30	40	60	120	∞
					NUMERATOR DEGREES OF FREEDOM					
1	6055.8	6106.3	6157.3	6208.7	6234.6	6260.6	6286.8	6313.0	6339.4	6365.9
2	99.399	99.416	99.433	99.449	99.458	99.466	99.474	99.482	99.491	99.499
3	27.229	27.052	26.872	26.690	26.598	26.505	26.411	26.316	26.221	26.125
4	14.546	14.374	14.198	14.020	13.929	13.838	13.745	13.652	13.558	13.463
5	10.051	9.8883	9.7222	9.5526	9.4665	9.3793	9.2912	9.2020	9.1118	9.0204
6	7.8741	7.7183	7.5590	7.3958	7.3127	7.2285	7.1432	7.0567	6.9690	6.8800
7	6.6201	6.4691	6.3143	6.1554	6.0743	5.9920	5.9084	5.8236	5.7373	5.6495
8	5.8143	5.6667	5.5151	5.3591	5.2793	5.1981	5.1156	5.0316	4.9461	4.8588
9	5.2565	5.1114	4.9621	4.8080	4.7290	4.6486	4.5666	4.4831	4.3978	4.3105
10	4.8491	4.7059	4.5581	4.4054	4.3269	4.2469	4.1653	4.0819	3.9965	3.9090
11	4.5393	4.3974	4.2509	4.0990	4.0209	3.9411	3.8596	3.7761	3.6904	3.6024
12	4.2961	4.1553	4.0096	3.8584	3.7805	3.7008	3.6192	3.5355	3.4494	3.3608
13	4.1003	3.9603	3.8154	3.6646	3.5868	3.5070	3.4253	3.3413	3.2548	3.1654
14	3.9394	3.8001	3.6557	3.5052	3.4274	3.3476	3.2656	3.1813	3.0942	3.0040
15	3.8049	3.6662	3.5222	3.3719	3.2940	3.2141	3.1319	3.0471	2.9595	2.8684
16	3.6909	3.5527	3.4089	3.2587	3.1808	3.1007	3.0182	2.9330	2.8447	2.7528
17	3.5931	3.4552	3.3117	3.1615	3.0835	3.0032	2.9205	2.8348	2.7459	2.6530
18	3.5082	3.3706	3.2273	3.0771	2.9990	2.9185	2.8354	2.7493	2.6597	2.5660
19	3.4338	3.2965	3.1533	3.0031	2.9249	2.8442	2.7608	2.6742	2.5839	2.4893
20	3.3682	3.2311	3.0880	2.9377	2.8594	2.7785	2.6947	2.6077	2.5168	2.4212
21	3.3098	3.1730	3.0300	2.8796	2.8010	2.7200	2.6359	2.5484	2.4568	2.3603
22	3.2576	3.1209	2.9779	2.8274	2.7488	2.6675	2.5831	2.4951	2.4029	2.3055
23	3.2106	3.0740	2.9311	2.7805	2.7017	2.6202	2.5355	2.4471	2.3542	2.2558
24	3.1681	3.0316	2.8887	2.7380	2.6591	2.5773	2.4923	2.4035	2.3100	2.2107
25	3.1294	2.9931	2.8502	2.6993	2.6203	2.5383	2.4530	2.3637	2.2696	2.1694
26	3.0941	2.9578	2.8150	2.6640	2.5848	2.5026	2.4170	2.3273	2.2325	2.1315
27	3.0618	2.9256	2.7827	2.6316	2.5522	2.4699	2.3840	2.2938	2.1985	2.0965
28	3.0320	2.8959	2.7530	2.6017	2.5223	2.4397	2.3535	2.2629	2.1670	2.0642
29	3.0045	2.8685	2.7256	2.5742	2.4946	2.4118	2.3253	2.2344	2.1379	2.0342
30	2.9791	2.8431	2.7002	2.5487	2.4689	2.3860	2.2992	2.2079	2.1108	2.0062
40	2.8005	2.6648	2.5216	2.3689	2.2880	2.2034	2.1142	2.0194	1.9172	1.8047
60	2.6318	2.4961	2.3523	2.1978	2.1154	2.0285	1.9360	1.8363	1.7263	1.6006
120	2.4721	2.3363	2.1915	2.0346	1.9500	1.8600	1.7628	1.6557	1.5330	1.3805
∞	2.3209	2.1847	2.0385	1.8783	1.7908	1.6964	1.5923	1.4730	1.3246	1.0000

Denominator degrees of freedom

TABLE A.5
F Distribution (α = 0.025 in the right tail)

NUMERATOR DEGREES OF FREEDOM

df_2 \ df_1	1	2	3	4	5	6	7	8	9
1	647.79	799.50	864.16	899.58	921.85	937.11	948.22	956.66	963.28
2	38.506	39.000	39.165	39.248	39.298	39.331	39.335	39.373	39.387
3	17.443	16.044	15.439	15.101	14.885	14.735	14.624	14.540	14.473
4	12.218	10.649	9.9792	9.6045	9.3645	9.1973	9.0741	8.9796	8.9047
5	10.007	8.4336	7.7636	7.3879	7.1464	6.9777	6.8531	6.7572	6.6811
6	8.8131	7.2599	6.5988	6.2272	5.9876	5.8198	5.6955	5.5996	5.5234
7	8.0727	6.5415	5.8898	5.5226	5.2852	5.1186	4.9949	4.8993	4.8232
8	7.5709	6.0595	5.4160	5.0526	4.8173	4.6517	4.5286	4.4333	4.3572
9	7.2093	5.7147	5.0781	4.7181	4.4844	4.3197	4.1970	4.1020	4.0260
10	6.9367	5.4564	4.8256	4.4683	4.2361	4.0721	3.9498	3.8549	3.7790
11	6.7241	5.2559	4.6300	4.2751	4.0440	3.8807	3.7586	3.6638	3.5879
12	6.5538	5.0959	4.4742	4.1212	3.8911	3.7283	3.6065	3.5118	3.4358
13	6.4143	4.9653	4.3472	3.9959	3.7667	3.6043	3.4827	3.3880	3.3120
14	6.2979	4.8567	4.2417	3.8919	3.6634	3.5014	3.3799	3.2853	3.2093
15	6.1995	4.7650	4.1528	3.8043	3.5764	3.4147	3.2934	3.1987	3.1227
16	6.1151	4.6867	4.0768	3.7294	3.5021	3.3406	3.2194	3.1248	3.0488
17	6.0420	4.6189	4.0112	3.6648	3.4379	3.2767	3.1556	3.0610	2.9849
18	5.9781	4.5597	3.9539	3.6083	3.3820	3.2209	3.0999	3.0053	2.9291
19	5.9216	4.5075	3.9034	3.5587	3.3327	3.1718	3.0509	2.9563	2.8801
20	5.8715	4.4613	3.8587	3.5147	3.2891	3.1283	3.0074	2.9128	2.8365
21	5.8266	4.4199	3.8188	3.4754	3.2501	3.0895	2.9686	2.8740	2.7977
22	5.7863	4.3828	3.7829	3.4401	3.2151	3.0546	2.9338	2.8392	2.7628
23	5.7498	4.3492	3.7505	3.4083	3.1835	3.0232	2.9023	2.8077	2.7313
24	5.7166	4.3187	3.7211	3.3794	3.1548	2.9946	2.8738	2.7791	2.7027
25	5.6864	4.2909	3.6943	3.3530	3.1287	2.9685	2.8478	2.7531	2.6766
26	5.6586	4.2655	3.6697	3.3289	3.1048	2.9447	2.8240	2.7293	2.6528
27	5.6331	4.2421	3.6472	3.3067	3.0828	2.9228	2.8021	2.7074	2.6309
28	5.6096	4.2205	3.6264	3.2863	3.0626	2.9027	2.7820	2.6872	2.6106
29	5.5878	4.2006	3.6072	3.2674	3.0438	2.8840	2.7633	2.6686	2.5919
30	5.5675	4.1821	3.5894	3.2499	3.0265	2.8667	2.7460	2.6513	2.5746
40	5.4239	4.0510	3.4633	3.1261	2.9037	2.7444	2.6238	2.5289	2.4519
60	5.2856	3.9253	3.3425	3.0077	2.7863	2.6274	2.5068	2.4117	2.3344
120	5.1523	3.8046	3.2269	2.8943	2.6740	2.5154	2.3948	2.2994	2.2217
∞	5.0239	3.6889	3.1161	2.7858	2.5665	2.4082	2.2875	2.1918	2.1136

Denominator degrees of freedom

TABLE A.5 (cont.)

NUMERATOR DEGREES OF FREEDOM

Denominator degrees of freedom

$df_2 \backslash df_1$	10	12	15	20	24	30	40	60	120	∞
1	968.63	976.71	984.87	993.10	997.25	1001.4	1005.6	1009.8	1014.0	1018.3
2	39.398	39.415	39.431	39.448	39.456	39.465	39.473	39.481	39.490	39.498
3	14.419	14.337	14.253	14.167	14.124	14.081	14.037	13.992	13.947	13.902
4	8.8439	8.7512	8.6565	8.5599	8.5109	8.4613	8.4111	8.3604	8.3092	8.2573
5	6.6192	6.5245	6.4277	6.3286	6.2780	6.2269	6.1750	6.1225	6.0693	6.0153
6	5.4613	5.3662	5.2687	5.1684	5.1172	5.0652	5.0125	4.9589	4.9044	4.8491
7	4.7611	4.6658	4.5678	4.4667	4.4150	4.3624	4.3089	4.2544	4.1989	4.1423
8	4.2951	4.1997	4.1012	3.9995	3.9472	3.8940	3.8398	3.7844	3.7279	3.6702
9	3.9639	3.8682	3.7694	3.6669	3.6142	3.5604	3.5055	3.4493	3.3918	3.3329
10	3.7168	3.6209	3.5217	3.4185	3.3654	3.3110	3.2554	3.1984	3.1399	3.0798
11	3.5257	3.4296	3.3299	3.2261	3.1725	3.1176	3.0613	3.0035	2.9441	2.8828
12	3.3736	3.2773	3.1772	3.0728	3.0187	2.9633	2.9063	2.8478	2.7874	2.7249
13	3.2497	3.1532	3.0527	2.9477	2.8932	2.8372	2.7797	2.7204	2.6590	2.5955
14	3.1469	3.0502	2.9493	2.8437	2.7888	2.7324	2.6742	2.6142	2.5519	2.4872
15	3.0602	2.9633	2.8621	2.7559	2.7006	2.6437	2.5850	2.5242	2.4611	2.3953
16	2.9862	2.8890	2.7875	2.6808	2.6252	2.5678	2.5085	2.4471	2.3831	2.3163
17	2.9222	2.8249	2.7230	2.6158	2.5598	2.5020	2.4422	2.3801	2.3153	2.2474
18	2.8664	2.7689	2.6667	2.5590	2.5027	2.4445	2.3842	2.3214	2.2558	2.1869
19	2.8172	2.7196	2.6171	2.5089	2.4523	2.3937	2.3329	2.2696	2.2032	2.1333
20	2.7737	2.6758	2.5731	2.4645	2.4076	2.3486	2.2873	2.2234	2.1562	2.0853
21	2.7348	2.6368	2.5338	2.4247	2.3675	2.3082	2.2465	2.1819	2.1141	2.0422
22	2.6998	2.6017	2.4984	2.3890	2.3315	2.2718	2.2097	2.1446	2.0760	2.0032
23	2.6682	2.5699	2.4665	2.3567	2.2989	2.2389	2.1763	2.1107	2.0415	1.9677
24	2.6396	2.5411	2.4374	2.3273	2.2693	2.2090	2.1460	2.0799	2.0099	1.9353
25	2.6135	2.5149	2.4110	2.3005	2.2422	2.1816	2.1183	2.0516	1.9811	1.9055
26	2.5896	2.4908	2.3867	2.2759	2.2174	2.1565	2.0928	2.0257	1.9545	1.8781
27	2.5676	2.4688	2.3644	2.2533	2.1946	2.1334	2.0693	2.0018	1.9299	1.8527
28	2.5473	2.4484	2.3438	2.2324	2.1735	2.1121	2.0477	1.9797	1.9072	1.8291
29	2.5286	2.4295	2.3248	2.2131	2.1540	2.0923	2.0276	1.9591	1.8861	1.8072
30	2.5112	2.4120	2.3072	2.1952	2.1359	2.0739	2.0089	1.9400	1.8664	1.7867
40	2.3882	2.2882	2.1819	2.0677	2.0069	1.9429	1.8752	1.8028	1.7242	1.6371
60	2.2702	2.1692	2.0613	1.9445	1.8817	1.8152	1.7440	1.6668	1.5810	1.4821
120	2.1570	2.0548	1.9450	1.8249	1.7597	1.6899	1.6141	1.5299	1.4327	1.3104
∞	2.0483	1.9447	1.8326	1.7085	1.6402	1.5660	1.4835	1.3883	1.2684	1.0000

TABLE A.5
F Distribution ($\alpha = 0.05$ in the right tail)

df_2	df_1 1	2	3	4	5	6	7	8	9
1	161.45	199.50	215.71	224.58	230.16	233.99	236.77	238.88	240.54
2	18.513	19.000	19.164	19.247	19.296	19.330	19.353	19.371	19.385
3	10.128	9.5521	9.2766	9.1172	9.0135	8.9406	8.8867	8.8452	8.8123
4	7.7086	6.9443	6.5914	6.3882	6.2561	6.1631	6.0942	6.0410	5.9988
5	6.6079	5.7861	5.4095	5.1922	5.0503	4.9503	4.8759	4.8183	4.7725
6	5.9874	5.1433	4.7571	4.5337	4.3874	4.2839	4.2067	4.1468	4.0990
7	5.5914	4.7374	4.3468	4.1203	3.9715	3.8660	3.7870	3.7257	3.6767
8	5.3177	4.4590	4.0662	3.8379	3.6875	3.5806	3.5005	3.4381	3.3881
9	5.1174	4.2565	3.8625	3.6331	3.4817	3.3738	3.2927	3.2296	3.1789
10	4.9646	4.1028	3.7083	3.4780	3.3258	3.2172	3.1355	3.0717	3.0204
11	4.8443	3.9823	3.5874	3.3567	3.2039	3.0946	3.0123	2.9480	2.8962
12	4.7472	3.8853	3.4903	3.2592	3.1059	2.9961	2.9134	2.8486	2.7964
13	4.6672	3.8056	3.4105	3.1791	3.0254	2.9153	2.8321	2.7669	2.7144
14	4.6001	3.7389	3.3439	3.1122	2.9582	2.8477	2.7642	2.6987	2.6458
15	4.5431	3.6823	3.2874	3.0556	2.9013	2.7905	2.7066	2.6408	2.5876
16	4.4940	3.6337	3.2389	3.0069	2.8524	2.7413	2.6572	2.5911	2.5377
17	4.4513	3.5915	3.1968	2.9647	2.8100	2.6987	2.6143	2.5480	2.4943
18	4.4139	3.5546	3.1599	2.9277	2.7729	2.6613	2.5767	2.5102	2.4563
19	4.3807	3.5219	3.1274	2.8951	2.7401	2.6283	2.5435	2.4768	2.4227
20	4.3512	3.4928	3.0984	2.8661	2.7109	2.5990	2.5140	2.4471	2.3928
21	4.3248	3.4668	3.0725	2.8401	2.6848	2.5727	2.4876	2.4205	2.3660
22	4.3009	3.4434	3.0491	2.8167	2.6613	2.5491	2.4638	2.3965	2.3419
23	4.2793	3.4221	3.0280	2.7955	2.6400	2.5277	2.4422	2.3748	2.3201
24	4.2597	3.4028	3.0088	2.7763	2.6207	2.5082	2.4226	2.3551	2.3002
25	4.2417	3.3852	2.9912	2.7587	2.6030	2.4904	2.4047	2.3371	2.2821
26	4.2252	3.3690	2.9752	2.7426	2.5868	2.4741	2.3883	2.3205	2.2655
27	4.2100	3.3541	2.9604	2.7278	2.5719	2.4591	2.3732	2.3053	2.2501
28	4.1960	3.3404	2.9467	2.7141	2.5581	2.4453	2.3593	2.2913	2.2360
29	4.1830	3.3277	2.9340	2.7014	2.5454	2.4324	2.3463	2.2783	2.2229
30	4.1709	3.3158	2.9223	2.6896	2.5336	2.4205	2.3343	2.2662	2.2107
40	4.0847	3.2317	2.8387	2.6060	2.4495	2.3359	2.2490	2.1802	2.1240
60	4.0012	3.1504	2.7581	2.5252	2.3683	2.2541	2.1665	2.0970	2.0401
120	3.9201	3.0718	2.6802	2.4472	2.2899	2.1750	2.0868	2.0164	1.9588
∞	3.8415	2.9957	2.6049	2.3719	2.2141	2.0986	2.0096	1.9384	1.8799

NUMERATOR DEGREES OF FREEDOM

Denominator degrees of freedom

TABLE A.5 (cont.)

NUMERATOR DEGREES OF FREEDOM

df_2 \ df_1	10	12	15	20	24	30	40	60	120	∞
1	241.88	243.91	245.95	248.01	249.05	250.10	251.14	252.20	253.25	254.31
2	19.396	19.413	19.429	19.446	19.454	19.462	19.471	19.479	19.487	19.496
3	8.7855	8.7446	8.7029	8.6602	8.6385	8.6166	8.5944	8.5720	8.5494	8.5264
4	5.9644	5.9117	5.8578	5.8025	5.7744	5.7459	5.7170	5.6877	5.6581	5.6281
5	4.7351	4.6777	4.6188	4.5581	4.5272	4.4957	4.4638	4.4314	4.3985	4.3650
6	4.0600	3.9999	3.9381	3.8742	3.8415	3.8082	3.7743	3.7398	3.7047	3.6689
7	3.6365	3.5747	3.5107	3.4445	3.4105	3.3758	3.3404	3.3043	3.2674	3.2298
8	3.3472	3.2839	3.2184	3.1503	3.1152	3.0794	3.0428	3.0053	2.9669	2.9276
9	3.1373	3.0729	3.0061	2.9365	2.9005	2.8637	2.8259	2.7872	2.7475	2.7067
10	2.9782	2.9130	2.8450	2.7740	2.7372	2.6996	2.6609	2.6211	2.5801	2.5379
11	2.8536	2.7876	2.7186	2.6464	2.6090	2.5705	2.5309	2.4901	2.4480	2.4045
12	2.7534	2.6866	2.6169	2.5436	2.5055	2.4663	2.4259	2.3842	2.3410	2.2962
13	2.6710	2.6037	2.5331	2.4589	2.4202	2.3803	2.3392	2.2966	2.2524	2.2064
14	2.6022	2.5342	2.4630	2.3879	2.3487	2.3082	2.2664	2.2229	2.1778	2.1307
15	2.5437	2.4753	2.4034	2.3275	2.2878	2.2468	2.2043	2.1601	2.1141	2.0658
16	2.4935	2.4247	2.3522	2.2756	2.2354	2.1938	2.1507	2.1058	2.0589	2.0096
17	2.4499	2.3807	2.3077	2.2304	2.1898	2.1477	2.1040	2.0584	2.0107	1.9604
18	2.4117	2.3421	2.2686	2.1906	2.1497	2.1071	2.0629	2.0166	1.9681	1.9168
19	2.3779	2.3080	2.2341	2.1555	2.1141	2.0712	2.0264	1.9795	1.9302	1.8780
20	2.3479	2.2776	2.2033	2.1242	2.0825	2.0391	1.9938	1.9464	1.8963	1.8432
21	2.3210	2.2504	2.1757	2.0960	2.0540	2.0102	1.9645	1.9165	1.8657	1.8117
22	2.2967	2.2258	2.1508	2.0707	2.0283	1.9842	1.9380	1.8894	1.8380	1.7831
23	2.2747	2.2036	2.1282	2.0476	2.0050	1.9605	1.9139	1.8648	1.8128	1.7570
24	2.2547	2.1834	2.1077	2.0267	1.9838	1.9390	1.8920	1.8424	1.7896	1.7330
25	2.2365	2.1649	2.0889	2.0075	1.9643	1.9192	1.8718	1.8217	1.7684	1.7110
26	2.2197	2.1479	2.0716	1.9898	1.9464	1.9010	1.8533	1.8027	1.7488	1.6906
27	2.2043	2.1323	2.0558	1.9736	1.9299	1.8842	1.8361	1.7851	1.7306	1.6717
28	2.1900	2.1179	2.0411	1.9586	1.9147	1.8687	1.8203	1.7689	1.7138	1.6541
29	2.1768	2.1045	2.0275	1.9446	1.9005	1.8543	1.8055	1.7537	1.6981	1.6376
30	2.1646	2.0921	2.0148	1.9317	1.8874	1.8409	1.7918	1.7395	1.6835	1.6223
40	2.0772	2.0035	1.9245	1.8389	1.7929	1.7444	1.6928	1.6373	1.5766	1.5089
60	1.9926	1.9174	1.8364	1.7480	1.7001	1.6491	1.5943	1.5343	1.4673	1.3893
120	1.9105	1.8337	1.7505	1.6587	1.6084	1.5543	1.4952	1.4290	1.3519	1.2539
∞	1.8307	1.7522	1.6664	1.5705	1.5173	1.4591	1.3940	1.3180	1.2214	1.0000

Denominator degrees of freedom

TABLE A.6
Critical Values of the Pearson Correlation Coefficient r

n	$\alpha = .05$	$\alpha = .01$
4	.950	.999
5	.878	.959
6	.811	.917
7	.754	.875
8	.707	.834
9	.666	.798
10	.632	.765
11	.602	.735
12	.576	.708
13	.553	.684
14	.532	.661
15	.514	.641
16	.497	.623
17	.482	.606
18	.468	.590
19	.456	.575
20	.444	.561
25	.396	.505
30	.361	.463
35	.335	.430
40	.312	.402
45	.294	.378
50	.279	.361
60	.254	.330
70	.236	.305
80	.220	.286
90	.207	.269
100	.196	.256

NOTE: To test H_0: $\rho = 0$ against H_1: $\rho \neq 0$, reject H_0 if the absolute value of r is greater than the critical value in the table.
SOURCE: From Triola, *Elementary Statistics*, 5/e, © 1992 Addison-Wesley Publishing Co., Reading, MA. Reprinted by permission.

TABLE A.7
Critical Values for the Sign Test

	α			
n	.005 (ONE TAIL) .01 (TWO TAILS)	.01 (ONE TAIL) .02 (TWO TAILS)	.025 (ONE TAIL) .05 (TWO TAILS)	.05 (ONE TAIL) .10 (TWO TAILS)
1	*	*	*	*
2	*	*	*	*
3	*	*	*	*
4	*	*	*	*
5	*	*	*	0
6	*	*	0	0
7	*	0	0	0
8	0	0	0	1
9	0	0	1	1
10	0	0	1	1
11	0	1	1	2
12	1	1	2	2
13	1	1	2	3
14	1	2	2	3
15	2	2	3	3
16	2	2	3	4
17	2	3	4	4
18	3	3	4	5
19	3	4	4	5
20	3	4	5	5
21	4	4	5	6
22	4	5	5	6
23	4	5	6	7
24	5	5	6	7
25	5	6	7	7

NOTES:
1. * indicates that it is not possible to get a value in the critical region.
2. The null hypothesis is rejected if the number of the less frequent sign (x) is less than or equal to the value in the table.
3. For values of n greater than 25, a normal approximation is used with

$$z = \frac{(x + 0.5) - \left(\frac{n}{2}\right)}{\frac{\sqrt{n}}{2}}$$

TABLE A.8
Critical Values of T for the Wilcoxon Signed-Rank Test

	α			
	.005 (ONE TAIL)	.01 (ONE TAIL)	.025 (ONE TAIL)	.05 (ONE TAIL)
n	.01 (TWO TAILS)	.02 (TWO TAILS)	.05 (TWO TAILS)	.10 (TWO TAILS)
5				1
6			1	2
7		0	2	4
8	0	2	4	6
9	2	3	6	8
10	3	5	8	11
11	5	7	11	14
12	7	10	14	17
13	10	13	17	21
14	13	16	21	26
15	16	20	25	30
16	19	24	30	36
17	23	28	35	41
18	28	33	40	47
19	32	38	46	54
20	37	43	52	60
21	43	49	59	68
22	49	56	66	75
23	55	62	73	83
24	61	69	81	92
25	68	77	90	101
26	76	85	98	110
27	84	93	107	120
28	92	102	117	130
29	100	111	127	141
30	109	120	137	152

NOTE: Reject the null hypothesis if the test statistic T is less than or equal to the critical value found in this table. Fail to reject the null hypothesis if the test statistic T is greater than the critical value found in this table.
SOURCE: From *Some Rapid Approximate Statistical Procedures,* Copyright © 1949, 1964, Lederle Laboratories Division of American Cyanamid Company. Reprinted with the permission of the American Cyanamid Company.

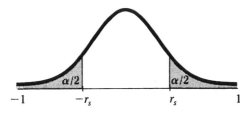

TABLE A.9
Critical Values of Spearman's Rank Correlation Coefficient r_s

n	$\alpha = 0.10$	$\alpha = 0.05$	$\alpha = 0.02$	$\alpha = 0.01$
5	.900	—	—	—
6	.829	.886	.943	—
7	.714	.786	.893	—
8	.643	.738	.833	.881
9	.600	.683	.783	.833
10	.564	.648	.745	.794
11	.523	.623	.736	.818
12	.497	.591	.703	.780
13	.475	.566	.673	.745
14	.457	.545	.646	.716
15	.441	.525	.623	.689
16	.425	.507	.601	.666
17	.412	.490	.582	.645
18	.399	.476	.564	.625
19	.388	.462	.549	.608
20	.377	.450	.534	.591
21	.368	.438	.521	.576
22	.359	.428	.508	.562
23	.351	.418	.496	.549
24	.343	.409	.485	.537
25	.336	.400	.475	.526
26	.329	.392	.465	.515
27	.323	.385	.456	.505
28	.317	.377	.448	.496
29	.311	.370	.440	.487
30	.305	.364	.432	.478

NOTE: For $n > 30$ use $r_s = \pm z/\sqrt{n-1}$, where z corresponds to the level of significance. For example, if $\alpha = 0.05$, then $z = 1.96$.

To test H_0: $\rho_s = 0$
against H_1: $\rho_s \neq 0$

SOURCE: From "Distribution of sums of squares of rank differences to small numbers of individuals," *The Annals of Statistics* Vol. 9, No. 2. Reprinted with permission of the Institute of Mathematical Statistics.

TABLE A.10
Critical Values for Number of Runs G

Value of n_2

Each cell lists two critical values: the upper number is the smaller (lower) critical value and the lower number is the larger (upper) critical value.

Value of n_1		2	3	4	5	6	7	8	9	10	11	12	13	14	15	16	17	18	19	20
2	lower	1	1	1	1	1	1	1	1	1	2	2	2	2	2	2	2	2	2	2
	upper	6	6	6	6	6	6	6	6	6	6	6	6	6	6	6	6	6	6	6
3	lower	1	1	1	1	2	2	2	2	2	2	2	2	2	3	3	3	3	3	3
	upper	6	8	8	8	8	8	8	8	8	8	8	8	8	8	8	8	8	8	8
4	lower	1	1	1	2	2	2	3	3	3	3	3	3	3	3	4	4	4	4	4
	upper	6	8	9	9	9	10	10	10	10	10	10	10	10	10	10	10	10	10	10
5	lower	1	1	2	2	3	3	3	3	3	4	4	4	4	4	4	4	5	5	5
	upper	6	8	9	10	10	11	11	12	12	12	12	12	12	12	12	12	12	12	12
6	lower	1	2	2	3	3	3	3	4	4	4	4	5	5	5	5	5	5	6	6
	upper	6	8	9	10	11	12	12	13	13	13	13	14	14	14	14	14	14	14	14
7	lower	1	2	2	3	3	4	4	5	5	5	5	5	6	6	6	6	6	6	6
	upper	6	8	10	11	12	13	13	14	14	14	14	15	15	15	16	16	16	16	16
8	lower	1	2	3	3	3	4	4	5	5	5	6	6	6	6	6	7	7	7	7
	upper	6	8	10	11	12	13	14	14	15	15	16	16	16	16	17	17	17	17	17
9	lower	1	2	3	3	4	4	5	5	5	6	6	6	7	7	7	7	8	8	8
	upper	6	8	10	12	13	14	14	15	16	16	16	17	17	18	18	18	18	18	18
10	lower	1	2	3	3	4	5	5	5	6	6	7	7	7	7	8	8	8	8	9
	upper	6	8	10	12	13	14	15	16	16	17	17	18	18	18	19	19	19	20	20
11	lower	1	2	3	4	4	5	5	6	6	7	7	7	8	8	8	9	9	9	9
	upper	6	8	10	12	13	14	15	16	17	17	18	19	19	19	20	20	20	21	21
12	lower	2	2	3	4	4	5	6	6	7	7	7	8	8	8	9	9	9	10	10
	upper	6	8	10	12	13	14	16	16	17	18	19	19	20	20	21	21	21	22	22
13	lower	2	2	3	4	5	5	6	6	7	7	8	8	9	9	9	10	10	10	10
	upper	6	8	10	12	14	15	16	17	18	19	19	20	20	21	21	22	22	23	23
14	lower	2	2	3	4	5	5	6	7	7	8	8	9	9	9	10	10	10	11	11
	upper	6	8	10	12	14	15	16	17	18	19	20	20	21	22	22	23	23	23	24
15	lower	2	3	3	4	5	6	6	7	7	8	8	9	9	10	10	11	11	11	12
	upper	6	8	10	12	14	15	16	18	18	19	20	21	22	22	23	23	24	24	25
16	lower	2	3	4	4	5	6	6	7	8	8	9	9	10	10	11	11	11	12	12
	upper	6	8	10	12	14	16	17	18	19	20	21	21	22	23	23	24	25	25	25
17	lower	2	3	4	4	5	6	7	7	8	9	9	10	10	11	11	11	12	12	13
	upper	6	8	10	12	14	16	17	18	19	20	21	22	23	23	24	25	25	26	26
18	lower	2	3	4	5	5	6	7	8	8	9	9	10	10	11	11	12	12	13	13
	upper	6	8	10	12	14	16	17	18	19	20	21	22	23	24	25	25	26	26	27
19	lower	2	3	4	5	6	6	7	8	8	9	10	10	11	11	12	12	13	13	13
	upper	6	8	10	12	14	16	17	18	20	21	22	23	23	24	25	26	26	27	27
20	lower	2	3	4	5	6	6	7	8	9	9	10	10	11	12	12	13	13	13	14
	upper	6	8	10	12	14	16	17	18	20	21	22	23	24	25	25	26	27	27	28

NOTE: The entries in this table are the critical G values assuming a two-tailed test with a significance level of $\alpha = 0.05$. The null hypothesis of randomness is rejected if the total number of runs G is less than or equal to the smaller entry or greater than or equal to the larger entry.

SOURCE: From "Tables for testing randomness of groupings in a sequence of alternatives," *The Annals of Mathematical Statistics* Vol. 14, No. 1. Reprinted with permission of the Institute of Mathematical Statistics.

Appendix B: Data Set

TABLE B.1
Real Estate Data (150 randomly selected homes recently sold in Dutchess County, N.Y.)

SELLING PRICE (DOLLARS)	LIVING AREA (SQ. FT)	LOT SIZE (ACRES)	NUMBER OF ROOMS	NUMBER OF BATHS
179,000	3,060	0.75	8	2
126,500	1,600	0.26	8	1.5
134,500	2,000	0.7	8	1
125,000	1,300	0.65	5	1
142,000	2,000	0.75	9	1.5
164,000	1,956	0.5	8	2.5
146,000	2,400	0.4	7	2.5
129,000	1,200	0.33	6	1
141,900	1,632	3	6	3
135,000	1,800	0.5	7	2
118,500	1,248	0.25	7	1
160,000	2,025	1.1	7	2
89,900	1,660	0.21	7	1
169,900	2,858	0.79	9	3
127,500	1,296	0.5	9	1
162,500	1,848	0.5	7	2.5
152,000	1,800	0.68	7	1.5
122,500	1,100	0.37	7	1
220,000	3,000	1.15	10	3.5
141,000	2,000	0.65	7	1
80,500	922	0.3	5	1
152,000	1,450	0.3	6	1.5
231,750	2,981	1.3	10	3.5
180,000	1,800	1.52	8	2.5
185,000	2,600	0.75	8	2
265,000	2,400	2	7	2
135,000	1,625	0.36	7	1.5
203,000	2,653	1.8	9	3
141,000	3,500	1	10	2.5
159,000	1,728	0.5	8	1.5
182,000	2,400	0.5	8	2.5
208,000	2,288	1.2	8	2.5
96,000	864	0.32	4	1

NOTE: This data set is available on disk in the Minitab format.

TABLE B.1 (*cont.*)

SELLING PRICE (DOLLARS)	LIVING AREA (SQ. FT)	LOT SIZE (ACRES)	NUMBER OF ROOMS	NUMBER OF BATHS
156,000	2,300	0.65	7	3
185,500	2,800	1.68	9	1.5
275,000	2,820	1	9	2.5
144,900	1,900	0.44	6	2
155,000	2,100	0.58	8	1.5
110,000	1,450	0.3	6	2
154,000	1,800	0.679	7	2
151,500	1,900	0.75	7	2
141,000	1,575	0.25	7	1.5
119,000	1,200	0.25	7	1
108,500	1,540	0.18	7	2
126,500	1,700	0.3037	8	2
302,000	2,130	11.91	8	1.5
130,000	1,800	0.3	7	1.5
140,000	1,650	0.5	8	2.5
123,500	1.362	0.4	7	2
153,500	3,700	1.1	10	3
194,900	2,080	1	8	2.5
165,000	2,320	0.4	8	2.5
179,900	2,790	0.75	13	2.5
194,500	2,544	0.28	9	2.5
127,500	1,850	0.26	9	2
170,000	2,277	0.8	8	3
160,000	1,900	1	8	2.5
135,000	1,400	0.35	6	2
117,000	1,248	0.3	6	1
235,000	3,150	0.3	11	4
223,000	1,680	14.37	8	2
163,500	2,276	1	8	2.5
78,000	821	2.3	4	1
187,000	2,080	1.23	8	2.5
133,000	1,100	0.33	6	1
125,000	1,200	0.33	5	1
116,000	1,100	1.1	6	1
135,000	1,800	1	8	2.5
194,500	2,300	0.91	8	2.5
99,500	1,000	0.49	4	1
152,500	1,786	0.3	8	2
141,900	1.950	0.75	8	2.5
139,900	1,839	2.6	7	1.5
117,500	1,300	0.29	6	1
150,000	1,564	0.3328	6	2
177,000	2,010	0.68	8	1.5
136,000	1,300	0.3	7	1
158,000	1,500	0.54	5	2.5
211,900	2,310	0.46	8	2.5
165,000	1,725	1.528	8	2.5
183,000	2,016	0.78	8	2.5
85,000	875	0.26	5	1
126,500	1,092	0.259	6	1
162,000	2,496	0.75	9	2.5
169,000	1,930	3	9	3

TABLE B.1 (*cont.*)

SELLING PRICE (DOLLARS)	LIVING AREA (SQ. FT)	LOT SIZE (ACRES)	NUMBER OF ROOMS	NUMBER OF BATHS
175,000	2,400	0.7	8	3
267,000	1,950	18.7	7	2.5
150,000	1,122	3.09	5	2
115,000	1,080	0.31	5	1
126,500	1,500	0.5	7	1.5
215,000	2,100	0.5	8	2.5
190,000	2,300	5.63	7	2.5
190,000	2,473	1.25	9	2.5
113,500	1,624	1.8	7	1.5
116,300	1,050	0.43	5	1.5
190,000	2,100	1.3	8	1.5
145,000	1,800	0.658	8	2.5
269,900	2,500	0.92	8	3
135,500	1,526	0.3	7	1.5
190,000	1,745	0.58	7	2.5
98,000	1,165	0.12	6	1
137,900	1,856	0.33	7	1.5
108,000	1,036	0.948	6	1
120,500	1,600	0.4	6	2
128,500	1,344	0.936	6	2
142,500	1,552	0.46	6	1.5
72,000	600	0.5	3	1
124,900	1,248	0.22	7	1
134,000	1,502	0.35	7	1.5
205,406	2,465	1.55	8	2.5
217,000	3,100	0.54	10	3.5
94,000	850	0.11	4	1
189,900	2,464	0.43	8	2.5
168,500	1,900	1.0636	7	2.5
133,000	2,000	0.5	8	2
180,000	2,272	0.41	9	2.5
139,500	1,610	0.45	8	1.5
210,000	2,100	0.5	8	2.5
126,500	1,050	1	5	1
285,000	2,516	8.1	7	2.5
195,000	2,265	0.85	8	2.5
97,000	1,300	0.37	5	1
117,000	1,008	0.5	6	1
150,000	1,600	1.84	7	2
180,500	2,000	0.6	9	2.5
160,000	1,760	0.05	7	2
181,500	2,250	0.33	9	2.5
124,000	1,783	0.22	8	1.5
125,900	1,118	0.56	7	1.5
165,000	2,680	0.5	9	3
122,000	1,950	0.5	7	1.5
132,000	2,000	0.108	8	2
145,900	1,680	0.5	6	1.5
156,000	3,000	0.5	11	2.5
136,000	1,750	0.5	7	2
142,000	1,500	0.41	7	1
140,000	1,403	0.5	6	2

TABLE B.1 (*cont.*)

SELLING PRICE (DOLLARS)	LIVING AREA (SQ. FT)	LOT SIZE (ACRES)	NUMBER OF ROOMS	NUMBER OF BATHS
144,900	1,450	0.3	7	1
133,000	1,908	0.46	7	2
196,800	1,960	1.33	8	2.5
121,900	1,300	0.78	6	1
126,000	1,232	0.314	6	2
164,900	1,980	0.7	8	2.5
172,000	2,100	1	8	2.5
100,000	1,338	0.12	6	1
129,900	1,070	1.69	5	1
110,000	1,289	0.25	6	1
131,000	1,066	0.33	5	1
107,000	1,100	0.17	5	1
165,900	1,840	1.162	8	2

Appendix C: Answers to Odd-Numbered Exercises

Chapter 1 Section 1.2

1. Discrete
3. Continuous
5. Continuous
7. Discrete
9. Continuous
11. Ordinal
13. Nominal
15. Nominal
17. Ratio
19. Interval
21. a. Ratio
    b. Interval (or possibly ordinal)
23. Fahrenheit temperatures are at the interval level of measurement so that ratios are not meaningful. Three times 300° F is not the same as 900° F.

Section 1.3

1. Because the graph does not start at the zero point, the differences are exaggerated.
3. The maker of shoe polish has an obvious interest in the importance of the product and there are many ways this could affect the survey results.
5. 62% of 8% of 1875 is 93.
7. One answer: In recent years a large proportion of women with no prior experience has entered the job market.
9. Since many persons have unlisted numbers, if the telephone directory is used to obtain a sample, all such persons will have no chance of being included. Also, the sample is going to contain many people who probably have no familiarity with fax machines since they have not used them. A sample of users/potential users of fax machines is

probably more appropriate.
11. a. $320
    b. $384
    c. No
13. The implication is that the stable marriage *causes* lower monetary worth, but that isn't necessarily true. Also, it isn't necessarily true that higher monetary worth is the *cause* of an unstable marriage. Other factors could be causes.
15. Since there are groups of 20 subjects each, all percentages of success should be multiples of 5. The given percentages cannot be correct.
17. According to the *New York Times*, "It would have to remove all the plaque, remove it again and then remove it for a third time plus some more still."

Review Exercises

1. a. Continuous
   b. Ratio
3. In order to determine whether the customers of the bank are receiving prompt service, the overall picture in time of how the employees of the bank are servicing the customers is needed. Hence the numbers must be treated as part of an overall process.
5. a. Discrete
   b. Continuous
   c. Continuous
7. They probably based their figure on the retail selling price, but they could have used cost, wholesale price, and so on. They might want to exaggerate in order to appear more effective.

Chapter 2 Section 2.2

1. Class width: 8. Class marks: 83.5, 91.5, 99.5, 107.5, 115.5. Class boundaries: 79.5, 87.5, 95.5, 103.5, 111.5, 119.5.

3. Class width: 5.0. Class marks: 18.65, 23.65, 28.65, 33.65, 38.65. Class boundaries: 16.15, 21.15, 26.15, 31.15, 36.15, 41.15.

5.

IQ	CUMULATIVE FREQUENCY
LT 88	16
LT 96	53
LT 104	103
LT 112	132
LT 120	146

7.

WEIGHT	CUMULATIVE FREQUENCY
LT 21.2	16
LT 26.2	31
LT 31.2	43
LT 36.2	51
LT 41.2	54

9.

IQ	RELATIVE FREQUENCY
80- 87	0.110
88- 95	0.253
96-103	0.342
104-111	0.199
112-119	0.096

11.

WEIGHT	RELATIVE FREQUENCY
16.2-21.1	0.296
21.2-26.1	0.278
26.2-31.1	0.222
31.2-36.1	0.148
36.2-41.1	0.056

13. 80-84, 85-89, 90-94, 95-99, 100-104, 105-109, 110-114, 115-119

15. 16.0-19.9, 20.0-23.9, 24.0-27.9, 28.0-31.9, 32.0-35.9, 36.0-39.9, 40.0-43.9

17. $0-$1999

19. 17.3-19.4

21.

AGE (YEARS)	FREQUENCY
0.0- 1.9	3
2.0- 3.9	4
4.0- 5.9	3
6.0- 7.9	4
8.0- 9.9	1
10.0-11.9	3
12.0-13.9	3
14.0-15.9	2
16.0-17.9	4
18.0-19.9	1
20.0-21.9	2
22.0-23.9	6
24.0-25.9	2
26.0-27.9	2

23.

ENERGY (kWh)	FREQUENCY
700-734	4
735-769	4
770-804	6
805-839	10
840-874	4
875-909	3

25. The relative frequencies for men are: 0.019, 0.071, 0.118, 0.171, 0.087, 0.273, 0.142, 0.118. The relative frequencies for women are: 0.010, 0.072, 0.173, 0.265, 0.042, 0.279, 0.060, 0.100.

27. The third guideline is clearly violated since the class width varies. While the class limits don't appear to be convenient numbers (fifth guideline), they do correspond to special classes, including preschool (under 5), elementary school (5-13), and high school (14-17).

Section 2.3

1. 3.

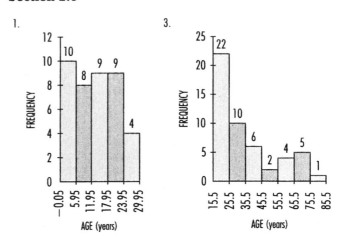

5.

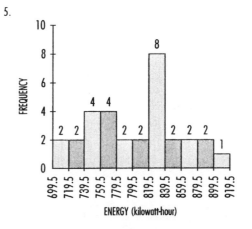

7.

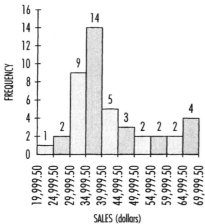

9. a.   A: Lines shorted by trees
   B: Improper grounding
   C: Ice on lines
   D: Accidents
   E: Others
   F: Power surge

It would allow the utility company to determine the cause of power outage that occurs most often and improve it. For example, trim trees.

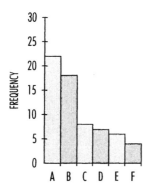

b.

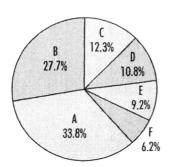

c.   The Pareto chart does a better job of depicting the relative sizes of the components.

11. a.   A: Other
   B: Japan
   C: Canada
   D: Germany
   E: Taiwan
   F: United Kingdom

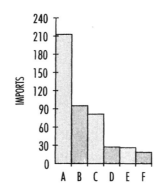

b.

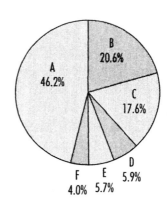

13. The heights of the bars will be approximately halved. Also, depending on the data, the general shape may be changed.

15.

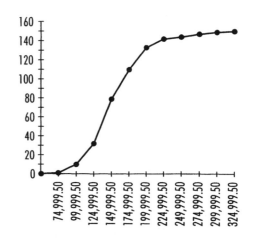

Section 2.4

1. The run chart reveals a cycle with higher values on Mondays.
3. There seems to be an upward trend in the process.
5. There seems to be some form of cyclical variation in the process and the third shift seems to have more defects.
7. There is an upward shift in the process.
9. There seems to be a downward shift in the process.
11. There is an upward trend in the process.
13. There is increasing variation in the process.
15. The process seems to be stable.
17. The process seems to be stable.
19. There is a downward trend in the process.
21. No, reducing variability is good. Management would be wise to ensure that the reasons for the decreasing variability are understood and continued.

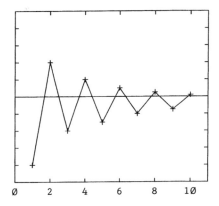

Section 2.5

1. Mean = 2.40
   Median = 2.20
   Mode = 0.0, 2.0, 2.1, 2.4, 4.4
   Midrange = 2.25
3. Mean = 7.5
   Median = 8 min
   Mode = 10
   Midrange = 6.5
5. Mean = 6.00
   Median = 6.0
   Mode = 6.0
   Midrange = 6.00
7. Mean = 7.2
   Median = 7
   Mode = 7, 8.
   Midrange = 7.5
9. Mean = 13.41
   Median = 13.05
   Mode = 23.1
   Midrange = 13.70

11. Mean = 806.9
    Median = 818.0
    Mode = 752, 774
    Midrange = 811.0
13. a. 19.5, 59.5, 99.5, 139.5, 179.5
    b. 95.7
15. a. 18, 25, 34.5, 44.5, 54.5, 64.5
    b. 40.6
17. Company 1:
    Mean = 1.960
    Median = 1.750
    Mode = 2.00
    Midrange = 2.625
    Company 2:
    Mean = 1.930
    Median = 1.975
    Mode = 2.25
    Midrange = 1.945
    I would choose company 2 since the median dividend is higher, even though the mean of company 1 is slightly higher.
19. a. 79.0   b. 2.929
21. From exercise 1: mean > median. Hence the data are skewed to the right.
    From exercise 2: mean > median. Hence the data are skewed to the right.
    From exercise 3: mean < median < mode. Hence the data are skewed to the left.
    From exercise 4: mean > median > mode. Hence the data are skewed to the right.
    From exercise 5: mean = median = mode. Hence, the data are symmetric.
23. $147,606

Section 2.6

1. Range = 4.50
   Variance = 1.67
   Standard deviation = 1.29
3. Range = 11
   Variance = 13.7
   Standard deviation = 3.7
5. Machine 1:
   Mean = 6.00
   Range = 0.6
   Variance = 0.035
   Standard deviation = 0.19
   Machine 2:
   Mean = 6.00
   Range = 0.2
   Variance = 0.005
   Standard deviation = 0.07
   The second machine is better since it has less variation than the first.

7. Range = 7
   Variance = 4.4
   Standard deviation = 2.1
9. 27.20 68.64 8.28
11. 194.0 2763.1 52.6
13. 219.6 14.8
15. 1451.0 38.1
17. a.

ENERGY	FREQUENCY
700-749	4
750-799	10
800-849	10
850-899	6
900-949	1
	31

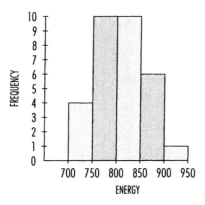

   b. 649.199, 964.601
   c. At least 89%
   d. 99.8%
   e. 100%
   f. The empirical rule gives a better estimate if the data set has a roughly bell-shaped distribution. This is the case for this data set.
   g. $s \approx$ range/4 = 48.5
      Actual standard deviation is 52.6
      The range rule of thumb seems to work quite well in this case.
19. Mean = 12.00
    Range = 22.50
    Variance = 41.75
    Standard deviation = 6.45
    General conclusion: When all the data values are multiplied by a constant:
    —the mean gets multiplied by the value of the constant
    —the range and the standard deviation also get multiplied by the value of the constant.
    —the variance gets multiplied by the square of the value of the constant
21. a. At least 3/4 of the scores are between 300 and 700.
    b. At least 8/9 of the scores are between 200 and 800.

23. a. $41,610.80
    b. $42,384.50; Error is $773.70.
25. a. 95%
    b. 1.05

Section 2.7

1. a. $z = 2.00$
   b. $z = -2.00$
   c. $z = 0.50$
   d. $z = 3.10$
   e. 3.10 is most unusual
3. 0.55; no
5. a. $z = 1.40$ (ordinary)
   b. $z = 2.10$ (unusually heavy)
   c. $x = (0.1)(3.5) + 6 = 6.35$ ounces
7. a. $z = -3.20$. Yes
   b. 500, 1000
   c. $x = 1250$
9. Test b since $z = 0.60$ is greater than $z = 0.30$.
11. Test b since $z = 3.00$ is greater than 2.00 or 2.67.
13. 9
15. 73
17. $117,500
19. $184,000
21. $126,500
23. $179,000
25. 8
27. 72
29. 6400
31. 13,450
33. 7470
35. 7930
37. a. $52,500
    b. $152,750
    c. $96,703
    d. Yes; yes
    e. No
39. Answer varies.

Section 2.8

1. 20, 20, 23, 25, 28
3. 406, 406, 407, 408, 410, 419, 419, 419, 419, 421, 423, 424, 426, 426, 430, 438, 438

5.

6	48
7	5679
8	000112334444569
9	0012233447

7.
```
1 | 1
1 | 5 6 7 9
2 | 1 2 3 4 4
2 | 5 6 8 8 8 9
3 | 1 1 2 3 4
3 | 7
```

9.

17.2   18.7 19.3   20.05   26.3

11.

106   181 198 221   350

13. a. Machine 2 seems to be better since there is less variation in the data when compared to machine 1.
   b. Machine 1 will make some containers noticeably underfilled, resulting in customer complaints, as well as some overfilled containers.
   c. data set B.

15. a. Shift 1:
   Median = 12
   Hinge 1 = 10
   Hinge 2 = 17
   Minimum = 9
   Max = 20
   Shift 2:
   Median = 7
   Hinge 1 = 6
   Hinge 2 = 7.5
   Min = 4
   Max = 8

   b. Shift 2 seems to produce significantly fewer typing errors and there is less variation in the number of errors as well. Shift 2 seems better.

17. a.

ACTORS' AGES	STEM	ACTRESSES' AGES
	2	146667
998753221	3	00113344455778
8876543322100	4	11129
6651	5	
210	6	011
6	7	4
	8	0

b.

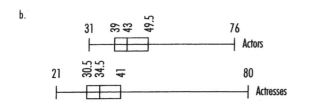

c. Females who win Oscars tend to be younger than males.

Review Exercises

1. a. 16.0
   b. 17.0
   c. 8.0
   d. 16.5
   e. 17.0
   f. 39.1
   g. 6.3

3.

NUMBER	FREQUENCY
0–9	2
10–19	4
20–29	10
30–39	5
40–49	7
50–59	2
60–69	6
70–79	2
80–89	7
90–99	5

5.

7. Mean is 50.1 and standard deviation is 27.8.

9.

8   27.5   45   72   97

11.
```
1 | 200 248 300 600 632 800 956
2 | 000 000 025 400
3 | 060
```

13.

1200   1600 1878 2000   3060

15.

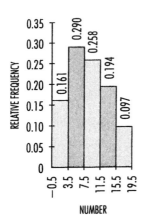

b. Mean = 16.110
    Median = 16.10
    Modes = 15.96, 16.02, 16.06, 16.07, 16.10, 16.14, 16.17, 16.19;
    The data set is multimodal.
    Midrange = 16.105
    Range = 0.37
    Variance = 0.0096
    s.d = 0.098

c. Quite well. The difference is only 0.005

d. The machine seems to be filling the jars with only about 0.1 gm
    excess jam than the desired value.

e.
x	z
16.10	−0.10
16.29	1.84
15.95	−1.63

17. a. There are two extremely high values so the process does not seem
    stable.

b.
```
1 | 6  7  7
1 | 8  8  8  9  9  9
2 | 0  0  0  0  1  1  1  1  1
2 | 3  3  3
2 | 5
2 |
2 |
3 |
3 | 3
3 |
3 | 7
```

c. Median = 20
    Hinge 1 = 19
    Hinge 2 = 21
    Minimum = 16
    Maximum = 37

19. $\bar{x}$ = 25.25; s = 4.78

x	z	
18	−0.68	ordinary
23	0.37	ordinary
33	2.46	unusual
37	3.29	very unusual

21. a. Range = 0.37
        s.d = 0.093

Chapter 3 Section 3.2

1. 1.2, 77/75, −1/2, 5, 1.001, $\sqrt{2}$
3. 0.750
5. 0.382
7. 0.361
9. 0.280
11. 0.0261
13. 237/600
15. 0.340
17. 0.0896
19. P(fraud resulted from a lost card) = 85/500 = 0.170
21. 0.0460
23. 0.600
25. This reasoning is not correct. We can assign any event a probability
    of 0.5 only when we know for sure that it has a 50% chance of
    occurring. We cannot assign a probability of 0.5 to an event just
    because we know nothing about its occurrence.

Section 3.3

1. Mutually exclusive: d, e
3. 4/5
5. 0.520

7. 30/43

9. 0.217

11. 0.824

13. 0.438

15. 0.710

17. 69/758

19. 453/758

21. 17/60

23. a. $P(A \text{ or } B) = 0.9$

   b. $P(A \text{ or } B) < 0.9$

   c. $0.5 \leq P(B) \leq 0.8$ and they may or may not be mutually exclusive.

Section 3.4

1. Independent: a, b, e

3. a. $P(\text{store cannot open}) = (0.06)(0.06)(0.06) = 0.000216$. No, the owner should not be concerned about opening.

   b. Yes, the owner should be concerned about opening because they may all take off together.

      This problem is different from part (a) because this close friendship may indicate that the employees may not operate independently of each other.

5. 0.00766

7. $P(6 \text{ o-rings work correctly}) = 0.977^6 = 0.870$

   No, we want the probability to be much higher to conclude that the design is safe.

9. 55/96

11. a. $P(2 \text{ males live to age 30}) = 0.968$

    b. $P(2 \text{ males die}) = 0.000256$

13. 0.787

15. $P(4 \text{ non-smoking reservations}) = 0.179$

17. 0.0896

19. 0.477

21. a. 5/8

    b. 3/8

    c. 5/18

    d. 5/8

23. a. 4/5

    b. 1/5

    c. 2/5

    d. 3/5

    e. 8/25

    f. 16

    g. Yes; 24, 4, 6

Section 3.5

For problems 1–10 refer to run charts

1. The process is statistically unstable. There seems to be a downward shift in the data.

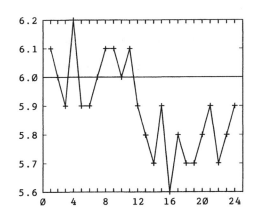

3. The process is statistically stable according to the run of 8 rule, but there seems to be one high value.

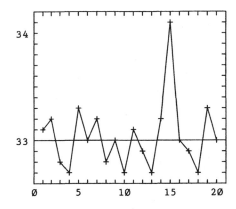

5. The process is statistically stable according to the run of 8 rule. There seems to be a cyclical pattern because Monday is always later.

7. The process is statistically stable according to the run of 8 rule.

9. a. The process is statistically unstable.

    b. Yes. The observations taken after the new proofreader took over are concentrated above the mean. ($\bar{x} = 1.18$)

(continued)

9.

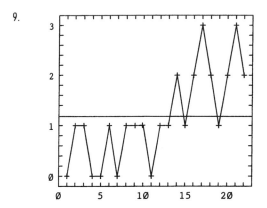

11. a. P(7 items below mean or 7 above mean) = 0.0156

   b. P(9 items below mean or 9 above mean) = 0.00391

Section 3.6

1. 5040
3. 4830
5. 720
7. 30
9. 120
11. 1326
13. $_5P_5 = 5!/(5-5)! = 120$
15. $_5C_0 = 5!/[(5-0)! \cdot 0!] = 1$
17. 6
19. 5040
21. 646,646
23. $10! = 3,628,800$
25. a. 5040
   b. 1/5040
27. a. $(10)^9$
   b. $(10)^{16}$
29. 43,680
31. a. 125,000
   b. permutations
33. 18,720
35. a. 2002
   b. 0.675
37. 2,095,681,645,538 (about 2 trillion)
39. a. 2
   b. $(n - 1)!$
41. Calculator: 3.0414093×10^{64}; approximation: 3.0363452×10^{64}.

Review Exercises

1. a. 0.60
   b. 0.85
   c. 0.635

3. A: getting a stock from NYSE
   B: did not declare dividends
   a. 0.370
   b. 0.775
   c. A: stock from NYSE
      B: declared dividends
      $P(A) = 120/200$; $P(B) = 127/200$
      $P(A) \cdot P(B) = 0.381$
      $P(A \text{ and } B) = 0.465$
      Since $P(A) \cdot P(B)$ is not equal to $P(A \text{ and } B)$, the events A and B are not independent.
   d. P(dividend declared among NYSE stocks) = 93/120 = 0.775
      P(dividend declared among ASE stocks) = 26/50 = 0.520
      P(dividend declared among OTC stocks) = 8/30 = 0.267
      Since the probability that dividend is declared among NYSE stocks is more, I would choose NYSE stocks.

5. 11/19
7. 0.00830
9. a. 0.442
   b. 0.507
   c. 0
11. 1/18,595,558,800
13. a. 0.08
   b. 0.6
   c. 0.8
15. a. 0.300
   b. 0
   c. P(getting A) = 60/400
      P(student is a management major) = 100/400
      P(selecting student with A and student is management major) = 0
      Since P(getting A) $\cdot P$(student is a management major) is not equal to P(student gets an A and student is a management major), the events are not independent.
17. 0.0380
19. 0.000000531
21. 0.0268

Chapter 4 Section 4.2

1. Probability distribution
3. No, $\Sigma P(x) \neq 1$
5. This is not a probability distribution because there is a negative probability. All probabilities should be between 0 and 1.
7. No, $\Sigma P(x) \neq 1$
9. Probability distribution
11. a. $x = 0, 1, 2$
   b. $P(0) = 1/4$, $P(1) = 1/2$, $P(2) = 1/4$

c.

x	P(x)
0	1/4
1	1/2
2	1/4

d.

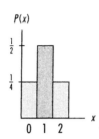

13. a. x = 0, 1, 2, 3
    b. P(0) = 0.45, P(1) = 0.25,
        P(2) = 0.20, P(3) = 0.10

c.

x	P(x)
0	0.45
1	0.25
2	0.20
3	0.10

d.

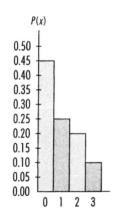

15. a. x = −5, 0, 5, 10, 15
    b. P(−5) = 0.10, P(0) = 0.20, P(5) = 0.30, P(10) = 0.20, P(15)
        = 0.20

c.

x	P(x)
−5	0.10
0	0.20
5	0.30
10	0.20
15	0.20

d.

P(x)

0.4 ┤
0.3 ┤
0.2 ┤
0.1 ┤
0.0 ┤
        −5 0 5 10 15   x

17. a. Yes
    b. No, $\Sigma P(x) > 1$

19. a. Need to check two things:
        $0 \leq P(x) \leq 1$
        $\Sigma P(x) = 1$
        Both are satisfied, so it is a probability distribution.
    b. $P(Y < 5) = P(0) + P(1) + P(2) + P(3) + P(4)$
        $= 0.05 + 0.10 + 0.15 + 0.20 + 0.20$
        $= 0.70$
    c. $P(Y \leq 5) = P(0) + P(1) + P(2) + P(3) + P(4) + P(5)$
        $= 0.05 + 0.10 + 0.15 + 0.20 + 0.20 + 0.15$
        $= 0.85$
    d. $P(4 \leq Y \leq 6) = P(4) + P(5) + P(6)$
        $= 0.20 + 0.15 + 0.10$
        $= 0.45$
    e. $P(Y = 4.5) = 0$

Section 4.3

	MEAN	VARIANCE	STANDARD DEVIATION
1.	1.1	0.5	0.7
3.	2.5	0.5	0.7
5.	21.3	304.7	17.5

7. $\mu = 3.9$, $\sigma^2 = 1.362$, $\sigma = 1.167$, $\mu - 2\sigma = 1.566$, $\mu + 2\sigma$
    $= 6.234$, $Z = -0.77$, $Z = -3.34$. Yes, $x = 0$ is very unusual.

9. Commuter Train Line 1:

x_1	$P(x_1)$	$x_1 \cdot P(x_1)$	x_1^2	$x_1^2 \cdot P(x_1)$
−4	0.10	−0.40	16	1.60
−2	0.20	−0.40	4	0.80
0	0.40	0	0	0
2	0.20	0.40	4	0.80
4	0.10	0.40	16	1.60
	Total	0		4.80

$$\mu = \Sigma x_1 \cdot P(x_1) = 0$$

$$\sigma = \sqrt{4.8 - 0^2} = \sqrt{4.8} = 2.19$$

$$\sigma = \frac{\text{Range}}{4} = \frac{4 - (-4)}{4} = 2$$

Commuter Train Line 2:

x_2	$P(x_2)$	$x_2 \cdot P(x_2)$	x_2^2	$x_2^2 \cdot P(x_2)$
-2	0.10	-0.20	4	0.40
0	0.80	0	0	0
2	0.10	0.20	4	0.40
Total		0		0.80

$$\mu = \Sigma x_2 \cdot P(x2) = 0$$

$$\sigma = \sqrt{0.80 - 0^2} = \sqrt{0.80} = 0.89$$

$$\sigma = \frac{\text{Range}}{4} = \frac{2 - (-2)}{4} = 1$$

Commuter Train Line 2 seems to provide higher quality service because the standard deviation is smaller so that there is more consistent service.

The supervisor is ignoring the variation in times.

11. 0.044   0.224

13. a. $\mu = 3.048$, $\sigma = 1.09$, $\mu - 2\sigma = 0.868$.
    b. 0.009
    c. 0.025 or 2.5%
    d. -2.80, -0.96
    e. Yes
    f. No

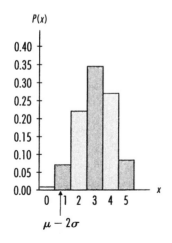

$\mu - 2\sigma$

15.

x	$P(x)$	$x \cdot P(x)$	x^2	$x^2 \cdot P(x)$
0	0.705	0	0	0
1	0.115	0.115	1	0.115
2	0.090	0.180	4	0.360
3	0.090	0.270	9	0.810
	Total	0.565		1.285

$$\mu = 0.565$$

$$\sigma^2 = 1.285 - (0.565)^2 = 0.97$$

$$\sigma = \sqrt{0.97} = 0.98$$

$100(0.565) = 56.5$ vacant seats would be expected on 100 such flights.

17. a. 31.25
    b. 0.05
    c. 1.25
    d. 1.25

Section 4.4

1. a. Yes, the trials are independent, same probability of success and two possible outcomes.
   b. No, the trials are not independent when performing the experiment without replacement.
   c. Yes, independent trials, same probability of success, and two possible outcomes.
   d. Yes, trials are independent and two possible outcomes.
   e. Yes, trials are independent and two possible outcomes.

3. a. 0.117
   b. 0.215

5. a. 10
   b. 1

7. a. 45/512
   b. 8/27

9. 0.346

11. 0.2816

13. 0.3980
    No, with the 20% rate you can easily (0.3980) get fewer than 3.

15. a. 0.105
    b. 0.243
    c. 0.274

17. 0.000297

19.

x	$P(x)$
0	0.296
1	0.444
2	0.222
3	0.037

21. 0.246

23. a. $P(x > 8) = 0.0053 + 0.0005 = 0.0058$

  b. $P(x \geq 8) = 0.0278 + 0.0058$
  $= 0.0336$

25. 0.0524

27. 0.417

Section 4.5

	MEAN	VARIANCE	STANDARD DEVIATION
1.	32.0	16.0	4.0
3.	4.8	1.9	1.4
5.	9.0	6.8	2.6
7.	92.4	76.4	8.7
9.	3.2	2.6	1.6
11.	168.7	56.2	7.5

13. $\mu = np = 50(1/2) = 25$

  $\sigma^2 = npq = 50(1/2)(1/2) = 12.5$

  $\sigma = \sqrt{12.5} = 3.54$

15. $\mu = 10(0.75) = 7.5$

  $\sigma^2 = 10(0.75)(0.25) = 1.88$

  $\sigma = \sqrt{1.88} = 1.37$

17. 105.6   31.3   5.6

19. 4.4   1.7

21. 2.4, 1.5

23. $\mu = 25(0.95) = 23.75$

  $\sigma^2 = 25(0.95)(0.05) = 1.19$

  $\sigma = \sqrt{1.19} = 1.09$

  $\mu - 2\sigma = 23.75 - 2(1.09) = 21.57$

  $\mu + 2\sigma = 23.75 + 2(1.09) = 25.93$

No, it is not unusual to find 22 good pens.
Yes, it is unusual to find 16 good pens.

25. $\mu = 40(0.80) = 32$

  $\sigma^2 = 40(0.80)(0.20) = 6.4$

  $\sigma = \sqrt{6.4} = 2.53$

  $\mu + 3\sigma = 32 + 3(2.53) = 39.59$

  $\mu - 3\sigma = 32 - 3(2.53) = 24.41$

27 or 34 rooms occupied on a weekend are not unusual because they do not lie 3 standard deviations beyond the mean.

27. Yes, it's more than 2 standard deviations away from the mean.

Review Exercises

1. a. Mean is 7.9 and standard deviation is 1.6

  b. 0.238

3. a. 0.060

  b. 1.0

  c. 1.0

5. No, $\Sigma P(x) \neq 1$

7. a. $\mu = 20(0.44) = 8.8$

  b. $\sigma^2 = 20(0.44)(0.56) = 4.93$

  c. $\sigma = \sqrt{4.93} = 2.22$

  $\mu - 2\sigma = 8.8 - 2(2.22) = 4.36$

  $\mu + 2\sigma = 8.8 + 2(2.22) = 13.24$

Yes, it would be unusual to get all of the pieces in box damaged.

9. a.

x	P(x)
0	0.20
1	0.70
5	0.10

  b. $\mu = 1.20$

  c. $\sigma = \sqrt{3.2 - (1.20)^2} = 1.33$

  d.

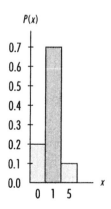

11. 0.9230, 0.077, 0.9960

Chapter 5 Section 5.2

1. 0.0987
3. 0.4332
5. 0.3413
7. 0.4599
9. 0.1587
11. 0.0336
13. 0.1587
15. 0.1814
17. 0.8413
19. 0.9989
21. 0.8185
23. 0.9104
25. 0.1359
27. 0.0954
29. 0.1017
31. 0.3128
33. 0.5
35. 0.3753
37. 0.0049
39. 0.8997
41. 0.2843
43. 0.0843
45. 0.3621
47. 0.9929
49. a. 68.26%
    b. 95.00%
    c. 99.74%
    d. 81.85%
    e. 4.56%
    f. 0.0000005734
51. a. 2.01
    b. 1.23
    c. 1.84
    d. −1.04
    e. −2.50

Section 5.3

1. 0.4987
3. 0.0038
5. 0.1596
7. 0.5
9. 0.0336
11. 0.6406
13. (a) 0.1493
    (b) 5000(0.1493) = 746.5 or 747
15. 0.9266

17. a. 0.00069
    b. 0.0000034
    c. 0.000000001
    d. for a. 690   b. 3.4   c. 0.001
19. a. 0.2119
    b. 0.0918
    c. 0.0516
21. 94.84%
23. a. 0.0574
    b. 0.00275
25. a. 103
    b. 0.8558
    c. 0.0446
27. a. $\bar{x} = 3.275$
       $s = 1.402$
    b. 2/20 = 0.10 or 10%
    c. 0.1093.
       Assumed a normal population.

Section 5.4

1. yes
3. no
5. statistically stable; normal
7. statistically stable; not normal
9. Yes, the sample comes from a population having a normal distribution.

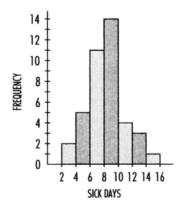

11. Yes, the sample is drawn from a population that is approximately normal.
13. This is a process. Yes, the sample does appear to be approximately normally distributed.
15. At least 40.
    The sample is from a population.

Section 5.5

1. 1.645
3. −1.645
5. −1.645, 1.645
7. −1.645, 1.28
9. 0.25
11. 0.67
13. 153.4
15. a. 525, 60% of the scores are below 525
    b. 552
17. 27,563 mi
19. a. 602.62 (10:03)
       99% of the delivery times are before 10:03 AM.
    b. 563.12 (9:23)
       30% of the delivery times are before 9:23 AM.
21. 13th percentile: 24.874
    Top 7th percentile: 25.396
23. 3.470, 5.756
25. 50.14 years
27. a. No, the data are not normally distributed.
    b. 8.2
    c. 5.4

Section 5.6

1. Yes; $\mu = 6.25$, $\sigma = 2.17$
3. No; $\mu = 79.8$; $\sigma = 2.00$
5. a. 0.121
   b. 0.1173
7. a. 0.194
   b. 0.1922
9. 0.0043
11. 0.5871
13. 0.5160
15. a. 0.0039
    b. No, from part (a) the error rate would appear to be less than 15%.
17. 0.0000002867
19. 0.6119
21. a. 0.782
    b. 0.782722294
    c. 0.7852
23. 262
25. a. at least 500
    b. 0.0119
    c. 0.0038
    d. 0.9843
    e. No, because the calculated probability of 0.0119 is very unlikely if the error rate is really 1%.
    f. No, the error rate is not likely to be 1% because the calculated probability is 0.0038.

Section 5.7

1. a. 0.1179
   b. 0.4641
3. a. 0.6844
   b. 0.9987
5. a. 0.6826
   b. 0.975
7. 0.7734
9. a. No, it is not possible to find the probability that a single guest will spend between $1500 and $2200.
   b. 0.9999999620
   c. 0.000000001. No, the marketing firm's claim is not believable.
11. a. 0.3543
    b. 0.0918
    c. $10{,}000(00.0918) = 918$
    d. 0.8017
    e. 0.00007
13. a. 1.06
    b. 0.454
    c. 0.628
    d. 0.217
    e. 2.12
15. a. 0.1428
    b. 0.4314
    c. 0.6970
17. 0.000000001
19. a. $\mu = 8.0$, $\sigma = 5.4$
    b. 2, 3 2, 6 2, 8 2, 11 2, 18 3, 6 3, 8 3, 11 3, 18 6, 8 6, 11 6, 18 8, 11 8, 18 11, 18
    c. 2.5, 4.0, 5.0, 6.5, 10.0, 4.5, 5.5, 7.0, 10.5, 7.0, 8.5, 12.0, 9.5, 13.0, 14.5
    d. $\mu_{\bar{x}} = 8.0$, $\sigma_{\bar{x}} = 3.4$
21. a. The standard error of the mean decreased from 2 (for $n = 100$) to 1 (for $n = 400$).
    b. 2.5 (for $n = 64$)
       5 (for $n = 16$)
       The standard error of the mean increased from 2.5 (for $n = 64$) to 5 (for $n = 16$).

Section 5.8

1.

SAMPLE	$\bar{x}$
1	100.33
2	99.67
3	99.00
4	103.17
5	100.67

Yes, the process is statistically stable.

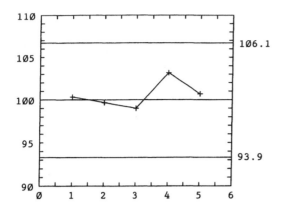

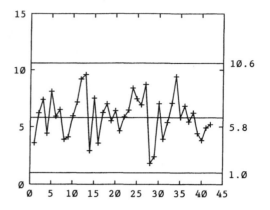

3. Yes, the process is statistically stable.

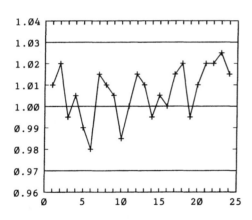

5. Answer varies.

Review Exercises

1. 0.7292
3. a. 0.4090
   b. 0.0764
5. a. 0.2643
   b. 0.0239
   c. 0.00016
7. 0.0034
9. 0.99995
11. 0.1398
13. Yes, the process is statistically stable.

Chapter 6 Section 6.2

1. a. 1.96
   b. 2.33
   c. 2.05
   d. 2.093
   e. 2.977
3. 2.94
5. 20.6
7. 3.8625
9. $68.8 < \mu < 72.0$
11. $97.45 < \mu < 99.75$
    Must have Normal Distribution.
13. $40.0 < \mu < 43.6$
15. $47.18 < \mu < 57.46$
17. $1.79 < \mu < 3.01$
19. 110
21. a. $\bar{x} = 6000$, $s = 1000$
    b. $5231.33 < \mu < 6768.67$
    c. Yes
    d. 97
23. a. $37.5 < \mu < 42.1$
    b. 60
25. 107
27. a. $s = range/4 = 12.50$
       $n = 151$
    b. $18.8 < \mu < 23.8$
29. b. 52

Section 6.3

1. a. 0.2
   b. 0.8
   c. 0.2
   d. 0.0351
3. a. 0.304
   b. 0.696
   c. 0.304
   d. 0.0276

5. $0.208 < p < 0.292$

7. $0.755 < p < 0.925$

9. 625

11. $0.0527 < p < 0.0812$

13. $0.243 < p < 0.311$

15. $70.3\% < p < 73.7\%$

17. 553

19. a. $0.0354 < p < 0.198$

   b. $np = 7.2$

     $nq = 52.8$

     Yes, the sample size is large enough.

   c. 110

21. a. 350

   b. $0.0267 < p < 0.0683$

   c. The rubber grippers seem to be effective since the 95% confidence interval for (b) is less than 0.09.

23. $0.721 < p < 0.779$

25. b. 231

27. 89%

29. $p > 0.818$; 81.8%

Section 6.4

1. a. 12

   b. 97

   c. 9.886, 45.559

3. a. 3.247, 20.483

   b. 1335

   c. 1.44

5. $4.0 < \sigma^2 < 11.3$

7. $58.5 < \sigma^2 < 208.5$

9. $14.01 < \sigma < 23.88$

11. $7.3 < \sigma < 12.3$

13. a. $0.00745 < \sigma < 0.0111$

   b. The sample is collected from a normally distributed population.

   c. 192

15. a. $s = 41.6685$; $756.9 < \sigma^2 < 6331.3$

   b. $27.5h < \sigma < 79.6h$

   c. 22

17. $1.73 < \sigma < 3.33$ $(s = 2.2814)$

19. 98%

21. $2.7 < \sigma < 2.9$

23. Answer varies

Review Exercises

1. a. 83.2

   b. $82.2 < \mu < 84.2$

3. 423

5. 404

7. a. $22.6 < \mu < 33.8$

   b. $1.4 < \sigma < 11.9$

9. a. $0.0696 < p < 0.110$

   b. $n = 1393$

11. a. 1.645

   b. 2.700, 19.023

   c. 2.262

   d. 0.25

13. a. 16.81

   b. $3.0 < \sigma < 6.3$

15. $0.215 < p < 0.265$

17. a. 2.05

   b. 2.947

   c. 6.844, 38.582

   d. 99%

19. $0.911 < p < 0.949$

Chapter 7 Section 7.2

1. a. H_0: $\mu \leq 30$; H_1: $\mu > 30$

   b. H_0: $\mu \leq 3$

     H_1: $\mu > 3$

   c. H_0: $\mu \geq \$250$

     H_1: $\mu < \$250$

   d. H_0: $\mu = \$14,700$

     H_1: $\mu \neq \$14,700$

   e. H_0: $\mu = 3271$

     H_1: $\mu \neq 3271$

3. a. Type I error: Reject the claim that the mean age of accountants is 30 years or less when their mean is actually 30 years or less. Type II error: Fail to reject the claim that the mean age of accountants is 30 years or less when that mean is actually greater than 30 years.

   b. Type I error: Reject the claim that the mean length of time spent on paperwork is 3 h or less when the mean is actually 3 h or less. Type II error: Fail to reject the claim that the mean length of time spent on paperwork is 3 h or less when that mean is actually greater than 3 h.

   c. Type I error: Reject the claim that the mean amount charged by credit card users each month is at least $250 when it is actually at least $250. Type II error: Fail to reject the claim that the mean amount charged by credit card users each month is at least $250 when it is actually less than that amount.

   d. Type I error: Reject the claim that the mean annual household income equals $14,700 when it is that amount. Type II error: Fail to reject the claim that the mean annual household income is $14,700 when it is actually different than that amount.

e. Type I error: Reject the claim that the mean monthly maintenance cost of an aircraft is $3271 when it does actually equal that amount.

Type II error: Fail to reject the claim that the mean monthly maintenance cost of an aircraft is $3271 when that cost does not equal $3271.

5. Right-tailed: a, b. Left-tailed: c. Two tailed: d, e.

7. a. 1.645
   b. 2.33
   c. ± 1.96
   d. ± 2.575
   e. -1.645

9. Test statistic: $z = 1.44$. Critical value: $z = 2.33$. Fail to reject H_0: $\mu \le 100$.
   There is not sufficient evidence to warrant rejection of the claim that the mean is less than or equal to 100.

11. Test statistic: $z = -4.33$. Critical values: $z = -1.96, 1.96$. Reject H_0: $\mu = 20$.
    There is sufficient evidence to warrant rejection of the claim that the mean is 20.

13. Test statistic: $z = 1.73$. Critical values: $z = \pm 1.645$. Reject H_0: $\mu = 500$.
    There is sufficient evidence to warrant rejection of the claim that the mean is equal to 500.

15. Test statistic: $z = 1.77$. Critical value: $z = 1.645$. Reject H_0: $\mu \le 40$.
    There is sufficient evidence to support the claim that the mean exceeds 40.

17. Test statistic: $z = -0.45$. Critical values: $z = \pm 1.96$. Fail to reject H_0: $\mu = 14.00$.
    There is not sufficient evidence to warrant rejection of the claim that the mean age is equal to 14 years.

19. Test statistic: $z = 2.47$. Critical value: $z = 1.645$. Reject H_0: $\mu \le 90,000$.
    There is sufficient evidence to support the claim that the mean is more than 90,000 mi.

21. Test statistic: $z = -1.31$. Critical value: $z = -1.645$ (assuming a 0.05 significance level). Fail to reject H_0: $\mu \ge 7.5$.
    There is not sufficient evidence to support the claim that the mean is less than 7.5 years.

23. Test statistic: $z = -8.63$. Critical value: $z = 1.645$. Fail to reject H_0: $\mu \le 420$.
    There is not sufficient evidence to support the claim of improved reliability. In fact, it appears that reliability actually deteriorated.

25. Test statistic: $z = 3.00$. Critical values: $z = -1.96, 1.96$. Reject H_0: $\mu = 500$.
    There is sufficient evidence to warrant rejection of the claim that the mean expense is equal to $500.

27. $\bar{x} = 31.946$, $s = 0.533$.
    Test statistic: $z = -0.61$. Critical values: $z = \pm 1.96$. Fail to reject H_0: $\mu = 32$.

29. The exact value of σ is not known. Use $\sigma = 12$.
    Test statistic: $z = 1.48$. Critical values: $z = -1.96, 1.96$. Do not reject H_0: $\mu = 100$.
    There is insufficient evidence to warrant rejection of the claim that the mean equals 100.

31. 13.25

Section 7.3

1. Reject the null hypothesis.

3. Fail to reject the null hypothesis.

5. P-value: 0.0322. Since the P-value of 0.0322 is less than $\alpha = 0.05$, we reject the null hypothesis.

7. P-value: 0.0262. Reject the null hypothesis.

9. P-value: 0.0970. Fail to reject the null hypothesis.

11. P-value: 0.0524. Fail to reject the null hypothesis.

13. Test statistic: $z = -2.24$.
    P-value: 0.0125. Reject H_0:
    $\mu \ge 100$.
    There is sufficient evidence to warrant rejection of the claim that the mean is greater than or equal to 100.

15. Test statistic: $z = 2.40$. P-value: 0.0164. Fail to reject H_0: $\mu = 75.6$.
    There is not sufficient evidence to warrant rejection of the claim that the mean is 75.6.

17. Test statistic: $z = -0.45$. P-value: 0.6528. Fail to reject H_0:
    $\mu = 14.00$.
    There is not sufficient evidence to warrant rejection of the claim that the mean is equal to 14 years.

19. Test statistic: $z = 2.47$. P-value: 0.0068. Reject H_0: $\mu \le 90,000$.
    There is sufficient evidence to support the claim that the mean is more than 90,000 mi.

21. a. Test statistic: $z = -1.31$.
       P-value: 0.0951. Fail to reject H_0: $\mu \ge 7.5$.
       There is not sufficient evidence to support the claim that the mean is less than 7.5 years.
    b. $6.40 < \mu < 7.63$

23. Test statistic: $z = 3.00$. P-value: 0.0026. Reject H_0: $\mu = \$500$.
    There is sufficient evidence to warrant rejection of the claim that the mean dental expense is $500.

25. Test statistic: $z = 3.16$. P-value: 0.00138. Reject H_0: $\mu = 5$.
    There is sufficient evidence to warrant rejection of the claim that the mean is equal to 5 oz. Now that we reject the null hypothesis, the difference between the desired mean (5 oz) and the actual mean (estimated to be 5.03 oz) needs to be evaluated to determine if the difference is significant from a practical viewpoint. There may not be a need to adjust the process.

27. $24,696

Section 7.4

1. a. ± 2.056
   b. 1.337
   c. -3.365

3. Test statistic: $t = 2.310$. Critical value: $t = 1.860$. Reject H_0: $\mu \le 10$. P-value $= 0.025$.
   There is sufficient evidence to warrant rejection of the claim that the mean is 10 or less.

5. Test statistic: $t = 2.014$. Critical values: $t = \pm 2.145$. P-value is approximately 0.06. Fail to reject H_0: $\mu = 75$.
   There is not sufficient evidence to warrant rejection of the claim that the mean equals 75.

7. Test statistic: $t = -6.241$. Critical values: $t = \pm 2.500$. Reject H_0: $\mu = 157.6$.
   There is sufficient evidence to warrant rejection of the claim that the mean is equal to 157.6 cm.

9. Test statistic: $t = -4.845$. Critical value: $t = -2.861$. Reject H_0: $\mu \ge 154$.
   The new tires will be purchased.

11. Test statistic: $t = 1.667$. Critical value: $t = \pm 2.064$. Fail to reject H_0: $\mu = 20$.
    There is not sufficient evidence to warrant rejection of the claim that the mean is equal to 20 mg.

13. Test statistic: $t = 1.518$. Critical value: $t = 2.064$. Fail to reject H_0: $\mu \le 1500$.
    There is not sufficient evidence to support the claim that the mean amount charged is greater than $1500.

15. Test statistic: $t = 0.472$. Critical value: $t = 1.314$. Fail to reject H_0: $\mu \le 5$.
    There is not sufficient evidence to support the claim that the mean is greater than 5 years.

17. a. Test statistic: $t = -1.657$. Critical value: $t = -2.110$. Fail to reject H_0: $\mu = 23$.
    There is not sufficient evidence to warrant rejection of the claim that the mean is 23 oz.
    b. $22.43 < \mu < 23.07$

19. $\bar{x} = 15.889$, $s = 0.257$.
    Test statistic: $t = -1.296$. Critical value depends on significance level, but the test statistic is not in the critical region for any reasonable choice. Fail to reject H_0: $\mu \ge 16$.
    There is not sufficient evidence to conclude that the consumer is being cheated.

21. The critical z score from Table A-2 will be less than the corresponding t score from Table A-3 so that the critical region will be larger than it should be, and you are more likely to reject the null hypothesis.

23. Using $z = 1.645$, the table and the approximation both result in $t = 1.833$.

Section 7.5

1. Test statistic: $z = 3.27$. Critical values: $z = \pm 1.96$. Reject: H_0: $p = 0.3$.
   There is sufficient evidence to warrant rejection of the claim that the proportion of defects is equal to 0.3. In fact, it seems to be significantly higher.

3. Test statistic: $z = 3.59$. Critical value: $z = 2.33$. Reject H_0: $p \le 0.7$.
   There is sufficient evidence to support the claim that more than 70% of the population supports the ban.

5. Test statistic: $z = 1.48$. Critical values: $z = \pm 1.645$. Fail to reject H_0: $p = 0.71$.
   There is not sufficient evidence to warrant rejection of the claim that the actual percentage is 71%.

7. Test statistic: $z = 6.91$. Critical value: $z = 2.05$. Reject H_0: $p \le 1/4$.
   There is sufficient evidence to support the claim that more than 1/4 of all white-collar criminals have attended college.

9. Test statistic: $z = 3.73$. Critical value: $z = 2.33$. Reject H_0: $p \le 0.784$.
   There is sufficient evidence to support the claim that the on-time arrival rate is higher than 78.4%.

11. Test statistic: $z = 2.78$. Critical value: $z = 1.645$. Reject H_0: $p \le 0.01$.
    There is sufficient evidence to warrant rejection of the claim that no more than 1% of the vitamin bottles are incorrectly sealed.

13. Test statistic: $z = 1.02$. Critical value: $z = 1.645$. P-value: 0.1539. Fail to reject H_0: $p \le 0.50$.
    There is not sufficient evidence to support the claim that more than half of buyers of compact cars are men.

15. a. Test statistic: $z = -2.68$. Critical value: $z = -2.33$. Reject H_0: $p \ge 0.04$.
    There is sufficient evidence to support the claim that the default rate is less than 4%.
    b. P-value: 0.0038
    c. $0.0191 < p < 0.0331$

17. 1.977%

19. a. To get $np = 5$, n must be 125. The condition $nq \ge 5$ will also be satisfied with $n = 125$.
    b. Test statistic: $z = -1.48$. Critical value: $z = -1.28$. Reject H_0: $p \ge 0.05$.
    There is sufficient evidence to support the claim that the rate of scratch defects is under 4%.
    c. $0.0062 < p < 0.0404$

Section 7.6

1. a. 8.907, 32.852
   b. 10.117
   c. 40.289

3. Test statistic: $\chi^2 = 50.440$. Critical value: $\chi^2 = 38.885$. Reject H_0: $\sigma^2 \le 100$.
   There is sufficient evidence to support the claim that the variance is greater than 100.

5. Test statistic: $\chi^2 = 108.889$. Critical value: $\chi^2 = 101.879$. Reject H_0: $\sigma^2 \leq 9.00$.

   There is sufficient evidence to warrant rejection of the claim that the variance is equal to or less than 9.00.

7. Test statistic: $\chi^2 = 114.586$. Critical values: $\chi^2 = 57.153$, 106.629. Reject H_0: $\sigma = 43.7$ ft.

   There is sufficient evidence to warrant rejection of the claim that the standard deviation is equal to 43.7 ft.

9. Test statistic: $\chi^2 = 44.800$. Critical value: $\chi^2 = 51.739$. Reject H_0: $\sigma \geq 0.15$. P-value: about .005.

   There is sufficient evidence to support the claim that the standard deviation is less than 0.15 oz.

11. Test statistic: $\chi^2 = 24.576$. Critical value: $\chi^2 = 43.188$. P-value: Less than 0.005. Reject H_0: $\sigma \geq 0.75$.

   There is sufficient evidence to support the claim that the standard deviation is less than 0.75 lb.

13. Test statistic: $\chi^2 = 122.513$. Critical value: $\chi^2 = 90.531$. Reject H_0: $\sigma \leq 4.00$.

   There is sufficient evidence to support the claim that the standard deviation is more than 4.00 h.

15. The sample standard deviation is $s = 1026.718$. Test statistic: $\chi^2 = 6.325$. Critical values: $\chi^2 = 1.635$, 12.592. Fail to reject H_0: $\sigma = 1000$ kWh.

   There is not sufficient evidence to warrant rejection of the claim that the standard deviation is equal to 1000 kWh.

17. a. Estimated values: 73.772, 129.070
       Table A–4 values: 74.222, 129.561
    b. 116.643, 184.199

19. a. Test statistic: $\chi^2 = 15.327$. Critical value: $\chi^2 = 16.919$. Fail to reject H_0: $\sigma \leq 2$.

       There is not sufficient evidence to support the claim that the standard deviation is greater than 2 grams.

    b. Test statistic: $\chi^2 = 83.851$. Critical value: $\chi^2 = 67.505$. Reject H_0: $\sigma \leq 2$.

       There is sufficient evidence to support the claim that the standard deviation is greater than 2 grams.

    c. The first conclusion states that the evidence is not sufficient to support the claim that the standard deviation is greater than 2 grams, and the second conclusion states that there is sufficient evidence to make that conclusion. The first P-value is between 0.05 and 0.10; the second P-value is less than 0.005.

Review Exercises

1. a. $z = -1.645$
   b. $z = 2.33$
   c. $t = \pm 3.106$
   d. $\chi^2 = 10.856$
   e. $\chi^2 = 16.047$, 45.722

3. a. H_0: $\mu \geq 20.0$
   b. Left-tailed

c. Rejecting the claim that the mean is at least 20.0 min when it really is at least 20.0 min.

d. Failing to reject the claim that the mean is at least 20.0 min when it really is less than 20.0 min.

e. 0.01

5. Test statistic: $z = -1.71$. Critical value: $z = -1.645$. Reject H_0: $p \geq 0.15$.

   There is sufficient evidence to support the claim that the proportion of fraudulent credit card applicants is less than 0.15.

7. Test statistic: $t = -5.45$. Critical value: $t = -2.492$. Reject H_0: $\mu \geq 55$.

   There is sufficient evidence to support the claim that the lawnmower produces less than 55 g of smog-producing emissions. (Data must be normal, and can be checked with a histogram.)

9. Test statistic: $z = -1.03$. Critical value: $z = -1.645$. Fail to reject H_0: $p \geq 0.25$.

   There is not sufficient evidence to support the claim that fewer than 1/4 of all income tax returns have the presidential donation box checked.

11. a. Test statistic: $t = 5.472$. Critical value: $t = 1.701$. Reject H_0: $\mu \leq 0.75$.

       There is sufficient evidence to support the claim that the mean is greater than 0.75 s.

    b. P-value: less than 0.005.

    c. Test statistic: $\chi^2 = 222.380$. Critical value: $\chi^2 = 37.916$. Reject H_0: $\sigma \leq 0.22$.

       There is sufficient evidence to support the claim that the standard deviation is greater than 0.22 s.

    d. P-value: less than 0.005 (so reject null hypothesis).

    e. The consumption of the four beers increased the mean reaction times and also increased variation of reaction times. Based on the hypothesis tests performed, the mean braking reaction time is greater than 0.75 s and the standard deviation is greater than 0.22 s.

13. Test statistic: $z = -1.79$. Critical value: $z = -1.645$. Reject H_0: $p \geq 0.5$.

   There is sufficient evidence to support the claim that less than half of all adults are annoyed by violence on television.

15. a. $\bar{x} = 29.64$, $s = 9.05$
    b. Test statistic: $t = -0.132$. Critical value: $t = -2.228$, 2.228. Fail to reject H_0: $\mu = 30$.

       There is not sufficient evidence to reject the claim that the mean is 30.

    c. Test statistic: $\chi^2 = 32.761$. Critical value: $\chi^2 = 18.307$. Reject H_0: $\sigma \leq 5$.

       There is sufficient evidence to support the claim that the standard deviation is greater than 5.

d. The behavior of the process is not meeting up to the specifications of the Houston Bakery. Based on the hypothesis test, they seem to be getting a mean of 30, but the standard deviation seems much larger than desired so that some cookies will have too few chips and others will have too many.

Chapter 8 Section 8.2

1. Assignable type
   a. Monitoring customer service time by a run chart or $\bar{x}$ chart; monitoring errors in transactions.
   b. Having tellers work in shifts.

3. Random

5. Assignable type
   a. Monitoring the tax preparation time with a run chart or $\bar{x}$ chart.
   b. Giving adequate training to new recruits.

7. Random

9. A Pareto chart can be made for failed components so that the most important problem can be identified.

11. The average time required to take orders, the average time taken to assemble the computers, the average time required to test the computers or the average time taken for the computers to reach the consumers can be determined.

13. Plotting a run chart of the individual values for order or shipping time will give an indication of how the process is proceeding—whether the process is statistically stable or not.

15. The $\bar{x}$ chart will give an indication of whether the process averages are in control or not.

17. Stable.

19. Not stable. 8 consecutive points above the center line (criterion 2).

21. a. The run chart will show an upward trend in the data.
    b. More and more points will fall above the center line. Some may even fall beyond the upper control line.
    c. The height of the bar for large values of x will progressively increase.
    d. The process mean will shift up.
    e. The standard deviation of the process may or may not change, but the standard deviation of the set of data taken over time will appear to increase.

Section 8.3

[For exercises 1 through 9 refer to control charts]

1. $n = 6, k = 24$
   CL $= 20.306$
   LCL $= 20.306 - (1.287)5.960 = 12.64$
   UCL $= 20.306 + (1.287)5.960 = 27.98$
   The process mean seems to be statistically stable.

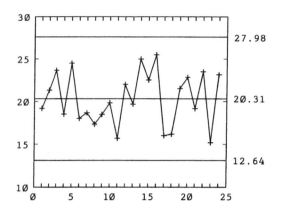

3. $k = 20, n = 4$ $\bar{s} = 0.152$
   CL $= 15.983$
   LCL $= 15.983 - (1.628)0.152 = 15.74$
   UCL $= 15.983 + (1.628)0.152 = 16.23$
   The process mean seems to be statistically stable.

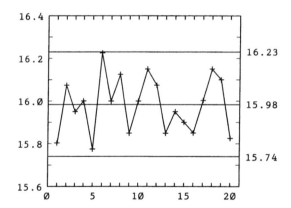

5. $k = 24, n = 4, \bar{R} = 7.46$
   CL $= 14.68$
   LCL $= 14.68 - (0.729)7.46 = 9.24$
   UCL $= 14.68 + (0.729)7.46 = 20.12$
   The process mean seems to be in statistical control.

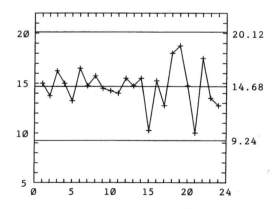

7. $\bar{s} = 4.98$
   CL $= 499.3$
   LCL $= 499.3 - (1.427)4.98 = 492.19$
   UCL $= 499.3 + (1.427)4.98 = 506.41$
   The process mean is not in control. Observation 20 is below the LCL.

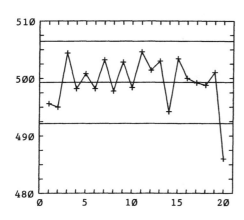

9. CL $= 20.306$
   LCL $= 20.306 - 3[5.960/\text{sqrt}\,(6)] = 13.01$
   UCL $= 20.306 + 3[5.660/\text{sqrt}(6)] = 27.61$
   The process is still stable. The control limits are slightly closer together than in exercise 1 but slightly wider than those in Exercise 2.

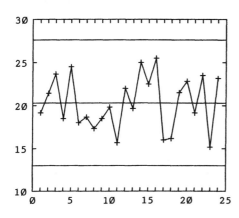

11. a. The bicycle frame would not hold together, which could result in injury to the rider.
    b. None of the sample mean values are less than or equal to 485 lb. 3 of the individual spot welds are less than or equal to 485 lb. No, the process mean has dropped in the last sample and while that mean is greater than 485, we now have a process with some individual bikes that don't meet specification.

Section 8.4

[For exercises 5 through 14 refer to control charts]

1. Out of control. Sample 19 lies beyond the upper control line. (criterion 1)

3. Out of control. Sample 12 lies beyond the upper control line. Also there are 8 consecutive points below the center line. (criteria 1 and 2)

5. CL $= 14.958$
   LCL $= D_3\bar{R} = 0(14.958) = 0$
   UCL $= D_4\bar{R} = 2.004(14.958) = 29.98$
   Process variation in control.

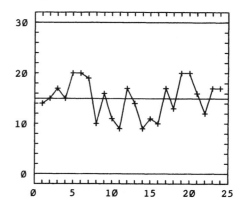

7. CL $= 0.152$
   LCL $= B_3\bar{s} = 0(0.152) = 0$
   UCL $= B_4\bar{s} = 2.266(0.152) = 0.34$
   Process variation in control.

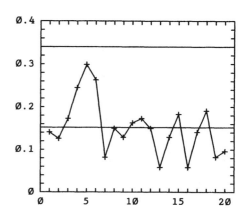

9. CL $= 7.46$
   LCL $= D_3\bar{R} = 0(7.46) = 0$
   UCL $= D_4\bar{R} = 2.282(7.46) = 17.02$
   Process variation out of control. Run of 8 points below the center line. (criterion 2)

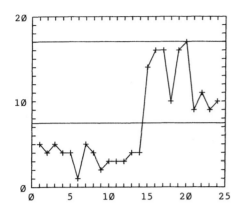

11. CL = 4.98
$$LCL = B_3\bar{s} = 0(4.98) = 0$$
$$UCL = B_4\bar{s} = 2.089(4.98) = 10.403$$
Process variation in control.

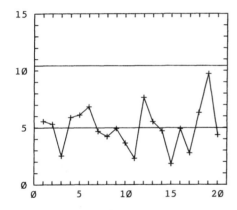

13. CL = 0.525
$$LCL = D_3\bar{R} = 0(0.525) = 0$$
$$UCL = D_4\bar{R} = 2.114(0.525) = 1.109$$
Process variation out of control. Run of 8 points below the center line. Also observations 12, 15, 16 and 19 lie beyond the upper control line. (criteria 1 and 2).

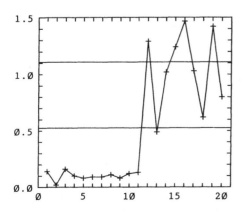

15. a. Test statistic: $z = 9.922$. Critical value: $z = 1.645$.
Reject H_0: $\mu \leq 15$
b. $19.3 < \mu < 21.4$
c. Test statistic: $x^2 = 654.271$
Critical value: $x^2 = 171.6$ (approx.)
Since the test statistic is in the critical region, reject H_0: $\sigma \leq 3$:

17. The process variation has shifted up and is out of statistical control. The mean also seems to have shifted and seems to be out of control. The process variation must be brought under control before examining the mean. Once the process variation is in control, the mean can be examined for stability and corrective measures taken if necessary to bring it under control.

Section 8.5

[For exercises 5 through 8 and 10 refer to control charts]
1. In control
3. Out of control. Sample 20 lies beyond the upper control line. Also there is an upward trend in the data. (criteria 1 and 3)
5. $n = 300$
CL = 0.017
$$LCL = 0.017 - 0.022 = -0.005 = 0$$
$$UCL = 0.017 + 0.022 = 0.039$$
Out of control. Samples 6 and 7 lie beyond the control lines. (criterion 1)

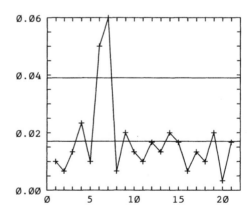

7. $n = 120$
CL = 0.041
$$LCL = 0.041 - 0.054 = -0.013 = 0$$
$$UCL = 0.041 + 0.054 = 0.095$$
Out of control. Observation 8 lies beyond the upper control line. (criterion 1)

(continued)

7.

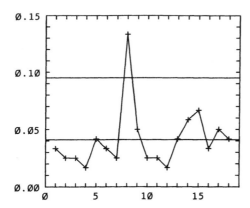

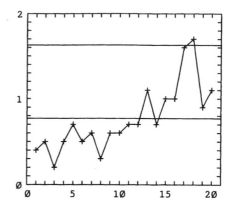

9. a. $0.016 < p < 0.022$
   b. $H_0 : p \leq 0.01$
       $H_1 : p > 0.01$
       Test statistic =
       $(0.019 - 0.01)/[\text{sqrt } (0.01 \times 0.99/400 \times 20)] = 8.09$
       Z (from tables) $= 1.645$
       Since $8.09 > 1.645$ reject H_0.

11. $\bar{p} = 0.05$
   a. $\text{LCL} = 0.05 - 0.065 = 0$
       $\text{UCL} = 0.05 + 0.065 = 0.115$
   b. $\text{LCL} = 0.012$
       $\text{UCL} = 0.088$
   c. As n increases the control lines get closer. The advantage is that
       even very small shifts in the process can be readily detected.
       The disadvantage is that more items must be sampled.
       The chart in b would be better for detecting changes from 5% to
       10%.

Review Exercises

[For exercises 5 through 10 refer to control charts]
1. Out of control. Sample 7 beyond the lower control line. (criterion 1)
3. Out of control. Run of 8 points above the middle line. (criterion 2)
5. Center line: 0.770
   $\text{LCL} = D_3\bar{R} = 0$
   $\text{UCL} = D_4\bar{R} = 1.628$
   Process variation out of control. Run of 8 points below the center line.

7. $\text{CL} = 0.084$
   $\text{LCL} = 0.084 - 0.083 = 0.001$
   $\text{UCL} = 0.084 + 0.083 = 0.167$
   Out of control. A sample point lies below the lower control limit.
   (criterion 1)

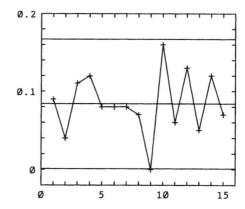

9. $\text{CL} = 0.902$
   $\text{LCL} = B_3\bar{s} = 0(0.902) = 0$
   $\text{UCL} = B_4\bar{s} = 2.266(0.902) = 2.044$
   The process variation does seem to be in control.

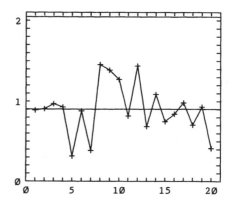

Chapter 9 Section 9.2

1. Test statistic: $F = 2.0000$. Critical value: $F = 4.0260$. Fail to reject H_0: $\sigma_1^2 = \sigma_2^2$.
There is not sufficient evidence to warrant rejection of the claim that the variances are equal.

3. Test statistic: $F = 169.0000$. Critical value: $F = 3.8919$. Reject H_0: $\sigma_1^2 = \sigma_2^2$
There is sufficient evidence to warrant rejection of the claim that the variances are equal.

5. Test statistic: $F = 4.0000$. Critical value: $F = 3.1789$. Reject H_0: $\sigma_1^2 \leq \sigma_2^2$.
There is sufficient evidence to support the claim that the variance of Population A exceeds that of Population B.

7. Test statistic: $F = 1.4063$. Critical value: $F = 1.6664$. Fail to reject H_0: $\sigma_1^2 \leq \sigma_2^2$.
There is not sufficient evidence to support the claim that the variance of Population A exceeds that of Population B.

9. Test statistic: $F = 1.4246$. Critical value: $F = 2.1946$. Fail to reject H_0: $\sigma_1^2 = \sigma_2^2$.
There is not sufficient evidence to warrant rejection of the claim that the two production methods yield the same variance.

11. a. Test statistic: $F = 3.7377$. Critical value: $F = 1.9005$. Reject H_0: $\sigma_1^2 \leq \sigma_2^2$.
There is sufficient evidence to support the claim that the first line has a larger standard deviation.

    b. Smaller standard deviation will increase the consistency of the filling process. There will be fewer overfilled and underfilled containers, thus improving quality.

13. Test statistic: $F = 1.1352$. Critical value of F is between 3.5257 and 3.4296. Fail to reject H_0: $\sigma_1^2 = \sigma_2^2$.
There is not sufficient evidence to warrant rejection of the claim that both time periods have the same variance.

15. Test statistic: $F = 8.2915$. Critical value of F: between 2.4645 and 2.5731. Reject H_0: $\sigma_1^2 = \sigma_2^2$.
There is sufficient evidence to warrant rejection of the claim of equal variances. Hence the method used by Telstar should be recommended because it seems to have a smaller variation.

17. a. $F_L = 0.2484$, $F_R = 4.0260$
    b. $F_L = 0.2315$, $F_R = 5.5234$
    c. $F_L = 0.1810$, $F_R = 4.3197$
    d. $F_L = 0.3071$, $F_R = 4.7290$
    e. $F_L = 0.2115$, $F_R = 3.2560$

19. a. No
    b. No
    c. No

Section 9.3

1. Test statistic: $z = -3.18$. Critical values: $z = -1.96, 1.96$. Reject H_0: $\mu_1 = \mu_2$.
There is sufficient evidence to warrant rejection of the claim of equal means.

3. F-test results: Test statistic: $F = 4.1927$. Critical value: $F = 2.6171$. Reject H_0: $\sigma_1^2 = \sigma_2^2$.
There is sufficient evidence to warrant rejection of the claim that the variances are equal.
Test of means: Test statistic: $t = -3.069$. Critical values: $t = -2.132, 2.132$. Reject H_0: $\mu_1 = \mu_2$.
There is sufficient evidence to warrant rejection of the claim that the two population means are equal.

5. $-13.9 < \mu_1 - \mu_2 < -3.3$

7. $-12.2 < \mu_1 - \mu_2 < -2.2$

9. $3.9 < \mu_d < 19.9$

11. F-test results: Test statistic: $F = 1.4246$. Critical value: $F = 2.1946$. Fail to reject H_0: $\sigma_1^2 = \sigma_2^2$.
There is not sufficient evidence to warrant rejection of the claim that the variances are equal.
Test of means: Test statistic: $t = -3.213$. Critical values: $t = -1.96, 1.96$. Reject H_0: $\mu_1 = \mu_2$.
There is sufficient evidence to warrant rejection of the claim that there is no difference between the population means. P-value < 0.005

13. Test statistic: $z = -1.45$. Critical values: $z = \pm 1.645$. Fail to reject H_0: $\mu_1 = \mu_2$.
There is not sufficient evidence to warrant rejection of the claim that the two populations have the same mean.

15. $27 < \mu_1 - \mu_2 < 121$

17. F-test results (assuming a 0.02 significance level): Test statistic: $F = 2.0669$. Critical value: $F = 2.7608$. Fail to reject H_0: $\sigma_1^2 = \sigma_2^2$.
There is not sufficient evidence to warrant rejection of the claim that the variances are equal.
Test of means: Test statistic: $t = 0.943$. Critical values: $t = -2.327, 2.327$. Fail to reject H_0: $\mu_1 = \mu_2$.
There is not sufficient evidence to reject the claim of equal means.

19. F-test results: Test statistic is $F = 1.3010$. Critical value of F is between 3.5257 and 3.4296. Fail to reject H_0: $\sigma_1^2 = \sigma_2^2$.
Test of means: Test statistic is $t = -4.337$. Critical values: $t = \pm 2.074$. Reject H_0: $\mu_1 = \mu_2$.
There is sufficient evidence to warrant rejection of the claim that the mean is the same for each brand.

21. $\bar{d} = 9.67$, $s_d = 5.83$. Test statistic: $t = 4.974$. Critical values: $t = -2.306, 2.306$. Reject H_0: $\mu_d = 0$.
There is sufficient evidence to warrant rejection of the claim that the training program had no effect on the number of defects.

23. Test statistic: $t = 2.931$. Critical values: $t = -1.96, 1.96$. Reject H_0: $\mu_1 = \mu_2$.
There is sufficient evidence to warrant rejection of the claim that shifts 1 and 2 have the same mean.

25. Test statistic: $t = -2.706$. Critical values: $t = -2.064, 2.064$.
    Reject H_0: $\mu_2 = \mu_3$.
    There is sufficient evidence to warrant rejection of the claim that shifts 2 and 3 have the same mean.
27. $-0.67 < \mu_1 - \mu_3 < 0.19$
29. 501
31. a. 50/3
    b. 2/3
    c. 52/3

Section 9.4

1. a. -2.05
   b. $-1.96, 1.96$
   c. Reject H_0: $p_1 = p_2$
   d. 0.0404
   e. $-0.244 < p_1 - p_2 < -0.006$
3. Test statistic: $z = 4.46$. Critical values: $z = \pm 2.575$. Reject H_0: $p_1 = p_2$.
   There is sufficient evidence to warrant rejection of the claim that the central city refusal rate is the same as the refusal rate in other areas.
5. Test statistic: $z = 2.51$. Critical value: $z = 1.28$. Reject H_0: $p_1 \leq p_2$.
   There is sufficient evidence to support the claim that the error rate is lower after training sessions.
   P-value = 0.0060
7. $-0.0045 < p_1 - p_2 < 0.0445$
9. Test statistic: $z = 2.94$. Critical values: $z = -1.645, 1.645$. Reject H_0: $p_1 = p_2$.
   There is sufficient evidence to warrant rejection of the claim that modifications had no effect. P-value = 0.0032
11. Test statistic: $z = 1.61$. Critical values: $z = \pm 1.96$. Fail to reject H_0: $p_1 = p_2$.
    There is not sufficient evidence to warrant rejection of the claim that 4-year public and private colleges have the same freshman dropout rate.
13. Test statistic: $z = -6.74$. Critical value: $z = -2.33$. Reject H_0: $p_1 \geq p_2$.
    There is sufficient evidence to support the claim that the Salk vaccine is effective.
15. Test statistic: $z = 0.47$. Critical values: $z = -1.96, 1.96$. Fail to reject H_0: $p_1 = p_2$.
    There is not sufficient evidence to support the claim that the proportions are different. P-value = 0.6384
17. $0.158 < p_1 - p_2 < 0.322$
19. Test statistic: $z = -2.40$. Critical values: $z = \pm 1.96$. Reject H_0: $p_1 - p_2 = 0.25$.
    There is sufficient evidence to warrant rejection of the claim that the California percentage exceeds the New York percentage by an amount equal to 25%.
21. $n = 2135$ in each sample

Review Exercises

1. a. $\bar{x}_1 = 16.325$, $s_1 = 1.378$; $\bar{x}_2 = 16.105$, $s_2 = 0.633$
   b. Test statistic: $F = 4.7390$. Critical value: $F = 2.5731$. Reject H_0: $\sigma_1^2 = \sigma_2^2$.
      There is sufficient evidence to warrant rejection of the claim that both populations have the same variance.
   c. Test statistic: $t = 0.593$. Critical values: $t = -2.132, 2.132$. Fail to reject H_0: $\mu_1 = \mu_2$.
      There is not sufficient evidence to warrant rejection of the claim that both populations have the same mean.
   d. By reducing humidity there does not seem to be any significant change in the mean amount of cake mix in the box. The variance seems to be lower after the humidity has been reduced. The bakery should lower the humidity since the process would become more consistent.
3. Test statistic: $z = 0.39$. Critical value: $z = 1.645$. Fail to reject H_0: $p_1 \leq p_2$.
   There is not sufficient evidence to support the claim that the campaign was successful in lowering the rate of commuters who ride alone.
   P-value = 0.3483
5. (Nonunion = 1; Union = 2)
   a. Test statistic: $F = 1.3527$. Critical value: $F = 2.4523$. Fail to reject H_0: $\sigma_1^2 = \sigma_2^2$.
      There is not sufficient evidence to warrant rejection of the claim that the variances are equal.
   b. Test statistic: $t = 1.656$. Critical value: $t = 1.282$. Reject H_0: $\mu_1 \leq \mu_2$.
      There is sufficient evidence to support the claim that union workers have higher mean hourly wages.
      $0.025 <$ P-value < 0.05
   c. $-0.09 < \mu_2 - \mu_1 < 1.09$
7. a. Test statistic: $F = 27.5625$. Critical value of F is close to 2.1952. Reject H_0: $\sigma_A = \sigma_B$.
      There is sufficient evidence to warrant rejection of the claim that the standard deviations are equal.
   b. F-test results: Test statistic is $F = 27.5625$. Critical value of F is close to 2.1952. Reject H_0: $\sigma_A^2 = \sigma_B^2$.
      Test of means: Test statistic is $t = -4.843$. Critical values: $t = \pm 2.093$. Reject H_0: $\mu_A = \mu_B$.
      There is sufficient evidence to warrant rejection of the claim that the means are equal.
   c. $-3.3 < \mu_A - \mu_B < -1.3$
9. (Before = 1; After = 2)
   a. $\bar{x}_1 = 3.28$, $s_1 = 1.09$; $\bar{x}_2 = 2.44$, $s_2 = 0.94$
   b. Test statistic: $F = 1.3446$. Critical value: $F = 2.2693$. Fail to reject H_0: $\sigma_1^2 = \sigma_2^2$.
      There is not sufficient evidence to warrant rejection of the claim that the variance in time was not affected by changes.
   c. Test statistic: $t = 2.918$. Critical values: $t = -1.96, 1.96$. Reject H_0: $\mu_1 = \mu_2$.

There is sufficient evidence to support the claim that the mean time has changed.

 d. $0.37 < \mu_1 - \mu_2 < 1.31$.

  Since zero is not contained in the interval, we conclude (at the 90% level) that the mean time has changed.

 e. The waiting time after the changes seems to have reduced significantly. Also, there does not seem to be any significant difference in the variances. Hence, the changes should be kept.

11. (Before 1) Test statistic: $t = -10.615$. Critical value: $t = -2.365$. Reject H_0: $\mu_1 \geq \mu_2$.

 There is sufficient evidence to support the claim that the training session was effective in increasing test scores.

Chapter 10 Section 10.2

1. The expected frequencies are 20, 20, 20, 20, 20.

 a. 5.900

 b. 13.277

 c. Because the test statistic is not in the critical region, fail to reject the null hypothesis. There is not sufficient evidence to warrant rejection of the claim that absences occur on the five days with equal frequency.

3. Test statistic: $\chi^2 = 156.500$. Critical value: $\chi^2 = 21.666$.

 Reject H_0: $p_1 = p_2 = p_3 = p_4 = p_5 = p_6 = p_7 = p_8 = p_9 = p_{10}$. There is sufficient evidence to warrant rejection of the claim that the last digits occur with the same frequency. There is sufficient evidence to reject Dr. Lindson's claim that she weighs patients.

5. Test statistic: $\chi^2 = 25.634$. Critical value: $\chi^2 = 11.071$.

 Reject H_0: $p_1 = p_2 = p_3 = p_4 = p_5 = p_6 = 1/6$.

 There is sufficient evidence to warrant rejection of the claim that all six outcomes are equally likely.

7. Test statistic: $\chi^2 = 3.567$. Critical value: $\chi^2 = 9.488$.

 Fail to reject the claim that the defects are equally distributed among the different production lines.

9. Test statistic: $\chi^2 = 7.512$. Critical value: $\chi^2 = 7.815$.

 Fail to reject the claim that the actual frequencies agree with the expected rates.

11. Test statistic: $\chi^2 = 9.013$. Critical value: $\chi^2 = 9.488$.

 Fail to reject the claim that the given percentages are correct.

13. Test statistic: $\chi^2 = 21.310$. Critical value: $\chi^2 = 7.815$.

 Reject H_0: $p_0 = 0.78$, $p_1 = 0.12$, $p_2 = 0.07$, and $p_3 = 0.03$. There is sufficient evidence to warrant rejection of the claim that the new form doesn't affect the error rates.

15. Combining time slots 1 and 2, 5 and 6, 7 and 8, and 9 and 10, we get a test statistic of $\chi^2 = 4.118$ and a critical value of $\chi^2 = 11.071$ (assuming that $\alpha = 0.05$). Fail to reject the claim that observed and expected frequencies are compatible.

17. a. 0.296, 0.444, 0.222, 0.037

 b. 88.9, 133.3, 66.7, 11.1

 c. Test statistic: $\chi^2 = 23.241$. Critical value: $\chi^2 = 7.815$.

Reject H_0: $p_0 = 0.296$, $p_1 = 0.444$, $p_2 = 0.222$, and $p_3 = 0.037$. There is sufficient evidence to warrant rejection of the claim that the observed frequencies fit the given binomial distribution.

 d.

$$\Sigma \frac{(O-E)^2}{E} = \Sigma \frac{O^2 - 20E + E^2}{E}$$

$$\Sigma \left(\frac{O^2}{E} - 20 + E \right) = \Sigma \frac{O^2}{E} - 2n + n$$

$$\Sigma \left(\frac{O^2}{E} \right) - n$$

Using the above formula of the test statistic, we obtain $\chi^2 = 89.100 + 132.701 + 40.540 + 60.901 - 300 = 23.241$. The conclusion remains the same as in part (c) (within rounding).

Section 10.3

1. Test statistic: $\chi^2 = 1.174$. Critical value: $\chi^2 = 3.841$.

 Fail to reject the claim that the treatment is independent of the reaction.

3. Test statistic: $\chi^2 = 1.261$. Critical value: $\chi^2 = 5.991$.

 Fail to reject H_0: The item purchased and the gender of the shopper are independent.

 There is not sufficient evidence to warrant rejection of the claim that the item purchased and the gender of the shopper are independent.

5. Test statistic: $\chi^2 = 1.505$. Critical value: $\chi^2 = 3.841$.

 Fail to reject the claim that the accident rate is independent of the use of cellular phones.

7. Test statistic: $\chi^2 = 26.721$. Critical value: $\chi^2 = 9.488$.

 Reject the claim that the category of defect and shift are independent.

9. Test statistic: $\chi^2 = 4.803$. Critical value: $\chi^2 = 7.815$.

 Fail to reject the claim that the type of college is independent of the dropout rate.

11. Test statistic: $\chi^2 = 25.007$. Critical value: $\chi^2 = 13.277$.

 Reject the claim that the consumer's opinion and the region are independent.

13. 58.050; 54.478 (with correction)

 In general, the test statistic decreases.

15. a. The row totals are $a + b$ and $c + d$. The column totals are $a + c$ and $b + d$. The grand total is $a + b + c + d$. Use these values to find the expected frequencies and then calculate the test statistic using $\Sigma (O - E)^2 / E$ to obtain the given expression.

 b. $z^2 = \dfrac{\left(\dfrac{a}{a+c} - \dfrac{b}{b+d} \right)^2}{\dfrac{a+b}{a+b+c+d} \cdot \dfrac{c+d}{a+b+c+d} \left(\dfrac{1}{a+c} + \dfrac{1}{b+d} \right)}$

 = same result for χ^2 given in part a.

Review Exercises

1. Test statistic: $\chi^2 = 0.855$. Critical value: $\chi^2 = 5.991$.

 Fail to reject the claim that $p_A = 0.50$ and $p_B = 0.25$ and $p_C = 0.25$.

3. Test statistic: $\chi^2 = 7.607$. Critical value: $\chi^2 = 5.991$.
   Reject the claim that the occurrence of headaches is independent of the group.

5. Test statistic: $\chi^2 = 11.825$. Critical value: $\chi^2 = 9.488$ (assuming a 0.05 significance level). $0.01 < P$-value < 0.025
   Reject the claim that the day of the week and product quality are independent.

Chapter 11 Section 11.2

1. Test statistic: $F = 6.2385$. Critical value: $F = 3.2317$. Reject the claim of equal means.

3. Test statistic: $F = 5.3276$. Critical value: $F = 3.4668$. Reject the claim of equal means.

5. $0.6 < \mu_2 - \mu_3 < 3.2$

7. Test statistic: $F = 2.6435$. Critical value: $F = 3.2874$. Fail to reject the claim of equal means.

9. $5.5 < \mu_3 < 6.2$

11. Test statistic: $F = 49.6301$. Critical value: $F = 2.8951$. Reject the claim of equal means.

13. $172 < \mu_5 - \mu_3 < 284$

15. Test statistic: $F = 0.1587$. Critical value: $F = 3.3541$. Fail to reject the claim of equal means.

17. Test statistic: $F = 5.0793$. Critical value: $F = 3.3541$. Reject the claim of equal means.

19. $SSTreatment = 34.3$; $SSError = 32.617$; $SSTotal = 66.917$

21. $SSTreatment = 2.17$, df treatment $= 2$, $MSTreatment = 1.085$, df error $= 16$, df total $= 18$, $MSError = 7.036$. Test statistic: $F = 0.1542$. Critical value: $F = 3.6337$. Fail to reject the claim of equal means.

23. a. Test statistic: $t = 1.069$. Critical value: $t = \pm 2.101$. Fail to reject the claim of equal means.
    b. Test statistic: $F = 1.1429$. Critical value: $F = 4.4139$. Fail to reject the claim of equal means.
    c. Test statistic: $1.069^2 = 1.1428 \approx 1.1429$
       Critical value: $2.101^2 = 4.414 \approx 4.4139$

Section 11.3

1. Test statistic: $F = 42.0420$. Critical value: $F = 4.7571$. Reject the claim that the plug types have the same fuel consumption mean.

3. $-4.2 < \mu_B - \mu_C < -1.8$

5. $20.8 < \mu_3 < 22.2$

7. Test statistic: $F = 35.9273$. Critical value: $F = 5.4120$. Reject the claim of equal means.

9. $1.53 < \mu_2 - \mu_3 < 3.23$
   Mean starting salaries for accounting majors is greater than the mean starting salary for marketing majors.

11. $3.30 < \mu_1 - \mu_4 < 4.82$
    Majors with a 3.5 or above have a higher mean starting salary than those in the 2.0–2.5 category.

13. Test statistic: $F = 144.0839$. Critical value: $F = 5.1433$. Reject the claim of equal means.

15. Test statistic: $F = 17.5851$. Critical value: $F = 4.7571$. Reject the claim of equal means.

17. $SSTotal = 13,968$, $SSTreatment = 728$, $SSBlock = 13,182$, $SSError = 58$

19. The results are not affected. We have only switched the roles of treatments and blocks.

21. $SSBlock = 1,318,200$, $SSTreatment = 72,800$, $SSTotal = 1,396,800$
    The sums of squares are all multiplied by 100, but the ANOVA results are not affected.

Review Exercises

1. Test statistic: $F = 10.3634$. Critical value: $F = 2.6802$. Reject the claim of equal means.

3. $2.14 < \mu_3 - \mu_1 < 5.46$
   Method 3 seems to have a larger mean than method 1.

5. Test statistic: $F = 19.4000$. Critical value: $F = 6.9443$. Reject the claim of equal means.

7. Test statistic: $F = 13.4000$. Critical value: $F = 6.9443$. Reject the claim of equal means.

Chapter 12 Section 12.2

1. a. Negative association.
   b. Positive association.
   c. No association.
   d. Positive association.
   e. Negative association.

3. a. $\hat{y} = 1840$
   b. $\hat{y} = 2730$

5. $\hat{y} = 0.655 + 0.480x$

7. $\hat{y} = 29.4 - 2.09x$

9. b. $n = 7$
      $\Sigma x = 20$
      $\Sigma x^2 = 72$
      $\Sigma y = 37$
      $\Sigma y^2 = 259$
      $\Sigma xy = 130$
      $SSxy = 24.286$
      $SSx = 14.857$
   c. $\hat{\beta}_1 = 1.63$
   d. $\hat{\beta}_0 = 0.615$
   e. $\hat{y} = 0.615 + 1.63x$

11. b. $n = 5$
       $\Sigma x = 9$
       $\Sigma x^2 = 31$
       $\Sigma y = 21$
       $\Sigma y^2 = 95$
       $\Sigma xy = 47$

$SSxy = 9.2000$

$SSx = 14.800$

c. $\hat{\beta}_1 = 0.622$

d. $\hat{\beta}_0 = 3.08$

e. $\hat{y} = 3.08 + 0.622x$

13. $n = 8$

$\Sigma x = 16.8$

$\Sigma x^2 = 40.540$

$\Sigma y = 1334$

$\Sigma y^2 = 241,394$

$\Sigma xy = 3060.7$

$SSxy = 259.30$

$SSx = 5.26$

$\hat{\beta}_1 = 49.3$

$\hat{\beta}_0 = 63.2$

$\hat{y} = 63.2 + 49.3x$

$235.78

15. $n = 7$

$\Sigma x = 105$

$\Sigma x^2 = 3225$

$\Sigma y = 48.3$

$\Sigma y^2 = 339.67$

$\Sigma xy = 636.50$

$SSxy = -88$

$SSx = 1650$

$\hat{\beta}_1 = -0.0533$

$\hat{\beta}_0 = 7.70$

$\hat{y} = 7.70 - 0.0533x$

7.70 lb, 6.10 lb

17. $n = 8$

$\Sigma x = 4.63$

$\Sigma x^2 = 2.8391$

$\Sigma y = 73.700$

$\Sigma y^2 = 881.61$

$\Sigma xy = 47.457$

$SSxy = 4.8031$

$SSx = 0.15948$

$\hat{\beta}_1 = 30.1$

$\hat{\beta}_0 = -8.22$

$\hat{y} = -8.22 + 30.1x$

6.84

19. b. $\hat{y} = 9.60 + 0.00x$

$\hat{y} = 9.60$

d. Since the value of the slope is zero, there is no linear association between the x and y variables. This indication of no association is evident from the scatter diagram.

21. a. $\bar{x} = 165/8 = 20.625$

$\bar{y} = 1334/8 = 166.75$

$y = 71.0 + 4.64 (20.625) = 166.7 = \bar{y}$

b. In $\hat{y} = \hat{\beta}_0 + \hat{\beta}_1 x$, substitute $\bar{x}$ for x, $\bar{y}$ for $\hat{y}$, then replace $\hat{\beta}_0$ by $\bar{y} - \hat{\beta}_1 \bar{x}$ to get $\bar{y} = \bar{y} - \hat{\beta}_1 \bar{x} + \hat{\beta}_1 \bar{x}$ or $\bar{y} = \bar{y}$.

Section 12.3

1. a. Possible value for R^2 and the regression line seems to fit the data well since the value is large. (close to 1)

b. Possible value for R^2 but the regression line does not seem to fit the data well since the value is rather small. (close to 0)

c. Not a possible value for R^2.

d. Possible value for R^2 and the regression line seems to fit the data well since the value is large (close to 1).

e. Not a possible value for R^2.

f. Possible value for R^2 but the regression line does not seem to fit the data well since the value is small (close to 0).

3. a. $SSy = 63.429$

b. $SSxy = 24.286$

c. $SSError = 23.730$

d. $\hat{\sigma}_e = 2.1785$

e. $SSRegression = 39.698$

f. $R^2 = 0.626$

5. a. $SSy = 6.8$

b. $SSxy = 9.2$

c. $SSError = 1.0811$

d. $\hat{\sigma}_e = 0.60030$

e. $SSRegression = 5.7189$

f. $R^2 = 0.841$

7. a. $SSy = 18949.5$

b. $SSxy = 259.30$

c. $SSError = 6166.8$

d. $\hat{\sigma}_e = 32.059$

e. $SSRegression = 12,783$

f. $R^2 = 0.675$

9. a. $SSy = 6.4$

b. $SSxy = -88$

c. $SSError = 1.7067$

d. $\hat{\sigma}_e = 0.58424$

e. $SSRegression = 4.6933$

f. $R^2 = 0.733$

11. a. $SSy = 202.65$

b. $SSxy = 4.8031$

c. $SSError = 57.999$

d. $\hat{\sigma}_e = 3.1091$

e. $SSRegression = 144.65$

f. $R^2 = 0.714$

13. a. $R^2 = 0.833$

$\hat{\sigma}_e = 7.07$

This indicates a good fit of the regression line to the data.

b. $R^2 = 0.200$

$\hat{\sigma}_e = 15.5$

This indicates a bad fit of the regression line to the data.

15. a. $SSRegression = \hat{\beta}_1 SSxy$

       $SSError = SSy - \hat{\beta}_1 SSxy$

       Substitute into the $SSError$ equation and get $SSError =$

       $SSy - SSRegression$

       Then

       $SSy = SSError + SSRegression$

  b. $SSx = 100$

       $SSxy = 200$

       $SSy = 1650$

       $\hat{\beta}_1 = 2$

       $\hat{\beta}_0 = 5$

  c.

x	$\hat{y}$
10	25
10	25
20	45
20	45

Section 12.4

1. a. $\bar{x} = 12.167$

  b. $\bar{y} = 6.5$

  c. $SSx = 46.833$

  d. $SSy = 11.5$

  e. $SSxy = 22.5$

  f. $\hat{\beta}_1 = 0.48043$

       $\hat{\beta}_0 = 0.65474$

       $\hat{y} = 0.655 + 0.480x$

       $H_0: \beta_1 = 0$

       $H_1: \beta_1 \neq 0$

       Test statistic: $t = 7.914$. The critical values are $t = -2.776$ and $t = 2.776$ with $n - 2 = 6 - 2 = 4$ degrees of freedom. The test statistic of $t = 7.914$ does fall within the critical region, so we reject the null hypothesis. Because we reject $\beta_1 = 0$, we conclude that the regression line fits the data well and it is usable for prediction.

3. a. $\bar{x} = 6.125$

  b. $\bar{y} = 16.625$

  c. $SSx = 19.375$

  d. $SSy = 129.875$

  e. $SSxy = -40.425$

  f. $\hat{\beta}_1 = -2.0865$

       $\hat{\beta}_0 = 29.405$

       $\hat{y} = 29.4 - 2.09x$

       $H_0: \beta_1 = 0$

       $H_1: \beta_1 \neq 0$

       Test statistic: $t = -3.334$. The critical values are $t = -2.447$ and $t = 2.447$ with $n - 2 = 8 - 2 = 6$ degrees of freedom. The test statistic of $t = -3.334$ does fall within the critical region, so we reject the null hypothesis that $\beta_1 = 0$. Because we reject $\beta_1 = 0$, we conclude that the regression line fits the data well and it is usable for prediction.

5. $0.312 < \beta_1 < 0.649$

7. $-3.62 < \beta_1 < -0.555$

9. a. $H_0: \beta_1 = 0$

       $H_1: \beta_1 \neq 0$

       Test statistic: $t = 2.892$. The critical values are $t = -2.571$ and $t = 2.571$ with $n - 2 = 7 - 2 = 5$ degrees of freedom. The test statistic of $t = 2.892$ does fall within the critical region, so we reject the null hypothesis $\beta_1 = 0$. We conclude that the regression line fits the data well and it is usable for prediction.

  b. $0.181 < \beta_1 < 3.09$

11. a. $H_0: \beta_1 = 0$

       $H_1: \beta_1 \neq 0$

       Test statistic: $t = 3.984$. The critical values are $t = -3.182$ and $t = 3.182$ with $n - 2 = 5 - 2 = 3$ degrees of freedom. The test statistic of $t = 3.984$ does fall within the critical region, so we reject the null hypothesis. Because we reject $\beta_1 = 0$, we conclude that the regression line fits the data well and it is usable for prediction.

  b. $0.125 < \beta_1 < 1.12$

13. a. $H_0: \beta_1 = 0$

       $H_1: \beta_1 \neq 0$

       Test statistic: $t = 3.527$. The critical values are $t = -2.447$ and $t = 2.447$ with $n = 6$ degrees of freedom. The test statistic of $t = 3.527$ does fall within the critical region, so we reject the null hypothesis. Because we reject $\beta_1 = 0$, we conclude that the regression line fits the data well and it is usable for prediction.

  b. $15.1 < \beta_1 < 83.5$

15. a. $H_0: \beta_1 = 0$

       $H_1: \beta_1 \neq 0$

       Test statistic: $t = -3.708$. The critical values are $t = -2.571$ and $t = 2.571$ with $n - 2 = 7 - 2 = 5$ degrees of freedom. The test statistic of $t = -3.708$ does fall within the critical region, so we reject the null hypothesis. Because we reject $\beta_1 = 0$, we conclude that the regression line fits the data well and it is usable for prediction.

  b. $-0.0903 < \beta_1 < -0.0164$

17. a. $H_0: \beta_1 = 0$

       $H_1: \beta_1 \neq 0$

       Test statistic: $t = 3.868$. The critical values are $t = -2.447$ and $t = 2.447$ with $n - 2 = 8 - 2 = 6$ degrees of freedom. The test statistic of $t = 3.868$ does fall within the critical region, so we reject the null hypothesis. Because we reject $\beta_1 = 0$, we conclude that the regression line fits the data well and it is usable for prediction.

  b. $11.1 < \beta_1 < 49.2$

19. $H_0: \beta_0 = 0$

    $H_1: \beta_0 \neq 0$

    $s_{\beta_0} = 40.470$

    Test statistic: $t = 1.755$. The critical values are $t = -2.447$ and $t = 2.447$ with $n - 2 = 8 - 2 = 6$ degrees of freedom. The test statistic of $t = 1.755$ does not fall within the critical region, so we do not reject the null hypothesis that $\beta_0 = 0$.

21. a. H_0: $\beta_1 = 5.00$
    H_1: $\beta_1 \neq 5.00$
    Test statistic: $t = -0.195$. The critical values are $t = -2.447$ and $t = 2.447$ with $n - 2 = 8 - 2 = 6$ degrees of freedom. The test statistic of $t = -0.195$ does not fall within the critical region, so we do not reject the null hypothesis that $\beta_1 = 5.00$.

    b. H_0: $\beta_0 = 50$
    H_1: $\beta_0 \neq 50$
    Test statistic: $t = 0.520$. The critical values are $t = -2.447$ and $t = 2.447$ with $n - 2 = 8 - 2 = 6$ degrees of freedom. The test statistic of $t = 0.520$ does not fall within the critical region, so we do not reject the null hypothesis that $\beta_0 = 50$.

Section 12.5

1. a. $\hat{y} = 187$
   b. $147.8 < \mu_y < 226.3$
   c. $83.4 < y < 290.7$
3. a. $\hat{y} = 164$
   b. $129.8 < \mu_y < 197.9$
   c. $62.1 < y < 265.6$
5. a. $\hat{y} = 161.82$
   b. $133.9 < \mu_y < 189.8$
   c. $78.5 < y < 245.1$
7. a. $\hat{y} = 7.70$
   b. $6.9 < \mu_y < 8.5$
   c. $6.0 < y < 9.4$
9. a. $\hat{y} = 6.84$
   b. $3.76 < \mu_y < 9.92$
   c. $-1.37 < y < 15.05$
11. a. Yes, based on the scatter diagram, there does appear to be a linear relationship between the glue nozzle pressure and the amount of glue.
    b. H_0: $\beta_1 = 0$
    H_1: $\beta_1 \neq 0$
    Test statistic: $t = 8.816$. The critical values are $t = -2.306$ and $t = 2.306$ with $n - 2 = 10 - 2 = 8$ degrees of freedom. Since the value of the test statistic does fall within the critical region, we reject the null hypothesis that $\beta_1 = 0$.
    c. $0.0946 < \beta_1 < 0.162$
    d. Based on the Minitab regression results, the regression equation could be used to make predictions. $R^2 = 90.7\%$.
    e. The nozzle pressure which seems to be the best is 25 based upon the 95% confidence interval and prediction interval.

Section 12.6

1. H_0: $\rho = 0$
   H_1: $\rho \neq 0$
   The test statistic is $t = 6.388$. The critical values are $t = -2.101$

and $t = 2.101$ with $n - 2 = 20 - 2 = 18$ degrees of freedom and 0.05 in two tails. Since the test statistic falls in the critical region, we reject H_0 and conclude that there is a significant linear correlation.

3. H_0: $\rho = 0$
   H_1: $\rho \neq 0$
   The test statistic is $t = 3.403$. The critical values are $t = -1.96$ and $t = 1.96$ with $n - 2 = 75 - 2 = 73$ degrees of freedom and 0.05 in two tails. Since the test statistic falls in the critical region, we reject H_0 and conclude that there is a significant linear correlation.

5. H_0: $\rho \leq 0$
   H_1: $\rho > 0$
   The test statistic is $t = 2.791$. The critical value is $t = 1.714$ with $n - 2 = 25 - 2 = 23$ degrees of freedom and 0.05 in the upper tail. Since the test statistic falls in the critical region, we reject H_0 and conclude that there is a significant positive linear correlation.

7. H_0: $\rho \geq 0$
   H_1: $\rho < 0$
   The test statistic is $t = -0.868$. The critical value is $t = -1.771$ with $n - 2 = 15 - 2 = 13$ degrees of freedom and 0.05 in the lower tail. Since the test statistic does not fall in the critical region, we do not reject H_0. There is not sufficient evidence to support the claim of a negative correlation.

9. a. $r = 0.791$
   b. H_0: $\rho = 0$
   H_1: $\rho \neq 0$
   The test statistic is $t = 2.891$. The critical values are $t = -2.571$ and $t = 2.571$ with $n - 2 = 7 - 2 = 5$ degrees of freedom and 0.05 in two tails. Since the test statistic falls in the critical region, we reject H_0 and conclude that there is a significant linear correlation.
   c. Yes, there is a significant linear correlation between advertising units and sales units.
   d. $r^2 = (0.791)^2 = 0.626 = R^2$

11. a. $r = 0.917$
    b. H_0: $\rho = 0$
    H_1: $\rho \neq 0$
    The test statistic is $t = 3.982$. The critical values are $t = -3.182$ and $t = 3.182$ with $n - 2 = 5 - 2 = 3$ degrees of freedom and 0.05 in two tails. Since the test statistic falls in the critical region, we reject H_0 and conclude that there is a significant linear correlation.
    c. Yes, there is a significant linear correlation between number of telephone inquiries and number of mail orders.
    d. $r^2 = (0.917)^2 = 0.841 = R^2$

13. a. $r = 0.821$
    b. H_0: $\rho = 0$
    H_1: $\rho \neq 0$
    The test statistic is $t = 3.522$. The critical values are $t = -2.447$ and $t = 2.447$ with $n - 2 = 8 - 2 = 6$ degrees of freedom and 0.05 in two tails. Since the test statistic falls in the

critical region, we reject H_0 and conclude that there is a significant linear correlation.

  c. Yes, there is a significant linear correlation between taxes and selling price.

  d. $r^2 = (0.821)^2 = 0.674 = R^2$

15. a. $r = -0.856$

  b. $H_0: \rho = 0$
    $H_1: \rho \neq 0$

    The test statistic is $t = -3.702$. The critical values are $t = -2.571$ and $t = 2.571$ with $n - 2 = 7 - 2 = 5$ degrees of freedom and 0.05 in two tails. Since the test statistic falls in the critical region, we reject H_0 and conclude that there is a significant linear correlation.

  c. Yes, there is a significant linear correlation between cigarettes smoked per day and weight of baby (pounds).

  d. $r^2 = (-0.856)^2 = 0.733 = R^2$

17. a. $r = 0.845$

  b. $H_0: \rho = 0$
    $H_1: \rho \neq 0$

    The test statistic is $t = 3.871$. The critical values are $t = -2.447$ and $t = 2.447$ with $n - 2 = 8 - 2 = 6$ degrees of freedom and 0.05 in two tails. Since the test statistic does fall in the critical region, we reject H_0 and conclude that there is a significant linear correlation.

  c. Yes, there is a significant linear correlation between hydrocarbon and carbon monoxide levels.

  d. $r^2 = (0.845)^2 = 0.714 = R^2$

19. a. $H_0: \rho = 0$
    $H_1: \rho \neq 0$

    The test statistic is $t = 0.014$. The critical values are $t = -2.306$ and $t = 2.306$ with $n - 2 = 10 - 2 = 8$ degrees of freedom and 0.05 in two tails. Since the test statistic does not fall in the critical region, we do not reject H_0 and conclude that there is not a significant linear correlation.

  b. $\bar{y} = 25.0$

21. a. $H_0: \rho = 0$
    $H_1: \rho \neq 0$

    The test statistic is $t = 9.212$. The critical values are $t = -2.069$ and $t = 2.069$ with $n - 2 = 25 - 2 = 23$ degrees of freedom and 0.05 in two tails. Since the test statistic falls in the critical region, we reject H_0 and conclude that there is a significant linear correlation.

  b. $\hat{y} = 110$

23. a. $r = 0.982$

  b. $r = -0.982$

25. a. $r = 0.952$

  b. $H_0: \rho = 0$
    $H_1: \rho \neq 0$

    The test statistic is $t = 8.796$. The critical values are $t = -2.306$ and $t = 2.306$ with $n - 2 = 10 - 2 = 8$ degrees of

freedom and 0.05 in two tails. Since the test statistic falls in the critical region, we reject H_0 and conclude that there is a significant linear correlation.

  c. Yes, there is a significant linear relationship between the two variables because the Minitab display shows that when testing for β_1 the P-value is 0.000 which is less than 0.05. This indicates a significant linear relationship, as well as the results of the test performed in part (b).

27. b. $\hat{y} = 2.17 + 0.111x$

  c. $\hat{y} = 18.82$ hundred sq ft

  d. $r = 0.717$

29. Show

$$\frac{\hat{\beta}_1 - 0}{\sqrt{\dfrac{SSError}{n-2}\Big/ SSx}} = \frac{r - 0}{\sqrt{\dfrac{1 - r^2}{n - 2}}}$$

$$\frac{\hat{\beta}_1^2}{\dfrac{SSError}{n-2}\Big/ SSx} = \frac{r^2}{\dfrac{1 - r^2}{n - 2}}$$

$$\frac{(SSx)\,\hat{\beta}_1^2}{SSError} = \frac{r^2}{1 - r^2}$$

$$\frac{(SSx)\,\hat{\beta}_1^2}{SSy - \hat{\beta}_1\, SSxy} = \frac{r^2}{1 - r^2}$$

$$\frac{(SSx)\left(\dfrac{SSxy}{SSx}\right)^2}{SSy - \left(\dfrac{SSxy}{SSx}\right)SSxy} = \frac{\dfrac{SSxy^2}{(SSx)(SSy)}}{1 - \left[\dfrac{SSxy^2}{(SSx)(SSy)}\right]}$$

$$\frac{SSxy^2}{(SSx)(SSy) - SSxy^2} = \frac{SSxy^2}{(SSx)(SSy) - SSxy^2}$$

Review Exercises

1. Yes, there appears to be a relationship.

3. $SSRegression = 1.57$
  $SSError = 0.394$
  $R^2 = 0.799$
  $r = 0.894$

5. $H_0: \beta_1 = 0$
  $H_1: \beta_1 \neq 0$

  Test statistic: $t = 4.882$. Critical value: $t = -2.447, 2.447$. Reject the claim that $\beta_1 = 0$. Conclude that the regression line fits the data well.

7. a. $\hat{y} = 5.24$

  b. $4.98 < \mu_y < 5.50$

  c. $4.56 < y < 5.92$

9. $\hat{\beta}_1 = 0.0341$
   $\hat{\beta}_0 = 3.88$
   $\hat{y} = 3.88 + 0.0341x$
11. $-0.0286 < \beta_1 < 0.0967$
13. $H_0: \rho = 0$
    $H_1: \rho \neq 0$
    Test statistic: $t = 1.175$. Critical values: $t = -2.160, 2.160$. Do not reject the claim that $\rho = 0$.
15. a. $H_0: \rho = 0$
       $H_1: \rho \neq 0$
       Test statistic: $t = -1.868$. Critical values: $t = -2.101, 2.101$. Do not reject the claim that $\rho = 0$.
    b. Since we conclude from part (a) that the regression line does not fit the data well, use $\bar{y} = 40$.

Chapter 13 Section 13.2

1. 85
3. 75
5. $\hat{y} = 9.49 - 0.0899x_1 + 0.483x_2 + 0.0240x_3$
7. 7.66 (or $7660)
9. $\hat{y} = 34.5 + 3.00x_1 - 3.00x_2$; 13.5
11. $\hat{y} = 24.3 - 1.81x_2 + 3.41x_3$; 18.24
13. a. Taxes $= -0.088 + 0.0185$ (selling price) $- 0.0432$ (living area)
    b. 2.61 (or $2610)
15. a. Taxes $= 3.21 + 0.306$(living area) $- 0.984$(acreage) $- 0.776$(rooms)
    b. 2.25 (or $2250)
17. a. 142.14, 230.61, 147.10, 126.00, 129.83, 132.28, 176.35, 249.68
    b. 2698.4283
    c. 146, 212, 142, 128, 132, 138, 176, 248
       $SSError = 3130$

Section 13.3

1. $\hat{y} = -0.48 + 6.17x_1 - 0.076x_2$
3. Test statistic: $F = 608.82$. Critical value: $F = 4.7374$. Reject $H_0: \beta_1 = \beta_2 = 0$. P-value: 0.000.
5. a. Test statistic: $F = 45.24$. Critical value: $F = 4.7571$. Reject $H_0: \beta_1 = \beta_2 = \beta_3 = 0$.
   b. P-value: 0.0000
   c. 95.8%
7. a. Test statistic: $F = 67.57$. Critical value: $F = 4.7374$. Reject $H_0: \beta_1 = \beta_2 = 0$.
   b. P-value: 0.000
   c. 95.1%
9. a. Test statistic: $F = 7.61$. Critical value: $F = 5.7861$. Reject $H_0: \beta_1 = \beta_5 = 0$.
   b. P-value: 0.030
   c. 75.3%

11. a. Test statistic: $F = 1.33$. Critical value: $F = 6.5914$. Fail to reject $H_0: \beta_1 = \beta_3 = \beta_4 = 0$.
    b. P-value: 0.383
    c. 49.9%
13. b. $SSRegression = 10,021$; $SSError = 8929$; $R^2 = 0.5288$
    c. Test statistic: $F = 2.81$. Critical value: $F = 5.7861$. Fail to reject $H_0: \beta_1 = \beta_3 = 0$.
15. b. $\hat{y} = 3.96 + 0.0120x_1$; $R^2 = 0.788$; P-value $= 0.003$
    c. $\hat{y} = 4.47 + 0.000029x_2$; $R^2 = 0.567$; P-value $= 0.031$
    d. $\hat{y} = 3.35 + 0.0327x_1 - 0.000060x_2$; $R^2 = 0.953$, P-value $= 0.000$
    e. While all three models are significant, the best model includes x_1 and x_2 (which equals x_1^2). It is best because 95.3% of the variation is explained by the variables x_1 and x_2.

Section 13.4

1. Test statistic: $t = 2.535$. Critical values: $t = -2.571, 2.571$. Fail to reject $H_0: \beta_1 = 0$.
3. Test statistic: $t = 0.752$. Critical values: $t = -2.571, 2.571$. Fail to reject $H_0: \beta_2 = 30$.
5. $16.08 < \beta_2 < 60.50$
7. $-31.28 < \beta_0 < 79.62$
9. Test statistic: $t = -11.15$. Critical values: $t = -2.447, 2.447$. Reject $H_0: \beta_1 = 0$. There is sufficient evidence to warrant rejection of the claim that the mileage coefficient is zero.
11. $8.47 < \beta_0 < 10.5$
13. $-0.0353 < \beta_3 < 0.0833$
15. $0.206 < \beta_2 < 0.761$
17. a. Selling price $= 9.97 - 0.0895$(mileage) $+ 0.450$(cruise control)
    b. 0.951, 0.958
    c. First test: Test statistic: $t = -11.13$. Critical values: $t = -2.365, 2.365$.
       Reject $H_0: \beta_1 = 0$. (β_1: mileage)
       Second test: Test statistic: $t = 4.17$. Critical value: $t = 1.895$.
       Reject $H_0: \beta_2 \leq 0$. (β_2: cruise control)
    d. The multiple regression equation with age excluded seems better. All of its coefficients are significant and the two values of R^2 are close.

Section 13.5

1. a. 7.156 (or $7156)
   b. $6.784 < \mu_y < 7.528$
   c. $6.597 < y < 7.715$
3. MTB > REGRESSION C4 3 C1 C2 C3;
   SUBC> PREDICT 27 0 16.
5. a. 138.88 (or $138,880)
   b. $112.550 < \mu_y < 165.200$
   c. $73.600 < y < 204.150$

7. a. 161.60 (or $161,600)

   b. $133.800 < \mu_y < 189.410$

   c. $95.720 < y < 227.490$

9. a. 214.150 (or $214,150)

   b. $180.270 < \mu_y < 248.040$

   c. $145.480 < y < 282.830$

11. a. 136.80 (or $136,800)

   b. $109.530 < \mu_y < 164.070$

   c. $77.140 < y < 202.460$

13. If the living area is held constant at 1800 sq ft and the tax bill is $1500, the confidence interval and prediction interval are: $109.560 < \mu_y < 162.170$; $70.590 < y < 201.130$. If the living area is held constant at 1800 sq ft and the tax bill is $1600, the confidence interval and prediction interval are: $114.760 < \mu_y < 164.620$; $74.960 < y < 204.420$. As the tax bill increases from $1500 to $1600 while the living area is held constant at 1800 sq ft, both the confidence interval and the prediction interval become narrower.

15. a. There were no residuals that were marked by Minitab as having a large standard residual.

   b. Only the first data point is marked with a large residual (2.19).

   c. Only the sixth data point is marked with a large residual of -2.05.

Section 13.6

1. Extrapolation: Because the value for $x_2 = 50$ is beyond the range of the given x_2 values, there may be an extrapolation problem. This is seen in the 95% prediction interval where Minitab noted a row with very extreme values.

3. Estimability: The number of coefficients to be estimated is greater than the number of data points for each variable. Multicollinearity: There are high correlations between x_1 and x_2 and between x_2 and x_4.

5. Extrapolation: The values for living area and tax bill are beyond the range of the data points.

7. Extrapolation: Values for mileage and age are far beyond the range of the data.

Review Exercises

1. $\hat{y} = 27.6 + 1.69x_1 - 2.46x_2 - 6.04x_3 - 4.20x_4$

3. 10.13

5. a. Test statistic: $F = 3.31$. Critical value: $F = 5.1922$. Fail to reject H_0: $\beta_1 = \beta_2 = \beta_3 = \beta_4 = 0$.

   b. P-value: 0.111

7. $-1.32 < \beta_1 < 4.71$

9. $\hat{y} = 14.7 + 2.41x_1 - 2.57x_2$

11. 9.08

13. a. Test statistic: $F = 3.28$. Critical value: $F = 4.7374$. Fail to reject H_0: $\beta_1 = \beta_2 = 0$.

   b. P-value: 0.099

15. $-0.546 < \beta_1 < 5.36$

Chapter 14 Section 14.2

1. 96.5

3. 74.8

5. 98.0

7. 140.7

9. 100.8

11. 110.3

13. 102.2

15. 79.7

17. 100.8

19. 79.4

21. $0.97

23. $1.06

25. 25.7%

27.

Year	1981	1982	1983	1984	1985	1986	1987	1988	1989	1990
CPI	80.0	85.0	87.7	91.5	94.7	96.5	100.0	104.2	109.2	115.0

29. a. 82.8

   b. 82.6

   c. 82.7

   d. 103.9

Section 14.3

1. Seasonal variation

3. Irregular variation

5. Trend

7. Cyclical variation

9. Seasonal variation

11. Trend

13. Cyclical variation

15. Irregular variation

17. Trend

19. Irregular variation

21. Seasonal variation

23. Cyclical variation

25. Irregular variation

27. Trend

Section 14.4

1.

	QUAR	$T \times C$ $S \times I$	MOVING TOTALS	MOVING AVERAGES	$T \times C$
1st Year	1	149			
	2	152			
			634	158.50	
	3	161			162.1
			663	165.75	
	4	172			170.8
			703	175.75	

			MOVING TOTALS	MOVING AVERAGES	T × C
2nd Year	1	178	744	186.00	180.9
	2	192	784	196.00	191.0
	3	202	825	206.25	201.1
	4	212	859	214.75	210.5
3rd Year	1	219	892	223.00	218.9
	2	226	925	231.25	227.1
	3	235	952	238.00	234.6
	4	245	979	244.75	241.4
4th Year	1	246	1004	251.00	247.9
	2	253	1024	256.00	253.5
	3	260			
	4	265			

3.

MOVING TOTALS	MOVING AVERAGES	T × C
17.2	4.3000	4.319
17.35	4.3375	4.413
17.95	4.4875	4.530
18.29	4.5725	4.634
18.78	4.6950	4.741
19.15	4.7875	4.928
20.27	5.0675	5.184
21.2	5.3000	5.369
21.75	5.4375	5.496
22.22	5.5550	5.628
22.8	5.7000	5.783
23.46	5.8650	5.853
23.36	5.8400	

5.

MOVING TOTALS	MOVING AVERAGES	T × C
404.7	101.175	101.78
409.5	102.375	103.20
416.1	104.025	104.91
423.2	105.800	106.88
431.8	107.950	109.03
440.4	110.100	110.61
444.5	111.125	111.40
446.7	111.675	111.70
446.9	111.725	111.75
447.1	111.775	110.96
440.6	110.150	109.83
438.0	109.500	109.50
438.0	109.500	109.51
438.1	109.525	110.40
445.1	111.275	111.74
448.8	112.200	111.78
445.4	111.350	110.60
439.4	109.850	108.70
430.2	107.550	106.28
420.0	105.000	104.14
413.1	103.275	

7.

MOVING TOTALS	MOVING AVERAGES	T × C
817.7	204.425	207.03
838.5	209.625	212.56
862	215.500	218.89
889.1	222.275	226.29
921.2	230.300	234.93
958.2	239.550	244.70
999.4	249.850	253.99
1032.5	258.125	262.29
1065.8	266.450	269.96
1093.9	273.475	276.66
1119.4	279.850	284.35
1155.4	288.850	292.39
1183.7	295.925	298.94
1207.8	301.950	305.11
1233.1	308.275	310.28
1249.1	312.275	313.66
1260.2	315.050	

9. (1) Calculate the moving totals by finding the sum of each sequence of 52 consecutive weeks. (2) Calculate the moving averages by dividing each moving total by 52. (3) Isolate T × C by finding the centered moving averages. This is done by calculating the average (mean) of each pair of consecutive moving averages.

11.

MOVING TOTALS	MOVING AVERAGES	T × C
1245.5	103.792	104.14
1253.9	104.492	104.83
1261.9	105.158	105.60
1272.4	106.033	106.42
1281.7	106.808	107.23
1291.9	107.658	108.14
1303.5	108.625	109.01
1312.8	109.400	109.68
1319.4	109.950	110.17
1324.6	110.383	110.44
1326	110.500	110.63
1329.1	110.758	110.85
1331.2	110.933	110.90
1330.3	110.858	111.04
1334.7	111.225	111.25
1335.3	111.275	111.21
1333.7	111.142	111.05
1331.5	110.958	110.87
1329.3	110.775	110.60
1325.2	110.433	110.29
1321.8	110.150	110.08
1320.2	110.017	110.02
1320.2	110.017	109.95
1318.5	109.875	109.91
1319.3	109.942	109.89
1318.1	109.842	109.57
1311.6	109.300	109.05
1305.6	108.800	108.58

1300.4	108.367	108.09
1293.8	107.817	107.52
1286.7	107.225	106.98
1280.9	106.742	106.43
1273.5	106.125	105.73
1264.1	105.342	105.02
1256.4	104.700	104.44
1250.2	104.183	103.79
1240.8	103.400	

13. 16.0, 16.28, 16.77, 17.19, 17.42, 17.90, 18.49, 18.90, 19.09, 19.49, 20.01, 20.39, 20.60, 21.12, 21.83

Section 14.5

1. a. $T = 50.0 + 2x$
   b. T: 52.0, 54.0, 56.0, 58.0, 60.0, 62.0, 64.0, 66.0, 68.0, 70.0, 72.0, 74.0
   c. C: All twelve values of C are 1.000.
3. a. $T = 703.4 + 5.20x$
   b. T: 709, 714, 719, 724, 729, 735, 740, 745, 750, 755, 761, 766, 771, 776, 781, 787
   c. C: 1.001, 1.002, 0.999, 1.002, 0.998, 0.998, 0.999, 1.000, 1.002, 0.999, 1.000, 1.000, 0.997, 1.001, 1.001, 1.000
5. Trend equation: $T = 156.5 + 8.49x$
   TREND T:
   165.0 173.5 181.9 190.4 198.9 207.4 215.9 224.4 232.9 241.4 249.8 258.3
   CYCLICAL COMPONENT C:
   .983 .985 .994 1.003 1.011 1.015 1.014 1.012 1.007 1.000 .992 .981
7. $T = 4.09 + 0.152x$
   TREND T:
   4.240 4.391 4.543 4.694 4.846 4.997 5.149 5.300 5.452 5.604 5.755 5.907
   CYCLICAL COMPONENT C:
   1.019 1.005 .997 .987 .978 .986 1.007 1.013 1.008 1.004 1.005 .991
9. $T = 107.0 + 0.163x$
   TREND T:
   107.18 107.35 107.51 107.67 107.84 108.00 108.16 108.33 108.49 108.65 108.82 108.98 109.14 109.31 109.47 109.63 109.80 109.96 110.12 110.29
   CYCLICAL COMPONENT C:
   .950 .961 .976 .993 1.011 1.024 1.030 1.031 1.030 1.021 1.009 1.005 1.003 1.010 1.021 1.020 1.007 .989 .965 .944
11. $T = 198.9 + 7.57x$
   TREND T:
   206.47 214.04 221.61 229.18 236.75 244.32 251.90 259.47 267.04 274.61 282.18 289.75 297.32 304.89 312.46 320.03
   CYCLICAL COMPONENT C:
   1.003 .993 .988 .987 .992 1.002 1.008 1.011 1.011 1.007 1.008 1.009 1.005 1.001 .993 .980
13. The same procedure will apply to monthly data.

15. $T = 109.3 - 0.0388x$

TREND T BEGINNING WITH THE 7TH MONTH:

109.27	109.23	109.20	109.16	109.12	109.08	109.04	109.00	108.96
108.92	108.89	108.85	108.81	108.77	108.73	108.69	108.65	108.61
108.58	108.54	108.50	108.46	108.42	108.38	108.34	108.30	108.27
108.23	108.19	108.15	108.11	108.07	108.03	107.99	107.96	107.92

CYCLICAL COMPONENT C BEGINNING WITH THE 7TH MONTH:

.953	.960	.967	.975	.983	.991	1.000	1.006	1.011
1.014	1.016	1.018	1.019	1.021	1.023	1.023	1.022	1.021
1.019	1.016	1.015	1.014	1.014	1.014	1.014	1.012	1.007
1.003	.999	.994	.990	.985	.979	.972	.967	.962

Section 14.6

1. a. 0.9943
   b. 0.904, 1.129, 1.117, 0.850
3. a. 1.0212
   b. 0.814, 0.974, 1.039, 1.173
5. a. 0.996, 0.995, 1.013, 1.000, 0.998, 0.998, 1.008, 1.005, 1.005, 0.985, 1.009, 0.989
   b. 1.000, 0.992, 1.010, 0.998, 1.000, 0.992, 1.010, 0.998, 1.000, 0.992, 1.010, 0.998
   c. 0.996, 1.003, 1.003, 1.002, 0.998, 1.005, 0.998, 1.007, 1.006, 0.992, 0.999, 0.991
7. a. 0.991, 0.987, 1.008, 1.009, 1.001, 0.992, 1.014, 1.006, 1.006, 0.995, 0.991, 0.996
   b. 1.000, 0.992, 1.005, 1.004, 1.000, 0.992, 1.005, 1.004, 1.000, 0.992, 1.005, 1.004
   c. 0.991, 0.996, 1.003, 1.005, 1.001, 1.000, 1.009, 1.002, 1.007, 1.003, 0.987, 0.992
9. $S \times I$:
   .993 1.007 .984 1.005 1.004 1.007 1.000 .995 1.002 1.015 .992 .998
   S:
   .999 1.009 .992 .999 .999 1.009 .992 .999 .999 1.009 .992 .999
   I:
   .994 .998 .992 1.006 1.005 .998 1.009 .996 1.002 1.005 1.000 .999
11. $S \times I$:
   1.530 1.027 .472 1.008 1.466 1.019 .484 1.078 1.434 .990 .515 1.088
   S:
   1.463 1.002 .486 1.048 1.463 1.002 .486 1.048 1.463 1.002 .486 1.048
   I:
   1.046 1.024 .972 .961 1.002 1.016 .996 1.029 .980 .987 1.060 1.038
13. $S \times I$:
   1.024 .960 .983 1.026 1.021 .974 1.003 1.019 1.016 .972 1.019 .980 1.013 .977 1.002 1.023 1.036 .961 .997 1.009
   S:
   1.021 .968 1.000 1.011 1.021 .968 1.000 1.011 1.021 .968 1.000 1.011 1.021 .968 1.000 1.011 1.021 .968 1.000 1.011

I:

1.003 .992 .983 1.016 1.000 1.006 1.003 1.008 .995 1.004 1.019 .970 .992 1.009 1.002 1.012 1.015 .993 .997 .999

15. *SxI*:

1.002 .995 .994 .997 .999 .996 1.002 1.017 .992 1.001 .994 .999 1.016 1.000 .988 1.012

S:

1.002 .998 .994 1.006 1.002 .998 .994 1.006 1.002 .998 .994 1.006 1.002 .998 .994 1.006

I:

1.000 .997 .999 .991 .997 .998 1.008 1.011 .990 1.003 1.000 .993 1.014 1.003 .994 1.006

17. (1) Beginning with the original time series data, find the centered moving averages. (See the solution to Exercise 13 from the preceding section.) (2) Divide all values of $T \times C \times S \times I$ by the estimated values of $T \times C$ to get the estimated values of $S \times I$. (3) For each of the twelve months, find the mean of the $S \times I$ values. (4) Adjust each of the preceding twelve means by multiplying by the adjustment factor: 12/(sum of the twelve monthly averages).

19. *SxI* BEGINNING WITH THE 7TH MONTH:

.986 1.030 1.020 .990 .990 1.007 1.057 1.029 .998 .977 .970 1.005 1.010 1.032 1.015 .960 .984 1.001 1.033 1.064 1.004 .966 .956 .994 .982 1.015 1.021 .984 .995 1.040 1.057 1.041 .988 .963 .943 .984

S (Beginning with the 7th month of the first year):

.990 1.023 1.016 .976 .988 1.013 1.046 1.042 .994 .966 .954 .992 .990 1.023 1.016 .976 .988 1.013 1.046 1.042 .994 .966 .954 .992 .990 1.023 1.016 .976 .988 1.013 1.046 1.042 .994 .966 .954 .992

I (Beginning with the 7th month of the first year):

.996 1.007 1.004 1.015 1.003 .994 1.010 .988 1.004 1.011 1.017 1.014 1.020 1.009 .999 .984 .997 .988 .988 1.021 1.010 1.000 1.002 1.002 .992 .992 1.005 1.008 1.008 1.026 1.010 .999 .994 .996 .989 .992

Section 14.7

1. $724,218

3. $94,616, $94,604, $94,618, $94,556

5. 53.7

7. 61.53, 57.37, 67.84, 85.76

9. SEASONALLY ADJUSTED VALUES (BEGINNING WITH THE 3RD QUARTER):
161 170 179 192 202 210 221 226 235 243 248 253
FORECAST VALUES FOR THE FOLLOWING YEAR:
282 292 301 312

11. SEASONALLY ADJUSTED VALUES (BEGINNING WITH THE 3RD QUARTER):
4.52 4.52 4.40 4.46 4.75 5.01 5.16 5.52 5.39 5.56 6.13 6.08
FORECAST VALUES FOR THE FOLLOWING YEAR:
3.09 6.83 9.75 6.83

13. SEASONALLY ADJUSTED VALUES (BEGINNING WITH THE 3RD QUARTER):
102.1 102.4 103.1 108.5 109.0 111.3 111.7 112.6 111.2 111.5 111.9 106.1 108.6 111.5 112.0 113.1 112.2 108.0 106.0 104.0
FORECAST VALUES FOR THE FOLLOWING YEAR:
110.8 112.1 113.4 107.7

15. SEASONALLY ADJUSTED VALUES (BEGINNING WITH THE 3RD QUARTER):
207.1 211.9 218.8 224.2 234.1 244.1 256.0 265.1 267.2 277.5 284.3 290.5 303.1 305.8 308.6 315.6
FORECAST VALUES FOR THE FOLLOWING YEAR:
340.8 352.4 358.6 364.6

17. Once the trend equation and seasonal indexes are found, both methods are essentially the same.

19. SEASONALLY ADJUSTED VALUES (BEGINNING WITH THE 7TH MONTH):
103.7 105.6 106.0 108.0 107.5 107.5 110.1 108.3 110.6 111.7 112.5 112.3 113.1 112.0 111.1 109.5 110.7 109.5 109.2 112.6 111.2 110.0 110.2 110.1 109.0 108.7 109.6 109.5 109.0 110.3 108.1 106.3 105.1 104.6 103.3 103.0
FORECAST VALUES FOR THE NEXT YEAR:
112.7 112.1 106.9 103.9 102.5 106.5 106.4 109.9 109.0 104.7 105.9 108.7

Review Exercises

1. Seasonal variation

3. Irregular variation

5. Cyclical variation

7. Irregular variation

9. CENTERED MOVING AVERAGES ($T \times C$):
105.128 107.303 111.144 116.595 123.370 129.274 130.585 128.344 124.339 118.598 116.170 118.638

11. CYCLICAL COMPONENT C:
.933 .943 .966 1.003 1.051 1.091 1.091 1.062 1.019 .962 .934 .945

13. *S*:
1.007 1.031 .976 .986 1.007 1.031 .976 .986 1.007 1.031 .976 .986

15. SEASONALLY ADJUSTED VALUES (BEGINNING WITH THE 3RD QUARTER):
107.85 104.54 107.26 116.18 125.63 129.47 136.47 135.17 117.45 120.07 113.57 111.26

17. CENTERED MOVING AVERAGES ($T \times C$):
4.769 4.735 4.678 4.604 4.578 4.626 4.714 4.820 4.908 4.969 4.991 4.969

19. CYCLICAL COMPONENT C:
1.035 1.020 1.001 .979 .967 .971 .983 .999 1.010 1.016 1.014 1.004

21. *S*:
1.012 1.141 .883 .963 1.012 1.141 .883 .963 1.012 1.141 .883 .963

23. SEASONALLY ADJUSTED VALUES (BEGINNING WITH THE 3RD QUARTER):
4.79 4.86 4.61 4.55 4.54 4.57 4.75 4.83 4.96 4.93 5.06 5.05

25. 85.9

27. 109.3

Chapter 15 Section 15.2

1. The test statistic $x = 1$ is less than or equal to the critical value of 1. Reject the claim that there is no difference between the filling weights of the two nozzles.

3. The test statistic $x = 1$ is less than or equal to the critical value of 1. Reject the null hypothesis of no difference between the two tests.

5. The test statistic $x = 2$ is not less than or equal to the critical value of 1. Fail to reject the null hypothesis that the course does not affect scores. It appears to have little or no effect.

7. The test statistic $x = 4$ is not less than or equal to the critical value of 0. Fail to reject the null hypothesis of no difference. There appears to be little or no difference between the ages of husbands and wives.

9. The test statistic $x = 3$ is not less than or equal to the critical value of 1. Fail to reject the null hypothesis that at most half of all dentists favor Covariant toothpaste.

11. The statistic $x = 18$ is converted to the test statistic $z = -1.84$. The critical value is $z = -1.645$. Since the test statistic is less than or equal to the critical value, reject the null hypothesis that production was unchanged or lowered by the new fertilizer. It appears that production was increased.

13. Test statistic: $z = -2.08$. Critical values: $z = -1.645$. Reject the claim that the median is two knots or less.

15. The statistic $x = 22$ is converted to the test statistic $z = -0.71$. The critical value is $z = -1.28$. Fail to reject the null hypothesis that at most half of the voters favor the bill. There is not sufficient evidence to support the claim that the majority favor the bill.

17. With $k = 3$ we get $6 < M < 17$.

19. 78

Section 15.3

1. The given entries 5, 8, 10, 12, 15 correspond to ranks 1, 2, 3, 4, 5.

3. The given entries of 6, 8, 8, 8, 9, 12, 20 correspond to ranks 1, 3, 3, 3, 5, 6, 7.

5. a. 3, −7, −2, −4, −1, 0 (discard), −10, −15
   b. 3, 5, 2, 4, 1, 6, 7
   c. +3, −5, −2, −4, −1, −6, −7
   d. $T = 3$ (the smaller of 3 and 25)

7. a. 25; reject H_0
   b. 25; reject H_0

9. a. 35; reject H_0
   b. 8; reject H_0

11. $T = 6.5$, $n = 9$. The test statistic $T = 6.5$ is greater than the critical value of 6 so fail to reject the null hypothesis of equal results.

13. The test statistic of $T = 3.5$ is less than or equal to the critical value of 21. Reject the claim of no difference between the two types of paint.

15. Assume $\alpha = 0.05$. The test statistic $T = 1$ is less than or equal to the critical value $T = 14$. Reject the claim that the program has no effect on the anxiety level.

17. The test statistic $T = 2$ is less than or equal to the critical value of $T = 14$. Reject the claim that there is no difference.

19. a. $T = 51.5$. $n = 36$. Test statistic $z = -4.42$ is less than or equal to the critical value of $z = -2.575$, so reject the null hypothesis that both systems require the same times. (It appears that the scanner system is faster.)

b. $T = 51.5$, $n = 36$. Test statistic $z = -4.42$ and the critical value is $z = -2.33$, so reject the null hypothesis that the distribution of scanner times is the same as (or to the right of) the distribution of times for the manual system. There is sufficient evidence to support the claim that the distribution of scanner times is shifted to the left of the distribution of times for the manual system. It appears that the scanner times are lower.

21. 1954

Section 15.4

1. $\mu_R = 174.0$, $\sigma_R = 21.54$, $R = 175$, $z = 0.05$.
   Test statistic: $z = 0.05$. Critical values: $z = \pm 1.96$.
   Fail to reject the null hypothesis that the states have the same salaries.

3. $\mu_R = 175$, $\sigma_R = 17.08$, $R = 235.5$, $z = 3.54$.
   Test statistic: $z = 3.54$. Critical values: $z = \pm 1.96$.
   Reject the null hypothesis that the populations of salaries are identical.

5. $\mu_R = 115$, $\sigma_R = 15.17$, $R = 55$, $z = -3.96$.
   Test statistic: $z = -3.96$. Critical values: $z = \pm 1.96$.
   Reject the null hypothesis that there is no difference between the lives of batteries from each method.

7. $\mu_R = 121$, $\sigma_R = 14.20$, $R = 169.5$, $z = 3.42$.
   Test statistic: $z = 3.42$. Critical values: $z = \pm 1.96$.
   Reject the claim that both sides have identical populations of pedestrian traffic.

9. $\mu_R = 144$, $\sigma_R = 16.25$, $R = 84$, $z = -3.69$.
   Test statistic: $z = -3.69$. Critical values: $z = \pm 1.96$.
   Reject the null hypothesis of no difference between mail order and store prices.

11. $\mu_R = 150$, $\sigma_R = 17.32$, $R = 213.5$, $z = 3.67$.
    Test statistic: $z = 3.67$. Critical values: $z = \pm 1.96$.
    Reject the claim that the new drying technique results in the same population as the old technique.

13. a. $\mu_R = 232.5$, $\sigma_R = 24.11$, $R = 120$, $z = -4.67$.
    Test statistic: $z = -4.67$. Critical values: $z = \pm 1.96$.
    Reject the null hypothesis that both groups come from the same population.
    b. $\mu_R = 232.5$, $\sigma_R = 24.11$, $R = 225$, $z = -0.31$.
    Test statistic: $z = -0.31$. Critical values: $z = \pm 1.96$.
    Fail to reject the null hypothesis that both groups come from the same population.

15. a. *ABAB* 4
    ABBA 5
    BBAA 7
    BAAB 5
    BABA 6

b.

R	P
3	1/6
4	1/6
5	2/6
6	1/6
7	1/6

c. No, the most extreme rank distribution has a probability of at least 1/6 and we can never get into a critical region with a probability of 0.10 or less.

Section 15.5

1. a. $H = 0$.
   b. With a test statistic of $H = 0$ and a critical value of $\chi^2 = 5.991$, fail to reject the claim of identical populations. The three treatments appear to have yields which are not significantly different.

3. Test statistic: $H = 14.35$. Critical value: $\chi^2 = 5.991$.
   Reject the null hypothesis that the samples come from identical populations.

5. Test statistic: $H = 7.980$. Critical value: $\chi^2 = 5.991$.
   Reject the null hypothesis that the receipts are the same.

7. Test statistic: $H = 1.589$. Critical value: $\chi^2 = 5.991$.
   Fail to reject the null hypothesis that the living areas are the same in all three zones.

9. Test statistic: $H = 1.732$. Critical value: $\chi^2 = 5.991$.
   Fail to reject the null hypothesis that the taxes are the same in all three zones.

11. a. $H = \dfrac{1}{1176}(R_1^2 + R_2^2 + \cdots + R_8^2) - 147$
    b. No change
    c. No change

13. Dividing the unrounded value of H by the correction factor results in $1.1375604 \div 0.99923077$, which is rounded off to 1.138, the same value obtained without the correction factor.

Section 15.6

1. a. ± 0.450
   b. ± 0.280
   c. ± 0.373
   d. ± 0.475
   e. ± 0.342

3. $d = 3, 0, 0, 3; \Sigma d^2 = 18; n = 4; r_s = -0.8$

5. $r_s = 0.261$. Critical values: $r_s = \pm 0.648$.
   No significant correlation.

7. $r_s = -0.964$. Critical values: $r_s = \pm 0.786$.
   Significant correlation.

9. $r_s = 0.190$. Critical values: $r_s = \pm 0.738$.
   No significant correlation.

11. $r_s = 0.494$. Critical values: $r_s = \pm 0.738$.
    No significant correlation.

13. $r_s = 0.458$. Critical values: $r_s = \pm 0.738$.
    No significant correlation.

15. $r_s = -0.903$. Critical values: $r_s = \pm 0.648$.
    Significant correlation.

17. a. 123, 132, 213, 231, 312, 321
    b. 1, 0.5, 0.5, −0.5, −0.5, −1
    c. 1/6 or 0.167

19. a. The rank correlation coefficient, because the trend is not linear.
    b. Sign changes.
    c. Both will be the same.
    d. Test statistic: $r_s = 0.855$. Critical value: $r_s = 0.564$.
       Reject H_0: $\rho_s \leq 0$. There is sufficient evidence to support the claim that there is a positive correlation.

Section 15.7

1. $n_1 = 5, n_2 = 3, G = 3$, critical values: 1, 8.

3. $n_1 = 10, n_2 = 10, G = 9$, critical values: 6, 16.

5. $\bar{x} = 11.0$; BBBBBABAAA; $n_1 = 6, n_2 = 4, G = 4$.
   The critical values are 2, 9. Fail to reject randomness.

7. $\bar{x} = 9.2$; $n_1 = 6, n_2 = 8, G = 2$.
   The critical values are 3, 12. Reject randomness.

9. Median is 9.5, $n_1 = 5, n_2 = 5, G = 2$.
   Critical values are 2, 10. Reject randomness.

11. Median is 9 so delete the three 9s to get BBBBBBBAAAAAAA. $n_1 = 7$, $n_2 = 7, G = 2$. Critical values are 3, 13. Reject randomness.

13. $n_1 = 30, n_2 = 15, G = 14, \mu_G = 21, \sigma_G = 2.94$.
    Test statistic: $z = -2.38$. Critical values: $z = \pm 1.96$. Reject randomness.

15. Median is 834. $n_1 = 8, n_2 = 8, G = 2$.
    Critical values are 4, 14. Reject randomness. (There appears to be a downward trend.)

17. The median is 0.145, $n_1 = 10, n_2 = 10, G = 4$.
    Test statistic: $G = 4$. Critical values: 6, 16.
    Reject randomness above and below the median.

19. $n_1 = 50, n_2 = 37, G = 48, \mu_G = 43.53, \sigma_G = 4.532$.
    Test statistic: $z = 0.99$. Critical values: $z = \pm 1.96$.
    Fail to reject randomness.

21. a. $\bar{x} = 11.075, n_1 = 29, n_2 = 11, G = 12. \mu_G = 16.95; \sigma_G = 2.473$.
       Test statistic: $z = -2.00$. Critical values: ± 1.96.
       Reject randomness.
    b. Majority of the customers arrive at 12:00 and a lesser number at 1:00. At other hours of the day, the number of customers varies considerably.

23. $\mu_G = 21, \sigma_G = 3.12$, so that $G = 27.12$, which is consistent with the interpretation of the table value of $G = 28$. Discrepancies can be explained by the fact that the normal distribution is an approximation to the true distribution of G and it uses a continuous scale while the values in Table A-10 are discrete.

25. a. Ten sequences have 3 runs.
    b. $P(3 \text{ runs}) = 10/220 = 0.045$.

c. No

d. 2

e. $\mu_G = 5.5$, $\sigma_G = 1.197$. Using these values and $z = -1.96$ in Formula 12-8, we solve to get $G = 3.154$, or 3 if we use only discrete values. The correct lower critical G value is 2, but the normal approximation yields 3 in this case.

Review Exercises

1. $n_1 = 25$, $n_2 = 8$, $G = 5$, $\mu_G = 13.12$, $\sigma_G = 2.05$.
    Test statistic: $z = -3.96$. Critical values: $z = \pm 1.96$. Reject randomness.

3. $r_s = 0$. Critical value: $r_s = \pm 0.786$.
    No significant correlation.

5. Test statistic: $H = 6.181$. Critical value: $\chi^2 = 5.991$ (assuming a 0.05 significance level). Reject the null hypothesis that the three precincts have the same response times.

7. Test statistic: $x = 5$. Critical value: 2. There is not sufficient evidence to support the claim that the median score is greater than 78.

9. $\mu_R = 137.50$, $\sigma_R = 17.26$, $R = 177.5$, $z = 2.32$.
    Test statistic: $z = 2.32$. Critical values: $z = \pm 1.96$. Reject the null hypothesis of no difference.

11. a. $r_s = 0.976$. Critical values: $r_s = \pm 0.648$.
        Significant correlation.
    b. Even though there is a significant correlation between bars and churches this does not prove that one causes the other. It only serves to indicate a significant statistical association between the two variables.

13. $T = 4$, $n = 12$. The test statistic of $T = 4$ is less than or equal to the critical value of 14, so reject the null hypothesis that the tune-up has no effect on fuel consumption.

15. Discard the two zeros to get 11 negative signs and 1 positive sign so that $x = 1$, which is less than the critical value of 2 found from Table A-7. Reject null hypothesis of no effect.

17. $\mu_R = 126.5$, $\sigma_R = 15.23$, $R = 155.5$, $z = 1.90$.
    Test statistic: $z = 1.90$. Critical values: $z = \pm 1.96$. Fail to reject null hypothesis that both brands are the same.

19. Test statistic: $H = 8.756$. Critical value: $\chi^2 = 9.488$ (assuming a 0.05 level of significance). Fail to reject the null hypothesis that the methods are equally effective.

21. $T = 12$, $n = 7$. The test statistic of $T = 12$ is greater than the critical value of 2, so fail to reject the null hypothesis that there is no difference between the scores of Judge A and Judge B.

23. a. $n_1 = 57$, $n_2 = 13$, $G = 26$, $\mu_G = 22.17$, $\sigma_G = 2.49$, $z = 1.54$.
        Critical values are ± 1.96. Fail to reject randomness.
    b. Defects occur at every sixth observation.

Chapter 16 Section 16.2

1. Actions: 1. The man buys the insurance.
             2. The man doesn't buy the insurance.
    States of Nature: 1. The man lives through the year.
                       2. The man doesn't live through the year.

CASE	OUTCOME
Man buys policy and lives	−$87
Man buys policy and dies	$49,913
Man doesn't buy policy and lives	0
Man doesn't buy policy and dies	0

Objective variable: Net change in wealth

3. Actions: 1. Settle out of court.
             2. Go to trial.
    States of Nature: 1. Determined to be guilty
                       2. Determined to be not guilty

CASE	OUTCOME
Settle, and would be found guilty	−$150,000
Settle, and would be found not guilty	−$150,000
Go to trial and found guilty	−$500,000
Go to trial and found not guilty	0

Objective variable: Amount of payment

5. Actions: 1. Use TV only
             2. Use print media only
             3. Use TV and print media
    States of Nature: 1. Campaign is successful
                       2. Campaign is not successful

CASE	OUTCOME
Use TV only and campaign is successful	$250,000
Use print only and campaign is success.	$175,000
Use TV and print; campaign successful	$300,000
Use TV only and campaign is unsuccessful	−$80,000
Use print only and campaign is unsuccess.	−$60,000
Use TV and print and campaign is unsuc.	−$140,000

Objective variable: Increase in profits

7. Actions: 1. Buy the safe blue chip stock
             2. Buy the speculative stock
    States of Nature: 1. Economy is healthy
                       2. Economy is unhealthy

CASE	OUTCOME
Buy safe stock and economy is healthy	$5,000
Buy speculative stock in healthy econ.	$12,000
Buy safe stock in unhealthy economy	−$3,000
Buy speculative stock in unhealthy econ.	−$12,000

Objective variable: Amount of money earned on stock

9. Actions: 1. Use the outdoor stadium
             2. Use the indoor arena
   States of Nature: 1. Weather is good
                     2. It rains

CASE	OUTCOME
Outdoor stadium used and weather is good	$200,000
Indoor arena used and weather is good	$40,000
Outdoor stadium used and it rains	−$100,000
Indoor arena used and it rains	$40,000

Objective variable: Amount of profit

11. Actions: 1. 0 units ordered
             2. 5 units ordered
             3. 10 units ordered
             4. 15 units ordered
    States of Nature: 1. Signal changes
                      2. Signal doesn't change

CASE	OUTCOME
0 units ordered and signal changes	0
5 units ordered and signal changes	−$450
10 units ordered and signal changes	−$900
15 units ordered and signal changes	−$1350
0 units ordered and signal doesn't change	0
5 units ordered and signal doesn't change	$300
10 units ordered and signal doesn't change	$600
15 units ordered and signal doesn't change	$900

Objective variable: Amount of profit

13. a.

	S1	S2
A1	$40,000	$0
A2	$45,000	−$5000
A3	$50,000	−$70,000

   b.

	S1	S2
A1	$40,000	$0
A2	$45,000	−$5000
A3	$50,000	−$70,000
A4	$47,000	−$10,000

   c.

	S1	S2
A1	$40,000	$0
A2	$45,000	−$5000
A3	$50,000	−$70,000
A4	$47,000	−$10,000
A5	$60,000	−$80,000

   d. No, there is not a maximum number

15. No, it does not necessarily follow that one of rows A2 and A3 must dominate the other if we assume that row A1 dominates both rows A2 and A3. An example could be taken from Table 16.1 as follows:

	S1	S2
A1	$55,000	$0
A2	$45,000	−$5000
A3	$50,000	−$70,000

Section 16.3

1.

	S1	S2
A1	0	5
A2	4	0

3.

	S1	S2	S3
A1	0	4	6
A2	0	0	0

5.

	S1	S2	S3
A1	10	0	0
A2	15	10	5
A3	0	20	10

7.

	S1	S2	S3	S4
A1	0	0	0	0
A2	12	4	11	8

9.

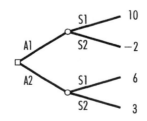

11.

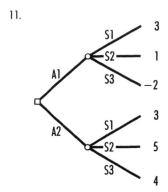

13.

	S1	S2
A1	0	4
A2	8	0

15.

	S1	S2
A1	8	0
A2	6	1
A3	0	2

17.

	LIVES	DIES
Buys insurance	$87	0
Doesn't buy	0	$49,913

19.

	NOT GUILTY	GUILTY
Settle out	$150,000	0
Go to trial	0	$350,000

21.

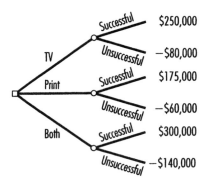

23.

25. a.

	S1	S2	S3
A1	3	8	0
A2	0	0	7

b.

	S1	S2	S3
A1	3	8	0
A2	0	0	7

c. No. From parts *a* and *b* we see that different payoff tables can lead to the same opportunity loss table, so there can be no way to reverse the process.

27. a. Eliminate A2 and A3.

b. Eliminate A1 and A3. Always choose A2.

Section 16.4

1. a. A1
   b. A2
   c. A2
3. a. A2
   b. A2
   c. A2
   (Note: A2 dominates A1)
5. a. A3
   b. A1
   c. A1
7. a. A1
   b. A1
   c. A1
   (Note: A1 dominates)
9. a. Buy
   b. Don't Buy
   c. Buy
11. a. Go to trial
    b. Settle
    c. Settle
13. a. Use both
    b. Use print
    c. Use TV
15. a. Buy speculatively
    b. Buy safe
    c. Buy safe
17. a. Outdoors
    b. Indoors
    c. Outdoors
19. a. Order 15
    b. Order 0
    c. Order 5
21. No, the values in any column of an opportunity loss table are relative to each other, but they don't relate to values in other columns. It is impossible to identify the action corresponding to the maximum payoff, and it is impossible to find a minimum payoff for an action.

23. Yes. One possible example:

	S1	S2	S3
A1	10	9	8
A2	7	6	5
A3	4	3	2

Section 16.5

1. 268
3. 0.6604
5. −$106
7. $213,000
9. 5.2 (A1); 4.8 (A2); A1 is the best
11. 1.007 (A1); 3.797 (A2); A2 is the best
13. 3.00 (A1); 10.50 (A2); 12.00 (A3); A1 is the best
15. 0.0 (A1); 8.867 (A2); A1 is the best
17. E(don't buy insurance) = 0; E(buy insurance) = $913
    Best action: buy insurance
19. E(settle out) = −$150,000; E(go to trial) = −$100,000
    Best action: go to trial
21. E(TV only) = $118,000; E(print only) = $81,000; E(both) = $124,000
    Best action: Use both TV and print
23. E(safe) = −$600; E(speculative) = −$6900
    Best action: Buy the safe stock
25. E(indoor) = $40,000; E(outdoor) = $162,500
    Best action: Schedule the concert outdoors
27. E(0 ordered) = 0; E(5 ordered) = $150; E(10 ordered) = $300
    E(15 ordered) = $450
    Best action: Order 15 cable TV decoders
29. Opportunity Loss table:

	S1	S2	S3
A1	29.8	0	0
A2	1.8	19.7	8.5
A3	0	26.2	1.7

Expected value of payoff for each action:
E(A1) = 6.57; E(A2) = 4.72; E(A3) = 5.64
Expected opportunity loss for each action:
E(A1) = 8.49; E(A2) = 10.34; E(A3) = 9.42
Best action: A1

31. a. Expected values are multiplied by the same constant
    b. Expected values are multiplied by the same negative constant. The action that was originally best will now become the worst choice.

Review Exercises

1. a. Maximax
   b. Maximin
   c. Maximin

3. a. A1
   b. A3
   c. A3
5. Actions: 1. Pay the bill
             2. Contest the bill
   States of Nature:
             1. Court ruling is favorable
             2. Court ruling is unfavorable

CASE	OUTCOME
Bill is paid/favorable ruling	−$10,000
Bill is paid/unfavorable ruling	−$10,000
Bill is contested/favorable ruling	−$2,000
Bill is contested/unfavorable ruling	−$12,000

Objective variable: Net change in wealth

7.

	FAVORABLE	UNFAVORABLE
Bill is paid	$8000	0
Bill is contested	0	$2000

9. a. Contest the bill
   b. Pay the bill
   c. Contest the bill
11. a. Actions: 1. Fix the pump
                 2. Replace the pump
                 3. Leave the pump alone
    States of Nature:
                 1. The truck is kept
                 2. The truck is sold

CASE	OUTCOME
Pump is fixed & truck is kept	−$300
Pump is replaced & truck is kept	−$1000
Pump left alone & truck kept	−$2000
Pump is fixed and truck is sold	−$300
Pump is replaced and truck is sold	−$800
Pump is left alone and truck is sold	0

Objective variable: Net change in wealth

13.

	TRUCK KEPT	TRUCK SOLD
Pump fixed	0	$300
Pump replaced	$700	$800
Pump left alone	$1700	0

15. a. Leave pump alone
    b. Fix the pump
    c. Fix the pump

Index

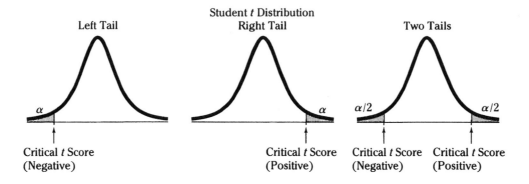

Left Tail

Student *t* Distribution
Right Tail

Two Tails

α

Critical *t* Score
(Negative)

α

Critical *t* Score
(Positive)

$\alpha/2$

Critical *t* Score
(Negative)

$\alpha/2$

Critical *t* Score
(Positive)

TABLE A.3
t Distribution

				α		
DEGREES OF FREEDOM	.005 (ONE TAIL) .01 (TWO TAILS)	.01 (ONE TAIL) .02 (TWO TAILS)	.025 (ONE TAIL) .05 (TWO TAILS)	.05 (ONE TAIL) .10 (TWO TAILS)	.10 (ONE TAIL) .20 (TWO TAILS)	.25 (ONE TAIL) .50 (TWO TAILS)
1	63.657	31.821	12.706	6.314	3.078	1.000
2	9.925	6.965	4.303	2.920	1.886	.816
3	5.841	4.541	3.182	2.353	1.638	.765
4	4.604	3.747	2.776	2.132	1.533	.741
5	4.032	3.365	2.571	2.015	1.476	.727
6	3.707	3.143	2.447	1.943	1.440	.718
7	3.500	2.998	2.365	1.895	1.415	.711
8	3.355	2.896	2.306	1.860	1.397	.706
9	3.250	2.821	2.262	1.833	1.383	.703
10	3.169	2.764	2.228	1.812	1.372	.700
11	3.106	2.718	2.201	1.796	1.363	.697
12	3.054	2.681	2.179	1.782	1.356	.696
13	3.012	2.650	2.160	1.771	1.350	.694
14	2.977	2.625	2.145	1.761	1.345	.692
15	2.947	2.602	2.132	1.753	1.341	.691
16	2.921	2.584	2.120	1.746	1.337	.690
17	2.898	2.567	2.110	1.740	1.333	.689
18	2.878	2.552	2.101	1.734	1.330	.688
19	2.861	2.540	2.093	1.729	1.328	.688
20	2.845	2.528	2.086	1.725	1.325	.687
21	2.831	2.518	2.080	1.721	1.323	.686
22	2.819	2.508	2.074	1.717	1.321	.686
23	2.807	2.500	2.069	1.714	1.320	.685
24	2.797	2.492	2.064	1.711	1.318	.685
25	2.787	2.485	2.060	1.708	1.316	.684
26	2.779	2.479	2.056	1.706	1.315	.684
27	2.771	2.473	2.052	1.703	1.314	.684
28	2.763	2.467	2.048	1.701	1.313	.683
29	2.756	2.462	2.045	1.699	1.311	.683
Large (*z*)	2.575	2.327	1.960	1.645	1.282	.675

k	number of samples; number of independent or predictor variables in a regression equation	r^2	coefficient of determination
		R^2	multiple coefficient of determination
$\bar{\bar{x}}$	mean of sample means	P_o	price in base time period
$\bar{s}$	mean of sample standard deviations	P_t	price in time period t
$\overline{R}$	mean of sample ranges	Q_o	quantity in base time period
d	difference between two paired scores	Q_t	quantity in time period t
$\overline{d}$	mean of the differences d found from paired sample data	T	trend component in time series; rank sum in Wilcoxon signed-rank test
s_d	standard deviation of the differences d found from paired sample data	C	cyclical component in time series
s_p	pooled standard deviation for two samples	S	seasonal component in time series
t	number of treatment types or number of populations being compared	I	irregular (or random) component in time series
b	number of blocks	T	rank sum used in Wilcoxon signed-rank test
$\overline{B_i}$	mean of values in ith block	H	Kruskal-Wallis test statistic
SS	sum of squares, as in SSx, SSy, $SSTotal$, $SSTreatment$, $SSError$, $SSRegression$	R	sum of the ranks for a sample; used in the Wilcoxon rank-sum test
$\hat{y}$	predicted value of y	μ_R	expected mean rank; used in the Wilcoxon rank-sum test
β_i	constant or slope coefficient in regression equation	σ_R	expected standard deviation of ranks; used in the Wilcoxon rank-sum test
$\hat{\beta_i}$	estimate of β_i	r_s	Spearman's rank correlation coefficient
$\hat{\sigma}_e$	estimate of standard deviation of error in regression	G	number of runs in runs test for randomness
r	sample linear correlation coefficient	μ_G	expected mean number of runs; used in runs test for randomness
ρ	(rho) population linear correlation coefficient	σ_G	expected standard deviation for the number of runs; used in runs test for randomness